Less managing. More teaching. Greater learning.

INSTRUCTORS...

Would you like your **students** to show up for class **more prepared**?
(Let's face it, class is much more fun if everyone is engaged and prepared...)

Want ready-made application-level **interactive assignments,** student progress reporting, and auto-assignment grading? *(Less time grading means more time teaching...)*

Want an **instant view of student or class performance** relative to learning objectives? *(No more wondering if students understand...)*

Need to **collect data and generate reports** required for administration or accreditation? *(Say goodbye to manually tracking student learning outcomes...)*

Want to **record and post your lectures** for students to view online?

With **McGraw-Hill's *Connect® Plus Business Law,***

INSTRUCTORS GET:

- Interactive Applications – **book-specific interactive assignments** that require students to APPLY what they've learned.

- Simple **assignment management**, allowing you to spend more time teaching.

- **Auto-graded** assignments, quizzes, and tests.

- **Detailed Visual Reporting** where student and section results can be viewed and analyzed.

- Sophisticated **online testing** capability.

- A **filtering and reporting** function that allows you to easily assign and report on materials that are correlated to accreditation standards, learning outcomes, and Bloom's taxonomy.

- An easy-to-use **lecture capture** tool.

STUDENTS...

Want an online, **searchable version** of your textbook?

Wish your textbook could be **available online** while you're doing your assignments?

Connect® Plus Business Law eBook

If you choose to use *Connect® Plus Business Law*, you have an affordable and searchable online version of your book integrated with your other online tools.

Connect® Plus Business Law eBook offers features like:

- Topic search
- Direct links from assignments
- Adjustable text size
- Jump to page number
- Print by section

STUDENTS...

Want to get more **value** from your textbook purchase?

Think learning Business Law should be a bit more **interesting**?

Check out the STUDENT RESOURCES section under the *Connect®* Library tab.

Here you'll find a wealth of resources designed to help you achieve your goals in the course. You'll find things like **quizzes, PowerPoints, and Internet activities** to help you study. Every student has different needs, so explore the STUDENT RESOURCES to find the materials best suited to you.

Dynamic Business Law

THE ESSENTIALS

Second Edition

Dynamic Business Law

THE ESSENTIALS

Second Edition

Nancy Kubasek
Bowling Green State University

M. Neil Browne
Bowling Green State University

Daniel J. Herron
Miami University

Lucien J. Dhooge
Georgia Institute of Technology

Linda Barkacs
University of San Diego

McGraw-Hill Irwin

McGraw-Hill
Irwin

DYNAMIC BUSINESS LAW: THE ESSENTIALS

Published by McGraw-Hill/Irwin, a business unit of The McGraw-Hill Companies, Inc., 1221 Avenue of the Americas, New York, NY, 10020. Copyright © 2013, 2010 by The McGraw-Hill Companies, Inc. All rights reserved. Printed in the United States of America. No part of this publication may be reproduced or distributed in any form or by any means, or stored in a database or retrieval system, without the prior written consent of The McGraw-Hill Companies, Inc., including, but not limited to, in any network or other electronic storage or transmission, or broadcast for distance learning.

Some ancillaries, including electronic and print components, may not be available to customers outside the United States.

This book is printed on acid-free paper.

1 2 3 4 5 6 7 8 9 0 QVR/QVR 1 0 9 8 7 6 5 4 3 2

ISBN 978-0-07-352497-9
MHID 0-07-352497-2

Vice president and editor-in-chief: *Brent Gordon*
Editorial director: *Paul Ducham*
Executive editor: *John Weimeister*
Executive director of development: *Ann Torbert*
Development editor II: *Megan Shultz*
Editorial coordinator: *Heather Darr*
Vice president and director of marketing: *Robin J. Zwettler*
Marketing director: *Amee Mosley*
Executive marketing manager: *Sarah Schuessler*
Vice president of editing, design, and production: *Sesha Bolisetty*
Senior project manager: *Diane L. Nowaczyk*
Senior buyer: *Carol A. Bielski*
Lead designer: *Matthew Baldwin*
Senior photo research coordinator: *Keri Johnson*
Photo researcher: *Michelle Buhr*
Media project manager: *Rachel Townsend*
Media project manager: *Balaji Sundararaman, Hurix Systems Pvt. Ltd.*
Cover and interior design: *Matthew Baldwin*
Typeface: *10/12 Times Roman*
Compositor: *Laserwords Private Limited*
Printer: *Quad/Graphics*

Library of Congress Cataloging-in-Publication Data

Dynamic business law : the essentials / Nancy Kubasek ... [et al.]. — 2nd ed.
 p. cm.
 Includes index.
 ISBN-13: 978-0-07-352497-9 (alk. paper)
 ISBN-10: 0-07-352497-2 (alk. paper)
 1. Business law—United States. I. Kubasek, Nancy.
KF390.B84D963 2013
346.7307—dc23

2011041532

www.mhhe.com

About the Authors

Nancy K. Kubasek received her JD from the University of Toledo College of Law in 1981 and her BA from Bowling Green State University in 1978. She joined the BGSU faculty in 1982 and became an associate professor in 1988 and a full professor in 1993.

During her tenure at Bowling Green State University, she has primarily taught courses in business law, legal environment of business, environmental law, health care law, and moral principles. She has published over 75 articles, primarily in law reviews and business journals. Most of her substantive articles focus on environmental questions, and she writes a quarterly column about environmental issues for the *Real Estate Law Journal.* She has helped get students involved in legal research, and a number of her articles are co-authored with students. She has also published a number of pedagogical articles in teaching journals, focusing primarily on the teaching of critical thinking and ethics.

She wrote the first environmental law text for undergraduate students, *Environmental Law,* and co-authored *The Legal Environment of Business: A Critical Thinking Approach.* She has written supplemental materials, such as study guides, test banks, and instructors' manuals.

Active in many professional organizations, she has served as president of the Academy of Legal Studies in Business, the national organization for professors of legal studies in colleges of business. She has also served as president of the Tri-State Academy of Legal Studies in Business, her regional professional association.

In her leisure time, she and her husband, Neil Browne, fish for halibut and salmon in Alaska, as well as large-mouth bass in Florida. In addition, they are regular participants in polka, waltz, zydeco, and Cajun dance festivals in Europe and the United States. For almost 30 years, they have been successful tournament blackjack players as well. Both are avid exercisers—lifting weights, doing yoga, and running almost every day.

M. Neil Browne is senior lecturer and research associate and a distinguished teaching professor emeritus at Bowling Green State University. He received his BA in history and economics at the University of Houston, his PhD in economics at the University of Texas, and his JD from the University of Toledo. He has been a professor at Bowling Green for more than four decades.

Professor Browne teaches courses in jurisprudence, ethical reasoning, critical thinking, and economics at both the undergraduate and graduate levels. He has received recognition as the Silver Medalist National Professor of the Year, the Ohio Professor of the Year, and Distinguished Teacher and Master Teacher at Bowling Green State University, as well as numerous research awards from his university and from professional organizations. His consulting activities with corporate, government, and educational institutions focus on improving the quality of critical thinking in those organizations. In addition, he serves as a Rule 26 expert with respect to the quality of the reasoning used by expert witnesses called by the party opponent in legal actions.

Professor Browne has published 20 books and over 130 professional journal articles in law journals, as well as economics, sociology, and higher education journals. His current research interests focus on the relationship between orthodox economic thinking and legal policy. In addition, he is in the midst of writing books about the power of questionable assumptions in economics, the usefulness of asking questions as a learning strategy, and the importance of critical thinking in environmental arguments.

Professor Browne tries to find time for a broad array of outside activities. He and his wife, Nancy Kubasek, fish for halibut and salmon in Alaska, as well as large-mouth bass in Florida, as frequently as possible. In addition, they are regular participants in polka, waltz, zydeco, and Cajun dance festivals in Europe and the United States. For almost 30 years, they have been successful tournament blackjack players as well. Both are avid exercisers—lifting weights, doing yoga, and running almost every day.

Daniel J. Herron is a professor of business legal studies at Miami University in Oxford, Ohio. He received his law degree from Case Western Reserve University School of Law in 1978 and is a member of the Ohio and federal bars. He has taught at Miami University, his alma mater, since 1992, having previously taught at the University of Wyoming, Western Carolina University, the University of North Carolina–Wilmington, and Bowling Green State University. He has been a member of the Academy of Legal Studies in Business for nearly 25 years and has served as its executive secretary since 1991. His research interests focus on law and ethics, employment law, and legal history.

He has been married for over 30 years to his wife Deborah, and they have two children, Elisabeth and Christopher, and a daughter-in-law, Amanda, and one grandchild, Jack. Herron and his wife reside in Oxford, Ohio, with their two beagles, Max and Missy.

Lucien J. Dhooge is the faculty director of the Global Executive MBA Program and is the Sue and John Staton Professor of Law at the Georgia Institute of

Technology. He teaches business law, real estate law, and ethics.

After completing an undergraduate degree in history at the University of Colorado in 1980, Professor Dhooge attended the University of Denver College of Law, where he received his JD in 1983. He received his LL.M. in 1995 from Georgetown University Law Center, where he specialized in international and comparative law. Before coming to the College of Management at the Georgia Institute of Technology, Professor Dhooge spent 11 years in private law practice and 12 years serving on the faculty of the University of the Pacific in California.

Professor Dhooge has authored more than 50 scholarly articles, coauthored seven books, and presented research papers and courses throughout the United States, as well as in Asia, Europe, and South America. Professor Dhooge is the recipient of numerous research awards given by the Academy of Legal Studies in Business, including seven Ralph C. Hoeber Awards for excellence in research. He was designated the outstanding junior business law faculty member in the United States by the Academy in 2002 and received the Kay Duffy Award for outstanding service in 2005. He was designated as an International Scholar by the Soros Foundation in 2006. Professor Dhooge was the program chair for the Academy's 2009 international conference in Denver and served as the Academy's president from 2009–2010. He is a past editor-in-chief of the *American Business Law Journal* and the *Journal of Legal Studies Education*.

A native of Chicago but raised in Denver, Professor Dhooge enjoys spending time with his family and following the fortunes of the Chicago Cubs and Colorado Rockies professional baseball teams.

Linda L. Barkacs

received her JD from the University of San Diego in 1993. She also has a BA in political science from San Diego State University and an AA in accounting from Irvine Valley College.

Upon graduating from law school and passing the California bar exam, Professor Barkacs became an associate at a downtown San Diego law firm. During her time with that firm, she was involved in a number of high-profile trials, including a sexual harassment case against the City of Oceanside that resulted in a $1.2 million verdict. In 1997, Professor Barkacs and her husband Craig (also a professor at USD) started their own law firm specializing in business and civil litigation (in both federal and state courts), employment law cases, and appeals. They were also involved in numerous mediations and arbitrations.

Professor Barkacs began teaching at USD in 1997 and was tenured in 2011. As an educator, she has designed and taught numerous courses on law, ethics, and negotiation. She teaches in USD's undergraduate and graduate programs, including the Master of Science in Executive Leadership (a Ken Blanchard program), the Master of Science in Global Leadership, and the Master of Science in Supply Chain Management. Professor Barkacs often teaches in USD's study-abroad classes and has traveled extensively throughout Europe, Asia, and South America.

Professor Barkacs has received numerous awards for her teaching at USD, including USD's 2010 Professor Impaact (MSCM Program); the 2008 USD School of Business Outstanding Undergraduate Business Educator of the Year; and the 2008 and 2007 Professor of the Year, USD Senior Class (universitywide)

She and her husband are principals in The Barkacs Group (www.tbgexecutivetraining.com), a consulting firm that provides negotiation, ethics, and team training for the private sector. Professor Barkacs has published numerous journal articles in the areas of law, ethics, and negotiation. She and her husband are coauthoring a book on negotiation. She has been the president, vice president, conference chair, and treasurer for the Pacific Southwest Academy of Legal Studies in Business (www.pswalsb.net).

Professor Barkacs currently spends her time teaching, publishing, consulting for The Barkacs Group, and doing volunteer work for various civic causes. She enjoys walking, weight-lifting, and spending her free time with her husband and their three cats, Phoenix, Violet, and Vanessa.

Preface

We wrote this book because our primary sense of who we are as professionals is that we are teachers. We play various roles in our careers, but we are especially dedicated to our students. We want them to listen, read, create, and evaluate more effectively as a result of their experience in a business law class. Above all, we want them to sense the importance and excitement of the law.

We tried to construct a book that contains the basics of business law but does not get bogged down in the kind of details that would be more appropriate in an upper-level law class.

It is our pedagogical features that provide the distinctive value of this book. Each feature stands by itself as an aid to the kind of learning we hope to encourage. Yet the features are also a cohesive unit, contributing both to the liberal education of the students who read it and to their skills as decision makers in a market economy.

Specifically, we provide what competing texts deliver, an examination of the basic questions, concepts, and legal rules of business law. Our text must address the power and authority of constitutions, statutes, case law, and treaties as sources of law. Together the various elements of what we call "the law" make up the foundation and structure of the market exchange process.

Decisions to trade and produce require trust—trust that consumers, firms, workers, financial institutions, and asset owners will do as they promise and that violations of such promises will be unacceptable in the marketplace. Without guarantees that promises will be kept, market exchanges would grind to a halt. Business law provides these guarantees and the boundaries within which certain promises can be made and enforced.

Market decisions are made in a context—a persistently changing context. The law, in turn, is dynamic in response. New technologies and business practices bring new disputes over rights and responsibilities in a business setting.

Future business leaders need knowledge of existing business law, as well as a set of skills permitting them to adjust efficiently and effectively to new legal issues as they arise over the course of their careers.

We are excited about the contents of our features and want to explain the function of each of them in preparing students for leadership positions in business.

A. Global Boxes

This first feature highlights the emerging, interconnected market. Where relevant, the chapters contain Global Context boxes. Because so many market decisions are made in an international context, learners need to familiarize themselves with the likelihood that a particular legal principle essential to doing busi-

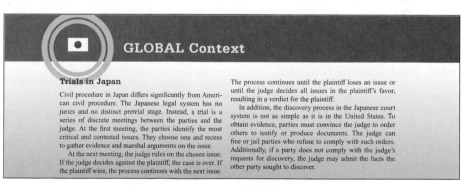

GLOBAL Context

Trials in Japan

Civil procedure in Japan differs significantly from American civil procedure. The Japanese legal system has no juries and no distinct pretrial stage. Instead, a trial is a series of discrete meetings between the parties and the judge. At the first meeting, the parties identify the most critical and contested issues. They choose one and recess to gather evidence and marshal arguments on the issue.

At the next meeting, the judge rules on the chosen issue. If the judge decides against the plaintiff, the case is over. If the plaintiff wins, the process continues with the next issue.

The process continues until the plaintiff loses an issue or until the judge decides all issues in the plaintiff's favor, resulting in a verdict for the plaintiff.

In addition, the discovery process in the Japanese court system is not as simple as it is in the United States. To obtain evidence, parties must convince the judge to order others to testify or produce documents. The judge can fine or jail parties who refuse to comply with such orders. Additionally, if a party does not comply with the judge's requests for discovery, the judge may admit the facts the other party sought to discover.

ness in one country may not be appropriate in other countries. The Global Context boxes illustrate how unique the law in a certain country often is. After reading these "stories of difference," readers will certainly better understand the need to discover relevant law in all jurisdictions where their market decisions have legal implications.

We believe that students learn innumerable valuable lessons about American business law by contrasting the concepts of our business law system with those of our primary trading partners. We typically use Canada, Japan, China, Russia, Mexico, and the European Union for our comparisons because modern business managers will more likely be interacting with the law in those particular jurisdictions.

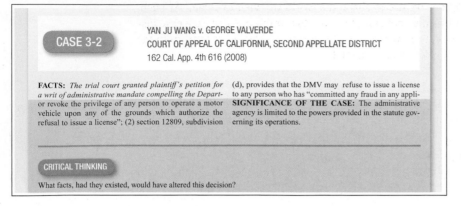

B. Critical Thinking

After each case in the book, we have provided critical thinking questions to highlight the need to think critically about the reasoning used by the court. In addition, we include in every chapter a Point/Counterpoint problem that encourages the reader to evaluate the conflicting reasoning surrounding a key issue in the chapter.

But we do much more than just ask a lot of critical thinking questions at particular locations throughout the chapters. We encourage the use of a step-by-step critical thinking approach that has been developed and used in classrooms in many countries. We do not just repeatedly urge students to "think critically." Instead, we describe for them what is meant by that phrase in the context of business law.

We include this step-by-step approach in Appendix 1A at the end of Chapter 1. Instructors who wish to emphasize critical thinking can use that appendix as a structured approach for learning how to evaluate legal reasoning.

C. Ethical Reasoning

Our book emphasizes consideration of all stakeholder interests in every market decision. Business ethics should never be an afterthought or something firms consider only because they think they must.

Instead, business ethics is what provides the social legitimacy for markets, what distinguishes markets from the life of the jungle. While market decisions are calculating and purposeful, they must at the same time reflect awareness that the good and the right provide social borders that elevate those decisions above simple greed and egoism.

Ethical discussion focuses on the basic observation that we are socially and globally interdependent as entrepreneurs, asset owners, workers, businesspeople, and consumers. Our inescapable contact with one another requires that our aspirations be defined, at least in part, by their impact on others.

Our text has several ethical reasoning possibilities in each chapter. But for the reader to make use of this emphasis requires a practical step-by-step approach. In other words, students need more than just a discussion about values or ethics.

They need to have some sense that the discussion is headed somewhere. They want to know, "How will my behavior be any more ethical after I have read the chapter and participated in the class discussions?" Our text answers their question.

Chapter 1 provides a clear explanation of our approach—an approach that students can use on a regular basis. The language and organization of our model of ethical reasoning leans implicitly on standard ethical theories. But it meets the challenge of a fast-paced business world. It pushes stakeholders to the forefront of market decisions, where they belong, and does so in a manner that is both powerful and doable without becoming tedious.

The WPH Framework for Business Ethics

A useful set of ethical guidelines requires the recognition that managerial decisions must meet the following primary criteria (Exhibit 1-3):

- The decisions affect particular groups of stakeholders in the operations of the firm. The pertinent question is thus, *Whom* would this decision affect?
- The decisions are made in pursuit of a particular *purpose*. Business decisions are instruments toward an ethical end.
- The decisions must meet the standards of action-oriented business behavior. Managers need a doable set of guidelines for *how* to make ethical decisions.

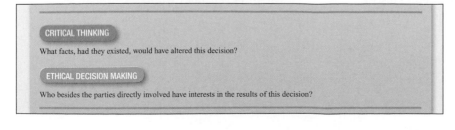

Business ethics serve as the guidelines we use to shape the world we wish to create. As such, they provide guidance for the kind of business behavior we want to reinforce. After each case discussion, we pause to think about the ethics of business law by asking a question derived from the practical approach to business ethics developed in Chapter 1.

D. E-Commerce Boxes

A central feature of modern business decisions is new technology, specifically the rapid spread of electronic commerce. This development has created new challenges and opportunities that were unforeseeable until very recently. By including boxes that call attention to these challenges, we think we can best convince students of the pervasive influence of this new, complicating aspect of business decisions.

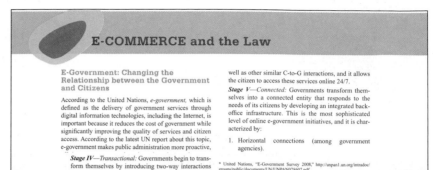

E-COMMERCE and the Law

E-Government: Changing the Relationship between the Government and Citizens

According to the United Nations, *e-government*, which is defined as the delivery of government services through digital information technologies, including the Internet, is important because it reduces the cost of government while significantly improving the quality of services and citizen access. According to the latest UN report about this topic, e-government makes public administration more proactive,

Stage IV—Transactional: Governments begin to transform themselves by introducing two-way interactions between "citizen and government" (C to G). This includes options for paying taxes and applying for ID cards, birth certificates, passports, and license renewals, as well as other similar C-to-G interactions, and it allows the citizen to access these services online 24/7.

Stage V—Connected: Governments transform themselves into a connected entity that responds to the needs of its citizens by developing an integrated back-office infrastructure. This is the most sophisticated level of online e-government initiatives, and it is characterized by:

1. Horizontal connections (among government agencies).

* United Nations, "E-Government Survey 2008," http://unpan1.un.org/intradoc/groups/public/documents/UN/UNPAN028607.pdf.
† Ibid., p. 20.
‡ Robert D. Atkinson (Progressive Policy Institute), "Unsatisfactory Progress: The Bush Administration's Performance on E-Government Initiatives," October 14, 2004, www.ppionline.org/ppi_ci.cfm?knlgAreaID=140&subsecID=290&contentID=4252960.

Walkthrough

We have designed our features around the things we do in our classes to encourage excitement about business law. We believe they provide Business Law Plus.

We also have a variety of supplementary material available for instructors, to aid in course development, and for students, to provide additional study.

Online Learning Center (www.mhhe.com/kubasekess2e)

With all of the possibilities that technology can offer, we've organized our Online Learning Center for ease of use for both instructor and student. Password-protected instructor materials can be found in the *Instructor Center,* including the Instructor's Manual, Testbank, PowerPoint presentation options, additional resources for classroom exercises, and notes on how to incorporate them all into the classroom. *You Be the Judge Online* (detailed below) is linked for accessibility and convenience. The *Student Center* offers opportunities for independent study, such as chapter quizzes and additional cases. Premium content includes narrated PowerPoint slides, iPod content, and streaming video.

Instructor's Manual
Written by our fellow co-author Lucien Dhooge, this resource includes lecture notes, case briefs, answers to all questions in each chapter, assignment ideas, teaching assistance (emphasizing practical tips that new or part-time teachers can try right away), and suggested handouts.

Test Bank
Prepared by Vonda Laughlin, of Carson-Newman College, our test bank contains a variety of true/false, multiple-choice, and essay questions, as well as "scenario-based" questions, which are application-based and use a situation described in a narrative, with three to five multiple-choice test questions based on the situation.

EZ Test Online
McGraw-Hill's EZ Test Online is a flexible and easy-to-use electronic testing program. The program allows instructors to create tests from book-specific items, accommodates a wide range of question types, and enables instructors to add their own questions. Multiple versions of the test can be created, and any test can be exported for use with course management systems such as WebCT, Blackboard, or any other course management system. EZ Test Online is accessible to busy instructors virtually anywhere via the web, and the program eliminates the need for them to install test software. Utilizing EZ Test Online also allows instructors to create and deliver multiple-choice or true/false quiz questions using iQuiz for iPod. For more information about EZ Test Online, please see the website at www.eztestonline.com.

PowerPoint Presentation Slides
Developed by Jeff Penley at Catawba Valley Community College, two different sets of slides are available for instructors. The Basic set consists of an outline of each chapter. The Premium set expands on this outline to include hypotheticals and ethical dilemmas, allowing the instructor to incorporate application into the lecture.

You Be the Judge Online (www.mhhe.com/ybtj)

This interactive product includes 18 hypothetical business law cases. All the cases are based on real cases within our business law texts. Each case allows you to watch interviews of the plaintiff and defendant before the courtroom argument, see the courtroom proceedings, view relevant evidence, read other actual cases relating to the issues in the case, and then create your own ruling. After your verdict is generated, you can view what an actual judge ruled (unscripted) in the case and then get the chance to defend or change your ruling.

McGraw-Hill *Connect®* Business Law

Less Managing. More Teaching. Greater Learning.

McGraw-Hill *Connect Business Law* is an online assignment and assessment solution that connects students with the tools and resources they'll need to achieve success.

McGraw-Hill *Connect Business Law* helps prepare students for their future by enabling faster learning, more efficient studying, and higher retention of knowledge.

McGraw-Hill Connect Business Law Features

Connect Business Law offers a number of powerful tools and features to make managing assignments easier, so faculty can spend more time teaching. With *Connect Business Law*, students can engage with their coursework anytime and anywhere, making the learning process more accessible and efficient. *Connect Business Law* offers you the features described below.

Simple Assignment Management

With *Connect Business Law*, creating assignments is easier than ever, so you can spend more time teaching and less time managing. The assignment management function enables you to:

- Create and deliver assignments easily with selectable end-of-chapter questions and test bank items.
- Streamline lesson planning, student progress reporting, and assignment grading to make classroom management more efficient than ever.
- Go paperless with the eBook and online submission and grading of student assignments.

Smart Grading

When it comes to studying, time is precious. *Connect Business Law* helps students learn more efficiently by providing feedback and practice material when they need it, where they need it. When it comes to teaching, your time also is precious. The grading function enables you to:

- Have assignments scored automatically, giving students immediate feedback on their work and side-by-side comparisons with correct answers.
- Access and review each response; manually change grades or leave comments for students to review.
- Reinforce classroom concepts with practice tests and instant quizzes.

Instructor Library

The *Connect Business Law* Instructor Library is your repository for additional resources to improve student engagement in and out of class. You can select and use any asset that enhances your lecture. The *Connect Business Law* Instructor Library includes:

- *Ebook*
- *Instructor's Manual*
- *PowerPoint files*
- *Videos and Instructional Notes*
- *Business Law Newsletter archives*
- *Access to interactive study tools*

Student Study Center

The *Connect Business Law* Student Study Center is the place for students to access additional resources. The Student Study Center:

- Offers students quick access to lectures, practice materials, eBooks, and more.
- Provides instant practice material and study questions, easily accessible on the go.
- Gives students access to the Personalized Learning Plan described below.

Student Progress Tracking

Connect Business Law keeps instructors informed about how each student, section, and class is performing, allowing for more productive use of lecture and office hours. The progress-tracking function enables you to:

- View scored work immediately and track individual or group performance with assignment and grade reports.
- Access an instant view of student or class performance relative to learning objectives.
- Collect data and generate reports required by many accreditation organizations, such as AACSB.

Lecture Capture

Increase the attention paid to lecture discussion by decreasing the attention paid to note taking. For an additional charge Lecture Capture offers new ways for students to focus on the in-class discussion, knowing they can revisit important topics later. Lecture Capture enables you to:

- Record and distribute your lecture with a click of a button.
- Record and index PowerPoint presentations and anything shown on your computer so that it is easily searchable, frame by frame.
- Offer access to lectures anytime and anywhere by computer, iPod, or mobile device.
- Increase intent listening and class participation by easing students' concerns about note taking. Lecture Capture will make it more likely you will see students' faces, not the tops of their heads.

McGraw-Hill *Connect Plus Business Law*

McGraw-Hill reinvents the textbook learning experience for the modern student with *Connect Plus Business Law*. A seamless integration of an eBook and *Connect Business Law, Connect Plus Business Law* provides all of the *Connect Business Law* features plus the following:

- An integrated eBook, allowing for anytime, anywhere access to the textbook.

- Dynamic links between the problems or questions you assign to your students and the location in the eBook where that problem or question is covered.

- A powerful search function to pinpoint and connect key concepts in a snap.

In short, *Connect Business Law* offers you and your students powerful tools and features that optimize your time and energies, enabling you to focus on course content, teaching, and student learning. *Connect Business Law* also offers a wealth of content resources for both instructors and students. This state-of-the-art, thoroughly tested system supports you in preparing students for the world that awaits.

For more information about Connect, go to **www.mcgrawhillconnect.com**, or contact your local McGraw-Hill sales representative.

Tegrity Campus: Lectures 24/7

 Tegrity Campus is a service that makes class time available 24/7 by automatically capturing every lecture in a searchable format for students to review when they study and complete assignments. With a simple one-click start-and-stop process, you capture all computer screens and corresponding audio. Students can replay any part of any class with easy-to-use browser-based viewing on a PC or Mac.

Educators know that the more students can see, hear, and experience class resources, the better they learn. In fact, studies prove it. With Tegrity Campus, students quickly recall key moments by using Tegrity Campus's unique search feature. This search helps students efficiently find what they need, when they need it, across an entire semester of class recordings. Help turn all your students' study time into learning moments immediately supported by your lecture.

To learn more about Tegrity, watch a 2-minute Flash demo at **http://tegritycampus.mhhe.com**.

Assurance of Learning Ready

Many educational institutions today are focused on the notion of *assurance of learning,* an important element of some accreditation standards. *Dynamic Business Law: The Essentials,* Second Edition, is designed specifically to support your assurance of learning initiatives with a simple, yet powerful, solution.

Each test bank question for *Business Law* maps to a specific chapter learning outcome/objective listed in the text. You can use our test bank software, EZ Test and EZ Test Online, or *Connect Business Law* to easily query for learning outcomes/objectives that directly relate to the learning objectives for your course. You can then use the reporting features of EZ Test to aggregate student results in similar fashion, making the collection and presentation of assurance of learning data simple and easy.

The **Best** of **Both Worlds**

McGraw-Hill and Blackboard

McGraw-Hill Higher Education and Blackboard have teamed up. What does this mean for you?

1. **Your life, simplified.** Now you and your students can access McGraw-Hill's *Connect* and *Create* right from within your Blackboard course—all with one single sign-on. Say goodbye to the days of logging in to multiple applications.

2. **Deep integration of content and tools.** Not only do you get single sign-on with *Connect* and *Create*, but you also get deep integration of McGraw-Hill content and content engines right in Blackboard. Whether you're choosing a book for your course or building *Connect* assignments, all the tools you need are right where you want them—inside Blackboard.

3. **Seamless gradebooks.** Are you tired of keeping multiple gradebooks and manually synchronizing grades into Blackboard? We thought so. When a student completes an integrated *Connect* assignment, the grade for that assignment automatically (and instantly) feeds into your Blackboard grade center.

4. **A solution for everyone**. Whether your institution is already using Blackboard or you just want to try Blackboard on your own, we have a solution for you. McGraw-Hill and Blackboard can now offer you easy access to industry-leading technology and content, whether your campus hosts it or we do. Be sure to ask your local McGraw-Hill representative for details.

AACSB Statement

McGraw-Hill Companies is a proud corporate member of AACSB International. Understanding the importance and value of AACSB accreditation, the authors of *Dynamic Business Law: The Essentials,* Second Edition, recognize the curricula guidelines detailed in the AACSB standards for business accreditation by connecting selected questions in the test bank to the six general knowledge and skill guidelines in the AACSB standards.

The statements contained in *Dynamic Business Law: The Essentials,* Second Edition, are provided only as a guide for the users of this textbook. The AACSB leaves content coverage and assessment within the purview of individual schools, the mission of the school, and the faculty. While *Dynamic Business Law: The Essentials,* Second Edition, and the teaching package make no claim of any specific AACSB qualification or evaluation, we have within *Dynamic Business Law: The Essentials,* Second Edition, labeled selected questions according to the six general knowledge and skill areas.

McGraw-Hill Customer Care Contact Information

At McGraw-Hill, we understand that getting the most from new technology can be challenging. That's why our services don't stop after you purchase our products. You can e-mail our Product Specialists 24 hours a day to get product-training online. Or you can search our knowledge bank of Frequently Asked Questions on our support website. For Customer Support, call **800-331-5094**, e-mail **hmsupport@mcgraw-hill.com**, or visit **www.mhhe.com/support**. One of our Technical Support Analysts will be able to assist you in a timely fashion.

Acknowledgments

This final component of the Preface contains a palpable tone of gratitude and humility. Any project the scope of *Dynamic Business Law: The Essentials*, Second Edition, is a collective activity; the authors are but the visible component of a remarkably large joint effort. We want to thank several contributors by name, but there are doubtlessly many other students, colleagues, and friends who made essential contributions to these pages.

Our largest gratitude goes to the dozens of business law colleagues who saved us from many embarrassing errors, while tolerating our stubborn reluctance to adhere to certain of their suggestions. In addition, the book could not have been written without the competent and dedicated research assistance we received from Lauren Biksacky, Andrew Reed, and Amanda Bunner.

We'd like to thank the following people for helping us with their comments and feedback on various stages of our manuscript:

William H. Bradley, *Azusa Pacific University*

Carol Brady, *Milwaukee Area Technical College*

Patrick Creehan, *Flagler College–Tallahassee Branch*

Peter Dawson, *Collin College*

Cheryl Davisson Gracie, *Washtenaw Community College*

Armand Grunberger, *American University– Washington, D.C.*

Marc Hall, *Auburn University–Montgomery*

Mark E. Handley, *Delaware Technical & Community College*

Cheryl L. Head, *Central Piedmont Community College*

Sarah Holcomb, *Northern Arizona University*

Russell E. Holmes, *Des Moines Area Community College*

Catherine G. Jones-Rikkers, *Grand Valley State University*

Steven C. Kaber, *Baldwin-Wallace College*

Christine W. Lewis, *Auburn University–Montgomery*

Darryll Lewis, *University of Nebraska–Omaha*

Jessica A. Magaldi, *Pace University*

Linda B. Meltzer, *Queensborough Community College*

Christine Mooney, *Queensborough Community College*

Sandra Mullings, *Baruch College, CUNY*

Tonia Murphy, *University of Notre Dame*

Michael J. O'Hara, *University of Nebraska–Omaha*

Michael Rogers, *Albany State University*

Sean D. Scott, *St. Petersburg College*

Bonnie S. Shane, *Sinclair Community College*

Harvey Slentz, *Florida State College–Jacksonville*

Michael Spagnoli, *American International College*

Dr. Robert J. Woods, *Texas Woman's University*

Finally, a book is but a raw, unsold manuscript until the skilled team at a publishing house starts to refine it. Our manuscript benefited immeasurably from the guidance of the multiple levels of skill provided to us by McGraw-Hill/Irwin. We respect and honor our Executive Editor, John Weimeister; our Development Editor, Megan Shultz; the book's Executive Marketing Manager, Sarah Schuessler; and its Senior Project Manager, Diane Nowaczyk.

Brief Contents

Contents

Appendixes

List of Cases

PART

1

CHAPTER

1

An Introduction to the Fundamentals of Dynamic Business Law and Business Ethics

LEARNING OBJECTIVES

After reading this chapter, you will be able to answer the following questions:

LO 1-1 What is business law?

LO 1-2 How does business law relate to business education?

LO 1-3 What are the purposes of law?

LO 1-4 What are alternative ways to classify the law?

LO 1-5 What are the sources of the law?

LO 1-6 What are the various schools of jurisprudence?

LO 1-7 What are business ethics and the social responsibility of business?

LO 1-8 How are business law and business ethics related?

LO 1-9 How can we use the WPH framework to make ethical business decisions?

LO 1-1

business law
The enforceable rules of conduct that govern the actions of buyers and sellers in market exchanges.

LO 1-2

This book is for future business managers, especially those who wish to be leaders. An essential factor in preparing for that career is awareness of the legal issues arising in business. Businesses need to finance capital growth, purchase inputs, and hire and develop employees. In addition, they must sell to consumers, please owners, and comply with government rules. All these activities are full of potential legal conflicts.

Business law consists of the enforceable rules of conduct that govern commercial relationships. In other words, buyers and sellers interact in market exchanges within the rules that indicate the boundaries of legal business behavior. Constitutions, legislatures, regulatory bodies, and courts spell out what market participants may or may not legally do.

Understanding business law is necessary for future businesspeople because there simply is no market transaction that occurs outside legal guidelines. All contracts, employment decisions, and payments to a supplier are limited and protected by business law. Each of the six functional areas of business—management, production and transportation, marketing, research and development, accounting and finance, and human resource management—sits on a foundation of business law.

Law and Its Purposes

LO 1-3

law
Rules of conduct in any organized society that are enforced by the governing authority of the community.

Many of us might like to impose rules on others, defining their rights and responsibilities. Few of us can do this as individuals, but a majority of citizens in a democracy can agree to establish rules for business behavior. They can permit certain authorities to make and enforce rules describing what behavior is permitted and encouraged in their community. These rules are what we refer to as the **law,** and they are enforceable in the courts of that community. Exhibit 1-1 lists a few of the numerous purposes fulfilled by the law.

Each purpose of the law is important, but taken as a unit, Exhibit 1-1 is a reminder of why we are very proud when we say we are a society of laws. The respect we give to the law as a source of authority is in part a recognition of the fact that in the absence of law, we would rely solely on the goodwill and dependability of one another. Most of us greatly prefer the law to that option.

Classification of the Law

LO 1-4

private law
Law that involves suits between private individuals or groups.

public law
Law that involves suits between private individuals or groups and their government.

civil law
The body of laws that govern the rights and responsibilities either between persons or between persons and their government.

There are many ways of thinking about the law. For example, we can divide law into *national* versus *international* law, *federal* versus *state* law, and *public* versus *private* law. **Private law** involves disputes between private individuals or groups. As an illustration, if a businessperson owns a computer equipment store and is delinquent in paying rent to the landlord, the dispute between them entails private law. **Public law** involves disputes between private individuals or groups and their government. For instance, if a computer store dumps waste behind its building in violation of local, state, or federal environmental regulations, the resulting dispute focuses on public law.

Another distinction among types of laws is civil law versus criminal law. **Civil law** involves the rights and responsibilities found in relationships between persons and between persons and their government. It also involves the remedies available when someone's rights are violated. One example of a civil law case involving a large business organization occurred in 1993. The

Exhibit 1-1

Purposes of the Law

- Providing order such that one can depend on a promise or an expectation of obligations.
- Serving as an alternative to fighting.
- Facilitating a sense that change is possible, but only after a rational consideration of options.
- Encouraging social justice.
- Guaranteeing personal freedoms.
- Serving as a moral guide by indicating minimal expectations of citizens and organizations.

restaurant chain Jack-in-the-Box was ordered to pay damages after a two-year-old child died of food poisoning from *E. coli* and several other people became ill from eating the tainted meat.

In contrast to civil law, **criminal law** applies to situations in which someone commits an act against the public as a unit. These crimes are prosecuted not by individuals but by the state or federal government.

One example of a criminal law is the prohibition against insider trading on the stock exchange. Insider trading occurs when an individual uses insider, or secret, company information to increase her or his own finances or those of family or friends. For example, several years ago an IBM secretary allegedly told her husband, who told several other people, that the company was going to take over operations of Lotus Development. This information was spread among a number of individuals before it was publicly announced.

On the basis of this leak, 25 people bought stock that increased greatly in value following IBM's public announcement. The Securities and Exchange Commission filed charges against the 25 stock purchasers because they were creating an unfair trading environment for the public.

criminal law
The body of laws that involve the rights and responsibilities an individual has with respect to the public as a whole.

Sources of Business Law

LO 1-5

How is law created, and where do we look to find the laws?

CONSTITUTIONS

The United States Constitution and the constitution of each state establish the fundamental principles and rules by which the United States and the individual states are governed. The term **constitutional law** refers to the general limits and powers of the federal and state governments as stated in their written constitutions. The U.S. Constitution is the supreme law of the land, the foundation for all laws in the United States. It is the primary authority when we are trying to identify the relationship between business organizations and government.

constitutional law
The general limits and powers of a government as interpreted from its written constitution.

STATUTES

Legislative actions, called *statutes,* are another important source of law. The assortment of rules and regulations put forth by legislatures is what we call **statutory law.** These legislative acts can be found in the United States Code when they are passed by Congress or in the various state codes when they are enacted by state legislatures. The codes are a collection of all the laws in one convenient location.

Because so much business activity occurs within the jurisdiction of state courts, business managers must be familiar with the local city and county ordinances that govern matters not covered by federal or state codes. These ordinances address important business considerations such as local taxes, environmental standards, zoning ordinances, and building codes.

For example, if you want to open a Krispy Kreme franchise in Santa Fe, New Mexico, you must follow local guidelines regarding the area where you may build your store, the materials that you may use to build, and the state minimum wage that you must pay to employees making donuts. The regulations will be different if you want to open your franchise in Toledo, Ohio, or in Seattle, Washington.

While they are not a source of law in the same sense as constitutions and statutory law, **model** or **uniform laws** serve as a basis for some statutory law at the state level. Business activity is made more difficult when state laws vary. To prevent such problems, a group of legal scholars and lawyers formed the National Conference of Commissioners on Uniform State Laws (NCC). The NCC regularly urges states to enact model laws to provide greater uniformity of law. The response is entirely in the hands of the state legislatures. They can ignore a suggestion or adopt part or all of the proposed model law.

The proposals of the NCC, while not laws themselves, have been adopted on more than 200 occasions by state legislatures. The NCC is an especially important influence on business law. Paired with the publications of the American Law Institute, the NCC became the source of the *Uniform Commercial Code (UCC).* The UCC is a body of law so significant for business activities

statutory law
The assortment of rules and regulations put forth by legislatures.

model laws
Laws created to account for the variability of laws among states. These laws serve to standardize the otherwise different interstate laws. Also called *uniform laws.*

that it will be the focus of intensive study in several chapters of this text. The UCC laws include sales laws and other regulations affecting commerce, such as bank deposits and collections, title documents, and warranties. For example, these laws govern the different types of warranties that companies such as Microsoft, Sony, and Honda provide with their products.

CASES

Constitutions, legislatures, and administrative agencies encourage certain behavior and prevent other actions. But the boundaries of these laws are seldom self-explanatory. Consequently, law must be interpreted.

Case law is the collection of legal interpretations made by judges. An alternative name for case law is **common law.** These interpretations are law unless they are revoked later by new statutory law.

Case law is especially significant for businesses because a modern business often operates in multiple legal jurisdictions. Because statutory laws are subject to interpretation, one court may have interpreted particular laws one way at one business location and a second court may interpret a similarly worded statute differently at a second business location.

Courts issue judicial decisions that often include interpretations of statutes and administrative regulations. These decisions contain the reasoning used by the courts to arrive at their decisions. The reasoning depends heavily on **precedent,** the use of past decisions to guide future decisions. An earlier decision in a similar fact pattern is a precedent that guides later decisions, thereby providing greater stability and predictability to the law.

It is crucial that business managers pay attention to changes in the law and cases in which new precedents are set. These precedents must be taken into account when making future business decisions. For instance, courts sometimes make new rulings regarding the kinds of warnings companies should be required to provide to consumers about potential harm that could result from their products.

One example was a case filed against McDonald's. After a woman was severely burned by very hot coffee, the company was found negligent for failing to provide a warning label on its hot-beverage cups. Now many retailers of hot beverages provide warning labels on their beverage cups because of the precedent that was set by this case.

When courts rely on precedent, they are obeying **stare decisis** ("standing by the decision"). Following stare decisis creates greater predictability for both businesses and individuals that look to the courts for the rules on which they should rely when they engage in market exchanges. In accordance with stare decisis, rulings that are made in higher courts become binding precedent for lower courts. If an issue is brought before a state court, the court will ascertain whether the state supreme court has made a decision on a similar issue, which would have then set a binding precedent that the lower court would need to follow.

Even though this practice is meant to create a consistent and reliable justice system, different judges may view the facts of a case in different ways. In addition, courts are sometimes presented with a new issue and do not have a binding decision to follow. In such instances, they may look to decisions made in similar cases by nonbinding courts in other states or jurisdictions.

If a new issue comes before two state courts and there is no binding decision from the state supreme court, both state courts need to look for other rulings on similar cases. They are not bound by each other's decision, and so they might have different decisions on the same subject. The decisions in these lower courts can be appealed to the state appeals court, however, and the appeals court's decision can be appealed to the state supreme court. If the state supreme court rules on the case, its decision is binding for the state but does not affect earlier decisions made by state courts. The state supreme court's decision affects only the decision being appealed and any future cases brought in the state on that particular subject.

One example of a case that has been used in accordance with stare decisis as a binding precedent is *Brown v. Board of Education,*[1] which abolished discriminatory policies for individuals of different racial backgrounds. For instance, in *Regents of the University of*

case law

The collection of legal interpretations made by judges. They are considered to be law unless otherwise revoked by a statutory law. Also known as *common law.*

precedent

A tool used by judges to make rulings on cases on the basis of key similarities to previous cases.

stare decisis

"Standing by the decision"; a principle stating that rulings made in higher courts are binding precedent for lower courts.

[1] 347 U.S. 483 (1954).

California v. Bakke,[2] the plaintiff, a white male, had applied to the University of California at Davis medical school two years in a row and been denied admittance. He alleged that the admissions process was discriminatory because out of 100 slots 16 were reserved for members of minority races.

The U.S. Supreme Court found that the school's admissions policy was not legal, referencing *Brown* and stating that the basic principle behind it and similar cases was that individuals could not be excluded on the basis of race or ethnicity. The Court wrote, "Preferring members of any one group for no reason other than race or ethnic origin is discrimination for its own sake."

Just as state statutes have been strongly influenced by the suggestions of the NCC, common law evolves with the assistance of a mechanism called **Restatements of the Law.** These Restatements are summaries of the common law rules in a particular area of the law that have been enacted by most states. The American Law Institute prepares the Restatements for contracts, agency, property, torts, and many other areas of law that affect business decisions. While the Restatements are not themselves a source of business law, judges frequently use them to guide their interpretations in a particular case.

In addition to the Restatements, many influences are at work in the minds of judges when they interpret constitutions, statutes, and regulations. For example, the values and social backgrounds of the judges function as lights and shadows, moving the judges toward particular legal decisions.

Restatements of the Law
Summaries of common law rules in a particular area of the law. Restatements do not carry the weight of law but can be used to guide interpretations of particular cases.

ADMINISTRATIVE LAW

Constitutions and statutes are never complete in the sense of covering all the detailed rules that affect government and business relations. The federal government, as well as state and local governments, has dozens of administrative agencies, whose task is to perform a particular government function. For example, the Environmental Protection Agency (EPA) has broad responsibilities to enforce federal statutes in the area of environmental protection.

Administrative law is the collection of rules and decisions made by all these administrative agencies. Just glance at Exhibit 1-2 to get a sense of the scope of a few of the major federal administrative agencies.

Businesses function within the rules established by agencies like these. For example, the Occupational Safety and Health Administration (OSHA) oversees health and workplace safety and makes sure that employees are working in conditions that are not hazardous. One instance in which OSHA exercised its authority occurred in 1994, when OSHA settled a complaint with United Parcel Service (UPS). The company was not providing adequate safety measures and equipment for workers who handled hazardous waste, and OSHA was responsible for making sure that UPS adapted its practices to follow federal safety guidelines.

administrative law
The collection of rules and decisions made by administrative agencies to fill in particular details missing from constitutions and statutes.

INDEPENDENT AGENCIES	EXECUTIVE AGENCIES
Commodity Futures Trading Commission (CFTC)	Federal Deposit Insurance Corporation (FDIC)
Consumer Product Safety Commission (CPSC)	Occupational Safety and Health Administration (OSHA)
Equal Employment Opportunity Commission (EEOC)	General Services Administration (GSA)
Federal Trade Commission (FTC)	National Aeronautics and Space Administration (NASA)
Federal Communications Commission (FCC)	
Interstate Commerce Commission (ICC)	Small Business Administration (SBA)
National Labor Relations Board (NLRB)	International Development Cooperative Agency (IDCA)
National Transportation Safety Board (NTSB)	National Science Foundation (NSF)
Nuclear Regulatory Commission (NRC)	Veterans Administration (VA)
Securities and Exchange Commission (SEC)	Office of Personnel Management (OPM)

Exhibit 1-2

Major Federal Administrative Agencies

[2] 438 U.S. 265 (1978).

TREATIES

A *treaty* is a binding agreement between two states or international organizations. Treaties may be called several things: international agreements, covenants, exchanges of letters, conventions, or protocols. In the United States, a treaty is generally negotiated by the executive branch. To be binding, it must then be approved by two-thirds of the Senate.

A treaty is similar to a contract in two important ways. Both treaties and contracts are attempts by parties to determine rights and obligations among themselves. In addition, when a party fails to obey a treaty or an international contract, international law imposes liability on that party.

EXECUTIVE ORDERS

The president and state governors can issue directives requiring that officials in the executive branch perform their functions in a particular manner. The Code of Federal Regulations (CFR) contains all the executive orders created by the president. (The CFR is online at www.gpoaccess .gov/cfr/index.html.) Presidents claim the power to issue such orders on the basis of their Article II, Section 1, constitutional power to "take care that the laws be faithfully executed."

An illustration of an especially controversial executive order is Order 9066, issued by President Franklin Roosevelt during World War II. On the basis of this order, Japanese-Americans on the West Coast, as well as thousands of Italian-American and German-American families, were sent to internment camps for the duration of the war.

LO 1-6

SCHOOLS OF LEGAL INTERPRETATION

When legislators or courts make law, they do so guided by certain habits of mind and specific beliefs about human nature. These views guide them toward particular legal solutions and away from others. This section briefly describes several of the more common guides to legal interpretation.

natural law
A school of jurisprudence that recognizes the existence of higher law, or law that is morally superior to human laws.

Natural Law The term **natural law** refers to the idea that there are certain ethical laws and principles that are morally right and "above" the laws devised by humans. This concept suggests that individuals should have the freedom to disobey a law enacted by a majority of people if their individual conscience goes against the law and they believe the law is wrong. The idea that people have basic human rights, for example, is rooted in the concept of natural law.

For instance, Dow Chemical wants its suppliers to conform to U.S. environmental and labor laws, not just the local laws in the supplier's country, where regulations may not be as stringent. This reaction reflects the beliefs that people have a right to be treated fairly in their jobs and that they have a right as human beings to a clean environment.

legal positivism
A school of jurisprudence which holds that because society requires authority, a legal and authoritarian hierarchy should exist. When a law is made, therefore, obedience is expected because authority created it.

Legal Positivism **Legal positivism** is an interpretive guide that urges us, as its followers, to design our legal system on the basis of the belief that legitimate political authority deserves our obedience when it issues a rule. This idea stresses that society requires authority and the hierarchy that such authority demands. When a duly authorized branch of government issues a law, positivism would urge us to see our proper role as obedience. The law is then a set of appropriate commands.

This view sees law as something quite distinct from morality. Moral questions about the law should not interfere with our inclination to obey it. A judge with leanings in the direction of legal positivism, for example, might write that she is deciding to enforce the law in question but that her decision does not necessarily mean that she sees the law as the morally correct rule.

identification with the vulnerable
A school of jurisprudence which holds that society should be fair. Particular attention is therefore paid to the poor, the ill, and the elderly.

Identification with the Vulnerable Closely linked to pursuing legal change through natural law is pursuing change through **identification with the vulnerable**. Some members of our society are able to take care of themselves in terms of most life situations. Others, especially the ill, children, the aged, the disabled, and the poor, require assistance to meet their fundamental needs of life, health, and education.

This guide to legal change is tied closely to the pursuit of fairness in our society. The metaphor of a level playing field is linked with some higher law or body of moral principles that connects all of us in the human community. We might look at a particular employment contract, for example, and react by observing that "it is just not fair." Our caring impulse as a human feels outrage

at that legal arrangement. That outrage can be a stimulus for legal change. One example of identification with the vulnerable is minimum-wage laws. They reflect the beliefs that workers should receive a minimum hourly wage and that employers should not be allowed to pay them less.

Historical School: Tradition One of the most often used guidelines for shaping the law is **tradition,** or *custom,* which is also called the **historical school.** Stare decisis is rooted in this perspective. When we follow tradition, we attempt to link our future behavior to the behavior of those who faced similar problems in earlier historical periods. The logic of the approach is that we need not reinvent the wheel each time a legal problem arises. Past practice is assumed to have been the product of careful thought.

Legal Realism **Legal realism** is based on the idea that, when ruling on a case, judges need to consider more than just the law. This school of thought dictates that they also take factors such as social and economic conditions into consideration when making a judgment. Followers of legal realism argue that the law must not be the sole factor in deciding a case since legal guidelines were designed by humans and exist in an ever-changing society.

Judges who follow this school of thought are more likely to depart from past court decisions to account for the fact that our society is constantly shifting and evolving. Those who subscribe to legal realism also believe that the law can never be enforced with complete consistency. They argue that because judges are human, they will bring different methods of reasoning to very similar cases.

One example of a law that has been enacted to reflect changes in our society is the Family and Medical Leave Act (FMLA). This act mandates that businesses employing more than 50 people must provide their workers with up to 12 weeks' unpaid leave every year to take care of family-related affairs such as caring for ill parents, adopting a child, or having a child. The FMLA protects pregnant women who take time off work, as their employers must provide them with the same pay and the same or an equivalent job when they return to work. This act reflects the fact that more mothers are working outside the home and more women are returning to work soon after they have a child. The FMLA also protects new parents against some types of employer discrimination that might occur after they return to work.

Cost-Benefit Analysis From this perspective, we need to examine all the costs and benefits for alternative laws or decisions and place monetary values on those costs and benefits. If we possessed those calculations, we could use **cost-benefit analysis** as a guide to legal change, choosing the legal alternatives that maximized the ratio of benefits to costs. For instance, in a contract dispute someone using this approach would attempt to attach responsibility for the problem in such a way that total benefit is maximized in relation to costs.

This approach to legal change is tied closely to the pursuit of efficiency. If a law yields more benefits than costs, then we have saved resources. Those resources can, in turn, be used to provide us with more goods and services. Our economy is thus more efficient in the sense of producing more for less.

For example, regulations enacted by the EPA can affect costs and benefits in the national economy. Polluted land is an economic loss because it cannot be used for farming or recreation. Polluted water can be toxic for fish and cannot be used for drinking. Polluted air can cause health problems and result in higher health care costs. While EPA regulations may end up costing companies more initially in order to control pollutants, the cost of environmental cleanup, and the loss of productivity in the economy as a whole, may be greater than the resources companies expend to control pollution.

Global and Comparative Law

Comparative and international law is extremely important for future business managers. Because of advances in technology and transportation, trade with other countries is far easier today than it was in past years. Now it is possible to make different components for the same product in various countries all over the world and then assemble them in another country. It is possible to operate an antique store in Poughkeepsie but sell to customers in Moscow or Taipei through a website.

As a result of this ease in trade, business managers must be familiar with global trade laws that regulate business practices among nations. For instance, the United States and other countries have entered into agreements such as the North American Free Trade Agreement (NAFTA)

historical school
A school of jurisprudence that uses traditions as the model for future laws and behavior. Also called *tradition* or *custom.*

legal realism
A school of jurisprudence which holds that context must be considered as well as law. Context includes factors such as economic conditions and social conditions.

cost-benefit analysis
An economic school of jurisprudence in which all costs and benefits of a law are given monetary values. Laws with the highest ratios of benefits to costs are then preferable to those with lower ratios.

and the General Agreement on Tariffs and Trade (GATT). These agreements help establish the conditions of trade between countries.

It is also important that future business managers understand comparative law, comparing and studying the laws in different countries. Business managers need to be aware of various trade laws and restrictions in different countries so that they can act accordingly when they set out to do business in those countries. The European Union, for example, has laws that differ from those of the United States in terms of regulating the taxes on Internet sales and the amount of pollution that can be released into the environment. Companies doing business in the EU must take these standards into account.

An example of a company that has conformed to a foreign country's laws is the search engine company Google, which has agreed to restrict the content of searches performed on Google.cn, the Chinese version of the company's search engine. Google took this action to satisfy regulations set by the Chinese government, which did not want its citizens to have access to certain websites or pieces of information. To do business in China, Google had to conform to these standards. This loss of freedom of information or access to information was considered by some to be such an "evil" that they felt Google had violated its own mission statement: "Do no evil."

Modern business managers must have an ongoing fascination with the law to function effectively. Business law tells business managers the basic rules of the business game. Play any game without having first studied the rules, and you will probably fail.

But, unlike an ordinary game, the business game has a rule book that is changing dynamically. In addition, increased globalization requires that business leaders be alert to legal differences among national jurisdictions.

LO 1-7 Business Ethics and Social Responsibility

ethics

The study and practice of decisions about what is good or right.

business ethics

The use of ethics and ethical principles to solve business dilemmas.

ethical dilemma

A question about how one should behave that requires one to reflect on the advantages and disadvantages of the optional choices for various stakeholders.

social responsibility of business

The expectations that a community places on the actions of firms inside that community's borders.

Ethics is the study and practice of decisions about what is good or right. Ethics guides us when we are wondering what we should be doing in a particular situation. **Business ethics** is the application of ethics to the special problems and opportunities experienced by businesspeople. An **ethical dilemma** is a problem about what a firm should do for which no clear, right decision is available. Reasonable people can expect to disagree about optimal solutions to ethical dilemmas.

Closely related to ethical dilemmas arising in business situations is the concept of the social responsibility of a business. The **social responsibility of business** consists of the expectations the community imposes on firms doing business within its borders. These expectations must be honored to a certain extent, even when a firm wishes to ignore them, because firms are always subject to the implicit threat that legislation will impose social obligations on them. So, if the community expects businesses to obey certain standards of fairness even when the standards interfere with profit maximization, firms that choose to ignore this expectation do so at their peril.

The definition of business ethics refers to *standards* of business conduct. *It does not result in a set of correct decisions.* Business ethics can improve business decisions by serving as a reminder to not simply choose the first business option that comes to mind or the one that enriches the firm in the short run. But business ethics can never produce a list of correct business decisions that all ethical businesses will make.

LO 1-8 Business Law and Business Ethics

Before business managers consider the social responsibilities of firms in their communities, they need to gather all the relevant facts. Experienced managers know that assembling the facts is just the beginning of a thoughtful business decision. Next, it makes sense to ask, *Is it legal to go forward with this decision?*

The legality of the decision is the minimal standard that must be met. But the existence of that minimum standard is essential for the development of business ethics. To make this point, let's take a look at the growing practice of bribery in the absence of legal standards. In some countries businesses must pay bribes to receive legitimate supplies. Although the businessperson may be morally opposed to paying the bribes, the supplies are necessary to stay in business and there may be no other means of obtaining them.

Thus, foreign companies face an ethical dilemma: They must decide whether to pay bribes or find alternative sources of supplies. For instance, when McDonald's opened its doors in Moscow, it made arrangements to receive its supplies from foreign providers. These arrangements ensured that the franchise did not have to engage in questionable business practices.

At the same time that business ethics guides decisions within firms, ethics helps guide the law. Law and business ethics serve as an interactive system—informing and assessing each other. For example, our ethical inclination to encourage trust, dependability, and efficiency in market exchanges shapes many of our business laws. The principles of contract law, for instance, facilitate market exchanges and trade because the parties to an exchange can count on the enforceability of agreements. Legal rules that govern the exchange have been shaped in large part by our sense of commercial ethics.

Of course, different ethical understandings prevail in different countries. Thus, ethical conceptions shape business law and business relationships uniquely in each country. Increasingly, business leaders require sensitivity to the differences in legal guidelines in the various countries in which they operate. These differences are based on somewhat different understandings of ethical behavior among businesspeople in diverse countries.

As we mentioned above, business ethics does not yield one "correct" decision. So how are business managers to chart their way through the ethical decision-making process? One source of assistance consists of the general theories and schools of thought about ethics. Each ethical system provides a method for resolving ethical dilemmas by examining duties, consequences, or virtues.

In the interest of providing future business managers with a practical approach to business ethics *that they can use,* we suggest a three-step process: the **WPH approach.** This approach provides future business managers with some **ethical guidelines,** or practical steps, that serve as a dependable stimulus to ethical reasoning in a business context. Appendix 1A provides the theoretical basis for the WPH approach used in this book.

> **WPH approach (to ethical decision making)**
> A set of ethical guidelines that urges us to consider whom an action affects, the purpose of the action, and how we view its morality.
>
> **ethical guideline**
> A simple tool that helps determine whether an action is moral.

LO 1-9

> **stakeholders**
> The groups of people affected by a firm's decisions.

The WPH Framework for Business Ethics

A useful set of ethical guidelines requires the recognition that managerial decisions must meet the following primary criteria (Exhibit 1-3):

- The decisions affect particular groups of stakeholders in the operations of the firm. The pertinent question is thus, *Whom* would this decision affect?
- The decisions are made in pursuit of a particular *purpose.* Business decisions are instruments toward an ethical end.
- The decisions must meet the standards of action-oriented business behavior. Managers need a doable set of guidelines for *how* to make ethical decisions.

WHO ARE THE RELEVANT STAKEHOLDERS?

The **stakeholders** of a firm are the many groups of people affected by the firm's decisions. Any given managerial decision affects, in varying degrees, the following stakeholders:

1. Owners or shareholders.
2. Employees.

Exhibit 1-3

The WPH Process of Ethical Decision Making

1. **W—WHO (Stakeholders):**
 Customers
 Owners or investors
 Management
 Employees
 Community
 Future generations
2. **P—PURPOSE (Values):**
 Freedom
 Security
 Justice
 Efficiency
3. **H—HOW (Guidelines):**
 Public disclosure
 Universalization
 Golden Rule

3. Customers.
4. Management.
5. The general community where the firm operates.
6. Future generations.

Managers should make sure they consider all relevant stakeholders when they engage in ethical reasoning.

WHAT ARE THE ULTIMATE *PURPOSES* OF THE DECISION?

values

Positive abstractions that capture our sense of what is good and desirable.

When we think about the ultimate reason or purpose that we make decisions in a business firm, we turn to the basic unit of business ethics—values. **Values** are positive abstractions that capture our sense of what is good or desirable. They are *ideas* that underlie conversations about business ethics. We derive our ethics from the interplay of values. Values represent our understanding of the purposes we will fulfill by making particular decisions.

For example, we value honesty. We want to live in communities where the trust we associate with honesty prevails in our negotiations with one another. Business depends on the maintenance of a high degree of trust. No contract can protect us completely against every possible contingency. So we need some element of trust in one another when we buy and sell.

If we think about the definition of values for a moment, we realize two things. First, a huge number of values pull and push our decisions. Second, to state that a value is important in a particular situation is to start a conversation about what is meant by that particular value.

To help make WPH useful to you as a manager, Exhibit 1-4 outlines an efficient way to apply this second step in the WPH framework. The exhibit identifies four of the most important values influencing business ethics and presents alternative meanings for each. This table should not only help clarify the importance of values in your own mind but also enable you to question others who claim to be acting ethically.

For instance, a manager might be deciding whether to fire an employee whose performance is less than impressive. In making the decision, the manager explores alternative visions of key values such as justice and efficiency and then makes choices about which action to take. Values and their alternative meanings are often the foundation for different ethical decisions.

Exhibit 1-4

Primary Values and Business Ethics

VALUE	ALTERNATIVE MEANINGS
Freedom	1. To act without restriction from rules imposed by others
	2. To possess the capacity or resources to act as one wishes
	3. To escape the cares and demands of this world entirely
Security	1. To possess a large-enough supply of goods and services to meet basic needs
	2. To be safe from those wishing to interfere with your property rights
	3. To achieve the psychological condition of self-confidence to such an extent that risks are welcome
Justice	1. To receive the products of your labor
	2. To treat all humans identically, regardless of race, class, gender, age, and sexual preference
	3. To provide resources in proportion to need
	4. To possess anything that someone else is willing to grant you
Efficiency	1. To maximize the amount of wealth in society
	2. To get the most from a particular output
	3. To minimize costs

Business Ethics and Swedish Advertising Law

Recall from the WPH approach to ethical decision making that when businesses make decisions, they should consider *all* the relevant stakeholders. One relevant stakeholder is the customer, or consumer. In Sweden, consumers are assumed to be vulnerable in the marketplace; therefore, protecting the consumer is considered to be the job of the government. Unlike the case in the United States, in Sweden public policy acknowledges that "there exist large groups of consumers who, owing to low incomes, deficient education and knowledge of the market, etc., are less well equipped than the average citizen for their role as consumers." One group of consumers less equipped than the average citizen in Sweden is children.

The government considers children to be extra vulnerable and impressionable and thus in need of even more protection than the average consumer. Swedish laws ban all television advertising targeting children below the age of 12. The ban includes not only toy advertisements but also commercials for foods high in fat and sugar, such as sweets and fast food. Advertisements for such products can be aired if the targets of the advertisements are not children. For example, commercials for toys, sweets, and foods high in fat may be aired if they are designed to attract and inform adults, as opposed to children. What may surprise many Americans is that almost 90 percent of Swedish advertising professionals are in favor of the ban on advertising to children because they recognize that such advertising is misleading since children do not understand the commercial nature and purpose of advertising.

HOW DO WE MAKE ETHICAL DECISIONS?

Making ethical decisions has always been one of our most confusing *and* important human challenges. In the process of meeting this challenge, we have discovered a few general, ethical guidelines to assist us. An *ethical guideline* provides one path to ethical conduct. Notice that all three ethical guidelines below reflect a central principle of business ethics: consideration of stakeholders.

The Golden Rule The idea that we should interact with other people in a manner consistent with the way we would like them to interact with us has deep historical roots. Both Confucius and Aristotle suggested versions of that guideline. One scholar has identified six ways the Golden Rule can be interpreted:

1. Do to others as you want them to gratify you.
2. Be considerate of others' feelings as you want them to be considerate of yours.
3. Treat others as persons of rational dignity like you.
4. Extend brotherly or sisterly love to others, as you would want them to do to you.
5. Treat others according to moral insight, as you would have others treat you.
6. Do to others as God wants you to do to them.

Regardless of the version of the Golden Rule we use, this guideline urges us to be aware that other people—their rights and needs—matter. The focus on others that is the foundation of the Golden Rule is also clearly reflected in a second ethical guideline: the public disclosure test.

Public Disclosure Test One way to think of the public disclosure test is to view it as a ray of sunlight that makes our actions visible, rather than obscured. The public disclosure test is sometimes called the "television test," for it requires us to imagine that our actions are being broadcast on national television. The premise behind this general guideline is that ethics is hard work, labor that we might resist if we did not have frequent reminders that we live in a community. Given our role as a member of a community, our self-concept is tied, at least in part, to how that community perceives us.

Universalization Test A third general guideline shares with the other two a focus on the "other"—the stakeholders whom our actions affect. Before we act, the **universalization test** asks us to consider what the world would be like were our decision copied by everyone else. Applying

universalization test
The ethical guideline that urges us to consider, before we do an action, what the world would be like if everyone acted in this way.

11

the universalization test causes us to wonder aloud: "Is what I am about to do the kind of action that, *were others to follow my example,* makes the world a better place for me and those I love?"

In summary, business managers can apply the WPH approach to most ethical dilemmas. The WPH framework provides a practical process suited to the frequently complex ethical dilemmas that business managers must address quickly in today's society.

Questions & Problems

1. What is the difference between private law and public law?

2. What are the main distinctions between the different schools of legal interpretation?

3. How do business ethics and business law interact with each other?

4. How does the WPH approach to ethics respond to an ethical problem?

5. Jarold Daniel Friedman worked as a temporary computer contractor for a pharmaceutical warehouse. The warehouse offered him a permanent position, but the warehouse required that he get a mumps vaccine, grown in chicken embryos, as a condition of his permanent employment. Friedman, a vegan, believed that the vaccination would violate his religious beliefs and declined to be vaccinated. As a result, the warehouse withdrew its offer of employment. Friedman claimed that the warehouse discriminated against him on the basis of religion. Do you agree with Friedman? Do employers have a duty to respect the beliefs of their employees? If so, what happens when that duty conflicts with employers' duty to provide a safe and healthy work environment? [*Friedman v. Southern California Permanente Medical Group,* 102 Cal. App. 4th 39 (2002).]

6. In 1999, an 18-year-old computer science student, Shawn Fanning, started an Internet website and file-sharing service that enabled users to download digital music files, or MP3s, from other users' computers across the Internet. Fanning's Napster included a centralized server that indexed files and created a searchable list of the music available across Napster's network. Through this software, users were able to find and download copyrighted digital song files for free. The plaintiffs, led by A&M Records, alleged copyright infringement by Napster, and filed a motion for a preliminary injunction to stop the exchange of copyrighted music on Napster immediately. The judge agreed and granted a preliminary injunction that prohibited Napster from engaging in or facilitating others in copying, downloading, uploading, transmitting, or distributing plaintiffs' copyrighted musical compositions and sound recordings, protected by either federal or state law, without express permission of the rights owner. On appeal, the circuit court agreed and ordered a stay of the district court's injunction, pending resolution. What values do you think influenced the court's decision granting the injunction against sharing copyrighted material? Do you agree with the court's decision? If not, what values are guiding your decision? [*A&M Records, Inc. v. Napster, Inc.,* 239 F.3d 1004 (2001).]

7. Tyco International, a manufacturing company, sued its former CEO, Dennis Kozlowski, in regard to his receipt of unauthorized bonuses from the company profits. Among his other wrongdoings, Kozlowski awarded unauthorized "special bonuses" to himself and over 40 other Tyco employees. In sum, he misappropriated from company funds over $100 million that he was not authorized to receive. Included in this misappropriation was the use of company funds for personal expenditures, such as $18 million to buy and redecorate his New York City apartment and $1 million for his wife's 40th birthday party, held on the Italian island of Sardinia. The extravagant party featured an ice sculpture of the statue of David urinating Stolichnaya vodka. Based on these and other corporate misdeeds in related criminal proceedings, Kozlowski is currently serving 8.33 to 25 years at the Mid-State Correctional Facility in New York. How do you think Kozlowski would have acted had he considered the public disclosure test before engaging in these corporate misdeeds? What if he applied the universalization test? [*Tyco Intl, Ltd. v. Kozlowski,* 2005 DNH 68; 2005 U.S. Dist. LEXIS 6867 (April 21, 2005.)]

8. In Arkansas, methamphetamine (meth) was manufactured primarily in small toxic labs (STLs) located in homes, tents, barns, or hotel rooms. According to the plaintiffs (a number of counties in Arkansas), Arkansas had one of the highest numbers of STLs in the nation. The counties alleged that they had spent significant amounts of taxpayer dollars combating the manufacture of methamphetamine, including law enforcement costs for locating, eliminating, and

cleaning up STLs; prison and jail costs for housing illegal users, dealers, and manufacturers; addiction treatment costs for users and addicts; payments to family service agencies for housing and treating children whose parents were arrested on meth-related charges; and costs for treating the physical side effects of meth use and exposure to its production. To recoup these costs, the plaintiffs sought compensation from Pfizer, Inc., and other manufacturers of cold and allergy medicines. They brought the suit against these manufacturers because meth cannot be produced without ingredients from their cold and allergy medicines. What ethical duties, if any, do you think the drug manufacturers owe to the state or people in this case? Apply the WPH framework to help reach your conclusions. [*Ashley County et al. v. Pfizer, Inc.,* 552 F.3d 659; 2009 U.S. App. LEXIS 19.]

9. Jennifer Erickson sued her employer, Bartell Drug Company, contending that its decision not to cover prescription contraceptives under its employee prescription drug plan constituted sex discrimination. Bartell argued that its decision was not sex discrimination because contraceptives were preventive, were voluntary, and did not treat an illness. With whom do you agree? Why? What values did you use to reach your conclusion? [*Erickson v. Bartell Drug Co.,* 141 F. Supp. 2d 1266 (2001).]

10. Entertainment Network, Inc. (ENI), a business that provided news, entertainment, and information via the Internet, sued government officials who prohibited the company from filming the execution of Oklahoma City bomber Timothy McVeigh and selling the footage of the execution online. The government officials argued that a Justice Department regulation prohibiting audio and visual recording devices at federal executions applied in the case at hand. ENI, however, argued that the regulation violated the company's First Amendment right to free speech. How do you think the court should have ruled in this case? Do you think ENI might have altered its decision to broadcast the execution if it had applied the Golden Rule? [*Entm't Network, Inc. v. Lappin,* 134 F. Supp. 2d 1002 (2001).]

11. Titan Distribution, Inc., had subcontracted with a company that provided employees, but Titan later decided to hire its own employees and end the subcontracting contract. Robert Chalfant worked for the subcontracted company, and when Titan made this change, Chalfant sought the same position with Titan that he had held while employed by the subcontractor. Although Titan initially indicated that Chalfant passed his physical examination and would be hired, the company subsequently decided that he failed the physical and it did not hire him. The evidence indicated that Titan mistakenly believed that Chalfant's physical ailments substantially limited his ability to work, that he previously performed and remained able to perform the functions of the job, and that the refusal to hire him on the basis of the allegedly failed physical was linked to his disability. Further, Titan's inconsistent and unexplained decision-making process, with knowledge of the federal discrimination laws, was sufficient to support an award of punitive damages. Later you will learn about discrimination, but right now consider the ethical issues of this case. What ethical issues do you think should be considered? Recall the "P" of the WPH framework: What is the purpose, or values, in the decision? What values are at odds in the dilemma outlined in this case? [*Chalfant v. Titan Distribution, Inc.,* 475 F.3d 982 (2007).]

Looking for more review material?

The Online Learning Center at **www.mhhe.com/kubasekess2e** contains this chapter's "Assignment on the Internet" and also a list of URLs for more information, entitled "On the Internet." Find both of them in the Student Center portion of the OLC, along with quizzes and other helpful materials.

Critical Thinking and Business Law

critical thinking skills
The ability to understand the structure and worth of an argument by evaluating the facts, issue, reasons, and conclusion of that argument.

Success in the modern business firm requires the development of **critical thinking skills**—the ability to understand what someone is saying and then to apply a set of evaluative criteria to determine the worth of what was said. In other words, businesspeople need to be able to sort sense from nonsense by evaluating arguments about relevant business law.

A critical thinker is always asking, "Now does that make sense?" And there is no better context in which to develop critical-thinking skills than in the study of the laws that affect business. Critical-thinking skills learned in the study of business law will be easily transferred to the decisions of business stakeholders.

Legal reasoning is similar to other reasoning in some ways and different in others. When people, including lawyers and judges, reason, they do so for a purpose. Some problem or dilemma bothers them. The stimulus that gets them thinking is a *legal issue*. It is stated as a question because it is a call for action. It requires us to *do* something, to think about answers.

For instance, we may be interested in such issues as the following:

- When are union organizers permitted under the National Labor Relations Act to trespass on an employer's property?
- Do tobacco manufacturers have liability for the deaths of smokers?
- Must a business fulfill a contract when the contract is made with an unlicensed contractor in a state requiring that all contractors be licensed?

Each of these questions has several potential answers. Which answer best accomplishes a particular business objective? Which answers are consistent with the law? Here is where critical thinking is essential to business success. Some answers can get the decision maker into trouble; others will advance the intended purpose. Each answer is called a *conclusion*.

Business firms often come into contact with such conclusions in the form of laws or court decisions. Business managers are therefore both consumers of and contributors to these legal conclusions. As businesspeople learn about and react to decisions or conclusions made by courts, they have two primary methods of response:

1. Memorizing and understanding the conclusions or rules of law as a guide for future business decisions.
2. Making judgments about the quality of the conclusions.

This book encourages you to do both. There are many forms of critical thinking, but they all share one characteristic: They focus on the quality of someone's reasoning. Critical thinking is active; it challenges each of us to form judgments about the quality of the link between a set of reasons and the conclusion supposedly derived from them. In particular, we will be focusing on the link between a court's reasons and its conclusions.

Our reactions to legal arguments shape our efforts to either support the status quo in the legal environment of business or offer support for particular changes.

The following structure for critical thinking is a thoroughly tested method used by successful market decision makers. Every time you read a case, try to follow this pattern of careful thinking.

1. Find the facts.

 Facts: Here we are looking for the most basic building blocks in a legal decision or argument. These building blocks, or facts, provide the environment or context in which the legal issue is to be resolved. Certain events occurred; certain actions were or were not taken; particular persons behaved or failed to behave in specific ways. All of these and many more possibilities together make up the intricate setting for the playing out of the issue in question. We always wonder, What happened in this case?

2. Look for the issue.

 Issue: In almost any legal conflict, finding and expressing the issue is an important step in forming our reaction. The issue is the question that caused the lawyers and their clients to enter the legal system. Usually, there are several reasonable perspectives concerning the

correct way to word the issue in dispute. Don't let the possibility of *multiple* useful ways to word the issue cause you any confusion. The legal issue is certainly not just anything that we say it is.

3. Identify the judge's reasons and conclusion.

Reasons and conclusion: Judges do not form legal conclusions on the basis of whim. They have support for their decisions. That support consists of their reasons. When we ask someone *why* a judge formed a particular conclusion, we are showing our respect for reasons as the proper basis for any assertion. We want a world rich with opinions so that we can have a broad field of choice. But we should agree with only those legal opinions that have convincing reasons supporting the conclusion. Asking "Why?" is our way of saying, "I want to believe you, but you have an obligation to help me by sharing the reasons for your conclusion."

4. Locate in the decision the rules of law that govern the judge's reasoning.

Rules of law: Judges cannot offer just any reasoning that they please. They must always look back over their shoulders at the laws and previous court decisions that together provide an anchor for current and future decisions. What makes legal reasoning so complex is that statutes and legal findings are never *crystal* clear. They may seem very clear, but judges and businesspeople have room for interpretive flexibility in their reasoning.

5. Apply critical thinking to the reasoning.

Evaluation of the reasoning: A judge's reasoning, once it has been laid before us by following the steps discussed here, is a message that we may either accept or reject. One of the most exciting things about our legal system is its potential for change. **Critical thinking in the legal context** consists of examining the legal opinion in search of potential problems in the reasoning.

critical thinking in the legal context
Examining a legal opinion to search for potential problems in the reasoning.

Here is a small sample of some especially useful critical-thinking guidelines for business managers to apply when thinking about business law:

- *Look for potential ambiguity in the reasoning.* The term *ambiguity* refers to a lack of clarity in a word or phrase in the reasoning. Many words have multiple meanings; until the intended meaning is discovered, we cannot tell whether we want to agree or disagree with the reasoning.

- *Ask whether the analogies used in the decision are strong.* When judges follow particular precedents, they are saying that the key similarities between the facts in the precedent and those in the case at hand are so similar that it makes sense to apply the same rule of law in both. Are there key differences in the factual situations that raise questions about the quality of that analogy?

- *Check the quality of the judge's use of evidence in his or her reasoning.* Is the evidence used by the judge to support the opinion both abundant enough and reliable enough that we should agree with the reasoning?

- *Think about the extent to which important missing information prevents you from being totally confident about the judge's reasoning.* Is there important missing information that you would need to have before making up your mind?

- *Consider the possibility of rival causes.* When the judge claims that one action caused another, think about whether some alternative cause may have been responsible.

The U.S. Legal System and Alternative Dispute Resolution

Questionable Jurisdiction over Caterpillar

James Lewis, a resident of Kentucky, sustained an injury while operating a Caterpillar bulldozer. He filed suit against Caterpillar, a company incorporated in Delaware but with its principal place of business in Illinois. Lewis also filed suit against the supplier of the bulldozer, Whayne Supply Company, whose principal place of business was Kentucky. Lewis filed his case in a Kentucky state court, alleging defective manufacture, negligence, failure to warn, and breach of warranty. Lewis and Whayne Supply Company agreed to settle out of court. Caterpillar then filed a motion to exercise its right of removal (its right to move the case from the state to the federal court system), arguing that the federal court had jurisdiction over the case because Caterpillar and Lewis were from different states. Lewis disagreed with Caterpillar's contention, claiming that because he had not completed his settlement with Whayne, the case still included a defendant (Whayne) from Lewis's state, Kentucky. Thus, Lewis argued, federal courts did not have jurisdiction over the case.

The court agreed with Caterpillar's argument and moved the case to a federal district court. Shortly thereafter, Lewis and Whayne finalized their settlement agreement, and the district court dismissed Whayne from the lawsuit. The federal district court granted Caterpillar a favorable judgment. Lewis, however, appealed the district court's decision, renewing his argument that the district court did not have jurisdiction over the case. The court of appeals agreed with Lewis, holding that because Whayne was a defendant in the case at the time that Caterpillar moved the case from state to federal court, the diversity of citizenship necessary to give the federal court jurisdiction over the case was absent. Thus, a state court should have resolved the dispute. Consequently, the appellate court vacated the district court's decision. Caterpillar then appealed to the U.S. Supreme Court.

1. What factors determine whether the state or federal court system hears a case?
2. If you were a businessperson with Caterpillar, why might you prefer that a federal court hear the dispute with Lewis, rather than a state court?

After reading this chapter, you will be able to answer the following questions:

LO 2-1 What types of jurisdiction must a court have to render a binding decision in a case?

LO 2-2 What is venue?

LO 2-3 What are the threshold requirements that must be met before a court will hear a case?

LO 2-4 What are the steps in civil litigation?

LO 2-5 How are the various forms of alternative dispute resolution used by businesses today?

As the Case Opener illustrates, when a dispute arises, parties in this country do not simply go "to court." They often must choose between federal and state court systems. This chapter examines these systems, as well as the trial procedures that apply in civil cases.

Jurisdiction

A useful way to understand jurisdiction is to think of it as courts' power to hear cases and render decisions that bind the parties before them. A court must have several types of jurisdiction to decide any particular case.

ORIGINAL VERSUS APPELLATE JURISDICTION

Trial courts, or **courts of original jurisdiction,** have the power to hear and decide cases when they first enter the legal system. In these courts, the parties present evidence and call witnesses to testify. In most states, these courts are called *courts of common pleas* or *county courts.* In the federal system, these trial courts are called *federal district courts.*

Courts of appellate jurisdiction, or **appellate courts,** have the power to review previous judicial decisions to determine whether trial courts erred in their decisions. Appellate courts do not hold trials. Instead, appellate judges review transcripts of trial court proceedings and occasionally consider additional oral and written arguments from each party.

Appellate courts handle only questions of law, not questions of fact. A **question of law** is an issue concerning the interpretation or application of a law. In contrast, a **question of fact** is a question about an event or characteristic in the case. For example, whether a white student yelled racial slurs on a college campus is a question of fact. On the other hand, whether the First Amendment protects the student's right to utter racial slurs is a question of law.

Only judges can decide questions of law. Trial courts determine questions of fact. In a bench trial (a trial with no jury), the judge decides questions of fact; in a jury trial, the jury decides questions of fact. Appellate courts can, however, overrule trial courts' decisions on questions of fact, but only when the trial court's finding was clearly erroneous or when no trial evidence supports the trial court's finding.

To see how the choice-of-forum issue relates to the preparation of the articles of incorporation discussed in your finance class, please see the **Connecting to the Core** activity on the text website at www.mhhe.com/kubasekess2e.

trial court
A court in which most civil or criminal cases start when they first enter the legal system. The parties present evidence and call witnesses to testify. Trial courts are referred to as *courts of common pleas* or *county courts* in state court systems and as *district courts* in the federal system. Also called *court of original jurisdiction* and *court of first instance.*

appellate court
A higher court, usually consisting of more than one judge, that reviews the decision and results of a lower court (either a trial court or a lower-level appellate court) when a losing party files for an appeal. Appellate courts do not hold trials but may request additional oral and written arguments from each party; they issue written decisions, which collectively constitute case law or the common law. Also called *court of appellate jurisdiction.*

question of law
An issue concerning the interpretation or application of a law.

question of fact
A question about an event or characteristic in a case.

LO 2-1

in personam jurisdiction

The power of a court to require that a party (usually the defendant) or a witness come before the court. The court must have personal jurisdiction to enforce its judgments or orders against a party. *In personam* jurisdiction extends only to the state's borders in the state court system and across the court's geographic district in the federal system.

plaintiff

The person or party who initiates a lawsuit (also known as an *action*) before a court by filing a complaint with the clerk of the court against the defendant(s). Also known as *claimant* or *complainant*.

defendant

The person or party against whom a civil or criminal lawsuit is filed in a court of law.

complaint

A formal written document that begins a civil lawsuit; contains the plaintiff's list of allegations against the defendant, along with the damages the plaintiff seeks.

summons

A legal document issued by a court and addressed to a defendant that notifies him or her of the lawsuit and how and when to respond to the complaint. A summons may be used in both civil and criminal proceedings.

long-arm statute

A statute that enables a court to obtain jurisdiction against an out-of-state defendant as long as the defendant has sufficient minimum contacts within the state, such as committing a tort or doing business in the state.

JURISDICTION OVER PERSONS AND PROPERTY

In personam **jurisdiction** (literally, "jurisdiction over the person") is a court's power to render a decision affecting the rights of the specific persons before the court. Generally, a court's power to exercise *in personam* jurisdiction extends only over a specific geographic region. In the state court system, a court's *in personam* jurisdiction usually extends to the state's borders. In the federal system, each court's jurisdiction extends across its geographic district.

A court acquires *in personam* jurisdiction over a person (the **plaintiff**) when she files a lawsuit with the court. The court acquires jurisdiction over the person the plaintiff is suing (the **defendant**) when it gives him a copy of the complaint and a summons. The **complaint** specifies the factual and legal basis for the lawsuit and the relief the plaintiff seeks. The **summons** is a court order that notifies the defendant of the lawsuit and explains how and when to respond to the complaint.

Service of process is the procedure by which courts present these documents to defendants. Traditionally, courts used personal service: An officer of the court handed the summons and complaint to the defendant. Recently, however, courts have employed other methods of service, including *residential service,* in which a court representative leaves the summons and complaint with a responsible adult at the defendant's home, and *service by certified* or *ordinary mail.*

If the defendant is a corporation, courts generally serve either the president of the corporation or an agent whom the corporation has appointed to receive service. Most states require that corporations appoint an agent for service when they incorporate. Corporations are subject to *in personam* jurisdiction in three locations: the state of their incorporation, the location of their main offices, and the geographic areas in which they conduct business.

Courts have *in personam* jurisdiction over persons only within a specific geographic region. In the past, a state court could not acquire *in personam* jurisdiction over out-of-state defendants unless it served the defendants within the court's home state. Thus, defendants who injured plaintiffs could evade legal action by leaving the state and remaining outside its borders.

To alleviate this problem, most states have enacted **long-arm statutes** that enable the court to serve defendants outside the state as long as the defendant has sufficient minimum contacts within the state. Each state has its own minimum-contact requirements, but most state statutes hold that acts like committing a tort or doing business in the state are sufficient to allow the state to serve a defendant. In the Caterpillar case, the company sold products in Kentucky, and its products caused an injury in that state. These two facts were sufficient minimum contacts to allow the Kentucky court to serve Caterpillar, even though it was an out-of-state company. Contrast the facts in the Caterpillar case with those in the Case Nugget.

If a defendant has property in a state, a plaintiff may file suit against the defendant's property instead of against the owner. For example, suppose a Utah resident had not paid property taxes on a piece of land she owned in Idaho. Idaho courts have *in rem* **jurisdiction** (Latin for "jurisdiction over the thing") over the property. Thus, an Idaho state court has the power to seize the property and sell it to pay the property taxes in an *in rem* proceeding.

Courts can also gain **quasi *in rem* jurisdiction,** or *attachment jurisdiction,* over a defendant's property that is *unrelated* to the plaintiff's claim. For example, suppose Charlie, a Massachusetts resident, ran a red light while he was vacationing in California and collided with Jessica's car. Suppose further that Jessica suffered extensive injuries from the accident and successfully sued Charlie for $200,000 in a California state court. The California court can exercise quasi *in rem* jurisdiction over Charlie's California vacation home by seizing it, selling it, and transferring $200,000 to Jessica to satisfy her judgment against Charlie. If Charlie's vacation home is worth more than $200,000, however, the court must return the excess proceeds to Charlie.

SUBJECT-MATTER JURISDICTION

Subject-matter jurisdiction is a court's power to hear certain kinds of cases. Most industrialized countries have a single court system, with courts that have the power to hear both national law cases and local law cases. In contrast, the United States has both a state and a federal court system. Subject-matter jurisdiction determines which court system may hear a particular case. Cases may fall under state jurisdiction, exclusive federal jurisdiction, or concurrent jurisdiction. Figure 2-1 illustrates the subject-matter-jurisdiction divisions.

CASE Nugget

A Question of Minimum Contacts

Hagan v. Field

Court of Appeals of Texas, Fifth District, Dallas

2006 Tex. App. LEXIS 393

The plaintiff, a Texas resident, and the defendants, Colorado residents, were cat breeders who met at a cat show in Colorado. Subsequently, the plaintiff sent two cats to the defendants in Colorado for breeding and sent a third cat to them to be sold. A dispute over the return of the two breeding cats arose, and the plaintiff filed suit against the defendants in Texas. The defendants alleged that the Texas court lacked personal jurisdiction over them because they did not have minimum contacts within the state of Texas. The trial court disagreed, and the defendants appealed. The court of appeals reversed the decision of the trial court, finding that under the Texas long-arm statute, the Texas court could exercise jurisdiction over an out-of-state defendant only if (1) the defendant has purposefully established minimum contacts with the forum state and (2) the exercise of jurisdiction comports with traditional notions of fair play and substantial justice.

In this case, the defendants were not residents of Texas and had no business in Texas. The only contact the defendants had with Texas was a single trip they made to Texas to pick up two other cats, not related to the litigation, that they were going to take to a cat show. During that same visit, the defendants took a cat unrelated to the lawsuit to see a Texas veterinarian, and the plaintiff's husband assisted the defendants with a web page for their business. These actions, even in combination with the defendants' sending the plaintiff a check for the proceeds from the breeding, were not found to constitute sufficient minimum contacts to give the Texas court jurisdiction. The defendants were not availing themselves of the benefits of the state of Texas, nor were their contacts sufficient to put them on notice that they could be subject to the court's jurisdiction.

in rem **jurisdiction**
The power of a court over the property or status of an out-of-state defendant when that property or status is within the court's jurisdiction area.

quasi *in rem* jurisdiction
A type of jurisdiction exercised by a court over an out-of-state defendant's property that is within the jurisdictional boundaries of the court. It applies to personal suits against the defendant in which the property is not the source of the conflict but is sought as compensation by the plaintiff. Also called *attachment jurisdiction*.

subject-matter jurisdiction
The power of a court over the type of case presented to it.

Exclusive Federal Jurisdiction
- Admiralty cases
- Bankruptcy cases
- Federal criminal prosecutions
- Cases in which one state sues another state
- Claims against the United States
- Other claims involving federal statutes that specify exclusive federal jurisdiction

Concurrent Jurisdiction
- Federal-question cases
- Diversity-of-citizenship cases

Exclusive State Jursidiction
- All other cases

Figure 2-1

Subject-Matter-Jurisdiction Divisions

The Sliding-Scale Standard for Internet Transactions

Does a business that has Internet contact with a plaintiff in a different state satisfy the minimum-contacts standard?

A federal district court established the following "sliding-scale" standard in a 1997 case:*

> [T]he likelihood that personal jurisdiction can be constitutionally exercised is directly proportionate to the nature and quality of commercial activity that an entity conducts over the Internet. This sliding scale is consistent with well developed personal jurisdiction principles.

At one end of the spectrum are situations where a defendant clearly does business over the Internet. If the defendant enters into contracts with residents of a foreign jurisdiction that involve the knowing and repeated transmission of computer files over the Internet, personal jurisdiction is proper.

At the opposite end are situations where a defendant has simply posted information on an Internet website that is accessible to users in foreign jurisdictions. A passive website that does little more than make information available to those who are interested in it is not grounds for the exercise of personal jurisdiction.

The middle ground is occupied by interactive websites through which a user can exchange information with the host computer. In these cases, the exercise of jurisdiction is determined by examining the level of interactivity and the commercial nature of the exchange of information that occurs on the website.

* *Zippo Mfg. Co. v. Zippo Dot Com, Inc.*, 952 F. Supp. 1119 at 1124 (1997).

Exclusive Federal Jurisdiction　The federal court system has exclusive jurisdiction over very few cases: admiralty cases, bankruptcy cases, federal criminal prosecutions, lawsuits in which one state sues another state, claims against the United States, and patent, trademark, and copyright cases. Additionally, federal courts have exclusive jurisdiction over claims arising under federal statutes that specify exclusive federal jurisdiction.

State Jurisdiction　The state court system has a broad range of jurisdiction; state courts have the power to hear all cases not within the exclusive jurisdiction of the federal court system. State courts also have exclusive jurisdiction over certain cases, such as cases concerning adoption and divorce. Most cases, therefore, fall under state court jurisdiction. The Caterpillar case fell under state court jurisdiction because its subject matter—product liability and negligence—did not place the case under the exclusive jurisdiction of the federal court system.

Concurrent Federal Jurisdiction　Concurrent federal jurisdiction means that both state and federal courts have jurisdiction over a case. Concurrent jurisdiction covers two types of cases: federal-question and diversity-of-citizenship cases. *Federal-question* cases require an interpretation of the U.S. Constitution, a federal statute, or a federal treaty. For example, suppose a plaintiff alleges that a Florida campaign-financing law violates his First Amendment free speech rights. Because this case raises a federal question, it falls under concurrent jurisdiction, and both state and federal courts have the power to hear it.

A *diversity-of-citizenship* case must satisfy two conditions: (1) The plaintiff(s) does (do) not reside in the same state as the defendant(s), and (2) the controversy concerns an amount in excess of $75,000. Courts use the location of a party's residence to determine whether diversity of citizenship exists. Most federal court cases are based on diversity of citizenship.

A business may reside in two states: the state of its incorporation and the state of its principal place of business. Thus, in the Case Opener, Caterpillar was a resident of Delaware, the state where it incorporated, and of Illinois, the state of its primary place of business.

While the rule for determining what state a defendant is a citizen of may sound simple, determining where a corporation's principal place of business was caused a lot of controversy initially. Was it the place where most of the states' business activities occurred? Or was it the state where its headquarters was located? In Case 2-1, the Supreme Court finally clarified how courts should determine a corporation's "principal place of business."

HERTZ CORPORATION v. FRIEND
UNITED STATES SUPREME COURT
130 S. Ct. 1181 (2010)

FACTS: *California employees sued their employer, Hertz Corporation, in state court, alleging violations of the state's wage and hour laws. Defendant Hertz, claiming diversity of citizenship, removed the case to the federal district court. Hertz argued that it was a citizen of New Jersey because New Jersey is its principal place of business. It is its principal place of business because Hertz has facilities in 44 states but its leadership is at its corporate headquarters in New Jersey and its core executive and administrative functions are primarily carried out there. Hertz also stated that California accounted for only a small portion of its business activities.*

The District Court concluded that it lacked diversity jurisdiction because Hertz was a California citizen under Ninth Circuit precedent, which asks whether the amount of the corporation's business activity is "significantly larger" or "substantially predominates" in one state. Finding that California was Hertz's "principal place of business" under that test because a plurality of the relevant business activity occurred there, the District Court remanded the case to state court. Hertz appealed and the Ninth Circuit Court of Appeals affirmed. Hertz then appealed to the U.S. Supreme Court.

ISSUE: For purposes of establishing citizenship of a corporation to determine whether there is diversity of citizenship to give the federal court jurisdiction, what test should the courts use to determine a corporation's principal place of business, a "nerve center" test or a "predominance of business activity" test?

REASONING: "Principal place of business" is best read as referring to the place where a corporation's officers direct, control, and coordinate the corporation's activities. In practice it should normally be the place where the corporation maintains its headquarters—provided that the headquarters is the actual center of direction, control, and coordination, i.e., the "nerve center," and not simply an office where the corporation holds its board meetings.

Three reasons support use of the "nerve center" approach. The first is that the approach is consistent with the language of the jurisdictional statute. The statute's word "place" is singular, not plural. Its word "principal" requires that the main, prominent, or most important place be chosen. And the fact that the word "place" follows the words

"State where" means that the "place" is a place within a State, not the State itself. A corporation's "nerve center," usually its main headquarters, is a single place. The public often considers it the corporation's main place of business. And it is a place within a State. By contrast, the application of a more general business activities test has led some courts to look, not at a particular place within a State, but incorrectly at the State itself, measuring the total amount of business activities that the corporation conducts there and determining whether they are significantly larger than in the next-ranking State.

Second, administrative simplicity is desired in a jurisdictional statute. A "nerve center" approach, which ordinarily equates that "center" with a corporation's headquarters, is simple to apply comparatively speaking.

Third, the statute's legislative history suggests that the words "principal place of business" should be interpreted to be no more complex than an earlier, numerical test that was criticized as too complex and impractical to apply. A "nerve center" test offers such a possibility. A general business activities test does not.

This test is relatively easier to apply and does not require courts to weigh corporate functions, assets or revenues different in kind, one from the other. This test may produce results that seem to cut against the basic rationale of diversity jurisdiction; accepting occasionally counterintuitive results is the price the legal system must pay to avoid overly complex jurisdictional administration while producing the benefits that accompany a more uniform legal system.

DECISION AND REMEDY: For purposes of federal-court diversity jurisdiction, a corporation's "principal place of business" refers to the place, often called "nerve center," from which the corporation's high level officers directed, controlled and coordinated corporation's activities. While it appeared from the evidence that Hertz corporate offices and its "nerve center" are located in New Jersey, the respondents should have a fair opportunity on remand to litigate this issue in light of this holding as to the applicable rule.

SIGNIFICANCE OF THE CASE: The case settles a long-standing conflict among the circuits as to what test to apply to determine where a corporation's "primary place of business" is.

It is important to note that diversity must be complete for a case to fall under concurrent jurisdiction. In the Caterpillar case, Lewis argued that diversity was not complete because both he and the supply company, the second defendant he originally sued, were residents of Kentucky. The appellate court agreed with his argument and overturned the district court's decision because the district court lacked subject-matter jurisdiction.

When a plaintiff files a case involving concurrent jurisdiction in state court, the defendant has a *right of removal*. This right entitles the defendant to transfer the case to federal court. Thus, either party to a case involving concurrent jurisdiction can put the case in the federal court system: The plaintiff can file the case in federal court initially; or if the case was initially filed in state court, the defendant can transfer the case to federal court by exercising her right of removal. In the Case Opener, Caterpillar exercised its right of removal, and the state trial court moved the case to a federal district court.

LO 2-2

Venue

venue

(1) The place where a hearing takes place. Its geographic location is determined by each state's statutes and based on where the parties live or where the event occurred or the alleged wrong was committed. (2) A legal doctrine relating to the selection of a court with subject-matter and personal jurisdiction that is the most appropriate geographic location for the resolution of the dispute.

Once a case is in the proper court system, **venue** determines which trial court in the system will hear the case. Venue is a matter of geographic location that each state's statutes determine. Usually, the trial court for the county where the defendant resides is the appropriate venue. If a case involves property, the trial court where the property is located is also an appropriate venue. Finally, if the focus of the case is a particular incident, the trial court where the dispute occurred is an appropriate venue. The plaintiff initially chooses from among the appropriate venues when she files the case.

If the location of the court where the plaintiff filed the case is an inconvenience to the defendant or if the defendant believes it will be difficult to select an unbiased jury in that venue, he may request that the judge move the case by filing a motion for a change of venue. The judge has the discretion to grant or deny the motion.

The Structure of the Court System

The U.S. legal system has two parallel court structures: a federal system and a state system. Once a plaintiff files a case in one of the systems, the case remains in that system throughout the appeals process. The only exception to this rule occurs when a party to a lawsuit appeals the decision of a state supreme court to the U.S. Supreme Court.

THE FEDERAL COURT SYSTEM

The federal court system derives its power from Article III, Section 2, of the U.S. Constitution and consists of three main levels: trial courts, intermediate appellate courts, and the court of last resort. Figure 2-2 illustrates this system.

Figure 2-2 The Federal Court System

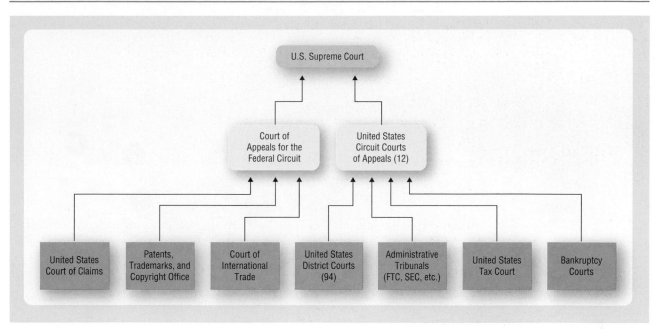

Federal Trial Courts In the federal court system, the trial courts, or courts of original jurisdiction, are U.S. district courts. The United States has 94 districts; each district has at least one trial court of general jurisdiction. Courts of general jurisdiction have the power to hear a wide range of cases and can grant almost any type of remedy. Almost every case in the federal system begins in one of these courts.

A small number of cases, however, do not begin in trial courts of general jurisdiction. For cases concerning certain subject matter, Congress has established special trial courts of limited jurisdiction. The types of cases heard by these special trial courts include bankruptcy cases, claims against the U.S. government, and copyright, patent, and trademark cases.

In an extremely limited number of cases, the U.S. Supreme Court functions as a trial court of limited jurisdiction. These cases include controversies between states and lawsuits against foreign ambassadors.

Intermediate Courts of Appeal The U.S. circuit courts of appeal make up the second level of courts in the federal system. The United States has 12 circuits, including a circuit for the District of Columbia. Each circuit court hears appeals from district courts in its geographic area. Additionally, a federal circuit court of appeals hears appeals from government administrative agencies. Figure 2-3 illustrates the geographic circuit divisions.

The Court of Last Resort The U.S. Supreme Court is the final appellate court in the federal system. Nine justices, who have lifetime appointments, make up the high court. Figure 2-4 identifies the nine justices on the U.S. Supreme Court.

The U.S. Supreme Court hears appeals of cases from the court of last resort in a state system. The Court will not, however, hear cases considering questions of pure state law. The Court also functions as a trial court on rare occasions.

STATE COURT SYSTEMS

No uniform state court structure exists because each state has devised its own court system, but most states have a structure similar to the federal court system's structure.

Figure 2-3 The Circuits of the Federal Court System

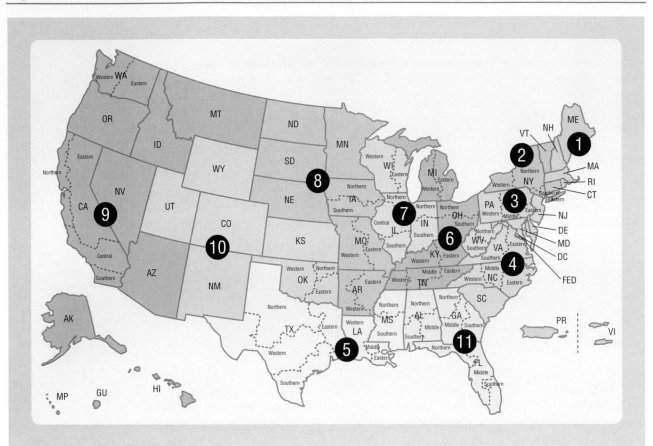

State Trial Courts In state court systems, most cases begin in a trial court of general jurisdiction. As in the federal system, state trial courts of general jurisdiction have the power to hear all cases over which the state court system has jurisdiction except those cases for which the state has established special trial courts of limited jurisdiction. Most states have a trial court of general jurisdiction in each county. The names of these courts vary by state, but most states refer to them as *courts of common pleas* or *county courts.* In some states, these courts have specialized divisions such as domestic relations and probate.

Most states also have trial courts of limited jurisdiction. Usually, these courts can grant only certain remedies. For example, small claims courts, a common type of court of limited jurisdiction in most states, may not grant damage awards larger than a specified amount. Other courts of limited jurisdiction have the power to hear only certain types of cases. For example, probate courts hear only cases about asset and obligation transfers after an individual's death.

Intermediate Courts of Appeal Intermediate courts of appeal, analogous to federal circuit courts of appeal, exist in approximately half the states. These courts usually have broad jurisdiction, hearing appeals from courts of general and limited jurisdictions, as well as from state administrative agencies. The names of these courts vary by state, but most states call them *courts of appeal* or *superior courts.*

Courts of Last Resort Appeals from the state intermediate courts of appeal lead cases to the state court of last resort. Most states call this court the *supreme court,* although some states refer to it as the *court of appeals.* Because approximately half of the states lack intermediate courts of appeal, appeals from trial courts in these states go directly to the state court of last resort.

The Court Structure in England

Even though we trace the roots of the U.S. legal system back to England, changes have occurred in both countries' court structures; as a result, the court structures in the United States and England share similarities but also have distinct features. The lowest criminal courts in England are the magistrates courts, which hear minor offenses. More serious cases are tried before a judge and jury in the crown court, which also hears cases appealed from the magistrates courts on factual points. The high court (in the Queen's Branch Division) hears appeals on points of law, and the court of appeal in the Criminal Division hears appeals on sentences and convictions.

Civil cases are first heard in the county courts (for minor claims) or the high court, which is divided into three divisions: Queen's Bench, Family, and Chancery. Cases may be appealed to the court of appeal (Civil Division). Cases may also be appealed from the county court to the high court.

The House of Lords is the supreme court of appeal. Its cases are heard by up to 13 senior judges known as *law lords*. In addition to the courts, there are specialized tribunals, which hear appeals on decisions made by various public bodies and government departments in areas such as employment, immigration, social security, tax, and land.

Figure 2-4

U.S. Supreme Court Justices

Associate Justice

Elena Kagan
Appointed in 2010 by President Obama

Associate Justice

Antonin Scalia
Appointed in 1984 by President Reagan

Associate Justice
Anthony M. Kennedy
Appointed in 1988 by President G.H.W. Bush

Associate Justice

Sonia Sotomayor
Appointed in 2009 by President Obama

Chief Justice

John G. Roberts
Appointed in 2005 by President G.W. Bush

Associate Justice

Clarence Thomas
Appointed in 1991 by President G.H.W. Bush

Associate Justice

Ruth Bader Ginsburg
Appointed in 1993 by President Clinton

Associate Justice

Stephen G. Breyer
Appointed in 1994 by President Clinton

Associate Justice
Samuel Alito
Appointed in 2006 by President G.W. Bush

Threshold Requirements

Before a case makes it to court, it must meet three *threshold requirements.* These requirements ensure that courts hear only cases that genuinely require adjudication. The three requirements are standing, case or controversy, and ripeness. (See Figure 2-5.)

STANDING

standing

The legal right of a party or an individual to bring a lawsuit by demonstrating to the court sufficient connection to and harm from the law or action challenged (i.e., the plaintiff has to demonstrate that he or she is harmed or will be harmed). Otherwise, the court will dismiss the case, ruling that the plaintiff "lacks standing" to bring the suit.

A person who has the legal right to bring an action in court has **standing** (or *standing to sue*). For a person to have standing, the outcome of a case must personally affect him or her. Thus, if you hire a landscaper to mow your lawn every week and he fails to show up every other week, you have standing to sue your landscaper. But if your friend hired the landscaper, you lack the standing to sue on your friend's behalf because you do not have a personal stake in the outcome of the case.

The reason the American legal system requires this personal stake in the outcome is the belief that the plaintiff's personal stake stimulates her to present the best possible case. The requirements for standing, according to the 2000 U.S. Supreme Court case *Friends of the Earth v. Laidlaw Environmental Services,*[1] are (1) the plaintiff must have an injury in fact that is concrete and actual or imminent; (2) the injury must be fairly traceable to the challenged action of the defendant; and (3) it must be likely that the injury will be redressed by a favorable decision.[2] In applying those criteria to the Laidlaw case, the Supreme Court found that FOE members' testimony that they were afraid to fish and swim in a river they previously enjoyed satisfied the first two criteria. The Court held that although the FOE members would not directly receive money from a penalty against Laidlaw, they would benefit because the penalties would deter Laidlaw and other companies from polluting the river in the future.[3] The Court ruled in FOE's favor and assessed Laidlaw a $405,800 penalty payable to the U.S. Treasury.

Figure 2-5

Threshold
Requirements

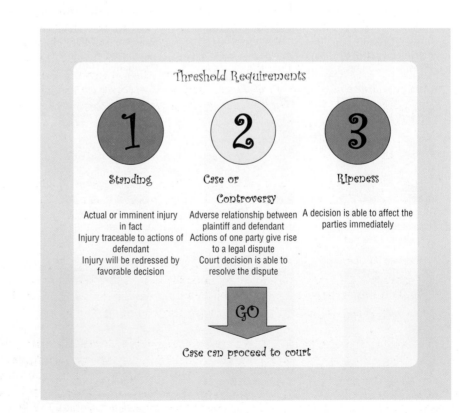

¹ 120 S. Ct. 923 (2000).
² Ibid.
³ Ibid.

CASE OR CONTROVERSY

The **case-or-controversy** (or *justifiable controversy*) requirement ensures that courts do not render advisory opinions. Three criteria are necessary for a case or controversy to exist. First, the relationship between the plaintiff and the defendant must be adverse. Second, actual or threatened actions of at least one of the parties must give rise to an actual legal dispute. Third, courts must have the ability to render a decision that will resolve the dispute. In other words, courts can give final judgments that solve existing problems; they cannot provide rulings about hypothetical situations.

RIPENESS

The case-or-controversy requirement is closely linked to the **ripeness** requirement. A case is *ripe* if a judge's decision is capable of affecting the parties immediately. Usually the issue of ripeness arises when one party claims that the case is moot—in other words, there is no point in the court's hearing the case because no judgment can affect the situation between the parties.

In the *Laidlaw* case, Laidlaw argued that the case was moot because by the time the case went to trial, the company had complied with the requirements of its discharge permits. The Supreme Court disagreed, ruling that the fact that a defendant voluntarily ceases a practice once litigation has commenced does not deprive a federal court of its power to determine the legality of the practice, because such a ruling would leave the defendant free to return to his old unlawful practices. Thus, the Court found the case was not moot because imposing a penalty on the defendant would have an important deterrent effect.[4]

Steps in Civil Litigation

The U.S. litigation system is an adversary system: A neutral fact finder—a judge or jury—hears evidence and arguments that opposing sides present and then decides the case on the basis of the facts and law. Strict rules govern the types of evidence fact finders may consider. Theoretically, fact finders make informed and impartial rulings because each party has an incentive to find all relevant evidence and make the strongest possible arguments on behalf of her or his position.

Critics of the adversary system, however, point out several drawbacks: the time and expense each lawsuit requires, the damage a suit may cause to the litigating parties' relationship, and the unfair advantage to those with wealth and experience using the court system

THE PRETRIAL STAGE

The *rules of civil procedure* govern civil case proceedings. The Federal Rules of Civil Procedure apply in all federal courts. Each state has its own set of rules, but most states' rules are very similar to the Federal Rules of Civil Procedure. In addition, each court usually has its own set of local court rules.

Informal Negotiations The initial attempt to resolve a business dispute is usually informal: a discussion or negotiation among the parties to try to find a solution. If the parties are unable to resolve their dispute, one party often seeks an attorney's advice. Together, the attorney and client may be able to resolve the dispute informally with the other party.

Pleadings The first formal stage of a lawsuit is the *pleading stage*. The plaintiff's attorney initiates a lawsuit by filing a *complaint* in the appropriate court. The complaint states the names of the parties to the action, the basis for the court's subject-matter jurisdiction, the facts on which the plaintiff bases her claim, and the relief the plaintiff seeks. The pleadings prevent surprises at trial; they allow attorneys to prepare arguments to counter the other side's claims. Exhibit 2-1 shows a typical complaint.

[4] Ibid.

case or controversy
A term used in the U.S. Constitution to describe the structure and requirements of conflicting claims of individuals that can be brought before a federal court for resolution. A case or controversy requires an actual dispute between parties over their legal rights that remains in conflict at the time the case is presented and that is a proper matter for judicial determination. Also referred to as *justifiable controversy.*

ripeness
The readiness of a case for a decision to be made. The goal is to prevent premature litigation for a dispute that is insufficiently developed. A claim is not ripe for litigation if it rests on contingent future events that may not occur as anticipated or may not occur at all.

LO 2-4

Exhibit 2-1

A Typical Complaint

THE COURT OF COMMON PLEAS OF CLARK COUNTY, NEVADA

Bob Lyons and Sue Lyons, Plaintiffs

v.

Christine Collins, Defendant

COMPLAINT FOR NEGLIGENCE

Case No. _____

Now come the plaintiffs, Bob Lyons and Sue Lyons, and, for their complaint, allege as follows:

1. Plaintiffs, Bob Lyons and Sue Lyons, both of 825 Havercamp Street, are citizens of Clark County, in the state of Nevada, and defendant, Christine Collins, 947 Rainbow Ave., is a citizen of Clark County in the state of Nevada.
2. On May 1, 2001, the defendant built a wooden hanging bridge across a stream that runs through the plaintiffs' property at 825 Havercamp Street.
3. Defendant negligently used ropes in the construction of the bridge that were not thick enough to sustain human traffic on the bridge.
4. At approximately 4:00 p.m., on May 20, 2001, the plaintiffs were attempting to carry a box of landscaping stones across the bridge when the ropes broke, and the bridge collapsed, causing plaintiffs to fall seven feet into the stream.
5. As a result of the fall, plaintiff, Bob Lyons, suffered a broken arm, a broken leg, and a skull fracture, incurring $160,000 in medical expenses.
6. As a result of the fall, plaintiff, Sue Lyons, suffered two broken cervical vertebrae, and a skull fracture, incurring $300,000 in medical expenses.
7. As a result of the fall, the landscaping stones, which had cost $1,200, were destroyed.
8. As a result of the foregoing injuries, plaintiff, Bob Lyons, was required to miss eight weeks of work, resulting in a loss of $2,400 in wages.
9. As a result of the foregoing injuries, plaintiff, Sue Lyons, was required to miss twelve weeks of work, resulting in a loss of $3,600 in wages.

WHEREFORE, plaintiffs demand judgment in the amount of $467,200, plus costs of this action.

> Harlon Elliot
>
> Attorney for plaintiffs
>
> 824 Sahara Ave.
>
> Las Vegas, Nevada, 89117

JURY DEMAND

Plaintiffs demand a trial by jury in this matter.

service of process

The procedure by which a court delivers a copy of the statement of claim or other legal documents, such as a summons, complaint, or subpoena, to the defendant.

default judgment

Judgment for the plaintiff that occurs when the defendant fails to respond to the complaint.

Service of Process To obtain *in personam* jurisdiction over a defendant and to satisfy due process, a court must notify the defendant of the pending lawsuit. **Service of process** occurs when a representative of the court serves (delivers) a copy of the complaint and a summons to the defendant.

The complaint explains the basis of the lawsuit to the defendant. The summons tells the defendant that if he or she does not respond to the lawsuit within a certain period of time, the plaintiff will receive a default judgment. A **default judgment** is a judgment in favor of the plaintiff that occurs when the defendant fails to answer the complaint and the plaintiff's complaint alleges facts that would support such a judgment.

Defendant's Response The defendant responds to the complaint with an **answer.** In this document, the defendant denies, affirms, or claims no knowledge of the accuracy of the plaintiff's allegations.

A defendant uses an *affirmative defense* when his or her answer admits that the facts contained in the complaint are accurate but also includes additional facts that justify the defendant's actions and provide a legally sound reason to deny relief to the plaintiff. For example, if a woman sued a man for battery because he punched her in the face, he might claim that he hit her only because she aimed a gun at him and threatened to shoot. His claim that he was acting in self-defense is an affirmative defense.

If the defendant plans to raise an affirmative defense, he must raise it in his answer to give the plaintiff adequate notice. If he fails to raise an affirmative defense in the answer, the judge will likely not allow him to raise it during the trial.

Upon receiving the complaint, if the defendant believes that even though all the plaintiff's factual allegations are true, the law does not entitle the plaintiff to a favorable judgment, the defendant may file a **motion to dismiss,** or *demurrer.* (A **motion** is a request by a party for the court to do something; in this instance, the request is to dismiss the case.) In deciding whether to grant a motion to dismiss, a judge accepts the facts as stated by the plaintiff and rules on the legal issues in the case. Judges generally grant motions to dismiss only when it appears beyond a doubt that the plaintiff cannot prove any set of facts to justify granting the judgment she seeks.

If the defendant believes he has a claim against the plaintiff, he includes this **counterclaim** with the answer. As Exhibit 2-2 shows, the form of a counterclaim is identical to the form of a complaint. The defendant states the facts supporting his claim and asks for relief.

If the defendant files a counterclaim, the plaintiff generally files a reply. A **reply** is an answer to a counterclaim. In the reply, the plaintiff admits, denies, or claims a lack of knowledge as to the accuracy of the facts of the defendant's counterclaim. If the plaintiff plans to use an affirmative defense, she must raise it in the reply.

Pretrial Motions The early pleadings establish the legal and factual issues of the case. After the pleadings, the plaintiff or defendant may file a motion to conclude the case early, eliminate some claims, or gain some advantage. A party may move, or request, that the court do almost anything pertaining to the case. For example, if the plaintiff files a suit about the right to a piece of property, she may move that the court prohibit the current possessor of the land from selling it. Courts may grant or deny such motions at their discretion.

When a party files a motion with the court, the court sends a copy to the opposing attorney, who may respond to the motion, usually by requesting that the judge deny the motion. In many cases, the judge rules on the motion immediately. In other cases, the judge holds a hearing at which the attorneys for both sides argue how the judge should decide the motion.

Two primary pretrial motions are a motion for judgment on the pleadings and a motion for summary judgment. Once the parties file the pleadings, either party can file a **motion for judgment on the pleadings.** The motion is a request for the court to consider that all the facts in the pleadings are true and to apply the law to those facts. The court grants the motion if, after this process, it finds that the only reasonable decision is in favor of the moving party.

Either party can file a **motion for summary judgment** after the discovery process (described below). The motion asserts that no factual disputes exist and that if the judge applied the law to the undisputed facts, her only reasonable decision would be in favor of the moving party. The difference between this motion and a motion for judgment on the pleadings is that in a motion for summary judgment, the moving party may use affidavits (sworn statements from the parties or witnesses), relevant documents, and depositions or interrogatories (a party's sworn answers to written questions) to support his motion. The judge grants the motion if, after examining the evidence, she finds no factual disputes. If, however, she finds any factual issues about which the parties disagree, she denies the motion and sends the case to trial.

answer

The response of the defendant to the plaintiff's complaint.

motion to dismiss

A request by the defendant that asks a judge or a court in a civil case to dismiss the case because even if all the allegations are true, the plaintiff is not entitled to any legal relief. Also called *demurrer.*

motion

An application by a party to a judge or a court in a civil case requesting an order in favor of the applicant.

counterclaim

A claim made by the defendant against the plaintiff that is filed along with the defendant's answer.

reply

A response by the plaintiff to the defendant's counterclaim.

motion for judgment on the pleadings

In a civil case, a request made by either party, after pleadings have been entered, that asks a judge or a court to issue a judgment.

motion for summary judgment

In a civil case, a request made by either party that asks a judge or a court to promptly and expeditiously dispose of a case without a trial. Any evidence or information that would be admissible at trial under the rules of evidence, such as affidavits, interrogatories, depositions, and admissions, may be considered on a motion for summary judgment. A court may hold oral arguments or decide the motion on the basis of the parties' briefs and supporting documentation alone.

Exhibit 2-2

Defendant's Answer
and Counterclaim

THE COURT OF COMMON PLEAS
OF CLARK COUNTY, NEVADA

Bob Lyons and Sue Lyons, Plaintiffs v. Christine Collins, Defendant
ANSWER AND COUNTERCLAIM FOR BREACH OF CONTRACT
Case No. _____

Now comes the defendant, Christine Collins, and answers the complaint of plaintiffs herein as follows:

FIRST DEFENSE

1. Admits the allegations in paragraphs 1 and 2.
2. Denies the allegation in paragraph 3.
3. Is without knowledge as to the truth or falsity of the allegations contained in paragraphs 4, 5, 6, 7, 8, and 9.

SECOND DEFENSE

4. If the court believes the allegations contained in paragraph 3, which the defendant expressly denies, plaintiffs should still be denied recovery because they were informed prior to the construction of the bridge that there should be no more than one person on the bridge at one time, and that no individual weighing more than 200 pounds should be allowed to walk on the bridge.

COUNTERCLAIM

5. On April 15, the parties agreed that defendant would build a wooden hanging bridge across a stream that runs through the defendant's property at 825 Havercamp Street, in exchange for which plaintiffs would pay defendant $2,000 upon completion of construction.
6. On May 1, 2001, the defendant built the agreed upon ornament, wooden, hanging bridge across a stream that runs through the defendant's property at 825 Havercamp Street, but plaintiffs failed to pay the agreed upon price for the bridge.
7. By their failure to pay, plaintiffs breached their contract and are liable to defendant for the contract price of $2,000.

 WHEREFORE, defendant prays for a judgment dismissing the plaintiffs' complaint, and granting the defendant a judgment against plaintiffs in the amount of $2,000 plus costs of this action.

Melissa Davenport
Attorney for Defendant
777 Decatur Ave.
Las Vegas, Nevada 89117

discovery

The pretrial phase in a lawsuit during which each party requests relevant documents and other evidence from the other side in an attempt to "discover" pertinent facts and avoid any surprises in the courtroom during the trial. Discovery tools include requests for admissions, interrogatories, depositions, requests for inspection, and document production requests.

interrogatories

A formal set of written questions that one party to a lawsuit asks the opposing party as part of the pretrial discovery process in order to clarify matters of evidence and help determine in advance what facts will be presented at any trial in the case. The questions must be answered in writing under oath or under penalty of perjury within a specified time. Also called *requests for further information.*

Discovery After filing the initial pleadings and motions, the parties gather information from each other through **discovery.** The discovery process enables the parties to learn about facts surrounding the case so that they are not surprised in the courtroom. Three common discovery tools are interrogatories, requests to produce documents, and depositions.

Interrogatories are written questions that one party sends to the other to answer under oath. Frequently, a *request to admit certain facts* accompanies interrogatories. Attorneys work with their clients to answer interrogatories and requested admissions of facts. Sometimes interrogatories are called *requests for further information.*

A **request to produce documents** (or other items) forces the opposing party to produce (turn over) certain information unless it is privileged or irrelevant to the case. Parties may request documents such as photographs, contracts, written estimates, medical records, tax forms, and other government documents. In tort cases, the defendant frequently asks the plaintiff to submit a mental- or physical-examination report.

Finally, the parties may obtain testimony from a witness before trial through a **deposition.** At a deposition, attorneys examine a witness under oath. A court reporter (stenographer) records every word the witness and attorneys speak. Both parties receive a copy of the testimony in document form. Depositions provide information and may also set up inconsistencies between a witness's testimony at the deposition and his testimony at trial. If a party discovers an inconsistency in the testimony of one of the other party's witnesses, she can bring the inconsistency to the fact finder's attention to diminish the witness's credibility. The parties may also use depositions when a witness is elderly, moving, or ill and thus may be unavailable at the time of the trial.

If a party does not comply with requests for discovery, the court may admit the facts the other party sought to discover. Attorneys who feel that certain material is outside the scope of the case often argue that the material is irrelevant to the case. If the court disagrees, however, the party must supply the requested information. Although these discovery tools are important in the United States, many countries do not have a discovery process.

Pretrial Conference A pretrial conference precedes the trial. A **pretrial conference** is an informal meeting of the judge with the attorneys representing the parties. During this conference, the parties try to narrow the legal and factual issues and possibly work out a settlement. If the parties cannot reach a settlement, the attorneys and the judge discuss the administrative details of the trial: its length, witnesses, and any pretrial stipulations of fact or law to which the parties agree.

THE TRIAL

If a plaintiff seeks at least $20 in monetary damages, the Seventh Amendment to the U.S. Constitution entitles the parties to a jury trial. The plaintiff must, however, demand a jury trial in her or his complaint. Some types of trials require 12-person juries, but 6-person juries hear most civil cases. If the plaintiff seeks an equitable remedy (an injunction or other court order) or if the parties have waived their right to a jury, a judge serves as the fact finder in the case.

Trials have six stages: jury selection, opening statements, examination of witnesses, closing arguments, conference on jury instructions, and posttrial motions. The following sections describe these stages.

Jury Selection The jury selection process begins when the clerk of the courts randomly selects a number of potential jurors from the citizens within the court's jurisdiction. Once the potential jurors have reported for jury duty, the **voir dire,** or jury selection, process begins. The voir dire process selects the jurors who will decide the case, as well as two or three "alternate jurors" who will watch the trial and be available to replace any juror who, for some legitimate reason, must leave jury duty before the trial ends.

During voir dire, the judge and/or attorneys question potential jurors to determine whether they are able to render an unbiased opinion in the case. If a potential juror's response to a question indicates that she or he may be biased, either attorney may challenge, or ask the court to remove, that potential juror "for cause." For example, a lawyer could challenge for cause a potential juror who was a college roommate of the defendant. In most states, each party has a certain number of **peremptory challenges.** These peremptory challenges allow a party to challenge a certain number of potential jurors without giving a reason.

Peremptory challenges, however, may lead to abuse. For example, in the past, attorneys have used peremptory challenges to eliminate a certain class, ethnic group, or gender from the jury. In the 1986 case *Batson v. Kentucky,*[5] the U.S. Supreme Court ruled that race-based peremptory challenges in criminal cases violate the equal protection clause of the Fourteenth Amendment to the U.S. Constitution. (Chapter 4 discusses the amendments to the Constitution in more detail.) The Supreme Court later extended the ban on race-based challenges to civil cases. In Case 2-2, the U.S. Supreme Court addressed the issue of whether the equal protection clause covers gender-based challenges.

request to produce documents

In a lawsuit, the right of a party to examine and copy papers of the opposing party that are relevant to the case. A legal request may be made and the categories of the documents must be stated to allow the other party to know what documents he or she must produce.

deposition

A pretrial sworn and recorded testimony of a witness that is acquired out of court with no judge present.

pretrial conference

An informal meeting of the judge with the attorneys representing the parties before the actual trial begins.

voir dire

The process of questioning potential jurors to ensure that the jury will be made up of nonbiased individuals.

peremptory challenge

In a jury trial, the right of the plaintiff and the defendant in jury selection to reject, without stating a reason, a certain number of potential jurors who appear to have an unfavorable bias.

[5] 476 U.S. 79 (1986).

J.E.B. v. ALABAMA, EX. REL. T.B.

UNITED STATES SUPREME COURT

114 S. Ct. 1419 (1994)

FACTS: *The State of Alabama filed a complaint for paternity and child support against J.E.B. on behalf of T.B., the unwed mother of a minor child. The court called a panel of 12 males and 24 females as potential jurors. Only 10 males remained after three individuals were removed for cause. The state used its peremptory challenges to remove nine male jurors and J.E.B. removed the tenth, resulting in an all-female jury. The trial court rejected J.E.B.'s objection to the gender-based challenges, and the jury found J.E.B. to be the father. J.E.B. appealed, and the court of appeals affirmed the trial court's ruling that the equal protection clause of the Fourteenth Amendment does not prohibit gender-based challenges. The Alabama Supreme Court declined to hear the appeal, and J.E.B. appealed to the U.S. Supreme Court.*

ISSUE: Does the equal protection clause prohibit removing possible jurors during voir dire on the basis of their gender?

REASONING: Justice Blackmun delivered the opinion of the Court:

> Discrimination in jury selection, whether based on race or on gender, causes harm to the litigants, the community, and the individual jurors who are wrongfully excluded from participation in the judicial process. The litigants are harmed by the risk that the prejudice which motivated the discriminatory selection of the jury will infect the entire proceedings. The community is harmed by the State's participation in the perpetuation of invidious group stereotypes and the inevitable loss of confidence in our judicial system that state-sanctioned discrimination in the courtroom engenders.

As with race-based *Batson* claims, a party alleging gender discrimination must make a prima facie showing of intentional discrimination before the party exercising the challenge is required to explain the basis for the strike. When an explanation is required, it need not rise to the level of a "for cause" challenge; rather, it merely must be based on a juror characteristic other than gender and the proffered explanation may not be pretextual.

Equal opportunity to participate in the fair administration of justice is fundamental to our democratic system. It reaffirms the promise of equality under the law—that all citizens, regardless of race, ethnicity, or gender, have the chance to take part directly in our democracy. When persons are excluded from participation in our democratic processes solely because of race or gender, this promise of equality dims, and the integrity of our judicial system is jeopardized.

DECISION AND REMEDY: Yes, to remove a potential juror based solely on gender is a violation of the equal protection clause. The court of appeals decision was reversed, and the case was remanded in favor of J.E.B.

SIGNIFICANCE OF THE CASE: This case extended protection against being peremptorily removed from a jury on the basis of gender alone, thus putting gender protections on par with the protections for race and ethnicity. Although historically the extension of the Fourteenth Amendment's equal protection clause to gender has been used to protect women's equal rights, the court found that the clause was equally applicable when a man's equal rights were being violated.

CRITICAL THINKING

The defendant was contesting the removal of males from the jury. Does this fact affect your assessment of the quality of the Court's reasoning? Explain.

ETHICAL DECISION MAKING

Which ethical norm does the case decision serve?

Despite *Batson* and *J.E.B.,* it is still not easy to challenge a dismissal as being based on race or gender. And in a 2006 case, the U.S. Supreme Court said that in order to find a dismissal unconstitutional, there must be no alternative to a gender- or race-based reason for dismissing a juror.[6]

[6] *Rice, Warden et al. v. Collins,* 126 S. Ct. 969 (2006).

The voir dire process has become more sophisticated over time. In cases involving significant amounts of money, rather than relying on their instinct or experience during jury selection, attorneys use professional jury selection services to identify demographic data to help select ideal jurors. Jury selection firms also provide additional services, including **mock trials,** in which mock jurors who are demographically similar to the real jurors hear the arguments and give feedback prior to the case, and **shadow juries,** in which shadow jurors sit in during the actual trial and deliberate at the end of each day to evaluate for the attorneys how each side is doing. Critics argue that jury selection services give an unfair advantage to one side when only one party can afford these services.

Opening Statements

Once the attorneys have impaneled, or selected, a jury, the case begins with opening statements. Each party's attorney explains to the judge and jury what facts he or she intends to prove, the legal conclusions to which these facts lead, and how the fact finder should decide the case based on those facts.

The Examination of Witnesses and Presentation of Evidence

Following opening statements, the plaintiff and defendant, in turn, present their cases-in-chief by examining witnesses and presenting evidence. The plaintiff has the burden of proving the case, meaning that if neither side presents a convincing case, the fact finder must rule in favor of the defendant. Thus, the plaintiff presents her case first.

The procedure for each witness is the same. First, the plaintiff's attorney questions the witness in *direct examination.* The plaintiff's attorney asks the witness questions to elicit facts that support the plaintiff's case-in-chief. Questions must relate to matters about which the witness has direct knowledge. Attorneys cannot elicit "hearsay" from the witnesses. *Hearsay* is testimony about what a witness heard another person say. Hearsay is impermissible because the opposing attorney cannot question the person who made the original statement to determine the statement's veracity.

The federal rules of evidence also prohibit attorneys from asking leading questions. Leading questions are questions that imply a specific answer. For example, an attorney cannot ask a witness, "Did the defendant come to your office and ask you to purchase stock from him?" Instead, attorneys must ask questions such as, "When did you first encounter the defendant?"

After direct examination, opposing counsel may *cross-examine* the witness. Opposing counsel, however, may ask only questions related to the witness's direct examination. On cross-examination, attorneys can ask leading questions. Attorneys try to show inconsistencies in the witness's testimony, cast doubt on the claims of the plaintiff's case, and elicit information to support the defendant's case.

After cross-examination, the plaintiff's attorney may conduct a *redirect examination,* a series of questions aimed at repairing damage done by the cross-examination. At the judge's discretion, opposing counsel has an opportunity to *re-cross* the witness to question her testimony on redirect examination. The parties follow this procedure for each of the plaintiff's witnesses.

Immediately following the plaintiff's presentation of her case, the defendant may move for a **directed verdict.** This motion is a request for the court to direct a verdict for the defendant because even if the jury accepted all the evidence and testimony presented by the plaintiff as true, the jury would still have no legal basis for a decision in favor of the plaintiff. The federal court system refers to a motion for a directed verdict as a *motion for a judgment as a matter of law.* Courts rarely grant motions for a directed verdict because plaintiffs almost always present at least *some* evidence to support each element of the cause of action.

If the court denies the defendant's motion for a directed verdict, the defendant then presents his case. The parties question the defendant's witnesses in the same manner as they questioned the plaintiff's witnesses, except that the defendant's attorney conducts direct and redirect examination and the plaintiff's attorney conducts cross-examination and re-cross-examination.

Closing Arguments

After the defendant's case, the attorneys present closing arguments. In closing arguments, each attorney summarizes evidence from the trial in a manner consistent with his or her client's case. The plaintiff's attorney presents her closing argument first, followed by the

mock trial

A contrived or imitation trial, with a jury recruited by a jury selection firm, that attorneys sometimes use in preparing for an actual trial to test theories, experiment with arguments, and try to predict the outcome of the real trial.

shadow jury

An unofficial jury, provided by a jury selection firm, that sits in during the actual trial and deliberates at the end of each day to evaluate for the attorneys how each side is doing.

directed verdict

A ruling by the judge, after the plaintiff has put forward his or her case but before any evidence is put forward by the defendant, in favor of the defendant because the plaintiff has failed to present the minimum amount of evidence necessary to establish his or her claim.

Trials in Japan

Civil procedure in Japan differs significantly from American civil procedure. The Japanese legal system has no juries and no distinct pretrial stage. Instead, a trial is a series of discrete meetings between the parties and the judge. At the first meeting, the parties identify the most critical and contested issues. They choose one and recess to gather evidence and marshal arguments on the issue.

At the next meeting, the judge rules on the chosen issue. If the judge decides against the plaintiff, the case is over. If the plaintiff wins, the process continues with the next issue.

The process continues until the plaintiff loses an issue or until the judge decides all issues in the plaintiff's favor, resulting in a verdict for the plaintiff.

In addition, the discovery process in the Japanese court system is not as simple as it is in the United States. To obtain evidence, parties must convince the judge to order others to testify or produce documents. The judge can fine or jail parties who refuse to comply with such orders. Additionally, if a party does not comply with the judge's requests for discovery, the judge may admit the facts the other party sought to discover.

defendant's attorney, and the plaintiff has the option to present a rebuttal of the defendant's closing argument.

Jury Instructions In a jury trial, the judge "charges the jury" by instructing the jurors on how the law applies to the facts of the case. Both sides' attorneys submit statements to the judge explaining how they believe she should charge the jury. The judge's instructions are usually a combination of both sides' suggestions.

After the judge charges the jury, the jurors retire to the jury room to deliberate. Once they reach a decision, they return to the courtroom, where the judge reads their verdict and discharges them from their duty. Trial procedures in the United States are quite different from trial procedures in other countries, as the Global Context box illustrates.

POSTTRIAL MOTIONS

Once the trial ends, the party who received the favorable verdict files a *motion for a judgment in accordance with the verdict.* Until the judge enters the judgment, the court has not issued a legally binding decision for the case.

The party who loses at trial has a number of available options. One option is to file a *motion for a judgment notwithstanding the verdict,* or *judgment non obstante verdicto,* asking the judge to issue a judgment contrary to the jury's verdict. To grant the motion, the judge must find that, when viewing the evidence in the light most favorable to the nonmoving party, a reasonable jury could not have found in favor of that party. In other words, as a matter of law, the judge must determine that the trial did not produce sufficient evidence to support the jury's verdict. This motion is similar to a motion for a directed verdict, except the parties cannot make this motion until *after* the jury issues a verdict. The federal court system refers to this motion as a *motion for judgment as a matter of law.*

The losing party can also file a *motion for a new trial.* Judges grant motions for a new trial only if they believe the jury's decision was clearly erroneous but they are not sure that the other side should necessarily have won the case. A judge often grants a motion for a new trial when the parties discover new evidence, when the judge made an erroneous ruling, or when misconduct during the trial may have prevented the jury from reaching a fair decision.

APPELLATE PROCEDURE

Either party may appeal the judge's decision on posttrial motions or on her or his final judgment. Sometimes, both parties appeal the same decision. For example, if a jury awarded the plaintiff $10,000 in damages, the plaintiff and the defendant may both appeal the amount of the judgment. Appellate courts, however, reverse only about 1 out of every 10 trial court decisions on appeal.

prejudicial error
An error of law that is so significant that it affects the outcome of the case.

To be eligible for appeal, the losing party must argue that a *prejudicial error of law* occurred during the trial. A **prejudicial error** is a mistake so significant that it likely affected the outcome

of the case. For example, a prejudicial error could occur if the judge improperly allowed hearsay evidence that enabled the plaintiff to prove an element of her case.

To appeal a case, the attorney for the appealing party (the appellant) files a notice of appeal with the clerk of the trial court within a prescribed time. The clerk then forwards the record of appeal to the appeals court. The record of appeal typically contains a number of items: the pleadings, a trial transcript, copies of the trial exhibits, copies of the judge's rulings on the parties' motions, the attorneys' arguments, jury instructions, the jury's verdict, posttrial motions, and the judgment order.

The appellant then files a **brief,** or written argument, with the court. Appellants file briefs to explain why the judgment in the lower court was erroneous and why the appeals court should reverse it. The attorney for the party who won in the lower court (the appellee) files an answering brief. The appellant may then file a reply brief in response to the appellee's brief. Generally, however, appellants do not file reply briefs.

The appeals court then usually allows the attorneys to present oral arguments before the court. The court considers these arguments, reviews the record of the case, and renders a decision.

There are four possible decisions an appellate court can render. The court can accept the lower court's judgment by **affirming** its decision. Alternatively, the appellate court may conclude that the lower court's decision was correct but the remedy was inappropriate, in which case it **modifies** the remedy. If the appellate court decides that the lower court was incorrect, it **reverses** the lower court's decision. Finally, if the appeals court thinks the lower court committed an error but does not know how that error affected the outcome of the case, it **remands** the case to the lower court for a new trial.

An appellate court usually has a bench with at least three judges. Appellate courts do not have juries; rather, the judges decide the case by majority vote. One of the judges who votes with the majority records the court's decision and its reasons in the *majority opinion.* These decisions have precedential value—that is, judges use these prior appellate court decisions to make decisions in future cases. Also, these decisions establish new guidelines in the law that all citizens must follow. If a judge agrees with the majority's decision but for different reasons, she may write a *concurring opinion,* stating the reasons she used to reach the majority's conclusion. Finally, judges disagreeing with the majority may write a *dissenting opinion,* giving their reasons for reaching a contrary conclusion. Attorneys arguing that a court should change the law frequently cite dissenting opinions from previous cases in their briefs. Likewise, appellate judges who change the law often cite dissenting opinions from past cases.

For most cases, only one appeal is available. In states with both an intermediate and a final court of appeals, a losing party may appeal from the intermediate appellate court to the state supreme court. In a limited number of cases, the losing party can appeal the decision of a state supreme court or a federal circuit court of appeals to the U.S. Supreme Court.

Appeal to the U.S. Supreme Court Every year thousands of individuals file appeals with the U.S. Supreme Court, but the Court hears, on average, only 80 to 90 cases each year. To file an appeal to the U.S. Supreme Court, a party files a petition asking the Court to issue a **writ of certiorari,** an order to the lower court to send to the Supreme Court the record of the case. The Court issues very few writs.

The justices review petitions and issue a writ only when at least four justices vote to hear the case (the *rule of four*). The court is most likely to issue a writ in four instances: (1) The case presents a substantial federal question that the Supreme Court has not yet addressed; (2) multiple circuit courts of appeal have decided the issue of the case in different ways; (3) a state court of last resort has ruled that a federal law is invalid or has upheld a state law that may violate federal law; or (4) a federal court has ruled that an act of Congress is unconstitutional. If the Supreme Court does not issue a writ of certiorari, the lower court's decision stands.

Alternative Dispute Resolution

Many firms find that using **alternative dispute resolution (ADR)** methods to resolve their legal problems offers many benefits. The term *ADR* refers to the resolution of legal disputes through methods other than litigation, such as negotiation, mediation, arbitration, summary jury trials, minitrials, neutral case evaluations, and private trials.

brief
A written legal argument, which a party presents to a court, that explains why that party to the case should prevail.

affirm
An appellate court decision that accepts a lower court's judgment in a case that has been appealed.

modify
An appellate court decision that grants an alternative remedy in a case; rendered when the court finds that the decision of the lower court was correct but the remedy was not.

reverse
An appellate court decision that overturns the judgment of a lower court, concluding that the lower court was incorrect and its verdict cannot be allowed to stand.

remand
An appellate court decision that returns a case to the trial court for a new trial or for limited hearing on a specified subject matter; rendered when the court decides that an error was committed that may have affected the outcome of a case.

writ of certiorari
A Supreme Court order, issued after the Court decides to hear an appeal, mandating that the lower court send to the Supreme Court the record of the appealed case.

alternative dispute resolution (ADR)
The resolution of legal problems through methods other than litigation.

Why might a business prefer ADR to litigation? First, ADR methods are generally faster and cheaper. According to the National Arbitration Forum, the average time from filing a complaint to judgment through litigation is 25 months.[7] Because ADR is faster, it is usually cheaper. According to the American Intellectual Property Law Association, for cases valued in the $1 million to $25 million range, the average total cost of patent litigation for each party through the close of discovery is $1.9 million.[8] Through the end of trial, the average cost to each party is $3.5 million. Thus, if a party can resolve a dispute through alternative dispute resolution, this can save significant money.

Second, a business may want to avoid the uncertainty associated with a jury decision; many forms of ADR give the participants more control over the resolution of the dispute. Specifically, the parties can select a neutral third party, frequently a person with expertise in the area of the dispute, to help facilitate resolution of the case. Third, a business may want to avoid setting a precedent through a court decision. Fourth, a business may prefer ADR because it is confidential. Fifth, because many forms of ADR are less adversarial than litigation, ADR allows the parties to preserve a business relationship.

Courts also generally support the use of ADR, which alleviates some of the pressure on the overwhelming court dockets. Congress has recognized the benefits of ADR methods through its enactment of the Alternative Dispute Resolution Act of 1998. This act requires that federal district courts have an ADR program along with a set of rules regarding the program. Additional evidence of congressional support for ADR comes from the passage of the Administrative Dispute Resolution Act, which mandates that federal agencies create internal ADR programs.

LO 2-5 Primary Forms of ADR

NEGOTIATION

negotiation
A bargaining process in which disputing parties interact informally to attempt to resolve their dispute.

Many business managers make frequent use of **negotiation,** a bargaining process in which disputing parties interact informally, either with or without lawyers, to attempt to resolve their dispute. No neutral third party is involved. Thus, negotiation differs from other methods of dispute resolution because the parties maintain high levels of autonomy. Some courts require that parties negotiate before they bring their dispute to trial.

Before negotiation begins, each side must determine its goals for the negotiation. Moreover, each side must identify the information it is willing to give the other party. Because negotiation generally occurs in every case before a more formal dispute resolution method is chosen, negotiation is not necessarily considered an alternative to litigation.

MEDIATION

mediation
A type of intensive negotiation in which disputing parties select a neutral party to help facilitate communication and suggest ways for the parties to solve their dispute.

An extension of negotiation is mediation. In **mediation,** the disputing parties select a neutral party to help facilitate communication and suggest ways for the parties to solve their dispute. Therefore, the distinguishing feature of mediation is that the parties voluntarily select a neutral third party to help them work together to resolve the dispute. The neutral third party frequently has expertise in the area of the dispute.

Mediation begins when parties select a mediator. Each party then typically writes a mediation brief to explain why it should win. An important feature of mediation is that it allows multiple parties to participate in a dispute. The parties take turns explaining the dispute. One of the mediator's main goals is to help each party listen carefully to the opposing party's concerns. The mediator asks the parties to identify any additional concerns. The parties begin generating alternatives or solutions for the disputed points. The mediator helps the parties evaluate the alternatives by comparing the alternatives with the disputed points and interests identified earlier. Finally, the mediator assists the parties in agreeing on a solution.

[7] National Arbitration Forum, *Business-to-Business Mediation/Arbitration vs. Litigation: What Courts, Statistics, & Public Perceptions Show about How Commercial Mediation and Commercial Arbitration Compare to the Litigation System,* January 2005, p. 3.
[8] AIPLA, *Report of the Economic Survey,* pp. 1-109–1-110.

The mediation concludes when the agreement between the parties is reached. The agreement is then usually put into the form of a contract and signed by the parties. The mediator may participate in the drafting of the contract. If one of the parties does not follow the agreement, that party can be sued for breach of contract. However, parties typically abide by the agreement because they helped to create it.

If mediation is not successful, the parties can turn to litigation or arbitration to resolve their dispute. However, nothing said during the mediation can be used in another dispute resolution method; the mediation process is confidential.

Advantages and Disadvantages of Mediation The primary advantage of mediation is that it helps the disputing parties preserve their relationships; this is especially attractive for businesses with a working relationship they would like to continue. A second advantage is the possibility of finding creative solutions. The goal of mediation is to find a compromise between the needs of various parties, rather than to find one party right and all the others wrong. A third advantage is the high level of autonomy mediation gives the participants. Instead of a neutral third party pronouncing a solution, the interested parties work together to create a solution, and this can make them more committed to following the agreement afterward.

These benefits can obviously be very worthwhile. However, we need to pay attention to the critics of the mediation process. One criticism of mediation is that it creates an image of equal parties working toward an equitable solution and thereby hides power imbalances that can lead to the party with greater power getting an agreement of greater benefit. A second criticism is that some people who enter mediation have no intention of finding a solution but, instead, use mediation as a tactic to draw out the dispute.

Uses of Mediation Mediation is most commonly used in collective bargaining disputes, because it allows the workers to maintain a relationship with their employer while still having their needs addressed. Under the National Labor Relations Act (NLRA), a union must contact the Federal Mediation and Conciliation Services to attempt to mediate its demands before beginning a strike to achieve higher wages or better working hours.

Similarly, the Equal Employment Opportunity Commission (EEOC) encourages the mediation of employment discrimination claims. The EEOC has a mediation program that uses mediators employed by the EEOC, as well as external mediators trained in mediation and discrimination law. Mediation is also used extensively in environmental law, because environmental disputes are often best served by finding a compromise between the frequently multiple parties.

ARBITRATION

One of the most frequently used methods of dispute resolution is **arbitration,** the resolution of a dispute by a neutral third party outside the judicial setting. Arbitration is frequently used in disagreements between employees and employers, and it is increasingly being used between consumers and businesses. Arbitration is often a voluntary process in that parties have a contractual agreement to arbitrate any disputes. This agreement may stipulate how the arbitrator will be selected and how the hearing will be administered.

Lawyers, professors, and other professionals typically serve as arbitrators. The general qualifications for being an arbitrator are honesty, impartiality, and subject-matter competence. Additionally, arbitrators are expected to follow the Arbitrator's Code of Ethics. Typically, parties choose arbitrators from the Federal Mediation and Conciliation Services (FMCS), a government agency, or the American Arbitration Association (AAA), a private, nonprofit organization.

arbitration
A type of alternative dispute resolution in which disputes are submitted for resolution to private nonofficial persons selected in a manner provided by law or the agreement of the parties.

The Arbitration Hearing The arbitration hearing is similar to a trial. Both parties present their cases to a neutral third party; parties may represent themselves or use legal counsel. During this presentation, the parties may introduce witnesses and documentation, cross-examine the witnesses, and offer closing statements. The fact finder offers a legally binding decision. However,

arbitration is also different from a trial in several ways. First, the arbitrator often takes a much more active role in an arbitration hearing than a judge takes in a trial, and the arbitrator can question witnesses. Second, no official written record of the hearing is kept in most arbitrations. Third, the rules of evidence applicable in a trial are typically relaxed in arbitration.

The Arbitrator's Award The arbitrator typically provides a decision within 30 days of the arbitration hearing. The arbitrator's decision is called an *award,* even if no monetary compensation is awarded. The arbitrator's decision differs from a judge's decision in several ways. The arbitrator does not have to state any findings of fact, conclusions of law, or reasons to support the award, and he or she is not as bound by precedent as a judge is. Also, because the arbitrator was hired to resolve a dispute between two parties, the arbitrator is more likely to make a compromise ruling instead of a win-lose ruling.

Unlike the case in most other forms of ADR, the arbitrator's decision is legally binding. In certain cases, a decision may be appealed to the district court. However, few of these cases are appealed. The courts give extreme deference to arbitrators' decisions.

The Federal Arbitration Act (FAA), the federal law enacted to encourage the use of arbitration, explicitly lists four grounds on which an arbitrator's award may be set aside: (1) The award was the result of corruption, fraud, or other undue means; (2) the arbitrator displayed bias or corruption; (3) the arbitrator refused to postpone the hearing despite sufficient cause, refused to hear relevant evidence, or otherwise misbehaved to prejudice the rights of one of the parties; (4) the arbitrator exceeded his or her authority or failed to use that authority to make a mutual, final, and definite award. In a 2008 decision, the U.S. Supreme Court held that these grounds are the only grounds for appeal and that the parties in an arbitration proceeding do not have the ability to give the courts additional grounds to set aside a decision.[9]

Consequently, in the United States, arbitration decisions are generally upheld. In fact, the Fifth Circuit recently held that "manifest disregard of the law and contrary to public policy are the only nonstatutory bases recognized by this circuit for the vacatur of an arbitration award."[10]

Advantages and Disadvantages of Arbitration Arbitration may be preferable to litigation for several reasons. First, arbitration is more efficient and less expensive. Second, parties have more control over the process of dispute resolution through arbitration. They choose the arbitrator and determine how formal the process will be. Third, the parties can choose someone to serve as the arbitrator who has expertise in the specific subject matter. Fourth, the arbitrator has greater flexibility in decision making than a judge has. Unlike judges, who are bound by precedent, arbitrators generally do not have to offer reasons for their decisions.

However, arbitration is not without its critics. First, arbitration panels are being used more frequently, resulting in a loss of some of the prior advantages of arbitration, such as efficiency and lower cost. Second, because appealing an arbitration award is so difficult, some scholars argue that injustice is more likely to occur. Third, some individuals are concerned that by agreeing to give up one's right to litigate, one may be losing important civil rights or giving up important potential remedies without really understanding which rights are being given up. Fourth, some scholars are afraid that if more and more employers and institutions turn to mandatory arbitration, it will become more like litigation. Fifth, some scholars are concerned about the privacy associated with arbitration. Companies and employers are able to "hide" their disputes through arbitration.

Binding Arbitration Clause Given the benefits associated with arbitration, parties may voluntarily submit their cases to arbitration. The primary method of securing arbitration is through a **binding arbitration clause,** a provision in a contract that mandates that all disputes arising under the contract must be settled by arbitration. The clause also typically states how the arbitrator will be selected. If parties have a binding arbitration agreement, the parties *must* resolve the dispute through arbitration. Both federal and state courts must uphold agreements to arbitrate. The Case Nugget illustrates the courts' willingness to enforce binding arbitration agreements.

binding arbitration clause

A contract provision mandating that all disputes arising under the contract must be settled by arbitration.

[9] *Hall Street Associates v. Mattell,* 2008 U.S. LEXIS 2911.
[10] *Kergosien et al. v. Ocean Energy, Inc.,* 390 F.3d 346 (5th Cir. 2004).

CASE Nugget

The Validity of Binding Arbitration Agreements

Preston v. Ferrer
United States Supreme Court

128 S. Ct. 978 (2008)

Under the FAA, is an administrative proceeding the same as a trial?

It has long been held that under the FAA, even if state statutes refer a state law controversy initially to a judicial forum, if the parties have agreed to submit that dispute to arbitration, the dispute must be arbitrated. Until 2008, however, the question existed of whether the same rule would apply when the state law directed that the first mode of resolution be an administrative proceeding rather than a court hearing. In this case, the U.S. Supreme Court ruled that for purposes of the FAA, an administrative proceeding was the equivalent of a judicial proceeding. In *Preston v. Ferrer,* the two had included a binding arbitration agreement in a contract for Preston to represent Ferrer. When Preston attempted to collect his fees, a question arose as to whether the matter had to be resolved by the California Labor Commission, which had jurisdiction over issues arising under the California Talent Agencies Act. The high court agreed with Ferrer that the dispute must be resolved through arbitration because the FAA preempted the state law. Even if a state law provides that an administrative forum has jurisdiction over a specific type of dispute, a binding arbitration agreement will supersede the forum declared by the state law.

A constraint on binding arbitration clauses is that they must be drafted in such a way as to ensure that the courts do not see them as being unconscionable. An *unconscionable contract provision* has been defined as one in which the terms are "manifestly unfair or oppressive and are dictated by a dominant party."[11] The doctrine has been used most often to strike down binding arbitration clauses in consumer and employment contracts. Exhibit 2-3 offers tips on creating a binding arbitration clause.

Exhibit 2-3

Tips for Creating a Binding Arbitration Clause

Overall, make sure the clause treats both parties fairly.

1. Be clear and unmistakable about what you wish to arbitrate.
2. The arbitration clause must be bilateral.
3. State explicitly which party will pay the arbitrator's fees, and make sure that it will not cost the non-drafting party more to arbitrate than it would have cost to litigate. Specify how the arbitrator will be selected.
4. Spell out the costs associated with the arbitration.
5. Avoid limitations on the remedies available to the parties.
6. Consider other potential parties when determining where to hold the arbitration.

[11] *Farris v. County of Camden,* 61 F. Supp. 2d 307, 341 (D. N.J. 1999).

Other ADR Methods

MED-ARB

med-arb

A type of dispute resolution process in which both parties agree to start out in mediation and, if unsuccessful, to move on to arbitration.

Med-arb is a dispute resolution process in which the parties agree to start out in mediation and, if the mediation is unsuccessful on one or more points, to move on to arbitration. In some cases, the same neutral third party may participate in both the mediation and the arbitration. Some critics argue that if parties know that the mediator may become the ultimate decision maker, they will be less likely to disclose information during the mediation stage. Others argue that having the same neutral mediator-arbitrator offers faster resolution because the third party is familiar with the facts of the case.[12]

SUMMARY JURY TRIAL

summary jury trial

An abbreviated trial that leads to a nonbinding jury verdict.

A **summary jury trial** is an abbreviated trial that leads to a nonbinding jury verdict. Two advantages are inherent in this method of dispute resolution. First, it is quick; a summary jury trial lasts only a day. Second, because a jury offers a verdict, both parties get a chance to see how their case would fare before a jury of their peers. Each judge can set his or her own rules. The judge advises the jury on the law, and each party's lawyer presents an opening statement and a limited amount of evidence before the jury. The lawyers have limited time for their presentations, and witnesses do not usually testify. The jury reaches an advisory verdict, although the jury does not know that its verdict is nonbinding. The parties then enter into a settlement conference, where they decide either to accept the jury verdict, reject the verdict, or settle on some compromise. Approximately 95 percent of cases are settled at this time. However, if the case is not settled, it will go to a regular trial. At that trial, nothing from the summary jury trial is admissible as evidence.

MINITRIAL

minitrial

A type of conflict resolution in which lawyers for each side present their arguments to a neutral adviser, who then offers an opinion as to what the verdict would be if the case went to trial. This decision is not binding.

A **minitrial** is similar to arbitration and mediation because it involves a neutral third party. However, despite the presence of a neutral third party, business representatives of the disputing corporations participate and have settlement authority. Lawyers for each side present their arguments before these executives and the neutral adviser, who then offers an opinion as to what the verdict would be if the case went to trial. The neutral adviser's opinion, like the jury's verdict in a summary jury trial, is not binding. Next, the corporate executives discuss settlement options. If they reach an agreement, they enter into a contract that reflects the terms of the settlement.

EARLY NEUTRAL CASE EVALUATION

With *early neutral case evaluation,* the parties select a neutral third party and explain their respective positions to this neutral, who then evaluates the strengths and weaknesses of the case. The parties use this evaluation to reach a settlement. Eighteen federal district courts currently use early neutral case evaluation.[13]

PRIVATE TRIALS

private trial

An ADR method in which a referee is selected and paid by the disputing parties to offer a legally binding judgment in a dispute.

Several states allow **private trials,** an ADR method in which a referee is selected and paid by the disputing parties to offer a legally binding judgment in a dispute. The referees do not have to have any specific training; however, because retired judges often serve as referees, this method is often referred to as "rent-a-judge." The cases are often heard privately to ensure confidentiality. The referee writes a report and files it with the trial judge, but a dissatisfied party reserves the right to request a new trial before a trial court judge. Private jury trials with experienced jury members are becoming more popular today as well. Private trials have been criticized because they seem to provide faster and cheaper justice for those who can afford the initial fee and because they "hide" the trial from the public eye.

[12] See Gerald F. Phillips, *Same Neutral Med-Arb: What Does the Future Hold?* Dispute Resolution Journal 60 (May–July 2005), p. 24.
[13] Michael H. Diamant et al., *Strategies for Mediation, Arbitration, and Other Forms of Alternative Dispute Resolution,* SK074 ALI-ABA 205 (2005) [citing the CPR Institute for Dispute Resolution, www.cprador.org].

SUMMARY

Jurisdiction	*In personam jurisdiction* is the power of a court to render a decision affecting a person's legal rights.
	Subject-matter jurisdiction is the power of a court to render a decision in a particular type of case. The three forms of subject matter jurisdiction are state, exclusive federal, and concurrent.
Venue	*Venue* is the geographic location of the trial.
The Structure of the Court System	The United States has two parallel court structures: the state and federal systems. The federal structure has *district courts* (trial courts), *circuit courts of appeal,* and the *U.S. Supreme Court.* The state court structure varies by state but generally includes courts of common pleas (trial courts), state courts of appeal, and a state supreme court.
Threshold Requirements	*Standing:* For a party to have the legal right to file a case, the outcome of the case must personally affect that party.
	Case or controversy: There must be an issue before the court that a judicial decision is capable of resolving. Parties cannot ask the judge for an "advisory opinion."
	Ripeness: The case cannot be moot; it must be ready for a decision to be made.
Steps in Civil Litigation	The stages of a civil trial include the pretrial, trial, posttrial, and appellate stages.
	Pretrial includes consultation with attorneys, pleadings, the discovery process, and the pretrial conference.
	The *trial* begins with jury selection, followed by opening statements, the plaintiff's case, the defendant's case, closing arguments, jury instructions, jury deliberations, the jury's verdict, and the judgment.
	After the trial, parties may file *posttrial motions.*
	The parties may then file *appeals* to the appropriate appellate court and, in some cases, to the U.S. Supreme Court.
Alternative Dispute Resolution	*Alternative dispute resolution* is a way to settle problems without having to go to a costly and time-consuming trial.
Primary Forms of ADR	The primary forms of ADR are *negotiation, mediation,* and *arbitration.*
Other ADR Methods	Other methods of ADR include *med-arb, summary jury trials, minitrials, early neutral case evaluation,* and *private trials.*

Point/Counterpoint

Should Companies Be Allowed to Include Binding Arbitration Clauses in Consumer Contracts?

YES	NO
Arbitration is a much faster way to resolve a likely small dispute. Through the discovery process, a defendant could draw out a case for two to three years before the case would actually go to trial. Thus, the consumer benefits from the binding arbitration clause by forcing the defendant to resolve the dispute quickly.	Arbitration may require that the consumer pay more up-front costs to begin the dispute resolution process. For example, the consumer may have to pay for the costs of the arbitrator. To file a complaint, a consumer has to pay filing fees only, which cost around $150. To file a claim through the American Arbitration Association, a consumer has to pay between $500 and $1,000, and the consumer is required to advance the arbitrator's fees.
According to a recent study by Ernst & Young, 55 percent of consumer arbitrations were resolved in the consumer's favor.* Another study suggested that 93 percent of people who participated in arbitration thought that they were treated fairly.† Consumers	Many consumers are not likely to read all the fine print when applying for a credit card or purchasing

receive fair and fast treatment through mandatory arbitration.

Consumers have a choice as to whether to purchase a good or service, and in some cases the purchase may include a requirement on how disputes will be resolved. If a consumer is opposed to a mandatory arbitration clause, the consumer can purchase the good or service from another provider.

In conclusion, companies should be permitted to include binding arbitration clauses in their consumer contracts.

a service. A consumer has no bargaining power to remove a mandatory arbitration clause from the contract; consequently, the consumer has no choice. It is unfair to force a consumer to submit a dispute to arbitration when she or he has no power to bargain regarding that aspect of the sales or service contract.

Finally, because arbitration is secret, a company can "hide" its disputes from the general public. The public exposure associated with lawsuits encourages companies to better respond to and resolve disputes.

In conclusion, consumers are harmed more than helped by binding arbitration clauses in consumer contracts.

* Ernst & Young, "Outcomes of Arbitration: An Empirical Study of Consumer Lending Cases," www.adrforum.com/rcontrol/documents/ResearchStudiesAndStatistics/2005ErnstAndYoung.pdf.

† "Report to the Securities and Exchange Commission Regarding Arbitrator Conflict Disclosure Requirements in NASD and NYSE Securities Arbitrations," www.nyse.com/pdfs/arbconflict.pdf.

Questions & Problems

1. Explain the two types of jurisdiction that a court must have to hear a case and render a binding decision over the parties.

2. Explain the differences between trial courts and appellate courts.

3. Identify and define the alternative tools of discovery.

4. Explain the three threshold requirements a plaintiff must meet before he or she can file a lawsuit.

5. The citizens of each state elect state court judges. The president, on the other hand, appoints federal court judges for lifetime positions. Why might this difference lead to different rulings on similar cases? Which method—election or appointment—do you like better? Why? What are the advantages and disadvantages of each method?

6. Missouri was International Shoe Corporation's principal place of business, but the company employed between 11 and 13 salespersons in the state of Washington who exhibited samples and solicited orders for shoes from prospective buyers in Washington. The state of Washington assessed the company for contributions to a state unemployment fund. The state served the assessment on one of International Shoe Corporation's sales representatives in Washington and sent a copy by registered mail to the company's Missouri headquarters. International Shoe's representative challenged the assessment on numerous grounds, arguing that the state had not properly served the corporation. Is the corporation's defense valid? Why or why not? [*International Shoe Co. v. Washington,* 326 U.S. 310 (1945).]

7. The Robinsons, residents of New York, bought a new Audi car from Seaway Volkswagen Corp., a retailer that was incorporated in New York and had its

principal place of business there. World-Wide Volkswagen, a company incorporated in New York and doing business in New York, New Jersey, and Connecticut, distributed the car to Seaway. Neither Seaway nor World-Wide did business in Oklahoma, and neither company shipped cars there. The Robinsons were driving through Oklahoma when another vehicle struck their Audi in the rear. The gas tank of the Audi exploded, injuring several members of the family. The Robinsons brought a product liability suit against the manufacturer, distributor, and retailer of the car in an Oklahoma state court. Seaway and World-Wide argued that the Oklahoma state court did not have *in personam* jurisdiction over them. After the state's trial court and supreme court held that the state did have *in personam* jurisdiction over Seaway and World-Wide, they appealed to the U.S. Supreme Court. How do you think the Court decided in this case? Why? [*World-Wide Volkswagen Corp. v. Woodson,* 444 U.S. 286 (1980).]

8. Central West Virginia Energy Company, a West Virginia coal sales company, along with Massy Coal Company, a Virginia corporation, filed a lawsuit in federal district court against Mountain State Carbon and its member companies, one of which, Severstal Wheeling, was located in Wheeling, West Virginia. The plaintiffs alleged that the defendants, all of which were in the steel business, refused to accept shipments of coal in breach of their supply agreement with Central Energy. The defendants filed a motion to dismiss for lack of diversity, claiming that both Severstal and Central Energy had their principal places of business in West Virginia. The district court dismissed the complaint for lack of diversity, citing

the fact that Severstal's self-described day-to-day operations such as "purchasing, sales, transportation, engineering, human resources, and accounting/financial functions are all handled in Wheeling" and noting Severstal's "visibility in and involvement with the Wheeling community." The plaintiffs appealed, arguing that the court misinterpreted *Hertz* and that the district court failed to consider the importance of the fact that Severstal's officers control the company's policies and high-level decisions from the corporate offices in Dearborn, where seven of the company's eight corporate officers maintain their offices. The plaintiffs also noted that in Severstal's corporate filings with the states of Ohio, Michigan, and West Virginia, the company listed a Dearborn, Michigan, address as its principal place of business. How do you think the court ruled on the appeal? Why? [*Central West Virginia Energy Company, Inc. v. Mountain State Carbon LLC,* Case No. 10-1486, 4th Cir. Ct. of Appeals, 2011 U.S. App. LEXIS 7557.]

9. Attorneys, journalists, media, and legal and human rights organizations brought action against the Central Intelligence Agency, challenging the constitutionality of Section 702 of the Foreign Intelligence Surveillance Act (FISA). In particular, they objected to a recent change to FISA, through the FISA Amendments Act, that shifted the party-monitoring compliance with the act's limitations from the judiciary to the executive branch, eliminating the power of the judiciary to review the surveillance procedures. The government argued that the plaintiffs lacked standing to bring the case to court. The plaintiffs argued that the recent change to FISA created a reasonable fear of future injury and that they had incurred costs to avoid that future injury. How do you think the court ruled in this case? Why? [*Amnesty International United States et al. v. Clapper, Alexander, and Holder,* 2011 U.S. App. LEXIS 5699.]

10. After Joel Varela died due to a work-related accident, his spouse and children filed a wrongful death action against his employee, Igloo Products Corp. Igloo filed a motion to compel arbitration under the terms of the arbitration agreement that Varela had signed in connection with his participation in an employee injury benefit plan. The trial court denied the motion to compel arbitration. What do you think happened on appeal? Why? [*In re Igloo Products Corp.,* 238 S.W.3d 574 (Tex. App. 2007).]

Looking for more review material?

The Online Learning Center at **www.mhhe.com/kubasekess2e** contains this chapter's "Assignment on the Internet" and also a list of URLs for more information, entitled "On the Internet." Find both of them in the Student Center portion of the OLC, along with quizzes and other helpful materials.

Administrative Law

CASE OPENER

Does the EPA Have an Obligation to Regulate Automobile Emissions?

On October 20, 1999, a group of 19 private organizations filed a rule-making petition asking the Environmental Protection Agency (EPA) to regulate "greenhouse gas emissions from new motor vehicles" under the Clean Air Act.[1] The petitioners cited the fact that 1998 was the "warmest year on record," that greenhouse gas emissions have significantly accelerated climate change, and that carbon dioxide is the most important man-made contribution to climate change. Fifteen months after the petition was filed, the EPA requested public comment on the issues. Then, on September 8, 2003, the EPA entered an order denying the rule-making petition, citing two reasons: (1) The Clean Air Act does not authorize the EPA to issue mandatory regulations to address global climate change; and (2) even if the agency had authority, it would be unwise to do so at this time. The case, *Massachusetts v. EPA*, eventually worked its way up to the U.S. Supreme Court, which had to decide whether the EPA was improperly failing to regulate carbon dioxide gas in automobile exhaust as a climate-changing pollutant.

1. What government entity is the final determiner of whether a particular type of rule will be issued by an agency?
2. Did the EPA err in not regulating greenhouse gases under the Clean Air Act?

[1] *Massachusetts v. EPA*, 549 U.S. 497 (2007).

LEARNING OBJECTIVES

After reading this chapter, you will be able to answer the following questions:

LO 3-1 What is administrative law?

LO 3-2 What is an administrative agency?

LO 3-3 How and why are administrative agencies created?

LO 3-4 What types of powers do administrative agencies have?

LO 3-5 What is the difference between an executive agency and an independent agency?

LO 3-6 What is the Administrative Procedures Act?

LO 3-7 How do formal, informal, and hybrid rule making differ from one another?

LO 3-8 What are the limits on agency power?

Introduction to Administrative Law

WHAT IS ADMINISTRATIVE LAW?

As a business owner or manager, you will need to be aware of regulations that affect your business. In addition to learning about laws passed by Congress, you will also need to know about rules passed by administrative agencies. **Administrative law** consists of the substantive and procedural rules created by **administrative agencies** (bodies of the city, county, state, or federal government), involving applications, licenses, permits, available information, hearings, appeals, and decision making.

An administrative agency is generally defined as any body created by the legislative branch (e.g., Congress, a state legislature, or a city council) to carry out specific duties. Agencies have three types of power: *legislative, judicial, and executive.* They may make rules for an entire industry, adjudicate individual cases, and investigate corporate misconduct. Because legislative, judicial, and executive powers have traditionally been placed in separate branches of government by the Constitution, the role of administrative agencies has led some to refer to agencies as the unofficial "fourth branch of government." Although there is a semblance of truth to that characterization, administrative agencies are not in fact another branch, primarily because all their authority is simply delegated to them and they remain under the control of the three traditional branches of government.

The first federal administrative agency, the **Interstate Commerce Commission (ICC),** was created by Congress near the end of the 19th century. Congress felt that the anticompetitive conduct of railroads could best be controlled by a regulatory body. The ICC no longer exists as a separate agency,[2] but for over 100 years the ICC regulated passenger and freight transportation. Following the crash of the stock market and the Great Depression of the 1930s, Congress saw a need for additional agencies to regulate business in the public interest. Since then, numerous agencies have been created whenever Congress believed there was an area that required more intense regulation than Congress could provide. In fact, after the Enron scandal there was talk that Congress might create a new agency to regulate the accounting industry. To date, no such agency has materialized.

WHY AND HOW ARE AGENCIES CREATED?

When Congress sees a problem that it believes needs regulation, it may create an administrative agency to deal with that problem. The idea is that the agency can be staffed with people who have special expertise in the area the agency is regulating and therefore are capable of knowing what types of regulations are necessary to protect the citizens in that area. Agencies typically act more swiftly than Congress in creating and enacting new laws. Today, administrative agencies actually create more rules than Congress and the courts combined.

Administrative agencies are created by Congress through passage of **enabling legislation,** which is a statute that specifies the name, functions, and specific powers of the administrative

LO 3-1

administrative law
The collection of rules and decisions made by administrative agencies to fill in particular details missing from constitutions and statutes.

LO 3-2

administrative agency
Any government body created by the legislative branch (e.g., Congress, a state legislature, or a city council) to carry out specific duties.

Interstate Commerce Commission (ICC)
The first federal administrative agency; created to regulate the anticompetitive conduct of railroads.

LO 3-3

enabling legislation
A statute that specifies the name, functions, and specific powers of an administrative agency and grants the agency broad powers for the purpose of serving the public interest, convenience, and necessity.

[2] The functions of the ICC were transferred to the Transportation Department by Congress as part of a cost-saving measure.

agency. Enabling statutes grant agencies broad powers for the purpose of serving the "public interest, convenience, and necessity." These broad powers include rule making, investigation, and adjudication.

LO 3-4

Rule Making Enabling statutes permit administrative agencies to issues rules that control individual and business behavior. These rules have the same effect as laws. If an individual or business fails to comply with agency rules, there are often civil, as well as criminal, penalties. Agencies may enact three types of rules: procedural, interpretive, and legislative.

Procedural rules are rules regarding the internal operations of an agency. *Interpretive rules* are rules that explain how the agency views the meaning of the statutes for which the agency has administrative responsibility. Finally, *legislative rules* are policy expressions that have the effect of law. The various rule-making processes are discussed later in this chapter.

subpoena

An order to appear at a particular time and place and provide testimony.

subpoena *duces tecum*

An order to appear and bring specified documents.

administrative law judge (ALJ)

A judge who presides over an administrative hearing; may attempt to get the parties to settle but has the power to issue a binding decision.

consent order

A statement in which a company agrees to stop disputed behavior but does not admit that it broke the law.

order

A binding decision rendered by a judge.

Investigation Enabling statutes grant executive power to agencies to investigate potential violations of rules or statutes. Many times, companies cooperate with agencies and voluntarily furnish information. Other times, however, agencies must use their investigative powers, defined in their enabling legislation, to gather information. Such powers typically include the power to issue a **subpoena** (i.e., an order to appear at a particular time and place and provide testimony) and a **subpoena *duces tecum*** (i.e., an order to appear and bring specified documents).

Adjudication Enabling statutes delegate judicial power to agencies to settle or adjudicate individual disputes that an agency may have with businesses or individuals. After investigation, the agency holds an administrative hearing before an **administrative law judge (ALJ)**. The ALJ will try to convince the parties to reach a settlement via a **consent order,** but the judge also has the authority to render a binding decision (an **order**) after a hearing (administrative law matters are heard only by an ALJ, as there is no right to a jury trial in administrative agencies). An appeal to the full commission or the head of an agency may then be filed. That decision may be appealed to the circuit court of appeals. If there are no appeals, the ALJ's initial order becomes the final order. Decisions of ALJs are typically upheld.

Example of an Administrative Problem. The EPA administrator, using the congressional mandate under the Clean Air Act, sets forth rules governing the amount of certain hazardous air pollutants that may be emitted into the atmosphere. Using these standards, another branch of the EPA sends investigators to inspect a plant suspected of violating the act. If the inspector finds a violation and the EPA imposes a penalty, the plant operator will most likely contest the imposition of the fine, and a hearing will be held before an ALJ employed in another division of the EPA. If the matter is not settled at the hearing, the ALJ will preside over another hearing and render a binding order. That order may be appealed within the agency and finally to the federal court. The courts, however, typically defer to the expertise of the agency and the associated ALJ. In other words, most orders by an ALJ are upheld.

Types of Administrative Agencies

executive agency

An agency that is typically located within the executive branch, under one of the cabinet-level departments. The agency head is appointed by the president with the advice and consent of the Senate.

independent agency

An agency that is typically not located within a government department. It is governed by a board of commissioners, who are appointed by the president with the advice and consent of the Senate.

Agencies are classified as either executive or independent. The administrative head of an **executive agency** is appointed by the president with the advice and consent of the U.S. Senate. Executive-agency heads may be discharged by the president at any time, for any reason. When a new president is elected, he will typically place his appointees in charge of executive agencies. These agencies are generally located within the executive branch, under one of the cabinet-level departments. Hence, executive agencies are referred to as *cabinet-level agencies.* Examples of traditional executive agencies are the Federal Aviation Agency (FAA), located within the Department of Transportation, and the Food and Drug Administration (FDA), located within the Department of Health and Human Services.

Independent agencies are governed by a board of commissioners, one of whom is the chair. The president appoints the commissioners of independent agencies with the advice and consent

Exhibit 3-1

Major Administrative Agencies

INDEPENDENT AGENCIES	EXECUTIVE AGENCIES
Commodity Futures Trading Commission (CFTC)	Federal Deposit Insurance Corporation (FDIC)
Consumer Product Safety Commission (CPSC)	General Services Administration (GSA)
Equal Employment Opportunity Commission (EEOC)	International Development Corporation Agency (IDCA)
Federal Communications Commission (FCC)	National Aeronautics and Space Administration (NASA)
Federal Trade Commission (FTC)	National Science Foundation (NSF)
National Labor Relations Board (NLRB)	Occupational Safety and Health Administration (OSHA)
Nuclear Regulatory Commission (NRC)	Office of Personnel Management (OPM)
Securities and Exchange Commission (SEC)	Small Business Administration (SBA)
	Veterans Administration (VA)

of the Senate, but these commissioners serve fixed terms and cannot be removed except for cause. No more than a simple majority of an independent agency can be members of any single political party (e.g., if the board consists of seven members, no more than four may be from the same political party). Serving fixed terms is said to make the commissioners less accountable to the will of the executive (thus the term *independent* agency). These agencies are generally not located within any department. Examples of independent agencies are the Federal Trade Commission (FTC), the Securities and Exchange Commission (SEC), and the Federal Communications Commission (FCC).

Another difference between these two types of agencies is the scope of their regulatory authority. Executive agencies tend to have responsibility for making rules covering a broad spectrum of industries and activities. Independent agencies, often called *commissions,* tend to have more narrow authority over many facets of a particular industry, focusing on such activities as rate making and licensing. Executive agencies have a tendency to focus more on *social* regulation, whereas independent agencies are more often focused on what we refer to as *economic* regulation. Exhibit 3-1 lists the major administrative agencies.

Some agencies do not fall clearly into one classification or the other. These agencies are typically referred to as **hybrid agencies.** Created as one type of agency, the body may share characteristics of the other. The EPA, for example, was created as an independent agency, not located within any department of the executive branch. Yet it is headed by a single administrator who serves at the whim of the president. During the early 1990s, in fact, there were discussions of the need to transform the EPA into a cabinet-level executive agency. (These initiatives did not get beyond the discussion stage.) Another example is the "independent" Federal Energy Regulation Commission (FERC), which has the typical structure of an independent agency yet is located within the Department of Energy.

LO 3-5

hybrid agency
An agency that has characteristics of both executive and independent agencies.

LO 3-6

Administrative Procedures Act (APA)
Federal legislation that places limitations on how agencies are run and contains very specific guidelines on rule making by agencies.

How Are Agencies Run?

In 1946 Congress passed the **Administrative Procedures Act (APA)** as a major limitation on how agencies are run. Prior to passage of APA, agencies could decide on their own how to make rules, conduct investigations, and hold hearings and trials. Under APA, there are very specific guidelines on rule making by agencies. The two most common types of rule making are *informal* and *formal,* and there is a third type known as *hybrid.* Each is discussed below, along with a few exemptions.

INFORMAL RULE MAKING

The primary type of rule making used by administrative agencies is **informal rule making,** or **notice-and-comment rule making.** Informal rule making applies in all situations in which the agency's enabling legislation or other congressional directives do not require another form. An

LO 3-7

informal rule making
A type of rule making in which an agency publishes a proposed rule in the *Federal Register,* considers public comments, and then publishes the final rule. Also called *notice-and-comment rule making.*

Federal Register
The government pub-
lication in which an
agency publishes each
proposed rule, along
with an explanation of
the legal authority for
issuing the rule and a
description of how the
public can participate in
the rule-making process,
and later publishes the
final rule.

agency initiates informal rule making by publishing the proposed rule in the *Federal Register,* along with an explanation of the legal authority for issuing the rule and a description of how the public can participate in the rule-making process. The *Federal Register* is the official daily publication for rules, proposed rules, and notices of federal agencies and organizations, as well as executive orders and other presidential documents.[3]

After publication, opportunity is provided for all interested parties to submit written comments. The comments may contain data, arguments, or other information a person believes might influence the agency in its decision making. Although the agency is not required to hold hearings, it has the discretion to receive oral testimony if it wishes to do so. While the agency is not required to respond to all comments it receives, it is required to respond to comments that significantly concern the proposed rule. After considering the comments, the agency may alter the rule. It publishes the final rule, with a statement of its basis and purpose, in the *Federal Register.* This publication also includes the date on which the rule becomes effective, which must be at least 30 days after publication. Informal rule making is most often used because it is more efficient for the agency in terms of time and cost. No formal public hearing is required, and no formal record need be established. Some people believe that informal rule making is unfair because parties who are interested in the proposed rule have no idea what types of evidence the agency has received from other sources with respect to that rule. Thus, if the agency is relying on what one party might perceive as flawed or biased data, that party has no way to challenge that data.

LO 3-7

FORMAL RULE MAKING

formal rule making
A type of rule making
that is used when legis-
lation requires a formal
hearing process with
a complete transcript;
consists of publication of
the proposed rule in the
Federal Register, a pub-
lic hearing, publication
of formal findings, and
publication of the final
rule if adopted.

The APA requires **formal rule making** when an enabling statute or other legislation mandates that all regulations or rules be enacted by an agency as part of a formal hearing process that includes a complete transcript. The first step in formal rule making is publication in the *Federal Register* of a notice of proposed rule making by the agency.

The second step is a public hearing at which witnesses give testimony on the pros and cons of the proposed rule and are subject to cross-examination. An official transcript of the hearing is kept. On the basis of information received at the hearing, the agency makes and publishes formal findings. On the basis of these findings, an agency may or may not promulgate a regulation. If a regulation is adopted, the final rule is published in the *Federal Register.* Because of the expense and time involved in obtaining a formal transcript and record, most enabling statutes do not require a formal rule-making procedure when promulgating regulations. If a statute is drafted in a manner that is at all ambiguous with respect to the type of rule making required, the court will *not* interpret the law as requiring formal rule making.

In the following case, the court had to decide whether to require formal rule making for substantive rules adopted by an agency.

LO 3-7

HYBRID RULE MAKING

hybrid rule making
A type of rule making
that combines features
of formal and informal
rule making; consists
of publication in the
Federal Register, a
written-comment period,
and an informal public
hearing with restricted
cross-examination.

After agencies began regularly making rules in accordance with the appropriate procedures, the flaws of each type of rule making became increasingly apparent. In response to these problems, a form of hybrid rule making became acceptable to the courts and legislature. **Hybrid rule making** is an attempt to combine the best features of both formal and informal rule making. The starting point, publication in the *Federal Register,* is the same. Publication is followed by the opportunity for submission of written comments, and then there is an informal public hearing with a more restricted opportunity for cross-examination than that in formal rule making. The publication of the final rule is done in the same manner as it is for other forms of rule making.

Exhibit 3-2 compares formal, informal, and hybrid rule making procedures.

EXEMPTED RULE MAKING

The APA contains an exemption from rule making that allows an agency to decide whether public participation will be allowed. Exemptions include rule-making proceedings with regard to "military or foreign affairs" and "agency management or personnel." Exemptions are also granted for

[3] *Federal Register,* www.gpoaccess.gov/fr/.

CASE Nugget

Do Substantive Rules Require Formal Procedure?

Alexis Perez v. John Ashcroft
U.S. District Court for the Northern District of Illinois, Eastern Division

236 F. Supp. 2d 899 (2002)

Perez, a native and citizen of Venezuela, had been a member of the Good Shepherd Church since November 1996. Beginning in December 1996 he worked as that congregation's music director, a full-time paid position. Under the law, a limited number of visas are available to an immigrant who, among other things, seeks to enter the United States to work for an organization in a professional capacity in a religious vocation or occupation. The Immigration and Naturalization Service (INS) denied Perez's visa application on the basis of his lack of religious training. Perez argued that the INS adopted the requirement of religious training in violation of the Administrative Procedures Act (APA), because it is a substantive rule adopted without the use of notice and comment or other formal rule-making procedures. Perez argued that he met all the requirements specified by the APA and INS regulations and, further, that the regulations contained no mention of a formal-religious-training requirement. INS countered that its imposition of the formal-training requirement—and its denial of Perez's visa request because he lacked that training—simply represented a reasonable interpretation of the regulations and that Perez's visa application was properly denied because he had no such training. There is no dispute that INS did not engage in any sort of formal rule-making process before adopting the requirement of formal religious training. The INS argued that the formal-training requirement was simply an interpretation of the regulations—more specifically, of the definition of "religious occupation"—and that therefore no formal rule making was necessary. The court disagreed.

All substantive rules adopted by an agency, that is, rules that create law, must be implemented through formal rule-making procedures.

Exhibit 3-2

Rule-Making Procedures

PROCEDURE	Type of Rule Making		
	FORMAL	INFORMAL	HYBRID
Public hearing	Yes	No	Yes
Formal record	Yes	No	No
Publication of proposed rule in *Federal Register*	Yes	Yes	Yes
Written comments from the public and interested parties	Yes	Yes	Yes
Oral testimony and cross-examination	Yes	No (agency discretion)	Yes (limited)
Publication of final rule in *Federal Register*	Yes	Yes	Yes

rule-making proceedings relating to "public property, loans, grants, benefits or contracts" of an agency. Military and foreign affairs often need speed and secrecy, which are incompatible with public notice and hearings. Other exemptions are becoming more difficult to justify in the eyes of

interpretive rule
A rule that does not create any new rights or duties but is merely a detailed statement of an agency's interpretation of an existing law, including the actions a party is to take to be in compliance with the law.

the courts unless they meet one of the exemptions of the Freedom of Information Act (discussed later in this chapter).

Also exempted from the rule-making procedures are interpretive rules and general policy statements. An **interpretive rule** is a rule that does not create any new rights or duties but is merely a detailed statement of the agency's interpretation of an existing law. Interpretive rules are generally very detailed, step-by-step statements of what actions a party is to take to be considered in compliance with an existing law. Case 3-1 demonstrates the courts' deference to reasonable agency interpretations of arguably unclear statutes.

 CASE 3-1

NATIONAL CABLE & TELECOMMUNICATIONS ASSN. v. GULF POWER CO.
UNITED STATES SUPREME COURT
122 S. Ct. 782 (2002)

FACTS: *The Pole Attachments Act . . . requires the Federal Communications Commission (FCC) to set reasonable rates that can be charged by owners of utility poles, such as telephone and electric poles, for certain attachments to their poles. Under [the act] a "pole attachment" includes "any attachment by a cable television system or provider of telecommunications service" to a utility pole. Some pole-owning utilities challenged, in various Federal Courts of Appeals, an FCC order that interpreted the act to cover attachments that provided commingled cable television and high-speed Internet services and to cover attachments by wireless telecommunications providers. . . . [T]he United States Court of Appeals for the Eleventh Circuit, in reversing the FCC on both points, held that (1) attachments for commingled services were not covered by either of the Act's two specific rate formulas . . . and (2) attachments for wireless communications were excluded from the Act by negative implication, where 224(a)(1) defined a "utility" as the owner of a pole that was used for wire communications.*

ISSUE: Is the FCC's interpretation of the Pole Attachments Act reasonable and entitled to deference by the federal courts?

REASONING: The Court stated, "The attachments at issue in this suit—ones which provide commingled cable and Internet service and ones which provide wireless telecommunications—fall within the heartland of the Act." In the Court's reasoning:

(1) The FCC's assertion of jurisdiction under the Act to regulate rates charged for attachments that provided commingled cable television and high-speed Internet access was reasonable and, therefore, entitled to deference, because the term "any attachment by a cable television system" in 224(a)(4) covered at least those attachments that provided cable television service.

(2) The FCC's assertion of jurisdiction under the Act to regulate rates charged for attachments by wireless telecommunications providers was reasonable and, therefore, entitled to deference, because the term "any attachment by a . . . provider of telecommunications service" covered at least those that provided telecommunications. . . .

The agency's decision, therefore, to assert jurisdiction over these attachments is reasonable and entitled to deference.

DECISION AND REMEDY: On certiorari, the U.S. Supreme Court reversed and remanded.

SIGNIFICANCE OF THE CASE: This case demonstrates the deference of the courts to the interpretations of statutes by administrative agencies.

CRITICAL THINKING

Why is the concept of deference less helpful than it seems at first glance? In other words, does any habit of deference also have its limits?

ETHICAL DECISION MAKING

What values are advanced by a doctrine of deference in this case? What values are downplayed when courts uphold the doctrine of deference?

The following case demonstrates, once again, the deference federal courts give to agency interpretation of ambiguous statutes.

CASE Nugget

What Is the Authority of Agency Interpretation of Statutes?

Warner-Lambert Company v. United States
U.S. Court of Appeals for the Federal Circuit

425 F.3d 1381 (2005)

Warner-Lambert imports and sells lozenges in packages under the name "Halls Defense™ Vitamin C Supplement Drops." The drops are composed primarily of sugar and glucose syrup, which together constitute more than 95 percent of each drop. Vitamin C constitutes just under 2 percent of each drop, with the remaining small percentage consisting of citric acid, flavors, and color. The Customs Service reclassified imported vitamin C supplement drops from their previous duty-free status as medicaments to dutiable status as sugar confectionery. As a result, the drops were subject to a duty of 6.1 percent. Warner-Lambert sued in the Court of International Trade. On appeal, the Customs Service reclassification was upheld. In a six-page detailed letter ruling, Customs explained the reasons for its action, including that its prior classification of the drops was "based upon the belief that Vitamin C imparted therapeutic or prophylactic character to the merchandise" but that "additional research indicates that Vitamin C has not been shown in the U.S. to have substances which imbue it with therapeutic or prophylactic properties or uses." The Court of International Trade held that Customs justifiably concluded that although the merchandise "may possess medical properties, it is being marketed as much for its flavor as for its medicinal value. Thus, it cannot be said that this merchandise is suitable only for medical purposes." The drops are marketed to provide users with their requirement of vitamin C, not to prevent or cure disease.

If a statute is ambiguous and if the implementing agency's construction is reasonable, the federal courts must accept the agency's construction of the statute, even if the agency's reading differs from what the court believes is the best statutory interpretation.

Policy statements are general statements about the directions in which an agency intends to proceed with respect to its rule-making or enforcement activities. Again, these statements have no binding impact on anyone; they do not directly affect anyone's legal rights or responsibilities.

A final exemption applies when public notice and comment procedures are "impracticable, unnecessary, or contrary to the public interest." This exemption is used most commonly either when the issue is so trivial that there would probably be very little, if any, public input or when the nature of the rule necessitates immediate action. Whenever an agency chooses to use this exception, it must make a "good-cause" finding and include in its publication of the final rule a statement explaining why there was no public participation in the process.

REGULATED NEGOTIATION

The exceedingly high number of challenges to regulations, as well as a growing belief that structured bargaining among competing interest groups might be the most efficient way to develop rules, has stimulated interest among a number of agencies in a relatively new form of rule making, often referred to as **reg-neg**. Each concerned interest group and the agency itself sends a representative to bargaining sessions led by a mediator. After the parties achieve a consensus, that agreement is forwarded to the agency.

policy statement
A general statement about the directions in which an agency intends to proceed with respect to its rule-making or enforcement activities; has no binding impact on anyone.

reg-neg
A type of rule making in which representatives of concerned interest groups and of the involved government agency participate in mediated bargaining sessions to reach an agreement, which is forwarded to the agency.

The agency is then expected to publish the compromise as a proposed rule in the *Federal Register* and follow through with the appropriate rule-making procedures. The agency, however, is not bound to do so. If it does not agree with the proposal the group negotiated, the agency is free to try to promulgate a completely different rule or a modification of the one obtained through the negotiation. The reasoning behind reg-neg is similar to that supporting the increased use of mediation. If the parties can sit down and try to work out a compromise solution together, that solution is much more likely to be accepted than one handed down by some authority. The parties who hammered out the agreement now have a stake in making it work because they helped to create it.

Admittedly, reg-neg is not possible in all situations. If there is an unmanageably large group of interests that would have to be represented, if any possible compromise would have to result from one group's backing away from a fundamental principle, or if two groups feel so antagonistic toward each other that they would be unable to rationally sit down and talk, reg-neg would probably not even be worth trying.

PROBLEMS ASSOCIATED WITH RULE MAKING

Agency employees are not subject to the same political pressures as legislators, but they are also not unbiased. Often the people with the necessary expertise to regulate specific areas come from the industry they are now going to be regulating. There is some concern that it will be difficult for regulators to ignore their past ties to industry and pass regulations that are in the public interest, especially when the regulations would increase costs to the industry or are opposed by the industry for other reasons. When people are discussing an agency in which they perceive this problem as existing, they often refer to the agency as being a "captured" agency. The counterargument is that those who have been deeply involved in an industry know it best. To prevent such actions during his administration, President Obama issued the *Executive Order on Ethics Commitments by Executive Branch Personnel*. The order prohibits executive-branch employees from accepting gifts from lobbyists; closes the revolving door that allowed government officials to move to and from private-sector jobs in ways that gave that sector undue influence over government; and requires that government hiring be based on qualifications, competence, and experience, not political connections.[4] Regulators must be sensitive to the role the economy plays in the public's willingness to accept or support certain regulations. When the economy is flourishing and unemployment is low, there is much greater acceptance of regulations. When unemployment is high, people are much more reluctant to accept regulations that they believe might cause some workers to lose their jobs and/or cause the prices of products to rise.

OTHER ADMINISTRATIVE ACTIVITIES

Agencies perform a variety of less well known but equally important tasks. These include advising, conducting research, issuing permits, and managing property. One of the most common situations in which individuals come into contact with agencies occurs when an agency advises businesses and individuals on whether the agency considers an activity legal or illegal. Agencies also conduct studies of industries and markets. For example, the FTC, OSHA, and FDA conduct studies to determine, respectively, the level of economic concentration, safety in the workplace, and safety of drugs. Also, agencies provide information to the general public on various matters through hotlines, publications, and seminars. Agencies also devote much of their time to issuing licenses or permits. The EPA, for example, helps protect the environment by requiring certain environmentally sound activities before granting permits. Local agencies are responsible for issuing liquor licenses and cabaret (dancing) permits to local bars and restaurants. Finally, agencies often are responsible for managing government property.

Case 3-2 illustrates limitations on an agency's use of its powers to issue, and in this case revoke, a driver's license.

[4] For a full text of the executive order, see www.whitehouse.gov/the_press_office/ExecutiveOrder-EthicsCommitments/.

YAN JU WANG v. GEORGE VALVERDE
COURT OF APPEAL OF CALIFORNIA, SECOND APPELLATE DISTRICT
162 Cal. App. 4th 616 (2008)

FACTS: *The trial court granted plaintiff Wang's petition for a writ of administrative mandate compelling the defendant, Department of Motor Vehicles (DMV), to set aside its revocation of Wang's class C driver's license. On appeal, the DMV argued that, as a matter of law, it had the authority to revoke Wang's class C license because it allegedly caught her cheating on an examination for a class B license. Wang, the holder of a valid class C (noncommercial) driver's license, applied for a class B (commercial) driver's license. She was given a written examination to determine whether she was qualified for a class B license, but she was not permitted to complete that examination because she was allegedly cheating in the taking of the examination by using crib notes. Wang was never criminally prosecuted for using crib notes, under Vehicle Code section 14610.5, because the DMV determined that there was insufficient evidence to support criminal action. The only administrative action taken against Wang by the DMV was to order the revocation of her class C (noncommercial) driver's license.*

ISSUE: Does the Vehicle Code empower the state to revoke a driver's license if the driver cheated on the test for a different driver's license?

REASONING: The DMV appealed the Appeals Court's concurring opinion that "[n]o such action is authorized by the Vehicle Code." The DMV argues that, as a matter of law, the DMV does have authority to revoke Wang's class C license because it allegedly caught her cheating on the examination for a class B license. The DMV purports to derive that authority from the Vehicle Code as follows: (1) Section 13359 provides that the DMV "may suspend or revoke the privilege of any person to operate a motor vehicle upon any of the grounds which authorize the refusal to issue a license"; (2) section 12809, subdivision

(d), provides that the DMV may refuse to issue a license to any person who has "committed any fraud in any application"; (3) an examination is part of an application; (4) the use of a crib sheet in taking an examination is a fraudulent act; so (5) by using the crib sheet, Wang committed a fraud in an application, which therefore authorized refusal to issue a class B license, which therefore authorized revocation of her class C license, because any ground for refusal to issue a license is also a ground for revocation of a license.

The DMV's argument thus depends upon the DMV's contention that under section 13359 *any* ground for refusal to issue *one* license is also sufficient to justify revocation of a *different* license. The DMV cites no authority for its construction of section 13359. We have found no case on point, but we conclude that the DMV's interpretation cannot be correct, because it would lead to untenable results. In general, the DMV's interpretation of the statute would authorize revocation of a class C license held by *any* unsuccessful applicant for a class B license. The statutory requirements for a class B license, however, are more demanding than the statutory requirements for a class C license, so statutory ineligibility for a class B license has no tendency, in itself, to show lack of statutory entitlement to a class C license. . . . Because the DMV's interpretation of section 13359 turns every unsuccessful application for a class B license into an authorization to revoke the applicant's class C license, it effectively negates the lower statutory threshold for entitlement to a class C license.

DECISION AND REMEDY: Affirmed, and respondent recovered the costs of her appeal.

SIGNIFICANCE OF THE CASE: The administrative agency is limited to the powers provided in the statute governing its operations.

CRITICAL THINKING

What facts, had they existed, would have altered this decision?

ETHICAL DECISION MAKING

Who besides the parties directly involved have interests in the results of this decision?

Limitations on Agency Powers

There are four basic limits on agency power: political, statutory, judicial, and informational (see Exhibit 3-3). The hope is that these limitations will keep the agencies and their thousands of employees from abusing their discretion.

POLITICAL LIMITATIONS

As discussed earlier in this chapter, the president appoints the administrative heads of all executive agencies with the advice and consent of the Senate. If the president is unhappy with the head of such an agency, that person may be fired at any time for any (or no) reason. As such, executive agencies are particularly accountable to the executive branch. Moreover, the political slant (liberal or conservative) of the agency is significantly influenced by the president.

Congress also has significant control over agencies, as the Senate must approve presidential nominees for them to become the administrative heads of agencies. Moreover, Congress has control over the budgets of all agencies. If Congress decides that a particular agency is not performing as it wishes, that agency's budget may be cut or even defunded. Just before the Enron crisis, Congress, after being heavily lobbied by the accounting industry, threatened to defund the Securities and Exchange Commission (SEC). In effect, Congress did not like the SEC's proposal that stock options be charged as earnings. Arthur Levitt, then head of the SEC, heard the warning loud and clear and decided to walk away from his firmly held position. In later interviews, Levitt said it was his biggest regret as head of the SEC.[5]

STATUTORY LIMITATIONS

Congress has the power to create or dissolve an agency. If Congress is unhappy with an agency, it may amend the agency's enabling legislation and limit the agency's power. Moreover, in 1996 legislation was signed into law that gives Congress 60 days to review proposed agency rules. Congress may override those rules before they become effective. In addition, the APA (passed by Congress in 1946) sets forth guidelines that all agencies must follow when engaged in rule making.

substantial evidence
Refers to evidence that a reasonable mind could accept as adequate to support a conclusion. It is defined as "more than a scintilla but less than preponderance" and consists of "such relevant evidence as a reasonable person would accept as adequate to support a conclusion."[7]

JUDICIAL LIMITATIONS

An individual or business that believes itself harmed by an administrative rule may challenge that rule in federal court once all administrative procedures have been exhausted.[6] This is probably the biggest constraint on agency power. If a rule is subjected to judicial review, the court will consider the following:

1. *The facts of the case:* Courts typically defer to an agency's fact finding. The facts must be supported by **substantial evidence**.

Exhibit 3-3

Limits on Agency Power

TYPE OF LIMIT	SPECIFIC LIMITATIONS
Political	The Senate must approve agency heads; Congress has power over agency budgets.
Statutory	Congress may create or eliminate agencies and amend enabling legislation (i.e., powers of agencies); Congress reviews and may override agency rules.
Judicial	Interested parties may challenge administrative rules in the courts, which may review the agency's finding of facts, its interpretation of the rule, and the scope of the agency's power in making the rule.
Informational	The Freedom of Information Act, Government in Sunshine Act, and Privacy Act of 1974 specify agencies' responsibilities regarding public access to information.

[5] PBS video, *Bigger than Enron—How Greed and Politics Undercut America's Watchdogs,* 1999.
[6] In a few situations, a court may not review an agency action. These include situations involving politically sensitive issues and those in which the agency's enabling legislation prohibits judicial review.
[7] *Mareno v. Apfel,* 1999 U.S. Dist. LEXIS 8575 (S.D. Ala., Apr. 8, 1999).

2. *The agency's interpretation of the rule:* Once again, the courts typically defer to the expertise of the agency and uphold the agency's interpretation of the rule.

3. *The scope of the agency's authority:* Has the agency exceeded the authority granted it by its enabling legislation?

While we typically think of judicial limitations as reining in overly zealous administrative regulators, the Case Opener illustrates that sometimes the judiciary is called on to restrict inaction by an agency. In *Massachusetts v. EPA,* the agency had resisted regulating greenhouse gases, arguing that carbon dioxide and similar gases are not pollutants under the Clean Air Act and, therefore, that the agency had no power to regulate them. When the high court reviewed the legislative mandate, however, it held that U.S. motor-vehicle emissions make a "meaningful contribution to greenhouse gas concentrations" and hence to global warming—and therefore the agency did have the authority to regulate such gases as air pollutants under the Clean Air Act.

INFORMATIONAL LIMITATIONS

Agency power is limited by the Freedom of Information Act (FOIA), the Government in Sunshine Act, and the Privacy Act of 1974.

Freedom of Information Act The **Freedom of Information Act (FOIA),** passed in 1966, requires that federal agencies publish in the *Federal Register* places where the public can get information from the agencies. The act requires similar publication of proposed rules and policy statements. It requires that agencies make such items as staff manuals and interpretations of policies available for copying to individuals, on request. Finally, all federal government agencies must publish records electronically.

Any individual or business may make a FOIA request to a federal government agency. Information may be obtained regarding how the agency gets and spends its money. Statistics and/or information collected by the agency on a given topic is also available. Perhaps most important, citizens are entitled to any records that the government has about them. For example, you could contact the Internal Revenue Service (IRS) and request all information that it has collected about you. FOIA does not apply to Congress, the federal courts, the executive staff of the White House, state or local governments, and private businesses. Exemptions to FOIA include, but are not limited to, national security, internal agency matters (e.g., personnel issues), criminal investigations, financial institutions, and an individual's private life.

Immediately after taking office, President Obama issued a Memorandum for the Heads of Executive Departments and Agencies indicating that FOIA should be administered with a clear presumption: In the face of doubt, openness prevails.[8] The memorandum directs that information should not be withheld simply because it is legal to do so and that if an agency cannot make full disclosure of information, it should consider making a partial disclosure.

Government in Sunshine Act The Government in Sunshine Act requires that agency business meetings be open to the public if the agency is headed by a collegiate body. A *collegiate body* consists of two or more persons, the majority of whom are appointed by the president with the advice and consent of the Senate. This open-meeting requirement applies only when a quorum is present. The law also requires that agencies keep records of closed meetings.

Privacy Act Under the Privacy Act of 1974, a federal agency may not disclose information about an individual to other agencies or organizations without that individual's written consent. This law guarantees three primary rights:

1. The right to see records about oneself, subject to the Privacy Act's exemptions.
2. The right to amend a nonexempt record if it is inaccurate, irrelevant, untimely, or incomplete.
3. The right to sue the government for violations of the statute, such as permitting unauthorized individuals to read your records.[9]

Freedom of Information Act (FOIA)
Federal legislation that mandates and facilitates public access to government information and records, including records about oneself. Sensitive information (e.g., on national security) is excluded.

[8] U.S. Department of Justice, www.usdoj.gov/ag/foia-memo-march2009.pdf.

[9] FCIC, "Your Right to Federal Records," www.pueblo.gsa.gov/cic_text/fed_prog/foia/foia.htm.

E-Government: Changing the Relationship between the Government and Citizens

According to the United Nations, *e-government,* which is defined as the delivery of government services through digital information technologies, including the Internet, is important because it reduces the cost of government while significantly improving the quality of services and citizen access. According to the latest UN report about this topic, e-government makes public administration more proactive, efficient, transparent, and service-oriented. Annual surveys by the UN indicate that nations throughout the world have made significant progress in e-government development, with the United States and Europe being among the leaders in this development.

The UN has characterized the development of e-government into the following stages:

Stage I—Emerging: A government's online presence mainly consists of a web page and/or an official website; links to ministries or departments of education, health, social welfare, labor, and finance may or may not exist. Much of the information is static, and there is little interaction with citizens.

Stage II—Enhanced: Governments provide more information on public policy and governance. They have created links that enable citizens to easily access archived information such as documents, forms, reports, laws and regulations, and newsletters.

Stage III—Interactive: Governments deliver online services such as downloadable forms for tax payments and applications for license renewals. In addition, the beginnings of an interactive portal or website with services to enhance the convenience of citizens are evident.

Stage IV—Transactional: Governments begin to transform themselves by introducing two-way interactions between "citizen and government" (C to G). This includes options for paying taxes and applying for ID cards, birth certificates, passports, and license renewals, as well as other similar C-to-G interactions, and it allows the citizen to access these services online 24/7.

Stage V—Connected: Governments transform themselves into a connected entity that responds to the needs of its citizens by developing an integrated back-office infrastructure. This is the most sophisticated level of online e-government initiatives, and it is characterized by:

1. Horizontal connections (among government agencies).
2. Vertical connections (central and local government agencies).
3. Infrastructure connections (interoperability issues).
4. Connections between governments and citizens.
5. Connections among stakeholders (government, private sector, academic institutions, NGOs, and civil society).

In addition, governments support and encourage e-participation and citizen engagement in the decision-making process.*

The most recent ranking of nations in terms of their progress toward development of effective e-government was as follows: (1) Sweden, (2) Denmark, (3) Norway, (4) United States, (5) Netherlands, (6) Republic of Korea, (7) Canada, (8) Australia, (9) France, and (10) United Kingdom.† Sadly, the United States was at the top of the list in 2001, but because the Bush administration failed to make a serious commitment to transforming the federal government through information technology and failed to develop an overall e-government plan detailing where the government wants to go and how it wants to get there, other nations have made much more rapid progress in this area than has the United States.‡

*United Nations, "E-Government Survey 2008," http://unpan1.un.org/intradoc/groups/public/documents/UN/UNPAN028607.pdf.

† Ibid., p. 20.

‡ Robert D. Atkinson (Progressive Policy Institute), "Unsatisfactory Progress: The Bush Administration's Performance on E-Government Initiatives," October 14, 2004, www.ppionline.org/ppi_ci.cfm?knlgAreaID=140&subsecID=290&content.ID=4252960.

The Privacy Act applies only to records about individuals maintained by agencies in the executive branch of the federal government. There are 10 exemptions to the Privacy Act under which an agency can withhold certain kinds of information from you. Examples of exempt records are those containing classified information on national security and those concerning criminal investigations.[10]

[10] Ibid.

Federal and State Administrative Agencies

Currently more than 100 federal agencies are in operation, as well as countless state agencies. Often, when there is a federal agency, there are also comparable state agencies to which the federal agency delegates much of its work. For example, the most important federal agency affecting environmental matters is the Environmental Protection Agency. Every state has a state environmental protection agency to which the federal EPA delegates primary authority for enforcing environmental protection laws. However, if at any time the state agency fails to enforce these laws, the federal EPA will step in to enforce them.

SUMMARY

Introduction to Administrative Law	*Administrative law* consists of the substantive and procedural rules created by administrative agencies (government bodies of the city, county, state, or federal government) involving applications, licenses, permits, available information, hearings, appeals, and decision making.
	An *administrative agency* is generally defined as any body created by the legislative branch (e.g., Congress, a state legislature, or a city council) to carry out specific duties.
	Administrative agencies are created by Congress through passage of *enabling legislation,* which is a statute that specifies the name, functions, and specific powers of the administrative agency. Enabling statutes grant agencies broad powers for the purpose of serving the "public interest, convenience, and necessity."
	An agency holds an administrative hearing before an *administrative law judge (ALJ).* The ALJ may attempt to get the parties to settle but has the power to issue a binding decision.
Types of Administrative Agencies	*Executive agency:* The administrative head of an executive agency is appointed by the president with the advice and consent of the U.S. Senate. Executive-agency heads may be discharged by the president at any time, for any reason. Executive agencies are generally located within the executive branch, under one of the cabinet-level departments (and thus are referred to as *cabinet-level agencies*). Examples are the Federal Aviation Agency (FAA) and the Food and Drug Administration (FDA).
	Independent agency: Independent agencies are governed by a board of commissioners. The president appoints the commissioners with the advice and consent of the Senate. Commissioners serve fixed terms and cannot be removed except for cause. No more than a simple majority of an independent agency can be members of any single political party.
	Hybrid agency: Hybrid agencies do not fall clearly into classification as an independent or an executive agency. Created as one type of agency, the body may share characteristics of the other type. The EPA, for example, was created as an independent agency, not located within any department of the executive branch, yet the head of the EPA serves at the whim of the president.
How Are Agencies Run?	In 1946 Congress passed the *Administrative Procedures Act (APA)* as a major limitation on how agencies are run. APA provides very specific guidelines on rule making by agencies.
	• *Informal rule making:* Under APA, the proposed rule is published in the *Federal Register,* and there is opportunity for public comment.
	• *Formal rule making:* All rules must be enacted by an agency as part of a formal hearing process that includes a complete transcript. The process begins with publication in the *Federal Register* of a notice of proposed rule making by the agency. Next, there is a public hearing at which witnesses give testimony on the pros and cons of the proposed rule and are subject to cross-examination. The agency makes and publishes formal findings. If a regulation is adopted, the final rule is published in the *Federal Register*.
	• *Hybrid rule making:* Hybrid rule making is an attempt to combine the best features of formal and informal rule making. The starting point is publication in the *Federal Register,*

followed by the opportunity for submission of written comments and then an informal public hearing with a more restricted opportunity for cross-examination than that in formal rule making.

- *Exempted rule making:* APA contains an exemption from rule making that allows an agency to decide whether public participation will be allowed. Exemptions include rule-making proceedings with regard to military or foreign affairs, agency management or personnel, and public property, loans, grants, benefits, or contracts of an agency.

Interpretive rules are rules that do not create any new rights or duties but merely state the agency's interpretation of an existing law. They are generally very detailed, step-by-step statements of what actions a party is to take to be considered in compliance with an existing law.

In reg-neg, each concerned interest group and the agency itself sends a representative to bargaining sessions led by a mediator. If the parties achieve a consensus, that agreement is forwarded to the agency. The agency is then expected to publish the compromise as a proposed rule in the *Federal Register* and follow through with the appropriate rule-making procedures. If the agency does not agree with the proposal the group negotiated, the agency is free to try to modify or replace it.

Limitations on Agency Powers

There are four basic limits on agency power: political, statutory, judicial, and informational.

Freedom of Information Act: Passed in 1966, FOIA requires that federal agencies publish in the *Federal Register* places where the public can get information from the agencies. Any individual or business may make a FOIA request to a federal agency for information on how the agency gets and spends its money, statistics and/or information collected by the agency on a given topic, and any records the government has about the individual seeking the information. Exemptions to FOIA include, but are not limited to, national security, internal agency matters (e.g., personnel issues), criminal investigations, financial institutions, and an individual's private life.

Government in Sunshine Act: This act requires that agency business meetings be open to the public if the agency is headed by a collegiate body (i.e., two or more persons, the majority of whom are appointed by the president with the advice and consent of the Senate). The law also requires that agencies keep records of closed meetings.

Privacy Act: Under the Privacy Act, a federal agency may not disclose information about an individual to other agencies or organizations without that individual's written consent.

Federal and State Administrative Agencies

Administrative agencies exist at the federal and state levels.

Point/Counterpoint

Do Agencies Have Too Much Power?	
YES	NO
The U.S. government is founded on separation of powers. That is why we have three branches of government: executive, legislative, and judicial. Giving administrative agencies all three powers—executive, legislative, and judicial—gives the agencies power to do anything they want with virtually no oversight. Agencies hire people who formerly worked in industry. Thus, these people often view regulation skeptically, yet they are the same people who run the agencies.	Administrative agencies came into existence because Congress, as well as state and local governments, did not have the expertise, time, or resources to deal with specialized problems such as air pollution, securities regulation, and banking administration. Without administrative agencies, these problems would not be addressed. An agency employs professionals with expertise and experience in the area the agency regulates. These people understand the industry and the ways in which it needs to be regulated.

Questions & Problems

1. What is enabling legislation?
2. What are the limits on agency power?
3. What are the three main powers given to agencies?
4. List the three categories of agencies.
5. Describe the various types of rule making.
6. T. J. Management operates Gabby's Saloon and Eatery in Minneapolis, Minnesota. In 1986, the Minneapolis City Council issued Gabby's a class B on-sale liquor license and annually renewed the license for 21 years without condition. Under its unconditional liquor license, Gabby's may stay open for business until 2 a.m. and maintain a maximum occupancy of 689 patrons. On August 7, 2006, a city council member e-mailed a number of city personnel, stating that she had received complaints about misconduct in the neighborhood surrounding Gabby's, that Gabby's violated its capacity limits, that its owners were regularly out of town, and that the neighborhood had "not had a homicide, yet [sic] but it is a recipe for one." Among the recipients were the city's deputy director for licensing and consumer services and the commander of the second police precinct, where Gabby's is located. At the deputy director's request, a city of Minneapolis license inspector conducted an inspection of Gabby's on the evening of September 30, 2006. Between the hours of 11:45 p.m. and 2:45 a.m., the inspector observed people littering, urinating in public, and yelling, and he heard vehicles with amplified music in the vicinity of Gabby's. The license inspector made no mention in his report of overcrowding or lack of appropriate management personnel. The commander of the second police precinct met with Gabby's owner Jeff Ormond on August 8, 2006, to discuss the neighborhood disruption issues that the commander believed were caused by Gabby's customers. On August 30, 2006, the council member, the precinct commander, the deputy director, and other city personnel convened to discuss conditions that could be placed on Gabby's liquor license to reduce disruptive activity in the neighborhood. At the hearing before the ALJ, the deputy director acknowledged that the proposed license conditions would require the voluntary cooperation of the owners of Gabby's and testified that the group discussed the challenges in trying to revoke the license if Gabby's refused to voluntarily agree to the license conditions. The deputy director also testified that despite the council member's complaint about overcrowding, he had determined that overcrowding was not an issue at Gabby's. On March 23, 2007, the Minneapolis City Council's Public Safety & Regulatory Services Committee recommended that the following adverse actions be taken against Gabby's: (1) a financial penalty of $25,000 be levied against Gabby's; (2) the occupancy limit of Gabby's be reduced to 400 customers at any given time; (3) Gabby's submit a comprehensive management plan to the city; (4) a properly trained manager or owner be on site during business hours; (5) Gabby's discontinue the sale of alcohol at 11:00 p.m.; (6) Gabby's agree to close at midnight every day of the week; (7) Gabby's increase the cover charge to at least $15; and (8) Gabby's eliminate free-drink events, such as "Ladies Night," and replace them with reduced-price drink specials. On March 31, 2007, two license inspectors conducted an inspection in response to neighborhood residents' complaints about noise and disturbances at Gabby's. Around 2 a.m., the inspectors videotaped the neighborhood surrounding Gabby's and recorded customers urinating in public; customers playing loud music in their cars; customers smoking in groups of 4-5 people around parked cars; a vehicle accident; cars "burning rubber"; police vehicle lights flashing in residential windows; and customers fighting. Gabby's challenged the adverse actions and argued that the scope of the Minneapolis law was limited solely to the license premises, including parking areas, and did not apply to off-premises activity. May Gabby's license be revoked for activities by its customers that occur outside Gabby's premises? Why or why not? [*In the Matter of the On-Sale Liquor License, Class B, Held by T. J. Management of Minneapolis d/b/a Gabby's Saloon and Eatery,* 763 N.W.2d 359 (Minn. Ct. App. 2009).]

7. Greenwood, an OSHA inspector, was driving by a construction site and thought that perhaps the site was unsafe. He got out of his car and videotaped the site, causing the foreman to ask him to leave. Greenwood also took measurements at the site and ultimately filed a report on OSHA violations of construction rules. The company running the construction site was assessed $49,000 in fines for OSHA violations. The company petitioned the court for review of the decision, arguing that an inspection by OSHA without a warrant was a violation of the right to privacy under the Fourth Amendment. How do you think the court decided? Explain your reasoning. [*Lakeland Enterprises of Rhinelander, Inc. v. Chao,* 402 F.3d 739 (7th Cir. 2005).]

8. Morales, a native and citizen of Mexico, was arrested in 1994 for entering the United States without inspection. He was released and served with a mail-out order to show cause why he should not be sent back to Mexico. Eventually, a removal hearing was

scheduled, and Morales was notified via certified mail of the time and place of the hearing. When Morales failed to attend the hearing, he was ordered removed in absentia. The INS apprehended and removed Morales from the United States in 1998. He attempted to reenter illegally in January 2001—this time using a false border-crossing card. He was apprehended at the port of entry and was expeditiously removed. Undaunted, Morales reentered the United States undetected the following day. Sometime between his 1998 and 2001 removals, Morales married a U.S. citizen. In March 2001, Morales's wife filed an I-130 alien relative petition based on his marriage to a U.S. citizen. When Morales and his wife met with the INS in January 2003, an immigration officer served them with a denial of the I-130 petition and a notice of intent to reinstate Morales's removal order. The case came before a three-judge panel, which held that the regulation authorizing immigration officers to issue reinstatement orders is invalid and Morales's removal order could be reinstated only by an immigration judge. Until 1997, removal orders could be reinstated only by immigration judges (i.e., not immigration officers). In 1997, the attorney general changed the applicable regulation to delegate this authority, in most cases, to immigration officers. Does the attorney general have the authority to change an INS regulation? Why or why not? [*Raul Morales-Izuierdo v. Alberto R. Gonzales, Attorney General,* 2007 U.S. App. LEXIS 10865 (9th Cir. 2007).]

9. Six conservation organizations filed a petition in Thurston County Superior Court asking that court to hold, pursuant to a provision in the Administrative Procedures Act (APA), that the Washington Forest Practices Board, the Washington Department of Ecology, and the Washington Department of Natural Resources (agencies) "failed to promulgate forest practice rules that advanced the environmental protection purposes and policies of the Forest Practices Act of 1974." The agencies countered by arguing that a formal petition for rule making must precede any petition for judicial review. Must an interest group exhaust administrative remedies before suing in a state or federal court? Why or why not? [*Northwest Ecosystem Alliance v. Washington Forest Practices Board,* 66 P.3d 614 (2003).]

10. This is an unusual case involving an effort to obtain judicial review of a Veterans Administration (VA) publication that was issued in 1978. The publication concerned the processing of claims filed by veterans who were seeking to establish service connection to certain diseases that they claimed had developed as a result of exposure to defoliants during their service in Vietnam. During the Vietnam War, the U.S. government sprayed herbicides over portions of Vietnam to

defoliate dense jungle areas. The most widely sprayed herbicide was known as Agent Orange, a name that referred to the orange stripes identifying the drums in which it was stored. Agent Orange contained dioxin, a toxic contaminant. In 1978, Vietnam veterans began to file claims for disability benefits based on their exposure to Agent Orange. Veterans claimed that Agent Orange exposure resulted in a variety of disabilities, including cancer, neurological dysfunction, psychiatric problems, persistent joint pain, chronic fatigue, and genetic damage manifested in birth defects among the veterans' children. In response to those claims, the Veterans Administration issued a "ratings practices and procedures" document entitled "Disability—Vietnam Defoliant Exposure." The document, which is dated April 17, 1978, became known as the Agent Orange Program Guide. After issuing the Program Guide, the VA denied many claims alleging service connection between defoliant exposure and most disabilities. Petitioners are veterans or survivors of veterans who allege they are suffering disability from exposure to Agent Orange. When petitioners' initial complaint was filed in 1979, no court had statutory authority to review VA regulations for compliance with APA procedural requirements. It was not until 1988 that Congress authorized judicial review of procedural challenges to such regulations under the APA. The petitioners contend that the long delay in the resolution of their original lawsuit should not, in itself, create a time bar to relief. The government cites the six-year limitations period for civil actions brought against the United States in district courts. Do you believe that the court should toll the statute of limitations and review the publication? Or should the court dismiss the claim as time-barred? Why? [*Block v. Sec'y of Veterans Affairs,* 2011 U.S. App. LEXIS 7685 (2011).]

11. On January 21, 2003, Robbins filed an application for site plan approval to construct an asphalt plant within the town limits of Hillsborough. Robbins had entered into a contract to purchase the property prior to submitting his application for site plan review, and subsequently he purchased the property. At the time he filed his application, an asphalt plant was a permitted use in a general industrial (GI) district subject to a site plan review. The property on which the asphalt plant was to be constructed was zoned GI. In reliance on the zoning ordinance in effect at the time of his application, Robbins spent approximately $100,000 to engineer and submit a site plan to comply with the conditional-use requirements set forth in the ordinance and to prepare for the required public hearings before the Town of Hillsborough Board of Commissioners. Three public hearings were held. The board received evidence but reached no decision. At the close of the third hearing, the board scheduled a

fourth hearing. Before the fourth hearing, the board amended the zoning ordinance to temporarily suspend review, consideration, and issuance of permits for manufacturing processes. Robbins's fourth hearing was canceled. Eventually, the suspension became a moratorium on permits until the end of the year. Robbins filed a complaint in Orange County Superior Court, alleging that he was entitled to rely on the language of the zoning ordinance in effect at the time he applied for the permit; that the board violated the law by failing to give notice of a public hearing or hold a public hearing prior to its decision to extend the moratorium; and that the defendant's decision to permanently prohibit asphalt plants was arbitrary and capricious. How should the court decide? Explain your answer. [*Robbins v. Town of Hillsborough,* 625 S.E.2d 813 (N.C. Ct. App. 2006).]

12. Tommy Robinson, a 60-year-old black male employee of the Food Safety and Inspection Service (FSIS), a division of the U.S. Department of Agriculture, alleged that the department discriminated against him on account of his age, sex, and race, in violation of Title VII of the Civil Rights Act of 1964, when it refused to promote him to the position of customer safety officer. The district court concluded that the complaint failed to state a claim for relief and dismissed it because Robinson failed to contact an equal employment opportunity (EEO) counselor and complain about the alleged discrimination. Federal-sector employees, such as Robinson, who believe that they have been subject to discrimination must initiate contact with an EEO counselor within 45 days of the effective date of the personnel action. An agency, however, "shall extend the 45-day time limit in paragraph (a)(1) of this section when the individual shows that . . . he or she did not know and reasonably should not have known that the discriminatory matter or personnel action occurred." In an attempt to get around the limitations bar, Robinson made two arguments: First, he said that he did not learn of the unlawful discrimination until November 15, 2001; second, he said that he did not learn that the person who obtained the position was white until sometime after he filed his grievance with the union on October 16, 2001. Robinson failed to make either argument

to the district court. On appeal, he argued that the court of appeals should extend the 45-day time limit. How did the court of appeals rule? Why? [*Robinson v. Jojanns, Secretary of Agriculture,* 2005 U.S. App. LEXIS 19561 (11th Cir. Ct. App. 2005).]

13. The respondent, the Public Company Accounting Oversight Board, was created as part of a series of accounting reforms in the Sarbanes-Oxley Act of 2002. The board is composed of five members appointed by the Securities and Exchange Commission (SEC). It was modeled on private self-regulatory organizations in the securities industry—such as the New York Stock Exchange—that investigate and discipline their own members subject to SEC oversight. Unlike these organizations, however, the board is a government-created entity with expansive powers to govern an entire industry. Every accounting firm that audits public companies under the securities laws must register with the board, pay it an annual fee, and comply with its rules and oversight. The board may inspect registered firms, initiate formal investigations, and issue severe sanctions in its disciplinary proceedings. The parties agree that the board is "part of the Government" for constitutional purposes. While the SEC has oversight of the board, it cannot remove board members at will but can do so only "for good cause shown," "in accordance with" specified procedures. The parties also agree that the commissioners, in turn, cannot themselves be removed by the president except for "inefficiency, neglect of duty, or malfeasance in office." The board inspected the petitioner accounting firm, released a report critical of its auditing procedures, and began a formal investigation. The firm and the petitioner Free Enterprise Fund, a nonprofit organization of which the firm is a member, sued the board and its members, seeking, *inter alia,* a declaratory judgment that the board is unconstitutional and an injunction preventing the board from exercising its powers. The petitioners argued that the Sarbanes-Oxley Act contravened the separation of powers by conferring executive power on board members without subjecting them to presidential control. Is the Public Company Accounting Oversight Board constitutional? Why or why not? [*Free Enter. Fund v. Pub. Co. Accounting Oversight Bd.,* 130 S. Ct. 3138 (2010).]

Looking for more review material?

The Online Learning Center at **www.mhhe.com/kubasekess2e** contains this chapter's "Assignment on the Internet" and also a list of URLs for more information, entitled "On the Internet." Find both of them in the Student Center portion of the OLC, along with quizzes and other helpful materials.

Constitutional Law

CASE OPENER

Regulations on Interstate Wine Sales: A Violation of the Commerce Clause?

Michigan and New York passed state statutes allowing in-state, but not out-of-state, wineries to sell wine directly to state residents. The statutes permitted out-of-state wine wholesalers, on the other hand, to sell to state residents. Thus, out-of-state wineries wishing to sell wine to Michigan and New York residents had to sell through a wholesaler. Because many small wineries produce insufficient quantities of wine to sell via wholesaler, however, the statutes effectively prohibited them from selling to Michigan and New York residents.

Michigan residents and an out-of-state winery challenged the statutes as violating the commerce clause of the U.S. Constitution. Michigan and New York argued that the Twenty-First Amendment protected the statutes. The Twenty-First Amendment states that "[t]he transportation or importation [of intoxicating liquors] into any state . . . for delivery or use therein, in violation of the laws thereof, is . . . prohibited." Moreover, the states argued that the statutes advanced legitimate public purposes: curbing wine sales to minors via the Internet, stemming tax evasion on wine sales, protecting public health and safety, and ensuring regulatory accountability.

The district court agreed with the states' argument, but on appeal the appellate court ruled that the statutes violated the commerce clause. Michigan and New York then appealed the case to the U.S. Supreme Court.

1. Do you think the Michigan and New York statutes violate the commerce clause? Why?
2. Would your answer to the previous question change if the state statutes regulated the sale of corn instead of wine? Why?

After reading this chapter, you will be able to answer the following questions:

LO 4-1 What is federalism?

LO 4-2 What is the function of each branch of government, and how does each branch serve to check the others?

LO 4-3 What is the relationship between the supremacy clause and preemption?

LO 4-4 How does the commerce clause affect the power of both the state and federal governments to regulate?

LO 4-5 What is the difference between commercial and political speech, and why is that difference important?

LO 4-6 How do the rights guaranteed by the Bill of Rights affect business managers?

The U.S. Constitution sets forth the framework of our nation's government; it establishes a system of government that divides power between the federal government and the states. This system of government provides the focus for this chapter.

In this chapter we examine the constitutional provisions that affect business. Then we turn our focus to the primary source of the federal government's authority to regulate business: the commerce clause. We next examine the federal government's authority to tax and spend. Finally, in the last part of the chapter, we focus on how several amendments to the Constitution affect business.

The U.S. Constitution

LO 4-1

The U.S. Constitution establishes a system of government based on the principle of **federalism,** according to which the authority to govern is divided between federal and state governments. According to the Tenth Amendment to the Constitution, all powers that the Constitution neither gives exclusively to the federal government nor takes from the states are reserved for the states. Because the federal government has only those powers granted to it by the Constitution, federal legislation that affects business must be based on an expressed constitutional grant of authority.

In addition to allocating authority between state and federal governments, the Constitution allocates the power of the federal government among the three branches of government. The first three articles of the Constitution establish three independent branches of the federal government: the legislative, executive, and judicial branches. The Constitution ensures that each branch maintains a separate sphere of power to prevent any one branch from obtaining undue power and monopolizing control of government.

The Constitution also establishes a system of *checks and balances.* Each branch's powers keep the other branches from dominating the government. For example, Congress, the legislative or lawmaking branch, has the power to enact legislation, but the president can veto a law that Congress passes. The legislature, however, can overturn a presidential veto with a two-thirds vote of the members of Congress. And if Congress

federalism
A system of government in which power is divided between a central authority and constituent political units.

To see how the concept of separation of powers can be analogized to a concept taught in accounting, internal controls, go to the **Connecting to the Core** activity on the text's website at www.mhhe.com/kubasekess2e.

Figure 4-1 The System of Checks and Balances

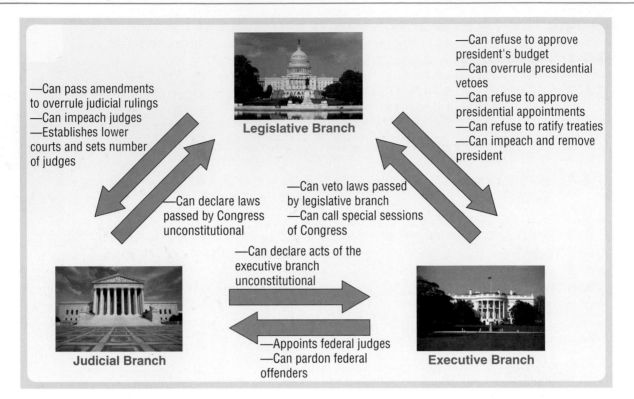

—Can pass amendments to overrule judicial rulings
—Can impeach judges
—Establishes lower courts and sets number of judges

—Can refuse to approve president's budget
—Can overrule presidential vetoes
—Can refuse to approve presidential appointments
—Can refuse to ratify treaties
—Can impeach and remove president

Legislative Branch

—Can declare laws passed by Congress unconstitutional

—Can veto laws passed by legislative branch
—Can call special sessions of Congress

—Can declare acts of the executive branch unconstitutional

—Appoints federal judges
—Can pardon federal offenders

Judicial Branch

Executive Branch

judicial review

The power of a court to review legislative and executive actions, such as a law or an official act of a government employee or agent, to determine whether they are constitutional.

LO 4-2

passes a bill and the president signs it, the judiciary can strike it down as unconstitutional. Figure 4-1 illustrates the system of checks and balances in more detail.

JUDICIAL REVIEW

Although the Constitution does not explicitly allow courts to review legislative and executive actions to determine whether they are constitutional, early common law established this process, known as **judicial review.** In the landmark 1803 U.S. Supreme Court case *Marbury v. Madison,* Chief Justice John Marshall wrote for the majority:

> [I]f a law be in opposition to the constitution; if both the law and the constitution apply to a particular case, so that the court must either decide that case [conforms] to the law, disregarding the constitution; or [conforms] to the constitution, disregarding the law; the court must determine which of these conflicting rules governs the case. This is of the very essence of judicial duty.

Judicial review also allows courts to review the constitutionality of lower courts' decisions.

LO 4-3

supremacy clause

Article VI, Paragraph 2, of the U.S. Constitution, which states that the Constitution and all laws and treaties of the United States constitute the supreme law of the land. Thus, any state or local law that directly conflicts with the U.S. Constitution or federal laws or treaties is void.

The Supremacy Clause and Federal Preemption

The **supremacy clause,** located in Article VI of the Constitution, provides that the Constitution, laws, and treaties of the United States constitute the supreme law of the land, "any Thing in the Constitution or Laws of any State to the Contrary notwithstanding." Any state or local law that directly conflicts with the Constitution, federal laws, or treaties is void. Federal laws include rules passed by federal administrative agencies. For example, the Federal Aviation Administration has banned the use of cell phones on airplanes. If a Missouri law permitted cell phone usage on airplanes, it would be unconstitutional according to the supremacy clause.

In some areas, the state and federal governments have concurrent authority; that is, both governments have the power to regulate the same subject matter. In such cases, the states may regulate in the area as long as a person's compliance with the state regulation would not cause her or him to be in violation of a federal regulation. For example, Congress has established a number of environmental standards, but some states have passed even more protective standards.

Sometimes, however, in areas where the state and federal governments have concurrent authority, the federal government can decide to regulate that area exclusively. In such a situation, according to the doctrine of **federal preemption,** the state law is unconstitutional. To determine whether Congress intended to provide exclusive regulation, courts look to the language of the statute and transcripts of congressional hearings.

federal preemption

A principle asserting the supremacy of federal legislation over state legislation when both pertain to the same matter.

The Commerce Clause

The primary source of authority for federal regulation of business is the **commerce clause,** located in Article I, Section 8, of the Constitution. This clause states that the U.S. Congress has the power to "regulate Commerce with foreign Nations, and among the several States, and with the Indian Tribes." This allocation of authority simultaneously empowers the federal government and restricts the power of state governments.

commerce clause

Clause 3 of Article I, Section 8, of the U.S. Constitution, which authorizes Congress to "regulate Commerce with foreign Nations, and among the several States, and with the Indian Tribes."

THE COMMERCE CLAUSE AS A SOURCE OF AUTHORITY FOR THE FEDERAL GOVERNMENT

LO 4-4

Today, most federal regulations are exercises of congressional authority according to the commerce clause. As long as a law affects commerce among the states, or interstate commerce, in some way, the regulation is generally constitutional. Congress, however, has not always enjoyed such extensive power.

In many cases, legislatures change the law by replacing statutes with different ones. In many other cases, however, the law changes even when statutes do not change because courts often interpret statutes differently over time. For example, although the text of the commerce clause has not changed since 1787, courts' interpretations of the meaning of the commerce clause have morphed over time. In particular, the phrase "among the several States" has been subject to changing interpretations throughout U.S. history. Prior to the 1930s, courts interpreted the clause very strictly, requiring that the regulated activity actually involve trade between states. This interpretation limited federal regulation of business.

In the 1930s, however, the Supreme Court began to interpret the commerce clause more broadly. The 1937 case *NLRB v. Jones & Laughlin Steel Corp.* was a turning point in the Supreme Court's interpretation of the commerce clause. In that case, the Court ruled that Congress could regulate labor relations at a manufacturing plant because a work stoppage at the plant would seriously affect interstate commerce. The Court stated that "[a]lthough activities may be intrastate in character when separately considered, if they have such a close and substantial relationship to interstate commerce that their control is essential or appropriate to protect that commerce from burdens or obstructions, Congress cannot be denied the power to exercise that control." Since that case, Congress has regulated a broad range of business activities according to the commerce clause, through legislation such as the Federal Mine Safety and Health Act, which sets standards for safety in coal mines; the Americans with Disabilities Act, which prohibits firms from discriminating against employees and potential employees who have disabilities; and the Consumer Protection Act, which criminalizes certain loan-sharking activities. Although businesses have challenged these statutes as being beyond the scope of congressional power, courts have upheld the statutes as valid exercises of congressional authority according to the commerce clause.

When the law changes, however, its movement is not always unidirectional. In fact, sometimes courts revert to standards and methods of interpretation that they rejected in the past. For example, the 1995 case *United States v. Lopez* marked a significant change in the nearly 60-year trend in the Supreme Court's interpretation of the commerce clause. In *Lopez,* the Court ruled

that Congress had exceeded its commerce clause authority when it passed the Gun-Free School Zone Act, a law banning the possession of guns within 1,000 feet of any school. In its ruling, the Court said that Congress could not regulate in an area that had "nothing to do with commerce, or any sort of enterprise."

Case 4-1 illustrates how the Supreme Court applies the commerce clause to determine the constitutionality of statutes passed by Congress.

CASE 4-1

CHRISTY BRZONKALA v. ANTONIO J. MORRISON ET AL.
UNITED STATES SUPREME COURT
120 S. Ct. 1740 (2000)

FACTS: *Petitioner Christy Brzonkala and respondents Antonio Morrison and James Crawford were students at Virginia Polytechnic Institute (Virginia Tech). Brzonkala met the respondents at a campus party, where they allegedly assaulted and raped her; according to Brzonkala, Morrison subsequently made boasting, debasing, and vulgar remarks on campus about what he would do to women. Brzonkala claimed to be emotionally disturbed and depressed as a result. She was treated by a university psychiatrist, and soon after the rape she withdrew from the university.*

Brzonkala filed a complaint against the respondents under Virginia Tech's Sexual Assault Policy. Morrison was initially found guilty and suspended for two semesters, but his punishment was ultimately set aside.

Brzonkala then sued Morrison, Crawford, and Virginia Tech in federal court, alleging, among other claims, that Morrison's and Crawford's attack violated the Violence against Women Act. Morrison and Crawford moved to dismiss this complaint on the grounds that it failed to state a claim and that the act's (§13981) civil remedy was unconstitutional.

The district court dismissed the complaint on grounds that Congress lacked authority to enact the section. The U.S. court of appeals affirmed the district court's conclusion.

ISSUE: Did Congress have the power under the commerce clause to enact the Violence against Women Act?

REASONING: Congress can regulate three broad categories of activities under its commerce powers. It can regulate the use of the channels of interstate commerce. It can regulate and protect the instrumentalities of interstate commerce, or persons or things in interstate commerce, even though the threat may come only from intrastate activities. It can regulate those activities that substantially affect interstate commerce. The act is properly analyzed as a potential regulation of an activity that substantially affects commerce.

The most relevant precedent is *Lopez,* in which the Supreme Court held that the Gun-Free School Zones Act of 1990, which made it a federal crime to knowingly possess a firearm in a school zone, exceeded Congress's authority under the commerce clause. That statute was struck down because, first, by its terms it was unrelated to commerce, and whenever the courts have sustained federal regulation of intrastate activity based on the activity's substantial effects on interstate commerce, the activity in question has been some sort of economic endeavor.

Second, the statute had no express jurisdictional element to limit its reach to a discrete set of firearm possessions that additionally have an explicit connection with or effect on interstate commerce. Third, Congress had no findings about the effect of gun possession at school on interstate commerce. Fourth, the link between gun possession and a substantial effect on interstate commerce was attenuated. To uphold the law would have meant that there were no limits on what Congress could regulate.

Likewise, gender-motivated crimes of violence are not economic activity, and there was no jurisdictional element showing that the federal cause of action is in pursuance of Congress's power to regulate interstate commerce. There were some statistics showing the impact of gender-related crime on victims and their families, but the Court had to decide whether these statistics demonstrate a substantial impact on interstate commerce, and the Court did not believe they do. The Court found that the congressional finding relied on a method of reasoning the Court had already rejected as unworkable if any limit on congressional powers is to be maintained. It is not sufficient to find that gender-motivated violence affects interstate commerce "by deterring potential victims from traveling interstate, from engaging in employment in interstate business, and from transacting with business, and in places involved in

interstate commerce; . . . by diminishing national productivity, increasing medical and other costs, and decreasing the supply of and the demand for interstate products." Allowing such reasoning would give Congress the power to regulate almost any crime.

DECISION AND REMEDY: The Court affirmed the lower courts' decisions, holding that Congress may not regulate noneconomic, violent criminal conduct solely on

the basis of that conduct's aggregate effect on interstate commerce.

SIGNIFICANCE OF THE CASE: The case clearly demonstrates an increasing willingness of the Court to limit congressional authority under the commerce clause. Note that the Court is not passing judgment on the quality of the law but is just saying that such a law would need to be passed by the state, not the federal, legislature.

CRITICAL THINKING

This case was a 5-4 decision. What reasoning do you think supported the dissent's opinion?

ETHICAL DECISION MAKING

Recall the WPH framework. What values led the majority to rule that Congress lacks authority to enact § 13981 of the Violence against Women Act? Do you think the values you listed are appropriate in this situation in spite of the individuals who are harmed by the decision?

The issue of whether the commerce clause has authorized Congress to act is an issue that still arises today. Currently, there is debate over whether the health care reform legislation passed under President Obama is unconstitutional. Two lower courts found it constitutional. One court found one section of it unconstitutional but felt that section could simply be struck down and the rest of the legislation could stand. A fourth court found the same provision unconstitutional but found that it was so intertwined with the legislation that the entire law must be struck down.

THE COMMERCE CLAUSE AS A RESTRICTION ON STATE AUTHORITY

The federal government's authority to regulate interstate commerce sometimes conflicts with the states' authority to regulate intrastate commerce. Courts have attempted to resolve this conflict by distinguishing between regulations of commerce and regulations under states' police power. **Police power** consists of the residual powers retained by each state to safeguard the health and welfare of its citizenry. Typical exercises of a state's police power include state criminal laws, building codes, zoning laws, sanitation standards for restaurants, and regulations for the practice of medicine.

Sometimes a state's use of its police power affects interstate commerce. If the purpose of a state law is to regulate interstate commerce or to discriminate against interstate commerce, the law is usually unconstitutional. Likewise, if a law substantially interferes with interstate commerce, it is generally unconstitutional. This restriction on states' authority to pass laws that substantially affect interstate commerce is called the **dormant commerce clause.**

Most cases are not so simple, however, and courts must balance the states' interest in protecting their citizens against the impact on interstate commerce. In balancing these competing interests, a court generally asks whether the state regulation is rationally related to a legitimate state end. If it is, the court then asks whether the regulatory burden imposed on interstate commerce is outweighed by the state's interest in enforcing the legislation. The court may also inquire whether there is a less drastic alternative available to attain the legitimate state purpose.

Although the supremacy clause establishes the sovereignty of federal law, courts generally presume that laws passed in accordance with states' police power are valid. For example, the city

police power
Power retained by each state to pass laws that protect the health, safety, and welfare of its citizens.

dormant commerce clause
A restriction on states' authority that is implied in the commerce clause of the U.S. Constitution: The power given to Congress to enact legislation that affects interstate commerce in effect prohibits a state from passing legislation that improperly burdens interstate commerce.

of Chicago passed an ordinance banning spray paint in the city as a means of reducing graffiti. Paint manufacturers challenged the legislation as a violation of the dormant commerce clause, but the U.S. court of appeals upheld the legislation.

Case 4-2 illustrates an attempt to challenge a state regulation on the grounds that it places an undue burden on interstate commerce.

CASE 4-2

BLACK STAR FARMS, LLC, ET AL. v. JERRY OLIVER, ARIZONA DEPARTMENT OF LIQUOR LICENSE AND CONTROL ET AL.
U.S. COURT OF APPEALS FOR THE NINTH CIRCUIT
600 F.3d 1225 (9th Cir. 2010)

FACTS: *Arizona generally requires all alcoholic beverages sold to consumers in the state to pass through a three-tier distribution system comprised of producers, wholesalers, and retailers. However, Arizona has carved out two exceptions to its system that allow wineries under specified circumstances to bypass the three-tier distribution system. First, all wineries that produce less than 20,000 gallons of wine per year—whether located in-state or out-of-state—are allowed to ship an unlimited amount of wine directly to consumers, regardless of how the order is placed, and to sell directly to retailers. Second, all wineries—whether located in-state or out-of-state—are allowed to ship two cases of wine per year directly to consumers who purchase wine while they are physically present at the winery.*

Black Star Farms, a Michigan winery, produced approximately 35,000 gallons of wine in 2006. Thus, the small-winery exception was not available to Black Star Farms, and wholesalers would not handle their wine in a cost-effective manner because they did not sell enough in the state. Nevertheless, the in-person exception did allow Black Star Farms to ship up to two cases per year to a consumer who purchased the wine while he was physically present at the winery in Michigan. Black Star Farms contended that these challenged exceptions to the three-tier system violated the dormant commerce clause, and sued the State Liquor Control Board because the winery could not ship directly to consumers who do not physically go to Michigan to purchase the wine.

They were joined in their action by a couple who wished to purchase Black Star Farms wine in Arizona without going to the Michigan winery. These consumer plaintiffs contended that it was economically and practically impossible for them to visit wineries located far from Arizona, including those in Michigan, Napa, and Oregon, in order to purchase wine in person and have it shipped home.

Black Star Farms and defendants each filed motions for summary judgment, and the district court denied Black Farms' motion but granted defendants' cross-motions for summary judgment, concluding that Black Star Farms failed to carry its burden of showing that the challenged statutory scheme discriminates against out-of-state wineries in practical effect. Black Farms appealed.

ISSUE: Do the exceptions to the state of Arizona's three-tier distribution system violate the dormant commerce clause?

REASONING: For the purposes of the dormant commerce clause, discrimination means differential treatment of in-state and out-of-state economic interests that benefits the former and burdens the latter. If such discrimination is found, the court will apply strict scrutiny. The party challenging the statute must prove discrimination.

This act at issue is intended to provide for a separate method of regulating only the sale and delivery of wine produced by small wineries, and allowing small wineries to bypass the wholesalers. Before the changes to the law, the "small-wineries exception" applied only to small wineries at which 75 percent of the grapes used were grown within the state of Arizona, making that exception facially unconstitutional, as it treated in-state and out-of-state wineries differently. The exception now applies to all small wineries, regardless of where their grapes are grown, so the law is facially neutral. The in-person exception likewise applies to in- and out-of-state wineries and is also facially neutral, and thus appears facially constitutional.

While Black Star Farms Winery contends that the law is discriminatory in its effect, (1) there was no indication that the exception creates a system under which local goods constitute a larger share, and goods with an out-of-state source constitute a smaller share, of the total sales in the market, and (2) more than half of all U.S. wineries can take advantage of the exception, and as of the time the case was

heard, more out-of-state than in-state wineries had taken advantage of it. Further, there is no indication whatsoever that the in-person exception has any effect on the flow of interstate commerce.

Thus, the law does not discriminate on its face or practically against interstate commerce.

DECISION AND REMEDY: The court of appeals concluded that Arizona's statutory exceptions to its three-tier distribution system, which treat similarly situated in-state and out-of-state wineries the same and impose no new impermissible burdens on out-of-state wineries, do not have the practical effect of favoring in-state economic interests over out-of-state interests. Therefore, the appellate court affirmed the district court's decision.

SIGNIFICANCE OF THE CASE: The case illustrates how the court responds to a challenge to a state statute based on grounds that the law violates the dormant commerce clause.

CRITICAL THINKING

What different facts might have led the court to a different conclusion?

ETHICAL DECISION MAKING

Identify the primary stakeholders helped and hurt by the outcome of this case.

Taxing and Spending Powers of the Federal Government

No government can function without a source of revenue. Article I, Section 8, of the Constitution gives the federal government the "Power to lay and collect Taxes, Duties, Imports and Excises." The taxes laid by Congress, however, must be uniform across the states. In other words, the government cannot impose higher taxes on residents of one state than it imposes on those of another.

Although tax collection allows the government to provide essential services, the government can also use taxes for other purposes. For example, to encourage the development of certain industries and discourage the development of others, the government can provide tax credits for firms entering favored industries. As long as the "motive of Congress and the effect of its legislative action are to secure revenue for the benefit of the general government," the credit is constitutional. The fact that it also has a regulatory impact does not affect the constitutionality of the credit.

Article I, Section 8, also grants Congress spending power by authorizing it to "pay the Debts and provide for the common Defense and general Welfare of the United States." As with its power to tax, Congress can use its spending power to achieve social welfare objectives. For example, in *South Dakota v. Dole,* the Supreme Court upheld a federal statute that grants federal funds for state highways to only those states in which 21 is the legal drinking age.

Other Constitutional Restrictions on Government

THE PRIVILEGES AND IMMUNITIES CLAUSE

Article IV, Section 2, of the Constitution states that "Citizens of each State shall be entitled to all Privileges and Immunities of Citizens in the several States." This provision, called the **privileges and immunities clause,** prohibits states from discriminating against citizens of other states when those nonresidents engage in ordinary and essential activities. These activities include buying

privileges and immunities clause

Clause in the U.S. Constitution requiring that a state grant citizens of other states the same legal benefits that it grants its own citizens.

and selling property, seeking employment, and using the court system. States may treat residents and nonresidents differently only when they have substantial reason for doing so.

For example, according to the privileges and immunities clause, a state cannot prohibit non-residents from opening restaurants in the state. States can, however, allow state universities to charge higher tuition to out-of-state students because residents pay taxes that fund state universities, while out-of-state students do not.

THE FULL FAITH AND CREDIT CLAUSE

full faith and credit clause

The clause of the U.S. Constitution (Article IV, Section 1) mandating that each state must recognize, respect, and enforce the public records, legislative acts, and judicial decisions of the other states.

Article IV, Section 1, of the Constitution contains the **full faith and credit clause.** This clause states, "Full Faith and Credit shall be given in each State to the public Acts, Records, and judicial Proceedings of every other State." This provision requires that courts in all states uphold contracts and public acts established in other states. For example, this clause protects wills, marriage and divorce decrees, and judgments in civil courts. Courts have held, however, that states do not have to give full faith and credit to laws that violate their "public policy." Thus, for example, although Massachusetts permits same-sex marriage, the full faith and credit clause does not require that other states recognize such marriages.

THE CONTRACT CLAUSE

contract clause

The clause in the U.S. Constitution that prohibits the government from unreasonably interfering with an existing contract.

Article I, Section 9, contains the **contract clause,** which states that government may not pass any "Law impairing the Obligation of Contract." In application, courts interpret this clause to mean that no law can be passed that will unreasonably interfere with existing contracts. For example, in the 1934 U.S. Supreme Court case *Home Building & Loan Association v. Blaisdell,* the Home Building & Loan Association challenged Minnesota's Mortgage Moratorium Act as a violation of the contract clause. The act, implemented temporarily during the Great Depression, authorized courts to extend the redemption periods of mortgages to delay foreclosures of mortgages on real estate. The Court ruled that the act's provisions were within the state's police power to protect its citizens and did not violate the contract clause. Although the act impaired contractual obligations between lenders and borrowers, the Court held that courts must balance even substantial contractual impairments against states' interest in protecting the welfare of their citizens.

The Amendments to the Constitution

The first 10 amendments to the U.S. Constitution, known as the Bill of Rights, substantially affect government regulation of business. These amendments prohibit the federal government from infringing on individual freedoms. Moreover, the Fourteenth Amendment extends most of the provisions in the Bill of Rights to the states, prohibiting state interference in citizens' exercise of their rights. Thus, the federal and state governments cannot deprive individuals of the freedoms protected by the Bill of Rights. Remember, however, that the amendments are a limit only on actions of the government—they do *not* limit the behavior of private employers. This distinction is commonly misunderstood by many citizens.

Many other countries do not have constitutional provisions to protect citizens from the government. The Australian constitution, for example, creates the framework for government in Australia. In many of the countries that do have individual protections in their constitutions, these protections have emerged recently. Some other countries' constitutions provide rights that American citizens do not have, as the Global Context box on Belarus's constitution illustrates.

Courts apply many amendments to corporations because corporations are treated, in most cases, as "artificial persons." The remainder of this chapter describes the amendments that most significantly affect the regulatory environment of business. Exhibit 4-1 summarizes the first 10 amendments.

THE FIRST AMENDMENT

Freedom of Speech and Assembly The First Amendment guarantees freedom of speech, including gestures and other forms of expression, and of the press. It prohibits abridgment of the right to assemble peacefully and to petition the government for redress of grievances. Finally, it

Constitution of Belarus

We think of the Constitution as establishing our system of government and guaranteeing certain rights to us. But some nations' constitutions actually impose duties on their citizens. For example, the constitution of Belarus requires that everyone protect the environment, preserve the nation's historical and cultural heritage and other cultural treasures, and respect the dignity, rights, liberties, and legitimate interests of others.

In addition, while the U.S. Constitution's Bill of Rights primarily restricts the government from interfering with our freedoms, some constitutions go much further in terms of giving people rights. For example, under the Belarus constitution, everyone has the right to an education, housing, and health care. Working people are entitled to work no more than 40 hours per week.

AMENDMENT	PROVISIONS
First	• Protects freedom of religion, press, speech, and peaceable assembly. • Ensures that citizens have the right to ask the government to redress grievances.
Second	• Finds that a well-regulated militia is necessary for security. • States that government cannot infringe on citizens' right to bear arms.
Third	• Provides that government cannot house soldiers in private residences during peacetime, or during war except for provisions in the law.
Fourth	• Protects citizens from unreasonable search and seizure. • Ensures that government issues warrants only with probable cause.
Fifth	• Ensures that government does not put citizens on trial except by the indictment of a grand jury. • Gives citizens the right not to testify against themselves. • Prevents government from trying citizens twice for the same crime. • Creates due process rights. • Provides that government cannot take private property for public use without just compensation.
Sixth	• Provides the right to a speedy public trial with an impartial jury, the right to know what criminal accusations a citizen faces, the right to have witnesses both against and for the accused, and the right to have an attorney.
Seventh	• States that in common lawsuits where the monetary value exceeds $20, citizens have the right to a trial by jury.
Eighth	• Provides that government will not set bail at excessive levels. • Prohibits government imposition of excessive fines. • Prohibits cruel and unusual punishment.
Ninth	• Provides that although the Bill of Rights names certain rights, this does not remove other rights retained by citizens.
Tenth	• Provides that powers that the Constitution does not give to the federal government are reserved for the states.

Exhibit 4-1

Summary of the Bill of Rights

prohibits the government from aiding the establishment of religion and from interfering with the free exercise of religion.

Like other rights, First Amendment rights are not absolute. For example, a person does not have the right to yell "Fire!" in a crowded theater. Nor does the First Amendment protect false statements about another that are injurious to that person's reputation. Due to the difficulty of determining the boundaries of individual rights, courts hear a large number of First Amendment cases.

LO 4-5

political speech
Speech that is used to support political candidates or referenda. It is given a high level of protection by the First Amendment as compared to other types of speech.

Political Speech. The First Amendment protections also apply to corporations. Courts do not, however, treat all corporate speech the same. Sometimes corporations engage in **political speech;** that is, they support political candidates or referenda. At one time, states restricted firms' political advertising because they feared that corporations, with their large assets, would drown out other voices. In the 1978 case *First National Bank of Boston v. Bellotti,* however, the U.S. Supreme Court considered the constitutionality of a Massachusetts law that prohibited certain corporations from spending money to influence voters on issues that did not materially affect the corporation. The Court held that the law was unconstitutional, stating, "The concept that the government may restrict speech of some elements of our society in order to enhance the relative voice of others is wholly foreign to the First Amendment." The Court ruled that the First Amendment protects corporate political speech to the same extent as ordinary citizens' political speech.

LO 4-6

commercial speech
Speech made by businesses about commercial matters, such as the sale of goods and services. It is protected by the First Amendment.

Commercial Speech. Not all corporate speech is political speech. **Commercial speech** is speech that conveys information related to the sale of goods and services. Courts analyze government restrictions on commercial speech according to a four-part test established in *Central Hudson Gas & Electric Corp. v. Public Service Commission of New York.* The *Central Hudson* test is illustrated in Figure 4-2.

Figure 4-2

The *Central Hudson* Test for Commercial Speech

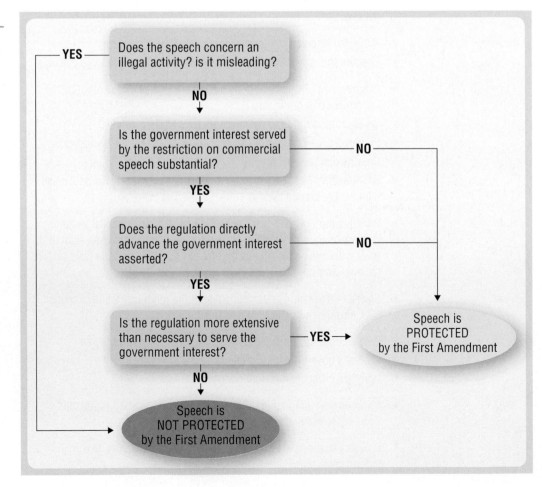

In Case 4-3, the Supreme Court applied this test to several New York regulations.

CASE 4-3	BAD FROG BREWERY v. NEW YORK STATE LIQUOR AUTHORITY U.S. COURT OF APPEALS FOR THE SECOND CIRCUIT 134 F.3d 87 (1998)

FACTS: *Bad Frog, a Michigan corporation, manufactures and markets alcoholic beverages under its "Bad Frog" trademark. Each label prominently features an artist's rendering of a frog holding up its middle "finger." Versions of the label feature slogans such as "He just don't care," "An amphibian with an attitude," "Turning bad into good," and "The beer so good . . . it's bad."*

In May 1996, Bad Frog's New York distributor applied to the New York State Liquor Authority for brand-label approval and registration pursuant to Section 107-a(4)(a) of New York's Alcoholic Beverage Control Law. NYSLA denied the application in July. Explaining its rationale for the rejection, the authority found that the label "encourages combative behavior" and that the gesture and the slogan, "He just don't care," placed close to and in larger type than a warning concerning potential health problems, foster a defiance to the health warning on the label, entice underage drinkers, and invite the public not to heed conventional wisdom and to disobey standards of decorum.

In addition, the authority said that it considered that approval of this label means that the label could appear in grocery and convenience stores, with obvious exposure on the shelf to children of tender age, and that it is sensitive to the label's adverse effects on a youthful audience.

Bad Frog filed suit against the NYSLA in October 1996 and sought a preliminary injunction barring NYSLA from taking any steps to prohibit the sale of beer by Bad Frog under the controversial labels.

ISSUE: Is the picture of a frog "behaving badly" on a product label entitled to protection as commercial speech?

REASONING: In the words of the court:

Bad Frog's label attempts to function, like a trademark, to identify the source of the product. Though the label communicates no information beyond the source of the product, the minimal information suffices to invoke the protections for commercial speech, articulated in the Central Hudson Case.

Central Hudson sets forth the analytical framework for assessing government restrictions on commercial speech:

[I]t at least must concern lawful activity and not be misleading. Next, we ask whether the asserted government interest is substantial. If both inquiries yield positive answers, we must

determine whether the regulation directly advances the government interest asserted, and whether it is not more extensive than is necessary to serve that interest. The last two steps in the analysis have been considered, somewhat in tandem, to determine if there is a sufficient "'fit' between the [regulator's] ends and the means chosen to accomplish those ends." The burden to establish that "reasonable fit" is on the governmental agency defending its regulation, though the fit need not satisfy a least-restrictive-means standard.

Applying the test, the labels concern lawful activity and not be misleading. The state claims two interests to support its asserted power to ban Bad Frog's labels: (i) the State's interest in "protecting children from vulgar and profane advertising," and (ii) the State's interest "in acting consistently to promote temperance, i.e., the moderate and responsible use of alcohol among those above the legal drinking age and abstention among those below the legal drinking age."

Both of the asserted interests are "substantial" because states have a compelling interest in protecting the physical and psychological well-being of minors, which includes shielding minors from the influence of literature that is not obscene by adult standards. The state also has a substantial interest in regulating alcohol consumption.

To meet the "direct advancement" requirement, a state must demonstrate that the law will directly restrict harms to that interest. In terms of protecting children from vulgarity, the restriction fails. Because of the wide range of vulgar displays throughout contemporary society, including comic books targeted directly at children, barring such displays from labels for alcoholic beverages cannot realistically be expected to reduce children's exposure to such displays to any significant degree. Attacking an almost insignificant part of a substantial problem is not sufficient.

As to the state interest in temperance, there was no evidence that viewing that gesture on a beer label will encourage disregard of health warnings or encourage underage drinking. Thus the law fails the third prong.

Finally, the law is more extensive than necessary to serve the asserted interest in insulating children from vulgarity. Less restrictive alternatives include restrictions on specific locations where children are more likely to view it, such as on billboards or on television advertising; restrictions on over-the-air advertising; and segregation of the product in the store.

DECISION AND REMEDY: The court concluded that "the State's prohibition of the labels from use in all circumstances does not materially advance its asserted interests in insulating children from vulgarity or promoting temperance, and is not narrowly tailored to the interest concerning children." The court therefore reversed the lower court's denial of Bad Frog's request for injunctive relief with respect to the disapproval of its labels.

SIGNIFICANCE OF THE CASE: The case illustrates the application of the Central Hudson test.

CRITICAL THINKING

What law do you think would advance the state's articulated interests without running afoul of the First Amendment?

ETHICAL DECISION MAKING

Which stakeholders' interests are advanced by this ruling? Which ones are harmed?

Unprotected Speech. The First Amendment right to free speech is not absolute. In the 1942 case *Chaplinsky v. New Hampshire,* the U.S. Supreme Court held:

> There are certain well-defined and narrowly limited classes of speech, the prevention and punishment of which have never been thought to raise any Constitutional problem. These include the lewd and obscene, the profane, the libelous, and the insulting or fighting words—those which by their very utterance inflict injury or tend to incite an immediate breach of the peace.

Thus, for example, the First Amendment does not protect defamation, or speech that harms the reputation of another. Moreover, as you will learn in Chapter 6, courts may require that an individual who uses such speech compensate the person whose reputation was harmed by the speech.

The First Amendment does not protect obscenity, either, although in many cases courts find it difficult to determine whether particular speech constitutes obscenity. In the 1973 case *Miller v. California,* the U.S. Supreme Court established a three-part standard to determine whether speech is obscene:

1. Would the average person, applying contemporary community standards, find that the speech, taken as a whole, appeals to the prurient (marked by or arousing an immoderate or unwholesome interest or desire) interest?
2. Does the speech depict or describe, in a patently offensive way, sexual conduct specifically defined by law?
3. Does the speech, taken as a whole, lack serious literary, artistic, political, or scientific value?

If the answer to all three questions is yes, the First Amendment does not protect the speech in question. Can you identify any significant ambiguities in the *Miller* standard?

Fighting words are a third class of unprotected speech. In *Chaplinsky v. New Hampshire,* a man protesting the government called the city marshal a "damned racketeer" and a "damned Fascist." The city arrested him for violating a statute prohibiting the use of offensive, derisive, or annoying words toward another in a public place. The U.S. Supreme Court held: "The English language has a number of words and expressions which by general consent are 'fighting words' when said without a disarming smile. . . . Such words, as ordinary men know, are likely to cause a fight." The Court further held that "'damned racketeer' and 'damned Fascist' are epithets likely to provoke the average person to retaliation, and thereby cause a breach of the peace." Thus, the Court determined that the First Amendment did not protect the man's speech.

Many universities believe that "hate speech," or derogatory speech directed at members of another group, such as another race, satisfies the definition of fighting words. Thus, 60 percent

Free Speech in China

The Chinese constitution does not guarantee freedom of speech or assembly, nor does it recognize any form of natural rights or human rights. Instead, it recognizes citizens' rights, which are specifically enumerated in the Chinese constitution or laws. Not only does the Chinese constitution not provide protections for expressive activity, but numerous Chinese laws prohibit citizens from engaging in political acts directed against the regime—acts that are protected in the United States. For example, Article 25 of China's Publishing Control Act prohibits the publication of any material that opposes the basic rules of the constitution. Articles 7 and 12 of the Law on Assemblies, Processions, and Demonstrations prohibit assemblies, processions, and demonstrations that oppose these basic rules.

of universities have banned verbal abuse and verbal harassment, and 28 percent have banned advocacy of an offensive viewpoint. State and federal appellate courts have struck down many of these hate-speech codes, but no cases have reached the Supreme Court yet. The international community, however, is less protective of hate speech. For example, a United Nations declaration and a number of foreign laws state that hate speech is not a protected form of expression.

Freedom of Religion The First Amendment contains two provisions that protect citizens' freedom of religion. The **establishment clause** maintains that government "shall make no law respecting an establishment of religion." In the 1971 case *Lemon v. Kurtzman,* the U.S. Supreme Court codified the following three tests to determine whether a particular government statute violates the establishment clause:

1. Does the statute have a secular legislative purpose?
2. Does the statute's principal or primary effect either advance or inhibit religion?
3. Does the statute foster an excessive government entanglement with religion?

To determine whether the statute fosters an excessive government entanglement with religion, courts examine the character and purposes of the institutions benefited, the nature of the aid that the government provides, and the resulting relationship between the government and the religious authority.

The **free-exercise clause** states that government cannot make a law "prohibiting the free exercise" of religion. Although government must remain neutral in matters of religion, determining whether a government action advances religion or merely allows free exercise of religion is often difficult. Likewise, determining whether a government action establishes religion or simply avoids interference with free exercise of religion is also difficult.

Issues concerning the establishment clause and the free-exercise clause often arise in workplace settings. In government workplaces, this conflict sometimes raises difficult issues. For example, in 1966, Tucker, an employee of the California Department of Education, insisted on signing office memos with his name and the letters "SOTLJC," an abbreviation for "Servant of the Lord Jesus Christ." In an attempt to avoid workplace disruptions and the appearance of government support for religion, Tucker's supervisor prohibited all displays of religious symbols in the workplace. The supervisor suspended Tucker for refusing to comply with the restrictions. When Tucker challenged the suspension on grounds that the rules interfered with his free exercise of religion, the appellate court agreed.

In private workplaces, issues related to free exercise of religion most often arise under Title VII, the federal law prohibiting employment discrimination. We discuss this important legislation in detail in Chapter 24.

THE FOURTH AMENDMENT

Freedom from Unreasonable Searches and Seizures The Fourth Amendment guarantees citizens the right to be "secure in their persons, their homes, and their personal property." Thus, it prohibits government from conducting unreasonable searches of individuals and seizing their property to use as evidence against them.

establishment clause
One of two provisions in the First Amendment of the U.S. Constitution that protect citizens' freedom of religion. It prohibits (1) the establishment of a national religion by Congress and (2) the preference of one religion over another or of religion over nonreligious philosophies in general.

free-exercise clause
A clause in the First Amendment of the U.S. Constitution which states that government (state and federal) cannot make a law "prohibiting the free exercise" of religion. This clause is interpreted to include absolute freedom to believe and freedom to act that may face state restriction.

search warrant

A court order that authorizes law enforcement agents to search for or seize items specifically described in the warrant.

A search is unreasonable if the government official conducting the search does not first obtain a search warrant from a court. A **search warrant** is a court order that authorizes law enforcement agents to search for or seize items specifically described in the warrant. Government officials can obtain search warrants only if they can show *probable cause* to believe that the search will uncover specific evidence of criminal activity. In other words, the government officials must have a sufficient reason based on known facts to obtain a warrant.

The Supreme Court has ruled, however, that in certain circumstances, government officials do not need a search warrant. For example, when law enforcement officials believe it is likely that the items sought will be removed before they can obtain a warrant, they may conduct a search without a warrant. Law enforcement officials frequently conduct automobile searches without a warrant according to this rule.

In most other cases, though, law enforcement officials must obtain a warrant before conducting a search. For example, an Ohio law required that buyers of five or more beer kegs provide the beer distributor with the address of the party where the kegs would be consumed. Additionally, the law required that the buyers sign a form allowing police and liquor agents to enter their property without a warrant to search the premises to enforce state liquor laws. In 2001, a college professor challenged the law on grounds that it infringed on citizens' Fourth Amendment rights. Before the court decided the case, Ohio repealed the law.

In addition to protecting individuals and their homes, the Fourth Amendment also protects corporations and places of business. This protection generally applies in criminal cases, but Fourth Amendment issues also arise when government regulations authorize administrative agencies to conduct warrantless searches.

Although administrative searches usually require search warrants, courts have established an exception to this rule: If an industry has a long history of pervasive regulation, a warrantless search is not unreasonable. In such industries, administrative agencies can use warrantless searches to ensure that firms uphold regulations.

This *pervasive-regulation exception,* however, is not always easy to interpret. Courts have ruled that warrantless searches authorized by the Federal Mine Safety and Health Act are legal because the federal regulatory presence is comprehensive and well defined. Thus, reasonable commercial-property owners ought to know that their property is subject to periodic inspections. A warrantless search based on the Occupational Safety and Health Act, however, may violate the Fourth Amendment because no significant legislation of working conditions existed before Congress passed that act in 1970. Hence, businesspeople covered by the law cannot reasonably anticipate warrantless searches.

THE FIFTH AMENDMENT

The Fifth Amendment protects individuals in several important ways. First, it protects against *self-incrimination,* meaning that in a criminal case, the defendant does not have to testify in court as a witness against himself or herself. The Fifth Amendment also protects against *double jeopardy.* Thus, government cannot try a person more than once for the same crime.

due process clause

A clause in the Fifth Amendment of the U.S. Constitution providing that the government cannot deprive an individual of life, liberty, or property without a fair and just hearing.

procedural due process

The requirement that a government must use fair procedures before depriving a person of his or her life, liberty, or property.

Due Process For businesspeople and corporations, the Fifth Amendment's **due process clause** provides extensive protection. This clause states that government cannot deprive a person of life, liberty, or property without *due process* of law.

The due process clause guarantees two types of due process: procedural and substantive. **Procedural due process** requires that the government use fair procedures when taking the life, liberty, or property of an individual or corporation. At a minimum, procedural due process entitles a person to notice of any legal action against her and to a hearing before an impartial tribunal. Originally, courts interpreted the due process clause as protecting an individual's right of procedural due process only in federal criminal proceedings. The subsequent passage of the Fourteenth Amendment extended the requirement of due process to criminal proceedings by state governments. Today, courts apply the due process clause to diverse situations, including the termination of welfare benefits, food stamps, or Social Security benefits; the suspension of a driver's license; the discharge of a public employee from his job; and the suspension of a student from school.

CASE Nugget

How Does Technology Affect the Fourth Amendment?

United States v. Kyllo
United States Supreme Court

533 U.S. 27 (2001)

Technological improvements have raised new issues in the application of the Fourth Amendment. New technologies have made eavesdropping and other covert activities easier. For example, in a 2001 U.S. Supreme Court case, police had information suggesting that Danny Kyllo grew marijuana in his home. Growing marijuana indoors requires heat lamps that use large amounts of electricity, and Kyllo had unusually high electric bills. The police used a thermal imager, an instrument that detects heat emissions, to provide them with the evidence necessary to obtain a warrant to physically search his house.

The Court addressed the issue of whether the use of thermal-imaging instruments on private property constituted a "search." Judges analyze cases by comparing them to past cases to see how other judges determined similar cases. Thus, in this case, the Court asked whether using thermal-imaging instruments is more like going through someone's garbage or more like using a high-powered telescope to look through someone's window. Previous Supreme Court cases held that the former behavior does not constitute a search but the latter scenario does constitute a search and therefore requires a warrant. The appellate court, examining the use of this technology for the first time, ruled that using thermal imaging was not a search prohibited by the Fourth Amendment without a warrant.

On appeal, however, the U.S. Supreme Court ruled that police use of thermal-imaging devices to detect heat patterns emanating from private homes constitutes a search that requires a warrant. The Court held, further, that the warrant requirement applies not only to the relatively crude thermal-imaging device but also to any "more sophisticated systems" that give the police knowledge that in the past would have required physical entry into the home. In explaining the Court's decision, Justice Scalia wrote that in the home, "all details are intimate details, because the entire area is held safe from prying government eyes." He added that the Court's precedents "draw a firm line at the entrance to one's house."

This case, however, is not necessarily the final word on the use of technology. The Court relied heavily on the fact that police used thermal imaging to see inside Kyllo's *home*. Thus, courts may in the future uphold thermal imaging of other locations.

The procedures that government must follow when taking an individual's life, liberty, or property vary according to the nature of the taking. Generally, more procedures are necessary as the magnitude of potential deprivation increases.

Substantive due process refers to the basic fairness of laws that may deprive an individual of her life, liberty, or property. To satisfy the substantive due process requirement, government must have a proper purpose for enacting laws that restrict individuals' liberty or the use of their property. The standard for determining whether a law violates substantive due process depends on the nature of the potential deprivation. Laws affecting fundamental rights must bear a substantial relationship to a compelling government purpose. These fundamental rights generally include the rights protected in the Constitution: the right to vote, the right to travel freely from state to state, the right to privacy, and so on. Compelling state interests include, for example, public safety and national security.

Not all laws, however, affect fundamental rights. To show that a law that does not affect fundamental rights satisfies the substantive due process requirement, government must prove only that the law bears a rational relationship to a legitimate state interest. Courts uphold most government

substantive due process
The requirement that laws depriving an individual of life, liberty, or property be fair and not arbitrary.

regulations according to this *rational-basis test.* For example, courts have upheld minimum-wage laws, rent control laws, banking regulations, environmental laws, and regulations prohibiting unfair trade practices according to the rational-basis test.

The Prohibition against Uncompensated Takings The Fifth Amendment provides that when government takes private property for public use, it must pay the owner *just compensation,* or fair market value, for her property. This provision is called the **takings clause,** and it applies to corporations. Several significant issues have arisen with respect to the takings clause. For example, what constitutes a "public use" for which government can take private property? This issue is explored in depth in Chapter 6.

> **takings clause**
> A clause in the Fifth Amendment of the U.S. Constitution requiring that when government uses its power to take private property for public use, it must pay the owner just compensation, or fair market value, for the property.

The takings clause has prompted other issues as well. What happens, for instance, when a government regulation interferes so substantially with an individual's use of her property that it effectively "takes" her property? For example, environmental regulations often affect the way landowners can use their property. Under the case of *Lucas v. South Carolina Coastal Commission,* the Supreme Court held that if a regulation is so extensive that it leaves the property owner with no economically viable use of his land, the regulation constitutes a taking and the owner is entitled to compensation for the value of his property, even though the state did not seek to take title to his land.

The Privilege against Self-Incrimination Although most provisions of the Fifth Amendment apply to corporations, corporations do not enjoy the Fifth Amendment's protection against self-incrimination. Sole proprietors, however, are entitled to this protection. Thus, different businesses have different constitutional rights depending on their form of business organization.

For example, in the 1988 U.S. Supreme Court case *Braswell v. United States,* the Court distinguished between the rights of corporate-record custodians and sole proprietors. Braswell was both the operator and the sole shareholder of his business. When a grand jury issued a subpoena requiring that he produce corporate books and records, Braswell argued that the subpoena violated his Fifth Amendment privilege against self-incrimination. The Court denied Braswell's claim, writing that "subpoenaed business records are not privileged, and as a custodian for the records, the act of producing the records is in a representative capacity, not a personal one, so the records must be produced." The Court held that the subpoena would have violated Braswell's privilege against self-incrimination if his business had been a sole proprietorship.

THE NINTH AMENDMENT

The Right to Privacy The Ninth Amendment states, "The enumeration in the Constitution, of certain rights, shall not be construed to deny or disparage others retained by the people." Although this amendment does not expressly guarantee the right to privacy, courts have interpreted the Ninth Amendment, together with the First, Third, Fourth, and Fifth Amendments, as providing individuals with a right to privacy.

In the 1965 case *Griswold v. Connecticut,* the Supreme Court ruled that a Connecticut law prohibiting the use of contraceptives was unconstitutional because it violated individuals' right to privacy. Justice Douglas wrote:

> Specific guarantees in the Bill of Rights have penumbras [fringes]. . . . Various guarantees create zones of privacy. The right of association contained in the penumbra of the First Amendment is one. . . . The Third Amendment in its prohibition against the quartering of soldiers "in any house" in time of peace without the consent of the owner is another facet of that privacy. The Fourth Amendment explicitly affirms the "right of the people to be secure in their persons, houses, papers, and effects, against unreasonable searches and seizures." The Fifth Amendment in its Self-Incrimination Clause enables the citizen to create a zone of privacy which government may not force him to surrender to his detriment.

THE FOURTEENTH AMENDMENT

> **equal protection clause**
> A clause in the Fourteenth Amendment of the U.S. Constitution that prevents states from denying "the equal protection of the laws" to any citizen. This clause implies that all citizens are created equal.

Equal Protection The Fourteenth Amendment contains the **equal protection clause,** which prevents states from denying "the equal protection of the laws" to any citizen. This clause combats discrimination because it applies whenever government treats certain individuals differently than other similarly situated individuals, usually through a classification scheme.

As with the due process clause, to determine whether a law violates the equal protection clause, courts use different standards based on the nature of the rights the classification affects. Three different standards of scrutiny apply: strict scrutiny, intermediate scrutiny, and the rational-basis test.

If a law prevents individuals from exercising a fundamental right, or if the law's classification scheme involves suspect classifications, the action will be subject to **strict scrutiny.** *Suspect classifications* include classifications based on race, national origin, and citizenship. Courts uphold suspect classifications only if they are necessary to promote a compelling state interest. In cases involving suspect classifications, courts do not begin their analysis with a presumption that the classification is constitutional, so few laws pass the strict-scrutiny standard. For example, in the 1954 case *Brown v. Board of Education,* the U.S. Supreme Court ruled that the classification scheme used to racially segregate public schools violated the equal protection clause.

Several courts have held, however, that in some cases, remedying past discrimination against a group is a compelling state interest. Chapter 24 discusses this issue in detail.

If the law's classification scheme is based on gender or on the legitimacy of children, courts use **intermediate scrutiny.** According to this standard, the law is constitutional only if it is substantially related to an important government objective.

When a classification scheme involves other matters, courts apply a **rational-basis test.** According to this test, courts ask whether there is any justifiable reason to believe that the classification scheme advances a legitimate government interest. Because courts begin their analysis with a strong presumption that the government action is constitutional, almost all laws pass this test.

strict scrutiny
The most exacting standard of review used by the courts in determining the constitutionality of a statute; requires a compelling government interest and the least restrictive means of attaining that objective.

intermediate scrutiny
A standard of review under which a law must be necessary to achieve a substantial, or important, government interest and it must be narrowly tailored to that interest.

rational-basis test
The lowest standard of review; requires that a law be designed to protect a legitimate state interest and be rationally related to that interest.

SUMMARY

The U.S. Constitution	*Federalism:* The authority to govern is divided between two sovereigns, or supreme lawmakers: the federal government and the states.
	Separation of powers: The Constitution divides power among the legislative, executive, and judicial branches of government. The system of checks and balances allocates specific powers to each branch to keep the other branches from dominating government.
The Supremacy Clause and Federal Preemption	*Federal supremacy:* Any state or local law that directly conflicts with the U.S. Constitution or federal laws or treaties is void.
	Concurrent authority: Both state and federal governments have the power to regulate certain matters; generally, the federal government defers to the state.
	Federal preemption: The federal government uses this doctrine to strike down laws that do not directly conflict with a federal law but attempt to regulate an area within federal legislative jurisdiction.
The Commerce Clause	The *commerce clause* grants the federal government the authority to pass regulations that significantly affect interstate commerce. Today, this clause provides the basis for most federal government regulations.
	Police powers are the residual powers retained by states to pass laws to safeguard the health and welfare of their citizens.
	The *dormant commerce clause* prohibits states from passing laws that significantly interfere with interstate commerce.
Taxing and Spending Powers of the Federal Government	Congressional taxes must be uniform across all states. Congress can use taxes and spending for purposes other than generating revenue; e.g., it can use them to indirectly promote social goals.
Other Constitutional Restrictions on Government	The *privileges and immunities clause* prohibits states from discriminating against citizens of other states.
	The *full faith and credit clause* states that in civil matters, courts in all states must uphold rights established by legal documents.
	The *contract clause* states that Congress cannot pass laws that unreasonably interfere with existing contracts.

The Amendments to the Constitution

First Amendment:

- Protects corporate speech in certain circumstances. It protects corporate political speech to the same extent that it protects individuals' political speech. The Central Hudson test determines whether the First Amendment protects particular corporate commercial speech.
- Contains the *establishment clause,* which states that Congress may not make laws respecting an establishment of religion, and the *free-exercise clause,* which states that Congress may not make laws prohibiting the free exercise of religion.

Fourth Amendment:

- Protects both corporations and individuals from unreasonable government searches and seizures. Although administrative searches generally require a warrant, administrative agencies may inspect some industries without a warrant to ensure compliance with industry regulations.

Fifth Amendment:

- States that government cannot take an individual's life, liberty, or property without due process of law. There are two types of due process: *procedural due process,* which focuses on rules for enforcing laws and entitles individuals to notice of legal action against them, and *substantive due process,* which requires that government have a proper purpose for enacting laws that restrict individuals' liberty or the use of their property.
- States that if government takes private property for public use, it must compensate the owner. The extent to which some government regulations constitute takings, however, generates much litigation.
- Includes a privilege against self-incrimination, although the provision does not apply to corporations. Only individual citizens and sole proprietorships may exercise this right.
- Guarantees individuals equal protection under the law. Courts use three different standards of scrutiny in equal protection cases: (1) *strict scrutiny,* to analyze government actions that abridge fundamental rights or that include suspect classifications; (2) *intermediate scrutiny,* to analyze classifications based on gender or on legitimacy of children; (3) the *rational-basis test,* to analyze classifications involving other matters.

Ninth Amendment:

- Along with the First, Third, Fourth, and Fifth Amendments, this amendment provides individuals with a right to privacy.

Fourteenth Amendment:

- Applies the due-process clause to state governments and contains the equal protection clause, which prohibits states from denying the equal protection of the laws to any citizens.

Point/Counterpoint

Is Judicial Review Consistent with Our System of Democracy?	
NO	YES
Our system of government is one of popular sovereignty: Voters have the liberty to make the laws under which they will live. As established in *Marbury v. Madison,* judicial review permits the Supreme Court to strike down laws passed by Congress—laws that ostensibly represent the will of a majority of Americans. The	Judicial review has an important role to play in ensuring that our democracy functions. Without the possibility of judicial review, elected representatives could pass laws to insulate themselves from political pressure. For example, Congress could pass a law making it a crime to criticize congresspersons.

Supreme Court, however, is not politically accountable. By declaring a law unconstitutional, the Supreme Court makes it enormously difficult for voters to overturn that decision; only an amendment to the Constitution (requiring approval of two-thirds of Congress and three-quarters of the state legislatures) can override it. Judicial review stymies voters' liberty to govern themselves.

Proponents of judicial review argue that it is necessary to protect the ideals in the Constitution. But the Constitution represents the values a majority of Americans held more than two centuries ago. The acts of the political branches of government, on the other hand, are more likely to accurately reflect the values of a majority of Americans today. Thus, to promote the values of a majority of Americans, the Supreme Court should refrain from judicial review.

Judicial review is especially problematic because the nine unelected justices of the Supreme Court are not likely to reflect the views of the nation as a whole. A vast majority of the justices throughout American history have been white, male, and wealthy. Thus, the values they promote when they strike down legislative acts are likely to differ from the values of a majority of Americans.

Such laws inhibit democracy from functioning well. The Supreme Court, insulated from political pressure, should exercise its power of judicial review to ensure participation and reinforce representation in the political process. Judicial review also allows the Supreme Court to transcend legislative preoccupation with immediate results and protect values at the center of our political system (e.g., protection of minority rights).

Our system, moreover, has many countermajoritarian features. The Constitution established the Senate, in which Wyoming and California are on equal footing; and the electoral college, not a popular majority, elects the president. Senate rules permit *filibustering,* allowing one senator to obstruct a proposed piece of legislation unless a supermajority of senators override the filibuster. In short, our system is *republican,* not majority rule. Judicial review is not inconsistent with this form of government.

Additionally, the Supreme Court has a high turnover rate. On average, a Supreme Court vacancy opens up every 22 months, so a one-term president can expect to fill two Supreme Court seats. This high turnover rate tends to ensure that the Court stays in step with the national pulse. And the political branches of government are not exactly the paradigms of deliberative democracy that high school textbooks make them out to be.

Questions & Problems

1. Explain how each branch of the government checks the power of the other branches.

2. How can both Sue and Sam be correct when Sue claims the commerce clause increases government's power and Sam claims the commerce clause reduces government's power?

3. What is the purpose of the contract clause?

4. How does the contract clause affect state regulation?

5. How does the First Amendment protection of corporate political speech differ from the protection of corporate commercial speech?

6. Taxpayers in the state of Kentucky alleged that a tax on out-of-state municipal bonds that excluded interest from in-state bonds was a violation of the commerce clause. Representatives of the state argued that the tax reflected a traditional government function that could persist without any differential treatment of local interests against the similar interests of out-of-state entities. Additionally, because Kentucky itself participates in the bond market, its potential discrimination should be found allowable. How would you have ruled in this case? Why? [*Department of Revenue of Kentucky v. George W. Davis*, 553 U.S. 328 (2008).]

7. The city of Concord, New Hampshire, enacted an ordinance prohibiting all electronic messaging centers (EMCs), which are signs that display electronically changeable messages—illuminated text that can be changed frequently by scrolling or flashing. The city had found EMCs to be detrimental to traffic safety and community aesthetics.

 Plaintiff Naser Jewelers, Inc., wanted to install an EMC at his store in Concord because after he had installed one at his store in Dover, his business increased by 18 percent. When he was denied a permit to install an EMC because of the ordinance, he sought a preliminary injunction against the enforcement of the ordinance on grounds that it was facially unconstitutional under the First Amendment. A magistrate judge denied the request, and the denial was upheld by the district court. The district court upheld the ordinance under the rule that content-neutral regulations are constitutional provided that they are narrowly tailored to serve a significant government interest and allow for reasonable alternative channels of communication. The plaintiff appealed. How do you think the court of appeals ruled in this case and why? [*Naser Jewelers v. City of Concord, New Hampshire,* No. 07-2098, 1st Cir. Ct. of Appeals (2008).]

8. The Entertainment Software Association (ESA), representing video game developers such as Sony Computer Entertainment and Nintendo, filed a motion for a permanent injunction in Illinois, claiming that the Illinois Sexually Explicit Video Game Law (SEVGL) was a content-based restriction on speech. The ESA argued that the law requiring the marking "18" on games containing sexually explicit images was subjective and failed to meet the Central Hudson test. The district court agreed. Representatives of the state, including then-governor Rod Blagojevich, appealed the decision, arguing that the law was narrowly tailored to promote a legitimate state interest. Using the four steps of the Central Hudson test, how do you think the court of appeals decided the case? [*Entertainment Software Association v. Blagojevich et al.,* 469 F.3d 641 (2006).]

9. An interstate trucking company filed suit against the state of Michigan, alleging that Michigan's $100 annual fee on trucks involved in intrastate commerce violates the dormant commerce clause. The trucking company argued that the fee discriminates against trucks involved in both intrastate and interstate commerce because they spend less time carrying cargo in Michigan than do trucks involved with solely intrastate commerce. The state argued that the fee is a valid exercise of its police power, intending to defray the costs of regulating the size and weight of trucks in Michigan. With whom do you think the U.S. Supreme Court sided in this case? Why? [*Am. Trucking Ass'ns v. Mich. PSC,* 125 S. Ct. 2419 (2005).]

10. Delaware enacted an apprentice regulatory scheme to "develop and conduct employee training and registered apprenticeship programs" and to provide "for the establishment and furtherance of standards of apprenticeship and training to safeguard the welfare of apprentices and trainees." Under the state's prevailing wage regulations, contractors who participated in the program could pay their apprentices significantly lower wages on certain public works projects. One of the requirements for having a registered apprenticeship training program that would qualify a contractor to pay these lower wages was to be a "Delaware Resident Contractor" or hold and maintain a "Delaware Resident Business License." "The Registrant must hold and maintain a permanent place of business, not to include site trailers or other facilities serving only one contract or related set of contracts." Thus, out-of-state contractors were basically excluded from participating in the program and qualifying for paying the lower wages. Tri-M, an out-of-state contractor who could not participate in the apprenticeship program and thus take advantage of paying lower wages to apprentices unless he established a permanent facility in the state of Delaware, sought a declaratory judgment and injunctive relief against enforcement of the Delaware prevailing wage law and the Delaware apprenticeship and training law. On what constitutional grounds do you think Tri-M sought this injunction? Why do you believe Tri-M should have won or lost its case? [*Tri-M Group v. Sharp,* 2011 U.S. App. LEXIS 5660, ___ 3d Cir. Ct of Appeals ___ (2011).]

11. Harris County arrested Carl Pruett for violating a law prohibiting bail-bond businesses from soliciting individuals with outstanding arrest warrants. The purpose of the law, according to the county, was to prevent individuals from fleeing the county when notified of their outstanding arrest warrants by bail-bonding companies. Pruett argued that the law was an unconstitutional restriction of his right to free speech. How do you think the court ruled in this case? Why? [*Harris County Bail Bond Bd. v. Pruett,* 2005 Tex. App. LEXIS 1912 (2005).]

12. The city of Toledo, Ohio, passed the Clean Indoor Air Ordinance, which required, among other provisions, that smoking be prohibited in bars and restaurants, except in separate smoking lounges that met very specific criteria. The lounge could not constitute more than 50 percent of the establishment's square footage into which the public is invited, must have a separate ventilation system, and cannot be located in an area where employees are required to work or be an area that the public must walk through to go to the restroom. An association of bar and restaurant owners challenged the law as a regulatory taking. The district court denied the claim and the association appealed. How do you think the appellate court ruled and why? [*D.A.R.E. Inc. v. City of Toledo,* 393 F.3d 692 (2005).]

13. In April 1986 the FBI arrested Larry Dean Dusenbery in his home. After the FBI removed Dusenbery from the premises and placed him in custody, it obtained and executed a search warrant for his property. During the search, FBI agents seized drugs, drug paraphernalia, weapons, an automobile, and $21,939 in currency. Dusenbery pleaded guilty to a charge of possession with intent to distribute. The trial court sentenced him to 12 years in prison and a 6-year special parole. Two years later, the FBI began to administratively forfeit the seized possessions. This process required that the FBI send written notice of the forfeiture procedures to Dusenbery. The FBI, in accordance with this policy, sent letters to Dusenbery by certified mail to the federal corrections institution where he was incarcerated. The FBI sent identical letters to his home address and his mother's address. The FBI received no response, but nevertheless it proceeded with the forfeiture of his assets. Five years later, Dusenbery filed a motion requesting that the FBI return his property to him. He received a response from the U.S. government informing him that the FBI

had returned all property not used in the drug business and had forfeited the rest of it. Dusenbery filed a civil suit claiming that the FBI denied his right of due process when it forfeited his property because he had never received the letter from the FBI. The district court ruled that the FBI had not violated his due process rights; the FBI satisfied his rights when it sent the notice. How do you think the appellate court ruled in this case? Why? [*Dusenbery v. United States,* 534 U.S. 161 (2002).]

14. In 1996 Congress passed the Telecommunications Act. This legislation addressed growing public concern that children could access, at least in part, sexually explicit programming through a phenomenon called "signal bleed." Signal bleed occurs when visual or audio portions of programs can be seen or heard despite cable providers' attempt to scramble the programs. The act required that cable providers fully scramble or otherwise fully block those channels or limit transmission to hours when children are unlikely to watch television. Most cable operators adopted the latter approach, broadcasting programs only during an eight-hour period at night. Playboy Entertainment Group, a firm that transmitted sexually explicit programming to cable television operators, filed suit against the federal government. The suit claimed that the Telecommunications Act violated the First Amendment, and it asked for an injunction prohibiting the act's enforcement. The district court ruled that the act imposed a content-based restriction on speech; the court concluded that although the government interests were compelling, the government could further those interests in a less restrictive way. How do you think the U.S. Supreme Court ruled in this case? Why? [*United States v. Playboy Entertainment Group,* 529 U.S. 803 (2000).]

Looking for more review material?

The Online Learning Center at **www.mhhe.com/kubasekess2e** contains this chapter's "Assignment on the Internet" and also a list of URLs for more information, entitled "On the Internet." Find both of them in the Student Center portion of the OLC, along with quizzes and other helpful materials.

CHAPTER

5

Criminal Law and Business

Untenable Trading

In late 1997, John Freeman, employed at Goldman Sachs & Co., Inc., began misappropriating nonpublic information concerning impending mergers and acquisitions. Rather than using that information to make trades himself, Freeman began disclosing the insider information to James Cooper and Benton Erskine, with the understanding and agreement that they would share a portion of their trading profits with him.

During the course of the scheme, Cooper received Freeman's permission to tip other individuals who might be able to assist them. Freeman knew of two people to whom Cooper gave the tips. Cooper, however, also tipped certain individuals without Freeman's knowledge or consent, including Chad Conner, a stockbroker. Cooper began regularly tipping Conner, who, in turn, tipped numerous other brokerage clients.

In the early fall of 1998, Freeman left Goldman Sachs to work part-time for Credit Suisse First Boston (CSFB), another investment bank. While Freeman continued to misappropriate information from CSFB, Conner and his clients believed the information they were now receiving was not as profitable as it had been in the past. Conner told Cooper that one of his clients was willing to pay the "New York source" $100,000 to return to Goldman Sachs. Cooper communicated this offer to Freeman.

Prior to receiving this offer, Freeman had been apprehended by the FBI and had agreed to assist the agency. On February 23, 2000, Conner and Cooper participated in a three-way telephone and online conversation with an FBI agent posing as Freeman. During this telephone conversation, Conner reiterated his offer to pay Freeman $100,000 to return to Goldman Sachs. The agent posing as Freeman asked Conner to personally deliver $5,000 to Atlantic City, and Conner agreed. On March 4, 2000, FBI agents arrested Conner in Atlantic City and seized an envelope containing $5,000. Conner was subsequently charged with commercial bribery and 81 counts of insider trading.[1]

1. Do you believe Conner did anything illegal? Anything unethical?
2. If a person has inside information and does not trade on it himself but passes it on to another who uses it to trade, is the person who passed on the information guilty of insider trading?

[1] *United States v. Geibel,* 369 F.3d 682 (2004).

After reading this chapter, you will be able to answer the following questions:

LO 5-1 What are the basic elements of a crime?

LO 5-2 How are crimes classified?

LO 5-3 Who can be held responsible when a corporate crime is committed?

LO 5-4 What are the basic steps of a criminal proceeding?

LO 5-5 What laws attempt to prevent white-collar crime?

This chapter helps the future business manager recognize when conduct has become criminal. The discussion begins by introducing the elements of a crime and explaining some common crimes that occur in the business context. After discussing how liability can be imposed on corporations and corporate executives, the chapter sets forth the steps of criminal procedure. The chapter concludes by discussing some of the laws used to fight business crime.

As the Case Opener illustrates, criminal behavior can come in many forms and affect large numbers of people. Also, crimes can quickly expand in terms of the number of people involved. It is important to note that Freeman, Cooper, Conner, and everyone Conner told made large sums of money at the expense of other investors. Although some crimes in commercial settings might seem like victimless ones at first, crimes always have victims, even if they are not readily identifiable.

The Nature and Elements of a Crime

LO 5-1

The purpose of criminal law is to punish an offender for causing harm to public health, safety, or morals. In a criminal proceeding, the *government* files the charges against the defendant. Thus, the government is always a party to a criminal action. Government involvement distinguishes criminal trials from civil proceedings. As you may recall from Chapter 3, an individual person or corporation can file a civil lawsuit. This difference exists because in a criminal trial society is seen as the victim, whereas in a civil trial there is an individual victim or victims.

In many situations, a particular course of conduct may lead a defendant to be prosecuted for committing a crime and also be sued in civil court for compensation by the victims of the crime. The outcome of the two cases may not be the same, however, for a number of reasons. As you will learn, the precise elements needed to prove the resulting criminal and civil cases will be different, and while many of the steps of civil and criminal procedure are the same, the defendant has additional protections in the criminal case. For example, the burden of proof in the criminal case is beyond a reasonable doubt, which is a much higher standard than that of a civil case, which, as you learned in Chapter 3, is a preponderance of the evidence. You will learn about many of the additional protections afforded criminal defendants later in this chapter.

ELEMENTS OF A CRIME

Criminal laws usually define criminal behavior and set guidelines for punishment. To punish an individual for criminal behavior, the government must demonstrate the two elements of a crime:

1. Wrongful behavior, that is, *actus reus* (guilty act).
2. Wrongful state of mind, also known as *mens rea* (guilty mind).

actus reus

Latin for "guilty act"; a wrongful behavior that is associated with the physical act of a declared crime.

mens rea

Latin for "guilty mind"; the mental state accompanying a wrongful behavior.

The government thus must show that a defendant committed a prohibited act with a wrongful intent.

To prove the first element, *actus reus* (guilty act), the government must establish the nonmental elements of the crime. That is, the government must demonstrate that a prohibited act or a prohibited consequence resulted because of the behavior of the defendant.

To prove the second element, *mens rea* (guilty state of mind), the government must prove that the defendant acted with the state of mind required by the law defining the relevant offense. The state of mind required by an offense may be purposeful, knowing, reckless, or negligent. The defendant's type of wrongful state of mind helps determine the seriousness of the punishment for the crime.

A defendant can *purposefully* commit a crime by engaging in a specific wrongful behavior to bring about a specific wrongful result. A defendant can *knowingly* commit a wrongful act if the person knows the act is wrongful or believes that the act is wrongful yet does nothing to confirm or disconfirm this belief. A defendant is *reckless* if a criminal act occurs when the individual consciously ignores substantial risk. Finally, a defendant is *negligent* if he or she does not meet a standard of care that the reasonable person would use in the context that led to the criminal act.

In certain cases, liability may be assessed even without establishing the guilty-mind criterion discussed above. Only certain crimes, typically violations of regulatory statutes, allow punishment to be assessed without having to prove a guilty mind. When liability is assessed without the guilty-mind criterion, it is known as **liability without fault,** or **strict liability.** Liability without fault involves actions that, regardless of the care taken, are deemed illegal to engage in; such acts are specifically prohibited regardless of state of mind. Liability without fault would apply, for example, if a business were to sell cigarettes or alcohol to a minor. Although the business might not have intended to sell cigarettes or alcohol to a minor (thus lacking a guilty mind), the statutory violation still allows liability to be imposed.

CLASSIFICATION OF CRIMES

Crimes are divided into categories based on the seriousness of the offense. Today, the categories used are felonies, misdemeanors, and petty crimes. **Felonies** include serious crimes, such as murder, that are punishable by imprisonment for more than one year in a penitentiary or death. **Misdemeanors** are less serious crimes punishable by fines and/or imprisonment for less than one year. **Petty offenses,** such as violating a building code, are minor misdemeanors and are usually punishable by a jail sentence of less than six months or a small fine. The statute defining the crime usually establishes whether the crime is a felony, misdemeanor, or petty offense. Crimes may also be federal or state, depending on whether they are created by the state or federal legislature.

White-Collar Crime

Originally, white-collar crimes were distinguished from other crimes because of the social status of the offender. The more modern approach is to define **white-collar crime** as a variety of nonviolent illegal acts against society that occur most frequently in the business context. Clearly, the crimes described in the Case Opener fall under this broad definition of white-collar crime.

Mail fraud, bribery, embezzlement, and computer crimes are examples of offenses typically classified as white-collar crimes. These crimes occur more frequently than you might think. According to some estimates, one in three American households is the victim of white-collar crime every year.

The consequences of white-collar crimes are far-reaching. First, the cost of white-collar crimes can be tremendous. According to some estimates, fraud in the health care industry alone costs society over $100 billion each year. Second, in cases where company employees commit the crime, many companies fail to report the crime to avoid publicity. Third, white-collar crimes can be costly to the environment. For example, improper disposal of chemicals, such as dumping

liability without fault
A legal term that imposes responsibility for damages regardless of the existence of negligence. Also called *strict liability.*

LO 5-2

felony
A serious crime, such as murder, rape, or robbery, that is punishable by imprisonment for more than one year or death.

misdemeanor
A crime that is less serious than a felony and is punishable by a fine and/or imprisonment for less than one year.

petty offense
A minor crime that is punishable by a small fine and/or imprisonment for less than six months in a jail.

LO 5-3

white-collar crime
A variety of nonviolent illegal acts against society that occur most frequently in the business context.

chemicals in a stream, has long-term repercussions for marine life, the surrounding ecosystem, and any humans who may come in contact with the contaminated water source.

Of course, the amount of money collected in fines from corporate executives engaged in criminal activity has not been insignificant either. For example, in 2010, the federal government collected $2.8 billion in restitution, criminal fines, and felony assessments in criminal cases.[2] Fines, however, are only one way that those found guilty of fraud and other white-collar crimes might be punished.

There are at least four other ways to punish white-collar criminals. First, incarceration has been mandated for certain types of white-collar crimes. As the prevalence of white-collar crime has increased, so too has the number of white-collar offenders who are in jail. Second, white-collar criminals may be ordered to do community service, such as giving speeches about business crime. For instance, junk-bond king Michael Milliken was compelled to give speeches about corporate crime after he was convicted of insider trading. Third, judges may disqualify the individual from employment. For instance, the judge may prohibit the offender from engaging in an occupation where the same or a similar criminal act could occur again. Fourth, the offender can be placed under house arrest. Individuals must wear a sensor so that the government can monitor whether they have left their houses.

With changes in technology, and governments that are increasingly pressed financially, governments are increasingly looking for sentences other than imprisonment for nonviolent offenders. People in the criminal justice field are also starting to recognize that there is something wrong with a system that results in a higher incarceration rate in the United States than in other industrialized nations. According to the most recent statistics, the United States was incarcerating 770 persons per 100,000, whereas the rate in Europe was around 110 per 100,000.

SPECIFIC WHITE-COLLAR CRIMES

Bribery One of the better-known white-collar crimes is bribery. **Bribery** is the offering, giving, soliciting, or receiving of money or any object of value for the purpose of influencing the judgment or conduct of a person in a position of trust. *Bribery of a public official* is a statutory offense under federal law. The purpose of this law against bribery is to maintain the integrity of the government. This statute also covers bribes offered to witnesses in exchange for testimony. Perhaps one of the most publicized examples of bribery was the 2002 Winter Olympics bribery scandal in Salt Lake City, Utah. The Salt Lake City Olympics Bid Committee allegedly gave International Olympic Committee members between $4 million and $7 million in cash and other benefits. These benefits included college tuition assistance payments, shopping trips for bathroom fixtures and doorknobs, and trips to the Super Bowl.

More common, however, is the simple cash bribe to obtain a government contract. For example, in 2008, the CEO of a multimedia communications company was convicted of paying over $200,000 in bribes to the technology director of Atlanta Public Schools to secure contracts to help connect schools in poor and rural areas to the Internet. He was sentenced to a five-year prison term and payment of restitution. The government official who had accepted the bribe, and ultimately testified against the man who bribed him, was sentenced to three years in prison.[3]

To demonstrate bribery under this statute, the government must show three elements: (1) Something of value was offered, given, or promised to (2) a federal public official with (3) intent to influence that person's judgment or conduct. The "thing of value" element has been construed very liberally; actual commercial value is not necessary. For instance, had the Salt Lake City Olympics Bid Committee given a member of the International Olympic Committee shares of stock in a new Silicon Valley start-up called BellyUp.com but the shares turned out to be worthless because the start-up was never established, this act may constitute bribery even though the

bribery
A corrupt and illegal activity in which a person offers, gives, solicits, or receives money, services, or anything of value in order to gain an illicit advantage.

[2] Department of Justice, "U.S. Attorneys Contributed to $6.68 Billion in Civil & Criminal Collections in Fiscal Year 2010," December 16, 2010, www.justice.gov/usao/cae/news/docs/2010/12-16-10CollectionsPressreleaseFY2010.pdf.
[3] "Georgia Man Sentenced for E-Rate Bribery," AsianFanaticsForum, December 28, 2008, asianfanatics.net/forum/topic/612815-georgia-man-sentenced-for-e-rate-bribery/..

stock is commercially worthless. Ultimately, the Department of Justice was unable to prove any of the 15 charges of bribery that it had filed against two members of the Salt Lake City Olympics Bid Committee. Several members of the committee resigned, however. As a result of investigations into the matter, 10 members of the International Olympics Committee were fired and another 10 were sanctioned.

Additionally, the definition of "public official" is also expansive. The statute defines *public officials* as members of Congress, government officers and employees, and anyone "acting for or on behalf of" the federal government "in any official function, under or by authority of" a federal government department or agency. For example, individuals who work for private corporations that have some degree of responsibility for carrying out federal programs or policies are considered public officials. The Case Nugget provides an interesting twist on the crime of bribery.

CASE Nugget

A Question of Bribery?

United States of America, Plaintiff-Appellee, v. Sonya Evette Singleton, Defendant-Appellant
Circuit Court of Appeals for the Tenth Circuit

165 F.3d 1297 (1999)

Often, when two defendants are charged with a crime, a prosecutor might offer to give one defendant leniency in exchange for truthful testimony against the other. Are such prosecutor plea deals really bribes and thus violative of federal bribery law, which prohibits the exchange of anything of value for testimony? The Tenth Circuit did not think so in this case.

Sonya Singleton was charged with money laundering and conspiring to distribute cocaine. Her co-conspirator, Napoleon Douglas, entered into a plea agreement with the prosecuting attorney under which he agreed to testify truthfully. In exchange, the prosecuting attorney promised leniency; the government would not prosecute him for related offenses, and the attorney would advise the sentencing court of Douglas's cooperation. Singleton argued that such an agreement violated the "anti-gratuity" statute, U.S.C. §201(c)(2). The district court allowed Douglas's testimony and convicted Singleton. A panel of the Tenth Circuit Court reversed the conviction, arguing that the attorney's promise for leniency did violate federal bribery law. The full circuit voted to rehear the case.

On rehearing, the court reinstated the defendant's conviction, noting that to hold otherwise would "deprive the sovereign of a recognized or established prerogative, title, or interest." The court held that from the common law, we have a long-standing practice sanctioning the testimony of accomplices against their confederates in exchange for leniency, and this long-standing practice created a vested sovereign prerogative in the government. In light of the long-standing practice of leniency for testimony, the court had to presume that if Congress had intended to overturn this ingrained aspect of American legal culture, it would have done so in clear, unmistakable, and unarguable language.

Another type of bribery is *commercial bribery*, which includes a bribe in exchange for new information or payoffs. For example, suppose Comdac Computers is looking for a company that manufactures a certain type of computer part. Jane Devlon owns such a company and realizes that if Comdac gets the computer parts from her, she will potentially make a lot of

money. When Comdac sends its contractor to the Devlon factory, Devlon offers the contractor $500,000 in exchange for the contractor's promise that Comdac will buy all such parts from only her factory for the next year. Alternatively, she might offer the contractor $5,000 to disclose the dollar amounts of the competing bids so that she can offer a better bid to earn the contract. This chapter's Case Opener also involves commercial bribery. Conner's offer of money to Freeman to return to his old job, so that he could provide better tips, is a commercial bribe.

One final type of bribery is the *bribery of foreign officials.* The purpose of the Foreign Corrupt Practices Act (FCPA) is to combat such bribery. The FCPA prohibits payments to foreign officials to corruptly influence an official act or decision or to influence a foreign government. You might think of the FCPA as an extension of the law to prevent bribery of a public official. The FCPA allows the government to prosecute those who bribe foreign officials.

But Congress does not pass laws affecting foreign affairs in a vacuum. Laws governing white-collar crime, like all laws, are dynamic, and one source of change in these laws is international law. Multinational organizations in which the United States is a member often pressure the United States to alter American law so that it conforms to certain international standards. Thus, for example, Congress amended the FCPA in 1998 to conform to the antibribery convention adopted by the Organization for Economic Cooperation and Development (OECD). The amendments broaden the scope of actions covered by the FCPA and the definition of a public official. As of this writing, it is expected that 30 OECD countries—such as Japan, South Korea, and Brazil—will adopt similar antibribery statutes.

Extortion Often confused with bribery, but completely different, is the crime of extortion. **Extortion,** otherwise known as *blackmail,* is the making of threats for the purpose of obtaining money or property. Whereas bribery is offering someone something to obtain a desired result, extortion involves the threat of doing something if the target of the extortion does not relinquish money or a specific piece of property. For example, if Conner in the Case Opener threatened to tell the government about Freeman's actions if he did not return to Goldman Sachs, then Conner would have committed extortion. Conner's actions would have been extortion because he would have issued a threat (to tell the government about Freeman's insider trading) for the purpose of obtaining money (to get Freeman to behave in a way that would enable Conner to make more money by receiving the more profitable tips from Goldman Sachs).

extortion

A criminal offense in which a person obtains money, property, and/or services from another by wrongfully threatening or inflicting harm on the other's person, property, or reputation. Also called *blackmail.*

Fraud Criminal **fraud** encompasses a variety of means by which an individual intentionally uses some sort of misrepresentation to gain an advantage over another person. Fraud generally requires the following three elements: (1) a material false representation made with intent to deceive *(scienter),* (2) a victim's reasonable reliance on the false representation, and (3) damages. Both the federal and the state governments have passed a number of statutes codifying specific types of fraudulent schemes. These schemes to defraud include a multitude of frauds, such as credit card fraud, insurance fraud, and securities fraud. Exhibit 5-1 summarizes the fraudulent acts that might occur in the corporate setting, many of which are discussed below.

fraud

An intentional deception that causes harm to another.

One of the FBI's largest *securities fraud* crackdowns occurred in June 2000, when it arrested a group of Mafia leaders for a series of scams that cost investors an estimated $25 million. Government officials claimed that the Mob bought large stakes in small companies and then bribed and coerced brokers to promote the stocks to other investors at inflated prices.

The Enron scandal also involved securities fraud, with Enron's top executives allegedly overstating its earnings to maintain high stock prices. Complex accounting methods were used to hide the corporation's debt. Enron's top executives and big investors sold their stocks while encouraging employees to continue buying company stocks. With the drastic decline in the company's stock value, many Enron employees lost much of their 401(k) investments.

Another specific type of securities fraud involved in the Enron case, as well as in this chapter's Case Opener, is insider trading. Illegal **insider trading** is generally a person's

insider trading

The illegal buying or selling of a corporation's stock or other securities by corporate insiders such as officers and directors, in breach of a fiduciary duty or some other relationship of trust and confidence, while in possession of material, nonpublic information about the security.

Exhibit 5-1

Selected Fraudulent Crimes

1. *Forgery:* The fraudulent making or altering of any writing in a way that changes the legal rights and liabilities of another.
2. *Defalcation:* The misappropriation of trust funds or money held in a fiduciary capacity.
3. *False entries:* The making of an entry into the books of a bank or corporation that is designed to represent the existence of funds that do not exist.
4. *False token:* A false document or sign of existence used to perpetrate a fraud, such as making counterfeit money.
5. *False pretense:* A designed misrepresentation of existing facts or conditions by which a person obtains another's money or goods, such as the writing of a worthless check.
6. *Fraudulent concealment:* The suppression of a material fact that a person is legally bound to disclose.
7. *Mail fraud:* The use of mails to defraud the public.
8. *Health care fraud:* Any fraudulent act committed in the provision of health care products or services.
9. *Telemarketing fraud:* Any scheme, including cramming and slamming, using the telephone to commit a fraudulent act.
10. *Ponzi scheme:* An investment swindle in which high profits are promised from fictitious sources and early investors are paid off with funds raised from later ones.
11. *Check kiting:* Drawing checks on an account in one bank and depositing them in an account in a second bank when neither account has sufficient funds to cover the amounts drawn. Just before the checks are returned for payment to the first bank, the kiter covers them by depositing checks drawn on the account in the second bank. Due to the delay created by the collection of funds by one bank from the other, known as the "float" time, an artificial balance is created.
12. *Pretexting:* Using fraudulent means to obtain information about someone's phone use.

buying or selling of a security, in breach of a fiduciary duty or some other relationship of trust and confidence, while in possession of material, nonpublic information about the security. Insider-trading violations also include "tipping" such information, securities trading by the person "tipped," and securities trading by those who misappropriate such information.[4] Enron's big investors and top executives knew the stock prices were overinflated due to the overstated earnings. They then used their knowledge, which was not public knowledge, to decide to sell off their stock before the price lowered drastically, thus engaging in insider trading. Consider how insider trading might violate each of the ethical norms we have previously discussed.

In March 2011, another apparent insider-trading scheme came to light when it was alleged that a corporate lawyer and a trader operated an insider-trading scheme that lasted decades and earned the two $32 million. The lawyer worked for a mergers and acquisitions firm, and he gave nonpublic information about deals the firm was working on to his partner, the trader, so that he could make appropriate stock trades using this information. One of their alleged profitable inside trades occurred when information that the lawyer acquired in April 2009 about Oracle's proposed bid for Sun Microsystems led the trader to purchase more than 4 million shares of the target company, which he was then able to make a handsome profit on when the deal closed in 2010.[5]

Another example of insider trading involves Qwest Communications, a Denver-based local phone provider in 14 western and midwestern states. Qwest has been under investigation over the past few years for various white-collar crimes, including insider training. Robin Szeliga, Qwest's former chief financial officer, is the highest-ranking official at Qwest to admit

[4] U.S. Securities and Exchange Commission, www.sec.gov/answers/insider.htm.
[5] Ben Protess, "Two Charged in Insider Trading Scheme Linked to Law Firms," *The New York Times,* April 6, 2011.

wrongdoing in the scandal. She admits to selling 10,000 shares of Qwest stock in 2001 for a net profit of $125,000. Szeliga knew some of Qwest's business units would not meet their targets. She also knew Qwest had illegally used nonrecurring revenue to try to meet its goals. Because the information Robin acted on was not public, and because she gained substantially by acting on the private information, Szeliga recently pleaded guilty to a single count of insider trading.

Stock-option backdating is yet another type of securities fraud that the SEC has been increasingly cracking down on. Backdating occurs when an employee falsifies documents to make it appear as though the company had granted options on certain dates, but the dates are selected after the fact by looking backward for dates on which the stock price was low, thereby falsely inflating the net profits of the company. In 2007, Myron F. Olesnyckyj, the former general counsel of Monster Worldwide, Inc., pleaded guilty to securities fraud for participating in a multiyear scheme with other Monster executives to secretly backdate stock options granted to thousands of Monster officers, directors, and employees, including himself. By backdating and improperly accounting for options, Monster granted undisclosed compensation to its employees, failed to recognize compensation expenses, and overstated its net income by $340 million from 1997 through 2005. Olesnyckyj personally made $381,000 from the scheme, which he agreed to forfeit.

An additional type of fraud is false pretense. **False pretense** is the illegal obtaining of property belonging to another through materially false representation of an existing fact, with knowledge of the falsity of the representation and with the intent to defraud. For example, Jim goes door-to-door selling vacuum cleaners at an amazing discount. To obtain the discount, the customers must pay immediately, and the vacuum cleaner will be delivered in three to five business days. However, Jim possesses no vacuum cleaners and does not plan on delivering any. Jim has committed the crime of false pretense, as he illegally obtained another's property (the money he received as payment) by making a false representation (telling the "customers" they would be receiving a vacuum) with the knowledge of the falsity (he knew there were no vacuum cleaners) and the intent to defraud (he did not plan on delivering any vacuum cleaners).

Forgery, the fraudulent making or altering of any writing in a way that changes the legal rights and liabilities of another, is another type of fraud. If you sign your colleague's name to the back of a check made out to your colleague, you have committed forgery.

One of the most frequently prosecuted frauds is *mail fraud,* which is the use of mails to defraud the public. The Mail Fraud Act of 1990 makes mail fraud a federal crime. To prove mail fraud, the government must demonstrate two elements: (1) an intent to defraud and (2) the use of or causing the use of mails to further the fraudulent scheme. Case 5-1 demonstrates the consideration of these two elements.

false pretense

The illegal obtaining of another's property by making a materially false representation of an existing fact, with knowledge of the falsity of the representation and with the intent to defraud.

forgery

A criminal falsification by imitating, impersonating, or altering a real document with the intent to deceive or defraud.

CASE 5-1

UNITED STATES OF AMERICA v. SVETE
COURT OF APPEALS FOR THE ELEVENTH CIRCUIT
556 F.3D 1157 (2009)

FACTS: *Svete, Girardot, and their agents were in the business of selling financial products based on agreements with viators, or persons who have terminal illnesses and sell their life insurance policies to third parties for* *less than the mature value of the policies. Investors who purchased these financial interests from agents of Svete and Girardot testified at trial that the sales agents made fraudulent statements and provided them with mail that*

contained false statements regarding the life expectancies of viators, the status of the contracts, and risks associated with investments.

The invested plaintiffs claimed that the defendants included statements by "medical specialists who had access to the viators medical records," but that these statements were false. The plaintiffs commented that, in fact, these viators were not terminally ill, and the information provided by "medical professionals" was incomplete.

Companies controlled by Svete obtained more than $100 million from more than 3,000 investors. Several of the investors that signed contracts with the defendants testified to not reading or understanding the contracts.

Nanette Zima, who served as the president of the brokerage company formed by Svete, LifeTime Capital, Inc., testified that Svete and Girardot instructed her to alter contracts that had been signed by investors without the knowledge or consent of the investors who had signed them.

In defense, Svete and Girardot argued that a person of "ordinary prudence and sophistication" would have read the contracts and disregarded the false statements. The defendants requested a jury instruction based on this argument. Instead of providing the requested jury instruction, the district court gave the pattern jury instruction of mail fraud.

ISSUE: Does the crime of mail fraud require proof that the scheme be capable of deceiving a reasonably prudent person?

REASONING: The district court gave a mail fraud pattern jury instruction that defined a "scheme to defraud" as including any plan or course of action intended to deceive or cheat someone out of money or property by means of false or fraudulent pretenses, representations, or promises. This jury instruction relied on the precedent of *United States v. Brown*. The Court of Appeals overruled the precedent of *United States v. Brown* that was relied on by the district court to give a mail fraud pattern jury instruction, instead of the jury instruction requested by the defendants. The Eleventh Circuit held that the precedent of *Brown* was inconsistent with the mail fraud statute's plain language and Supreme Court precedent, which instructed courts to reject common law elements that clearly were inconsistent with statutes Congress enacted.

DECISION AND REMEDY: The defendants' appeal to not include the jury instruction about mail fraud was affirmed. The Eleventh Circuit overruled the precedent of *United States v. Brown* and ordered a new trial.

SIGNIFICANCE OF THE CASE: This case shows what prosecutors must prove in a mail fraud case. This theory is important to prosecutors because it is important for them to know how to use the theory effectively. In addition, this case highlights the importance of relying on precedent that is consistent with a statute's plain language.

CRITICAL THINKING

Are you persuaded that Svete and Girardot were using the mails to perpetuate a fraudulent scheme? Why or why not? In other words, which reasons are responsible for your conclusion?

ETHICAL DECISION MAKING

Return to the WPH process of ethical decision making. Whom does this decision affect? In other words, who are the stakeholders in this decision?

Congress amended the mail fraud statute in 1994 to include commercial carriers and courier services as substitutes for the U.S. mail. Thus, using FedEx or UPS to further a fraudulent scheme can be prosecuted as mail fraud. Similarly, the wire fraud statute attempts to prevent the use of wire, radio, or television transmissions to defraud the public.

Other types of fraud include health care fraud, telemarketing fraud, and bankruptcy fraud. The Department of Justice recently named health care fraud its top priority after violent crime. An example of health care fraud is the submission of false claims to insurance plans such as Medicare or Medicaid. Additionally, some doctors prescribe unneeded equipment to patients and then receive kickbacks from the manufacturers of the equipment.

Telemarketing fraud has also gained much attention recently. The National Fraud Information Center reported that telephone cramming was the top telemarketing fraud of 1998. Cramming is a scheme in which companies bill consumers for optional services that the consumers did not order. Another frequent telemarketing scheme is slamming, in which consumers are tricked into changing their phone service to another carrier without their consent.

The elderly, who have been more susceptible to telemarketing fraud, are often the specific targets of telemarketing schemes. Thus, the Department of Justice and the FBI have been collaborating on various undercover operations, such as Operation Senior Sentinel, to investigate and prosecute fraudulent telemarketers.

Another type of fraud involves bankruptcies. In 2004, more than 1.6 million bankruptcy filings occurred. An individual can file for bankruptcy to be relieved of oppressive debt. Yet claims need to be carefully reviewed to prevent bankruptcy fraud. For example, an individual might hide some assets so that they will not be considered during the proceedings. Conversely, a creditor (a party to whom another owes money) might file a false claim against a debtor (the party who owes money to a creditor). Thus, bankruptcy fraud can occur on the part of the debtor or the creditor. The U.S. Department of Justice estimates that 10 percent of all bankruptcy petitions contain some elements of fraud. However, between the year 2000 and the year 2005, only a few more than 1,000 defendants faced bankruptcy fraud charges. Expect the number of defendants facing bankruptcy fraud to be on the rise with the culmination of the Justice Department's Operation Truth or Consequences. In October 2006, the Justice Department created an Internet hotline for the public to report suspected bankruptcy fraud to the U.S. Trustee Program. This hotline is just one aspect of the Department of Justice's revitalized commitment to combating bankruptcy fraud and protecting the integrity of the bankruptcy system.

Sometimes fraud cases can be very complex and involve multiple types of fraud. For example, in one recent case, a Beverly Hills lawyer was convicted of three counts of mail fraud, seven counts of wire fraud, and five counts of lying in a court hearing. In an elaborate fraudulent scheme, the lawyer had purchased a yacht for $1.9 million, sold it to two other partners to drive up its insurance value, and then had a company he owned repurchase the yacht and insure it for $3.5 million. Finally, he and his partners sunk the yacht and tried to collect the insurance.

A fraudulent crime that has recently come into the public eye is pretexting. *Pretexting* can be defined as using or causing others to use false pretenses, fraudulent statements, fraudulent or stolen documents, or other misrepresentations, including posing as an account holder or employee of a telecommunications carrier, to obtain the telephone records of another. Pretexting entered the national lexicon in 2006 when news broke that the investigators hired by Hewlett-Packard's board of directors to locate the source of several leaks to the media were engaging in this practice. Under the federal Telephone Records and Privacy Protection Act of 2006, anyone convicted of employing fraudulent tactics to persuade phone companies to hand over confidential data about a customer's calling habits can be sent to prison for up to 10 years. Some states also have statutes outlawing pretexting.

Both individuals and businesses can be victims of fraud. To minimize the chances that your firm will be a victim of fraud, review the fraud prevention tips in Exhibit 5-2 very carefully.

Embezzlement Joe is Kathleen's attorney. Kathleen gave Joe $5,000 to put in escrow, an account where Joe will have access to the money, although the money is not his to use as he pleases. Suppose Joe takes some of that money out of the account and uses it to gamble, and he "fixes" the records to cover up the fact that he has used some of the money for his personal use. He has committed the crime of **embezzlement,** the wrongful conversion of another's property by one who is lawfully in possession of that property. Embezzlement is distinguished from larceny because the individual did not take the property from another; he was already in possession of the property.

Embezzlement usually occurs when an employee steals money. Thus, it is often employees in banks who commit the crime. However, as the recent embezzlement of $6.9 million from the American Cancer Society demonstrates, even nonprofit organizations are vulnerable to the crime of embezzlement. White-collar crimes such as embezzlement are a problem in many countries. For example, the Chinese government, which has been focusing on economic crimes, caught

embezzlement

A wrongful conversion of another's funds or property by one who is lawfully in possession of those funds or that property.

Exhibit 5-2

Fraud Prevention
Tips

Red Flags Suggesting Possible Fraud

When you are looking at a brochure offering an investment opportunity that seems almost too good to be true, it may indeed not be as good as it seems, especially if it contains these red flags of fraud:

- *No independent proof of profitability:* The brochure provides the investment strategy but includes no details that can be verified, such as names and addresses of specific companies in which it invests.
- *Control by a single person.*
- *No audited financial statements and no evidence of internal controls.*
- *Unusually high rates of return:* The rates of return are significantly higher than those for other funds with a similar investment strategy.
- *New investors' reliance primarily on existing investors in deciding to invest.*

False "Assurances" That an Investment Opportunity Is Not Fraudulent

- *Long-time existence of investment opportunity:* A Ponzi scheme can operate for a long time. As long as the company keeps getting new investors, it can continue to use the new investors to pay off the few who insist on collecting their returns. Many investors may be content to accumulate paper profits, especially if there is a financial incentive for reinvestment of profits. For example, the Financial Advisory Fund had been in business for almost 20 years before its fraudulent foundation was uncovered.
- *A list of names and addresses of satisfied investors you can contact:* All such schemes will have some satisfied investors who have received payments from the new investment money.
- *Membership in the Better Business Bureau:* Any company can pay to join. If most of the investors have not attempted to withdraw their funds and the company is still getting new investments, there will be no disgruntled investors to complain to the BBB.
- *A report of profitability from Dun & Bradstreet:* Dun & Bradstreet does not do an independent financial audit of a company's profits. As stated on its Web site, Dun & Bradstreet simply provides the information regarding profits that it receives from companies.
- *Acceptance of money rolled over from IRAs:* There is no government check on the soundness of firms that roll over IRAs.
- *Bank references:* If a firm simply has a large amount of money in a checking account in a bank and has never sought a loan from the bank, the bank would have no reason to do any due diligence on the firm. Also, if the owner of the firm is personable and the account has never been overdrawn, the bank personnel may well give the firm a good reference.
- *Glossy brochures and television ads:* All you need for both is some money and the knowledge that many people may be overly impressed by a fancy brochure or ad campaign.

These tips come from Barry Minkow, who went from starting his own carpet cleaning business at the age of 16, to taking this multimillion-dollar company public at the age of 20, to facing a 23-year prison sentence and $26 million victim restitution payment at the age of 21 for massive fraud and theft perpetuated on behalf of his company, to now being a pastor and the cofounder of the Fraud Discovery Institute.

The fascinating story of how Barry Minkow, through fraudulent Ponzi schemes, check kiting, and theft, managed to build the multimillion-dollar ZZZZ Best Carpet Cleaning Company by the age of 20 is contained in his book, *Cleaning Up.* The book also provides insights into why some people may commit white-collar crimes, and it describes many of the long-running frauds Minkow has helped to uncover since deciding to use his understanding of the perpetuation of fraud to help uncover and prevent it.

Embezzlement and Bribery in China

On March 8, 1982, in response to a concern about a rise in white-collar crimes, Chinese officials added a resolution entitled "Severely Punishing Criminals Who Do Great Damage to the Economy" to the Chinese Criminal Code. The provision targeted top-ranking officials by providing that any state functionaries who extort, accept bribes, or exploit their office will no longer receive the fixed-term punishment (usually 10 years) allocated for bribery and extortion. Instead, those officials found guilty of extortion and accepting bribes would be sentenced to life imprisonment or possibly put to death.

Bank fraud is another white-collar crime that may be punishable by death. In 2004, China executed four people, including employees of two of its Big Four state banks, for fraud totaling $15 million. Three of the cases involved China Construction Bank.

A former accounting officer at this bank worked with others to steal 20 million yuan ($2.4 million) from the bank using fake papers. He and an accomplice were executed, along with another Construction Bank employee who was found to have taken 20 million yuan from the bank in an unrelated case. Additionally, an official employed by the Bank of China was executed for cheating.

The precise number of people executed in China is not made available to the public. Estimates range from 5,000 to 10,000 a year, for crimes including murder, corruption, and on occasion even bottom-pinching. Most are executed by a single shot in the back of the head.

Such punishments may seem extreme, but the reaction of the Chinese to the increase in white-collar crime reflects the culture's unusually great concern for social harmony.

employees in two major Chinese banks altering deposit slips and bank orders to direct the money to personal accounts throughout China. Those employees received death sentences for embezzlement, as discussed in the Global Context box.

Computer Crimes The term **computer crime** refers broadly to any wrongful act that (1) is directed against computers, (2) uses computers to commit a crime, or (3) involves computers. Computer crime is not necessarily a new kind of crime but is, instead, a new way of committing traditional crimes. Consider fraud, a crime that has existed for centuries. Today, online auctions, such as eBay, are a common source of fraud in the United States. Indeed, some statistics suggest that, compared with nonelectronic methods, using computers is a more profitable method of committing crimes. According to federal officials, the average loss in a nonelectronic embezzlement is $23,500; in contrast, in a computer fraud case, the average loss is almost $500,000.[6]

Computer crimes are often difficult to prosecute, in large part because they are difficult to detect. A computer crime could be committed by an insider, such as an employee, or by an outsider, such as a **hacker**—a person who illegally accesses or enters another person's or a company's computer system to obtain information or to steal money. In addition, computer systems are quite open to attack. The American Society for Industrial Security has reported that the losses from computer crimes in a single year were more than $250 billion for U.S. companies. Furthermore, the attacks are frequent. The IRS alone detects 800 to 1,200 cases of computer system misuse annually.

A **cyber terrorist** is a hacker whose intention is the exploitation of a target computer or network to create a serious impact, such as the crippling of a communications network or the sabotage of a business or organization. The activity of a cyber terrorist can have an impact on millions of citizens if the terrorist's attack is successful, particularly if it involves the computer systems of a major stock exchange, any bank, or any federal agency or government.

In an attempt to aid prosecutions of computer crimes, Congress passed the Counterfeit Access Device and Computer Fraud and Abuse Act of 1984 (also know as the Computer Fraud and Abuse Act, or CFAA). The act prohibits six broad categories of computer crimes:

1. Unauthorized use of or access to a computer to obtain classified military or foreign policy information with the intent to harm the United States or to benefit a foreign country.

computer crime
Crime committed using a computer.

hacker
A person who illegally accesses or enters another person's or a company's computer system to obtain information or to steal money.

cyber terrorist
A hacker whose intention is the exploitation of a target computer or network to create a serious impact, such as the crippling of a communications network or the sabotage of a business or organization, which may have an impact on millions of citizens if the terrorist's attack is successful.

[6] Charles Alexander, "The Wells Fargo Stick-Up," *Time.com,* www.time.com/time/magazine/article/0,9171,954673-3,00.html (accessed May 1, 2007).

E-COMMERCE and the Law

Computer Use and Ethics

The use of computers to store and transfer important business information has resulted in a new set of ethical concerns. How private is the computer screen? Are companies allowed to collect information about their customers? Who owns the information customers give to e-businesses? E-commerce law is gradually adjusting to such questions. But, as the beginning of Chapter 1 pointed out, knowing the law is just the first step in discovering the ethical business decision.

One case that considered questions related to e-commerce and privacy involved Toysmart.com and its privacy policy. In 2000, the Federal Trade Commission (FTC) filed a complaint against Toysmart.com, charging the online retailer with selling customer lists despite its earlier privacy statements that claimed its customers' personal data would never be shared with a third party. The customer lists were included as assets to be sold as part of the company's bankruptcy proceedings. The FTC issued a settlement with Toysmart.com allowing the lists to be sold as long as (1) the sale occurred before July 2001, (2) the lists would be sold to a family-oriented company, and (3) the buyer would agree to abide by the original Toysmart.com privacy policy. After the FTC imposed these restrictions, the end result was that customers' personal information was not sold.

The Toysmart.com case makes it clear that, for both ethical and legal reasons, companies that adopt a privacy policy need to think that policy through before announcing it to customers.

2. Unauthorized use of a computer to collect financial or credit information protected under federal privacy law.

3. Unauthorized access to a federal computer and the use, modification, destruction, or disclosure of data it contains or the prevention of an authorized person's use of such data.

4. Alteration or modification of data in financial computers causing a loss of $1,000 or more.

5. Modification of data that impedes medical treatment to individuals.

6. Fraudulent transfer of computer passwords or other similar data that could aid unauthorized access that either (a) affects interstate commerce or (b) permits access to a government computer.

Computer crimes falling into the first category are felonies, whereas the others are misdemeanors.

The National Information Infrastructure Protection Act of 1996 amended the Computer Fraud and Abuse Act. One of the major changes to the CFAA is the substitution of the term *protected computers* for *federal interest computers* so that the statute now protects any computer attached to the Internet.

In a further attempt to aid prosecution of computer crimes, the U.S. Department of Justice formed the Computer Crime and Intellectual Property Section (CCIPS) in its Criminal Division. Attorneys in this division prosecute only federal computer crimes. They also coordinate their activities with numerous government entities, the private sector, scholars, and foreign representatives in an attempt to develop a global response to computer crime.

virus

A computer program that rearranges, damages, destroys, or replaces computer data.

Destruction of data is one of the most serious problems facing companies today. A **virus** is a computer program that rearranges, damages, destroys, or replaces computer data. Thus, if an employee or a hacker creates and releases a virus, a company can easily lose vital information.

The most economically destructive computer crime to date was the creation of the "love bug" virus. In May 2000, the virus spread rapidly throughout the world by e-mail. Once the e-mail was opened, it destroyed files on the user's computer, and then the virus sent itself to every address in that computer's e-mail address book. In the end, the virus caused over $10 billion in damages and halted computers in major companies and government agencies worldwide.

Companies can try to prevent the destruction of data by installing virus detection programs on their computers. However, the detection programs recognize only previously existing harmful files. As a result, if someone creates a new virus, the detection program is useless.

When an employee uses his or her computer in a manner not authorized by the employer, the employee has committed a crime. Employers, then, must clearly communicate with employees about authorized versus unauthorized behavior. For example, if an employee uses her work

computer to run her own personal business on the side, her employer may argue that she is engaging in theft because she is not using her computer in an authorized manner. Thus, when you become a business manager, you will want to make sure that you explicitly list acceptable computer uses, along with the penalties associated with unauthorized use.

Corporate Criminal Liability

LO 5-3

An individual or a corporation can be charged with and convicted of a crime. However, there has been much debate over whether corporations should be held criminally responsible. Under the common law, a corporation could not be considered a criminal because it was not an actual person and thus did not have a "mind." Consequently, it could not meet the *mens rea* (guilty-mind) requirement for a crime. Slowly, however, courts began to impose liability on corporations for **strict-liability offenses,** those offenses that do not require state of mind. Next, courts imposed liability on corporations by imputing the state of mind of the employee to the corporation.

strict-liability offense
Offense for which no *mens rea* is required.

Currently, corporations can be held criminally accountable for almost any crime. However, they cannot be held liable for crimes that are punishable only by a prison sentence. For a corporation to be held criminally liable for the acts of an employee, the prosecutor must show that (1) the employee was acting within the scope of her or his employment; (2) the employee was acting with the purpose of benefiting the corporation; and (3) the act was imputed to the corporation.

In addition to corporations having criminal liability, corporate executives may also be personally liable for a business crime. The beneficiary of the crime is irrelevant, as corporate executives and officers can be found to be personally liable regardless of whether the crimes were committed for their personal benefit or for the benefit of the corporation.

Also, under the "responsible corporate officer" doctrine, a court may assess criminal liability on a corporate executive or officer even if he or she did not engage in, direct, or even know about a specific criminal violation. As Case 5-2 demonstrates, corporate executives sometimes have the responsibility and power to ensure the company's compliance with the law. If the executive fails to meet this responsibility, the executive can be held criminally liable.

CASE 5-2

UNITED STATES v. PARK
UNITED STATES SUPREME COURT
421 U.S. 658 (1975)

FACTS: *Defendant Park, the president of a national food-chain corporation, was charged, along with the corporation, with violating the Federal Food, Drug, and Cosmetic Act by allowing food in the warehouse to be exposed to rodent contamination. Park had conceded that his responsibility for the "entire operation" included warehouse sanitation, but he claimed that he had delegated the responsibility for sanitation to dependable subordinates. He admitted at trial that he had received a warning letter from the Food and Drug Administration regarding the unsanitary conditions at one of the company's warehouses. The trial court found the defendant guilty. The court of appeals reversed. The case was appealed to the U.S. Supreme Court.*

ISSUE: Can corporate executives be criminally liable for failing to ensure a company's compliance with the law?

REASONING: The Supreme Court has noted that the only way corporations can act is through their individual employees. The act in question, the Federal Food, Drug, and Cosmetic Act, requires stringent, affirmative actions on the part of corporate executives, but these standards are justified by the public interest in food safety. We expect executives such as Park to exercise appropriate authority and demonstrate supervisory responsibility. There is considerable evidence that Park had a duty to ensure sanitary conditions and that he violated that duty by failing to ensure that those to whom he delegated responsibility did their jobs.

The Court said: "[T]he requirements of foresight and vigilance imposed on responsible corporate agents are beyond question, demanding, and perhaps onerous, but they are not more stringent than the public has a right to expect of those who voluntarily assume positions of authority in business enterprises whose services and products affect the health and well-being of the public that supports them."

DECISION AND REMEDY: The U.S. Supreme Court reversed the appellate court's reversal of the trial court's conviction, finding that corporate executives can be criminally liable for failing to ensure a company's compliance with the law.

SIGNIFICANCE OF THE CASE: This case signaled to corporate officials that they could no longer use ignorance as a defense, because a court will hold high-level corporate actors responsible for their company's failure to comply with the law, even if they were unaware of what was going on within their company.

CRITICAL THINKING

Given the rule laid down in this case, would there have been any evidence that the defendant could have presented that would have led to a different decision?

ETHICAL DECISION MAKING

Suppose you were in Park's position in this case. You allegedly allowed food in your warehouse to be exposed to rodent contamination. If you were guided by the public disclosure test, what would you decide to do?

vicarious liability
The liability or responsibility imposed on a person, a party, or an organization for damages caused by another; most commonly used in relation to employment, with the employer held vicariously liable for damages caused by its employees.

Since *United States v. Park,* the general rule that corporate executives may be held accountable for the crimes arising from their failure to meet their responsibility has remained intact. The rule has, in fact, broadened so that now executives can be held criminally liable for offenses that we generally do not think of as crimes. For example, in *United States v. Iverson,*[7] a corporate officer of a waste treatment facility was convicted and sentenced for violating the Clean Water Act after he ordered employees to illegally dispose of wastewater. This case demonstrates that corporate executives can be sentenced not only for committing the common law crimes that we have traditionally understood to be criminal offenses but also for violating provisions of regulatory statutes that permit criminal sanctions. In such cases, **vicarious liability**, or liability imposed on one person for the acts of another, is assessed to the corporate executive. In fact, courts have held that employers are vicariously liable for the wrongful acts of their employees if the employer directed, partook in, or authorized the wrongful act.

LO 5-4 Criminal Procedure

Criminal procedure differs from civil procedure in several key ways. First, the government, referred to as the *prosecutor,* always brings the criminal case, whereas in a civil case, the party filing the case, the plaintiff, can be an individual, business, or government entity. Second, the outcome of each is different. In a criminal case, the objective is punishment, so the defendant may be fined or imprisoned; in a civil case, the objective is to remedy a wrong done to the plaintiff, so the defendant either will have to provide compensation to the plaintiff or may be subject to an equitable remedy such as an injunction or order for specific performance. Third, because the potential impact of losing a criminal case is so much more serious than the impact of losing a civil case, the Constitution provides a number of safeguards for the criminal defendant. These safeguards are set forth in Exhibit 5-3.

[7] 162 F.3d 1015 (1998).

AMENDMENT	PROVISIONS
Fourth	• Protection from unreasonable search and seizure.
	• Restrictions on warrants.
Fifth	• Prohibition of double jeopardy.
	• Right not to incriminate oneself.
	• Right to due process.
Sixth	• Right to a speedy and public trial.
	• Right to a trial by an impartial jury of one's peers.
	• Right to be informed of the accusations against oneself.
	• Right to confront witnesses.
	• Right to have witnesses on one's side.
	• Right to counsel at various stages of the proceedings.
Eighth	• Freedom from excessive bail.
	• Freedom from excessive fines.
	• Freedom from cruel and unusual punishment.
Fourteenth	• Extension of the right to due process to all state matters.
	• Extension of most constitutional rights to defendants at the state level.

Exhibit 5-3

Constitutional Provisions That Safeguard Criminal Defendants' Rights

PRETRIAL PROCEDURE

Prior to an arrest, grand juries may conduct criminal investigatory proceedings or issue a grand jury subpoena for company records. Criminal proceedings generally begin when an individual is **arrested** for a crime. A law enforcement officer must perform the arrest. This officer is often a police officer but may also be an agent of another government agency, such as the Bureau of Alcohol, Tobacco and Firearms; the Federal Bureau of Investigation; or the Immigration and Naturalization Service.

A law enforcement officer should obtain an arrest warrant before an individual is taken into custody. Ordinarily, to obtain an arrest warrant, the law enforcement agent must demonstrate that there is **probable cause,** or a likelihood, that a suspect committed or is planning to commit a crime. A *magistrate,* the lowest-ranking judicial official, issues the arrest warrant. In certain circumstances, however, courts have recognized that law enforcement agents can arrest a suspect without a warrant if the officer believes there is probable cause but not enough time to obtain the warrant.

When law enforcement agents arrest individuals, the officers must inform the individuals of their **Miranda rights.** If they fail to do so, any information a defendant offers at the time of the arrest is not admissible at trial. To comply with the Supreme Court's requirements for protecting a citizen's rights, a law enforcement officer must inform the defendant of the following facts before questioning:

1. "You have the right to remain silent and refuse to answer any questions."
2. "Anything you say may be used against you in a court of law."
3. "You have the right to consult an attorney before speaking to the police and have an attorney present during any questioning now or in the future."
4. "If you cannot afford an attorney, one will be appointed for you before the questioning begins."
5. "If you do not have an attorney available, you have the right to remain silent until you have had an opportunity to consult with one."
6. "Now that I have advised you of your rights, are you willing to answer any questions without an attorney present?"

arrest
The action in which a police officer or a person acting under the law takes a person into custody.

probable cause
Any essential element and/or standard by which a lawful officer may make a valid arrest, conduct a personal or property search, or obtain a warrant.

Miranda rights
The rights that are read to an arrested individual by a law enforcement agent before the individual is questioned about the commission of a crime.

booking

After an individual is arrested, the procedure during which the name of the defendant and the alleged crime are recorded in the investigating agency's or police department's records.

first appearance

The initial appearance of an arrested individual before a judge who determines whether there was probable cause for the arrest. If the judge ascertains that probable cause did not exist, the individual is freed.

bail

A thing of value, such as a money bail bond or any other form of property, that is given to the court to temporarily allow a person's release from jail and to ensure his or her appearance in court.

information

A document, prepared by the prosecutor and presented to the magistrate, which demonstrates that there is enough evidence to charge the defendant and bring him or her to trial.

indictment

Finding by the grand jury that there is adequate evidence to charge the defendant and bring him or her to trial.

arraignment

The first appearance in court by the defendant, at which the defendant is advised of the pending charges, the right to counsel, and the right to trial by jury and he or she enters a plea to the charge.

nolo contendere

A plea in which the defendant does not admit guilt but agrees not to contest the charges.

petit jury

A group of 6 or 12 citizens who are summoned to and sworn by the court to hear evidence presented by both sides and render a verdict in a trial.

The Miranda rights are not absolute. In fact, the Supreme Court has several times created exceptions to the Miranda rights. For example, in *New York v. Quarles,*[8] the Court created a "public safety" exception to the Miranda rights. This exception allows statements to be used at trial, even if a person was not informed of his or her Miranda rights, if the need to protect the public is served by the admissibility of the statements in question.

After being arrested and read their Miranda rights, defendants are taken to the police station for **booking,** a procedure during which the name of the defendant and the alleged crime are recorded in the investigating agency's or police department's records. After the prosecutor files the complaint, the defendant makes the **first appearance,** which is the appearance before a magistrate who determines whether there was probable cause for the arrest. If the magistrate ascertains that probable cause did not exist, the individual is freed.

If the defendant committed a minor offense and pleads guilty, the magistrate sentences the individual. However, if the defendant claims innocence, the magistrate ensures that the defendant has a lawyer, or appoints one, if necessary, for an indigent defendant, and sets bail. **Bail** is the amount of money defendants pay to the court on release from custody as security that they will return for trial.

Next, the prosecutor has a choice: Should the case be prosecuted? The *Principles of Federal Prosecution,* established by the U.S. Department of Justice, suggest that at the federal level the decision to prosecute depends on two primary factors: (1) whether the evidence is sufficient to obtain a conviction and (2) whether prosecuting the case serves a federal interest. If the prosecutor decides not to go forward with the case, the defendant may still be liable for his or her actions in civil court.

If the prosecutor chooses to proceed with a criminal action, the prosecutor must demonstrate the likelihood that the defendant's actions and intent meet the elements of a crime by charging the defendant with a crime through an *information* or an *indictment.* For a misdemeanor, the prosecutor must present to the magistrate evidence sufficient to justify prosecution of the defendant. This is done through a written document called an **information,** a formal accusation stating the facts and specifying the violation of criminal law.

However, for a felony, the prosecutor must present a grand jury with evidence adequate to justify bringing the defendant to trial. If the grand jury agrees that the evidence is adequate, it issues an **indictment,** a written accusation of the crime allegedly committed by the defendant.

Note that the grand jury does not determine guilt. It is simply a group of citizens who consider evidence of criminal conduct presented by the prosecutor and then determine whether there is enough evidence to try the defendant for the crime.

In federal cases, a defendant accused of a felony has a constitutional right to a grand jury indictment. However, a felony prosecution may proceed by information if the defendant waives that right. For instance, in a high-profile case in which the defense attorney is trying to work out a deal with the prosecution, the defendant may ask that the case proceed by information. Federal misdemeanor cases may proceed by indictment or information.

If the criminal trial takes place in state court, the defendant may or may not have access to a grand jury. The U.S. Supreme Court has held that indictment by a grand jury is not a fundamental right, and thus states are not required to offer grand juries. About half the states still require that felony prosecutions be initiated by grand jury indictments; most of the rest use information as the method for commencing prosecution.

If the grand jury issues an indictment, the defendant appears in court to answer the indictment in a proceeding called the **arraignment.** At this time, the defendant enters a plea of guilty or not guilty. A defendant may also enter a plea of **nolo contendere,** whereby the defendant does not admit guilt but agrees not to contest the charges. The advantage of a nolo contendere plea over a guilty plea is that the former cannot be used against the defendant in a civil suit. If the defendant pleads not guilty, his case will be heard before a **petit jury,** which is a fact-finding jury.

[8] 467 U.S. 649 (1984).

At any time, the prosecutor and defendant can make a **plea bargain,** an agreement in which the prosecutor agrees to reduce charges, drop charges, or recommend a certain sentence if the defendant pleads guilty. Plea bargaining benefits both parties. The defendant gets a lesser sentence, and the prosecution saves time and resources by not trying the case. Businesspeople who commit crimes that affect business often engage in plea bargaining to avoid the publicity associated with a trial and the risk of a severe sentence.

plea bargain

An agreement in which the prosecutor agrees to reduce charges, drop charges, or recommend a certain sentence if the defendant pleads guilty.

TRIAL PROCEDURE

If the case goes to trial and the crime is a felony or a misdemeanor punishable by six months or more in prison, the defendant has a constitutional right to a jury trial. In most states, if the defendant waives the right to a jury trial, the judge will hear the case. When a judge is the fact finder in a case, the trial is called a **bench trial.**

In a criminal trial, the prosecutor has the burden of proof and the defendant does not have to prove anything. The **burden of proof** has two elements: the burden of production of evidence and the burden of persuasion. To meet the *burden of production of evidence,* the prosecution must produce any tangible evidence and testimony that prove the elements of the crime that the defendant allegedly committed. Along with producing evidence, the prosecution also has the *burden of persuasion:* The prosecutor must persuade the jury *beyond reasonable doubt* that the defendant committed the crime. The burden of proof, then, is higher in a criminal case than in a civil case, because in a civil case the burden of persuasion requires only that the claim be supported by a preponderance of the evidence.

The prosecution presents the government's case first, introducing evidence and examining witnesses to prove beyond a reasonable doubt that the defendant committed the crime. Once the prosecutions rests its case, it is the defendant's turn. The defendant either (1) can show, through examination of witnesses and introduction of evidence, that the prosecution did not meet its burden of proof or (2) can present an affirmative defense. An *affirmative defense* is a reason why the defendant, even though he or she did the physical acts alleged by the prosecution, should be excused from responsibility for those actions. Exhibit 5-4 lists some common affirmative defenses.

bench trial

A trial before a judge, with the judgment decided by the judge rather than a jury; occurs when the defendant has waived his or her right to a jury trial.

burden of proof

The duty of the plaintiff or prosecution to establish a claim or allegation by admissible evidence and to prove that the defendant committed all the essential elements of the crime to the jury's or court's satisfaction beyond any reasonable doubt, in order to convict the defendant.

Infancy	A person who is not yet a legal adult may use this defense to defuse the guilty-mind requirement of a crime.
Mistake	The defendant says his or her honest and reasonable mistake negates the idea of a guilty mind.
Intoxication	The defendant says he or she took an intoxicant without awareness of its likely effect, mistook its identity, or took the intoxicant under force.
Insanity	The defendant had a severe mental illness that substantially impaired the defendant's capacity to understand and appreciate the moral wrongfulness of the act.
Duress	The defendant says he or she was forced to perform an act against his or her will.
Entrapment	The defendant would not have committed the crime or broken the law if not induced or tricked into doing so by law enforcement officers.
Necessity	The defendant was acting to prevent imminent harm, and there was no legal alternative to the action he or she took.
Justifiable use of force	Use of force was necessary to prevent imminent death or great bodily harm to the defendant or to another or to prevent the imminent commission of a forcible felony.

Exhibit 5-4

Affirmative Defenses to Crimes

Figure 5-1

Steps in a Criminal
Procedure

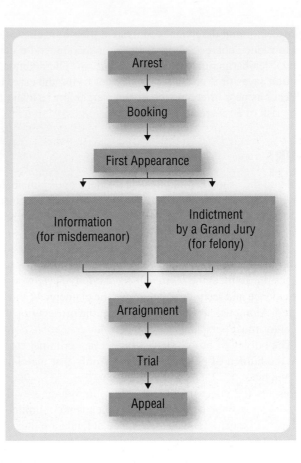

After the jury hears the case, it deliberates and tries to reach a verdict. A jury that is unable to reach a verdict is known as a "hung jury." If the jury finds the defendant not guilty, the accused is acquitted and released. If the jury returns a guilty verdict, the judge sets a date for sentencing.

POSTTRIAL PROCEDURE

If the petit jury returns a verdict of not guilty, the government cannot appeal the acquittal. However, if the verdict is guilty, the defendant may appeal the verdict by claiming that a prejudicial error of law occurred at the original trial. If there is no appeal, the defendant will be sentenced after the judge has received additional information relevant to sentencing.

Figure 5-1 summarizes the steps of a criminal procedure.

LO 5-5 Tools for Fighting Business Crime

While there are clearly a significant number of business-related crimes that can be committed, there are certain federal laws that help fight such crime. Three federal laws that have been somewhat successful in this battle are RICO, the False Claims Act, and the Sarbanes-Oxley Act of 2002. While these laws are currently extremely powerful white-collar-crime laws, RICO and the False Claims Act were created with different purposes in mind. Sarbanes-Oxley, however, was created to specifically combat white-collar crime.

RICO

One of the most important tools for fighting white-collar crime is Title IX of the Organized Crime Control Act of 1970: the **Racketeer Influenced and Corrupt Organizations (RICO) Act.** Although the statute was originally enacted to combat organized crime, in effect it prevents legitimate businesses from serving as covers for racketeering. This statute prohibits persons employed by or associated with an enterprise from engaging in a pattern of racketeering activity. Anyone whose business or property has been damaged by this pattern of racketeering activity can sue to recover treble damages and attorney fees in a civil action.

> **Racketeer Influenced and Corrupt Organizations (RICO) Act**
> A U.S. law that provides extended penalties for criminal acts performed as part of an ongoing criminal organization.

Demonstrating a claim under RICO requires proof of a pattern of racketeering. Courts have defined a pattern as more than one action. Thus, a one-time violator could not be prosecuted under RICO because there could be no pattern as yet. Some courts additionally have found that a pattern requires continued criminal activity over a "substantial" period of time. Although *pattern* is restricted to more than one act, racketeering has been defined broadly to include almost all criminal actions, such as acts of violence, fraud, bribery, securities fraud, and the provision of illegal goods and services. Therefore, RICO is an extremely effective tool in combating white-collar crimes.

In addition to being held civilly liable under RICO, a violator may also be subject to RICO's criminal penalties. A person found to have violated the act may be subject to a fine of up to $25,000 per violation, imprisonment for up to 20 years, or both.

THE FALSE CLAIMS ACT

Since 1986 private citizens have been using the **False Claims Act** to sue employers on behalf of the government for fraud against the government. For example, an employee in a health care facility might realize that his employer is submitting fraudulent claims to Medicare. The employee can bring a suit against the employer on behalf of the government for fraud against the government.

> **False Claims Act**
> An act that allows employees to sue employers on behalf of the federal government for fraud against the government. The employee retains a share of the recovery as a reward for his or her efforts.

If an employee realizes that her employer is committing fraud against the government, she must first notify the government of her intent to file the case on behalf of the government. If the government chooses to intervene and prosecute the case itself, with the help of the employee, the citizen would receive 25 percent of the amount recovered. If the government opts to not get involved, and the citizen continues with the case on behalf of the government, she receives 30 percent.

Certainly, an employee who brings a suit against his employer might be worried about retaliation, such as being fired or demoted. Thus, the act provides protection for employees who use the law. If an employer is found guilty of retaliation, the employer may be forced to pay the employee twice the amount of back pay plus special damages.

The biggest reward thus far under the act was the approximately $51 million share that four whistle-blowers and their attorneys received for blowing the whistle on a Swiss drug company, Serono, for participating in a marketing scheme that resulted in physicians' illegally prescribing over $11.5 million worth of a drug that was paid for by Medicaid. The government settled the case against the company for $704 million. The reward in this case, however, was far above the norm. In 2010, the Justice Department recovered a total of $53.7 billion under the False Claims Act, up from $53.5 billion collected in 2009[9].

Despite the fact that some of these cases might not have been pursued had it not been for the False Claims Act, there are many people who are opposed to the act. Some argue that the whistle-blowers are receiving money that should belong to the taxpayers, while others say that the act prompts people to not report fraud right away but wait until the value of the case grows. Still others complain that the act results in frivolous lawsuits as employees try to find an "easy" way to make money.

Defenders of the False Claims Act point out that the act has led to some significant cases of fraud being reported that otherwise might have cost the government millions of dollars. They also point out that when an employee does report a fraudulent employer, it is going to be very

[9] Fiscal Year 2012 Budget Request, Civil Division, http://www.justice.gov/jmd/2012justification/pdf/fy12-civ-justification.pdf (accessed July 1, 2010).

Protecting Whistle-Blowers in the United Kingdom

One way in which the United Kingdom fights white-collar crime is through the use of a national whistle-blower statute, the Public Interest Disclosure Act of 1998 (PIDA), which protects the whistle-blower from firing or retaliation if he or she makes a good-faith disclosure based on genuine concerns about crime, civil offenses, miscarriage of justice, danger to health and safety or the environment, and the cover-up of any of these.

The emphasis of PIDA is on fixing the problem within the company. The most protected, and preferred, disclosure is one that is made to a manager within the company, so the first step is often to disclose the possible violation to a manager in the company. Sometimes such disclosures are not always advisable or possible, so disclosures to the appropriate ministry are protected, when applicable, as well as disclosures to the appropriate regulatory agency, such as the Health and Safety Executive. Rather than just having a suspicion of wrongdoing, whistle-blowers must believe that their allegations are substantially true before disclosing them to a regulator.

If the whistle-blower reasonably believed that he or she would be victimized for disclosure to the company or regulator, reasonably believed that a cover-up was likely and there was no prescribed regulator, or had already raised the issue internally or with a regulator and no action had been taken, he or she would be protected for a wider disclosure.

The whistle-blowers do not get monetary rewards. They may be protected and compensated if action is taken against them, but they do not receive anything for their revelations.

difficult for that employee to get a job in the same field in the future and thus a significant incentive needs to be offered to get employees to report such fraud.

A number of False Claims Act cases have been filed against universities, including an interesting case filed in 2006 against Chapman University. In this case, three faculty members alleged that the institution for years encouraged early dismissals, resulting in many students' not getting the minimum classroom training required in several subjects. If the college had admitted that it had engaged in this practice, it would never have been accredited and thus never have received millions of dollars in federal grants and student aid, which the lawsuit claimed it took under false pretenses.[10] The case was ultimately dismissed by a Summary Judgment in 2007, and in 2011, the plaintiff's appeal to the U.S. Supreme Court was denied. Other False Claims Act cases against universities have been more successful. For example, in 2009, the University of Phoenix settled a FCA suit for $67.5 million for violating federal law that prohibits colleges from paying admissions counselors incentives based on the number of students recruited.

> To learn more about the impact of the disallowance provision of the IRS Code, which you learned about in your accounting classes, on white collar crime, please go to the **Connecting to the Core** activity on the text's website at www.mhhe.com/kubasekess2e.

THE SARBANES-OXLEY ACT

Sarbanes-Oxley Act
An act that criminalizes specific nonaudit services when provided by a registered accounting firm to an audit client; also increases the punishment for a number of white-collar offenses. Also known as the *Public Company Accounting Reform and Investor Protection Act of 2002.*

Unlike RICO and the False Claims Act, the **Sarbanes-Oxley Act** of 2002 was intended to curb white-collar crime. Congress passed Sarbanes-Oxley largely in response to the business scandals of the early 2000s, such as Enron, WorldCom, and Global Crossing, as well as the accounting firm Arthur Andersen. While much of the act consists of new rules and regulations for accounting firms, part of the act specifically addresses the issue of white-collar crime.

Sarbanes-Oxley makes it illegal for registered public accounting firms to provide nonaudit services to an audit client. Section 201 of the act specifically names as illegal:

1. Bookkeeping or other services related to the accounting records or financial statements of the audit client.

2. Financial information systems design and implementation.

3. Appraisal or valuation services, fairness opinions, or contribution-in-kind reports.

4. Actuarial services.

5. Internal audit outsourcing services.

[10] Martin Van Der Werf, "Lawsuit U.: The Growing Reach of the False Claims Act Has Lawyers Fearing Trouble Everywhere," *Chronicle of Higher Education,* August 4, 2006, http://chronicle.com/weekly/v52/i48/48a02301.htm.

6. Management functions or human resources.

7. Broker or dealer, investment adviser, or investment banking services.

8. Legal services and expert services unrelated to the audit.

9. Any other service that the board determines, by regulation, is impermissible.

In addition to criminalizing the activities listed above, Sarbanes-Oxley has amended the penalties associated with other white-collar crimes. Under Sarbanes-Oxley, it is now a felony to willfully fail to maintain proper records of audits and work papers for at least five years, and the punishment for not maintaining these records is up to 10 years' imprisonment. Also, the destruction of documents received updated punishments. The destruction of documents involved in a federal bankruptcy investigation is now a felony with possible sentences of up to 20 years' imprisonment. Similarly, the punishment for securities fraud has been increased to 25 years' imprisonment.

In addition, Sarbanes-Oxley has extended the statute of limitations regarding the discovery of fraud. The statute of limitations now extends to two years from the date of discovery of the fraud and five years from the criminal act. The old statute was one year from discovery and three from the act. Also, much like the False Claims Act, Sarbanes-Oxley has taken affirmative steps toward further protecting whistle-blowers.

SUMMARY

The Nature and Elements of a Crime	The elements of a crime are:
	• *Actus reus:* Wrongful behavior (guilty act).
	• *Mens rea:* Wrongful state of mind or intent (guilty mind).
	Crimes are classified into three categories:
	• *Felonies:* Serious crimes punishable by imprisonment for more than one year or death.
	• *Misdemeanors:* Less serious crimes punishable by fines or imprisonment for less than one year.
	• *Petty offenses:* Minor misdemeanors punishable by small fines or short jail sentences.
White-Collar Crime	White-collar crimes include:
	1. Bribery.
	2. Extortion.
	3. Fraud.
	4. Embezzlement.
	5. Computer crimes (destruction of computer data, unlawful appropriation of data or services).
Corporate Criminal Liability	Both corporations, as legal entities, and the corporate officers and managers can be held liable for crimes committed on behalf of the corporation.
Criminal Procedure	*Pretrial procedure:* The arrest, booking, first appearance, indictment, and arraignment.
	Trial procedure: Jury selection, trial with burden of proof on prosecution, jury deliberations, jury verdict, and (if guilty) sentencing hearing.
	Posttrial procedure: Appeal.
Tools for Fighting Business Crime	*RICO:* Prohibits persons employed by or associated with an enterprise from engaging in a pattern of racketeering activity. Anyone whose business or property has been damaged by this pattern of activity can sue under RICO to recover treble damages and attorney fees in a civil action.
	False Claims Act: Allows employees to sue employers on behalf of the federal government for fraud against the government. The employee retains a share of the recovery as a reward for his or her efforts.
	Sarbanes-Oxley Act: Criminalizes specific nonaudit services when provided by a registered accounting firm to an audit client; also increases the punishment for a number of white-collar offenses.

Point/Counterpoint

As you are considering this issue, you might want to think about statistics that would help you resolve it.

How Severely Should the Law Punish Individuals Convicted of White-Collar Crime?

LESS SEVERELY THAN VIOLENT CRIMINALS

Street crimes are different in kind from white-collar crimes. Whereas white-collar crime affects only individuals' property, street crime threatens individuals' lives and health. The law ought to recognize that protecting lives is more important than protecting property.

Moreover, white-collar crime tends to affect higher-income individuals, whereas street crime tends to affect lower-income individuals who lack the resources to protect themselves. Street crime disproportionately affects lower-income individuals who cannot afford the private security measures that higher-income individuals use to protect their persons and their property. The law ought to protect those who lack the power to protect themselves.

A third reason to punish white-collar crime less heavily than street crime is that white-collar criminals are more likely to engage in careful cost-benefit analysis when determining whether to commit white-collar crime. If the severity of the punishment, discounted by the chance they will get caught, is less than the expected payoff from the white-collar crime, rational individuals won't see the crime as a profitable enterprise. We assume that street criminals do not engage in the same kind of careful cost-benefit analysis before deciding, for example, whether to use illegal drugs. The most effective punishment for street crimes is likely to be severe punishment that incapacitates the criminals so that they are unable to commit more street crime. White-collar crime, on the other hand, can effectively be curbed by setting the punishment just high enough to make the crime unprofitable, which would often mean the punishment for white collar crime is less than the stringent punishment necessary for street crime.

MORE SEVERELY THAN VIOLENT CRIMINALS

It is far from clear that white-collar crime has less serious consequences than street crime. For example, individuals who defraud the government in effect steal taxes paid by all members of society, whereas individuals in possession of small amounts of marijuana may never adversely affect other members of society.

Indeed, white-collar crime affects all groups in society in both direct and indirect ways. Companies victimized by white-collar crime often must raise the prices of their goods to recoup the costs of the crime. Everyone in society feels the effects of the higher prices. Street crime, while by no means negligible, tends to affect smaller circles of people. Thus, to get the biggest bang for our buck, we should punish white-collar crime more heavily than street crime.

Another reason to punish white-collar crime more heavily than street crime focuses on the underlying causes of crime. Much street crime has its roots in other social problems. Often, individuals commit street crime because of the poor environments in which they were raised. Much white-collar crime, however, is committed by well-off individuals out of avarice. The law ought to dole out more severe punishments for crimes caused by individual responsibility, and society ought to use other mechanisms to address crime caused by aleatory factors.

Questions & Problems

1. Name and explain the two elements of a crime.
2. Identify the distinguishing features of white-collar crime.
3. List and define the primary affirmative defenses used in criminal cases.
4. List and describe the main types of fraud committed in the business context.

5. What is meant by reading a defendant his Miranda rights, and why are these rights important?
6. Explain the steps of a criminal prosecution.
7. Explain the federal laws that are currently being used to try to fight white-collar crime.
8. Defendants Schaffer and Arvidson were charged with conspiracy to commit computer fraud and to transport

stolen property interstate. In 2002, when contacted by an undercover FBI agent who was interested in the defendants' abilities in infiltrating wireless computer networks, Arvidson indicated a willingness to infiltrate the network of a Department of Defense contractor in Texas. In 2003, the FBI agent paid for the defendants' transportation to Texas from Ohio to acquire files from the contractor's computer. Upon the successful completion of the operation, the defendants were paid $100,000. Nearly five years later, in 2008, the defendants were indicted by a grand jury. The defendants sought dismissal based on entrapment. How do you think the court ruled? Why? [*Schaffer v. United States,* 586 F.3d 414 (6th Cir. 2009).]

9. Chester Jones was the committee chairman of the Perry County Democratic Party and a candidate for the Perry County School Board. Jones used money given to the Kentucky Democratic Party to hand out seventy-five $100 checks to Perry County voters, in an effort to persuade families to vote for Jones and Neace. In 2009, a grand jury in the Eastern District of Kentucky charged Jones with one count of aiding and abetting mail fraud and one count of conspiring to commit mail fraud and vote buying. Jones signed a plea agreement in which he pleaded guilty to one count of aiding and abetting mail fraud. The district court then sentenced Jones to 12 months' imprisonment. After Jones's conviction, a U.S. Supreme Court ruling in *Skilling v. United States* narrowed the scope of "honest services" fraud. Jones then contested that he wanted to vacate his conviction in the aftermath of the Skilling case. Jones argued that he had pleaded guilty to "conduct that has been determined by the Supreme Court not to be a crime." The court affirmed the district court's decision. Do you agree with the court's affirmation? Why or why not? [*United States v. Jones,* 2011 U.S. App. LEXIS 2269 (6th Cir. Ky. 2011).]

10. John and Tahir Ramin were indicted on charges of conspiracy to commit mail fraud and conspiracy to commit bribery, among other charges. They were alleged to have bribed Army Major Christopher West in order to secure a bunkers and barriers contract, which would enable them to provide bunkers and barriers to the airfield that West was responsible for. The defendants were then alleged to have inflated the number of bunkers and barriers that they actually provided to the airfield. In response to the charges, the defendants provided a defense to the bribery charge based on economic duress. The government filed a motion to exclude the evidence related to economic duress, arguing that economic duress was not a valid defense for bribery. Do you think the district court granted the government's motion to exclude evidence? Why or why not? [*United States v. West et al.,* 2010 U.S. Dist. LEXIS 33294 (N.D. Ill. 2010).]

11. Defendants driver Holland and Kelley, his passenger, were charged with drug possession with the intent to sell. Officers had arrested the driver on a misdemeanor, for changing lanes without signaling, after the officers had been advised by High-Intensity Drug Trafficking Area undercover officers to prevent the defendants from potentially robbing a confidential informant of narcotics. Upon arrest, officers had searched the center console of the vehicle, finding evidence that suggested their intent to sell drugs. The officers admitted to having no factual basis for believing that there was evidence of either defendant's drug possession within the vehicle at the time of arrest. Holland and Kelley argued that the search of the vehicle that ensued after the driver's arrest was unlawful and that evidence obtained through the arrest should be found inadmissible. The government argued that the arrest and search was lawful pursuant to the "good-faith exception" and the "inevitability exception." Whom do you think the court found in favor of? Why? [*United States v. Kelley and Holland,* 2011 U.S. Dist. LEXIS 5261 (S.D. Tex. 2011).]

12. The defendant, Raul Pol-Flores, referred two investors to Luis Herrero-Rovira. The two investors were then defrauded of their entire $290,000 investment, and Pol received nearly $20,000 of the funds. When the two investors had deposited the $290,000 in the bank, Pol told the bank that the funds were for investments but that he was not authorized to engage in the activity. Herrero returned the funds to the investors but convinced them to engage in another investment option, CLEIGG. The investors reinvested their $290,000 but saw only $3,622 in interest payments. The CLEIGG account funded numerous wire transfers, totaling $119,072, to banks in Puerto Rico. Herrero withdrew a total of $125,000 from the CLEIGG account. Two of the wire transfers, totaling $20,000, were made to Pol's company, Polarco. Pol was found guilty on 10 counts of wire fraud. Pol argued there was insufficient evidence presented at trial to convict him as an aider and abettor to wire fraud. The court affirmed the district court's decision that a reasonable jury could have concluded beyond a reasonable doubt that Pol had participated in Herrero's wire fraud scheme. Do you agree with the court's affirmation? Why or why not? [*United States v. Pol-Flores,* 2011 U.S. App. LEXIS 8885 (2011).]

13. Sistrunk was involved in committing an armed robbery at a residence being used as a "stash house." This residence, however, was actually a police setup, organized by an anonymous informant as well as an undercover agent, Juan Sanchez. Sistrunk attended meetings concerning the robbery and was informed that participants would be armed. The confidential informant met with Sistrunk to travel to the stash

house. When the confidential informant, Sistrunk, and the other defendants arrived, they were arrested. Sistrunk's argument did not initially mention entrapment or refer to the jury instruction for the entrapment defense; however, Sistrunk's closing attorney included the facts that Sistrunk now argues serve as the evidentiary basis for the entrapment instruction. The district court ruled that the entrapment defense did not apply as a matter of law, and the court withdrew the entrapment instruction as to count seven of the indictment for Sistrunk. One of the arguments that Sistrunk raised on appeal was that he had in fact been entrapped and the District Court for the Southern District of Florida was incorrect in ruling that the entrapment defense did not apply. Do you think Sistrunk's conviction should have been overturned on grounds that he had been entrapped? Why or why not? [*United States of America v. Sistrunk,* 622 F.3d 1328, 2010 U.S. App. LEXIS 20738 (2010).]

Looking for more review material?

The Online Learning Center at **www.mhhe.com/kubasekess2e** contains this chapter's "Assignment on the Internet" and also a list of URLs for more information, entitled "On the Internet." Find both of them in the Student Center portion of the OLC, along with quizzes and other helpful materials.

Tort Law

Rubin v. U.S. News

Richard Rubin, chief executive of Republic Metals, a gold-refining company, agreed to be interviewed and photographed for a *U.S. News & World Report* article.[1] Rubin argued that he had been told the article was about the Peruvian value tax, a rebate given to those who export gold from Peru. However, when the article appeared in the magazine, it was titled "The Golden Age of Crime: Why International Drug Traffickers Are Invading the Global Gold Trade." The author of the article explained how the gold trade is used as a tool for money laundering, and Rubin, also pictured, was quoted as saying, "There's a dual economic system. There's on the books and there's off the books."

When Rubin discovered that the article was about money laundering, he brought suit against *U.S. News & World Report.* Rubin argued that the story implied he is or has been involved in money laundering through his gold-refining business and that this implication hurt his reputation. *U.S. News* issued a clarification stating that the purpose of the article was not to imply Rubin was involved in illegal activity.

1. Suppose you are Rubin. You are concerned that the article has damaged your gold-refining business. What do you do? Why?

2. Now suppose you are a manager at a company that does business with Rubin's refining company. You read the story in *U.S. News.* Does the story lead to any change in your business with Rubin? Why?

[1] See Susan R. Miller, "*U.S. News* Sued by Gold Trader," quoted in "Money Laundering Story," *Broward Daily Business Review,* May 25, 2000, p. A1; "News Magazine Sued," *National Law Journal,* June 12, 2000, p. B2.

After reading this chapter, you will be able to answer the following questions:

LO 6-1 How are torts classified?

LO 6-2 What are some of the most common intentional torts, and what are the elements needed to prove these torts?

LO 6-3 What are the elements that must be proved to win a negligence case?

LO 6-4 What are the doctrines that help a plaintiff win a negligence case?

LO 6-5 What defenses are available in a negligence case?

LO 6-6 How does a party prove a strict-liability case?

LO 6-7 What types of damages are available in tort cases?

As a future business manager, you will likely be involved in a situation where one party believes he or she has been injured by the actions of another party, in the same way Rubin believed he had been injured by the *U.S. News & World Report* article. Wrongs such as these are often referred to as *torts*. A **tort** is commonly defined as a wrong or injury to another, other than a breach of contract. In fact, *tort* is a French word meaning "wrong." This chapter first examines the goals of tort law and the three primary classifications of torts. Next, the chapter examines each of the categories of torts. It concludes by discussing damages that may be available in tort cases.

tort
A violation of another person's rights or a civil wrongdoing that does not arise out of a contract or statute; primary types are intentional, negligent, and strict-liability torts.

Introduction to Tort Law

Chapter 5 introduced criminal law and explained the punishment individuals may receive for committing crimes. Most of the actions that give rise to criminal prosecutions also provide the basis for a tort claim by the victim of the crime.

While the primary objectives of criminal law are to punish wrongdoers and preserve order in society, the primary objective of tort law is to provide compensation for injured parties. Tort law also contributes to maintaining order in society because it discourages private retaliation by injured persons and their friends. After all, we do not want to live in a community where vigilantes with tempers are roaming about righting some harm they believe has occurred to them.

A third objective of tort law is to give citizens a sense that they live in a just society. Our collective sense of right and wrong suggests that someone who creates harm should make things right by compensating those who were harmed. The recognition that one will have to pay for the personal injuries she or he causes may also serve to deter the commission of torts.

Although this chapter discusses torts as if they were the same everywhere, tort law is primarily state law, so states may have slightly different definitions of each tort. In describing torts, this chapter uses the definitions common in most states, noting the instances where there seems to be a significant difference in the way certain states define the tort.

Despite the public impression of a tort litigation explosion often conveyed by the media, because tort law is state law, there is no entity that regularly compiles and publishes an annual report of the total number of tort cases filed nationwide. Writers for a legal publication, *Lawyer's Weekly USA*, however, do keep track of the top 10 jury verdicts every year. What they have found was that after years of decline since 2000, the top 10 jury verdicts rose dramatically in 2008 and increased by a lesser amount in 2009, with the average of the top 10 jury verdicts increasing from $112 million to nearly $145 million. But the very top award in 2009 was slightly lower, at $370 million, versus $388 million in 2008. In 2010, the average increased less than the prior year, however, rising from nearly $145 million to just under $157 million, but the top award was significantly higher in 2010. A Las Vegas attorney won a judgment of $505 million, with $500 million being punitive damages, against a manufacturer and distributor whose oversized vials of a drug led to an outbreak of Hepatitis C at outpatient surgical centers.[2] Given what we do know

[2] Lawyers USA Online, "Top Ten Jury Verdicts of 2010," http://lawyersusaonline.com/free-white-paper-top-ten-jury-verdicts-of-2010.

about tort litigation and damages, we know that potential tort liability should concern a competent business manager.

Classification of Torts

Torts are most commonly classified as intentional, negligent, or strict-liability torts. Each category differs in terms of the elements needed to prove the tort, the available damages, the available defenses, and the degree of willfulness of the actor. **Intentional torts** occur when the defendant takes an action intending certain consequences will result or knowing certain consequences are likely to result. **Negligent torts** occur when the defendant acts in a way that subjects other people to an unreasonable risk of harm. In other words, the defendant is careless to someone else's detriment. Finally, **strict-liability torts** occur when the defendant takes an action that is inherently dangerous and cannot ever be undertaken safely, no matter what precautions the defendant takes. It is important to remember that when we discuss these classifications, we are referring to their use in the United States. The Chinese legal system, for example, narrowly defines the activities actionable under tort law.

Intentional Torts

Intentional torts are the most "willful" of torts. Intentional torts are predicated on the common element of intent. The intent at issue is not intent to harm but, rather, is intent to engage in a specific act, which ultimately results in an injury, physical or economic, to another. In fact, one does not need to establish a motive when proving liability in an intentional tort case. Moreover, in tort law it is assumed that people intend what could be considered the normal consequences of their actions. For example, were Rob to throw a rock toward a group of people, it would be assumed under the law that he intended to hit someone with the rock and that the person hit would be hurt, regardless of Rob's intention merely to scare the group of people.

As a general rule, each specific intentional tort has a set of elements that must be proved to establish the tort, along with specific defenses that can be raised against each tort. However, not all harms intentionally committed will fall neatly into an existing category of torts. Therefore, a general theory of intentional tort liability has been created to aid judges in their decision making. In Section 870 of the Restatement (Second) of Torts, the general theory is explained this way:

> One who intentionally causes injury to another is subject to liability to the other for that injury, if his conduct is generally culpable and not justifiable under the circumstances. This liability may be imposed although the actor's conduct does not come within a traditional category of tort liability.

Intentional torts are divided into the following three categories: (1) torts against persons, (2) torts against property, and (3) torts against economic interests. The following sections discuss a number of specific torts that fall into each category, along with the defenses for each.

INTENTIONAL TORTS AGAINST PERSONS

Torts against persons are intentional acts that harm an individual's physical or mental integrity. There are a significant number of these torts. Assault and battery are two of the most common. Imagine that after searching for a parking space for 20 minutes you finally pull into a spot. However, as soon as you turn off your car, a man who looks like Mike Tyson starts pounding on your car window. He angrily yells, "You took my spot! If you don't move your car now, I'm going to hit you so hard you won't remember what your car looks like!" The man has just assaulted you.

An **assault** occurs when one person places another in fear or apprehension of an immediate, offensive bodily contact. Therefore, in the above example, if you think the man is just joking and you start laughing, no assault has taken place because there is no fear or apprehension. Not only must you feel fear or apprehension, but that feeling must be reasonable under the circumstances.

LO 6-1

intentional tort
A civil wrong resulting from an intentional act committed on the person, property, or economic interest of another. Intentional torts include assault, battery, conversion, false imprisonment, intentional infliction of emotional distress, trespass to land, and trespass to chattels.

negligent tort
A civil wrong that occurs when the defendant acts in a way that subjects other people to an unreasonable risk of harm (i.e., the defendant is careless, to someone else's detriment). Negligence claims are usually used to achieve compensation for accidents and injuries.

strict-liability tort
A civil wrong that occurs when the defendant takes an action that is inherently dangerous and cannot ever be undertaken safely, no matter what precautions the defendant takes. In such situations, a defendant is liable for the plaintiff's damages without any requirement that the plaintiff prove that the defendant was negligent.

LO 6-2

assault
A civil wrong that occurs when one person intentionally and voluntarily places another in fear or apprehension of an immediate, offensive physical harm. Assault does not require actual contact.

battery

A civil wrong that occurs when one person intentionally and voluntarily brings about a nonconsented harmful or offensive contact with a person or something closely associated with him or her. Battery requires an actual contact.

An assault is often, but not always, followed by a **battery,** an intentional, unwanted, offensive bodily contact. Almost any unwanted, intentional contact constitutes a battery. Even contacts that are harmless, if unwanted, are batteries. And even if a touch is intended as a joke, if the reasonable person would be offended, the contact is deemed "offensive."[3] To return to the example of the parking-space incident, if the man actually hit you, his action would constitute a battery. In contrast, if you both happened to be getting out of your respective cars at the same time and consequently bumped into each other, no battery would have occurred because there was no *intentional* bodily contact.

There are a limited number of defenses available to an action for a battery. A party charged with a battery may argue that the offended party consented to the contact. *Consent,* as a defense, mitigates the element of unwanted. A person cannot commit a battery if the contact was consented to and therefore wanted.

The most common defense to battery is *self-defense,* responding to the force of another with comparable force in order to defend oneself. In our parking-space example, if the man took a swing at you and you shoved him to try to keep him from hitting you, causing him to fall backward and hit his head on the street, he would not succeed in a case against you for battery because you could raise the defense of self-defense. To use this defense, you cannot use a greater level of force than is being used against you.

A third defense, *defense of others,* allows you to defend another by using the same degree of force that you could use to defend yourself. A final defense, *defense of property,* allows you to use reasonable force to defend your property from an intruder. The use of deadly force in defense of property is rarely, if ever, considered justified.

defamation

A false statement or an action that harms the reputation or character of an individual, business, product, group, government, or nation.

The tort alleged in this chapter's opening case was **defamation,** which is the intentional publication (communication to a third party) of a false statement harmful to an individual's reputation. In addition to the person who publishes a false statement, anyone who republishes, or in any manner repeats, a defamatory statement is also liable for defamation, even if he or she cites the original source of the defamation.

If the defamation is published in a permanent form, such as printed in a magazine or newspaper, it is known as *libel.* Defamation through television and radio broadcasts is also considered libel, since the broadcasts are permanently recorded. In the case of libel, "general damages" are presumed. Thus, the victim would be entitled to compensation for the damages that are presumed to flow from defamation yet are hard to prove, such as the humiliation the victim would feel.

If the defamation is made orally, it is *slander.* To recover damages in a case of slander, the plaintiff must prove "special damages"; that is, the plaintiff must show specific monetary loss that resulted from the defamatory statements. While libel is contained in a permanent form, slander, by virtue of being spoken, is not. It is the lack of permanence that gives way to the special damages involved with slander. If the people who heard the slander do not act in a way to cause harm to the slandered person, there is no cause for compensation, which is one of the main goals of tort law.

One exception to the requirement of special damages occurs if the false statements constitute *slander per se.* Slander per se statements are considered to be so inherently harmful that general damages are presumed. The kinds of statements considered slander per se are claims that an individual (1) has a loathsome, communicable disease (traditionally, venereal disease or leprosy); (2) has committed a crime for which imprisonment is a possibility; (3) is professionally incompetent; or (4) if a woman, has engaged in sexual misconduct.

If you say your boss is a tyrant or your roommate is a slob, are you in danger of being sued for defamation? You probably are not because such statements are not really statements of fact; rather, they are opinions, and subjective opinions that are not capable of being proved are generally not actionable.

One of the important elements of defamation is that the defamatory statement must be damaging to someone's reputation. For example, when a convicted criminal serving three life sentences attempted to sue a journalist for alleged errors in an article detailing his criminal history, the journalist filed a motion to dismiss on grounds that the defendant was

[3] Restatement (Second) of Torts, sec. 19.

libel-proof as a matter of law regarding claims about his criminal background. Upholding the dismissal, the court said the plaintiff's public reputation at the time the articles were published was so diminished with respect to a specific subject (his kidnapping and murder convictions) that he could not be further injured by allegedly false statements on that subject.[4]

The increase in communication over the Internet has presented new questions for the law of defamation to answer. First, does a false statement made over this information network constitute defamation? Second, who can be held liable if defamation does exist?

The court first attempted to answer these issues in the case of *Cubby v. CompuServ.*[5] In that case, CompuServ was sued because of defamatory statements published on one of the forums available through its online information service. In holding that CompuServ could not be held liable, the court made an analogy between an online information service provider such as CompuServ and bookstores, saying, "CompuServ's CIS product is in essence an electronic, for profit library." The court went on to say that once CompuServ decides to carry a given publication such as a news forum, it has little or no editorial control over that forum. It would therefore be no more feasible for CompuServ to examine every publication it carries for defamatory material than it would be for libraries or booksellers to do so.

Since *Cubby* was decided, the Communications Decency Act of 1996 was passed. One section of this act gives immunity to providers of interactive computer services for liability they might otherwise incur on account of material disseminated by them but created by others.

A person who is accused of defamation can raise two defenses: truth and privilege. *Truth* is frequently considered to be an absolute defense. That is, one cannot be held liable for defamation, regardless of whether damages result, if the statement made was the truth. If I say Bill is a convicted felon, and he is, I have not committed defamation. Under ordinary circumstances, the fact that you *thought* a statement was true is not a defense. So if I honestly believe Bill is a convicted felon and I tell others he is, but he is not, then I have committed slander.

Privilege is an affirmative defense in a defamation action. An affirmative defense occurs when the defendant admits to the accusation but argues that there is a reason why he should not be held liable. A privilege is either absolute or conditional. When an **absolute privilege** exists, one cannot be sued for defamation for any false statements made, regardless of intent or knowledge of the falsity of the claim. Absolute privilege arises in only a limited number of circumstances. The speech and debate clause of the U.S. Constitution gives an absolute privilege to individuals speaking on the House and Senate floors during congressional debate. This privilege exists because Congress wants to get to the truth of matters before it, and if people testifying before Congress had to fear they might be sued, they might be afraid to testify. Absolute privilege also arises during a judicial proceeding. Again, we do not want people to be afraid to testify in court, so we prohibit their being sued for whatever occurs within the courtroom. As the following Case Nugget illustrates, the concept of a judicial proceeding can extend beyond a traditional courtroom.

Conditional privilege is the second type. Under a conditional privilege, a party will not be held liable for defamation unless the false statement was made with **actual malice.** A statement is made with actual malice if it is made with *either* knowledge of its falsity or reckless disregard for its truth. Businesspersons should be most concerned about the conditional privilege that arises with respect to job recommendations. To encourage employers to give honest assessments of their former employees, this privilege protects an employer who makes a false statement about a former worker: The employer will not be held liable as long as the statement was made in good faith and was made only to those who had a legitimate interest in the information being communicated.

Another conditional privilege is the **public figure privilege.** Public figures are individuals who are in the public eye, typically politicians and entertainers. Because these individuals have a significant impact on our lives, we want to encourage free discussion about them, so we do not hold people liable for making false statements about them as long as the statements

absolute privilege
A special right, immunity, permission, or benefit given to certain individuals that allows them to make any statements about someone without being held liable for defamation for any false statement made, regardless of intent or knowledge of the falsity of the claim.

conditional privilege
A special right, immunity, permission, or benefit given to certain individuals that allows them to make any statements about someone without being held liable for defamation for any false statement made without actual malice.

actual malice
In defamation, either a person's knowledge that his or her statement or published material is false or the person's reckless disregard for whether it is false.

public figure privilege
A special right, immunity, or permission given to people that allows them to make any statements about public figures, typically politicians and entertainers, without being held liable for defamation for any false statement made without malice.

[4] *Thomas P. Lamb v. Tony Rizzo,* 391 F.3d 1133 (2004).
[5] 77b F. Supp. 135 (1991).

were not made with malice. This privilege does not seem to place an unfair burden on the public figure because such an individual can easily respond publicly to any false claims given that he or she is already in the public eye and has appropriate outlets available for giving his or her opinion.

There are those who believe a conditional privilege should apply when the defamatory statement is posted somewhere on the Internet. The reasoning behind application of the privilege in this context is that the person who has been defamed over the Internet can respond to the defamatory remarks in the same forum with minimal effort. Thus, there is less need for the stronger legal protection we ordinarily give to private parties who are defamed. In addition, we want to encourage free expression and the exchange of ideas on the Internet. One way to do so is to allow people to openly respond to criticisms on the Internet. When people are overly concerned about making errors, free exchange is hindered. Relaxing defamation standards in regard to the Internet can encourage people to speak their minds freely. Thus far, however, no such privilege has been established. And when a person is found to have committed defamation on an online bulletin board or website, the damages can be significant. For example, a jury awarded $3 million to a university professor who sued a former student who had accused him of being a pedophile on a website she maintained.

CASE Nugget

The Applicability of an Absolute Privilege

Hartman and Swinehart v. Keri
Supreme Court of Indiana

2008 Ind. LEXIS 265, 883 N.E.2d 774

On May 12, 2003, graduate students Virginia Hartman and Suzanne Swinehart filed formal complaints alleging sexual harassment by Dr. Gabe Keri, an assistant professor at Indiana University–Purdue University Fort Wayne (IPFW) from whom they had taken courses. IPFW charged Dr. Elaine Blakemore with the task of investigating the allegations; Blakemore submitted a report on June 30, 2003, that concluded Hartman and Swinehart's allegations were credible and commended their willingness to report the behavior. Furthermore, Blakemore suggested Keri be immediately removed from teaching positions. These findings and recommendations were further investigated by a three-person panel and Chancellor Wartell. Blakemore's report was supported and Keri was given a 100 percent research position with no use of his university office.

Keri appealed to the president of Purdue, who upheld the chancellor's decision. In response, Keri filed suit against Hartman and Swinehart in the Allen Superior Court, claiming libel, slander, and malicious interference. Hartman and Swinehart moved for summary judgment, claiming their statements were protected by absolute privilege. This motion was denied. Hartman and Swinehart appealed.

In finding that the students' statements were entitled to absolute privilege, the state supreme court judges explained that administrative proceedings that are quasi-judicial in nature are entitled to absolute protection. They applied the factors courts use to determine whether a proceeding is quasi-judicial in nature. These factors include whether the body has the power to (1) exercise judgment and discretion; (2) hear and determine or to ascertain facts and make decisions; (3) make binding orders and judgments; (4) affect the personal or property rights of private persons; (5) examine witnesses and hear the litigation of issues on a hearing; or (6) enforce decisions or impose penalties.

INTENTIONAL TORTS AGAINST PROPERTY

Because businesses own property, anyone who manages a business should be concerned about torts against property. The most common torts a businessperson might be involved with are trespass to realty, nuisance, trespass to personalty, and conversion.

Trespass to Realty The tort of **trespass to realty,** also called *trespass to real property,* occurs when a person intentionally (1) enters the land of another without permission; (2) causes an object to be placed on the land of another without the landowner's permission; (3) stays on the land of another when the owner tells him to depart; or (4) refuses to remove something he placed on the property that the landowner asked him to remove.

> **trespass to realty**
> A tort that occurs when someone goes on another's property without permission or places something on another's property without permission.

It is no defense for a person to argue that she thought she had a legal right to be on the property or she thought the land belonged to someone else. The intent refers to intentionally being on that particular piece of land. In a recent, unusual case heard in a small claims court in Westchester County, a plaintiff sued the defendant for trespass to realty when the defendant entered the plaintiff's property to serve the plaintiff with a reply affidavit for another legal action. The defendant had previously been barred from entering the plaintiff's property. The plaintiff argued that the defendant could not dictate how legal papers are served. The plaintiff sued for $3,000 in compensatory, nominal, and punitive damages. While the court ruled that the defendant committed trespass to realty, it awarded only nominal damages in the sum of $1.

Because guests are welcomed onto one's property, they are not considered trespassers. However, if a guest is asked to leave and he or she refuses, the person immediately becomes a trespasser and no longer maintains a right to be on the property in question. If charges were brought against such a person, that person could not raise the defense that he or she was a guest.

Also, when a trespasser is on someone's property, the trespasser is liable for damages she or he might cause to the property. Furthermore, under common law, a trespasser cannot hold an owner of property liable for damages the trespasser sustains while on the property. However, as of late, courts have been shifting away from this common law rule. Now, courts typically maintain that owners owe a reasonable duty to anyone who may end up on their property. The specifics of the duty vary by jurisdiction, as well as by the status of the parties. In some jurisdictions, it is possible, although rare, for owners to be liable for trespassers who were injured while trying to steal property from the owners.

Private Nuisance A **private nuisance** occurs when a person uses her property in an unreasonable manner that harms a neighbor's use or enjoyment of his property. Using one's property in a manner that caused the neighbor to be subjected to flooding, vibrations, excessive noise, or smoke could lead to a nuisance claim.

> **private nuisance**
> A nuisance that affects only a single person or a very limited number of individuals.

Trespass to Personal Property A person commits **trespass to personal property,** also called *trespass to personalty,* by temporarily exerting control over another's personal property or interfering with the true owner's right to use the property. Under trespass to personal property, the trespasser is responsible for damages caused to the property, as well as for damages caused to the owner related to the trespasser's wrongful possession of the property. For example, if I take someone's bike from his garage and use it for a week, I have committed trespass to personalty. If I return the bike after it has a flat tire, I will have to compensate the owner for the cost of repairing the tire and any other expenses that resulted from my having the bike for a week. Also, if the bike was the only means the person had for getting to work, I would be responsible for the person's lost wages resulting from the missed work, because I took the person's means of transportation.

> **trespass to personal property**
> Temporary interference with another's use or enjoyment of his or her personal property.

> **conversion**
> Permanent interference with another's use and enjoyment of his or her personal property.

Conversion **Conversion** occurs when a person permanently removes personal property from the owner's possession and control. When conversion occurs, the true owner can no longer regain the property. The owner usually recovers damages for the full value of the converted item, plus any additional damages that resulted from the loss.

It is not a defense to conversion for a person to argue that she believed she had a legal claim to the goods. For example, if Brittany accidentally takes Melvin's suitcase believing it to be hers

and then loses it, she is still liable for conversion. Moreover, the possession of stolen goods also makes a person liable for conversion. Therefore, buying goods in good faith without knowledge of any impropriety also is not a defense to conversion. Even if a person bought the goods believing the purchase was legal, the person with the stolen goods is liable to the legal owner of the goods.

An illustration of conversion comes from a recent case heard in the Westchester County Supreme Court. An amateur race-car driver left her race car at a service station. While the car was in the possession of the service station, an employee of the station, with a known drinking problem, apparently drove the car, wrecked it, and totally destroyed it. The car could never be returned in the condition it was in when brought to the station. The owner sued for conversion and recovered the value of the car in damages.

INTENTIONAL TORTS AGAINST ECONOMIC INTERESTS

All businesspersons should be familiar with the torts against economic interest. The five most common torts against economic interests, frequently referred to as "business torts," are disparagement, intentional interference with contract, unfair competition, misappropriation, and fraudulent misrepresentation. The first tort, **disparagement,** is similar to defamation, but it is a business's or product's reputation that has been tarnished.

The plaintiff in a disparagement case must prove that the defendant published a false statement of a material fact about the plaintiff's product or service that resulted in a loss of sales. When such statements are criticisms of the quality, honesty, or reputation of the business or product, the tort is sometimes called **slander of quality** (if spoken) or **trade libel** (if in printed form). If the statements relate to the ownership of the business property, the term **slander of title** is used.

Damages for disparaging are ordinarily based on a decrease in profits that can be linked to the publication of the false statement. An alternative, although less common, way to prove damages is to demonstrate that the plaintiff had been negotiating a contract with a third party but the third party lost interest shortly after the publication of the false statement. The profits the plaintiff would have made on the contract would be the damages.

Some interesting variations of the tort of disparagement have developed. For example, in 2007, California became the thirteenth state to recognize the tort of **food disparagement,** which critics call "veggie libel." Such laws provide ranchers and farmers with a cause of action when someone knowingly makes false, damaging statements about a food product. The California law was drafted in response to an incident during 2006 in which Taco Bell executives wrongly identified green onions grown at Boskovich Farms in Oxnard as the source of an *E. coli* outbreak that sickened 70 of the fast-food chain's customers.

A second tort against economic interests is the tort of **intentional interference with contract.** To successfully bring a claim of intentional interference with contract, the plaintiff must prove that (1) a valid and enforceable contract between the two parties existed; (2) the defendant party knew of the existence of the contract and its terms; (3) the defendant intentionally undertook steps to cause one of the parties to breach the contract; and (4) the plaintiff was injured as a result of the breach.[6]

When a contract exists, clear liability is placed on third parties for inducing a party to the contract to breach the contract. However, when a prospective contract exists, a third party might be liable for inducing a party to pull out of the contract before it is formed. Because the essence of business involves competition, simply offering a better deal is not enough to create liability when a prospective contract exists. However, if a party uses illegal means to cause another party not to enter into a contract, the party who acted illegally is liable for interfering with contractual relations.[7]

The most common situation involving intentional interference with a contract in the business context occurs when one employer tries to lure an employee away from another employer. Liability in such a situation, however, is limited to the case where the employee has a contract for a set period of time and the prospective employer actually knows of the contract.

disparagement

A business tort that occurs when a statement is intentionally used to defame a business product or service.

slander of quality

A business tort that occurs when false spoken statements criticize a business product or service and result in a loss of sales.

trade libel

A business tort that occurs when false printed statements criticize a business product or service and result in a loss of sales.

slander of title

A business tort that occurs when false published statements are related to the ownership of the business property.

food disparagement

A tort that provides ranchers and farmers with a cause of action when someone spreads false information about the safety of a food product.

intentional interference with contract

The tort that occurs when someone intentionally takes an action that will cause a person to breach a contract that she or he has with another.

[6] Restatement (Second) of Torts, sec. 766.
[7] Restatement (Second) of Torts, sec. 766B.

When a third party interferes with a contract, injured parties may recover damages for what was directly lost through the breached contract. They may also recover any losses suffered related to the breached contract, in addition to damages for emotional distress and harm to reputation.[8]

A third tort against economic interests, **unfair competition,** exists because of American views about the purpose of a business. Americans believe a business is intended to make a profit, and the law protects businesses acting on this profit motive. Therefore, when someone enters a business with the sole intent of driving another firm out of business, the law punishes this act as unfair competition. For example, if there is only one jewelry store in town, Mark cannot come in and set up a store where he makes no profits, just to drive the other store out of business, so that an acquaintance of his can then move in and open up a legitimate jewelry store once the competition has been eliminated.

A fourth tort against economic interests is **fraudulent misrepresentation,** which occurs when one uses intentional deceit to facilitate personal gain. To establish that a fraudulent misrepresentation exists, a party must demonstrate all the following:

1. A party knowingly, or with reckless disregard for the truth, misrepresented material facts and conditions.
2. The party intended to have other parties rely on the misrepresentations.
3. The injured party reasonably relied on the misrepresentations.
4. The injured party suffered damages because of relying on the misrepresentations.
5. A direct link exists between the injuries suffered and a reliance on the misrepresentations.[9]

As in the criminal act of fraud, in the civil act of fraudulent misrepresentation a party materially misrepresents something and thereby causes another party to suffer damages. Typically, fraudulent misrepresentation applies only to the misrepresentation of material facts. However, when a party with expert knowledge regarding a specific matter states an opinion, any party reasonably relying on the statement, although it is an opinion and not fact, may recover damages under the tort of fraudulent misrepresentation.

Negligence

LO 6-3

Negligence is behavior that creates an unreasonable risk of harm to others. Unlike intentional torts, which result from a person's willfully taking actions that are likely to cause injury, negligent torts involve the failure to exercise reasonable care to protect another's person or property.

Sometimes, however, harm occurs because an individual suffers an unfortunate accident, an incident that simply could not be avoided, even with reasonable care. For example, suppose Jonathan is driving on the highway when he suffers a stroke. Because of the stroke, he crashes into two other vehicles. He is not, however, liable for damages caused by the accident because he was not negligent. Yet if Jonathan had some type of warning that the stroke was going to occur, he might be liable for the accident.

To win a negligence case, the plaintiff must prove four elements: (1) duty, (2) breach of duty, (3) causation, and (4) damages. (See Exhibit 6-1.) A plaintiff who cannot establish all four of these elements will be denied recovery.

DUTY

The plaintiff must first establish that the defendant owes a *duty* to the plaintiff. In some particular situations, the law specifies the duty of care one individual owes to another. In most cases, however, the courts use the reasonable person standard to determine the defendant's duty of care. The **reasonable person standard** is a measurement of the way members of society expect an individual to act in a given situation. To determine the defendant's duty of care, the judge or jury must determine the degree of care and skill that a reasonable person would exercise under similar circumstances. The judge or jury then uses this standard to evaluate the actions of the individual in the case.

unfair competition
The act of competing with another not to make a profit but for the sole purpose of driving that other out of business.

fraudulent misrepresentation
The tort that occurs when a misrepresentation is made with the intent to facilitate personal gain and with the knowledge that it is false.

negligence
Behavior that creates an unreasonable risk of harm to others.

reasonable person standard
A measurement of the way members of society expect an individual to act in a given situation.

[8] Restatement (Second) of Torts, sec. 774A.
[9] Restatement (Second) of Torts, sec. 525.

Exhibit 6-1

Elements of
Negligence

To prove negligence, a plaintiff must demonstrate:
1. Duty
2. Breach of duty
3. Causation—actual and proximate
4. Damages

When courts attempt to determine whether a reasonable person would have owed a duty to others, they consider four questions:

1. How likely was it that the harm would occur?
2. How serious was the potential harm?
3. How socially beneficial was the defendant's conduct that posed the risk of harm?
4. What costs would have been necessary to reduce the risk of harm?

In many situations, it is far from clear what a reasonable person would do. For example, if a reasonable person saw an infant drowning in a shallow swimming pool, what would she do? In most situations like this one, the law holds that individuals have no duty to rescue strangers from perilous situations.

In some cases, however, the courts hold that individuals have a duty to aid strangers in certain types of peril. For example, if Sam negligently hits Janice with his car and, as a result, Janice is lying in the street, Sam has a duty to remove her from that dangerous position. Similarly, employers have a special duty to protect their employees from dangerous situations.

The courts generally hold that landowners have a duty of care to protect individuals on their property. Similarly, businesses have a duty of care to customers who enter business property. It is important, therefore, for future business managers to be knowledgeable about this duty. Businesses should warn customers about risks they may encounter on business property. Some risks, however, are obvious, and businesses need not warn customers about them. For example, a business need not inform customers that they could get a paper cut from the pages of a book.

The courts generally hold that businesses have a duty of care to protect their customers against foreseeable risks about which the owner knew or reasonably should have known. For example, in *Haywood v. Baseline Construction Company,* a woman who tripped over lumber on the front porch of the House of Blues restaurant in Los Angeles sued for negligence. The business's attempt to warn customers by marking the lumber with yellow construction tape was insufficient to avoid the determination of negligence; the woman was awarded $91,366 in damages.

The liability of businesses grew out of the traditional common law, under which the duty of owners and occupiers of real property depends primarily on the status of the injured party. The injured party may be an invitee, a person who enters another's premises as a result of an express or implied invitation of the owner for their mutual benefit, with a business invitee being one who is invited onto the property for the purpose of doing business; a licensee, a person who enters another's premises with the occupier's consent for his or her benefit alone; or a trespasser, one who is on the property without the owner's or occupier's permission, as described earlier in this chapter. Under this approach, the owner owes the greatest duty to the invitee, a duty to inspect the premises to ensure that they are reasonably safe and to warn of any hidden dangers. The owner has a duty to a licensee to warn of any hidden dangers of which he knows, but has no affirmative duty to inspect for hidden problems. The owner owes no duty to trespassers except to not intentionally harm them.

In 1968, however, the California Supreme Court rejected this rigid division[10], substituting a general duty of reasonable care in its place, under which a duty of reasonable care is owed any entrant onto the land, regardless of status. More than 25 states have now moved to this standard, with a few using this standard for both the invitees and the licensees, while maintaining the traditional approach to trespassers. The trend is toward the use of this unitary standard. But given the lack of uniformity among the states, it is important to know which approach is being used by the state in which you live and do business.

Professionals have more training than ordinary people. Thus, when professionals are serving in their professional capacity, courts generally hold that they have a higher duty of care to clients than does the ordinary person. A professional cannot defend against a negligence suit by

[10]Rowland, 443 P.2d 561 (Cal. 1968).

Negligence on the Internet

A commonly offered explanation for the increasing occurrence of violence is the increased violence portrayed in the media. Some plaintiffs try to hold owners of certain websites liable under negligence theories for violent acts committed by teenagers. For example, in *James v. Meow Media,* a 14-year-old boy took six guns to school and shot three of his classmates to death. The parents of the deceased classmates brought suit against several Internet websites and the creators and distributors of various video games. The parents argued that these defendants had a duty of ordinary care to the slain girls.

The courts have been consistent, however, in finding that it was not foreseeable that a boy who played certain video games and viewed certain websites would murder three of his classmates. In similar cases, courts have ruled that defendants (such as website owners, creators and distributors of video games, and directors and producers of movies) do not have a duty to protect a person from the criminal acts of a third party unless there is a special relationship that requires that the defendant act with that duty.

Although it appears that website owners, manufacturers, and producers will not be held liable, plaintiffs continue to bring suits against these groups of people. Can you think of an argument for why these groups of people might owe a duty of care to these plaintiffs?

claiming ignorance of generally accepted principles in her or his field of expertise. Clients who feel that they have suffered damages as a result of a professional's breach of her duty of care can bring a negligence case against her. These actions are frequently referred to as *malpractice cases.*

BREACH OF DUTY

Once the plaintiff has established that the defendant owes her a duty of care, she must prove that the defendant's conduct violated that duty. This violation is called a *breach of duty.* For example, the driver of an automobile owes the other passengers in his car a duty of care to obey traffic signs. If he fails to stop at a stop sign, he has violated his duty to follow traffic signs and has therefore breached his duty of care.

CAUSATION

Causation is the third element of a successful negligence claim, and it has two separate elements: actual cause and proximate cause. The plaintiff must prove both elements of causation to be able to recover damages.

The first element, **actual cause** (also known as *cause in fact*), is the determination that the defendant's breach of duty resulted directly in the plaintiff's injury. The courts commonly determine whether a breach of duty actually caused the plaintiff's injury by asking whether the plaintiff would have been injured if the defendant had fulfilled his or her duty. If the answer is no, then the actual cause of the plaintiff's injury was the defendant's breach. Actual cause is sometimes referred to as "but-for" causation because the plaintiff argues that the damages she suffered would not have occurred *but for* (except because of) the actions of the defendant.

Proximate cause, sometimes referred to as *legal cause,* refers to the extent to which, as a matter of policy, a defendant may be held liable for the consequences of his actions. In most states, proximate cause is determined by foreseeability. Proximate cause is said to exist only when both the plaintiff and the plaintiff's damages were reasonably foreseeable at the time the defendant breached his duty to the plaintiff. Thus, if the defendant could not reasonably foresee the damages that the plaintiff suffered as a result of his action, the plaintiff's negligence claim will not be sustained because it lacks the element of proximate causation.

You must be able to foresee that either the plaintiff himself or herself or a person in the plaintiff's position would be hurt. If you are running a red light, it is foreseeable that a person will be crossing with the light. If you hit a person crossing with the light, we say the person hit was foreseeable. If it makes more sense, we could say "both a person in the plaintiff's position" and the "plaintiff's damages," but most people refer simply to "the plaintiff and the plaintiff's damages."

For example, if a defective tire on a vehicle blows out, it is foreseeable that the driver may lose control and hit a pedestrian. It is not foreseeable, however, that the pedestrian may be a scientist carrying a briefcase full of chemicals that may explode on impact, causing a third-floor window

actual cause
The determination that the defendant's breach of duty resulted directly in the plaintiff's injury.

proximate cause
The extent to which, as a matter of policy, a defendant may be held liable for the consequences of his or her actions. In the majority of states, proximate cause requires that the plaintiff and the plaintiff's damages were foreseeable at the time of the accident. In the minority of states, proximate cause exists if the defendant's actions led to the plaintiff's harm.

Negligence in Germany

German law is concerned with the defendant's ability to foresee, understand, and avoid danger. Both mental and physical capabilities are taken into account. For example, the duty-of-care standard stipulates that "physical and mental disabilities or defects, panic, or confusion" exempt the defendant from being found negligent. Also, although the distinction is not recognized by a statute, the courts distinguish between conscious and unconscious negligence. *Conscious negligence* requires knowledge that the offense is about to occur and that it is an actual offense. *Unconscious negligence* occurs when the defendant is either unaware that the act constitutes an offense or unaware that the act is occurring at all. In such cases, the defendant is found not liable by reason of unconscious negligence.

to shatter, injuring an accountant at his desk. In most states, the accountant would not succeed if he sued the tire manufacturer for negligence. The tire failure is not considered a proximate cause of the accountant's injury because the contents of the pedestrian's briefcase were highly unusual. The pedestrian, however, would be eligible to recover damages from the tire manufacturer because hitting a pedestrian is a foreseeable consequence of tire failure. Thus, the defect in the tire is a proximate cause of the pedestrian's injury.

Palsgraf v. Long Island Railroad Company is a well-known case in which the majority opinion set forth the rule of foreseeability in determining proximate cause. The dissent, however, set forth an alternative definition of proximate cause that is accepted today in a small minority of states. Courts following the minority definition do not distinguish actual cause from proximate cause. In these states, if the defendant's action constitutes an actual cause, it is also considered the proximate cause. Therefore, in these few states, both the pedestrian-scientist and the third-floor accountant would be able to recover damages from the tire manufacturer in the previous example.

DAMAGES

Damages are the final required element of a negligence action. The plaintiff must have sustained compensable injury as a result of the defendant's actions. Because the purpose of tort law is to compensate individuals who suffer injuries as a result of another's action or inaction, a person cannot bring an action in negligence seeking only nominal damages. Rather, a person must seek **compensatory damages,** or damages intended to reimburse a plaintiff for her or his losses.

In typical negligence cases, courts rarely award **punitive damages,** or *exemplary damages,* which are imposed to punish the offender and deter others from committing similar offenses. Instead, courts usually award punitive damages in cases in which the offender has committed **gross negligence,** an action committed with extreme reckless disregard for the property or life of another person.

Plaintiff's Doctrines

The plaintiff has the burden of proving all four elements of a negligence case. Direct evidence of negligence by the defendant, however, is not always available. For example, there may have been no witnesses to the negligent conduct, and other evidence may have been destroyed. Therefore, two doctrines have been adopted by courts to aid plaintiffs in establishing negligence claims: *res ipsa loquitur* and negligence per se.

RES IPSA LOQUITUR

Res ipsa loquitur literally means "the thing speaks for itself." The plaintiff uses this doctrine to allow the judge or jury to infer that, more likely than not, the defendant's negligence was the cause of the plaintiff's harm, even though there is no direct evidence of the defendant's lack of due care. To establish *res ipsa loquitur* in most states, the plaintiff must demonstrate that:

1. The event was a kind that ordinarily does not occur in the absence of negligence.
2. Other responsible causes, including the conduct of third parties and the plaintiff, have been sufficiently eliminated.
3. The indicated negligence is within the scope of the defendant's duty to the plaintiff.

compensatory damages

Money awarded to a plaintiff as reimbursement for her or his losses; based on the amount of actual damage or harm to property, lost wages or profits, pain and suffering, medical expenses, disability, etc.

punitive damages

Compensation awarded to a plaintiff that goes beyond reimbursement for actual losses and is imposed to punish the defendant and deter such conduct in the future.

gross negligence

An action committed with extreme reckless disregard for the property or life of another person.

LO 6-4

res ipsa loquitur

A doctrine that allows the judge or jury to infer that, more likely than not, the defendant's negligence was the cause of the plaintiff's harm, even though there is no direct evidence of the defendant's lack of due care.

Proof of these three elements does not require a finding of negligence, however; it merely permits it. Once the plaintiff has demonstrated these three elements, the burden of proof shifts to the defendant, who must prove that he was not negligent to avoid liability.

One of the earliest uses of *res ipsa loquitur* was the case of *Escola v. Coca Cola.*[11] In that case, the plaintiff, a waitress, was injured when a bottle of Coca-Cola that she was removing from a case exploded in her hand. From the facts that (1) bottled soft drinks ordinarily do not spontaneously explode and (2) the bottles had been sitting in a case, undisturbed, in the restaurant for approximately 36 hours before the plaintiff simply removed the bottle from the case, the jury reasonably inferred that the defendant's negligence in the filling of the bottle resulted in its explosion. The plaintiff therefore recovered damages without direct proof of the defendant's negligence. Plaintiffs in numerous accident cases have subsequently used the doctrine where there has been no direct evidence of negligence. The defendant's best response to this doctrine is to demonstrate other possible causes of the accident. Case 6-1 illustrates the use of this doctrine.

> To read about the tax consequences of receiving a punitive damages award, as discussed in your personal accounting class, please see the **Connecting to the Core** activity at www.mhhe.com/kubasekess2e.

[11] 24 Cal. 2d 453, 150 P.2d 436 (1944).

SANDRA MORRIS v. WALMART STORES, INC.
U.S. COURT OF APPEALS FOR THE SIXTH DISTRICT
330 F.3d 854 (2003)

FACTS: *On September 27, 1998, the Plaintiff and her husband, Michael Morris, were shopping in the defendant's "Sam's Club" when the plaintiff slipped and fell on a substance thought to be water next to a small portable freezer known as a "spot box." After the fall, some of the defendant's employees approached to lend the Plaintiff assistance. At this point, the Plaintiff noticed that her clothes were soaked in what she believed to be water from the nearby freezer. When the store manager arrived at the scene, he ordered the water to be cleaned up. He pointed out to the Plaintiff and her husband that the plug in the bottom of the freezer was out. The Plaintiff testified that the store manager additionally said that the spot box was new and that he feared it might not be functioning properly. As a result of her injury, the Plaintiff was severely bruised and advised to stay in bed and off of her feet for a week.*

The Plaintiff subsequently filed suit against the defendant in Shelby County, Tennessee. The defendant removed the matter to District Court on the basis of diversity of citizenship. Following the Plaintiff's case-in-chief, the defendant moved for a judgment as to law, arguing that the Plaintiff failed to provide evidence that the defendant had notice of the water, and that the Plaintiff could not rely upon the doctrine of res ipsa loquitur. *The Plaintiff argued that she was not attempting to and could not show notice. She claimed instead that she provided evidence that the* defendant created a dangerous condition by placing the new spot box out without a plug in it, and that the doctrine of res ipsa loquitur applied. The District Court granted the defendant's motion. The Plaintiff appealed.

ISSUE: Should a plaintiff be allowed to use *res ipsa loquitur* to recover from injuries suffered by a defendant's malfunctioning product?

REASONING: A plaintiff should be allowed to use *res ipsa loquitur* to allow the jury to infer negligence when the plaintiff can demonstrate two conditions. First, the plaintiff was injured by an instrumentality that was within the defendant's exclusive control; second, the injury would not ordinarily have occurred in the absence of negligence.

To satisfy the first condition, Tennessee courts require that establishing "exclusive control" involves proving the defendant had a duty of care over the instrument that caused the harm. This standard should not be applied strictly, as then the standard would become overly restrictive. Instead, showing that the negligence was more likely than not that of the defendant and not another person will satisfy this condition. The second condition would be satisfied if the plaintiff proves that the injury more likely than not occurred because of some negligent conduct. This standard does not require that all possible alternatives be disproved.

The defendant moved for a judgment as to law, which required the trial court to look at the evidence in the most favorable light possible to the nonmoving party, the plaintiff. If a reasonable jury could find in favor of the plaintiff after evaluating all the evidence, then the trial court's granting of the motion was in error.

In this case, the plaintiff provided evidence that the manager believed that the freezer was malfunctioning and subsequently wanted to remove it from the public space, that the freezer did not have a plug properly installed, and that the substance that she slipped on was likely water emanating from the freezer. The evidence regarding where the liquid was from was corroborated by the plaintiff's written statement at the scene as well as the testimony of the employee tasked with cleaning the liquid, who said that the water was about 10 inches in diameter and "right there under the drain of the freezer." This evidence would be sufficient to allow a reasonable jury to find both elements of *res ipsa loquitur* satisfied and infer negligence on the part of the defendant.

DECISION AND REMEDY: The court reversed the trial court's granting of summary judgment in favor of the defendant and ordered a new trial at which *res ipsa loquitur* may be used.

SIGNIFICANCE OF THE CASE: This case provides an illustration of the type of conditions that can lead a jury to infer negligence.

CRITICAL THINKING

Given a negligence action like this one, what evidence could the defendant provide that might convince a jury to not find the defendant negligent?

ETHICAL DECISION MAKING

How does the court's ruling demonstrate that the law is based on the ethical concern for future customers of business firms?

NEGLIGENCE PER SE

negligence per se
A doctrine that allows a judge or jury to infer duty and breach of duty from the fact that a defendant violated a criminal statute that was designed to prevent the type of harm that the plaintiff incurred.

Negligence per se (literally, "negligence in or of itself") is another doctrine that helps plaintiffs succeed in negligence cases. Negligence per se applies to cases in which the defendant has violated a statute enacted to prevent a certain type of harm from befalling a specific group to which the plaintiff belongs. If the defendant's violation causes the plaintiff to suffer from the type of harm that the statute intends to prevent, the violation is deemed negligence per se. The plaintiff does not have to show that a reasonable person would exercise a certain duty of care toward the plaintiff. Instead, the plaintiff can offer evidence of the defendant's violation of the statute to establish proof of the negligence.

For example, if Ohio passes a statute prohibiting the sale of alcohol to minors, and a minor runs a red light and kills two pedestrians while driving under the influence of alcohol sold to him illegally, the liquor store's violation of the statute prohibiting the sale of alcohol to minors establishes negligence per se on the part of the store. The families of the pedestrians do not need to establish that a reasonable person would have a duty not to sell alcohol to a minor. The Case Nugget provides another illustration of negligence per se.

LO 6-5 Defenses to Negligence

The courts' doctrines of *res ipsa loquitur* and negligence per se help the plaintiff in a negligence case, but the courts permit certain defenses that relieve the defendant from liability even when the plaintiff has proved all four elements of negligence. Defendants can successfully rebut negligence claims with contributory negligence, comparative negligence, assumption of the risk, and other special negligence defenses.

CASE Nugget

A Clear Illustration of Negligence per Se

O'Guin v. Bingham County
Superior Court of Idaho

122 P.3d 308 (Sup. Ct. Id. 2005)

Shaun and Alex O'Guin cut across a field on their way home from school and entered the back of a landfill that was not fenced off, despite a law that required it to be fenced. A portion of a wall of the landfill collapsed, killing the boys. The boys' parents sued the county that operated the landfill, alleging that failure to have the landfill properly fenced constituted negligence per se.

The court agreed, explaining that the following four elements of negligence per se had been met: (1) The statute or regulation clearly defines the required standard of conduct, (2) the statute or regulation must have been intended to prevent the type of harm the defendant's act or omission caused, (3) the plaintiff must be a member of the class of persons the statute or regulation was designed to protect, and (4) the violation must have been the proximate cause of death.

CONTRIBUTORY NEGLIGENCE

Contributory negligence, a defense once available in all states but replaced today in some states by the defense of comparative negligence (discussed in the next section), applies in cases in which both the defendant and the plaintiff were negligent. The defendant must prove that (1) the plaintiff's conduct fell below the standard of care needed to prevent unreasonable risk of harm and (2) the plaintiff's failure was a contributing cause of the plaintiff's injury. How can defendants use contributory negligence in a case? Some defense lawyers argue that if a plaintiff involved in a car accident failed to wear her seat belt, that failure constitutes contributory negligence because her action contributed to her injuries.

If the defendant successfully proves contributory negligence, no matter how slight the plaintiff's negligence, the plaintiff will be denied any recovery of damages. Because this defense seems unfair, many states have adopted the **last-clear-chance doctrine.** This doctrine allows the plaintiff to recover damages despite proof of contributory negligence as long as the defendant had a final clear opportunity to avoid the action that injured the plaintiff.

For example, suppose that Samantha and Nicole, in their cars, are facing each other while stopped at a red light. The light turns green, and Nicole starts to turn left at the intersection. Samantha sees Nicole start to turn, but she still continues to travel straight through the intersection and crashes into Nicole's car. Although Samantha had the right-of-way at the intersection, she could have avoided hitting Nicole's car by braking or swerving. Thus, according to the last-clear-chance doctrine, Nicole could recover damages.

COMPARATIVE NEGLIGENCE

Most states have replaced contributory negligence with comparative negligence, because the adoption of the last-clear-chance doctrine still left many situations in which an extremely careless defendant can cause a great deal of harm to a plaintiff who is barred from recovery due to minimal contributory negligence. There are two forms of comparative negligence: pure and modified. According to a **pure comparative negligence** defense, the court determines the percentage of fault of the defendant. The defendant is then liable for that percentage of the plaintiff's damages.

contributory negligence
A defense to negligence whereby the defendant can escape all liability by proving that the plaintiff failed to act in a way that would protect him or her from an unreasonable risk of harm and that the plaintiff's negligent behavior contributed in some way to the plaintiff's accident.

last-clear-chance doctrine
A doctrine used by the plaintiff when the defendant establishes contributory negligence. If the plaintiff can establish that the defendant had the last opportunity to avoid the accident, the plaintiff may still recover, despite being contributorily negligent.

pure comparative negligence
A defense accepted in some states whereby the defendant is not liable for the percentage of harm that he or she can prove is due to the plaintiff's own negligence.

modified comparative negligence

A defense accepted in some states whereby the defendant is not liable for the percentage of harm that he or she can prove is due to the plaintiff's own negligence if the plaintiff's negligence is responsible for less than 50 percent of the harm; if the defendant establishes that the plaintiff's negligence caused more than 50 percent of the harm, the defendant has no liability.

Courts calculate damages according to **modified comparative negligence** in the same manner, except that the defendant must be more than 50 percent at fault before the plaintiff can recover.

Twenty-eight states have adopted modified comparative negligence, thirteen have adopted pure comparative negligence, and nine have adopted contributory negligence. Every state has adopted one of these three defenses. Thus, the parties to a negligence suit cannot choose among them.

ASSUMPTION OF THE RISK

assumption of the risk

A defense whereby the defendant must prove that the plaintiff voluntarily assumed the risk the defendant caused.

Another defense available to defendants facing negligence claims is called **assumption of the risk.** To use this defense successfully, a defendant must prove that the plaintiff voluntarily and unreasonably encountered the risk of the actual harm the defendant caused. In other words, the plaintiff willingly assumed as a risk the harm she suffered. There are two types of this defense. *Express assumption of the risk* occurs when the plaintiff expressly agrees (usually in a written contract) to assume the risk posed by the defendant's behavior. In contrast, *implied assumption of the risk* means that the plaintiff implicitly assumed a known risk.

The most difficult part of establishing this defense is showing that the plaintiff assumed the risk of the *actual* harm she suffered. A 1998 case against the Family Fitness Center illustrates an unsuccessful attempt to use assumption of the risk as a defense against a negligence claim.[12] In that case, the plaintiff was injured when a sauna bench on which he was lying collapsed beneath him at the defendant's facility. The trial court granted summary judgment in favor of the defendant on the basis of assumption of the risk. The plaintiff had signed a contract that included the following provision: "Buyer is aware that participation in a sport or physical exercise may result in accidents or injury, and Buyer assumes the risk connected with the participation in a sport or exercise and represents that Member is in good health and suffers from no physical impairment which would limit their use of FFC's facilities." The appellate court overturned the trial court's decision because the type of injury the plaintiff suffered was not the type of risk he had assumed. The court held that anyone signing a membership agreement could be deemed to have waived any hazard known to relate to the use of the health club facilities, such as the risk of a sprained ankle due to improper exercise or overexertion, a broken toe from a dropped weight, injuries due to malfunctioning exercise or sports equipment, or injuries from slipping in the locker room shower. No patron, however, could be charged with realistically appreciating the risk of injury from simply reclining on a sauna bench. Because the collapse of a sauna bench, when properly used, is not a "known risk," the court concluded that the plaintiff did not assume the risk of this incident as a matter of law.

SPECIAL DEFENSES TO NEGLIGENCE

Many states have additional ways to defend against a claim of negligence. For example, laws in some states hold that people in peril who receive voluntary aid from others cannot hold those offering aid liable for negligence. These laws, commonly called **Good Samaritan statutes,** attempt to encourage selfless and courageous behavior by removing the threat of liability.

Good Samaritan statute

A statute that exempts from liability a person, such as a physician passerby, who voluntarily renders aid to an injured person but negligently, but not unreasonably negligently, causes injury while rendering the aid.

The defendant in a negligence suit can also avoid liability by establishing a superseding cause. A *superseding cause* is an unforeseeable event that interrupts the causal chain between the defendant's breach of duty and the damages the plaintiff suffered. For example, suppose Jennifer is improperly storing ammonia in her garage when a meteor strikes her garage, spilling the ammonia into a stream nearby. Will, living downstream, drinks water from the stream and becomes dangerously ill. Because the meteor was unforeseeable, Jennifer is not liable for Will's injuries, even though she breached her duty of care to Will. Superseding causes allow the defendant to avoid liability because they are evidence that the defendant's breach of duty was not the proximate cause of the plaintiff's injuries. In other words, superseding causes disprove the causation element necessary to sustain a negligence claim.

[12] *Leon v. Family Fitness Center, Inc.,* 61 Cal. App. 4th 1227 (1998).

Strict Liability

LO 6-6

Strict liability is liability without fault. The law holds an individual liable without fault when the activity in which she engages satisfies three conditions: (1) It involves a risk of serious harm to people or property; (2) it is so inherently dangerous that it cannot ever be safely undertaken; and (3) it is not usually performed in the immediate community. Instead of banning such activities, the law allows people to engage in these activities but holds them liable for all resulting harm.

Inherently dangerous activities include dynamite blasting in a populated area and keeping animals that have not been domesticated. If an animal has shown a "vicious propensity," strict liability applies and the owner of the animal is responsible for any injuries suffered in an attack by the animal. If an individual keeps an animal that has shown vicious propensity, he has a duty to warn and protect individuals who come into contact with the animal. Today, the theory of strict liability is used most commonly in cases where the plaintiff is claiming to have been injured by a product that was unreasonably dangerous.

strict liability
Liability in which responsibility for damages is imposed regardless of the existence of negligence. Also called *liability without fault*.

Damages Available in Tort Cases

LO 6-7

There are three types of damages available in tort cases: compensatory, nominal, and punitive (see Exhibit 6-2). You will see this system of classifying damages again when we talk about damages in other contexts, such as in cases involving the breach of a contract.

COMPENSATORY DAMAGES

As the primary objective of tort law is to compensate victims, the primary type of damages are *compensatory damages,* damages designed to compensate the victim for all the harm caused by the person who committed the tort, often referred to as the **tortfeasor.** While we seem to hear a lot about "runaway jury" awards, there does not seem to be evidence of a trend toward increasingly huge jury awards. The overall median jury award for personal injury cases from 1998 to 2004 was $35,298. And that amount actually fell from $37,086 in 2003 to $35,000 in 2004.[13] In 2010, the median jury verdict award in personal injury cases was $40,000, which is not a huge jump over a six-year time span.[14]

Compensatory damages are typically awarded for pain and suffering, costs of repairing damaged property, medical expenses, and lost wages. For example, suppose Rubin, in the Case Opener, could demonstrate that he and his company lost money because of the *U.S. News & World Report* article. He might be able to recover the losses from *U.S. News.* Surprisingly, attorney fees are *not* recoverable as compensatory damages, despite the fact that most plaintiffs could not bring an action against the tortfeasor without hiring an attorney. Because the plaintiffs in personal injury cases must usually pay their attorneys anywhere from one-third to one-half

tortfeasor
A person who commits an intentional or through-negligence tort that causes a harm or loss for which a civil remedy may be sought.

TYPE	PURPOSE	AMOUNT
Compensatory	To make the plaintiff whole again.	An amount equivalent to all losses caused by the tort, including compensation for pain and suffering, but not attorney fees.
Nominal	To recognize that the defendant committed a tort against the plaintiff.	A trivial amount, typically $1 to $5.
Punitive	To punish the defendant and deter future wrongdoers.	An amount based on two factors: the severity of the wrongful conduct and the wealth of the defendant.

Exhibit 6-2

Types of Tort Damages

[13] JVR news release, www.juryverdictresearch.com/Press_Room/Press_releases/Verdict_study/verdict_study41.html (accessed October 10, 2006).
[14] Indiana Jury Verdicts, Accident and Injury Lawyer Blog, www.accidentinjurylawyerblog.com/2011/08/indiana_jury_verdicts.html, August 8, 2011.

of their recovery, some argue that compensatory damages fail to meet the intended goal of properly compensating victims. Others point out that one of the ways plaintiffs can, in essence, recover their attorney fees is by increasing their pain and suffering damages enough to cover these expenses.

NOMINAL DAMAGES

nominal damages
Monetary damages awarded to a plaintiff in a very small amount, typically $1 to $5, to signify that the plaintiff has been wronged by the defendant even though the plaintiff suffered no compensable harm.

Nominal damages are a small amount of money given to recognize that a defendant did indeed commit a tort in a case where there were no compensable damages suffered by the plaintiff. A plaintiff may receive nominal damages by simply failing to prove actual damages.

PUNITIVE DAMAGES

Punitive damages are awarded to punish the defendant. They are given only when the defendant's conduct is extremely outrageous. The purposes of punitive damages are both to punish the defendant and to deter him and others who are similarly situated from engaging in that kind of activity again. In awarding punitive damages, juries usually consider the egregiousness or willfulness of the tort and the wealth of the defendant. Obviously, the more wrongful the nature of the defendant's act, the greater the desire to send a message that such behavior will not be tolerated; and the greater the wealth of the defendant, the higher the damages must be to actually punish the defendant.

While the threat of large punitive damages is seen by many groups, including consumer advocates, as a good method for encouraging manufacturers to produce the safest possible products, others disagree. They believe that no threat beyond compensatory damages is required; and they argue that the main effect of punitive damages is to discourage innovation, because manufacturers will be afraid of the risk of producing a defective product, which could cost them millions in punitive damages.

Since the late 1970s, insurance companies and "tort reform" groups have been trying to limit the amount of punitive damages that can be assessed, using both the legislative process and the courts. The 1994 case of *Honda Motor Company v. Oberg*[15] provided tort reformers with their first judicial victory. In this case, the U.S. Supreme Court finally struck down a punitive-damage award as being a violation of due process. *Oberg,* however, was a limited victory because of two unique aspects of the case. First, the punitive damages were over 500 times the amount of the compensatory damages, which is extraordinarily rare. Second, the state law under which the damages were awarded was the only state law in the country that had no provision for judicial review of the amount of punitive-damage awards, and it was the denial of this safeguard that violated the due process clause. Because of its unusual facts, *Oberg* did not provide much guidance as to when punitive damages were so excessive as to violate due process.

A few years later, however, in *BMW v. Gore,*[16] the Supreme Court set forth a test that a number of commentators thought would substantially curb punitive-damage awards. The Court said three factors should be considered in determining whether an award was grossly excessive: "the degree of reprehensibility of the nondisclosure; the disparity between the harm or potential harm suffered by [the plaintiff] and his punitive damages award; and the difference between this remedy and the civil penalties authorized or imposed in comparable cases." However, a 1999 study found that the year after *BMW v. Gore,* punitive-damage awards across the country were not reduced any more frequently than they had been the year before the decision.[17]

Since *BMW v. Gore,* the Supreme Court has continued to encourage the courts to carefully scrutinize punitive-damage awards. In the 2001 case of *Cooper Industries, Inc. v. Leatherman Tool Group, Inc.,*[18] the high court ruled that appellate courts must review the trial court's decision on the constitutionality of an award *de novo,* meaning they should no longer give deference to the trial court's determination that the jury award was not unconstitutionally excessive and uphold it unless there was a clear abuse of discretion on the part of the trial court judge.

[15] 114 S. Ct. 2331 (1994).
[16] *BMW of North America v. Ira Gore, Jr.,* 116 S. Ct. 1589 (1995).
[17] James Dam, "Large Punitives Mostly Upheld, but $5B Award Overturned," *Lawyer's Weekly,* November 12, 2001, p. A1.
[18] 532 U.S. 424 (2001).

Punitive Damages in Canada and Japan

Those who believe the U.S. tort system is in need of reform with respect to its treatment of punitive damages may look to their Canadian neighbors with envy. Punitive-damage awards in Canada are both rare and small.

A study in 1990 reported on punitive-damage awards in Ontario. The researchers found that the highest award was $50,000. The majority of punitive-damage awards were less than $25,000; the median award was approximately 20 percent of the compensatory-damage award in the particular case.

Following English common law, Canadian courts have traditionally restricted punitive damages to two situations: cases involving oppressive, arbitrary, or unconstitutional actions by government servants and cases in which the defendant's conduct was calculated to have made a profit in excess of compensatory damages. In 1989, the Canadian Supreme Court recognized that punitive damages could also be awarded for conduct deserving punishment because of its "harsh, vindictive, reprehensible, and malicious manner."

Two reasons seem to explain the differences in Canadian and American treatment of punitive damages. First, Canadians see something undignified about the flamboyant punitive-damage awards in the United States. Second, civil juries are much less common in Canada, and, in general, judges tend to be much more conservative than juries in making punitive-damage awards.

Another country that would be even more heroic to those opposed to punitive damages is Japan. Several times, the Japanese Supreme Court ruled that punitive damages violated Japan's public policy. Recently, following the lead of the courts, the Japanese legislature forbade the acceptance of punitive damages, even those awarded by foreign courts.

In the 2003 case *State Farm v. Campbell,*[19] the Supreme Court once again addressed the issue of how to properly determine punitive damages. The Campbells had won a jury verdict for $1 million in compensatory damages and $145 million in punitive damages after State Farm failed to settle what was clearly a valid claim. The high court ruled that punitive-damage awards should bear some relationship to the actual harm caused and should not focus on the wealth of the defendants. While refusing to draw a firm line as to what ratio of compensatories to punitives was acceptable, the Court did say that "in practice, few awards exceeding a single-digit ratio between punitive and compensatory damages, to a significant degree, will satisfy due process."[20] The Court also stated that damages should not focus on deterrence based on wealth or on actions unrelated to the case at hand. Case 6-2 demonstrates how the courts are applying these guidelines today.

[19] 123 S. Ct. 1513 (2003).
[20] Ibid., p. 1524.

CASE 6-2

CLARK v. CHRYSLER CORPORATION
U.S. COURT OF APPEALS FOR THE SIXTH CIRCUIT
2006 U.S. App. LEXIS 2435

FACTS: *Charles Clark was fatally injured in an automobile accident when he pulled into an intersection in front of an oncoming vehicle and collided with it. He was not wearing a seat belt and was consequently ejected from his vehicle. His wife sued Chrysler, claiming that its pickup truck was defectively and negligently designed.*

After a three-day trial, the jury rendered a unanimous verdict in favor of Mrs. Clark on claims of strict liability, negligence, and failure to warn. The jury found Chrysler and Mr. Clark each 50 percent at fault, returning a verdict of $471,258.26 in compensatory damages and $3 million in punitive damages. The court entered a judgment against Chrysler for $3,235,629.13, reflecting 50 percent of the compensatory damages plus the $3 million punitive damages award. After a series of appeals, the last being an appeal of the trial court's motion to deny the defendant's

motion to send the case back to the district court for a reduction of damages, the case finally landed at the circuit court of appeals on the issue of whether the jury verdict was constitutionally excessive.

ISSUE: Should the plaintiff's $3 million punitive-damage award be struck down as constitutionally excessive when the amount of the compensatory damages is $471,258.26?

REASONING: Application of the *Gore* guideposts to this case renders the punitive-damage award excessive. According to *Gore,* five criteria are used to determine the reprehensibility of the defendant's conduct: (1) The harm caused was physical as opposed to economic; (2) the tortious conduct evinced an indifference to or a reckless disregard for the health or safety of others; (3) the target of the conduct had financial vulnerability; (4) the conduct involved repeated actions or was an isolated incident; and (5) the harm was the result of intentional malice, trickery, or deceit or mere accident. In this case, the physical harm suffered by Mr. Clark weighed strongly in favor of finding Chrysler's conduct reprehensible, but considering the four other factors leads to the conclusion that the factors as a whole show that Chrysler's conduct was not sufficiently reprehensible to warrant a $3 million punishment.

The second guidepost is the disparity between the actual or potential harm inflicted on the plaintiff and the punitive-damage award. Because the compensatory-damage award here is relatively small, a 1:1 ratio is inappropriate; but because of the lack of reprehensibility, a ratio higher than 2:1 would be unwarranted.

The third guidepost is the difference between the punitive-damage award and the civil or criminal penalties that could be imposed for comparable misconduct. Given *State Farm*'s focus on civil penalties, a $3 million punitive-damage award is excessive in light of comparable civil penalties.

DECISION AND REMEDY: The damage award was excessive. Chrysler's motion was reversed and remanded, with instructions to enter a punitive-damage award in the amount of $471,258.26.

SIGNIFICANCE OF THE CASE: This case gives the courts a little more guidance as to when punitive damages may be considered excessive.

CRITICAL THINKING

Which of the criteria used by the judge seems ambiguous? How might that ambiguity have affected the outcome of the case?

ETHICAL DECISION MAKING

What values are guiding the judge's decision that the punitive-damage award was excessive? Do you think that the values promoted by the decision are appropriate for the situation? Why or why not?

SUMMARY

Introduction to Tort Law	*Tort:* A civil wrong giving the injured party the right to bring a lawsuit against the wrongdoer to recover compensation for the injuries.
Classification of Torts	Torts are classified as intentional, negligent, and strict liability.
Intentional Torts	*Torts against persons* include assault, battery, and defamation.
	Torts against property include trespass to realty, private nuisance, trespass to personal property, and conversion.
	Torts against economic interest include disparagement, intentional interference with contract, unfair competition, misappropriation, and fraudulent misrepresentation.

Negligence	The plaintiff must prove four elements: duty, breach of duty, causation (actual and proximate), and damages.
Plaintiff's Doctrines	Doctrines used to establish negligence:

- *Res ipsa loquitur*
- Negligence per se

Defenses to Negligence	• Contributory negligence

- Modified comparative negligence
- Pure comparative negligence
- Assumption of the risk

Strict Liability	Persons who engage in activities that are so inherently dangerous that no amount of due care can make them safe are strictly liable, regardless of the degree of care they used when undertaking the activity.
Damages Available in Tort Cases	*Compensatory damages,* to make the plaintiff whole again.

Punitive damages, to punish the defendant and deter future wrongdoers.

Nominal damages, to recognize that the defendant committed a tort against the plaintiff.

Point/Counterpoint

Should Punitive Damages Be More Strictly Limited?

YES	NO
Excessive punitive damages are fundamentally unfair.	**The BMW standard for excessive punitive damages strikes a fair balance, protecting the interests of both consumers and firms.**

YES

Excessive punitive damages are fundamentally unfair.

Punitive damages are not a normal part of the tort system. Tort law is supposed to be a way to compensate victims. Punitive damages are almost quasi-criminal in nature; they are designed to punish the defendant. And they reward a plaintiff with, in some cases, riches far beyond what any reasonable person would see as compensation. Tort cases, with the possibility of huge punitive-damage awards, have turned into nothing but litigation lotteries, which have nothing to do with the purposes of our tort system.

The possibility of a huge punitive-damage award causes people to bring all sorts of loony lawsuits in hopes of striking it rich. If punitive damages were more reasonable, you would not see people, for example, suing the phone company for publishing false information about a physician that led to a botched liposuction or suing NBC for millions because a *Fear Factor* episode that involved eating rats made a viewer "dizzy and lightheaded and caused him to vomit and run into a doorway."

NO

The BMW standard for excessive punitive damages strikes a fair balance, protecting the interests of both consumers and firms.

In the 20 years prior to the BMW case, courts handed down a number of huge punitive-damage awards, some even exceeding $100 million. However, in the years since the BMW case, we have seen that the court's three-pronged test has resulted in punitive-damage awards being much lower, generally staying below a 9-to-1 ratio of punitive to compensatory damages. They now appear to be much more reasonable and to fulfill their necessary function. If we examine the top 10 jury verdicts of 2005, the awards are significantly lower than those of 2004 and previous years. There is no longer any need to further limit punitive damages, as they are now reasonably related to the harm the defendant has caused and they are still large enough to deter behavior.

Punitive damages, in their current manifestation, fulfill two important functions. First, they represent an important way for a significantly harmed plaintiff to recover costs and attorney fees. Without the possibility of large punitive-damage awards, the plaintiff

Besides, unfair punitive-damage awards can ruin a defendant's good name and, in some cases, run target companies out of business. We must bring fairness back to our tort system by limiting punitive damages. Sure, damage awards have fallen since the BMW and State Farm cases, but they were so exorbitant that they could hardly have gone any higher! Besides, the fact that they have fallen does not mean that they have fallen to reasonable levels.

We need more stringent standards for punitive damages to bring predictability, efficiency, and fairness to our civil justice system. We must all work together for these necessary changes.

may not actually be compensated for his or her losses because so much of the recovery goes to the attorneys and costs of litigation.

Second, punitive damages perform a necessary deterrence function. If corporations no longer have to fear punitive-damage awards that will hurt them, they will lose some of their motivation to produce safe products and behave as responsible citizens.

With the *BMW* rule, as clarified by *State Farm,* we now have a system in which punitive damages can serve their intended purpose without posing an unreasonable risk to potential defendants.

Questions & Problems

1. Distinguish the three types of damages available in tort cases.

2. Explain why some people see punitive damages as a necessary aspect of our tort system, while others want to restrict their availability.

3. List five intentional torts, and explain the elements needed to prove each.

4. List and define the elements that are necessary to prove a case of negligence.

5. Explain the differences between contributory and comparative negligence.

6. Explain the relationship between negligence per se and *res ipsa loquitur.*

7. Kerns, a home owner, sued defendant contractor Sealy for negligence, breach of contract, wantonness, and *res ipsa loquitur* in connection with a fire that occurred during the contractor's application of foam-installation in the plaintiff's attic. The contractor knew that applying the foam at a thickness over 2 inches created a risk of fire, and he applied the foam at a thickness exceeding 4 inches. He then left the scene for lunch. When he returned, Sealy discovered a haze indicative of fire and attempted to remove the foam. At trial, the defendant made a motion of summary judgment to dismiss all charges. Which charges, if any, do you think survived summary judgment in district court? [*Kerns et al. v. Sealy et al.,* 496 F. Supp. 2d 1306 (2007).]

8. David Burton smoked Camel cigarettes for 43 years, and, in 1993, he developed serious circulatory problems in his legs. His doctor informed him that smoking was causing his circulatory problems. Two other doctors confirmed his doctor's diagnosis and recommended vascular bypass surgery, which

Burton underwent unsuccessfully. After the operation, Burton had both of his legs amputated below the knee. Burton brought suit against the R.J. Reynolds Tobacco Company, alleging that the company negligently failed to warn him of the health hazards caused by smoking. R.J. Reynolds argued that it did not have a duty to warn Burton of the hazards that smoking posed to his health. What do you think? Should R.J. Reynolds be found negligent? Why? [*Burton v. R.J. Reynolds Tobacco Co.,* 397 F.3d 906 (2005).]

9. Vernon Hendrickson, an inmate at an Indiana correctional facility, sued correctional officer Scott Cooper for violation of the Eighth Amendment protections against cruel and unusual punishment after Cooper threw Hendrickson against a wall, slammed him onto the concrete floor of his housing unit, and then pressed his knees against Hendrickson's back while another officer cuffed Hendrickson. The jury found Cooper liable for excessive force and awarded Hendrickson $75,000 in compensatory damages and an additional $125,000 in punitive damages. Cooper appealed the decision, arguing that the jury did not have enough evidence to make its finding of excessive force and that the damage awards were excessive. Using the analysis discussed in this chapter, do you think that the punitive damages awarded to Hendrickson were excessive? What other facts might help inform your decision? [*Hendrickson v. Cooper,* 589 F.3d 887 (2009).]

10. Jaymie Quigley was a tenant of David Winter, renting a home with her husband and four children. In 2002, she contacted Winter about the possibility of moving to a larger home. While she was looking at Winter's other houses, Winter moved his hand down Quigley's arm and asked "Well, how do you like it?" In 2004,

Quigley learned that Winter had been in her home without prior notice when she was not home. Winter claimed he was there to replace a screen that was neither broken nor actually replaced. Other events illustrated similar behavior. Quigley successfully sued Winter under a theory of sexual harassment under the Fair Housing Act. The jury awarded Quigley with $13,685 in compensatory damages and $250,000 in punitive damages. The court reduced the punitive damages to $20,527.50 and awarded attorney fees of $20,000. Quigley appealed the decision to restore the original award. Was her punitive-damage award restored? Why or why not? [*Quigley v. Winter,* 598 F.3d 938 (2007).]

11. Erica Aponte, age seven, attended Thanksgiving dinner at the home of Michael and Deborah Castor, her aunt and uncle. Following dinner, Erica, accompanied by her cousin, went outside and crawled under/ through an electric wire fence that enclosed Castor's horse paddock area. Erica was subsequently kicked in the face by Castor's horse, sustaining injury. Teresa Aponte, Erica's mother, filed suit against Castor, seeking damages for Erica's injuries. Castor filed a motion for summary judgment, arguing that because Erica did not have permission to leave the house or enter the paddock area, and did so without her parents' or Castor's knowledge, Erica was a trespasser and, therefore, he should not be held liable for her injuries. Aponte responded that Erica was a social guest, not a trespasser; Castor should have warned Aponte regarding the dangerous nature of the horse; and genuine issues of material fact existed that would preclude the granting of summary judgment. The trial court granted summary judgment. Aponte appealed. How did the court rule on appeal? Why? [*Aponte v. Castor,* 155 Ohio App. 3d 553 (2003).]

12. The Bank of New York (BONY) sued the defendant insurance company, Fremont General Corporation, for intentional interference with contract and conversion. BONY sought to recover damages from the defendant's withdrawal of $14 million from BONY, which BONY alleged interfered with the New York Insurance Company's ability to pay claims of its policyholders. BONY had a valid contract with Fremont Indemnity, a compensation fund that was managed by the defendant. The defendant was aware of the contract between Fremont Indemnity and BONY. By transferring $14 million to another bank, the defendant breached the custodian agreement. The district court granted Fremont General's motion for summary judgment on both claims. BONY appealed the decision, arguing that it had met the evidentiary standards required to prove both claims. Do you agree with the district court? What additional information might alter your decision? [*Bank of New York v. Fremont General Corporation,* 523 F.3d 902 (2008).]

Looking for more review material?

The Online Learning Center at **www.mhhe.com/kubasekess2e** contains this chapter's "Assignment on the Internet" and also a list of URLs for more information, entitled "On the Internet." Find both of them in the Student Center portion of the OLC, along with quizzes and other helpful materials.

CHAPTER

7 Real, Personal, and Intellectual Property

Economic Redevelopment in Poletown

General Motors wanted to expand its facility but was unable to acquire the land it needed, so it approached the Detroit Economic Development Corporation (DEDC) with a request that the DEDC use its power of eminent domain to acquire a large parcel of land on which members of the plaintiff organization, Poletown Neighborhood Council, resided and had small businesses. Once the DEDC had acquired the land, it would be conveyed to General Motors for its plant expansion. The justification for the use of eminent domain in the case would be that the acquisition and transfer of the property would create jobs for the economically depressed area.

The plaintiffs, who did not want their community destroyed, sued the city and the development council on the grounds that they were attempting to abuse their power of eminent domain to take private property for a private use.

1. Can business managers ask the city to buy real property for them when the owners do not wish to sell it?
2. What would determine whether the government can legally take the property for a corporation?

LEARNING OBJECTIVES

After reading this chapter, you will be able to answer the following questions:

LO 7-1 How are the topics of real, personal, and intellectual property related?

LO 7-2 How does real property law balance private and public rights?

LO 7-3 What are the interests in real property that one can hold?

LO 7-4 What are the types of personal property?

LO 7-5 How do you transfer personal property?

LO 7-6 How does intellectual property law balance private and public rights?

LO 7-7 What are the similarities and differences among the methods for protecting various types of intellectual property?

Most Americans cherish the right to own property. For most Americans, this means the right to own real property, such as a house. Increasingly, Americans also cherish the right to own "intellectual property," the fruits of the mind, such as a manuscript for a novel. In this chapter we examine the nature of both real and intellectual property. The chapter starts by exploring how the three areas of law are related. Then, for each of these types of property, the chapter considers what interests individuals can hold and how the laws governing these types of property balance private and public rights. The Case Opener considers a real property issue. By the end of the chapter, you will see that disputes like the General Motors–Poletown dispute can arise not only when the property in question is land but also when it is personal or intellectual property.

The Nature of Real, Personal, and Intellectual Property

LO 7-1

Real property, commonly referred to as *realty,* is land and everything permanently attached to it. The type of ownership interest a person has in a piece of property determines his or her rights to the property. **Personal property** consists of tangible, movable objects. **Intellectual property** consists of the fruits of one's mind. The laws of intellectual property protect property that is primarily the result of mental creativity rather than physical effort. When we are thinking about property rights of any kind, it is important to remember that society, through laws, decides what rights individuals and communities have with regard to property.

real property
Land and everything permanently attached to it.

One metaphor often used with regard to property is that of a bundle of sticks. Each stick represents a distinct right an individual can have with regard to property. The rights to possess property, use it, give it away, or take it away are all sticks. With regard to all types of property, one of the most important rights is the right to exclude others. For example, with regard to real property, an individual can put a fence around the land and ask others to stay off the land. With personal property, you may simply keep it in a place where no one else has access to it. For intellectual property, an individual can accomplish the same thing with a trademark or patent—the holder can put a virtual fence around the idea trademarked or patented and ask others to refrain from using the property.

intellectual property
Intangible property that is the product of one's mind and not one's hands.

With regard to real property, some other important sticks are the rights to sell, lease, or mortgage land and the right to allow someone limited access. The public also has important sticks, such as the right to take land, regulate it, and/or tax it. In the next section, the various types of interests a person may have in real property are described in detail. These interests may be conveyed or transferred under legal guidelines for property rights. Most transfers of property are voluntary. However, for the benefit of the public, and to protect public health, safety, and welfare, the government may require involuntary transfers of property.

Real Property

LO 7-2

There are a number of different types of interests in land, ranging from temporary to permanent to future. The duration of one's ownership interest and the power one has over using the land depend on the type of *estate* one is said to hold. The section below on interests in real property describes the various estates in detail. First, though, this chapter explores the landowner's rights that pertain to areas beyond the surface of the land itself.

EXTENT OF OWNERSHIP

When a person owns land, she or he owns more than just the surface. The airspace above the land, extending to the atmosphere, is also part of the legal concept of real property. Rights to airspace generally do not generate much controversy, but occasionally disputes arise that involve aircraft flying "too low" over individuals' property. Alternatively, a tree's branches may hang over into the airspace of the property next door, and the owner of that airspace may want to cut the overhanging branches.

In dense, commercial urban areas, airspace may actually be an asset. Owners of two commercial buildings might want to build an overhead walkway joining their buildings across a parking lot that you own. They will have to pay you handsomely for the right to build in your airspace.

In addition to having airspace rights, the owner of real property also has *water rights,* the legal ability to use water flowing across or underneath the property. However, these rights are somewhat restricted; one cannot deprive the landowners downstream from the use of the water by diverting the water elsewhere.

Finally, ownership of real property extends to *mineral rights;* these rights involve the land below the surface. The landowner has the legal ability to dig or mine the materials from the earth, and he may sell or give these rights to another person. Ownership of these *subsurface rights* includes the right to enter onto the property to remove the underground materials.

All these additional rights are illustrated in Figure 7-1.

LO 7-3

INTERESTS IN REAL PROPERTY

Various interests in land are discussed below and summarized in Exhibit 7-1.

fee simple absolute
An ownership interest in which the holder has exclusive rights to ownership and possession of the land; the most comprehensive type of estate.

conditional estate
An ownership interest in which the holder has the same interest as that in a fee simple absolute except that this interest is subject to a condition.

Fee Simple Absolute With regard to estates in land, a **fee simple absolute** is the most complete estate a person may have. Exclusive rights to ownership and possession of the land belong to the person who has a fee simple absolute. It is this type of estate to which most people refer when they speak of "buying" a house or piece of land. A fee-simple-absolute interest is passed to the owner's heirs when the owner of such an estate dies.

Conditional Estate The owner of a **conditional estate** possesses the same interest as the owner of a fee simple absolute except that this interest is subject to a condition: Should a certain required event fail to occur, or should a specific prohibited event occur, the interest will be terminated. For example, Todd may be given property rights to a Victorian house on the condition that he is to preserve it in its original form. If he violates this condition by turning the house into a piano showroom or a beer hall, the house either will revert to the original owner or will be

Figure 7-1

Extent of Rights

Exhibit 7-1

Possessory Estates
in Land

INTEREST	EXTENT OF RIGHTS
Leasehold estate	Right to possess property for an agreed-on period of time.
Life estate	Right to possess property until death, subject to restriction against waste.
Conditional estate	Right to possess property until death, subject to restriction against waste.
Fee simple absolute	Right to possess property for life and pass it to heirs on death; the most encompassing interest.

transferred in accordance with the terms of the deed (the *deed* is the instrument used to convey real property).

Life Estate A **life estate** is granted for the lifetime of an individual; the right to possess the property terminates at the individual's death. On the death of the holder of the life estate, the property will go to another party as designated by the original grantor. Thus, this future owner has an interest in seeing that the life tenant does not *waste* the property; in other words, the life holder is not allowed to neglect or abuse the property in such a way that the property value is diminished. Should the life tenant fail to make necessary repairs, or should he or she use the property in ways damaging to its future value, the future holder could bring legal action against the holder of the life estate to recover damages for waste.

life estate

An ownership interest in which the holder has the right to possess the property until her or his death.

Future Interest A **future interest** is a person's present right to property ownership and possession in the future. Such an interest usually exists in conjunction with a life estate or a conditional estate. For example, Joe owns a life estate in Oak Hills Apartments, and on his death the property will pass to Sarah with fee-simple-absolute rights. Sarah, in this case, holds a future interest in Oak Hills Apartments, and if Joe allows the buildings to deteriorate from neglect, Sarah may sue Joe to enjoin him from engaging in waste of the property.

future interest

A person's present right to property ownership and possession in the future.

Leasehold Estate The interest of a **leasehold** differs from the interests previously described in that the holder of such an estate has a possessory interest but not an ownership interest. This interest is transferred by a contract known as a *lease.* Both the owner of the property (the lessor, or landlord) and the tenant (the lessee) sign the lease. The contract generally specifies the property to be leased, the amount of the rent payments and when they are due, the duration of the leasehold, and any special rights or duties of either party. A leasehold gives the lessee, or tenant, exclusive rights to the use and possession of the land, including the right to exclude the property owner under most circumstances, for the term specified by the lease.

leasehold

A possessory interest, but not an ownership interest, transferred by contract.

The tenant's and landlord's rights and obligations may vary according to the lease, but some states have statutes requiring that landlords keep the property in good condition for the tenant's use and giving the tenant the right to withhold rent payments should the landlord fail to maintain the premises. However, should the tenant fail to make the agreed-on payments without such grounds, the landlord may evict the tenant. The landlord is not allowed to enter the property, except when there is an emergency or when the tenant has given permission to enter to make repairs. Near the end of the leasehold, the landlord may enter with notice to the tenant for the purpose of showing the property to a potential tenant.

Subleasing of the property by the tenant to another party is permissible unless specifically prohibited by the lease. However, the initial tenant is liable throughout the entire term of the lease for payment of the rent to the landlord.

Nonpossessory Estates While most people think of interests in land as being possessory in nature, some estates do not include the right to possess the property. Such interests include easements, profits, and licenses. Easements and profits are similar in that they are neither ownership nor possessory interests and they are subject to similar rules, but they are not exactly the same.

Property Interests in Vietnam

In the United States, we take for granted the right to go out and purchase a piece of property if we have the money to do so. Property is not so freely available and transferable in all nations. Vietnam's new constitution, written in 1992, provides guidelines for the allocation, transfer, and sale of private property. However, the constitution still asserts that the people, or the state, own all the land. Thus, if individuals or private enterprises want to use land, they must pay tax on it as a form of rent. Those who agree to pay the tax on the land are granted a "use of right," which entitles them to extended use. The use of right also gives the renter the freedom to transfer the property. Technically, it is not the property that is being transferred but, rather, the right to use the property.

Transference of property can occur only with the approval of a state official. The official ensures that the new owner intends to use the land for the original, state-approved purpose. Moreover, the new owner can never be given a longer term of right or more extensive rights over the land than the original owner had. Finally, the state official determines the price at which the property will be transferred. The government has specified certain prices depending on how the land is used. Considering the involvement of the state in such property transactions, the extent to which the Vietnamese enjoy private property rights is limited.

easement

An irrevocable right to use some part of another's land for a specific purpose without taking anything from it.

profit

The right to go onto someone's land and take part of the land or a product of it away from the land.

An **easement** is an irrevocable right to use some part of another's land for a specific purpose without taking anything from it. A **profit** is the right to go onto someone's land and take part of the land or a product of it away from the land. For example, if Bill has the right to drive his car across Jenny's property to get to his property, he has an easement; but if he has the right to go onto her property and remove the topsoil he needs from it for his landscaping business, he has a profit. Easements and profits can be transferred in multiple ways: by express agreement, inheritance, necessity, implication, or prescription. If the land that benefits from the easement or profit is sold, the nonpossessory interest goes with the property. Thus, if Bill sold his land to Sonny, Sonny would also receive the easement across Jenny's property. Similarly, if Jenny sold her property, the new owner would have the burden of Bill's easement as long as it had been properly recorded. Of course, just as easements and profits can be created, they can also be terminated, with the most common method of termination being by agreement. The easement holder may simply deed the easement back to the property owner. If the easement arose by necessity and the necessity no longer exists, the easement would terminate.

license

A revocable right to temporarily use another's property.

A **license** is a right to use another's property that is both temporary and revocable. For example, when a person purchases a theater ticket, he or she has the right to a specific use of the property for a limited time, subject to good behavior. No property interest goes to the license holder.

PROPERTY TRANSFER

The owner's ability to transfer real property is part of the value of property. Any or all of the owner's property may generally be transferred to anyone for any price or no price, as the owner desires.

However, to effectuate such a transfer, the owner must follow certain legal procedures. These procedures are *execution, delivery, acceptance,* and *recording* (see Figure 7-2), the last of which is required to protect the recipient of the property. Such a transfer is presumed to be the conveyance of a fee simple absolute, unless the contrary is stated.

The transfer of the owner's interest in real property is not always voluntary. Transfer of property may also take place without the owner's knowledge and even, in some cases, against his or her will, by either adverse possession or condemnation. In **adverse possession** a person takes ownership of property by treating a piece of real property as his or her own, without protest or permission from the owner. Most states have established statutes determining a length of time after which such a possessor receives the ownership interest in the property. The exact lengths of time vary from state to state, but adverse possession must be *actual* (the person lives on or uses the land as an owner would), *open* (not secretive), and *notorious* (without the owner's permission). In some states, the adverse possessor must have performed certain acts such as the payment of real estate taxes. In other states, such possession must have taken place "under color of

adverse possession

An involuntary property transfer in which a person acquires ownership of property by treating a piece of real property as his or her own, without protest or permission from the owner.

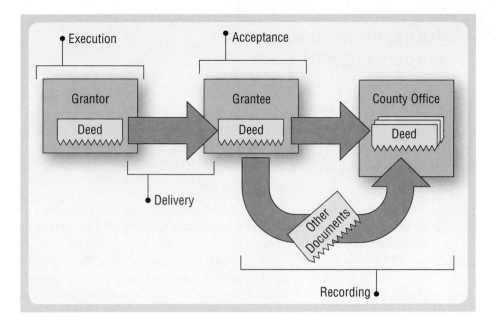

Figure 7-2

Steps in a Voluntary
Transfer

title"; in other words, the adverse possessor was operating under the assumption that he or she actually held the title to the land.

Condemnation is the legal process by which a transfer of property is made against the protest of the property owner. As you will remember from Chapter 4's discussion of the takings clause of the Fifth Amendment, the government has a constitutional right to take private property for the use of the public provided it pays the owner fair compensation. This right may be exercised at any government level, and sometimes it is exercised on behalf of a private company operating to benefit the public. For example, in the Case Opener about Poletown, a private business argued that the creation of new jobs was essential to the economic future of the area, and reducing unemployment through job creation took precedence over the residents' individual property rights.

When the government decides to exercise its power of eminent domain, it will first make an offer to purchase the property for what it believes is the fair market value. If the owner either does not want to sell or feels the price is too low, the government will initiate a condemnation proceeding and the court will determine whether the government body bringing the action has a valid claim that the taking is for a legitimate public purpose. If the court determines that, in fact, the taking of the property will benefit the public interest, the court will then determine the fair market value of the property. This price will be paid to the owner, and the property will be transferred to the government.

It is sometimes difficult to determine whether the exercise of eminent domain is actually for the public's benefit when the property will be conveyed by the government to another private individual. In the Poletown case, we see that a private corporation will clearly benefit from the government's taking of the property of the residents of the Poletown community. Could this benefit be described as being for a public use? Since the 1980s, businesses increasingly have been appealing to cities to use their power of eminent domain to assist the businesses in acquiring land that the owners have not wanted to sell. As this transference of property from one private individual to another is for the alleged public use of economic development, an increasing number of state supreme courts began to address the issue of whether economic development was a public use under the constraints of the Fifth Amendment. Some state supreme courts found that job creation and expansion of the tax base did constitute public use, while other courts found that they did not constitute public use. The U.S. Supreme Court finally settled the issue—at least for the present time—in the 5–4 decision summarized in Case 7-1. As you read this case, ask yourself whether there are any significant differences between the facts in *Poletown* and those in Case 7-1.

condemnation
The legal process by which a transfer of property is made against the protest of the property owner.

KELO v. CITY OF NEW LONDON
UNITED STATES SUPREME COURT
126 S. Ct. 326 (2005)

FACTS: *New London, a city in Connecticut, used its eminent domain authority to seize private property to sell to private developers. The city said developing the land would create jobs and increase tax revenues. Kelo Susette and others whose property was seized sued New London in state court. The property owners argued that the city violated the Fifth Amendment's takings clause, which guarantees that the government will not take private property for public use without just compensation. Specifically, the property owners argued that taking private property to sell to private developers was not public use. The Connecticut Supreme Court ruled for New London.*

ISSUE: Does a city violate the Fifth Amendment's takings clause if the city takes private property and sells it for private development, with the hopes the development will help the city's bad economy?

REASONING:

- The city's taking of private property to sell for private development qualified as a "public use" within the meaning of the takings clause.

- The city was not taking the land simply to benefit a certain group of private individuals but was following an economic development plan. Such justifications should be given deference.

- The takings here qualified as "public use" despite the fact that the land was not going to be used by the public.

- The Fifth Amendment did not require "literal" public use, the majority said, but the "broader and more natural interpretation of public use as 'public purpose.'"

O'Connor's dissent:

- An unelected (therefore voter-unaccountable) private nonprofit corporation was the primary beneficiary of the government taking.

- "Any property may now be taken for the benefit of another private party, but the fallout from this decision will not be random. The beneficiaries are likely to be those citizens with disproportionate influence and power in the political process, including large corporations and development firms."

- The decision eliminates "any distinction between private and public use of property—and thereby effectively delete[s] the words 'for public use' from the Takings Clause of the Fifth Amendment."

DECISION AND REMEDY: The city has not violated the Fifth Amendment. Affirmed, for New London.

SIGNIFICANCE OF THE CASE: The U.S. Supreme Court expanded significantly what constitutes "public use." Many people believe the Supreme Court went too far—they agree with Justice O'Connor's opinion.

CRITICAL THINKING

When you examine the reasoning in both the majority and dissenting opinions, you can see that a significant conflict between the opinions exists because of the ambiguity of a key term. Identify this term, and explain how its interpretation affects the reasoning. How do you think the courts should define the term?

ETHICAL DECISION MAKING

Who are the primary stakeholders involved in this case? How are they affected by the ruling? What are the implications of this ruling in terms of the distinction between public and private property? Further, this case highlights an important value conflict. Can you explain how certain values would lead one to support the majority opinion, whereas different values would lead one to support the dissenting opinion? How might holding a different value determine how one predicts the implications of this ruling?

Eminent Domain in Germany

Germany has both federal and state *(Lander)* regulations governing eminent domain. The federal system is similar to that in the United States, but one difference is that most of its eminent domain laws are incorporated through statutes, not through cases as in the United States.

The German federal government may expropriate land for the public good as long as it provides compensation. Germany's basic law provides: "Such compensation shall be determined by establishing an equitable balance between the public interest and the interests of those affected." Compensation in the German system is not based on fair market value alone but must also take the interests of those affected into consideration.

Germans may dispute the amount of compensation in the ordinary courts.

A taking requires that the government have the legal authority for the taking. The taking must also be appropriate for accomplishing the government's purpose and must be done in the least intrusive way possible, meaning that the government cannot take property before it needs it and the government can take only the property it needs. The taking must also pass a balancing test, showing that the public's interest is greater than the owner's interest.

One other difference in Germany is that if the property is no longer needed by the German government, it must revert to its former owner. In the United States, once the government has provided just compensation for the property, it belongs to the government.

Whereas the Kelo and Poletown cases involve government attempts to take property from individuals to sell to companies, sometimes governments seek to take the property of one company for use by another company. For instance, in June 2000, Costco, a large retail chain, wanted to expand its warehouse in Lancaster, California. Afraid of losing the large store, which threatened to move if it could not expand, the city considered using its eminent domain powers to acquire an adjacent 99 Cents Only store so that Costco could obtain the property. This example demonstrates that even businesses may be at risk of losing their property to larger, more powerful businesses.

The response to the *Kelo* decision was widespread. President Bush issued an executive order limiting the taking of private property by the federal government to "situations in which the taking is for public use, with just compensation, and for the purpose of benefiting the general public, and not merely for the purpose of advancing the economic interest of private parties to be given ownership or use of the property taken." During the year and a half after *Kelo,* 30 state legislatures enacted statutes limiting the use of eminent domain. Additionally, in 2006, nine states passed ballot measures restricting the definition of public use for purposes of eminent domain. Thus, it appears that the ultimate impact of the *Kelo* decision will be the opposite of what that decision held; by statute, a much more restrictive definition of public use will govern government takings. The case is also important because it shows how constitutional issues directly affect areas of the law, such as property law.

> To understand more about the relationship between the role of economic forces, which you learned about in your economics classes, and eminent domain, go to the **Connecting to the Core** activity on the text's website at www.mhhe.com/kubasekess2e.

Personal Property

LO 7-4

All property that is not land or not permanently affixed to land is personal property. Personal property may be either tangible or intangible. *Tangible property* is property that can be identified by the senses. It is property that you can see or touch. Tangible property includes items such as furniture, cars, and other goods.

Books are typically thought of as personal property. The owner of a book may write in it and generally do what he or she wants with it, and the law protects the owner against having the book taken by someone else. However, the growing popularity of e-books has raised questions about what rights e-book users have to their e-books. In July 2009, Amazon deleted copies of George Orwell's *1984* and *Animal Farm* directly off people's Kindles (Amazon's e-book reader) and

refunded their money. This action has sparked massive controversy over whether Amazon has the right to remove content that customers had bought from their Kindles. At least one lawsuit has already been filed as a result of this incident. Much of the outrage has been due to the fact that people do not see e-books and physical books as different types of property. Businesses that offer digital content should be clear about what rights customers have to the content, and they should make that information well known and visible to avoid problems like the one Amazon is currently facing.

Intangible property includes such items as bank accounts, stocks, and insurance policies. Because most intangibles (with the exception of some that are classified as intellectual property and discussed later in this chapter) are evidenced by writings, most of the following discussion applies to both tangible and intangible property. The primary issues that arise in conjunction with personal property involve the means of acquiring ownership of the property, which is discussed in the next section.

LO 7-5 VOLUNTARY TRANSFER OF PROPERTY

Voluntary transfer, as a result of either a purchase or a gift, is the most common means by which property is acquired. Ownership of property is referred to as *title,* and title to property passes when the parties so intend. When transfer of the property is by purchase, the acquiring party gives some consideration to the seller in exchange for title to the property.

Such a transfer of ownership usually requires no formalities, but in a few cases changes of ownership must be registered with a government agency. Sales of motor vehicles, watercraft, and airplanes are among the primary transfers requiring registration. To transfer such property, a certificate of title must be signed by the seller, taken to the appropriate government agency, and then reissued in the name of the new owner.

Gifts are another voluntary means of transferring ownership. They differ from purchases in that a promise to make a gift is unenforceable. Once properly made, however, a gift is irrevocable.

Three elements are necessary for a valid gift. First, there must be a *delivery* of the gift. Delivery may be actual, which is the physical presentation of the gift itself, or constructive, which entails the delivery of an item that gives access to the gift or represents it, such as the handing over of the keys to a car. Second, the delivery must be made with *donative intent* to make an immediate gift. The donor makes the delivery with the purpose of turning over ownership at the time of delivery. Third, there must be *acceptance,* a willingness of the donee to take the gift from the donor. Usually, acceptance is not a problem, although a donee may not want to accept a gift because of a desire to not feel obligated to the donor or because of a concern that ownership of the gift may impose some unwanted legal liability.

Sometimes, however, it can be difficult to determine whether something is a gift or a loan, especially when proper documentation is not filed at the time of the transaction. This was the scenario faced by Don Whittington when he disputed ownership of a 1979 Kremer Porsche displayed at the Indianapolis Motor Speedway Hall of Fame Museum. Whittington believed that he was the owner of the Porsche and that he had merely loaned it to the museum in 1980. The Indianapolis Motor Speedway Foundation believed that Whittington had given the car as a gift to the museum, and the foundation had even applied for and been granted a title to the car in 2001. In 2004, when Whittington requested the return of the car, he had to prove that he had a possessory interest in the car. Although the museum did not have a record of receiving the car as a gift or a loan, and Whittington had never applied for a tax reduction for giving the car as a gift and was able to produce one document in which he listed the car as an asset, the trial court found in favor of the foundation. The court determined that Whittington's behavior after the museum took possession of the car was more consistent with giving the car as a gift rather than as a loan.

The gifts we have been discussing so far have been what are called inter vivos gifts, gifts that are made by a person during his or her lifetime. Another type of gift that can be made is a gift *causa mortis,* a gift that is made in contemplation of one's immediate death. It can be revoked any time before the death of the donor, and it is automatically revoked if the donor recovers.

Litigation over gifts *causa mortis* often arises because the three elements of delivery, donative intent, and acceptance still have to occur before the gift is complete, and that means before the death of the donor. It can sometimes be difficult to determine whether in fact all the elements of a gift *causa mortis* have been met.

INVOLUNTARY TRANSFER OF PERSONAL PROPERTY

Involuntary transfers of ownership occur when property has been abandoned, lost, or mislaid. The finder of such property *may* acquire ownership rights to such property through possession.

Property that the original owner has discarded is *abandoned* property. Anyone finding such property becomes its owner by possessing it. For example, Karen is on vacation and decides that she doesn't really need her umbrella and doesn't want to carry it the rest of the trip, so she leaves the umbrella on a seat in the airport. If Bill then picks it up and takes it with him, he is now the lawful owner of the umbrella.

Lost property is property that the true owner has unknowingly or accidentally dropped or left somewhere. He or she has no way of knowing how to retrieve it. In most states, the finder of lost property has title to the lost good against all except the true owner.

Mislaid property differs from lost property in that the owner has intentionally placed the property somewhere but has forgotten its location. The person who owns the realty on which the mislaid property was placed has the right to hold the mislaid property. The reason is that it is likely that the true owner will return to the realty looking for the mislaid property.

In some states, the law requires that before becoming the owner of lost or mislaid property, a finder must place an ad in the paper that will give the true owner notice that the property has been found and/or must leave the property with the police for a statutorily established reasonable period of time.

OTHER MEANS OF ACQUIRING OWNERSHIP OF PROPERTY

There are additional means by which people acquire title to property. One such means is by creation: If a person creates a piece of property, then he or she owns that property. One exception to this rule occurs when a person is paid to create property for someone else, in which case the property is owned by the person who paid for its creation. Another means of acquiring ownership is by court order. In a number of different types of cases, the court will determine who is entitled to ownership of property. For example, in a divorce case the court may award ownership of certain property to different parties, or in a bankruptcy case the court may award ownership of certain property to a creditor.

A far less common means of acquiring ownership is confusion, which involves only fungible goods. *Fungible goods* are goods for which one unit of the good is essentially the same as every other unit, such as grains of wheat or gallons of oil. If two people accidentally commingle their fungible goods, or if the goods are commingled because of the actions of a third party, each party is entitled to the percentage of the fungible goods that he contributed.

However, if one of the parties was responsible for the commingling and that person cannot prove what percentage of the commingled goods she contributed, then the innocent party acquires title to all the goods. For example, if a farmer had stored grain in a rented storage elevator and another farmer wrongfully added his grain to the elevator, the innocent farmer would be entitled to the entire amount in the silo.

Intellectual Property

LO 7-6

Intellectual property, property that comes from creativity, also carries a bundle of sticks, both for the creator of the property and for the community. The creators of intellectual property often want to keep the property to themselves. For example, creators of copyrighted work (creative work in a fixed form) do not want others to copy that work without permission.

At times, intellectual property is more complicated than real property. For example, copyright often impacts freedom of speech. If a songwriter creates a song, others may think they

have the "right" to express themselves through this song, but a copyright may prevent this expression. Thus, copyright law and freedom of speech sometimes clash. Legislators and courts play an important role in responding to potential conflicts. They also balance the rights of innovators who create intellectual property with the interests of the community, especially interests in competition and freedom of expression. Courts and legislators decide what "sticks" to set aside for creators of intellectual property. They also decide what is left for the public, including artists and other businesses. The following sections describe specific types of intellectual property.

LO 7-7

TRADEMARKS

trademark

A distinctive mark, word, design, picture, or arrangement that is used by a producer in conjunction with a product and tends to cause consumers to identify the product with the producer.

A **trademark** is a distinctive mark, word, design, picture, or arrangement that is used by a producer in conjunction with a product and tends to cause consumers to identify the product with the producer. Even the shape of a product or package may be a trademark if it is nonfunctional.

Even though the description of a trademark is very broad, there has still been substantial litigation over precisely what features can and cannot serve as a trademark. In one case, discussed in the Case Nugget, the U.S. Supreme Court grappled with the issue of whether a color can be a trademark.

CASE Nugget

Color as a Trademark?

Qualitex Co. v. Jacobson Products Co.
United States Supreme Court

514 U.S. 159 (1995)

For years, the plaintiff, Qualitex Co., had colored the dry-cleaning press pads it manufactured a special shade of green-gold. When Jacobson Products, a competitor, started coloring its pads the same shade of green-gold, Qualitex sued Jacobson Products for trademark infringement. The defendant challenged the legitimacy of the trademark, arguing that color alone should not quality for registration as a trademark.

The district court found in favor of the plaintiff, but the Ninth Circuit reversed, holding that color alone could not be registered as a trademark. The plaintiff appealed to the U.S. Supreme Court.

In writing for the majority that a color could constitute a trademark, Justice Breyer said that both the language of the Lanham Act and the basic underlying principles of trademark law would seem to include color within the universe of things that could qualify as a trademark. He noted that the broad language used to describe trademarks included "any word, name, symbol, or device, or any combination thereof." Human beings might use as a "symbol" or "device" almost anything at all that is capable of carrying meaning. Justice Breyer noted that a particular shape (of a Coca-Cola bottle), a particular sound (of NBC's three chimes), and even a particular scent (of plumeria blossoms on sewing thread) could be trademarked, and he reasoned that if a shape, a sound, and a fragrance can act as symbols, it made sense that so could a color.

He also noted that a color, if unusual enough in the context, could in fact come to identify goods with their source, just as descriptive words on a product could. The Court concluded that the green-gold color acts as a symbol that has developed secondary meaning (i.e., customers identified the green-gold color as Qualitex's) and identifies the press pads' source. The high court therefore reversed the decision in favor of the plaintiff.

A trademark used *intrastate* is protected under state common law. To be protected in *interstate* use, the trademark must be registered with the U.S. Patent Office under the Lanham Act of 1947. If a mark is registered, the holder of the mark may recover damages from an infringer who uses it to pass off goods as being those of the mark owner. The owner may also obtain an injunction prohibiting the infringer from using the mark. (Only the latter remedy is available for an unregistered mark.) Once the mark is registered, the registration must be renewed between the fifth and sixth years. After that initial renewal, the mark holder must renew the registration every 10 years. (If the mark was initially registered before 1990, however, renewal is necessary only every 20 years.)

> To see how marketing relies on the use of trademarks, go to the **Connecting to the Core** activity on the text's website at www.mhhe.com/kubasekess2e.

To register a mark with the Patent Office, one must submit a drawing of the mark and indicate when it was first used in interstate commerce and how it is used. The Patent Office conducts an investigation to verify those facts and will register a trademark as long as it is not generic, descriptive, immoral, deceptive, the name of a person whose permission has not been obtained, or substantially similar to another's trademark. Even though we know the criteria for a trademark, it is not always easy to predict when a trademark will be granted or whether, even if granted, the trademark will stand up to a legal challenge. For example, immediately after actor Charlie Sheen was terminated from his role on the hit television program *Two and a Half Men* and began receiving a lot of media coverage, he started producing products marked with phrases that were beginning to be identified with his role on the program, namely "Duh, Winning," "Vatican Assassin," "Tiger Blood," and "Rock Star from Mars." It is uncertain whether these terms will be found by the courts to meet the criteria for trademarks as described above.

Case 7-2 demonstrates a typical analysis used in a trademark infringement suit.

CASE 7-2

TOYS "R" US, INC. v. CANARSIE KIDDIE SHOP, INC.
DISTRICT COURT OF THE EASTERN DISTRICT OF NEW YORK
559 F. Supp. 1189 (1983)

FACTS: *In 1961, plaintiff Toys "R" Us, Inc., obtained a trademark for "Toys 'R' Us" and aggressively advertised its products, children's toys and clothing, in stores across the country. In the late 1970s, defendant Canarsie Kiddie Shop opened two clothing shops called "Kids 'r' Us" within 2 miles of a Toys "R" Us shop. The defendant never tried to register its name. Toys "R" Us sued for trademark infringement in federal district court.*

ISSUE: Does "Kids 'r' Us" infringe on the mark "Toys 'R' Us"?

REASONING: To determine the likelihood of confusion associated with the defendant's mark, the court considered these factors:

- *Strength of the senior user's mark:* A mark can fall into one of four general categories, which, in order of

ascending strength, are (1) generic (is entitled to no protection); (2) descriptive (has a secondary meaning and informs public about uses of product); (3) suggestive (suggests qualities of product but requires imagination); and (4) arbitrary or fanciful (does not describe the qualities of the product). The plaintiff's mark has a strong secondary meaning as a source of children's products, so the court determines the mark has medium strength. But it falls short of the arbitrary or fanciful protection.

- *Degree of similarity between the two marks:* The key question is, Do consumers have the impression that purchasing from the junior user is purchasing from the senior user? Both parties use the phrase "R Us." However, the plaintiff uses an inverted capitalized "R," while the defendant uses a noninverted lowercase "r." The

plaintiff uses "Toys" while the defendant uses "Kids." The plaintiff's letter is usually multicolored.

- *Proximity of the products:* Both the plaintiff and the defendant sell children's clothing and are direct competitors.
- *The likelihood that plaintiff will "bridge the gap":* First, the senior user will expand sales efforts to compete with the junior user. Second, consumers will assume that both parties are related companies.
- *Evidence of actual confusion:* When there is proof that consumers are actually confused by the use of the name, the senior user has a stronger case.
- *Junior user's good faith:* The owner of Kids 'r' Us asserted that he did not recall whether he was aware of the plaintiff's mark. The court does not believe him and concludes that the defendant adopted the "Kids 'r' Us" mark with knowledge of the plaintiff's mark.

- *Quality of the junior user's product:* The court is much more concerned about the possible violation if the quality of the clothing is poor because such clothing would then reflect poorly on the senior user.
- *Sophistication of the purchasers:* Because children's clothing is not a major expenditure, customers will not exercise the same degree of care in evaluating the clothes.
- *Junior user's goodwill:* The junior user did not expend a lot of money advertising and promoting its own name. Thus, the defendant doesn't have a strong equitable interest in retaining its name.

DECISION AND REMEDY: Judgment for the plaintiff. The defendant's use of its mark creates the likelihood of confusion and constitutes trademark infringement.

SIGNIFICANCE OF THE CASE: This case clarifies the factors to consider in a trademark infringement case.

CRITICAL THINKING

How does this case depend to a large extent on the definitions of a few particular terms? How good are the definitions used? What standard are you using to determine whether the definitions are good?

ETHICAL DECISION MAKING

If you were the owner of Canarsie Kiddie Shop, Inc., how would your decision to refer to your store as "Kids 'r' Us" change if you were to act in accordance with the Golden Rule? What values are in conflict when considering the decisions of the owner of Canarsie Kiddie Shop, Inc., and of one who follows the Golden Rule?

trade dress

The overall appearance and image of a product.

The term **trade dress** refers to the overall appearance and image of a product. Trade dress is entitled to the same protection as a trademark. The main focus of a case of trade-dress infringement is usually on whether there is likely to be consumer confusion. For example, in a recent case,[1] Tour 18, Ltd., a golf course, copied golf holes from famous golf courses without permission of the course owners. In copying a hole from one of the most famous courses in the country, Harbour Town Hole 19, Tour 18 even copied the Harbour Town lighthouse, which is the distinctive feature of that hole. In its advertising, Tour 18 prominently featured pictures of this hole, including the lighthouse. The operator of the Harbour Town course sued Tour 18 for trade-dress infringement. The court found that there was infringement and made Tour 18 remove the lighthouse and disclaim in its advertising any affiliation with the owner of the Harbour Town course.

COPYRIGHTS

copyright

The protection of the expression of a creative work; i.e., protection of the fixed form that expresses the ideas.

Copyrights protect the *expression* of creative ideas. That is, they do not protect the ideas themselves but protect only the fixed form that expresses the ideas. Copyrights protect a diverse range of creative works, such as books, periodicals, musical compositions, plays, motion pictures, sound recordings, lectures, works of art, and computer programs. Titles and short phrases may not be copyrighted.

[1] *Pebble Beach Co. v. Tour 18, Ltd.,* 942 F. Supp. 1513.

E-COMMERCE and the Law

Domain Names and Trade Names

If you have a very strong trademark, what better domain name to have than that trademark? Unfortunately, the same trademark may be owned by two companies selling noncompeting goods, yet there can be only one user of any single domain name. For example, "apple" is a trademark owned by both a computer company and the company that produces the Beatles' records. Both cannot establish a site identified as apple.com.

Domain names are important because they are the addresses by which people and businesses are located on the web. A domain name is made up of a series of domains separated by periods. Most websites have two domains. The first-level domain, the one that the address ends with, generally identifies the type of site. For example, if it is a government site, the domain name will end in *gov;* an educational site, in *edu;* a network site, in *net;* an organization site, in *or;* and a business site, in *com.* These top-level domain names are the same worldwide.

The second-level domain is usually the name of whoever maintains the site. For a college, for example, it would be an abbreviation of the college name, such as *bgsu.* Businesses generally want to use their firm name or some other trademark associated with their product, because that name will obviously make it easiest for their customers to find them.

So how does a firm go about securing a domain name that reflects its trademark? Network Solutions, Inc. (NSI), which is funded by the National Science Foundation, is responsible for registering domain names. This entity acts on behalf of the Internet Network Information Center, which handles the daily administration of the domain name system in the United States.

Initially, a person applied to the NSI to use a specific domain name, and as long as no one else held that name, registration was granted. Since 1995, however, the NSI has been a little more careful in handing out names. Anyone seeking to register a domain name must now state in the application that the name will not infringe on anyone else's intellectual property rights and that the registrant intends to use the name on a regular basis on the Internet.

A party may lose registration of a name by not using it for more than 90 days. Or the domain name may be canceled if the registrant lied on the registration application. If you have a registered trademark and you find that a party is using your trademark as a domain name and that party does not also have ownership of that mark, you may give written notice to the NSI; under its domain dispute policy, it will most likely put the name "on hold," meaning that no one can use the name. Of course, if that party had registered its domain name before you obtained the trademark, there is probably nothing you can do. The party will be entitled to retain the domain name.

Some firms have tried to get the domain name they desire by going to another country. That alternative is certainly a possibility. However, many countries require that your firm be incorporated within their borders before you can gain the right to the domain name there. An additional problem is that trademark law relating to domain names is even more unclear abroad.

For the new entrepreneur, the best advice is to try to simultaneously apply for federal trademark protection and register the domain name. And for those not yet on the web, the sooner you get your domain name, the more likely you are to get the name you want. If you feel that your mark is being violated by another's domain name, you may want to sue the party for infringement, because the unauthorized use of another's trademark in a domain name has been found to be illegal. But you may be in for quite a fight because this is a new area of the law.

There are three criteria for a work to be copyrightable. First, it must be *fixed,* which means set out in a tangible medium of expression. Second, it must be *original.* Third, it must be *creative.* A copyright automatically arises under common law when the idea is expressed in tangible form. However, if the work is freely distributed without notice of copyright, the work falls into the public domain. A copyrighted work that is reproduced with the appropriate notice affixed is protected for the life of its creator plus 70 years.

Under the common law of copyright, an infringer may be enjoined only from reproducing a copyrighted work. For the creator to be able to not only seek an injunction but also recover damages arising from the infringement, the copyrighted work must be registered. One may register a work by filing a form with the Register of Copyright and providing two copies of the copyrighted material to the Library of Congress. Whenever the work is reproduced, the appropriate notice of copyright *should* accompany it, although such notice is no longer required by law. Printed works, for example, should be published with the word *copyright* and the symbol © or the abbreviation *copr.,* followed by the first date of publication and the name of the copyright owner. Once the work is registered, as long as it is always accompanied by the notice of copyright when reproduced, the holder of the copyright has the additional right to sue an infringer for damages caused by the infringer's use of the copyrighted material and to recover any profits made by the infringer on the copyrighted material.

It is not always easy to determine whether a copyright has been infringed, even when two works are similar. After all, if we are talking about creative works, such as photographs of a

famous scene, two people might independently take a very similar picture at completely different times and without even knowing of each other's work. The following Case Nugget illustrates the court's reasoning in a successful copyright infringement case.

CASE Nugget

A Question of Whether there was copying

Ty, Inc. v. GMA Accessories, Inc.
U.S. Court of Appeals, Seventh Circuit

45 U.S.P.Q. 1519 (1998)

Ty began selling Beanie Babies, and then GMA started selling bean-bag stuffed animals three years later. Ty sought an injunction under the Copyright Act to stop the sale of GMA's "Preston the Pig" and "Louie the Cow." Ty argued that these animals violated its copyrights for "Squealer" (a pig) and "Daisy" (a cow). Ty was successful in obtaining an injunction for copyright after the court asked the following questions: Did the alleged copier have access to the work he or she potentially copied? Did he or she actually copy the work? The court found that access (and copying) may be inferred when the two works are so similar and unlike anything in the public domain that it is likely the second user copied the first. This inference can be rebutted by disproving access or showing independent creation. Looking at pictures of the two cows compels an inference of copying. If GMA must have had access to Ty's cow, it must have had access to the pig, too. GMA's pig is strikingly similar to Ty's pig but not to anything in the public domain (e.g., a real pig). The only evidence GMA presented was an affidavit by the designer, who swears she never looked at Squealer. However, the actual bean-bag animal looks more like Ty's design than the designer's drawing.

fair-use doctrine
The lawful use of a limited portion of another's work for purposes of criticism, comment, news reporting, teaching, scholarship, and research that does not reduce the commercial value of the protected property.

The **fair-use doctrine** provides that a portion of a copyrighted work may be reproduced for purposes of "criticism, comment, news reporting, teaching (including multiple copies for classroom use), scholarships, and research." In determining whether the fair-use doctrine provides a valid defense to a claim of copyright infringement, Section 107 of the Copyright Act requires that the court weigh the following four factors: the purpose and character of the use, the nature of the copyrighted work, the amount and substantiality of the portion used in relation to the copyrighted work as a whole, and the effect of the use on the potential market for or value of the copyrighted work. Case 7-3 provides an example of the fair-use doctrine.

CASE 7-3

GAYLORD v. UNITED STATES
FEDERAL CIRCUIT COURT OF APPEALS
595 F.3d 1364 (Fed. Cir. 2010)

FACTS: *Congress enacted legislation to create a memorial for the Korean War. Cooper-Lecky Architects, P.C. was the contractor selected for the creation and construction of the memorial. Cooper-Lecky held a competition to select the sculptor for the memorial, and in 1990, Frank Gaylord, a nationally known sculptor, won*

the competition and began working on the Korean War Memorial. Specifically, he created a design where 19 statues represented a platoon of soldiers in formation for war. Gaylord registered copyrights for these soldier sculptures. In 1995, John Alli took photographs of the memorial as a gift for his father, who was a Korean War veteran. When Alli later decided to sell prints of the photo, he approached Cooper-Lecky for permission, and the parties agreed Alli would pay Cooper-Lecky a 10 percent royalty on his sales of the photo. In 2002, the U.S. Postal Service decided to use Alli's photo as a stamp commemorating the end of the Korean War. Alli told the Postal Service that it would need to get permission from Lecky, who he understood held the copyright on the statues. The Postal Service did not get permission from Lecky or from Gaylord. The Postal Service sold approximately $17 million worth of the stamps, and an estimated $5 million of that $17 million was from collectors who would not use the stamps. Gaylord sued the government in 2006 for copyright infringement in the Court of Federal Claims, where the court determined that the stamp made fair use of the sculptures. Gaylord appealed.

ISSUE: Was the Postal Service's use of Gaylord's sculpture on a postage stamp fair use?

REASONING: The Federal Circuit considered the four factors under Section 107 of the Copyright Act. First, the court considered the purpose and character of the infringing use. Specifically, the court evaluates whether the new work adds something new, such as a new expression, meaning, or message, and is transformative. The Federal Circuit determined that the stamp did not communicate any

"further purpose" than the memorial. It was not intended to provide commentary or criticism. Furthermore, the stamp had a commercial purpose. Consequently, the court determined this factor weighed against fair use.

Second, the Federal Circuit considered the nature of the copyrighted work, the memorial. Under this factor, courts consider (1) whether the work is more creative or more factual, and (2) whether the work is published or unpublished. Works that are more factual and works that are unpublished are more likely to be found as fair use. The memorial was both a creative and published work, so this factor weighed against fair use.

Third, the Federal Circuit considered the amount and substantiality of the portion used. The stamp included 14 of the 19 soldier sculptures. Furthermore, the stamp had the same focus as the memorial, so this factor weighed against fair use.

Finally, the Federal Circuit considered the effect of the use on the potential market. Here, the court considered the market for the copyrighted work as well as the market for the potentially infringing works. The Court of Federal Claims determined that the stamp did not harm either market and noted that Gaylord agreed that the stamp increased the memorial's value. The Federal Circuit did not disagree with the Court of Federal Claims' findings.

DECISION: The Federal Circuit determined that the factors led to the conclusion that the stamp's use was not a fair use.

SIGNIFICANCE OF THE CASE: The case clearly sets forth how the elements of the fair-use doctrine are applied.

Critical Thinking

Create a series of facts that, had they been true, would have caused the court to have decided that the stamp's use was a fair use.

Ethical Decision Making

What value conflict is responsible for the arguments surrounding the issue of fair use of intellectual property?

PATENTS

A **patent** protects a product, process, invention, machine, or a plant produced by asexual reproduction. For this protection to be granted, three criteria must be satisfied. First, the object of the patent must be *novel,* or new. No one else must have previously made or published the

patent
Protection that grants the holder the exclusive right to produce, sell, and use the object of the patent for 20 years; can be obtained for a product, process, invention, machine, or a plant produced by asexual reproduction.

plans for this object. Second, the object must be *useful,* unless it is a design. It must provide some utility to society. Third, the object must be *nonobvious.* The invention must not be one that a person of ordinary skill in the trade could have easily discovered. When a patent is issued for an object, it gives its holder the exclusive right to produce, sell, and use the object of the patent for 20 years from the date of application. The holder of the patent may *license,* or allow others to manufacture and sell, the patented object. In most cases, patents are licensed in exchange for the payment of *royalties,* a sum of money paid for each use of the patented process.

The only restriction on the patent holder is that he or she may not use the patent for an illegal purpose. The two most common illegal purposes are tying arrangements and cross-licensing. A **tying arrangement** occurs when the holder issues a license to use the patented object *only* if the licensee agrees to buy some nonpatented product from the holder. **Cross-licensing** occurs when two patent holders license each other to use their patents *only* on the condition that neither licenses anyone else to use his or her patent without the other's consent. Both of these activities are unlawful because they tend to reduce competition.

To obtain a patent, one generally contacts an attorney licensed to practice before the U.S. Patent Office. The attorney does a *patent search* to make sure that no other similar patent exists. If none exist, the attorney fills out a patent application and files it with the Patent Office. The Patent Office evaluates the application, and if the object meets the criteria already described, a patent is issued within approximately two years. While two years may seem like a long time, it is short compared to the six years it typically takes to secure a patent in Japan.

Once the patent is issued, the holder may bring a patent infringement suit in a federal court against anyone who uses, sells, or manufactures the patented invention without the permission of the patent holder. A successful action may result in an injunction prohibiting further use of the patented item by the infringer and also an award of damages. Sometimes, however, the result of the case is that the holder loses the patent. This loss would occur if the infringer is able to prove that the Patent Office should not have issued the patent in the first place.

TRADE SECRETS

A **trade secret** is a process, product, method of operation, or compilation of information that gives a businessperson an advantage over his or her competitors. Inventions and designs may also be considered trade secrets. A trade secret is protected by the common law from unlawful appropriation by competitors as long as it is kept secret and consists of elements not generally known in the trade.

Competitors may discover a "secret" by any lawful means, such as by doing reverse engineering or by going on public tours of plants and observing the use of trade secrets. Lawful discovery of a secret means there is no longer a trade secret to be protected.

If a competitor acquires a trade secret by unlawful means, the originator of the secret can take legal action. To enjoin such a competitor from continuing the use of a trade secret and/or to recover damages caused by the use of the secret, a plaintiff must prove that a trade secret actually existed, that the defendant acquired it through unlawful means, and that the defendant used the trade secret without the plaintiff's permission.

A common dilemma facing an inventor is whether to protect an invention through patent or trade-secret law. If the inventor successfully patents the invention and defends the patent, the inventor has a guaranteed exclusive monopoly on the use of the invention for 20 years, a substantial period of time. The problem is that once this period is over, the patented good goes into the public domain and everyone has access to it. There is also the risk that the patent may be successfully challenged and the protection lost prematurely.

Trade-secret law, on the other hand, could protect the invention in perpetuity. The problem is that once someone discovers the secret lawfully, the protection is lost.

tying arrangement

An illegal agreement in which the sale of one product is tied to the sale of another.

cross-licensing

An illegal contractual arrangement in which two or more parties license each other to use their specified intellectual property *only* on the condition that neither licenses anyone else to use the property without the other's consent.

trade secret

A process, product, method of operation, or compilation of information that gives a businessperson an advantage over his or her competitors.

SUMMARY

The Nature of Real and Intellectual Property	*Real property* is land and anything permanently affixed to the land. *Intellectual property* is property that is primarily the result of mental creativity rather than physical effort.
Real Property	*Fee simple absolute:* Right to possess for life and devise to heirs on death; the most encompassing interest. *Conditional estate:* Right that is comparable to a fee simple absolute except that the interest will terminate on the happening or nonhappening of a specified condition. *Leasehold estate:* Right to possess property for an agreed-on period of time. *Easement:* Irrevocable right to use a portion of someone else's land for a specified purpose. *License:* Right to temporarily use another's property.
Personal Property	*Personal property* is all property that is not land or permanently affixed to land. *Voluntary transfer of personal property:* Property can be transferred by purchase or by gift. *Involuntary transfer of property:* If property is lost, mislaid, or abandoned, a new owner acquires title to the property through possession.
Intellectual Property	A *trademark* is a distinctive mark, word, design, picture, or arrangement that is used by a producer in conjunction with a product and tends to cause the consumer to identify the product with the producer. Trademarks used in interstate commerce can be protected under the Lanham Act. A *copyright* protects the fixed form of the expression of an original, creative idea. The most common defense to an allegation of copyright infringement is the fair-use doctrine, which provides that a portion of a copyrighted work may be reproduced for purposes of "criticism, comment, news reporting, teaching (including multiple copies for classroom use), scholarships, and research." A *patent* protects a product, process, invention, machine, or plant produced by asexual reproduction that meets the criteria of being novel, useful, and nonobvious. Obtaining a patent under the Lanham Act allows the holder to license the use of his or her patented idea for royalties as long as the holder does not enter into a tying arrangement or engage in cross-licensing.

Point/Counterpoint

The process of applying for a patent and keeping a patent can be difficult and costly. As you know, an alternative to patenting an invention is to protect it through trade-secret law.

Should Inventors Avoid the Hassles of Patent Protection and Protect Their Inventions through Trade-Secret Law?

YES	NO
Inventors should choose to protect their inventions through trade-secret law. Trade-secret protection does not require registration with government agencies. Unlike patent protection, whereby the owner of the patent has exclusive rights to produce, sell, and use the object of the patent only for a limited time,	Inventors should not choose to protect their inventions through trade-secret law. Protection through trade-secret law is risky. It is the responsibility of the owner of the trade secret to take precautionary measures to maintain the privacy of the trade secret. With technological advances, the chance of competitors' using

trade-secret protection offers the owner of the trade secret exclusive rights indefinitely. For example, the unique process by which Coca-Cola makes its soft drink has been protected as a trade secret for over 100 years. This approach has prevented competitors from duplicating Coca-Cola's product. A patent holder also risks the chance of losing the patent if a challenger is able to show that the patent should not have been issued. Because trade-secret protection is not limited by registration requirements, inventors should use trade-secret law to protect their products.

legal methods such as reverse engineering to discover the trade secret is likely. An owner of a patent may bring a patent infringement suit if the patent has been used without permission. If a trade secret is discovered through lawful means, it is no longer a secret and the owner cannot bring actions against those using the product or process. Through patent protection the owner can decide whether to license the patent and can earn a profit from those who choose to use the product. The risks associated with trade-secret protection are too great to make it a desirable choice.

Questions & Problems

1. Explain the bundle-of-sticks idea as it relates to real property.

2. Explain the five possessory interests in land.

3. Explain the bundle-of-sticks idea as it relates to intellectual property.

4. How are trademarks and patents different?

5. Explain copyright infringement.

6. Willard W. Smith had owned a salvage yard since 1980. In 1984, the county enacted a zoning ordinance requiring a permit for salvage yards. Because the operation of Smith's yard predated the 1984 ordinance, he was not subjected to the permit requirement. A relevant regulation stated, "Any salvage yard which was licensed prior to June 12, 1988, may continue to be operated and maintained in accordance with the statutes and regulations in effect at the time the yard was initially licensed." In 1992, Smith sold the yard to Poole. Poole continued to use the property as a salvage yard. The use and operation of the property did not change. After Poole failed to apply for a permit, the circuit court found that the previous lawful, nonconforming use of the property was terminated when Smith sold the land to Poole. Poole appealed the court's decision. Do you think he was successful? Why or why not? [*Poole v. Berkeley County Planning Com'n,* 488 S.E.2d 349 (1997).]

7. Plaintiff homeowners purchased a parcel of land in the homeowners association's (HOA's) subdivision. Their real estate agent requested that the attached-garage requirement be waived, and when the owners did not receive a response from the HOA, they worked out a plan to construct one. The owners purchased a modular home to which they could attach a garage without first obtaining an architectural review pursuant to a restrictive covenant in the HOA declarations. One member of the HOA unilaterally disapproved of the home. The owners filed suit, and a

meeting of the HOA was held regarding the owners' home. However, the dispute was not resolved. Plaintiff homeowners then filed a request for a permanent injunction to prevent the defendant homeowners association from applying the architectural review covenant that led to the disapproval of the owners' planned home. The HOA counter-filed, seeking a permanent injunction upholding its application of the architectural review standards and also seeking damages. On the basis of the facts presented, to whom do you think the court awarded a permanent injunction and why? [*Ronald Bobbie Lawhon v. Winding Ridge Homeowners Association, Inc.,* 2008 Del. Ch. LEXIS 195.]

8. Thomas A. Carella filed for Chapter 7 bankruptcy. At the time, HSBC Bank USA held the sum of $16,540.94 on deposit in a joint bank account in the names of Carella and his father, Thomas J. Carella. The son sought to protect the money in the bank account, arguing that it was his father's account. The father had set up the joint account after finding out he needed to undergo heart bypass surgery. The father argues that he set up the joint account for convenience so that his son would have access to the money should the father pass away. The father survived the surgery and continued to manage the joint account. Only the father deposited or withdrew money from the account at any time. The son's bankruptcy trustee argued that the account was a gift *causa mortis* and thus is available as part of the bankruptcy. Did the joint account constitute a gift *causa mortis?* What are the necessary elements for establishing the joint account as a gift *causa mortis?* [*In re Thomas A. Carella,* 340 B.R. 710 (Bankr. W.D.N.Y. 2006).]

9. Defendant Tubbs met her fiancé, Church, over the Internet. After several years of correspondence and visits, they became engaged in February 2000. Church and Tubbs planned to be married in Las Vegas

in July 2000. Two months before the engagement, Church paid off $4,100 of Tubbs's credit card debt. He also gave Tubbs an engagement ring that he purchased for $7,274.42. On March 15, 2000, he deposited $194,852.56 in Tubbs's bank account to fund the purchase of land and a residential home in Michigan. Tubbs purchased the home in both of their names as joint tenants, on Church's instructions, and in April she moved in. Church moved some personal property to the residence, including a family heirloom diamond ring. On June 5, 2000, Tubbs e-mailed Church stating that their relationship was over because she was horrified after seeing his "bizarre and abnormal behavior" on the Internet and because she had discovered that he led a "risqué lifestyle as a cross-dresser and bi-sexual." Tubbs rejected Church's demands to repay the $4,100 and to return the engagement ring, his personal property, and her interest in the Michigan home. On July 24, 2000, Church died in England. Church's estate subsequently filed suit to recover the property. The court entered a final judgment entitling the estate to the rings or a money judgment for their values; the real property, partitioned as a matter of law to account for its appreciation; complete right, title, interest, and possession of the land and residential home, free and clear of any claim, right, title, or interest of Tubbs; and a money judgment in the amount of $75,000 (the amount of Tubbs's home equity mortgage), less credits to Tubbs of $13,000 for property taxes she paid from 2000 through 2005, or a modified money judgment in the amount of $62,000. Tubbs appealed. What arguments might she have made on appeal? How do you think the appellate court ruled in this case, and why? [*Salens v. Tubbs,* 2008 WL 4072342 (C.A. 6 Mich.).]

10. The plaintiff, Lone Star Steakhouse, operates over 30 Lone Star Steakhouse & Saloon restaurants in the United States. The trademarks "Lone Star Café" and "Lone Star Steakhouse & Saloon" are owned by Lone Star Steakhouse. Clothing and accessories with the logo are sold in the restaurant. In 1991 the defendant, Alpha, opened a restaurant named "Lone Star Grill" in Arlington, Virginia. Alpha conducted extensive advertising in the Virginia and Washington, D.C., area. The advertisements featured coupons with the words *Lone Star* and a five-pointed star similar to the one used by Lone Star Steakhouse. Lone Star Steakhouse operates four restaurants in Virginia and one restaurant in Washington, D.C. It testified that on several occasions customers presented coupons for Lone Star Grill. To prevent customer dissatisfaction, Lone Star Steakhouse would give customers free drinks, coupons, or meal discounts. Lone Star Steakhouse & Saloon brought a trademark infringement action against Lone Star Grill. How do you think the court

decided, and why? [*Lone Star Steakhouse & Saloon v. Alpha of Virginia,* 43 F.3d 922 (1995).]

11. The Stop & Shop Supermarket and Big Y Foods are supermarkets offering the same services and competing for the same customers. In an advertisement introducing its new, easy-to-use scan saver cards, Stop & Shop Supermarket used the slogan "It's that Simple." The supermarket used the slogan in radio, television, and print advertisements. The service mark was licensed to the supermarket by plaintiff Fullerton, who owns the right to the service mark. After Stop & Shop started using the slogan, Big Y Foods began to use a similar slogan, "We Make Life Simple." Both service marks are always accompanied by the name of the store. Fullerton and Stop & Shop Supermarket brought an action alleging infringement of the service mark. Do you think that the court granted the injunction? Why or why not? [*The Stop & Shop Supermarket Company and Fullerton Corp. v. Big Y Foods Inc.,* 943 F. Supp. 120 (1996).]

12. Smith, a satirist and outspoken critic of Walmart, created websites displaying designs and slogans that negatively parodied Walmart's registered marks. These designs and slogans incorporated the word *Walocaust*, a word Smith invented by combining the first three letters of Walmart's name with the last six letters of the word *holocaust*.

 Smith also sold novelty items online that were printed with graphics that parodied the retailer's slogans, with the disclaimer that he was unaffiliated with the retailer. One design depicted a blue stylized bird modeled to resemble a Nazi eagle grasping a yellow smiley face in the same manner that a Nazi eagle is typically depicted grasping a swastika. Above the bird image, the word *WAL*OCAUST* was printed in a blue font comparable to that commonly used by Walmart.

 The lower court found that Walmart had failed to establish that a smiley-face icon it used for advertising was distinctive enough to merit trademark protection and that Smith's slogans and graphics were scathing parodies and therefore did not violate any Walmart trademarks or cause dilution of its marks. Do you think the court of appeals upheld Smith's defense that he was engaged in parody and that such parody precluded claims of trademark infringement and dilution? [*Smith v. Wal-Mart Stores, Inc.,* 475 F. Supp. 2d 1318, 2007 U.S. Dist. LEXIS 13335 (N.D. Ga. 2007).]

13. Superior Form Builders held a copyright for animal mannequins. The sculpted animal forms were used to mount animal skins. The owner of Superior Form Builders, Tommy Knight, considers the mannequins to be a form of artistic expression. The defendant, Dan Chase Taxidermy Supply Company, ordered four

of Knight's mannequins from the Superior Form catalog. Chase, a competitor of Superior Form, ordered under a fictitious name. He used the mannequins to mount animal skins and made few changes to the forms. When Knight realized that Chase was using the Superior Form mannequins, he sued for copyright infringement. Chase argued that the copyright should never have been granted because the mannequins were useful and unoriginal. How do you think the court decided? [*Superior Form Builders, Inc. v. Chase Taxidermy Supply Co.,* 74 F.3d 488 (4th Cir. 1996).]

14. GoTo.com's logo features a green circle surrounded by a yellow background, with the words *Go* and *To* printed in the circle. Disney Corp. started to use its logo, a green circle surrounded by a yellow background with the word *Go* printed inside, on its GoNetwork page. GoTo.com filed suit against Disney Corp., seeking an injunction. Do you think the court granted the injunction? What factors would it have considered in making its decision? [*GoTo.com, Inc. v. Walt Disney Corp.,* 202 F.3d 1199, 1207 (9th Cir. 2000).]

Looking for more review material?

The Online Learning Center at **www.mhhe.com/kubasekess2e** contains this chapter's "Assignment on the Internet" and also a list of URLs for more information, entitled "On the Internet." Find both of them in the Student Center portion of the OLC, along with quizzes and other helpful materials.

Introduction to Contracts and Agreement

The Problematic Promotion

Pepsi had a promotion whereby consumers were encouraged to collect "Pepsi points" by consuming Pepsi products. They could then redeem the points for merchandise. If they did not have quite enough points for the prize they wanted, they could buy the needed additional points for 10 cents each; however, at least 15 original Pepsi points had to accompany each order.

At the climax of an early commercial for the promotion, three young boys are sitting in front of a high school building, one reading his Pepsi Stuff catalog while the others drink Pepsi, all gazing in awe at an object rushing overhead as the military march in the background builds to a crescendo. A Harrier jet swings into view and lands by the side of the school building, next to a bicycle rack. Several students run for cover, and the velocity of the wind strips one hapless faculty member down to his underwear. While the faculty member is being deprived of his dignity, the voice-over announces: "Now the more Pepsi you drink, the more great stuff you're gonna get."

A teenager opens the cockpit of the fighter and can be seen, without a helmet, holding a Pepsi. He exclaims, "Sure beats the bus," and chortles. The military drumroll sounds a final time, as the following words appear: "Harrier Fighter 7,000,000 Pepsi Points." A few seconds later, the following appears in more stylized script: "Drink Pepsi—Get Stuff."

John Leonard decided to accept Pepsi's offer of the Harrier fighter jet for 7 million Pepsi points. He quickly realized that it would be easier to raise the money to buy points than to collect the 7 million points. In early March 1996, he filled out an order form requesting the jet and submitted it to Pepsi, along with 15 Pepsi points and a check for $700,000.

In response, Pepsi sent him a letter saying, "The item that you have requested is not part of the Pepsi Stuff collection. It is not included in the catalogue or on the order form, and only catalogue merchandise can be redeemed under this program." John then sued for breach of contract.

1. Did Pepsi offer to sell the Harrier jet for 7 million points?
2. Did Leonard's submission of the order form constitute an acceptance?
3. Was the alleged contract in this case a bilateral or unilateral contract?

After reading this chapter, you will be able to answer the following questions:

LO 8-1 What is a contract?

LO 8-2 What are the sources of contract law?

LO 8-3 How can contracts be classified?

LO 8-4 What are the rules that guide the interpretation of contracts?

LO 8-5 What are the elements of a valid offer and valid acceptance?

LO 8-6 How does an offer terminate?

LO 8-1

The Definition of a Contract

contract

A promise or set of promises for the breach of which the law gives a remedy or the performance of which the law in some way recognizes a duty.

This part of the text focuses on contracts. A **contract,** according to the Restatement (Second) of Contracts, is "a promise or set of promises for the breach of which the law gives a remedy or the performance of which the law in some way recognizes a duty."[1] Another, perhaps simpler, way to think of a contract is that it is a set of legally enforceable promises.

ELEMENTS OF A CONTRACT

agreement

One of the four elements necessary for a contract; consists of an offer made by one party, the offeror, and the acceptance of the offer by another party, the offeree.

A contract has four elements: the agreement, the consideration, contractual capacity, and a legal object. The **agreement** consists of an **offer** by one party, called the *offeror,* to enter into a contract, and an **acceptance** of the terms of the offer by the other party, called the *offeree.* The agreement is discussed in more detail in the latter part of this chapter.

The second element of a contract is the **consideration,** which is defined as the bargained-for exchange. Another way to think of the consideration is that it is what each party gets in exchange for his or her promise under the contract. Consideration is further discussed in Chapter 9.

offer

A key factor in the agreement element of a contract; consists of the terms and conditions set by one party, the offeror, and presented to another party, the offeree.

The third element is **contractual capacity,** the legal ability to enter into a binding agreement. Most adults over the age of majority have the legal ability to enter into binding contracts, but Chapter 9 explains when people have either limited or no capacity to enter into these agreements. Persons who do not have the capacity to enter into legally binding contracts include those who are under the age of majority, intoxicated, or suffering from mental illness. Chapter 9 also discusses the fourth element of a binding, legal contract, **legal object.** The contract cannot be either illegal or against public policy.

The elements of a contract, as well as defenses to its enforcement, are listed in Exhibit 8-1.

acceptance

A key factor in the agreement element of a contract; consists of the agreement of one party, the offeree, to the terms of the offer in the contract made by the other party, the offeror.

DEFENSES TO THE ENFORCEMENT OF A CONTRACT

Sometimes the parties may enter into what appears to be a legally binding and enforceable contract because all four elements of a contract are present, but one of the parties may have a defense to the contract's enforcement. Such defenses fall into two categories. The first, discussed in Chapter 11, is a **lack of genuine assent.** A contract is supposed to be entered into freely by both parties, but sometimes the offeror secures the acceptance of the agreement through improper means, such as fraud, duress, undue influence, or misrepresentation. In these situations, there

[1] Restatement (Second) of Contracts, sec. 1.

ELEMENTS OF A CONTRACT	DEFENSES TO A CONTRACT
Agreement	Lack of genuine assent
Consideration	Lack of proper form
Legal purpose	
Capacity	

Exhibit 8-1

A Valid Contract Has Four Elements, and No Defenses Can Be Raised against It

really is no genuine assent to the contract, and the offeree may be able to raise the lack of genuine assent as a defense to enforcement of the agreement.

The second defense, discussed in Chapter 12, is that the contract lacks the *proper form,* which typically means it lacks a writing. Certain contracts require a writing, and if there is none, the agreement will not be enforced. Chapter 13 discusses the performance and discharge of contracts, as well as remedies arising when a contract is breached.

Sources of Contract Law

LO 8-2

There are two primary sources of contract law: case law and the Uniform Commercial Code (UCC). A third source of law, which has become more important with increasing globalization, is the Convention on Contracts for International Sales of Goods (CISG). Chapters 8 through 13 of this book focus primarily on the law of contracts as established by the common law, and Chapters 14 and 15 focus on the law as established by the UCC and CSIG.

COMMON LAW

Today's law of contracts actually originated in judicial decisions in England, which were followed by the early courts in the United States. Since then, contract law has been modified by our legislatures and by rulings of our courts. The law of contracts is primarily common law, and so to find out what the law is, one could go to the Reporters and read the decisions, but an easier way to know the law would be to go to the Restatement (Second) of the Law of Contracts. Prominent legal scholars, recruited by the American Law Institute, organized the principles of the common law of contracts into the original *Restatement of the Law, Contracts.* The compilation has subsequently been revised and published as *Restatement of the Law Second, Contracts.*

The Restatement (Second) is not actually the law itself, although judges frequently cite it in cases because it is an authoritative statement of what the law is. As the common law of contracts evolved in the various states, not all states interpreted all aspects of the law in the same way, so while we can generalize about the law of contracts, one would of course always want to know exactly what the law at issue is in one's own state. In the Restatement (Second), the drafters often explain what the law about a particular matter is in the majority of states and then provide alternative approaches that other states have adopted.

UNIFORM COMMERCIAL CODE

Having different laws governing contracts in different states did not make interstate commerce flow smoothly. To remedy some of the difficulties created by a patchwork of different laws governing commercial transactions, the National Conference of Commissioners on Uniform State Laws and the American Law Institute drafted a set of commercial laws that could be applicable to all states. This effort was called the **Uniform Commercial Code (UCC).** The UCC became law in each state that adopted it completely or partially as part of its state code. Thus, for example, if a firm enters into a contract governed by the Uniform Commercial Code in Ohio, it would be operating under the Ohio Uniform Commercial Code.

consideration
The bargained-for exchange; what each party gets in exchange for his or her promise under a contract.

contractual capacity
The legal ability to enter into a binding agreement.

legal object
A purpose that does not violate a statute or public policy.

lack of genuine assent
A defense to the agreement of a contract in which the offeree claims that the offeror secured the agreement through improper means, such as duress, fraud, undue influence, or misrepresentation.

Uniform Commercial Code (UCC)
A statutory source of contract law in the United States applicable to transactions involving the sale of goods. The UCC was created in 1952 and adopted by all 50 states, the District of Columbia, and the Virgin Islands; it may be modified by each state to reflect the wishes of the state legislature.

Contract Law in the European Union

If you are doing business with a member state of the European Union, there is one source to turn to in order to understand how the various member states regulate contracts, and that is the *Principles of European Contract Law.* The principles were drafted by an independent body of experts from each member state of the European Union under a project supported by the European Commission. The principles are stated in the form of articles with a detailed commentary explaining the purpose and operation of each article. Comments to each article provide illustrations, short cases that show how the rules are to operate in practice. Each article also has comparative notes surveying the national laws and other international provisions on the topic.

The part of the Uniform Commercial Code that is relevant to contracts is Article 2, which governs contracts for the sale (exchange for a price) of goods (tangible, movable objects). This part of the book will sometimes point out important differences between the UCC and the common law, but the UCC is discussed primarily in Chapters 14 and 15.

LO 8-3

Classification of Contracts

Contracts are classified in a number of different ways. Different classifications are useful for different purposes, as the following discussion demonstrates.

BILATERAL VERSUS UNILATERAL CONTRACTS

All contracts can be classified as either bilateral or unilateral. Knowing whether a contract is bilateral or unilateral is important because that classification determines when the offeree is legally bound to perform. Whether a contract is bilateral or unilateral depends on what response the offeror (the party proposing the contract) expects from the offeree (the person agreeing to or accepting the contract).

bilateral contract
A promise exchanged for a promise.

If the offeror wants a promise from the offeree to form a binding contract, the contract is a bilateral contract. A bilateral contract is commonly defined as a promise in exchange for a promise. As soon as the promises are exchanged, a contract is formed and the parties' legal obligations arise. For example, when Shannon promises to pay Gary $1,000 in exchange for his promise to paint her car on July 1, they have a bilateral contract. If either party fails to perform, the other may sue for breach.

unilateral contract
A promise exchanged for an act.

In a unilateral contract, the offeror wants a performance to form the contract. The offeror wants the offeree to do something, not promise to do something. The most common unilateral offer is a reward. If Jim loses his dog, he may post a sign stating "$50 reward for the safe return of my Poodle, Frenchie." If Rita calls Jim and says, "Don't worry, I'll find your dog," she is not making a contract because the unilateral offer calls for an action, not a promise. Once she finds Frenchie and takes the dog to Jim, a contract is formed and Jim must pay.

Just as the offeree is under no obligation to actually do the act called for by the offeror, the offeror may revoke the offer at any time before performance. However, to prevent injustice, once an offeree begins performance, the offeror must hold the offer open for a reasonable time to allow the offeree to complete the performance.

In the Case Opener, the plaintiff would argue that Pepsi appeared to be making an offer for a unilateral contract. In its television commercial, Pepsi promised to provide a prize for a performance, the presentation of a set number of points. By submitting the requisite number of points, the plaintiff believed he was accepting a unilateral offer.

EXPRESS VERSUS IMPLIED CONTRACTS

express contract
A contract in which all the terms are clearly set forth in either written or spoken words.

Contracts are classified as express or implied, depending on how they are created. Express contracts have all their terms clearly set forth in either written or spoken words. The contract in the Case Opener was an express contract, as the terms were set forth in the ad and the catalog.

Implied contracts, in contrast, arise not from words but from the conduct of the parties. For instance, when you have a dental emergency and your dentist pulls your severely infected tooth without prior negotiation about payment, or even any mention of payment, you have an implied contract for payment for his services.

As a general rule, three conditions must be met for the courts to find an implied, or as it is sometimes called, an *implied-in-fact,* contract. First, the plaintiff provided some property or service to the defendant. Second, the plaintiff expected to be paid for such property or service and a reasonable person in the position of the defendant would have expected to pay for such property or services. Third, the defendant had an opportunity to reject the property or services but did not.

implied contract

A contract that arises not from words of agreement but from the conduct of the parties.

QUASI-CONTRACTS

Quasi-contracts are sometimes called *implied-in-law contracts,* but they are not actually contracts. Rather, to prevent one party from being unjustly enriched at the expense of another, the courts impose contractual obligations on one of the parties, as if that party had entered into a contract.

For example, assume Jones hears a noise out in his driveway. He looks out and sees a group of workers apparently getting ready to resurface his driveway. The doorbell rings, and he does not answer it. He goes down into his basement office and stays there until the workers have gone and he has a resurfaced driveway. When he receives a bill from the paving company, he refuses to pay on grounds that he did not ask to have the driveway done. In such a case, where Jones knew that the company was getting ready to bestow on him a benefit to which he was not entitled, the court will probably impose a quasi-contract, requiring that Jones pay the paving company the fair market value of the resurfacing. Imposing such a duty prevents Jones from being unjustly enriched at the expense of the paving company.

There are limits to the doctrine, however; specifically, the enrichment must be unjust. Sometimes a benefit may simply be conferred on you because of a mistake by the other party, and the courts will not make people pay for others' mistakes. In our example, had Jones been out of town when his driveway was repaved, he would have just gotten lucky. The courts are not going to make him pay for the pavers' mistake when he could have done nothing to prevent the benefit from being bestowed on him.

quasi-contract

A court-imposed contractual obligation to prevent unjust enrichment.

VALID, VOID, VOIDABLE, AND UNENFORCEABLE CONTRACTS

What everyone hopes to enter into, of course, is a valid contract. A **valid** contract is one that contains all the legal elements of a contract, as set forth in Exhibit 8-1. As a general rule, a valid contract is one that will be enforced. However, sometimes a contract may be valid yet unenforceable.

A valid contract may be **unenforceable** when there is some law that prohibits the courts from enforcing it. For example, the statute of frauds, discussed in Chapter 12, requires that certain contracts must be evidenced by a writing before they can be enforced. Similarly, the statute of limitations mandates that an action for breach of contract must be brought within a set period of time, thereby limiting the enforceability of the contract.

A **void** contract is, in effect, not a contract at all. Either its object is illegal or it has some defect that is so serious that it is not a contract. If you entered into a contract with an assassin to kill your business law professor, that would be a void contract because it is obviously illegal to carry out the terms of the agreement.

A contract is **voidable** if one or both of the parties have the ability to either withdraw from the contract or enforce it. If the parties discover that the contract is voidable after one or both have partially performed, and one party chooses to have the contract terminated, both parties must return anything they had already exchanged under the agreement so that they will be returned to the condition they were in at the time they entered into the agreement.

Certain types of errors in the formation of a contract lead to its being voidable. Typically, the person who can avoid the contract is the person whom the court is attempting to protect, or the party the court believes might be taken advantage of by the other party. For example, contracts

valid

A term applied to a contract that includes all four elements of a contract: agreement (offer and acceptance), consideration, contractual capacity, and legal object.

unenforceable

A term applied to a contract that, because of a law, cannot be enforced by the courts.

void

A term applied to a contract that is not valid because its object is illegal or it has some defect that is so serious that it is not a contract.

voidable

A term applied to a contract that one or both parties have the ability to either withdraw from or enforce.

by minors are usually voidable by the minor, as discussed in Chapter 10. Contracts entered into as a result of fraud, duress, or undue influence—a problem with the validity of the acceptance, as described in Chapter 11—may be avoided by the innocent party.

EXECUTED VERSUS EXECUTORY CONTRACTS

executed
A term applied to a contract in which all of the terms have been fully performed.

executory
A term applied to a contract in which not all of the terms have been fully performed.

Once all the terms of the contract have been fully performed, the contract is said to have been **executed.** As long as some of the duties under the contract have not yet been performed, the contract is considered **executory.** For example, if Randolph hires Carmine to paint his garage on Saturday for $800, with $200 paid as a down payment and the balance due on completion of the job, the contract becomes executory as soon as the agreement is reached. When the down payment has been made and the painting is halfway completed, the contract is still executory. Once the painting has been finished and the final payment made, the contract is an executed contract.

LO 8-4

FORMAL VERSUS INFORMAL CONTRACTS

formal contract
A contract that must have a special form or must be created in a specific manner.

contract under seal
A contract that has a seal certifying its legality. Such contracts require no consideration for them to be legal.

recognizance
An obligation in which a party acknowledges in court that he or she will perform some specified act and/or pay a price on failure to do so.

letter of credit
A binding document that a buyer can request from a bank to guarantee that the payment for goods will be made to the seller.

negotiable instrument
A written document signed by a person who makes an unconditional promise to pay a specific sum of money on demand or at a certain time to the holder of the instrument; an acceptable medium for exchanging value from one person to another.

Contracts may also be classified as formal or informal. **Formal contracts** are those that have a special form or must be created in a specific manner. The Restatement (Second) of Contracts identifies the following four types of formal contracts: (1) contracts under seal, (2) recognizances, (3) letters of credit, and (4) negotiable instruments.

When people hear the term *formal contract,* what often comes to mind is a **contract under seal.** The term *under seal* comes from the days when a contract was literally sealed by a piece of soft wax into which an impression was made. Today, sealed contracts may still be literally sealed with wax or some other soft substance, but they are more likely to be simply identified with the word *seal* or the letters *L.S.* (an abbreviation for *locus sigilli,* which means "the place for the seal") at the end of the document. Preprinted contract forms with a seal printed on them can also be purchased today, and parties using such documents are presumed, without evidence to the contrary, to be adopting the seal for the contract.

States today do not require that contracts be under seal. However, 10 states still allow a contract without consideration to be enforced if it is under seal.

A **recognizance** arises when a party acknowledges in court that he or she will perform some specified act and/or pay a price on failure to do so. An example of a recognizance is a bond used as bail in a criminal case. The person agrees to return to court for trial or forfeit the bond.

A **letter of credit** is an agreement by the person or institution that issues the letter to pay a sum of money on receipt of an invoice and other documents (typically documents indicating that the goods were insured against damage in transit). The Uniform Commercial Code governs letters of credit.

A **negotiable instrument** is a written document signed by a person who makes an unconditional promise to pay a specific sum of money on demand or at a certain time to the holder of the instrument. The most common forms of negotiable instruments are checks, notes, drafts, and certificates of deposit. They are governed primarily by the UCC. (Negotiable instruments are discussed in greater detail in Chapters 16 and 17.)

Any contract that is not a formal contract is an **informal contract,** also called a *simple contract.* Informal contracts may in fact be quite complex, but they are called "simple" because no formalities are required in making them.

LO 8-5

The Agreement

informal contract
A contract that requires no formalities.

The first element of a contract is the agreement. As noted earlier, this chapter focuses on contracts governed by common law, that is, contracts other than those for the sale of goods. Under the common law, the agreement begins when one party, the offeror, makes an offer to another party, the offeree.

Elements of the Offer

An offer has three elements. Under the common law, these elements are intent, definite and certain terms, and communication to the offeree.

INTENT

The first element of the offer is **intent.** The offeror must manifest an intent to be bound by the offeree's acceptance. Contracts are interpreted using an objective standard, meaning that the courts are concerned with only the party's outward manifestations of his or her intent, not what is going on in that party's mind. The courts interpret the words and actions of the parties the way a reasonable person would interpret them.

intent
The intended purpose or goal of an action, especially in a contract.

Thus, if an individual is clearly joking or speaking out in anger, the reasonable person would not think that the individual seriously intended to make an offer and the courts would consequently not treat the words as an offer. If someone attempts to accept such an offer, the courts will not find that a contract has been made.

Sometimes an offeror may try to avoid a contract by later claiming that he was only joking when he made the offer, but the courts are not interested in one's hidden intent. As Case 8-1 demonstrates, if you joke too well, you may find yourself in an unwanted contract.

CASE 8-1

LUCY v. ZEHMER
SUPREME COURT OF APPEALS OF VIRGINIA
196 Va. 493, 84 S.E.2d 516 (1954)

FACTS: *Plaintiffs W. O. and J. C. Lucy had wanted to purchase Ferguson Farm from the Zehmers for at least eight years. One night, Lucy stopped by the establishment the Zehmers operated and said that he bet Zehmer wouldn't accept $50,000 for the place. Zehmer replied that he would, but he bet that Lucy would not pay $50,000 for it. Over the course of the evening, the parties drank whiskey and engaged in casual conversation, with the talk repeatedly returning to the sale of Ferguson Farm. Eventually Lucy got Zehmer to draw up a contract for the sale of the farm for $50,000.*

When Lucy later attempted to enforce the agreement, Zehmer refused to complete the sale, arguing that he had been drunk and that the agreement to sell the property had been made in jest. Lucy sued to enforce the agreement.

ISSUE: Had Lucy and Zehmer entered into a legally binding agreement?

REASONING: The mental assent of the parties is not a requirement for the formation of a contract. If the words or other acts of one of the parties have but one reasonable meaning, that party's undisclosed intention is immaterial

unless the other party somehow knows that the party does not mean what his words and actions would clearly indicate to any reasonable observer.

In this case, not only did Lucy believe that Zehmer was serious when he drew up the contract, but there was no evidence to indicate that any action taken by Zehmer would have indicated that he was not serious. When Zehmer asked his wife to sign the writing that he drew up containing the terms of the sale, he whispered to her that he was joking, but whispered so quietly that Lucy could not and did not hear it. What happened appeared to be a good-faith offer and a good-faith acceptance, followed by the execution and apparent delivery of a written contract. Therefore, the parties would be held to their outward manifestations of entering into a binding agreement.

DECISION AND REMEDY: The parties had entered into a binding agreement, and the court enforced the agreement.

SIGNIFICANCE OF THE CASE: This case demonstrates that the courts look at the circumstances surrounding the alleged making of a contract and focus

on the outward manifestations of a person's intent. It clearly sends the message that people need to be careful when joking about entering into a contract because a person who jokes too well might find herself or himself bound to an agreement that she or he did not really want to make.

CRITICAL THINKING

Why must a joke be visibly a joke to a reasonable observer for there to be no acceptance?

ETHICAL DECISION MAKING

What stakeholders are being protected by the reasoning that supports the rule the court applied in this case?

Preliminary Negotiations An invitation to negotiate or an expression of possible interest in an exchange is not an offer. For example, if Rachael asked Bill whether he would sell his car for $5,000, she is not making an offer; she is just inquiring about his potential willingness to sell. Likewise, when a firm or government entity requests bids for a construction project, the request is just an invitation for contractors to make offers. Thus the bids would be the offers.

Advertisements Another illustration of the invitation to make an offer is the advertisement. If a custom furniture maker places an advertisement in the paper that reads, "Old-fashioned, hand-crafted cedar rocking chairs only $250 the first week in May," the store is merely inviting potential customers to come to the store and offer $250 for a rocker. Because no reasonable person would expect the store to be able to sell a rocking chair to every person who might see the ad, the court would interpret the intent of the store as being to invite readers to make an offer.

Under limited circumstances, however, an ad can be treated as an offer. If it appears from the wording of the ad that the store did in fact intend to make an offer, the courts will treat it as an offer. In general, when the ad specifies a limited quantity and provides a specific means by which the offer can be accepted, the courts will treat the ad as an offer, as demonstrated by the Case Nugget.

The plaintiff in the Case Opener tried to rely on the *Lefkowitz* case to argue that the Pepsi commercial was an offer because it was "clear, definite, explicit and left nothing to negotiation." After all, the commercial clearly stated that 7 million points earned a Harrier jet, and the catalog provided an additional means of buying the points for cash.

The court in that case, however, found that the commercial could not be regarded as sufficiently definite because it specifically reserved the details of the offer to a separate writing, the catalog. Also, the commercial itself made no mention of the steps a potential offeree would be required to take to accept the alleged offer of a Harrier jet.

The court further found that the only offer in this scenario was the plaintiff's letter of March 27, 1996, along with the order form and the appropriate number of Pepsi points. As Pepsi rejected this offer with its letter, there was no contract.

To prevent possible bait-and-switch advertising, some states have consumer protection laws requiring that advertisers state in their ads either that quantities of the item are limited to the first *X* number of people or that rain checks will be available if the item sells out.

CASE Nugget

When Is an Ad an Offer?

Lefkowitz v. Great Minneapolis Surplus Store, Inc.
Supreme Court of Minnesota

251 Minn. 188, 86 N.W.2d 689 (1957)

In this case, the defendant had published a newspaper announcement stating: "Saturday 9 AM Sharp, 3 Brand New Fur Coats, Worth up to $1,000.00, First Come First Served $1 Each." Morris Lefkowitz arrived at the store, dollar in hand, but was informed that under the defendant's "house rules," the offer was open to ladies but not gentlemen. The court ruled that because the plaintiff had fulfilled all the terms of the advertisement and the advertisement was specific and left nothing open for negotiation, a contract had been formed.

From this case came the often-quoted exception to the rule that advertisements do not create any power of acceptance in potential offerees: an advertisement that is "clear, definite, and explicit, and leaves nothing open for negotiation." In that circumstance, "it constitutes an offer, acceptance of which will complete the contract."

Auctions Another situation in which what seems to be an offer may not be is the auction. When a person places a good with an auctioneer for sale by auction, is the seller making an offer or is the bidder? The answer depends on what kind of auction is taking place.

If nothing is stated to the contrary in the terms of the auction, an auction is presumed to be *with reserve.* In an auction with reserve, the seller is merely expressing an intent to receive offers. The auctioneer may withdraw the item from auction at any time before the auctioneer's hammer falls, signaling the acceptance of the bid. Similarly, at any time before the hammer falls, the bidder may also revoke the bid.

In an auction *without reserve,* the seller is treated as making an offer to accept the highest bid. Thus, the seller must accept the highest bid. Not surprisingly, very few auctions are without reserve.

DEFINITE AND CERTAIN TERMS

Under the common law, the terms of the offer must be definite and certain. In other words, all the material terms must be included. The *material terms* are those terms that allow a court to determine what the damages are in the event that one of the parties breaches the contract.

Sometimes an offer contains not the material term itself but a method for determining the term. For example, Guy's Sailboats is building Sara a sailboat, and the parties want to make it possible for her to pay one-third of the price of the boat in advance, one-third on delivery, and one-third in 12 monthly payments, with interest, beginning a month after delivery. Rather than stipulating an interest rate to be charged on the monthly payments, the contract might specify an external standard according to which the interest rate would be set through the course of the 12-month payment period.

The question of whether the terms of an alleged offer were adequate for the formation of a valid contract often arises in cases where one party believes that a contract had been formed and the other believes that there had been no contract because the terms of the alleged offer were not definite enough. That issue is the focus of Case 8-2.

JANKY v. BATISTATOS, LAKE COUNTY CONVENTIONS & VISITATIONS BUREAU ET AL.

U.S. DISTRICT COURT FOR THE NORTHERN DISTRICT OF INDIANA, HAMMOND DIVISION

559 F. Supp. 2d 923 (2008)

FACTS: *Janky originally sued defendant Lake County Conventions & Visitations Bureau (LCCVB), Henry Farag, and Street Gold Records in 2003 over the rightful use and ownership of a song written by Janky titled "Wonders of Indiana." She alleged primarily that the song had been sold to LCCVB by Farag, her one-time band-mate, without her knowledge. The jury initially awarded Janky $100,000 for LCCVB's copyright infringement, which LCCVB appealed. The parties litigated through two federal cases, three appeals, one judicial recusal, and several court-imposed sanctions. In 2007, LCCVB and Janky appeared to be on the verge of agreeing on a settlement.*

On November 20, 2007, Janky's attorney sent an e-mail to one of LCCVB's attorneys, providing a list of terms for settling, including the plaintiff's withdrawal of both complaints and one appeal and LCCVB's withdrawal of one appeal, as well as stipulating all parties' responsibility for their own attorney fees. On December 2, 2007, the LCCVB lawyer responded via e-mail accepting the offer with the inclusion of a stipulated "mutual global release."

In January 2008, attorneys for the defendant sent a draft to Janky of what the mutual global release would entail. This list included that Janky post a $100,000 bond to secure against future claims against the defendants, that Janky admit she was in error in pursuing litigation, that Janky pay all court sanctions, and that she convey ownership of the disputed song to the defendants. Janky filed a motion to enforce the settlement on February 15, 2008, claiming that the December 2 e-mail constituted acceptance of the settlement offer.

ISSUE: Did a valid settlement agreement exist between the defendant LCCVB and the plaintiff?

REASONING: Taking the December 2 e-mail as a stand-alone document, the court found that the contract did not provide specific-enough material terms for the court to determine damages. The December 2 e-mail explicitly alluded to future documents that would detail the meaning of the term *mutual global release* rather than defining the term within the e-mail. In the words of the court:

> Along with needing to state all essential terms, preliminary agreements which incorporate future written agreements are only enforceable if the essential terms they do include are definite. Wolvos, 668 N.E.2d at 675. . . . Without definite terms, the Court is left without anything to enforce. Definiteness is necessary because "the contract must provide a basis for determining the existence of a breach and for giving an appropriate remedy." McLinden v. Coco, 765 N.E.2d 606, 613 (Ind. Ct. App. 2002).

DECISION AND REMEDY: A valid contract did not exist because the term *mutual global release* is not definite enough to be enforceable.

SIGNIFICANCE OF THE CASE: This case illustrates the importance of making sure that all the essential terms of a proposed contract are definite and, if necessary, defined in the offer.

CRITICAL THINKING

What other reasons might the court have to find the contract invalid?

ETHICAL DECISION MAKING

Think about the conduct of the parties in this case. How much blame should the parties receive for their conduct? How might the outcome of this case have been different if the parties had acted in accordance with the Golden Rule?

COMMUNICATION TO THE OFFEREE

The offer must be communicated to the offeree or to the offeree's agent. Only the offeree to whom the offer was directed can accept the offer. If Bill overhears Sam offer to sell his car to Helen for $5,000, he cannot walk over and form a contract by accepting the offer. If he says to Sam, "I'll give you $5,000 for your car," he is not accepting the offer but, rather, is making a new offer.

Termination of the Offer LO 8-6

At some point in time, offers terminate; when an offer terminates, it can no longer be accepted to form a binding contract. There are five ways to terminate an offer: revocation by the offeror, rejection by the offeree, death or incapacity of the offeror, destruction or subsequent illegality of the subject matter of the offer, and lapse of time or failure of other conditions stated in the offer.

REVOCATION BY THE OFFEROR

The offeror is said to be the "master of his offer" and, as such, can revoke it at any time, even if he says he will hold the offer open for a stated period of time. If Jim sends Carol a letter offering to mow her yard every week during the summer for the price of $20 a week as long as she responds to his offer within the next month, he can still change his mind and tell her at any time before she responds that he is no longer interested in working for her, thereby revoking his offer.

If a person wishes to ensure that an offer will in fact be held open for a set period of time, the person may do so by entering into an option contract with the offeror. An **option contract** is an agreement whereby the offeree gives the offeror a piece of consideration in exchange for the offeror's agreement to hold the offer open for the specified period of time.

There is no requirement as to the value of the consideration. If the consideration is money, the parties may agree that if the offer is eventually accepted and a contract is formed, the consideration for the option contract will become part of the payment for the contract. This situation frequently arises in contracts involving real estate. Jones may be considering opening a restaurant and would like to have the option of purchasing a lot owned by Smith, so he gives Smith $1,000 for a 30-day option to purchase the lot, with the provision that the $1,000 will be deducted from the purchase price if Jones purchases the property. In the event that Jones does not buy the property, Smith will keep the $1,000.

The UCC imposes an additional limitation on the offeror's ability to revoke the offer. A promise to hold an offer for the sale of a good open for a specified period cannot be revoked if it is made in writing and signed by a merchant.

> To see how the six components of communication, which you studied in your marketing class, would be relevant to entering into a contract, go to the **Connecting to the Core** activity on the text's website at www.mhhe.com/kubasekess2e.

As a general rule, the revocation of an offer is effective when it is received by the offeree. Because of this rule, if it is really important to the offeror to know that his offer has been revoked, he should personally deliver the revocation to the offeree.

option contract
An agreement whereby the offeree gives the offeror a piece of consideration in exchange for the offeror's agreement to hold the offer open for the specified period of time.

REJECTION BY THE OFFEREE

The second means by which an offer can be terminated is rejection by the offeree. Regardless of how long the offer was stated to be open, once the offeree rejects it, it is terminated. In our earlier example, if Carol calls Jim and says that she is not interested in his working for her this summer or any summer because of the poor quality of the work he has done for her in the past but then calls him back an hour later to say that she has changed her mind and would like to hire him in accordance with his proposed terms, it is too late. There is no offer for her to accept because her rejection terminated the offer.

DEATH OR INCAPACITY OF THE OFFEROR

The offer terminates immediately if the offeror dies or loses the legal capacity to enter into the contract. This termination occurs even if the offeree does not know of the terminating event. The exception to this rule occurs when the parties had already entered into an option contract to hold the offer open for a set period of time. If an option contract exists, the administrator of the offeror's estate or the guardian of the offeror must hold the offer open until it expires in accordance with the option contract.

DESTRUCTION OR SUBSEQUENT ILLEGALITY OF THE SUBJECT MATTER

If the subject matter of the offer is destroyed or becomes illegal, the offer immediately terminates. For example, if Jamie offers Bill a job managing the riverboat casino he plans to open on January 1 but, before Bill accepts the offer, the state decides to no longer allow riverboat casinos to operate in the state, the offer of employment terminates.

LAPSE OF TIME OR FAILURE OF ANOTHER CONDITION SPECIFIED IN THE OFFER

As noted earlier, the offeror has the power to revoke the offer at any time, even if the offer states that it will be held open a set amount of time. But if the offer states that it will be held open for only a certain time, the offer will terminate when that time expires. In the absence of a time condition in the offer, the offer will expire after the lapse of a reasonable amount of time. What constitutes a reasonable amount of time varies, depending on the subject matter of the offer. For example, an offer by a retailer to purchase seasonal goods from a wholesaler would lapse before an offer to purchase goods that could be easily sold all year long.

Elements of the Acceptance

Once an offer has been made, the offeree has the power to accept that offer and form a contract. In examining the acceptance under the common law, the basic requirements for a valid acceptance parallel those for a valid offer. There should be a manifestation of intent to be bound by the acceptance to the contract, agreement to the definite and certain terms of the offer, and communication to the offeror.

MANIFESTATION OF INTENT TO BE BOUND TO THE CONTRACT

In general, there are two ways an offeree can manifest her or his intent to enter into the contract: by performance or by a return promise. The offeree must either do something or say something to form the contract.

Recall the distinction between a bilateral contract and a unilateral contract. If the offer is for a unilateral contract, the offeree can accept only by providing the requested performance. If Bill offered to pay $500 to anyone who returned his lost dog to him, Mary could accept the offer only by returning the dog. Bill did not want her promise, and if she called and promised to return the dog to him, that promise would have no legal effect because the only way to accept a unilateral offer is by performance.

With a bilateral contract, what the offeror wants to form the contract is not performance but, rather, a return promise. Sometimes, however, it is not clear whether the offeror wants performance or a return promise. In such a case, the offeree has the option of either performing or making a return promise.

Silence as a Form of Acceptance Silence, as a general rule, cannot be used to form a contract. For example, Lisa and Marie both work at a local diner where the manager is very flexible and lets the waitresses trade shifts. Marie calls Lisa and leaves her a voice-mail message saying,

Contracts in Japan

The Japanese tend to view contracts as ongoing relationships in which the parties work with each other to smooth out any problems that arise in performance of the contract. The Japanese tend to be suspicious of long, detailed contracts. They have a distinct preference for short, flexible contracts that leave a number of terms to be decided later.

When negotiating a contract with a Japanese businessperson, an American businessperson must recognize how the Japanese will interpret his attempts to include more details in the agreement. The American should think about which details are essential for inclusion.

"I can't work my three night shifts this week. If you can cover them for me, I'll pay you an extra $40 on top of the money you'll receive from the boss for working my shifts. If I don't hear from you by 7 p.m. tomorrow, I'll assume we have a deal and you will work for me. Thanks so much!" If Lisa does not call back, no contract has been formed because silence under these circumstances would not constitute an acceptance,

The Restatement of Contracts, however, offers three circumstances under which silence can be an acceptance. First, the offeree receives the benefits of the offered services with reasonable opportunity to reject them and knowledge that some form of compensation is expected, yet the offeree remains silent. Second, the offeror tells the offeree that silence or inaction will constitute an acceptance, and the offeree, by remaining silent, *intends* to accept. Third, the parties, by their previous course of dealing with each other, have established a pattern of behavior whereby it would be reasonable to assume that silence was intended to communicate acceptance. For example, a wholesaler and retailer have a long-standing relationship in which the wholesaler routinely ships a certain type of merchandise to the retailer, who rejects a shipment if it does not meet his needs. After such a pattern of behavior has been established, it is reasonable for the wholesaler to assume that when a shipment is not sent back, the retailer means to accept it.

ACCEPTANCE OF DEFINITE AND CERTAIN TERMS: THE MIRROR-IMAGE RULE

When a bilateral contract is being formed under the common law, the mirror-image rule applies to the acceptance. The **mirror-image rule** says that the terms of the acceptance must mirror the terms of the offer. If the terms of the acceptance do not mirror the terms of the offer, no contract is formed. Instead, the attempted acceptance is a counteroffer.

The mirror-image rule has caused a significant amount of trouble for businesses because often a buyer would make an offer on one form that contained not only the essential terms of the contract but also a number of additional, somewhat minor terms. Generally, the offer was on a standard form that had a place where the essential terms were written in. The seller would often return his standard form with its preprinted terms, along with the essential terms written in to match the terms of the offer. The problem was that because these preprinted forms did not match, there was legally no contract. If both parties performed their contracts, no problems arose; but the fact that there was no contract meant that on occasion one party could decide to simply not perform, leaving the other party with no remedy. Or, if the parties did perform, the buyer might perform according to the terms on the buyer's form and be sued for breach by the seller, who believed that the terms on the seller's form were the terms of the agreement.

To eliminate this problem of the "battle of the forms," UCC Section 2-207 significantly modified the mirror-image rule by providing that, as a general rule, an offeree may include in the acceptance terms that are additional to or different from the terms of the offer as long as (1) the offeror did not explicitly state in the offer that all terms of the offer must be accepted exactly as proposed; (2) the offeror does not promptly reject the new terms on receipt of the acceptance; and (3) the new terms do not materially change the terms of the original offer.

mirror-image rule
The principle which holds that the terms of the acceptance must mirror the terms of the offer; if the terms of the acceptance do not mirror the terms of the offer, no contract is formed and the attempted acceptance is a counteroffer.

In the case of additional terms—terms related to issues not addressed in the original offer—if none of the foregoing conditions occur, a contract is formed and the terms of the agreement are those of the acceptance, as long as the parties are merchants. If the parties are not merchants, the additional terms are merely proposals for additions to the contract and must be accepted by the offeror.

If the terms of the acceptance are different from those in the offer, various states treat the terms differently. In most states, the terms are said to cancel each other out, and the courts then look to the UCC for neutral terms to insert into the contract.

COMMUNICATION TO THE OFFEROR

An offeror has the power to control the means by which the acceptance is communicated, and if the offeror specifies that only a certain means of communication will be accepted, then only that method of communication forms a valid offer. Suppose, for example, that Jennifer offers to paint Bill's car for $500 but says that he must accept the offer by telephone before midnight on Thursday. If he sends her an e-mail Thursday morning accepting her offer, there is no valid contract. Even though e-mail might be a valid means of accepting a contract offer if no means is specified, when the offer is limited to a specific means of communicating the acceptance, only that means results in a valid contract. Thus Bill's attempted acceptance was simply a new offer.

If no means of communicating the acceptance is specified, any reasonable means is generally acceptable. Telephone, telegraph, mail, fax, and e-mail are all valid means of accepting an offer. If a person drafting an offer wants acceptance to be only by a particular means, the offer must make it clear that only a certain means is allowed. As Case 8-3 illustrates, courts will carefully interpret provisions specifying the means of acceptance.

CASE 8-3

OSPREY L.L.C. v. KELLY-MOORE PAINT CO.

SUPREME COURT OF OKLAHOMA

984 P.2d 194, 1999 Okla. LEXIS 64

FACTS: *The plaintiff leased commercial premises to the defendant. The lease required that the defendant provide notice of its intent to renew the lease at least six months prior to the lease's expiration, and notice was to be given in writing and delivered personally or through registered first-class mail. The defendant attempted to extend the lease by faxing a renewal letter on the last day of the six-month notification period. Although fax records and telephone records confirmed that the fax was transmitted, the plaintiff denied receiving the fax.*

The plaintiff refused to renew the lease and demanded that the defendant vacate the premises at the end of the current lease term. The defendant refused to vacate the premises, so the plaintiff filed an action for forcible entry and detainer.

The trial court found that the faxed notice effectively renewed the lease, and the appeals court reversed. The supreme court granted certiorari.

ISSUE: In this case, was the fax of a notice of renewal on a lease sufficient communication when the lease contract specified that renewal must be delivered personally or by mail?

REASONING: The court noted that the issue of whether faxes can constitute sufficient notice of acceptance had been decided by a number of different courts with varying results. The majority had generally recognized that, despite the contention that there must be strict compliance with the notice terms of a lease option agreement, use of an alternative method does not render the notice defective if the substituted method performed the same function or served the same purpose as the authorized method.

The court in this case agreed with the reasoning of Kelly-Moore that language in a contract is given its plain and ordinary meaning, unless some technical term is used in a manner meant to convey a specific technical concept.

The lease in this case specified that notice of acceptance "shall" be in writing and that delivery "may" be either in person or by certified or registered mail. Given the ordinary interpretation of *shall* as mandatory and *may* as permissive, the notice of acceptance of the lease at issue must be in writing, and that writing may be by the methods specified but may also be through other modes of transmission that would be just as effective.

The purpose of providing notice by personal delivery or registered mail is to ensure the delivery of the notice and to settle any dispute that might arise between the parties concerning whether the notice was received. A substituted method of notice that performs the same function and serves the same purpose as an authorized method of notice is not defective.

In this case, the contract provided that time was of the essence. The fax activity report and telephone company records confirm that the fax was transmitted successfully and that it was sent to Osprey's correct facsimile number on the last day of the deadline to extend the lease. The fax provided immediate written communication similar to personal delivery and, like a telegram, would be timely if it were properly transmitted before the expiration of the deadline to renew. Kelly-Moore's use of the fax served the same function and the same purpose as the two methods suggested by the lease, and it was transmitted before the expiration of the deadline to renew.

DECISION AND REMEDY: The court concluded that the faxed delivery of the written notice to renew the commercial lease was sufficient to exercise timely the renewal option of the lease given that this method of delivery fulfilled the same purpose as the permissive methods of delivery specified in the lease. The court therefore reversed in favor of the defendant.

SIGNIFICANCE OF THE CASE: The case illustrates that sometimes, in interpreting a contract's specifications for means of acceptance, the court may be willing to look beyond the methods of delivery identified in the contract and instead focus on the intent of the parties in identifying potential means of communicating the acceptance.

CRITICAL THINKING

What line of reasoning might another court have followed to lead to a different outcome in this case?

ETHICAL DECISION MAKING

Consider Osprey's denial of receiving the fax in question from Kelly-Moore. If this denial does amount to a false claim, what is the motivation for the commission of this falsehood?

The Mailbox Rule Because not all acceptances are made in person, a rule needed to be developed to determine the point at which an acceptance made through the mail became effective. The courts settled on the **mailbox rule,** which provides that an acceptance is valid when it is placed in the mailbox, whereas a revocation is effective only when received by the offeree. Today, the mailbox rule has been expanded to apply to faxes in some jurisdictions, with courts holding that once the fax has been transmitted, the acceptance is effective.

The Effect of an Acceptance after a Rejection As previously stated, if an acceptance is received after a rejection is received, the acceptance is not valid because the rejection terminated the offer. However, sometimes a rejection is dispatched, but before it is received, the acceptance is communicated to the offeror. In that case, a valid contract has been formed because the rejection is not effective until it is received. Suppose Brenda e-mails an offer to Harry, and he puts a rejection in the mail. Then, before the rejection is received, Harry calls Brenda and tells her he accepts. A valid contract has been formed, and the rejection will have no effect when it is received. However, if the telephone call had been made after Brenda had received the rejection, there would have been no contract.

mailbox rule

The principle which holds that an acceptance is valid when it is placed in the mailbox, whereas a revocation is effective only when received by the offeree. In some jurisdictions the mailbox rule has been expanded to faxes.

E-COMMERCE and the Law

The Mailbox Rule and E-Commerce

The future of the mailbox rule is in question, at least as it applies to electronic acceptances. In the case of computer information transactions, such as acceptances via e-mail, the law is clear: Electronic acceptance is effective when received. For all other transactions, though, the law is unclear.

In a recent article, Valerie Watnick, a professor of business law at Baruch College, offered reasons why the mailbox rule should apply as a default rule in e-commerce cases in which the law is unclear. She offers justifications for her view:

1. The mailbox rule fosters certainty and helps courts avoid complex factual inquiries that are likely in electronic acceptance cases.

2. The mailbox rule is practical in that it supplies the date the contract was formed without sorting out circular communications.

3. Electronic communication is very much like mail, only faster. It is not instantaneous. Messages are broken into "packets" of information, which are sent along different routes to a final destination. Sometimes, it takes hours for a complete message to reach its final destination.

Watnick concludes: "[A] dispatch rule in electronic contracting will allow parties to freely contract through electronic means, without regard to whether both parties have knowledge of the existence of the contract at the moment of its formation." Do you agree with Watnick?

Source: Valerie Watnick, "The Electronic Formation of Contracts and the Common Law 'Mailbox Rule,'" *Baylor Law Review* 50 (2004), p. 175.

SUMMARY

The Definition of a Contract	Contracts at their simplest level are legally enforceable agreements. A *valid contract* is generally viewed as one that has the following elements: agreement, consideration, legal object, and parties with legal capacity.
Sources of Contract Law	There are two sources of contract law: the Uniform Commercial Code and state common law. The Uniform Commercial Code, in Article 2, governs contracts for the sale of goods. All other contracts are also governed by the UCC.
Classification of Contracts	Contracts may be classified in a number of ways. Every contract is either unilateral or bilateral; express or implied; valid, voidable, or void; executed or executory; and formal or informal.
The Agreement	The *agreement* is the first element of a contract. It begins when one party, the offeror, makes an offer to another party, the offeree.
Elements of the Offer	A valid offer contains the manifestation of the offeror's intent to be bound to the definite and certain terms that are communicated to the offeree.
Termination of the Offer	An offer can be terminated by revocation by the offeror, rejection by the offeree, death or incapacity of the offeror, destruction or subsequent illegality of the subject matter of the offer, or lapse of time or failure of other conditions stated in the offer.
Elements of the Acceptance	An acceptance is valid when a manifestation of intent to be bound to the terms of the offer is communicated to the offeror by the offeree.

Point/Counterpoint

Recovery based on quasi-contract allows the court to impose liability on a party that did not enter into a contract; three conditions must exist: (1) A benefit was conferred on the defendant; (2) the defendant appreciated the benefit; and (3) because of the circumstances under which the defendant received the benefit, it would be unjust to allow the defendant to retain the benefit without compensating the party that conferred it.

Does the Third Prong of the Test for Imposition of Recovery in a Quasi-Contract Unjustifiably Limit the Court's Ability to Impose Relief Where It Is Needed?

YES	NO
Limiting the application of the doctrine to those circumstances in which the imposition of liability is required to prevent unjust enrichment is unfair. Looking at the case law, the "circumstances" that justify imposition of liability all focus on what the recipient of the benefit did. If he did not in some way acquiesce to the imposition of the benefit, no liability can be imposed. Such a limitation makes an artificial distinction based on the point in time at which the recipient discovers the conferral of the benefit. If there was some possible way for the recipient to have prevented the conferral, he has to pay; but if he had no way to prevent it, he does not have to pay. This distinction sounds fair enough at first glance, but it overlooks the fact that in either situation the recipient gets something he did not pay for and the other party conferred a benefit for no compensation. What if the benefit is really significant? What if ABC Construction builds a new garage for the Smiths, who were on vacation, instead of for their neighbors, who ordered the garage? Is it really fair for the Smiths to get that garage for free?	The limitation is a necessary one, preventing those knowledgeable about the law from taking unfair advantage of those with less knowledge. While it may seem unfair for someone to receive a benefit from another party when she did not give any value for that benefit, if she did not ask for the benefit and did not encourage the other party to provide it, there is no justification for making her pay for what is essentially the acting party's mistake. If we presume that neither party is acting with the intent of getting something undeserved, the recipient is still the most innocent party in the situation and, as such, should not be required to pay for the other party's mistake. Further, while we say that one party is receiving a benefit, that recipient may be receiving a legal "benefit" that is of no value to her. It seems especially unfair to make someone pay for a "benefit" that she had no desire to obtain in the first place, even though many others may find that benefit highly desirable.

Questions & Problems

1. Explain why the first question a person should ask when getting ready to analyze a contract problem is, "Is this alleged contract a contract for the sale of a good?"

2. What is the difference between an offer for a unilateral contract and an offer for a bilateral contract? Why might that difference be important to understand?

3. What must a party prove to recover under the theory of quasi-contract?

4. What is the mirror-image rule?

5. What is the mailbox rule?

6. Anthony Maglica and Claire Halasz, as boyfriend and girlfriend, lived together, held themselves out as a married couple, and acted as companions toward each other. In fact, Claire changed her last name to "Maglica," even though the couple never married. Together, the couple worked in a business owned solely by Anthony, although Claire participated in a substantial part of the work. The company, Mag Instrument, was incorporated in 1974, and all shares went to Anthony. However, both Anthony and Claire were paid equal salaries. After the company began manufacturing flashlights, the company grew rapidly, now exceeding hundreds of millions of dollars in net worth. In 1992, Claire and Anthony separated, and subsequently Claire filed suit against Anthony for breach of contract and claimed damages under a theory of quasi-contract. No contract existed between Anthony and Claire. Does Claire have any remedy under a theory of quasi-contract? If so, what must she prove? [*Maglica v. Maglica,* 1998 Cal. App. LEXIS 750.]

7. Business Systems agreed to provide supplies to IBM as a subcontractor to a deal to update computer systems of the Chicago Transit Authority. The budget for this deal was set at $3.6 million; however, only $2.2 million of services were actually performed under the contract. Business Systems sued IBM, believing that it was entitled to an additional $1.4 million that it had not received in the performance of the project. As evidence of contract, Business Systems produced a

spreadsheet detailing the ways in which the $3.6 million would be spent and an e-mail claiming "mutual agreement" to the $3.6 million budget. IBM claimed that it had performed all of its obligations under the contract and that Business Systems was not entitled to the $1.4 million because there was no contract as to the specific amount that Business Systems was entitled to. Do you think that Business Systems was entitled to the $1.4 million? What consideration was exchanged between the two parties? [*Business Systems v. IBM,* 547 F.3d 882 (2008).]

8. Theresa Polk discussed selling her residence and 181 acres of land to BHRGU Avon Properties, LLC. Avon presented an offer for the land. Polk responded by providing two counteroffers, both stipulating that Avon accept before February 7, 2005, at 5 p.m. Avon responded by providing an offer that materially changed terms in the counteroffers and delivered it before the February 7 deadline. Avon also delivered a $25,000 check. Polk's attorney accepted the check but later wrote "VOID" on it instead of cashing it. Avon filed a suit seeking specific performance. The trial court found in favor of Avon, determining that the counteroffers constituted option contracts. Polk appealed, arguing that the counteroffers were not enforceable contracts because they lacked consideration and were therefore offers that required Avon's acceptance. Avon argued that the $25,000 check constituted consideration for the option contracts, making the contracts enforceable. Do you believe that an option contract was formed? Why or why not? [*Polk v. BHRGU Avon Properties, LLC,* 2006 Fla. App. LEXIS 20760.]

9. Dr. Griffith allowed his life insurance to lapse after May 15, 2007. According to US Life's life insurance policy, he was granted a 31-day grace period after which he would be able to reinstate his insurance by paying the balance of the unpaid bill and receiving written approval from US Life of the required evidence of insurability. According to a reminder notice, Griffen had 60 days to make a full payment. On or around June 15, 2007, the insurance provider sent Griffith a lapse notice which included a reinstatement form and a self-addressed envelope and required that payment and the reinstatement form be received by the policy provider within 30 days from the lapsed coverage. On July 23, 2007, Griffith electronically directed payment to American Medical Association Insurance Agency (AMAIA), which acted as a third-party administrator for US Life. AMAIA acted on US Life's behalf to bill and collect premiums. AMAIA received the check from Griffith on July 30, 2007. On July 28, 2007, Griffith was kneeling beside his bicycle at Bethany Beach,

Delaware, when he was struck by a car that had drifted off the road when the driver fell asleep at the wheel. Do you think Griffith was insured at the time of his death? Why or why not? [*US Life Insurance Company v. Wilson,* 2011 Md. App. LEXIS 52.]

10. Sally Hilkene, owner of a grocery and goods store called Churchill's, signed a lease with Crestwood Shops to expand her store into the neighboring shop formerly occupied by a bookstore. Upon her inspection of the store, she discovered the presence of mold, a faulty foundation due to leaky water, and a defective HVAC system. She notified Crestwood of these problems and requested their resolution before she could begin conducting business at the location. Crestwood policy required that it acquire three bids for any project over $2,500, and it began soliciting bids for the problems. Hilkene became impatient and sent an e-mail to Scott Pardon, an agent for Crestwood. Among other concerns, Hilkene wrote, "I wish to release myself from the lease by March 24th, if the owners can't resolve the issues which cause concern for myself, Andy Fritzel, and my workers. More specifically the stachybotris [the mold] present in the space." Crestwood responded by accepting this statement as an offer to terminate the lease for the former bookstore. Hilkene filed a declaratory judgment requesting a declaration that the lease had not been terminated, arguing that Crestwood's "acceptance" did not comply with the mirror-image rule by immediately releasing the parties whereas the offer to terminate was reliant on a condition precedent. Do you agree with Hilkene's argument? Why or why not? [*Crestwood Shops, LLC v. Hilkene and Churchill in Crestwood,* 2006 Mo. App. LEXIS 1188.]

11. Sarah and Eddie Hogan wanted to sell 2.5 acres of land through their real estate agent, Darita Richardson. On December 10, 2001, Warren Kent offered to purchase the land for $52,500. An "Agreement to Buy or Sell" was created, which Kent signed right away. One term of the agreement was that the offer would expire on December 11, 2001, at 3 p.m., and it stated additionally, "Time is of the essence and all deadlines are final except where modifications, changes, or extensions are made in writing and signed by all parties." Although Richardson scheduled a meeting on December 11, 2001, at 2 p.m. with the Hogans, the Hogans failed to appear. However, the parties agreed to a two-day extension, lasting until December 13, 2001, at 3 p.m., and the extension was binding and irrevocable according to the "Addendum to Agreement to Purchase or Sell." The Hogans signed both documents at 9 a.m. on December 13, 2001. At about 11 a.m., Kent also

signed the addendum. However, neither Kent's agent nor Richardson contacted the Hogans prior to 3 p.m. about Kent's acceptance. After 3 p.m., Richardson realized that the Hogans had not placed the date and time next to their signatures. When she met with the Hogans, they placed the date and the time as 4:48 p.m., informing Richardson that they, the Hogans, had changed their minds about the sale. Kent sued for specific performance of the contract. What effect, if any, did the failure to communicate the acceptance of the offer prior to 3 p.m. have in terms of whether a contract was formed? What do you think the appellate court's reasoning was? [*Kent v. Hogan,* 2004 La. App. LEXIS 2539.]

Looking for more review material?

The Online Learning Center at **www.mhhe.com/kubasekess2e** contains this chapter's "Assignment on the Internet" and also a list of URLs for more information, entitled "On the Internet." Find both of them in the Student Center portion of the OLC, along with quizzes and other helpful materials.

Consideration

CASE OPENER

Upper Deck—Contract Liability or Gift?

In 1988 the Upper Deck Company was a baseball card company with an idea for a better baseball card: one that had a hologram on it. By the 1990s Upper Deck was a major corporation whose value was at least a quarter of a billion dollars. In 1988, however, the outlook wasn't bright for Upper Deck, which lacked the funds for a $100,000 deposit it needed to buy some special paper by August 1. Without that deposit its contract with the major-league baseball players' association would have been jeopardized.

Upper Deck's corporate attorney, Anthony Passante, Jr., loaned the company the money. That evening, the directors of the company accepted the loan and, in gratitude, agreed to give Passante 3 percent of the firm's stock. Passante never sought to collect the gift of stock, and later the company reneged on its promise. Passante sued for breach of oral contract.[1]

1. If you were on the jury, how would you decide the case? (The law of consideration will determine the outcome.) Was the offer of 3 percent of the firm's stock legal consideration for the loan? Or was it a mere gift?
2. Does Upper Deck have a moral obligation to give Passante the stock? If so, is this legally enforceable?

[1] *Passante v. McWilliam*, 53 Cal. App. 4th 1240 (1997).

LEARNING OBJECTIVES

After reading this chapter, you will be able to answer the following questions:

LO 9-1 What is consideration?

LO 9-2 When is consideration required?

LO 9-3 What is promissory estoppel and when can it be used?

LO 9-4 What is adequacy of consideration?

What Is Consideration?

LO 9-1

Rule: *Consideration is what a person will receive in return for performing a contract obligation.* Suppose, for example, that Dan agrees to purchase Mary's car for $1,000. Dan's payment of $1,000 is the consideration Mary will receive for her car. Title to and possession of the car is the consideration Dan will receive in exchange. Consideration can be anything, as long as it is the product of a bargained-for exchange. In a business context it is often (but not always) money. Other examples of consideration are presented in Exhibit 9-1.

Is a promise to refrain from something you are legally entitled to do appropriate consideration for a contract? In Case 9-1, the court considers whether a nephew's promise to refrain from certain vices is adequate consideration for his uncle's promise to pay him $5,000.

Rules of Consideration

LO 9-2

The key to understanding consideration is understanding the rules that govern it and their exceptions. We explore these principles below.

LACK OF CONSIDERATION

Rule: *For a promise to be enforced by the courts, there must be consideration.* A court will enforce one party's promise only if the other party promised something (an act, money, etc.) in exchange. For example, in a bilateral contract (a promise for a promise), the "consideration" for each promise is a return promise. Consider this example: Sue promises to pay Mike $2,000 for his car. Mike promises to sell Sue his car for $2,000. The exchange will be done tomorrow.

Exhibit 9-1

Examples of Consideration

TYPE OF CONSIDERATION	EXAMPLE
A benefit to the promisor	A promise to stay in a job until a particular project is complete (This is a benefit to the employer.)
A detriment to the promisee	A promise to your football coach to refrain from riding your motorcycle during football season even though you love riding it
A promise to do something	A promise to cook dinner for your roommate for the next six months
A promise to refrain from doing something	A promise to stop drinking alcohol during exam week

CASE 9-1

HAMER v. SIDWAY
NEW YORK COURT OF APPEALS
124 N.Y. 538 (1891)

FACTS: *William E. Story and his nephew, William E. Story, 2d, agreed that the uncle would pay his nephew $5,000 if the nephew would refrain from drinking, using tobacco, swearing, and playing cards and billiards for money until he turned 21. When the nephew turned 21, his uncle sent him a letter that indicated that the nephew had earned the $5,000 and that he would hold the money with interest until the nephew became capable of taking care of it responsibly. The nephew accepted the terms. The uncle died 12 years later without having transferred the funds to his nephew.*

The nephew assigned the funds to Louisa Hamer, who brought suit against the executor of the uncle's estate, Franklin Sidway, to collect the money. Sidway, however, argued that the contract was without consideration to support it, and, therefore, invalid. He asserts that the nephew, by refraining from the use of liquor and tobacco, was not harmed but benefited; that that which he did was best for him to do independently of his uncle's promise, and insists that it follows that unless the uncle was benefited, the contract was without consideration.

At trial judgment was entered in Hamer's favor but was reversed on appeal in Sidway's favor. Hamer appealed.

ISSUE: The issue before the court is whether a promise of forebearance (e.g., to not engage in particular activities) can be deemed valid and lawful consideration for a contract.

REASONING: Defendant contended that the contract was invalid because it lacked consideration and that there is no consideration unless the promisor is benefited. Such a rule could not be tolerated, and is without foundation in the law. Consideration means not so much that one party is profiting as that the other abandons some legal right in the present or limits his legal freedom of action in the future. Now, applying this rule to the facts before us, the promisee used tobacco, occasionally drank liquor, and he had a legal right to do so. He abandoned that right for a period of years based upon the promise of his uncle that for such forbearance he would give him $5,000. We need not speculate on the effort which may have been required to give up the use of those stimulants. It is sufficient that he restricted his lawful freedom of action within certain prescribed limits upon the faith of his uncle's agreement. Now, having fully performed the conditions imposed, it makes no difference whether such performance was actually a benefit to the promisor, and the court will not inquire into it.

DECISION AND REMEDY: It is deemed established for the purposes of this appeal, that on January 31, 1875, defendant's testator was indebted to William E. Story, 2d, in the sum of $5,000. All concur.

SIGNIFICANCE OF THE CASE: Forbearance is sufficient consideration for a valid and enforceable contract.

CRITICAL THINKING

What difference would it have made in this case had the nephew not had the legal right to drink or smoke? Why is this question crucial to the decision?

ETHICAL DECISION MAKING

What values is the idea of consideration upholding?

There is an oral contract. Sue's promise to pay Mike $2,000 for the car is her consideration to Mike. Mike's promise to sell Sue the car for $2,000 is his consideration to Sue. There has been a mutual exchange of something of value—a promise to pay $2,000 and a promise to sell the car for $2,000.

Another example of a bilateral contract, or a promise for a promise, occurred when the U.S. government seized control of insurance giant American International Group (AIG). The U.S. agreed to lend AIG up to $85 billion in exchange for nearly 80 percent of AIG's stock. The

Exhibit 9-2

Type of
Consideration Based
on Type of Contract

TYPE OF CONTRACT	PROMISOR	PROMISEE
Bilateral	A promise	A promise
Unilateral	A promise	An act

consideration AIG received was the promise of up to $85 billion in U.S. government loans. The consideration the U.S. received was the promise of almost 80 percent of AIG's stock.[2]

In a unilateral contract (a promise for an act), one party's consideration is the promise and the other party's consideration is the act. Suppose your professor made the following statement in class: "If any student shows up at my house on Saturday and does the gardening, I will pay that student $100." You show up and do the gardening. The professor's consideration to you is the promise of the payment of $100 on completion of the gardening, and your consideration to the professor is the act of completing the gardening. Once again, there has been a mutual exchange of something of value.

Exhibit 9-2 summarizes the consideration in bilateral and unilateral contracts.

In Case 9-2, the court must decide whether continued employment is consideration for signing a noncompete agreement.

[2] "U.S. Seizes Control of AIG with $85 Billion Emergency Loan," *Washington Post,* September 17, 2008, www.washingtonpost.com/wp-dyn/content/article/2008/09/16/AR2008091602174 (retrieved May 25, 2009).

CASE 9-2

ANTHONY A. LABRIOLA v. POLLARD GROUP, INC.

SUPREME COURT OF WASHINGTON

152 Wn. 2d 828; 100 P.3d 791 (Sup. Ct. Wash. 2004)

FACTS: *Employer hired Employee to work as a salesperson. Under the employment agreement, Employer could terminate Employee without cause. Employee's compensation consisted of a base salary and commission from sales. The agreement also contained a restrictive covenant not to compete in the custom printing business for a period of three years after employment ended. The agreement had no geographic limitations. Nearly five years later, Employer requested and Employee executed a noncompete agreement requiring that Employee refrain from accepting employment with a competitor for a period of three years within 75 miles of Employer's business. Employee remained an "at-will" employee and received no additional benefits. A few months later, Employer announced a new commission sales compensation schedule. Employee determined that the new schedule would reduce his income by about 25 percent and sought employment for a similar position elsewhere. Employer discovered Employee's intention to seek employment with a competitor and terminated Employee.*

Employer sent a letter to the competitor interested in hiring Employee, stating its intent to enforce Employee's noncompete agreement. The competitor did not hire Employee. Employee remains unemployed despite actively seeking a position similar to the one he had held with Employer. Employee initiated suit against Employer, seeking a declaratory judgment that the noncompete agreement was null and void and that Employer tortiously interfered with Employee's business. The trial court ruled against Employee and upheld the agreement. The trial court also denied Employee's motion that the trial court modify the noncompete agreement's time restriction from three years to six months. Employee sought direct review of this court, which was granted.

ISSUE: Is there consideration for the formation of a contract when an employee, already employed by the employer, executes a noncompete agreement but receives no new benefit?

REASONING: In the court's own words (abridged and slightly modified):

> Employee claims that the noncompete agreement fails for lack of consideration; in other words, a contract was not formed. Employer contends that the noncompete agreement is enforceable because future and continued employment and/or job training served as the Employer's consideration in exchange for Employee's execution of the noncompete agreement. The general rule in Washington is that consideration exists if the employee enters into a noncompete agreement when he or she is first hired. A noncompete agreement entered into after employment will be enforced if it is supported by independent consideration. Independent, additional consideration is required for the valid formation of a modification or subsequent agreement. There is no consideration when "one party is to perform some additional obligation while the other party is simply to perform that which he promised in the original contract." Independent consideration may include increased wages, a promotion, a fixed term of employment, and so on. Independent consideration involves new promises or obligations previously not required of the parties.

In the present case, Employer contends that continued employment served as consideration for the later noncompete agreement; however, Employee's noncompete agreement made no promises as to future employment and wages. Employer's president conceded that "no extra benefits or consideration or promises [were] made to [Employee] if he signed the noncompete."

Consideration is a bargained-for exchange of promises. A comparison of the status of the employer before and after the noncompete agreement confirms that the noncompete agreement was entered into without consideration. Employer did not incur additional duties or obligations from the noncompete agreement. Prior to execution of the noncompete agreement, Employee was an "at-will" employee. After Employee executed the noncompete agreement, he still remained an at-will employee terminable at Employer's pleasure. We hold that continued employment in this case did not serve as consideration by Employer in exchange for Employee's promise not to compete.

DECISION AND REMEDY: The trial court's decision was reversed. The noncompete agreement lacked independent consideration and was not enforceable against the employee.

SIGNIFICANCE OF THE CASE: This case illustrates that for a contract to be binding, there must be consideration.

CRITICAL THINKING

What is the reasoning used by the court to support its decision? Are there any ambiguous words or phrases in that reasoning that you would want defined before you decided whether to agree with the court's ruling?

ETHICAL DECISION MAKING

Return to the WPH framework. Who are the stakeholders in this case? Is the decision of the employer consistent with how one would act when using the Golden Rule as one's guide?

LO 9-3

promissory estoppel
The legal enforcement of an otherwise unenforceable contract due to a party's detrimental reliance on the contract.

Rule: *Promissory estoppel is the legal enforcement of an otherwise unenforceable contract due to a party's detrimental reliance on the contract.*

One exception to the rule requiring consideration is **promissory estoppel.** Promissory estoppel occurs when three conditions are met:

- One party makes a promise knowing the other party will rely on it.
- The other party does rely on the promise.
- The only way to avoid injustice is to enforce the promise.

How does this work? Suppose that on graduation from college, Amanda receives a job offer across the country. She gives up her apartment, cancels all her other job interviews, and moves all her possessions. After arriving, she rents a new apartment and shows up for work. The only problem is that Amanda is told there is no job! May Amanda sue the employer? The answer in most states is yes, under the theory of promissory estoppel. She spent a lot of money in reliance on the job offer. She also moved across the country. Amanda may be able to recover her

reliance damages (i.e., money she spent in "reliance" on the job offer). Promissory estoppel is not awarded regularly, but in the right case it can provide a remedy where no other remedy exists.

In a recent case, the Ninth Circuit Court of Appeals held that Yahoo's promise to remove a nude photo from its website was subject to a claim of promissory estoppel. In that case, the plaintiff learned that her ex-boyfriend, pretending to be her, had posted nude photos of her on Yahoo. He also included all her contact information and an invitation for men to contact her for sexual purposes.[3] The plaintiff contacted Yahoo (in accordance with its established policies) and requested that the photo be removed. Yahoo agreed but, despite repeated requests, did not remove the photo for six months. The court held that Yahoo's promise to de-post the profile meant that Yahoo had a duty to the plaintiff. As such, the plaintiff's claim of promissory estoppel could be maintained. If the plaintiff is able to prove that she reasonably relied on Yahoo's promise to her detriment, she may well prevail on her claim.

ADEQUACY OF CONSIDERATION

LO 9-4

Rule: *The court seldom considers adequacy of consideration.* What this rule means is that the court does not weigh whether you made a good bargain. Example: Donna purchases a stereo from Celia, a friend in her business law class. Donna pays $500 for the stereo but later realizes that the stereo is not worth $100. May Donna sue Celia? Typically, the answer is no. It is Donna's responsibility to do her research and determine what price she should pay. The court will not set aside the sale because she made a bad deal.

There is an exception to this rule. Suppose that you are on the verge of bankruptcy, and your creditors are threatening legal action. You know that if you default on your mortgage, car payment, bank loans, credit card payments, and other bills, the court may order that your assets be sold to pay the creditors. Instead of risking this result, you decide to "sell" your assets. You sell your BMW to your best friend for $50 and your vacation house to your sister for $500. Now, asset-free, you declare bankruptcy, knowing that your creditors will be able to collect nothing. Is this permissible? The answer, of course, is no. In such a case, the court will look at "adequacy of consideration." If it appears that the "sale" of the assets was done to avoid payment to creditors, the court may set aside each sale and sell the assets to pay your creditors. In Case 9-3, the court had to consider whether $1 plus "love and affection" was adequate consideration for the transfer of property.

[3] "Do Interactive Websites Have a Legal Duty to Remove Malicious Content?" http://writ.news.findlaw.com/scripts/printer_friendly.pl?page=/ramasastry/20090519.html (retrieved May 25, 2009). This article discusses *Barnes v. Yahoo, Inc.*, 2009 U.S. App. LEXIS 10940 (9th Cir. 2009).

CASE 9-3

THELMA AGNES SMITH v. DAVID PHILLIP RILEY
COURT OF APPEALS OF TENNESSEE, EASTERN SECTION, AT KNOXVILLE
2002 Tenn. App. LEXIS 65

FACTS: *Smith and Riley lived together out of wedlock for several years. They opened a joint checking account and, over time, both Smith and Riley deposited money into the account. In addition, Riley entered into a lease with Jerry Strickland and Wanda Strickland with respect to a residence owned by them. The lease was accompanied by an option to purchase. Almost four months later, Smith and Riley asked their attorney to prepare a bill of sale and an assignment. In the bill of sale, Riley transferred to Smith a one-half undivided interest in seven items of personal property. Riley also assigned to Smith a one-half undivided interest in the lease and option to purchase with the*

Stricklands; this interest included a right of survivorship in the one-half interest retained by Riley. The property Riley sold and assigned to Smith in the two agreements was stated in each to be "for and in consideration of the sum of One Dollar ($1.00) and other and good and valuable consideration, the sufficiency of which is hereby acknowledged." When the relationship ended, Smith filed suit against Riley in the trial court, seeking the dissolution of their "domestic partnership" and seeking to enforce the two written agreements with Riley regarding the sale and assignment of property to her. The trial court enforced the agreements and divided the parties' property. The defendant appealed, arguing that the agreements lacked consideration and were void as they were against public policy.

ISSUE: Is $1 plus love and affection adequate consideration for the two agreements between Smith and Riley?

REASONING: In the court's own words (abridged and slightly modified):

> It is a well-settled principle of contract law that in order for a contract to be binding, it must, among other things, be supported by sufficient consideration. In expounding on the adequacy of consideration, the court has stated that it is not necessary that the benefit conferred or the detriment suffered by the promisee shall be equal to the responsibility assumed. Any consideration, however small, will support a promise. In the absence of fraud, the courts will not undertake to regulate the amount of the consideration. The parties are left to contract for themselves, taking for granted that the consideration is one valuable in the eyes of the law.

Quoting the United States Supreme Court, the court went on to state that "[a] stipulation in consideration of $1 is just as effectual and valuable a consideration as a larger sum stipulated for or paid." Indeed, the consideration of love and affection has been deemed sufficient to support a conveyance. Both the bill of sale and the assignment recite that they are undertaken "for and in consideration of the sum of One Dollar ($1.00) and other and good and valuable consideration, the sufficiency of which is hereby acknowledged." Facially, the documents are therefore supported by sufficient consideration, as clearly recognized by the Supreme Court. Moreover, Smith's "society and consortium"—a concept comparable to the love and affection—is further evidence of sufficient consideration to support these conveyances.

DECISION AND REMEDY: The judgment of the trial court was affirmed. The case was remanded for enforcement of the judgment and for collection of costs. Costs on appeal were taxed to the appellant, Riley.

SIGNIFICANCE OF THE CASE: This case demonstrates that courts will generally not consider the adequacy of consideration.

CRITICAL THINKING

What is the reasoning of the appellant in terms of why the consideration was not adequate to cause the contracts to be enforceable? What key rule of law did this reasoning overlook?

ETHICAL DECISION MAKING

What values are being advanced by the logic of the relevant rule of law in this case? In other words, what values prevent the rule of law from being that "consideration must be in an amount similar in value to the item or services being transferred in order for the contract to be enforceable"?

LO 9-5

illusory promise
A situation in which a party appears to commit to something but really has not committed to anything. It is not a promise and thus not consideration.

ILLUSORY PROMISE

Rule: *An illusory promise is not consideration.* What is an illusory promise? Suppose Shawn offers to sell Molly his skis for $300. Molly responds, "I'll look at them in the morning, and if I like them, I'll pay you." At this point, Molly has not committed to doing anything. The law considers this an **illusory promise**—that is, it is not a promise at all. Moreover, an illusory promise is not consideration.

LO 9-6

PAST CONSIDERATION

Rule: *Past consideration is no consideration at all.* Consideration is an essential element of a contract. For a court to enforce a promise, both sides must offer consideration. Imagine that you have graduated from college and gotten a great job. After you have worked at the company for

Lack of Consideration in Japan

In the United States, a contract that lacks consideration is unenforceable. For example, if Anne promises to pay Gene $5,000 for all he has done for her over the years but Anne does not pay, Gene has no ability to collect the $5,000. The rule in the United States is clear—past consideration is no consideration at all. Unless there is consideration on both sides of the transaction, there is no contract.

In Japan, however, a promise to give property to one party gratuitously is enforceable. "Gifts shall become effective by the manifestation by one of the parties of his/her intention to give his/her property to the other party gratuitously, and the acceptance of the other party thereof" (CC Art 549).* In this way, depending on the disclosed intent agreed by the donor and the donee, gifts also form a contract under Japanese law. Therefore, the donor has an obligation to deliver the promised property to the donee. However, unlike a contract where there is a value relationship between the parties, in a gift contract the donee receives the property at no cost. Article 550 of Japan's Civil Code provides that a gift not in writing can be canceled. Moreover, any portion of a gift that was not in writing for which performance has already been completed cannot be canceled.

*Hiroto Dogauchi, "Transparency of Japanese Law Project," www.tomeika.jur. kyushu-u.ac.jp/transaction/contract.html (retrieved May 21, 2011).

five years, your boss says to you, "Because you have done such a great job the last five years, I am going to give you 5 percent of the company stock." Six months later, you still have not received the stock. May you sue your boss to enforce the promise? The answer is no. For a promise to be enforceable, there must be bargaining and an exchange. In this example, there was no exchange. Work done in the past, by definition, has already been performed. As such, you have given nothing in exchange, and the court will not enforce the promise. You are at the mercy of your boss's goodwill to keep her promise. A promise cannot be based on consideration that was provided before the promise was made.

PREEXISTING DUTY

LO 9-7

Rule: *A promise to do something that you are already obligated to do is not valid consideration.* There are actually two parts to this rule. First, *performance of a duty you are obligated to do under the law is not good consideration.* For example, a police officer is sworn to uphold the law. Part of that public duty involves catching suspected criminals. If someone offers a reward for the capture of a suspected criminal, the police officer may not collect the reward, as he or she was already obligated to apprehend the suspect. Second, *performance of an existing contractual duty is not good consideration.* Gene decides to have a pool built in his backyard. Under the existing contract, the pool is to be completed by June 1, just in time for summer. The pool contractor comes to Gene and explains that due to a shortage of workers, the completion date cannot be met; however, if Gene were to pay an extra $5,000, additional workers could be hired and the pool would be completed on time. Gene tells the contractor that he will pay the $5,000. On June 1, the pool is completed, and the contractor asks for the additional $5,000 payment. Is Gene legally obligated to pay? The answer is no. The pool contractor had a preexisting contractual duty to complete the pool by June 1. Gene is under no obligation to pay the additional money.

Exceptions to the Preexisting-Duty Rule There are exceptions to the preexisting-duty rule:

- Unforeseen circumstances
- Additional work
- UCC—sale of goods

If **unforeseen circumstances** cause a party to make a promise regarding an unfinished project, that promise is valid consideration. Let's once again consider the pool example. Suppose that Gene's pool contractor has been building pools in Gene's neighborhood for the last 20 years. During all that time, the contractor has never had any problem with rocks—until now. While bulldozing the hole for the pool in Gene's backyard, the pool contractor hits solid rock. It is

unforeseen circumstances
Events that a reasonable person would not be expected to anticipate.

estimated that it will cost an additional $5,000 to clear the rock by using jackhammers and possibly even dynamite. The contractor explains that he is sorry, but unless Gene agrees to pay the additional money, he will not be able to finish the pool. Gene agrees to pay. When the pool is completed, the contractor asks for the additional $5,000. Will a court enforce this promise? The answer is yes. Even though the contractor is completing only what he was obligated to do under the contract, neither party knew of the solid rock. The contractor has given additional consideration (removal of the rock), and Gene will be held to his promise to pay the additional money.

If a party to a contract agrees to do additional work (i.e., more than she is obligated to do under the contract), the promise is valid consideration. Using the pool example, if the contractor asks Gene for an additional $10,000 but agrees to add a waterfall and a deck to the pool, the promise to do the additional work is consideration. If Gene agrees to pay the $10,000, that is his consideration. Both parties are now bound.

LO 9-8

The rules and exceptions we have been discussing fall under the common law of contracts. The Uniform Commercial Code (UCC) has changed the common law in significant ways. Rule: *Under Article 2 of the UCC (sale of goods), an agreement modifying a contract needs no consideration to be binding.* This is an exception to the preexisting-duty rule. Under UCC Section 2-209:[4]

1. An agreement modifying a contract within this Article needs no consideration to be binding.
2. A signed agreement which excludes modification or rescission except by a signed writing cannot be otherwise modified or rescinded, but except as between merchants such a requirement on a form supplied by the merchant must be separately signed by the other party.

Gary is a manufacturer of blow-dryers. He sends a purchase order for 10,000 white on/off switches to a switch manufacturer. Later, Gary telephones the switch manufacturer and changes his order to 5,000 white switches and 5,000 red switches. Under the UCC, no additional consideration is required for the modification of the agreement to be binding. Moreover, unless stated otherwise, such an agreement need not be in writing.

UNIFORM COMMERCIAL CODE: REQUIREMENT AND OUTPUT CONTRACTS

requirement contract

An agreement whereby the buyer agrees to purchase all of his or her goods from one seller and no quantity is stated in the contract; valid under the UCC but not under common law.

output contract

An agreement whereby the seller guarantees to sell everything he or she produces to one buyer and no quantity is stated; valid under the UCC but not under common law.

Rule: *Under UCC Section 2-306, requirement and output contracts are permitted for the sale of goods.* A **requirement contract** is an agreement whereby the buyer agrees to purchase all of his goods from one seller. No quantity is stated in the contract. Under common law, such a contract would be void because the buyer has made no commitment and, therefore, there is no consideration. An **output contract** is an agreement whereby the seller guarantees to sell everything she produces to one buyer. Once again, no quantity is stated, and under common law, there is lack of consideration. Because such contracts are valued by merchants, under the UCC both requirement and output contracts are valid with the limitation that the output or requirement must be made in "good faith." The consideration, then, is that the party act in good faith. Neither party may take advantage of the other party either by requiring more than was expected when the deal was signed or by producing more than was expected when the deal was signed.

LO 9-9

Partial Payment of a Debt

liquidated debt

Debt for which there is no dispute between the parties about the fact that money is owed and the amount of money owed.

Partial payment of a debt may or may not be valid consideration, depending on whether the debt is liquidated or unliquidated. In a **liquidated debt,** there is no dispute about the fact that money is owed and the amount of money owed. Example: Natalie owes $3,000 on her credit card. She calls the credit card company and explains that she is a poor student and cannot afford to pay the entire $3,000. The credit card company agrees to accept $2,000 as payment in full. The following month, Natalie receives her new credit card statement showing that she owes the remaining $1,000. May the credit card company collect the additional $1,000? Yes! A creditor's promise to accept less than owed, when the debtor is already obligated to pay the full amount, is not binding.

[4] www.law.cornell.edu/ucc/2/article2.htm#s2-209.

CASE Nugget

Requirement Contracts

Mast Long Term Care v. Forest Hills Rest Home et al.
Court of Appeals of North Carolina

156 N.C. App. 556 (N.C. Ct. App. 2003)

Mast Long Term Care and Forest Hills Rest Home entered into an agreement whereby the rest home was to buy from Mast all the drugs needed for its patients that were not commonly stocked at the rest home. The rest home argued that the agreement was not a valid contract since it contained vague purchasing terms, obligating it to buy only those drugs not commonly stocked.

At the hearing, Forest Hills Rest Home argued that the vendor-pharmacist agreement between the parties lacked consideration. The agreement did not state any price terms with respect to the pharmaceuticals to be supplied. The court ruled that North Carolina law permitted requirement contracts and that the sale of drugs was governed by the North Carolina Uniform Commercial Code (UCC). Under the UCC, the omission of certain material terms did not invalidate the contract, because courts were permitted to read good-faith requirements into a contract. No definite amount needed to be stated in the agreement. Moreover, consideration need not consist of a promise to pay money for goods or services. Instead, it can take the shape of mutual promises to perform some act or to forbear from taking some action.

In this case, the consideration for the parties' agreement consisted of the plaintiff's promise to supply the defendant with certain pharmaceuticals and the defendant's counter-promise to stock the plaintiff's products at its pharmacy and sell them to its patients. Accordingly, the agreement does not fail for either lack of consideration or lack of specificity.

The exception to the rule regarding liquidated debt occurs when the debtor offers different performance. Suppose Natalie offered the credit card company her car in full settlement of the $3,000 debt. If the credit card company accepts, regardless of the value of the car, the debt is paid in full and the credit card company may not sue Natalie for any additional money.

In an **unliquidated debt,** the parties either dispute the fact that any money is owed or agree that some money is owed but dispute the amount. A dispute over an unliquidated debt may be settled for less than the full amount if the parties enter into an **accord and satisfaction.** For an accord and satisfaction to be enforceable, three requirements must be met:

1. The debt is unliquidated (i.e., the amount or existence of the debt is in dispute).
2. The creditor agrees to accept as full payment less than the creditor claims is owed.
3. The debtor pays the amount they have agree on.

Rule: *An accord and satisfaction is an arrangement between contracting parties whereby one of the parties substitutes a different performance for his or her original duty under the contract.* The promise to perform the new duty is the *accord,* and the actual performance of that new duty is the *satisfaction.*

To see how an accord and satisfaction relates to income taxation, please see the **Connecting to the Core** activity on the text website at www.mhhe.com/kubasekess2e.

LO 9-10

unliquidated debt

Debt for which the parties either dispute the fact that any money is owed or agree that some money is owed but dispute the amount.

accord and satisfaction

An arrangement between contracting parties whereby one of the parties substitutes a different performance for his or her original duty under the contract.

Under such circumstances, the debt is fully discharged. The *accord* is the new agreement to pay less than the creditor claims. The *satisfaction* is the payment, by the debtor, of the reduced amount. If the debtor fails to pay the new amount, the creditor may then sue for the full amount of the original debt. It pays to keep your word.

One way that people sometimes attempt to create an accord and satisfaction is by sending a check to the creditor and writing "paid in full" on the check. Under common law, in many states this did create an accord and satisfaction, and if the creditor cashed the check, he or she was bound to accept the lesser amount as payment in full. The UCC, however, has changed the scope of this rule. Under UCC Section 3-311, effective in 30 states, the rule remains in place but has two major exceptions.

First, in cases of business organizations, thousands of checks may be received each day. To protect themselves, businesses may notify their debtors that any offer to settle a claim for less than the amount owed must be sent to a particular address and/or person. If you check the terms printed on your credit card statement, you will likely find language directing you to send such payments to a different address and person than those to which regular payments are sent. This safeguard protects businesses from inadvertently creating accord-and-satisfaction agreements. Here is an example of the wording you might find on a credit card statement:

> *Conditional Payments:* Any payment check or other form of payment that you send us for less than the full balance that is marked "paid in full" or contains a similar notation, or that you otherwise tender in full satisfaction of a disputed amount, must be sent to [address omitted]. We reserve all rights regarding these payments (e.g., if it is determined that there is no valid dispute or if any such check is received at any other address, we may accept the check and you will still owe any remaining balance).[5]

Second, if a business does inadvertently cash a "paid-in-full" check, the business has 90 days from the date it cashed that check to offer repayment in the same amount to the debtor. For example, if John owed $3,000 to his credit card company and he sent the company a $2,000 check marked "paid in full" and mailed to the correct address and person, the credit card company has 90 days to offer to repay John the $2,000. Once the offer has been made by the business, no accord and satisfaction exists.

[5] From Chase Visa statement.

SUMMARY

What Is Consideration? *Consideration* is something of value given in exchange for something else of value; it must be the product of a mutually bargained-for exchange.

Rules of Consideration For a promise to be enforced by the courts, there must be *consideration.* A court will enforce one party's promise only if the other party promised something (an act, money, etc.) in exchange.

Promissory estoppel occurs when one party makes a promise knowing the other party will rely on it, the other party does rely on it, and the only way to avoid injustice is to enforce the promise.

The court seldom considers *adequacy of consideration.* What this means is that the court does not weigh whether you made a good bargain.

An *illusory promise* is not consideration (i.e., it is not a promise at all).

Past consideration is generally no consideration at all. A promise cannot be based on consideration that was provided before the promise was made.

The *preexisting-duty rule* provides that when a party does what it is already legally obligated to do, there is no consideration because there has been no detriment.

A *requirement contract* is an agreement whereby the buyer agrees to purchase all his goods from one seller. No quantity is stated in the contract.

An *output contract* is an agreement whereby the seller guarantees to sell everything she produces to one buyer. Once again, no quantity is stated.

Partial Payment of a Debt

In a *liquidated debt,* there is no dispute about the fact that money is owed and the amount of money owed.

In an *unliquidated debt,* the parties either dispute the fact that any money is owed or agree that some money is owed but dispute the amount.

For an *accord and satisfaction* to be enforceable, three requirements must be met: (1) The debt is unliquidated (i.e., the amount or existence of the debt is in dispute); (2) the creditor agrees to accept as full payment less than the creditor claims is owed; and (3) the debtor pays the amount they have agree on. The accord is the agreement, and the satisfaction is the payment of the reduced amount.

Point/Counterpoint

Should the Courts Evaluate Adequacy of Consideration?	
YES	NO
Allowing courts to review adequacy of consideration would be a deterrent to those who want to take advantage of parties to a contract. Allowing courts to review adequacy of consideration would give parties an avenue for relief that would be easier to prove than fraud, which is currently the only recourse for parties who believe they were taken advantage of.	When two parties agree to a contract, the court should not intervene to determine if the parties got a fair deal. The courts have never considered the adequacy of consideration and there is no reason to begin now. Precedent should be followed. The value of the consideration received is subjective, and the court should not substitute its judgment for that of the parties to the contract.

Questions & Problems

1. List the four types of consideration described in the text.
2. What is required to prove promissory estoppel when consideration is missing?
3. Can $1 be adequate consideration? Why or why not?
4. List and describe the three exceptions to the preexisting-duty rule.
5. List the three elements of accord and satisfaction.
6. When Holloman applied for a job at Circuit City, she signed a "Dispute Resolution Agreement" (DRA) that stated: "This agreement requires you and Circuit City to arbitrate certain legal disputes related to your application for employment or employment with Circuit City." The job application then added, "Circuit City will consider your application only if this agreement is signed." Finally, the DRA stated, "I understand that my employment, compensation and terms and conditions of employment can be altered or terminated, with or without cause, and with or without notice, at any time, at the option of either Circuit City or myself." Holloman was hired, but she later quit and sued Circuit City, claiming she had been discriminated against and constructively discharged. Holloman argued that the arbitration agreement was illusory and not supported by consideration because

of Circuit City's unilateral ability to terminate or modify the agreement. How should the court rule? Explain your reasoning. [*Holloman v. Circuit City Stores*, 162 Md. App. 332 (Md. Ct. App. 2005).]

7. Cece Hylton and Edward Meztista had a partnership, MMD, which had an advertising account with a grocery store. Pursuant to the partnership agreement, Hylton and Meztista would equally divide the profits MMD earned once expenses were paid. They also agreed to equally divide the partnership's liabilities. From the record, it appears that the grocery store, which paid MMD $30,000 a month, was the only account the partnership handled. When the grocery store was sold, MMD lost the account. In January 1998, Meztista provided Hylton with a two-page document, which he said was an accounting of MMD's profits and expenses. The bottom line showed a balance of $35,235.67, of which Hylton was owed $17,617.84. Hylton, however, questioned certain expenses included in the accounting and asked Meztista to let her review the partnership's books. Hylton was never given the opportunity to see the books. Meztista did not return her telephone calls, nor did he provide her with an explanation regarding the expenses shown on the accounting. In April 1998, Meztista gave Hylton a check for $17,617.84, which was drawn on MMD's account. The face of the check stated that it was "final payment/payment in full." Hylton cashed the check, but wrote on it that she was doing so "under protest." She added: "Cashing this check does not constitute my acceptance of this amount as payment in full." Did writing "final payment/payment in full" on the check create an accord and satisfaction? What, if any, was the effect of Hylton's cashing the check after writing "under protest" on it? If you were the court, how would you decide and why? [*Ex parte Meztista*, 845 So. 2d 795 (2001).]

8. On February 1, 2004, Zhang entered into a contract to buy former realtor Frank Sorichetti's Las Vegas home for $532,500. The contract listed a March closing date and a few household furnishings as part of the sale. On February 3, Sorichetti told Zhang that he was terminating the sale "to stay in the house a little longer" and that Nevada law allows the rescission of real property purchase agreements within three days of contracting. Sorichetti stated that he would sell the home, however, if Zhang paid more money. Zhang agreed. Another contract was drafted, reciting a new sales price, $578,000. This contract added to the included household furnishings drapes that were not listed in the February 1 agreement, and it set an April, rather than March, closing date. The primary issue before the court was whether a real property purchase agreement is enforceable when it is executed by the buyer only because the seller would not perform under an earlier purchase agreement for a lesser price. Should the court enforce the second contract? Why or why not? [*Zhang v. The Eighth Judicial District Court of the State of Nevada*, 103 P.3d 20 (Sup. Ct. Nev. 2004).]

9. In 2001, Joseph Toscano, who was employed as the general manager of a Fields Pianos store in Santa Ana, was very unhappy with his job and decided to find other employment. Toscano contacted Michael Greene, the president of San Diego–based Greene Music, because he had heard that Greene was considering buying Fields's Riverside store. During the course of several conversations in June and July of 2001, Michael Greene offered Toscano a sales management position with Greene to start on September 1, 2001. On August 1, 2001, Toscano resigned from Fields in reliance on Michael Greene's promise of employment. In mid-August, however, Greene withdrew the employment offer. Toscano later found lower-paying jobs; the first at a piano store in Mission Viejo and then at another piano store in Utah. Toscano sued Greene for promissory estoppel. Should Toscano prevail on his claim for promissory estoppel? Why or why not? [*Toscano v. Greene Music*, 124 Cal. App. 4th 685 (2004).]

10. Five employees of American Electric Power Service Corp. (AEP) invented a new product. "In consideration of the sum of One Dollar (1.00), and of other good and valuable consideration paid to the undersigned Assignor," each employee signed an agreement giving AEP exclusive patent rights to the invention. Some of the employees sued, alleging that there was no contract because AEP never paid the one dollar. How do you think the court ruled? Explain your reasoning. [*Bennett et al. v. American Electric Power Service Corporation*, 2001 Ohio App. LEXIS 4357 (Ohio Ct. App. 2001).]

11. This appeal arises out of the trial court's division of property in a divorce case. Vincent Simmons appeals from the trial court's order awarding to his wife, Dorothy Simmons, a one-half interest in land that he inherited from his parents. Vincent contends that the land is nonmarital property and, consequently, should have remained his separate property. Vincent and Dorothy Simmons were married in 1976. Vincent's mother executed a trust in order to convey the land in Florida to her children, Vincent and his sister, upon her death. Louise Simmons died on April 1, 1999, but the land remained in trust for several years after her death. After Louise died, Dorothy became concerned that she would not receive an interest in the Florida land if Vincent died before the trust was distributed, so she hired an attorney in Monticello, David Chambers,

to prepare a document to protect her interest. In the document, Vincent says, in part, "It is my intention, through this affidavit, to convey to my said wife marital interest in said real property. If I should die prior to the above-stated Trust being dissolved, then my said wife shall receive my share of said real property as her own property." In 2003, Dorothy filed for divorce. Vincent argued that there was a total absence of consideration to support a contract in this case. Dorothy argued that her ongoing marriage to Vincent constituted adequate consideration to support the contract. Who is correct? Why? [*Vincent Simmons v. Dorothy Simmons*, 98 Ark. App. 12 (Ark. Ct. App. 2007).]

12. Martin was employed as a retail associate by UPS for over two years. He had no written employment agreement. On December 5, 2004, Martin's boss called him at his home and told him that he was terminating Martin's employment. The parties disagreed, however, as to the content of the rest of the conversation. Martin testified that his boss had said that he was fired because the other employees felt intimidated by him and that he would give him a severance package of two week's pay if Martin would not litigate. Martin's mother corroborated this version of the conversation. In contrast, Martin's boss stated that he told Martin that he was fired because of his continued use of company computers for personal use and because of the multiple downloads on company computers. The boss claims he indicated that he would give Martin his last week's pay and his November bonus and that he would consider giving him two weeks of severance pay in a few weeks. Martin never received severance pay from the company. The company now argues that the offer of severance pay was not supported by consideration and that Martin was not prejudiced by his boss's rescission of his offer to pay severance. How should the court decide? Why? [*Richard A. Martin v. Ost Mark, Inc.*, 2006 Ohio App. LEXIS 3938 (Ohio Ct. App. 2006).]

13. In February 2000, CNS International Ministries, Inc., signed a contract with Eiman Brothers Roofing Systems. Under the contract, Eiman would provide CNS with a clay tile roof for one of its properties. On the basis of the size of the roof provided in CNS's plans, the total amount of the contract was $52,731. In May 2000, Eiman realized that the plan provided by CNS underestimated the roof's actual size, which required an additional 20 to 25 squares. Eiman, demanding a second contract, recalculated and rebid the project. In May 2000, CNS signed a contract modification proposal sent by Eiman, adding $23,000 in costs. With the work substantially complete, CNS noted problems in Eiman's performance and its alleged failure to deliver on assurances to correct those problems. Consequently, CNS ordered Eiman to stop working on the roof. Eiman then brought a breach-of-contract action. At the time of the alleged breach, CNS had paid a total of $29,000 on the contract. CNS claimed that the contract was unenforceable for lack of consideration, in that Eiman had a preexisting duty to CNS. Specifically, CNS argues that the May 2000 proposal called for Eiman to perform in exactly the same manner as that specified in the original contract. Did Eiman have a preexisting duty to CNS? Why or why not? [*Eiman Brothers Roofing Systems, Inc. v. CNS International Ministries, Inc.*, 158 S.W.3d 920 (2005).]

Looking for more review material?

The Online Learning Center at **www.mhhe.com/kubasekess2e** contains this chapter's "Assignment on the Internet" and also a list of URLs for more information, entitled "On the Internet." Find both of them in the Student Center portion of the OLC, along with quizzes and other helpful materials.

CHAPTER

10 Capacity and Legality

A Wasted Education

Ten months before attaining the age of majority, the plaintiff paid for and received a course in elementary aviation from the defendant. Five months later, he purchased and received a limited commercial pilot's course from the defendant. Two months later, he entered into a contract with the defendant for an advanced course of instruction to become a transport pilot, but he withdrew from the course within the month and paid nothing. He reached the age of majority on July 20.

Six months after attaining the age of majority, he received a bill from the defendant for the balance due on his course. He visited the defendant's attorney and denied liability but said nothing about disaffirmance. He took no further action until a few days shy of a year from the day he attained the age of majority. At that time, he filed suit against the defendant, seeking to disaffirm his contracts for the aviation courses and seeking a return of the money he had paid for them on grounds that he had entered into the contracts as a minor and had the right to disaffirm them and recover what he had given up under the contracts. The defendant argued that the courses were necessaries and, as such, that the plaintiff was not entitled to disaffirm the contracts for them.[1]

1. Were the contracts for necessaries and, as such, not subject to being disaffirmed?
2. Even if the plaintiff had the right to disaffirm the contracts, was almost a year too long to wait to disaffirm them?

[1] *John P. Adamowski v. The Curtiss-Wright Flying Service, Inc.,* 300 Mass. 281; 15 N.E.2d 467; 1938 Mass. LEXIS 942.

LEARNING OBJECTIVES

After reading this chapter, you will be able to answer the following questions:

LO 10-1 When would a minor have only limited capacity to enter into a contract?

LO 10-2 How can a contract created when one is a minor be ratified after one is no longer a minor?

LO 10-3 Under what conditions is a contract unenforceable by law?

LO 10-4 When does unfairness affect a contract's enforceability?

LO 10-5 What is the legal effect of entering into a contract for an illegal purpose?

LO 10-6 Why would anyone care whether a contract was severable?

Capacity

This chapter examines the third and fourth elements of a contract. **Capacity** is the third element of a legally binding contract. A person who has legal capacity to contract is one who has the mental ability to understand his or her rights and obligations under a contract and therefore will presumably be able to understand how to comply with the terms of the agreement. *Incapacity,* or *incompetence,* as it is sometimes called, is some sort of mental or physical defect that prevents a natural person from being able to enter into a legally binding contract. Depending on the nature and extent of the defect, a person may have either no capacity, and therefore any attempted contract is void, or limited capacity, resulting in the ability to form only voidable contracts.

Historically, people with limited or no capacity included married women, minors, and insane persons. Through statutes, other categories were added for classes of people for whom guardians had been appointed, such as habitual drunkards, narcotic addicts, spendthrifts, the elderly, and convicts. Today, married women have been removed from the category of those lacking contractual capacity, although in a few states their capacity to enter into certain kinds of contracts is still limited. In this section of the chapter, we explain the current law limiting the capacity of some categories of persons to enter into legally binding agreements.

capacity
The legal ability to enter into a binding contract.

MINORS

LO 10-1

One of the oldest limitations on capacity is the ability of minors to enter into only voidable contracts. Today, in all but three states, a *minor* is someone under the age of 18.[2] In most states, however, a person is given full legal capacity to enter into contracts when he or she becomes emancipated before reaching the age of majority. *Emancipation* occurs when a minor's parents or legal guardians give up their right to exercise legal control over the minor, typically when the minor moves out of the parents' house and begins supporting himself or herself. Often the minor will petition the court for a declaration of emancipation. In most cases, when a minor marries, she or he is considered emancipated.

Disaffirmance of the Contract Because their contracts are voidable, minors have the right, until a reasonable time after reaching the age of majority, to disaffirm, or avoid, their contracts. There are no formalities required to disaffirm the contract; the minor need only manifest an intention to rescind the contract, either by words or by actions. However, the minor must avoid the entire contract; he or she cannot choose to disaffirm only a portion of it.

The obligations of the minor on disaffirmance vary from state to state. Traditionally, most states simply required that the minor notify the competent party of the intent to disaffirm and return to the competent party any consideration received under the contract that was still under the minor's control, regardless of the condition of the consideration. If the consideration has been destroyed or damaged, the minor returns whatever is left of it, and the other party has no recourse against the minor under most circumstances. For instance, if William, a minor, purchased a stereo receiver from Sound Systems, Inc., under a six-month contract and dropped it a week after he took it home, he could return it to the store in its broken condition and tell the owner that he wished to rescind the contract. He would be entitled to the return of his down payment and would owe no further obligations to the store.

[2] In Alabama, Nebraska, and Wyoming, full capacity to contract does not arise until the person reaches the age of 19, which is the age of majority in those states. In Mississippi, the age of majority is still 21.

Capacity of a Minor in China

United States law allows minors to void certain contracts. The mentality behind this law is that individuals below a certain age cannot be entirely accountable for their decisions. Chinese law holds minors accountable for their contracts in more situations than contracts for necessities. Children between 10 and 18 are deemed competent for entering into certain contracts, appropriate to each child's mental state. The validity of the contracts made by these minors is normally conditioned on the retrospective approach of a parent or guardian unless the contract is merely beneficial to the child or is an appropriate contract for the child's age, intelligence, and mental state. Some of these contracts involve agreements for necessities such as food or clothing, while others might involve agreements to purchase a bicycle, depending on the minor's intelligence and mental state. The contract is void when the mental state of a minor is not sufficient to claim that the minor is a competent party to the contract.

Such a rule makes sense if you view minors as innocents in need of protection from competent adults who would otherwise take advantage of minors. However, the rule is not going to encourage competent parties to enter into contracts with minors, and some observers argue that it allows a knowledgeable and unethical minor to take advantage of a competent party. Consequently, a number of states have modified the duty of the minor on disaffirmance, holding that the minor has a duty of restitution that requires that she or he place the competent party back in the position that party was in at the time the contract was made.

Thus, continuing with the stereo receiver example, in some states William would have a duty of restoration that would require that he compensate the store owner for the difference between the value of the receiver in the condition it was in when given to William and its value in the condition it was in when returned. Case 10-1 illustrates the application of the majority rule for return of consideration on disaffirmance.

CASE 10-1

SWALBERG v. HANNEGAN
UTAH COURT OF APPEALS
883 P.2d 931 (Utah App. 1994)

FACTS: *The parties entered into a contract for the sale and purchase of an automobile. The minor's age was not discussed, and there was no allegation that the minor misrepresented his age. The minor made a down payment and promised to pay the remaining balance three months later. Thereafter, the minor disaffirmed the contract on the basis of his minority. The seller filed the complaint asking to have the contract enforced or to be put back into his precontractual state. The seller argued that the minor did not properly restore the automobile under Utah Code Ann. § 15-2-2 (1986) because it was returned in a condition that was worth substantially less than the purchase price. Utah Code Ann. § 15-2-2 (1986) states as follows:*

> A minor is bound not only for the reasonable value of necessities but also for his contracts, unless he disaffirms them before or within a reasonable time after he obtains his majority and restores to the other party all money or property received by him by virtue of said contracts and remaining within his control at any time after attaining his majority.

The trial court awarded a sum to the seller representing the remaining balance owed minus the value of the automobile when it was returned. The plaintiff appealed.

ISSUE: Is a minor who disaffirms a contract required to restore the full value of the property received under the contract?

REASONING: The judge found that, from examining the plain and unambiguous language of the law, it is clear that disaffirmance requires only that the minor return the property he has in his possession in whatever condition it is in.

The court stated that in previous analogous cases the courts clearly pointed out that the purpose of the statute

was to protect minors, and therefore any adult entering into a contract with a minor does so at her or his own risk because the law does not require that the minor return the adult to her or his precontract status.

DECISION AND REMEDY: The appellate court reversed the decision of the trial court, finding in favor of the minor and holding that a minor need not restore the contracting party to that party's precontract position in order to disaffirm a contract.

SIGNIFICANCE OF THE CASE: This case shows that the courts are willing to uphold a minor's right to avoid a contract even when the minor cannot return the consideration he or she received in its original condition.

CRITICAL THINKING

What facts about this case could you change that might have led the judge to a different conclusion?

ETHICAL DECISION MAKING

Does this case reflect a consideration of the interests of all the relevant stakeholders? What values do you think influenced the judge in deciding this case?

The disaffirmance must occur before or within a reasonable time of the minor's reaching the age of majority. What constitutes a reasonable time is determined on a case-by-case basis. For example, in the situation described in the Case Opener, the court found that it was not unreasonable for the defendant to disaffirm his contracts almost a year after attaining the age of majority.

In deciding to allow the disaffirmance, the court explained that the contracts were wholly executed and that there was no evidence that an earlier disaffirmance would have benefited the defendant or saved it from any harm. The court further noted that the plaintiff had made no use of his education in aviation, which had been of no apparent benefit to him. Under such circumstances, the court felt that a year was a reasonable time period within which to disaffirm a contract.

Exceptions to the Minor's Right to Disaffirm the Contract The minor's right to disaffirm is designed to protect the minor from competent parties that might otherwise take advantage of the minor. But there are certain situations in which, primarily for public policy reasons, either the courts or state legislatures have determined that the minor should not have the right to disaffirm the contract. As a general rule, most states will not allow a minor to disaffirm contracts for life insurance, health insurance, psychological counseling, the performance of duties related to stock and bond transfers and bank accounts, education loan contracts, child support contracts, marriage contracts, and contracts to enlist in the armed services.

Most of these exceptions apply in most, but not all, states. Another contractual issue on which the states disagree is the minor's misrepresentation of his or her age. While the majority rule is that misrepresentation does not affect a minor's right to disaffirm a contract, some states hold that when a minor who appears to be of the age of majority misrepresents his or her age and a competent party relies on that misrepresentation in good faith, the minor gives up the right to disaffirm the agreement. One justification for this rule is that any minor who is going to misrepresent his or her age does not need the protection that disaffirmance is designed to provide.

Other states have found a compromise between the two extreme positions either by requiring that the minor restore the competent party to that party's precontract position before allowing the disaffirmance or by allowing the minor to disaffirm but then giving the competent party the right to sue the minor in tort and recover damages for fraud.

Liability of Minors for Necessaries Contracts for necessaries are sometimes considered an exception to the rule that minors can disaffirm their contracts. Technically, a minor can disaffirm contracts for necessaries; however, the minor will be held liable for the reasonable value of the necessary. The purpose of this limitation is to ensure that minors are able to obtain the basic necessities of life when their parents will not provide them.

To compare how the law treats minors with how those in the marketing field treat minors, go to the **Connecting to the Core** activity on the text's website at www.mhhe.com/kubasekess2e.

A *contract for a necessary* is a contract that supplies the minor with the basic necessities of life, generally thought of as food, clothing, shelter, and basic medical services. It is sometimes difficult, however, to determine whether something is in fact a necessary. Some courts define a necessary as what is needed for the minor to maintain his or her standard of living and financial and social status, but this can lead to a problem when an item that may be considered a necessary for a child of upper-income parents might be considered a luxury to a child of lower-income parents.

Whether an item is considered a necessary is also related to whether the minor's parents are willing to provide the item in question for the minor. For example, in a recent case, a minor chose to live independently, but her parents kept her bedroom open for her and were willing to have her return home any time. When she chose to return home after having fulfilled only two months of a year-long lease, the court found that the lease for the apartment was not a necessary because her parents had always been willing to provide a home for her.[3]

One of the issues raised in the Case Opener was whether the aviation classes constituted a necessary. The court found that, given the defendant's social class, it would be difficult to find that instruction in aviation was really a necessary. Although perhaps some forms of education might constitute a necessary under certain circumstances, the defendant's circumstances did not merit such a finding.

LO 10-2

Ratification Once a person reaches the age of majority, he or she may ratify, or legally affirm, contracts made as a minor. Once ratified, the contract is no longer voidable. Ratification may be either express or implied.

An *express ratification* occurs when, after reaching the age of majority, the person states, either orally or in writing, that he or she intends to be bound by the contract entered into as a minor. For example, when she is 17, Marcy enters into an agreement to purchase an automobile from Sam for 10 monthly payments of $1,000. After making the fifth payment, Marcy turns 18 and decides to move out of state. She e-mails Sam and tells him not to worry because even though she is moving, she still intends to make her monthly payments to purchase the car. She has expressly ratified the contract.

An *implied ratification* occurs when the former minor takes some action after reaching the age of majority that is consistent with an intent to ratify the contract. Going back to the previous example, if the day after she turns 18, Marcy enters into an agreement with Joe to sell him the car in six months, that action is obviously consistent with an intent to finish purchasing the car, so she has impliedly ratified the contract. Most courts find that continuing to act in accordance with the contract, such as continuing to make regular payments under a contract after reaching the age of majority, constitutes ratification. For example, if Marcy continued using the car and making payments on it for several months after reaching the age of majority, the courts would probably find that she had ratified the contract.

Parents' Liability for Their Children's Contracts, Necessaries, and Torts As a general rule, parents are not liable for the contracts entered into by their minor children. Because of this rule, merchants are often reluctant to enter into contracts with minors unless some competent person is willing to agree to cosign the contract. In that way, the competent person will be legally bound to perform the obligations undertaken by the minor if the minor no longer wishes to live up to the terms of the contract.

[3] *Kim Young v. Phillip Weaver,* 883 So. 2d 234 (Ala. Civ. App. 2003).

Parents do, however, have a legal duty to provide their children with the basic necessities of life, such as food, clothing, and shelter. Thus, they may be held liable in some states for the reasonable value of necessaries for which their children enter into contracts.

In most states, parents are not liable for the torts of their minor children; minors are liable for their own personal torts. In many states, however, parents may be liable in cases where a child causes harm because the parent failed to properly supervise the child, thereby subjecting others to an unreasonable risk of harm from the child.

MENTALLY INCAPACITATED PERSONS

Persons suffering from a mental illness or deficiency may have full, limited, or no legal capacity to enter into a binding contract, depending on the nature and extent of their mental deficiency. If a person suffers from mental problems yet still understands the nature of the contract and the obligations imposed by it, the person may enter into a binding, legal agreement. Suppose, for example, that Gina suffers from the delusion that she is a rock star. When an encyclopedia salesperson comes to her door, she buys a set of encyclopedias from him because she believes that it is important that she be knowledgeable to set a good example for her fans. As long as she understands that she is binding herself through a contract to make monthly payments for two years to pay for the encyclopedias, she is bound to the contract. If, after making a year of payments, she no longer suffers from her delusions and wishes to disaffirm the contract, she will not be able to do so because her delusions did not affect her understanding of what she was legally agreeing to do.

However, a person has only limited capacity to enter into a contract if he suffers from a mental illness or deficiency that prevents him from understanding the nature and obligations of the transaction he is entering into. If, in the above scenario, Gina's delusions prevented her from understanding that she was signing a contract, and she thought she was giving the salesperson her autograph when she signed the contract, the contract is voidable. She may disaffirm it at any time until a reasonable time after she no longer suffers from the mental deficiency. Once the mental deficiency has been removed, she may also choose to ratify the contract.

As with contracts of minors, a contract of a person suffering from a mental deficiency that is for necessaries can be enforced for the reasonable value of the necessary.

If a person's mental deficiencies have resulted in his being adjudicated insane and a guardian has been appointed for him, he has no capacity to enter into contracts and any contract he attempts to enter into is void. Guardians may be appointed not only for those who are adjudicated insane but also for those who are adjudicated habitual drunkards and those whose judgment has been impaired because of a condition such as Alzheimer's. In any case, although the person for whom the guardian has been appointed no longer has the legal capacity to enter into contracts, the guardian has the legal capacity to enter into contracts on that person's behalf.

INTOXICATED PERSONS

For purposes of determining capacity, intoxicated persons include those under the influence of alcohol or drugs. There is some variation among states in the treatment of the capacity of intoxicated persons to enter into contracts. As a general rule, most states follow the Restatement of Contracts, Section 16, which provides that contracts of an intoxicated person are voidable by the intoxicant if the other party had reason to know that because of the intoxicated person's condition, that person was unable to understand the nature and consequences of the transaction or is unable to act in a reasonable manner in relation to the transaction. If the intoxication merely causes someone to exercise poor judgment, the person's capacity to enter into a legally binding contract is not affected.

Likewise, if one party has no way of knowing that the other was intoxicated at the time the agreement was made, and the agreement is a fair one, it will be upheld by most courts. For example, Lisa e-mails Rob and offers to buy his antique car from him for $8,000. Rob has just broken up with his girlfriend and has been drinking nonstop all day. He gets the e-mail message and immediately responds in the affirmative. Lisa had no way of knowing Rob was intoxicated, and so they would have a valid contract in most states.

Once sober, the intoxicant has the ability to either ratify or disaffirm the contract. Because public policy does not favor intoxication, the courts tend to not be sympathetic to intoxicants and will fairly liberally interpret behavior that seems like ratification as ratifying the contract. If Jim became intoxicated at a bar one evening, and Randi took advantage of the situation by getting him to sign a contract to sell her his 2004 SUV for $8,000, any act Jim takes consistent with ratification after becoming sober will result in a binding contract. If Randi appears at his house the next morning with the cash, shows him the contract drafted on a napkin that he signed, and asks for the keys and the title, then by giving her the keys and saying, "I knew I shouldn't have drunk that much," Jim has entered into a binding contract.

If the contract is disaffirmed on the basis of intoxication, each party to the contract must return the other to the condition she or he was in at the time the contract was entered into. Also, as with contracts of other persons who have limited capacity, a contract of an intoxicated person for necessaries will be enforced for the reasonable value of the necessaries.

LO 10-3 Legality

To be enforceable, a contract must have a legal exchange as its subject and must be able to be performed legally. In the event of a contract with an illegal subject, it is the agreement or the bargain that is illegal, not the contract. By definition, contracts are legal. That is why when a contract is overturned due to being contrary to law, the contract is frequently declared void, as if it never existed, as opposed to being declared illegal. It is important to recognize, however, that contracts can be determined illegal even if they are not against a specific statute. When contracts are against generally accepted public policy, these agreements are determined to be **unenforceable**, and not void. No remedy is available for unenforceable agreements.

unenforceable
A term applied to a contract that, because of a law, cannot be enforced by the courts.

CONTRACTS THAT VIOLATE STATE OR FEDERAL STATUTES

As previously stated, certain agreements are illegal because either the subject or the performance of the agreement violates a state or federal statute. Given the various state and federal statutes, there are a large number of possible ways in which contracts can violate a statute. Some of the more common ways are discussed below.

Agreements to Commit a Crime or Tort Contracts cannot be for an illegal subject or be carried out by illegal means. Therefore, any agreement to commit a crime or tort is illegal and unenforceable. However, should a legal contract be formed and then the subject of the contract becomes illegal under a new statute, the contract is considered to be discharged by law. For example, Jim agrees to work for Heather for one year as a poker dealer at her casino. After Jim and Heather enter into this employment agreement, the state government passes a law saying that poker may no longer be offered in casinos in the state. Because it would now be illegal for Jim to work as a dealer, the contract is discharged by law.

Licensing Statutes All 50 states have statutes requiring that people working in certain professions obtain a license before practicing their craft. For example, doctors of all varieties, plumbers, cosmetologists, lawyers, electricians, teachers, and stockbrokers are all required to obtain a license before practicing. While this list of professions is far from exhaustive, it demonstrates how widespread the licensing requirement can be in various states.

When licensing is required by law, people in certain fields must obtain a license before they can legally enter into an agreement to perform the restricted services. Frequently, such licenses can be obtained only after extensive schooling or training. The requirement of schooling and licensing demonstrates the concern society places on proper performance of duties in the designated professions.

In addition to indicating concern with proper performance, licensing statutes have two main purposes. The first is to give the government an avenue by which to regulate the specific industries. By requiring that professionals obtain a license, the government has some say over who can perform which jobs, as well as how many people can perform these jobs.

The second main purpose of licensing statutes is more closely related to the public interest. This second purpose is to protect the public's health, safety, and welfare. By imposing legal standards on a profession, the government is attempting to prevent people from being harmed due to substandard work. For example, surgery is a delicate, complicated process. It is not in the public's best interest to allow an unqualified person to perform surgery. Therefore, to limit the number of people who might be harmed during surgery, the government steps in and requires that surgeons, even after extensive schooling, obtain a license.

Given the different reasons for licensing various professionals, there are different outcomes when someone enters into an agreement with a person who is not lawfully licensed. The state in which the unlicensed person is practicing is also relevant because many licensing statutes occur at the state level and thus vary from state to state. For example, in some states, the statutes specify "no license, no contract." These states will not enforce any agreement with an unlicensed professional.

However, in a state that does not explicitly bar the enforcement of all contracts with unlicensed professionals, the courts typically examine the profession in question to determine why professionals in that field are required to be licensed. If the purpose of licensing is to provide government control over the profession, most states allow enforcement of the contract. Although the unlicensed professional is acting in violation of the law, there are no grave reasons that the contract should not be carried out. Nonetheless, because the professional is in violation of the law, he or she is usually required to pay a fine for working without the necessary license.

Conversely, if the licensing statute is intended to protect the public's health, safety, or welfare, the agreement is typically deemed illegal and unenforceable. Licensing statutes do not protect the public if people without the necessary licenses are allowed to practice the restricted professions. Returning to the example of surgeons, the public is made safer by the government's allowing only licensed professionals to perform surgery. Therefore, people cannot enter into a contract for professional service with unlicensed professionals when the law requires a license and the statute is intended to protect the public.

Usury Almost as widespread as licensing statutes, statutes prohibiting usury exist in nearly every state. **Usury** occurs when a party gives a loan at an interest rate exceeding the legal maximum. The legal maximum interest rate varies from state to state, but it is easy to determine the rate in any given state.

usury
The lending of money at an exorbitant or unlawful rate of interest.

While usury statutes act as a ceiling in terms of setting a maximum possible rate, there are a few legal exceptions whereby loans may exceed the predetermined maximum. One exception relates to corporate loans. Most states with usury statutes allow corporations to lend and borrow at rates exceeding the maximum. The rationale behind the corporation exception is that if a business needs money to expand and is willing to pay the higher interest rate, the corporation should be afforded the opportunity to borrow. The converse is that if a corporation is willing to borrow at a high interest rate, parties should be allowed to lend at that rate for corporations only. The intent is to facilitate business transactions in order to keep the economy in a healthy state.

Another exception to usury statutes applies to smaller loans. Many states allow parties to make small loans at rates above the maximum to parties that cannot obtain a needed loan at the statutory maximum. The belief is that if people need money and the statutory maximum is not inducing people to lend, certain parties will make the necessary loans at a higher rate as long as the loan is "small," which is defined however the state chooses to define it. This exception is the principle that allows cash advancement institutions to operate.

In the event there is no exception allowing a usurious loan, the legal outcome varies by state. A minority of states declare all usurious loans void, which means the lending party is not entitled to recover either the interest or the principal. A larger number of states allow lenders to recover the principal amount they loaned, but these parties cannot collect any interest on the loan. In addition, a final group of states allow lenders to recover the principal as well as an amount of interest up to, but not exceeding, the statutory maximum. In essence, these states allow the lenders to recover all but the excess interest, as if the loan were given at the statutory maximum rate.

gambling
An agreement in which a party pays consideration (money placed during bets) for the chance, or opportunity, to obtain an amount of money or property.

Gambling As with licensing statutes, all states engage in at least some regulation of gambling. In this chapter, the term **gambling** refers to agreements in which parties pay consideration (money placed during bets) for the chance, or opportunity, to obtain an amount of money or property.

While gambling is still illegal in the vast majority of states, many states allow casino gambling. The states most notable for casino gambling are Nevada, New Jersey, and Louisiana. Some states allow certain other types of gambling, either intentionally or through legal loopholes. For example, given California's definition of gambling, betting on draw poker is legal. Some states make other exceptions, such as for horse tracks, casinos located on Native American reservations, or legal state-run lotteries.

Sabbath Laws A large number of states still have what are known as *Sabbath, Sunday,* or *blue* laws on the books. Sabbath laws limit the types of business activities in which parties can legally engage on Sundays.

In most states with Sabbath law restrictions, these laws date back to colonial times. In fact, the term *blue law* is a reference to the blue paper on which New Haven, Connecticut, printed its Sabbath laws in 1781. New Haven's 1781 law prohibited shops from being open, as well as prohibited all work, on the "Lord's day" (Sunday).

The activities restricted today by Sabbath laws vary from state to state. Most Sabbath laws pertain to the sale of alcoholic beverages. These laws tend to prohibit the sale of all alcohol or at least specific types either all day or at restricted times on Sundays. Some Sabbath laws go as far as to make it illegal to enter into any contractual relationship on a Sunday. However, an executed, or fully performed, contract created on a Sunday cannot be rescinded.

There are exceptions to Sabbath laws. Most states with Sabbath laws allow the performance of charity work on Sundays. In addition, Sabbath laws do not typically apply to contracts involving the obtaining of "necessities," typically defined as prescription medication, food, or anything else related to health or survival.

Regardless of how widespread Sabbath laws are, the vast majority of states do not enforce all, or at least some, of their Sabbath laws. In fact, some Sabbath laws have in the past been deemed unconstitutional according to the First Amendment. Nevertheless, if Sabbath laws are on the books, despite convention to the contrary, they can be applied, and some states do apply such laws. As a businessperson, you should always find out whether Sabbath laws exist and, if they do, whether authorities enforce these laws.

AGREEMENTS THAT VIOLATE PUBLIC POLICY

Unlike agreements that are precluded by statute, some types of agreements are not illegal per se, as they are not in violation of any statute or legal code, but are unenforceable because courts have deemed them to be against commonly held public policy. Public policy involves both the government's concern for its citizens and the beliefs people hold regarding the proper subject of business transactions. The focus is "what is in society's best interest."

Contracts in Restraint of Trade It is a widely held belief in economics, as well as in America in general, that competition drives down prices, which is good for consumers. Accordingly, agreements that restrain trade are viewed as being harmful to consumers and thus against public policy. These restraints on trade are also known as *anticompetitive agreements.* Not only are anticompetitive agreements against public policy, but they also frequently violate antitrust laws.

There is an exception that allows specific types of restraints on trade. When a restraint on trade is reasonable, as determined by the courts, and the restraint is part of a subordinate, or ancillary, clause, the restraint is typically allowed. Such restraints are known as covenants not to compete, or *restrictive covenants.* Covenants not to compete tend to come in two varieties. The first involves noncompetition in the sale of an ongoing business, and the second involves noncompetition in employment, both of which are discussed below.

The first category of permissible restraints on trade is covenants not to compete that involve the sale of an ongoing business. *Ongoing* refers to the status of the business being sold: The business is still running and will still run on its own; it is not being merged and is not closing down.

The public policy argument in favor of supporting restrictions with the sale of a business involves the fairness of the sale. Let us examine a hypothetical situation to see why this restraint on trade is allowed. Suppose you purchase a jewelry store from Ann Smith. Ann is a well-respected member of the community, and her business has been around for many years. The

Sabbath laws

Laws prohibiting the performance of certain activities on Sundays.

covenant not to compete

An agreement not to compete against a party for a set period of time within a designated geographic area.

people in the community know the store, and they trust Ann to provide fair exchanges. As a well-informed businessperson, you know about Ann's reputation. In fact, her good reputation made the purchase more appealing.

Now suppose Ann turns around and opens another jewelry store a block away one month later. Ann's loyal customers are likely to go to her new store because they still trust her. In the meantime, Ann's good name is no longer associated with your store, and your business suffers accordingly. You entered into the sales agreement thinking you would benefit from Ann's good name, but in the end you overpaid for a business that lacks the benefit of Ann's name because Ann took her name with her when she went into competition with your store.

In the interest of self-proclaimed fairness, courts are willing to impose restrictions preventing Ann, or others in her position, from going into immediate competition with you, or others in your position. Public policy requests fairness in business transactions, and this fairness does not occur when people profit from a business transaction and then start a new business that destroys the business they just sold.

Consequently, the restraints to trade being discussed with the sale of an ongoing business involve the seller's ability to open up another business within a certain geographic location within a designated time period. As previously mentioned, to be enforceable, a covenant not to compete needs to be in a *subordinate* clause in the contract. If the covenant not to compete is a part of the main agreement, and therefore not subordinate, the agreement is typically considered unenforceable and void as it goes against public policy by providing unreasonable restraints to trade. The unreasonableness arises because when the covenant is an integral part of the contract, it cannot be objected to. In contrast, when the covenant is subordinate, the specific noncompetition clause can be removed and the agreement can go forward as planned. Case 10-2 illustrates the analysis of the court in a case involving a covenant not to compete signed in conjunction with the sale of a business.

The second category of permissible restraints on trade is covenants not to compete that involve employment contracts. The covenants in employment contracts are similar to those in sales contracts. However, with employment, the employee is agreeing not to compete with her boss, if she leaves, for a designated period of time within a designated geographic area.

CASE 10-2

JOHN MILLER, APPELLANT v. JAY PREEFER, RICHARD PREEFER, COMPROMISED MANAGEMENT, INC. AND PALM BEACH ALE HOUSE AND RAW BAR, INC., APPELLEES

COURT OF APPEALS OF FLORIDA, FOURTH DISTRICT

1 So. 3d 1278, 2009 Fla. App. LEXIS 1281

FACTS: *Miller operates or has ownership interest in numerous restaurant and bar establishments in Florida under the "Ale House" name. Preefer also operates or has ownership in numerous restaurant and bar establishments throughout Florida, some under the name of "Ale House." In 1992, Miller and nine associated companies sued the Preefer defendants for trademark and service mark infringement. The parties agreed in 1994 to settle the dispute when they entered into a mediated settlement agreement. Part of the agreement included a covenant to not compete. Miller agreed not to conduct a restaurant-related* *business in Palm Beach County, Florida, for a period of fifty years. This agreement was incorporated into the final judgment of the dispute.*

In 2002, Preefer sued Miller, alleging violations of the 1994 agreement. Miller counterclaimed, in part alleging that the covenant to not compete was unenforceable because it was illegal restraint of trade against public policy. The parties settled this dispute as well. Shortly afterward, Miller filed suit against Preefer, alleging that the covenant not to compete provision within the 1994 settlement was unenforceable. In 2007, the trial court ruled in favor of Preefer,

finding that the covenant was valid and enforceable as being part of a valid final judgment. Miller appealed, arguing that the Florida law expressly prohibits all agreements not to compete except those defined in legislation.

ISSUE: Is a covenant not to compete illegal when signed in conjunction with a settlement agreement? If so, does the illegal covenant not to compete void the final judgment of a dispute?

REASONING: Florida law provides for four situations where covenants not to compete are enforceable: (1) the sale of the goodwill of a business; (2) an employment, agency, or independent contractor relationship; (3) a licensing relationship; or (4) a partnership. The situation in the settlement agreement met none of these four provided situations.

The inclusion of a void or illegal provision in a final judgment does not, in itself, render the final judgment void. Thus, the final judgment could not be attacked at any time. Because the settlement agreement contained an illegal restraint of trade, the final judgment in the 1994 case was voidable. Accordingly, Miller could have filed a timely appeal or timely motion and had the settlement agreement within the final judgment struck down. However, Miller did not act in a timely manner to dismiss the settlement agreement not to compete. Instead, he operated within the confines of the final judgment and enjoyed the benefits of the agreement for 13 years.

DECISION AND REMEDY: The case was affirmed in favor of the Preefer defendants in light of Miller's lack of timely appeal of the original settlement agreement.

SIGNIFICANCE OF THE CASE: The case illustrates a situation in which an illegal covenant not to compete will be upheld as being enforceable.

CRITICAL THINKING

Do you agree with the court's argument in this case? Why or why not?

ETHICAL DECISION MAKING

How do the classical ethical guidelines help explain why the timeliness of Miller's action led to the court's decision? In other words, what is the ethical aspect contained in the court's reasoning? These covenants in employment contracts are not unusual. In fact, many middle or upper-level managers enter into agreements not to compete with their employers. In such a covenant, the employee is agreeing not to work for competitors or to start his or her own competing business.

Covenants not to compete in employment contracts are legal in most states. However, to be legal, the covenant needs to protect a legitimate business interest. Furthermore, the covenant needs to be for a reasonable period of time and geographic area so that it does not unlawfully impinge on the employee's right to earn a living. The agreement must not be for a longer period of time or larger geographic region than is necessary to protect the employer's legitimate business interest.

Given the variations from state to state in other areas of the law, it should come as no surprise that the enforceability of covenants not to compete also varies from state to state. For example, California does not allow any covenants not to compete. On a different note, Texas requires that the employee gain a specific benefit from a contract, beyond employment, before its courts will enforce a covenant not to compete. The employee must be given, or gain, something even if the covenant not to compete is for a reasonable period of time and geographic region.

LO 10-4 **Unconscionable Contracts or Clauses** When courts are asked to review contracts, fairness is not usually high on the courts' lists of things for which to look. Instead, courts typically assume that the contracting parties are intelligent, responsible adults. The belief is, barring proof of coercion, that parties enter into contracts because they want to do so. Nevertheless, there are times when agreements are so one-sided, or heavy-handed against one party, that the courts will not make the

harmed, innocent person fulfill his or her contractual duties. These heavily one-sided agreements are known as **unconscionable** agreements. The term *unconscionable* refers to the fact that the agreement in question is so unfair that it is void of conscience.

Rules against unconscionable contracts exist in both the Restatement (Second) of Contracts and the Uniform Commercial Code. However, before the Restatement and the UCC existed, the common law would not enforce contracts the courts deemed to be too unfair, or unconscionable. Now UCC Section 2-302 states:

> (1) If the court as a matter of law finds the contract or any clause of the contract to have been unconscionable at the time it was made, the court may refuse to enforce the contract, or it may enforce the remainder of the contract without the clause, or it may so limit the application of any unconscionable clause as to avoid any unconscionable result; (2) When it is claimed or appears to the court that the contract or any clause thereof may be unconscionable, the parties shall be afforded a reasonable opportunity to present evidence as to its commercial setting, purpose, and effect to aid the court in making the determination.

Every state, with the exceptions of California and Louisiana, has incorporated the above UCC section into its state's UCC. Section 208 of the Restatement also incorporates the above section from the UCC.

There are two main types of unconscionable agreements, procedural and substantive. **Procedural unconscionability** relates to conditions that would impair one party's understanding of a contract, as well as to the integration of terms into a contract. Regarding impaired understanding of contractual terms, the factors can be anything from tiny, hard-to-read print on the back of an agreement to excessive use of legalese (unnecessarily technical legal language) or even the inability of a person to fully read over a contract and ask any questions before he or she was required to sign.

Most frequently, procedural unconscionability arises when one party presents the other with an adhesion contract. An **adhesion contract** is a contract created by a party to an agreement that is presented to the other party on a take-it-or-leave-it basis. That is, the contract is presented as complete and as the only chance the presented party (known as the *adhering party*) will have to enter into the agreement. While adhesion contracts are themselves legal, the presence of one does raise some potential problem indicators for courts. Given that adhesion contracts usually do not allow for debate regarding the agreement, courts tend to examine adhesion contracts to see if they can determine how voluntary the agreement really was.

Conversely, **substantive unconscionability** involves overly harsh or lopsided substance in an agreement. That is, if an agreement is terribly one-sided, it is probably invalid on the basis of substantive notions of fairness and fair dealing. Courts would find the following, for example, to be substantively unconscionable: high differences between cost and price in a sales agreement; agreements in which one party gains vastly more than the other; agreements in which one party is prevented from having any sort of equal benefit; agreements in which one party has little to no legal recourse, according to the agreement; and portions of an agreement that are completely unrelated to anything having to do with either party's business risk.

Exculpatory Clauses An **exculpatory clause** is a statement releasing one of the parties to an agreement from all liability, regardless of who is at fault or what the injury suffered is. Because tort law attempts to return the wronged party to the state he or she was in before the wrong occurred, anything preventing this corrective mechanism is against public policy. It does not benefit society to allow some parties to get away with not having to pay for wrongs they commit simply because they state they will not be liable in various contracts. In fact, the patently unfair nature of an exculpatory clause is closely tied to the idea of unconscionable contracts.

Exculpatory clauses frequently show up in rental agreements for commercial or residential property. These clauses are often found to be against public policy. The reasoning is that sometimes people are injured while on property they are renting from another and sometimes the injuries are due to the carelessness, negligence, or other wrongdoings of the owner. Once again, it does not serve the public's interest to allow landlords, especially when it comes to residential

unconscionable
A term applied to a contract in which one party has so much more bargaining power than the other party that the powerful party dictates the terms of the agreement and eliminates the other party's free will.

procedural unconscionability
Unconscionability that derives from the process of making a contract.

adhesion contract
A contract created by a party to an agreement that is presented to the other party on a take-it-or-leave-it basis. Such contracts are legal but are sometimes rescinded on the grounds of unconscionability and the absence of one party's free will to enter a contract.

substantive unconscionability
Unconscionability that derives from one-sided, unjust, or overly harsh substance in a contract.

exculpatory clause
A statement in a contract that frees one party (usually the drafter of the agreement) from all liability arising out of performance of the contract; generally based on factors such as consumer ignorance or a great deal of unexplained fine print that serve to deprive the less powerful party of a meaningful choice.

property, to simply disavow all liabilities in advance. Were they allowed to do so, there would be nothing requiring that landlords fix problems in their rental units, including potentially lethal problems, such as faulty electric wiring or lead-based paint.

A basic test to determine whether an exculpatory clause is unenforceable is to see if the enforcing party engages in a business directly related to the public interest. Examples of such businesses include banks, transportation providers, and public utilities. Courts believe it is against the public interest to allow businesses engaging in work in the public's interest to not be held accountable to the public they are serving.

Another concern with large businesses that are serving the public interest is the unfair bargaining power they can possess in negotiating a contract. Given the power these businesses have, they could simply demand that all customers accept the exculpatory clause, thus escaping all possible liability. While the idea of these businesses' not being liable is bad, what is worse is that there would be no punitive financial motive for them to carefully conduct their business operations, or so the argument goes. As a result, the potential for increased accidents would be large. Obviously, it is not in the public's interest to have unsafe businesses that are not accountable to the public. Thus, these businesses cannot enforce exculpatory clauses.

Case 10-3 details a court's determination that an illegal exculpatory clause existed.

CASE 10-3

ERIC LUCIER AND KAREN A. HALEY v. ANGELA AND JAMES WILLIAMS, CAMBRIDGE ASSOCIATES, LTD., AND AL VASYS
SUPERIOR COURT OF NEW JERSEY, APPELLATE DIVISION
841 A.2d 907 (2004)

FACTS: *Eric Lucier and Karen A. Haley, a young married couple, were first-time home buyers. They contracted with the Williams to purchase a single-family residence. Lucier and Haley engaged the services of Cambridge Associates, Ltd. (CAL), to perform a home inspection. Al Vasys had formed CAL and was its president. Lucier dealt directly with Vasys, and Vasys performed the inspection and issued the home inspection report on behalf of CAL.*

The home inspection agreement contained a provision limiting CAL's liability to "$500, or 50% of fees actually paid to CAL by Client, whichever sum is smaller." This provision, and several others in the form agreement prepared by CAL, was followed by a line for placement of the client's initials. Lucier initialed this provision. The fee for the home inspection contract was $385, which Lucier paid to CAL.

Lucier claims that when he began to read the agreement, in Vasys' presence, he felt that some of the language was unfair and confusing. According to Lucier, Vasys stated that he would not change any provisions, it was a standard contract based on home inspections done in New Jersey, and Lucier would have to sign the agreement "as-is" or

not at all. Vasys does not dispute this, but relies on Lucier's signing the agreement and initialing the limitation-of-liability clause. Likewise, Lucier does not deny signing the contract or initialing that clause.

Lucier and Haley obtained title to the property from the Williams. Shortly after, they noticed leaks in the house. They engaged the services of a roofing contractor and found out the roof was defective. Lucier and Haley argue that Vasys should have observed and reported the problem to them. The cost of repair was about $8,000 to $10,000.

Lucier and Haley brought suit against the Williams, CAL, and Vasys, seeking damages to compensate them for the loss occasioned by the alleged defect. CAL and Vasys moved for partial summary judgment, seeking a declaration that the limit of their liability in the action, if any, was one-half the contract price, or $192.50. The motion for partial summary judgment was granted. Lucier and Haley then filed an appeal, seeking review of the partial summary judgment order.

ISSUE: Was the limitation of liability clause in the home inspection contract unconscionable?

REASONING: The courts find unconscionability to be "an amorphous concept obviously designed to establish a broad business ethic."

To avoid a contract on grounds of unconscionability, a court must first find that the contract is one of adhesion. Then it will examine "the subject matter of the contract, the parties' relative bargaining positions, the degree of economic compulsion motivating the 'adhering' party, and the public interests affected by the contract." In a situation where the potentially unconscionable provision limits a party's liability, the court pays particular attention to any inequality in the bargaining power and status of the parties, as well as the substance of the contract, keeping in mind the public policy against allowing parties to immunize themselves from liability for their own negligence, meaning that any limitation on such liability should be sufficient to provide a realistic incentive for the party to act diligently.

In the words of the court:

> Applying these principles to the home inspection contract before us, we find the limitation of liability provision unconscionable. We do not hesitate to hold it unenforceable for the following reasons: (1) the contract, prepared by the home inspector, is one of adhesion; (2) the parties, one a consumer and the other a professional expert, have grossly unequal bargaining status; and (3) the substance of the provision eviscerates the contract and its fundamental purpose because the potential damage level is so nominal that it has the practical effect of avoiding almost all responsibility for the professional's negligence. Additionally, the provision is contrary to our state's public policy of effectuating the purpose of a home inspection contract to render reliable evaluation of a home's fitness for purchase and holding professionals to certain industry standards.
>
> This is a classic contract of adhesion. There were no negotiations leading up to its preparation. The contract was presented to Lucier on a standardized pre-preprinted form, prepared by CAL, on a take-it-or-leave-it basis, without any opportunity for him to negotiate or modify any of its terms.

The bargaining position between the parties was grossly disparate. Vasys has been in the home inspection business for twenty years. He has inspected thousands of homes. He has an engineering degree. He has served as an expert witness in construction matters. He holds various designations in the building and construction field. He advertises his company and holds it and himself out as possessing expertise in the home inspection field. Lucier and Haley, on the other hand, are unknowledgeable and unsophisticated in matters of home construction. They are consumers. They placed their trust in this expert. They had every reason to expect he would act with diligence and competence in inspecting the home they desired to purchase and discover and report major defects. The disparity in the positions of these parties is clear and substantial.

The foisting of a contract of this type in this setting on an inexperienced consumer clearly demonstrates a lack of fair dealing by the professional. The cost of homes in New Jersey is substantial.

The limitation of liability clause here is also against public policy. First, it allows the home inspector to circumvent the state's public policy of holding professional service providers to certain industry standards. Second, it contravenes the stated public policy of New Jersey regarding home inspectors.

With professional services, exculpation clauses are particularly disfavored. The very nature of a professional service is one in which the person receiving the service relies upon the expertise, training, knowledge and stature of the professional. Exculpation provisions are antithetical to such a relationship.

DECISION AND REMEDY: The contract was unconscionable, and therefore the court reversed the decision and remanded it back to the lower court for trial.

SIGNIFICANCE OF THE CASE: While courts do not frequently find contracts to be unenforceable due to unconscionability, this case provides a good illustration of when the court will find the doctrine applicable.

CRITICAL THINKING

From the facts you have about the case, does the judge seem to be making any assumptions without an adequate factual basis to support those assumptions?

ETHICAL DECISION MAKING

Examine the ethical nature of the parties to the case. Whose behavior was particularly blameworthy? Whose was praiseworthy? What facts from the case and what ethical guidelines support your characterizations?

While businesses closely linked to the public interest cannot enforce exculpatory clauses, not all exculpatory clauses are unlawful. To be able to enforce an exculpatory clause, the party seeking enforcement must be a private business or an individual and must *not* be important to the public interest. Such private businesses or individuals provide nonessential services and thus do

not have the same bargaining power as the previously discussed groups, such as banks, utilities, and airlines. Given their lack of huge bargaining power, it is assumed that private businesses and individuals will enter on relatively equal terms and will voluntarily agree on or decline the final contract.

Examples of private businesses that can enforce exculpatory clauses include skiing facilities such as resorts or rental places, private gyms or health clubs, any business offering skydiving or bungee jumping, and amusement parks, to name a few. Because the services provided by all these businesses, as well as others in this category, are not something related to the public interest and not something in which people must engage, these parties are allowed to deny liability if the party with which they are contracting agrees to the exculpatory clause. Just because these parties *might* be able to enforce an exculpatory clause, however, does not mean the clause is always automatically enforceable.

The following Case Nugget looks at an interesting situation involving an exculpatory clause.

CASE Nugget

Can Parents Enter into Contracts on a Minor's Behalf?

Trent Woodman v. Kera LLC
Supreme Court of Michigan

486 Mich. 228 (2010)

Five-year-old Trent Woodman was injured on his birthday at Bounce Party, an indoor play area operated by Kera LLC. Before Trent began playing at the play area, his father signed a liability waiver including an exculpatory clause on Trent's behalf. Mr. Woodman signed the form as the parent, and Trent's name was printed on the form as "participant," meaning he was the one participating in the activity for which the exculpatory clause was drafted. When Trent broke his leg after jumping off an inflatable slide, Trent's mother, as next friend, filed suit against Kera LLC, on behalf of her son, alleging negligence, gross negligence, and violation of the Michigan Consumer Protection Act (MCPA). Kera LLC filed a motion for summary judgment, claiming that the claims were barred by the exculpatory clause.

Michigan common law prevents parents from entering their children into contracts that waive, release, or compromise a minor's claims. Because parents' authority of a minor is limited to the care and custody of the minor, any contract that a parent might enter into on his or her minor's behalf is unenforceable.

The Michigan Supreme Court upheld the common law in this case by finding that the waiver that Trent's father signed was unenforceable. The court refused to change common law because it believed that the court lacked the tools to adequately measure the risks involved in such a policy change. Therefore, the better vehicle for changing the common law is through legislature. Trent's case was remanded for further proceedings.

EFFECT OF ILLEGAL AGREEMENTS

LO 10-5

in pari delicto
In equal fault.

Generally speaking, when an agreement is deemed illegal, courts will label the contract void. The reason most illegal agreements are void is that, in most cases, both parties are equally responsible for the illegal agreement. In the law, when both parties are equally responsible for an illegal agreement, the parties are said to be *in pari delicto.*

When both parties are at fault, it does not make sense for the courts to attempt to salvage the agreement or reward either party. Therefore, most illegal agreements are void, meaning neither party can enforce the agreement and neither party is entitled to recovery.

However, it is not always the case that both parties are at fault. In the event that one party is not responsible for an illegal agreement or that there are special circumstances forgiving the illegality, it makes sense sometimes to allow one party to an illegal agreement to recover various damages.

The first exception to the general rule occurs when a member of a protected class is involved in an agreement that contradicts a statute intended to protect the specific class. In the event of such a contradiction, the member of the protected class is allowed to sue for performance. The reasoning is that if a statute is intended to protect a specific class, the statute should not be allowed to be used by people outside the class to harm those inside the class.

For example, a work agreement between a truck driver and his or her employer may specify that the driver gets paid for the number of hours worked. Yet certain statutes limit the number of hours truck drivers may drive in a given time period. If the truck driver accidentally drives more than the allowable hours, the driver has technically violated a statute. However, this violation does not allow the employer to refuse to pay the driver for the extra hours. Rather, the driver may sue the employer to enforce the work agreement.

The second exception to the voiding of illegal agreements occurs when there is a justifiable ignorance of facts. A *justifiable ignorance of facts* is one party's lack of knowledge regarding a provision of the agreement that would make it illegal. While ignorance of the law does not excuse illegal behavior, not knowing that the other party to a contract intended to fulfill the agreement through illegal means does function as an excuse.

When one of the parties is relatively innocent in the whole deal, the court may give back any consideration that party gave or may require an exchange for partial performance such that both parties can be returned to the positions they were in before they entered into the agreement. Conversely, if one party is completely innocent of any illegality and has completed his or her portion of the contract, then—depending on the reason the contract is considered illegal and depending on which state's laws are in question—the court might enforce the entire agreement.

A third exception to the general rule occurs when one of the parties withdraws from an illegal agreement. The key to any recovery is that the party must have withdrawn before any illegality occurred. If this is the case and if part or full performance has occurred, the party may recover value for whatever portion has been completed. However, if the party is involved in any way in the illegal activity, the party cannot recover at all.

Severable Contracts A **severable contract,** also known as a *divisible contract,* contains multiple parts that can each be performed separately. In addition, separate consideration is offered for each individual part. In essence, a severable contract is like numerous contracts in one. Conversely, an **indivisible contract** requires complete performance by both parties, even if it appears as though the contract contains multiple parts, similar to a severable contract.

With respect to illegality, severable contracts have a huge advantage over indivisible contracts: If a severable contract has both legal and illegal portions, the court has the option of declaring void only those sections of the agreement that are illegal. The court can then enforce the remaining, legal portions of the contract. Indivisible contracts must be enforced or rejected in their entirety. For a court to be able to enforce parts of a severable contract, the parts that are enforced must still represent the main purpose of the original agreement. If declaring parts of a contract void substantially alters the contract, the court is not likely to enforce the remaining portions of the agreement. Courts ultimately want to facilitate business transactions and enforce the legal wishes of parties, and severable contracts enable courts to do so.

LO 10-6

severable contract
A contract that contains multiple parts that can each be performed separately.

indivisible contract
A contract that requires complete performance by both parties.

SUMMARY

Capacity

Natural persons over the age of majority are presumed to have the full legal capacity to enter into binding, legal contracts.

A person has only limited capacity to enter into a legally binding contract if the person is:

- A minor.
- Suffering from a mental deficiency that prevents the person from understanding the nature and obligations of contracts.
- Intoxicated.

A person has no capacity to enter into a contract if the person:

- Has been adjudicated insane.
- Has been adjudicated a habitual drunkard.
- Has had a legal guardian appointed to enter into contracts on his or her behalf.

Legality

Contracts that do not have a legal object are not valid.

Contracts may lack a legal object because they violate a statute or violate public policy.

If the illegal portion of a contract can be severed from the legal portion, the courts may simply refuse to enforce the illegal parts and enforce the remaining legal parts.

Point/Counterpoint

Should the Law Allow Mentally Incompetent Individuals to Void Their Contracts?

YES	NO
Holding mentally incompetent individuals to their contracts sharply increases the likelihood of fraud. If contract law bound such individuals to their contracts, unscrupulous sellers could legally encourage mentally incompetent individuals to enter into fraudulent contracts, and courts, bound to apply the law, would enforce those contracts. Hence, permitting mentally incompetent individuals to escape their contracts sends a message to opportunistic individuals that the law will not sanction their fraudulent practices.	The great majority of mentally incompetent individuals live with mentally competent relatives, friends, or guardians who watch out for their best interests. Compared to judges, these guardians are much more likely to be able to act in the best interests of the mentally incompetent.
In addition to discouraging fraud, contract laws that permit mentally incompetent individuals to void their contracts protect the most vulnerable members of society. The law binds mentally *competent* individuals to their contracts under the assumption that they are capable of looking out for their best interests. But mentally *incompetent* individuals lack the ability to protect their best interests. Critics call these types of laws paternalistic, but a major function of the law is to protect individuals such as the mentally incompetent who cannot protect themselves.	Moreover, this government regulation hurts mentally incompetent individuals more than it helps them. If mentally incompetent individuals can legally void their contracts, competent individuals will be less willing to enter into fair contracts with them. As a result, mentally incompetent individuals will have fewer opportunities to enter into contracts consistent with their best interests. Hence, although the purpose of allowing mentally incompetent individuals to escape their contracts is well meaning, the result is malicious to the very individuals the law intends to help.
Indeed, if the justification for contract law is rooted in our desire for individuals to be able to enter into	Proponents of allowing mentally incompetent individuals to void their contracts argue that doing so would discourage fraud. But their position encourages fraud against mentally competent individuals. If mentally incompetent individuals can escape their

mutually beneficial exchanges, allowing mentally incompetent individuals, who by definition cannot determine what is in their self-interest, to void their contracts is consistent with this justification.

contracts, they have an incentive to enter risky contracts with mentally competent individuals.

Finally, proponents of binding mentally incompetent individuals to their contracts highlight courts' lack of institutional competence to determine mental competence. How can courts, they ask, reliably determine which individuals lack the mental competence to look out for their own interests?

Questions & Problems

1. How does the concept of the age of majority in Great Britain differ from that in the United States?

2. Explain the obligations of a minor who chooses to disaffirm a contract.

3. Go back to the discussion of contracts that cannot be disaffirmed by minors, and explain the policy reasons that support each of the exceptions. Can you make an argument for any additional kinds of contracts that should not be subject to disaffirmance by minors?

4. If all you know about a man is that his neighbors think he is crazy, you do not know whether a contract he entered into was valid, voidable, or void. Why not?

5. What factors determine whether a covenant not to compete is legal or illegal?

6. What is the relationship between contracts in restraint of trade and unconscionable contracts?

7. Hansen, a passenger on an America West flight, put a robotic head worth approximately $750,000 in the overhead compartment for storage during his flight. When he changed planes, he forgot to bring his robot head with him. By the time he realized what had happened, the plane with the robot head had already departed on another flight. Airline officials said they would retrieve it when the plane landed, and would ship it to him in San Francisco, but Hansen never received the head. He sued for damages for conversion and negligence. The airline was granted its motion for summary judgment on grounds that the loss was covered by a valid limitation of liability clause contained in the contract of passage and that the airline had offered Hansen the opportunity to insure the head for a greater amount, but he had chosen not to. Do you think the award for summary judgment should have been upheld on appeal? Why or why not? [*Hanson v. American West Airlines,* F. Supp. 2d (2008 WL 926297, C.D., Calif., 2008).]

8. Battistella entered into a contract to sell her veterinarian business to Martin. The sales agreement included a covenant not to compete for a period of five years

and within a radius of 15 miles. This agreement included a prohibition on all veterinarian-related practices. Battistella filed a declaratory judgment regarding the enforceability of the noncompetition clause because she wanted to open a veterinary health resort. Martin filed a counterclaim alleging that Battistella would be in breach of contract if she opened the health resort because Martin would no longer receive the "goodwill" of the business, which amounted to $5,000 of the purchase price. Do you think that the noncompetition clause was void and unenforceable? Why or why not? [*Martin v. Battistella,* 9 So. 3d 1235 (2008).]

9. Priscilla Howard was 16 when she signed a binding arbitration agreement with her employer, Food, Folks & Fun, Inc. She later sued her former employer on grounds that she suffered sexual harassment during her employment and that she was constructively discharged because of her complaints about the work environment. The defendant employer filed a motion to compel arbitration regarding Howard's claims. Howard responded by arguing that her filing of the lawsuit amounted to disaffirmance of the contract regarding the arbitration agreement. Additionally, she argues that she did not understand when she signed the arbitration agreement what the ramifications of that agreement would mean and that the defendant never informed her of what arbitration even was. The defendant argued that Howard's disaffirmance was not timely because it came eight months after her eighteenth birthday and had the assistance of counsel. Do you think the binding arbitration agreement was enforceable? Why or why not? [*Howard v. Food, Folks & Fun, Inc.,* 2010 U.S. Dist. LEXIS 133190.]

10. Deanna Milligan was injured when she fell two stories while saving herself and her children from a fire that destroyed her apartment building. She sued the apartment owner (Chesterfield) and management company (McCormack), alleging negligence as to fire and city codes and ordinances, apartment rules

and policies, smoke alarm inadequacies, and other matters. Chesterfield and McCormack asserted an affirmative defense of release, claiming that Milligan had signed and initialed an exculpatory clause that waived all liability to harms or loss of property suffered by any cause whatsoever, even if that cause was alleged to be the fault of or caused by the lessor. The defendants moved for summary judgment. Milligan countermotioned for a partial summary judgment. She argued that the paragraph containing the exculpatory clause was too broad and included nonreleasable subject matter. The trial court eventually granted the defendants' motion and denied Milligan's. Do you think that the exculpatory clause was declared unenforceable on appeal? Why or why not? [*Milligan v. Chesterfield Village GP, LLC and McCormack Baron Ragan Management Services*, 232 S.W.3d 683 (Mo. App. S.D., 2007).]

Looking for more review material?

The Online Learning Center at **www.mhhe.com/kubasekess2e** contains this chapter's "Assignment on the Internet" and also a list of URLs for more information, entitled "On the Internet." Find both of them in the Student Center portion of the OLC, along with quizzes and other helpful materials.

Reality of Assent

A Disagreement over an Agreement

Wilson LeJeune was a manager/member of Tri-Lake of Louisiana and was interested in purchasing a mobile home.[1] Couteau Plateau had a mobile home it had been using as a temporary camp after its camp was destroyed in Hurricane Rita in 2006. LeJeune looked at the mobile home, negotiated a $25,000 purchase price with Couteau manager Frank Sadler, and decided to go forward with the purchase. LeJeune attempted to get the mobile home titled in Tri-Lake's name but was informed there were significant tax defects related to the original purchase of the mobile home.

LeJeune contacted Sadler about the outstanding taxes, and the parties disagreed about whether the taxes were actually owed. According to Sadler, he offered to refund the $25,000 but LeJeune refused. According to LeJeune, the matter was left up in the air when Sadler left for vacation. Before Sadler returned from vacation, Hurricane Ike had made landfall and the mobile home was destroyed by floodwaters.

LeJeune filed suit seeking the return of the purchase price, arguing the existence of taxes was a mutual mistake. The trial court entered judgment in favor of LeJeune in the amount of the purchase price. Sadler appealed, arguing in part that there was a tax exemption for which he was eligible. The exemption paperwork could have been filed at any time and would have resulted in a full waiver of the taxes. The defendant filed this paperwork almost a full year after the mobile home was destroyed.

1. Imagine you were the judge in this case. Was the payment of taxes a part of the original agreement between LeJeune and Sadler? If not, was it something that materially altered the agreement?
2. Under which ethical system should LeJeune be able to recover the full $25,000 purchase price?

[1] *Tri-Lake of Louisiana, LLC v. Couteau Plateau, LLC*, 2011 WL 832502 (La. App. 3d Cir. 2001).

After reading this chapter, you will be able to answer the following questions:

LO 11-1 Why is genuine assent important?

LO 11-2 What are the elements of mistake?

LO 11-1

The Importance of Genuine Assent

When two people talk to each other in the hope that an exchange will take place, all kinds of things can go wrong. Global business needs dependability. Just imagine what it would be like if "Yes" meant "Maybe"! Deals would be closed only to be reopened again and again. The costs of all purchases would soar. Businesses would be forced to charge extra to pay for all the extra time they had to spend to finally get to the point where "Yes" really meant "Yes."

To make business transactions smoother and more dependable, the law has developed rules about when "Yes" means "Yes." As Chapter 8 explained, you need an offer and an acceptance to form a contract. Sometimes, however, there is a problem with the acceptance. Certain problems with the acceptance, or the *yes,* may give rise to the claim that the acceptance was not really genuine and, therefore, that the resulting contract is not valid. In this chapter we are going to examine the problems that may arise with an acceptance that will make the resulting contract **voidable.** When a contact is voidable, it may be **rescinded,** or canceled.

The cancellation of a contract permits the person who canceled it to require the return of everything she gave the other party. At the same time, the person who rescinds the contract must herself return whatever she has received from the other party. A major theme of this chapter is that good business managers aim for genuine assent in their contracts. This chapter shows you how to achieve genuine assent. It explains the major obstacles to genuine assent: *mistake, misrepresentation, undue influence,* and *duress.* Knowing about these potential problems will help you to avoid them.

voidable
A term applied to a contract that one or both parties have the ability to either withdraw from or enforce.

rescind
To cancel a contract.

LO 11-2

Mistake

When people agree to buy or sell, they do so with a particular understanding about the nature of the good or service they are about to exchange. However, one or both parties may think they consented to exchange a particular thing only to find out later that no meeting of the minds had occurred. People may misunderstand either some fact about the deal or the value of what is being exchanged. We focus on misunderstandings about facts because they are the only issues that raise the potential of rescission in American courts.

European courts take a different approach to mistakes about *the value of performance* of a contract. In general, they agree with the reluctance of American courts to interfere with a contract just because the value of the item in question has changed since the agreement. The parties are assumed to have accepted the risk, when they made the contract, that the value might change later. However, European courts permit rescission of the contract for a mistake of value when the mistake involves more than 50 percent of the value at the time of the contract.

Legal assent is absent when a legal mistake occurs. The term *mistake* in contract law has a special meaning that deserves special attention because it is not quite the same as the ordinary use of the term. A **mistake** is an erroneous belief about the facts of a contract *at the time the contract is concluded.*

There is one more important aspect of the definition of mistake. Later in this chapter, when we discuss misrepresentation, our focus will be on incorrect beliefs about the facts of the contract

mistake
An erroneous belief about the facts of a contract at the time the contract is concluded. When a mistake occurs, legal assent is absent.

206

caused by the other party's untrue statements. Mistakes in contract law do not result from the untrue statements of the other party to the contract.

Mistakes may be **unilateral,** the result of an error by *one* party about a material fact, that is, a fact that is important in the context of the particular contract. Alternatively, they may be **mutual,** shared by both parties to the agreement. This distinction is important in determining which contracts are voidable.

UNILATERAL MISTAKE

In general, a unilateral mistake does not void a contract. Courts are hesitant to interfere with a contract in a situation where one of the parties has a correct understanding of the material facts of the agreement. For instance, a widow seeking to rescind her and her husband's election to have his retirement benefits paid out over *his life* was not permitted to receive survivor's pension benefits. The court held that representatives of the retirement system had provided sufficient information to the plaintiff and her husband before they elected that particular form of payout.[2]

Sometimes, however, rescission is permitted for even unilateral mistakes. Because our economic well-being depends so heavily on reliable contracts, we want to be fully aware of the circumstances under which unilateral mistakes permit rescission. Any of the following conditions would permit a court to invalidate a contract on grounds of unilateral mistake:

1. One party made a mistake about a material fact and the other party either knew or had reason to know about the mistake.
2. The mistake was caused by a clerical error that did not result from gross negligence.
3. The mistake was so serious that the contract is unconscionable, that is, so unreasonable that it is outrageous.

These situations are rare, but it is important to be aware of them because any rescission can be costly in terms of time and lost opportunities.

Returning to the Case Opener, suppose LeJeune committed a unilateral mistake when he agreed to the terms of the sale. What would he have to prove to demonstrate that a unilateral mistake was made such that the decision should be corrected? Would LeJuene's lack of awareness about the taxes amount to a unilateral mistake?

MUTUAL MISTAKE

In cases where both parties to a contract are mistaken about either a current or a past material fact, either party can choose to rescind the contract. Rescinding such a contract is fair because any agreement between the parties was an illusion: An ambiguity in some key fact prevented the parties from being in actual agreement.

The famous story of the ship *Peerless*[3] has taught generations of students the importance of being very clear in defining material facts in any contract. The parties to the contract that led to the contract disagreement had agreed that the vessel *Peerless* would deliver the cotton they were exchanging. Unfortunately for them, there were two ships named *Peerless*. So when the deal was made, one party had one *Peerless* in mind while the other meant the second *Peerless*. The times the ships sailed were materially different, so the court rescinded the contract. *Warning:* Anticipate ambiguity in the material facts, and clarify them in advance to save yourself headaches later.

For a mutual mistake to interfere with legal consent, it must involve all the following:

1. A basic assumption about the subject matter of the contract.
2. A material effect on the agreement.
3. An adverse effect on a party that did not agree to bear the risk of mistake at the time of the agreement.

[2] *Ricks v. Missouri Local Government Employees Retirement System,* 1999 WL 663217 (Mo. App. WD).
[3] *Raffles v. Wichelhaus,* 159 Eng. Rep. 375 (1864).

unilateral mistake
The result of an error by one party about a material fact, i.e., one that is important in the context of a particular contract.

mutual mistake
The result of an error by both parties about a material fact, i.e., one that is important in the context of a particular contract.

CASE Nugget

A Questionable Mistake

Mary w. Scott (Respondent-Appellant) v. Mid-Carolina
Homes, Inc. (Appellant-Respondent)
Court of Appeals of South Carolina

293 S.C. 191 (1987)

Mary Scott signed a contract to purchase a repossessed 1984 mobile home from Mid-Carolina Homes, Inc., for $5,644, to be paid in full before delivery. She gave the salesperson a check for $2,913.71 and agreed to pay the balance before the end of the month. Within the next week, the salesman called and told her he could not sell her the home because it had a bent frame, and the South Carolina Manufactured Housing Board would not permit him to sell a home with a bent frame. She offered to buy it as is and sign a waiver, but the salesman said that would not be legal. A few weeks later, Mid-Carolina sold the mobile home to another couple for $9,220. Scott sued and was awarded $3,600 actual damages and $6,400 punitive damages for breach of contract accompanied by a fraudulent act and $3,000 actual damages for violation of a state consumer protection law. The appeals court upheld the award.

On appeal, Mid-Carolina argued that it was entitled to rescind the contract because the salesperson was acting under a mistake of fact when he gave Scott the sales price. In upholding the award, the state supreme court explained that a contract may be rescinded for unilateral mistake only when the mistake has been induced by fraud, deceit, misrepresentation, concealment, or imposition of the party opposed to the rescission, without negligence on the part of the party claiming rescission, or when the mistake is accompanied by very strong and extraordinary circumstances that would make it a great wrong to enforce the agreement. Mid-Carolina had not demonstrated the presence of any of the circumstances that would justify a rescission. The salesperson was in the superior bargaining position to know the price, and the buyer's reliance on a salesperson's representation of the price was reasonable.

Courts will not void contracts for reason of mutual mistake if even one of the preceding attributes is missing.

For instance, to rise to the level of a basic assumption, the mistake would need to be about the existence, quality, or quantity of the items to be exchanged. To meet the second condition, the mistake must involve the essence of the agreement. A fact is material when it provides a basis for a person's agreeing to enter into the contract. The second element is not satisfied when the person attempting to avoid the contract simply claims that the item to be exchanged is not the one he had intended to exchange.

The third condition is necessary to protect those who bargain with someone who agreed, at the time of the agreement, to bear the risk of mistake but then later wants to avoid that risk when the contract does not work out as well as he or she had planned. This situation might arise, for instance, if the adversely affected party had agreed in the contract to accept the items "as is" but later felt they were not worth the price paid. For example, the Case Opener may have led to a different result if LeJeune had agreed to purchase the mobile home for $25,000 and had agreed to accept responsibility for any monies currently owed on the property. Case 11-1 offers you the opportunity to see the elements of mutual mistake analyzed in the sale of a business.

CASE 11-1

CALIBER ONE INDEMNITY COMPANY, A FOREIGN CORPORATION, PLAINTIFF-APPELLEE, V. WADE COOK FINANCIAL CORPORATION, A FOREIGN CORPORATION, DEFENDANT, AND DIANA K. CAREY, TRUSTEE-APPELLANT

U.S. COURT OF APPEALS FOR THE NINTH CIRCUIT

491 F.3d 1079 (2007)

FACTS: *Wade Cook Financial Corporation purchased commercial property insurance from Caliber One Indemnity Company in 1998 that included $5,000,000 in earthquake coverage. In 1999, Cook renewed the policy, with the instructions to renew "under exactly the same terms" as the 1998 policy. Due to a clerical error, the earthquake coverage was changed to $500,000. Neither Cook nor Caliber One noticed this mistake. In 2000, Cook once again renewed the policy with terms identical to the 1999 policy. The $500,000 earthquake coverage mistake was replicated. On February 28, 2001, the Cook headquarters were damaged in an earthquake, and Cook filed a claim with Caliber One. At this time, Caliber One discovered the clerical error that had resulted in the reduction of the earthquake coverage, and it notified Cook that it would seek to be held only to the $500,000 limit. The federal district court granted summary judgment for Caliber One on the $500,000 limit, and Cook appealed, claiming the amount was a mutual mistake.*

ISSUE: Is the mutual-mistake doctrine applicable in this case even though both parties approved the contract containing the mistake?

REASONING: Both parties believed that they were renewing the contract under the original terms, including $5 million in earthquake coverage. Neither party was aware of the clerical error in 1999 or the reproduction of the error in 2000. According to *Washington Mutual Savings Bank v. Hedreen,* "Negligence in failing to observe that a writing does not express what has been assented to 'is not a bar to reformation of a contract when the reformation claim is based upon mutual . . . mistake." Therefore, simply because both parties had been negligent in catching the mistake does not mean that the mutual-mistake doctrine is not applicable in this case. Because the mistake was "relate[d] to a basic assumption on which both parties relied when making the contract" *(Denaxas v. Sandstone Court of Bellevue),* the mutual-mistake doctrine is applicable in this case. Both parties believed that the contract was being renewed according to the original 1998 terms.

DECISION AND REMEDY: The decision of the district court was reversed, and the case was remanded to have the terms of the contract altered to fit the original terms of the 1998 contract.

SIGNIFICANCE OF THE CASE: This case demonstrates that a mutual mistake can occur even on a straightforward matter, such as the amount of insurance coverage, and that the parties should be held to their original joint assumption rather than the mistake included in the contract.

CRITICAL THINKING

What is fundamentally at issue in this dispute? That is, what basic question do the two sides disagree on? Do you agree with the court's finding of which side's argument was superior? Why or why not?

ETHICAL DECISION MAKING

On the basis of the provided information, do your best to sketch the ethical considerations taken into account by each side in this dispute before the lawsuit. Does your projection paint either side as approaching matters from the ethical high ground? What facts of the case led to your stance, and what ethical guidelines did you use to reach your conclusion? Did you find yourself making any assumptions about behaviors not justified in terms of available information? If so, what do you think caused you to make these assumptions? Why is this sort of phenomenon important to consider in thinking critically about the court's decision?

LO 11-3 # Misrepresentation

Misrepresentations are similar to mistakes. In both cases, at least one of the parties is in error about a fact material to the agreement. But a **misrepresentation** is an untruthful assertion by one of the parties about a material fact. One party said something that prevented the parties from having the mental agreement necessary for a legal contract. The parties only appeared to agree, so their contract lacked legal assent.

> To see how packaging and labeling, as discussed in your marketing class, can be related to legal assent, go to the **Connecting to the Core** activity on the text's website at www.mhhe.com/kubasekess2e.

The courts are insistent that there must be a meeting of the minds for a valid contract. Thus, they might rescind a contract even though the person making the false assertion was entirely innocent of any intentional deception.

INNOCENT MISREPRESENTATION

misrepresentation
An untruthful assertion by one of the parties about a material fact.

innocent misrepresentation
A false statement about a fact material to an agreement that the person who made the statement believed to be true.

scienter
Deliberately or knowingly.

negligent misrepresentation
A false statement of material fact made by a party who thinks it is true but who would have known the truth about the fact had he or she used reasonable care to discover or reveal it.

An **innocent misrepresentation** is a false statement about a fact material to an agreement that the person who made the statement believed to be true. The person who made the false statement had no knowledge of the falsity of the claim. We say the person lacked **scienter.**

Innocent misrepresentations permit the party that was misled by the false statement to rescind the contract. However, because the party that made the false statement had no intent to mislead, the aggrieved party cannot sue for damages. The reasoning in such cases is similar to the arguments in a mutual-mistake case, as you might expect.

NEGLIGENT MISREPRESENTATION

In some contract negotiations, one party makes a statement of material fact that he thinks is true, but he is negligent in making the assertion. Such a **negligent misrepresentation** results when the party making the statement would have known the truth about the fact had he used reasonable care to discover or reveal it.

Even though there was no actual intent to deceive, the party making the false statement is treated in contract law as if the intent were present. If this standard seems unfair to you, remember that the courts find negligent misrepresentation only when the party making the false statement should have known the truth had she used the skills and competence required of a person in her position or profession. The impact of negligent misrepresentation is identical to that of fraudulent misrepresentation, discussed next.

FRAUDULENT MISREPRESENTATION

fraudulent misrepresentation
A false representation of a material fact that is consciously false and is intended to mislead the other party.

intentional misrepresentation
A false representation of a material fact made by a party who either knows or believes that the factual claim is false or knows that there is no basis for the assertion. Scienter is clear.

Any fraud on the part of a party to a contract provides a basis for rescission. The parties cannot be said to have assented when one of the parties was tricked into the "agreement" by a fraudulent misrepresentation. Thus, the agreement was not voluntary and can be rescinded on the grounds that there was no meeting of the minds.

Even in countries that are trying to encourage joint ventures and global commercial activity, such as the People's Republic of China, fraudulent claims can end the country's hospitality to agreements with outsiders.[4] In China, accusations of outsiders' fraudulent misrepresentation have resulted in heavy fines and even refusals to allow the fraudulent party to enter into any more agreements with Chinese firms. The point is that in most, if not all, cultures there is little judicial sympathy for those who consciously mislead others in commercial activities.

A **fraudulent misrepresentation** is a false representation of a material fact that is consciously false and is intended to mislead the other party. Fraudulent misrepresentation is **intentional misrepresentation.** Here scienter is clear. The party making the misrepresentation

[4] Charles D. Paglee, "Contracts and Agreements in the People's Republic of China," www.qis.net/chinalaw/explan1.htm, updated March 6, 1998.

either knows or believes that the factual claim is false or knows that there is no basis for the assertion.

To understand the requirements for a finding of fraudulent misrepresentation, start with the two elements from the definition:

1. *A false statement about a past or existing fact that is material to the contract.*
2. *Intent to deceive.* Intent can be inferred from the particular circumstances.

Then add a third necessary element:

3. *Justifiable reliance on the false statement by the innocent party to the agreement.* Justifiable reliance is generally present unless the injured party knew, or should have known by the extravagance of the claim, that the false statement was indeed false. For example, a person could not justifiably rely on a claim by another that a hair on her head, while worth $1,000, was available for $10.

Finally, if damages are sought, the defrauded party must have been injured by the misrepresentation.

Each of these elements can become a source of debate in any attempt to rescind a contract on grounds of fraudulent misrepresentation. Thus, it is your responsibility as a person who will be involved with dozens of contracts in your business activities to know these elements. A rescinded contract is a time-consuming and expensive business opportunity that has gone wrong.

Pay careful attention to the facts in Case 11-2, and decide whether you believe the defendant committed fraud.

CASE 11-2

MANDERVILLE V. PCG&S GROUP, INC.
COURT OF APPEAL OF CALIFORNIA, FOURTH APPELLATE DISTRICT, DIVISION ONE
146 Cal. App. 4th 1486 (2007)

FACTS: *The plaintiff-buyers, the Mandervilles and the Rinears, were looking for a property they could purchase and subdivide so that they could build two homes. Through their agent, Fowler, they found a property in El Cajoh, California. The second MLS listing for the property stated, in part, "All Useable 2.62 Acres County States 1 Acre Min. Lot Size Could Be Split." The listing was placed by the sellers, through the defendant brokers, PCG&S Group, Inc. One of the brokers, Clark, placed the language in the listing after talking to a county representative, whose name and gender he could not recall.*

The plaintiffs had seen the first MLS listing, which had been posted for 347 days, but did not inquire about the property at that time because it did not contain the language about splitting. Because this language was new, the plaintiffs asked their agent to confirm that the property could be split. The agent called one of the defendant brokers, who told her that the split had been approved by the county. Two days later, the plaintiffs made an offer

on a California standard agreement form that included a statement that the buyer had the right to inspect and investigate the property and that the brokers did not guarantee the condition of the property. The form also contained the following paragraph: "All understandings between the parties are incorporated in this Agreement. Its terms are intended by the parties as a final, complete and exclusive expression of their Agreement with respect to its subject matter and may not be contradicted by evidence of any prior agreement or contemporaneous oral agreement."

During the escrow period, the plaintiffs received a disclosure package from the defendant that contained documents indicating that the property was the correct size for splitting but that it had a 24 zoning, which, under the county's master plan, meant the land was "impact-sensitive." After the close of escrow, the buyers hired a civil engineer to submit their request for permission to split the property. The engineer informed them that, in

preparing the request, he had discovered that because of the property's designation as impact-sensitive, it could not be split.

The buyers then sued for intentional misrepresentation. The trial court granted summary judgment for the brokers on grounds that the buyers did not reasonably rely on the misrepresentations because they had not diligently investigated the legal condition of the property and that their agreement contained a clause stating that all representations were incorporated into the agreement. The buyers appealed.

ISSUE: Should a lack of diligence and the existence of an exculpatory clause prohibit a buyer from raising a claim of intentional misrepresentation?

REASONING: Reliance exists when a defendant's misrepresentations are an immediate cause of his taking an action that altered his legal relations, and without which he would not have undertaken such an action. As a general rule, a plaintiff's negligence in failing to investigate a defendant's intentional misstatement is not sufficient to eliminate the possibility that a plaintiff's reliance on the statement was reasonable. The fact that a contract says a plaintiff has a right to investigate the condition of property that is the subject matter of the suit does not mean that he has a duty to do so. And any provision of a contract that would render a defendant not liable for fraud, that is, an exculpatory clause, would be void as a matter of public policy. Thus, the void exculpatory clause cannot render the plaintiff's reliance unreasonable as a matter of law. In this case it was indisputable that the brokers knew that the ability to split the property was questionable and that the ability to split the property might move a property that had sat on the market for a long period of time. Under the circumstances, the plaintiffs should have the opportunity to attempt to prove that they entered into the agreement because of the fraudulent misrepresentations of the defendants.

DECISION AND REMEDY: The summary judgment was reversed, and the plaintiffs will have the opportunity to prove the elements of fraudulent misrepresentation.

SIGNIFICANCE OF THE CASE: This case shows that misrepresentation is serious enough that courts will not let defendants hide behind an exculpatory clause.

CRITICAL THINKING

The issue this case focused on was one aspect of proving fraudulent misrepresentation: reasonable reliance. List the other elements the plaintiffs must prove, and use the available facts to show how they might prove misrepresentation.

ETHICAL DECISION MAKING

What stakeholders are most affected by the outcome of this case?

Let's now revisit each of the elements of fraudulent misrepresentation. While the elements may have seemed relatively straightforward when they were presented, they become more complicated in the context of actual disagreements among parties to a contract.

False Assertion of Fact For fraudulent misrepresentation to be the basis for a contract rescission, the statement of fact need not be an actual assertion. Either concealment or nondisclosure can be treated as the equivalent of an actual assertion. **Concealment** involves the *active* hiding of the truth about a material fact, for example, removing 20,000 miles from the odometer on your car before selling it to me. **Nondisclosure** is different because it involves a failure to provide pertinent information about the projected contract. The courts have until recently been hesitant to use nondisclosure as a basis for rescinding a contract because it is a passive form of misleading conduct. Under ordinary situations associated with a legal bargain, it is not the obligation of one party to bring up any and all facts he or she might possess. Each individual is, to a large extent, treated as a responsible decision maker.

concealment

The active hiding of the truth about a material fact.

nondisclosure

A failure to provide pertinent information about a projected contract.

Consumer Contracts Law in Japan

In 1997, after studying the application of civil law in the country, the Japanese Social Policy Council, an advisory body to the prime minister, recognized that the environment surrounding consumers was growing more diversified and there was a significant gap between consumers and businesses in their access to information and knowledge as well as in their negotiating power. Because it cannot honestly be said that consumers and businesses are equal, as contracting parties are presumed to be under the country's Civil Code, the council developed a special Consumer Contracts Law. This legislation is considered to place consumers and businesses on a more equal footing in transactions.

Under the Consumer Contracts Law, if a business fails to provide a consumer with information or makes misrepresentations concerning basic or other important contractual matters that are necessary for the consumer to make a judgment about the contract, and if the consumer would not have entered into the contract had the information been provided or the misrepresentation not been made, the consumer may cancel the contract. This provision is applicable whenever a business, in trying to induce a consumer to enter into a contract, (1) fails to provide information about the contents of the contract, (2) fails to provide important information necessary for the consumer to make the decision to enter into the contract, or (3) makes misrepresentations. In many such cases, the consumer would not have been entitled to relief under the Civil Code because of its strict requirements for the application of fraud.

However, courts will now find nondisclosure as having the same legal effect as an actual false assertion under certain conditions:

1. *A relationship of trust exists between the parties to the contract.* In this situation the relationship provides a reasonable basis for one person's expectation that the other would never act to defraud him or her.

2. *There is failure to correct assertions of fact that are no longer true in light of events that have occurred since the initial consent to the terms of the agreement.* An illustration is my failing to inform you of the recent outbreak of rust on my "rust-free" car that you have agreed to purchase next month.

Nondisclosure is especially likely to provide the basis for rescission when one party has information about a basic assumption of the deal that is unavailable to the other party. As a result of this logic, sellers have a special duty to disclose because they know more about the structural makeup of the item being purchased.

Intent to Deceive Scienter is present when the party accused of making the fraudulent assertion believed that the assertion was false or made the claim without any regard for whether it was true or false. Alternatively, intent to deceive is present when the party making the false statement claims or implies that he or she has personal knowledge of the accuracy of the assertion. Any resulting assent is not legal because the injured party was not allowed to join the mind of the deceiving party. The party with scienter or intent to deceive wanted the contract to be fulfilled on the basis of a falsehood.

Justifiable Reliance on the False Assertion What responsibilities does the injured party have in instances where a false assertion was made by the other party? As we said earlier, the injured party has no justifiable claim of fraud when he or she relied on assertions that should have been obviously false. Anyone who pays for a house in reliance on the claim that it was "built before the founding of our country" cannot later try to rescind the contract on grounds of fraudulent misrepresentation.

In addition, parties to contracts cannot successfully claim they justifiably relied on a false assertion of fact when the error in the statement would have been clear to anyone who had inspected the item being exchanged. However, even this duty to inspect is declining in modern contract law. Increasing responsibility is being placed on the person who made the erroneous assertion.

Duress in India

In Indian law, duress is referred to as *coercion,* or the committing of, or threatening to commit, any act forbidden by the Indian Penal Code to force a person into entering an agreement. To prove coercion, the plaintiff must establish that (1) there was a clear utterance of threat; (2) the threat referred to an act forbidden by the Indian Penal Code; (3) the act was committed with the intention of causing the plaintiff to enter into an agreement; (4) there was unlawful detaining of or threatening to detain any property; (5) coercion was employed by a party or by his agent; and (6) the plaintiff is a party or any other person with some interest in the agreement.

Indian contract law distinguishes between physical coercion and moral coercion. Physical coercion may include threats to commit suicide. In contrast, moral coercion is synonymous with *undue influence*. The Indian Contract Act states that a contract is induced by undue influence when the relations subsisting between the parties are such that one of the parties is in a position to dominate the will of the other and the dominating party uses that position to obtain an unfair advantage over the other.

Quite unlike the concept of duress in the United States, the Indian concept of moral coercion, or undue influence, includes the unique consideration of *pardanashin*

ladies in contract law. In India, a pardanashin woman is a woman who lives in seclusion without communication with any male except for specific male relatives. Indian law gives protection to pardanashin ladies on the grounds that "they are ignorant so far as the worldly knowledge goes." Any contract with a pardanashin woman is automatically presumed to have been induced by undue influence.

In India, a major difference between acts of coercion and acts of undue influence is the legal consequence of each action. In cases of coercion, the agreement obtained by coercion is automatically voidable. In cases of undue influence, the contract is either voidable or is "set aside." Factors that enter into the finding of undue influence include the following:

1. Inadequacy of consideration.
2. Inequality between the parties in regard to age, inteligence, or social status.
3. Fiduciary relationship between the parties.
4. Unconscionable bargains.
5. Pardanashin women.

The more of these factors present, the more likely a court is to rescind the contract on grounds of undue influence.

undue influence
The situation in which one person has taken advantage of his or her dominant position in a relationship to unduly persuade the other person to the extent that the dominant person's persuasive efforts have interfered with the other person's ability to make his or her own decision.

LO 11-4

Before leaving this section about misrepresentation, consider what would have happened if Sadler, in the Case Opener, had known he owed taxes on the original purchase of the mobile home but failed to tell LeJeune. Would LeJeune be able to claim the contract lacked assent because of Sadler's misrepresentation? What if, instead of saying nothing, Sadler affirmatively asserted that all payments, taxes, and other monies related to the mobile home were paid? Would LeJeune then be able to claim the contract lacked assent because of Sadler's misrepresentation?

Undue Influence

When legal assent is present, both parties to the agreement are assumed to have made their own choices based on complete freedom to consent to or reject the terms of the bargain. However, many factors in our lives can work together to make our choices anything but free. **Undue influence** refers to those special relationships in which one person has taken advantage of his or her dominant position in the relationship to unduly persuade the other person. The persuasive efforts of the dominant person must have interfered with the ability of the other person to make his or her own decision. When people are bargaining with their attorney, doctor, guardian, relative, or anyone else in a relationship involving a high degree of trust, they can be persuaded by unusual pressures unique to that relationship.

DURESS

Duress is a much more visible and active interference with free will than is undue influence. **Duress** is found when one party was forced into the agreement by the wrongful act of another.

The wrongful act may come in various forms. Any of the following would trigger a successful request for rescission on grounds of duress:

duress

Any unlawful act or threat exercised on a person whereby the person is forced to enter into an agreement or to perform some other act against his or her will.

- One party threatens physical harm or extortion to gain consent to a contract.
- One party threatens to file a criminal lawsuit unless consent is given to the terms of the contract. (Threats to file a civil case against a party do not constitute duress unless the suit is frivolous.)
- One party threatens the other's economic interests (this is known as *economic duress*). For instance, Jim refuses to perform according to a contract unless Ellen either signs another contract with him or pays him a higher price than that specified in the original agreement.

The injured party makes the case for duress by demonstrating that the threat left him or her no reasonable alternatives. The point is that the free will necessary for legal consent had been removed by the specifics of the threat.

Consider the extent to which the threat in Case 11-3 left the plaintiff no reasonable options other than signing the agreement.

CASE 11-3

TELEKENEX IXC, INC. v. CHARLOTTE RUSSE, INC.
COURT OF APPEALS OF WASHINGTON, DIVISION ONE
158 Wash. App. 1037 (2010)

FACTS: *In December 2004, Charlotte Russe entered into a Master Service Agreement with AuBeta Network Corporation for communication services at its retail stores. The agreement was renewed several times. Just before it was to terminate in March of 2009, Tom Hunsinger from AuBeta e-mailed Giri Durbhakula, Charlotte's Vice President of Technology. Hunsinger stated that Charlotte would need to "make a commitment to Telekenex to avoid service disruption." Telekenex was taking over the contract. Durbhakula then received a proposed amendment to the Master Service Agreement. Charlotte only had two days to respond. Durbhakula signed the Amendment, but pointed out that nobody had explained to Charlotte why the existing Agreement was no longer valid. Durbhakula stated that "it has been made clear repeatedly that our service would be shut off if we do not sign up to a long term commitment."*

Two months later, Durbhakula told Chaney that Charlotte believed the Amendment was unenforceable. Charlotte obtained a Temporary Restraining Order, enjoining Telekenex from terminating Charlotte's service. Meanwhile, Telekenex sued Charlotte for breach of contract. Pleadings were served on Charlotte, but the papers were lost and Charlotte did not answer. The trial court entered a default judgment against Charlotte. Charlotte appealed, arguing that it had presented substantial evidence of a strong defense of duress to Telekenex's claims.

ISSUE: Is economic loss in the business setting sufficient to establish a defense of duress?

REASONING: In Washington, "business compulsion" is a type of duress in which a party is left with a choice between suffering a serious business loss or making a detrimental payment. Typically, duress will serve as a

defense to a breach of contract claim only if the breaching party was left with no reasonable alternative but to agree to the terms demanded by the other party. Moreover, the defense will fail if the party claiming duress contributed to his own vulnerability. For example, a party who actively tries to sell his business, seeks out a purchaser, and accepts a very low bid will be unlikely to claim duress. However, when a party, such as Russe, is operating under a contract that is not expiring, the party does not have notice of termination under the terms of the contract, and there is no indication of self-imposed pressure to enter into the agreement, the defense may succeed. Finally, the defense is available when a party who does not immediately accept the terms will suffer an immediate and substantial business loss. Here, Russe established that if it had failed to agree to the terms, it would have had 185 stores unable to connect to the Internet, connect to the company data center, use the telephone, process customer purchases, track inventory, keep employee time cards, or access company e-mail. Russe's inability to perform its business would have resulted in financial harm as well as harm to the company's goodwill and reputation.

DECISION AND REMEDY: The case was originally decided on a motion for default judgment. The court found that Russe had established a prima facie defense of duress and remanded for further proceedings.

SIGNIFICANCE OF THE CASE: This case demonstrates that duress in the business setting must amount to more the simple pecuniary loss. To establish the duress defense, one must be able to prove significant business loss.

CRITICAL THINKING

If this case establishes when the defense of duress may succeed, what are some examples of when the defense is most likely to fail even though a business will suffer a loss?

ETHICAL DECISION MAKING

Why would there be different rules for economic duress when the case involves a business as opposed to an individual? What ethical norms support this distinction?

GLOBAL Context

Defects in Assent in the Philippines

The law in the Philippines is somewhat unusual in the way it limits the time for rescinding a contract. In the Philippines, if consent is given through mistake, violence, intimidation, undue influence, or fraud, contracts are valid until they are annulled. The period within which to annul such a contract is four years. In cases of intimidation, violence, or undue influence, the time period is measured from the time the defect in the assent ceases. In cases of mistake or fraud, it is measured from the time of the discovery of the defect.

SUMMARY

The Importance of Genuine Assent	If assent is not genuine, or legal, a contract may be voidable. For purposes of planning, it is important for people to understand the circumstances under which failure of assent may render their contracts voidable.
Mistake	*Mistakes* are erroneous beliefs about the material facts of a contract at the time the agreement is made. They may be either unilateral or mutual. Only under certain rare conditions are unilateral mistakes a basis for rescinding a contract. However, if both parties to a contract are mistaken about a material fact, either can opt to rescind the contract. In cases of mutual mistake, the agreement was not based on a meeting of the minds, a basic criterion for legal assent.
Misrepresentation	*Misrepresentation* is an intentional untruthful assertion by one of the parties about a material fact. An innocent misrepresentation occurs when the party making the false assertion believes it to be true. The misled party may rescind the contract. When a misrepresentation is fraudulent, any assent that is given is gained by deceit. The courts permit rescission for fraudulent misrepresentation. In addition to requiring false assertion and the intent to deceive, fraudulent misrepresentation also requires justifiable reliance on the assertion by the innocent party.
Undue Influence	*Undue influence* refers to the persuasive efforts of a dominant party who uses a special relationship with another party to interfere with that other's free choice of the terms of a contract. Any relationship in which one party has an unusual degree of trust in the other can trigger concern about undue influence in gaining the assent of the more dependent party.
Duress	*Duress* occurs when one party threatens the other with a wrongful act unless assent is given. Such assent is not legal assent because coercion interferes with the threatened party's free will. For a court to rescind the agreement, the injured party must demonstrate that the duress left no reasonable alternatives to agreeing to the contract.

Point/Counterpoint

The principles of legal assent are based on the belief that, in the main, each person can look out for himself or herself. Thus, parties are usually held to the agreements they make on the grounds that the terms were reached by decisions guided by the free wills of both parties. But we live in a world of rapid technological change, where chemicals, fibers, and services come in a blinding array of complexity, that could make decision making more difficult for some people.

Should Courts Provide More Protection from Agreements Based on Lack of Knowledge on the Part of the Buyer?	
YES	**NO**
Courts should protect buyers from assent that is based on ignorance. For an assent to be worthy of legal protection, the buyer must appreciate what he or she has agreed to purchase. Otherwise, contract law protects the strong from the weak.	Existing contract law already contains adequate protection against severe cases of buyer confusion. Much of this chapter contains reasoning that buyers could use in certain instances to rescind an agreement.
For assent to be a cornerstone of a fair legal framework, it must flow from something other than large-scale misunderstanding about the safety, composition, and longevity of what we purchase.	What is especially disturbing about the suggestion that courts should provide more protection for parties to a contract is the danger the suggestion poses for personal liberty and independence. What will happen to our incentive to learn and grow as individuals if we know that the local judge and jury are ready to protect us from our own failures to discover more about goods and services that we plan to purchase?
Just go to any grocery store and ask yourself, "How much do I know about what I am about to assent to purchase?"	

Questions & Problems

1. Explain the difference between a unilateral mistake and a mutual mistake.

2. Explain when a unilateral mistake can lead to a contract's being voidable.

3. Distinguish innocent misrepresentation from fraudulent misrepresentation.

4. Explain how nondisclosure can be treated as misrepresentation.

5. Explain the primary differences between duress and undue influence.

6. Olga Mestrovic, the wife of an internationally known sculptor and artist, died owning a number of his works of art. Her will directed that all the artwork be sold, with the proceeds split among the surviving family members. She also owned real estate that, likewise, was to be sold. The executor, 1st Source Bank, sold the real estate to Wilkins, along with specified pieces of personal property that were in the house, such as the refrigerator, stove, and French scones. When Wilkins took possession of the property, he complained to the bank that the property was a mess. The bank said it would either hire a rubbish removal service or allow Wilkins to clean it up and pay him for doing so.

 In the process of cleaning up, Wilkins discovered eight drawings and one sculpture done by the artist. Wilkins claimed that he owned these items under his agreement with the bank, but the bank sought to recover them. The probate court ruled that there was no contract for the sale of the works of art. What argument do you think Wilkins made on appeal? How do you think the court ruled? Why? [*Wilkins v. 1st Source Bank,* 548 N.E.2d 170 (Ind. Ct. App. 1990).]

7. A dealer in Seminole County, Florida, contacted Harley-Davidson to secure authorization to sell the dealership to PowerSports. Harley had questions about PowerSports' business model to make sure it would meet the requirements Harley-Davidson had established for its dealers. Based on the answers provided by PowerSports, the transfer of the dealership was approved. Shortly after approving the transfer, Harley-Davidson discovered that PowerSports had not intended to operate its dealership in accordance with the Harley business model, which the firm required all dealerships to follow. Harley sued to rescind the transfer of the dealership on grounds that providing false answers to Harley-Davidson's queries during the negotiation of the transfer constituted misrepresentation. Harley also sought compensatory damages and punitive damages. The trial court held for PowerSports, and Harley-Davidson appealed. How do you

think the appellate court resolved the appeal? Why? [*Harley-Davidson Motor Co. v. PowerSports, Inc.,* 319 F.3d 973 (7th Cir. 2003).]

8. In 2007, Mewhinney decided to sell the contents of his wine cellar. Kurtz, as president of The London Wineman, Inc., contacted Mewhinney about the sale. London Wineman was in the business of purchasing wine from individuals and reselling it through an auction house. Mewhinney sent a list of what was available, which indicated that the cellar contained five bottles of 1945 Chateau Mouton Rothschild. Kurtz arranged to visit the wine cellar to inspect the wines to ensure the bottles were in sufficient condition for resale. After the brief inspection, Kurtz identified which bottles he wanted to purchase, including the five bottles of the purported 1945 Chateau Mouton Rothschild priced at $6,000 per bottle. When the bottles arrived, Kurtz discovered that four of the five bottles were actually labeled as 1955 wines.

 After hearing all the evidence, the trial jury found Mewhinney made a negligent misrepresentation upon which Kurtz had justifiably relied. The jury awarded $24,000 in damages. Mewhinney appealed the judgment. What was the negligent misrepresentation at issue? What do you think the outcome of the appeal was? Why? [*Mewhinney v. London Wineman, Inc.,* 2011 WL 989058 (Tex. App.).]

9. Audrey Vokes was a 51-year-old widow who wanted to become an "accomplished dancer." She was invited to attend a "dance party" at J. P. Davenports' School of Dancing, an Arthur Murray franchise. She subsequently signed up for dance classes, at which she received elaborate praise. Her instructor initially sold her eight half-hour dance lessons for $14.50 each, to be used one each month. Eventually, after being continually told that she had excellent potential and that she was developing into a beautiful dancer—when in fact she was not developing her dance ability and had no aptitude for dance—she ended up purchasing a total of 2,302 hours' worth of dance lessons for a total of $31,090.45. When it finally became clear to Vokes that she was not developing her dance skills, in part because she had trouble even hearing the musical beat, she sued Arthur Murray. What would be the basis of her argument? Her case was initially dismissed by the trial court. What do you think the result of her appeal was? [*Vokes v. Arthur Murray,* 212 So. 2d 906 (1968).]

10. The Lower Yukon School District provides public education in the region that includes the village of Scammon Bay in Alaska. Askinuk Corporation is the Scammon Bay native village corporation created by

the Alaska Native Claims Settlement Act. In October 2003 the school district proposed leasing from Askinuk 20 acres of land to build and operate a new public school. The proposed lease indicated that the school district would pay $1 per year. Askinuk's attorney reviewed the proposed lease and sent a letter to the board of directors cautioning the board about accepting the $1-per-year rate. The attorney drafted a new proposed lease containing a proposed rate of $400 per month for the first 10 years, after which the rate would be adjusted. The parties then met to discuss the lease. The school board indicated that $1 per year was all they could afford to pay and that the rate could be subject to renegotiation after 10 years. The proposed lease was approved by shareholder vote. Askinuk filed suit alleging, among other things, that the lease should be reformed as a result of a mistake in the price. According to Askinuk, the school board knew all along that the corporation would need to recover the fair market value of the land. Should the contract be reformed? Why or why not? [*Askinuk Corp. v. Lower Yukon School Dist.,* 214 P.3d 259 (2009).]

11. Robert McNeel was married twice during his life. McNeel had two stepdaughters from his first marriage and a son from his second. In 1998, McNeel moved to a ranch near Big Piney. The ranch consisted of approximately 4,015 acres of deeded land and 31,000 acres of grazing-permitted land, 420 cattle, and two homes. By 2002, McNeel's physician confirmed that he was suffering from progressive Alzheimer's dementia. Just one year later, McNeel was divorced and his stepdaughters appeared to reestablish a relationship. McNeel had had virtually no contact with his stepdaughters for 18 years. Both of the stepdaughters moved to the ranch to live with their stepfather.

In 2005, the ranch house where his stepdaughter Mrs. Kelly had been living with her family burned down. A few days later Mr. Kelly drove McNeel to his attorney's office. Mr. Kelly stayed in the room while McNeel changed his estate plan from leaving equal shares to his two stepdaughters and his son to leaving two-thirds to Mrs. Kelly and one-third to his other stepdaughter. Just a few short months later, doctors diagnosed McNeel with advanced dementia. After a short stay in a psychiatric hospital, McNeel was released into the care of the Kellys. Mrs. Kelly was substituted as guardian for McNeel. A few days later, Mrs. Kelly signed a contract for construction of a half-million-dollar house on the ranch. McNeel's son filed suit. What do you think was the basis of the son's suit? Who do you think prevailed? [*Kelly v. McNeel,* 2001 WL 1743922 (Wyo.).]

12. Horst Grasz reached an agreement with Bert Allen Toyota, Inc., to purchase a 2003 Toyota Tacoma for $16,971, less a $1,000 rebate, plus taxes and fees. The sales manager entered the numbers into a computer and came back with a final price of $15,017.50. If the computations had been correct, the total would have been $17,017.50. Grasz wrote a check to cover the $500 deposit and the sales manager manually wrote on the sales agreement, "$14,517.50 due @ delivery." It wasn't until the truck arrived at the dealership approximately four weeks later that the sales manager discovered the error. The manager insisted Grasz pay an additional $2,000 over the agreed-on price to take delivery of the truck. Grasz filed suit. Bert Allen defended by arguing mutual mistake or, in the alternative, unilateral mistake. Who do you think prevailed? Why? [*Bert Allen Toyota, Inc. v. Grasz,* 909 So. 2d 763 (2005).]

Looking for more review material?

The Online Learning Center at **www.mhhe.com/kubasekess2e** contains this chapter's "Assignment on the Internet" and also a list of URLs for more information, entitled "On the Internet." Find both of them in the Student Center portion of the OLC, along with quizzes and other helpful materials.

CHAPTER

12 Contracts in Writing and Third-Party Contracts

CASE OPENER

Fallout from a Forgettable Fight

On June 28, 1997, in Las Vegas, Nevada, heavyweight boxers Mike Tyson and Evander Holyfield met for what was to be a night to remember. During the third round of the fight, a desperate Tyson bit off a piece of Evander Holyfield's ear. The fight continued until moments later when Tyson bit Holyfield's other ear.[1] Tyson was disqualified, and numerous fans were unhappy with the outcome. Some fans were so outraged they decided to sue Tyson, the fight promoters, and the telecasters, seeking a refund.[2] The fans sued on the basis of, among other theories, a claim to being third-party beneficiaries to various contracts into which the defendants had entered.

1. Are the fans entitled to refunds based on a theory of third-party beneficiary rights? What type of beneficiaries would the fans have to be to enforce contractual rights?

2. If you were one of the fight promoters, what sorts of contractual duties would you have to the viewers?

[1] CNN/SI, "Year in Review 1997," http://sportsillustrated.cnn.com/features/1997/yearinreview/topstories.
[2] *Castillo v. Tyson,* 268 A.D.2d 336 (2000).

LEARNING OBJECTIVES

After reading this chapter, you will be able to answer the following questions:

LO 12-1 What types of contracts fall within the statute of frauds?

LO 12-2 What are the requirements for a writing to satisfy the statute of frauds?

LO 12-3 What does the parol evidence rule do?

LO 12-4 What is the difference between an assignment and a delegation?

LO 12-5 What does it mean to say that the assignee stands in the shoes of the assignor?

LO 12-6 What is the difference between an intended and an incidental beneficiary?

LO 12-7 What is the difference between a creditor beneficiary and a donee beneficiary?

Written contracts provide certain advantages that oral contracts lack. In situations where disputes may arise regarding the specifics of the terms of an oral contract, such disputes are easier to settle when the contractual terms are solidified in writing. In addition, when parties to a contract write down their terms, the moment of writing allows both parties to reconsider their terms and ensure that the parties are advocating what they desire in the contract. In general, written contracts help business contracting flow more smoothly.

The idea of requiring that certain contracts be in writing comes from the English "Act for the Prevention of Frauds and Perjuries," passed in 1677. To prevent disputes over the existence of a contract, the act required that certain types of contracts, to be legally enforced, must be in writing and be signed by the party denying the existence of the contract. In the United States, the term *statute of frauds* is somewhat misleading, because there is no federal statute of frauds; rather, such legislation exists at the state level, with the exception of Louisiana. Maryland and New Mexico have statutes of frauds created by judicial decision rather than legislation. Interestingly, the English have repealed almost all their requirements for writing, while American states and courts are still expanding the requirements for what falls within the statute of frauds. The term *statute of frauds* is also misleading in another way: The statute of frauds does not relate to fraudulent contracts, nor does it address the issue of illegal contracts. Rather, the statute addresses the enforceability of contracts that fail to meet the requirements set forth in the statute. Furthermore, the statute serves to protect promisors from poorly considered oral contracts by requiring that certain contracts be in writing.

This chapter addresses some commonalities among the statutes of frauds of different states, while referring simply to the "statute of frauds" as if it were a unitary law. The chapter examines which contracts need to be in writing, as well as exceptions to the rule. Then the chapter examines the parol evidence rule, which discusses what types of oral evidence are admissible, and when, as related to contracts within the scope of the statute of frauds.

Although a contract is typically an agreement between two parties, sometimes third parties have rights in the contract as well, either through assignments or as beneficiaries. The second half of this chapter focuses on how third parties gain rights to contracts.

Statute of Frauds

The **statute of frauds** has three main purposes. The first is to ease contractual negotiations by requiring sufficiently reliable evidence to prove the existence and specific terms of a contract. The second is to prevent unreliable oral evidence from interfering with a contractual relationship. Requiring a written contract prevents the admittance of oral evidence denying or substantially altering the contract. (This chapter discusses the admissibility, or lack thereof, of oral evidence later, in the section on the parol evidence rule.) The third is to prevent parties from entering into contracts with which they do not agree. The statute's requirements impose on parties the need to carefully consider the terms, agree to them, write them down, and sign the contract.

statute of frauds
State-level legislation that addresses the enforceability of contracts that fail to meet the requirements set forth in the statute; serves to protect promisors from poorly considered oral contracts by requiring that certain contracts be in writing.

Contracts Falling within the Statute of Frauds

LO 12-1

As previously stated, only specific types of contracts fall within the statute of frauds and thus are required to be evidenced in writing (see Figure 12-1). These types of contracts are (1) contracts whose terms prevent possible performance within one year, (2) promises made in consideration of marriage, (3) contracts for one party to pay the debt of another if the initial party fails to pay,

Figure 12-1

Contracts Falling
within the Statute
of Frauds

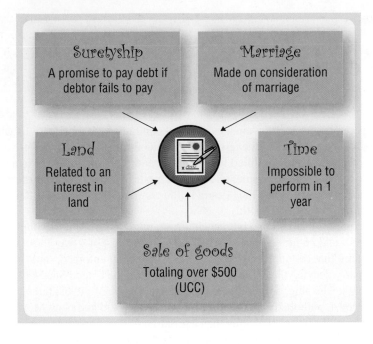

and (4) contracts related to an interest in land. Although required to be in writing under the Uniform Commercial Code (UCC), and not the statute of frauds, a related fifth category is contracts for the sale of goods totaling more than $500.[3]

CONTRACTS WHOSE TERMS PREVENT POSSIBLE PERFORMANCE WITHIN ONE YEAR

Contracts whose performance, based on the terms of the contract, could not possibly occur within one year fall within the statute of frauds and, therefore, must be in writing.[4] It is important to realize that the one-year period begins to run the day after the contract is created, *not* when the contract is scheduled to begin.

 The test for compliance with the one-year rule is not related to the likelihood of the completion of the contract within one year. Rather, the test considers the *possibility* of completing the contract within one year. For example, if Robert contracts with Elise for lifetime employment, they do not have to write and sign the agreement because it is possible for the contract to be completed within one year: Robert could die after two days of work. Moreover, Robert and Elise's contract, if oral, would be enforceable, as it is not within the statute of frauds. The possibility that a contract's terms could be performed within one year removes the contract from the statute's written requirements. Similarly, contracts for complex construction projects need not be in writing because, theoretically, they can be completed within one year if the crew works around the clock every day, even if the scenario is highly unlikely.

PROMISES MADE IN CONSIDERATION OF MARRIAGE

Agreements regarding marriage in which one party is gaining something other than a return on his or her promise to marry are within the statute of frauds and must be in writing.[5] In other words, when one party promises something to the other as part of an offer of marriage, the contract must be in writing to be enforceable.

 It is important to realize that mutual promises to marry do not fall within the statute of frauds. For example, if Ed and Jeanie promise each other they will get married, this agreement does not need to be in writing, as it does not fall within the statute.

[3] UCC § 2-201.
[4] Restatement (Second) of Contracts, sec. 130.
[5] Restatement (Second) of Contracts, sec. 124.

While a mutual promise to marry does not fall within the statute of frauds, prenuptial agreements do. A **prenuptial agreement** is an agreement two parties enter into before marriage that clearly states the ownership rights each party enjoys in the other party's property. To be enforceable, prenuptial agreements must be in writing. Furthermore, although consideration is not legally required, courts tend to privilege prenuptial agreements that involve consideration. The reason consideration is privileged is that a prenuptial agreement is not automatically enforceable just because it is in writing. Although writing is required, it is not sufficient to establish enforceability. Consideration at least offers evidence that both parties understand and agree to the terms of the contract and that the contract is not biased in favor of one of the parties.

prenuptial agreement
An agreement two parties enter into before marriage that clearly states the ownership rights each party enjoys in the other party's property. To be enforceable, the agreement must be in writing.

CONTRACTS FOR ONE PARTY TO PAY THE DEBT OF ANOTHER IF THE INITIAL PARTY FAILS TO PAY

The contracts involving promises to pay a debt that are within the statute of frauds are of a very limited kind. These promises are referred to as *secondary promises, collateral promises,* or *suretyship promises.* All of these terms refer to agreements in which a third party agrees to pay the debt owed by another party if that other party fails to pay his or her debt. For example, Helen enters into a contract with Tom to sell Tom her car. Subsequently, Diana agrees to pay Tom's debt if he fails to pay Helen the money he owes her. To be enforceable, Diana's promise needs to be in writing because it is within the statute.

It is important to understand the distinction between primary and secondary obligations to know when the statute necessitates a written agreement. *Primary obligations* are debts entered into in an initial contract. Using our car-sale example, the primary obligation is Tom's promise to pay Helen for the car. Primary obligations are not within the statute of frauds and, therefore, need not be in writing to be enforceable.

Secondary obligations, however, are within the statute and need to be in writing. A *secondary obligation,* as explained above, arises when a party outside a primary agreement promises to fulfill one of the original party's (the primary debtor's) obligations if the original party (primary debtor) fails to fulfill his or her obligation.

A specific instance of a secondary obligation involves the administrator or executor of an estate. Administrators and executors of estates are responsible for paying the debts of an estate and then dividing the remaining wealth among the heirs. While an agreement to pay the estate's debts with the estate's funds need not be in writing, promises the administrator or executor makes to pay those debts personally are within the statute of frauds and must be in writing. Because the administrator or executor is paying with his or her own money, and not the estate's, the promises must be in writing to be enforceable—the administrator or executor has assumed a secondary obligation.

There is an exception as to when a promise to pay someone else's debt needs to be in writing: *the main-purpose rule.* If the main purpose for incurring a secondary obligation is to obtain a personal benefit, the promise does not fall within the statute and need not be in writing.[6] The assumption is that a party attempting to achieve a personal benefit will not back out of the agreement, and thus there is no need for a written record of the agreement. The court's job is to use the context surrounding the agreement to determine the third party's main purpose for entering the agreement.

CONTRACTS RELATED TO AN INTEREST IN LAND

Under the statute of frauds, land is considered real property, such as the land and soil itself, as well as anything attached to the land, such as trees or buildings. The statute is intended to prevent oral claims to the existence of a contract for the sale of land. That is, because the statute requires a writing as evidence of the contract, a claim to an oral contract for the sale of land is not enough to prove such a contract existed.

In addition to contracts for the sale of land, contracts transferring other interests in land are also within the statute of frauds. Mortgages and leases are within the statute of frauds because they are considered transfers of interest in land.

Determining exactly what constitutes an interest in land under the statute of frauds is difficult. While the sale of land and the transfer of mortgages and leases are within the statute, a number

[6] Restatement (Second) of Contracts, sec. 116.

England and the Statute of Frauds

As stated in the text, England gave birth to the statute of frauds. While the United States, in addition to numerous other Western countries, has subsequently adopted versions of the 1677 English act, the English have gone in the opposite direction. Instead of expanding the powers and use of the 1677 act, the English have severely limited the number of cases falling within their statute of frauds.

Although formal complaints were levied against the English statute of frauds as early as 1937, no action was taken until 1953. In that year, the Law Reform Committee addressed numerous arguments that had been made in 1937 in favor of repeal of the statute of frauds. The 1953 committee recommended that Parliament repeal Section 4 of the 1677 act, the section that identified the specific types of contracts that must be in writing. The Law Reform Act of 1954 subsequently repealed Section 4, with one cautionary exception: The 1954 act still required that promises to pay for the debt of others be in writing. In other words, the only provision still active (requiring a writing) under the statute of frauds in the country that invented the statute is what we would call *suretyship* or *collateral promise*.

of things that seem as if they are interests in land do not fall within the statute. For example, promises to sell crops annually, agreements between parties for profit sharing from the sale of real property, and boundary disputes that have been settled through the use of land are not within the statute of frauds and, therefore, do not require evidence in writing. The Case Nugget presents a case related to land in which the parties disagreed as to whether a writing was needed.

CASE Nugget

What Is an "Interest in Land"?

Shelby's, Inc. v. Sierra Bravo, Inc.
Court of Appeals of Missouri, Southern District

68 S.W.3d 604 (2002)

Shelby's and Sierra entered into a written agreement in which Shelby's granted Sierra permission to use Shelby's land as disposal for waste and debris Sierra removed as part of the construction of a new highway. Shelby's claimed that the parties also entered into an oral contract for Sierra to construct a waterway and building pad on Shelby's property. Sierra never completed the construction and denied that an oral contract existed. Shelby's sued, and the jury found in its favor.

Sierra appealed on the basis that the oral agreement was within the statute of frauds and therefore unenforceable. Sierra saw the alleged oral agreement as involving a sale of an interest in land, which is within the statute of frauds. Therefore, the agreement, to be enforceable, would have had to be in writing.

The court firmly disagreed with Sierra's argument. The court stated:

> We agree with the well-reasoned argument of Respondent [Shelby's]. The contract in this case was not a "sale," much less a sale of an interest in lands. . . . Here, there was no transfer of ownership or title. The written agreement gave Appellant [Sierra] permission to deposit debris and soil on Respondent's land, not the right to do so. The oral contract was for the construction of a waterway and building pad and passed no interest in the land. . . . We decline to create a new category to which the statute of frauds applies, that of a contract for services for the deposit of dirt and soil on land. The trial court did not err in denying Appellant's motion for judgment notwithstanding the verdict. Appellant's point is denied and the judgment of the trial court is affirmed.

CONTRACTS FOR THE SALE OF GOODS TOTALING MORE THAN $500

Agreements in which the total price for a sale is $500 or more are required by the UCC, Section 2-201, to be recorded in a written contract or a memorandum. To satisfy this UCC requirement, the contract or memorandum need only state the quantity to be sold. Buyer, seller, price, and method of payment do not need to be included in the writing according to the UCC. Contractual terms beyond quantity may be written, but they need not be. In fact, terms other than quantity can be inexact or be left out of the writing as long as what is written does not contradict the parties' agreement. The contract will be enforceable for the stated quantity and not a unit more. Furthermore, for the contract to be enforceable against a party, the party against whom action is sought must have signed the written document.

In addition to sales contracts for $500 or more, there are other specific situations under the UCC for contracts that need to be in writing. These situations are contracts involving the sale of securities[7] and personal property[8] if the sale is greater than $5,000 in price.

FURTHER REQUIREMENTS SPECIFIC TO CERTAIN STATES

As discussed at the beginning of the chapter, the statute of frauds is actually state law. Consequently, certain states have various requirements not found in other states. While these requirements are not universal, it is important to note some of the distinctive elements of the statutes of frauds in a minority of the states.

Some states require a writing within the statute of frauds under what is called the *equal dignity rule.* Under the **equal dignity rule,** contracts that would normally fall under the statute and need a writing if negotiated by the principal must be in writing even if negotiated by an agent.

equal dignity rule
A rule requiring that contracts that would normally fall under the statute of frauds and need a writing if negotiated by the principal must be in writing even if negotiated by an agent.

Within their statutes of frauds, a minority of states have special provisions related to promises to pay debt. One example pertains to a promise to pay a debt that has already been discharged because of bankruptcy. For such an agreement to be enforceable, it must be in writing to prevent the promisor from hiding behind the fact that the debt has been discharged. Another example involves a promise to pay a debt where collection of the debt is barred by a statute of limitations. As in the first example, if the agreement is not in writing, the promisor can easily prove that he or she does not need to pay. Therefore, the statutes of frauds in certain states require that both of these types of promises be in writing to be enforceable.

Exceptions to the Statute of Frauds

As with most legal rules, there are certain exceptions to which the statute of frauds does not apply, even though under normal circumstances it would. These exceptions are (1) admission, (2) partial performance, (3) promissory estoppel, and (4) although not under the statute of frauds, exceptions under the UCC.

ADMISSION

An **admission** is a statement made in court, under oath, or at some stage during a legal proceeding in which a party against whom charges have been brought admits that an oral contract existed, even though the contract was required to be in writing.[9] All states except Louisiana and California adhere to the admission exception. To the extent that the statute of frauds is intended to necessitate proper evidence of agreements, the admission exception is well reasoned. However, to the extent that the statute of frauds is intended to cause people to be cautious about clearly establishing the specifics of their agreements, the admission exception seems to unnecessarily punish honest parties while rewarding dishonest ones.

admission
A statement made in court, under oath, or at some stage during a legal proceeding in which a party against whom charges have been brought admits that an oral contract existed, even though the contract was required to be in writing.

[7] UCC § 8-319.
[8] UCC § 81-206.
[9] Restatement (Second) of Contracts, sec. 133.

Similar to the statute of frauds, the UCC makes a comparable exception in cases where parties admit to the existence of an oral contract. However, unlike the statute of frauds, the UCC specifies that an oral contract required to be in writing but admitted to in court will be enforceable only for the quantity admitted.[10]

PARTIAL PERFORMANCE

partial performance
An exception to the statute of frauds in which the performance of portions of an unwritten agreement by one or both parties can constitute proof that an oral contract exists between the parties.

Although the statute of frauds requires a writing for sales of interests in land, there is an exception based on the theory of partial performance. Under **partial performance,** if the buyer in an alleged contract for the sale of land has paid any portion of the sales price and either has begun to permanently improve the land or has taken possession of the land, the courts will consider the contract partially performed, and this partial performance will amount to proof of the contract.

Accordingly, partial performance can override the statute's requirement for a written agreement. The logic is that the actions of both parties demonstrate the existence of their agreement, so the agreement no longer needs to be in writing to be enforceable, even though a writing would otherwise be needed. Under similar sections of the UCC, a buyer or seller is responsible for an oral contract that should have been in writing to the extent that he or she accepts payment or delivery of the goods in question.[11]

PROMISSORY ESTOPPEL

promissory estoppel
The legal enforcement of an otherwise unenforceable contract due to a party's detrimental reliance on the contract.

Under certain circumstances, when a party relies on an oral contract that is within the statute of frauds, and therefore should have been in writing, the reliance can create a situation in which the contract is enforceable. **Promissory estoppel** is the legal enforcement of an otherwise unenforceable contract due to a party's detrimental reliance on the contract.

For promissory estoppel to be in effect, the party's reliance must be to his or her own detriment. Furthermore, the reliance must have been reasonably foreseeable; that is, the party who did not rely on the contract should have known that the other party was going to rely on it.[12]

Suppose that, after accepting an offer on your current house, you enter into a contract to buy a house. However, the new house costs more than the sales price of your old house, and the person from whom you are buying knows about the sale of your old house and the difference in the prices. To pay for the price difference, you sell your collection of rare coins. Unfortunately, during this whole process, you forgot to create a written contract for the purchase of the new house. The other person now refuses to sell the house to you. You are now homeless and have sold off your only real assets. Because the other person reasonably should have known you were relying on the contract, and because you did so to your own detriment, under promissory estoppel you could win performance of the oral sales contract.

EXCEPTIONS UNDER THE UCC

In addition to the exceptions under the statute of frauds, exceptions also exist under the UCC as to when a contract ordinarily required to be in writing need not be in writing. For instance, under the UCC, oral contracts between merchants need not be in writing to be enforceable. Therefore, if one merchant agrees to sell goods to another, the contract is enforceable even if it is not in writing.

To learn more about the link between concepts studied in your management class and the statute of frauds, go to the **Connecting to the Core** activity on the text's website at www.mhhe.com/kubasekess2e.

Likewise, oral contracts for customized goods are enforceable even if they would normally have to be in writing. The reasoning is that customized goods are not likely to be able to be sold to a general audience. Accordingly, if one party backs out of an oral arrangement for the sale of customized goods, the party that did not back out probably incurred unreasonable costs due to the negated contract. To prevent one party from bearing the cost of a canceled contract, the UCC allows oral agreements to be enforced when they are for customized goods.

[10] UCC § 2-201(3)(b).
[11] UCC § 2-201(3)(c).
[12] Restatement (Second) of Contracts, sec. 139.

Sufficiency of the Writing

Although there are no specific requirements for the form of a written contract under the statute of frauds, certain elements need to be present for a writing to constitute proper evidence of a written contract under the statute. It is worth mentioning that, in the absence of a single standard form, multiple documents can together evidence the existence of a written agreement under the statute.

Required elements in the writing include the identification of the parties to the contract, the subject of the agreement, the consideration if any is given, and any pertinent terms of the contract. Furthermore, the contract must be signed, but the signature does not need to be located at the end, which is the traditional location for a signature. In fact, the signature need not be the full signature; a mark, such as an initial, is permissible as long as the mark is placed with the intent that it function as a signature. While it is standard for both parties to sign the agreement, because the writing is being offered as proof of an agreement, only the party against whom action is sought needs to have signed the writing. If only one party signed, the agreement is enforceable against the signing party but not against the nonsigning party. The required elements can be contained in a memorandum, a written document, or a compilation of several written documents.

The requirements under the UCC for sales contracts vary slightly from those under the statute of frauds. The UCC does not require that the parties be named in the agreement. Rather, the UCC requires that the writing clearly state the quantity to be sold. Similar to the statute of frauds, the UCC allows a variety of written documents to constitute a writing. Some documents that count include faxes, e-mails, invoices, bills of lading, sales slips, checks, or any combination of these documents.

Also noteworthy is the fact that oral testimony can be elicited that establishes the existence of a writing that would meet the requirements under the statute of frauds. For example, testimony regarding an invoice for products sold, when the actual invoice is not produced, is enough in certain states to meet the requirements under the statute.

Case 12-1 demonstrates how judges determine what constitutes oral testimony that establishes the existence of a writing and when a writing is sufficient under the statute of frauds.

 CASE 12-1

MARTHA A. NIX AND CHARLES E. UPHAM v. SKIP WICK, CHRISTIE WICK, AND JAMES OLDFIELD

SUPREME COURT OF ALABAMA

2010 Ala. LEXIS 250

FACTS: *Skip Wick and wife Christie Wick owned a house with approximately 4½ acres of land at 296 West Shugart Ridge in Gardendale. Christie Wick and her brother James Oldfield owned several acres of land adjacent to and surrounding the Wicks' property. On April 2, 2008, the Wicks signed an agreement with Charles Upham and Martha Nix (a married couple) to sell the home and 4½ acres to the Upham couple. On the same day, the Wicks and Uphams signed an addendum to the April 2 contract stating "this agreement is for the additional at*

least 5 acres at a price of $32,500 per acre. . . . This is an option for the Uphams to purchase this adjoining acreage." The contract was closed on April 16, 2008. On April 22, 2008, the Wicks and Uphams signed an agreement stating: "The Uphams hereby agree to purchase and the Wicks hereby agree to sell the following described lot or other unimproved land and appurtenances thereto situated in the City of Gardendale, County of Jefferson, Alabama on the terms stated below: Address: adjacent to 296 West Shugart Ridge. . . . This contract is per agreement

written on Addendum sheet on 4/2/08." The April 22 contract stated that the addendum was attached; however, no copies of that contract included the addendum.

Skip Wick testified that prior to the making of the initial April 2 contract, the Wicks and the Uphams met and discussed the purchase of the 5 adjacent acres. Wick testified that they "discussed that the potential property lines would run forty feet to the left of the mailbox as you are facing the house, and then would run back to the right corner of the property." This description was not included in either the addendum or the April 22 contract. It is an undisputed fact that Skip Wick did not own the 5 acres to the left of the mailbox that he had described to the Uphams. The Uphams deny that Wick told them that Oldfield was joint owner of the left 5 acres. Wick denied any intent to mislead the Uphams.

Oldfield, the joint owner of the 5 acres, refused to sell the land. The Uphams contended that they would not have purchased the Wicks' house and 4½ acres if they had known they could not also purchase the left 5 acres. The purchasing of the "left five acres" was determined via oral testimony between the Uphams and the Wicks. The Uphams sued the Wicks and Oldfield and filed for breach of contract, fraudulent misrepresentation, suppression, and fraudulent inducement. The Wicks and Oldfield raised a defense appealing to the Statute of Frauds. They argued that the April 22 contract was void under the Statute of Frauds because it did not sufficiently describe the land to be purchased, that the Uphams' tort claims failed because they were based on the void April 22 contract, and that the Uphams' tort claims were not supported by sufficient evidence. The trial court ruled in favor of the Wicks and Oldfield, holding that the April 22 contract was void under the Statute of Frauds. The Uphams appealed.

ISSUE: Does oral testimony constitute a writing that satisfies the statute of frauds?

REASONING: The court commented that the Uphams failed to show that the trial court erred in entering a summary judgment against them on all of their claims against the Wicks and Oldfield. The court noted that the statute of frauds voids both written contracts with insufficient descriptions of land and oral agreements to sell land. Additionally, the Uphams contended that the Wicks and Oldfield engaged in fraud by attempting to sell land that they did not own outright. The court referred to the precedent of *DeFriece v. McCorquodale, Bruce v. Cole,* and *Holman v. Childersburg Bancorporation* to appeal to past decisions which involved legal circumstances similar to that of the Uphams. These cases state that "regardless of whether the misrepresentations allegedly made are viewed as contractual in nature or as simply fraudulent, they are subject to the Statute of Frauds because they concern the conveyance of an interest of land." When the Uphams asserted that "the Court blew it in *DeFriece, Bruce,* and *Holman*" on appeal, the court disregarded this statement as the Uphams did not "provide a sufficient basis upon which we could, even if we were so inclined, overrule *DeFriece, Bruce,* and *Holman.*" Finally, the Uphams raised additional arguments on their appeal which contended that the statute of frauds does not bar their tort claims and that they have satisfied the elements of promissory fraud. The court asserted that the Uphams did not cite authority to support any of those claims. The court concluded that "it is not the function of this Court to do a party's legal research or to make and address legal arguments for a party based on undelineated general propositions not supported by sufficient authority or argument." Most important, the court noted that *the April 22 contract "does not describe the contract with such certainty that it can be identified without resort to oral evidence" and that this circumstance is subject to the statute of frauds.*

DECISION AND REMEDY: The court affirmed the trial court's judgment, stating that the April 22, 2008, contract was void under the statute of frauds.

SIGNIFICANCE OF THE CASE: This case demonstrates the requirements included in the statute of frauds that establish oral testimony as a writing.

CRITICAL THINKING

How does this case demonstrate the importance of ensuring your argument is supported by evidence? Is there anything the Uphams could have included in their argument on appeal to make their position more convincing to the court?

ETHICAL DECISION MAKING

What ethical considerations do you think the judge relied on in making the decision in this case?

Parol Evidence Rule

A problem arises with a written contract when a party asserts that the writing is in some way deficient. In order to smooth transactions by limiting the types of evidence admissible to address the written agreement, the courts rely heavily on the parol evidence rule. The **parol evidence rule** is a common law rule that specifically addresses the admissibility of oral evidence as it relates to written contracts. The parol evidence rule states that oral evidence of an agreement made prior to or contemporaneously with a written agreement is inadmissible when the parties intend to have the written agreement be the complete and final version of their agreement.[13] *Parol* in *parol evidence rule* means "speech" or "words," specifically words outside the original writing.

The purpose of the parol evidence rule is to restrict evidence from being admitted that substantially contradicts the agreement in its written form. Therefore, evidence of prior agreements and negotiations, as well as of contemporaneous agreements and negotiations, is typically excluded under the parol evidence rule. A written agreement is assumed to be complete, and evidence contradicting this final agreement usually impedes business transactions, which is why the parol evidence rule exists.

However, when a court determines that the written agreement does *not* represent a complete and final version of the agreement, evidence may be admissible to further the court's understanding of the agreement. The admissible evidence is limited to additional elements, missing in the writing, that are consistent with the written agreement. These elements may be terms typically included in similar transactions that were left out of the specific writing, or they may be separate agreements in which consideration was offered.

A cautionary note is in order: "Parol evidence rule," on its face, is a misnomer. First and foremost, parol evidence applies to both parol (spoken words) and written speech. The parol evidence rule covers evidence extrinsic to the original writing and is not limited to spoken words. Second, the parol evidence rule is *not* a rule of evidence but, rather, relates to substantive legal issues, namely, what constitutes a legally binding agreement and how do we know what the agreement is. Third, the parol evidence rule is not a unitary concept or rule but an amalgamation of different rules and conditions.

Although the parol evidence rule applies to writings created at the same time as the written agreement, these writings tend to be treated differently than prior or contemporaneous oral agreements. That is, the writings are more readily admitted as part of the written agreement than is oral evidence regarding conditions or terms in the final agreement. The reasoning is that judges are allowed discretion in determining which documents constitute the final contract. As long as the contemporaneous written documents do not substantially contradict what is in the final writing, judges can deem these other writings to be part of the final written agreement. Consequently, the parol evidence rule does not usually exclude extrinsic written evidence.

Sometimes parties take the initiative and attempt to signal to judges that the written agreement is intended to be the final and complete statement of the agreement. A **merger clause** is a clause parties include in a written agreement within the statute of frauds that states that the written agreement accurately reflects the final, complete version of the agreement. Not all courts consider merger clauses to be conclusive proof of a contract. Nonetheless, where merger clauses are accepted, they greatly reduce the amount of guesswork courts must do in determining whether a written agreement was in fact intended to be the final statement of the agreement.

Exceptions to the Parol Evidence Rule

As with the statute of frauds, there are exceptions to the general applicability of the parol evidence rule. That is, there are situations where parol evidence, which is normally excluded, may be admissible in court. These exceptions pertain to (1) contracts that are subsequently modified, (2) contracts conditioned on orally agreed-on terms, (3) contracts that are not final as they are

parol evidence rule
A common law rule which states that oral evidence of an agreement made prior to or contemporaneously with a written agreement is inadmissible when the parties intend to have the written agreement be the complete and final version of their agreement.

merger clause
A clause in a written agreement within the statute of frauds which states that the written agreement accurately reflects the final, complete version of the agreement.

[13] Restatement (Second) of Contracts, sec. 213.

part written and part oral, (4) contracts with ambiguous terms, (5) incomplete contracts, (6) contracts with obvious typographical errors, (7) voidable or void contracts, and (8) evidence of prior dealings or usage of trade.

CONTRACTS THAT HAVE BEEN SUBSEQUENTLY MODIFIED

Although parol evidence contradictory to the final terms is inadmissible, evidence regarding a contract's subsequent modification is admissible. To be admissible, the modification must have been made after the writing and the evidence must clearly indicate this later modification.

Despite the allowance of evidence to demonstrate modifications, not all evidence of modification is admissible. If the agreement is required to be in writing under the statute of frauds, oral modifications are unenforceable. However, oral evidence of a subsequent written agreement is admissible. In addition, if the contract's terms require that modification be in writing, oral modifications are inadmissible and unenforceable.[14]

CONTRACTS CONDITIONED ON ORALLY AGREED-ON TERMS

The parol evidence rule does not prevent parties from introducing evidence proving the written agreement was conditioned on terms agreed to orally. The reason the parol evidence rule does not apply is that the evidence being elicited does not substantially modify the written agreement. Rather, what is at issue with such evidence is the enforceability of the contract as written. No terms are altered, so the parol evidence rule does not apply.

condition precedent
In a contract, an event that must occur in order for a party's duty to arise.

When an entire contract is conditioned on something occurring first, that first thing is known as a **condition precedent.** Evidence of the existence of a condition precedent agreed to orally is admissible, as stated previously, because the contract is not modified by such evidence; rather, its enforceability is called into question. Since the statute of frauds is concerned primarily with the enforceability of agreements, it logically follows that the parol evidence rule does not apply to evidence of condition precedents.

NONFINALIZED, PARTIALLY WRITTEN AND PARTIALLY ORAL, CONTRACTS

When a contract consists of both written and oral elements, judges tend to treat the agreement as nonfinalized. Accordingly, the judge makes the assumption that the parties do not intend to have the written agreement represent the entire agreement. Therefore, oral evidence related to the contract is admissible because the written document is not the complete and final representation of the agreement.

CONTRACTS CONTAINING AMBIGUOUS TERMS

When a contract contains what the court deems to be ambiguous terms, the court is faced with a dilemma in interpretation. To attempt to reach the most accurate interpretation of the original agreement, the court allows evidence, even if it is oral, for the sole purpose of clarifying ambiguous terms. As with evidence regarding orally agreed-on condition precedents, evidence used to clarify ambiguity is believed not to modify the contract but, rather, to clarify it. Accordingly, oral evidence related to ambiguity is admissible *only* to clarify, and not to change, any of the contractual terms.

INCOMPLETE CONTRACTS

When a contract is fundamentally flawed because it is missing critical information, courts can allow parol evidence to provide the missing information. Typically, the missing information is related to essential terms of the contract. Parol evidence will be admitted to clarify the contract by filling in the missing parts while not modifying, in any substantial way, the written agreement. Parol evidence is used to attempt to facilitate business transactions, as opposed to forcing the parties to enter into a new, complete agreement.

[14] UCC § 2-209(2), (3).

CONTRACTS WITH OBVIOUS TYPOGRAPHICAL ERRORS

Whenever a written agreement under the statute of frauds contains a serious, and obvious, typographical error, parol evidence is admissible to demonstrate that the typo was a typo, as well as to set forth the proper term. Allowing parol evidence to correct typos does not fundamentally alter the written agreement because the typo is not an accurate reflection of the parties' agreement. The agreement is not altered by correcting a typo; rather, the agreement is granted better clarity.

VOID OR VOIDABLE CONTRACTS

Certain conditions can make an otherwise valid contract void or voidable. (Refer to Chapter 8 for an in-depth discussion of what makes a contract void or voidable.) While the contract does not list these conditions, the courts allow parol evidence to demonstrate that the contract is void or voidable. As with the vast majority of the exceptions to the parol evidence rule, allowing evidence that proves a contract is void or voidable does not fundamentally alter the terms of the contract. Rather, the parol evidence would address the enforceability of the agreement, which is not the same as changing the terms of the agreement. Furthermore, evidence of a defense against a contract is admissible to prove a contract is void or voidable.

EVIDENCE OF PRIOR DEALINGS OR USAGE OF TRADE

This final exception, although directly related to those already mentioned, actually falls under the UCC and not the statute of frauds. Regardless, this exception also allows otherwise inadmissible parol evidence for a specific reason.

According to the UCC, parol evidence is admissible for the sake of clarification if the evidence addresses prior dealings between the parties or usages of trade in the same business field as that which the parties are in.[15] Evidence related to past dealings can help clarify missing or ambiguous terms by examining how the parties had previously interacted. The assumption is that parties will continue to interact in a similar manner, because repeated interactions tend to indicate pleasant interactions between the parties. Therefore, if a term is missing or ambiguous, the courts rely on evidence of what was done between the parties in the past to attempt to gauge what was intended in the contract in question.

Similarly, when a contract is ambiguous or incomplete, the courts examine the standard practices in the business. Here, the courts are assuming that businesses intend to engage in standard transactions. Furthermore, the courts believe that common business practices might sometimes be overlooked and, therefore, not be included when these common practices accurately reflect the intentions of the parties involved. Once again, an exception to the applicability of the parol evidence rule is made to allow evidence to clarify a contract, as opposed to changing any material terms of the contract.

Integrated Contracts

Integrated contracts are written contracts intended to be the complete and final representation of the parties' agreement. When the courts deem a contract integrated, unless one of the above exceptions applies, parol evidence is inadmissible. With partially integrated contracts, parol evidence is admissible to the extent it clarifies part of the contract or addresses the enforcement of the contract.[16] Therefore, the easiest test to determine the admissibility of parol evidence is to check whether the written contract, within the statute of frauds, is an integrated contract.

integrated contract
A written contract intended to be the complete and final representation of the parties' agreement.

As previously discussed, one way parties can indicate their desire to create an integrated contract is through the use of a merger clause. A merger clause explicitly states that the written contract is intended to be the complete and final version of the contract between the parties and that other possible agreements between the parties, besides the one in question, are not part of the final written agreement. In essence, a merger clause seeks to blend other agreements either

[15] UCC §§ 1-205 and 2-202.
[16] Restatement (Second) of Contracts, sec. 216.

into the final agreement or into something explicitly stated as being outside the final agreement. Most states will allow a merger clause to constitute the stated intent of the parties involved unless proof of a personal defense against the contract is offered by one of the parties. However, it is worth mentioning that some states consider merger clauses to be recommendations, but not necessarily binding on the parties involved.

LO 12-4

Third-Party Rights to Contracts

obligor
A contractual party who agreed to do something for the other party.

obligee
A contractual party who agreed to receive something from the other party.

assignment
A contracting party's transfer of his or her rights to a contract to a third party.

assignor
In a contract, the party who transfers his or her rights to the contract to a third party (an assignee), giving the assignee the right to collect what was contractually agreed on in the original contract.

assignee
In a contract, the party who receives the rights of another party (an assignor) to collect what was contractually agreed on in the original contract.

As you read in Chapter 8, contracts involve agreements between two parties in which each party agrees to give something to or do something for the other party. Contracts are typically private agreements, in the sense that the focus of the contract is the two parties involved and no one else. Accordingly, parties not in *privity of contract* (i.e., parties other than the contracting parties) usually do not have rights to a contract. However, as frequently is the case in the law, there are exceptions to the general rule.

There are two main situations in which a third party gains rights to a contract to which she or he is not a party. In the first, one of the contracting parties transfers rights or duties to a third party. In the second, the third party is a direct beneficiary of a contract involving two other parties. The remainder of this chapter examines both of these situations.

Assignments and Delegations

Contracts typically involve an agreement between two parties in which each party agrees to do something for the other. That is, both parties are **obligors** (contractual parties who agreed to do something for each other) and **obligees** (contractual parties who agreed to receive something from each other). Consequently, contracts create a situation in which each party has a duty to perform the agreed-on action and a right to be the recipient of the other party's duty. These rights and duties can be transferred to *third parties*—parties not part of the original contract. The sections below discuss both the transferring of rights (assignment) and the transferring of duties (delegation) to third parties.

ASSIGNMENT

Assignment occurs when a party to a contract (an **assignor**) transfers her rights to a contract to a third party (an **assignee**). In other words, the assignor gives to the assignee the right to collect what was contractually agreed on in the original contract (see Figure 12-2). For example, Lisa agrees to sell her car to Luke for $8,000. Lisa then assigns her right to receive Luke's payment to

Figure 12-2

Assignment of Rights

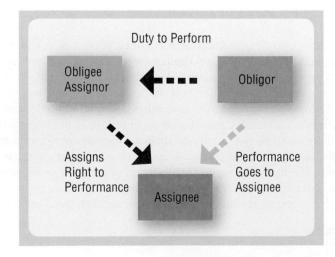

Assignment of Rights in Russia

Almost all developed market economies permit the free assignability of contract rights. Assignments are important because they play a crucial role in business financing. Banks and businesses make loans and pay debts through assignments. In Russia, civil law is operated primarily by the Russian Civil Code. The Russian law does not address the "assignment of a contract" in the same manner as does U.S. law. Instead, the Russian Civil Code refers to the assignment of rights as an "assignment of claim." The economic or monetary rights of the assignor may be transferred to another person; however, the Russian Civil Code states that "rights which are closely related with the personality of the creditor, such as alimony rights or rights for compensation of personal injury," are not permitted to be assigned to another person. Unlike the case in the United States, where assignments can be given orally or in writing, in Russia the Civil Code requires that assignments be produced in writing. The debtor (or obligor) is not required to perform the obligation to the new assignee until he or she receives written proof that the assignment took place. The assignment of rights, or "assignment of claims," in Russia is highly regulated by the Russian Civil Code.

Kelly. Kelly, who was not part of the original contract between Luke and Lisa, is an assignee and now has the right to receive payment from Luke for Lisa's car.

LO 12-5

When an assignor transfers her rights to an assignee, the assignor legally gives up all rights she previously had to collect on the contract.[17] Now the assignee may legally demand performance from the other party to the original contract. Returning to our example, once Lisa transfers her right to Kelly, Lisa can no longer require that Luke pay her for her car; however, Kelly can request that Luke pay her for Lisa's car.

The assignee essentially fills in for the assignor as the legal recipient of the contractual duties. As such, the assignee acquires the same rights the assignor had. The assignee is offered no additional protections. Moreover, the obligor (the other party to the contract, who owes a duty to the assignee) may raise any of the same defenses for nonperformance to the assignee as he would have been able to raise against the assignor. Thus, if Lisa failed to deliver her car to Luke, he can legally refuse to pay Kelly on the basis of Lisa's breach of contract. It does not matter that Kelly had no duty in the original contract; she is subject to the same defense Luke had against Lisa, and therefore Kelly would not be paid in this situation.

Although there is no legally required wording to be used or forms to be filled out for assignments to be valid, certain restrictions exist. First, although assignments may be given orally or in writing,[18] the UCC requires that assignments be in writing when the amount being assigned is greater than $5,000.[19] Furthermore, assignments covered by the statute of frauds also must be in writing. Because it is difficult to prove the existence of assignments given orally, it is usually suggested that assignments be in writing.

Second, an assignee must agree to accept the assigned rights. An assignee may decline an assignment if he has not legally agreed to the assignment and he declines in a timely fashion after learning about the assignment and its terms.[20] There is no protocol an assignee must follow to reject an assignment, but once the assignment is rejected, it is considered rejected from the time it was first offered. Third, in some situations contractual rights cannot be assigned.[21]

Rights That Cannot Be Assigned Exhibit 12-1 lists the four situations in which contractual rights cannot be assigned to a third party. We discuss each of them below.

First, the rights to a contract cannot be assigned when the contract is personal in nature. For a contract to be personal in nature, the obligor must have promised something specific to the

[17] Restatement (Second) of Contracts, sec. 317.
[18] Restatement (Second) of Contracts, sec. 324.
[19] UCC § 1-206.
[20] Restatement (Second) of Contracts, sec. 327.
[21] Restatement (Second) of Contracts, sec. 317(2).

Exhibit 12-1

Contractual Rights
That Cannot Be
Assigned

1. Rights that are personal in nature.
2. Rights that increase the obligor's risk or duties.
3. Rights whose assignment is prohibited by contract.
4. Rights whose assignment is prohibited by law or public policy.

person receiving it. Because the subject matter of the contract is personal, a third party cannot legally become the recipient. The one exception occurs when the only part of a contract left to be fulfilled is the payment,[22] because rights to payment can always be assigned. Case 12-2 demonstrates a situation in which a contractual duty cannot be assigned because the courts deemed it personal in nature.

[22] Restatement (Second) of Contracts, secs. 317 and 318.

CASE 12-2

TRAFFIC CONTROL SERVICES v. UNITED RENTALS NORTHWEST, INC.
SUPREME COURT OF NEVADA
87 P.3d 1054 (2004)

FACTS: *Phillip Burkhardt was a former United employee who took a job with NES. As a condition of employment with NES, he signed noncompetition and nondisclosure covenants. On June 30, 2002, United and NES entered into an asset purchase agreement. The purchase agreement was limited to certain assets and provided that "all contracts and agreements that are not listed as 'Assumed Contracts' are 'Excluded Assets.'" While the agreement listed other noncompetition covenants as assumed contracts, Burkhardt's noncompetition covenant was not on the list. The purchase agreement also stated that "none of the Assumed Contracts requiring a consent to assignment have been obtained prior to the Closing Date."*

A week before closure of the asset purchase, United requested or demanded that Burkhardt and a number of other employees sign new one-year noncompetition and nondisclosure covenants. Burkhardt refused.

On August 5, 2002, Burkhardt accepted employment with Traffic Control. United terminated Burkhardt's employment on August 8, 2002, after which he returned all his work-related items to company officials. NES and United filed a complaint alleging that Burkhardt obtained confidential information during his employment with them and subsequently used and disclosed NES/United confidential information, contacted United's clients, and attempted to solicit United's customers. The district court ultimately ruled in favor of United, enforcing the noncompetition covenant. Burkhardt appealed.

ISSUE: Are employee noncompetition covenants assignable?

REASONING: In the words of the court:

When an employee enters into a covenant not to compete with his employer, he may consider the character and personality of his employer to determine whether he is willing to be held to a contract that will restrain him from future competition with his employer, even after termination of employment. This does not mean, however, the employee is willing to suffer the same restriction with a stranger to the original obligation. Certainly, the sale of a business fundamentally alters the nature of an employment relationship.

Burkhardt testified, by way of deposition, to his concern about working for a company other than NES, especially United. In this, he covenanted specifically with NES not to compete with NES. At the hearing on the motion for a preliminary injunction, the district court agreed with Burkhardt the noncompetition covenant was personal in nature but concluded, because the covenant held value, it was assignable. Testimony also established that United enjoyed a much greater volume of business in the trench-shoring business than did NES. Therefore, Burkhardt's obligation materially changed when the covenant was assigned. Burkhardt was thus "foreclosed from competing on any level with a much larger business entity."

DECISION AND REMEDY: Employee noncompetition agreements are of a personal nature and cannot be assigned without the express consent of an employee. The decision was reversed.

SIGNIFICANCE OF THE CASE: This case demonstrates why certain contracts are personal and therefore not automatically assignable.

CRITICAL THINKING

What evidence did the judge rely on in this case to make his decision? How would you judge the quality of this evidence?

ETHICAL DECISION MAKING

What ethical considerations do you think the judge relied on in making the decision in this case?

Second, rights cannot be assigned when the assignment would increase the risk or duties the obligor would face in fulfilling the original contract. For example, Ben agrees to replace the siding on Erin's two-bedroom ranch. Erin cannot assign her right to Ben's services to Chris, who lives in a three-story, five-bedroom house, because Ben's (the obligor's) duties would be greatly increased from the work required in the original contract with Erin to the work required in an agreement with Chris.

Third, rights cannot be assigned when the contract expressly forbids assignments. When parties include an *antiassignment clause* in their contract, the parties are attempting to limit their ability to assign their rights under the contract. However, the wording of the antiassignment clause is determinative regarding the effectiveness of the clause. That is, if worded improperly or ambiguously, the clause does not effectively limit assignments.

Most courts consider contractual prohibitions against assignments to be promises. Consequently, courts consider an assignment made despite an antiassignment clause to be effective, but the party who makes the assignment will still be liable for breaching the terms of the contract. Moreover, unless the clause is very specific in what it prohibits, the court will generally interpret the antiassignment clause as preventing delegation of duties, not assignment of rights.[23] A clause stating "All assignments are void under this contract" would be considered effective. In contrast, when a contract includes a clause explicitly permitting assignments, the parties may assign rights, even when assignments would normally be considered improper because of an increased duty, risk, or burden to the obligor.[24]

Even in the presence of an antiassignment clause, there are exceptions in which assignments can still be made. For instance, antiassignment clauses do not affect assignments made by operation of law. That is, if a law necessitates an assignment, such as in bankruptcy cases, the assignment is effective regardless of any contractual agreement to the contrary. Likewise, as previously stated, the right to assign monetary payments cannot be denied. Therefore, even when a contract has an antiassignment clause, either party may still assign his or her right to receive payment.[25] Part of the reason the law does not bar the right to receive payment is that businesses often transfer rights to payments in the regular course of business. Also, one's duty to pay is not affected when the party to whom one must make a payment changes. That is, no added burden is placed on the obligor when the recipient of a payment changes, requiring that payment be sent to a different party.

In addition, assignments for the right to receive damages for a breach of contract to sell goods or services are unaffected by antiassignment clauses.[26] Therefore, if one party breaches the contract, the other party can sue the breaching party and transfer the right to recovery to a third party.

[23] Restatement (Second) of Contracts, sec. 323(1), and UCC § 2-210(3).
[24] Restatement (Second) of Contracts, sec. 323(1).
[25] UCC § 9-318(4).
[26] UCC § 2-210(2).

Fourth, rights cannot be assigned when law or public policy forbids such assignments. Various state and federal statutes prohibit the assigning of specific rights. Even when no statute prohibits an assignment, if the assignment is determined to be against public policy, the assignment is deemed ineffective.

Except as outlined in this section, all other rights are presumed to be assignable. Once it has been established that an assignment is valid, notice should be given to the obligor regarding the assignment.

Notice of Assignment Although notice need not be given for a valid assignment, it is usually a good idea for the assignor or the assignee to notify the obligor of the assignment. Assignments are effective immediately, regardless of notice, but by providing notice the assignor can help avoid two serious complications with assignments.

The first complication involves the obligor's fulfilling of the contractual duty. Without notice of assignment, the obligor can discharge his contractual duties simply by fulfilling his duties to the assignor. Because fulfilling the contract discharges the obligor's duties, the act also constitutes a discharge of the assignee's claim on the assignor's right. However, after the obligor has been given notice, the obligor can discharge his contractual obligations only by fulfilling the contract for the assignee.

The second complication regarding a lack of notice involves the granting of multiple assignments of the same right. When an assignor assigns two or more parties the same right, confusion arises as to which party has the right to the contract. Most states use the **first-assignment-in-time rule,** which states that the first party granted the assignment is the party correctly entitled to the contractual right. By giving proper notice, a party can ensure that there is no confusion over when the assignment was made. Furthermore, a minority of states have adopted the **English rule,** which states that the first assignee to give notice of assignment to the obligor is the party with rights to the contract. Consequently, especially when living in a state using the English rule, parties are well advised to give notice of assignments to ensure they maintain their assigned rights.

The Restatement (Second) of Contracts states a view between the first-assignment-in-time rule and the English rule.[27] The Restatement grants legal right to the first assignee in most situations. However, if the first assignment is legally voidable or revocable by the assignor, subsequent assignments are considered evidence of the voiding or revocation of the first assignment. In such situations, the later assignee has legal right to the contract. Also, the later assignee is considered the legal owner of the contractual right if she offers something to the assignor as consideration and then obtains (1) performance by the obligor on his duty, (2) judgment requiring performance by the obligor, (3) a new contract with the obligor, or (4) evidence frequently used to signify a contractual right (e.g., a writing indicating a contractual obligation).

DELEGATION

A **delegation** occurs when a party to a contract (a **delegator**) transfers her duty to perform to a third party who is not part of the original contract (a **delegatee**). Whereas assignments transfer rights to a contract, delegations transfer duties. (See Figure 12-3.) Instead of the third party's receiving something, as in an assignment, delegations require that the delegatee fulfill the delegator's contractual obligation to the obligee—the party to the contract to whom a duty is owed. For example, John contracts with Teresa to have her deliver machinery to his factory. Teresa then delegates her duty to Bill, who delivers the machinery to John.

One important distinction between assignments and delegations involves the rights of the transferring party—the assignor or the delegator. In assignments, after the assignment is made, the assignor has no right left to the original contract. Conversely, with delegations, the delegator is not relieved of his duty to perform by making a delegation. If the delegatee fails to fulfill the contract, the delegator is still liable to the obligee for fulfillment of the contract. In our example, if Bill fails to deliver the machinery to John, Teresa is liable to John for damages.

first-assignment-in-time rule

A rule which states that the first party granted the assignment is the party correctly entitled to the contractual right.

English rule

A rule which states that the first assignee to give notice of assignment to the obligor is the party with rights to the contract.

delegation

A contracting party's (a delegator's) transfer of his or her duty to perform to a third party who is not part of the original contract (a delegatee).

delegator

A party in a contract who transfers his or her duties to perform to a third party who is not a part of the original contract (a delegatee).

delegatee

A third party who is not part of the original contract but to whom duties to perform are transferred by one of the contracting parties (a delegator).

[27] Sec. 342.

Figure 12-3

Assignment of Duties

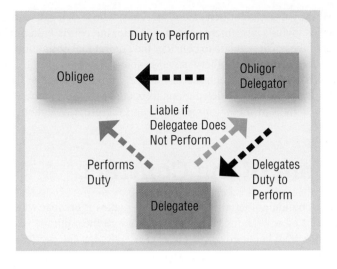

Duties That Cannot Be Delegated As with assignments, the starting assumption is that duties to a contract can be delegated. However, courts tend to examine delegations more closely than assignments. The reasoning is that an assignment usually does not affect the party to the contract who is not involved in the assignment (the obligor), whereas a delegation forces the party to the contract who is not involved in the delegation (the obligee) to receive performance of the contract from a party with whom the obligee did not directly contract.

Also, just as with assignments, in certain situations duties cannot be delegated to a third party (see Exhibit 12-2).[28] The first type of duty that cannot be delegated, mirroring assignments, is any duty of a personal nature. A duty is personal in nature when it requires the specific talents, skills, or expertise of the obligor. An interesting situation arises when the initial contract bears an implicit assumption that work will be performed by others. In such situations, if supervision is important to the task, the supervision could be considered to be a personal duty that the obligor may not delegate to others. For example, suppose you are planning to have a new building built and you contract with a well-respected construction manager. He will not build the building; the contract is for his management skills. His contractual duties would be considered personal and therefore cannot be delegated.

Delegation for personal duties is admissible where otherwise not allowed when there is an explicit or implicit contractual agreement to allow delegations. Usually, for a delegation of personal duties to be effective, the contract must state that delegations are permitted.

While personal duties typically cannot be delegated, any nonpersonal duties in a contract can be delegated. For example, the delivering of goods, mowing of one's lawn, paying of money, or painting of a house are all considered nonpersonal duties. These duties are nonpersonal because they do not require particular skill or expertise and therefore can be completed by most people. Accordingly, one can delegate these nonpersonal duties.

The second type of duty one cannot delegate is a duty whose performance by the delegatee would vary significantly from its performance by the delegator. To protect the obligee, who is a part of the original contract, when performance would differ substantially from that to which the obligee contractually has the right, courts will rule that the delegation is ineffective.

> To contrast the delegation of duties is a contract with the concept of delegation as discussed in your management class, go to the **Connecting to the Core** activity on the text's website at www.mhhe.com/kubasekess2e.

Exhibit 12-2

Duties That Cannot Be Delegated

1. Duties that are personal in nature.
2. Duties for which the delegatee's performance will vary significantly from the delegator's.
3. Duties in contracts that forbid delegations.

[28] Restatement (Second) of Contracts, sec. 318, and UCC § 2-210.

The third type of duty one cannot delegate is any duty whose delegation is prohibited by the contract. When parties include agreements not to delegate, the courts typically treat these inclusions as indications of the parties' desire to consider the contractual obligations as personal. Consequently, the courts frequently find otherwise-allowable delegations to be inappropriate when an agreement not to delegate is in the contract. However, even if a clause prohibiting delegations exists, the courts will probably allow delegations to occur if they are impersonal. For example, courts consider the payment of money impersonal, and therefore delegable, even if a contract prohibits delegations.

Assignment of the Contract

Frequently, contracts contain ambiguous language that makes it unclear what is being assigned or delegated. Examples of ambiguous language are "I assign the contract" or "I assign all of my rights under the contract." When a court cannot clearly tell what the parties intended, the court usually considers the assignment to be both of rights and of duties. In other words, when ambiguous language is used, the court considers that the assignor has assigned his rights, as well as delegated any duties he had under the contract. (See Figure 12-4.) Doing so removes any right the assignor had to collect under the contract, but he is still liable to the obligee for any duties the delegatee, who is also the assignee, fails to perform.

third-party benefi-
ciary contract
A contract created when
two parties enter into a
contract agreement with
the intended purpose of
benefiting a third party.

intended beneficiary
A third party to a con-
tract whom the contract-
ing parties intended to
benefit directly from their
contact.

Third-Party Beneficiary Contracts

We have thus far learned about one of the ways in which third parties may obtain rights to a contract: through assignments or delegations. We now move on to the other way, which is that the third party is an intended beneficiary of a third-party beneficiary contract. A **third-party beneficiary contract** is created when two parties enter into a contract with the intended end purpose of benefiting a third party. To be an intended third-party beneficiary, the third party does not need to be explicitly named in the contract, as long as the terms of the contract or events occurring after the creation of the contract make it clear who the intended recipient of the contractual benefits is.

LO 12-6 ## INTENDED BENEFICIARIES

Early in the common law, courts had difficulty when contracts were written to benefit third parties. The courts were not sure how to treat these contracts and usually deemed third parties to have no rights to contracts to which they were not in privity. Now, however, third parties who are intended beneficiaries have the right to enforce contracts. An **intended beneficiary** is a third party to a contract whom the contracting parties intended to benefit directly from their contract.

Figure 12-4

Assignment of the
Contract

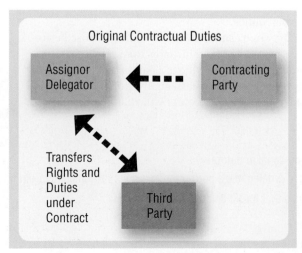

Intended beneficiaries may enforce their rights to a contract when both parties to the contract intended for the third party to benefit. In determining whether a third party is an intended beneficiary, courts ask if the contracting parties intended that the third party be the "direct," "primary," or "express" beneficiary of the contract.

The **promisor** in a third-party beneficiary contract is the party to the contract who made the promise that benefits the third party. The **promisee** is the party to the contract who owes something to the promisor in exchange for the promise made to the third-party beneficiary. For example, Amanda contracts with Alex to clean his house. In exchange, Alex will pay Amanda's credit card debt. The credit card company is the third-party beneficiary, as the contract is created to benefit the company. Alex is the promisor, for he made the promise to pay the third-party beneficiary. Amanda is the promisee because she owes a duty to the promisor, Alex.

In a third-party beneficiary contract, the intended beneficiary may sue the promisor to enforce the contract. Although the promisee typically owes something to the third-party beneficiary before the contract with the promisor exists, if the third party sues the promisee after the promisor does not fulfill his or her obligations, the promisee can then sue the promisor for breach of contract. Therefore, courts allow the third-party beneficiary to sue the promisor, thus eliminating the litigation that would ensue if the promisee sued the promisor. In our example, if Alex fails to pay the credit card company for Amanda's debt, the credit card company has the right to sue Alex, even though it is Amanda's debt.

Let us return to the Case Opener. The fans of the Tyson fight argued that they were third-party beneficiaries and therefore had rights under several contracts that were violated when Tyson was disqualified early in the fight. Boxing matches are widely viewed events, and one can argue that the fights are organized for the enjoyment of the fans. Does the idea of boxing matches being organized for the fans make the fans the "direct," "primary," or "express" beneficiaries of contracts involved in the fight? In other words, are the fans of the Tyson fight intended beneficiaries to the contracts Tyson entered when agreeing to the fight? What else do we need to know before we can determine whether the fans have a legal right to a refund?

There are two types of intended beneficiaries: creditor beneficiaries and donee beneficiaries.

Creditor Beneficiaries A **creditor beneficiary** is a third party who benefits from a contract in which the promisor agrees to pay the promisee's debt. In our previous example, because Alex (the promisor) agreed to pay the debt of Amanda (the promisee), Amanda's credit card company is a creditor beneficiary.

Case 12-3 is a famous dispute in which the courts began to recognize the rights of third parties to sue promisors for performance.

promisor
In a third-party beneficiary contract, the party to the contract who made the promise that benefits the third party.

promisee
In a third-party beneficiary contract, the party to the contract who owes something to the promisor in exchange for the promise made to the third party.

creditor beneficiary
A third party who benefits from a contract in which the promisor agrees to pay the promisee's debt.

CASE 12-3	LAWRENCE v. FOX
	COURT OF APPEALS OF NEW YORK
	20 N.Y. 268 (1859)

FACTS: *In November 1857, Holly, at the request of Fox, loaned him $300. Before loaning the money, Holly informed Fox that Holly owed Lawrence $300, due the next day. In consideration of the loan, at the time of the loan, Fox agreed to pay Lawrence for Holly the next day. Fox did not pay, and Lawrence sued him. Fox sought to dismiss the charges because there was no proof tending to show that Holly was indebted to Lawrence, Fox's agreement with Holly to pay Lawrence was void for want of consideration, and there was*

no privity between Lawrence and Fox. Fox's motion to dismiss was denied. The jury ultimately found in favor of Lawrence for the sum of the loan plus interest. Fox appealed and the judgment was affirmed. Fox then appealed again.

ISSUE: Does Lawrence have the right to sue Fox, the promisor, for payment?

REASONING: There is a principle of law, found in English law as well as the law of many states, that if one

person makes a promise to another for the purpose of benefiting a third party, that third person may "maintain an action upon it." Although many of the preceding cases in which this principle was applied were trust cases, nothing about the law requires that the case be a trust case. Fox's duty to pay Lawrence in return for the loan he received from Holly was a clear condition of the loan. The spoken promise is equal to a written promise in this case. Therefore, Lawrence should receive payment from Fox in the interest of justice, even if the law could be more narrowly interpreted.

DECISION AND REMEDY: The decision of the earlier court was affirmed. Fox was required to pay Lawrence as he had promised Holly.

SIGNIFICANCE OF THE CASE: This case was one of the earliest cases that upheld the rights of third parties to sue promisors to have agreements enforced.

CRITICAL THINKING

Form an opinion about the contemporary relevance of this ruling. Given the widespread and extremely significant changes in U.S. society and the world over the last 150 years, what is the justification for consideration of such an old case? How does this type of process aid our legal system? How might it detract from the reasonableness of modern deliberations?

ETHICAL DECISION MAKING

Consider the actions of Fox, both leading up to and through the course of the legal dispute. From an ethical standpoint, which stakeholders was Fox considering? What values was he attempting to uphold?

The fans in the Tyson case argued that they are intended beneficiaries. If the fans are correct, and we know Tyson did not have a debt to the fans, then they must be donee beneficiaries. Does an agreement to perform create a situation in which the audience members become the intended beneficiaries of the performance?

donee beneficiary

A third party who benefits from a contract in which a promisor agrees to give a gift to the third party.

Donee Beneficiaries The other type of intended beneficiaries is donee beneficiaries. **Donee beneficiaries** are third parties who benefit from a contract in which a promisor agrees to give a gift to the third party. The most common form of donee beneficiary contracts is life insurance policies. Someone (the promisee) pays premiums on a life insurance plan to have the insurer (the promisor) agree to pay a third party (the donee beneficiary) on the promisee's death.

vest

To mature, as in the maturing of rights such that a party can legally act on the rights.

Vesting of Rights Although an intended beneficiary can enforce her rights to a contract, she cannot do so until her rights to the contract **vest,** that is, until the rights mature such that a party can legally act on the rights. Before a third party's rights have vested, the original contracting parties can make changes to the original contract without the permission of the third party. For example, third-party rights in a life insurance policy do not vest until the promisee's death. Consequently, Jane (the promisee) can change the intended beneficiary of her life insurance policy from Mary to Peter. Jane does not need Mary's permission, and Mary cannot sue Jane, because Mary's rights have not vested.

Generally, one of three things must occur for a third party's right to a contract to vest.[29] First, under certain circumstances, third-party rights vest immediately. When rights vest immediately,

[29] Restatement (Second) of Contracts, sec. 311.

the third party can enforce the contract at any time. These rights take effect instantaneously, even if the beneficiary does not know about the contract.

Second, rights may vest when the beneficiary decides to accept the rights to the contract. Sometimes the beneficiary must positively accept the rights, such as by notifying the contracting parties of acceptance. However, in the absence of an overt act of rejecting the rights to a contract, acceptance is assumed when the beneficiary becomes aware of the contract.

Third, rights may vest when the beneficiary changes his position because of reliance on the contractual rights. In other words, the beneficiary must take some action he would not have taken otherwise because he is expecting to benefit from the contract. For example, Vince is a third-party beneficiary to a contract. When he finds out about the contract, he decides to lease a new car because he is expecting to benefit from the contract. Obtaining the lease would cause his rights to the contract to vest because doing so demonstrates a change in position based on reliance on the contract.

If a contract specifies that the original contracting parties maintain the right to alter or rescind the contract, the vesting of the third party's rights does not preclude the promisor or the promisee from changing the original contract.

Many states hold that donee beneficiary rights vest before creditor beneficiary rights. The rationale is that even if the contract is altered when there is a creditor beneficiary, the creditor beneficiary still maintains her rights against the debtor (the promisee). Donee beneficiaries do not have the same rights as creditor beneficiaries, and thus many states allow their rights to vest more quickly than those of creditor beneficiaries.

Creditor versus Donee Beneficiaries There are two main distinctions between creditor beneficiaries and donee beneficiaries (see Exhibit 12-3). The first distinction is based on the reason the third-party beneficiary contract was created. If the promise in the contract is intended to release a party from an obligation to a third party, such as the paying of one's debt, the contract involves a creditor beneficiary. Conversely, if the contract intends to grant a gift to a third party, the third party is a donee beneficiary.

LO 12-7

The second distinction involves the conditions under which an intended beneficiary can enforce her rights under a contract. Creditor beneficiaries can enforce their rights under a contract whenever the contract is valid. Donee beneficiaries can enforce their rights to most contracts. However, some jurisdictions do not allow donee beneficiaries to enforce their contractual rights in all situations.

When a donee beneficiary can enforce his rights under a contract, he may do so only against the promisor. The reason the donee beneficiary cannot sue the promisee is that the promisee had no duty to the donee beneficiary. In contrast, creditor beneficiaries can sue the promisor or the promisee for performance, as both parties owed a duty to the creditor beneficiary. However, if the creditor beneficiary wins a judgment against one party, she may not seek judgment against the other party. In addition, if a creditor beneficiary wins judgment

CREDITOR BENEFICIARY	DONEE BENEFICIARY
Purpose of the Contract	
Contractual performance fulfills an obligation to a third party.	Contractual performance gives a gift to a third party.
Enforcement of Rights	
Beneficiary can enforce rights to a contract if the contract is valid and the rights have vested.	Beneficiary has limited ability to enforce contracts, depending on the jurisdiction.
Beneficiary can enforce rights against the promisor or the promisee.	Beneficiary can enforce rights against the promisor.

Exhibit 12-3

Creditor versus Donee Beneficiaries

against the promisee, the promisee may sue the promisor to recover under a theory of breach of contract.[30]

It is not always easy to determine when someone is a creditor or a donee beneficiary. Sometimes a contract is created for reasons that are intended both to be charitable and to pay a debt. Given the lack of clear distinction as to when someone is a creditor beneficiary and when he is a donee beneficiary, the Restatement (Second) of Contracts takes a different approach.[31] The Restatement focuses on the distinction between intended and incidental beneficiaries.

Creditor and donee beneficiaries are both intended beneficiaries, and according to the Restatement, intended beneficiaries have the right to enforce a contract. When it is clear that the contract was created for the benefit of a third party and that performance of the contractual duties will pay off the payee's debt or give a gift as the payee intended, the third party is an intended beneficiary.

INCIDENTAL BENEFICIARIES

incidental beneficiary
One who unintentionally gains a benefit from a contract between other parties.

Similar to intended beneficiaries, incidental beneficiaries are third-party beneficiaries to contracts. However, unlike the case with intended beneficiaries, the contracting parties do not *intend* to benefit incidental beneficiaries. An **incidental beneficiary** is one who unintentionally gains a benefit from a contract between other parties. (See Exhibit 12-4.) One significant difference between intended and incidental beneficiaries is that incidental beneficiaries cannot sue to enforce a contract. Incidental beneficiaries maintain no rights to enforce other people's contracts.

In determining whether a party is an incidental beneficiary, the courts take a reasonable person approach: They ask if a reasonable person in the position of the party in question would believe that the contracting parties intended to benefit him or her. If the reasonable person would believe that the contracting parties consciously intended to benefit him or her, the courts will consider the party an intended beneficiary. If the reasonable person would not find such intent, the third party is an incidental beneficiary.

As a thought experiment, consider the reasonable person test in the context of the Tyson dispute in the Case Opener. For the fans to be able to receive refunds, the reasonable person in the position of the fans would have to believe that Tyson intended to benefit him or her with Tyson's performance. Do the fans meet the reasonable person test?

The courts consider other elements besides the reasonable person approach when determining whether a party is an intended or incidental beneficiary. One factor the courts consider is whether performance of the contract is done directly to the third party. If nothing is explicitly done for or given to the third party, she or he cannot be an intentional beneficiary. The courts also examine the third-party's ability to control the specifics of performance of the contract. That is, if a third party has the ability to provide input regarding how the contractual duties are fulfilled, the third party is probably an intended beneficiary. For example, Dianne (the promisee) agrees to pay Charles (the promisor) to paint Henry's (the third party's) house. Henry tells Charles what color he wants the house, as well as when Charles should be there to paint. Henry's ability to control how Charles paints the house demonstrates his

Exhibit 12-4

Intended versus Incidental Beneficiaries

INTENDED BENEFICIARIES	INCIDENTAL BENEFICIARIES
Contracting parties intended to benefit the third party with their contract.	Contracting parties did not intend to benefit the third party with their contract.
Beneficiary has the right to enforce the contract.	Beneficiary does not have the right to enforce the contract.
Beneficiary benefits from direct reception of contractual performance.	Beneficiary benefits from indirect circumstances created by contractual performance.

[30] Restatement (Second) of Contracts, sec. 310.
[31] Restatement (Second) of Contracts, sec. 302.

status as an intended beneficiary. In addition, note that Charles renders performance directly to Henry, so the explicit-performance factor also indicates Henry's status as an intended beneficiary.

A third factor the courts examine in determining the type of third-party beneficiary is whether the contract directly states that the third party is the benefiting party. In our example, because Charles agreed in the contract to paint Henry's house, the contract lists Henry as the beneficiary. Consequently, Henry is an intended beneficiary. Although Henry meets all three additional tests (besides the reasonable person test), it is not necessary to meet all three. If a third party meets at least one of the last three tests, he is usually an intended beneficiary.

SUMMARY

Statute of Frauds	The term *statute of frauds* refers to various state laws modeled after the 1677 English Act for the Prevention of Frauds and Perjuries. These state laws are intended to (1) ease contractual negotiations by requiring sufficient reliable evidence to prove the existence and specific terms of a contract, (2) prevent unreliable oral evidence from interfering with a contractual relationship, and (3) prevent parties from entering into contracts with which they do not agree.
Contracts Falling within the Statute of Frauds	1. Contracts whose terms prevent possible performance within one year. 2. Promises made in consideration of marriage. 3. Contracts for one party to pay the debt of another if the initial party fails to pay. 4. Contracts related to an interest in land. 5. Under the Uniform Commercial Code, contracts for the sale of goods totaling more than $500.
Exceptions to the Statute of Frauds	The exceptions include (1) admission, (2) partial performance, (3) promissory estoppel, and (4) various exceptions under the UCC.
Sufficiency of the Writing	A sufficient writing under the statute of frauds must clearly indicate (1) the parties to the contract, (2) the subject of the agreement, (3) the consideration given for the contract, (4) all relevant contractual terms, and (5) at least the signature of the party against whom action is brought. Under the UCC, a writing must clearly indicate (1) the quantity to be sold and (2) the signature of the party being sued. Under neither the statute of frauds nor the UCC must the writing be contained within one document.
Parol Evidence Rule	The *parol evidence rule* is a common law rule stating that oral evidence of an agreement made prior to or contemporaneously with a written agreement is inadmissible when the parties intend to have the written agreement be the complete and final version of their agreement.
Exceptions to the Parol Evidence Rule	1. Contracts that are subsequently modified. 2. Contracts conditioned on orally agreed-on terms. 3. Contracts that are not final as they are part written and part oral. 4. Contracts with ambiguous terms. 5. Incomplete contracts. 6. Contracts with obvious typographical errors. 7. Voidable or void contracts. 8. Evidence of prior dealings or usage of trade.
Integrated Contracts	*Integrated contracts* are written contracts, within the statute of frauds, intended to be the complete and final representation of the parties' agreement, thus precluding the admissibility of parol evidence other than in the exceptions listed above.
Third-Party Rights to Contracts	There are two main situations in which a third party gains rights to a contract to which she or he is not a party: (1) One of the contracting parties transfers rights or duties to the third party. (2) The third party is a direct beneficiary of a contract involving two other parties.

Assignments and Delegations

Contracts typically involve an agreement between two parties:

Obligor: Contractual party who owes a duty to the other party in privity of the contract.

Obligee: Contractual party who is owed a duty from the other party in privity of the contract.

An *assignment* is the transfer of rights under a contract to a third party.

Assignor: The party to a contract who transfers his or her rights to a third party.

Assignee: A party not in privity to a contract who is the recipient of a transfer of rights to a contract.

Contractual rights that cannot be assigned:

1. Rights that are personal in nature.
2. Rights that would increase the obligor's risks or duties.
3. Rights in a contract that expressly forbids assignment.

A *delegation* is the transfer of a duty under a contract to a third party.

Delegator: The party to a contract who transfers his or her duty to a third party.

Delegatee: A party not in privity to a contract who is the recipient of a transfer of a duty in a contract.

Contractual duties that cannot be assigned:

1. Duties that are personal in nature.
2. Duties whose performance by the delegatee would be substantially different from that which the obligee originally contracted.
3. Duties in a contract that expressly forbids delegation.

Assignment of the Contract

When ambiguous language is used, courts interpret the transfer to consist of an assignment of rights and a delegation of duties.

Third-Party Beneficiary Contracts

An *intended beneficiary* is a third party to a contract whom the contracting parties intended to benefit directly from their contract.

Promisor: A party to a contract who made the promise that benefits the third party.

Promisee: A party to a contract who owes something to the promisor in exchange for the promise made to the third-party beneficiary.

Creditor beneficiary: A third party who benefits from a contract in which the promisor agrees to pay the promisee's debt.

Donee beneficiary: A third party who benefits from a contract in which a promisor agrees to give a gift to the third party.

Vest: The maturing of rights such that a party can legally act upon the rights. An incidental *beneficiary* is a third party who unintentionally gains a benefit from a contract between other parties. That is, it was never the conscious objective of the contracting parties to benefit the third party.

Point/Counterpoint

Does the United States Still Benefit from Having a Statute of Frauds?	
YES	NO
The statute of frauds provides great benefit to America. The rule serves as a social lubricant aiding business transactions. Because it requires that certain	The United States does not benefit from the statute of frauds, and the states should repeal the relevant sections of their laws.

types of contracts be in writing, we know that such a contract either will have enough evidence to prove its existence and terms or will be unenforceable. Since only certain contracts are required to be in writing, the rule does not preclude oral contracts, but it ensures that the most important contracts can be enacted without complications.

Another way in which the statute of frauds benefits America is by preventing unreliable evidence from being used in court. Human memories are notoriously weak and faulty, and it does not make sense to base important legal decisions on what someone says he or she remembers. Furthermore, people with a vested interest can change their testimony on the basis of changed circumstances in order to gain personally from the changed circumstances. However, with the requirement that certain contracts be in writing, the parties become bound to what they wrote and need not rely on faulty memory or biased testimony.

Finally, the act of writing gives people time to pause for reflection. No one benefits when parties hastily rush into an agreement they later regret. The problem of hasty agreement is lessened when the parties are required to take time to write out the terms of their agreement. Thoughtful reflection prevents parties from entering into contracts with which they do not agree, and this means fewer cases are brought due to one party's entering an unfair, or otherwise defective, agreement.

One of the greatest problems with the statute of frauds is that it acts as an impediment to contractual agreements. When parties agree, why should they be subjected to unnecessary formalities? The written requirements of the statute of frauds get in the way of business transactions more often than they help.

Furthermore, the required writing frequently imposes additional costs on the parties to an agreement. When even simple agreements (although this applies to the more technical ones as well) must be written, parties have to spend more time with the agreement. The time spent writing down an agreement in which neither party contests any of the terms is time *not* spent conducting other business. Frequently, the parties have to hire attorneys to write their contracts. The attorney fees impose additional costs on the parties to the agreement, helping to decrease whatever benefit might have been gained from the original agreement before the writing took place.

In addition, the statute of frauds provides unnecessary loopholes for unscrupulous people. Although most parties enter agreements in good faith, it is not uncommon for parties to seek a way out of contracts they cannot perform. The writing requirements are not always accurately fulfilled, and when this occurs, unethical parties can exploit minor technicalities to have a contract declared void. In the end, the innocent party is harmed by the writing requirement, and the unethical party escapes a bad situation with little to no harm. America is not served by a system that enables such behavior.

Questions & Problems

1. Explain how the requirements of the statute of frauds under the UCC are different from those under the common law.

2. List the kinds of contracts that require a writing under the statute of frauds.

3. Identify the exceptions to the parol evidence rule, and explain why some people might argue that the parol rule is not very effective.

4. Integrate the concept of assignments with the concept of delegations.

5. Why is it that incidental beneficiaries cannot enforce rights under a contract? Should they be able to enforce such rights?

6. Explain the difference between an assignor's liability and a delegator's liability after rights have been transferred to a third party.

7. Explain the desirability to business of allowing a transfer of rights or duties to third parties.

8. The McCartheys owned stock in a corporation that controlled the *Salt Lake City Tribune.* When that company merged with another company, as part of the deal, the McCartheys were told that they would have the right to repurchase the newspaper for five years after the merger. The detailed merger agreement did not mention the right to repurchase. When the company sold the newspaper to Newsmedia in five years instead of allowing the McCartheys to repurchase the paper, the McCartheys sued for breach of contract. The trial court dismissed the claim on grounds that the statute of frauds barred enforcement of the oral agreement. How do you believe the appellate court ruled on the McCartheys' appeal? Why? [*MediaNews Group v. McCarthey,* 494 F.3d 1254 (10th Cir. 2007).]

9. The Laths were the owners of a farm that they wanted to sell. Mrs. Mitchell considered purchasing the land but found that an ice house located across

the road was objectionable. Mitchell argued that the Laths orally agreed to remove the ice house in consideration of her promise to purchase the property, which she agreed to purchase for $8,400 in a written contract. After Mitchell moved into her new home and made several improvements to the land, the Laths never removed the ice house and expressly communicated their intention not to do so. Mitchell sued the Laths for breach of contract. What effect does the parol evidence rule have on the admissibility of the oral agreement to remove the ice house? Why this effect? [*Mitchell v. Lath*, 247 N.Y. 377 (1928).]

10. A seller agreed to give a buyer the first right to purchase the remainder of her property if she chose to sell it. When the seller became deceased, the buyer filed suit against the estate, seeking the option to purchase. The two parties entered into a settlement agreement that was disapproved by the probate court. After the probate court's disapproval, the parties continued to attempt to negotiate a sale. They then entered into a second settlement agreement that was never signed. The buyer took possession of the keys and property. The buyer then attempted to renegotiate a lower price. The estate filed suit to compel specific performance, and the district court granted the estate's request. The buyer challenged the order of the district court, which enforced an oral settlement agreement requiring that the buyer purchase the real estate, on the grounds that the statute of frauds precluded the enforcement of agreements that were not in writing or signed by both parties. On appeal the court applied the doctrine of partial performance to its decision, stating that the doctrine of partial performance took the agreement outside the statute of frauds because the estate tendered possession of the property and the buyer took and retained possession, used the property, and never denied that the parties had reached an agreement. The court affirmed the district court's ruling. Do you agree with the argument of the appellate buyer or the argument of the state supreme court? Why? [*Simek v. Tate*, 231 P.3d 891, 2010 Wyo. LEXIS 68.]

11. A company sued a meat distribution market, claiming breach of contract following the market's failure to pay money owed on five notices of purchase (NOPs), as well as collection of accounts under the Uniform Commercial Code, Article 9. The district court held that the market did in fact breach its contract because the NOPs were valid and enforceable contracts. The meat distribution market appealed the order of the U.S. District Court for the District of New Jersey, which found the market liable for

$1,010,435. The appellant meat market argued that the NOPs were not valid and enforceable contracts because the invoices "were false and unattached to the NOPs when the plaintiff company received the signed and delivered copies." On appeal, the court noted that the general manager of the meat distribution market did in fact sign the NOPs and that the NOPs were valid and enforceable despite missing invoices; both parties agreed that the dollar amount indicating the money the meat market owed the plaintiff company was clear and present on the face of each NOP, and thus "the essential term at issue was conspicuously available for interpretation by both parties." Do you agree with the rulings of the district and appeal courts, which determined that Madison Financial LLC had an enforceable contract claim under the statute of frauds? Why or why not? [*Hunts Point Cooperative Market, Inc. v. Madison Financial LLC*, 2009 U.S. App. LEXIS 19382.]

12. The plaintiff and defendant engaged in phone calls and e-mails that unambiguously indicated an intent to be bound to all necessary terms of a transaction. The district court recognized these recorded communications between parties as enforceable contracts, and thus the statute of frauds was inapplicable. When the plaintiff abandoned the deal, the court recognized the plaintiff's actions as a breach of contract. The plaintiff appealed. The reviewing court disagreed with part of the summary judgment, stating that "a trier of fact could have decided either way on the question of whether the email included an implication that there was a binding agreement that would have been supplemented by customary terms as a mere formality, or whether the parties were only engaged in ongoing negotiations that could have ultimately fallen apart." Further, the reviewing court concluded that the plaintiff did not produce sufficient evidence of industry standards to persuade the court that the disputed e-mail was not definite enough to represent an enforceable agreement. Since the reviewing court found ambiguity in the "agreement" on April 20, the court concluded that the case was not properly resolved at summary judgment; the court stated that "because [the ambiguity] has not been briefed or argued before us, we leave to the good judgment of the district court the issue of whether either side may now demand fact-finding on liability before a jury instead of at a bench trial." The reviewing court concluded that there was no error in the district court's damage award, or the district court's ruling of the inapplicability of the statute of frauds, but that it was up to the district court whether to revisit its findings. The court remanded

for proceedings consistent with the court's opinion. If you were the reviewing court, what information would convince you that the agreement between the two parties was an enforceable contract? Why? [*Aps Capital Corp. v. Mesa Air Group Inc.*, 580 F.3d 265 (2009).]

13. California farmers and farming entities purchase water from Westlands Water District, which receives its water from the U.S. Bureau of Reclamation under a 1963 contract between Westlands and the bureau. In 1993, Westlands and other water districts sued the bureau for reducing their water supply. The farmers, though not parties to the 1963 contract, intervened as plaintiffs. After negotiations, all parties except the farmers stipulated to dismissal of the districts' complaint. The farmers pressed forward with, as relevant here, the claim that the United States had breached the contract. They contended they were third-party beneficiaries entitled to enforce the contract. The district court ultimately held that the farmers were neither contracting parties nor intended third-party beneficiaries of the contract. The Ninth Circuit affirmed. If you were on the Supreme Court, how would you rule on appeal? Justify your legal decision. [*Orff v. United States*, 125 S. Ct. 2606 (2005).]

14. The farmers are former customers of Ron Kaufman, the owner and operator of Southeast Implements, Inc., a Case International Harvester equipment dealership. Between 1996 and 1998, they agreed to purchase or lease various items of farm equipment from Southeast. In each instance, the farmers and Kaufman orally negotiated the terms of the purchases/leases, and Kaufman then prepared written purchase agreements for each transaction, assigning his rights thereunder to Case. Case, in turn, after approving the assignments and agreeing to finance the purchases/leases, paid Kaufman for the equipment and looked to the farmers, as debtors, for payment. The written purchase agreements, however, were prepared and assigned without the farmers' knowledge and did not reflect the terms of the oral contracts. Kaufman inflated the purchase/lease prices and forged the farmers' signatures, thereby obtaining thousands of dollars in overpayments from Case. When Case became aware of Kaufman's fraud, it sent representatives to meet with the individual farmers. After verifying that the farmers were in possession of equipment covered by the forged purchase agreements, Case attempted to enforce the terms of the forged contracts. The farmers alleged that Case's assignment was improper because the rights assigned were not the ones to which the farmers agreed. The farmers filed suit against Case and Southeast.

The court found in favor of Case, and the farmers appealed. Is Kaufman's assignment made to Case binding? What defenses might the farmers have against Case? [*Day v. Case Credit Corp.*, 427 F.3d 1148 (2005).]

15. CEI and NU were planning a multibillion-dollar merger. Among the terms and conditions of the underlying merger agreement, CEI agreed to purchase all of NU's outstanding shares for $3.6 billion—$1.2 billion over the prevailing market price. Shortly before the scheduled closing, CEI declared that NU had suffered a material adverse change that "dramatically lowered" NU's valuation, and CEI declined to proceed with the merger unless NU would agree to a lower share price. NU rejected the share price reduction, treated CEI's demand as an anticipatory repudiation and breach of the agreement, and declared that the merger was "effectively terminated." Both parties brought suit. The district court ruled that NU could sue on behalf of its shareholders for the $1.2 billion. The court reasoned that the merger agreement expressly designated NU's shareholders as intended third-party beneficiaries. Due to subsequent legal actions, both parties appealed. The appellate court then decided the issue of whether any NU shareholders were intended third-party beneficiaries. If you were on the court, how would you have ruled? Why? [*Consol. Edison, Inc. v. Northeast Utils.*, 426 F.3d 524 (2005).]

16. Spouses Kenneth and Betty Herman hired an attorney, Byrd, to create an amendable trust on their behalf. The Hermans intended the trust to include that after the death of one spouse, the surviving spouse would have control of the assets, including the power to change beneficiaries. Byrd drafted three amendments to the trust. At the time of the first spouse's (Mr. Herman's) death, the trust stated that all assets were to be distributed to Michael and Don Dyer. Then, in 1996, Mrs. Herman hired a separate attorney, Stuart, who drafted further amendments to the trust. In the fourth amendment, Littell was designated as a joint successor trustee. Eventually, after Mr. Herman and Mrs. Herman died, Littell was the sole trustee, the beneficiary of a yacht, and the residual beneficiary of the trust assets. After Mrs. Herman's death, the previously named beneficiaries, the Dyers, brought suit, challenging the validity of the amendments made to the trust following Mr. Herman's death. The probate court ruled in favor of the Dyers and held that all amendments to the trust executed by Mrs. Herman were invalid. Littell filed a suit of legal malpractice, arguing that he was an intended beneficiary of the trust and was frustrated by the

negligence of the defendant attorneys as his share in the trust was lost as a direct result of such negligence. The district court dismissed his legal malpractice claim, and Littell appealed. The court of appeals confirmed the district court's ruling that the plaintiff was not an intended beneficiary of the trust and lacked third-party beneficiary standing. Do you believe Littell should have been granted third-party beneficiary standing? Why or why not? [*Littell v. Law Firm of Byrd,* 2009 U.S. App. LEXIS 19596.]

Looking for more review material?

The Online Learning Center at **www.mhhe.com/kubasekess2e** contains this chapter's "Assignment on the Internet" and also a list of URLs for more information, entitled "On the Internet." Find both of them in the Student Center portion of the OLC, along with quizzes and other helpful materials.

CHAPTER

13

Discharge and Remedies

The Battle of the Pharmacies

Walgreen operated a pharmacy in a mall in Milwaukee, Wisconsin, owned by the Sara Creek Property Company. Under Walgreen's lease, Sara Creek promised not to rent space in the mall to anyone else who wanted to operate a pharmacy. Several years into the lease, Sara Creek informed Walgreen that it intended to buy out the anchor tenant in the mall and install a Phar-Mor discount store in its place. This store would include a pharmacy the same size as Walgreen's and would be within 200 feet of Walgreen's store. The Phar-Mor pharmacy would sell pharmaceuticals at a deeper discount than that of Walgreen. Walgreen was granted an injunction against the new lease by the Seventh Circuit Court of Appeals. Sara Creek appealed, claiming that monetary damages would be a more appropriate remedy and then the Phar-Mor pharmacy could be allowed to move in.[1]

1. Do you think monetary damages alone would be an adequate remedy for Walgreen?
2. What kind of remedy should the court grant Walgreen?

[1] *Walgreen Co.* v. *Sara Creek Property* Co., U.S. Court of Appeals for the Seventh Circuit, 966 F.2d 273 (1992).

LEARNING OBJECTIVES

After reading this chapter, you will be able to answer the following questions:

LO 13-1 What are the primary methods for discharging a contract?

LO 13-2 What are the primary legal remedies available for a breach of contract?

LO 13-3 What are the primary equitable remedies available for a breach of contract?

LO 13-1 Methods of Discharging a Contract

The previous five chapters focus primarily on how parties enter into a legally binding agreement. Once a party has entered into a binding agreement, how does the party terminate his or her obligation under the contract? That question is the focus of this chapter. When a party's obligations under a contract are terminated, they are said to be discharged. There are a number of ways by which a party's contractual obligations can be terminated, or discharged. The first, and the one most parties hope to secure from the other when they enter into an agreement, is performance. The others are the happening of a condition or its failure to occur, material breach by one or both parties, agreement of the parties, or operation of law. The chapter explains each of these methods.

CONDITIONS

conditional contract
A contract that becomes enforceable only on the happening or termination of a specified condition.

Under ordinary circumstances, a party's duty to perform the promise agreed to in a contract is absolute. Sometimes, however, a party's duty to perform may be affected by whether a certain condition occurs. Contracts containing conditions affecting the performance obligations of the parties are called **conditional contracts**. The conditions may be either implied by law or expressly inserted into the contract by the parties.

condition precedent
In a contract, an event that must occur in order for a party's duty to arise.

Discharge by Conditions Precedent, Subsequent, and Concurrent There are three types of conditions: condition precedent, condition subsequent, and concurrent conditions. A **condition precedent** is a particular event that must occur in order for a party's duty to arise. If the event does not occur, the party's duty to perform does not arise. Frequently, real estate contracts are conditioned on an event such as the buyer's being able to sell his current home by a certain date. If the home does not sell, the condition does not arise, and the parties have no duty to perform and are thus discharged from the contract.

Another common example of a contract containing a condition precedent is an insurance contract. If Bill purchases a life insurance contract, he is obligated to pay the monthly premiums specified in the contract, but the insurance company's obligation to perform arises only when he dies. Bill's death is the condition that triggers the company's duty to pay his beneficiary. The key to this concept is that the condition must occur before a duty to perform arises.

condition subsequent
In a contract, a future event that terminates the obligations of the parties when it occurs.

A **condition subsequent** is a future event that terminates the obligations of the parties when it occurs. For example, John may enter into an agreement to lease an apartment for five years, conditioned on his not being called to active duty in the National Guard. If he is called to serve, his obligation to be bound by the lease is discharged.

concurrent conditions
In a contract, terms under which each party's performance is conditioned on the performance of the other; occur only when the parties are required to perform for each other simultaneously.

Concurrent conditions occur when each party's performance is conditioned on the performance of the other. They occur only when the parties are required to perform for each other simultaneously. For example, when a buyer is supposed to pay for goods on delivery, the buyer's duty to pay is impliedly conditioned on the seller's duty to deliver the goods, and the seller's duty to deliver the goods is impliedly conditioned on the buyer's duty to pay for the goods. The legal effect of a contract's being concurrently conditioned is that each party must offer to perform before being able to sue the other for nonperformance.

express condition
A condition specifically and explicitly stated in a contract and usually preceded by words such as *conditioned on, if, provided that,* or *when.*

Express and Implied Conditions Conditions in contracts are also described as being express or implied. **Express conditions** are explicitly stated in the contract and are usually preceded by words such as *conditioned on, if, provided that,* or *when.* For example, in a situation involving a potential sale of a house, the offer expressly required that the buyer make a deposit of $1,000 "on acceptance." The buyer wrote "accepted" on the offer and returned it but did not include the deposit. No deposit of money was ever made. The seller then canceled the transaction. Several weeks later, the buyer attempted to tender payment to the seller. The court found that under the terms of the contract, payment of the $1,000 was an express condition of acceptance and since the acceptance was incomplete, there was no contract.[2]

implied condition
A condition that is not specifically and explicitly stated but is inferred from the nature and language of the contract.

Implied conditions are those that are not explicitly stated but are inferred from the nature and language of the contract. For example, if a man enters into a contract with a builder to replace the

[2] *Smith v. Holmwood*, 231 Cal. App. 2d 549 (1965).

windows in his house, there is an implied condition that the builder will be given access to the home so that she may fulfill her obligations under the contract.

DISCHARGE BY PERFORMANCE

In most situations, parties discharge their obligations by doing what they respectively agreed to do under the terms of the contract; this is called *discharge by performance.* Parties also discharge their duty by making an offer to perform and being ready, willing, and able to perform. This offer of performance is known as a **tender.** If a painter shows up at Sherry's house with his paint and ladders and is ready to start painting the garage, he has tendered performance. If Sherry refuses to let him start, the painter has now discharged his duties under the contract by his tender of performance and he may sue Sherry for material breach (discussed in detail later in this chapter).

Types of Performance There are two primary kinds of performance: complete performance and substantial performance. Performance may also be conditioned on the satisfaction of a party to the contract or of a third party.

 Complete performance occurs when every aspect of the parties' duties under the contract is carried out perfectly. In many instances, complete performance is difficult, if not impossible, to attain, and courts today generally require only substantial performance.

 Substantial performance occurs when the following conditions have been met: (1) completion of nearly all the terms of the agreement, (2) an honest effort to complete all the terms, and (3) no willful departure from the terms of the agreement. Substantial performance discharges the party's responsibilities under the contract, although the court may require that the party compensate the other party for any loss in value caused by the failure to meet all the standards set forth in the contract. For example, if a contract called for all bedrooms of a house to be painted blue but one was inadvertently painted green, the court may require that the contractor compensate the buyer with the amount that it will cost the buyer to have that room repainted. The difficulty of determining whether there has in fact been substantial performance is illustrated in the Case Nugget.

Performance Subject to Satisfaction of a Contracting Party Sometimes the performance of the contract is subject to the satisfaction of one of the contracting parties. In such a case, a party is not discharged from the contract until the other party is satisfied. Satisfaction is considered an express condition that must be met before the other party's obligation to pay for the performance arises.

 Satisfaction may be judged according to either a subjective or an objective standard. When the judgment involved is a matter of personal taste, such as when a woman is having a dress custom-made for her, the courts apply a subjective satisfaction standard. As long as the person, in good faith, is not satisfied, the other party is deemed to have not met the condition.

 If the performance is related to a mechanical or utility standard, the objective satisfaction standard applies. Also, if the contract does not clearly specify that the satisfaction is to be personal, the objective standard applies. When an objective standard is used, the courts ask whether the reasonable person would be satisfied with the performance.

 Sometimes a contract is conditioned on the satisfaction of a third party. Usually, such provisions arise in construction contracts specifying that before a buyer accepts a building, an architect must provide a certificate stating that the building was constructed according to the plans and specifications.

DISCHARGE BY MATERIAL BREACH

A *breach* occurs whenever a party fails to perform her obligations under the contract. If the breach is a minor one, it may entitle the nonbreaching party to damages but it does not discharge the nonbreaching party from the contract.

 A **material breach,** however, discharges the nonbreaching party from his obligations under the contract. A material breach occurs when a party unjustifiably fails to substantially perform his obligations under the contract. It is often difficult to know when the court is going to determine that a breach is material. Case 13-1 demonstrates the analysis a court may use to determine whether a defendant's behavior constitutes material breach.

tender
An offer by a party in a contract to perform, along with being ready, willing, and able to perform, a duty outlined in that contract.

complete performance
Contract performance that occurs when all aspects of the parties' duties under the contract are carried out perfectly.

substantial performance
Contract performance that occurs when nearly all the terms of the agreement have been met, there has been an honest effort to complete all the terms, and there has been no willful departure from the terms of the agreement.

material breach
A substantial breach of a significant term or terms of a contract that excuses the nonbreaching party from further performance under the contract and gives the nonbreaching party the right to recover damages.

CASE Nugget

A Substantial or Insubstantial Performance?

Larry Pettit et al. v. Hampton and Beech, Inc., et al.
Court of Appeals of Connecticut

101 Conn. App. 502, 922 A.2d 300 (2007)

The plaintiffs contracted for construction of a new house with the defendant. They wanted their home to be a reverse image of the house depicted in the defendant's advertisement, and they also modified the plans by widening the kitchen and great room and extending the rear of the house. There were some delays in the construction. At the time of the issuance of the certificate of occupancy, which was one day after the closing date specified in the contract, the plaintiffs gave the defendants a punch card of items to be fixed, placed $20,000 of the purchase price in escrow, refused to set a new closing date, moved into a motel, and sued the defendant, claiming the defendant failed to substantially perform the contract.

The trial court found, pursuant to expert testimony, that reading and comprehending the blueprints provided by the plaintiffs were difficult for the framers and probably led to some of the shortcomings in the construction process. The court found that there were surface cracks in the concrete front porch because expansion joints were not installed and that the front steps, which were built to industry standards, had settled. The court further found that the porch could be repaired by resurfacing it and that the gap between the steps and the porch was a minor repair. The court awarded $3,238 to the plaintiffs to repair both problems.

There were cracks in the foundation, not uncommon after construction, which could be repaired for $700. Rather than following the blueprint requirement, the defendant used an alternate construction that provided better structural support and complied with the building code. The court awarded $105 to attach a joist to an existing one to add additional support, although this might not be necessary structurally. The court found that a beam needed to be installed under the kitchen and awarded $250 for the repair. Joint hangers were missing on the header and stringers of the stairway to the basement. Their omission was not a structural defect, and they easily could be installed at a cost of $75. Bridging and blocking were omitted or not nailed where ducts and pipes passed through joists, another nonstructural defect, and this could be remedied at a cost of $60. Settlement cracks in the walls, a common postconstruction phenomenon, could be repaired for $1,265. The court also awarded the plaintiffs $219.34 to replace a window over the garage.

The plaintiffs appealed on grounds that the proper standard for substantial performance was not applied and thus they were entitled to more damages. In affirming the lower court's judgment that the defendant had substantially performed, the appeals judge said that issuance of a certificate of occupancy may be evidence of substantial performance; it is not dispositive of the question. Other factors include the extent to which the injured party will be deprived of the benefit reasonably expected, the extent to which that party can be adequately compensated for the deficiency of performance, the extent to which the performing party will suffer forfeiture, the likelihood that the performing party will cure his failure in light of the circumstances and his reasonable assurances, and the extent of good faith and fair dealing on the part of the performing party. Applying the factors to the case, the ruling of the trial court judge was not clearly erroneous, and therefore his judgment was affirmed.

CASE 13-1

ALLSTATE INSURANCE COMPANY v. HERRON
NINTH CIRCUIT COURT OF APPEALS
634 F.3d 1101 (9th Cir. 2011)

FACTS: *Herron got into a single-car accident that severely injured his passenger, Angelia Trailov. At the time of the accident, Allstate Insurance Company provided car insurance to Herron under a policy obtained by Herron's parents, which provided a maximum of $100,000 bodily injury coverage for each person involved. Allstate conducted an investigation of the accident, including requests for medical information from Trailov.*

In February of 2003, Trailov's attorney, Michele Power, sent a letter to Allstate requesting that Allstate pay full policy limits for Trailov's injury. The letter did not specify a deadline for Allstate's response. Allstate forwarded the letter to Herron, informing him that his policy does not cover punitive damages. Herron's attorney urged Allstate to accept the policy-limits offer. In April, Power wrote to Allstate stating that the offer to settle would be revoked on May 16 unless there is some discussion regarding pre-filing resolution.

On May 12, Allstate paid Trailov $25,000 to compensate a portion of her medical expenses. On May 16, Allstate faxed Power a letter indicating that it had not yet completed its investigation, but that it would do so and respond to her settlement offer by the end of the month. On May 30, Allstate faxed Power a letter offering to settle at the $100,000 policy limit in addition to $12,500 in attorney fees. That same day, Allstate received a letter from Douglas Johnson indicating that he had been retained as co-counsel to file suit against Allstate.

Allstate filed a complaint in U.S. District Court against Herron, seeking declaratory relief. Allstate sought a declaration that its good-faith effort to settle Trailov's claims satisfied its obligation to the insured and that it was not obligated to pay any amount that exceeded the limit of the bodily injury coverage afforded to Herron. Prior to being served with this complaint, Herron confessed to judgment in the amount of $1,937,500 against himself in favor of Trailov in Alaska Superior Court. In light of Herron's actions, Allstate amended its complaint to seek additional declarations that (1) Herron breached the cooperation clause of the insurance contract; (2) Herron's breach was not excused by any prior material breach by Allstate; (3) Herron's breach voided the insurance contract; and (4) either Allstate's liability is limited to the amount of bodily injury coverage, or Herron's breach voided the contract and all liability coverage.

The jury found Allstate's actions to settle with the May 30 settlement offer to be in good faith. Allstate sought to amend the judgment to stipulate that (1) Herron's breach of contract was not excused by any breach on Allstate's part; (2) Herron's breach voided the insurance policy's liability coverage; and (3) Herron's assignment of rights against Allstate to Trailov was null and void because Allstate has no liability. The District Court granted Allstate's request. Herron filed a timely appeal.

ISSUE: Did the lower court abuse discretion to find Herron materially breached the insurance policy contract with Allstate?

REASONING: Under Alaska law, a material breach is one that will or may result in the other party not receiving substantially what that party bargained for. This breach must have an adverse impact on the relationship between the parties. Herron alleges that Allstate breached its contract with Herron by failing to settle by Power's May 16 deadline. However, that failure was found by jury to be a reasonable attempt on Allstate's part to uphold its obligations to Herron.

Allstate alleges that a material breach of contract occurred when Herron confessed to a certain amount of liability to Trailov. This confession directly contributed to an adverse relationship between the insurer and the insured and is undeniably a breach of the cooperation clause. On these two bases, the breach is material. However, under Alaska law, a material breach of the cooperation clause relieves only a prejudiced insurer from liability under a policy. The breach of the cooperation clause does not, in this case, equate to a material breach of the insurance contract because Allstate had not shown that it suffered harm as a direct result of Herron's breach of the cooperation clause. Such a ruling required the decision of a finder of fact, and cannot be resolved as a matter of law.

DECISION AND REMEDY: The lower court's decision to amend the ruling was affirmed with respect to Herron's material breach of the cooperation clause. The court of appeals overruled and remanded the lower court's decision with respect to the second and third points.

SIGNIFICANCE OF THE CASE: This case illustrates the importance of the difference between a material breach of a contract and a material breach of a separable clause of a contract.

CRITICAL THINKING

What is the reasoning that explains why a material breach requires harm to the insurer? Why would not just any breach be material to the ongoing responsibilities under the contract?

ETHICAL DECISION MAKING

Think about the Alaska law regarding material breaches of the cooperation clause for insurance policies. Whom do you think such a law is meant to protect? Why do you think the Alaskan law protects those people unless they harm the insurer?

In the Walgreen's dispute in the Case Opener, there was no question of whether the defendant had materially breached the contract. A key term of the 30-year lease between Walgreen and the defendant was the exclusivity clause. Walgreen would never have entered into the lease if it could not have been the only drugstore in the shopping center. To allow not just another discount drugstore in the shopping center but a deeper-discount drugstore that would open up right next door to Walgreen was clearly a material breach of the agreement.

Anticipatory Repudiation Sometimes a contracting party may decide not to complete the contract before the actual time of performance. This situation often arises when market conditions change and one party realizes that it will not be profitable to carry out the terms of the contract. The breaching party may convey the anticipatory breach to the nonbreaching party either by making an express indication of her intent to no longer perform or by taking an action that would be inconsistent with her ability to carry out the contract when performance was due.

Once the contract has been anticipatorily repudiated, the nonbreaching party is discharged from his obligations under the contract. He is free to go ahead and sue for breach, as well as find another, similar contract elsewhere. However, if the nonbreaching party wishes, he may decide to give the party who repudiated the opportunity to change her mind and still perform.

DISCHARGE BY MUTUAL AGREEMENT

Sometimes the parties to a contract agree to discharge each other from their obligations. They may do so through four primary means: discharge by mutual rescission, discharge by a substituted contract, discharge by accord and satisfaction, or discharge by novation.

Mutual Rescission Parties may agree that they simply wish to discharge each other from their mutual obligations and therefore may rescind or cancel the contract. For example, if James agreed to cater a graduation reception for Bill's son but it appears that the child is not going to graduate when planned, James could agree to no longer hold Bill responsible for paying him the agreed-on cost for the catering in exchange for Bill's agreement to no long expect James to cater the reception.

Substituted Contract Sometimes, instead of canceling the contract and terminating their relationship, the parties want to substitute a new agreement in place of the original. The substituted contract immediately discharges the parties from their obligations under the old contract and replaces those obligations with the new obligations imposed by the substituted contract.

Accord and Satisfaction An accord and satisfaction is used when one of the parties wants to substitute a different performance for his original duty under the contract. The promise to perform the new duty is called the *accord,* and the actual performance of that new duty is called the *satisfaction.*

The party's duty under the contract is not discharged until the new duty is actually performed. Thus it is the satisfaction that discharges the party.

Novation Sometimes the parties to the agreement want to replace one of the parties with a third party. This substitution of a party is called a **novation.** The original duties remain the same under the contract, but one party is discharged and the third party now takes that original party's place. All three parties must agree to the novation for it to be valid.

To understand more about the link between building consensus, which you studied in your management class, and its role in performance of contracts, see the **Connecting to the Core** activity for Chapter 13 on the text's website at www.mhhe.com/kubasekess2e.

DISCHARGE BY OPERATION OF LAW

Sometimes a contract may be discharged not by anything the parties do but, rather, by operation of law. Alteration of the contract, bankruptcy, tolling of the statute of limitations, impossibility, commercial impracticability, and frustration of purpose are all situations in which a contract may be discharged by operation of law.

novation
In a contract, the substitution of a third party for one of the original parties; the duties remain the same under the contract, but one original party is discharged and the third party takes that original party's place.

Alteration of the Contract The courts want to uphold the sanctity of contracts. Therefore, if one of the parties materially alters a written contract without the knowledge of the other party, the courts have held that such alteration allows the innocent party to be discharged from the contract. For example, if a seller, without knowledge of the buyer, changes the price of the contract, the buyer can treat the contract as terminated.

Bankruptcy When a party files bankruptcy, the court allocates the assets of the bankrupt among the bankrupt's creditors and then issues the party a discharge in bankruptcy. Once the assets have been distributed, all the bankrupt's debts are discharged. (Bankruptcy is discussed in detail in Chapter 18.)

Tolling of the Statute of Limitations The tolling of the statute of limitations, that is, the expiration of the time allowed by the statute, does not technically discharge a party's obligations under the contract. However, once the statute of limitations has tolled, neither party can any longer sue the other for breach, so for all practical purposes the parties are no longer bound to perform.

Impossibility of Performance Sometimes an unforeseen event occurs that makes it physically or legally impossible for a party to carry out the terms of the contract. In such a situation, the parties will be discharged on grounds of impossibility of performance. Courts distinguish between *objective impossibility,* meaning it is in fact not possible to lawfully carry out one's contractual obligations, and *subjective impossibility,* meaning it would be very difficult to carry out the contract. Objective impossibility but not subjective impossibility discharges the parties' obligations under the contract.

For example, if farmer Gray has a contract with the Hunts Corporation to provide it with 100 bushels of tomatoes on August 30 and a flood wipes out Gray's crop, it is not physically impossible for him to comply with the agreement. He has to go out on the market and purchase 100 bushels of tomatoes to ship to the Hunts Corporation. It may be inconvenient, and perhaps subjectively impossible, but it is not objectively impossible.

In contrast, suppose farmer Jones owns a historic farmhouse built in 1827 and he agrees to sell it to Smith, but the night before the parties are to exchange money for the title, lightning strikes the farmhouse and it burns to the ground. It is now objectively impossible to comply with the terms of the contract, so the parties are discharged from their obligations. The historic farmhouse is not like tomatoes; the subject matter of the contract is forever destroyed and cannot be re-created.

There are three main situations in which the courts find objective impossibility. The first is *destruction of the subject matter,* as in the example of the historic farmhouse destroyed by fire. If we go back to the example of the tomatoes, note that we said the farmer still had to perform because it was still possible for him to obtain tomatoes elsewhere. To protect himself in the event that his crop was destroyed, farmer Gray could have drafted the contract to identify the subject matter as 100 bushels of tomatoes grown on the Smith family farm. In that case, if Smith's fields were flooded, it would be objectively impossible to comply with the contract because there would be no tomatoes from the Smith farm in existence.

The second situation of objective impossibility is the *death or incapacity of a party whose personal services are necessary* to fulfill the terms of the contract. For example, if a famous artist is commissioned to paint a portrait and the artist dies, the contract is discharged. The artist's style is unique, and there is no way for anyone to take over the artist's role.

The third situation is *subsequent illegality*. If the law changes after the contract was made, rendering the performance of the contract illegal, the contract is discharged. For example, Bill orders a case of a nutritional supplement from Osco Drugs and Supplements. Before his order can be filled, the nutritional supplement is banned because of recently discovered harmful side effects. The parties are now discharged from their duties because to sell the banned substance would be to violate the law.

Commercial Impracticability Commercial impracticability is seen by some as a response to a somewhat unfair harshness of the objective impossibility standard. Commercial impracticability is used when performance is still objectively possible but would be extraordinarily injurious or expensive to one party. Commercial impracticability arises when, because of an unforeseeable event, one party would incur unreasonable expense, injury, or loss if that party were forced to carry out the terms of the agreement.

According to the Restatement (Second) of Contracts, Section 261 (1981), discharge by reason of impracticability requires that the party claiming discharge prove the following three elements:

1. That an event occurred whose nonoccurrence was a basic assumption of the contract.
2. That continued performance is not commercially practicable.
3. That the party claiming discharge did not expressly or impliedly agree to performance in spite of impracticability that would otherwise justify his nonperformance.

It is sometimes difficult to know whether the potential harm to the party seeking to avoid the contract is sufficient to give rise to the use of commercial impracticability. The doctrine is most commonly used in situations where raw materials needed for manufacturing goods under the contract become extraordinarily expensive or difficult to obtain because of an embargo, war, crop failure, or unexpected closure of a plant. Case 13-2 illustrates how the courts sometimes struggle to determine whether to apply the doctrine of commercial impracticability to discharge a contract.

 CASE 13-2

THRIFTY RENT-A-CAR SYSTEM v. SOUTH FLORIDA TRANSPORT
U.S. DISTRICT COURT FOR THE NORTHERN DISTRICT OF OKLAHOMA
2005 U.S. Dist. LEXIS 38489

FACTS: *The plaintiffs, Thrifty Rent-A-Car System and its affiliates DTG and Rental Car Finance Corp., allowed South Florida Transport (SFT), the defendant, to establish a Thrifty franchise. In 2003, they entered into four agreements, providing SFT the right to use Thrifty's trademark and business methods in exchange for payment to Thrifty of licensing and administrative fees and requiring SFT to maintain a fleet of automobiles for rent.*

In July 2004, SFT provided DTG with a check as payment, but it was returned for insufficient funds. SFT continued to make delinquent payments, and by August SFT owed Thrifty and DTG $1,134,819.40. Due to SFT's failure

to make payments, Thrifty and DTG informed SFT that they were going to terminate the licensing agreements and repossess the vehicles, to which DTG had legal title. However, DTG agreed to postpone repossession due to predictions of severe weather and allowed SFT to continue renting vehicles until repossession was completed.

When DTG repossessed the vehicles, DTG noticed that numerous cars were missing, to which SFT notified DTG that it had sold 51 vehicles without authorization. By August 2005, SFT owed Thrifty and DTG $4,238,249.53. SFT claimed that several hurricanes rendered its business operations commercially impracticable. The plaintiffs filed

a motion for summary judgment, seeking full reimbursement for the debts owed by SFT.

ISSUE: Under what circumstances will commercial impracticability excuse nonperformance of a contract?

REASONING: In the words of the court:

The doctrine of commercial impracticability is typically invoked in cases involving the sale of goods.

Codified in section 2-615 of the Uniform Commercial Code (UCC), which has been adopted by the Oklahoma legislature, the doctrine of commercial impracticability provides a defense to a seller for a delay in delivery or nondelivery of promised goods if performance has been made impracticable by a contingency, the nonoccurrence of which is an assumption of the contract.

Commercial impracticability may excuse a party from performance of his obligations under a contract where performance has become commercially impracticable because of unforeseen supervening circumstances not within the contemplation of the parties at the time of contracting. UCC commentary provides that a party pleading commercial impracticability must demonstrate the "basic assumption" prong of the test also found in the impracticability of performance context, that is, that the nonoccurrence of the supervening event was a basic assumption of the parties at the time of contracting. A rise or a collapse in the market standing alone does not constitute a justification for failure to perform. A contract is deemed commercially impracticable when, due to unforeseen events, performance may only be obtained at "an excessive and unreasonable cost . . . or when all means of performance are commercially senseless." In applying the doctrine of commercial impracticability, the crucial question is "whether the cost of performance has in fact become so excessive and unreasonable that failure to excuse performance would result in grave injustice."

. . .The evidence strongly suggests that the non-occurrence of hurricanes was not a basic assumption of the parties' agreements. Moreover, defendant provides no evidence to support a suggestion that the event of the hurricanes made the cost of performance of the terms of the agreements unduly burdensome, or even remotely more expensive. Finally, the Court observes, again, that SFT was behind on its payments to Thrifty and DTG before the arrival of the hurricanes in August 2004. No genuine issue of material fact exists, and the Court holds that the defense of commercial impracticability is unavailable to defendant.

DECISION AND REMEDY: The plaintiffs' motion for summary judgment was granted.

SIGNIFICANCE OF THE CASE: This case illustrates how strictly courts look at the circumstances to determine whether to apply the doctrine of commercial impracticability.

CRITICAL THINKING

Especially given the increased rates of severe weather and natural disasters witnessed recently around the world, to what extent can parties entering into contracts reasonably be expected to plan for the effects of a rapidly changing global climate?

ETHICAL DECISION MAKING

What values do you think are furthered by the decision in this case? What values are being subordinated by this decision?

Frustration of Purpose Closely related to impracticability is frustration of purpose. Sometimes, when a contract is entered into, both parties recognize that the contract is intended to fulfill a particular purpose, and the happening of that purpose is said to be a basic assumption on which the contract is made. If, due to factors beyond the control of the parties, the event does not occur, and neither party had assumed the risk of the event's nonoccurrence, the contract may be discharged.

This doctrine arose from the so-called coronation cases in England. Numerous parties had contracted for rooms along the parade route for the king's coronation, but the king became ill and the coronation was canceled. The courts held that the parties' duties under the room contracts should be discharged and that any payments made in advance should be returned as the essential purposes of the contracts could no longer be fulfilled, through no fault of any of the parties.

Again, this doctrine is not frequently used. For example, if you contract for an organist to play at your daughter's wedding but the groom gets cold feet at the last moment and the wedding is canceled, you cannot use frustration of purpose to discharge the contract because the groom's changing his mind was a foreseeable event, even though it was unlikely. The following Case Nugget illustrates how the courts sometimes struggle with whether to apply the frustration of purpose document.

CASE Nugget

An Unforeseeable Event?

Liggett Restaurant Group, Inc. v. City of Pontiac
Michigan Court of Appeals

260 Mich. App. 127, 676 N.W.2d 633 (Mich. App. 2003)

Elias Brothers Restaurants, Inc., had a contract with the defendant, City of Pontiac Stadium Building Authority, to provide concessions at the Silverdome until 2000. The parties renegotiated the contract in 1990, and Elias Brothers agreed to pay additional consideration for the option to extend the contract until 2005 to coordinate with the end of the Detroit Lions' sublease. The additional consideration involved paying the city a higher percentage on profits from sales. This option was exercised on December 1, 1998, and the Detroit Lions prematurely discontinued playing in the Silverdome after the 2001 football season.

The plaintiff sought to use the frustration-of-purpose doctrine to discharge its obligations under the contract extension and therefore have returned to it the additional consideration it had paid under the extension. The plaintiff argued that the contract was made on the assumption that the Lions would play in the Silverdome until their lease ran out and thus that their early departure frustrated the purpose of the extension.

The court said the doctrine was inapplicable in this case. The court first set forth the conditions under which the doctrine applied: (1) The contract must be at least partially executory; (2) the frustrated party's purpose in making the contract must have been known to both parties when the contract was made; (3) this purpose must have been basically frustrated by an event not reasonably foreseeable at the time the contract was made, the occurrence of which was not due to the fault of the frustrated party and the risk of which was not assumed by him.

Then the court noted that the situation clearly did not meet the third criterion. Far from being an unforeseen event, the Lions leaving prematurely was expressly addressed in the original contract by a paragraph specifying a reduction in the guaranteed minimum annual payment for each year in which the Lions did not play a minimum of eight games in the stadium.

LO 13-2 Remedies

The fact that one party has breached a contract does not necessarily mean that the nonbreaching party will sue. A number of factors go into the decision of whether it makes sense to file suit. Some of those considerations are (1) the likelihood of success, (2) the desire or need to maintain an ongoing relationship with the potential defendant, (3) the possibility of getting a better or faster resolution through some form of alternative dispute resolution, and (4) the cost of litigation or some form of ADR as compared to the value of the likely remedy.

The remedies the potential plaintiff will be thinking about can generally be classified as either *legal remedies* (also known as *money damages*) or *equitable remedies,* some form of court-ordered action. The distinction between legal and equitable remedies can be traced back to a time in our legal system's English roots when, instead of one unitary legal system, there were two separate courts, a court of law and a court of equity. When parties were seeking money damages, they went to the court of law; but when parties needed any remedy other than money damages, they went to the High Court of Chancery, which was a court of equity. When the United States was establishing its legal system, it combined both these types of powers in a unitary system. The reasons for this joinder are not known, but it seems likely that the primary reason

was that the early colonists simply did not have the resources to support two separate systems. The courts did, however, still maintain the distinction between legal and equitable remedies. However, unlike judges in the old English courts, judges in the U.S. system have the power to award both legal and equitable remedies in the same case. This section discusses these various remedies.

LEGAL REMEDIES (MONETARY DAMAGES)

Monetary damages are also referred to as *legal damages,* and they include compensatory, punitive, nominal, and liquidated damages. Whenever possible, courts award monetary damages rather than some form of equitable relief.

Compensatory Damages The most frequently awarded damages are **compensatory damages,** damages designed to put the plaintiff in the position he would have been in had the contract been fully performed. These damages are said to compensate the plaintiff for his loss of the benefit of the bargain. He can recover, however, only for those provable losses that were foreseeable at the time the contract was entered into. Sometimes, the plaintiff actually may have no losses. Suppose, for example, that Dr. Wilcox hires Jeremy to work exclusively as his research assistant during the fall semester, for a salary of $2,000 per month. If Wilcox breaches the contract and terminates Jeremy for no reason with two months left on the contract, and the only job Jeremy can get as a substitute pays only $500 per month, Jeremy is entitled to compensatory damages of $3,000. However, if Jeremy gets a new job that pays $2,500 per month, he is actually better off now, so he has no compensatory damages. Sometimes these damages are referred as *expectation damages* because they compensate a person for the benefit she or he expected to gain as a result of entering into the contract.

In addition to losing the benefit of the bargain, the plaintiff may suffer other losses caused directly by the breach. These losses may be compensated as *incidental damages.* For example, because Jeremy was unfairly terminated before his contractual term was over, he may have to spend money to find another job. His job search expenditures would be considered incidental damages.

Some kinds of contracts have special rules for determining their compensatory damages, namely, contracts for the sale of goods, contracts for the sale of land, and construction contracts. Each of these is discussed in a little more detail below.

Contracts for the sale of goods are governed today by the Uniform Commercial Code. If the seller breaches the contract, compensatory damages are generally calculated as the difference between the contract price and the market price on the day the goods were supposed to be delivered,[3] plus any incidental damages resulting from the breach. In other words, this measure of damages is the difference between what the buyer would have paid for the goods under the contract and what he or she is now going to have to pay to obtain the goods from another seller. Occasionally, however, the buyer may have no damages because the market price of the goods is lower than the parties had anticipated it would be at the date of delivery and so the buyer can now actually purchase the goods at a lower price than the contract price.

If the buyer breaches before accepting the goods, the seller would be able to resell the goods and recover as compensatory damages the difference between the price he sold the goods for and the contract price, plus any incidental expenses associated with the sale.[4] If the seller is unable to sell the goods to another buyer, as might be the case, for example, with shirts embroidered with a company's monogram, then the seller may be entitled to the contract price as damages. If the buyer breaches before the goods are even manufactured, the seller's damages would typically be based on the profits that would have been made from the sale.

In construction contracts, contracts whereby an owner enters into an agreement to have a building constructed, damages are calculated differently depending on who the breaching party is and what stage the construction is in when the breach occurs. If the contract is breached by the owner

compensatory damages
Money awarded to a plaintiff as reimbursement for her or his losses; based on the amount of actual damage or harm to property, lost wages or profits, pain and suffering, medical expenses, disability, etc.

[3] UCC §§ 2-708 and 2-713.
[4] UCC §§ 2-706 and 2-710.

before the construction is begun, damages are simply lost profits, which are calculated by subtracting the projected costs of construction from the contract price. For example, if Cameron Construction Company anticipates building a warehouse for the Johnson Corporation and the contract price is $500,000 and the cost of raw materials and labor is $420,000, Cameron could recover $80,000 in lost profits if Johnson were to breach the contract before performance had begun.

If, however, Cameron Construction had already expended $20,000 on materials and labor on the job when the breach occurred, the company would be able to recover $100,000 in damages because the amount of damages when construction is in progress is measured by the lost profits plus any money already invested in the project. And if the breach by Johnson had occurred after construction was completed, then Cameron would be entitled to recover the entire contract price, plus interest from the time payment for the project was due.

If the construction company, or contractor, breaches the contract before or during the construction, the owner's damages are generally measured by the cost of hiring another company to complete the project, plus any incidental costs associated with obtaining a new contractor, as well as any costs arising from delays in the construction project. If the contractor completes the job but finishes after the date for completion, the owner is entitled to damages for the loss of the use of the building that she would have had if the contract had been completed in a timely manner.

consequential damages

In a contract, foreseeable damages that result from special facts and circumstances arising outside the contract itself. The damages must be within the contemplation of the parties at the time the breach occurs. Also called *special damages*.

Consequential Damages It should be apparent by now that contract law requires greater certainty in the proof of damages than does tort law. Damages are not recoverable for breach of contract unless they can be proved with a high degree of certainty. One type of damages in contract cases that is often especially difficult to prove is what are called **consequential** or **special damages.** Consequential damages are foreseeable damages that result from special facts and circumstances arising outside the contract itself. These damages must be within the contemplation of the parties at the time the breach occurs.

In the Case Nugget that follows, the court distinguishes consequential damages from the damages that arise naturally from a breach of contract.

punitive damages

Compensation awarded to a plaintiff that goes beyond reimbursement for actual losses and is imposed to punish the defendant and deter such conduct in the future.

Punitive Damages Just as in tort law, **punitive damages** in contract law are designed to punish the defendant and deter him and others from engaging in similar behavior in the future. Because the primary objective of contract law, however, is to ensure that parties' expectations are met, punitive, or exemplary, damages are rarely awarded. Most jurisdictions award them only when the defendant has engaged in reprehensible conduct such as fraud. The primary factor in determining the amount of punitive damages is how much is necessary to "punish" the defendant; thus the amount depends on matters such as the wealth and income of the defendant.

nominal damages

Monetary damages awarded to a plaintiff in a very small amount, typically $1 to $5, to signify that the plaintiff has been wronged by the defendant even though the plaintiff suffered no compensable harm.

Nominal Damages In a case where no actual damages resulted from the breach of contract, the court may award the plaintiff **nominal damages.** The award is typically for $1 or $5, but it serves to signify that the plaintiff has been wronged by the defendant.

liquidated damages

Damages specified as a term of the contract, before a breach of contract occurs.

Liquidated Damages Typically, the court determines the amount of damages to which a nonbreaching party is entitled. Sometimes, however, the parties recognize that if there is a breach of contract, it will probably be somewhat difficult for the court to determine exactly what the damages are. To prevent a difficult court battle, the parties specify in advance what the **liquidated damages** will be if there is a particular kind of breach. The parties specify these damages in what is called a *liquidated-,* or *stipulated-, damage clause* in the contract. The damages may be specified as either a fixed amount or a formula for determining how much money is due. Such clauses are frequently used in construction contracts when the buyer needs to know that the property is going to be available by a specific date so that she can make her plans for moving in. In such a case, the parties may estimate in advance what it will cost the buyer for storage and temporary housing if the property is not ready by the specified date. The courts generally enforce such clauses as long as they appear to bear a reasonable relationship to what the actual costs will be. If the amount specified is so unreasonable as to not bear any logical relationship to foreseeable

costs, the courts declare the clause a penalty clause and do not enforce it. In Case 13-3, the court had to decide whether the clause at issue was an unenforceable penalty clause or a valid liquidated-damage clause.

CASE Nugget

A Classic Case of Consequential Damages

Hadley v. Baxendale
Court of Exchequer

156 Eng. Rep. 145 (1854)

The plaintiffs were millers whose mill was stopped when the crankshaft of the mill broke. They sent the shaft to Greenwich to be used as a model for a new crank. The plaintiffs' servant took the shaft to the defendant, a common carrier, and told the defendant's clerk that the mill was stopped and that the shaft must be sent immediately. At the time, however, most mills would have had extra crankshafts around somewhere, so without more being said, the clerk would not have known that the mill would not be soon back and running on a spare shaft. The clerk said the shaft would be delivered at Greenwich on the following day. The defendant's clerk was told that a special entry, if required, should be made to hasten the shaft's delivery. The delivery of the shaft at Greenwich was delayed by some neglect, and, consequently, the plaintiffs did not receive the new shaft for several days after they would otherwise have received it. During that time the mill was shut down, and the plaintiffs thereby lost the profits they would have received had the shaft been delivered on time. They sought to recover damages for lost profits during that time. The defendant argued that the lost profits were "too remote." The court decided for the plaintiffs and allowed the jury to consider the lost profits in awarding damages. The defendant appealed.

On appeal, the appellate judge set forth what has come to be the standard for consequential damages:

> Where two parties have made a contract which one of them has broken, the damages which the other party ought to receive in respect of such breach of contract should be such as may fairly and reasonably be considered either arising naturally, i.e., according to the usual course of things, from such breach of contract itself, or such as may reasonably be supposed to have been in the contemplation of both parties, at the time they made the contract, as the probable result of the brveach of it. Now, if the special circumstances under which the contract was actually made were communicated by the plaintiffs to the defendants, and thus known to both parties, the damages resulting from the breach of such a contract, which they would reasonably contemplate, would be the amount of injury which would ordinarily follow from a breach of contract under these special circumstances so known and communicated. But, on the other hand, if these special circumstances were wholly unknown to the party breaking the contract, he, at the most, could only be supposed to have had in his contemplation the amount of injury which would arise generally, and in the great multitude of cases not affected by any special circumstances, from such a breach of contract. For, had the special circumstances been known, the parties might have specially provided for the breach of contract by special terms as to the damages in that case; and of this advantage it would be very unjust to deprive them.

In this case, the judge did not believe that the special circumstances had been communicated to the defendant. Thus it would have been unjust to hold the defendant liable for the damages, which he would not have contemplated as arising from the delayed delivery of a shaft.

**S. BROOKE PURLL, INC., T/A PURLL
CONSTRUCTION v. PATRICK DARRELL VAILES
DISTRICT OF COLUMBIA COURT OF APPEALS**

850 A.2d 1135 (2004)

FACTS: *The plaintiff hired the defendant to renovate his house and paid him a $5,000 initial payment under the construction contract but failed to do initial demolition work required under the contract. The contract contained a clause stating:*

> *The [owner] further agrees that if he shall cancel this Contract for any reason, whatsoever, then he shall pay to the contractor as fixed and liquidated damages, without proof of loss, the sum of money equal to Thirty Five Percent (35%) of the full contract price hereinabove stated. Furthermore, if it becomes necessary for the Contractor to file suit or take other legal action on this Contract because of a breach on the part of the party of the second part, the party of the second part agrees to pay reasonable attorney fees and court cost.*

The plaintiff sued the defendant contractor for return of his deposit, and the defendant counterclaimed for $36,102 and attorney fees, the amount that would be required under the liquidated-damage clause. The trial court held that the plaintiff had breached the contract, but it found the liquidated-damage clause to be an unenforceable penalty clause and awarded the contractor $1,722. The defendant appealed.

ISSUE: Was the clause imposing a payment of 35 percent of the contract value for breach by the owner a penalty clause or a valid liquidated-damage clause?

REASONING: Today, the trend is toward furthering freedom of contract through the enforcement of stipulated-damage provisions as long as they do not clearly disregard the principle of compensation. Such clauses simplify the resolution of a breach-of-contract dispute, as well as give the parties an opportunity to resolve the damage question without resorting to litigation, by setting the measure of damages at the outset, before a breach even occurs. Such provisions are especially appropriate when the parties enter into a contract in which the damages to be ascertained are uncertain in amount and cannot be easily ascertained. Thus, the courts tend to uphold these clauses unless they are clearly unreasonable. The liquidated sum must simply bear a reasonable relation to the damages foreseeable at the time the contract was made. The burden of proof is on the breaching party to demonstrate that the damage clause is disproportionate to the foreseeable damages.

In this case, the plaintiff provided no such evidence. The full contract price was $103,148.71. The contractor testified without contradiction that two-thirds of the contract price represented materials and labor and one-third represented his profit. The contractor explained that he consulted the Ames Construction Guide for the D.C. metropolitan area, which was customarily used in the industry for pricing construction jobs, in establishing his price. Thus, there was no evidence that the clause was unreasonable. The trial court had inappropriately struck the clause down because the contractor had failed to introduce evidence of his out-of-pocket expenses; such proof is not required to uphold a liquidated-damage clause.

DECISION AND REMEDY: The lower court's decision was reversed, in favor of the defendant contractor.

SIGNIFICANCE OF THE CASE: This case illustrates the preference for upholding liquidated-damage clauses.

CRITICAL THINKING

What evidence could the plaintiff have presented that might have changed the outcome of this case?

ETHICAL DECISION MAKING

The courts place the burden of proving the unreasonableness of a liquidated-damage clause on the breaching party. Which stakeholders benefit by this approach? Which stakeholders are disadvantaged by it?

Liquidated Damages in Japan

Under Japanese contract law, there are basically two types of contract damages, those that would ordinarily arise from the breach and those that arise because of some special circumstances that should have been reasonably foreseeable to the parties at the time of contract. In regard to the latter type, Japanese law provides for liquidated damages, similar to those available in the United States.

Under Article 420 of the Japanese Code, parties to a contract may specify in advance the amount of compensation payable when contractual obligation is not performed at all or not performed by a specified date. However, unlike in the United States, a party can raise a defense that he did not intentionally or negligently breach the contract. Using a form of comparative negligence, the court may reduce the amount of the liquidated damages to reflect the degree of negligence of the complainant. Japanese courts have also, on rare occasions, eliminated or reduced liquidated damages when they believed the amount violated public policy or constituted a windfall profit.

Mitigation of Damages When a contract has been breached, the nonbreaching party is often angry at the breaching party and may want to make the breaching party "pay through the nose." However, the courts do not allow a nonbreaching party to intentionally increase his damages. In fact, to recover damages in a breach-of-contract case, the plaintiff must demonstrate that he used reasonable efforts to minimize the damage resulting from the breach. This obligation is referred to as the *duty to mitigate one's damages.*

Thus, if you are the manager of a hotel, and a person who had booked 10 rooms for the week calls to cancel all the reservations, you have a duty to attempt to rent the rooms to minimize the damages. The mitigation must be reasonable, however, and no one is expected to settle for less than what was contemplated under the contract in order to mitigate the damages.

One area where interesting mitigation issues arise is cases in which an employee is wrongfully discharged and must seek new employment to mitigate her damages. If the employee does not seek alternative employment, the amount of lost wages recovered as damages will be reduced by the amount the employee reasonably could have earned in another job. If the employee does not find another job, the court must decide whether the employee could have found comparable alternative employment with reasonable effort. For example, in 1970, the California Supreme Court considered a classic case that involved an actress who was contracted to star in a musical motion picture that was to be filmed in the United States but was canceled prior to production. The court held that the requirement to mitigate damages did not require that the actress accept as an alternative a starring role in a western drama being filmed in Australia.[5]

EQUITABLE REMEDIES

LO 13-3

As noted earlier, equitable remedies grew out of the English court's authority to fashion remedies when the existing laws did not provide adequate ones. These remedies were typically unique solutions specifically crafted to the demands of the situation. Today, the most common equitable remedies include rescission and restitution, orders for specific performance, and injunctions.

As a carryover from the days of the English courts of law and equity, a party seeking equitable relief must meet five requirements. The party must prove that (1) there is no adequate legal remedy available; (2) irreparable harm to the plaintiff may result if the equitable remedy is not granted; (3) the contract is legally valid (except when seeking relief in quasi-contract); (4) the contract terms are clear and unambiguous; and (5) the plaintiff has "clean hands," that is, has not been deceitful or done anything in breach of the contract.

rescission
The termination of a contract.

Rescission and Restitution Sometimes the parties simply want to be returned to their precontract status; they want to have the contract terminated and to have any transferred property returned to its original owner. That is, they want rescission and restitution. **Rescission** is the termination of the contract, and **restitution** is the return of any property given up under the contract.

restitution
The return of any property given up under a contract.

[5] *Parker v. Twentieth Century-Fox Film Corp.*, 3 Cal. 3d 176, 474 P.2d 689 (1970).

Restitution and rescission are most frequently awarded in situations in which there is a lack of genuine assent (discussed in Chapter 11). When a party enters into a contract because of fraud, duress, undue influence, or a bilateral mistake, the contract is voidable and the party who wants out may seek to avoid the contract or, in other words, may seek rescission and restitution.

specific performance
An order of the court requiring that a non-breaching party fulfill the terms of the contract.

Specific Performance **Specific performance** is sometimes called *specific enforcement.* It is an order requiring that the breaching party fulfill the terms of the agreement. Courts are very reluctant to grant specific performance and will do so only when monetary damages simply are not adequate, typically because the subject matter of the contract is unique. If the subject matter of the contract is unique, then even if the nonbreaching party is given compensation, he cannot go elsewhere to buy the object from someone else, so this renders any kind of money damages inadequate. Primarily for historical reasons, every piece of real property is considered unique. Therefore, an order for specific performance would often be the appropriate remedy for the breach of a contract for the sale of a piece of real estate.

Under the UCC, orders for specific performance of a contract for the sale of goods may be awarded "where the goods are unique or in other proper circumstances."[6] While the other circumstances have not been delineated by the UCC, the case law reveals that a commonly accepted circumstance is one in which the good is scarce or is no longer being produced and therefore would be difficult to obtain on the open market.

injunction
A court order either forcing a party to do something or prohibiting a party from doing something.

Injunction An **injunction** is an order either forcing a person to do something or prohibiting a person from doing something. Most commonly, injunctions are prohibitions against actions. Such an injunction might be used, for example, as a remedy in a contract case involving a personal service. Mandy is a lounge singer, and she has a contract to perform at JZ's Lounge every weekend night from January through June. Two months into her contract she decides to go work for Bally's Lounge instead because Bally's will pay her twice as much money. There is no way to adequately calculate the damages that would arise from the singer's going over to the other club to perform, so money damages would not really be an adequate remedy. Instead, the owner of JZ's may obtain an injunction prohibiting Mandy from performing in any lounge until the end of June, when her term of performance under the contract will have been completed.

In the Walgreen's dispute in the Case Opener, the appellate court agreed with the trial court judge that it would be extremely difficult for the court to calculate how to adequately determine the damages that Walgreen would sustain if Sara Creek were allowed to simply violate the contract's exclusivity clause and lease space to another drugstore. The court would have had to determine how much business the new store would take from Walgreen over the course of the next 10 years, and it felt that such a calculation would be almost impossible to figure. Hence, the court agreed that money damages would not be adequate and that an injunction prohibiting the leasing of the space in violation of the exclusivity clause would be the only adequate remedy.

Sometimes, when a party is suing another for breach of contract, one of the parties is concerned that before the court has had a chance to decide the case, the other party will do something to make it impossible for the concerned party to get the relief he would be entitled to. In such a situation, the concerned party may ask for a preliminary injunction to prohibit the other party from taking any action during the course of the lawsuit that would cause irreparable harm to any of the parties to the contract. For example, Jim agrees to sell Bob a very rare antique car for $15,000 but then says he is not going to comply with the terms of the agreement. Bob sues Jim for breach of contract, but before the case goes to trial, Bob finds out that Sara has told Jim that she is willing to pay him $20,000 for the car. Bob may seek a preliminary injunction to prohibit Jim from selling the car to anyone else until the court decides whether Bob is entitled to an order for specific performance forcing Jim to sell the car to him. Thus the preliminary injunction fulfills the purpose of maintaining the status quo until the case can be finally decided.

Reformation Sometimes a written contract does not reflect the parties' actual agreement, or there may be inconsistencies in the contract, such as the price being listed as "$200,000 (twenty thousand dollars)." In such a case, the written document may be rewritten to reflect what the parties had agreed on.

[6] UCC § 2-716.

Recovery Based on Quasi-Contract When an enforceable contract does not in fact exist, the court may grant a recovery based on quasi-contract; that is, the court may impose a contractlike obligation on a party to prevent an injustice from occurring. Recovery in quasi-contract is often sought when a party thought a valid contract existed and gave up something of value in relying on the existence of a contract. To recover under a theory of quasi-contract, a plaintiff must prove that (1) the plaintiff conferred a benefit on the defendant; (2) the plaintiff had reasonably expected to be compensated for the benefit conferred on the defendant; (3) the defendant would be unjustly enriched from receiving the benefit without compensating the plaintiff for it.

SUMMARY

Methods of Discharging a Contract	Contracts may be discharged in a number of different ways, including:

Contracts may be discharged in a number of different ways, including:

- The happening of a condition subsequent or the nonhappening of a condition precedent.
- Complete or substantial performance.
- Material breach.
- Mutual agreement.
- Operation of law.

Remedies

Courts may grant parties in a breach-of-contract action legal or equitable remedies. *Legal remedies,* or money damages, include:

- Compensatory damages.
- Nominal damages.
- Punitive damages.
- Liquidated damages.

Equitable remedies, which are granted only when legal remedies are inadequate, include:

- Restitution and rescission.
- Specific performance.
- Injunction.

Point/Counterpoint

Should Nonbreaching Parties Be Required to Mitigate Damages?	
YES	NO
Courts' requiring nonbreaching parties to mitigate damages provides the most equitable solution when a contract is breached. Although a nonbreaching party could understandably be frustrated with the breaching party, such a breach does not license the nonbreaching party to force the breaching party to provide full payment for the contract, especially when many costs could have been avoided. For example, if a city contracts with a company to construct a bridge across a river and the city later learns that the roads that would connect to	Courts' requiring nonbreaching parties to mitigate damages is unfair. Contract law is designed to reward both parties for the agreement that they have reached. If one party is irresponsible and cannot perform as agreed, why should courts then punish the nonbreaching party by requiring him or her to mitigate damages? After all, the nonbreaching party likely made decisions subsequent to the contract on the assumption that the contract terms would be carried out, and mitigating damages introduces stress regarding those decisions.

the bridge would disrupt a nesting bald eagle, the company should not be permitted to still build the bridge and demand full payment. The city would then have to pay for a useless bridge, even though the company could have avoided the costs of building the bridge.

In this example and similar contexts, the breaching parties would have an incentive to do nothing and still demand payment, even though damages could have been reduced. For instance, if a person entered a two-year employment contract to work for a company but the company could not honor the contract, the nonbreaching party should not be entitled to sit at home for two years and still receive compensation. In other words, if nonbreaching parties were not required to mitigate damages—either by discontinuing performance, as in the bridge example, or by finding a reasonable replacement, such as a different job, in the employment example—nonbreaching parties would run up the costs by completing performance under the contract or doing nothing. In the context of finding a reasonable alternative, nonbreaching parties would actually have an incentive to do nothing.

Finally, mitigating damages promotes better relationships between contracting parties, making both parties more willing to contract again in the future.

For instance, if a hotel owner entered a contract with a person who agreed to rent 50 hotel rooms and a conference room for a weekend, the hotel owner would focus his time and energy on advertising for other weekends. To require the hotel owner, after learning that the person no longer wanted the rooms, to mitigate damages places stress on the owner that he would not have otherwise experienced. Instead of completely focusing on booking rooms for other weekends, the hotel owner must now take time away from advertising those rooms so that he can try to fill the 50 vacant rooms and conference room, even if he wants to sue for breach of contract.

In addition, requiring nonbreaching parties to mitigate damages encourages irresponsible behavior on the part of contracting parties. If a party knows she can breach a contract as long as she provides enough notice, she may be able to avoid most, if not all, liability. Returning to the hotel example, if the person who contracted to rent the 50 rooms notifies the hotel owner of the breach two months before the weekend she contracted for, the hotel owner could fill the rooms and the breaching party would likely not be liable for any damages, even though the hotel owner incurred greater expense and spent additional time filling the rooms with other guests. "Mitigating damages," therefore, is just a fancy way of saying that the burden shifts back to the nonbreaching parties, rewarding the very people who should bear the costs of breaching contract.

Questions & Problems

1. Explain the difference between legal and equitable remedies.

2. Explain how the existence of conditions subsequent and precedent affects the discharge of a contract.

3. Explain the relationship between commercial impracticability and frustration of purpose.

4. When Barry Meyer asked Robyn Mitnick to marry him, he gave her an engagement ring that cost $19,500. Before the marriage, he asked her to sign a prenuptial agreement. She refused, and the engagement was broken. He asked her to return the ring, saying it was a gift conditioned on marriage. She refused, arguing that it was an unconditional gift. The trial court agreed with Meyer, finding the engagement ring to be a conditional gift. Mitnick appealed. How do you think the court of appeals ruled, and why? [*Meyer v. Mitnick,* 244 Mich. App. 697, 2001 WL 171453 (Ct. App. Mich. 2001).]

5. Janelle Rederford suffered from systemic lupus erythematosus when she was terminated from US Airways. Rederford brought suit against US Airways under the Americans with Disabilities Act (ADA), alleging that she had been wrongfully terminated because of her condition. Concurrently, US Airways filed a petition for relief under Chapter 11 with the bankruptcy court. Through the bankruptcy proceedings, Rederford was required to request a hearing to establish her personal injury tort, which was covered by US Airways' insurance policy. Rederford did not file any such request with the bankruptcy court. The bankruptcy court accordingly disallowed any litigation pertaining to personal injuries US Airways caused prior to its bankruptcy proceedings. Rederford later filed suit in federal court against US Airways to seek compensation. US Airways filed a motion to dismiss, claiming that the case had been discharged in bankruptcy court. Rederford argued that because she

sought an equitable remedy of reinstatement to her position that her case could not have been resolved in bankruptcy court. Do you find Rederford's argument convincing? Why or why not? [*Rederford v. US Airways, Inc.,* 2009 U.S. App. Lexis 27258.]

6. Posh Pooch Inc., which designs couture pet carriers and accessories, convinced the Italian corporation Nieri Argenti to manufacture various fine leather and related goods for Posh Pooch. Posh Pooch picked up some of the goods in Italy, but at least seven shipments were sent to its store in New York. At the bottom of 12 invoice forms sent to Posh Pooch from Nieri Argenti was a seven-line paragraph written in tiny type in Italian, under the heading "Condizioni Generali Di Vendita." The last sentence of this paragraph stated, "Per controversie e competente il Foro di Firenze," which translates as, "The courts of Florence have jurisdiction over disputes." Other than this paragraph, most of the invoice was either written in English or translated into English. There is no evidence that the parties otherwise discussed the forum for resolution of disputes.

 Posh Pooch brought an action in New York against Nieri Argenti. At oral argument, the parties seemed to presume the existence of a contract between them for the sale of goods, but apparently they had not signed any written purchase contract. The parties did enter into two written confidentiality and nondisclosure agreements in 2003 that were written in English. Both agreements provided that New York law and international law would govern the construction of those agreements.

 Nieri Argenti contends that the court should dismiss the action on the basis of the forum selection clause contained on the invoices sent to Posh Pooch. The court found that additional terms to a contract for the sale of goods "are to be construed as proposals for addition to the contract" and do not become part of the contract between merchants if they "materially alter it," unless both parties explicitly agree to the alteration. Do you believe the term in the contract requiring that the dispute be resolved in Italy should be enforced? Why or why not? [*Posh Pooch Inc. v. Nieri Argenti,* 2006 N.Y. Slip Op 50224U; 11 Misc. 3d 1055A (2006).]

7. In 1991, EnerSys entered into an agreement with Exide Technologies to purchase substantially all of Exide's battery business for about $135 million. To formalize this sale, the parties entered into more than 23 agreements. Under the collection of agreements, Exide agreed to allow EnerSys to use the Exide trademark without royalties in the industrial battery business, while Exide retained the right to use the Exide trademark outside the industrial battery business. In 2000, Exide wished to reenter the North American industrial battery business. Both parties agreed to the termination of the 10-year noncompetition agreement, but Exide was unable to regain the Exide trademark from EnerSys. In 2002, when Exide filed for bankruptcy protection, Exide attempted to reject various agreements it had made with EnerSys in 1991, including the right to use Exide's trademark. The bankruptcy court granted an order finding that the agreement was an executory contract, a contract that was so underperformed that failure of either party to complete performance would result in a material breach excusing performance of the other. The Bankruptcy Code allows debtors to reject any executor contract. EnerSys appealed the bankruptcy court's decision, arguing that it had substantially performed its obligations under the 1991 agreement, including paying the full $135 million and operating the industrial battery business the 11 years prior to the 2002 bankruptcy ruling. The district court affirmed the bankruptcy court's holding that EnerSys's obligation for trademark use and quality standards provision amounted to elements of the agreement that would cause a material breach if they were not observed. EnerSys again appealed, arguing that any obligations EnerSys had under the 1991 agreement were not material. How do you think the court of appeals ruled? What standard would you use to determine whether an element of the agreement between the two parties was material? [*In re Exide Techs.,* 2010 U.S. App. LEXIS 11029.]

8. Andrew Finch, a stockbroker at Morgan Stanley Dean Witter & Co., assumed that his role in making Morgan Stanley the lead underwriter on the initial public offering (IPO) of Webmethods stock would allow him to allocate 75,000 shares of the stock to his clients. He prematurely acted on this belief by telling clients they could purchase the IPO shares through him. Several investors set up a vehicle at Morgan Stanley (Twin Fires) to purchase these funds through Finch.

 Before the IPO of Webmethods was issued, Finch learned that his allotment was only 225 shares. Too embarrassed to tell his clients, Finch pretended that trading of the stock had been delayed. As the price of the stock shot up from $35 to $212 on the first day, the clients were celebrating—until they realized that they had never purchased as much stock as Finch led them to believe they had. The clients argued that an equitable remedy would be for Morgan Stanley to compensate them for the gains they would have made (nearly $12 million) had they purchased the stock as they had intended. Do you think the court ultimately agreed with the plaintiffs? Why or why not? If not, what remedy do you believe the plaintiffs would

have been entitled to? [*Twin Fires Inv., LLC v. Morgan Stanley Dean Witter & Co.,* 445 Mass. 411, 837 N.E.2d 1121 (Mass. 2005).]

9. Williams owns two trucks that he uses to transport, under contract, frozen produce. Williams drives one truck himself and employs a driver to drive the other one. He provides the driver with a CB radio, cell phone, and expense money so that the driver can stay in communication with him. As a carrier, Williams is subject to the rules of the Department of Transportation for common carriers. One of these rules requires that all drivers be tested for drug use. Williams hired Hall as a driver but did not require that he take a drug test.

Williams had a contract with Mountaire Farms to pick up frozen-chicken produce from suppliers and deliver it to specific locations in New York and New Jersey. Williams assigned the delivery to Hall, who picked up the poultry but failed to deliver it because he was high on illegal drugs. Hall was arrested and the poultry recovered, but by the time it was recovered, the produce had spoiled, a loss valued at $33,373.63. Williams argued that he should be excused from liability under the contract on the grounds of commercial impracticability; the unforeseen drug use of his driver was an intervening circumstance beyond his control that prevented the fulfillment of the contract. Do you believe the doctrine of commercial impracticability is applicable in this case? Why or why not? [*Mountaire Farms, Inc. v. Williams,* not reported in A.2d, 2005 WL 1177569 (Del. Super. 2005).]

10. Hunt Construction Corporation hired National · Wrecking Corporation as a subcontractor to a larger project that Hunt oversaw. National Wrecking agreed to finish its work by February 12, 2004. Around the deadline, Hunt learned that the work would be delayed. Hunt complained to National Wrecking and incurred additional expenses for the delay in the work. National Wrecking completed its work on April 6, 2004. Even though Hunt knew of the impending delay since early February, Hunt failed to notify National Wrecking's sureties of the default until July 2004. When it filed suit against National Wrecking for breach of contract and added National Wrecking's sureties, National Wrecking's sureties sought summary judgment, arguing that Hunt had failed to provide timely notice of the default. The district court granted summary judgment in National Wrecking's favor. Hunt appealed, arguing that the surety bond contract did not require notice as a condition precedent to recovery. No reference to notice is provided in the bond form in question. How do you think the court of appeals ruled? Do you think that National Wrecking's sureties needed to state notice as

a condition precedent to collection? [*Hunt Construction Group, Inc. v. National Wrecking Company et al.,* 388 U.S. App. D.C. 361, 587 F.3d 1119 (2009).]

11. Energy cooperative Hoosier Energy sought to move depreciation deductions that it could not use to John Hancock Life Insurance Company. Under the transaction, John Hancock would pay Hoosier Energy $300 million for a 63-year lease of an undivided two-thirds interest in Hoosier Energy's Merom generation plant. Hoosier Energy agreed to lease the plant back from John Hancock for 30 years, making periodic payments with a present value of $279 million. The difference represented some of the value of the deductions that John Hancock could take as the long-term lessee of the plant. Because of the risks to John Hancock in the case of Hoosier Energy's default, Hoosier agreed to provide John Hancock with additional security in the form of a credit-default swap and a surety loan of about $120 million. Ambac Assurance Corporation agreed to be the surety bond holder. As stipulated by the parties, if Ambac's credit rating fell below a certain threshold, Hoosier would be required to find a different surety bond holder.

In 2008, Ambac's credit rating fell below the stipulated threshold. In accordance with their agreement, John Hancock gave Hoosier 60 days to find a replacement. When Hoosier reported having trouble finding a replacement, John Hancock extended the deadline to 120 days. At the end of this second deadline, Hoosier reported that it was "in negotiations" with Berkshire Hathaway to replace Ambac. Hoosier contended that immediately replacing Ambac as a surety bondholder was impossible, in light of the changes in the credit market. John Hancock argued that Hoosier was capable of finding a replacement but found the offered fees too high.

Hoosier filed a preliminary injunction to prevent John Hancock from requesting the surety from Ambac, which claims that it was ready, willing, and able to pay the surety bond. Hoosier argued that a temporary commercial impracticability existed in the market that made the situation unfair for Hoosier, which would be required to default on its loan immediately upon Ambac's payment of the surety fee. Do you agree? Why or why not? [*Hoosier Energy Rural Elec. Coop. v. John Hancock Life Ins. Co.,* 2009 U.S. App. LEXIS 20759.]

12. Brad Gupta formed two companies, Ameriquest Holdings and Ananya Aviation, for which he purchased three airplanes that were in lease agreements with US Airways and Continental Airlines. However, after the events of September 11, 2001, the two airlines did not renew their leases for the three planes

now owned by Gupta. Consequently, Gupta could not continue his loan repayments, and U.S. Bancorp Equipment Finance foreclosed and sold the planes. U.S. Bancorp sought to enforce the loan agreements for the millions of dollars still owed for Gupta's debt after the proceeds from the sale of the airplanes had been deducted. Gupta, however, argued that the events of September 11, 2001, resulted in immense losses to the airline industry and that performance of the loan agreements (i.e., repayment) was impossible. Did Gupta properly raise the defense of impossibility? What was the court's reasoning? [*U.S. Bancorp Equip. Fin., Inc. v. Ameriquest Holdings,* 2004 U.S. Dist. LEXIS 24709.]

Looking for more review material?

The Online Learning Center at **www.mhhe.com/kubasekess2e** contains this chapter's "Assignment on the Internet" and also a list of URLs for more information, entitled "On the Internet." Find both of them in the Student Center portion of the OLC, along with quizzes and other helpful materials.

CHAPTER

14 Formation and Performance of Sales and Lease Contracts

CASE OPENER

Who Is Liable for Ears Falling Off: The Farmers, the Seed Company, or the Weather?

In the spring of 1981 Robert and William Peterson bought Migro Seed Company, Inc., corn seeds from John Sandall. Both Petersons were local farmers, and John Sandall, also a farmer, was Migro's area dealer. Migro produces hybrid seeds for sale, and the corn seeds bought by the Petersons were a "product of scientific genetic cross-breeding to produce a seed having desirable germination, growing, and production qualities."[1]

Around July 23, 1981, the Petersons discovered that nearly 70 percent of their corn, grown from the Migro seeds, had broken off at the ear level after a typical Nebraskan thunderstorm the evening before. However, corn growing from non-Migro seeds had not suffered such damage.

It turns out that silica in the sandy soil in this particular area of Nebraska had been absorbed by these plants, causing them to develop a brittle stalk and thus break at about the first-ear-of-corn level. No other variety of corn seed had this problem. When John Sandall, the neighboring farmer and Migro dealer, sold the Petersons the 102 bags of seed, the literature accompanying the seed indicated that one of the Migro seed's attributes was "excellent stalk quality." When the crop was harvested, the Petersons harvested approximately 19½ bushels per acre of the Migro corn while averaging 114¾ bushels per acre of corn grown from seed provided by other seed companies. The Petersons brought a lawsuit for breach of contract.

1. Is the sale of seed a contract for the sale of goods when it was the resulting plant that may have been defective? Does this contract fall under UCC Article 2 or under common law?
2. Are the parties involved here merchants under the UCC and thus subject to a higher standard of care?

[1] See *Peterson v. North American Plant Breeders,* 218 Neb. 258, 354 N.W.2d 625 (1984).

LEARNING OBJECTIVES

After reading this chapter, you will be able to answer the following questions:

LO 14-1 What kinds of contracts fall under the UCC interpretations?

LO 14-2 What is a sales contract under the UCC?

LO 14-3 What is a merchant, and why is that designation significant?

LO 14-4 What is a lease contract?

LO 14-5 What is the CISG?

LO 14-6 What is the concept of title? How does it pass?

LO 14-7 What is risk of loss?

Businesses and organizations that purchase products need to be aware of which laws govern their purchases because the laws can differ. Three sources of laws that interpret sales contracts exist: state common law, the Uniform Commercial Code, and state statutory law. There is very little, if any, federal law that governs contracts for the buying and selling of items, and when such law does exist, it is highly specialized (e.g., the buying and selling of stock under laws created by the Securities and Exchange Commission).

This chapter introduces the Uniform Commercial Code. It explains the scope and significance of the UCC, discusses sections of the UCC that govern both sales and lease contracts, and reviews how these contracts are formed and executed.

The Uniform Commercial Code

THE SCOPE OF THE UCC

In some areas of law, federal statutes ensure that the same law applies in all the states. Federal statutes do not govern the formation of sales and lease contracts. Instead, each state passes its own laws to outline rules in this area. Consequently, laws vary from state to state. While all states (except Louisiana) follow the English common law, over 200 years of legal precedent that has developed in each separate state can create differences in contract interpretation and application. With the development of interstate commercial activities, these differences began to pose problems for parties from different states entering into a contract with each other. What was needed was some kind of uniform law for business transactions that all the states could adopt.

The **Uniform Commercial Code (UCC)** was created in 1952 and has been adopted in part by all 50 states, the District of Columbia, and the Virgin Islands. Louisiana, not having the English common law heritage, has adopted only portions of the UCC that do not conflict with its historically French-based code law. When a state adopts the UCC, that code becomes part of the law of that particular state; it becomes the commercial code for that state. The UCC is divided into sections known as *articles*. These articles cover a wide range of topics, from sales contracts to secured transactions (see Exhibit 14-1).

Uniform Commercial Code (UCC)

A statutory source of contract law in the United States applicable to transactions involving the sale of goods. The UCC was created in 1952 and adopted by all 50 states, the District of Columbia, and the Virgin Islands; it may be modified by each state to reflect the wishes of the state legislature.

THE SIGNIFICANCE OF THE UCC

The UCC is significant because it clarifies sales law and makes this area of law more predictable to businesses that engage in transactions in more than one state. Essentially, the UCC facilitates commercial transactions. This is an important point to remember. When in doubt, judges will try to interpret the UCC in order to keep an agreement in force. As the drafters of the UCC intended, the UCC is designed to facilitate commercial transactions, not construct ways to impede them.

However, it is important to emphasize that the UCC does not pertain to all business transactions. Under UCC Article 2, the subject matter of this chapter, the UCC explains the creation and interpretation of sales contracts.

Exhibit 14-1

An Outline of the UCC

ARTICLE	TOPIC
1	General provisions
2	Sales
2(A)	Leases
3	Negotiable instruments
4	Bank deposits and collections
4(A)	Wire transfers
5	Letters of credit
6	Bulk transfers
7	Documents of title
8	Investment securities
9	Secured transactions

LO 14-1 Articles 2 and 2(A) of the UCC

Article 2 of the UCC governs sales contracts, while Article 2(A) governs lease contracts. Specifically, Article 2 focuses on contracts for the sale of goods; Article 2(A) focuses on contracts for the lease of goods. For the purpose of "selling something," the UCC divides all the items that can be bought and sold into three categories: goods, realty, and services (including intangible goods such as securities). Article 2 pertains only to the sale of goods. Nonetheless, Article 2 is not a comprehensive guide to sales contract formation.

When Article 2 is silent on an issue of sales contract formation or interpretation, the common law rules apply. Of course, if a state has passed statutory law regarding contracts, that law always supersedes the common law. Additionally, it is important to note that under the UCC the rules for transactions involving merchants differ from those for transactions involving regular buyers and sellers. Merchants will generally be held to a higher standard of care and behavior than nonmerchants. Every state except Louisiana[2] has adopted Article 2 of the UCC.

> To see how Article 2 applies to transactions of goods, please see the **Connecting to the Core Activity** on the text's website at www.mhhe.com/kubasekess2e.

If you are not sure whether a contract falls under common law or under the UCC, the decision tree in Exhibit 14-2 can help you make a determination. To use this rubric, consider the following definitions of many of its terms.

LO 14-2 ARTICLE 2 OF THE UCC

sale

The passing of title from a seller to a buyer for a price.

Sale Section 2-106(1) of the UCC states that a **sale** "consists of the passing of title from the seller to the buyer for a price." Thus, in the transaction involving the Petersons and Migro Seed Company, the sale consisted of the passing of title (right of ownership) of the seeds themselves from Migro to the Petersons for a price.

goods

All physically existing things that are movable at the time of identification to the contract for sale

Goods Section 2-105 of the UCC defines **goods** as "all [tangible] things . . . which are movable at the time of identification to the contract for sale." Items are tangible if they exist physically. The issue in the Case Opener is whether the goods being bought are the seeds or the subsequent plants, which were defective. Note that Section 2-105 reads "at the time of identification to the

[2] Louisiana's civil tradition is based on the Code Napoleon, or the French Civil Code.

Exhibit 14-2

Common Law or
UCC?

1. Does the transaction involve a sale or lease (as opposed to, let's say, a gift)?

 If yes → go to question 2.

 If no → apply the appropriate area of common or statutory law.

2. Is the transaction for the sale or lease of a good?

 If yes → go to question 3.

 If no → apply common law.

3. If the contract is for the sale or lease of both goods and nongoods, which type of item is predominant in the contract?

 If goods → UCC Article 2 applies; go to question 4.

 If nongoods (real estate or services) → common law applies.

4. If this is a UCC Article 2 transaction, is either party a merchant?

 If yes → pay close attention to when the special rules on merchants apply.

 If no → then only "reasonable" care applies to the parties; no special or heightened duty of care applies to a party deemed to be a merchant.
 From the UCC's perspective, everything that can be bought and sold falls into three categories: goods, services, and realty. Think of it this way:

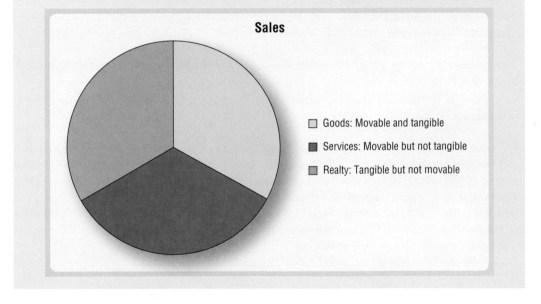

Sales

☐ Goods: Movable and tangible

■ Services: Movable but not tangible

■ Realty: Tangible but not movable

contract." At the time that the contract was created by the Petersons, the items being sold were the seeds. Seeds are goods because they are tangible and can be moved. Some items are not goods under Article 2. For example, corporate stocks and copyrights are not tangible, so they are not goods. Real estate cannot be moved, so it is not a good. Yet items attached to real estate that are used for business activities are known as *trade fixtures* and are treated as goods under the UCC.

Items taken from real estate may be treated as goods. Minerals, clay, and soil can all be treated as goods, with their sales contract governed by Article 2, if the owner takes these items out of the ground and then sells them to the buyer. Should the owner sell the buyer the right to come and remove the items, the contract would be governed not by the UCC but by common law for the sale of an interest in realty, in this case, an interest known as a "profit." Crops that are sold while

CASE Nugget

A "Mixed" Sale

John Sherman and Joann Sherman, Husband and Wife, Jointly and Severally, Plaintiffs and Appellants, v. Geralyn M. Sherman, Defendant and Appellee Supreme Court of South Dakota

2000 S.D. 117; 616 N.W.2d 393; 2000 S.D. LEXIS 118; 42 U.C.C. Rep. Serv. 2d (Callaghan) 491 (2000)

In this case, the defendants, a husband and wife, owned a feed store. At the time of their divorce, they owed a debt of nearly $147,000 to the plaintiffs for the purchase of feed to be resold in their store. To satisfy the debt, the husband and wife agreed to sell the feed store to the plaintiffs and have, as part of the cost of buying the store, the outstanding debt partially satisfied. The store cost less than the $147,000 debt, so the defendants still owed money to the plaintiffs. When the defendants defaulted on payment, the plaintiffs brought an action for breach five years after it arose. The question raised was whether the four-year statute of limitations under the UCC applied or whether the six-year statute of limitation for real estate contracts applied. This question hinged on whether the sales contract was for goods or for real estate. Both parties moved for summary judgment; the trial court granted the defendants' motion and denied the plaintiffs' motion. On appeal, the court affirmed. The feed was considered "goods" under UCC Article 2 because it was movable and was not money or a thing in action. Therefore, since the debt originated from the sale of feed, it was subject to the four-year statute of limitations for the sale of goods.

still growing in the field are also considered goods, and their sales contracts are subject to UCC interpretation.

Mixed Goods and Services Contracts Sometimes, it is not easy to tell whether something is a good because a tangible item is tied to or mixed with something intangible, such as a service. For instance, if Migro had sold not just the seeds but also seminars on efficient crop management and crop rotation and if the Petersons had bought a "package deal" that included the seeds and the seminars, it would not have been as clear that the contract was for the sale of a good. A contract that combines a good with a service is a **mixed sale.** Article 2 applies to mixed sales if the goods are the predominant part of the transaction.

Consider the Case Nugget below on the sale of grain and real estate.

Merchants UCC Article 2 pertains to anyone buying and selling goods. However, the UCC distinguishes **merchants** from regular buyers and sellers; thus it contains provisions that either apply only to merchants or impose greater duties on merchants. The drafters of the UCC assumed that merchants have a greater ability to look out for themselves than do ordinary buyers and sellers. The definition in the margin can be used to determine whether a seller or a buyer is a merchant under the UCC.

Think of questions about merchants as they relate to the transaction between the Petersons, Migro Seed Company, and John Sandall. Specifically, can any part of UCC Section 2-104(1) be used to argue that John Sandall is a merchant? What about the Petersons? Also, consider the possibility that if the Petersons are merchants, a court will assume that they need less protection than they would if they were nonmerchant buyers of the seeds. There is no question that Migro Seed Company is a merchant. However, if the Petersons sue John Sandall as well, is he a merchant and thus subject to a higher standard of care? If the Petersons are merchants, then as merchants in the business of farming, should they have known that their sandy soil, rich in silica, could pose a problem?

mixed sale
A contract that combines a good with a service or real estate.

LO 14-3

merchant
Under the UCC, a person who regularly sells goods as his or her business or trade or employs people to sell those goods; anyone who works for a person selling those goods; or anyone who holds himself or herself out as a "merchant" or a "dealer."

The UCC and the Internet

The Uniform Commercial Code was designed to address the sale of tangible goods such as scooters, electric power tools, and jeans. Because the UCC was written long before the Internet and e-commerce boom, this legislation was not designed for transactions related to less tangible things, such as software and information. Not surprisingly, the UCC does not respond well to certain legal issues that arise in today's marketplace. For example, the UCC does not tell us the answers to these questions: What rules should govern computer software, which is likely to be licensed rather than sold as a good? What about downloadable software files? What rules should govern information providers like America Online (AOL), which provides a continuing service? What rules should govern the exchange of information, such as stock quotes? What rules cover travel reservations a person makes online?

The National Conference of Commissioners on Uniform State Laws (NCCUSL) has adopted the Uniform Commercial Information Transactions Act (UCITA), which answers the questions above and many more. This law promises to do for electronic contracting what the UCC did for transactions in physical goods: protect consumers by providing predictability, uniformity, and clear rules. As with the UCC, states will choose whether to adopt UCITA. In 2001, Virginia became the first state to enact UCITA, probably because major Internet-related companies (i.e., AOL, UUNET Technologies) are headquartered in northern Virginia.

Sources: Robert Holleyman, "Updating Contract Law for the Digital Age," *USA Today* (magazine), March 1, 2000 (2000 WL 9014770); and Scott W. Burt, "Controversial New Rules for Computer Contracts," *Metropolitan Corporate Counsel* 8 (June 2000), col. 1.

ARTICLE 2(A) OF THE UCC

Every state except Louisiana has adopted Article 2 of the UCC. Article 2(A) covers contracts for the lease of goods. This section of the UCC is increasingly important, as consumers (both individuals and businesses) are more likely to lease goods today than ever before. Consumers lease cars, equipment, and machines. Article 2(A) does not cover leases related to real property.

Leases UCC Section 2A-103(j) defines a **lease** as "a transfer of the right to possession and use of goods for a term in return for consideration." A **lessor** is "a person who transfers the right to possession and use of goods under a lease."[3] A **lessee** is "a person who acquires the right to possession and use of goods under a lease."[4] Thus, if you lease a car, the company that leases the car to you (the lessor) transfers the right of possession and use of the car to you (the lessee) in return for consideration (money). If, as part of the contract with Migro Seed Company, the Petersons had leased a machine that plows the fields and plants the seeds, the Petersons would have been lessees for that equipment rather than purchasers.

lease
A transfer of the right to possession and use of goods for a term in return for consideration.

LO 14-4

lessor
A person who transfers the right to possession and use of goods under a lease.

lessee
A person who acquires the right to possession and use of goods under a lease.

LO 14-5

Contracts for the International Sale of Goods

THE SCOPE AND SIGNIFICANCE OF THE CISG

By the 1970s, it became clear that, increasingly, businesses planned to conduct commercial transactions not only across state lines but also across country borders. In 1980, the **United Nations Convention on Contracts for the International Sale of Goods (CISG)** was offered as a treaty that countries could sign, indicating their willingness to allow this treaty to govern international business-to-business sales contracts.

The CISG is important because if a problem arises with an international sale and a party to the transaction initiates litigation, the UCC does not provide guidance in the litigation; instead, the CISG preempts the UCC. The CISG covers the same general topics as the UCC. For instance, the CISG covers offers, acceptances, and other contract topics. However, specific provisions of the CISG differ from the UCC. For example, the CISG requirements related to the

United Nations Convention on Contracts for the International Sale of Goods (CISG)
The legal structure for international sales, including business-to-business sales contracts.

[3] UCC § 2A-103(p).
[4] UCC § 2A-103(o).

statute of frauds are more lenient than those under the UCC. In particular, the CISG does not require that contracts be in writing.

How Sales and Lease Contracts Are Formed under the UCC

Earlier in this textbook, you studied the common law of contracts, from the rules for agreements to the remedies for breaches. Sales and lease contracts require the same components as general contracts, but some UCC provisions that govern contracts for the sale or lease of goods are not identical to the common law requirements you learned about in Part 2. This section highlights the most important provisions of the UCC with regard to the formation of sales and lease contracts. Differences between the UCC and the CISG will be noted.

FORMATION IN GENERAL

Under both the UCC and the CISG, contracts for the sale or lease of goods may be made in any manner sufficient to show agreement.[5] A court will uphold a contract for the sale or lease of goods as long as the parties intended to make a contract and there is a reasonably certain basis for giving an appropriate remedy.[6]

OFFER AND ACCEPTANCE

Offer Under the UCC, if certain contract terms are left open, it is acceptable to fill them in. Exhibit 14-3 indicates what generally happens under the UCC when certain terms of a contract or lease are left open. While the quantity element is usually required, since without it the courts will have no guideline to determine the intent of the parties, the UCC does permit "output" and "requirement" terminology to determine quantity. If a farmer agrees to sell all the grain his fields will produce but is unable to determine a specific amount, then "quantity" has been satisfied under the UCC as an *output* contract. Conversely, if a buyer agrees to buy all of her "requirements" for a certain good but is unable to specifically identify an exact amount, then the UCC recognizes this as an enforceable *requirements* contract. See the Case Nugget on the next page for an interesting example of this.

 The UCC also creates a new category of offers: the firm offer. Under UCC Section 2-205, offers made by merchants are considered **firm offers** if the offer (1) is made in writing and (2) gives assurances that it will be irrevocable for up to three months despite a lack of consideration for the irrevocability. If a firm offer is silent as to time, the UCC assumes a three-month irrevocability period. This contrasts sharply with the common law, under which an offer is revocable

firm offer
An offer made in writing and giving assurances that it will be irrevocable for not longer than three months despite a lack of consideration for the irrevocability.

[5] UCC §§ 2-204(1) and 2A-204(1).
[6] Ibid.

Exhibit 14-3

The UCC and Open Terms

Exhibit 14-3

The UCC and Open Terms

TERM LEFT OPEN	INTERPRETATION UNDER UCC
Price	A "reasonable price" is supplied at the time of delivery.
Payment	Payment is due at the time and place at which the buyer is to receive the goods.
Delivery	The place for delivery is the seller's place of business.
Time	The contract must be performed within a reasonable time.
Duration	The party that wants to terminate an ongoing contract must use good faith and give reasonable notification.
Quantity	Courts generally have no basis for determining a remedy.

CASE Nugget

PMC Corporation v. Houston Wire & Cable Company

Supreme Court of New Hampshire

147 N.H. 685; 797 A.2d 125; 2002 N.H. LEXIS 68; 47 U.C.C. Rep. Serv. 2d (Callaghan) 1427 (2002)

PMC sells thermocouple wire. Houston entered into an agreement to buy a substantial or "major portion" of its wire from PMC. In the middle of the contract period, Houston informed PMC that it would still purchase wire from PMC but that the "bulk" of its purchase would be made through a competitor of PMC. PMC brought suit for breach of contract. The court refused the defendant's motion for summary judgment, and then the defendant appealed. The reviewing court found that there was sufficient evidence to find that the quantity element was sufficient for the contract to be enforceable under the statute of frauds. The writing expressed a quantity term when the distributor stated that it intended to purchase a major portion of the product from the supplier. This term was sufficient to afford a basis for believing that the offered evidence rested on a real transaction. There was sufficient evidence to reasonably determine the terms, including the quantity, of the contract. The reviewing court found that the agreement contained language from which a jury could have determined that the distributor agreed to purchase exclusively from the supplier up to a certain quantity.

at any time prior to acceptance unless a period of irrevocability (also known as an *option*) is supported by some kind of consideration.

Acceptance Under the UCC, an acceptance may be made by any reasonable means of communication,[7] and it is effective when dispatched. It is important to note that the **mirror-image rule** that applies under common law does not apply under the UCC. Recall that the mirror-image rule states that an offeree's acceptance must be on the exact terms of the offer. If the acceptance includes additional terms, the acceptance becomes a counteroffer instead of an acceptance.

Under the UCC, additional terms are permitted in contracts for the sale or lease of goods. Under UCC Section 2-207(1), additional terms do not negate acceptance unless acceptance is made expressly conditional on assent to the additional terms.

> **mirror-image rule**
> The principle which holds that the terms of the acceptance must mirror the terms of the offer; if the terms of the acceptance do not mirror the terms of the offer, no contract is formed and the attempted acceptance is a counteroffer.

CONSIDERATION

Sales and lease contracts require consideration. Under the common law, when a contract is modified, it must be supported by new consideration. The UCC eliminates that requirement for the modification of sales and lease contracts.[8] The UCC requires only that modifications be made in good faith.[9]

BATTLE OF THE FORMS

When parties are negotiating and offers and counteroffers are being exchanged, the UCC recognizes something we call the "battle of the forms." Essentially, it works like this: If the last set of negotiations is not specifically rejected, then the last terms standing, so to speak, are the ones that are applicable to the final transaction. The CISG tends to be less lenient with the battle of

[7] UCC §§ 2-206(1) and 2A-206(1).
[8] UCC §§ 2-209(1) and 2A-208(1).
[9] UCC § 1-203.

E-Commerce Sales in the Middle East

The Middle East seems to provide a potentially fertile ground for e-business start-ups. Why? Just one country, the United Arab Emirates (UAE), is a huge source of buyers interested in purchasing online. Commentator Dan Stuart notes that:

> 80% of respondents have a credit card; 70% of respondents use their credit card for online purchases; 40% of respondents buy online once per month or more; 56% of respondents are somewhat to very comfortable buying online from Europe, 59% from North America, but with the largest group of respondents from the GCC and Levant saying that buying from this region just hasn't even been an option; 49% of respondents cite the chief reason for hesitation or lack of online shopping from this region is the lack of options.

However, the fly in the ointment is the costs of the available payment providers. Consider that in North America, the requirements for setting up an e-commerce payment provider (such as PayPal) are $0 of collateral on account as a deposit with the merchant account provider, $199 setup fee, $420 yearly maintenance fee, and 2.6 percent and $0.25 on every transaction. In contrast, in the Middle East, these innocuous costs jump to $85,000 of collateral on account as a deposit with the merchant account provider (subtract from your operating capital), $1,000 setup fee, $5,000 yearly maintenance fee, and 3% on every transaction.

Source: www.danstuart.me/2010/02/24/the-state-and-opportunity-for-e-commerce-in-the-m-e/ (2010).

the forms and relies more on the old common law mirror-image rule; that is, if the parties did not expressly agree to certain terms, then those terms cannot be assumed. The UCC, focusing on its predisposition to facilitate commercial transactions, assumes that the terms found in the battle of the forms are part of the contract whether expressly agreed to or not.

REQUIREMENTS UNDER THE STATUTE OF FRAUDS

Under common law, the statute of frauds requires that all material terms to a contract be in writing. Under the UCC, contracts for the sale of goods must be in writing if the goods are priced at $500 or more;[10] lease contracts that require payments of $1,000 or more must be in writing to be enforceable.[11] There is a significant difference between the statute of frauds and the UCC as to what constitutes a **writing** that satisfies the statute. Common law requires some kind of writing created or signed by the party who is contesting the enforceability of the contract.

writing
A type of documentation that shows contractual intent and satisfies the statute of frauds requirement.

This rule holds true under the UCC unless the parties are merchants. If two merchants have an oral agreement, a written memo from either party to the other is deemed to satisfy the statute of frauds, even if it is not acknowledged by the receiving party. If the memo is not objected to within 10 days of receipt, the oral agreement, memorialized by the memo, is binding. The CISG has eliminated the statute of frauds. The CISG requires only credible and reasonable proof that a contract exists, regardless of whether the proof is documented or verbal.

UNCONSCIONABILITY

A contract or contract provision is *unconscionable* if it is so unfair that a court would be unreasonable if it enforced the contract. The UCC outlines actions a court can take if it discovers that a contract or lease provision or the contract or lease as a whole is unconscionable.[12] If a court finds that a contract or lease was unconscionable, in whole or in part, when it was made, the court either can refuse to enforce the contract or lease or can enforce the parts that are fair.

Title

Once the sales contract has been created and the parties are obligated to perform, the next issue to consider is the concept of title. *Title* means "ownership." The most important aspect of title is that a person must have title in order to pass title. In other words, you can't sell something that

[10] UCC § 2-201(1).
[11] UCC § 2A-201(1).
[12] UCC §§ 2-302 and 2A-108.

you don't own. Moreover, you can't give it away or use it as collateral for a loan. So what does it mean to have title?

THREE KINDS OF TITLE

There are three kinds of title: good title, void title, and voidable title. First, good title is title that is acquired from someone who already owns the goods free and clear. Next, void title is not true title. Someone who purchases stolen goods, knowingly or unknowingly, has void title. Finally, voidable title occurs in certain situations in which the contract between the original parties would be void but the goods have already been sold to a third party. The next few sections of the chapter discuss these types of title in detail.

Acquiring Good Title

LO 14-6

The most obvious way of attaining good title is acquiring it from someone who has good title, that is, the person who owns it free and clear, without any qualifications. In contrast, someone who has come into possession of stolen goods never has good title and can never pass a good title. A person in possession of stolen goods has void title.

However, problems may arise when someone thinks he or she has good title but actually has void title. Consider Case 14-1, which concerns the sale of a stolen vehicle and whether a car dealership's title was voidable or void.

good title
Title acquired from someone who already owns the goods free and clear.

void title
Not true title; e.g., the title held by someone who knowingly or unknowingly purchased stolen goods.

voidable title
Title that occurs in situations in which the contract between the original parties would be void but the goods have already been sold to a third party.

CASE 14-1

ALFONSO CANDELA, APPELLANT, V. PORT MOTORS, INC., RESPONDENT, ET AL., DEFENDANT

SUPREME COURT OF NEW YORK, APPELLATE DIVISION, SECOND DEPARTMENT

208 A.D.2d 486; 617 N.Y.S.2d 49 (1994)

FACTS: *Candela purchased a car for approximately $19,000 from Port Motors, Inc. The police later seized the car, claiming that it may have been stolen. Candela brought suit against Port Motors for breach of warranty of title. Port's defense was that it indeed passed a good title to Candela. New York's Supreme Court, which is New York's trial court level, granted Port Motors' motion for summary judgment, agreeing with Port that the car dealer had voidable title. The case went up on appeal and considered the issue of whether good title can ever pass for stolen goods.*

ISSUE: Can a good-faith seller of stolen goods pass a voidable or even good title to a good-faith innocent buyer?

REASONING: In a word, no. Good faith and innocence have no bearing whatsoever on this matter. Someone who

sells stolen goods, regardless of the degree of good faith, can never pass a voidable or good title to the buyer. The buyer has a void title, and therefore the rightful owner can reclaim the goods.

DECISION AND REMEDY: The court of appeals held that the only remedy is that, if the buyer did not receive a good title to the goods from the seller, the buyer could sue the seller for the money paid.

SIGNIFICANCE OF THE CASE: The significance of the decision is that if Port Motors purchased the vehicle from a thief, or from the successor to a thief, Port's title would be void and Port could not have conveyed good title to Candela.

CRITICAL THINKING

The appellate court reversed the trial court's decision, which had granted a summary judgment to Port. Candela is going to have the opportunity to have a court rule on whether Port Motors passed good title to him. What key facts will determine whether the title was void or voidable?

ETHICAL DECISION MAKING

Why would Port Motors, Inc., fight Candela in court? Shouldn't the car dealer want to make its customers happy? What ethical norm must be underlying Port Motors' behavior in contesting Candela's claim?

The key point to remember, which many people misunderstand, is that good faith is actually irrelevant when passing a void title. If a person has a void title (as in the best, and most frequent, example: a person has possession of stolen goods), then no matter how honorable the intentions of the seller are, that good-faith seller cannot pass anything to the buyer but another void title. The only exception to this is the entrustment situation, which is discussed later in the chapter.

VOIDABLE TITLE

When a seller transfers goods to a buyer, normally the buyer gets good title. However, the buyer gets only voidable title if any of the following apply:

- The buyer deceived the seller regarding his or her true identity.
- The buyer wrote a bad check for the goods.
- The buyer committed criminal fraud in securing the goods.
- The buyer and seller agreed that title would not pass until some later time.
- The buyer is a minor.

The first four of these situations that can create a voidable title are articulated in Section 2-403 of Article 2 of the UCC; the final one, the buyer is a minor, comes from common law. A seller who discovers any of these situations has the right to cancel the contract and reclaim the goods, even if they have already been delivered to the buyer. That is why the title is called *voidable.*

ENTRUSTMENT

entrustment

The transfer of goods to a merchant who ordinarily deals in that type of goods. If the merchant subsequently sells them to a good-faith third-party purchaser, the buyer acquires good title to the goods.

If an owner *entrusts* the possession of goods to a merchant who deals in goods of that kind, the merchant can transfer all rights in the goods to a buyer in the ordinary course of business. One form of **entrustment** occurs when someone entrusts the possession of a good (e.g., a car) to a merchant and asks him to repair that good. Suppose the merchant fraudulently or accidentally sells the item as if it were part of his inventory.

If the purchaser is a good-faith purchaser (i.e., did not know that the item belonged to someone else and paid a fair market value, not some unreasonable discounted value), then that purchaser gets a good title. The original owner's only recourse is to bring suit against the merchant. Again, the rationale behind this concept is the facilitation of commercial activity regarding good-faith purchasers in the marketplace.

TITLE VERSUS OTHER INTERESTS IN THE GOODS

The determination of who has good title does not always result in the expected and equitable solution to a problem. For example, suppose you purchased a couch at a furniture store. It is pretty safe to say that once you identify the couch and pay for it, you have "title" to it. Now suppose that when the store attempts to deliver the couch to your home, lightning hits the store's delivery truck and destroys the couch. Is the store legally obligated to replace the couch? Most of us would intuitively answer that it is. After all, you never took possession of the couch. However, as previously noted, *you* have title. Under pre-UCC law, this loss could have fallen on whoever had title at that time—and that person would be you. Under the UCC, if the store is a merchant, the risk of loss remains with the seller until the couch is actually delivered to you.

As a result of such dilemmas, the UCC breaks up the various issues traditionally correlated with title and treats them separately. Several different issues normally are thought of under the concept of title:

- *Ownership:* When does title actually transfer from the seller to the buyer, since the right to transfer ownership of the goods, whether through a subsequent sale or gift, is tied to title?
- *Encumbrance:* The right to encumber goods as collateral for a debt is dependent on who is holding title. When title passes is important because having title means that one can then sell or encumber the goods. In other words, having title means that one can pass title.
- *Loss:* In regard to the right to indemnification if the goods are damaged, when the risk of loss attaches is important. This is because, regardless of title passing, we need to know the seller's and buyer's responsibility to each other in the event that the goods are damaged or destroyed prior to the buyer's taking complete possession of the goods.
- *Insurable interest:* An *insurable interest* is the right to insure the goods against any risk exposure such as damage or destruction. When an insurable interest is created in the goods is important. Both the buyer and the seller can insure themselves for potential loss, in the event the goods are damaged or destroyed at some point in the transaction. A key point is identifying the earliest time in the transaction that the buyer can claim an insurable interest. The Case Nugget on the next page addresses that issue.

One very important point to note is that the parties are always free to create a contract that lays out and defines such issues as when title passes and when risk of loss passes. The UCC's rules are essentially the default rules for contracts that do not clearly spell out such provisions.

Let's look at each one of these issues within the context of the four kinds of sales contracts that Article 2 creates.

Types of Sales Contracts

The UCC lays out essentially four broad factual scenarios for the sale of goods:

1. *Simple delivery contract:* A simple delivery contract occurs when the purchased goods are transferred to the buyer from the seller at either the time of the sale or some time later by the seller's delivery.
2. *Common-carrier delivery contract:* This type of contract occurs when the goods are delivered to the buyer via a common carrier, such as a trucking line.
3. *Goods-in-bailment contract:* This type of contract occurs when the purchased goods are in some kind of storage under the control of a third party, such as a warehouseman.
4. *Conditional sales contract:* A conditional sales contract occurs when the sale itself is contingent on approval, for example.

In the sections that follow, this chapter answers questions about ownership, encumbrance, loss, and insurable interest as they relate to these four types of sales contracts.

CASE Nugget

When Does Insurable Interest Arise?

National Compressor Corp. v. Carrow and McGee
Federal Circuit Court of Appeals

417 F.2d 97 (1969)

National Compressor bought a large compressor from Davis, who had bought the compressor from Carrow and McGee. Title to the compressor was not to pass to National Compressor until the compressor was removed from Carrow and McGee's property. Prior to the compressor's being moved (and title passing to National Compressor) a fire broke out at the site, destroying the compressor. National Compressor had already paid the $12,000 purchase price. The issue before the court was whether National Compressor had any kind of insurable interest since clearly title had not yet passed. The defendants claimed that National Compressor had no standing to bring the lawsuit as it had no "interest" in the property since title had yet to pass.

The court ruled otherwise, stating that National Compressor had an insurable and special interest in the good, thus giving it standing to sue. The court ruled:

> Where a third party so deals with goods *which have been identified to a contract* for sale as to cause actionable injury to a party to that contract (a) a right of action against the third party is in either party to the contract for sale who has title to or a security interest or a special property or an insurable interest in the goods; and if the goods have been destroyed or converted a right of action is also in the party who either bore the risk of loss under the contract for sale or has since the injury assumed that risk as against the other. . . .

The buyer obtains a special property and an insurable interest in goods by identification of existing goods as goods to which the contract refers even though the goods so identified are nonconforming and he has an option to return or reject them. Such identification can be made at any time and in any manner explicitly agreed to by the parties. In the absence of explicit agreement, identification occurs (a) when the contract is made if it is for the sale of goods already existing and identified. [emphasis added]

SIMPLE DELIVERY CONTRACT

simple delivery contract

Type of contract in which purchased goods are transferred to the buyer from the seller either at the time of the sale or at some time later by the seller's delivery.

With a **simple delivery contract,** the buyer and seller typically execute an agreement, and the buyer leaves with the goods. To most of us, it appears that title, risk of loss, and insurable interest all pass to the buyer at the moment the transaction is consummated and the buyer walks out with the goods. However, under the UCC, there are three distinct steps: (1) Title transfers to the buyer on the goods' being identified to the contract, that is, when the contract is executed; (2) risk of loss transfers to the buyer when the buyer takes possession; and (3) insurable interest is created in the buyer when the goods are identified to the contract, in other words, at the same time that title passes.

But what happens if the buyer comes back later to pick up the goods or arranges to have the seller, or an agent of the seller, deliver the goods at a later time? For the purposes of title and insurable interest, nothing really changes. The dilemma occurs with risk of loss.

Let's suppose a buyer and seller execute a contract in which the seller is going to deliver a refrigerator later in the day to the buyer. Through no fault of the seller, the refrigerator is damaged in a fire at the seller's store. Who has the risk of loss if neither party is at fault? In

this case, the issue rests on the seller's status. If the seller is a merchant, as in this instance, the risk of loss remains with the seller until the goods are actually delivered to the buyer. If the seller is not a merchant, the risk of loss remains with the buyer under the rule of **tender of delivery.**

Simply put, tender of delivery is the moment the goods were available for the buyer to take. Consider this example: You purchase a dresser at a garage sale, but you want to go home and get your truck so that you can get it home easily. Unfortunately, a car hits the dresser and destroys it. You, the buyer, cannot get your money back because (1) the law does not consider the seller a merchant and (2) you could have taken the dresser with you when you bought it.

Note that the results are different if either party is at fault for the damage. In that case, the responsible person is liable under tort law for the damage caused. With a simple delivery contract whereby a seller transfers goods to a buyer without the middle-delivery common carrier, the various interests transfer as shown below. (Note: Even if the seller has its agent deliver the goods to the buyer, this is still a simple delivery.)

Simple delivery: seller → buyer

1. Title transfers on identification of the goods to the contract.
2. If the seller is a merchant, risk of loss transfers on delivery of the goods to the buyer; if the seller is not a merchant, risk of loss transfers when the goods are made available for the buyer to possess (tender of delivery).
3. The parties may buy insurance on their goods if they hold title or have any risk of loss or other economic interest.

COMMON-CARRIER DELIVERY CONTRACT

If a buyer and seller execute a contract and the seller subsequently places the goods with a common carrier for delivery to the buyer, the parties have executed a **common-carrier delivery contract.** Note that a common carrier is an independent contractor and not an agent of the seller. What makes the common carrier an independent contractor, rather than an agent, is that the carrier controls the primary aspects of performance, such as how the goods are actually delivered.

The UCC names two kinds of delivery contracts in this category: origin, or shipment, contracts and destination contracts. *Shipment contracts* require that the seller ship the goods to the buyer via a common carrier. The seller is required to make proper shipping arrangements and deliver the goods into the common carrier's hands. Title passes to the buyer at the time and place of shipment. Thus, the buyer bears the risk of loss while the goods are in transit. *Destination contracts* require that the seller deliver the goods to the destination stipulated in the sales contract. This may be the buyer's place of business or some other location. The seller bears the risk of loss until that time. Exhibit 14-4 identifies shipping terms that create the conditions of transit and delivery.

With a shipment contract whereby a seller transfers goods to a buyer with delivery of the goods effected by a common carrier, the various interests transfer as follows:

Shipment contract: seller → common carrier → buyer

1. If the shipment contract is an origin contract (if the contract is vague or ambiguous, an origin contract will be presumed), the title passes to the buyer when the goods are turned over by the seller to the common carrier.
2. If the shipment contract is a destination contract, the title transfers from the seller to the buyer when the common carrier delivers the goods to the buyer.
3. The risk of loss in either situation—origin or destination contract—transfers from the seller to the buyer simultaneously with the title.
4. An insurable interest is created when the buyer and/or seller holds title or retains a risk of loss.

tender of delivery
Requirement that the seller or lessor have and hold conforming goods at the disposal of the buyer or lessee and give the buyer or lessee reasonable notification to enable him or her to take delivery.

common-carrier delivery contract
A type of contract in which purchased goods are delivered to the buyer via an independent contractor, such as a trucking line.

LO 14-7

TERM	EXPLANATION
FOB (free on board)	The selling price includes transportation costs, and the seller carries the risk of loss to either the place of shipment or the place of destination.
FAS (free alongside)	The seller, at seller's expense, delivers the goods alongside the ship before the risk passes to the buyer.
CIF or C&F (cost, insurance, and freight; cost and freight)	The seller puts the goods in possession of a carrier before the risk passes to the buyer. Contracts are usually shipment contracts rather than destination contracts.
Delivery ex-ship (delivery from the carrying vessel)	Risk of loss passes to the buyer when the goods leave the ship.

GOODS-IN-BAILMENT CONTRACT

goods-in-bailment contract

A type of contract in which the purchased goods are in some kind of storage under the control of a third party, such as a warehouseman.

A **goods-in-bailment contract** involves goods that are in some kind of storage (e.g., in a warehouse or on board a ship), so the seller cannot transfer physical possession of them. Instead, the seller has one of three documents indicating ownership of the goods: a negotiable document of title, a nonnegotiable document of title, or a contract or other instrument showing ownership that is not a negotiable or nonnegotiable document of title. If the seller has a negotiable document (i.e., a document containing the words "deliver to the order of [seller]"), then both title and risk of loss transfer from the seller to the buyer as soon as that negotiable instrument is endorsed over to the buyer. On the other hand, if the document is nonnegotiable (i.e., a document lacking the words "to the order of"), then the title passes with the instrument of title but the risk of loss does not pass to the buyer until the bailee (the custodian of the goods) is notified of the transfer or a reasonable time has elapsed since the transaction. Finally, if there is neither a negotiable or a nonnegotiable document of title, then the title passes at the time the sales contract is executed but the risk does not pass to the buyer until the bailee is notified of the transaction and acknowledges such notification.

With goods in bailment, the three interests—title, risk of loss, insurable interest—pass in the following way:

> Seller → buyer, but the goods are elsewhere in some kind of storage and in a third party's possession and care.

1. Title passes from the seller to the buyer when the document of title (e.g., a warehouse receipt or a bill of lading) is actually endorsed or signed over to the buyer. If there is no document of title, then title passes when the goods are identified to the contract and the contract is executed.

2. Risk of loss passes to the buyer simultaneously with the document of title provided that the document of title is a negotiable one. If it is nonnegotiable, the risk does not pass until the bailee (the possessor or custodian of the goods) is notified or a reasonable time elapses. If there is no document of title, risk passes to the buyer on notification and acknowledgment by the bailee.

3. Insurable interest is created when either party has title, risk of loss, or some other economic interest attached to the goods (e.g., a creditor who secures a loan by taking the goods as collateral).

CONDITIONAL SALES CONTRACT

conditional sales contract

A type of contract in which the sale itself is contingent on approval; can be either a sale-on-approval contract or a sale-or-return contract.

sale-on-approval contract

A contract in which the seller allows the buyer to take possession of the goods before deciding whether to complete the contract by making the purchase.

Conditional sales contracts are either sale-on-approval contracts or sale-or-return contracts. A contract is a **sale-on-approval contract** if the seller allows the buyer to take possession of the goods before deciding whether to complete the contract by making the purchase. Title and risk of loss remain with the seller until the buyer notifies the seller about the approval of the contract.

A **sale-or-return contract** occurs when the seller and buyer agree that the buyer may return the goods at a later time. Such contracts usually occur when the buyer is buying inventory to resell. For example, suppose the seller is a dress wholesaler and the buyer is a retailer who is purchasing the dresses to sell in her store. In their sale-or-return agreement, the insurable interest is created in the buyer once the goods are identified in the contract. Title and risk of loss depend on whether the goods are in bailment, delivered by common carrier, or delivered by the seller himself. Without an agreement to the contrary, if the buyer subsequently returns the dresses, she does so at her own expense and risk.

<div style="float:right">**sale-or-return contract**

A contract in which the buyer and seller agree that the buyer may return the goods at a later time.</div>

Risk of Loss during a Breach of Contract

WHEN THE SELLER IS IN BREACH

The failure to deliver goods is the most common way a sales contract is breached. If the seller does not provide the goods that were described in the contract, the buyer may either (1) accept the nonconforming goods as is or (2) reject the goods subject to the seller's curing the deficiency in the goods. The buyer may reject the goods if no cure is possible or the seller fails to cure the deficiency within a reasonable time. In all these instances, the risk of loss remains with the seller until either the buyer accepts the goods or the seller cures the deficiency and provides the buyer with conforming goods.

If a cure is not possible or if the seller has failed to cure the deficiency within a reasonable time, the buyer has the option to revoke the contract. (The remedies are discussed in subsequent chapters.) However, the UCC creates a disincentive for buyers who do so: If the risk of loss would have transferred to the buyer had there not been a breach, the risk transfers to the buyer to the extent of any insurance the buyer has. The loss reverts to the breaching seller only to the extent that the buyer's insurance does not cover it.

WHEN THE BUYER IS IN BREACH

Most buyer breaches occur when a buyer refuses to accept conforming goods from the seller and then the goods are subsequently lost or damaged. With an origin or shipment contract, the risk would have already transferred to the breaching buyer. However, if the contract is a destination contract, the risk remains with the seller. To encourage sellers to create origin contracts, the UCC requires that the risk of loss remain with the seller to the extent of the seller's insurance. If the seller does not have insurance or the loss exceeds the seller's insurance, the remainder transfers to the breaching buyer.

SUMMARY

The Uniform Commercial Code	*Scope of the UCC:* The UCC is a uniform or model law that governs commercial transactions, from the sale of goods to secured transactions. *Significance of the UCC:* The UCC adds clarity and predictability to sales law.
Articles 2 and 2(A) of the UCC	*Article 2 (Sales)* covers contracts for the sale of goods. • *Sale:* The passing of title from the seller to the buyer for a price. • *Goods:* Tangible things that can be moved. • *Mixed goods and services contracts:* Contracts that include both goods and services. Courts apply Article 2 if the goods are the predominant part of the transaction. • *Merchants:* Buyers or sellers who (1) deal in goods of the kind, (2) by occupation, hold themselves out as having knowledge and skill unique to the practices or goods involved in the transaction, or (3) employ a merchant as a broker, agent, or other intermediary. Various provisions of the UCC distinguish merchants from ordinary buyers and sellers.

Article 2(A)(Leases) covers contracts for the lease of goods.

- *Leases:* Transfers of the right to possession and use of goods for a term in return for consideration.
- *Special kinds of leases:* Consumer leases and finance leases. The UCC outlines special rules and protections for each kind of lease.

Contracts for the International Sale of Goods

Scope of the CISG: The CISG is a treaty countries can sign to govern international business-to-business sales contracts. Many major trading nations have signed the CISG.

Significance of the CISG: The CISG is important because it, rather than the UCC, governs international sales contracts. The CISG provides clarity, predictability, and uniformity for businesses that operate in the global economy.

How Sales and Lease Contracts Are Formed under the UCC

Formation in general: The UCC is more lenient than common law regarding contract formation. Courts look at the intent of the parties to a sales or lease contract.

Offer and acceptance: Offers are valid even if terms are left open. The common law mirror-image rule does not apply to contracts for the sale or lease of goods. Courts look on a case-by-case basis to determine whether to allow additional terms.

Consideration: When sales and lease contracts are modified, these modifications do not need to be supported by new consideration.

Battle of the forms: The last "form" in either the offer or acceptance that a party sends to the other is presumed to control the final terms of the contract unless specifically objected to by the receiving party.

Statute of frauds: Contracts for the sale of goods must be in writing if the goods are priced at $500 or more. Lease contracts that require payments of $1,000 or more must be in writing. Exceptions exist for:

- Specifically manufactured goods.
- Contracts that parties admit exist.
- Situations in which partial performance has occurred.

Unconscionability: Under the UCC, a court can refuse to enforce the parts of a contract or lease that are unfair or one-sided.

Title

There are three kinds of title: good title, void title, and voidable title.

- *Good title* is title that is acquired from someone who already owns the goods free and clear.
- *Void title* is not true title. Someone who purchases stolen goods has void title.
- *Voidable title* occurs in certain situations in which the contract between the original parties would be void but the goods have already been sold to a third party.

Acquiring Good Title

Article 2 of the Uniform Commercial Code covers issues related to acquiring good title.

- The most obvious way to attain *good title* is to acquire it from someone who has good title.
- Someone who has come into possession of stolen goods never has title and can pass only *void title.*
- A buyer gets *voidable title* if he or she has deceived the seller regarding his or her true identity, written a bad check for the goods, committed criminal fraud in securing the goods, or is a minor or if the buyer and seller agreed that title would not pass until some later time.

Third-party purchasers generally get good title.

If an owner *entrusts* the possession of goods to a merchant who deals in goods of that kind, the merchant can transfer all rights in the goods to a buyer in the ordinary course of business.

The UCC provides recourse for situations in which good title may not be enough for an equitable result. The UCC responds to issues related to the following:

- *Ownership* refers to transfer of title.
- *Encumbrance* refers to when goods may be used as collateral for a debt.
- *Loss* refers to who has the risk of loss, which matters when someone is seeking indemnification for damaged goods.
- *Insurable interest* refers to the right to insure goods against any risk exposure.

Types of Sales Contracts

A *simple delivery contract* is formed when the buyer and seller execute an agreement and the buyer leaves with the goods. *Title* transfers to the buyer when the contract is executed. *Risk of loss* transfers to the buyer when the buyer takes possession. *Insurable interest* is created in the buyer at the same time title passes.

A *common-carrier delivery contract* exists when a buyer and seller execute a contract and the seller subsequently places the goods with a common carrier. There are two types of common-carrier delivery contracts: origin, or shipment, contracts and destination contracts.

- In *shipment contracts,* title transfers to the buyer at the time and place of shipment. The buyer bears the risk of loss while the goods are in transit.
- In *destination contracts,* the seller bears the risk of loss until the seller delivers the goods to the destination stipulated in the sales contract.

A *goods-in-bailment contract* is one that identifies goods that are in some kind of storage. Rules regarding passage of title, risk of loss, and insurable interest vary depending on whether the seller has a negotiable document of title, a nonnegotiable document of title, or a contract showing ownership that is neither a negotiable nor nonnegotiable document of title.

A *conditional sales contract* includes sale-on-approval or sale-or-return contracts.

- In a *sale-on-approval contract,* title and risk of loss remain with the seller until the buyer notifies the seller about the approval of the contract.
- In a *sale-or-return contract,* the insurable interest is created in the buyer once the goods are identified in the contract. Title and risk of loss depend on whether the goods are in bailment, delivered by common carrier, or delivered by the seller.

Risk of Loss during a Breach of Contract

When the seller is in breach by failing to deliver goods, the buyer may either accept the non-conforming goods as is or reject the goods subject to the seller's curing the deficiencies in the goods. Risk of loss remains with the seller until the buyer accepts the goods or the deficiencies are corrected.

When the buyer is in breach because he or she has refused to accept conforming goods and then the goods are subsequently lost or damaged, who bears the risk of loss depends on the type of contract that exists between the buyer and the seller.

Point/Counterpoint

If a merchant (bailee) is holding goods for someone for repair or storage and sells those goods to a good-faith purchaser, that good-faith purchaser gets good title and the previous owner may recover the loss only from the bailee by suing in the tort of conversion.

Is It Right That a Bailee Who Has Only Possession, Not Title, Can Pass a Good Title to a Purchaser?	
YES	NO
The primary purpose of the Uniform Commercial Code, in addition to attempting to "uniformize" manners and methods of commercial processes, is to facilitate and enable commercial activity.	The entrustment rule is an example of the Uniform Commercial Code's taking a principle to an illogical and inequitable conclusion.

To put it succinctly, purchasers should not have to look over their shoulders, so to speak, regarding every transaction for fear that the title may not be valid. The facilitation of commercial activity requires that a good-faith purchaser can rely on the sale to validate his or her title to the goods.

We see such a perspective in other areas of the Uniform Commercial Code. As we see in Article 9, on secured transactions, if a buyer in the ordinary course of business purchases an item that is encumbered, the purchaser gets title over the creditor.

This philosophy puts the greater goal of the Uniform Commercial Code ahead of any individualized inconvenience of losing title to goods in entrustment. The focus of the code is the facilitation of commerce, and therefore parties who put goods into entrustment must exercise due care in choosing a bailee.

There is no question that the focus of the Uniform Commercial Code is the facilitation of commerce, and the example (given by the opposing view) of the buyer in the ordinary course of business is valid except that it is misplaced. A merchant who has a voidable title can pass on a good title; a merchant who has a good title can obviously pass on a good title. But a merchant who has a void or bad title or no title at all cannot pass on a good title. This is a fundamental premise regarding the ability to pass title.

The entrustment rule is the exception to this title rule, and it is misplaced. First, common sense tells us that this situation occurs so infrequently as to negate the need for a special rule. Second, when it does occur, often the goods are unique or one of a kind and are not replaceable. Thus, the inequity in denying possession to the true owner of unique goods truly outweighs the need to facilitate commercial activity.

Questions & Problems

1. Explain what determines whether a contract is covered by the UCC.

2. How can good title be acquired?

3. What are the various types of sales contracts?

4. The defendant contracted with the plaintiff to design, maintain, and develop software and to host the defendant's web page. After a falling out, the defendant moved its web page to another site and refused to honor its contract with the plaintiff. The plaintiff sued. Did the contract fall under the UCC? Were the items—software, web hosting, website maintenance—"goods" under the UCC? [*Dennis Conwell and Frank Splittorff, D/B/A Piece of America, Appellant, v. Gray Loon Outdoor Marketing Group, Inc., Appellee,* No. 82S04-0806-CV-00309, Sup. Ct. Ind., 906 N.E.2d 805; 2009 Ind. LEXIS 465; 69 U.C.C. Rep. Serv. 2d (Callaghan) 71 (2009).]

5. The plaintiff, Betty Epstein, visited a beauty parlor to get her hair dyed. In the dying process, the beautician used a prebleach solution manufactured by Clairol, Inc., and then a commercial dye manufactured by Sales Affiliate, Inc. The treatment went awry, and the plaintiff suffered severe hair loss, injuries to both hair and scalp, and some disfigurement. She sued the beauty salon, Clairol, and Sales Affiliate under Article 2 of the UCC. The defendants claimed that the contract was predominantly for services rather than for the sale of a good. How would you construct arguments supporting each side? What difference does it make whether the beauty treatment was a good or a service? [*Epstein v. Giannattasio,* 197 A.2d 342 (1963).]

6. An agricultural cooperative sued Carroll Nelson for breach of contract under UCC Article 2. Nelson was a Texas wheat farmer and had an oral contract with the cooperative for the purchase of his wheat. The cooperative had forwarded to Nelson a written confirmation of the agreement, but Nelson did not acknowledge or sign any confirmation. When the cooperative initiated the lawsuit, Nelson raised the statute of frauds as a defense. He claimed that because he was not a merchant, a signed memorandum with his signature of some sort was needed for the contract to be enforceable. The cooperative claimed that because Nelson was a merchant, the unobjected-to memorandum satisfied the statute of frauds for agreements between merchants. Is farmer Nelson a merchant? [*Nelson v. Co-operative Exchange,* 548 S.W.2d 352 (1977).]

7. A manufacturer based in Argentina and an importer based in New Jersey entered into an oral agreement under which the importer agreed to sell the manufacturer's products in the United States. The district court found that the manufacturer's claim that the importer had failed to pay the full amount due was barred by the United Nations Convention on Contracts for the International Sale of Goods (CISG) because the agreement was not in writing. Although the CISG eliminated formal writing requirements for contracts, Argentina had made a declaration opting out of that provision. However, the United States had not made such a declaration. The court of appeals held that it was necessary to consider New Jersey choice-of-law rules to determine whether New Jersey or Argentine

form requirements governed the manufacturer's claim. Does the contract need documentation to be enforceable, or, if U.S. law applies with the adoption of the CISG, are the oral declarations satisfactory? [*Forestal Guarani S.A., Appellant, v. Daros International, Inc.,* No. 08-4488, 3d Cir. Ct. of Appeals, 614 F.3d 395; 2010 U.S. App. LEXIS 14969.]

8. Mitchell Aircraft Spares, Inc., has filed a lawsuit against European Aircraft Service (EAS) AG, asserting claims for breach of contract and breach of warranty. Mitchell, an Illinois corporation, is a broker in the market for surplus aircraft parts. EAS is a Swedish corporation that buys parts from companies in Western Europe and the United States and sells these parts to a wide variety of purchasers. At issue is Mitchell's claim that it suffered damages in the amount of $120,000 because EAS sent it integrated drive generators with the wrong part numbers. In Mitchell's industry, specific part numbers are important. What law is likely to govern this dispute? Explain. [*Mitchell Aircraft Spares, Inc. v. European Aircraft Service AB,* 23 F. Supp. 2d 915 (1998).]

9. Mitchell Coach Manufacturing Company, Inc., produces motor homes and sells them to other retail dealers and directly to customers. Ronny Stephens was a customer. WW, Inc., bought and sold motor homes from Mitchell. Under their agreement, WW would pay Mitchell either a down payment on a motor home before the motor home was purchased or the entire amount due for the completed product. Also under the agreement, the title of the motor home remained with WW until Stephens paid in full. WW paid Mitchell a down payment of $10,000 for the construction of the motor home. Upon completion, the motor home was to be picked up by Stephens at Mitchell's facility. WW paid the remaining balance to Mitchell, but the check was returned for lack of sufficient funds. Stephens, through a loan, had paid for the motor home in full, but WW had not paid Mitchell. Both Mitchell and Stephens claim title to the motor home. Who does title belong to? [*Mitchell Coach Manufacturing Company, Inc. v. Ronny Stephens,* 19 F. Supp. 2d 1277 (1998).]

10. Marilyn Thomas purchased an installed pool heater from Sunkissed. The pool heater was delivered to Marilyn's residence, but the delivery slip was signed by Nancy Thomas. Marilyn did not know of anyone by that name. She called Sunkissed to advise the company to move the heater. The neighborhood was not safe, and she was worried that the heater would be taken. The heater remained in her driveway for approximately four days. When Marilyn noticed that the heater was no longer in her driveway, she again contacted Sunkissed, but she was told "not to worry." Who was responsible for the loss of the heater? Did Sunkissed actually "deliver" the heater to Marilyn? How do you think the court decided? [*In re Marilyn Thomas,* 182 B.R. 347 (1995).]

11. In 1987, R. H. Love Gallery owned the title to a painting entitled *Marlton's Cove.* The gallery sold 50 percent of the painting to Altman Fine Arts, a New York art dealer, and 50 percent to Andre Lopoukhine, a Boston art dealer. In 1989, plaintiff Morgold, Inc., purchased Altman's 50 percent of the painting. Morgold and Lopoukhine decided to try to sell the painting. In 1990, Lopoukhine sold the painting to Mark Grossman. Lopoukhine did not pay Morgold the 50 percent due for the sale of the painting. Morgold argued that this lack of payment indicated that the title was never officially passed on to Grossman. Through an art dealer, Grossman sold the painting to Fred Keeler. In 1991, Morgold contacted Keeler and claimed to be the sole owner of the painting. Who do you believe owns title to the painting? [*Morgold, Inc. v. Keeler,* 891 F. Supp. 1461 (1995).]

12. MAN Roland agreed to sell Quantum Color Corporation a used press for $405,000. According to the contract, Quantum was supposed to pay $5,000 at the time of the contract, $265,000 at delivery, and the balance of $145,000 before the press was actually used. The first two payments were made, but MAN Roland did not receive the $145,000. MAN Roland alleged that Quantum had been using the press and, therefore, that Quantum was required to pay the balance. Quantum argued that MAN Roland breached the contract by delivering nonconforming goods. Part of the contract indicated that MAN Roland would provide standard equipment and installation, but MAN Roland did not install the equipment or provide Quantum with the standard equipment. How do you think the court settled this case? [*MAN Roland Inc. v. Quantum Color Corp.,* 57 F. Supp. 2d 576 (1999).]

13. Treibacher, an Austrian vendor of hard-metal powders, agreed to two contracts with the defendant TDY to sell specified quantities of tantalum carbide (TaC), a hard-metal powder, to TDY Industries, Inc., for delivery to "consignment." TDY planned to use the TaC in manufacturing tungsten-graded carbide powders at its plant in Gurney, Alabama. After it had received some of the amount of TaC specified in the November 2000 contract, TDY refused to take delivery of the balance of the TaC specified in both contracts, and, in a letter to Treibacher dated August 23, 2001, denied that it had a binding obligation to take delivery of or pay for any TaC that it did not want to use. Unbeknownst to Treibacher, TDY had purchased the TaC it needed from another vendor at lower prices than those specified in its contracts with Treibacher. Treibacher eventually sold the quantities

of TaC that TDY had refused to take delivery of, but at lower prices than those specified in its contracts with TDY. Treibacher then filed suit against TDY, seeking to recover the balance of the amount Treibacher would have received had TDY paid for all of the TaC specified in the November and December 2000 contracts. What is the appropriate remedy here for Treibacher if TDY is in breach? Does this case fall under the CISG or the UCC? Is there any significance to applying the CISG rather than the UCC? [*Treibacher Industrie, A.G., Plaintiff-Appellee, v. Allegheny Technologies, Inc., a Pennsylvania Corporation et al., Defendants, TDY Industries, Inc., Defendant-Appellant,* 464 F.3d 1235 (11th Cir. 2006); 2006 U.S. App. LEXIS 23252; 19 Fla. L. Weekly Fed. C 1046 (2006).]

14. Mr. and Mrs. Kahr donated a bag of clothing to Goodwill. Unbeknownst to them, mixed in with the clothing was a bag of antique sterling-silver silverware valued in excess of $3,000. When the Kahrs realized what they had done, they immediately called Goodwill. However, Goodwill had sold the silverware for $15 to a purchaser. The Kahrs brought suit against the purchaser for the return of the silverware. Did they get it back because the silver was "lost property," or was this a classic entrustment case? [*Kahr v. Markland,* 543 N.E.2d 579 (1989).]

15. The plaintiff and the defendant entered into a three-year contract in which the defendant would be the sole supplier of steel parts that the plaintiff used in its products. A dispute arose after the defendant sought to surcharge the parts sold to reflect increased costs. The plaintiff filed a lawsuit for breach of contract, and the jury returned a verdict in favor of the defendant, finding on a special verdict that there had been a valid modification to the contract, based solely on e-mails between the parties. Is this evidence enough to support a reformation of the contract? [*Copeland Corporation, Plaintiff-Appellant, v. Choice Fabricators Incorporated, Defendant-Appellee, No. 08-3194,* 6th Cir. Ct. of Appeals, 09a0622n.06; 345 Fed. Appx. 74; 2009 U.S. App. LEXIS 19986; 2009 FED App. 0622N (6th Cir.); 69 U.C.C. Rep. Serv. 2d (Callaghan) 802.]

Looking for more review material?

The Online Learning Center at **www.mhhe.com/kubasekess2e** contains this chapter's "Assignment on the Internet" and also a list of URLs for more information, entitled "On the Internet." Find both of them in the Student Center portion of the OLC, along with quizzes and other helpful materials.

Sales and Lease Contracts: Performance, Warranties, and Remedies

CASE OPENER

What a Difference a Day Makes!

Founded in 1966 as a trader of oil and oil products, Vitol is a company with no external shareholders. All shareholders are also employees. It is a conglomerate corporation of energy companies that work in oil transportation, energy market intelligence, refining, distribution, and trading and financing.[1] It is unencumbered by external shareholders and the need to answer to analysts and investment funds. Instead, Vitol is a group of separate companies, each staffed by energy professionals with a true depth of experience in the business of oil transportation, market intelligence, refining, distribution, marketing, trading and finance.

Vitol entered into a contract on January 13, 2000, with the defendant, Koch Petroleum Group, for the delivery of oil. Koch Petroleum Group is a component of Koch Industries, Inc., a Wichita, Kansas, private company with over $100 billion in worldwide revenues and over 70,000 employees. The sales contract required that Koch deliver 75,000 barrels of heating oil to a barge designated by Vitol between February 3 and 5, 2000. Later that January, Vitol sold the oil to a third party, Castle Oil Corporation. Castle Oil and Vitol agreed that the oil would be delivered to Castle Oil's barge on February 3, and they communicated that fact to Koch. Koch agreed. Koch was unable to deliver the oil on February 3 despite being told by Vitol that time was of the essence regarding that date for Castle Oil. When Koch failed to deliver the oil until February 4, Castle Oil canceled its contract with Vitol, sued Vitol for breach, and was awarded a $1.7 million arbitration judgment. Vitol now is suing Koch for recovery of the $1.7 million it had to pay Castle.[2]

The issue here is that of perfect tender. Koch claims that it substantially complied with the contract, as delivery of the oil was to be during the February 3 to 5 time window. Vitol argues that the contract was modified with Koch's acceptance to delivery specifically on February 3. The court must determine:

1. Did Koch's failure to deliver the oil on February 3 constitute something less than perfect tender and thus a breach of contract?
2. Did that one-day difference in delivery constitute a breach of the perfect tender rule?

[1] See Vitrol's web page at www.vitol.com/about.php.
[2] *Vitol S.A., Inc. v. Koch Petroleum Group, LP,* 2005 U.S. District Lexis 18688, 58 U.C.C. Rep. Serv. 2d (Callaghan) 2005.

After reading this chapter, you will be able to answer the following questions:

LO 15-1 What is the difference between conforming and nonconforming goods?

LO 15-2 What is the perfect tender rule?

LO 15-3 What is the right to cure?

LO 15-4 What is commercial impracticability?

LO 15-5 What are the implied warranties of title, merchantability, and particular purpose?

LO 15-6 How are third parties affected by implied warranties?

LO 15-7 How can implied warranties be disclaimed?

LO 15-8 What is cover and resale?

LO 15-9 When are money damages available?

When individuals and/or organizations like Vitol and Koch enter into sales contracts or leases with others, they need to know their rights and obligations so that they can engage in efficient business transactions. This chapter explains the performance obligations of sellers and buyers. In addition, it explains the performance obligations of lessors and lessees, which are similar to those of buyers and sellers. The chapter explains the perfect tender rule and exceptions to this rule. It also explains the buyer's general obligation to inspect, pay for, and accept goods, and it discusses exceptions to this general obligation. Moreover, it explains performance obligations under both express and implied warranties, breach of contract, and remedies available in the event of breach.

LO 15-1

The Basic Performance Obligation

The obligations of sellers/lessors and buyers/lessees are determined by (1) terms the parties outline in agreements, (2) custom, and (3) rules outlined by the Uniform Commercial Code (UCC). This chapter focuses on rules outlined by the UCC.

Under the UCC, sellers and lessors are *obligated to transfer and deliver conforming goods.* Buyers and lessees are *obligated to accept and pay for conforming goods in accordance with the contract.* Courts rely on UCC rules to clarify these obligations when the contract or lease the parties agreed to is unclear. In the Case Opener, is the window of time for delivery absolutely crucial to the performance of the contract, or can it deviate just a bit? Is any kind of deviation a breach of contract? This chapter addresses that topic and others after explaining how the idea of good faith places transactions in a particular context. What if there was an issue of mistake? Remember that at common law a unilateral mistake may still constitute a binding contract whereas a bilateral mistake will not. Issues of mistake often raise the corollary issue of unconscionability. In the Case Opener, Koch is obligated to deliver oil to a barge designated by Vitol. The window for such delivery is February 3 to 5, 2000. Vitol claims that it has the right to indicate within that time frame the exact date of delivery. It notifies Koch that delivery must be made on February 3. Koch does not

make the delivery until February 4. Has Koch breached the contract under the perfect tender rule? Is there perhaps some kind of mistake or misunderstanding between Vitol and Koch? If so, is that material to determining breach of contract? Did Koch act in good faith? If so, does that mitigate the delay of one day? Consider the following Case Nugget as you think about these issues.

CASE Nugget

Do Mistake and Unconscionability Affect the Enforceability of a Contract?

Donovan v. RRL Corporation
California Supreme Court

26 Cal. 4th 261 (2001)

The Donovans showed up at the defendant car dealership. After hearing the sales pitch, Mr. Donovan stated that he'd take the car at the price quoted in the newspaper, $25,995. The horrified salesman said that he could go as low as $37,995 but not $25,995. At that point, Donovan showed the salesman a copy of an ad that had been running in the local newspaper identifying the very same automobile for $25,995. The salesman responded that the advertisement had to be a mistake. Donovan said that he wanted the car at the $25,995 price. He subsequently brought an action in the municipal court in Orange County. The trial court found for RRL Corp. on mistake. However, the California court of appeals reversed, stating that all the material elements of a contract were clearly stated in the advertisement and that Donovan's acceptance of those terms constituted a good contract.

The California Supreme Court heard the case, reversing it on a combination of mistake and unconscionability. The supreme court found that a contract was indeed created but that the contract could be rescinded since the evidence showed that (1) the defendant's unilateral mistake was made in good faith; (2) the defendant did not bear the risk of the mistake; and (3) the enforcement of a contract with an erroneous price would be unconscionable as a matter of law.

GOOD FAITH

UCC Section 1-203 requires **good faith** in the performance and enforcement of every contract. *Good faith* means "honesty in fact." When the parties are merchants, the UCC imposes a higher standard. Between merchants, the UCC imposes not only honesty in fact but also reasonable commercial standards of fair dealing. This second requirement is often called **commercial reasonableness.** In the context of good faith, courts decide the specific obligations of sellers/ lessors and buyers/lessees. The next few sections of the chapter discuss these specific obligations.

Specific Obligations of Sellers and Lessors

THE PERFECT TENDER RULE

The UCC requires that sellers and lessors tender conforming goods to buyers and lessees. UCC Sections 2-503(1) and 2A-508(1) state that **tender of delivery** requires that the seller/lessor have and hold conforming goods at the disposal of the buyer/lessee and give the buyer/lessee

good faith
Honesty in fact.

commercial reasonableness
Reasonable commercial standards of fair dealing, required of merchants in addition to honesty in fact.

tender of delivery
Requirement that the seller or lessor have and hold conforming goods at the disposal of the buyer or lessee and give the buyer or lessee reasonable notification to enable him or her to take delivery.

GLOBAL Context

Choice of Law: "Religious Laws"?

It is a common practice for parties to any contract to indicate in the contract itself which laws will govern the transaction should a dispute arise. For example, if a merchant in Germany purchases goods from a seller in the United States and the goods are in a warehouse in France, the contract may state that the laws of France will govern the contract. It could just as easily state the laws of Germany or the United States. In some situations, the contract could state some other jurisdiction, however remote or tenuous the jurisdiction's connection may be to the parties or goods. Which laws govern a contract is up to the will of the parties, unless the jurisdiction has specific laws that decide the "choice of law" for the parties regardless of their intent. Hence it is always important to know the local laws governing transactions.

An interesting issue that is starting to arise is whether parties may choose religious laws to govern disputes. For example, may the parties to a contract choose *Sharia* law, that is, the religious law based on the Koran in the Muslim religion. We've not yet seen the use of Sharia law in UCC or CISG contracts, but a Florida trial judge ruled in March 2011 that a dispute regarding the ouster of trustees of a mosque should be determined under Sharia law. The issue raises questions; if, for example, a mediation clause in a contract calls for mediation by canon law, should or even could a court adhere to that provision? In our ever-shrinking world, this issue does give one cause for thought.

Source: www.tampabay.com/news/courts/civil/article1158818.ece.

conforming goods
Goods that conform to contract specifications.

> To see more on how conforming goods relate to customized purchases, visit the **Connecting to the Core** activity on the text's website at www.mhhe.com/kubasekess2e.

LO 15-2

perfect tender rule
Requirement that the seller deliver the goods in conformity with the contract, down to the last detail.

reasonable notification to enable the buyer/lessee to take delivery. **Conforming goods** are goods that conform to contract specifications. However, Article 49(1) of the CISG allows *avoidance* (the term used for the buyer's refusing to accept nonconforming goods) only if there is substantial and foreseeable nonconformity of the goods. In other words, the CISG follows more closely the common law concept of substantial performance than it does the perfect tender rule. In our Case Opener, is the exact time for delivery part and parcel of the perfect tender rule?

A common law rule known as the **perfect tender rule** required that the seller deliver goods in conformity with the terms of the contract, right down to the last detail. UCC Sections 2-601 and 2A-509 embrace the perfect tender rule. These sections indicate that if goods or tender of delivery fails *in any respect* to conform to the contract, the buyer/lessee has the right to accept the goods, reject the entire shipment, or accept part and reject part. Common law usually substitutes perfect tender with the doctrine of substantial performance. Substantial performance occurs when all the material elements of a contract are satisfied even if some nonmaterial requirements may not be satisfied. The perfect tender rule would not recognize the distinction between material and immaterial contractual requirements. The next Case Nugget considers how the perfect tender rule is affected when good faith is an issue.

Consider Case 15-1, which provides an illustration of a situation in which the UCC's version of the perfect tender rule was relevant when compared to the common law rule of material breach under the doctrine of substantial performance. In the Case Opener, does Koch's tender of delivery a day late constitute substantial performance under common law and perfect tender under the UCC? What about under the CISG?

EXCEPTIONS TO THE PERFECT TENDER RULE

The perfect tender rule is not as inflexible as it appears. Although the rule itself demands perfection, both courts and UCC drafters have created exceptions that reduce the rule's rigidity. These exceptions limit the seller's obligation to deliver conforming goods and/or limit the buyer's power to reject goods that do not conform. The exceptions allow sellers/lessors and buyers/lessees to ask questions such as:

- What are the norms in the particular industry, and/or what past dealings have the parties had with one another?

CASE Nugget

How Does Good Faith Affect Perfect Tender?

Y&N Furniture Inc. v. Nwabuoku
New York Court of Appeals

734 N.Y.S.2d 392 (2001)

The defendant, Nwabuoku, purchased $1,500 worth of furniture from the plaintiff, Y&N Furniture. Through an arrangement with the plaintiff, the defendant financed the purchase through a financing company named Beneficial. On receipt of the furniture, the defendant was to notify Beneficial that receipt was effected, and Beneficial would pay Y&N the $1,500 purchase price. Nwabuoku would then begin paying Beneficial the amount due plus interest according to their financing agreement.

Nwabuoku refused to acknowledge receipt to Beneficial and eventually rejected the goods, claiming that he did not want the furniture. The civil court of the City of New York found that Nwabuoku had rejected the goods, and the court cited the perfect tender rule as requiring "exact performance by the seller." Moreover, the court held that "rejection of goods must be within a reasonable time of their delivery or tender." The court indicated that Nwabuoku did indeed make a rightful rejection. However, the court noted that a rejection of goods must be based on some claim that the goods are in some way nonconforming. The defendant in this case had a disagreement over the terms of the financing (though the terms were clearly stated in the financing statements). The defendant made no claim of nonconforming goods. Thus, the court found that "in this case, too, we have a rejection that is not only 'wrongful,' but also in bad faith." A wrongful rejection is not necessarily in bad faith; the buyer may honestly believe that the goods fail to conform but may simply be mistaken. But a rejection that does not even purport to rest on an honest assessment of conformity of the goods has "the effect of destroying or injuring the right of the seller to receive the fruits of the contract."

- What does the parties' agreement say?
- Is it possible for the seller/lessor to cure or correct problems?
- What if the goods have been destroyed?
- What if nonconformity substantially impairs the value of goods?
- What if unforeseen circumstances make contract performance commercially impracticable?

usage of trade
Any practice that members of an industry expect to be part of their dealings.

course of dealing
Previous commercial transactions between the same parties.

course of performance
The history of dealings between the parties in the particular contract at issue.

Norms in the Industry and Past Dealings between the Parties When the buyer alleges that goods failed to conform to contract specifications, the buyer does not automatically have the right to reject the goods. The UCC requires that courts consider norms in a particular trade. Sometimes, the norms for a particular trade do not permit a buyer to reject goods with minor flaws. UCC Section 1-205(2) defines **usage of trade** as any practice that members of an industry expect to be part of their dealings.

In addition to its requirement on usage of trade, the UCC requires that courts consider the ideas of course of dealing and course of performance. UCC 1-205(1) defines **course of dealing** as previous commercial transactions between the same parties. Under UCC 208(1), **course of performance** refers to the history of dealings between the parties in the particular contract at issue.

Exceptions Outlined in the Parties' Agreement Sometimes, language in the parties' agreement limits the rigidity of the perfect tender rule. For instance, parties may agree that the seller must have the opportunity to repair or replace nonconforming goods within a particular period of time.

LO 15-3

ALASKA PACIFIC TRADING CO. V. EAGON FOREST PRODUCTS INC.
WASHINGTON APPELLATE DIVISION 1
933 P.2d 417 (1997)

FACTS: *Alaska Pacific Trading Company (ALPAC) and Eagon Forest Products, Inc., contracted to buy and sell raw logs. ALPAC and Eagon engaged in months of communications about a shipment of 15,000 cubic meters of logs from Argentina to Korea between the end of July and the end of August 1993. The delivery date passed without ALPAC shipping the logs. Eagon canceled the contract, alleging that ALPAC had breached the agreement by failing to deliver. ALPAC alleged that its failure to deliver was not a material breach and that the parties had modified the delivery date. Alternatively, ALPAC argued that Eagon breached the contract by failing to provide adequate assurances or repudiating the contract. The miscommunication between the parties occurred after the market for logs began to soften, making the contract less attractive to Eagon. ALPAC was reluctant to ship the goods because it was concerned that Eagon might not accept the shipment. However, Eagon never stated that it would not accept the cargo.*

ISSUE: The question for the court is whether to apply the common law doctrine of material breach or the UCC doctrine of perfect tender.

REASONING: In the court's own words:

As a contract for the sale of goods, this contract is governed by the Uniform Commercial Code, Article II (UCC II) which replaced the common law of material breach, on which ALPAC relies, with the "perfect tender" rule. Under this rule, "If the goods or the tender of delivery fail in any respect to conform to the contract, the buyer may . . . reject the whole." . . . Both the plain language of the rule and the official comments clearly state that, if the tender of the goods differs from the terms of the contract in any way, the seller breaches the contract and the buyer is released from its duty to accept the goods.

DECISION AND REMEDY: The court applied the literal language of the UCC, holding that the perfect tender rule applied and that ALPAC's failure to deliver was a breach of contract.

SIGNIFICANCE OF THE CASE: Though difficult to measure at times, the perfect tender rule is a departure from the common law rule of substantial performance. Any deviation from the contract may indeed constitute a breach of the perfect tender rule, materiality notwithstanding.

CRITICAL THINKING

Here, Eagon got lucky. The company got out of a contract that was unfavorable to it, given the softening market for logs. In what way did the judge simplify the case? Is it fair to say the judge oversimplified the case?

ETHICAL DECISION MAKING

What ethical norm or value underlies the judge's decision? Explain.

Alternatively, parties may agree with a level of performance that is less than perfect. They could indicate, by agreement, the expectation regarding performance.

The Seller's and Lessor's Right to Cure Under UCC Sections 2-508 and 2A-513, sellers and lessors have the right to **cure** or fix problems with nonconforming goods. In particular, sellers and lessors can repair, adjust, or replace defective or nonconforming goods as long as they give prompt notice of the intent to cure and go ahead and cure within the contract time for performance.

cure
A breaching party's right to provide conforming goods when nonconforming goods were initially delivered; subject to a reasonable time test.

Destroyed Goods Under UCC Sections 2-613 and 2A-221, if goods are identified at the time the parties entered into a contract and the goods are destroyed through no fault of the parties

before risk passes to the buyer or lessee, the parties are excused from performance. If the goods are only partially destroyed, the buyer can inspect the goods and decide whether to (1) treat the contract as void or (2) ask the seller for a reduction of the contract price and then accept the damaged goods.

Substantial Impairment Two sections of the UCC use the concept of **substantial impairment** to modify the perfect tender rule. The first applies when a buyer *revokes acceptance of goods*. UCC Section 2-608 indicates that a buyer who has accepted goods may later revoke the acceptance only if the buyer can show that the defects substantially impair the value of the goods. The second applies when the buyer and seller have entered into an *installment contract*. UCC 2-612(2) and 2A-510(1) indicate that a buyer/lessee may reject an installment of a particular item only if the defects substantially impair the value of the goods and cannot be cured.

Commercial Impracticability UCC Sections 2-615(a) and 2A-405(a) state that a delay in delivery or nondelivery, in whole or in part, is not a breach in circumstances in which performance has been made impracticable because a contingency has occurred that was not contemplated when the parties reached an agreement. For example, this rule would be relevant if a change in government regulation that neither party contemplated forbids the import or export of a particular item the parties had agreed would be shipped.

> **substantial impairment**
> A concept, used to modify the perfect tender rule, whereby a buyer can revoke acceptance of goods and, with installment contracts, a buyer/lessee can reject an installment of a particular item only if the defects substantially impair the value of the goods.

LO 15-4

Specific Obligations of Buyers and Lessees

THE BASIC OBLIGATION: INSPECTION, PAYMENT, AND ACCEPTANCE

Under UCC Sections 2-301 and 2A-516(1), buyers and lessees are obligated to accept and pay for conforming goods in accordance with the contract. Before paying for and accepting the goods, buyers/lessees ordinarily inspect the goods to make sure they conform to the specifications in the parties' agreement.

EXCEPTIONS TO THE BASIC OBLIGATION

Buyers/lessees do not always end up accepting and paying for goods. Sometimes, on inspection, the buyer or lessee decides to reject the goods and refrain from paying for them. In this section, we take a look at exceptions to the buyer's/lessee's basic obligation. These exceptions allow sellers/lessors and buyers/lessees to ask questions such as:

- What forms of payment are allowed under the UCC?
- In what circumstances can a buyer reject goods?
- Is the buyer allowed to accept part but not all of the goods?
- In what circumstances can a buyer revoke acceptance of goods?
- How and when can a buyer reject nonconforming goods?
- Are installment contracts treated differently than other kinds of contracts?

Problems on Inspection If all goes well in a transaction over the sale or lease of goods, the buyer or lessee inspects the goods and then pays by any means the parties have agreed on, including payment by cash, check, or credit card. Unless the parties have agreed otherwise, the buyer or lessee typically inspects the goods before paying. Under UCC Sections 2-513(1) and 2A-515(1), the seller or lessor must provide an opportunity for inspection before enforcing payment.

The concept of reasonableness governs the inspection process. For example, inspection must take place at a reasonable time and place, in a reasonable way. Once the buyer or lessee inspects

the goods, he or she decides whether to accept them. Sometimes, on inspection, the buyer or lessee decides not to accept the goods.

Problems with Acceptance When all goes well, UCC Sections 2-606(1) and 2A-515(1)(a) indicate that the buyer or lessee, after inspecting, signifies agreement to the seller or lessor that the goods are either (1) conforming or (2) acceptable even though they are nonconforming. UCC 2-602(1), 2-606(1), and 2A-515(1)(b) allow the seller or lessor to presume acceptance if the buyer or lessee fails to reject the goods within a reasonable period of time. UCC 2-601(c) and 2A-509(1) allow the buyer or lessee to make a partial acceptance when the goods are nonconforming and the seller or lessor has failed to cure the defects.

When goods are nonconforming, the buyer or lessee is allowed to revoke or withdraw acceptance of the goods. The previous section on specific obligations of sellers/lessors discussed this concept under the topic of substantial impairment. From the buyer's/lessee's perspective, the buyer or lessee may revoke acceptance if the nonconformity substantially impairs the value of the goods but only if he or she had a legitimate reason for the initial acceptance.

LO 15-5 Warranties

At common law, the obligations and responsibilities of the contractual parties are determined by the express terms of the contract. UCC contracts are the same but with a major addition: implied warranties. *Implied* means that the warranty or guarantee is automatically a part of the contract; the parties do not negotiate for it. At common law, the only implied warranty in a contract is the implied warranty of assignability. However, the UCC changes this part of contract law dramatically.

warranty

An assurance, either express or implied, by one party that the other party can rely on its representations of fact; in sales, a binding promise regarding a product in the event that the product does not meet the manufacturer's or seller's promises.

Let's look at the whole range of warranties in contract law. **Warranties** generally arise in conjunction with a sale or lease. They impose certain duties on the seller or lessor, and if the seller or lessor fails to live up to these duties, he or she may be sued for breach of warranty. There are three basic categories of warranties: warranties of title, express warranties, and implied warranties. Each is discussed in the following sections.

WARRANTIES OF TITLE

While no warranties automatically arise under the common law, the UCC assumes that the seller:

warranty of title

An assurance, inferred in every UCC sales transaction, that the seller has good and valid title to the goods and has the right to transfer title free and clear of any liens, judgments, or infringements of intellectual property rights of which the buyer does not have knowledge.

1. Has good and valid title to the goods.
2. Has the right to transfer title free and clear of any liens, judgments, or infringements of intellectual property rights of which the buyer does not have knowledge.

The UCC specifically permits buyers to recover from sellers who have breached these **warranties of title.** The only exceptions to title warranties occur if they are disclaimed or modified by specific language in the contract or if the seller is obviously unable to guarantee title, as would be the case, for instance, at a sheriff's sale of seized goods.

Clearly, if the buyer is aware of any problem with the transfer of goods, the buyer is indeed purchasing them at her own risk. Still, if the seller transfers goods to an unknowing buyer for which no good title passes or on which there are encumbrances or patent claims, the buyer may treat the contract as being in breach. Under such circumstances, the buyer may then avail herself of the remedies available under a breach situation.

EXPRESS WARRANTIES

express warranty

Any description of a good's physical nature or its use, in either general or specific circumstances, that becomes part of a contract.

Although the common law does not use the term *express warranties,* the concept and its application do exist in the common law. It seems only fair and equitable that promises made by a seller to induce a buyer to execute a sales contract should be enforceable. An **express warranty** is any description of a good's physical nature or its use, in either general or specific circumstances, that

becomes part of the contract. To use common law language, an express warranty is a material term of the sale or lease contract.

Express warranties may be found in advertisements or brochures (e.g., "This electric saw comes with a lifetime guarantee"). Such a warranty may also be part of a written sales or lease contract; or it may be a salesperson's oral promise concerning the good, made while he is attempting to close the deal. A sample or model may also provide an express warranty. Generally speaking, if the buyer relies on representations, those representations become part of the contract in the form of express warranties.

IMPLIED WARRANTIES OF QUALITY

Implied warranties arise by operation of law under certain circumstances. Earlier, you read about the implied warranties of title that arise under the UCC. This section focuses on the three warranties of quality that arise under the UCC.

Implied Warranty of Merchantability Consider the following scenario: You purchase a toaster from a local discount store. When you use the toaster, all you get is either burnt toast or bread that is only slightly warm. You take the toaster back to the store and are met with this answer: "Well, we don't guarantee how well the toaster will work. After all, it does toast, either very, very lightly or very, very burnt." This answer, of course, is nonsense. There is a reasonable expectation of how a toaster will perform. That reasonable expectation is codified in the UCC **implied warranty of merchantability.**

To invoke this implied warranty, the buyer or lessee must have purchased or leased the good from a merchant. Thus, a dirt bike purchased at a bicycle shop is covered by the warranty of merchantability, but a bike that is bought from a neighbor is not, unless the neighbor is a bicycle merchant.

Under the UCC, the goods must be *merchantable,* meaning that they must:

> **implied warranty of merchantability**
> An assurance, inferred in every sale unless clearly disclaimed, that merchantable goods will conform to a reasonable performance expectation. The purchaser must have purchased or leased the good from a merchant.

1. Be able to pass without objection in the trade or market for similar goods.
2. In the case of fungible goods, be of fair average quality within the description.
3. Be fit for the ordinary purposes for which such goods are used.
4. Be produced, within the variations permitted by the agreement, with even kind, quality, and quantity in each unit and among all units involved.
5. Be adequately contained, packaged, and labeled as the agreement may require.
6. Conform to the promises or affirmations made on the container or label, if any.

The quintessential case defining and illustrating the implied warranty of merchantability is that of the Blue Ship Tea Room and Ms. Webster (see Case 15-2). The case concerned the merchantability of food.

CASE 15-2	PRISCILLA D. WEBSTER V. BLUE SHIP TEA ROOM, INC. SUPREME JUDICIAL COURT OF MASSACHUSETTS 347 Mass. 421; 198 N.E.2d 309 (1964)

FACTS: *Priscilla Webster, a restaurant patron who ordered seafood chowder and choked on a fishbone, brought this case. She maintained that she would not have reasonably expected to find a bone in the chowder. As a result of the bone in the chowder, Webster suffered through several hospital procedures to remove the bone, at considerable cost and pain. At the trial, a jury found for Webster. The Blue Ship Tea Room, the defendant, appealed the*

case on the basis of the legal interpretation of the implied warranty of merchantability. The appellate decision has become a classic in American jurisprudential reasoning.

ISSUE: Does a fishbone found in fish chowder render the chowder inedible, thereby breaching the implied warranty of merchantability?

REASONING: The court, in great detail, discussed the rich culinary history of New England seafood chowders. In going through the details of exactly how "good" chowder is made, the court praised the richness of thick, plump, delicious pieces of fish and shellfish. Completely ridding the chowder of any possibility of bones would require that the cook finely mince the seafood, depriving the dish of one of its hallmark characteristics. Further, the court argued that anyone eating good New England seafood chowder would know or should know that fishbones are indeed a possibility.

DECISION AND REMEDY: As lamentable as Webster's injuries were, the court found that the Blue Ship Tea Room had not breached its implied warranty of merchantability.

SIGNIFICANCE OF THE CASE: Common sense needs to apply in defining "merchantability." Clearly, a piece of bone in a hamburger is unreasonable and would violate the implied warranty. However, in cases where the buyer should expect a problem, such as a possible fishbone in a seafood dish, the buyer must be prepared to accept the situation.

CRITICAL THINKING

As with most legal decisions, the critical-thinking activity that is most obvious is the need to examine possible analogies which could be used by the court in justifying its conclusion. Consider this analogy: Is the fish bone in the chowder the same as a shard of beef bone in a beef vegetable soup? What about a piece of chicken bone in a chicken salad sandwich? How about a small caterpillar in a fresh green salad? Would the aptness of the analogy depend at all on the size of the bone in the fish chowder?

ETHICAL DECISION MAKING

The judge mainly used assumption of risk to rule against Webster, though she suffered an injury in fact. Should the restaurant have somehow compensated her? What would the WPH framework indicate should be done?

implied warranty of fitness for a particular purpose

An assurance, inferred in any UCC sale, whereby when a seller or lessor knows or has reason to know (1) why the buyer or lessee is purchasing or leasing the goods in question and (2) that the buyer or lessee is relying on him or her to make the selection, the buyer or lessee has an enforceable warranty if such assurance is false.

Implied Warranty of Fitness for a Particular Purpose Another important UCC implied warranty is the **implied warranty of fitness for a particular purpose.** This warranty comes about when a seller or lessor knows or has reason to know (1) why the buyer or lessee is purchasing or leasing the goods in question and (2) that the buyer or lessee is relying on him or her to make the selection. Under this warranty, a seller or lessor does not have to be a merchant.

An implied warranty of fitness for a particular purpose should not be confused with an express warranty. If the buyer walks into a store and the salesclerk says, "This saw will cut through metal," the seller has created an express warranty. However, if the buyer comes into the store and asks the salesclerk for a saw to cut through some copper tubing and the salesclerk refers the customer to a wall of different saws, it is reasonable for the buyer to assume that all the saws on the wall will satisfy the *particular purpose* that the buyer has indicated. Thus, an implied warranty of fitness for a particular purpose has been created.

Implied Warranty of Trade Usage The UCC, always diligent in its goal to facilitate the flow and ease of commercial activity, recognizes that a well-accepted course of dealing or trade usage may create implied warranties dependent on the circumstances. For example, if it is generally accepted in the trade that a certain product is always preassembled and shrink-wrapped, the failure of the seller to deliver the goods in that condition would be a breach of the **implied warranty of trade usage.**

Warranty Rights of Third Parties

The idea of a seller's being in breach of an implied warranty raises an entirely new issue: Is the seller liable to anyone other than the buyer? This question may initially sound peculiar. After all, the seller and the buyer are bound together by contract and if either breaches, then the breaching party is liable to the nonbreaching party.

However, consider this possible scenario: Jane buys a blender from a local store. Prior to using the blender, she lends it to her cousin Valerie to use at a party. While Valerie is blending drinks at the party, the blades fly off the blender and injure her. What obligation, if any, does the seller have to the injured Valerie? No contractual relationship exists between Valerie and the seller. However, it seems to be patently unfair to conclude that Valerie has no cause of action against the seller. The UCC recognizes this unfairness and clearly states that Valerie may indeed have a cause of action based on breach of warranty against the seller. The states are given the following three choices regarding *third-party beneficiaries of warranties:*

1. Seller's warranties extend to the buyer's household members and guests.
2. Seller's warranties extend to any reasonable and foreseeable user.
3. Seller's warranties extend to anyone injured by the good.

Most states have adopted the second option.

implied warranty of trade usage

An assurance, inferred in the context of certain UCC sales, depending on the circumstances, that can be created through a well-accepted course of dealing or trade usage.

Warranty Disclaimers and Waivers

There really is no question as to whether an implied warranty may be disclaimed. The real question is *how* it is to be disclaimed. Generally speaking, if an implied warranty is to be disclaimed, the seller must do so in clear, unambiguous, conspicuous language. To disclaim the implied warranty of fitness for a particular purpose, the seller must disclaim the warranty in writing. The seller may disclaim the warranty of merchantability either orally or in writing; however, some states require that the term *merchantability* must be used in the disclaimer. Under the CISG, however, the term *merchantability* does not need to be specifically expressed in order to disclaim it. Any reasonable language disclaiming the warranty is acceptable.

To avoid potential liability, a seller of corn for feed, for example, might decide to include in any sales contract for feed corn a clause that states, "No guarantees are made, either expressly or implied, that this feed corn has not been contaminated by mold or the toxin Fumonisin. Buyer is advised to test the corn to determine the presence of these potential contaminants." Of course, such a disclaimer might certainly have a negative impact on the sales of one's product.

The buyer may also waive both implied and express warranties. A buyer may waive these rights by (1) failing to examine goods for which an express warranty was created by a sample or model or (2) failing to comply with the seller's request to inspect the goods. Suppose, for example, that a printer requests that the buyer come into the shop to proof letterhead and envelopes. The buyer refuses, claiming that he is too busy, and tells the printer to go ahead and run the stationery. On receipt of the stationery, the buyer discovers that the numbers in the phone number are transposed, making the stationery useless. Unfortunately, the buyer has indeed waived his rights due to his failure to inspect.

A buyer may also waive her warranty rights under the contract by failing to comply with the statute of limitations. Under the UCC, the buyer or seller must bring a lawsuit on a breached contract within four years of when the breach occurred or when the nonbreaching party became aware of it. The buyer and seller are free to negotiate contractually a shorter time period (as long as it is not less than one year), but they are not free to negotiate a longer time period than the four years.

While the UCC remains the primary codification of both state and federal laws regarding sellers' warranties, there has also been specific legislation pertaining to this issue. The 1975 federal law known as the Magnuson-Moss Act requires that if a seller decides to issue a written

warranty for a consumer good (the seller is not required to do so), the seller must indicate whether that warranty is a *full* warranty or a *limited* warranty. This applies to any consumer good sold for more than $10. If the written warranty is silent, it is presumed to be a full warranty, which means that if the good fails or is defective, the good or its defective part will be replaced. If replacement cannot be timely effected, the buyer has the right to a refund or a full replacement.

If the good is sold for more than $15, the written warranty must disclose a number of items of information—names and addresses of the warrantors, any limitations on the warranty, and the procedures required to activate the warranty remedies—all in readable and easily understood language, in other words, not in *legalese!*

The Goal of Contract Remedies

Of course, the laying out of these various contractual obligations gives rise to the question of what remedies are available if those obligations are breached. The obligations of sellers/lessors and buyers/lessees are determined by (1) terms the parties outline in agreements, (2) custom, and (3) rules outlined by the Uniform Commercial Code, such as the various implied warranties described previously.

Remedies Available to Sellers and Lessors under the UCC

CANCEL THE CONTRACT

UCC Sections 2-703(f) and 2A-523(1)(a) allow a seller or lessor to cancel the contract if the buyer or lessee is in breach. The UCC requires sellers/lessors to notify buyers/lessees of the cancellation. Then the seller or lessor pursues remedies available under the UCC. Remember, these remedies give the seller/lessor the benefit of the bargain, and no more.

WITHHOLD DELIVERY

Sometimes a buyer breaches the contract or lease before the seller has delivered the goods. For instance, the buyer or lessee might fail to pay according to the terms of the agreement. UCC Sections 2-703(a) and 2A-523(1)(c) allow sellers or lessors to withhold delivery of goods when the buyer or lessee is in breach.

RESELL OR DISPOSE OF THE GOODS

Sellers or lessors are also allowed to resell or dispose of the goods when the buyer is in breach and the goods have not yet been delivered. The seller or lessor then holds the buyer or lessee liable for any loss. UCC Section 2-706 allows the seller to recover the difference between the resale price and the contract price, plus incidental damages and minus expenses saved. Although buyers are liable for these damages, the seller gets to keep any profits it makes on the resale. UCC 2A-527(2) outlines a similar rule for lease agreements. The lessor is allowed to lease the goods to another party and recover unpaid lease payments and any deficiency between the lease payments due under the original lease contract and those due under the new contract. The lessor can also seek incidental damages.

SUE TO GET THE BENEFIT OF THE BARGAIN

In trying to give the seller or lessor the benefit of the bargain, and nothing more, courts often grant damages to recover the purchase price or lease payments due. Consider the following Case Nugget.

CASE Nugget

Price or Profit?

G. B. "Boots" Smith Corporation v. Henry R. Cobb, Jr. and Richard Cobb
Supreme Court of Mississippi

860 So. 2d 774; 2003 Miss. LEXIS 578; October 30, 2003, Decided

The plaintiff entered into a contract with the Cobbs for the sale of landfill dirt needed for a road project the defendants were undertaking. The language of the contract seemed to infer that the defendants would purchase all the dirt they required from the plaintiff. However, the defendants chose to buy some of the required fill dirt from another seller. The plaintiff brought suit under the UCC.

The court found the parties' agreement to be a requirements contract. Even though the language of the contract was not expressly clear, the court found that the language inferred a requirements contract, which therefore mandated that the defendants purchase all of the fill dirt from the plaintiff. The court awarded the purchase price of the dirt to the plaintiff. On appeal, the appellate court reversed the award of damages, holding that the purchase price was the incorrect damage measure. Since the plaintiff was still in possession of the fill dirt, the lost profit was the appropriate damage award, not the purchase price. Awarding the purchase price would essentially allow the plaintiff to have the potential windfall of a double award.

STOP DELIVERY

UCC Sections 2-705(1) and 2A-526(1) allow a seller or lessor to stop delivery of goods that are in transit. *In transit* means that the seller or lessor has delivered the goods to a carrier or bailee but the carrier or bailee has not yet turned them over to the buyer. Of course, the seller/lessor must give timely notice to the carrier/bailee so that the carrier/bailee is able to stop delivery. Also, the rules are different for insolvent and solvent buyers and lessees. If the buyer/lessee is insolvent, the carrier/bailee can stop delivery regardless of the quantity shipped. If the buyer/lessee is solvent, however, the carrier/bailee can stop delivery only if the quantity shipped is a large shipment (e.g., a carload or truckload).

RECLAIM THE GOODS

Under UCC Sections 2-709(1) and 2A-529(1), if the buyer or lessee has possession of the goods and is in breach, the seller or lessor can sue for the purchase price of the goods or for the lease payments due, plus incidental damages. In some circumstances, the UCC allows the seller or lessee to reclaim the goods. UCC 2-702(2) allows a seller to reclaim goods when the seller discovers the buyer is insolvent. UCC 2A-525(2) allows a lessor to reclaim goods when the lessee fails to make payments according to the lease terms.

Remedies Available to Buyers and Lessees under the UCC

CANCEL THE CONTRACT

Sometimes, sellers or lessors fail to deliver the goods or to deliver conforming goods and thus are in breach. UCC Sections 2-711(1) and 2A-508(1)(a) allow buyers and lessees to cancel the contract and then seek remedies that give them the benefit of the bargain.

LO 15-8

cover

A buyer's right to substitute goods for those due under a sales or lease agreement when the seller provides nonconforming goods.

LO 15-9

consequential damages

In a contract, foreseeable damages that result from special facts and circumstances arising outside the contract itself. The damages must be within the contemplation of the parties at the time the breach occurs. Also called *special damages*.

liquidated damages

Damages specified as a term of the contract, before a breach of contract occurs.

specific performance

An order of the court requiring that a nonbreaching party fulfill the terms of the contract.

OBTAIN COVER

Under UCC Sections 2-712 and 2A-518, buyers and lessees are allowed to **cover,** or substitute, goods for those due under the sales or lease agreement.

The buyer must (1) demonstrate good faith in obtaining the substitute goods, (2) pay a reasonable amount for the substitute goods, (3) act without unreasonable delay in purchasing the substitute goods, and (4) purchase goods that are reasonable substitutes.

SUE TO RECOVER DAMAGES

Buyers and lessees, are entitled to incidental and consequential damages. **Consequential damages** include damages for lost profits, as long as these damages are not too speculative. These monetary damages give the injured buyer or lessee the benefit of the bargain. There is also the availability of liquidated damages and even, under some situations, punitive damages.

Liquidated damages are damages identified *before* the breach occurs. The parties are free to negotiate, as part of the contract, a liquidated-damage clause in which the parties agree in advance what the damages will be for each party should a breach occur. Generally speaking, a court will enforce a liquidated-damage clause as long as it is not so far out of reasonable range as to be punitive in nature. Liquidated-damage clauses that are deemed to be punitive in nature are not enforceable.

The code provides for liquidated damages if the parties have not expressly negotiated a liquidated-damage clause. UCC Section 2-718 pertains to liquidated damages and allows the nonbreaching seller to claim against a breaching buyer 20 percent of the purchase price or $500, whichever is less, as liquidated damages.

Although the UCC does not mention the availability of punitive damages, other than in its voiding of liquidated damages that are punitive in nature, an issue that remains unsettled is the awarding of punitive damages against a breaching party who intentionally or egregiously breaches the contract. You will remember from tort law that when a tort is committed either intentionally or recklessly, the court may infer legal malice and instruct a jury that it may consider the awarding of punitive damages in addition to compensatory damages. Although this concept is well settled in tort law, it has never been widely applied in contract law. Yet there are some who argue that it should be, especially to deter intentional breaches of contract.

RECOVER THE GOODS

UCC Sections 2-502 and 2A-522 allow buyers and lessees to recover the goods identified in the contract if the seller or lessor becomes insolvent within 10 days after receiving the first payment due under the agreement. Buyers or lessees are obligated to pay the remaining balance according to the terms of the agreement.

OBTAIN SPECIFIC PERFORMANCE

UCC Sections 2-716(1) and 2A-521(1) allow buyers and lessees to seek the remedy of specific performance when either (1) the goods are unique or (2) a remedy at law is inadequate. **Specific performance** usually requires that the seller or lessor deliver the particular goods identified in the contract.

REJECT NONCONFORMING GOODS

UCC Sections 2-601 and 2A-519 allow the buyer or lessee to reject nonconforming goods. The buyer or lessee may then obtain cover or cancel the contract.

REVOKE ACCEPTANCE OF NONCONFORMING GOODS

UCC Sections 2-608 and 2A-517 sometimes allow the buyer or lessee to revoke acceptance of nonconforming goods.

E-COMMERCE and the Law

Computer Contracts

Sometimes, computer purchasers are surprised to find out they are bound to agreements that were created when sellers included contracts in the box in which the computer was delivered. Some of these agreements limit the purchaser's remedies. For instance, in *Hill v. Gateway 2000*,[*] Hill purchased a computer from Gateway 2000 by placing a telephone order. The computer arrived through the mail. Gateway had placed a contract in the computer's shipping box that indicated that the terms sent in the box were binding on the buyer unless the buyer returned the computer within 30 days. One of the terms in this contract was a provision which stated that any disputes between the parties would be resolved through arbitration. The order taker had not read any of the terms of the contract over the telephone when Hill placed the order. When the computer arrived, Hill did not read the contract. In an effort to avoid the arbitration clause, Hill asked the court to determine that Gateway 2000 could not limit buyers' remedies or avenues through which they seek remedies (i.e., through arbitration) by bundling hardware and legal documents. The court ruled that the contract was binding on the parties. The court stated, "A contract need not be read to be effective; people who accept take the risk that the unread terms may in retrospect prove unwelcome."[†]

[*] 105 F.3d 1157 (1997).
[†] Ibid., p. 1158.

ACCEPT THE NONCONFORMING GOODS AND SEEK DAMAGES

Under UCC Sections 2-607, 2-715, and 2A-519, buyers or lessees are allowed to accept nonconforming goods and then seek monetary damages to give them the benefit of the bargain. The buyer or lessee must give the seller or lessor reasonable notice of the defect.

Modifications or Limitations to the Remedies Otherwise Provided by the UCC

Parties to sales and lease contracts are allowed to modify or limit remedies. Under UCC Sections 2-719 and 2A-503, parties are allowed to create agreements that make it clear that the remedies outlined in the agreement are exclusive remedies. Courts uphold modifications or limitations to remedies unless the remedies fail in their essential purpose.

SUMMARY

The Basic Performance Obligation	Under the UCC, sellers and lessors are obligated *to transfer and deliver conforming goods.*
	Buyers and lessees are obligated *to accept and pay for conforming goods in accordance with the contract.*
	The UCC requires *good faith* in the performance and enforcement of every contract.
Specific Obligations of Sellers and Lessors	The *perfect tender rule* indicates that if goods or tender of delivery fail in any respect to conform to the contract, the buyer/lessee has the right to accept the goods, reject the entire shipment, or accept part and reject part.
	Exceptions to the perfect tender rule allow sellers/lessors and buyers/lessees to consider:

- Norms in the industry and past dealings between the parties.
- Exceptions outlined in the parties' agreement.
- The seller's/lessor's right to cure.

- Excuse from performance when identified goods are destroyed through no fault of the parties.
- The concept of substantial impairment as it relates to revocation of acceptance and installment contracts.
- The concept of commercial impracticability.

Specific Obligations of Buyers and Lessees

If all goes well in a transaction over the sale or lease of goods, the buyer or lessee inspects the goods and then *pays* according to the agreement.

The seller or lessor must provide an opportunity for *inspection.*

- The concept of reasonableness governs the inspection process.
- After inspection, the buyer or lessee decides whether to accept the goods.

After inspecting, the buyer/lessee signifies *acceptance* or partial acceptance.

- Sellers or lessors sometimes presume acceptance.
- Partial acceptance is allowed in some circumstances.
- Buyers or lessees are allowed to revoke or withdraw acceptance of nonconforming goods.
- Buyers or lessees must issue reasonable notice if they decide to reject goods.

Cases in which a buyer decides to assert his or her right to reject nonconforming goods are often categorized under the heading "rescission or revocation of acceptance by buyer."

Warranties

A *warranty* is a promise on the part of the seller with respect to certain characteristics of the good.
 Warranties of title:

- Passage of good title.
- Implied promise of no liens or judgments against title.
- Implied promise that title is not subject to any copyright, patent, or trademark infringement.

 Express warranties:

- Description of the good's physical nature or its use.
- Either general or specific.
- Material term of the contract.
- Reliance of buyer on representations.

 Implied warranties:

Implied warranty of merchantability: A warranty based on a reasonable expectation of performance of the purchased good. The good must:

- Pass without objection.
- Be of fair quality within the description.
- Be fit for ordinary uses.
- Have even quality.
- Be adequately packaged.
- Conform to promises made on the label.

Implied warranty of fitness: A warranty that arises when the seller knows the purpose for which the buyer is purchasing goods and the buyer relies on the seller's judgment.

Implied warranty of trade usage: A warranty that arises as a result of generally accepted trade practices.

Warranty Rights of Third Parties

The states have three choices regarding the warranty rights of third-party beneficiaries:

- Seller's warranties extend to the buyer's household members and guests.
- Seller's warranties extend to any reasonable and foreseeable user.
- Seller's warranties extend to anyone injured by the good.

Warranty Disclaimers and Waivers	Methods of waiving include:

- Seller does not make warranties in the first place (express warranty).
- Seller disclaims in clear, unambiguous, conspicuous language (implied warranty).
- Buyer fails or refuses to examine goods.
- Buyer fails to file suit within the time of the statute of limitations.

Magnuson-Moss Act: If a seller decides to issue a written warranty for a consumer good, the seller must indicate whether the warranty is full or limited.

The Goal of Contract Remedies	The goal of contract remedies is to give the parties the *benefit of the bargain they struck,* and nothing more.

Remedies Available to Sellers and Lessors under the UCC	When the buyer/lessee is in breach, the seller/lessor can:

- Cancel the contract.
- Withhold delivery.
- Sell or dispose of the goods.
- Sue to recover the purchase price, lease payments due, or some other measure of damages that gives the seller or lessor the benefit of the bargain.
- Stop delivery.
- Reclaim the goods.

Remedies Available to Buyers and Lessees under the UCC	When the seller/lessor is in breach, the buyer/lessee can:

- Cancel the contract.
- Obtain cover.
- Sue to recover damages.
- Recover the goods.
- Obtain specific performance.
- Reject nonconforming goods.
- Revoke acceptance of nonconforming goods.
- Accept the nonconforming goods and seek damages.

Modifications or Limitations to the Remedies Otherwise Provided by the UCC	Parties to sales and lease contracts are allowed to modify or limit remedies. Courts uphold modifications or limitations to remedies unless the remedies fail in their essential purpose.

Point/Counterpoint

According to its critics, the application of the perfect tender rule can be a hypertechnical application of contractual obligations that really have no bearing on the substance of the contract but allow a party to escape contractual obligations on second thought.

Should the Perfect Tender Rule Be Ignored by the Courts and Replaced with the Common Law and CISG Concept of Substantial Performance?	
YES	NO
Common law really got it right through its cases holding that only material obligations must be complied with and immaterial ones are just that—immaterial	The underlying concept that is the foundation of contract law worldwide is the notion that the parties are free to negotiate the terms and conditions

and inconsequential. Common law has perfected, so to speak, the substantial-performance rule to a very workable conclusion. It gives the trier of fact flexibility in determining the impact of nonperformance in the overall scheme of the contractual relationship while keeping the focus on the intent of the parties and the ultimate injury or harmlessness of the noncompliance.

Furthermore, as more and more countries are adopting the CISG, UCC concepts such as the perfect tender rule are out of sync with the rest of the commercial world. In the ever-accelerating venue of international transactions, uniformity is clearly the order of the day. We all need to be on the same page with contract interpretation.

of their respective contracts. Nothing in the UCC prohibits the parties from negotiating a substantial-performance definition in the performance obligation of the contract.

However, by creating something other than the perfect tender rule, the courts send the message that the will of the parties may be frustrated if the noncompliance is somehow lessened to some level of immateriality. But who is better-suited to determine this immateriality: the parties or the courts? By including specific performance requirements in the contract, the parties indicate what is material and what is not material. This determination should be left undisturbed by the courts and common law.

Questions & Problems

1. What determines the obligations of sellers/lessors and buyers/lessees?

2. Explain what the good-faith and commercial reasonableness obligations are.

3. Explain what the perfect tender rule is and how it can be modified.

4. Amboy Closeouts, Inc., agreed to purchase 25,000 Christmas ornaments from Polar Trading, Inc. Alcorn, president of Amboy, requested 15 cases of the ornaments as samples and agreed to purchase the samples if he was pleased with the quality. He received the samples and determined that they were in satisfactory condition, but the bill was never paid. Alcorn contacted Polar Trading to order more ornaments, but he was told that he needed to fax a copy of a deposit check in order to secure the shipment. Alcorn faxed a copy of the $2,000 deposit check to Polar Trading, but he did not mail the check. Polar Trading sent a total of 352 ornaments to Alcorn. After receiving the shipment, Alcorn contacted Polar Trading and reported that many of the cases were defective. He had already sold some of the ornaments, but the rest were sent back. Polar Trading sold some of the returned ornaments but was unable to sell the complete shipment. Amboy argued that, under the UCC, it had the right to reject all the goods, accept all the goods, or partially accept and reject some of the goods. Furthermore, Amboy argued that Polar Trading breached the contract by delivering defective goods and, therefore, no payment was due. How did the court decide? [*Polar Trading, Inc. v. Amboy Closeouts, Inc.,* 899 S.W.2d 577 (1995).]

5. The buyer purchased from a car dealer a used car that was made by the dealership's car manufacturer. The car was still under the car manufacturer's limited warranty. The car buyer, because of problems with the car that she alleged were not fixed, brought her claims under the Magnuson-Moss Warranty–Federal Trade Commission Improvement Act (Magnuson-Moss Act). What remedies are available? Why would the court grant damages but not allow the buyer to revoke the contract? [*Mydlach v. DaimlerChrysler Corp.,* Docket No. 102588, Sup. Ct. Ill., 226 Ill. 2d 307; 875 N.E.2d 1047; 2007 Ill. LEXIS 1162; 315 Ill. Dec. 760; 64 U.C.C. Rep. Serv. 2d (Callaghan) 44 (2007).]

6. Wilbur Reed operated a small greenhouse in Montana. He ordered most of his plants from McCalif Grower Supplies. Reed often supplied local Kmart and Ernst stores with his products. During the holiday season, he agreed to provide them with poinsettia plants. Reed ordered the plants from McCalif, and McCalif had growers send the plants to Reed from Colorado. Reed's employee accepted the boxes at the airport and did not note any damages to the packaging. However, when the boxes were opened, the poinsettias appeared damaged. Reed contacted McCalif and notified it that the poinsettias were damaged as a result of poor packing. McCalif advised Reed to report the damages to the carrier, Delta Airlines. Delta paid Reed $924.66 in compensation. McCalif was not able to supply Reed with more poinsettias before the holiday season. As a result, Reed lost accounts to many of the stores. McCalif sued Reed for payment for the poinsettias, $3,223.56. Reed refused to pay and argued that McCalif had failed to deliver according to their contract. Whom did the court agree with? [*McCalif Grower Supplies, Inc. v. Wilbur Reed,* 900 P.2d 880 (1995).]

7. Rockland Industries agreed to purchase three containers of antimony oxide at $1.80 per pound from Manley-Regan Chemicals. Rockland produces

drapes, and antimony oxide is used to fireproof the drapes. A representative from Manley-Regan, David Hess, worked with Conrad Ailstock, Rockland's purchasing agent. Hess informed Ailstock of a slight delay, but he assured Ailstock that the product, which was coming from China, was "on the water." Three months after the two companies had made the agreement, Hess contacted Ailstock to report that the product was not coming. According to Hess, Manley-Regan was considering legal claims against the Chinese supplier or the Chinese government. Rockland was forced to find another supplier, but the price was substantially higher. Rockland brought suit to recover the difference between Manley-Regan's quoted price and the price of the substitute antimony oxide. Is the commercial impracticability defense appropriate? Explain. [*Rockland Industries, Inc. v. Manley-Regan Chemicals Division*, 991 F. Supp. 468 (1998).]

8. The buyer contracted with the seller for the purchase of ribs. After delivery, the buyer refused to pay the contract price, claiming that the ribs arrived in an "off condition." The seller filed suit for breach of contract. The buyer claimed that when the ribs were defrosted and thawed, they were unfit for consumption. The seller claimed that the off condition occurred after delivery to the buyer. Who had to prove what? Did the buyer have to show that the off condition occurred before taking possession? Or could there have been some kind of assumption after the meat was defrosted? [*Chicago Prime Packers, Inc., Plaintiff-Appellee, v. Northam Food Trading Co., Defendant-Appellant*, No. 04-2551, 7th Cir. Ct. of Appeals, 408 F.3d 894; 2005 U.S. App. LEXIS 9355.]

9. David Cooper purchased a computer and software for his supermarket business. He was using a software program recommended and installed by the seller, Contemporary Computer Systems, Inc. The sales contract had a clause that stated that no refunds would be given after the 90-day warranty period. Cooper initially had problems with both the hardware and the software. Contemporary Computer Systems tried to remedy these problems. A pattern of problems and attempts to fix them went on for some time, far beyond the 90-day period expressly described in the contract. When Cooper had had enough, he decided to revoke the contract and demand his money back. Contemporary Computer Systems said the 90-day express clause in the contract precluded this action. Who won? [*David Cooper, Inc. v. Contemporary Computer Systems, Inc.*, 846 S.W.2d 777 (1993).]

10. Aubrey Reeves purchased a computer system for his business from Radio Shack Computer Center. Radio Shack is the local retailer for products sold by Tandy, its parent company. During negotiations, it became clear that Reeves needed software that Radio Shack could not provide. A Radio Shack salesperson referred Reeves to a software source book, let Reeves know he could choose compatible software from the source book, and informed him that Tandy did not support or service software from the source book. A disclaimer to this effect was in the source book. Reeves eventually purchased computers from Tandy, some software from Tandy, and more specialized software from a company called Lizcon. The Lizcon software did not meet Reeves's needs. Reeves subsequently sent a letter to Tandy, asking for rescission of the contract and damages. Could Reeves rescind? [*Aubrey's R.V. Center, Inc. v. Tandy Corporation*, 731 P.2d 1124 (1987).]

11. Landrum sold Gappelberg a big-screen television. The television had many defects, some of which Landrum and his service representatives fixed. Three weeks after the sale, the television stopped working altogether, and Gappelberg let Landrum know. Landrum promised to fix the television, but he did not. Gappelberg then requested return of consideration and asked the service representative to pick up the set but not to repair it because he would not accept it or a replacement. The question in the case was whether Gappelberg was allowed to prevent Landrum from curing the nonconforming television by his refusal to accept a replacement set. What did the court decide? Are you more sympathetic to Landrum or Gappelberg? [*Leitchfield Development Corp. v. Clark*, 757 S.W.2d 207 (1988).]

12. After living in their home for three years, Roger Nathaniel and Sharon Diamond sold the home to the plaintiffs, Marc Copland and Joan Lund. Nathaniel and Diamond hired a pest control company to inspect the home. The company reported that there was evidence of a previously treated infestation but that no evidence of active infestation was found. This report was provided to Copland and Lund prior to the sale of the home. The contract specified that the purchaser had inspected the premises and agreed to purchase it "as is." A year later, the plaintiffs discovered that levels of chlordane were present on the property. They also discovered that the home had been treated 10 years earlier for termites. At that time, chlordane was used to remove termites. Despite one toxicologist's report that the level of chlordane did not constitute a health concern, Copland and Lund spent $50,000 removing the contaminated soil from their property. They brought an action against the previous owners, Nathaniel and Diamond. How do you think the court decided? [*Copland v. Nathaniel*, 624 N.Y.S.2d 515 (1995).]

13. Grimberg sold a famous painting to Cohen for $785,000. Possession of the painting passed to Cohen but payment was never made. Despite various

and sundry attempts to resolve the issue, Grimberg never received payment or got the painting back. Cohen was subsequently convicted of fraud. Grimberg filed an insurance claim with his insurance company, which denied payment since, it claimed, Grimberg had transferred title to Cohen. Grimberg claimed that he transferred a voidable title and thus still retained an insurable interest in the painting. Who won? [*Zurich American Insurance Co., Subscribing to Policy Number IM 8338602, Certificate Number D279FL, Plaintiff-Counter-Defendant-Appellee, v. Felipe Grimberg Fine Art, Fine Arts Services, Inc., Doing Business as Felipe Grimberg Fine Art, Felipe Grimberg, John Does, A-Z, Defendants-Counter-Claimants-Appellants,* 08-1300-cv, 2d Cir. Ct. of Appeals, 324 Fed. Appx. 117; 2009 U.S. App. LEXIS 9937; 68 U.C.C. Rep. Serv. 2d (Callaghan) 690, May 7, 2009.]

14. A restaurant called "The Inn Between" entered into a contract to purchase a used restaurant computer system. The contract included installation and training from Remanco Metropolitan, Inc. The contract also required that Remanco keep the computer system in good operating order. The system was delivered and installed on March 29, 1995. The following day the computer malfunctioned and was down for three hours. Between March 30 and July 3, the restaurant contacted Remanco 48 times to report malfunctions. Though Remanco responded to each of the problems, the computer system continued to break down. Inn Between brought an action to revoke its acceptance of the computer system. It viewed the system as a nonconforming good. Remanco counterclaimed, seeking the unpaid price under the system maintenance agreement for nonreturn of the system. Which side got the remedy it sought? [*The Inn Between, Inc. v. Remanco Metropolitan, Inc.,* 662 N.Y.S.2d 1011 (1997).]

15. Shipping terms play an important role in determining when title, risk of loss, and insurable interest pass from seller to buyer. What is the significance of such terms as *CIF* and *FAS* in determining such issues? What happens when the contract is clearly CIF but the seller claims that the "CIF" was a typo and that the parties "knew" it should have been "FAS"? [*P & O Nedlloyd, Ltd., Plaintiff, v. Sanderson Farms, Inc.; Certain Underwriters at Lloyd's of London, Defendants, v. Sanderson Farms, Inc.; Third Party Plaintiff/Appellant v. Certain Underwriters at Lloyd's of London, Subscribing to Insurance Contract No. MC02ADKH, Third Party Defendant/Appellee,* No. 05-3766, 8th Cir. Ct. of Appeals, 462 F.3d 1015; 2006 U.S. App. LEXIS 22227; 60 U.C.C. Rep. Serv. 2d (Callaghan) 1051 (2006).]

Looking for more review material?

The Online Learning Center at **www.mhhe.com/kubasekess2e** contains this chapter's "Assignment on the Internet" and also a list of URLs for more information, entitled "On the Internet." Find both of them in the Student Center portion of the OLC, along with quizzes and other helpful materials.

CHAPTER

16

Negotiable Instruments: Negotiability and Transferability

Oral Agreements and Negotiable Instruments

As a gambling facility, MGM Desert Inn Inc. regularly holds and executes negotiable instruments. During a period of two months, customer William E. Shack, Jr., entered MGM and delivered eight checks to the casino in exchange for markers. These checks, which totaled $93,400, were signed by Shack and dated at the time of transfer. When MGM sent Shack's checks to the bank for payment, they were dishonored because the funds in Shack's account were insufficient.

MGM filed an action in district court to obtain the $93,400. Shack contended that a casino host had told him that he had sufficient remaining casino credit to receive the markers. The district court judge ruled in favor of MGM, affirming its argument that the checks were negotiable instruments and stating that no evidence of an oral agreement between the casino and Shack was provided. The checks contained Shack's signature, on a specified date, and were to be payable on demand from Shack's bank to MGM. Shack was ordered to pay MGM $5,000 for attorney fees in addition to the $93,400 originally owed on the checks.[1]

1. If you were employed at MGM, what would you do to avoid future disputes with your patrons about the nature of payment agreements?

2. Assuming that Shack's claims about an oral agreement with MGM were true, would this affect your decision as to whether the checks' payments were currently due?

[1] *MGM Desert Inn, Inc., dba Desert Inn Hotel & Casino v. William E. Shack*, U.S. District Court, District of Nevada, 809 F. Supp. 783 (1993).

After reading this chapter, you will be able to answer the following questions:

LO 16-1 Why is there a need for negotiable instruments?

LO 16-2 What are the types of negotiable instruments recognized by the UCC?

negotiable instrument
A written document signed by a person who makes an unconditional promise to pay a specific sum of money on demand or at a certain time to the holder of the instrument; an acceptable medium for exchanging value from one person to another.

Once a sales contract has been created and executed and the parties are aware of their respective obligations under the contract, the next phase is the *payment* by the buyer to the seller for the goods purchased. Payment is usually made in one of three ways: in cash, through credit arrangements (which are discussed in the chapter on secured transactions), or with a *substitute for cash.* It is this substitute for cash that is the focus of this chapter and the next one.

A substitute for cash, or a **negotiable instrument,** is a written document containing the signature of the creator, who makes an unconditional promise or order to pay a sum certain in money either at a time certain or on demand. Negotiable instruments are executed on a daily basis in the form of checks, certificates of deposit, drafts, and promissory notes in exchange for goods, services, or business financing.

LO 16-1 The Need for Negotiable Instruments

It is easy to figure out why using documents as payments greatly facilitates commercial transactions, especially in times when actual currency or cash is in short supply or when it is dangerous to transfer large amounts of currency or precious metals. These documents of payment are generically called *commercial paper,* and under Article 3 of the UCC they are specifically labeled *negotiable instruments.*

CONTRACTS AS COMMERCIAL PAPER

We have already discussed one common form of commercial paper: contracts. It does not matter whether the contract is a common law contract or a UCC Article 2 contract. Both kinds are examples of commercial paper. As such, through the process of assignment, these contracts may be circulated and transferred throughout the commercial world. Here is an illustration of assignment:

> Bob sells a bushel of apples to Betty; in exchange, Betty executes a contract to pay Bob $5 on demand. A few days later, Bob buys some oranges from Pat for $5. Instead of paying Pat the $5 in cash, Bob *assigns* Betty's obligation to pay Bob the $5 to Pat. When Pat demands the money from Betty, Betty will pay Pat the $5 and everyone will be square.

This illustration demonstrates the point that any contractual obligation, except personal ones and nonassignable ones, may be transferred and thus is classified as commercial paper.

PROBLEMS WITH COMMERCIAL PAPER

Even though the illustration with Bob, Betty, and Pat is a simple one, it still contains a potential problem. Consider that fact pattern again, only this time assume that the apples Bob sold to Betty were all rotten. Betty did not know the apples' condition at the time because they looked and felt fine. It was only after cutting into them that the problem became apparent.

When Pat demands the $5 from Betty, Betty naturally is going to refuse, claiming that Bob had breached their original contract by delivering to her defective apples. Betty would be justified and on legally safe ground to refuse to pay. Pat could do nothing against Betty and would have to go back and sue Bob. The commercial paper that Bob transferred to Pat was not acceptable. In other words, the whole reason for having the transferability of commercial paper as a substitute for currency is defeated under these circumstances.

Types of Negotiable Instruments

LO 16-2

Under Article 3, the UCC recognizes four specific types of negotiable instruments: notes and certificates of deposits, a highly specialized type of note; and drafts and checks, a highly specialized type of draft (UCC Section 3-104). A **note** is a promise by the *maker* of the note to pay a payee [UCC 3-103(a)(9)]. A **draft** is an order by a *drawer* to a drawee to pay a payee (in our example above, Bob could have drawn a draft ordering Betty to pay Pat $5, since Betty owed Bob $5) [UCC 3-103(a)(6)]. A note is a two-party instrument, whereas, by definition, a draft is a three-party instrument.

Notes and drafts can either be demand instruments or time instruments. With a **demand instrument,** the payee (or subsequent holder) can demand actual payment at any time. The UCC defines an instrument that is "payable on demand" as one that "(i) states that it is payable on demand or at sight, or otherwise indicates that it is payable at the will of the holder, or (ii) does not state any time of payment" [3-108(a)]. With a **time instrument,** payment can be made only at a specific time designated in the future. The UCC requires that an "instrument payable at a definite time" have a time easily determined from the document itself [3-108(b)].

Certificates of deposit and checks are specific illustrations of these distinctions. A **certificate of deposit** is a promise made by a bank to pay a payee a certain amount of money at a future time. The UCC defines a certificate of deposit as "an instrument containing an acknowledgment by a bank that a sum of money has been received by the bank and a promise by the bank to repay the sum of money. A certificate of deposit is a note of the bank" [3-104(j)]. Usually, a payee buys one of these instruments from a bank and then collects the principle plus a determined amount of interest in the future. However, because these instruments have a present value, even though they are not payable until some future time, the payee may transfer them or even sell them before the future date of payment.

A **check** is a specific draft, drawn by the owner of a checking account, ordering the bank to pay the payee from that drawer's account [UCC 3-104(f)]. A check is always a demand instrument and can never be a time instrument (postdating really does not affect the ability of the holder to cash the check before the post date). Types of checks include:

- *Cashier's check:* "[A] draft with respect to which the drawer and drawee are the same bank or branches of the same bank" [UCC 3-104(f)].
- *Traveler's check:* "[A]n instrument that (i) is payable on demand, (ii) is drawn on or payable at or through a bank, (iii) is designated by the term 'traveler's check' or by a substantially similar term, and (iv) requires, as a condition to payment, a countersignature by a person whose signature appears on the instrument" [UCC 3-104(i)].
- *Certified check:* "[A] check accepted by the bank on which it is drawn" [UCC 3-409(d)].

An Overview of the Law of Negotiable Instruments

For an instrument to be negotiable, specific requirements of *negotiability* must be met. However— and this is a very important concept that many people miss—if an instrument fails to qualify as a negotiable instrument, that does *not* mean that the instrument fails to be a perfectly good, perfectly enforceable contract. All it means is that the special rules regarding negotiable instruments

note
A promise by the maker of the note to pay the payee of the note.

draft
An instrument validating an order by a drawer to a drawee to pay a payee.

demand instrument
A type of draft that allows the payee to demand payment at any time from a holder.

time instrument
A type of draft that allows the payee to collect payment only at a specific time in the future.

certificate of deposit
A document whereby a bank promises to pay a payee a certain amount of money at a future time.

check
A special draft that orders a bank (the drawee) to pay a specified sum of money to the payee from the drawer's account.

do not apply. Once an instrument is a negotiable instrument, it has the potential of conferring on its possessor some special qualities. Let's go back to our example with Bob, Betty, and Pat. Use Figure 16-1 to follow the logic of the exchanges.

Figure 16-1

Potential Complexity of Negotiable Instruments

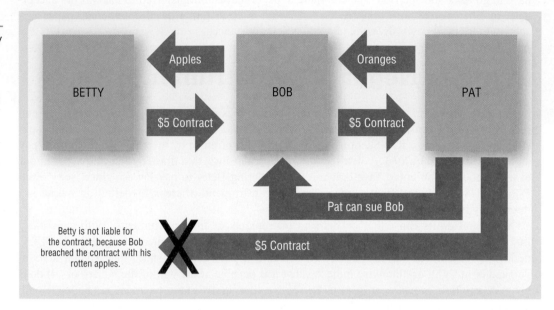

Betty buys apples from Bob for $5 and gives Bob a negotiable note promising to pay the $5 on demand. Bob then buys oranges from Pat for $5 and properly transfers (also known as *negotiates*) the $5 negotiable note to Pat. Pat presents the note to Betty for payment after Betty has found out that the apples she bought from Bob were all bad. Betty refuses to pay Pat the $5. Bob, that shady apple dealer, has disappeared. Pat sues Betty for the $5. Under the rules of negotiable instruments, Pat could very well prevail, and Betty, regardless of the awful apples she got from Bob, might just have to pay Pat.

That's an awful lot of information to jump in with right away, so we need to break down the steps. The following are the issues that have to be explored to understand this chain of events:

1. What constitutes a negotiable instrument?
2. How does one transfer a negotiable instrument?
3. What is the status of a holder of a negotiable instrument?
4. What happens when the person who created a negotiable instrument has a good defense for not honoring his or her paying on the instrument?

Clearly, when the contracts for such transactions are not in breach, everything works out fine. Potential problems, however, led to the evolution of the law surrounding negotiable commercial paper. The next section discusses the elements that make commercial paper a negotiable instrument. Remember that even when commercial paper does not meet the requirements for negotiability, it may still constitute an enforceable contract.

LO 16-3 REQUIREMENTS FOR NEGOTIABILITY

The UCC requires that for an instrument to be negotiable (do *not* equate *negotiable* with *enforceable*), the instrument must satisfy the six requirements in the following definition: A negotiable instrument is a written document that is signed by the maker or drawer with an unconditional promise or order to pay a sum certain in money on demand or at a time certain to the order of bearer [UCC 3-104(a)]. The six requirements are:

1. The instrument is a written document.
2. It is signed by the creator of the instrument.

Figure 16-2 Requirements of Negotiability in a Check

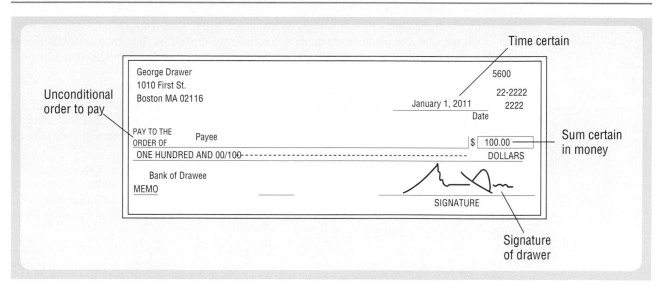

3. The instrument has an unconditional promise or order to pay.
4. The amount to be paid is a sum certain in money.
5. Payment is to be made either on demand or at a fixed future time (a time *certain*).
6. The document must contain either the words of negotiability—"to the order of"—or words indicating that it is a bearer instrument.

As you read through the following explanations pertaining to the requirements of negotiability, use Figure 16-2 as an example of the requirements as they apply to personal checks.

Written Document The written-document requirement is not as simple as it may appear. Clearly, the law does not permit an *oral* negotiable instrument. Telling someone that you unconditionally promise to pay her $50 next Tuesday does not create a negotiable instrument. However, under the right factual circumstances and when these words are provable, such a statement may be a binding, enforceable contract.

What makes the writing requirement a little complex is the mandate that the written document must have two characteristics: **relative permanence** and **movability**. Writing a negotiable instrument in the mud, for example, clearly lacks permanence; it will likely disappear as the mud dries. Thus, it is not a negotiable instrument. Likewise, the mud is something that one cannot move about in a commercially reasonable or expected manner. After all, one of the reasons for negotiable instruments is the ease with which they can be moved about.

Signature of the Maker or Drawer The UCC and cases interpreting the signature requirement are fairly liberal in interpreting what constitutes a signature. Anyone's affirmative mark, from a full-blown signature to an *X,* will suffice provided the party intended that the mark be placed on the instrument and uses that mark to identify himself [UCC 1-201(39)]. The UCC specifies that a signature "may be made (i) manually or by means of a device or machine, and (ii) by the use of any name, including a trade or assumed name, or by a word, mark, or symbol executed or adopted by a person with present intention to authenticate a writing" [3-401(b)].

Likewise, the signature of a duly authorized agent also satisfies this requirement. An agent's signature on behalf of her principal binds the principal and satisfies the signature requirement [UCC 3-401(b)].

A handwritten negotiable instrument satisfies the signature requirement even when no formal signature is present. The handwritten statement "I, John Smith, promise to pay Roberta Alexander, or to bearer, the sum of $20 on Tuesday July 4, 2008" would satisfy the signature

relative permanence
The quality of a negotiable instrument that ensures its longevity.

movability
The quality of a negotiable instrument that ensures it is mobile and available.

requirement because the handwriting affirms the maker's intent and, in that handwritten promise, the maker wrote his own name, John Smith.

Automated signatures, either by stamp or machine, satisfy the writing requirement as well. Even when the stamp or machine signature is fraudulently applied, such as by a person who had no authority to apply it, the signature may be valid if the maker or drawer intended that his or her name be affixed.

Unconditional Promise or Order to Pay The promise or order to pay must be specific and not implied. The language must be affirmative in nature [UCC 3-103(a)(9)]. For example, simply acknowledging a debt does not create language for payment; therefore, a common IOU is not a promise or an order to pay and thus cannot be a negotiable instrument.

The unconditional nature of the promise or order is often the controversial variable of this requirement of negotiability. Stated simply, the promise or order to pay cannot be contingent on something else's happening. An instrument stating "I promise to pay if the following occurs" is not a negotiable instrument. Remember: It may be a perfectly enforceable contract, but it fails to satisfy the terms of negotiability.

Sum Certain in Money Negotiable instruments must promise or order that payment be made in a national currency [UCC 3-104(a)]. For example, U.S. dollars, English pounds, euros, and Japanese yen all satisfy the currency requirement. Bushels of apples, gold, shares of stock, diamonds and rare gems, and the like, are not currencies. While promises to pay in apples or gold or stock may form a perfectly enforceable contract, the resulting instrument is not a negotiable instrument. An instrument promising payment in "German marks and rare French wine" would not be negotiable—even changing the *and* to an *or* would not salvage negotiability. Payment *must* be made in a currency. Case 16-1 establishes the idea that although the sum certain must be made in a currency, the specific type of currency is not relevant.

DIF BANK DEUTSCHE INVESTITIONS FINANZ GMBH v. FLUORMATIC CORPORATION OF AMERICA

U.S. DISTRICT COURT, NORTHERN DISTRICT OF ILLINOIS, EASTERN DIVISION

1991 U.S. Dist. LEXIS 520

FACTS: *DIF Bank is a company organized under the laws of the Federal Republic of Germany and is engaged in the business of banking. Fluormatic is a Delaware corporation with its principal place of business in Villa Park, Illinois. Multimatic Maschinen GmbH & Co. is a company organized under the laws of the Federal Republic of Germany and engaged in the manufacture of dry-cleaning equipment. Fluormatic is in the business of distributing and servicing dry-cleaning equipment. Multimatic and Fluormatic are both owned by Mr. H. F. Gustav Koetter.*

Between May 9, 1981, and July 11, 1986, Fluormatic regularly purchased dry-cleaning equipment from Multimatic. Fluormatic generally paid for the equipment either by promissory notes made payable to Multimatic in U.S.

dollars or by endorsing drafts in deutsche marks drawn by Multimatic. Two promissory notes and six drafts are at controversy here. Multimatic received the notes and drafts from Fluormatic and discounted them to DIF Bank, which credited funds to Multimatic. DIF Bank presented the notes and drafts on their due dates, and payment was not made. DIF Bank gave Fluormatic notice of the dishonor, and the drafts were duly protested. DIF Bank brought a two-count complaint against Fluormatic for recovery on the instruments.

In the judge's words:

> *Fluormatic . . . argues that the drafts are not negotiable because they are not payable in a "sum certain" as required by paragraphs 3-104 and 3-106 of the Code. Ill. Rev. Stat. ch. 26, paras.*

3-104 and 3-106 (1961). The drafts, while payable in German deutsche marks, do not specify an exchange rate. The failure to include an exchange rate, Fluormatic contends, requires the conclusion that the drafts are not payable in "a sum certain" as required under the Code.

ISSUE: Is a draft negotiable if it is not payable in a sum certain?

REASONING: Section 3-107(2) of the UCC provides:

(2) A promise or order to pay a sum stated in a foreign currency is for a *sum certain in money* and, unless a different medium of payment is specified in the instrument, may be satisfied by

payment of that number of dollars which the stated foreign currency will purchase at the buying sight rate for that currency on the day on which the instrument is payable or, if payable on demand, on the day of demand. If such an instrument specifies a foreign currency as the medium of payment the instrument is payable in that currency. [emphasis added]

DECISION AND REMEDY: The judge overruled Fluormatic's objection, finding for the plaintiff.

SIGNIFICANCE OF THE CASE: By basing its decision on the clear intent of Section 3-107(2), the court is avoiding a possible obstruction to foreign trade.

CRITICAL THINKING

Why was the evidence provided by Fluormatic unacceptable? What conditions would the company have had to have met for its argument to be seen as acceptable to the court?

ETHICAL DECISION MAKING

Fluormatic's defense in this case was not strong. What values would have led the company to choose to settle the matter with DIF Bank rather than try the issue in court?

Payable at a Time Certain or on Demand A negotiable instrument must be payable on demand or at a specific time that can be computed from the instrument itself. Obviously, if the instrument states a specific date, the instrument has stated a time certain. If the instrument is dated and then states that "payment will be made 10 days after above date," the instrument is negotiable because the specific date can be calculated. A dated instrument stating that "payment is to be made at some future time after the above date" is clearly nonnegotiable (although, again, it may be enforceable as a contract).

Likewise, an instrument that states that "payment will be made 10 days after delivery of the goods" but indicates nowhere in the instrument when delivery is to be made is not a negotiable instrument. (It might also be nonnegotiable if such a reference is construed to be a condition of payment as well.)

Demand instruments, such as checks, are payable as soon as they are issued. If an instrument is silent as to the time of payment, the UCC presumes that it is a demand instrument and thus it retains its negotiable status [3-108(a)].

Words of Negotiability Finally, for an instrument to be negotiable, the instrument must indicate that it was created for the purpose of being transferred. How can an instrument, or better yet its maker or drawer, indicate this purpose? It can do so by having the phrase "to the order of" near the payee's name. When a specific payee is named, this is known as an *order* instrument [UCC 3-109(b)]. For the maker or drawer to indicate that she anticipates the instrument she is creating will be circulated, she writes the phrase *to the order of* and then the name of the payee, or some variation of that wording. Examples of order negotiable-instrument language are "Pay to the order of Jim Smith" and "Pay to Jim Smith or his order."

Negotiable instruments payable to whomever is bearing them are known as *bearer instruments* [UCC 3-109(a)]. Bearer instruments are treated like cash. Accordingly, one who comes into possession of a bearer instrument by any means, including theft, may claim the payment due

LO 16-4

The End of the Float?

Consumers who rely on "float" (the time it takes for a check to go through the traditional check-clearing process) have a limited amount of time to enjoy the delayed payment afforded by the process. Businesses in many parts of the country are testing new technology that speeds up the check-clearing process. Soon, float might be an outdated tradition.

In Nevada, for instance, Nevada State Bank allows businesses that purchase a special service to scan checks, send them electronically, and get money for checks drawn on other banks much more quickly; the delay in check processing is cut by 40 percent. Other banks are testing similar products and services. In some states, businesses are substituting electronic images of checks for the checks themselves. Here's how the process works: (1) A customer gives a business a check in payment for a product or service, (2) the business scans the check and sends it to the bank providing the new check-clearing products and services, (3) the bank sends the image to the customer's bank, (4) the customer's bank prints a substitute check, and, quickly, (5) the customer's payment is deposited in the business's account at that business's bank.

It remains to be seen what kinds of litigation will emerge from this expedited process.

on the instrument. Also, endorsing an order instrument, such as a check, converts the instrument into a bearer instrument that may be claimed by anyone in possession of it. Instruments payable to no one, to "X," or to "cash" are also considered bearer instruments.

The phrase *to the order of* is then necessary to create a negotiable instrument. Wordings such as "Pay to bearer," "Pay to Jim Smith or bearer," "Pay to cash," and "Pay to the order of cash [or bearer]" would all result in the paper's being negotiable.

Once the six elements of negotiability are satisfied, the instrument created is indeed negotiable.

Negotiation

One important characteristic of negotiable instruments is the ease associated with transferring the instrument to a third party. Once a negotiable instrument is created, it can be transferred to another party through negotiation. **Negotiation** is the transfer of possession to a third party, who becomes the holder of the negotiable instrument (UCC Section 3-201). A party who possesses a negotiable instrument payable to the party or to the bearer of the instrument is a **holder** of the instrument [UCC 1-201(b)(21)].

When the rights to a negotiable instrument are transferred from one party to another, such a transfer is called a *negotiation.* It is important to understand that the rules of negotiation differ slightly depending on whether the instrument is an **order instrument** (i.e., an instrument payable to a specific, named payee) or a **bearer instrument** (an instrument payable to cash or to whoever is in possession of the instrument) (UCC 3-109). Bearer paper requires only a delivery of the instrument to the holder by the payee. In contrast, order paper requires delivery *and* an endorsement.

DELIVERY

Delivery simply requires the physical handing of an instrument from the person who is entitled to it to the person who is intended to receive it. Thus, a bearer instrument that falls out a window, blown off someone's desk by the wind, and lands in someone else's hand has not been properly negotiated. This lucky person cannot legally demand payment of that instrument because she is not a proper holder. However, she could pass it on to someone who could legally collect on it.

Drawers must be careful when delivering an instrument because if the drawer is negligent in how he or she makes the delivery, the drawer may be liable for notes paid with forged or unauthorized endorsements. For example, if the drawer of a check mails the check to the wrong business, the drawer may be liable for the amount of the check when the wrong business cashes the check.

negotiation
The transferring of the rights to a negotiable instrument from one party to another.

holder
A party in possession of a negotiable instrument.

order instrument
An instrument payable to a specific, named payee.

bearer instrument
An instrument payable to cash or to whoever is in possession of the instrument.

Negotiable Instruments in the Commonwealth

The law of negotiable instruments has its origins in English law. In the 14th century, merchants created the use of the draft, or bill of exchange, so that they could conduct business transactions without transporting large sums of money. Since 1882, negotiable-instrument transactions in England have been governed by the Bills of Exchange Act. It served as a model for the National Conference of Commissioners on Uniform State Laws (NCCUSL), which promulgated the Uniform Negotiable Instruments Law (NIL) in 1896. Subsequently, all of the U.S. states adopted the law by 1924, and the law of negotiable instruments and bank collections was revised and modernized through Articles 3 and 4 of the Uniform Commercial Code.

In the Commonwealth of Nations (formerly referred to as the British Commonwealth), almost all member states have codified their laws relating to negotiable instruments in Bills of Exchange acts, just as the United States used the original act when drafting its own negotiable-instrument laws. Notice the similarities between the UCC's regulations regarding negotiable instruments and the Bills of Exchange Act of England. The Bills of Exchange Act:

1. Defines a bill of exchange as "an unconditional order in writing, addressed by one person to another, signed by the person giving it, requiring the person to whom it is addressed to pay on demand, or at a fixed or determinable future time, a sum certain in money to or to the order of a specified person, or to bearer."

2. Defines a check as "a bill of exchange drawn on a banker payable on demand."

3. Defines a promissory note as "an unconditional promise in writing made by one person to another, signed by the maker, engaging to pay on demand, or at a fixed or determinable future time, a sum certain in money to or to the order of a specified person or to bearer."

ENDORSEMENT

Order paper must be *endorsed* as well as *delivered* to be negotiated. The person creating the endorsement is the **endorser,** and the person receiving the endorsement is the **endorsee.** Normally, there is a place on the negotiable instrument for endorsements (such as on the back of a check). If there is no room on the instrument or if all the room has been taken by previous endorsements, an **allonge** may be attached. An allonge is simply an additional piece of paper with the endorsements. It must be firmly attached (staples usually work; paper clips do not) [UCC 3-204(a)]. There are three kinds of endorsements that will affect the legal status of the negotiable instrument in different ways: unqualified, qualified, and restrictive endorsements.

Unqualified Endorsements: Blank and Special Endorsements There are two kinds of unqualified endorsements: blank and special. A **blank endorsement** is simply the payee's or last endorsee's signature, nothing else [UCC 3-205(b)]. The effect of this unqualified blank endorsement is that it turns an order paper into a bearer paper. An instrument with an unqualified blank endorsement may be negotiated by delivery only. A **special endorsement** consists of the signature of the endorser together with a named endorsee. An illustration would be "Pay to Jackie Jones" followed by the endorser's signature.

Note that in an endorsement, the words of negotiability, *to the order of,* are not needed. The instrument remains negotiable. However, adding those words keeps order paper as order paper and thus continues to require an endorsement and delivery for further negotiation.

NONCRIMINAL ENDORSEMENT PROBLEMS

In situations involving fraud or forgery, it should come as no surprise that problems with endorsements exist. These criminal endorsement issues are examined later in this chapter. However, even in situations not involving criminal offenses, endorsement problems may arise. We consider these problems below.

Misspelled Name One problem with endorsements occurs when a negotiable instrument contains a misspelled name. In the event of a misspelled name, the holder may endorse the document with the misspelled name, the holder's actual name, or both. The typical practice is for the holder

endorser
One who issues an endorsement.

endorsee
One who receives an endorsement.

allonge
Accompanying a negotiable instrument, a piece of paper that provides room for an endorsement if no room is available on the instrument itself.

blank endorsement
A payee's or last endorsee's signature on a negotiable instrument.

special endorsement
An endorser's signature accompanied by the name of the endorsee.

to endorse the instrument with the misspelled name followed by the holder's actual name, spelled properly.

Payable to a Legal Entity Another complication regarding endorsements involves instruments made payable to a legal entity. If the legal entity is an estate, organization, partnership, or the like, the instrument may be endorsed by any authorized representative of the entity. A variation of the same problem occurs when instruments are made payable to a public office. In such an event, the person holding the office may endorse the instrument. For example, when filing her local taxes, Sarah, not knowing whom to make her check payable to, filled in "pay to the order of County Tax Collector." Bill Deepockets, the county tax collector, may endorse the check, as he is the person currently holding the office listed on the check.

Alternative or Joint Payees A third endorsement problem arises when a negotiable instrument has been made payable to more than one person. Two possibilities arise when the instrument is payable to more than one person. The first possibility is that there are *alternative payees.* When the instrument reads "Pay to the order of Jones *or* Smith," the instrument contains alternative payees. In the event of alternative payees, the endorsement of any one of the listed payees is sufficient.

The second possibility is that there are *joint payees.* Joint payees exist when an instrument lists more than one person as a payee and the instrument is to be payable to *all* the listed payees, typically indicated by the word *and.* In the event of joint payees, the instrument would read "Pay to the order of Smith *and* Jones." Instruments bearing joint payees require the endorsement of all listed payees before the instrument may be negotiated.

Courts have held that when an instrument is silent as to the issue of whether the listed payees are joint or alternative, the instrument is to be interpreted as containing alternative payees. That is, when an instrument does not specify whether the payees are joint or alternative, the endorsement of only one listed payee is required to negotiate the instrument. The next Case Nugget illustrates a situation in which the check was silent on the issue of whether the payees were joint or alternative and the court interpreted the ambiguity as containing alternative payees.

This case illustrates how it is particularly important in cases where there are multiple payees for a negotiable instrument to be clear and explicit. By being less ambiguous, businesses attempt to avoid endorsement problems that arise when a negotiable instrument has been made payable to more than one person.

Banking

So far, this chapter has explained what a negotiable instrument is, how a negotiable instrument is transferred, and some of the problems associated with negotiable instruments. The following sections discuss the negotiable instruments with which you are probably most familiar: checks. You have most likely written, cashed, and deposited checks; but, as you may have guessed, your relationship with the bank is more complicated than you originally thought.

When you open an account at a bank, you create a contractual relationship with the bank. This relationship is governed by Article 4 of the UCC. Within this relationship, both you, as the customer, and the bank have certain rights and duties. For example, you have the right to order a stop payment on a check for any or no reason. The corresponding duty of the bank is to follow this order.

As we explained earlier in this chapter, checks are considered negotiable instruments under Article 3 of the UCC. However, Article 4 of the UCC is also relevant; this section of the UCC governs the transfer of checks between banks. Thus, both Article 3 and Article 4 are relevant to this chapter.

Article 3 of the UCC outlines the requirements that negotiable instruments, including checks, must meet. Article 3 also establishes the rights and responsibilities pertaining to parties to negotiable instruments. Article 4 creates a framework controlling deposit and checking agreements between banks and customers. In addition, Article 4 directs the relationships between banks as

CASE Nugget

Check with Slash Mark between Payees' Names

New Wave Technologies, Inc. v. Legacy Bank of Texas
U.S. Court of Appeals of Texas, Eighth District

WL 2553519, Ct. App. Tex. (2008)

Maxim Solutions Group, Inc., and New Wave Technologies entered into a joint purchase agreement under which New Wave would sell computer equipment to Maxim and afterward Maxim would sell it to United Services Automobile Association (USAA). On July 7, 2004, USAA ordered scanners and computer equipment from Maxim/New Wave. The two purchase orders were supposed to be paid from USAA directly to New Wave via negotiable instrument. However, USAA mailed the checks to Maxim instead of New Wave.

The checks were made payable to "Maxim Solutions Group/New Wave Techn" for $134,656.16 and $52,558.73, respectively. The back of each check stated, "Each Payee Must Endorse Exactly As Drawn." The checks were received by the president of Maxim, after Maxim had gone out of business, and were subsequently deposited in Maxim's bank account. The checks were accepted for deposit by a teller at Legacy Bank of Texas. Each check had only Maxim's account number as an endorsement written on the back. The checks were not endorsed at all by the other payee, "New Wave Techn." Legacy Bank cashed the checks anyway and argued that it did not convert the checks since both Maxim and New Wave were alternative payees by law.

In the opinion written by Judge David Chew, the Texas Court of Appeals determined that the bank was not liable for conversion because the "payable to" line with multiple payees and a slash mark was ambiguous under Texas Business and Commerce Code Ann. § 3.110(d) (2002). The front of the check used a slash mark, which was interpreted to mean "or." Furthermore, the printed instructions on the back of the check only increased the ambiguity. Due to this ambiguity, the instruments were payable alternatively. Therefore, the bank did not take the instruments from a person not entitled to enforce them.

checks are processed among different banks. Moreover, according to UCC Section 4-102(a), when conflicts arise between rules in Articles 3 and 4, Article 4 is to take precedence.

In 2003, Americans wrote approximately 70 billion checks. Clearly, checks are an enormous part of the bank-customer relationship. In fact, of all the negotiable instruments regulated by the UCC, checks are the most common type used. Thus, we begin our discussion of banking by taking a closer look at different types of checks. Then we examine the process of check collection: If the bank accepts a check, how is the money from one account actually transferred to another account? Next, we consider when a bank may charge a customer's account in the context of potential problems with checks, such as stale, postdated, and forged checks. Finally, we turn to an increasingly important element of the banking process: the electronic transfer of funds.

Checks LO 16-5

Although you have likely written a check, do you know what the actual characteristics of checks are? (The key terms and an illustration are provided in Exhibit 16-1 and Figure 16-3.) According to the UCC, a check is a special kind of draft. A *draft* is an instrument that is an order. Three

drawer
The party that writes an order or the person who writes a check.

drawee
The party that must obey an order. In the context of banking, the drawee is the bank that must pay the funds ordered by a customer's check.

payee
The party that receives the benefit of an order (check, etc.).

LO 16-6

cashier's check
A check for which both drawer and drawee are the same bank.

traveler's check
An order that is payable on demand, is drawn on or through a bank, is designated by the phrase *traveler's check,* and requires a counter-signature by the person whose signature appears on the check.

parties are related to this order. First, a **drawer** is the party that gives the order. Second, a **drawee** is the party that must obey the order. For example, in Figure 16-3, the bank is the drawee. Finally, the **payee** is the party that receives the benefit of the order. Thus, when you write a check at the grocery store, you are the drawer ordering the drawee (your bank) to make a payment to the payee (the grocery store).

A *check* is a special draft that orders the drawee, a bank, to pay a fixed amount of money on demand [UCC Section 3-104(f)]. The UCC defines a bank as "any business engaged in the business of banking" [4-105(1)]. Consequently, savings banks, savings and loans, credit unions, and trust companies are all considered banks. The drawer of a check writes the check and thus orders the bank to pay. The payee is the party to whom the check is written.

CASHIER'S CHECKS

A **cashier's check** is a check for which both the drawer and the drawee are the same bank [UCC 3-104(g)]. (See Figure 16-4 for an example.) The payee of the check is a specific person. In other words, the bank is drawing on itself and thus assumes the responsibility for paying the check to that specific person. Customers often purchase cashier's checks to give to creditors who want to be sure the funds represented by the check are available. Cashier's checks are useful because they are considered by many in the business community to be the near equivalent of cash.

TRAVELER'S CHECKS

A **traveler's check** (see Figure 16-5) is an instrument that must (1) be payable on demand, (2) be drawn on or through a bank, (3) be designated by the phrase *traveler's check,* and (4) be countersigned by the person whose signature appears on the instrument [UCC 3-104(i)]. The drawer of a traveler's check is usually a large financial organization, such as American Express. The person who signs the traveler's check must sign it when she buys the checks; then, when she is ready to use the traveler's check to make some kind of payment, the same person must sign the traveler's check again, in the presence of the acceptor.

Exhibit 16-1

Key Terms for Checks

Draft	An instrument whereby one party orders a second party to pay an amount of money to the party listed on the instrument. A check is a draft in which the bank is the drawee.
Drawer	The party giving the order to pay on a draft.
Drawee	The party ordered to pay on a draft.
Payee	The party receiving the money from the draft.

Figure 16-3

A Check

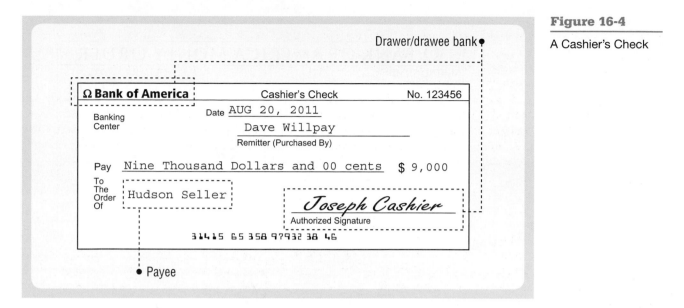

Figure 16-4

A Cashier's Check

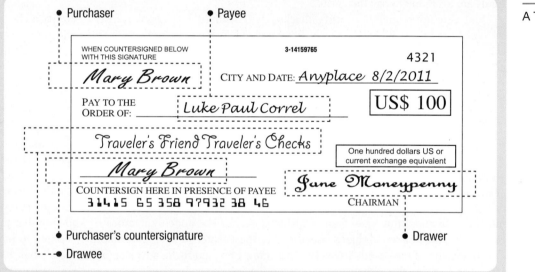

Figure 16-5

A Traveler's Check

MONEY ORDERS

Money orders (see Figure 16-6), particularly personal money orders, are usually in the same form as personal checks and are considered checks under UCC Section 3-104. Both banks and nonbanks sell money orders. The money order states that a certain amount of money is to be paid to a particular person. The amount of money to be paid is usually already imprinted on the money order. The person purchasing the money signs the money order as the drawer and fills in the name of the person who is to receive the money.

CERTIFIED CHECKS

A **certified check** is a check that is accepted at the bank at which it is drawn [UCC 3-409(d)]. For example, suppose Hope writes a check to Jeremiah from her account at Citizens National Bank (CNB). Hope asks CNB to certify her check. CNB then accepts the check, withdraws the money from Hope's account, and places that money in its certified-check account. CNB then signs or

certified check

A check that is accepted by the bank from which the funds are drawn.

Figure 16-6

A Money Order

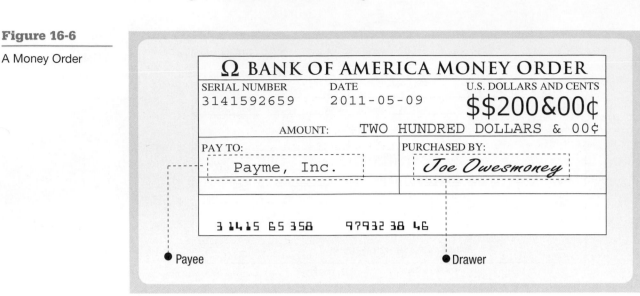

stamps the face of the check to indicate that it is certified. In other words, CNB is promising that funds are available to pay the check.

Banks are not required to certify checks [UCC 3-409(d)]. If a bank refuses to certify a check, the check is not considered dishonored; it merely lacks the extra protection of certification. However, once the bank does certify a check, the drawer of the check is no longer liable for the amount of the check [UCC 3-414(c)]. The bank has become primarily liable for the check.

WHY USE CASHIER'S OR CERTIFIED CHECKS?

There are a number of reasons to use a cashier's or certified check as opposed to a regular check when conducting business exchanges. While all of these types of drafts are different, one thing they have in common is an increased guarantee of being paid. That is, a cashier's or certified check is less likely to be denied by a bank.

Cashier's checks are a valuable business tool because the bank, and not the individual, is the drawer as well as the drawee. When a cashier's check is presented for payment, the bank, and not the individual, must pay for the cashier's check. The added guarantee of knowing that the bank is paying for the cashier's check makes the cashier's check a veritable guarantee to pay. One downside of the cashier's check is that it must be paid for in advance, including a small fee. However, because the cashier's check is paid for first, it can be purchased at any bank, regardless of whether one has an account at the bank.

Certified checks are useful in business because when a bank certifies a check, it essentially says that it cannot refuse liability on the check. A certified check is one the bank sets aside money for and agrees to pay when the certified check is presented. Despite the added guarantee, there are two main drawbacks to a certified check. The first is that a person must have an account at a specific bank to obtain a certified check. If the person does not have an account at the bank, he or she cannot obtain a certified check from that bank.

The second drawback is that banks do not have to certify checks. Banks may refuse to certify any check for any reason. Refusing to certify is not the same as dishonoring a check, but it does not provide the same guarantee that a certified check provides. While banks do not have to certify a check, they are not allowed to refuse to sell a cashier's check, as long as the payment is valid.

LOST, STOLEN, OR DESTROYED CASHIER'S OR CERTIFIED CHECKS

In the event a cashier's or certified check is lost, stolen, or destroyed, the UCC allows for recovery. According to UCC Section 3-312, the remitter (the party who purchased the check) or the payee may request a refund because the check was lost, stolen, or destroyed. With proper identification, the party should be able to obtain a full refund for the amount on the check.

The claim is enforceable at the later of (1) the time the claim is made, or (2) the 90th day following the date on the check if it is a cashier's check. For a certified check, it is enforceable at the later of (1) when the claim is made, or (2) the 90th day following the date of the acceptance of the check [UCC 3-312(b)(1)]. After the claim becomes enforceable, if no one presented the check for payment, a refund is issued and the bank is discharged of liability [UCC 3-312(b)(4)]. When a claim is made, the person making the claim warrants to the bank and any party who has an interest in the check that the check was really lost, stolen, or destroyed.

If the check was not lost, stolen, or destroyed, the holder barred from receiving payment on the check because of the claim may sue the person who made the claim for breach of warranty. A person filing a false claim is also subject to criminal penalties.

Accepting Deposits

LO 16-7

Charging a customer's account is only part of the bank-customer relationship; the bank must also credit a customer's account when the customer makes cash and check deposits to her account. This section considers the check collection process and examines several issues that focus on the availability of deposited money.

THE CHECK COLLECTION PROCESS

Suppose Jack Blackstone gives Molly Whetfield a check to pay her for her consulting services. When Molly deposits that check into her account, how does the money from Jack's account actually get transferred into Molly's account? This section considers the check collection process (see Figure 16-7) and examines several issues regarding deposits made to banks.

Check Collection within the Same Bank Sometimes the depositary bank is the same bank as the payor bank. When this is the case, the check is referred to as an "on-us item." For example, suppose Molly's and Jack's accounts are at the same bank. When Molly deposits Jack's check into her account, the check does not have to be sent to another bank because she and Jack share the same bank. Instead, the bank gives a "provisional" credit to Molly's account. If this bank does not

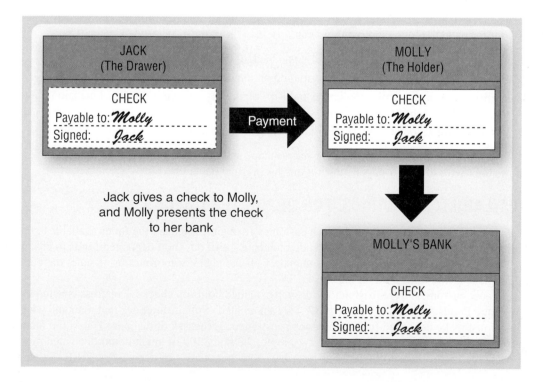

Figure 16-7

Illustration of the Check Collection Process

dishonor the check on the second day, the check is paid [UCC Section 4-215(e)(2)]. Finally, on the third day, the provisional credit becomes an actual payment.

Check Collection between Different Banks Suppose that Jack and Molly have accounts at different banks. Molly's account is in Los Angeles, while Jack's account is in Miami. When Molly deposits Jack's check at her bank in Los Angeles, her bank is the depositary bank. When a depositary bank receives a check, it must present the check at the payor bank or send it through intermediary banks to reach the payor bank. Once a bank receives a check, it must pass the check on before midnight of the next day [UCC 4-202(b)]. When the check finally reaches the payor bank, the payor bank must respond to the check by dishonoring it or becoming liable for the face amount of the check (UCC 4-302).

The UCC allows banks to establish cutoff hours for making entries on their books. For example, a bank may determine that 2 p.m. or later is the cutoff hour for handling checks (UCC 4-108). If the bank receives a check after this deadline, the bank will defer posting this check to its customer's account until the next day.

ELECTRONIC CHECK PRESENTMENT

In the past, checks were physically presented to each bank in the chain of collection. Now, checks are transmitted electronically from bank to bank (UCC 4-110). Through electronic check presentment, a check can be processed on the day on which it is deposited. An item is encoded with information that is transferred from one bank's computer to another bank's computer. The person who enters the information into the computer (i.e., encodes the information) warrants that the information is correct (UCC 4-209). Alternatively, the image of a check may be transmitted for payment to other banks.

Substitute Checks To help facilitate electronic presentment, in 2004 Congress passed the *Check Clearing for the 21st Century Act* (also known as *Check 21* or the *Check Truncation Act*). Check 21 allows banks to forgo sending original checks as part of the collection or return process and instead send a truncated version. In place of the original paper check, a bank may send (1) a substitute check or (2) by agreement, an electronic image of the check along with data from the magnetic ink character recognition (MICR) line on the original check.

A substitute check is similar to the electronic image that may be sent in lieu of the original paper check. Check 21 defines a *substitute check* as a paper reproduction of the original check that conforms to the following requirements:

1. Contains a clear replication of the front and back of the original paper check.
2. Bears an MICR line with all the information on the original check's MICR line.
3. Conforms with generally applicable industry standards for paper stock, dimensions, and other general qualities.
4. Is suitable for automated processing in the same manner as the original paper check.

Check 21 provides the guidelines for the issuance and use of substitute checks. The act also allows the use of digital or paper substitutions for original paper checks.

AVAILABILITY SCHEDULE FOR DEPOSITED CHECKS

Once a check is considered deposited in a customer's account, when are the funds available to the customer? In the past, banks placed extended holds (e.g., 10 days) on deposited funds to ensure that the payor bank would not dishonor the check. If the check was from out of state, the bank might place a two-week hold on the check.

Because customers were frustrated with such extended holds on checks, Congress enacted the Expedited Funds Availability Act of 1987. This act created explicit timelines that mandate when banks must make deposited funds available to customers. If the risk of dishonor is low, the funds must be made available very quickly. For example, the first $100 of any amount deposited must be available to the depositor on the business day following the day of deposit [12 C.F.R. Section

229.10(a)–(c)]. The availability of the rest of the funds depends on whether the check is local, what the amount of the check is, and how the depositor wants to withdraw the funds.

1. If the deposited check is drawn on a bank within the same Federal Reserve Bank area, the depositary bank must make the deposited funds available to the customer on the second business day following the deposit day [12 C.F.R. 229.10(b)].
2. If the deposited check is outside the same Federal Reserve Bank area, the depositary bank must make the funds available on the fifth business day following the day of deposit [12 C.F.R. 229.12(c)].

THE TRUTH-IN-SAVINGS ACT

In an effort to allow consumers to be better informed, Congress passed the Truth-in-Savings Act (TISA) in 1991. TISA requires that depositary institutions disclose, in great detail, the terms and conditions of their accounts. Depositary institutions include commercial banks, savings banks, credit unions, and savings and loan associations.

TISA requires that every bank inform its customers of a number of specific pieces of information relevant to the bank's accounts. This information is to be handed to the customer as a pamphlet, brochure, or handout before the customer opens a deposit account. The information that must be given to the customer includes:

1. The minimum balance required to open an account and to be paid interest.
2. The manner in which the balance of the account will be calculated.
3. The annual percentage yield of interest for the account.
4. The way interest on the account will be calculated.
5. Notification of any fees, charges, and penalties the account may be assessed and how they are calculated.
6. Notification of any limitations on withdrawals or deposits.

Furthermore, TISA and Regulation DD, which serves as the act's implementing regulation, require that banks pay interest based on the full balance of interest-bearing accounts daily. The requirement prevents banks from calculating interest on an account when the account is at its lowest balance.

When a Bank May Charge a Customer's Account

LO 16-8

The following sections consider certain problems related to a bank's accepting and paying a customer's check.

WRONGFUL DISHONOR

When a customer opens a checking account, both the customer and the bank accept certain duties and rights. Generally, the customer assumes a duty to keep sufficient funds in her account to cover the checks written on her account. If the customer does not have enough funds to cover a check, the bank will dishonor the check and the customer becomes liable for the amount of the check.

Similarly, under the *properly payable rule,* the bank has a duty to pay checks from the customer's account as long as the checks are "properly payable" [UCC Section 4-401(a)]. In other words, a check must be authorized by the drawer and must not violate agreement between the bank and the customer. Generally, for a check to be considered properly payable, it must:

1. Have the drawer's authorized signature on the check.
2. Be paid to a person entitled to enforce the check.

3. Not have been altered.

4. Not have been completed by addition of unauthorized terms if the check was incomplete.

5. Be paid on or after the date of the check.

6. Not be subject to a stop payment from the drawer.

If the bank wrongfully fails to pay a check—wrongfully dishonoring the check—the bank may be liable to the customer for damages. The UCC clearly states that banks can be held liable, but it does not cite a specific theory for recovery. Therefore, someone whose check was dishonored need prove only that the dishonoring was wrongful, and he or she will be entitled to recovery. Case 16-2 provides an example of the damages a customer may potentially recover from a bank for wrongful dishonor.

CASE 16-2

THE TWIN CITY BANK v. KENNETH ISAACS
SUPREME COURT OF ARKANSAS
672 S.W.2d 651 (1984)

FACTS: *The Issacs discovered their checkbook was missing on Sunday, May 13, 1979. They promptly reported the loss to Twin City Bank the next day. They learned that two checks totaling $2,050 had been forged and charged to their account. When they reported the lost checkbook, their account balance was approximately $2,000.*

Because Mr. Issacs had been previously convicted of burglary, the bank thought he might be involved with the forgeries. Thus, the bank froze the Isaacses' account. However, the individual who forged the checks was discovered and convicted at the end of May 1979. The police notified the bank that there was no evidence to connect the Isaacs to the forgeries. Yet the bank continued to keep the account frozen. The Isaacs filed suit for wrongful dishonor in June 1979. Their account was kept frozen for the next four years.

At trial, the jury awarded the Isaacs $18,500 in compensatory damages and $45,000 in punitive damages. The bank appealed. The appellate judge noted:

> On the issue of damages, the bank maintains there was insufficient evidence to support the $18,500 award for mental anguish, for loss of credit and loss of the bargain on a house, that the award of punitive damages should not have been given at all as there was not only insufficient proof of actual damages but insufficient evidence of malice or intent to oppress on the part of the bank.

ISSUE: When is a bank that wrongfully dishonors the checks of an account holder liable for damages to the account holder?

REASONING: In the court's own words:

> The bank does not challenge the sufficiency of the evidence of its wrongful dishonor, but contends only that there was no evidence to support an award of damages. These arguments cannot be sustained.

The statute upon which this suit was based is Ark. Stat. Ann. § 85-4-402:

> Bank's liability to customer for wrongful dishonor—A payor bank is liable to its customer for damages proximately caused by the wrongful dishonor of an item.

The jury was instructed that if they found the bank liable they were to fix the amount of money which would compensate the Isaacs "for any of the following elements of damage sustained which were proximately caused by the conduct of Twin City Bank: 1) Any amounts of money wrongfully held by the defendant and remaining unpaid, 2) any mental anguish and embarrassment suffered by the plaintiffs, 3) any financial losses sustained by the [Isaacs]."

Initially, there can be no serious question as to certain losses: the $2,000 wrongfully withheld by the bank for four years, and the value of two vehicles repossessed because the Isaacs did not have access to their funds, resulting in a loss of approximately $2,200. Additionally, after the account was frozen, the bank continued to charge the account a service charge and overdraft fees on checks written before the forgeries but presented after the account was frozen. . . .

Decisions upholding recovery for mental suffering under the code have found injury resulting from circumstances comparable to this case. In *North Shore Bank* v. *Palmer* for example, a $275 forged check was paid from Palmer's account. After the bank knew or should have known the check was forged, it charged Palmer with the $275 check and later wrongfully dishonored other checks. Part of the actual damages awarded was attributed to mental suffering for the "embarrassment and humiliation Palmer suffered from having been turned down for credit for the first time in his life." . . .

In this case, prior to the forgery incident the Isaacs' credit reputation with Twin City Bank was described by the bank as "impeccable" and the freezing of their funds had a traumatic effect on their lives. They obviously lost their credit

standing with Twin City, and were unable to secure credit commercially at other institutions because of their status at Twin City. The Isaacs had to borrow from friends and family, and were left in a precarious position financially. They did not have use of their $2,000 for four years. The allegation relative to the loss of a house resulted from the dishonor of an earnest money check for a home they were planning to buy, ending prospects for the purchase at that time. . . . Finally, the Isaacs lost equities in two vehicles repossessed as a result of the withholding of their funds.

DECISION AND REMEDY: The court found that in addition to the losses mentioned above, there was sufficient evidence to sustain damages for mental suffering and loss of credit, as well as sufficient demonstration of some loss attributable to the inability to pursue the purchase of a home. The judge affirmed for the plaintiff.

SIGNIFICANCE OF THE CASE: A bank that wrongfully dishonors a check of an account holder is liable for (1) any amounts of money wrongfully held by the bank and remaining unpaid, (2) any mental anguish and embarrassment suffered by the account holder, and (3) any financial losses sustained by the account holder.

CRITICAL THINKING

The judge uses *North Shore Bank* to make an analogy with the Isaacses' case. Do you think this analogy is effective?

ETHICAL DECISION MAKING

Return to the WPH framework. Suppose you are the bank manager who decided to keep a freeze on the Isaacses' funds for four years. If your actions are guided by the public disclosure test, would you have behaved differently?

STOP-PAYMENT ORDER

A customer can issue a **stop-payment order,** an order by a drawer that instructs the drawee bank not to pay a check that has been drawn on the customer's account (UCC 4-403). A customer issues a stop-payment order when he has issued a check that has not yet been accepted and he wants the check not to be accepted. If the bank pays a check in violation of a stop-payment order, the bank will incur liability for the damages suffered by the customer due to its violation of the stop payment [UCC 4-403(b)].

To be effective, the stop order must meet two requirements: (1) The customer must give the order in a reasonable time, and (2) the customer must describe the item with "reasonable certainty" [UCC 4-403(a)]. For example, the stop-payment order must be given promptly so that the bank has enough time to inform its tellers and other employees that they should not pay the check. Moreover, the UCC states that the stop-payment order must reach the bank by a certain cutoff time. Generally, the stop-payment order should list (1) the date of the check, (2) the name of the payee, (3) the amount of the check, (4) the number of the check, and (5) the checking account number.

stop-payment order
An order by a drawer that instructs the drawee bank not to pay an issued check.

POSTDATED CHECKS

Under previous versions of Articles 3 and 4 of the UCC, a check could not be charged to a customer's account until the date of the check. Thus, some customers attempted to hold off payment on a check by postdating the check and giving it to the payee. However, because banks generally use an automated system to process checks, checks are now frequently paid without regard to the date. If a bank pays a check before its date and thus depletes a customer's account, the bank could be liable to the customer for damages. Thus, some banks include certain clauses in their customer agreements that state they may pay checks regardless of the date.

The UCC presents a middle ground that protects a bank from liability while permitting customers to postdate checks. Section 4-401(c) states that customers can postdate checks but they must give the bank notice of the postdated check. Therefore, the bank can assume that it can pay all checks on presentment unless the bank has received notice. Most banks charge a processing fee for notice of a postdated check.

STALE CHECKS

If a check is not presented to a bank within six months of its date, the check is considered a stale check. Banks are not required to honor stale checks.

FORGERIES AND ALTERATIONS

In 1999, attempted check fraud in the United States rose to approximately $2.2 billion, while merchants and banks suffered actual losses approximating $679 million through check fraud. Thus, banks are clearly concerned about the acceptance of altered or forged checks.

Checks Bearing Forged Signatures Under the properly payable rule, the bank may pay a check only if it is authorized by the customer. Who is liable if a bank cashes a check signed by an unauthorized person? In other words, what happens when someone forges a drawer's signature on a check?

The UCC has established that a forged signature has no legal effect as a signature of the drawer [3-403(a)]. Consequently, in most cases, if a bank pays a check when the drawer's signature has been forged, the bank will be liable for the amount of the check.

However, there are some exceptions to this rule. First, if the customer's negligence substantially contributed to a forged signature and the bank pays the check in good faith, the bank is not required to repay the customer [UCC 3-406(a)]. For example, if the customer is an employer who keeps a rubber stamp of his signature in an unlocked drawer, and an employee uses the signature stamp to create a check payable to herself, the customer has substantially contributed to the forged signature and will likely not be able to recover the amount of the check.

Another exception to the forgery liability rule is related to the customer's duty to examine his or her bank statement. Banks make a customer's statement available to the customer approximately once a month. This statement lists or includes all the checks that have been charged against the customer's account over the past month. A customer must examine her bank statement reasonably promptly for any forgeries or unauthorized payments. If the customer discovers a forgery or unauthorized payment, she must notify the bank promptly [UCC 4-406(c)]. Under the UCC, if the customer does not notify the bank of an unauthorized signature within 30 days after the statement was made available, she cannot hold the bank liable for the payment [4-406(d)]. See the following Case Nugget, where this rule was applied.

The duty to examine the bank statement is particularly important in cases where there have been multiple forgeries by the same forger, or "same wrongdoer." If a customer examines a statement and does not notify the bank of the first forgery within 30 days, the customer will be liable for future forgeries on the customer's account by the same wrongdoer.

Again, if the bank was negligent in paying the forged checks, the customer's liability for the checks may be diminished through comparative negligence [UCC 4-406(e)]. Regardless of the 30-day requirement for multiple forgeries or the care used in cashing a check, a customer must report a forgery within one year from the date the statement is available to the customer or he will lose the right to recover this money [UCC 4-406(f)].

Checks Bearing Forged Endorsements If a bank pays a check that has been fraudulently endorsed, who is responsible? In the same way that a drawer is not responsible for a check that bears the drawer's forged signature, the drawer is similarly not responsible for a check that has been fraudulently endorsed. Generally, when an endorsement has been forged, the first party to accept the forged instrument is ultimately liable for the loss because a forged endorsement does not legally transfer title [UCC 4-207(a)(2)]. However, the drawer again has a duty to examine her statement for fraudulent endorsements and then notify the bank. The drawer must report all forged endorsements within three years of receiving the returned forged items or her statement

CASE Nugget

Thirty Days to Report

Fernando Tatis v. U.S. Bancorp
U.S. Court of Appeals for the Sixth Circuit

F.3d 672 (2007)

Plaintiff-appellant Fernando Tatis, a major-league baseball player, opened several banking accounts through U.S. Bank. One of the accounts Tatis opened was a personal checking account about which he had received the terms and conditions before becoming the primary signatory for the account. When the account was initially established, Tatis asked that all bank statements be held in the bank's Professional Sports Division. The personal checks were then sent to Tatis's residence in Montreal, where an employee proceeded to take the checks and forge several of them between August and November 2001. Tatis later brought suit against the bank to recover his lost funds. The defendant contested Tatis's accusations and moved for summary judgment.

The district court granted the defendant's motion for summary judgment, and when Tatis moved for reconsideration with the district court, his motion was denied. Tatis then appealed the district court's decision to the Sixth Circuit of the U.S. Court of Appeals.

In the opinion written by Alan Sharp, the Sixth Circuit found that Tatis did not have the right to recover the funds from the bank. When the account was opened, Tatis was notified by the terms and conditions he received that he had only 30 days after the bank statements became available to report any unauthorized signatures or alterations. Although Tatis was not given the statements directly, they were made available to him and held at the location that he had requested.

By not reporting the first forgery that appeared on the first bank statement, Tatis lost rights to all subsequent funds that were taken. As a result of payments being made on the checks previously written by Tatis's employee, the bank could claim that Tatis had failed to report that the employee was not an authorized signatory on the account. Hence, even after Tatis noticed the forgeries, he was not able to recover any funds.

containing the forged items. If the drawer does not report the forgery within three years, the bank is no longer liable for that customer's loss (UCC 4-111).

Altered Checks Remember, under the properly payable rule, a bank is to pay only those checks that are authorized. When a party makes an unauthorized change or alteration to a check, the check becomes unauthorized. The UCC defines **alteration** as a change (without consent) that modifies the obligation of a party to the instrument. Generally, if a bank pays a check that has been altered, the bank will be liable for the alteration.

A customer's substantial contribution to the alteration will limit the customer's ability to require that the bank credit his or her account. In other words, if the customer leaves large blank spaces open on the check and thus another party may easily alter the check, the customer will likely be liable for the altered amount of the check. Similarly, under the UCC, any drawer who leaves the dollar amount blank may not later protest paying whatever amount has been written on the check [4-401(d)(2)].

As in the case of forged signatures, the customer's duty to examine his bank statement also applies to looking for altered checks. Thus, if the customer does not discover the altered check or does not report the altered check within a reasonable time, the bank's liability for the altered check is reduced. Similarly, if both the customer and the bank are negligent in contributing to and paying an altered check, both parties will be responsible for a portion of the check.

alteration
An unauthorized change to an instrument that modifies the obligation of a party to the instrument.

Using Technology to Fight Check Fraud

Banks rely on advances in technology to try to stay ahead of thieves who use the new technology to forge or alter checks. In 1996, Keybank experienced new account fraud in 42 percent of its demand deposit accounts. In mid-1997, Keybank started using "Early Warning," a database that is a combination of commercially available databases. Early Warning compares Social Security numbers with birth dates and compares phone numbers with zip codes. In other words, Early Warning makes it easier for financial institutions to determine whether a customer is opening an account to perpetuate a fraud. The use of Early Warning has reduced check fraud in Keybank's demand deposit accounts from 42 to 13 percent.

Source: "Industry Focus: How Banks Are Using Technology to Help Control Check Fraud," *Preventing Business Fraud,* November 1999.

Electronic Fund Transfers

CONSUMER FUND TRANSFERS

electronic fund transfer (EFT)

The transfer of funds by an electronic terminal, telephone, or computer.

Consumer fund transactions are governed by the *Electronic Fund Transfer Act (EFTA) of 1978.* This act sets out the rights and liabilities of the parties involved in **electronic fund transfers (EFTs).** Regulation E of the act allows the Federal Reserve Board to issue rules and regulations to enforce EFTA. The following transactions are considered consumer fund transactions: transactions in which a retail customer pays for an item with a debit card that allows the customer's bank account to be instantly charged, ATM transactions, and direct deposits of paychecks.

Customer and Bank Rights and Responsibilities EFTA requires that merchants inform customers of their rights regarding EFTs. First, if a customer's ATM card is lost or stolen, the customer must notify the bank within two days. The customer is then liable for only the first $50 stolen. If the customer does not notify the bank, the customer will be held liable for up to $500 that is stolen. Second, the bank has a duty to provide a monthly statement that includes electronic fund transfers, and the customer has a duty to examine this bank statement for any unauthorized electronic fund transfers or errors. Third, the customer has a duty to notify the bank of any errors in the electronic transactions within 60 days of receiving the statement. Fourth, the bank is required to provide customers with receipts for electronic transactions. Fifth, the bank must notify the customer that preauthorized payments may be stopped; however, the customer must stop the payment by notifying the bank at any time up to three days before the preauthorized payment is scheduled. While a customer may stop a preauthorized payment, a customer cannot order a stop payment on an EFT because such transfers occur instantaneously.

> To see more on an alternative to checks, direct deposit, and financial accounting, please see the **Connecting to the Core** activity on the text's website at www.mhhe.com/kubasekess2e.

Unauthorized Transfers Under EFTA, an unauthorized electronic transfer is a federal felony punishable through criminal sanctions, such as a $10,000 fine or 10-year prison sentence. An electronic transfer is unauthorized if (1) it is initiated by a person who has no authority to transfer, (2) the customer receives no benefit from the transfer, and (3) the customer did not give his personal identification number to the unauthorized party.

When banks violate EFTA, consumers may recover actual and punitive damages, with the punitive damages totaling between $100 and $1,000.

COMMERCIAL FUND TRANSFERS

Because EFTA did not cover all situations where funds may be electronically transferred, Article 4(A) of the UCC was issued to address commercial fund transfers. An important type of commercial fund transfer is a wire transfer. Funds are "wired" between two commercial parties. There are two major payment systems that coordinate wire payments: the Federal Reserve wire transfer network (Fedwire) and the New York Clearing House Interbank Payments Systems

(CHIPS). These two systems account for the transfer of more than $1 trillion daily. This sum is substantially more than is transferred by any other means.

E-Money and Online Banking

With the rapid advancements in technology, the banking system is finding itself changing rapidly. Electronic payments, or e-payments, are becoming increasingly prevalent in daily life. Increasingly, bank transactions are being conducted electronically, marking a shift away from physical currency. In fact, it is possible for electronic forms of money to completely replace physical currency such as paper and coin money. **Digital cash,** money stored electronically on microchips, magnetic strips, or other computer media, would allow for the elimination of physical currency.

Helping to lead the digital banking revolution are the various forms of **e-money** (electronic money). The most common example of e-money is **stored-value cards.** Stored-value cards are typically plastic cards that contain magnetic strips. The magnetic strips, similar to those on credit cards or ATM cards, contain data regarding the value of the card.

Related to the expansion of technology in banking is the increase in use of online banking. With online banking, banks allow customers to have electronic access to their accounts so that they can check their accounts, transfer money, order payments, pay bills, check their investments, and, through some banks, even trade stock. While services vary from bank to bank, many banks are offering at least some form of online banking to their customers.

digital cash
Money stored electronically in place of physical currency.

e-money
Electronic money.

stored-value card
A plastic card that contains data regarding the value of the card, thereby allowing EFTs to be made.

ONLINE BANKING SERVICES

Although online banking services vary among banks, there are three services most banks with online banking offer: (1) bill consolidation and payment, (2) transfer of funds from one account to another, and (3) loan applications (an appearance at the bank to sign the loan is typically required to finalize the loan process). By offering these services, banks are able to cut down on their own costs as well as give customers greater control over their funds.

Despite the number of banking services offered online, not all banking services can be conducted over the Internet. For example, depositing and withdrawing funds are two services that cannot be conducted online.

REGULATORY COMPLIANCE

In the main, banks are in favor of the increased use of online banking. Part of the reason banks like online banking is that it helps reduce a bank's operating cost and thus increase its profits. One way online banking reduces cost is through paperless billing. By not having to send paper statements to their customers, banks save on paper, ink, envelopes, and postage. The bank posts all the information to the user's account online, and this does not cost the bank much at all.

Another reason banks are in favor of online banking is that it decreases what is known as "float" time. *Float time* is the period between the time a check is written and the time it is presented for final payment, during which a customer can still use his or her funds. As an electronic check does not have to physically transfer between banks, accounts can be credited or debited more quickly.

PRIVACY PROTECTION

Are e-money institutions the same as traditional financial institutions? Do the same laws apply? These two questions hold the key to the question: How secure are e-payments and e-money? The answer is, We do not know.

E-Money Payment Information Which laws apply to e-money is still mostly untested legal ground. That is, there is little clarity regarding which laws do apply to e-money. The Federal Reserve has explicitly stated that Regulation E, which regulates traditional electronic fund transfers, does not apply to e-money transactions. Nonetheless, laws regarding computer files, not

directly related to banking, might apply to e-money, such as laws against unauthorized access of electronic files or communication. There are several such laws, but it is not clear whether they apply to e-money.

E-Money Issuer's Financial Records In 1978, Congress passed the Right to Financial Privacy Act [12 U.S.C. Section 3401 et seq.]. Under this act, financial institutions, such as banks, may not give a federal agency information regarding a person's finances without either that person's explicit consent or a warrant. The Right to Financial Privacy Act may apply to digital cash providers if the provider is considered a legal bank or credit provider that supplies customers with a card considered to be similar to a credit or debit card. However, given the lack of a physical location for digital cash providers, it is also possible that the Right to Financial Privacy Act does not apply, in which case digital cash providers may release a person's financial information freely to any federal agency.

Consumer Financial Data In an effort to further protect people's financial privacy, Congress passed the Financial Services Modernization Act, also known as the Gramm-Leach-Bliley Act [12 U.S.C. Sections 24a, 248b, 1820a, 1828b]. The act's purpose is to control how financial institutions handle customer information, thereby ultimately providing greater privacy protections to financial institution customers. Financial institutions are prohibited from disclosing personal information about their clients to third parties unless certain requirements set forth in the act are met. In addition, each financial institution is legally required to present customers with its privacy policies and practices.

SUMMARY

The Need for Negotiable Instruments	*Contracts as commercial paper:* Any contractual obligation, except personal ones and nonassignable ones, may be transferred and thus is a form of commercial paper.
	Problems with commercial paper: A breach of the contract invalidates the commercial paper.

Types of Negotiable Instruments

Note: A promise by the maker to pay a payee (e.g., a certificate of deposit).

Draft: An order by the drawer to a drawee to pay a payee (e.g., a check).

A note or draft can be either of the following:

- *Demand instrument:* Payee can demand actual payment at any time.
- *Time instrument:* Payment will be made only at a specific designated time.

An Overview of the Law of Negotiable Instruments

Requirements for negotiability:

1. Written document:
 - Relative permanence
 - Movability
2. Signature of the maker or drawer:
 - Affirmative mark
 - Duly authorized agent
 - Handwritten, even without signature
 - Automated signature
3. Unconditional order or promise to pay:
 - Must be specific, not implied
4. Sum certain in money:
 - Currency only, any currency acceptable
5. Payable at a time certain or on demand:
 - Acceleration of payment
 - Extension of payment

6. Words of negotiability:
- To the order of
- Order instrument

The significance of negotiability: More than a two-party transaction.

Negotiation *Delivery:* The physical handing over of a negotiable instrument.

Banking Article 3 of the UCC outlines the requirements that negotiable instruments, including checks, must meet, and it establishes the rights and responsibilities pertaining to parties to negotiable instruments. Article 4 creates a framework controlling deposit and checking agreements between banks and customers, and it directs the relationships between banks as checks are processed among different banks.

Checks *Draft:* An instrument that is an order.

Drawer: The party that gives the order.

Drawee: The party that must obey the order.

Payee: The party that receives the benefit of the order.

Check: A special draft that orders the drawee, a bank, to pay a fixed amount of money on demand.

Cashier's check: A check in which both the drawer and the drawee are the same bank.

Traveler's check: An instrument that is payable on demand, is drawn on or through a bank, is designated by the phrase "traveler's check," and requires a countersignature by the person whose signature appears on the instrument.

Money order: An instrument stating that a certain amount of money is to be paid to a particular person.

Certified check: A check that is accepted at the bank at which it is drawn.

Accepting Deposits: The banking institution must take deposits for an existing account. Consequently, it must collect deposits and make the funds available for use.

When a Bank May Charge a Customer's Account *Properly payable rule:* A bank may pay an instrument only when it is authorized by the drawer and does not violate an agreement between the bank and the customer.

Wrongful dishonor: If a bank refuses to pay a properly payable check, the bank incurs liability.

Stop-payment order: A drawer orders the drawee bank to not pay a check that has been drawn on the drawer's account.

Postdated check: A customer can postdate a check but must give the bank notice of the postdated check.

Stale check: A check is not presented to a bank within six months of its date.

Forgeries and alterations:

1. *Check bearing a forged signature:* Generally, the drawer is not liable for a forged check unless the drawer substantially contributed to the forgery.
2. *Check bearing a forged endorsement:* Neither the drawer nor the drawer's bank is liable for a forged endorsement.
3. *Altered check:* If an unauthorized change modifies the obligation of a party to the instrument, the drawer is generally not liable for the altered amount unless he or she negligently contributed to the alteration.

Electronic Fund Transfers: These transfers are transactions in which a retail customer pays for an item with a debit card that allows the customer's bank account to be instantly charged, ATM transactions, and direct deposits of paychecks.

E-Money and Online Banking *Digital cash:* Money is stored electronically on microchips, magnetic strips, or other computer media.

Point/Counterpoint

Should a Company Be Allowed to Require That Employees Receive Payment through Direct Deposit?

YES	NO
A company should be allowed to require that employees receive payment through direct deposit because direct-deposit payment is the most efficient form of payment for both employers and employees. Direct deposit allows employers and employees security they would not have with mailed paychecks. Companies can keep track of employee payments more accurately when employees are paid through one payment method. Through direct deposit, employers are assured that *all employees* are paid at the same time, on the same day. Neither employees nor employers need to be concerned with lost, stolen, delayed, or damaged paychecks. Many people have already chosen the convenience of online banking for their other banking needs; adding direct deposit only simplifies their lives. In fact, studies show that the average worker spends between 8½ and 24 hours each year cashing and depositing his or her payroll checks.* Direct deposit allows for a separate payroll account and more exact bookkeeping. The losses normally associated with stolen and doubled paychecks can be reinvested in the company, eventually allowing for potential salary/wage increases for all. Furthermore, a company saves a lot of money on paper costs alone by switching to direct deposit. Many people willingly choose to directly deposit their paychecks. A company establishing a requirement of direct-deposit payment would only streamline and simplify the process for everyone involved.	A company should not be allowed to require that its employees receive payment through direct deposit. While direct deposit is a good option for employers to provide to employees, the choice of payment form should be left to the employees. First, very few guidelines have been established regarding direct-deposit procedures. Employees would not necessarily be provided an in-depth statement discussing the details of each pay period. With direct deposit, employees have more difficulty ensuring that pay statements are accurate. Wage-based employees, for example, need to know exactly what they are paid per hour, for how many hours, so that the employees know whether they need to be paid overtime wages. Some direct-deposit statements list only the amount of money transferred to the employee's account. Some employees simply prefer to literally hold and personally deposit a physical check. They also have a physical copy of their pay stub for paper records. The absence of a physical receipt creates "holes" in an individual's paper records. These holes can create problems when an individual gathers documents in preparation for tax season. While companies can and should present to employees a list of the advantages of direct deposit, the ultimate decision should be left to the employees, because the employees are most heavily affected if their paychecks are not deposited properly.

* www.msmoney.com.

Questions & Problems

1. Explain the reason behind the need for negotiable instruments.

2. Are negotiable instruments more similar to money or contracts? Explain.

3. Identify and define each of the elements of negotiability.

4. Evaluate the following statement: "Order paper and bearer paper must be delivered to be negotiated."

5. Who are the three parties involved in the transfer of money through a check?

6. Explain the reason for the following policy: A customer has a duty to examine her or his bank statement.

7. Evaluate the following statement: "If a signature on a check is forged, the customer will never be responsible for the amount on the check."

8. Doseung Chung, the plaintiff, a horse player, was at Belmont Park Racetrack, which is owned by the defendant, New York Racing Association. While at the track, Chung was using a voucher to place bets on the races through an automated betting machine. After placing a bet, Chung took his betting ticket but forgot his voucher, which had thousands of dollars left on it. A few minutes later, he returned to the machine, but the voucher was gone. Chung put an electronic stop on the voucher, but the voucher had been cashed out about one minute after it was left in the machine. Chung subsequently sued the racetrack, arguing that the track was negligent in not requiring proof of identity when patrons cash out their vouchers, which constitute negotiable instruments. How did the court rule? Why? [*Doseung Chung v. New York Racing Ass'n,* 714 N.Y.S.2d 429 (2000).]

9. Dr. Rick LaCombe, an optometrist, was practicing optometry as a sole proprietorship and doing business as LaCombe Eye Center. His business took in checks for services and products made out in various ways: Dr. Rick LaCombe; Rick LaCombe, O.D.; Rick LaCombe, M.D.; Rick LaCombe; and LaCombe Eye Center (all referred to collectively as LaCombe). Lana Slyfield was the business director at the Eye Care Center, and as such she was the individual in charge at the front desk. Slyfield started embezzling from LaCombe by stealing checks from the mail. She did this by simply placing her account number under forged endorsements on the checks and depositing the checks into her account at Bank One. On some checks Slyfield added LaCombe's initials as part of her forged endorsement, stating that LaCombe's signature "didn't really look like a signature, so I guessed that it would make it look like more of a signature." On others, she simply inscribed "For Deposit Only," followed by her account number. No employee of the bank ever questioned her regarding her depositing checks made payable to LaCombe into her personal account. How does the UCC treat forged signatures on checks? Who should be liable for the amount of the check? [*Dr. Rick LaCombe v. Bank One Corp.* 953 So. 2d 161 (2007).]

10. Abdul Matin returned from a lengthy trip abroad and discovered that an unknown person had used forged checks to empty his account at Chase Manhattan Bank. The person forged a change-of-address card, which caused the bank to send the monthly statements to a different address. Upon returning to the United States, Matin demanded that the bank reimburse him for his losses, and when the bank refused, he sued to recover his damages. Chase Manhattan claimed that Matin did not inform it of the forged signatures until more than one year after the issuance of the statements and therefore it is not liable. What is the general rule under the UCC regarding who is liable when a forged check is not reported within one year? Were there any special circumstances in this case that would lead the court to not uphold this general rule? How do you think the court ruled in this case? [*Matin v. Chase Manhattan Bank,* 10 A.D.3d 447 (2004).]

11. The plaintiff, U.S. Bank, filed a complaint to foreclose the defendant's mortgage because the defendant had failed to pay the monthly installments on the mortgage. However, the defendant purported to tender payment for the entire balance of the mortgage by an enclosed "Bonded Bill of Exchange." Attached to the bill were instructions on how to process it with the U.S. Treasury Department. The instructions stated that the defendant had established a "Personal Treasury UCC Contract Trust Account" through the Treasury Department and that the bill was a negotiable instrument that should be mailed to the secretary of the treasury for redemption. However, the bill tendered by the defendant was not made "payable to bearer or to order." Does the bill discussed in this case meet the six requirements for negotiability? If not, what requirement is not met? How do you think the court ruled? [*U.S. Bank N.A. v. Phillips,* 366 Ill. App. 3d 593 (2006).]

12. Wachovia, a bank, made a loan in 2003 to McNamee for $150,000, and he signed a promissory note for the loan. At some point, Wachovia misplaced, lost, or destroyed the original note. The note matured in 2005, and after the loan matured, Wachovia assigned its rights in and to the note to another company, Atlantic National Trust., which then sued McNamee for recovery. Atlantic demanded McNamee repay the remaining principal balance on the note, $138,620, plus interest. Atlantic had a copy of the original note but not the original. McNamee asserted that Atlantic had no right to enforce the note since it was never in possession of the original document and that the assignee of a lost note has no standing to sue the maker. Thus, McNamee contended that because the original note was destroyed, the note could not be enforced. Recall your ethical training from Chapter 1. What ethical concerns are at issue in this case regarding negotiable instruments? How do you think the court ruled? [*Atlantic National Trust, LLC v. McNamee,* 984 So. 2d 375 (2007).]

13. In 1792, Colonel Marinus Willett wrote a document stating that in 1781 he had entered into an agreement with 60 members of the Oneida tribe. In return for their help in fighting during the Revolutionary War, the colonel promised each of the 60 members a blanket, but he later found himself unable to fulfill

his commitment. In 2004, Andre Deeks filed suit against the U.S. government, claiming that he, as the possessor of Colonel Willett's note, was owed $3 million because the government had never paid its debt to the Oneida tribe. Deeks claimed that the document written by Colonel Willet was a "Bill of Credit in bearer form," which had transferred to him, the current possessor, the standing to sue for the document's enforcement. The text of the note reveals neither an intent that it be circulated as money nor an unconditional promise to pay a certain sum. Based on this information, is the document a negotiable instrument? Does it meet the standards for negotiability? [*Deeks v. United States,* 151 Fed. App. 936 (2005).]

Looking for more review material?

The Online Learning Center at **www.mhhe.com/kubasekess2e** contains this chapter's "Assignment on the Internet" and also a list of URLs for more information, entitled "On the Internet." Find both of them in the Student Center portion of the OLC, along with quizzes and other helpful materials.

CHAPTER

17

Holder in Due Course, Liability, and Defenses

CASE OPENER

Stolen Money Orders and Holder-in-Due-Course Status

In December 1990, Stacy Anne Dillabough presented two American Express money orders in the amounts of $550 and $650 to Chuckie's Enterprise, Inc., a check-cashing business in Pennsylvania.[1] Later, in February 1991, Robert Lynn presented an American Express money order in the amount of $200 to Chuckie's. All money orders were endorsed, and the payees showed photo identification when presenting the money orders. Consequently, Chuckie's cashed the money orders and gave the appropriate amounts of money to Dillabough and Lynn.

When Chuckie's presented these money orders for payment at the American Express bank, American Express refused to honor the money orders because it discovered that the numbers on the money orders had been logged as stolen.[2] Another individual, Robert Triffin, purchased the American Express money orders from Chuckie's and took assignment of all of Chuckie's rights in the money orders. Triffin thus brought suit against American Express, along with Dillabough and Lynn.

At trial, American Express argued that the money orders were nonnegotiable and that the language on the back of each money order stated that American Express would not pay if the money order was stolen. Triffin argued that by purchasing the money orders from Chuckie's, he gained a special legal status, called *holder-in-due-course* status, and, therefore, American Express's defense was not applicable to him.

1. Who do you think should bear the costs of the stolen money orders? In other words, should American Express be required to pay Triffin? Why or why not?
2. Suppose you are a business manager at Chuckie's. You learn that the court holds that American Express does not have to pay for the stolen money orders. Would you make any changes in your business? Would you be less likely to accept American Express money orders in the future?

[1] "Digests of Recent Opinions: Superior Court," *Pennsylvania Law Weekly,* February 19, 1996, p. 15.
[2] Michael A. Riccardi, "High Court to Decide Status of Money Orders; Is Amex Liable for Stolen Blank Papers?" *Legal Intelligencer,* July 10, 1996, p. 1.

After reading this chapter, you will be able to answer the following questions:

LO 17-1 What is a holder in due course?

LO 17-2 What requirements must be met to obtain holder-in-due-course status?

LO 17-3 What is the shelter principle?

LO 17-4 In what ways has the holder-in-due-course doctrine been abused?

LO 17-5 What information is needed to determine signature liability?

LO 17-6 What is warranty liability?

LO 17-7 How does one avoid liability for negotiable instruments?

LO 17-1

Holder-in-Due-Course Doctrine

Suppose you want to purchase computers for your office building. You contract with a computer seller, Data Corp., to buy 50 computers. As partial payment, you give Data Corp. a note for $30,000. Data Corp. negotiates the note to Data Corp.'s landlord, Morgan, for payment of rent.

Suppose Morgan meets all the requirements (which you will soon learn) to be a holder in due course. You discover your computers are damaged, and you claim that Data Corp. breached its contract with you. If Data Corp. still held the $30,000 note, you could refuse to honor the note and claim as a defense that Data Corp. breached the contract. However, remember that Data Corp. negotiated the note to Morgan. Since Morgan is a holder in due course, you must pay Morgan because a holder in due course has higher rights to a negotiated instrument. If Morgan were simply a holder, you could use the defense of breach of contract against Morgan.

REASON FOR HOLDER-IN-DUE-COURSE STATUS

Do you think the elevated holder-in-due-course status is fair? The purpose of holder-in-due-course status is to protect a financial intermediary. In other words, someone who processes a payment should not be required to shoulder the transaction risks. Thus, the legal system offers greater legal protection to certain parties to encourage them to engage in financial transactions.

LO 17-2

holder in due course (HDC)
An individual who acquires a negotiable instrument in good faith.

Requirements for Holder-in-Due-Course Status

To be considered a **holder in due course (HDC),** a party must meet four requirements regarding the taking of the instrument. These requirements are established in UCC Section 3-302:

1. The party must be a holder of a complete and authentic negotiable instrument.
2. The holder must take the instrument for value.
3. The holder must take the instrument in good faith.
4. The holder must take the instrument without notice of defects.

Meeting these requirements is very valuable, as the Case Nugget demonstrates.

CASE Nugget

HDC Status to the Rescue

Watson Coatings, Inc. v. American Express Travel Services, Inc.
U.S. Court of Appeals for the Eighth Circuit

436 F.3d 1036 (2006)

Christine Mayfield used to work for Watson Coatings, Inc., and part of her role there included that of company treasurer. During her time as treasurer, Mayfield wrote approximately 45 to 47 checks from Watson's account to American Express for personal debt totaling $745,969.39. With each check that was submitted, American Express credited Mayfield's personal account. After Mayfield was dismissed from Watson Coatings, the money she had taken was discovered and suit was filed against American Express for taking the money from Mayfield despite the checks' having been clearly labeled as belonging to Watson Coatings, Inc.

The district court granted American Express's motion for summary judgment, but Watson filed an appeal. In the opinion written by Judge Smith, the extent to which American Express can be considered a holder in due course of the checks written by Mayfield was considered. The judge explained that because a payee can be considered a holder in due course, American Express would qualify. However, the court also needed to decide whether holder-in-due-course status would offer any protection to American Express.

The appeals court found that even though Watson had brought forth several common law claims against American Express, the fact that American Express is a holder in due course can serve as a defense. The checks had been accepted by American Express in good faith, making it the holder in due course of the documents. Thus, the court affirmed the district court's grant of summary judgment to American Express.

BE A HOLDER OF A COMPLETE AND AUTHENTIC NEGOTIABLE INSTRUMENT

Party Must Be a Holder First, as we mentioned earlier in the chapter, to be a holder in due course, a party taking the instrument must be a **holder,** a party who is in possession of an instrument that is payable to the party or to the bearer of the instrument [UCC Section 1-201(20)]. For example, if Adam Brewer possesses a check that states "Payable to Adam Brewer," Adam is a holder. However, suppose Adam asked his bank for a cashier's check to buy a boat from his friend, Corey Baum. (See Figure 17-1.) Even though Adam possesses the cashier's check and his name appears on the check, he is not a holder of the check because it is payable to his friend. When Adam gives the cashier's check to his friend, Corey, the friend becomes the first holder of the cashier's check.

holder
A party in possession of a negotiable instrument.

Figure 17-1

Illustration of
the Relationship
between Being a
Payee and a Being a
Holder

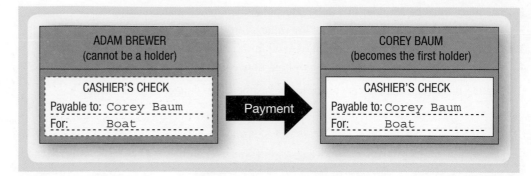

Similarly, if someone steals a check "Payable to Adam Brewer" and forges Adam's signature on the back of the check, this thief is not a holder of the check. (See Figure 17-2.) Because the check is payable to Adam Brewer and not the thief, the thief cannot be considered a holder, even if he forges Adam's name.

Instrument Must Be Negotiable Second, the instrument must be negotiable. A party cannot be a holder in due course of a nonnegotiable instrument. If an instrument lacks any of the requirements for negotiability, the holder cannot be a holder in due course.

Instrument Must Be Complete and Authentic Third, the negotiable instrument must be complete and authentic [UCC 3-302(a)(1)]. When the instrument is issued or negotiated, the note must appear complete and authentic. What happens if the instrument is incomplete? For example, suppose that someone writing a check forgets to write the date on the check.

The UCC allows the holder to complete the check as long as the completion is consistent with the intent of the issuer (3-115). For example, suppose you write a check to a company to purchase some business supplies. Although you write the company's name, you forget to write the date. Under the UCC, the company may complete the instrument—in this instance, the check—by writing the date. However, if the person completes the instrument in a way that is inconsistent with the intent of the issuer, the instrument is considered materially altered.

If an instrument has clearly been materially altered or is so irregular or incomplete that its authenticity is called into question, the UCC bars a person taking this flawed instrument from becoming a holder in due course [3-302(a)(1)].

Figure 17-2

Illustration of a
Failed Attempt to
Become a Holder
through Forgery

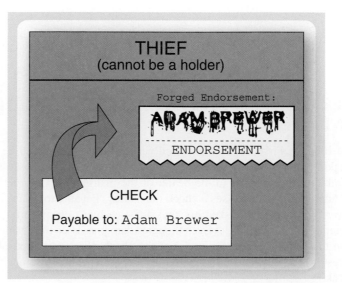

TAKE INSTRUMENT FOR VALUE

The holder in due course must take the negotiable instrument "for value." In other areas of the law, taking something for value usually means taking something with consideration, a bargained-for promise. However, the for-value requirement is more stringent than consideration: The party must take the instrument in exchange for a promise that has already been performed. The UCC explicitly excludes from "value" any promises that have not yet been performed. In other words, the party must suffer an out-of-pocket loss (3-303). Why? If a party has not yet performed the promise, he or she has not completely committed financially to the transaction and thus should not receive special legal protection. Therefore, when a party receives a negotiable instrument as a gift or acquires it through mistake, the party will be a holder instead of an HDC.

A holder can take an instrument for value if the holder:

1. Performs the promise for which the instrument was issued.
2. Acquires a security interest or some other lien in the instrument.
3. Takes the instrument for payment of a preceding claim.
4. Exchanges the instrument for another negotiable instrument.
5. Exchanges the instrument for an irrevocable obligation to a third party. [UCC 3-303(a)]

TAKE INSTRUMENT IN GOOD FAITH

The HDC must take the negotiable instrument in good faith [UCC 3-302(a) (2)(ii)]. What exactly is good faith? Historically, there has been some debate about whether *good faith* had an objective or subjective definition. For example, when determining whether a holder took an instrument in good faith in the objective sense, some courts would decide whether the holder purchased the instrument with a proper degree of caution through a usual and ordinary manner of conducting business. Looking at good faith in an objective sense means considering what the reasonable holder would have done.

However, other courts looked at good faith in a subjective sense by asking whether the holder acted honestly when taking the instrument. Looking at good faith in a subjective sense means considering the holder's actual behavior.

The UCC's definition of good faith is somewhere in the middle of the subjective and objective standards. The UCC defines good faith as "honesty in fact and the observance of reasonable commercial standards of fair dealing" [3-103(a)(4)]. Therefore, to act in good faith, a holder must not deviate from the reasonable commercial standards of fair dealing. The UCC drafters were most concerned with the fairness of the dealing.

TAKE INSTRUMENT WITHOUT NOTICE

Finally, a holder must take an instrument without notice of various claims to or defects of the negotiable instrument. If the holder has notice or is aware of any of the following defects, the holder cannot be an HDC [UCC 3-302(a)]:

1. The instrument is overdue.
2. The instrument has been dishonored.
3. The instrument was issued as part of a series that is in default.
4. The instrument has been altered or contains an unauthorized signature.
5. There is a claim to the instrument. (Such claims are described in UCC Section 3-306.)
6. Another party has a defense or claim in recoupment to the instrument.

What Does It Mean to Have Notice? According to the UCC, a person has notice of a fact in any one of the following circumstances:

1. The person has actual knowledge of the fact.
2. The person receives notice or notification of it.

3. The facts and circumstances known to the person at the time in question give the person reason to know that the fact exists [UCC 1-201(25)].

For example, suppose that Chuckie's, the check-cashing company in the Case Opener, received a letter from American Express that listed the numbers of the American Express money orders that had been stolen. As long as Chuckie's received this letter *before* it accidentally accepted the stolen money orders, Chuckie's would have notice of a defect and thus could not be a holder in due course. The UCC states that "to be effective, notice must be received at a time and in a manner that gives a reasonable opportunity to act on it" [3-302(f)].

Suppose that a person receives an instrument that has clearly been altered; however, the person taking the instrument does not inspect the instrument and thus does not notice the obvious alteration. As stated earlier, one of the requirements of becoming a holder in due course is that the holder accept a complete and authentic negotiable instrument [UCC 3-302(a)(1)]. Consequently, the question of a holder's awareness of such extreme irregularities does not matter; the very existence of such irregularities means that the holder cannot be a holder in due course.

If a person has notice of a defect before he or she gives value for the instrument but still gives value, the person will not be able to claim holder-in-due-course status.

Overdue Instruments Suppose you accept a check from a business associate. Unfortunately, the check falls behind your desk and is lost for the next four months. If you try to negotiate this instrument to another party, that party will not be permitted to claim holder-in-due-course status because the check is overdue. If a holder has notice that an instrument is overdue, the holder cannot claim holder-in-due-course status. How does a holder know whether an instrument is overdue? Overdue status is dependent on the type of instrument. The UCC explains how two types of instruments—demand and time instruments—may be overdue (3-304).

demand instrument
A type of draft that allows the payee to demand payment at any time from a holder.

Demand Instruments. A **demand instrument**, an instrument payable on demand, becomes overdue if it has been outstanding for an unreasonably long period of time after its date [UCC 3-304(a)(3)]. If the demand instrument is a check, the UCC states that the check is overdue 90 days after its date [3-304(a)(2)]. Thus, because your check has been outstanding for four months, it is overdue. The date on the check would give another party notice of its overdue status; thus, the party cannot claim HDC status.

time instrument
A type of draft that allows the payee to collect payment only at a specific time in the future.

Time Instruments. A **time instrument**, an instrument payable at a definite time, becomes overdue at any time after the expressed due date on the instrument. Most of the rules regarding whether a time instrument is overdue depend on the payment structure of the instrument. For example, a time instrument may or may not be payable in installments. If the instrument requires that a party make payment in a lump sum rather than in installments, the instrument is overdue if the party does not make the lump-sum payment by the due date [UCC 3-304(b)(2)].

However, how does nonpayment of installments affect whether the instrument is overdue? Overdue status depends on whether a late payment applies to the principal or the interest on the instrument. If a party misses payment of an installment on the principal of an instrument, the instrument is overdue until this installment is paid [UCC 3-304(b)(1)]. However, if a party misses a payment of interest on this instrument, the instrument is not overdue [UCC 3-304(c)].

Why might a party have reason to know that an installment payment of principal was not made and thus the instrument is overdue? This information is usually included on a credit report. For example, if a bank is considering purchasing a consumer note from a retailer, the bank can determine whether all payments have been made on the note by looking at the consumer's credit report. If the credit report indicates that an installment had not been paid, the bank would have notice that the instrument was overdue.

dishonored
Refused; specifically, a payment that has been refused despite a holder's presenting an instrument in a timely and proper manner.

Dishonored Instruments If a holder is aware that an instrument he or she is taking has been dishonored, the holder cannot become an HDC. An instrument is **dishonored** when a party refuses to pay the instrument. For example, suppose you deposit a check from a customer into your company's account at a Wells Fargo bank. The customer has an account at Chase Manhattan. Wells Fargo credits your account and later presents the check for payment at Chase.

Exhibit 17-1

Defenses and
the Holder in Due
Course

A holder in due course is generally free from personal defenses but is subject to real defenses.
The holder in due course is *free* from the following personal defenses:

1. Lack or failure of consideration.

2. Breach of contract.

3. Fraud in the inducement in the underlying contract.

4. Incapacity.*

5. Illegality.*

6. Duress.*

7. Unauthorized completion or material alteration of the instrument.

8. Unauthorized acquisition of the instrument.

The HDC is *subject to* the following real defenses:

1. Fraud in the essence.

2. Discharge of the party liable through bankruptcy.

3. Forgery.

4. Material alteration of a completed instrument.

5. Infancy—a party is below the legal age of consent.

* Although an HDC cannot normally be submitted to the defenses of incapacity, illegality, or duress, these defenses do sometimes apply. If the incapacity, illegality, or duress was significant enough for a court to deem the original contract void, the HDC will be subject to that defense. Once incapacity (or illegality or duress) is present to the extent that the contract is void, the defense of incapacity (or illegality or duress) is a real defense. In other words, if the contract is void due to incapacity, illegality, or duress, a party can use that defense against an HDC.

However, Chase refuses to pay because there are insufficient funds in your customer's account. Chase has dishonored the check and would likely stamp the phrase "insufficient funds" on your check. If you then tried to negotiate this check to another party, that party, seeing the words *insufficient funds,* would have notice that the check was dishonored.

However, if a party has no reason to know that a note has been dishonored, the party can become an HDC. Thus, if Chase did not stamp the phrase "insufficient funds" on the check, the new party would likely not have notice that the check was dishonored. Consequently, this new party could become an HDC.

Claims or Defenses If a party is aware of any claim or defense to an instrument, that party has notice and thus cannot become an HDC [UCC 3-302(a)(2)(v),(vi)]. However, if the party had no reason to know that various claims or defenses applied to an instrument even if the claims and defenses existed, the party would not be precluded from becoming an HDC.

Exhibit 17-1 provides a summary of the defenses that do and do not apply to the holder in due course.

The Shelter Principle and HDC

LO 17-3

shelter principle
The principle that when
an item is transferred,
the transferee acquires
all the rights the trans-
feror had to the item.

Generally, if an item is transferred from one person to another, the transferee acquires all the rights that the transferor had in the item. This idea is called the **shelter principle** [UCC Section 3-203(b)]. Therefore, following the shelter principle, even if a holder cannot attain holder-in-due-course status, the holder can acquire the rights and privileges of an HDC *if* the item is being transferred

from an HDC. Note that the instrument does not need to be transferred directly from an HDC for the recipient to have the rights of an HDC. Under the shelter principle, as long as the holder of an instrument can demonstrate that someone through the line of transfers had obtained the rights of an HDC, then all subsequent holders have the rights of an HDC.

Therefore, in the Case Opener, plaintiff Triffin received the American Express money orders from Chuckie's, a holder in due course. If Triffin did not qualify for HDC status on his own, he would have received the rights that Chuckie's, the transferor, had. In other words, Triffin is taking "shelter" in Chuckie's status as an HDC.

One exception to the shelter principle involves cases of fraud or other illegal activities. If a person engages in fraud or other illegal interference with an instrument, he or she may not become an HDC, even if obtaining the instrument later from an HDC.

The shelter principle may at first seem contrary to the idea of the HDC principle; however, the purpose of the shelter principle is to encourage the marketability of instruments. The greater protection offered to an HDC is very appealing; thus, allowing parties to achieve the rights of an HDC through the shelter principle encourages financial interactions.

LO 17-4 Abuse of the Holder-in-Due-Course Doctrine

While HDC status offers great protection to financial intermediaries, the intermediaries might attempt to abuse this protection. For example, suppose you are starting a small business and a salesperson for a company called Office Supplies Made Easy comes to your new office and wants to sell you high-quality office supplies. You pay for the office supplies with a negotiable installment note on which you are supposed to pay three installments of $1,000. However, the next day, the Office Supplies Made Easy salesperson negotiates the note to a finance company.

When you receive your office supplies, you discover that the supplies are extremely low-quality and certainly not worth the $3,000 you agreed to pay. You call Office Supplies Made Easy, saying that you want to return the office supplies. However, an employee tells you that your installment note has been negotiated to the finance company, which became a holder in due course.

Consequently, the finance company calls your office every day because you have refused to pay for the low-quality supplies. You later discover that the finance company is in the practice of negotiating all notes from all salespersons of Office Supplies Made Easy. It appears to you that Office Supplies Made Easy and the finance company have some kind of arrangement so that the finance company can attain HDC status. Claims or defenses you have against Office Supplies Made Easy do not apply to the finance company.

When cases like this arise, judges look at the connection between the transferor and the transferee. If the companies are closely connected, as in the Office Supplies Made Easy example, some judges apply the salesperson's knowledge of your claims and defenses to the finance company. Consequently, this application prevents the finance company from achieving HDC status.

To ensure that companies cannot abuse the HDC status, the FTC created several rules in the 1970s that help to protect consumers against HDC abuse, as in the Office Supplies Made Easy example. One FTC rule requires that every consumer credit contract or any purchase money loan must contain the following statement in 10-point, boldface type:

> **ANY HOLDER OF THIS CONSUMER CREDIT CONTRACT IS SUBJECT TO ALL CLAIMS AND DEFENSES WHICH THE DEBTOR COULD ASSERT AGAINST THE SELLER OF GOODS OR SERVICES OBTAINED PURSUANT HERETO OR WITH THE PROCEEDS HEREOF. RECOVERY HEREUNDER BY THE DEBTOR SHALL NOT EXCEED AMOUNTS PAID BY THE DEBTOR HEREUNDER.[3]**

Consequently, no subsequent holder of the contract will have the rights of an HDC.

[3] FTC Holder in Due Course Regulations, 16 C.F.R. 433.2 (1978).

Negotiable Instruments in England and Similarities to the HDC Doctrine in the United States

In England, the doctrine of privity of contract declares that contracts are exclusive to those who created them. However, this doctrine often limits and complicates business transactions. The problems created by privity of contract in England can be countered by using a negotiable instrument. Unlike contracts, in England bills of exchange, promissory notes, and checks can be negotiated between parties.

Negotiable instruments are used in business, in England as in the United States, to facilitate business transactions.

To ease the exchange and free flow of money in business transactions, businesses need to be able to transfer quickly money or other forms of payment. In the United States, companies can transfer their right to collect or their duty to perform under a contract. The English practice of privity prevents similar transfers. Accordingly, English businesses must be able to transfer money a different way in order to conduct regular business. It is the ease of transferability of negotiable instruments and the rights that come with a transferred negotiable instrument, as outlined in this chapter, that make negotiable instruments an ideal way for English businesses to avoid the problems created by the privity requirement.

Liability

As you have seen, it is not always clear who should bear responsibility for the amount of a negotiable instrument. The following sections explain the various ways a party may be liable for a negotiable instrument. First, when a person signs a negotiable instrument, he or she is potentially liable for the instrument. This type of liability is called **signature liability.** Second, in contrast, a party may be liable if the transfer of the instrument breaches a warranty associated with the instrument. This type of liability is called **warranty liability.** After we consider both signature and warranty liability, we examine the defenses to these types of liability. Finally, we investigate how liability for a negotiable instrument may be discharged.

signature liability
Liability attributed because of a party's signature on an instrument.

warranty liability
Liability attributed when the transfer of an instrument breaches a warranty associated with an instrument.

Signature Liability

LO 17-5

UCC Section 3-401(a) imposes liability if the party, or the party's agent, signs the instrument. If a party does not sign, the party cannot be held liable. Because the signature on an instrument leads to liability, it is important to know what counts as a signature. According to the UCC, a signature can be any name, word, mark, or symbol used by a party to authenticate a writing [3-401(b)]. Thus, if you wrote either your full name or an X with the intent to authenticate an instrument, either writing would constitute a signature.

PRIMARY LIABILITY OF MAKERS AND ACCEPTORS

A party who is **primarily liable** for an instrument must pay the stated amount on the instrument when it is presented for payment. This liability for the stated amount begins as soon as the instrument is issued. Moreover, the primarily liable party must pay without resorting to any other party. For example, suppose you own a business and write a check drawing on your funds in your business account at First National Bank. First National has primary liability for the check; it must pay the stated amount when the check is presented for payment.

primarily liable
Liable for paying the amount designated on an instrument when it is presented for payment.

The UCC establishes that certain parties—makers and acceptors—are primarily liable. First, a **maker** is a party who has promised to pay. For example, the maker of a promissory note is primarily liable for the amount of the note because that party has promised to pay the amount of the instrument. Moreover, UCC Section 3-412 states that a party who signs as an issuer of an instrument is liable for the amount of the instrument as soon as it is issued. For example, a bank that issues a cashier's check is primarily liable for the amount of the check as soon as the cashier's check is created (UCC 4-412).

maker
A person who has promised to pay a set sum to the holder of a promissory note or certificate of deposit.

Signatures and the Internet

On June 30, 2000, the Electronic Signatures in Global and National Commerce Act (the *E-Sign Act*) became federal law. The E-Sign Act gives legal force to digital signatures and online contracts in financial, business, consumer, personal, and government contexts. For example, the act covers loan transactions made, insured, or guaranteed by the federal government. The act applies to "transferable records" and states that any instrument that is a loan relating to real property and that would be considered a note under Article 3 of the UCC is considered a transferable record. Thus, students can now electronically sign their student loans. Furthermore, citizens can file and digitally sign their tax returns.

What exactly is a digital signature? A *digital signature* is a personal identifier that can be broken into electronic code. In other words, the signer "stamps" a document with his or her "signature" by placing data unique to the signer on it. Currently, there are two types of digital signatures: biometric and key-based signatures. Biometric digital signatures stamp the document with unique physical characteristics such as a fingerprint. Key-based signatures use digital "keys." The signer has a public key and a private key. These keys scramble information so that only parties with appropriate keys may read the information. The signer can use the private key to sign documents.

Source: David M. Nadler and Valerie M. Furman, "Landmark Electronic Signatures Legislation Becomes Effective," *Derivatives Litigation Reporter,* February 26, 2001.

acceptor

A person (drawee) who accepts and signs a draft to agree to pay the draft when it is presented.

secondarily liable

Liable for paying the amount designated on an instrument should the primarily liable party default.

endorser

One who issues an endorsement.

drawer

The party that writes an order or the person who writes a check.

presentment

The act of making a demand for the drawee to pay.

Second, an **acceptor,** a drawee of a draft who accepts and signs the draft to agree to pay the draft when it is presented, is primarily liable [UCC 3-413(a)]. A party who accepts a draft by signing on the face of the draft is primarily liable (UCC 3-413). For example, when a bank accepts a check, it is primarily liable for the amount of the check (UCC 3-409).

SECONDARY LIABILITY OF DRAWERS AND ENDORSERS

A party who is **secondarily liable** for an instrument must pay the amount on the instrument if the primarily liable party defaults. Drawers and endorsers are secondarily liable parties. An **endorser** is a party who signs an instrument to restrict payment of it, negotiate it, or incur liability [UCC 3-204(b)]. A **drawer** is a person who signs as a party ordering payment [UCC 3-103(a)(5)].

For example, if you write a check from your bank account that is payable to the electric company, you are the drawer of the check, the bank is the drawee, and the electric company is the holder of the check. The holder of the check (the electric company) presents the check to the drawee (the bank) for payment. **Presentment** is defined in the UCC as making a demand for the drawee to pay [3-501(a)]. The UCC creates specific rules that govern the time and manner of presentment.

Suppose the holder (the electric company) presented your check and the bank dishonored the check because of insufficient funds in your account. The UCC states that drawers of drafts are liable for an instrument only after it has been dishonored (3-414, 3-415). Thus, you (the drawer) are now liable for the check.

Three conditions must be met for a drawer or endorser to become liable. First, the holder of the instrument must present the instrument in a proper and timely fashion. Second, the instrument must be dishonored. Third, notice of the dishonor must be given to the drawer.

Presentment An instrument must be presented in a proper and timely manner. First, the instrument must be presented to the proper party. If the instrument is a note, the holder must present the note to the maker of the note. In contrast, if the instrument is a draft, the holder must present the instrument to the drawee. Thus, continuing our electric company example, the electric company must present the check to the bank (the drawee).

Second, the instrument must be presented to the proper party in a proper way. UCC Section 3-501(b) states that an instrument can be presented (1) by any commercially reasonable means, (2) through a clearinghouse procedure, or (3) at the place designated in the instrument.

Third, the instrument must be presented to the proper party in a timely manner. Thus, if the instrument is a note, the holder must present the note to the maker on the note's due

Exhibit 17-2

Summary of Process of Determining Secondary Liability

	NOTE	DRAFT
To whom must the holder present the instrument?	Maker	Drawee
When should the instrument be presented?	On due date	Reasonable time; if a check, within 30 days of date of check or within 30 days of time of endorsement
If the instrument is presented and dishonored, who is usually now liable for the instrument?	Any endorser	Drawer or endorser
What are the requirements for an instrument to be officially dishonored so that a holder may then turn to secondarily liable parties?	1. Present to maker for payment 2. Maker dishonors 3. Holder gives notice of dishonor to secondarily liable parties (endorsers)	1. Present to drawee for payment 2. Drawee dishonors 3. Holder gives timely notice of dishonor to drawer or endorsers

date. If the instrument is a draft, such as a check, the holder must present the instrument within a *reasonable* time. The failure to present an instrument on time is the most common reason that improper presentment occurs, ultimately discharging unqualified endorsers from secondary liability.

Dishonor When a holder presents an instrument within a timely and proper manner but acceptance or payment is refused, the instrument has been *dishonored*. The instrument must be explicitly dishonored; a refusal to pay does not necessarily mean that the instrument has been dishonored. For example, suppose you are a holder of a check that is payable to your business. You present this check for payment, but the bank refuses to pay the check because you cannot present identification [UCC 3-501(b)(2)]. Likewise, a bank may refuse to pay on an instrument because the endorsement of the instrument is not proper. Again, this refusal to pay does not dishonor the instrument. Remember, a secondarily liable party becomes liable *only* if a primarily liable party dishonors the instrument.

Notice of Dishonor The UCC provides a specific time line in which notice of dishonor of an instrument must be given to a secondarily liable party (3-503). (The process of determining secondary liability is summarized in Exhibit 17-2.) If the party that dishonors an instrument is a collection bank, it must give notice before midnight of the next day [UCC 3-503(c)]. Other parties must give notice of the dishonor within 30 days of the day on which they receive notice of dishonor. This notice can be given in any commercially reasonable manner: oral, written, or electronic communication [UCC 3-503(b)]. The notice must identify the instrument in question and state that this instrument has been dishonored. If the word *dishonored* appears on the instrument, this writing is enough to constitute notice. As long as the holder gives notice to the secondarily liable parties about the dishonor of the instrument, the holder can sue the other parties.

 If all three of these conditions are met, the holder can bring suit against a secondarily liable party. However, in most cases, while a secondarily liable party may have to pay a holder the amount of the instrument, the secondarily liable party can then seek recourse against the primarily liable party.

 In the event an instrument contains more than one endorsement, each endorser is liable for the full amount to any subsequent endorser or to any holder. The secondary liability established

through endorsement requires that an endorser pay anyone who endorses the instrument after him or her.

ACCOMMODATION PARTIES

accommodation party
A party who signs an instrument to provide credit for another party who has also signed the instrument.

Suppose that, after you graduate from college, you decide to start your own business. You need to borrow a significant amount of money from the bank, and you plan to create a promissory note. However, because you have never owned your own business and have little credit history, the bank is a little wary about whether you will be able to pay the note. Therefore, the bank decides to ask you to have a third party sign the note to ensure that the bank will be paid. Consequently, your business law professor cosigns your note. This third party is called an **accommodation party,** a party who signs an instrument to provide credit for another party who has also signed the instrument [UCC 3-419(a)].

Accommodation parties may be primarily or secondarily liable for an instrument and can sign as makers, drawers, acceptors, or endorsers. However, accommodation parties more frequently sign as makers or endorsers. As a maker, an accommodation party has primary liability, but as an endorser, the party has secondary liability.

Suppose you, in the example above, cannot pay your note, and your business professor, as an accommodation party, pays the note instead. This professor has a right of reimbursement to recover the money from you, the accommodated party [UCC 3-419(e)]. If, however, you, the accommodated party, pay the note when it is due, you cannot force the professor to contribute to the amount due on the loan.

UNAUTHORIZED SIGNATURES AND ENDORSEMENTS

As a general rule, if a signature to a negotiable instrument is unauthorized, the signature will not impose liability to the named party. This rule applies to two cases: forgery and unauthorized agents.

First, return to the accommodation party example above. Suppose you forged your business law professor's name to ensure that you would get your money to start your new business. If you could not pay on the note, your business law professor would not be forced to pay on the basis of the forged signature. Similarly, this rule applies to parties who forge the drawer's signature on a check. However, forgery in the employment context is treated differently, as we explain below in the section entitled "The Fictitious-Payee Rule."

ratify
To approve an unauthorized agent's signature on an instrument.

Second, if an agent is not authorized to sign a negotiable instrument on behalf of a principal, the principal will generally not be liable for the instrument. Consequently, the agent would be personally liable for the instrument. However, if the principal decides to **ratify,** or approve of, the unauthorized agent's signature, the principal will then become liable for the instrument while the agent will escape personal liability [UCC 3-403(a)].

How does a principal ratify an unauthorized signature? A principal could explicitly approve of the signature. For example, a Florida court held that a principal could not recover the amount of two checks he gave to his agent because the principal had ratified the signatures.[4] The agent, who was supposed to deposit two checks into the principal's account, forged the principal's signature and deposited the checks into the agent's account. The agent ultimately told the principal about the forged checks and the location of the money. The principal did nothing until the agent later ran away with the money, and the court ruled that the principal's inaction was the same as his approval of his signature.

Alternatively, if the principal accepts the benefits associated with this unauthorized signature, the principal in effect ratifies the signature by his or her conduct. For example, in *Rakestraw v. Rodriguez,*[5] a husband had forged his wife's signature in order to obtain a loan to start a grocery store. A few days later, the wife discovered the forgery, but she did nothing to correct it and even participated in the business over the next few years. Part of running the business included sharing in the profits from the grocery store. When the business failed, the wife tried to avoid liability,

[4] *Fulka v. Florida Commercial Banks, Inc.,* 371 So. 2d 521 (Fla. Dist. Ct. App. 1979).
[5] 500 P.2d 1401 (Cal. 1972).

claiming her husband forged her signature. The court ruled that her actions in sharing in profits and in helping run the business effectively ratified her signature.

This ratification of an unauthorized signature does not exclusively apply to the agent-principal relationship. Your business law professor could similarly choose to ratify your unauthorized signature of his name and thus would be liable for your promissory note.

However, these are some exceptions to the general rule that an unauthorized signature is not enforceable. Generally, the policy behind these exceptions is that courts want to place the burden on the parties who are in the best position to take a loss or take action to recover a loss. Moreover, particularly in regard to the last two rules that are discussed below (the imposter rule and the fictitious-payee rule), the court focuses on the intent of the party who is issuing the instrument.

Negligence In some cases, a party's negligence does not permit the party to escape liability for an unauthorized signature. If the party whose signature was forged behaved so negligently as to "substantially contribute to . . . the making of a forged signature," the party may be precluded from escaping liability (UCC 3-406).

For example, in *Thompson Maple Products v. Citizens National Bank,* Thompson[6] was a corporation that manufactured bowling pins from maple logs. Thompson would accept loads of logs from timber owners. When a load arrived at the mill, a Thompson employee filled out a scaling slip that listed the name of the owner, along with the quantity and grade of the logs. Thompson office employees then used the slips to prepare checks for the owners of the logs. A Thompson employee, Emery Albers, took blank scaling slips and filled them out for fictitious loads of logs. The office employees, thinking the slips represented real loads of wood, then prepared checks for payment. Albers took the checks, forged the name of the owner of the logs, and cashed the checks or deposited them into his bank account at Citizens National Bank. The court ruled that Thompson "substantially contributed" to the forgeries because the blank scaling slips used to record loads of logs were easily accessible. In fact, office employees gave Albers two entire pads of these slips. Moreover, even though it was company policy for the slips to be initialed by authorized employees who were accepting the loads, Thompson office employees created checks even for slips that were not authorized. Thus, Thompson's negligence led to the conclusion that Thompson should be liable.

The Imposter Rule Suppose that Jamaar, a business manager, has been communicating through e-mail with Carlie, a potential employee. Jamaar has scheduled a meeting with Carlie. However, Samantha, without Carlie's knowledge, decides to impersonate Carlie at the interview. Samantha (as Carlie) tells Jamaar she will strongly consider signing an employment agreement if Jamaar will issue her a $200 check as a presigning bonus. Jamaar agrees and issues the check to Carlie that day. Samantha forges Carlie's name and deposits the check into her own account. Will Jamaar be liable for the amount of the check?

Jamaar's signature has not been forged; he clearly signed the check with intent to transfer money to Carlie. But he did not know that Carlie was actually Samantha. Is Samantha's signature considered a forgery? No. Under the UCC's **imposter rule,** if a maker or drawer issues a negotiable instrument to an imposter, the imposter's endorsement will be effective [UCC 3-404(a)]. The court considers the intent of the drawer or maker when issuing the instrument. Because Jamaar intended for Samantha (as Carlie) to have the instrument, her endorsement of the instrument is considered valid. Moreover, it is easier for Jamaar as maker or drawer to identify the true identity of Carlie than it would be for a later holder of the check to do so. Perhaps you are surprised by the imposter rule. The UCC, as stated, places an immense responsibility on Jamaar to ensure that he is not being duped. What values are in conflict here? Should Jamaar be forced to shoulder this responsibility?

> **imposter rule**
> A rule which holds that if one obtains a negotiable instrument by impersonating another and endorses it with the impersonated party's signature, the loss falls on the drawer of the instrument.

The Fictitious-Payee Rule Suppose now that Jamaar, who has been authorized to write checks from the company account, draws bonus checks from the company account for five more potential employees. Unfortunately, Jamaar never actually interviewed these employees; thus, these people are not entitled to the bonuses. Jamaar takes these checks, which are made out to the

[6] 234 A.2d 32 (Pa. Super. Ct. 1967).

fictitious potential employees, endorses the checks in their names, and deposits these checks into his personal bank account. These potential employees have no interest (i.e., no right to payment) in the checks and are thus called **fictitious payees** (UCC 3-404, 3-405). As with the endorsement in the imposter case, Jamaar's endorsement of the fictitious payees is not considered forgery [UCC 3-404(b)(2)]. Jamaar's company will be liable for the checks.

Why is the company liable? Courts view the company as being in a better position to bear the loss of the checks. The loss has occurred because Jamaar, a company employee, has acted wrongly. Although the company is liable for the amounts of the checks, the company can recover the money from Jamaar.

LO 17-6

Warranty Liability

In the previous section, we explained how a party might be liable for an instrument on the basis of his or her signature on the instrument. In this section, we consider another type of liability: *warranty liability.* A party may be liable for an instrument because of a breach of warranty. There are two relevant types of warranties here: transfer warranties and presentment warranties.

TRANSFER WARRANTY

transfer warranties
Warranties regarding a negotiable instrument and its transfer; created by a party who transfers the instrument.

A negotiable instrument can be transferred from one party to another. A party who transfers a negotiable instrument to another party in good faith for consideration creates **transfer warranties** regarding the instrument and the transfer itself [UCC 3-416(a)]. Transfer warranties always apply to the party to whom the instrument is transferred (the transferee).

When a party transfers an instrument for consideration, he or she warrants:

1. The transferor is entitled to enforce the negotiable instrument.
2. Signatures on the instrument are authentic and authorized.
3. The instrument has not been altered.
4. The instrument is not subject to a defense or claim in recoupment.
5. The transferor has no knowledge of insolvency proceedings against the maker, acceptor, or drawer of the instrument. [UCC 3-416(a)]

If the transfer is through endorsement, these warranties apply to any future holders. However, if the transfer does not occur through endorsement, the warranties apply only to the transferee.

These rules on whether the warranties apply to future holders or only to the immediate transferee are important because liability can be imposed for breach of warranty. If the warranties apply and there is a breach of one of the warranties, the parties can bring suit against the transferor, the warrantor, for damages suffered as a result of the breach [UCC 3-416(b)].

To see how signature liability can affect ethical behavior in the workplace, see the **Connecting to the Core** activity on the text's website at www.mhhe.com/kubasekess2e.

As soon as a transferee discovers that a breach of warranty has occurred, he or she can bring suit against the transferor. However, the transferee must give notice of the breach-of-warranty claim to the transferor within 30 days of discovering the breach [UCC 3-416(c)]. If the transferee does not give notice within 30 days of discovering the breach, the warranty will be discharged to some extent. If the transferred instrument is a check, the warranties cannot be disclaimed [UCC 3-416(c)].

While warranties on checks cannot be disclaimed, they can be disclaimed on other instruments. When parties agree to a disclaimer, an endorser can disclaim warranties by including in the endorsement the phrase *without warranties. Without warranties* disclaims warranty liability.

PRESENTMENT WARRANTY

In the "Signature Liability" section, we discussed the requirements for a negotiable instrument to be properly presented for payment. Certain warranties are associated with the presentment of an instrument. Remember, presentment occurs when a party properly presents an

instrument for acceptance and the party to whom it was presented accepts the instrument or pays it in good faith.

Why are presentment warranties needed? Parties who accept or pay instruments may worry that they are not paying the proper party. Thus, while transfer warranties apply to the transferee, **presentment warranties** cover parties who accept instruments for payment. Both the party presenting the instrument and any previous transferor of the instrument make presentment warranties. Therefore, if there is a breach of presentment warranty, the acceptor can recover damages from the presenting party or previous transferors. As with the notice rule for transfer warranties, a party must give notice of a breach of presentment warranty within 30 days.

There are two types of presentment warranties. These types depend on what kind of instrument is being presented to a certain kind of party. When a party presents an unaccepted draft to a drawee, the holder guarantees:

presentment warranty
A warranty covering the parties accepting an instrument for payment; created to ensure that the accepting or paying party is paying the proper party.

1. The warrantor of the instrument is entitled to enforce the instrument.
2. The instrument has not been altered.
3. The warrantor has no knowledge that the drawer's signature or the draft is unauthorized. [UCC 3-417(a)]

These warranties apply only to a drawee who pays or accepts a draft in good faith.

If the instrument is not an unaccepted draft presented to a drawee, only one presentment warranty applies. The party presenting the instrument guarantees that the warrantor is or was entitled to payment or authorized to obtain payment [UCC 3-417(d)(1)]. In other words, only warranty 1 listed above applies to presentments of instruments other than unaccepted drafts.

Case 17-1 considers whether a bank that cashed forged checks gives presentment and transfer warranties.

HALLIBURTON ENERGY SERVICES, INC. V. FLEET NATIONAL BANK
U.S. DISTRICT COURT FOR THE SOUTHERN DISTRICT OF TEXAS, HOUSTON DIVISION
334 F. Supp. 2d 930 (2004)

FACTS: *On March 20, 2000, Halliburton issued a check, drawn on a Citibank account, to Arthur Andersen for $215,000. The check was deposited in the U.S. mail. An unknown person stole the check from the mail and then altered the payee to "Paul A. Schumacher."*

On March 27, 2000, a person claiming to be Paul A. Schumacher opened a Fleet brokerage account from the bank's Internet site. The person posing as Paul A. Schumacher endorsed the altered check by signing the name "Paul A. Schumacher" on the back and presented it to Fleet, which honored it. Fleet then presented the check to Citibank, the drawee/payor bank. On March 30, 2000, Citibank charged Halliburton's checking account the sum of $215,000 because Citibank had paid the check in full.

On May 15, 2000, Arthur Andersen informed Halliburton it had not received the $215,000 check. A Halliburton

employee working for Accounts Payable then contacted Citibank and learned that the check had been paid. On May 17, Halliburton requested the original check from Citibank. On receiving and examining the check, Halliburton saw that the payee's name had been altered and that the check had been endorsed by the fictitious payee, Paul A. Schumacher, "for deposit only."

On June 26, 2000, Citibank notified Fleet that Fleet had honored a fraudulently altered check and asked for prompt reimbursement of what Citibank deemed a wrongful payment. The request was denied. Citibank then assigned any claim it may have against Fleet to Halliburton. Halliburton sued, and filed for summary judgment.

ISSUE: When is a bank liable when it honors a check made out to a fictitious payee?

REASONING: In the court's own words:

An impostor is "one who pretends to be someone else to deceive others, esp. to receive the benefits of a negotiable instrument," or "a person who practices deception under an assumed character, identity or name."

The impostor rule applies when a bank has honored a check made out to a fictitious payee. If the impostor's endorsement is effective, the collecting bank then becomes a "holder in due course." . . . Even a forger can effectively endorse an instrument. Unless the depository bank knew about the forgery, there is no breach of presentment warranty when the depository bank presents it to the drawee. Therefore, in such circumstances, the presenting bank is not liable for the drawer's or drawee's loss.

. . . The drawee may override the depository/collecting/presenting bank's affirmative defense only if the collecting bank failed "to exercise ordinary care in paying or taking the instrument and that failure contributed to loss resulting from the payment of the instrument." The "ordinary care" standard is just that: It does not mandate that a depository bank engage in peculiar vigilance. . . .

If the drawee bank can establish that the collecting bank failed to exercise ordinary care, the drawee may recover from the presenting bank "to the extent the failure to exercise ordinary care contributed to the loss."

DECISION AND REMEDY: The court found that "Halliburton has not presented evidence that Fleet was anything other than a holder in due course. In other words, Halliburton has not offered evidence of Fleet's bad faith, e.g., that Fleet's employees connived with the forger. Nor has Halliburton provided any evidence that Fleet had reason to believe the check had been fraudulently altered." The summary judgment motion was denied.

SIGNIFICANCE OF THE CASE: This case spells out when a bank that accepts a forged check provides warranties.

CRITICAL THINKING

The motion for summary judgment was denied because there was too much omitted information. As a judge, what information would you deem relevant that was missing from the case? Why is the missing information relevant to this case?

ETHICAL DECISION MAKING

Ethical reasoning requires consideration of all the relevant parties affected by the action on question. Who besides the bank that honored the check and Halliburton are affected by the issue in this set of facts?

LO 17-7 Avoiding Liability for Negotiable Instruments

If a party tries to enforce a negotiable instrument, a defendant can try to avoid liability in two ways. First, the defendant can try to claim a defense to liability. Second, the defendant can try to claim that the liability has been discharged.

DEFENSES TO LIABILITY

Earlier in the chapter, we listed defenses to liability that do or do not apply to a holder in due course. Here, we return to these defenses to liability. There are two categories of defenses: real defenses and personal defenses. **Real defenses,** also called universal defenses, apply to all parties. **Personal defenses** do not apply to holders in due course.

real defense
A liability defense that applies universally to all parties.

personal defense
A liability defense that is not applicable to holders in due course.

Real Defenses A party's right to enforce a negotiable instrument is subject to the following real defenses:

1. Infancy (being below the legal age of consent), to the extent that it makes a contract void.
2. Duress, to the extent that it makes a contract void.
3. Lack of legal capacity, to the extent that it makes a contract void.

4. Illegality of the transaction, to the extent that it makes a contract void.
5. Fraud in the factum.
6. Discharge through insolvency proceedings (bankruptcy).
7. Forgery.
8. Material alteration.

The first six defenses are stated explicitly in UCC Section 3-305. As we discussed earlier in this chapter, the UCC establishes forgery as a defense to liability because a party must have signed the instrument to be held liable. Finally, a material alteration of an instrument discharges a party of a liability [UCC 3-407(a)].

Fraud in the Factum. When a party signs a negotiable instrument without knowing that it is, in fact, a negotiable instrument, the party can claim **fraud in the factum** (also called *fraud in the execution* and *fraud in the essence*) as a defense. For example, suppose Michael Jordan believes he is signing an autograph for a fan, but he is actually signing a promissory note. Because he did not intend to sign a negotiable instrument, he will not be held liable for the instrument.

Similarly, suppose you, a business manager, are negotiating with another company to purchase materials for your manufacturing business. After your negotiations, the company asks you to sign a document as a preorder for the materials. You hurriedly sign the document and leave. However, instead of signing a preorder, you have actually signed a note. Will you be held liable for this note? In this case, it depends on the extent to which you, as the signing party, had reason to know what you were signing.

For another illustration of these issues, see the Case Nugget.

fraud in the factum
A liability defense available to a party who signs a negotiable instrument without knowing that it is a negotiable instrument.

CASE Nugget

Defense of Ignorance?

Laborer's Pension Fund v. A & C Envtl., Inc.
U.S. Court of Appeals for the Seventh Circuit

301 F.3d 762 (2002)

A & C Environmental, Inc., is a corporation that transports and disposes of nonhazardous waste. In April 1999, A & C was asked to complete a job in Gary, Indiana, which prompted representatives from Laborer's Pension Fund to approach the company. Frattini of the fund asked Clark of A & C to sign a form that would guarantee the five individuals who would work in Gary, Indiana, the coverage of the local union. Clark was hesitant to sign the agreement because he feared that if someone within his company were covered under the union, the entire company would then be covered. It wasn't until after Frattini of the fund guaranteed Clark that the only employees of A & C who would be affected would be those working in Gary, Indiana, that the agreement was signed. When A & C did not pay dues for all of its employees, the fund brought suit for delinquent contributions.

The district court ruled against the fund as a result of the fraud-in-the-execution defense that was brought forth by A & C. The court decided that any reasonable juror would believe that Clark did not know that he was agreeing to pay the fund dues for each employee of A & C. The fund appealed to the U.S. Seventh Circuit Court of Appeals.

In the opinion written by Judge Ripple, the Seventh Circuit found that Clark may not have known what he was agreeing to. Unlike the district court, however, the appeals court found that Clark had a reasonable opportunity to review the document, which was written in English. Although Frattini of the fund had misrepresented the contents of the document to Clark, there was an opportunity to review the document that established dues for all employees of A & C. Thus, the court of appeals reversed the decision of the district court.

Although fraud in the factum is a real defense, courts have held that the signer's experience may determine whether the signer should have known what he or she was actually signing. Recall the situation with Jamaar in which he was solely responsible for ensuring the identity of the individual he was signing a check to. However, that level of responsibility is not required of Michael Jordan in the situation described earlier. Can you account for the difference in the two situations, pointing out the differing values and ethical norms?

As another example, consider *Schaeffer v. United Bank & Trust Co.*[7] United Bank sued Schaeffer to collect on a promissory note Schaeffer had signed as an accommodation maker. However, the Maryland court ultimately ruled that Schaeffer was not liable due to fraud in the factum. It turns out Schaeffer barely knew how to read, did not understand the document he was signing, and was lied to by the note's maker, who had told Schaeffer that Schaeffer's signature would serve as a character witness. The court ruled that United Bank was not a holder in due course and was subjected to Schaeffer's defense even if the bank were a holder in due course as the note was void due to fraud in the factum.

Material Alteration. The UCC defines a *material alteration* as "an unauthorized change in an instrument that purports to modify in any respect the obligation of a party, or an unauthorized addition of words or numbers or other change to an incomplete instrument relating to the obligation of a party" (3-407). Only unauthorized changes that affect the rights of the party are considered material alterations. Changes that typically fall under UCC Section 3-407 include changes to the parties to the instrument, the amount of the instrument, the date the instrument is due, and the applicable interest rate.

If the material alteration is fraudulent, the party whose rights have been affected by the change is completely discharged from the instrument [UCC 3-407(b)]. However, if the material alteration is not fraudulent, the instrument will be enforced only under the original terms.

Personal Defenses Personal defenses apply to holders, not holders in due course. Personal defenses can be divided into two categories. First, there are general defenses that can be asserted against the defendant on general contract theory. These defenses include:

1. Breach of contract or warranty.
2. Lack or failure of consideration.
3. Fraud in the inducement. (See the Case Nugget on the next page for an example of how the courts consider the defense of fraud in the inducement.)
4. Illegality.
5. Mental incapacity.

Second, the UCC lists specific personal defenses created by provisions of Article 3. These defenses, summarized in Exhibit 17-3, include the following:

1. Defense of nonissuance, conditional issuance, or issuance for a special purpose [3-105(b)].
2. Defense of modification or nullification of an obligation by a separate agreement (3-117).
3. Defense of nondelivery of the instrument [3-105(b)].
4. Defense of unauthorized, nonfraudulent completion of an instrument (3-115).

DISCHARGE OF LIABILITY ON INSTRUMENTS

discharged

Released from liability for a negotiable instrument.

When a party's liability for a negotiable instrument is terminated, this party's liability has been **discharged.** In other words, the party is released from liability. Discharge can occur through a variety of ways. For example, as stated earlier, discharge of endorsers can occur if a party who has a right to enforce an instrument has materially altered the instrument. Keep in mind that discharge is not effective against a holder in due course (UCC 3-601).

[7] 360 A.2d 461 (Md. Ct. Spec. App. 1976).

CASE Nugget

Fraud in the Inducement

Hugh L. Caraway v. Land Design Studio
Texas Court of Appeals

47 S.W.3d 696 (2001)

Internacional Realty hired Land Design to perform landscaping services on an apartment complex development known as the Deerfield Project, resulting in a debt owed to Land Design for work completed on the project. Land Design later told Caraway, the president of Realty, that it needed to remove Realty's account receivable from Land Design's books in order to continue receiving working capital from its lender. The parties created a promissory note that essentially replaced Realty's account receivable. In September 1998, the parties executed the note.

The note was to be paid in full no later than March 31, 1999; however, no payment was received. Land Design demanded payment and brought suit in July 1999 to collect the amount due. Land Design filed suit against Caraway. In response, Caraway denied liability, asserting several defenses, one being fraud in the inducement. Specifically, Caraway asserted that Land Design orally represented to him that the note would not be due until Realty closed on its Deerfield Project construction loan, thus fraudulently inducing him into signing the note. However, this type of parol evidence is generally inadmissible to alter the terms of a promissory note.

On the basis of the specifics of the case regarding parol evidence, the court determined that Caraway must show that some type of trickery, artifice, or device was employed by Land Design in addition to showing that Land Design represented to him that he would not be liable on the note. However, Caraway's summary judgment proof failed to present any evidence of trickery or artifice by Land Design. Caraway's only evidence was his repeated assertion in his affidavit (and two supplemental affidavits) that Land Design promised that the note would not be due until Realty closed on its construction loan. Even if correct, this was insufficient. A mere representation to a maker, without some accompanying trickery or artifice, will not defeat the application of the parol evidence rule.

Caraway's claim of fraudulent inducement was further weakened by the fact that the promissory note itself makes a reference to closing on the loan. The note states: "Should Debtor close on the property prior to March 31, 1999, payment shall be made within three (3) days of Debtor's receipt of funds. . . ." The deadline for payment was March 31, 1999. Therefore, trickery is unlikely when the note references the event that Caraway claims is the event triggering his obligation to pay.

Because of Caraway's reliance on the assertions in his affidavit regarding Land Design's promise and the fact that such evidence is inadmissible under the parol evidence rule, Caraway offered no evidence to raise a genuine issue of material fact. Therefore, the court concluded that no factual question existed as to fraudulent inducement.

Discharge through Payment and Tender of Payment Earlier in this chapter, we discussed how a party becomes liable for an instrument by signing the instrument. If a party (or another party on the first party's behalf) who has signed an instrument has an obligation to pay and then pays the full amount due, all parties who are liable will be discharged (UCC 3-602).

For example, Stuart creates a note in which he promises to pay Vanessa $1,000. If Stuart pays the $1,000 on the due date, he will be discharged from liability on the note. However, if Stuart

Exhibit 17-3

Summary of
Defenses to Liability
for a Negotiable
Instrument

Real (universal) defenses	Infancy (below the legal age of consent)*
	Duress*
	Lack of legal capacity*
	Illegality of the transaction*
	Fraud in the factum
	Discharge through insolvency proceedings
	Forgery
	Material alteration
Personal defenses	*Contract defenses:*
	Breach of contract or warranty
	Lack or failure of consideration
	Fraud in the inducement
	Illegality
	Mental incapacity
	Article 3 defenses:
	Nonissuance of an instrument
	Modification of an obligation by a separate agreement
	Nondelivery of the instrument
	Unauthorized, nonfraudulent completion of the instrument

* To the extent that it makes a contract void.

makes the payment on the note to John, knowing that John stole the note from Vanessa and is wrongfully possessing it, Stuart's obligation will not be discharged. Paying John does not discharge Stuart's liability because John, who stole the note, is not a holder and not entitled to the amount on the note [UCC 3-602(b)(2)].

Moreover, some parties' obligations on an instrument will be discharged if the obliged party tenders full payment on the due date but the holder of the instrument refuses to accept the money [UCC 3-603(b)]. If Stuart makes a proper tender of the full amount ($1,000) to Vanessa on the note's due date but she improperly refuses to accept the money, Stuart will still be liable for the $1,000 but will not have to pay interest on the amount. However, if any endorsers or accommodation parties are liable for Stuart's note, these parties' obligation will be discharged.

Discharge by Cancellation or Renunciation A party who is entitled to enforce an instrument may decide to cancel the instrument with or without consideration. Canceling the instrument discharges the obligation of a party who must pay the instrument (UCC 3-604). The party who decides to cancel the instrument may engage in an intentional voluntary act to cancel the instrument. For example, the party might write "Paid" on the instrument, intentionally destroy or mutilate the instrument, or give the instrument to the obliged party.

Alternatively, a party may renounce an instrument by promising not to sue to enforce the instrument. *Renunciation* occurs when a party agrees, in writing, not to sue the obliged party.

Discharge by Reacquisition *Reacquisition* occurs when a former holder of an instrument has the instrument transferred back to him or her by negotiation or other means. When reacquisition occurs, anyone who endorsed the instrument in between the initial acquisition and the reacquisition by the holder has his or her endorsement canceled. When an endorsement is canceled, discharge occurs. The holder who reacquired the instrument can further negotiate the instrument, but the intermediate endorsers will not be held liable (UCC 3-207).

Discharge by Impairment of Recourse A right to recourse is the ability of a party to seek reimbursement. Typically, when a holder presents an instrument to an endorser, the endorser can seek recourse from prior endorsers, the maker, the drawer, or accommodating parties. However, if the holder has in some way impaired the endorser's ability to seek recourse from any of these parties, the endorser is not liable on the instrument [UCC 3-605(i)].

Discharge by Impairment of Collateral If a party posts collateral to ensure his performance of the negotiable instrument and the holder of the collateral impairs the value of the collateral, the party to the instrument is discharged from the instrument to the extent of the damage to the collateral [UCC 3-605(d)].

SUMMARY

Holder-in-Due-Course Doctrine	The HDC doctrine provides incentive for financial intermediaries to engage in transactions because they receive greater legal protection.
Requirements for Holder-in-Due-Course Status	1. *Be a holder of a complete and authentic negotiable instrument.* 2. *Take the instrument for value:* The holder must suffer an out-of-pocket loss. 3. *Take the instrument in good faith:* The holder must take the instrument with "honesty in fact and the observance of reasonable commercial standards of fair dealing." 4. *Take the instrument without notice:* The holder must take the instrument without notice of the following defects: It is overdue, is dishonored, or is part of a series in default; it has been altered or has an unauthorized signature; or it is subject to claims or defenses.
The Shelter Principle and HDC	*Shelter principle:* If a holder cannot attain HDC status, the holder can acquire the rights and privileges of an HDC *if* the item is being transferred *from* an HDC.
Abuse of the Holder-in-Due-Course Doctrine Liability	*FTC rule:* Negotiation of consumer notes may not be subject to HDC status. It is not always clear who should bear responsibility for the amount of a negotiable instrument. A party may be liable for a negotiable instrument if he or she signs the instrument or if the transfer of the instrument breaches a warranty associated with the instrument.
Signature Liability	A party can be held liable for an instrument only if the party has signed the instrument. *Primary liability of makers and acceptors:* They must pay the stated amount on the instrument when it is presented for payment. *Secondary liability of drawers and endorsers:* They must pay the amount on the instrument if the primarily liable party dishonors the instrument and the following three conditions are met: 1. Presentment 2. Dishonor 3. Notice of dishonor *Accommodation parties:* An accommodation party is one who signs an instrument to provide credit for another party who has also signed the instrument. *Unauthorized signature:* If a signature to a negotiable instrument is unauthorized, this unauthorized signature will not impose liability to the named party. 1. Negligence 2. Imposter rule 3. Fictitious-payee rule
Warranty Liability	*Transfer warranty:* When a party transfers an instrument to another party for consideration, the transferring party makes certain promises or warranties regarding the instrument and the transfer itself.

Presentment warranty: When a party properly presents an instrument for acceptance, that party makes certain promises regarding the instrument and the party who is entitled to payment.

Avoiding Liability for Negotiable Instruments

1. *Defenses to liability:* The arguments as to why a party should not be held liable for an instrument include:

 a. Real (universal) defenses.

 b. Personal defenses.

2. *Discharge of liability:* Release from liability can occur through:

 a. Discharge by payment or tender of payment.

 b. Discharge by cancellation or renunciation.

 c. Discharge by reacquisition.

 d. Discharge by impairment of recourse.

 e. Discharge by impairment of collateral.

Point/Counterpoint

Should a Company Be Held Liable When an Employee's Work-Related Illegal Actions Include the Endorsement of Fraudulent Checks?

YES	NO
A company should always be held liable for an employee's work-related illegal actions. The company hired the employee and put him in the position to commit an illegal action, so the company should be held responsible.	Companies should not be held liable for an employee's fraudulent checks. The employees, not the companies, should be held liable.
A company benefits from the work of each of its employees. If employees are profitable, company profits increase, the value of shareholder stock increases, and salaries increase; everyone benefits. Thus, because the company *benefits* when the employee is *profitable,* the company should also experience *losses* when the employee is *unprofitable* or *harmful.*	Every employee is an individual who controls his or her own actions. Although a company can try to monitor employee activities, if an employee wants to commit an illegal act, she will. Most companies hire smart, well-qualified people. Smart people can always find a way around even the best company security systems.
One of the factors in assigning liability for fraudulent checks is the ability of a party to bear the loss of the checks. A company is better equipped to bear a loss of funds than an individual. The losses occurred because of the actions of a specific *company* employee. Therefore, a company should shoulder the blame and pay for the losses from the fraudulent checks. After the company bears the losses of the checks, the company can then assess how to penalize the employee who endorsed the fraudulent checks.	Employees also need to feel the consequences of their own actions. If a corporation always takes the hit for an employee's poor decision, the employee cannot learn to change his behavior.
A company should be held liable for an employee's actions because the company has the ability to monitor employee activities and the company chose to use the employee to represent the company.	Companies should not be blamed for an employee's fraudulent checks because, sometimes, the bank responsible for paying out the fraudulent checks should be held responsible. Banks are companies as well, and as such, they should be aware of suspicious activities. When cashing large checks, the bank could easily require a verification code that would be known only by someone authorized to give checks.
	Employees make their own decisions and are not forced to act against the law. Therefore, the employees should be held personally accountable.

Questions & Problems

1. Explain the rationale for the following statement: "The purpose of holder-in-due-course status is to encourage parties to engage in financial transactions."

2. What are the requirements of holder-in-due-course status?

3. What is the distinction between primary liability and secondary liability for a signed negotiable instrument?

4. Evaluate the following statement: "A party can never be held liable for a negotiable instrument if he or she did not sign the check."

5. What are the similarities and differences between transfer and presentment warranties?

6. How are real defenses different from personal defenses to liability for a negotiable instrument?

7. In this bankruptcy case, the court had to determine whether an LLC should have been considered a purchaser of instruments or a holder in due course under the UCC. Yale, the company that purchased the instruments through bankruptcy, did not establish that it acted in good faith in purchasing the instruments by observing reasonable commercial standards of fair dealing. However, Yale was a holder of a complete and authentic negotiable instrument and took the instrument for value. Based on these facts, can Yale be a holder in due course of the instruments? If not, what requirement(s) for being a holder in due course is (are) not met? [*In re Jersey Tractor Trailer Training Inc., Debtor; Wawel Savings Bank v. Jersey Tractor Trailer Training, Inc., and Yale Factors LLC,* 580 F.3d 14 (2009).]

8. At the end of January 2001, while cleaning out his self-storage locker, Kim Griffith found a certificate of deposit purportedly issued by Mellon Bank, N.A., of Pittsburgh, Pennsylvania, on July 3, 1975, for the amount of $530,000 plus interest to be payable to bearer on August 4, 1975. The CD was in one of several books Griffith had purchased from an unnamed buyer. On its face, the certificate of deposit had not been marked paid. On August 15, 2002, more than a year after finding the certificate of deposit, Griffith presented it for payment in person at a Mellon Bank office in Pennsylvania. Mellon refused to honor the certificate of deposit, arguing that because the bearer certificate of deposit matured 27 years earlier, the certificate was questionable on its face and thus was not genuine. On the basis of Mellon's refusal to honor the certificate of deposit, Griffith filed suit against Mellon. Mellon argues that it has no records of the CD as not being paid and that, under Pennsylvania law, it falls to Griffith to prove nonpayment. Griffith argues that he is a holder in due course and is entitled to payment regardless of any possible defenses Mellon might raise. Is Griffith a holder in due course? Should he be able to collect on the CD? Why or why not? [*Griffith v. Mellon Bank, N.A.,* 328 F. Supp. 2d 536 (2004).]

9. A business associate of an elderly man persuaded the man to issue a $10,000 check to recover a failed investment as part of a scam perpetrated on the maker of the check. The business associate (endorser) presented the check to the check-cashing center, which paid it to the endorser after unsuccessfully trying to contact the maker. The maker stopped payment on the check after realizing the check had been paid. The check for $10,000 was cashed by someone identifying himself as a broker; the transaction was not the typical type handled by the check-cashing center; and reasonable commercial standards required that more care be taken than was usual for the normal transactions that occurred at the center. By releasing funds without verifying the check with its maker, the center did not observe reasonable commercial standards. The issue in this case is whether the check-cashing store qualifies as a holder in due course so that it can collect on a $10,000 check written by the elderly man who was fraudulently induced to issue the check by the person who cashed it. How do you think the court ruled? Was the check-cashing store a holder in due course? Did the procedures it used meet the requirements for good faith to be an HDC? [*Any Kind Checks Cashed, Inc. v. Talcott,* 830 So. 2d 160 (2002).]

10. Joshua Herrera found a purse in a dumpster. He contacted the owner of the purse, and it was returned to its owner. After returning the purse, Herrera returned to the dumpster. He found a check written out to "cash." Herrera testified that he thought that meant that he "could get money for the check." He presented the check at a bank, and the bank teller instructed him to put his name on the payee line next to cash. Herrera added the words "to Joshua Herrera" to the payee line and endorsed the check. The trial court found Herrera guilty of forgery. On appeal Herrera argued that he did not alter the check because he did not change the legal efficacy of the check. Herrera claimed that the check was a bearer instrument and payable to anyone possessing the instrument. How do you think the court decided? [*State of New Mexico v. Joshua Herrera,* 2000 N.M. App. LEXIS 100 (2000).]

11. Donald Lynch purchased a check from Allied Irish Bank (AIB) in Ireland. The check was made payable to Advance Marketing and Investment Inc. (AMI) in the amount of U.S. $250.00, which was handwritten as "Two Hundred + Fifty" on the center line of the check and as "U.S. $250.00" on the upper right-hand side of the check. The drawee/payor on the check was HSBC Bank USA. Prior to the check's deposit into AMI's account at F&M Bank–Northern Virginia, the amount of the check was altered from $250.00 to $250,000.00 by adding three zeros and changing the period to a comma in the numerical portion of the check and adding the letters "Thoud" in the written portion. The alteration was unauthorized, and the check was endorsed "A.M.I., Inc." F&M presented the check for payment to HSBC. In so doing, F&M warranted that the check "had not been altered." HSBC honored the check as presented and paid $250,000.00 to F&M, and it debited AIB's account for that amount. HSBC then recredited AIB's account for the amount of the unauthorized alteration and brought suit alleging a claim for breach of presentment warranty. How do you think the court ruled? Was a presentment warranty violated by F&M? [*HSBC Bank USA v. F&M Bank–Northern Virginia,* 246 F.3d (2001).]

12. Olga Ensenat, an 88-year-old woman, had substantial investment accounts. Eventually her niece, Diana Flores, moved in to take care of Ensenat. While living with her, Flores withdrew on Ensenat's accounts, forged Ensenat's signature, and deposited the money into Flores's accounts. In the end Flores embezzled $157,386.30, all of which was deposited at Hancock Bank, where Flores had an account. Ensenat alleged that she did not herself withdraw or authorize any other person to withdraw retirement funds from her accounts. Ensenat sued Hancock Bank, claiming it was responsible because it allowed the checks to be paid or deposited without her endorsement, signature, or authorization. Did the court agree with Ensenat and find Hancock Bank liable for the deposited checks? Why or why not? [*Hancock Bank v. Ensenat,* 819 So. 2d 3 (2001).]

13. A customer of Foster Bank named Choi deposited in her account a check for $133,026 that listed her as the payee. The check had been drawn on Wachovia Bank by a company called MediaEdge that had an account with that bank. Foster presented the check to Wachovia for payment. Wachovia paid Foster and debited MediaEdge's account. Now, as it happened, the actual payee of the check as originally issued was not Choi; it was a company called CMP Media. When CMP Media told MediaEdge that it had not received the check, an investigation ensued and revealed that Choi had somehow gotten her name substituted for CMP Media on the check she deposited. By the time this was discovered, Choi had withdrawn the money from her account and vanished, and Wachovia had destroyed the paper check that Foster had presented to it for payment. It had done this in accordance with its normal practice, the lawfulness of which was not a question. It had retained a computer image of the check, but whether the image was of the original check drawn on Wachovia, with an alteration, or of a forged check could not be determined. The issuing bank's suit was based on the "presentment warranty," under which, when a depositary bank presented a check for payment by the bank that issued the check, it warranted that the check had not been altered. On the basis of these facts and the information you know regarding warranties, who do you think should be liable for the amount of the check? [*Wachovia Bank v. Foster Bancshares,* 457 F.3d 619 (2006).]

14. Michelle Campbell worked for Luiz Simmons as his secretary. After Campbell was hired, she formed an acquaintanceship with Simmons's outside bookkeeper, Denise Evans. Campbell began to forge Simmons's name to checks drawn on several of her employer's accounts. Because Evans was a participant in the scheme and because Simmons trusted his employees, Campbell's forgeries went undetected by Simmons for over two years. During this time, Michael Lennon sold Campbell his Chevrolet Blazer for $22,000. Campbell paid for the Blazer, in part, with a forged check from Simmons's account. Simmons and Lennon knew one another through a business relationship. Also, Lennon and Campbell were once romantically involved, during which time Campbell forged Lennon's name on credit card applications and accumulated $17,000 in credit card debt in Lennon's name. More than 15 months after the sale of the Chevrolet Blazer, Simmons discovered that Campbell, with the aid of Evans, had been embezzling funds from his accounts for over two years by forging his signature on checks. Simmons filed a complaint against Lennon to recover for the amount of the forged check he accepted as payment from Campbell. Simmons argued that Lennon should have known the check was a forgery because he knew Simmons, as well as had firsthand experience with Campbell's illegal actions. How did the court decide the case? Should Lennon have been more cautious in accepting a check from Campbell given their past interactions? [*Simmons v. Lennon,* 139 Md. App. 15 (2001).]

15. Cletus Onyekwere opened a checking account for his company, Weafri Well Services, with NatWest bank. Onyekwere and his wife were the only authorized signatories on the account. In January 1997,

the bank received a letter requiring that Onyekwere's future statements be sent to an address in Nigeria. The bank claimed that this letter was suspicious, and it faxed a letter to Onyekwere to confirm the letter. Onyekwere never responded to the fax, and his address was never changed. Starting in February 1997, the bank paid seven allegedly forged checks bearing what was believed to be Onyekwere's signature. The bank claimed that the forged signatures were not obvious; Onyekwere presented inadmissible evidence that the employees should have discovered that the signature was forged. The last forged check, check 120, was returned for insufficient funds. The check and a statement were mailed to Onyekwere in early March. Onyekwere did not respond to the bank until the end of June. The bank tried to recover the amounts paid on the seven checks, but no recovery was made. Onyekwere sued the bank to recover the amounts debited from his company's account under the allegedly forged checks. Do you think the bank acted in accordance with reasonable commercial standards when paying the checks? What other information might help you make this decision? [*Weafri Well Services, Co. v. Fleet Bank,* 2000 U.S. Dist. LEXIS 14394 (2000).]

Looking for more review material?

The Online Learning Center at **www.mhhe.com/kubasekess2e** contains this chapter's "Assignment on the Internet" and also a list of URLs for more information, entitled "On the Internet." Find both of them in the Student Center portion of the OLC, along with quizzes and other helpful materials.

CHAPTER

18 Secured Transactions and Bankruptcy

Case Opener

A Commercially Reasonable Sale?

On April 27, 1992, Darro and Tracy Long purchased a 1980 Ford Escort for $2,795 from Auto Credit, Inc. They made a cash down payment of $300 and financed the balance of the purchase price. The terms of the financing required that the Longs pay $38.84 each week for 84 weeks. The financing permitted Auto Credit to seize the automobile in the event payments became delinquent. The Longs made six timely payments but returned the automobile to Auto Credit on June 17, 1992, and made no further payments. The automobile as returned was in the same condition as it had been when it was purchased by the Longs with the exception of an additional 3,500 miles on the odometer.

At the time of the surrender, the remaining balance due on the automobile was $2,594.02. Auto Credit informed the Longs that their failure to pay this balance within 10 days would cause the automobile to be sold at a private sale. The automobile was ultimately sold by Auto Credit at the Billings Auto Auction on August 12, 1992, for $150. Auto Credit incurred $229.47 in expenses associated with the sale. Thus, after crediting the sales price and adding the costs associated with the sale, the Longs' indebtedness was increased by $79.47.

Auto Credit filed a lawsuit against the Longs, seeking recovery of the deficiency, which now totaled $2,934.15 with interest and penalties. The Longs filed a counterclaim in which they contended that the sale was unreasonable under the Uniform Commercial Code.[1]

1. If you were the judge deciding this case, would you grant Auto Credit the full $2,934.15 deficiency?

2. If you were the manager of Auto Credit, what steps would you undertake to secure the rights of your company to automobiles purchased on credit and its rights at auction sales of such vehicles subject to repossession?

[1] *Auto Credit, Inc. v. Long,* 971 P.2d 1237 (Mont. 1998).

After reading this chapter, you will be able to answer the following questions:

LO 18-1 What are the important definitions associated with secured transactions?

LO 18-2 How are secured interests created?

LO 18-3 How are secured interests perfected?

LO 18-4 What is the scope of a security interest?

LO 18-5 How are disputes regarding priority handled?

LO 18-6 What is default?

LO 18-7 What are the goals of the Bankruptcy Act?

LO 18-8 What specific types of relief are available through bankruptcy?

LO 18-9 How are the various creditors' claims prioritized in bankruptcy?

The agreement made between Auto Credit and the Longs regarding the automobile is a common component of business transactions. Such agreements are called *secured transactions.* A **secured transaction** is a transaction in which the payment of a debt is guaranteed by personal property owned by the debtor. In the Case Opener, the Longs guaranteed that they would pay the debt for the purchase of the automobile by giving Auto Credit rights to the vehicle, including the right to sell it upon repossession. In contrast, a creditor that does not have a secured interest must file a lawsuit, obtain a judgment, and execute on the judgment to recover money for an unpaid debt.

Article 9 of the Uniform Commercial Code (UCC) governs secured transactions in personal property (as opposed to real property). Thus, throughout the chapter, we refer to Article 9 of the UCC. As of 2009, with some variation, all states had enacted Article 9. Thus, while the law governing secured transactions is state law, the universal adoption of Article 9 permits us to discuss laws regarding secured transactions across state lines.

secured transaction
A transaction in which the payment of a debt is guaranteed by personal property owned by the debtor.

Important Definitions Associated with Secured Transactions

LO 18-1

It is important to understand the definitions of the terms used in secured transactions to understand how such transactions are created. These definitions generally come from the UCC's definitions of the terms:

1. A **secured interest** is an "interest in personal property or fixtures which secures payment or performance of an obligation" [UCC Section 1-201(37)]. Suppose Best Buy sells you a laptop on credit. Best Buy retains a secured interest in the laptop, which means that the store can repossess the laptop if you fail to make payments.

2. A **secured party** is the person or party that holds the interest in the secured property. Thus, in the example above, Best Buy is the secured party. The secured party is also known as the *secured creditor.*

secured interest
An interest in personal property or fixtures that secures payment or performance to a creditor.

secured party
The party that holds the interest in a secured property.

debtor

A party that owes money to another party.

security agreement

An agreement in which the debtor gives the secured interest to the secured party.

collateral

The property that is subject to a secured interest.

3. A **debtor** is the person or party that has an obligation to the secured party. You, the laptop owner, are the debtor because you have an obligation to make payments.

4. A **security agreement** is the agreement in which the debtor gives the secured interest to the secured party. Thus, when you made the agreement with Best Buy, you created a security agreement.

5. **Collateral** is the property that is subject to the security interest. In the Best Buy example, the laptop is the collateral. Collateral may include goods (consumer goods, farm products, inventory, and equipment), indispensable paper (documents of title, negotiable instruments, and chattel paper), intangibles (accounts, goodwill, and literary rights), and proceeds.

LO 18-2

Creation of Secured Interests

How does a creditor become a secured party? To become a secured party, the creditor must gain a security interest in the collateral of the debtor. There are three criteria for creating the security interest:

1. The two parties create a security agreement and either (a) there is a record of the security agreement (usually a written agreement that describes the collateral and is signed by the debtor) or (b) the secured party is in possession of the collateral.

2. The secured party must give value to get the security agreement.

3. The debtor has a right in or to the collateral. [UCC 9-203(b)].

Once these three criteria are met, the secured party's rights attach to the collateral. When **attachment** occurs, the creditor becomes a secured party with an interest in the collateral.

attachment

The point at which a creditor becomes the secured party that has a security interest in the collateral.

WRITTEN AGREEMENT

The written agreement, often referred to as the *security agreement,* must be signed by the debtor. Moreover, the agreement must describe the collateral. The description of the collateral must be accurate and detailed enough to reasonably identify the collateral. For example, in a description of a laptop that is serving as collateral, the serial number of the laptop might be listed in the written agreement. Let's revisit the Auto Credit case. The security agreement between the Longs and Auto Credit most likely included the following: (1) a statement that the Longs are buying the automobile on credit from Auto Credit; (2) a statement that Auto Credit is retaining a security interest in the automobile; (3) a description of the automobile, as well as its vehicle identification number; (4) the price of the automobile, as well as the amount of the monthly payments due to Auto Credit; and (5) a description of the process to be utilized in the event of the Longs' default and subsequent repossession of the vehicle by Auto Credit.

It is important that the collateral be described clearly in the written agreement because the creditor could otherwise lose its rights to the collateral.

VALUE

The secured party must give value. What exactly does it mean to "give value"? According to the UCC, value is consideration. Thus, in the Case Opener, the use of the automobile was considered the value that Auto Credit gave to the Longs. Alternatively, suppose you receive a loan from a company. The money is the value given by the company, the secured party.

DEBTOR RIGHTS IN THE COLLATERAL

The final criterion necessary for the attachment of the security interest is the debtor's rights in the collateral. The Longs, the purchasers of the automobile, had a legal right to the vehicle (the collateral) after they signed the agreement.

PURCHASE-MONEY SECURITY INTEREST

Now that we have discussed the criteria necessary for the creation of a security interest, we briefly consider one specific type of security interest, the **purchase-money security interest (PMSI),** which is formed when a debtor uses borrowed money from the secured party to buy the collateral.

According to the UCC, a PMSI exists when a security interest is retained or taken by (1) the seller of the collateral to secure part or all of the purchase price *or* (2) a person who gives something of value to the debtor so that the debtor can gain rights to or use of the collateral (9-103). In our laptop example, you bought the laptop on credit from Best Buy. Best Buy extended credit to you for the entire purchase price of the laptop. In other words, Best Buy is lending you the money to buy the laptop. Because the laptop is the collateral, Best Buy has a PMSI.

purchase-money security interest (PMSI)
A security interest formed when a debtor uses borrowed money from the secured party to buy the collateral.

Perfected Security Interest

LO 18-3

Suppose that you borrow money from a bank and the bank has a secured interest in your wedding ring. You are supposed to make monthly payments to the bank, but you lose your job and cannot make the payments. When you fail to make these payments, you **default** on the loan. Because the bank has a secured interest, it can repossess your ring.

But suppose you also borrowed money from another creditor, your boss, and you used your ring as collateral for that transaction as well. Your boss was unaware that you used the ring as collateral for your bank loan. Both your boss and your bank have an interest in your ring. Who gets the ring? The party that *perfects* its interest in the ring will have first claim.

When a party perfects its interest in collateral, it is legally protecting its claim to the collateral. **Perfection** is a series of legal steps a secured party takes to protect its right in the collateral from other creditors who want to have their debts satisfied through the same collateral. We consider below the various methods of perfection.

default
Failure to make payments on a loan.

perfection
The series of legal steps a secured party takes to protect its right in the collateral from the other creditors who want to have their debt returned through the same collateral.

PERFECTION BY FILING

The most common way to perfect an interest is to file a financing statement with a state agency. According to the UCC, a **financing statement** should list the names and addresses of all the parties involved, a description of the collateral, and the signature of the debtor (UCC Section 9-502). First, the names and addresses of the statement are important elements because someone looking for the financing statement may want to contact the secured party or the debtor. Second, the financing statement must be filed under the name of the debtor whether the debtor is an individual, an unincorporated business association, or a corporation. If the statement is filed under an incorrect name, the perfection is likely not effective. Third, the financing statement must include a description of the collateral. The purpose of including a description of the collateral is to inform other potential parties who might want to lend money to the debtor. The description of the collateral may be replicated from the description of the collateral in the security agreement.

Once the financing statement is filed, the statement becomes public knowledge. Parties considering making a loan to another party are expected to search for notification of secured interests. Consequently, if you ask to borrow money from your boss, your boss should check with state agencies to ensure that you have not already used your ring as collateral. If your boss discovers that your bank has perfected its interest in your ring, your boss should not agree to loan you money with the ring as your collateral because the bank's perfection of the security interest means that the ring will go directly to the bank. Your boss would have a claim against the ring only as an unsecured creditor.

financing statement
A document that lists the names and addresses of all the parties involved in the transaction, a description of the collateral, and the signature of the debtor.

Place and Duration of Filing Suppose you need to file a financing statement. Where should you file? For how long is the filing effective? The place of filing depends on whether the debtor is an individual or a business. If the debtor is an individual, the secured party files the financing

statement in the state in which the debtor resides. The actual place of filing changes from state to state. Sometimes the statements are filed with the secretary of state. Alternatively, the statements might be filed with the county clerk. Each state must establish a central filing office.

Once you have filed the financing statement with the correct agency, for how long is the statement valid? Under the UCC, the statement is valid for five years (9-515). After five years, the statement expires, and the security interest is not protected. However, within six months of the expiration date of the financing statement, the secured party can file a continuation statement, which is valid for another five years.

PERFECTION BY POSSESSION

pledge
The transfer of collateral to the secured party.

Sometimes a debtor gives a creditor the collateral to hold until the loan is paid off. For example, suppose that you borrow money from a bank and give the bank your diamond necklace to hold until you pay back the loan. The transfer of collateral to the secured party for the purpose of perfection is called a **pledge.** When the bank takes possession of the necklace, it has perfected its interest without filing a financing statement. Once you pay off the loan, the necklace is returned to you.

There are several advantages associated with perfection by possession. First, a secured party does not have to file a financing statement. In fact, the parties do not have to even create a written security agreement. Second, there is little chance that another party will loan money to the debtor relying on the collateral that another secured party possesses. Third, if the debtor defaults on the loan, the secured party already has possession of the collateral, so there are no difficulties associated with repossession.

Despite the many advantages of perfection by possession, it is often impractical because the debtor cannot benefit from the use of the collateral. For example, if you get a loan from a bank to purchase farm equipment, you likely need the farm equipment to produce crops that will enable you to make payments on the loan.

instrument
A writing that serves as evidence of the right to payment of money.

Certain types of collateral *must* be perfected through possession. These types of collateral include **instruments**—writings that serve as evidence of rights to payment of money, such as certificates of deposit—and stocks and bonds.

AUTOMATIC PERFECTION

consumer good
A good used or bought for use primarily for personal, family, or household purposes.

If a retailer had to file a financing statement every time it sold a laptop, a wide-screen television, or a washer and dryer on credit, the retailer would do nothing but file statements. Moreover, it does not make sense for the retailer to possess the collateral. Thus, when a creditor sells a consumer good to a debtor on a credit basis or a creditor extends a loan to a debtor for the purchase of a consumer good, the security interest in the good perfects automatically. Under the UCC, a **consumer good** is a good used or bought for use primarily for personal, family, or household purposes [9-102(23)]. Thus, if an item is purchased for business use, the security interest would not perfect automatically; the secured party would have to file a financing statement.

PERFECTION OF MOVABLE COLLATERAL

According to the UCC, a security interest in collateral that has been perfected in one state will generally transfer to another state for a period of four months from the date that the property is brought into the state. The secured party may reperfect the interest in the new state. However, if the interest is not reperfected, the secured party may lose its protection.

PERFECTION OF SECURITY INTERESTS IN AUTOMOBILES AND BOATS

We have now discussed various methods of perfection: perfection by filing, perfection by possession, automatic possession, and perfection of movable collateral. Exhibit 18-1 provides a summary of the methods of perfection. None of these methods apply to perfection of

Exhibit 18-1

Summary of
Methods of
Perfection by Type
of Collateral

Perfection by Filing	1. *Chattel paper:* Writing that indicates the debtor's monetary obligation as well as a secured interest
	2. *Documents of title:* Papers that demonstrate the owner's possession of the goods (e.g., warehouse receipts)
	3. *Accounts:* Rights to payments for goods sold or leased
	4. *General intangibles:* Trademarks, copyrights, patents
	5. *Equipment:* Goods purchased primarily for business use
	6. *Farm products:* Products of livestock or crops
	7. *Inventory:* Goods held for sale or lease
	8. *Fixtures:* Goods that have become attached to real estate
Automatic Perfection	Purchase-money security interests in consumer goods
Perfection by Possession	1. Chattel paper
	2. Documents of title
	3. Instruments (stocks, bonds, checks)
	4. Equipment
Perfection of Interests in Motor Vehicles	Notation of secured interest on certificate of title

automobiles and boats. Each state has created special laws that pertain to perfection of motor vehicles.

Almost every state requires a certificate of title for any motor vehicle. Perfection of a security interest in a motor vehicle occurs when the secured party makes a notation of this interest on the certificate of title. The rationale for noting the interest on the title is that the title will follow the car owner everywhere. Thus, the title would be the best place to note a secured interest. If a creditor examines a title and discovers no notation of a secured interest in the vehicle, the creditor can assume that no other creditors have a secured interest in the vehicle.

The Scope of a Security Interest LO 18-4

Generally, once a secured party perfects its interest in collateral, the perfection is effective until the collateral is sold, exchanged, or transferred. Our examination of security interests to this point has been concerned with property the debtor currently possesses. However, a security interest can also apply to personal property that is not yet in the debtor's possession.

AFTER-ACQUIRED PROPERTY

You borrow $60,000 from your bank to start an electronics store. However, you have recently graduated from college and have only your car, valued at $3,500, as collateral. The bank will take a security interest in your car, but it will also take a security interest in the materials that you will purchase to open your store. For example, you will need to create an inventory of televisions, computers, and stereos, which are **after-acquired property,** property acquired by the debtor after the security agreement is made. After-acquired property can be inventory, livestock, equipment, or almost any other kind of property. Under the UCC, a party may agree, through a clause in the security agreement, that the security interest will attach to after-acquired property. Whenever the debtor purchases new equipment or goods, the security interest is attached to the new good. Thus, whenever you buy a television to sell in your store, the bank's security interest in the television will attach.

after-acquired property
Property acquired by a debtor after the security arrangement is made.

PROCEEDS

proceeds
Something that is exchanged for a debtor's sold collateral.

When a debtor sells collateral, he or she receives **proceeds,** something that is exchanged for the collateral. The secured party automatically has an interest in the proceeds. Why? If you use a good as collateral for a bank loan and then sell that good, the bank has nothing to continue to secure its loan. Consequently, the security interest in the good also applies to the proceeds from the good.

Under the UCC, the secured party's interest in the proceeds lasts only 10 days after the debtor receives the proceeds. At that time, the secured party will typically need to file a new financing statement. The parties may also agree in the security agreement that there will be extended coverage of interest in the proceeds.

Termination of a Security Interest

termination statement
An amendment to a financing statement which states that the debtor has no obligation to the secured party.

Suppose that rather than defaulting on their loan payment, the Longs paid Auto Credit the full amount for the automobile as required under the agreement. If a secured party has filed a financing statement and the debtor has repaid the secured party, the secured party must file a termination statement with the filing office. A **termination statement** is an amendment to a financing statement which provides that the debtor has no obligation to the secured party [UCC Section 9-513(a)].

LO 18-5

Priority Disputes

We have spent much time discussing the perfection of a security interest. Why? Remember, perfection of an interest is supposed to serve as protection of the secured party's interest in collateral from other creditors. In this section, we consider various conflicts between creditors who claim interest in the same collateral. A conflict may arise in many circumstances; however, priority disputes are most likely to arise when a debtor files for bankruptcy.

SECURED VERSUS UNSECURED CREDITORS

Generally, secured parties have priority over unsecured creditors. Thus, if two parties provide a loan based on the same collateral, the party with the secured interest will have priority in repossessing the collateral over the party with the unsecured interest. This priority to the collateral does not depend on the perfection of a secured interest. Rather, the priority depends on the *attachment* of the secured interest.

SECURED VERSUS SECURED CREDITORS

Who has priority to the collateral when both parties are secured creditors? If both parties are secured, the determination of priority for claim to collateral moves to considerations of time and perfection.

If there is a dispute between a perfected secured party and an unperfected secured party, the creditor with the perfected interest has priority over the unperfected interest. But what if the dispute is between two secured parties with perfected interests? The party that perfected its interest first will have priority in claim to the collateral (UCC Section 9-317). Finally, if neither party has perfected its security interest, the party that attached its security interest first will have first claim to the collateral.

Exhibit 18-2 provides a summary of the priority of creditors' claims to collateral.

PMSI Conflicts There is an exception to these priority rules. Generally, if a PMSI is involved, the perfected PMSI will almost always have priority over other claims to collateral. The rules regarding PMSIs depend on whether the collateral is inventory or noninventory.

First, if the PMSI is in inventory, the perfected PMSI has priority over a previously perfected non-PMSI if the following two conditions are met: (1) The PMSI party perfects its interest before

DISPUTE	PREVAILING PARTY
Secured versus unsecured creditor	Secured creditor
Secured perfected creditor versus secured unperfected creditor	Secured perfected creditor
Secured perfected creditor versus secured perfected creditor	Party that perfected its interest first
Secured unperfected creditor versus secured unperfected creditor	Party that attached its interest first

Exhibit 18-2

Summary of Priority of Creditors' Claims to Collateral

or at the same time that the debtor receives his inventory; and (2) the PMSI party checks for previous secured interests and gives written notice to the holders of the PMSI [UCC 9-324(b)]. For example, General Electric Capital Commercial Automotive (GECC) Inc. entered into a security agreement with Spartan Motors, Ltd. GECC loaned Spartan over $1 million and secured this loan by attaching its rights to Spartan's entire inventory as collateral. GECC filed this agreement in New York. A few years later, Spartan signed another security agreement, but this time it was with General Motors Acceptance Corporation (GMAC). This agreement, however, was an agreement that involved a PMSI. GMAC loaned money to Spartan to purchase its inventory. Realizing that this was a PMSI, GMAC filed its agreement *and* notified GECC of its competing security interest.

The next year, Spartan filed a bankruptcy petition and went out of business. GMAC repossessed two BMWs that were purchased with the money it had loaned to Spartan and sold them in an auction for $194,500. GECC brought an action against GMAC on grounds that GECC's security interest had priority. In the end, the court found that because GMAC had a PMSI in inventory *and* notified GECC of the competing agreement, GMAC had priority to the profits from the sale of the BMWs.

SECURED PARTY VERSUS BUYER

If a debtor sells collateral in which a secured party has an interest, the security interest generally remains in effect. Suppose you obtain a loan from a bank and use your boat as collateral. You need more money, so you sell your boat. The bank's secured interest in the boat remains with the boat. If you default on the loan, the bank can seize the boat from the buyer. However, the UCC provides some exceptions to this general rule.

Buyers in the Ordinary Course of Business A **buyer in the ordinary course of business** is a person who routinely buys goods in good faith from a person who routinely sells such goods. Under the UCC, a buyer in the ordinary course of business can take the goods free of any security interest created by the seller of the good *even if* the security interest is perfected [9-320(a)]. What is the rationale for this rule? Asking buyers to determine whether a security interest in inventory exists is burdensome. Thus, the purpose of this rule is to encourage commerce. For example, if your company buys products from an electronics store in the ordinary course of business, you can take possession of these products free of any security interest created by the party who originally sold the products to the electronics store.

buyer in the ordinary course of business
A person who routinely buys goods in good faith from a person who routinely sells such goods.

Buyers of Consumer Goods Suppose you buy a digital camera for $800 on credit from Best Buy. Best Buy has a security agreement for a PMSI in the digital camera. (Remember, a PMSI in a consumer good perfects automatically.) However, you discover that you do not have enough money to pay your rent. Consequently, you sell your digital camera to your neighbor, who is unaware of Best Buy's secured interest in the camera. Can Best Buy repossess the camera? Under the UCC, as long as the buyer is not aware of the security interest, purchases the good for his or her personal use, and purchases the good before the secured party files a financial statement, the buyer obtains the good free of the security interest [9-320(b)]. Even though the secured party's interest perfects automatically, the secured party must have filed a financial statement to repossess a consumer good from another buyer.

Consider Case 18-1, in which the court considers the transfer of an automobile to a third party.

CASE 18-1

IN RE GIROLAMO AFONICA, DEBTOR
BANKRUPTCY COURT, NORTHERN DISTRICT OF OHIO
174 B.R. 242 (1994)

FACTS: *First of America Bank had a security interest in a 1966 Chevrolet Chevelle owned by Girolamo Afonica. The Chevelle secured a loan of $11,276.46 made by the bank to Afonica. Afonica transferred the Chevelle without a certificate of title for $25 to a friend who was a junk dealer. The reason for the transfer was the alleged objection to the Chevelle's continued presence on the driveway by Afonica's ex-wife. Afonica subsequently filed for Chapter 7 bankruptcy. As a result of the prior transfer, Afonica was unable to deliver the Chevelle to the bank as required by the security agreement.*

ISSUE: The bank moved the bankruptcy court for an order denying Afonica a discharge or the exclusion of its debt from his discharge on the basis that Afonica willfully and maliciously injured property in which the bank maintained a security interest.

REASONING: The court agreed with the bank and held Afonica's debt to be nondischargeable in bankruptcy. To succeed in denying a debtor a discharge, a creditor must establish that (1) the debtor transferred, or permitted to be transferred (2) property of the debtor (3) within one year before the petition in bankruptcy was filed (4) with the intent to hinder, delay, or defraud the creditor or in a willful and malicious manner. Although the transfer of the Chevelle violated the security agreement, the court could not assume that it was done with the specific intent to hinder, delay, or defraud the bank. Although the bank clearly demonstrated that the sale of the Chevelle was improper, it failed to demonstrate the requisite intent to conclude that fraud was committed. However, the court determined that

the bank proved that Afonica willfully and maliciously caused injury to the collateral. This conclusion was based on the intentional nature of the sale, the lack of notice to the bank, the lack of a valid justification for the sale, and Afonica's refusal to offer title to the purchaser (which fostered the impression that the Chevelle was clear of liens). The sale thus willfully and maliciously deprived the bank of its ability to collect the collateral to recover or offset Afonica's liability in the event of default. The debt was thus nondischargeable in the amount of the lesser of either the value of the converted property or the amount of the indebtedness.

DECISION AND REMEDY: The court ordered the bank and Afonica to provide evidence attesting to the fair market value of the Chevelle so that the court could enter an appropriate damage award.

SIGNIFICANCE OF THE CASE: This case illustrates the difficulty creditors may encounter in attempting to deny relief to a debtor in bankruptcy when a secured interest is at stake. Although Afonica clearly violated the security agreement, the court was unwilling to declare the sale of the Chevelle for $25 to be fraud on its face without further evidence. However, the case also demonstrates that a debtor should exercise considerable care when selling property in which his or her creditor maintains a secured interest as such sales may be subject to judicial examination at a later date. Obtaining fair market value for such property and disclosing the existence of the secured interest are of paramount importance in such circumstances.

CRITICAL THINKING

What are the issue and conclusion in this case? Why was the bank successful in its claim against Afonica even in the absence of fraud?

ETHICAL DECISION MAKING

As with any disagreement over what is fair, it is relatively easy to identify the primary interests involved in the dispute. But court rulings have a responsibility to look beyond the surface interests. In this case, whose interests are affected by the ruling and need to be taken into consideration when making a determination like the one the court made?

Buyers of Chattel Paper and Instruments If a buyer purchases **chattel paper,** a writing that indicates both a monetary obligation and a security interest in specific goods, or an *instrument,* a writing that demonstrates a right to payment of money, in the ordinary course of business, the buyer can obtain the good free of any security interest. The buyer must typically be unaware of the security interest in the good. Why is there an exception for buyers of chattel paper and instruments? Both chattel paper and instruments are easily transferable. Consequently, the UCC provides that these forms of collateral can be sold to a buyer free of the secured party's interest.

Sometimes, the issue with a secured creditor is not the simple repossession of the collateral in question but the collection of monies due on the collateral. In the following Case Nugget, the secured creditor repossessed collateral when the debtor filed bankruptcy. However, that property had been damaged and repaired by the debtor. The insurance policy covering the collateral had never been paid on the damaged property. The secured creditor argued that it should also receive the insurance money as well as the property itself.

chattel paper
A writing that indicates both a monetary obligation and a security interest in specific goods.

CASE Nugget

Rights of a Secured Party

In re Tower Air, Inc.
Third Circuit Court of Appeals

397 F.3d 191 (3d Cir. 2005)

May a secured party recover insurance proceeds for damage to collateral that had been repaired and returned to the lender? Tower, an airline, borrowed $21 million from Finova to purchase an aircraft and four aircraft engines. As part of the security agreement, Finova received a security interest in the aircraft and four engines. The security agreement also provided that Tower would insure the collateral and that Finova would also have a security interest in the insurance proceeds. The lender perfected its security interest in the planes, engines, and insurance proceeds.

In 1997, one of the engines was damaged in an accident. Using its own funds, Tower repaired the engine for $2.25 million (while $1.91 million was attributable to the accident). Tower did not submit an insurance claim.

Tower later filed for bankruptcy. Because Finova had a secured interest, all collateral, including the repaired engine, was returned to the lender. The bankruptcy trustee then discovered the insurance policy and filed a claim for $1.91 million in repairs. The insurance company settled the claim by paying approximately $950,000. Finova objected to the settlement and argued that it was entitled to the insurance proceeds pursuant to the security agreement. The bankruptcy court ruled that the insurance proceeds should be paid to Finova, and the district court agreed.

On appeal, the trustee argued that Finova should not recover the insurance proceeds because it had already recovered the fully repaired engine. Recovering both the insurance proceeds and the repaired engine would be unfair. The court ruled that Finova was permitted to recover the collateral and insurance money to the extent of the amount of the debt. Much of the collateral was damaged; thus, Finova was permitted to recover the full value of the insurance proceeds.

Default

LO 18-6

Generally, when a debtor fails to make payments on a loan or declares bankruptcy, the debtor has *defaulted* on the loan. However, the UCC does not define *default.* Consequently, each security agreement provides a specific definition of what is considered a default. Moreover, each agreement determines the procedures and consequences that occur in the event of default. Because the

creditor is usually in a better bargaining position, the creditor usually determines the definition of default.

What are a secured party's remedies to recover its money when a debtor defaults on a loan? The secured party can (1) take possession of the collateral or (2) ignore its rights in the collateral and proceed to judgment. However, the party is not limited to just one of these remedies. If one method is unsuccessful, the party can attempt to pursue the other method. Note that these remedies are limited if the debtor has filed for bankruptcy.

TAKING POSSESSION OF THE COLLATERAL

If a debtor defaults on a loan, the secured party can take possession of the collateral (UCC Section 9-609). While the secured party may act without any court order to retain possession of the property, the secured party may not "breach the peace" in repossessing the property. What exactly is *breaching the peace?* The UCC does not define the phrase. Generally, if the secured party can repossess the collateral without using force or committing trespass, the action is not a breach of the peace. If the secured party is unable to repossess the property without breaching the peace, the party will file suit against the debtor to obtain a court order for the debtor to turn over the property.

Generally, the security agreement will state that if the debtor defaults on the loan, the debtor must turn over the collateral in a reasonable time and manner. If the debtor refuses to turn over the property, the secured party will typically hire a repossession company to obtain the collateral. Once the secured party has possession of the collateral, the party can choose to retain or dispose of the collateral.

Disposition of the Collateral Under the UCC, the secured party can sell, lease, or transfer the collateral in any commercially reasonable method (9-610). The secured party may sell the collateral in a private or public sale. Regardless of where the collateral is sold, the secured party must strive to receive the best price for the collateral. Striving to receive the best price is part of the requirement to conduct every aspect of the sale in a "commercially reasonable manner." In addition to adhering to the commercial reasonableness requirement, the secured party must also notify the debtor of the sale. Additionally, the secured party must notify any other parties that have secured interests in the collateral.

Once the collateral is sold, the proceeds must be paid in the following order: (1) paying the reasonable expenses of retaking and disposing of the collateral (including attorney fees), (2) satisfying the debt of the secured party, and (3) satisfying remaining holders of junior security interests [UCC 9-615(a)].

Retention of the Collateral Instead of disposing of the collateral, the secured party may choose to keep the collateral in full or partial satisfaction of the debt. However, the secured party must notify the debtor of this intent by sending written notice. The debtor has 20 days to object to the secured party's retention of the collateral. If the debtor does not object to the retention, the secured party may retain the collateral (UCC 9-620-622). By retaining the collateral for full satisfaction of debt, the secured party gives up any claim to the debt. In other words, the secured party cannot demand additional money from the debtor. Consequently, if the collateral is not valued at the full amount of the money due to the secured party, the secured party has no right to additional money from the debtor. If the debtor objects to the secured party's retention of the collateral, the secured party must sell or dispose of the collateral.

PROCEEDING TO JUDGMENT

Another remedy for a defaulted loan is the secured party's rejection of the right in the collateral and the party's filing of a suit against the debtor. The secured party can sue the debtor for the entire amount of the debt. Rather than taking the time to organize the sale of the collateral, the secured party may choose to file suit. In contrast, an unsecured creditor has just one option: to file suit and seek a judgment in the amount of the debt.

Bankruptcy and Reorganization

When an entity is unable to pay its debts, bankruptcy law provides various options for the entity to resolve these debts. Bankruptcy remedies are available to individuals, partnerships, and corporations.

Generally, a debtor is an entity that owes money to another entity. However, the term *debtor* is defined differently under each type of bankruptcy remedy; thus, an individual or company that is eligible for one type of bankruptcy might not be eligible for another type of bankruptcy.

The remainder of this chapter explains the various bankruptcy remedies available to debtors. We begin with a discussion of the goals of bankruptcy law and an overview of the Bankruptcy Code. Then we consider specific types of bankruptcy relief under the code.

The Bankruptcy Act and Its Goals

LO 18-7

There are two general goals of bankruptcy laws. First, bankruptcy laws provide protection to **creditors**—entities to whom a debtor owes money. Bankruptcy laws ensure that creditors competing for a debtor's assets are treated equally and receive a fair share of the debtor's assets. Second, bankruptcy laws provide opportunities for debtors to gain a fresh financial start. In summary, bankruptcy law provides an organized method by which **insolvent debtors**—debtors who cannot pay their debts in a timely fashion—respond to their debts.

Bankruptcy law is federal law. Article I, Section 8, of the Constitution states: "The Congress shall have the power . . . to establish an uniform rule of naturalization and uniform laws on the subject of bankruptcies throughout the United States." Congress recently revised the Bankruptcy Code through the **Bankruptcy Abuse Prevention and Consumer Protection Act (BAPCPA) of 2005.** This revision includes the most comprehensive changes to bankruptcy law in over 25 years.

creditor
An entity to which a debtor owes money.

insolvent debtor
A debtor who cannot pay debts in a timely fashion.

Bankruptcy Abuse Prevention and Consumer Protection Act (BAPCPA) of 2005
A renovation in the system of bankruptcy enacted to address increased numbers of bankruptcy filings, significant losses associated with bankruptcy filings, loopholes and incentives that allowed for abuse, and the financial ability of debtors.

TITLE 11 OF THE UNITED STATES CODE

Title 11 of the United States Code (U.S.C.) contains the Bankruptcy Code, which is divided into chapters. Chapters 1, 3, and 5 provide the general definitions and provisions concerning bankruptcy case administration and debtors. These chapters apply to all types of bankruptcy relief. Chapters 7, 9, 11, 12, 13, and 15, briefly described in Exhibit 18-3, apply six specific types of bankruptcy relief.

Bankruptcy Proceedings

Most bankruptcy cases share a set of procedures, or certain actions that must be taken in every bankruptcy case. These actions are as follows:

1. All bankruptcy cases begin with the filing of a petition for bankruptcy.
2. Once the petition is filed, the court grants an automatic stay for creditor actions against the debtor's estate. In other words, creditors' legal actions against the debtor must cease.

Chapter 7	Sale of the debtor's assets by a trustee and the distribution of money to creditors
Chapter 9	Adjustment of a municipality's debts
Chapter 11	Reorganization of the debtor's financial affairs under supervision of the bankruptcy court
Chapter 12	Reorganization of a family farmer's debts
Chapter 13	Reorganization of an individual's debts
Chapter 15	Recognition of insolvency proceedings pending in a foreign country and relief for foreign debtors

Exhibit 18-3

Types of Bankruptcy Relief by Chapter

LO 18-8

Specific Types of Relief Available

Before a debtor files for one specific type of relief, the clerk of courts must give the debtor written notice of the other types of relief available. This requirement helps to ensure that the debtor has full information about the bankruptcy process.

Under BAPCPA, an individual may not be considered a debtor under any chapter unless within 180 days prior to filing, he or she receives credit counseling from a nonprofit budget and credit counseling agency. If the individual does not fulfill the credit-counseling requirement, the bankruptcy court will dismiss the bankruptcy petition—even if the individual faces immediate home foreclosure or wage garnishment.

Moreover, BAPCPA attempts to prevent "repeat filers" from filing one bankruptcy claim after another. If an individual was a debtor in a bankruptcy case that was dismissed within 180 days of the current case, the individual is generally not eligible to be a debtor under Chapters 7, 11, or 13. However, if the previous bankruptcy was completed rather than dismissed, the individual is generally permitted to file for bankruptcy again. If a party completes a Chapter 7 bankruptcy, the party is not permitted to seek a Chapter 7 bankruptcy again for eight years.

In the following sections we discuss the main types of relief available, including Chapter 7, 11, 12, and 13 bankruptcies.

CHAPTER 7: LIQUIDATION PROCEEDINGS

liquidation
The process in which a debtor turns over all assets to a trustee.

trustee
In bankruptcy proceedings, an individual who takes over administration of a debtor's estate.

The most familiar type of bankruptcy proceeding is liquidation, which is sometimes called *straight bankruptcy*. **Liquidation** occurs when a debtor turns over all assets to a **trustee**, an individual who takes over administration of the debtor's estate. Trustees are usually attorneys in private practice who specialize in bankruptcy law. Every Chapter 7 proceeding has a trustee who sells the nonexempt assets and distributes the proceeds of the sale among the creditors. Liquidation provides an organized method of selling the debtor's property to generate cash to pay creditors.

Who is defined as a debtor for liquidation purposes? Under Chapter 7 liquidation proceedings, individuals, partnerships, and corporations are considered debtors. Railroads, insurance companies, banks, savings and loan associations, industrial banks, credit unions, and health maintenance organizations are not eligible for Chapter 7 relief.

Petition Filing As is the case with most bankruptcies, liquidation begins when the petition is filed. Under Chapter 7, liquidation may be voluntary or involuntary; thus, a voluntary or involuntary petition is filed. The person filing the petition is also responsible for paying filing fees.

Voluntary Liquidation Petition. When the debtor decides to file for bankruptcy, he or she files a voluntary petition. The debtor must state that he or she understands the other types of bankruptcy relief available and chooses liquidation. Once the petition is filed, all the debtor's prepetition assets form the **bankruptcy estate.** Assets that the debtor gains after filing the petition are generally not part of the bankruptcy estate unless they fall under an exemption.

bankruptcy estate
The assets that are collected from a debtor who files for bankruptcy.

Involuntary Liquidation Petition. If a debtor is not paying debts as they come due, creditors can attempt to force the debtor into bankruptcy by filing an involuntary petition under Chapter 7. By filing the petition, the creditors attempt to force the debtor to surrender his or her assets so that the proceeds from the sale of the assets may be distributed among the creditors. If the judge believes that creditors are using involuntary liquidation proceedings frivolously, the court may force the creditors to pay the attorney costs, fees of the debtor, and even punitive damages.

Not everyone can be forced into bankruptcy through Chapter 7. Farmers, ranchers, and nonprofit organizations are examples of debtors that cannot be forced into liquidation. Also, debtors that are ineligible to voluntarily file for Chapter 7 bankruptcy (railroads, insurance companies, banks, savings and loan associations, credit unions, and health maintenance organizations) are excluded from forced bankruptcy.

Dismissal of Petition A bankruptcy judge may dismiss a voluntary or involuntary bankruptcy petition. Under BAPCPA, a bankruptcy judge may dismiss a petition "for cause." One cause for dismissal is failure of the *means test.* If an individual's debt is primarily consumer debt and if the

individual's income is above the median income in his or her state, the court may presume that the individual is abusing the bankruptcy provisions. However, the individual may continue with the petition under the presumption.

Automatic Stay Once a petition, voluntary or involuntary, is filed, the code provides for an **automatic stay,** or moratorium, for almost all creditor litigation against the debtor. During the stay, creditors cannot bring or continue legal action against the debtor or his property. For example, creditors cannot attempt to repossess property during bankruptcy proceedings. Moreover, if a creditor received a judgment against a debtor prior to the bankruptcy filing, the creditor may not enforce the judgment.

There are some exceptions to the stay. First, under BAPCPA, if the debtor was a debtor in a bankruptcy case that was dismissed within a year of the current bankruptcy case filing, the stay automatically terminates 30 days after the current filing. Second, legal actions to determine paternity or to collect child support or alimony payments are not subject to the stay. Third, the court may exclude secured creditors from the stay if they petition the court to show that they do not have "adequate protection" under the stay. If a creditor is aware of the stay and continues to engage in legal action against the debtor, the code provides that the debtor may recover damages, costs, attorney fees, and possibly even punitive damages.

Order of Relief After a bankruptcy petition has been filed, the next step is for the court to determine whether an order of relief is granted. An **order of relief** means that bankruptcy relief is ordered; that is, the bankruptcy proceedings can continue. If the filing of the voluntary petition is proper, the petition automatically becomes an order of relief. Similarly, if a debtor does not object to an involuntary bankruptcy, the order of relief is automatic.

Should the debtor challenge the involuntary petition for bankruptcy, a hearing will be held. At the hearing, the judge generally will grant the order of relief for involuntary bankruptcy if one of two conditions occurs:

1. The debtor is not paying debts as they become due.
2. The custodian took possession of almost all the debtor's property within 120 days before filing the petition.

After the court enters the order of relief, a U.S. trustee, a government official appointed by the attorney general, selects an interim trustee. A *trustee* is the person responsible for collecting the debtor's available assets and liquidating the property into cash for the creditors. The interim trustee is responsible for organizing the creditors' meeting.

Creditors' Meeting Between 20 and 40 days after the order of relief has been granted, the interim trustee calls a **creditors' meeting**—a meeting of all the creditors listed in the Chapter 7 required schedule for liquidation. While the debtor and the interim trustee also attend this meeting, the bankruptcy judge does not attend.

If the debtor fails to appear at the meeting, the court may refuse to grant the bankruptcy. The principal purpose of the creditors' meeting is to enable the creditors and trustee to examine the debtor under oath regarding her financial affairs. The debtor's filing of the Chapter 7 required schedules does not necessarily provide enough information. Creditors want to know more about the way the debtor is handling her assets and property. Moreover, they want to ensure that the debtor is not concealing property. Not only does the trustee ask the debtor questions regarding her financial status, but the trustee also ensures that the debtor is aware of the other forms of bankruptcy relief as well as the consequences of filing for bankruptcy.

Another important purpose of the creditors' meeting is the election of a permanent trustee. The interim trustee might become the permanent trustee, or the creditors might elect a different one. The creditors elect the trustee because the trustee generally represents the creditors.

The Trustee The general duty of the trustee is to collect the debtor's available assets (i.e., the debtor's prefiling assets) and to liquidate the property to cash that will be distributed among the creditors. Thus, the trustee takes possession of the debtor's property and has it appraised. Moreover, the trustee examines the debtor's records and might even temporarily take over the debtor's business. If someone else holds the debtor's property, the trustee has the power to require that the

automatic stay
After bankruptcy has been filed, a moratorium during which creditors cannot bring or continue action against the debtor or his or her property.

order of relief
An order stating that bankruptcy proceedings can continue.

creditors' meeting
A meeting of all the creditors listed in the Chapter 7 required schedule for liquidation.

person return that property. Next, the trustee separates the exempt property from the nonexempt property and sells the nonexempt property. In addition to selling the debtor's property, the trustee has a variety of powers that assist him in fulfilling his duties. First, the trustee has the power to sue and be sued. He can initiate collection actions but must also defend against creditor actions. He has the right to assume or reject executory contracts. Moreover, he has the right to obtain credit. Finally, the trustee has the power to void certain liens against the debtor's property. For example, a debtor's ability to exempt property is hindered by any liens against such possessions. Consequently, the trustee is permitted to void these liens.

Exempt Property A debtor is not required to give up her exempt property. The trustee sorts the exempt property from the nonexempt property. The exemptions are stated in the Bankruptcy Code and are adjusted every three years on the basis of the consumer price index.

There are federal exemptions as well as state exemptions. States, through legislation, can and have opted out of the federal exemptions to give debtors the option for state exemptions only. However, in some states, a debtor may choose whether to make state or federal exemptions; the debtor cannot make some state exemptions and some federal exemptions. Exhibit 18-4 lists the federal exemptions. In addition to having the exemptions in Exhibit 18-4, a debtor is entitled to 100 percent of Social Security benefits, veteran's benefits, and civil service retirement benefits. One exemption was recently added—retirement funds in an individual retirement account (IRA).

Why has Congress created such exemptions for property? Suppose that a debtor was forced to sell all his property through liquidation. Remember, one purpose of bankruptcy is to provide a debtor with a fresh start. If a debtor were forced to sell all his property, he would likely fall right back into debt again. Thus, the exemptions are for items considered necessary to earning a living.

Consider the dilemma regarding the retirement funds that are the focus of Case 18-2, which provides the Supreme Court's reasoning for why IRA funds are exempt.

CASE 18-2

ROUSEY v. JACOWAY
UNITED STATES SUPREME COURT
544 U.S. 320 (2006)

FACTS: *Richard and Betty Jo Rousey were employed by Northrup Grumman Corporation. When their employment was terminated, Northrup Grumman required them to take lump-sum distributions from their employer-sponsored retirement plans. The Rouseys deposited the lump sums in two IRAs, one in each of their names. Several years later, the Rouseys filed a joint Chapter 7 bankruptcy petition in which they listed the IRAs as exempt. The trustee objected to this exemption, and the bankruptcy court agreed with the trustee that the IRAs should be included in the bankruptcy estate. On appeal, the Bankruptcy Appellate Panel and Court of Appeals agreed that the IRAs were not exempt. The Rouseys appealed to the U.S. Supreme Court, which granted certiorari and heard the case.*

ISSUE: Do the individual IRA accounts satisfy two requirements under the Bankruptcy Code for exemption:

(1) the right to receive the compensation due to a pension plan, annuity, profit-sharing plan, and the like; and (2) the right to receive payment due to illness, disability, or minimum retirement age?

REASONING: The Court first held that the right to receive payment pursuant to the IRAs was on account of the Rouseys' age. The Court determined that "on account of" means "because of," thereby requiring a causal connection between the right to receive payment and age. Although the Rouseys could withdraw funds from the IRAs for any reason whatsoever as long as they were willing to pay a 10 percent penalty before the age of 59½ years, this did not mean that the right to payment was unrelated to old age. The Court held that the substantial tax penalty suggested that the U.S. Congress designed it to preclude early access to IRAs. It therefore limits the Rouseys' right to

payment of the balance of their IRAs. This limitation could be removed only by age, specifically, the account holder turning 59½ years old.

The Court then addressed the issue of whether the IRAs were a stock bonus, pension, profit-sharing, annuity, or similar plan or contract. To be "similar," an IRA must be like, though not identical to, the specific plans or contracts listed in the Bankruptcy Code and must share common characteristics. Although the Bankruptcy Code does not define any of these terms, their common feature is that they provide income that substitutes for wages. The Court concluded that the income the Rouseys would derive from their IRAs is income that substitutes for wages. First, the minimum-distribution requirements mandate that distribution begin, at the latest, in the calendar year after the year in which the account holder turns 70½, after which they are most likely retired and lacking wage income. Second, the Internal Revenue Code's

tax treatment of money held in IRAs encourages account holders to wait until retirement to withdraw the funds. Third, withdrawals before age 59½ are subject to a tax penalty, restricting preretirement access to the funds. Fourth, to ensure that the beneficiary uses the IRA in his retirement years, an account holder's failure to take the requisite minimum distributions results in a 50 percent tax penalty on funds improperly remaining in the account. All of these features show that IRA income substitutes for wages lost upon retirement and distinguish IRAs from typical savings accounts.

DECISION AND REMEDY: The U.S. Supreme Court reversed the bankruptcy appellate panel and the court of appeals and held that the IRAs were exempt.

SIGNIFICANCE OF THE CASE: This case put to rest one of the most compelling interests that employees have, specifically, protection of personal IRAs.

CRITICAL THINKING

One of the most controversial issues surrounding the judiciary is the notion of "judicial activism." "Judicial activism" is the claim that judges act outside their role as judges and begin to legislate through judicial opinions. Critics argue that this role should be left to the legislatures, not the judiciary. Others argue that such interpretation is necessary to keep the law relevant and up to date. Do you believe that this case, coming from a relatively conservative Supreme Court, is an example of judicial activism?

ETHICAL DECISION MAKING

We can certainly understand the interests advanced by the decision made by the Court in this case. But what stakeholders are potentially harmed by this decision?

Exhibit 18-4

Federal Bankruptcy Exemptions

1. Up to $15,000 for residence
2. Interest in a motor vehicle (not necessarily an automobile) up to $2,400
3. Interest, up to $400 for a particular item, in personal and household goods and furnishings, clothing, appliances, books, animals, crops, and musical instruments (aggregate total of all items limited to $8,000)
4. Interest in jewelry up to $1,000
5. $800 of any property the debtor chooses (functions as a "wild-card" exemption)
6. Tools of trade and professional books up to $1,500
7. Any unmatured life insurance contract owned by the debtor
8. Professionally prescribed health aids
9. Interest in any other property up to $800, plus any unused part of the homestead exemption up to $7,500
10. The right to receive certain personal injury awards up to $15,000
11. Retirement funds in an IRA or SEP

A debtor must file a list of the property that she or he claims is exempt. Under the Bankruptcy Code and the bankruptcy rules, creditors may file objections to the claimed exemptions. If a debtor improperly lists property as exempt and a creditor does not timely file an objection, the debtor will likely be permitted to claim the property as exempt.

Preferential Payments Because a major purpose of the Bankruptcy Code is to prevent debtors from making payments to one creditor and thus treating that creditor preferentially, the trustee has the power to recover **preferential payments,** or payments made by an insolvent debtor that give preferential treatment to one creditor over another. If the debtor made any payments within 90 days of the bankruptcy filing, the trustee can examine these payments as preferential payments. For a payment to be preferential, the trustee must show that the transfer gave the creditor more money than the creditor would have received through bankruptcy proceedings. Thus, other creditors are disadvantaged by the debtor's preferential payment.

> **preferential payment**
> A payment made by an insolvent debtor that gives preferential treatment to one creditor over another.

If the preferred creditor is an insider, such as a relative or partner, the trustee has the power to recover payments made within two years before the debtor's filing for bankruptcy. However, in such cases, the trustee must demonstrate the debtor's insolvency rather than assume insolvency. In contrast, the trustee may not recover preferential payments made for alimony or child support.

Fraudulent Transfers A trustee can recover preferential payments because these payments are not fair to creditors. Similarly, a trustee can void **fraudulent transfers** of property. These transfers can be actually or constructively fraudulent. An *actual fraudulent transfer* would be made with intent to defraud creditors. Generally, there is no direct evidence of intent to defraud (e.g., an e-mail written by a debtor who states that he is transferring assets to hide them). To show *constructive* fraud, a trustee would establish intent through circumstantial evidence.

> **fraudulent transfer**
> A transfer of property made with intent to defraud creditors or made for an amount significantly lower than the property's fair market value within two years of filing for bankruptcy.

Similarly, if a debtor transfers property for an amount significantly lower than its fair market value, he or she may have engaged in a fraudulent transfer. Suppose that you are unable to pay your debts and are preparing to file for bankruptcy. You decide to sell your $50,000 boat to your business partner for $50. The trustee of your case could recover the boat if the sale occurred within two years of your filing for bankruptcy. Furthermore, you could be subject to criminal penalties for your attempt to hide your assets. By punishing debtors who attempt to hide their assets, the Bankruptcy Code provides protection for creditors.

Suppose that, instead of selling your boat to your business partner, you sold your boat to a creditor. Because you are making a payment to a creditor, the trustee would analyze this payment as a preferential payment (assessing how the other creditors would be harmed by this payment) rather than a fraudulent transfer (assessing the reasonableness of consideration for the transfer).

LO 18-9

Creditors' Claims Within 90 days of the creditors' meeting, all creditors (except secured creditors) must file a proof of claim with the bankruptcy court clerk to receive a portion of the debtor's estate. This proof of claim lists the creditor's name and address and the amount of the debt owed to the creditor. If the creditor fails to file such a claim, the creditor may not receive a portion of the debt. However, the fact that the claim was filed does not mean that the creditor will automatically receive a portion of the proceeds from the sale of the debtor's assets. The trustee must permit that the claim be allowed, and there are numerous defenses to creditors' claims.

When the trustee is sorting and examining the property, the trustee must determine whether a creditor has a secured interest in the debtor's property. If a secured interest exists, the creditor has first claim to the property. The debtor may decide to surrender the property to the creditor to satisfy the debt. Alternatively, the creditor may foreclose on the property and use the proceeds of the sale to reduce the debt owed to the creditor. However, the secured party is secured only to the value of the collateral.

All creditors do not have equal claims to the proceeds of the sale. Secured parties have priority over all unsecured parties in receiving portions of the proceeds of the liquidation. Thus, secured parties are paid first. The code establishes classes of priority claims. One class must be completely paid before anyone in another class receives any payment. If there are insufficient

Exhibit 18-5

Classes of
Priority Claims for
Distribution

Class 1	Any unpaid domestic support obligations (alimony or child support)
Class 2	Court costs, trustee fees, attorney fees, and other administrative claims among expenses associated with the bankruptcy
Class 3	Unsecured claims in involuntary bankruptcy that arise through the debtor's ordinary business expenses from the date of filing the petition to the date of the appointment of the trustee
Class 4	Unsecured claims for unpaid wages, salaries, and commissions (up to $10,000 per individual) earned within 180 days of the filing of the petition
Class 5	Unsecured claims for contributions to employee retirement plans (up to $10,000 per employee)
Class 6	Unsecured claims by farmers and fishers (up to $4,000) against grain operators of grain storage facilities or fish storage or processing facilities
Class 7	Claims for deposits given to the debtor in connection with property or services never given
Class 8	Certain taxes and penalties due to government units
Class 9	Claims in bankruptcies related to federal depository institutions
Class 10	Unsecured claims for personal injuries and deaths caused by the debtor's operation of a motor vehicle while under the influence of alcohol or drugs

funds to fully pay all the creditors in one class, one class is paid proportionately and the lower classes get nothing.

The classes of priority claims among unsecured creditors are shown in Exhibit 18-5.

Discharge If a debtor has honestly dealt with her creditors during bankruptcy proceedings, the debtor is likely eligible for a discharge of her remaining debts. A **discharge** is a written federal court order signed by a bankruptcy judge stating that the debtor is immune from creditor actions to collect debts. When a debt is discharged, the debtor is essentially no longer responsible for the debt.

When is a discharge of debt appropriate? First, discharge of debt under Chapter 7 is available only to individuals, not partnerships or corporations. Second, discharge of debt is a privilege, not a right. A judge determines which debts are dischargeable. If the debtor has received a previous discharge of debt within eight years of the current filing for bankruptcy, the judge will likely refuse a new discharge of debt.

discharge

A written federal court order signed by a bankruptcy judge stating that the debtor is immune from creditor actions to collect debt; i.e., a release from liability.

Exceptions to Discharge. Generally, most debts are discharged unless there are objections to the discharge or the debts are ineligible for discharge. If a major goal of bankruptcy law is to give debtors a fresh start, why are some debts nondischargeable? Some of the debts that are not dischargeable are debts to those who are in a weak bargaining position with the debtor. For example, child support and alimony payments are nondischargeable. Children and ex-spouses often depend on payments; consequently, the court will not permit the discharge of these debts. Exhibit 18-6 lists the debts that are nondischargeable as established by the Bankruptcy Code.

Revocation of Discharge. While a debt might be discharged, the discharge is not necessarily permanent. If the trustee or a creditor discovers that the debtor has acted fraudulently or dishonestly during the bankruptcy proceedings, the court may revoke the discharge within one year. The revocation of discharge allows the creditors to bring action against the debtor.

Reaffirmation of Debt A debtor may wish to repay a dischargeable debt. The debtor might owe money to a family member or a longtime business associate. To maintain a good relationship with these people, a debtor might choose to repay the debt instead of having the debt discharged. This repayment can occur through a **reaffirmation agreement,** an agreement in which the debtor agrees to pay the debt even though it could be discharged.

reaffirmation agreement

An agreement in which the debtor agrees to pay a debt even though it could have been discharged in bankruptcy.

1. Claims for back taxes or government fines within three years of filing for bankruptcy
2. Claims for liabilities against the debtor for his or her obtaining money or property under false pretenses, false representation, or fraud
3. Claims by creditors who weren't listed on the schedule and did not have notification of the bankruptcy proceedings
4. Claims based on fraud, embezzlement, or larceny by the debtor while she or he was acting in a fiduciary relationship
5. Alimony, child support, and some property settlements
6. Claims of willful or malicious conduct by the debtor that caused injury to another person or property
7. Specific student loans, unless payment of the loans imposes undue hardship on the debtor
8. Judgments against a debtor for claims resulting from the debtor's drinking and driving
9. Debts not discharged in previous bankruptcies
10. Claims for money borrowed to pay a tax to the United States that would be nondischargeable
11. Cash advances beyond $1,500 on a credit card

Unfortunately, creditors may attempt to pressure a debtor into reaffirming a debt. Congress was worried that debtors were unwisely surrendering their ability to discharge their debts by making reaffirmation agreements. Thus, Congress created the following extensive rules so that a decision for reaffirmation of debt cannot be an impulsive one:

1. The reaffirmation agreement must be made before the debt is discharged.
2. The debtor must be able to cancel the agreement, and the agreement must contain explicit information regarding the time frame in which the debtor may cancel the agreement.
3. The agreement should contain a statement notifying the creditor that the law does not require the agreement.
4. The agreement must be filed with the bankruptcy court. Typically, the debtor's attorney files a form along with the agreement stating that the debtor is voluntarily entering the agreement and the agreement will not result in hardship to the debtor. Unless the attorney files this form, court approval for the agreement is needed.

CHAPTER 11: REORGANIZATIONS

The largest bankruptcy in U.S. history was the 2002 WorldCom bankruptcy filing. World-Com had over $103 billion in assets at the time of filing. WorldCom filed under Chapter 11, which allows the creditors and debtor to create a plan to reorganize the debtor's financial affairs under the supervision of the bankruptcy court instead of liquidating the assets. Generally, the creditors and debtor agree that part of the debt will be discharged while the other part is or will be paid. Creditors generally agree to these plans because they believe that the value of the operating business is greater than the value of the business broken up and sold in pieces.

Who is eligible for Chapter 11 reorganization? Corporate debtors most frequently use Chapter 11 reorganization because they are permitted to remain in business. However, the debtor does not have to be a business entity to use reorganization; the debtor can be an individual unrelated to business. Stockbrokers, commodities brokers, banks, and savings and loan companies are not permitted to file under Chapter 11.

Most of the Chapter 11 reorganization procedures are similar to Chapter 7 liquidation procedures. Like liquidation, reorganization may be voluntary or involuntary. The reorganization process begins with the filing of the reorganization petition.

When the petition is filed, an automatic stay prohibits legal action against the debtor during the reorganization process. The debtor is required to file a list of creditors. Next, the order

of relief is granted, and the court appoints a trustee, who appoints a creditors' committee of unsecured creditors. Because there may be hundreds of creditors, the creditors' committee is supposed to represent the interests of the range of creditors. The Bankruptcy Code contemplates seven creditors on the committee. The members of the creditors' committee have a fiduciary duty to the other creditors, and under BAPCPA, the creditors' committee must provide the other creditors with access to information.

Generally, the trustee is responsible for developing the reorganization plan to handle the creditors' claims. The *reorganization plan* is a contract between a debtor and his or her creditors. The goal of the plan is to rehabilitate the debtor while preserving the assets for the creditors. Reorganization plans usually state three things:

1. The classes of claims and interests in the debtor's property.
2. The treatment for each class of creditors.
3. A description of the means for execution of the agreement.

A debtor has an exclusive right to file a plan within the first 120 days of the case. If the debtor files a plan within this period, no one else may file a plan within the first 180 days after the debtor's filing. This period allows the debtor time to persuade the creditors to accept the plan. Once the plan has been developed, creditors must vote to accept the plan. For the plan to be accepted, two-thirds of the creditors of each class of creditors must vote to approve it. If the plan is approved, it will go before the court for confirmation. The court may decide to reject the plan if it is not in the best interests of the creditors. When the court confirms a plan, the debts not under the reorganization plan are discharged.

Collective Bargaining Agreements and Reorganization Through reorganization, a debtor can reject some contracts. In the early 1980s, legal scholars were concerned that debtors could use reorganization as a tool to avoid collective bargaining agreements. This issue became a serious concern when the Supreme Court held, in *National Labor Relations Board v. Bildisco & Bildisco,* that collective bargaining agreements are "executory contracts" and thus subject to rejection. In other words, a debtor was not required to engage in collective bargaining before rejecting part of the collective bargaining agreement through reorganization. However, in the opinion, the judge stated that rejection is not permitted unless the reorganization procedures would benefit through the rejection.

After the Supreme Court decision was handed down in 1984, Congress amended the code to prevent debtors from misusing Chapter 11 to reject collective bargaining agreements. The amendments set forth procedures under which collective bargaining agreements can be rejected or modified.

CHAPTER 13: INDIVIDUAL REPAYMENT PLANS

Chapter 13, "Adjustments of Debts for Individuals," permits individuals to pay their debts to creditors in installment plans under the supervision of the court. Repayment plans may seem similar to reorganization. Any debtor who files under Chapter 13 could also have filed under Chapter 11. However, Chapter 13 repayment plans are usually simpler and less expensive. By statute, these plans last between 36 and 60 months.

Who is defined as a debtor for a Chapter 13 repayment plan? Only individuals are permitted to file under Chapter 13; partnerships and corporations are not eligible. Individuals must have a regular income and must owe less than $307,675 for fixed unsecured debts or $922,975 for fixed secured debts.

Filing the Petition As with the other forms of bankruptcy relief, the repayment process begins only when the debtor files the petition. However, repayment is distinct from other types of relief because repayment is voluntary only. A debtor cannot be forced into a repayment plan. In the petition, the debtor states that he is unable to pay his debts. The debtor might request an extension of time to pay the debts or ask that the total amount of debt be reduced.

Alternatively, the debtor might request a combination of those options. As in liquidation proceedings, the debtor commonly files various schedules listing the creditors as well as the debtor's assets. Furthermore, an automatic stay on litigation against the debtor is granted when the debtor files the petition. However, one of the benefits of Chapter 13 is that this stay applies to creditors' attempts to collect from co-debtors.

Creditors' Meeting and the Repayment Plan Proceedings After the debtor files the petition, the court calls a creditors' meeting. At this meeting, the debtor submits a plan of payment for her debts. This plan is not required to provide for the full payment of all claims. However, the plan must treat all same-class creditors equally, and the plan for repayment must not exceed a three-year period, unless the court approves otherwise.

Creditors do not vote to approve a Chapter 13 plan; if the court approves of the plan, the plan is accepted. The court holds a hearing to determine whether to confirm the plan. Unsecured creditors may object to the plan at the hearing. However, the court can overrule their objections if all of the debtor's projected disposable income is used to make payments. If the court believes that the plan was created in good faith, the plan is accepted.

However, if the plan modifies a creditor's secured claim while proposing that the debtor keep the property securing the claim, the creditor may oppose the proposed plan. Court approval of an opposed plan that changes a secured claim is called a "cram down." Since BAPCPA, it has been harder for debtors to make changes to secured claims over the objections of creditors.

After the court approves the plan, the court appoints a trustee to carry out the repayment plan. Every Chapter 13 case has a trustee. The debtor makes monthly payments to the trustee based on his or her disposable income. The trustee then disburses payments to the creditors. Moreover, as payment for services, the trustee receives a percentage of the funds distributed to creditors.

Thirty days after the debtor files the plan, the debtor must begin making payments. The trustee must ensure that the debtor is making the payments. If the debtor fails to make payments, the court may decide to transfer the case to a liquidation bankruptcy or to refuse to grant the repayment plan.

Discharge of Debts under Repayment Proceedings After a debtor makes all payments under a repayment plan, the remaining debts are discharged. However, even if all payments are not made by the expiration of the plan, the court might discharge some of the debts if the debtor has experienced a severe hardship. Like liquidation, some debts, such as alimony and child support debts, are not dischargeable.

CHAPTER 12: FAMILY-FARMER PLANS

Chapter 12 provides for adjustment of the debts of family farmers. Chapter 12 was added to the code in the 1980s, in the midst of severe debt among large numbers of farmers. Many farmers had borrowed large amounts of money to increase their production; however, during that time there was a surplus of farm products. Consequently, many farmers faced serious financial problems. Congress addressed these problems with Chapter 12.

Not all farmers are eligible for Chapter 12 relief. A family farmer, under Chapter 12, must have regular annual income, and the farmer's gross income must be at least 50 percent farm-dependent. Moreover, 80 percent of the debt must be farm-related. Finally, the total debt must be under $1.5 million.

What are the family-farm relief proceedings? Congress modeled Chapter 12 after Chapter 13 relief. The procedure begins when the farmer files a Chapter 12 petition. Automatic stay is granted to protect the farmer from legal action. Within 90 days of the filing, the farmer must file a plan. A trustee is appointed to oversee the financial affairs and is permitted to sell unnecessary assets. The court holds a hearing to rule on the proposed plan. Unsecured creditors are entitled to at least liquidation value of the debt owed to them. Once the farmer fulfills his or her adjustment plan, the farmer will likely receive a discharge from his or her debts and retain possession of the farm.

SUMMARY

Important Definitions Associated with Secured Transactions	*Secured interest*: An interest in personal property or fixtures that secures payment or performance of an obligation.
	Secured party: The person or party that holds the interest in the secured property.
	Debtor: The person or party that has an obligation to the secured party, the person who owns interest in the property.
	Security agreement: The agreement in which the debtor gives the secured interest to the secured party.
	Collateral: The property that is subject to the security interest.
Creation of Secured Interests	Attachment of a security interest requires these three elements:
	Written agreement: An agreement that describes the collateral and is signed by the debtor.
	Value: An item of value given from the creditor to the debtor.
	Debtor rights in the collateral: The rights of the debtor over the collateral.
Purchase-Money Security Interest	A *purchase-money security interest* is formed when a debtor uses borrowed money (e.g., buying on credit) from the secured party to buy the collateral.
Perfected Security Interest	*A perfected security interest* is a security interest in which the creditor has legally protected his or her claim to the collateral. Methods of perfection include:
	1. *Perfection by filing:* Perfection of an interest by filing a financing statement with a state agency. • *Place and duration of filing:* Generally, the financial statements for consumer goods must be filed with the county clerk, and the statement is valid for five years. 2. *Perfection by possession:* Perfection of an interest by holding the collateral of the debtor until the loan is paid off. 3. *Automatic perfection:* Perfection that automatically occurs when a retailer sells a consumer good. 4. *Perfection of movable collateral:* Perfection of an interest in collateral moved to another state by "reperfecting" the interest after four months. 5. *Perfection of security interests in automobiles and boats:* Perfection of an interest in an automobile or boat by noting the interest on the certificate of title.
The Scope of a Security Interest	*After-acquired property:* A creditor has a security interest in property acquired by the debtor after the security agreement is made if a clause to this effect is included in the agreement.
	Proceeds: A creditor automatically has rights to the proceeds from the sale of collateral for 10 days.
Termination of a Security Interest	*Termination statement:* An amendment to a financing statement stating that the debtor has no obligation to the secured party.
Priority Disputes	A *priority dispute* occurs when two corporations or individuals claim rights to the same collateral.
	Secured versus unsecured: When an individual with a secured interest is disputing with an individual with an unsecured interest, the individual with the secured interest wins.
	Secured versus secured: When two individuals with secured interests are disputing, the individual who perfected his or her interest first wins.
	PMSI conflicts: If a party with a perfected purchase-money security interest disputes with another party, the PMSI party will almost always have a right to the collateral—regardless of when the agreement was perfected.
	Secured party versus buyer: If a debtor sells his collateral, the creditor may dispute with the buyer over the collateral.
	1. *Buyers in the ordinary course of business:* If a person buys the collateral in the ordinary course of business without realizing that it is collateral, she has a right to the good.

2. *Buyers of consumer goods:* As long as the consumer does not know that the product is secured, the buyer's new product is free of any security interest.

3. *Buyers of chattel paper and instruments:* If the buyer purchases chattel paper and instruments, he is free from any security interest.

Default

Default occurs when a debtor fails to pay back her or his loan. Remedies include:

1. *Taking possession of the collateral:* If a debtor defaults on a loan, the secured party can take possession of the collateral.

- *Disposition of the collateral:* The creditor may sell, lease, or transfer the collateral.
- *Retention of the collateral:* The creditor may choose to keep the collateral as payment of the debt.

2. *Proceeding to judgment:* A secured party may sue the debtor for the entire amount of the debt instead of dealing with the collateral.

Bankruptcy and Reorganization

A *debtor* is an entity that owes money to another entity. Bankruptcy law provides various options for debtors to resolve their debts. Bankruptcy remedies are available to individuals, partnerships, and corporations.

The Bankruptcy Act and Its Goals

Purpose:

1. To provide debtors with an opportunity to achieve a fresh financial start.

2. To offer protection to creditors.

Bankruptcy Proceedings

1. Every case begins with the filing of a petition for bankruptcy.

2. The court grants an automatic stay for creditor actions against the debtor's estate.

3. The court determines whether an order of relief should be granted.

4. The creditors meet with the debtor.

5. A payment plan is created and approved, usually by the creditors and the court.

6. Debts remaining after the plan is carried out are usually discharged.

Specific Types of Relief Available

Chapter 7: Sale of nonexempt assets and the distribution of money to the creditors.

Chapter 11: Reorganization of the debtor's financial affairs under supervision of the bankruptcy court.

Chapter 12: Adjustment of family farmer's debts.

Chapter 13: Adjustment of individual's debts.

Point/Counterpoint

Secured transactions give a creditor more assurance that it will be repaid even if the debtor is unable to pay. As you learned in this chapter, when a debtor has both secured and unsecured creditors, the secured creditors will be paid first. Some scholars have argued that secured credit unfairly transfers risk to unsecured creditors.

Should Secured Credit Be Limited?	
YES	NO
Suppose an unsecured creditor extended a loan to a debtor years before a secured creditor makes a loan. Later, a secured creditor extends credit to the debtor and gains an interest in the debtor's property. The debtor's financial situation has changed since the unsecured loan. Because of the secured creditor's interest, the likelihood that the unsecured creditor will be paid in full is now lower. The unsecured creditor's	Debtors and creditors are rational actors who have to make choices. An unsecured creditor makes a choice in extending credit to a debtor. The unsecured creditor makes money on the basis of the interest it charges the debtor. Frequently, the interest rate on an unsecured loan is much higher than the interest rate on a secured loan. The unsecured creditor is compensated for the higher risk it may face.

only response is to increase its interest rate; however, the unsecured creditor does not necessarily know about the secured creditor's interest in the collateral. Consequently, when the debtor is unable to pay, the unsecured creditor may get nothing.

Moreover, the availability of secured credit may force a debtor to encumber her assets to obtain credit. By limiting the availability of secured credit, both unsecured creditors and debtors will be treated more fairly.

Moreover, a debtor has a choice as to whether he wants to give the creditor an interest in his property. The debtor may choose a secured loan because of the lower interest rate. We should not restrict the debtor's choice.

Finally, many people who receive secured credit are economically disadvantaged. Limiting the availability of secured credit would harm these parties' ability to access credit.

Questions & Problems

1. What are the required elements of a security interest?

2. Describe the various ways in which secured interests are perfected.

3. How does bankruptcy law benefit debtors and creditors?

4. Under what circumstances would Chapter 11 be used rather than Chapter 7?

5. Indiana Auto Sales & Repair repossessed an automobile from one of its debtors. Indiana Auto paid an independent contractor $30 to repossess the car. The contractor's 15-year-old, unlicensed employee was directed to repossess the vehicle. During the repossession, the boy exceeded the speed limit and crashed into Birrell, the plaintiff (who is struck by the car). She sustained serious personal injuries as a result of the collision. Birrell brought a lawsuit against Indiana Auto Sales & Repair for the injuries she sustained during the repossession. The trial court found in favor of Indiana Auto Sales & Repair. Birrell appealed the decision. Do you think the court of appeals affirmed or reversed the decision? Why or why not? [*Birrell v. Indiana Auto Sales & Repair,* 698 N.E.2d 6 (Ind. Ct. App. 1998).]

6. Century Energy is a partnership in the business of producing oil and gas. Century received a loan from First Interstate Bank of Commerce. A security agreement was executed, and two of Century's oil pumps, the F pump and the E pump, served as the collateral. First Interstate Bank perfected its security interest by filing the appropriate financing statements. Century subsequently developed a second business entity, Limited. Limited became indebted to New Oil, Inc., and the F pump was transferred to New Oil to satisfy the debt. First Interstate Bank became aware that New Oil claimed ownership of the F pump. New Oil notified First Interstate Bank that it intended to sell the F pump. First Interstate Bank brought an action to have the rights of the F pump determined. The trial court found that First Interstate Bank had a perfected security interest in the pumping unit that was superior to any interest of New Oil. New Oil appealed the decision. How do you think the court decided on appeal? [*New Oil, Inc. v. First Interstate Bank of Commerce,* 895 P.2d 871 (Wyo. 1995).]

7. The Barretts purchased a 1982 Kenworth truck in June 1995 from Mary Harwood. The purchase price was $11,000, to be paid in monthly installments of $300 before the 10th of each month. Eighteen months after the sale, Harwood retained Smith to repossess the truck due to delinquent payments by the Barretts. Smith contacted the Village of Malone Police Department to request the presence of a police officer at the site of the repossession. The village subsequently dispatched Officer Durant to the scene. At the site of the repossession, Barrett produced the purchase agreement and signed receipts tending to prove the payments on the truck were current. Officer Durant examined these documents but advised the Barretts that this was a civil matter and that they should retain an attorney. A verbal and physical altercation ensued between the Barretts and Harwood, who was present at the scene. Durant subsequently warned Barrett, "If you start any trouble here, you'll be in the back seat of my car. Do you understand me, mister?" As a result, the Barretts surrendered the keys to the truck to Smith on the basis of Durant's perceived threat of arrest. Smith subsequently purchased the truck from Harwood for $3,500. The Barretts sued all of the parties involved in the allegedly unlawful repossession, including the Village of Malone, for violation of their due process rights under color of law in contravention of federal civil rights laws. How do you think the court decided? [*Barrett v. Harwood,* 189 F.3d 297 (2d Cir. 1999).]

8. For-Med, Inc., and David Anderson executed a loan and security agreement in the amount of $79,924.89 with First Westside Bank. Anderson offered his 1978 Blue Bird motor home as collateral. After Anderson and For-Med defaulted on the loan, First Westside repossessed the motor home and sold it for $60,000. The motor home was very large, and First Westside claimed that it could not be left on its parking lot for show. Therefore, First Westside did not officially advertise that the motor vehicle was for sale. Rather, bids were solicited by word of mouth from financial institutions, dealers, and customers. First Westside sued For-Med and David Anderson to collect the difference between the loan and the sale price of the motor home. The court found in favor of First Westside. On appeal, For-Med and Anderson argued that the sale of the collateral was not commercially reasonable because First Westside failed to adequately advertise the motor home. Therefore, For-Med and Anderson believed that First Westside failed to obtain the best price under the circumstances. How do you think the court decided on appeal? Was the sale price of the collateral commercially unreasonable? [*First Westside Bank v. For-Med, Inc.,* 529 N.W.2d 66 (Neb. 1995).]

9. Kevin Scott purchased a new Ford van on credit from Koons Ford of Baltimore, Inc. He made a down payment of $3,406 and agreed to make 60 monthly payments of $403.93 to pay off the balance. The contract was assigned by Koons Ford to Ford Motor Credit Company (FMCC). Scott's van was subsequently wrecked, and the cost of repair exceeded the value of the van. FMCC was paid the insurance proceeds, but Scott did not continue to make the installment payments. The van was repossessed and sold. FMCC notified Scott that he was responsible for a difference of $6,452.56. Scott never paid the balance of the payments, and four years later FMCC brought an action to reclaim the balance. Did FMCC, as the assignee of Koons Ford's security interest in the van, have the right to receive the monthly payments provided for in the agreement between Scott and Koons Ford? How do you think the court decided? [*Scott v. Ford Motor Credit Co.,* 691 A.2d 1320 (Md. 1997).]

10. Gergely, an obstetrician, performed an amniocentesis on Jordan Lee-Brenner's mother during her pregnancy. As a result of problems with the procedure, Jordan Lee-Brenner was blinded in one eye. After his birth, and through his guardian, Lee-Brenner brought an action against Gergely, claiming that Gergely had misrepresented the need for amniocentesis and had performed it negligently. Lee-Brenner received an award for $780,282, which he failed to collect prior to Gergely's filing a Chapter 7 bankruptcy petition. Lee-Brenner moved to have the judgment set aside as a nondischargeable debt. The bankruptcy court dismissed his petition, so he appealed. On what grounds could he argue that the debt should not have been discharged? Do you think his argument was successful before the appellate court? [*In re Gergely,* 110 F.3d 1448 (9th Cir. 1997).]

11. First Jersey Securities, Inc., filed a petition for Chapter 11 bankruptcy after the Securities and Exchange Commission (SEC) obtained a court order against the firm to repay $75 million in illegal proceeds. On the same day that its petition was filed, First Jersey transferred $600,000 in assets to its attorneys, the law firm RSW, to pay for previous and future legal services. The trustee and SEC both challenged the transfer of the assets to the debtor's lawyers. The bankruptcy court and district court upheld the transfer. The trustee and SEC appealed. Why do you believe the circuit court either upheld or overturned the district court's ruling? [*In re First Jersey Securities, Inc.,* 180 F.3d 504 (3d Cir. 1999).]

12. On August 2, 2000, Sheldon B. Toibb filed a voluntary petition for relief under Chapter 7 of the Bankruptcy Code, disclosing assets that included stock in an electric power company. When he discovered that the stock had substantial value, he decided to avoid its liquidation by moving to convert his Chapter 7 case to one under Chapter 11's reorganization provisions. After the bankruptcy court granted his motion and he filed his reorganization plan, the court dismissed his petition, finding that he did not qualify for relief under Chapter 11 because he was not engaged in an ongoing business. The district court and the court of appeals affirmed. Why do you believe the U.S. Supreme Court reversed or affirmed the lower court's ruling? [*In re Sheldon Baruch Toibb, Petitioner,* 501 U.S. 157, 111 S. Ct. 2197.]

13. Debtors Bill Brandon Beard and Peggy Jane Beard came up with a plan that permitted them to remit payments directly to an unsecured creditor, without having to transfer the funds to that creditor through the bankruptcy trustee. The two lower courts recognized that by granting the debtors the right to make these direct remittances and thus to bypass the standing trustee, the debtors would thereby avoid having to pay certain statutory fees that the standing trustee would normally receive in the course of administering the Chapter 12 bankruptcy estate. The bankruptcy court approved the plan, as did the district court. The trustee appealed. Why should the appellate court affirm or overturn the lower court decision? [*In re Bill Brandon Beard and Peggy Jane Beard,* 45 F.3d 113 (6th Cir. 1985).]

Looking for more review material?

The Online Learning Center at **www.mhhe.com/kubasekess2e** contains this chapter's "Assignment on the Internet" and also a list of URLs for more information, entitled "On the Internet." Find both of them in the Student Center portion of the OLC, along with quizzes and other helpful materials.

CHAPTER

19 Agency and Liability to Third Parties

National Farmers Union Insurance and an Independent Contractor

Elmer Oestman was an insurance agent for National Farmers Union Insurance Company. The company had a contract providing that the "local agent, acting solely as an independent contractor, is hereby authorized to solicit and submit written applications for insurance policies and other contracts of insurer strictly in accordance with the instructions and direction of insurer." The contract specifically stated that "[n]othing contained herein shall be construed as creating the relationship of employer and employee between the local agent and insurer." Oestman was commissioned through the insurer, filed his own taxes as a self-employed individual, set his own and his staff's working hours, had sole discretion in hiring and firing his staff, bore all expenses in selling insurance, and provided his own transportation and office equipment. When his employment was terminated, Oestman sued the insurance company, claiming a violation of the Age Discrimination in Employment Act of 1967.

1. On the basis of the agreement between Oestman and the insurance company, do you think Oestman is justified in filing a lawsuit against the insurance company for firing him? Why?

2. What rights does Oestman have as an independent contractor? How would these rights differ if he were an employee of the insurance company?

LEARNING OBJECTIVES

After reading this chapter, you will be able to answer the following questions:

LO 19-1 How is an agency relationship created?

LO 19-2 What are the different types of agency?

LO 19-3 What are the different types of agency relationships?

LO 19-4 What are the duties of the agent?

LO 19-5 What are the duties of the principal?

LO 19-6 What are the different types of authority of the agent?

LO 19-7 Do the principal and the agent have any contractual liability? How so?

LO 19-8 How can an agency relationship be terminated?

In the Case Opener, it is important to determine whether Oestman is an employee or an independent contractor of the insurance company because different legal obligations arise, depending on the nature of the relationship. One of the most important relationships in the business world is the *agency relationship,* in which the employee may be an agent of the employer, having the ability, among others, to bind that employer legally.

Agency relationships are crucial to running large businesses because the use of agents allows corporations to enter into contracts and therefore conduct business in multiple locations simultaneously. This chapter explores the nature and creation of the agency relationship, as well as the legal obligations that the parties take on when they form such a relationship.

Introduction to Agency Law

Agency is generally defined as a relationship between a principal and an agent. In an **agency relationship,** the **agent** is authorized to act for and on behalf of the **principal,** who hires the agent to represent him or her. The Restatement of Agency defines **agency** as "the fiduciary relation that results from the manifestation of consent by one person to another that the other shall act in his behalf and subject to his control, and consent by the other so to act."[1] (A **fiduciary** is a person who has a duty to act primarily for another person's benefit. A lawyer, for example, is a fiduciary for his or her client. We discuss fiduciaries in depth later in this chapter.)

Agency law is primarily state law. Thus, while there are similarities among the laws governing agency relationships, the laws may vary somewhat from state to state. For example, at least 27 states have enacted statutes governing the behavior of sports agents. Twenty-three of those states impose civil penalties or damages on agents for violations of the athlete-agent statutes. Twenty-four states (e.g., California and Florida) have established criminal penalties for sports agents who violate the state statute. In contrast, only five states have criminalized statute violations by the athletes themselves.

Agency law is especially important for modern firms doing business in foreign countries. More and more companies are expanding their commercial ventures to overseas markets. While foreign countries offer fresh markets and eager consumers, American companies often run into legal difficulties in other countries. These difficulties may arise from a language barrier or simply a lack of knowledge about local laws. To avoid such problems, many companies hire agents familiar with local laws, customs, and customers to help them function smoothly in foreign markets.

Creation of the Agency Relationship **LO 19-1**

Agency relationships are consensual relationships formed by informal oral agreements or formal written contracts. However, an agency relationship exists only when the principal takes action to ask another individual to act on behalf of the principal.

agency relationship
The association between one party and an agent who acts on behalf of that party.

agent
A party who has the authority to act on behalf of and bind another party.

principal
The party that an agent's authority can bind or act on behalf of.

agency
The fiduciary relationship that arises when one person consents to have another act on his behalf and subject to his control and the other consents to do so.

fiduciary
A person who has a duty to act primarily for another person's benefit.

[1] Restatement (Second) of Agency, sec. 1(1). The Restatement is a valuable reference that is well respected in the legal profession. It is frequently cited by judges as well as attorneys and scholars in making legal arguments. The Restatement provides a summary of agency law.

Exhibit 19-1

Creation of Agency
Relationships

Expressed agency	Formed by making a written or oral agreement
Implied authority	Formed by implication through the conduct of the parties
Agency by estoppel	Formed when a principal leads a third party to believe that another individual serves as his or her agent but the principal had made no agreement with the so-called agent
Agency by ratification	Exists when an individual misrepresents himself or herself as an agent for another party and the principal accepts or ratifies the unauthorized act

Under what circumstances can an agency relationship be created? First, an agency relationship can be created only for a lawful purpose in the same way that a contract cannot have an illegal purpose. Thus, a principal could not hire an agent to kill someone on behalf of the principal.[2] Second, almost anyone can act as an agent. A contract made by an agent is viewed as a contract between the principal and a third party. Therefore, a person can serve as an agent regardless of age or competency.[3] However, if an individual does not have contractual capacity, the individual could not hire an agent to make contracts on his or her behalf. For example, because a contract entered into by a minor is voidable, most states do not allow minors to hire agents.

LO 19-2

As long as these two criteria are met, agency relationships can be created on the basis of any of the following four forms of authority:

1. By expressed agency, or agency by agreement.
2. By implied authority.
3. By apparent agency, or agency by estoppel.
4. By ratification.

The following sections discuss the types of agency formation, and Exhibit 19-1 presents a summary.

EXPRESSED AGENCY (AGENCY BY AGREEMENT)

expressed agency

An agency created in a written or oral agreement. Also called *agency by agreement.*

When parties form an agency relationship by making a written or oral agreement, the agency is known as **expressed agency,** or **agency by agreement.** Expressed agency is the most common type of agency. As specified in the expressed agreement, the agent has the authority to contract on behalf of the principal. While a contract is not necessary, if an agency agreement is formed through a contract, the contract must meet all the elements of a contract discussed in Chapter 6. If a principal agrees to hire no other agent for a period of time or until a particular job is done, the principal and agent have entered into an exclusive agency contract.

power of attorney

A specific form of express authority that grants an agent specific powers.

One legal document that establishes agency relationships is a **power of attorney,** a document that gives an agent authority to sign legal documents on behalf of the principal. Power of attorney can be classified in several ways. First, a power of attorney can be general or specific. For example, with a general power of attorney, a principal gives an agent broad authority to sign legal documents on behalf of the principal. In contrast, with a specific power of attorney, a principal gives authority to an agent for only the specific areas or purposes listed in the agreement.

Powers of attorney are often given for business and health care purposes. In the health care instance, a principal gives power of attorney to an agent so that the agent can make decisions about the principal's medical care in case the principal cannot make those decisions. Given that a principal must have the ability to enter into contracts to enter into an agency relationship, a principal may not enact a power of attorney after becoming incompetent. Therefore, before incapacitation, a principal may create a durable power of attorney.

durable power of attorney

A document which specifies that an agent's authority is intended to continue beyond the principal's incapacitation.

A **durable power of attorney** is a written document, created by a principal, expressing his or her wishes for an agent's authority not to be affected by the principal's subsequent incapacity. Alternatively, a durable power of attorney might become active only after a principal becomes

[2] Restatement (Second) of Agency, sec. 19.
[3] Restatement (Second) of Agency, sec. 21.

incapacitated in any matter. Because the agreement is entered into before incapacitation, a power of attorney is legally binding after the principal becomes incapacitated.

It is important to note a few additional points. First, the Restatement states, "[A]n agency relation exists only if there has been a manifestation by the principal to the agent that the agent may act on his account, and consent by the agent so to act."[4] Therefore, in addition to the above criteria, there needs to be agreement by the principal to have the person act as an agent and by the agent to act for the principal. As noted below, this agreement can be reached in several different ways.

Second, agency agreements usually do not need to be in writing. However, there are two important exceptions. First, agency agreements need to be in writing whenever an agreement is reached for an agent to enter into a contract that under the statute of frauds must be in writing. For example, Janet wants Phil to act as her agent. She grants him the power to enter into contracts. The statute of frauds, or, more specifically, the equal dignities rule, mandates that the type of contracts Phil is allowed to enter into must be in writing. Therefore, Phil's agreement with Janet must also be in writing. Also, whenever an agent is given power of attorney (discussed below), the agreement must be in writing.

Third, agents may perform their services gratuitously. A **gratuitous agent** is one who acts without consideration; that is, the agent is not paid for his or her services. Gratuitous agents function much like regular agents, with a few specific exceptions noted later in this chapter.

gratuitous agent
An agent who acts without being paid for his or her services.

AGENCY BY IMPLIED AUTHORITY

In some cases, an agency relationship is not created by an expressed agreement but, rather, is implied by the conduct of the parties. The circumstances of a situation determine the extent of an agent's ability to conduct business on behalf of the principal. However, the implied authority cannot conflict with any express authority.

APPARENT AGENCY (AGENCY BY ESTOPPEL)

Suppose a principal leads a third party to believe that another individual serves as his or her agent but the principal has made no agreement with the so-called agent. Does an agency relationship exist? Yes, because by his or her conduct, the principal has created **apparent agency,** or **agency by estoppel.** According to the principal's conduct, the agent has apparent authority to act; thus, the principal is estopped, or prevented, from denying that the individual is an agent.[5] When a third party relies on the principal's conduct and makes an agreement with an apparent agent, the principal must uphold any agreements made by the agent. If the principal attempts to deny an agency relationship existed, the third party must demonstrate that he or she reasonably believed, on the basis of the principal's conduct, that an agency relationship existed. The court will consider the principal's conduct in determining whether an agency relationship existed.

apparent agency
An agency relationship created by operation of law when one party, by his actions, causes a third party to believe someone is his agent when that person actually has no authority. Also called *agency by estoppel.*

Suppose an executive of Emporium Carpet is interviewing a potential salesperson named Jose. In the course of the interview, the employer introduces Jose to some clients who are in the building. During the conversation, he says, "I cannot wait to have Jose in our firm. The sooner he works for us, the happier I will be." For some reason, Jose is not hired. But Jose happens to meet these clients later, and in the course of their conversations, the clients place an order with Jose, believing him to be an employee of Emporium Carpet. Emporium now has an obligation to fulfill the order because the third party reasonably believed Jose was an agent of Emporium.

The Case Nugget on the next page discusses the importance of apparent authority.

AGENCY BY RATIFICATION

Suppose Fred is driving home and sees a car with a "For Sale" sign in the window. He stops to look at the car because his friend wants to buy a used car. He's amazed at the price and quality of the car, so he tells the owner his friend wants to buy the car. The owner claims that another individual is coming to probably buy the car in an hour. So, to ensure that his friend gets this

[4] Restatement (Second) of Agency, sec. 15.
[5] Restatement (Second) of Agency, sec. 8B.

CASE Nugget

Apparent Authority and Agency

Steven A. B. Hannington, Appellant, v. Trustees of the
University of Pennsylvania and Dr. Mark Bernstein, Appellees
Superior Court of Pennsylvania

2002 Pa. Super. 314; 809 A.2d 406; 2002 Pa. Super. LEXIS 2873

Steven Hannington, a doctoral candidate at the University of Pennsylvania, was expelled for outstanding tuition fees, which he claimed had been waived in exchange for organizing a two-day conference on behalf of the university's Energy Management and Policy Program. Hannington filed suit against the university for breach of contract, and the university countersued for the outstanding tuition, fees, and interest. Before the case went to trial, Hannington and the university negotiated a settlement through their attorneys. Hannington's attorney notified the court that an agreement had been reached, and he filed an "Order to Settle, End, and Discontinue." One month later, Hannington obtained new counsel and filed a motion to restore the case to the trial list, claiming that his previous attorney had exceeded the scope of his authority by settling the case without his express authority. Hannington's motion was denied by the trial court, and he appealed.

The appellate court affirmed the trial court's decision, citing the doctrine of apparent authority for three reasons. First, the university was innocent and free from fault. Second, Hannington's attorney notified the university in a letter that Hannington had approved of the attached settlement release. Third, the negotiations took place over a six-month period, during which Hannington "had clothed his lawyer with the authority to communicate with the University on his behalf. Therefore, it was reasonable for the University and its lawyer to believe that Appellant had expressly authorized the settlement agreement." The court ruled that, regardless of Hannington's claims regarding the conduct of his attorney, the settlement was enforceable. If Hannington's attorney had not exceeded the scope of his authority, the settlement would be enforceable on its own. If Hannington's attorney had exceeded the scope of his authority, the doctrine of apparent authority would be applicable, giving the university the right to rely on the representation of Hannington's attorney to enter into a binding contract.

car, Fred signs a contract to purchase the car, but he notes on the contract that he is an agent of his friend. Because he is not an agent for his friend, the friend is not required to uphold the contract.

However, if Fred's friend agrees to purchase the car, the friend has accepted him as the agent for the contract. Fred's friend is now bound by the contract, and Fred cannot be held liable for misrepresenting himself as the agent. This type of agency relationship is **agency by ratification.** As suggested in the example above, there are two requirements for agency by ratification:

1. An individual must misrepresent himself or herself as an agent for another party.
2. The principal accepts or ratifies the unauthorized act.

For ratification to be effective, two additional requirements must be met:

1. The principal must have complete knowledge of all material facts regarding the contract.
2. The principal must ratify the entirety of the agent's act. (The principal cannot accept certain parts and reject other parts of the agent's act.)

agency by ratification
An agency relationship that arises when an individual misrepresents himself or herself as an agent for another party and that party accepts the unauthorized act.

Agency Relationships

LO 19-3

There are generally three types of business relationships to which agency laws are relevant: the principal-agent relationship, the employer–employee relationship, and the employer–independent contractor relationship. We discuss all three in the following sections and summarize them in Exhibit 19-2.

PRINCIPAL-AGENT RELATIONSHIP

The principal–agent relationship typically exists when an employer hires an employee to enter into contracts on behalf of the employer. This relationship is the most basic type of agency relationship. For example, suppose a salesclerk at Abercrombie & Fitch sells Amanda a shirt. The clerk is acting on behalf of the owner; consequently, any sales made by the salesclerk are binding on the owner of Abercrombie & Fitch. Similarly, think of all the advertisements seen on television in which a professional athlete speaks on behalf of a product. The athlete usually hires an agent to find and make agreements on behalf of the athlete to promote products.

EMPLOYER-EMPLOYEE RELATIONSHIP

Whenever an employer hires an employee to perform some sort of physical service, the parties have created an employer–employee relationship. The employee is subject to the control of the employer.[6] Generally, all employees are considered to be agents of the employer. Even employees not legally authorized to enter into contracts binding their employer or to interact with third parties are considered agents. While all employees are agents, the reverse is not true. That is, not all agents are employees.

EMPLOYER–INDEPENDENT CONTRACTOR RELATIONSHIP

Employers often hire **independent contractors,** persons who are not employees, to conduct certain tasks. The Restatement of Agency defines an independent contractor as "a person who contracts with another to do something for him but who is not controlled by the other nor subject to the other's right to control with respect to his physical conduct in the performance of the undertaking."[7] For example, building contractors, doctors, stockbrokers, and lawyers are independent contractors. Furthermore, building contractors, doctors, stockbrokers, and lawyers are agents, while not employees. However, not all independent contractors are agents. Independent contractors cannot enter into contracts on behalf of the principal unless authorized to do so by the principal.

independent contractor
A person who is hired to perform a task for another but who is not the other's employee.

Employee or Independent Contractor? The question of whether a worker is an employee or an independent contractor has important implications in terms of workers' compensation, workplace safety, and unemployment statutes. The employer–employee relationship is subject to the

[6] Restatement (Second) of Agency, sec. 2.
[7] Restatement (Second) of Agency, sec. 2.

RELATIONSHIP	HOW TO IDENTIFY	SIGNIFICANT FOR WHAT ISSUES?
Principal–agent	Parties have *agreed* that agent will have power to bind principal in contract.	Contract law
Employer–employee	Employer has right to *control* conduct of employees.	Tort law, tax law, wage law, discrimination law, copyright law
Employer–contractor	Employer has *no control* over details of conduct of independent contractor.	Tort law, tax law, wage law, discrimination law, copyright law

Exhibit 19-2

Types of Business Relationships and Their Significance for Agency

CRITERIA	EMPLOYEE	INDEPENDENT CONTRACTOR
Does the worker engage in a distinct occupation or an independently established business?	No	Yes
Is the work done under the employer's supervision, or does a specialist without supervision complete the work?	Employer supervision	Specialist without supervision
Does the employer supply the tools?	Yes	No
What skill is required for the occupation?	No specialized skill	Great degree of skill
What is the length of time for which the worker is employed?	Long time	Varies
Is the worker a regular part of the business of the employer?	Yes	No
How is the worker paid?	Regular payments according to time	When the job is completed

workers' compensation, workplace safety, employment discrimination, and unemployment statutes, while the employer–independent contractor relationship is not. Furthermore, as discussed later in this chapter, employers are generally liable in tort for the actions of their employees, while they are generally not liable for the actions of independent contractors.

When courts are deciding whether a worker is an employee or an independent contractor, perhaps the most important issue they consider is how much control the employer exerts over the agent.[8] If the employer has substantial control over day-to-day operations of the worker, the worker is generally considered an employee.

While the degree of control an employer maintains is the central factor courts look at in determining whether a person is an employee or an independent contractor, it is by no means the only factor examined. Exhibit 19-3 lists the additional criteria the court considers in deciding whether a worker is an employee or an independent contractor. These criteria were established in the Restatement of Agency.[9]

LO 19-4 Duties of the Agent and the Principal

An agency relationship is a fiduciary relationship of trust, confidence, and good faith. Thus, the formation of an agency relationship results in the creation of certain duties that the principal and agent owe each other. These duties are established in the agency agreement and are implied by the law. We discuss them in the following sections and present a summary in Exhibit 19-4.

LO 19-5 PRINCIPAL'S DUTIES TO THE AGENT

When a principal contractually agrees that another person can make agreements on his or her behalf, the principal owes certain duties to the agent. If these duties are not fulfilled, the principal has violated the agent's rights. Consequently, the agent can bring a suit against the principal. If the agent is successful in bringing a suit against the principal, the agent is entitled to contract or tort remedies. Furthermore, if the principal has failed to meet duties owed to the agent, the agent can refuse to act on behalf of the principal until the failure is remedied.

duty to compensate
A principal's obligation to pay an agent for his or her services.

Duty of Compensation The principal has a **duty to compensate** the agent for services provided unless the parties have agreed that the agent will act gratuitously. The agency contract usually specifies the type and amount of compensation as well as the time at which the compensation

[8] Restatement (Second) of Agency, sec. 2(3).
[9] Restatement (Second) of Agency, sec. 220.

PRINCIPAL TO AGENT	AGENT TO PRINCIPAL
Duty of compensation	Duty of loyalty
Duty of reimbursement and indemnification	Duty of performance
Duty of cooperation	Duty of notification
Duty to provide safe working conditions	Duty of obedience
	Duty of accounting

Exhibit 19-4

Summary of Duties in an Agency Relationship

will be given to the agent. Thus, if a person hires an attorney to represent her, she has a duty to pay that attorney, her agent. If there is no agreement on the amount the principal will compensate the agent, the courts suggest that compensation should be calculated according to the customary fee in the situation.[10]

Duty of Reimbursement and Indemnification The principal has a **duty of reimbursement and indemnification** to the agent. If an agent makes authorized expenditures in the course of working on behalf of the principal, the principal has a duty to reimburse the agent for the amount of money spent.[11] Thus, if an agent takes a trip on behalf of the principal, the principal must have authorized this trip if the agent is to be reimbursed by the principal.

Similarly, the principal has the duty to indemnify or reimburse the agent for any losses the agent incurs while working within the scope of authority on the principal's behalf.[12] For example, suppose an agent makes an agreement with a third party on behalf of the principal and the principal fails to uphold the agreement. The third party could sue the agent for damages because of the failure to uphold the agreement. The principal has a duty to indemnify the agent for the losses the third party regained.

duty of reimbursement and indemnification
A principal's obligation to reimburse an agent for any expenses or losses incurred by the agent on the principal's behalf.

Duty of Cooperation The principal also owes a **duty of cooperation** to the agent. Therefore, the principal must assist the agent in the performance of his or her duties. Furthermore, the principal can do nothing to interfere with the reasonable conduct of an agent. For example, suppose Suzy hired someone to sell her car for her. Suzy must be willing to let the agent show her car to interested buyers.

duty of cooperation
A principal's obligation to assist an agent in the performance of the agent's duties and not to interfere with reasonable conduct of the agent.

Duty to Provide Safe Working Conditions The principal has a **duty to provide safe working conditions** for the agent. This includes equipment, premises, and other working conditions. If the principal is aware of unsafe working conditions, the principal has a duty to warn the agent of the potential danger and make the necessary repairs. Federal and state statutes, such as the Occupational Safety and Health Act (OSHA), set specific standards for the working environment. If an employer violates these standards, the employer may be subject to fines.

duty to provide safe working conditions
A principal's obligation to provide proper equipment, suitable premises, and a safe working environment in accordance with federal and state statutes.

AGENT'S DUTIES TO THE PRINCIPAL

When an agent agrees to act on behalf of a principal, the agent is a *fiduciary,* a person in a position of trust and confidence, and as such owes certain duties to the principal. However, because the agent makes agreements on behalf of the principal, the agent is in a position to potentially harm the principal. If, for example, an agent makes numerous contracts the principal could not possibly carry out all at once, it is likely the third parties would sue the principal for not carrying out the agreements. If the agent breaches his or her fiduciary duties, the principal can sue the agent, and the principal may be entitled to a variety of contract and tort remedies beyond those stated in the contract.

[10] Restatement (Second) of Agency, sec. 443.
[11] Restatement (Second) of Agency, sec. 438.
[12] Restatement (Second) of Agency secs. 438 and 439.

duty of loyalty
An agent's obligation to act in the interest of the principal.

Duty of Loyalty Courts suggest that the **duty of loyalty** is perhaps the most important duty an agent owes to a principal. Because the agency relationship is a fiduciary relationship (i.e., a relationship of trust), the agent has a responsibility to act in the interest of the principal.[13] There are a number of ways the agent carries out her duty of loyalty to the principal, including avoiding conflicts of interest and protecting the principal's confidentiality.

An agent can in most situations represent and act on behalf of only one principal in an agreement. An agent usually cannot represent both the principal and a third party (who would then become another principal if represented by the same agent) in an agreement because there could be a conflict of interest. In addition, the agent has a duty to notify the principal of any offers from third parties.

For example, suppose Tony has hired a real estate agent to make land purchases for him. A third party notifies the real estate agent that some of her property will soon be going up for sale, and the third party wants to know whether Tony, the principal, would be interested in buying the property. The real estate agent cannot decide to buy that property for himself until (1) the agent has communicated the offer to Tony and (2) Tony has considered and rejected the offer.

The duty of loyalty also requires that the agent keep confidential any information about the principal during the course of agency, as well as after the agency relationship is terminated. The agent cannot disclose or misuse any information received during or after the agency relationship with the principal.

duty of notification
An agent's obligation to inform the principal of the agent's actions on the principal's behalf and of all relevant information.

Duty of Notification Not only does the agent have to communicate offers from third parties, but the agent must also communicate any information the agent thinks could be important to the principal. This duty is known as the **duty of notification**.[14] For example, if a third party has made an agreement through an agent with a principal and the third party has failed to meet the agreement, the agent must notify the principal of this information in a timely manner. It is critical for an agent to inform the principal of all relevant information because the law typically assumes the principal is aware of all information revealed to the agent, regardless of whether the agent shares all this information with the principal. In Case 19-1 pay special attention to the duties of the agent to the principal.

[13] Restatement (Second) of Agency, sec. 401.
[14] Restatement (Second) of Agency, sec. 381.

CASE 19-1

READING RADIO, INC. v. FINK
SUPERIOR COURT OF PENNSYVANIA
2003 Pa. Super. 353; 833 A.2d 199 (2003)

FACTS: *David L. Kline was the station manager/sales manager of Reading Radio, Inc., which was part of the WAGO Radio Station. One of Kline's work responsibilities was to supervise the station's sales representatives, including Molly Fink and Isaac Ulrich. Both Fink and Ulrich signed a covenant-not-to-compete agreement with WAGO that provided they would not seek or accept employment involving "any radio or television broadcasting station located within a fifty mile radius of Reading, Pennsylvania." However, Kline never signed a covenant-not-to-compete.*

In mid-1990, Reading Eagle expressed an interest in purchasing WAGO and its FM affiliate, WIOV, from Reading Radio. The two companies held negotiations, but the sale never came to fruition. However, in the midst of the sales negotiations, Reading Eagle offered Kline a position, which included in its duties management of Reading Eagle's A.M. station, WEEU. Kline accepted the position. He tendered his resignation as station manager of WAGO but agreed to remain in WAGO's employ for 30 days and made repeated assurances to his superiors at WAGO that he would continue to work as diligently for WAGO as he did in the past.

On the contrary, Kline canceled his bluegrass music program on WAGO without notice to his employers and transferred a significant car dealership advertising account to Reading Eagle. Also within the 30-day period, Kline solicited Fink and Ulrich to work for WEEU in identical sales positions that they held at WAGO. Kline then refused to enforce the covenants-not-to-compete even after questioned about his failure to do so. As a result, WAGO sued Kline for a breach of fiduciary duty of loyalty. At court, the jury sided with WAGO. The defendants appealed.

REASONING: In the words of the court:

To prevail on a claim of breach of fiduciary duty of loyalty, a plaintiff must demonstrate that his agent acted for a person or entity whose interests conflicted with the plaintiff. Restatement (Second) of Agency § 394 (1958). The jury found that Appellant Kline breached his fiduciary duty of loyalty to his principal, WAGO. We agree. The facts demonstrate that, while still employed by WAGO, Appellant Kline actively engaged in diverting Fink and Ulrich from WAGO to Appellant WEEU, and he refused to enforce the covenants-not-to-compete to which they were bound.

Appellant Kline was also aware at this time of the loss of a third sales representative due to maternity leave. Appellant Kline's failure to protect the integrity of the covenants-not-to-compete and the sales staff at WAGO were clear violations of his duty of loyalty, for which he was liable in damages.

DECISION AND REMEDY: The court was satisfied that the trial court did not err when it refused to enter judgment in the appellants' favor with respect to this claim. Therefore, the court affirmed the lower court's decision. The court found that Kline breached his duty of loyalty to his former employer.

SIGNIFICANCE OF THE CASE: When entering into agency relationships, all parties to the relationship need to understand their rights and duties. This case helps clarify an agent's duty of loyalty to his employer.

CRITICAL THINKING

Are any of the key terms in this court decision ambiguous? If so, how does the ambiguity affect the strength of the court's decision?

ETHICAL DECISION MAKING

What set of guidelines could Kline have followed in making a more ethical decision? What guidelines does the judge appear to be following in reaching his decision? Are the judge's guidelines ethically superior to those chosen by Kline? Why or why not?

Duty of Performance The agent owes a **duty of performance** to the principal. This duty is two-fold. First, the agent must perform the duties as specified in the agency agreement. For example, suppose an insurance agent contacts Bethany about purchasing a car insurance policy. Bethany agrees to purchase the policy, but for some reason the agent never obtains the policy for her. Bethany discovers the insurance agent's mistake when she gets into a car accident. The insurance agent did not meet the duty of performance. Consequently, Bethany could bring a claim against the insurance agent.

Second, the agent must perform the specified duties with reasonable skill and care. The agent is expected to provide the same standards of skill, care, and professionalism that a reasonable person in the same situation would provide. For example, when an attorney advertises that he is a specialist in a certain type of law, this lawyer will be held to the reasonable standard of care in that specialty of law.[15] A gratuitous agent cannot be found liable for a breach of contract for failure to perform because no contract exists between the principal and the agent. However, if a gratuitous agent begins to act as a regular agent, and the principal affirms the relationship, a duty to perform arises insofar as the agent has begun a specific task for the principal.

duty of performance
An agent's obligation to perform the duties specified in the agency agreement and to do so with reasonable skill and care.

[15] Restatement (Second) of Agency, sec. 379.

Duties of Agents and Principals in Iran

Principals in both Iran and the United States share many of the same duties to their agents. For example, in Iran, the principal must compensate the agent for his services, and indemnify him for expenses or losses incurred through no fault of the agent, if the agent was acting within the scope of his authority. Similarly, agents in these two countries share many of the same duties to the principal, including the duty of loyalty. In Iran, an agent is considered a trustee, and the nature of his trust requires a high degree of loyalty. However, a large difference exists between an Iranian agent's duty of loyalty and that of an American agent. In the United States, a breach-of-fiduciary-duty claim such as a breach of loyalty is a civil action. However, in Iran, a breach of an agent's trust is so serious it may be considered a criminal offense as well. That is why in Iran it is especially important for an agent to bear in mind the interests of his principal and give the principal a full accounting of his activities.

duty of obedience

An agent's obligation to follow the lawful instruction and direction of the principal.

Duty of Obedience Under the **duty of obedience,** the agent must follow the lawful instruction and direction of the principal.[16] Thus, if the agent makes an unauthorized agreement, the agent has failed to meet the duty of obedience. However, if the principal gives unlawful or unethical instructions, the agent is not required to behave in accordance with those instructions. For example, let's say a principal tells an agent to sell a basketball autographed by Michael Jordan; however, the agent knows that the principal forged the signature on the basketball. The agent is not required to obey the instructions of the principal.

duty of accounting

An agent's obligation to keep an accurate account of the transactions of money and property made on behalf of the principal.

Duty of Accounting Under the **duty of accounting,** the agent must keep an accurate account of the transactions of money and property made on behalf of the principal.[17] If the principal requests to see this accounting, the agent has a duty to provide the principal with the accounting. Part of the duty of accounting is the duty of the agent to keep separate accounts for the principal's funds and the agent's funds. The agent cannot allow the funds to "mix."

Rights and Remedies

PRINCIPAL'S RIGHTS AND REMEDIES AGAINST THE AGENT

Because the agency relationship generally *is* a contractual relationship, a principal has contract remedies available for breach of fiduciary duties. In addition, a principal may use tort remedies for an agent's misrepresentations, negligence, or other business failings that cause damage to the principal. Furthermore, when an agent breaches his or her fiduciary duties, the principal has the right to terminate the agency relationship. While numerous possible remedies are available to the principal, the three main remedies are constructive trust, avoidance, and indemnification.

Constructive Trust Agency relationships exist primarily for the benefit of the principal. Therefore, principals are the legal owners of anything an agent may come to possess through the employment or agency relationship. Accordingly, when an agent through deceit or other means retains profits or goods obtained through the employment or agency relationship, which by law belong to the principal, the agent has breached his or her fiduciary duties. For example, Joy is an agent of Sarah's selling real estate. Joy sells a piece of property for $2,000 more than Sarah anticipated. Joy then keeps the extra $2,000 and reports the sale at the price Sarah expected. By law the profits belong to Sarah, and Joy has breached her fiduciary duties by keeping the money.

Also, an agent may not use the agency relationship to obtain goods or property for himself when the principal desired to obtain the same goods or property. In an agency relationship, the

[16] Restatement (Second) of Agency, secs. 383 and 385.
[17] Restatement (Second) of Agency, sec. 382.

principal always has right of first refusal. That is, before an agent may use the relationship for a personal acquisition, the principal has the opportunity to buy whatever goods or properties are in question. Returning to Sarah and Joy, if Joy were to buy a piece of land she knew Sarah wanted to purchase, she again would have breached her fiduciary duties to Sarah.

When an agent illegally benefits from the agency relationship, the principal may enact a constructive trust on the profits, goods, or property in question. A **constructive trust** is an equitable trust imposed on a person who wrongfully obtains or holds legal right to property he or she should not possess. When a principal enacts a constructive trust, the court rules that the agent is merely holding the property or goods in trust for the principal, granting the principal legal right or possession.

constructive trust
An equitable trust imposed on a person who wrongfully obtains or holds legal right to property he or she should not possess.

Avoidance When an agency relationship exists through a contract and the agent breaches the agreement or his fiduciary duties, the principal may use her right of avoidance. *Avoidance* allows a principal to nullify any contract the agent negotiated. Which, if any, contracts are voided is at the discretion of the principal.

Indemnification Agents enter into contracts with third parties on behalf of the principal. If a third party believes that the agent is acting with actual or apparent authority, she may sue the principal for any breach of contract. However, when the breach was caused by the agent's negligence, the principal has a right to *indemnification.* That is, when sued by a third party, a principal may sue his agent to recover the amount assessed to the third party if the breach of contract is the agent's fault.

In addition to recovering for negligence, a principal can recover if an agent fails to follow the principal's instructions. Courts have had difficulty in determining when a principal gives limiting instructions and when he merely gives advice. Going against advice does not impose liability on an agent, but violating limiting instructions does. For a principal to avoid a potential lawsuit from a third party, he should notify the third party whenever a relationship with an agent ceases or limiting instructions are given.

AGENT'S RIGHTS AND REMEDIES AGAINST THE PRINCIPAL

While agency relationships are intended to benefit the principal, the agent is not without rights and remedies. Whenever a duty is imposed on the principal, a corresponding right exists for the agent. Agents have available tort and contract remedies, in addition to the right to demand an accounting.

Tort and Contract Remedies Agents, much like principals, have certain tort and contract remedies available for situations in which a principal violates an agency agreement. These remedies are the same as standard tort and contract remedies.

Demand for an Accounting When an agent feels she is not being properly compensated, especially when working on commission, the agent may *demand an accounting.* When an agent demands an accounting, she may withhold further performance of her duties until the principal supplies appropriate accounting data. For example, Hal is a used-car salesman working for Not a Lemon Car Dealers. When Hal receives his pay, he believes he has been shorted the appropriate amount he made on commission. Hal can request that Not a Lemon obtain an auditor to perform an audit and determine whether he was in fact paid the proper amount for his sales.

Specific Performance When a contract exists and a principal agrees to certain conditions but fails to perform, under contract remedies the agent may seek court assistance in forcing the principal to perform the contract as stipulated. However, when the agency relationship is not contractual or the contract is for personal services, an agent does not have the right to seek specific performance. In noncontractual relationships, an agent may recover for services rendered and/or future damages, but the agent may not force the principal to fulfill the specific contractual agreements or even to continue to employ the agent.

Authority of the Agent: The Link to the Principal's Liability

Earlier in the chapter, we discussed how an agency relationship and its resulting authority could be created. That section introduced the important concepts of (1) expressed agency, or agency by agreement; (2) implied agency; and (3) apparent agency, or agency by estoppel. Each of these avenues for creating agency includes a form of authority that attaches to that type of agency.

EXPRESS AUTHORITY

express authority

The authority of an agent that arises when the principal explicitly instructs the agent to do something. Also called *actual authority.*

In an expressed agency relationship, the agent has **express authority,** which is often referred to as *actual authority.* The principal has explicitly instructed the agent to do something. Therefore, if the principal requests that her agent sell her house for $100,000, the agent has explicit authority to sell the house for that amount. Express authority is binding in the sense that it gives the agent the power to make transactions and agreements with third parties. Because an agent with express authority has specific goals he or she is to achieve, the agent is also granted the use of other means, beyond the expressed agreement, reasonably necessary to achieve the desired goal.[18]

When express authority is granted for an agent to enter into a contract legally required to be in writing, most states require that the grant of authority also be in writing. This requirement is known as the **equal dignity rule.** When an agency agreement fails to adhere to the equal dignity rule, the subsequent contracts are typically considered to be voidable by the principal. This rule is based on the statute of frauds.

equal dignity rule

A rule requiring that contracts that would normally fall under the statute of frauds and need a writing if negotiated by the principal must be in writing even if negotiated by an agent.

There are two key exceptions to the equal dignity rule. The first pertains to executive officers. When an executive officer is conducting business in the usual course of her job, she need not obtain written approval from the corporation for every decision she makes. The second exception is rooted in common sense. The equal dignity rule does not apply to an agent when the agent is working in the direct presence of the principal.

IMPLIED AUTHORITY

implied authority

The authority of an agent that arises by inference from the words and actions of the principal.

In an implied agency relationship, the agent has **implied authority;** that is, the relationship is inferred from the conduct of the parties. Consequently, the authority of the agent is implied on the basis of words and actions of the principal to the agent.[19] An agent's implied authority is derived from an agent's express authority and consists of what is reasonably necessary for carrying out the agent's grant of express authority.

One way an agent may have implied authority is through custom. Therefore, it is important that third parties familiarize themselves with the trade. Furthermore, if an agent must make an agreement or transaction to carry out the transaction he or she has agreed to perform for the principal, we can generally infer the presence of the authority.

For example, suppose one agrees to serve as a manager for a store. The contract probably does not expressly give authority for every decision the manager might need to make. However, the manager has implied authority to make agreements and transactions that customarily go along with the manager's position.

Another example of implied authority revolves around anyone, such as a purchasing agent, who ordinarily is the person who everyone in the industry expects will make contracts for particular inputs. For someone to act as if the purchasing agent lacks authority to make such commitments on behalf of the firm would be to act contrary to the expected lines of authority.

APPARENT AUTHORITY AND ESTOPPEL

As you learned earlier in this chapter, apparent agency exists when a third party reasonably believes, on the basis of a *principal's* actions, that an agency relationship exists between the principal and another individual. Thus, if the third party reasonably believes that the agent has

[18] Restatement (Second) of Agency, sec. 35.
[19] Restatement (Second) of Agency, sec. 33.

authority to represent the principal, the principal must uphold any agreements made with the agent, who has apparent authority.[20] The principal is prevented (estopped) from acting as if the agent had no such authority.

Contractual Liability of the Principal and Agent

In addition to identifying the type of authority an agent has, courts must identify a few other factors when making decisions about an agency relationship's liability to third parties. First, the court must determine the classification of the principal. Second, the court must decide whether the principal authorized the actions of the agent.

CLASSIFICATION OF THE PRINCIPAL

Classifications are made from the perspective of the third party. In other words, the extent of the third party's knowledge about the principal determines the classification of the principal.

What are potential ethical issues arising from questions about the authority of a particular agent? The law of agency places special weight on the viewpoint of the agency relationship from the perspective of the third party (neither the agent nor the principal). But who are the other stakeholders in a managerial decision who might be affected by the assignment of a particular form of authority?

When a principal is classified as a **disclosed principal,** the third party is aware that the agent is making an agreement on behalf of a principal and the third party also knows the identity of the principal. In contrast, if a third party is aware that an agent is making an agreement on behalf of a principal but the third party is unaware of the identity of the principal, the principal is classified as a **partially disclosed principal** or an **unidentified principal.** Finally, if a third party does not know an agent is acting on behalf of a principal, the principal is classified as an **undisclosed principal.** Remember, the classification of the principal is important because it is a significant factor in determining the liability of the principal.[21]

AUTHORIZED ACTS

When an agent acts within the scope of her authority on behalf of a disclosed or partially disclosed principal, the agent is not liable for the acts of the principal.[22] The principal is liable only if the agent has some kind of authority to act on the principal's behalf. With a disclosed principal, the agent is not liable because he or she is not a party to the transaction.

Yet, if the principal is partially disclosed, the agent can be held liable herself because the courts generally treat the agent as a party to the contract. As a party to the contract, the agent may be found liable to the third party for contractual nonperformance.[23] Whether disclosed or partially disclosed, apart from any liability the agent might have, the principal is liable for the agreements made with the third party.

When the agent acts within her authority on behalf of an undisclosed principal, the law will likely hold the agent liable for the agreement. Remember, with an undisclosed principal, the third party is not aware of the existence of the principal. Thus, in the eyes of the third party, the agent is the only possible person who could be liable. Yet, if the agent is liable to the third party, then the undisclosed principal is liable to the agent. However, there are certain situations in which the agent is the only party liable for the contract. These situations are:

1. The contract expressly excludes the principal from the contract. In that the principal was not a party to the contract, he or she has no liability to the agent.

disclosed principal
A principal whose identity is known to a third party. The third party is aware that the agent is making an agreement on behalf of the principal.

partially disclosed principal
A principal whose identity is not known by a third party, although the third party is aware that the agent is making an agreement on behalf of a principal. Also called *unidentified principal.*

undisclosed principal
A principal whose existence is not known by a third party. That is, the third party does not know an agent is acting on behalf of a principal.

[20] Restatement (Second) of Agency, secs. 27 and 159.
[21] Restatement (Second) of Agency, sec. 4.
[22] Restatement (Second) of Agency, sec. 320.
[23] Restatement (Second) of Agency, sec. 321.

2. The agent enters into a contract that is a negotiable instrument. The Uniform Commercial Code (UCC) governs negotiable instruments and states that another party, that is, a principal, cannot be liable for a negotiable instrument if his name is not on the instrument or if the agent's signature does not indicate that the agreement was made in a representative capacity.[24]

3. The third party enters into a contract with the agent that requires the performance of the agent. In this case, the third party may reject the performance of the principal. For example, if the agent is a photographer and she enters into a contract for her principal without disclosing this fact, the third party may reject the principal's attempt to fulfill the contract by taking the third party's picture.

4. If the principal or agent knows a third party would not enter into a contract with the principal if the principal's identity were disclosed but the agent enters into a contract with the third party anyway, the agent will be the only party liable should the third party rescind the contract.

In situations in which a principal was undisclosed, a judgment for a third party against an agent, when the third party comes to know of the undisclosed principal's identity, releases the principal from liability.[25] Also, a judgment against a previously undisclosed principal frees the agent from liability.[26]

Exhibit 19-5 summarizes contractual liability to third parties for authorized acts of the agent.

UNAUTHORIZED ACTS

If an agent has no authority to act on behalf of a principal but the agent still enters into a contract with a third party, the principal, regardless of the classification, is not bound to the contract unless the principal ratifies the agreement.

When the agent exceeds his authority to act on behalf of the principal, the agent will likely be personally liable to the third party. Yet, when the third party is aware that the agent does not represent the principal, the law does not hold the agent liable for the agreement. In almost all other cases in which the agent claims to have authority to contract on behalf of the principal, the law holds the agent liable to the third party. If an agent enters into a contract knowingly misrepresenting his alleged authority, the agent is liable to the third party in a tort action.

Agents who go beyond their authority when the principal is disclosed or partially disclosed are liable for a breach of implied warranty, not for a breach of contract. The agent cannot be found liable for breach of contract because the agent is never an intended party to the contract, even when exceeding his or her authority. The agent can breach the implied warranty intentionally, through a knowing misrepresentation, or unintentionally, through a good-faith mistake such as simply misjudging his or her authority. In either case, the agent is liable if the third party acted relying on the agent's alleged status.

Exhibit 19-6 summarizes the contractual liability of principals and agents to third parties for unauthorized acts of the agent.

[24] UCC § 3-402(b)(2).
[25] Restatement (Second) of Agency, sec. 210.
[26] Restatement (Second) of Agency, sec. 337.

Exhibit 19-5

Contractual Liability to Third Parties for Authorized Agent Acts

CLASSIFICATION OF PRINCIPAL	AGENT LIABILITY?	PRINCIPAL LIABILITY?
Disclosed	No	Yes
Partially disclosed	Possibly	Yes
Undisclosed	Yes	Yes

THIRD-PARTY BELIEF	AGENT LIABILITY?	PRINCIPAL LIABILITY?
Believes that the agent has authority	Yes	No
Believes that the agent is mistaken about her authority	No	No

Exhibit 19-6

Contractual Liability to Third Parties for Unauthorized Acts of the Agent

Tort Liability and the Agency Relationship

If an agent commits a tort that injures a third party, the agent is personally liable for his or her actions, regardless of both the classification of the principal and the liability of the principal.[27] The principal may also be held liable for the agent's actions. This liability can arise from authorized or unauthorized acts. Furthermore, tortious liability of the principal can be established directly or indirectly. Finally, if an agent is an employee and the principal/employer controls the employee's behavior, the principal can be found liable. The next section explains these methods of establishing tortious liability.

PRINCIPAL'S TORTIOUS CONDUCT

The law holds a principal directly responsible for the tortious conduct of his agent under two conditions. First, if the principal directs the agent to commit a tort, the principal is liable for any damages caused by that tort. The principal is authorizing the agent's unlawful behavior; thus, the principal is held responsible.[28] Similarly, the principal is liable for an agent's tortious act if the principal, although not condoning the agent's conduct, ratifies the agent's actions knowing the agent acted improperly.[29]

Second, if the principal fails to provide proper instruments or tools or gives inadequate instructions to the agent concerning the necessity to employ competent agents, the law then holds the principal liable to a third party for negligence. Under this provision of liability, a principal is liable for his or her negligent hiring of an agent. Thus, a principal must use proper care in selecting an agent for a job. This doctrine of negligent hiring has been used when an agent commits a tort against a customer, who often argues that the principal is liable because he or she should have taken more care in hiring the agent.

Respondeat Superior The doctrine of *respondeat superior* (a Latin phrase meaning "let the superior speak") is used in the context of the principal/employer–agent/employee relationship. The principal/employer holds **vicarious liability** (i.e., liability assigned without fault) for any harm caused by the agent/employee during the time the agent/employee is working for the principal. In other words, the principal/employer is liable, not because he or she was personally at fault but because he or she negligently hired an agent.

The rationale behind this doctrine is that employers should be held liable for employees who commit torts because the employer is furthering his or her business through the work of the employee. If the employer is benefiting by the work of the employee, the employer should also be responsible for the harms caused by the employee.

Therefore, when a third party is injured through the negligence of an employee during the course of the employee's work, the third party can sue either the employee or the employer.[30] To establish employer liability, the third party must establish that the wrongful act occurred within

respondeat superior
Latin for "let the superior speak"; the principle by which liability for harm caused by an agent/employee is held by the principal/employer.

vicarious liability
The liability or responsibility imposed on a person, a party, or an organization for damages caused by another; most commonly used in relation to employment, with the employer held vicariously liable for damages caused by its employees.

[27] Restatement (Second) of Agency, sec. 343.
[28] Restatement (Second) of Agency, sec. 212.
[29] Restatement (Second) of Agency, sec. 218.
[30] Restatement (Second) of Agency, secs. 216 and 219.

the scope of employment. The courts consider the following elements in determining whether an act has occurred within the course and scope of employment:[31]

1. Did the employer authorize the employee's act?
2. Did the act occur within the time and space limits of employment?
3. Was the act performed, at least in part, on behalf of the employer?
4. To what extent were the employer's interests advanced by the act?
5. To what extent were the private interests of the employee involved?
6. Did the employer provide the means (i.e., tools) by which the act occurred?
7. Did the employee use force that was not expected by the employer?
8. Did the employer know that the act would involve the commission of a serious crime?

For example, if an employee is a delivery driver and negligently injures a third party while making deliveries on behalf of the employer, both the employee and the employer will be held liable.

Now suppose that the delivery driver is using the company vehicle when he stops at a drive-through at a fast-food restaurant to get some coffee. Could the employer be liable to a third party for an accident involving the delivery driver? If an agent makes a substantial departure from the course of the employer's business, the employer is not liable.

Courts often refer to a substantial departure as a "frolic of his own." However, if the deviation from the employer's business is *not* substantial, the employer can still be held liable. In Case 19-2, the court considers the scope of the employment relationship.

[31] Restatement (Second) of Agency, sec. 229.

CASE 19-2

IGLESIA CRISTIANA LA CASA DEL SENOR, INC., ETC. v. L.M.
COURT OF APPEAL OF FLORIDA, THIRD DISTRICT
783 So. 2d 353 (2001)

FACTS: *L.M. sued Ali Pacheco, the former pastor of Iglesia Cristiana la Casa del Senor, Inc. (the Church), as well as the Church, alleging that Pacheco had sexually assaulted her in July 1991 when she was a minor. The allegation of sexual assault formed the basis of L.M.'s claims against the Church based on respondeat superior. When the criminal act occurred, L.M. was 16 years old.*

Before the criminal act took place, Pacheco visited L.M.'s residence twice when L.M. had been left home alone. On another occasion, Pacheco visited L.M. at her school. L.M. told her mother about Pacheco's visit but did not advise anyone from the Church.

According to L.M., on July 8, 1991, Pacheco called her at work and invited her to lunch to discuss her parents' marital problems. L.M. accepted, and Pacheco picked her up from work. L.M. noticed a sandwich and soft drink in the car. Pacheco drove to a Marriott Hotel. L.M. testified that Pacheco led her to a room he had rented and told her not to worry because she would finally be cured. He then proceeded to sexually assault her. Pacheco testified that L.M. consented to having sex.

According to him, their meeting was prearranged. They had discussed the matter and had in fact been to the Marriot Hotel on the previous day intending to have sexual relations but had decided against it. Pacheco testified that he knew what he was doing was wrong, but he explained that it was a great temptation in his life.

The jury returned a verdict in L.M.'s favor, finding the Church liable for Pacheco's criminal act on the grounds of respondeat superior. The Church appealed.

ISSUE: Was Pacheco acting as an employee of the Church when he assaulted L.M.?

REASONING: The court stated that for the doctrine of *respondeat superior* to apply, Pacheco's employer could not be liable for the tortious or criminal acts of Pacheco "unless the acts were committed during the course of the employment and to further a purpose or interest, however

excessive or misguided, of the employer. An employee's conduct is within the scope of his employment, when (1) the conduct is of the kind he was employed to perform, (2) the conduct occurs substantially within the time and space limits authorized or required by the work to be performed, and (3) the conduct is activated at least in part by a purpose to serve the master."

In the case of L.M., the sexual assault did not occur on Church property, and what Pacheco did was not the kind of behavior the Church hired Pacheco to perform. In addition, his act was not an expression of Pacheco's desire to serve

the Church. Little counseling occurred on the day of the crime. The Church would have tried very hard to prevent his actions had it known of his plans.

DECISION AND REMEDY: The court reversed the trial court's judgment and entered judgment for the Church.

SIGNIFICANCE: *Respondeat superior* does not mean that the employer is responsible for whatever an employee might do while at work. This case spells out the requirements for such liability to be imposed on the principal.

CRITICAL THINKING

Assume that L.M.'s account of the crime is true. Examine the exception to the scope-of-employment criteria mentioned by the judge. How could the plaintiff make an argument, using that exception, that Pacheco's conduct was within the scope of his employment?

ETHICAL DECISION MAKING

The judge in this case outlines a doctrine for determining the liability of an employer for the actions of employees. What value preference is highlighted by that doctrine?

If the third party is able to establish employee negligence such that the employer is liable, the employer has the right to recover from the employee any damages the employer paid to the third party as a result of the employee's negligence. The right to recover damages is referred to as the *right of indemnification.* However, if the employee is innocent of negligence, the employer is also free of liability.

Intentional Torts and *Respondeat Superior* The agent is liable for any torts he or she commits. In the same way that the principal is responsible for the negligent acts of the employee under the doctrine of *respondeat superior,* the principal may be liable for any intentional torts of the employee. Furthermore, an employer may be responsible for any tortious acts of the employee if the employer knew or should have known that the employee had a tendency to commit a tortious act. Hence, a principal may be liable for negligent hiring if he or she fails to do a background check to learn about the tendencies of potential employees.

For example, the principal of an employee with a criminal background may be held liable for tortious acts committed by his or her hired agent, even though the employee may not recognize the wrongfulness of his act. Therefore, employers will most likely purchase liability insurance in case particular employees engage in tortious activities.

AGENT MISREPRESENTATION

If an agent misrepresents himself or herself to a third party, the principal may be tortiously liable for the agent's misrepresentation. Unlike tort liability, which is based on whether the agent/employee was acting in the scope of employment, *misrepresentation liability* depends on whether the principal authorized the agent's act. If the principal authorizes the agent to engage in an act

and the agent misrepresents herself intentionally or unintentionally, the principal is always tortiously liable to someone who relied on the agent's misrepresentation.

If an agent has misrepresented herself, the third party has two options:

1. The third party can cancel the contract with the principal and be compensated for any money lost.

2. The third party can affirm the contract and sue the principal to recover damages.

PRINCIPAL'S LIABILITY AND THE INDEPENDENT CONTRACTOR

As we discussed earlier in this chapter, an independent contractor is not an employee of the individual who hires him or her to do work. The individual doing the hiring does not control the details of the independent contractor's performance. Consequently, an individual who hires an independent contractor cannot be held liable for the independent contractor's tortious actions under the doctrine of *respondeat superior.*

Suppose that while working on the outside of the building he is renovating, an independent contractor accidentally injures an innocent bystander when he drops a pile of bricks on the bystander. The owner of the building is not liable for the innocent bystander's injuries; the independent contractor is liable.[32]

If, however, the independent contractor engages in extremely hazardous activities, such as blasting operations, for the principal, the principal will be responsible for any damages by the independent contractor. Certain activities are held strictly liable because of their inherently dangerous nature. Thus, an employer cannot escape the strict liability associated with those hazardous activities simply by hiring an independent contractor to complete the activities. In addition, the employer cannot escape liability for an independent contractor's tort if the employer directs the contractor to commit the tort.

The Case Nugget on the next page demonstrates the role of tort principles in establishing the liability of those who employ independent contractors to engage in inherently dangerous activities.

Termination of the Agency Relationship

There are multiple ways to end an agency relationship. The parties may act to terminate the relationship. Alternatively, some agencies terminate automatically by the lapse of time, fulfillment of purpose, or operation of law. If the agency relationship has ended, the agent no longer has authority to make agreements on behalf of the principal. However, the agent's apparent authority continues until the principal notifies third parties that the agency relationship has ended. What terminates the agency relationship?

Notice of the termination of an agency relationship can be given in two general forms: actual or constructive. **Actual notice** of termination is given when third parties are directly informed, orally or in writing, that an agency agreement has terminated.[33] Actual notice must be given to third parties who have had business interactions with the agent. Also, when the agent's authority was granted in writing, actual notice must be given in writing. Parties not directly related to an agency agreement may receive **constructive notice,** which is how notice of the termination of an agency agreement is generally announced.[34] Constructive notice is most frequently delivered through publication in a generally circulating newspaper for the area where the agency agreement existed.

The issue of termination of the agency is especially important for global commerce. When parties are forming a contract of agency in a foreign jurisdiction, it is extremely important that the parties include the conditions of termination within the contract.

Termination of an agency relationship involving persons from separate jurisdictions often results in complicated legal battles over compensation and liability. For example, principals must be aware of local labor laws because these laws can create agents' compensation and pension

actual notice

Notice of agency termination that is given by directly informing third parties, either orally or in writing.

constructive notice

Notice of agency termination that is usually given by publishing an announcement in a newspaper.

[32] Restatement (Second) of Agency, sec. 250.
[33] Restatement (Second) of Agency, sec. 136(2).
[34] Restatement (Second) of Agency, sec. 136(3).

CASE Nugget

Liability When Hiring Independent Contractors

Larry S. Lawrence v. Bainbridge Apartments et al.
Court of Appeals of Missouri, Western District

957 S.W.2d 400 (1997)

In 1989, Smart Way Janitorial offered a bid to Larry Lawrence to wash the windows of Bainbridge Apartments. In May 1989, when Larry went to look at the apartments, he was told that Bainbridge wanted the windows washed from outside the building so that the residents would not be disturbed. The Bainbridge property consisted of six buildings: two seven-story buildings and four four-story buildings. Even though Lawrence could not create a safety line for washing the outside of the windows of the four-story buildings, the building manager insisted that Lawrence wash the windows from the outside. When Lawrence started washing the windows from the outside, he fell from one of the shorter buildings and suffered injuries. He brought a suit against Bainbridge Apartments, arguing that Bainbridge was negligent based on the "inherently dangerous–activity" exception to the doctrine that landowners are not vicariously liable for injuries caused by the negligence of an independent contractor or his employees.

The trial court ruled that because Lawrence had recovered workers' compensation benefits, the injury was not covered by the inherently dangerous–activity exception. The trial court granted summary judgment to Bainbridge; however, when Lawrence appealed, the decision was reversed and remanded because the court of appeals ruled that Lawrence was not a covered employee entitled to workers' compensation benefits.

The court argued that in establishing the rule of liability in this case, it would look to which party can best avoid the harm and manage the risk of loss of the inherently dangerous activity in question. An independent contractor who knows he will not be compensated by the landowner for his injuries has a strong incentive to take additional care and avoid neglect in performing his duties. This encourages him to demand additional safety measures and compensation before he agrees to undertake an inherently dangerous activity. The independent contractor is free to bargain and negotiate without restraint with the landowner. An independent contractor holds himself out as an expert who is uniquely qualified and skilled to bid for and perform the acts in question. As an expert, he is in a better position to understand the risks and costs involved in a particular job, and he may demand sufficient remuneration and safety measures to cover what he believes the attendant risks to be. In return for his bargained-for price, he accepts the allocation of the risk. The court held that an injured independent contractor, although uninsured, cannot recover under the inherently dangerous–activity exception.

rights that are unknown to the principal. Local legal counsel should be especially knowledgeable about the provisions surrounding termination of agency in the particular jurisdiction and be able to help managers avoid unnecessary legal battles.

For example, if a manager has business transactions in one of the European Union countries and wants to terminate an agency relationship, he or she would want to have access to knowledge about the intricacies of Chapter IV of the Agency Relationship Law, which focuses on termination. After the termination of an agency contract in the EU countries, the agent receives help from the law in collecting damages. A released agent receives compensation if the agent has brought the principal new customers from whom the principal continues to profit, if the agent is unable to otherwise recover costs incurred through the performance of the contract, or if the agent dies.

Under certain circumstances, however, the law in European Union countries prohibits the agent's receiving compensation. For instance, if the principal has terminated the contract due to the incapacity of the agent, the principal is not obligated to dispense compensation. Also, compensation is not payable if the agent terminates the contract or assigns rights and duties under the agency contract to another person.

TERMINATION BY ACTS OF PARTIES

The agency relationship can be terminated following certain acts. Several possibilities are discussed below.

Lapse of Time If an agency agreement specifies that the agency relationship will exist for a certain amount of time, the relationship will end when the amount of time expires.[35] For example, an agency agreement might state that the agency relationship will begin on September 1 and end on September 30. While the agent and principal can agree to continue the agency relationship through October, they will have to make a new agreement. The agent's express authority ends when the relationship ends; thus, it is the responsibility of the principal to notify third parties that the former agent no longer has the ability to act on the principal's behalf.

Fulfillment of Purpose Suppose a homeowner enters into an agreement with a real estate agent to sell his house. In other words, the very basis for the relationship is a function or purpose—the selling of a piece of real estate. Once the house is sold, the agent no longer has the authority to act on the seller's behalf. The agent has fulfilled the purpose of the agency relationship.[36]

Occurrence of a Specific Event An additional means of ending an agency relationship is the occurrence of a specific event. For example, John chooses Claire as an agent to move his bed to another location. Once the move has been made, the agency relationship would terminate.

Mutual Agreement by the Parties Remember, agency is a consensual agreement between two parties. Consequently, if the two parties mutually decide they do not wish to continue in the agency relationship, they can cancel the agreement and therefore terminate the agency relationship.

Revocation of Authority At any time, a principal can revoke an agent's authority.[37] Again, the basis of agency law is consensual agreement. If the principal does not want the agent to act on his behalf, the principal can revoke the agent's authority. However, the principal's revocation might constitute a breach of contract with the agent. Therefore, the principal could be liable for damages due to the breach of contract.[38] If the agent has somehow breached her fiduciary duty to the principal, the principal can revoke the agent's authority without being liable for damages to the agent.

Renunciation by the Agent In the same way that a principal terminates an agency relationship by revoking authority, the agent can terminate the agency relationship by renouncing the authority given to the agent. The agent can be liable for breach of contract if the agency agreement has stated a specific amount of time the agency relationship is to exist.

agency coupled with an interest

An agency relationship that is created for the benefit of the agent, not the principal.

Agency Coupled with an Interest An **agency coupled with an interest** is a special kind of agency relationship. Unlike regular agency agreements, an agency coupled with an interest is created for the agent's benefit, not for the principal's. Given that the agent is the one who benefits, an agency coupled with an interest is also known as *power given as security.* Because the agency arrangement is created to benefit the agent, the principal may not terminate the relationship. Rather, the agency relationship is terminated when an event occurs that discharges the principal's obligation.

[35] Restatement (Second) of Agency, sec. 105.
[36] Restatement (Second) of Agency, sec. 106.
[37] Restatement (Second) of Agency, sec. 119.
[38] Restatement (Second) of Agency, sec. 118.

TERMINATION BY OPERATION OF LAW

LO 19-8

Certain events lead to automatic termination of the agency relationship. These events may involve a situation in which the agent is unable to fulfill his task or one in which the principal does not desire to continue with the performance. In addition, automatic termination may occur when further pursuit of the agency relationship's objectives would be illegal. These events are discussed below.

Death If either the principal or the agent dies, the agency relationship is automatically terminated. Even if one party is unaware of the other party's death, the agency relationship no longer exists. Suppose an agent has authority to buy antiques on behalf of a principal. However, without the agent's knowing it, the principal dies, but the agent continues to purchase items on behalf of the principal. Those transactions are not binding on the principal's estate because as soon as the principal died, the agent's authority to act was gone.

Insanity If a principal or agent becomes insane, the agency relationship is finished. Some states have modified this law so that unless the person has been adjudicated insane, the agency contract still exists.

Bankruptcy If the principal or agent files a bankruptcy petition, the agency relationship is generally no longer in existence. If the agent is filing for bankruptcy and the agent's credit is important to the agency relationship, the relationship will end. However, if the agent's financial history is not relevant to the agency relationship, the agency may continue. Insolvency, which is defined as the inability to pay debts or the condition of liabilities outweighing assets, does not necessarily result in the termination of the agency relationship.[39]

Changed Circumstances If there is an unusual change in circumstances that leads the agent to believe that the principal's instructions do not apply, the agency relationship terminates.[40] For example, suppose Smith contracts someone to act as her agent to sell a painting she found in her great-aunt's attic. Smith authorizes the agent to sell the painting for $5,000. However, in the course of showing the painting to several buyers, the agent learns the painting is a Van Gogh original. Thus, because the painting is worth much more than $5,000, the agent should infer that the principal does not want the original agency to continue.

Change in Law When a new law is passed subsequent to the formation of an agency agreement that makes the commission of the agency agreement illegal, the agency agreement is terminated. For example, Tyler hires Ryan to paint her house green. Then, after Ryan was hired, the city council passes a law making it illegal to paint one's house green. The new law automatically terminates the agency agreement.

Impossibility Suppose that while in the process of attempting to sell the painting in our earlier example, there is a fire in Smith's house and the painting is destroyed. Because it is impossible for the agent to sell the painting, it is impossible for the agency relationship to continue.[41]

Additionally, if the agent loses qualifications needed to perform duties for the principal, the agency relationship ends because of impossibility. For example, Jackson hires a lawyer to serve as his agent. However, the lawyer has unfortunately engaged in a series of illegal actions and is disbarred. Because the lawyer can no longer fulfill the functions Jackson has authorized him to perform, the agency relationship is terminated.

Disloyalty of Agent An agency agreement is terminated whenever the agent, unknown to the principal, acquires an interest against the principal's interest. The agency agreement is also terminated if the agent breaches the duty of loyalty he or she has to the principal.[42] For example,

[39] Restatement (Second) of Agency, sec. 113.
[40] Restatement (Second) of Agency, sec. 109.
[41] Restatement (Second) of Agency, sec. 124.
[42] Restatement (Second) of Agency, sec. 112.

E-COMMERCE and the Law

Agents and Electronic Contracts in Singapore

Many legislatures have found it necessary to add or create certain laws in response to technology. Singapore, for instance, addressed the growing use of electronic contracts with new legislation in 1997. Because of the possibility of e-mail and electronic fraud, certain risks are associated with forming electronic contracts. The new legislation attempts to combat those risks and specifies the consequences of such fraud.

The fourth section of this legislation pertains to the formation of agency contracts. Agency contracts made electronically will be valid and enforceable if the principal or a principal's designated agent sent the contract. As for contracts made between third parties, certain circumstances must exist for the third party to make the assumption that the electronic record is that of the principal.

Either the third party follows a procedure of clarification previously agreed on by the principal or he or she sees the message originated from an agent who has been endorsed by the principal. Under either of these circumstances, the third party is legally allowed to assume that the electronic message originated with the principal.

If an agent in Singapore sends an electronic record not approved by the principal, the third party has the right to act as a result of that message. In the event such actions result in injuries or damages to the third party, the principal is responsible under law. The principal cannot claim that he or she was unaware of the agent's actions. While there may have been no actual awareness, Singapore does not recognize the lack of awareness as a defense.

Singapore's new legislation intends to protect third parties from the poor judgment of principals by creating this direct link between them. Making the principal answerable and liable to the third party increases the pressure to employ reliable agents.

Mary is an attorney representing Lola in her suit against a pharmaceutical company. If the pharmaceutical company offers Mary a job and she accepts, the agency agreement would terminate because Mary has acquired an interest opposed to Lola's interests.

SUMMARY

Introduction to Agency Law	*Agency:* The relationship between a principal and an agent.
	Agent: One authorized to act for and on behalf of a principal.
	Principal: One who hires an agent to represent him or her.
	Fiduciary: One with a duty to act primarily for another person's benefit.
Creation of the Agency Relationship	*Expressed agency:* Agency formed by making a written or oral agreement.
	Power of attorney: Document giving an agent authority to sign legal documents on behalf of the principal.
	Durable power of attorney: Power of attorney intended to continue to be effective, or to take effect, after the principal has become incapacitated.
	Agency by implied authority: Agency formed by implication through the conduct of the parties.
	Agency by estoppel: Agency formed when a principal leads a third party to believe that another individual serves as his or her agent but the principal has made no agreement with the so-called agent.
	Agency by ratification: Agency that exists when an individual misrepresents himself or herself as an agent for another party and the principal accepts or ratifies the unauthorized act.
Agency Relationships	An *agency relationship* is a fiduciary relationship (a relationship of trust) in which an agent acts on behalf of the principal.
	A *principal–agent relationship* exists when an employer hires an employee to enter into contracts on behalf of the employer.
	An *employer–employee relationship* exists when an employer hires an employee to perform some sort of physical service.

An *employer–independent contractor relationship* exists when an employer hires a person other than an employee to conduct certain tasks.

Principal:

Duties of the Principal and the Agent

- Duty of compensation
- Duty of reimbursement and indemnification
- Duty of cooperation
- Duty of safe working conditions

Agent:

- Duty of loyalty
- Duty of performance
- Duty of notification
- Duty of obedience
- Duty of accounting

Principal:

Rights and Remedies

- Constructive trust
- Avoidance
- Indemnification

Agent:

- Tort and contract remedies
- Demand for an accounting
- Specific performance

Express authority: The principal has explicitly instructed the agent to do something.

Authority of the Agent: The Link to the Principal's Liability

Implied authority: The relationship is inferred from the conduct of the parties.

Apparent authority and estoppel: Apparent agency exists when a third party reasonably believes on the basis of a principal's actions that an agency relationship exists between the principal and another individual.

Classification of the principal: The principal must be classified as either disclosed, partially disclosed, or undisclosed.

Contractual Liability of the Principal and Agent

Authorized acts: These are acts within the scope of the agent's authority.

Unauthorized acts: These are acts that go beyond the scope of the agent's authority.

Principal's tortious conduct: The law holds a principal directly responsible for his or her own tortious conduct under two conditions: (1) The principal directs the agent to commit a tortious act and (2) the principal fails to provide proper instruments and tools or adequate instructions.

Tort Liability and the Agency Relationship

Agent misrepresentation: If an agent misrepresents himself or herself to a third party, the principal may be tortiously liable for the agent's misrepresentation

Respondeat superior: The principal/employer is liable not because he or she was personally at fault but because he or she negligently hired an agent.

Principal's liability and the independent contractor: An individual who hires an independent contractor cannot be held liable for the independent contractor's tortious actions under the doctrine of *respondeat superior* unless the contractor engages in hazardous activities.

Termination by acts of parties: This may occur by lapse of time, fulfillment of purpose, occurrence of a specific event, mutual agreement by the parties, revocation of authority, or renunciation by the agent.

Termination of the Agency Relationship

Termination by operation of law: The agency relationship may be terminated automatically due to death, insanity, bankruptcy, changed circumstances, change in law, impossibility, or disloyalty of the agent.

Point/Counterpoint

Should the Principal/Employer Be Indirectly Liable for the Actions of the Agent/Employee under the Doctrine of *Respondeat Superior?*

YES	NO
The employer should be held responsible for the actions of the employee while the employee is working for the employer. The employer gains from the benefits of the employee's work. Hence, there is a certain symmetry in requiring that the employer also accept the fruits of the negative behavior of the employee. In short, the benefits the employer experiences from the employee are paid for in part by the risk the employer must assume for the possible negligence of that same employee. When a company hires an employee for a position for which he or she is not competent, the company should be punished for any harm the agent causes while acting in his or her hired position. The agent would not be in a position to cause harm had the company not negligently hired him or her in the first place. For example, if a pizza company hires a person with a marred driving record as a pizza delivery driver, the pizza company should be held accountable for any harm caused by that pizza driver while at work delivering pizza. Harm should be compensated, and the employer is usually in a much more secure financial position than is the employee to provide that compensation	The employer should not be held responsible for the actions of an employee while the employee is working for the employer. Employees make daily choices using basic human judgment. These employees are hired and trusted for their competence. If an employee makes a poor decision, he or she needs to be held individually responsible. Without a model of individual responsibility, individual workers need never fear the full consequences of their actions. The employees always know their parent companies will be forced to "take care of them" under the doctrine of *respondeat superior.* With the knowledge that their employers will be held somewhat accountable, employees do not necessarily exercise the same amount of caution as they would if they were held personally accountable for every decision they make. Consider the example of the pizza delivery driver. The delivery driver injures a third party while delivering pizzas for her company, perhaps because she accidentally drove through a red traffic signal. Though she was delivering a pizza for her employer, it is the pizza delivery driver, not the pizza company, who ran a red light and injured a pedestrian. Individuals should be held accountable for individual choices. The parent companies need to be held responsible only for decisions that the parent companies make directly.

Questions & Problems

1. Who can serve as an agent or a principal?

2. What are the similarities and differences between the types of agency relationships?

3. Why is it important to determine whether a worker is an independent contractor or an employee?

4. How is apparent agency, or agency by estoppel, different from expressed agency?

5. What are the different types of authority an agent might have, and why is it important to identify the type of an agent's authority?

6. When might a principal be liable for torts committed by an agent?

7. Explain how the doctrine of *respondeat superior* affects agency relationships.

8. Ward Manufacturing, Inc., decided to construct a casting facility on its property located in Blossburg, Pennsylvania. Ward entered into a written contract with Welliver-McGuire, Inc. Under the terms of the contract, Welliver agreed to indemnify Ward for any and all claims for bodily injury and property damage arising out of the performance of the work identified in the contract. Welliver assumed control, possession, and responsibility over the construction site throughout the project. Ward did, however, maintain an on-site representative to act as liaison

and monitor the status of the project. Ward also had a safety representative on-site periodically to inspect the work site. Jonathon Olin worked as a carpenter for Welliver. Olin, while engaged in surveying activities on the Ward construction site, fell into an unbarricaded excavation pit allegedly covered with water and mud. As a result of the fall, Olin purportedly suffered severe injuries. Since the date of the accident, Olin has received total disability workers' compensation benefits from Welliver. Olin brought suit against Ward for negligence. Ward argued that Olin, through Welliver, was an independent contractor and that Ward therefore was not liable to Olin for damages. Furthermore, Ward argued that Welliver, and not Ward, was in charge of the site. Ward then moved for summary judgment. Was Ward successful in its motion for summary judgment? Why? [*Olin v. George E. Logue, Inc.,* 119 F. Supp. 2d 464 (2000).]

9. Scheerer, a licensed real estate agent, and Fisher, a manager of commercial real estate, worked together on past real estate deals and knew each other from their business relationship. Scheerer gave Fisher a tip that some commercial real estate was on the market that Fisher might be interested in purchasing. Fisher made an offer to buy the properties and, with this offer, orally contracted for a 2 percent commission for Scheerer from the seller and another 2 percent commission from himself. Unfortunately, that deal fell apart. Shortly thereafter, however, Fisher formed another company that purchased real estate and bought the very same property. Scheerer was not paid a commission on the deal and sued, contending that he was an agent for Fisher and that an implied contract for his services had been breached. Fisher argued that no formal contract in writing regarding the commission or Scheerer's agency relationship was ever created. Did the authority of the agent in this case need to be in writing to be legally binding? Does the fact that there was no separate, written agency contract between Fisher and Scheerer mean that an agency relationship did not exist? [*Scheerer v. Fisher,* 688 S.E.2d 472 (2010).]

10. Thomas Kimbro, a Department of Public Safety (DPS) officer, was the driver of a state-owned vehicle that struck Brystal McCloud's vehicle on April 1, 2005. Kimbro normally worked in Phoenix, where he lived, but at the time of the accident he was temporarily assigned to Douglas and surrounding areas, including Sierra Vista, where the accident occurred. While there, Kimbro stayed in a local motel. On the day of the accident, Kimbro had begun his workday at 4 a.m., ended his scheduled time at noon, and worked some overtime. Shortly before the accident, he stopped at the Sierra Vista DPS station and got

the name of a local restaurant. He and other members of his unit, including his supervisor, were driving to the restaurant at the time of the accident. Kimbro was looking for it as he drove, did not see traffic stopped in front of him, and struck McCloud's vehicle. McCloud suffered injuries, incurred medical expenses, lost earnings, and sustained damage to her vehicle. She filed an administrative claim against the state of Arizona, DPS, and Kimbro. The issue at court was whether Kimbro was acting within the scope of his employment at the time of the accident. In other words, should the Department of Public Safety be held vicariously liable for Kimbro's actions? Why or why not? [*McCloud v. Kimbro,* 2010 WL 1038782, Ct. App. Ariz. (2010).]

11. Brian Olander became a State Farm insurance agent in 1981. In August 1996, Olander was charged with murder after a violent altercation with a neighboring landowner. When Olander refused to take a leave of absence until the criminal charges were resolved, State Farm terminated his agency agreement and assigned other agents to serve the State Farm policyholders previously served by Olander's agency. In 1999, Olander brought suit against State Farm, alleging wrongful termination of the agency agreement. The district court granted State Farm's motion for summary judgment, concluding that Section III.A of the written State Farm Agent's Agreement unambiguously made the parties' contractual relationship terminable at will. On appeal, a divided panel of the court reversed. State Farm appealed. The issue on appeal may be quickly summarized: If the agreement was terminable at will by either party, then Olander has no wrongful-termination claim and his related claims were properly dismissed as well. Was the agency agreement one that could be terminated by either party? What duties did State Farm owe Olander when it terminated their agency agreement? [*Olander v. State Farm Mutual Automobile Ins. Co.,* 317 F.3d 807 (2003).]

12. International Airport Centers lent its employee, Citrin, a laptop to use for work. Some time later, Citrin decided to quit and go into business for himself, in breach of his employment contract. Before returning the laptop, Citrin deleted all the data in the computer by transmitting to the computer a secure-erasure program that was designed, by writing over the deleted files, to prevent their recovery. In violation of his duty of loyalty, he destroyed files that incriminated himself and other files that were also the property of his employer. After Citrin violated his duty of loyalty, did an agency relationship exist? In other words, was the agency relationship terminated then? Why or why not? [*International Airport Centers v. Citrin,* 440 F.3d 418 (2006).]

13. Julaju drove a taxi on a part-time basis for El Palmar Taxi, Inc., usually only on Sundays and sometimes on Mondays. He worked an unrelated job on the remaining days of the week. Julaju was given certain rules to follow—dress neatly, do not allow smoking in the car, do not allow passengers in front unless absolutely necessary, and ask the passengers to wear their seat belts. All cars driven for El Palmar had to be white and display the El Palmar logo. Julaju had obtained his taxi license from the city by filling out an application and giving it and the applicable fee to El Palmar. Julaju further testified that when he was driving a taxi, he did not have a set schedule and could work when he wanted and for as long as he wanted. While working, he drove either a car provided by El Palmar or a car owned by another taxi driver. To obtain a fare from El Palmar, Julaju would call the office to let them know he was working and then wait for them to give him an address to pick someone up. While he was waiting, Julaju was free to look for his own fares. In the case in question, El Palmar sent Julaju to pick up Maria Lopez and her children. Julaju got into an accident, and Lopez filed suit with El Palmar to recover damages. El Palmar argued it was not liable because Julaju was an independent contractor. Do you think the court ruled that Julaju was an employee or independent contractor? [*Lopez v. El Palmar Taxi, Inc.,* 297 Ga. App. 121; 676 S.E.2d 460 (2009).]

Looking for more review material?

The Online Learning Center at **www.mhhe.com/kubasekess2e** contains this chapter's "Assignment on the Internet" and also a list of URLs for more information, entitled "On the Internet." Find both of them in the Student Center portion of the OLC, along with quizzes and other helpful materials.

CHAPTER

Forms of Business Organization

20

The McDonald's Franchise Agreement

The McDonald's Corporation operates numerous fast-food restaurants worldwide, organizing many of them as franchises. One McDonald's franchise was sold to the Robertson family in 1971. The Robertsons operated their franchise restaurant in Jacksonville, Florida, for many years with few problems. The McDonald's Corporation later notified them, however, that the franchise had been violating part of the license agreement. After repeated incidents, McDonald's Corporation (the franchisor) demanded termination of the franchise.

1. Did McDonald's lawfully revoke the Robertsons' franchise?
2. What are some potential problems that a franchisor and a franchisee might experience in their relationship?

LEARNING OBJECTIVES

After reading this chapter, you will be able to answer the following questions:

LO 20-1 What are the major forms of business organization?

LO 20-2 What are the advantages of each alternative form of business organization?

LO 20-3 What is the special significance of the operating agreement in a limited liability company?

LO 20-4 What are the differences among the different forms of business organization?

LO 20-5 What are the specialized forms of business organization?

E-COMMERCE and the Law

Suppose that you get an idea to produce a novel product. You think that production of this new product could lead to enormous profits. But what is the best way to produce this product? Should you produce it yourself by creating your own business? Do you have enough money to create your own business? What are the legal ramifications for you if your business is not successful? What legal responsibilities do you have with respect to your business?

Maybe you share your idea for this new product with your best friend, who suggests that the two of you become partners in the production and sale of this product. What are the benefits associated with forming a partnership? What are the disadvantages? Are there other forms of businesses that you should consider?

Deciding what form of business to create is one of the most important decisions a business makes. The extent of liability, as well as the extent of the control the owner will have over the business, is dependent on the form of the business. However, the business world is not static, and businesses can, and do, change form over time. Accordingly, this chapter is relevant not only to new businesses but also to already existing businesses. The first section in this chapter introduces the major types of business organization, describing how these forms are both created and ended. The second section considers several types of business organization that are less well known but important nevertheless.

LO 20-1 Major Forms of Business Organization

SOLE PROPRIETORSHIP

sole proprietorship
A business in which one person (sole proprietor) is in control of the management and profits.

sole proprietor
The single person at the head of a sole proprietorship.

If you decide to go into business on your own, you are creating a **sole proprietorship,** a business organization in which you, as the **sole proprietor,** are in sole control of the management and the profits. Thus, if you wanted to open a lawn-mowing business or a sewing shop, you would likely be creating a sole proprietorship. It is a naturally occurring form of business organization in the sense that if you started doing business without thinking about the form, you would be a sole proprietor.

Why might an entrepreneur choose to create a sole proprietorship over other business organizations? First, a sole proprietorship requires very few legal formalities. Thus, one advantage of the sole proprietorship is the ease of creating such a business. Second, a sole proprietor has complete control of the management of the business. Consequently, the sole proprietor has great freedom to hire employees, determine business hours, and expand or change the nature of the business. Finally, the sole proprietor keeps all the profits from the business. These profits are taxed as the personal income of the sole proprietor.

However, sole proprietorships have disadvantages too. Suppose you are the sole proprietor of a restaurant in which someone is injured. This customer sues your business. You are personally liable for any losses or any obligations associated with the business. Consequently, if you accrue large debts because of your business, you might have to sell your home to cover those debts.

ADVANTAGES	DISADVANTAGES
1. Creation is easy.	1. Proprietor has personal liability for all losses.
2. Proprietor is in total control of management.	2. Funding is limited to personal funds and loans.
3. Proprietor keeps all profits.	

Exhibit 20-1

Advantages and Disadvantages of the Sole Proprietorship

Moreover, because the sole proprietorship is not considered a separate legal entity, you, as the owner and sole proprietor, can be personally sued. Sole proprietorships are terminated, however, when the sole proprietor dies.

Not only are you personally liable for any debts of the business, but the funding for your business is limited to your personal funds as well as loans you might be able to obtain. Thus, sole proprietorships often struggle in the initial stages of business because of large start-up costs in relation to the profits they make.

Sole proprietorships are by far the most popular form of business organization in the United States. Exhibit 20-1 summarizes their advantages and disadvantages.

An alternative form of business organization that retains many of the advantages of the sole proprietorship but that addresses the funding drawback in part is the partnership.

PARTNERSHIP

Suppose you and your best friend from college decide to create a business in which you plan to buy and sell used books and DVDs through the Internet. You both agree that you will share control of the Internet business and will split the profits equally. According to the Uniform Partnership Act (UPA), you have created a **partnership,** a voluntary association between two or more persons who co-own a business for profit. Except in a few cases, a partnership is not considered a separate legal entity and is dissolved when a partner dies. The UPA governs partnerships in most states in the absence of an express agreement.

What are the advantages associated with creating a partnership? First, the creation of a partnership is easy. The partners, each of whom is considered an agent of the partnership, are generally not required to create an official or even written agreement to create the partnership. Second, because the partnership is in most cases not considered a separate legal entity, the income from the business is taxed as individual income for each partner. Because the income is taxed as personal income, the partners can deduct the business losses.

While there are certain advantages to creating a partnership, there are also disadvantages associated with partnerships. Most importantly, the partners are personally liable for the debts of the partnership. For instance, suppose you are in a partnership with your best friend, who embezzles $50,000 through your partnership. Because of the partnership, you would likely be held personally liable for the debts of the partnership. In other words, you would likely be responsible for the $50,000. Exhibit 20-2 summarizes the advantages and disadvantages of partnerships.

Although it is not listed in Exhibit 20-2, one advantage of a partnership is the ability to choose the people with whom you want to be partners. As the Case Nugget demonstrates, the courts recognize the right to choose one's partners as a basis for partnership law.

partnership
A voluntary association between two or more people who co-own a business for profit.

ADVANTAGES	DISADVANTAGES
1. Creation is easy.	1. Each partner has personal liability for all losses, including those of another partner (in most cases).
2. Income of business is personal income.	
3. Business losses can be deducted from taxes.	

Exhibit 20-2

Advantages and Disadvantages of Partnerships

CASE Nugget

Do Partners Have a Duty to Remain Partners?

Colette Bohatch v. Butler & Binion
Supreme Court of Texas

977 S.W.2d 543

Colette Bohatch became an associate in the Washington, D.C., office of Butler & Binion in 1986. John McDonald and Richard Powers, both partners, were the only other attorneys in the office. After Bohatch was made a partner in February 1990, she became concerned that McDonald was overbilling Pennzoil, the main client of the office. Bohatch met with the law firm's managing partner, Louis Paine, to report her concern regarding McDonald's overbilling. In July 1990, McDonald met with Bohatch to report that Pennzoil was dissatisfied with her work.

The next day, Bohatch relayed her concern to Paine, as well as to two other members of the law firm's management committee. Paine led an investigation of Bohatch's complaint and discussed the billed hours with the in-house counsel at Pennzoil, who concluded that the bills were reasonable. In August 1990, Paine met with Bohatch, telling her that there was no basis for her claims against McDonald and that she should look for work elsewhere. The firm refused Bohatch a year-end partnership distribution for 1990. Finally, in August 1991, Bohatch was given until November to vacate her office. She filed suit in October 1991, and the firm voted to expel her from the partnership three days later.

At trial, the jury ruled that the firm breached the partnership agreement and its fiduciary duty and awarded Bohatch $57,000 for past lost wages, $250,000 for past mental anguish, $4,000,000 total in punitive damages (this amount was apportioned against several defendants), and attorney fees. Later, the trial court reduced the punitive damages to around $237,000. The court of appeals ruled that the firm's only duty to Bohatch was to not expel her in bad faith. When the court found no evidence that the firm fired Bohatch for self-gain, it ruled that Bohatch could not recover for breach of fiduciary duty. The case was appealed to the state supreme court.

The supreme court ruled that the firm did not owe Bohatch a duty to remain partners. While Bohatch presented a compelling argument that firms should not be permitted to expel partners who "whistle-blow" in good faith, the court could not ignore one basis of partnership law: a belief that partners should be allowed to choose their partners. The court found that forcing firms to keep whistle-blowing partners would cause partners to engage in business with people they could no longer trust, thereby undermining the viability of the partnership. Therefore, the supreme court affirmed the ruling of the court of appeals.

general partnership

A partnership in which the partners divide profits and management responsibility and share unlimited personal liability for the partnership's debts.

There are several types of partnerships: general partnerships, limited partnerships, and limited liability partnerships. A **general partnership** consists of an agreement that the partners will divide the profits (usually equally) and management responsibilities and share unlimited personal liability for the partnership's debts. Thus, in our Internet business example, you and your best friend would form a general partnership by agreeing to share the management responsibilities and profits as well as assuming unlimited personal liability.

Now imagine that your parents want to invest in your Internet business. Suppose that they want to share in the profits associated with the business but they do not want to share in the management responsibilities or assume personal liability for the debts of the partnership. Your parents can join your business as limited partners, and your partnership would become a limited

partnership. A **limited partnership (LP)** is an agreement between at least one general partner and at least one limited partner. The *general* partners, you and your best friend, assume unlimited personal liability for the debts of the partnership. However, your parents, the *limited* partners, assume no liability for the partnership beyond the capital they have invested in the business. Moreover, the limited partners do not have any part in the management of the company. However, limited partners pay taxes on their share of the business profit.

If a limited partner dies, the limited partnership is usually unaffected. If a general partner dies, however, the limited partnership is usually dissolved.

The limited partnership must meet certain requirements that are not expected of general partnerships. First, the limited partnership must use the word *limited* in its title. Second, to create a limited partnership, the parties must file a certificate of partnership with a state office. If the certificate of partnership is incorrectly filed, or simply not filed at all, the courts will rule that a general partnership exists. Consequently, all parties will be held personally liable for all the debts of the partnership.

Now suppose that you are an attorney and a partner in a law firm with 30 other partners. Suppose further that one of your partners is sued because he was negligent in his duties as an attorney. This partner has unlimited liability because of professional malpractice. But will you and the other partners at the firm be held liable for this partner's malpractice?

If you and your fellow partners have created a **limited liability partnership (LLP),** a different form of partnership than the LP, all the partners assume liability for any partner's professional malpractice to the extent of the partnership's assets. In other words, the limited liability partnership is different from other forms of partnership because the partners' liability for professional malpractice is limited to the partnership. If one partner in an LLP is guilty of malpractice, the other partners' personal assets cannot be taken. Therefore, professionals who do business together commonly use the LLP. It is the extra protection awarded partners in an LLP that makes the LLP a *separate* form of partnership from a limited partnership. Limited partnerships are not the same as limited liability partnerships.

Limited liability partnerships are fairly new; in 1991, Texas was the first state to enact a statute permitting the creation of LLPs. Almost all states now have similar statutes. Like the limited partnership, the LLP has several special requirements. First, the business name must include the phrase *Limited Liability Partnership* or the abbreviation *LLP.* Second, the parties must file a form with the secretary of the state to create the LLP.

The LLP is not considered a separate legal entity. Each partner pays taxes on his or her share of the income of the business.

An alternative form of business organization, the corporation, separates business ownership from business control.

> To see more on shareholders and corporations, please see the **Connecting to the Core** activity on the text's website at www.mhhe.com/kubasekess2e.

limited partnership (LP)

A partnership consisting of at least one general partner and at least one limited partner in which the general partners assume all liability for the partnership's debts and the limited partners assume no liability beyond their originally invested capital.

limited liability partnership (LLP)

A partnership in which all the partners assume liability for any partner's professional malpractice to the extent of the partnership's assets.

CORPORATION

When you hear the word *business,* you probably think about businesses such as Walmart, Kmart, McDonald's, and Nike. Perhaps the most dominant form of business organization is the **corporation,** a legal entity formed by issuing stock to investors, who are the owners of the corporation. The investor-owners are called **shareholders.** These shareholders elect a board of directors, which is responsible for managing the business. The board of directors, in turn, hires officers to run the day-to-day business.

The corporation is considered a separate legal entity; thus, the corporation can be sued. None of the other forms of business we have discussed are considered separate legal entities. How does a corporation become a separate legal entity? It must be created according to state law.

What are the consequences of a corporation's status as a separate legal entity? First, while the corporation can be held liable, shareholders cannot be held personally liable for the debts of the corporation. Their liability is usually limited to the amount they have invested. Second, the corporation is not dissolved when the shareholders die. Third, the corporation must pay taxes on its profits. In addition, the shareholders must pay taxes on the dividends they receive from the corporation.

corporation

A legal entity formed by issuing stock to investors, who are the owners of the corporation.

shareholders

Investors in a corporation, who own the corporation.

Exhibit 20-3

Advantages and
Disadvantages of
Corporations

ADVANTAGES	DISADVANTAGES
1. Limited liability for shareholders	1. Corporate income taxed twice
2. Ease of raising capital by issuing stock	2. Formalities required in establishing and maintaining corporate form
3. Profits taxed as income to the shareholders, not the partners	

Exhibit 20-3

Advantages and Disadvantages of Corporations

S corporation

A corporation that enjoys the tax status of a partnership.

One way that a corporation can avoid this double taxation is by forming an **S corporation,** a business organization formed under federal tax law that is considered a corporation yet is taxed like a partnership as long as it follows certain regulations. For example, the S corporation cannot have more than 100 shareholders. Any income of the corporation is taxed when it is distributed to the shareholders, who must report the income on their personal income tax forms. S corporations are always formed under federal law. S corporations cannot be formed under state law, whereas other forms of corporations are created under state law.

Exhibit 20-3 summarizes the advantages and disadvantages of the corporate form of business.

LIMITED LIABILITY COMPANY

limited liability company (LLC)

An unincorporated business that is taxed like a partnership, with the members paying personal income taxes, and has the limited liability of a corporation.

One of the newest forms of business organization in the United States is the **limited liability company (LLC),** an unincorporated form of business organization that many people see as combining the most advantageous features of partnerships and corporations. It combines the tax advantages and management flexibility of a partnership with the limited liability of a corporation.

This form of business organization was first recognized in the United States in 1977 in Wyoming and is now recognized in every state, although the rules regarding this new form did not evolve uniformly. As with other areas of law, the National Conference of Commissioners on Uniform State Laws recognized the desirability of bringing some uniformity to this area of law and drafted the Uniform Limited Liability Company Act (ULLCA) in 1995. In 2006, the commissioners revised the ULLCA. This act provides a model for states to follow, but it has not been uniformly adopted, so it is always necessary when establishing an LLC to check the exact requirement of the law for LLCs in the state in which you wish to create your company.

LO 20-2

Key Reasons for the Rapid Acceptance of LLCs As previously mentioned, the LLC form offers its members the same limited liability for business debts as that offered by the corporate form. However, unlike the corporate form, it does not require that profits and losses be allocated in proportion to ownership interests. Also unlike corporations, LLCs are not required to hold an annual meeting and draft meeting minutes, so record keeping is simpler and more flexible. Unlike the case in limited partnerships, to obtain limited liability, the owner (referred to as a *member*) does not have to give up his or her right to participate in management of the LLC. In fact, an additional advantage of the LLC form is the flexibility it offers members in terms of alternative ways to structure its management.

The most frequently cited advantage of the LLC is that it is generally treated by the IRS like a partnership or sole proprietorship, with members reporting their share of the profits and losses of the LLC on their personal tax returns and no separate tax being assessed on the company itself, thereby allowing its members to avoid the double taxation that owners of a corporation pay. However, if an LLC's members prefer, they may elect to have the entity taxed like a corporation. In a situation where most of the profits are going to be reinvested in the business, this option allows the profits to be taxed at the lower corporate rate. So, while we think of the opportunity to avoid double taxation as a key benefit of the LLC, more important perhaps is the fact that the members have the choice of how they want to be taxed.

In our global environment, an increasingly important advantage of LLCs is that members need not be citizens or permanent residents of the United States. Other organizational forms, such as the subchapter S corporation, are available only when all the owners are U.S. citizens. Finally, as

with a corporation, ordinary business expenses, such as salaries paid to owners, can be deducted from the profits of an LLC before the LLC's income is allocated to its owners for tax purposes.

Formation and Management of LLCs A limited liability company is formed by filing articles of organization in the state in which members want to establish their LLC. While precise requirements vary by state, typically the articles include the name of the business, which must include the words *Limited Liability Company* or the initials *LLC,* its principal business address, the name and address of a registered agent for service, the names of the owners, and information about how the company's management will be structured.

LO 20-3

LLCs typically want to do business in states other than the state in which they are formed, and they usually need to register in every additional state in which they want to operate, a process typically referred to as *qualification.* Qualification simply entails filing a certificate of authority or a similar document and getting a business license in each additional state in which the business plans to operate. The LLC will usually be referred to as a *foreign company* in the additional states, and under most state statutes the LLC will be governed by the LLC rules of the state in which it was created, regardless of where it is transacting business.

For purposes of jurisdiction, however, an LLC is considered a citizen of every state in which its members reside. Remember that a party can be sued in federal court over a matter involving more than $75,000 when diversity of citizenship exists, that is, when no plaintiff and defendant are residents of the same state. For determining whether diversity exists, a corporation is considered a resident of both the state in which it is incorporated and the state in which it has its primary place of business. However, this rule does not apply to LLCs, as their citizenship is determined by the residences of their members. Consequently, if parties want to be more likely to be able to avail themselves of the federal courts, they may want to either limit their membership to individuals of only one or a few states or use a different form of business organization.

When members form an LLC, they typically draft an operating agreement, which is the foundational contract among the entity's owners. It spells out such matters as how the company is to be managed, how the profits and losses will be allocated, how interests may be transferred, and how and when the LLC may be dissolved. Any matter not covered in the operating agreement will be resolved in accordance with the state LLC statute; if a matter is not covered by the relevant statute, the principles of partnership law are generally followed.

While there is no requirement for an LLC to have a detailed, written operating agreement, to ensure the smooth functioning of the company, it is a good idea to have such an agreement. Failure to have a detailed, written agreement may result in a court's imposing standards on the company that may be very different from what the members had in mind when forming the company.

It is very important, however, to make sure that everyone understands the terms of the operating agreement, because once the parties enter into such an agreement, the courts will enforce it.

One of the key issues to be determined in the operating agreement is how the company is to be managed. There are two options: member-managed and manager-managed. Under the ULLCA, unless the operating agreement specifies otherwise, LCCs are member-managed. In a *member-managed LLC,* all members participate in management, with decisions in the ordinary course of business activities made by a majority vote. The consent of all members, however, is required to sell, lease, exchange, or otherwise dispose of all, or substantially all, of the company's property; approve a merger or conversion to a different form; undertake any other act outside the ordinary course of the company's activities; and amend the operating agreement. The members in such an LLC all have the apparent and actual authority to enter into contracts on behalf of the LLC.

In a *manager-managed LLC,* the members select a group of managers to manage the affairs of the company. The managers may be selected from the members or may be nonmembers. The managers have the apparent and actual authority to enter into contracts on behalf of the LLC, while the members who are not managers do not have such authority. The managers owe the LLC and its members the same fiduciary duties as the officers and directors of a corporation owe to the corporation and its shareholders.

Dissolution of LLCs Under the ULLCA, an LLC dissolves on the happening of any event that the operating agreement specifies will cause dissolution, the consent of all the members, the

Exhibit 20-4

Comparison of Alternative Forms of Business Organization

	SOLE PROPRIETORSHIP	GENERAL PARTNERSHIP	LIMITED PARTNERSHIP	CORPORATION	LIMITED LIABILITY COMPANY
Legal Position	Not a separate legal entity.	Not a separate legal entity in most states.	A separate legal entity.	A separate legal entity.	A separate legal entity for purposes of liability but not always for taxes.
Control Considerations	Sole proprietor has total control.	Each partner is entitled to equal control.	Each partner is entitled to equal control.	Separation of ownership and control.	Members control allocation of control.
Liability	Sole proprietor has unlimited personal liability.	Each partner has unlimited personal liability for partnership debts.	Each partner has liability limited up to his or her capital contribution.	Liability is limited to loss of capital contribution.	Liability is limited to loss of capital contribution.
Lifetime	Limited to life of proprietor.	Limited by life of partners.	Limited to life of general partners.	Can have unlimited life.	Operating agreement spells out the lifetime.
Taxation	Profits are taxed directly as income to the sole proprietor.	Profits are taxed as income for partners.	Profits are taxed as income for partners.	Profits are taxed as income to corporation and as income to partners in the form of dividends.	Operating agreement spells out whether profits will be taxed as a corporation or partnership.
Transferability of Ownership Interest	Nontransferable.	Nontransferable.	Nontransferable.	Generally unlimited transfer.	Operating agreement spells out the transferability.

passage of 90 consecutive days during which the company has no members, or the issuance of a court order for dissolution. Under the ULLCA and most state LLC statutes, a member's voluntary withdrawal from the LLC, referred to as *dissociation,* does not terminate the LLC.

LO 20-4 Exhibit 20-4 provides a comparison of the alternative forms of business organization.

LO 20-5 # Specialized Forms of Business Organization

In addition to the more traditional forms of business organization mentioned above, the following specialized forms of business organization have become increasingly important: cooperatives, joint stock companies, business trusts, syndicates, joint ventures, and franchises.

COOPERATIVE

cooperative

An organization formed by individuals to market new products. Individuals in a cooperative pool their resources together to gain an advantage in the market.

A **cooperative** is an organization formed by individuals to market products. The cooperative is a business organization in which the members usually pool their resources together to gain some kind of advantage in the market. For instance, farmers might pool certain crops together to ensure that they get a high market price for their crops. Usually, members of the cooperative receive dividends in proportion to how many times a year they engage in business with the cooperative.

Partnerships under Islamic Law

Not all countries have forms of business organization that are similar to those used in the United States. Consider, for instance, Islamic partnerships. Under Islamic law, the partnership and its partners are one unit, not separate units. A person's personal wealth is the capital of the business, and upon it the contract for the company is formed. Because Islamic partnerships are not considered separate entities, they do not receive many of the unique advantages that partnerships receive in the United States.

For example, recall that in the United States, once a partnership has fulfilled all the legal requirements, it is then established and the partners become separate entities from the partnership, which becomes a legal entity in its own right. This means that, in the United States, a partnership is a physical "person" in that it is liable to pay its own taxes and can be taken to court and sued. However, the idea of a separate entity contradicts the concept of the Islamic partnership, as the partners are considered *the partnership*. Under Islamic law, if the company is taken to court, it is the individual partners that are liable. How do you think this difference in partnership liability affects the actions of the partners? Would partners likely be more careful or prudent if they knew they could be held personally liable for the actions of the partnership?

Cooperatives may be incorporated or unincorporated. Unincorporated cooperatives are treated like partnerships, meaning that the members share joint liability for the cooperative's actions. Members of incorporated cooperatives, on the other hand, enjoy limited liability just as do the shareholders of a corporation.

JOINT STOCK COMPANY

A **joint stock company** is a partnership agreement in which company members hold transferable shares while all the goods of the company are held in the names of the partners. Thus, the joint stock company is a mixture of a corporation and a partnership. As with the corporation, the members who hold shares of stock own the joint stock company. As with the partnership, the shareholders have personal liability, and in most cases the company is not a separate legal entity. The joint stock company is formed by agreement rather than statute.

joint stock company
A partnership agreement in which company members hold transferable shares while all the goods of the company are held in the names of the partners.

BUSINESS TRUST

A **business trust** is a business organization governed by a group of **trustees,** who operate the trust for the **beneficiaries.** A written trust agreement establishes the duties and powers of the trustees and the interests of the beneficiaries.

As with a corporation, the trustees and beneficiaries enjoy limited liability, and in most states business trusts are taxed like corporations.

business trust
A business organization governed by a group of trustees, who operate the trust for beneficiaries.

trustee
A person who operates a trust for beneficiaries in a business trust.

beneficiary
A person who can expect to benefit from a relationship.

SYNDICATE

An investment group that comes together for the explicit purpose of financing a specific large project is a **syndicate.** Syndicates are often used in the purchase of professional sports teams. The syndicate is quite useful in the sense that it can raise large amounts of money in a small amount of time. Syndicates are usually considered a type of joint venture, and thus they are almost always governed by partnership law.

syndicate
An investment group that comes together for the explicit purpose of financing a specific large project.

JOINT VENTURE

A **joint venture** is a relationship between two or more persons or corporations created for a specific business undertaking. This relationship may entail financing, producing, and selling goods, securities, and commodities. Participants in the joint venture usually share the profits and losses of the joint venture equally.

Joint ventures can be agreements between small businesses as well as agreements between very large businesses. For example, Nestlé and Häagen-Dazs entered into a joint venture to

joint venture
An association between two or more parties wherein the parties share profits and management responsibilities with respect to a specific project.

create Ice Cream Partners, USA. Generally, joint ventures are taxed like partnerships. In fact, from a legal standpoint, partnerships and joint ventures are virtually the same. Thus, courts frequently apply partnership law to joint ventures. Joint ventures differ from partnerships, however, because a joint venture is usually created for making and selling a single product while a partnership creates an ongoing full business. Once all the single products are sold, the joint venture is usually terminated. The members, however, can determine when the joint venture will end.

Despite the similarities, there are several minor differences between partnerships and joint ventures in the eyes of the law. First, if one of the members of a joint venture dies, the joint venture is not automatically terminated. Second, the members of a joint venture have less authority than general partners because members of a joint venture are not agents of the other members.

The parties who compose a joint venture usually share equal management of the task for which they have come together. They, however, can make an agreement to give one party greater management responsibilities. Furthermore, all the parties usually assume liability for the project. Each party can be held responsible for the liability of another party in the joint venture.

Like a partnership, a joint venture may be formed without drawing up a formal agreement. Case 20-1 illustrates how the courts determine whether a joint venture exists. What facts does the judge rely on to determine whether a joint venture existed between the Parkers?

CASE 20-1

KENNETH R. PARKER v. CONCELIA PARKER
SUPREME COURT OF NEW YORK
196 Misc. 2d 672; 766 N.Y.S.2d 315 (2003)

FACTS: *When Kenneth and Concelia Parker were married, they executed a prenuptial agreement whereby each party waived their respective rights in the separately held property of the other, whether arising before or subsequent to the marriage. "Marital property" was defined as property held jointly. During their marriage, Mrs. Parker purchased a lottery ticket that became the sole winning ticket of a $25 million New York State Lottery prize. A check in the amount of $8,590,077 was made payable to Mrs. Parker alone and was presented to her.*

Shortly after, Mrs. Parker purchased a condominium and put the remainder in an account under a living trust that was solely in her name. She also made gifts of the lottery winnings to her children from a prior marriage. However, she indicated therein that upon her death, her husband could reside in the marital residence and would receive income off a segregated amount of money during his lifetime. Her husband then filed for divorce. The husband moved for an order to restrain the wife from making any disposition of separate or marital funds, including the $8 million in lottery winnings, and to place $3 million of such winnings in an escrow account. Mr. Parker claimed the lottery money was joint property under a theory that the parties entered into a "joint venture." He claimed that,

in the past, the parties had purchased lottery tickets with joint funds and that it was he who contributed the funds with which the wife purchased the winning ticket.

ISSUE: Were Kenneth and Concelia Parker engaged in a joint venture?

REASONING: An oral agreement to share lottery winnings is valid and enforceable. Eventually, the husband would have the burden of proving at the trial that the parties made a certain and specific mutual promise to share the subject lottery winnings; that the purchase of the winning ticket by the wife was in furtherance of the parties' "joint venture"; and that the wife breached the parties' agreement by refusing to share the winnings with him.

In actions where the subject matter is a specific fund of money, such as lottery winnings, preliminary injunctive relief may lie upon the requisite showing of the likelihood of success on the merits and that the balance of the equities lies in the movant's favor. Here, the husband's allegations did not set forth sufficient detail to demonstrate a likelihood of success on the merits, as he has asserted nothing more than broad, vague generalizations about the ongoing purchase of lottery tickets by the wife with joint

funds, and the sharing of gambling winnings, all of which allegations are denied by the wife. Further, it was undisputed that the wife had separate funds available to her to use to purchase lottery tickets. Accordingly, if the husband had commenced a breach of contract action rather than a matrimonial action, he would not be entitled to preliminary injunctive relief.

However, pursuant to New York Domestic Relations Law (DRL) 234, a matrimonial litigant need only demonstrate that an interim restraint is required to preserve his or her right to an equitable share of marital assets. In this case, the husband asserted a "joint venture" claim to the lottery winnings in issue and in the event he succeeds on said claim, such winnings would constitute a marital asset subject to equitable distribution.

DECISION AND REMEDY: On the basis of the circumstances of the case, the court found that the husband is entitled to interim relief pursuant to DRL 234 as a matrimonial litigation. Accordingly, his motion was granted to the following extent:

It is hereby Ordered that pending further order of the Court, the wife, individually and as trustee of the defendant trust; her agents; attorneys and assigns are restrained from making any disposition of $3,000,000.00 of the lottery winnings that were on deposit . . . as of April 25, 2003.

In other words, it appears as though the husband's claim regarding the "joint venture" had some merit under Domestic Relations Law, and his motion was granted. He would still have to prove in trial court that a joint venture existed, however.

SIGNIFICANCE OF THE CASE: This case demonstrates the importance of parties' intent when conducting business together or when married. No formal agreement or written contract is required to form a joint venture, so parties may enter into a joint venture with relative ease. At the very least, engaged couples should consider an express statement in a prenuptial agreement that lotto prizes won by either party during the marriage are not marital property through a "joint venture" and are the separate property of the ticket holder.

CRITICAL THINKING

When a court tries to determine intent, it must of necessity look at the behavior of the relevant parties. In this case, what kind of actions would have raised serious questions about whether the parties were indeed engaged in a joint venture?

ETHICAL DECISION MAKING

Consider the primary stakeholders in the situation. Are there ethical problems with Mrs. Parker's actions, or is she justified in claiming the winnings all to herself?

FRANCHISE

When you go into McDonald's to eat lunch, what type of business are you patronizing? You are likely eating at a **franchise**, a business that exists because of an arrangement between the **franchisor**, an owner of a trade name or trademark, and the **franchisee**, a person who sells goods or services under the trade name or trademark.

What are the advantages and disadvantages for the franchisor and the franchisee? Exhibits 20-5 and 20-6 summarize these advantages and disadvantages. First, the franchisee enjoys the franchisor's help in opening the franchise. Second, think about how many times you have driven through a strange town and felt relieved when you saw a Burger King. Even though you may have never been to that town before and did not know who controlled that particular business, you know Burger King. Before you walk into the restaurant, you know almost exactly what will be on the menu. Thus, on the one hand, the franchisee benefits from the franchisor's strong trade name or trademark. Moreover, the franchisee benefits from the franchisor's worldwide advertising of the trade name or trademark. The franchisor, on the other hand, does not take a large risk in creating the franchise, yet it can greatly benefit from the income it receives from the franchisee.

franchise
A business arrangement between an owner of a trade name or trademark and a person who sells goods or services under the trade name or trademark.

franchisor
The owner of the trade name or trademark in a franchise.

franchisee
The seller of goods or services under a trade name or trademark in a franchise.

Exhibit 20-5

Advantages and Disadvantages to the Franchisee of Starting a Franchise

ADVANTAGES	DISADVANTAGES
1. Help from the franchisor in starting the franchise	1. Must meet the franchisor's standards or risk losing the franchise
2. Instant recognition due to the franchisor's strong trademark or trade name	2. Has little to no creative control over the business
3. Benefits from the franchisor's worldwide advertising	

Exhibit 20-6

Advantages and Disadvantages to the Franchisor of Starting a Franchise

ADVANTAGES	DISADVANTAGES
1. Low risk in starting a franchise	1. Has little control over the franchise
2. Increased income from franchises	2. Can become liable for the franchise if it exerts too much control

Exhibit 20-7

Types of Franchises

FRANCHISE TYPE	DESCRIPTION
Chain-style business operation	Franchisor helps franchisee set up a business run under the franchisor's business name according to the franchisor's usual methods and standards.
Distributorship	Franchisor licenses franchisee to sell the franchisor's product in a specific area.
Manufacturing arrangement	Franchisor provides the franchisee with the technical knowledge needed to manufacture the franchisor's product.

Exhibit 20-8

The Top 10 Global Franchises, 2011

1. Subway
2. McDonald's
3. KFC
4. 7-Eleven
5. Burger King
6. Snap-On Tools
7. Pizza Hut
8. Wyndham Hotel Group
9. ServiceMaster
10. Choice Hotels

Source: Ranked by *Entrepreneur Magazine* on the basis of financial strength and stability, growth rate, and size of the system, www.entrepreneur.com/franzone/listings/fran500/0,5831,00.html.

chain-style business operation

A type of franchise in which the franchise operates under the franchisor's business name and is required to follow the franchisor's standards and methods of business operation.

distributorship

A type of franchise in which the franchisor manufactures a product and licenses a dealer to sell the product in an exclusive territory.

manufacturing arrangement

A type of franchise in which the franchisor provides the franchisee with a formula or necessary ingredient to manufacture a product.

Generally, franchises fall into one of three categories. McDonald's and Burger King are examples of chain-style business operations. In a **chain-style business operation,** the franchise operates under the franchisor's business name and is required to follow the franchisor's standards and methods of business operation.

The second category of franchises is the distributorship. **Distributorships** are franchises in which the franchisor manufactures a product and licenses a dealer to sell the product in an exclusive territory. A car dealership is an example of a distributorship.

Finally, the third category of franchises is the manufacturing arrangement. In a **manufacturing arrangement,** the franchisor provides the franchisee with a formula or necessary ingredient to manufacture a product. The franchisee then manufactures the product and sells it according to the franchisor's standards.

Exhibit 20-7 describes the various types of franchises. Exhibit 20-8 provides a sense of just how important franchises are for the market economy.

Look at Case 20-2 to see how the supreme court of Arkansas determined whether a franchise agreement existed between Mary Kay Cosmetics and Janet Isbell.

MARY KAY, INC., A/K/A MARY KAY COSMETICS, INC. v. JANET ISBELL
SUPREME COURT OF ARKANSAS

338 Ark. 556; 999 S.W.2d 669; 1999 Ark. LEXIS 443

FACTS: *In 1980, Janet Isbell signed an agreement to become a beauty consultant for Mary Kay. This agreement established that she would sell products to customers at home demonstration parties, but she was prohibited from selling the products in retail establishments. In 1981 and 1991, Isbell signed agreements to become a unit sales director. In addition to serving as a beauty consultant, Isbell recruited beauty consultants. In 1994, she rented a space in a shopping mall to serve as a training center. In April 1994, Mary Kay's legal coordinator contacted Isbell, stating that the store space was not to be used to sell Mary Kay products. According to the agreement, Isbell's office could not look like a Mary Kay store. In September 1995, the vice president of sales development notified Isbell that Mary Kay was terminating its agreements with Isbell. Isbell filed suit against Mary Kay, claiming that she was a franchise under the Arkansas Franchise Practices Act. She argued that Mary Kay violated the Franchise Practices Act by refusing to comply with the FPA provisions for termination of a franchise. The trial court granted summary judgment to Isbell, but it did not explain why Isbell's relationship with Mary Kay could be considered a franchise. The trial court ruled as a matter of law that Mary Kay's termination of Isbell had violated the act, and a jury awarded Isbell $110,583.33. Mary Kay appealed.*

ISSUE: Was Janet Isbell a franchisee of Mary Kay?

REASONING: Sections 4-72-203 and 4-72-202 (6) of the Arkansas Franchise Practices Act establish that the act applies only to a franchise that contemplates or requires the franchise to establish or maintain a place of business in the state. A place of business is defined as "a fixed geographical location at which the franchisee [1] displays for sale and sells the franchisor's goods or [2] offers for sale and sells the franchisor's services." In this case, there was no evidence that Isbell sold Mary Kay products from a fixed geographic location. Isbell was, in fact, prohibited from selling products from her office or center. Isbell was to sell products in customers' homes. Additionally, the agreements signed by Isbell make no mention of a fixed geographic location as a place of business. There was no evidence that Mary Kay contemplated that Isbell would maintain a place of a business in Arkansas.

DECISION AND REMEDY: The Arkansas Franchise Practices Act did not apply to Isbell because Isbell did not meet the definition of a franchise. The trial court's ruling was reversed, and the case was dismissed.

SIGNIFICANCE OF THE CASE: This case raises questions about legal protections for people like Janet Isbell who sell products for companies that, like Mary Kay, don't require the sellers to maintain a fixed place of business. If those sellers are not franchisees, what is their role? Independent contractors? Agents? Employees? What legal protections are offered to the sellers?

What missing information would you call for when considering the facts of this case?

Would you interpret the Arkansas Franchise Practices Act and how it applies to the facts of the case differently than the judge did? Why or why not?

Consider the WPH framework. What values was Isbell promoting? What values were in conflict? Was the court fair in assessing her actions in light of these values?

Franchise Law Because franchisors are usually larger than franchisees and have more resources, they often have the upper hand in franchise relationships. Federal and state laws, however, have been established to protect the franchisee in the franchise relationship.

A franchise is a contractual relationship between the franchisor and the franchisee. Thus, contract law, and the Uniform Commercial Code in particular, applies to the franchise relationship. If the terms of the contract are not met, either side can sue for breach of contract. For example, in *Ford Motor Co. v. Lyons,*[1] Lyons sued Ford for breach of its dealer franchise obligations. In the franchise agreement, Ford had agreed to send factory representatives to the dealership, as well as offer Lyons assistance with his business. However, Ford failed to perform its duties. Lyons sued, bringing forth evidence showing that Ford had intentionally failed to perform its contractual duties because one of the other dealership franchises was jealous of the dealership territory Ford had given to Lyons as part of the franchise agreement.

In addition, several laws that are more specific have been established to govern the franchise relationship. For example, the Federal Trade Commission has a franchise rule requiring that franchisors present prospective franchisees with the material facts necessary for the franchisee to make an informed decision about entering a franchise relationship. Moreover, the Automobile Dealers' Franchise Act of 1965 prohibits car dealership franchisors from terminating franchise relationships in bad faith. Thus, for example, DaimlerChrysler could not terminate its franchise relationship with a dealer because the dealer failed to meet impossible standards. Finally, the Petroleum Marketing Practices Act of 1979 outlines the reasons for which a franchisor may terminate a gas station franchise. Franchises must also be aware of federal antitrust laws. Antitrust laws prohibit specific forms of anticompetitive behavior and might be applicable to franchises.

Many states have adopted additional laws to protect franchisees. Fifteen states, for example, require that franchisors provide prospective franchisees with a host of information about the franchise relationship before the agreement can be signed. What ethical standards do you think these 15 states are promoting in their decision to mandate franchise protections?

franchise agreement

A contract whereby a company (the franchisor) grants permission (a license) to another entity (the franchisee) to use the franchisor's name, trademark, or copyright in the operation of a business and associated sale of goods in return for payment.

Creation of the Franchise In the franchise relationship, the parties make a **franchise agreement** regarding various factors: the payment to the franchisor, the location of the franchise, the restrictions the franchisee must follow, and the method of termination of the franchise.

First, the franchise agreement usually states that the franchisee is to pay a large sum to the franchisor for use of the trade name or trademark. Moreover, the agreement determines what percentage of the income from the sales of the goods will go to the franchisor.

Second, the agreement usually determines where the franchise will be located. If the franchise requires a building, the agreement specifies who will pay for buying or renting the building. Similarly, if the building must be constructed, the agreement states who is responsible for the costs of the construction of the building.

Third, the franchisor usually includes in the agreement certain business practices that are forbidden and other business standards that must be met. For example, the franchisor might require that the business meet specific levels of cleanliness. Moreover, the franchisor can set certain sales quotas as well as requirements for record keeping by the franchisee. The franchisor can require that the franchisee purchase certain supplies from the franchisor at a set price, but the franchisor cannot attempt to establish the price at which the franchisee must sell the goods.

The disagreement in the Case Opener arose because of these second and third factors in franchise agreements. First, McDonald's offered the Robertsons a new franchise, to be located a block from the existing franchise. McDonald's purchased the property, agreed to income guarantees, and planned to give the Robertsons the new franchise in exchange for the existing franchise, which McDonald's would thereafter close. Negotiations between McDonald's and the Robertsons, however, were unsuccessful; the Robertsons continually refused the offer. Second, because

[1]405 N.W.2d 354 (Wis. Ct. App. 1987).

many McDonald's restaurants are owned by franchisees, McDonald's has established a "McDonald's System," which promotes business practices enhancing the quality of food and services at each restaurant. McDonald's also has quality, safety, and cleanliness (QSC) standards for each of its franchises. The Robertsons' franchise agreement stipulated that McDonald's could inspect the Robertsons' restaurant at any reasonable time.

Although the franchisor has the legal authority to ensure that the franchisee maintains the quality of goods and services associated with the franchise, the franchisor must be cautious. If it exercises too much authority in the day-to-day affairs of the business, the franchisor could be held liable for the torts of the franchisee's employees.

Termination of the Franchise The franchise agreement establishes how the franchise will be terminated. The franchise is usually established for a trial period, such as a year. If the franchisee does not meet the requirements established in the franchise agreement, the franchisor can terminate the franchise agreement, but the franchisor must give the franchisee sufficient notice of the termination. Furthermore, the termination usually must have cause. Much of the litigation associated with franchises regards wrongful termination of a franchise. The typical agreement gives the franchisor broad authority to terminate a franchise. In recent years, however, many states have been giving the franchisee greater termination protection.

The courts usually rely heavily on the written franchise agreement when determining whether a franchise was wrongfully terminated. Look at Case 20-3, which illustrates the importance of the written franchise agreement.

CASE 20-3

COUSINS SUBS SYSTEMS, INC. v. MICHAEL R. MCKINNEY
U.S. DISTRICT COURT FOR THE EASTERN DISTRICT OF WISCONSIN
59 F. Supp. 2d 816 (1999)

FACTS: *Cousins Subs Systems entered into an agreement with Michael McKinney, a Minnesota businessman who owned a company that operated a chain of gas stations, for McKinney to operate several Cousins submarine sandwich shops. The sub shops were to be placed in the gas stations. In April 1998, McKinney became disillusioned with the agreement and terminated the agreement. McKinney claimed that Cousins guaranteed him annual sales at each of his franchises ranging from $250,000 to $500,000. Furthermore, McKinney argued that Cousins promised to provide advertising for the franchises. McKinney also claimed that Cousins guaranteed it would provide assistance in recruiting other franchises. McKinney alleges that he terminated the agreement because Cousins failed to uphold these promises. In June 1998, Cousins filed suit against McKinney for wrongfully terminating the agreement with Cousins. Later in 1998, McKinney filed a counterclaim against Cousins. Cousins filed a motion to dismiss the counterclaim.*

ISSUE: Did Cousins Subs Systems make misleading statements of material facts?

REASONING: McKinney alleges that Cousins violated the Minnesota statute prohibiting businesses from using false statements of material facts (or omissions of material facts) to sell franchises. McKinney claims that Cousins made false verbal statements of material facts; however, when an alleged verbal statement contradicts a written contract, the written contract carries more weight. In this case, the written contracts, signed by McKinney and Cousins and later entered as exhibits, contradict the verbal statements McKinney claims Cousins made. The contracts state that no promises were made regarding the profit McKinney would earn, that advertising was McKinney's responsibility, and that the contracts contained all terms, conditions, and promises made by Cousins.

DECISION AND REMEDY: As demonstrated by the contracts McKinney signed, Cousins did not make any

misleading statements of material facts. The counterclaim was dismissed.

SIGNIFICANCE: It is unclear whether Cousins made the verbal promises alleged by McKinney. Regardless, McKinney did sign contracts that contradicted the alleged verbal promises. This case demonstrates how important it is for businesspeople to read contracts thoroughly and to ensure that all terms, conditions, and promises are contained in those contracts.

CRITICAL THINKING

What are the primary facts of this case? How would you word the issue of the case in your own words?

The judge stated that the written terms of the contracts between Cousins and McKinney were inconsistent with any alleged oral agreements that they made. Do you agree that written contracts should overrule oral agreements in most instances? Why or why not?

ETHICAL DECISION MAKING

The court ruled in favor of Cousins. Who are the primary stakeholders affected by the court's ruling for Cousins?

The decisions of a court have implications for business ethics. While Chapter 2 distinguishes between what the law requires of a manager and what ethics requires, the relationship between the law and ethics is reciprocal. While ethical judgments lie behind various laws, it is also the case that law has impacts on business ethics. For example, in Case 20-3, the court's decision is reminding us that business ethics must pay attention to the various stakeholders who feel the impacts of any business agreement.

SUMMARY

Major Forms of Business Organization	*Sole proprietorship*: The owner has total control and unlimited personal liability, and profits are taxed directly as income to the sole proprietor.
	General partnership: For most purposes, the partnership is not a legal entity, and each partner has equal control and unlimited liability, with profits that are taxed as income for partners.
	Limited partnership: Limited partnerships are similar to general partnerships, except that limited partners' liability is limited to the extent of their capital contributions.
	Corporation: A corporation is a separate legal entity wherein the owners' liability is limited to the amount of their contributions and the profits are taxed as income to the corporation.
	Limited liability company: A limited liability company combines the best tax and liability features of partnerships and corporations. In an LLC all members may participate in management of the business entity while enjoying a shield of limited liability for their personal assets.
Specialized Forms of Business Organization	The specialized forms are cooperatives, joint stock companies, syndicates, business trusts, joint ventures, and franchises.
	A *franchise* is a contractual relationship between the franchisor and the franchisee. Thus, contract law, and the Uniform Commercial Code in particular, applies to the franchise relationship. If the terms of the contract are not met, either side can sue for breach of contract.

Point/Counterpoint

Should a New Restaurateur Open a New Location of a Restaurant Franchise Rather Than Become a Sole Proprietor?

YES	NO
A businessperson new to the restaurant business should open a restaurant as part of an existing franchise rather than begin an individual restaurant as a sole proprietor.	A new restaurateur should open a new restaurant as a sole proprietor rather than a franchisee. A businessperson new to the restaurant business has greater potential for long-term success as a sole proprietor than as a franchisee.
A new restaurateur encounters substantial risks when opening a business as a sole proprietor. Sole proprietors have unlimited personal liability, meaning they are held solely accountable for the finances in their businesses. For example, a sole proprietor often needs to provide her house as collateral to obtain a small business loan.	The main appeal of a franchise is less personal risk and liability at the start of the business. However, with careful research and expert advice, sole proprietors can obtain low-risk, longer-term loans that are unlikely to jeopardize their personal assets. Additionally, sole proprietors always hold the option of later adding a full business partner or a limited partner. Franchisees, however, usually do not retain that right after entering business with the franchisor. To decrease liability, sole proprietors can implement additional safety measures.
Additionally, a restaurant sole proprietor can be held personally liable for injury in her restaurant. This personal liability means the restaurant owner could be personally sued for employee or customer injury. One main advantage of becoming a franchisee is that the franchisee usually is not held solely liable for an injury.	One major disadvantage of opening a new franchise is that the new franchise must pay the franchisor a percentage of profits for the duration the new franchise exists. For a sole proprietor, after debts are repaid, all profits are kept in the business for improvements and personal income.
One primary concern should be that the businessperson is *new* to the restaurant business. The franchisee encounters limited financial risk. Additionally, a franchisor can fulfill the vital role of supervision and provide crucial guidance to a new businessperson. Because restaurant franchises are already successful, the new franchisee has a clear idea of business practices that have been proved successful by the franchisor.	Franchises are extremely restrictive in creativity. A sole proprietor is truly her own boss. A sole proprietor can change the "look" of her restaurant at any time.
Further, most franchisors offer new franchisees a clear outline of forbidden practices that would endanger the new franchise, as well as minimum standards (cleanliness, service) that will assist the new franchise. Sole proprietors must experience a "trial-and-error" time period as they learn which business practices should be implemented. The franchisor's assistance eliminates the trial-and-error period because the franchisee is informed of and warned not to repeat past errors.	Sole proprietors can determine how many and which hours they would like to be in operation. Sole proprietors can also decide whether to hire a manager or manage their restaurants directly. Additionally, sole proprietors can decide how many and what kind of individuals they would like to employ at their restaurants. Franchisees often face restrictions and limitations regarding size, hours, management, and employment practices.
	Perhaps most important, a sole proprietor retains flexibility if the economy changes, which it frequently does. If need be, a sole proprietor can simply uproot the restaurant and move to a different location. Further, a sole proprietor can change her restaurant's menu and appearance if the customer constituency in her area changes.

Questions & Problems

1. What is the distinction between a general partnership and a limited partnership?

2. Explain why a cooperative could not claim to be a syndicate.

3. Suppose you were asked to review and assess a franchise agreement. What responsibilities would you expect to be included in that agreement?

4. Tracy Allen rented a home in which she had been residing since the summer of 1998. The landlord-owner of the house later failed to pay taxes on the property, and on March 16, 2000, Hard Assets LLC acquired the property from the owner in lieu of foreclosure. When Hard Assets obtained title, it did not intend to lease the property, nor were its members aware that Allen was living at the property. Once Hard Assets became aware that Allen was residing at the property, Hard Assets advised her and her family that they were not supposed to be there and that they had 30 days to vacate the premises. After 30 days, Allen had not vacated the property. While residing at the property, the children living with Allen suffered elevated blood-lead levels and were allegedly injured from lead paint exposure. As a result, the children's mother filed a suit against one of the members of the LLC for violations of the city's housing code and negligence. Should the member of the LLC be held personally liable for the alleged injuries of the children who lived at Allen's home? Why or why not? [*Allen v. Dackman,* 964 A.2d 210 (2009).]

5. The Meehans entered into a franchise agreement with Consumers Club. However, the Meehans' franchise failed. The Meehans alleged that, just before they entered into the franchise agreement, Consumers Club made false statements and misleading representations to them about (1) earnings, (2) success rates, (3) pricing, and (4) warranties, support, and service. The district court dismissed both counts, determining that the express disclaimers contained in the franchise agreement precluded the Meehans from proving justifiable reliance, if any misrepresentations were made. Meehan contended the disclaimers do not defeat the misrepresentation claim because they do not contain evidence of whether actual representations were made and relied on. How do you think the court ruled regarding the alleged false and misleading representations made regarding the Meehans' franchise? (*Hint:* Review the discussion on Case 20-3 and the power of written franchise agreements.) [*Meehan v. United Consumers Club Franchising Corp.,* 312 F.3d 909 (2002).]

6. Connie Steinle, accompanied by her seven-year-old daughter, left the family ranch for Douglas, Wyoming. The purpose of the trip was to purchase a calf for her daughter to raise on the ranch. While en route, the truck Connie was driving collided with a vehicle driven by Ronald Popejoy. Connie died as a result of the accident, and Ronald sustained injuries. One week after the accident, William Steinle (Connie's husband) completed the calf purchase for his daughter. She raised the calf on the family farm and later sold the calf for profit. Ronald Popejoy then began experiencing severe pain in his neck and back and underwent two separate neurosurgeries to fuse his cervical vertebrae. Ronald then filed a creditor's claim against William's estate, as he had died shortly after Connie's death. After his creditor's claim was rejected, he filed a complaint against the personal representatives of William's estate. The complaint was premised on the theory that William and Connie Steinle were engaged in a joint venture when Connie embarked on her "business trip" to pick up her daughter's calf. Do you think they were engaged in a joint venture? Why or why not? [*Ronald L. Popejoy and Doris J. Popejoy v. Carl Steinle and the Converse County Bank,* 820 P.2d 545 (1991).]

7. Between 8 p.m. on April 15, 2000, and 1:45 a.m. on April 16, 2000, Anthony Sulls was a patron of Silk Stockings and Cafe Del Mar. Silk Stockings and Cafe Del Mar are an adjoining bar and adult entertainment nightclub. Sulls was allegedly served and consumed large quantities of alcoholic beverages. Even though Sulls was visibly and obviously intoxicated, the defendants, acting by and through their agents, servants, and/or employees, continued to serve him. Sulls left Cafe Del Mar and Silk Stockings in a grossly intoxicated state and drove his vehicle until he lost control of it and drove off the roadway, resulting in injuries and death to the occupants of the vehicle. One of the passengers who was killed was William Ridgaway, Jr. Ridgaway's estate subsequently sued two members of Silk LLC, the owner of Silk Stockings and Cafe Del Mar. Are the two members of the LLC personally liable for the accident that occurred after Sulls was served alcohol at their bar and nightclub? [*Estate of William Ridgaway, Jr. et al. v. Silk, LLC et al.,* 2004 Conn. Super. LEXIS 548 (2004).]

8. Milburn Pierce was the sole proprietor of the Pierce Painting Company, a painting contracting company with two employees in addition to Pierce. Pierce bought workers' compensation insurance for his business through the Louisiana Workers' Compensation Corporation, but in the written agreement he chose to exclude himself from the policy's coverage. In August 2002, Pierce was working on a job for Tom Fullilove Construction Company when he fell off a roof. Pierce broke his left wrist and left femur and incurred more than $30,000 in medical bills for his treatment and therapy. Pierce filed a compensation claim in September 2002, and Fullilove paid his medical bills. In October 2002, Fullilove sued Pierce for reimbursement of the compensation payments. The Office of Workers' Compensation found for Fullilove. Pierce appealed, arguing that a Louisiana statute provided that a "sole proprietor with respect to such sole proprietorship may by written agreement elect not to be covered" under workers' compensation

insurance. Thus, Pierce argued, he had elected not to be covered with respect to his sole proprietorship, a separate legal entity. But with respect to Tom Ful-lilove Construction Company, Pierce argued that he never elected not to be covered. How do you think the appellate court ruled? Why? [*Pierce v. Tom Fullilove Constr. Co.,* 892 So. 2d 757 (2005).]

9. "YOU AND I" was a thoroughbred racehorse owned by a syndicate composed of 40 equal ownership shares. The syndicate agreement stated that if an acceptable offer was made to purchase the horse from the syndicate, each syndicate member had a "first right to purchase" under which he could sell his interest in the horse or buy the interests of the other syndicate members who had elected to sell their interests in the horse. The syndicate agree-ment, however, required that if a syndicate member planned to exercise his first right to purchase, he had to notify the syndicate manager of his intent within 10 days of his receiving notification of the acceptable offer. In September 2003, Brereton Jones, a syndicate member and the syndicate manager, received an offer from Blooming Hills Farms to buy YOU AND I for $500,000. Jones sent a memo to all the syndicate members notifying them that Blooming Hills Farms had made the offer, that he believed the offer to be fair, and that he planned to sell his interest. Jones received word from 39 of the 40 syndicate members that they planned to sell their interest in YOU AND I. The following day, Never Tell Farm, a syndicate member, notified Jones that it planned to exercise its first right to purchase. Jones and Never Tell pro-ceeded to negotiate over whether Never Tell would exercise its first right to purchase, and the 10-day window elapsed. When the negotiations fell through, Never Tell notified Jones of its intent to exercise its first right to purchase. Jones told Never Tell that it had not timely asserted its right and thus the horse had been sold to Blooming Hills Farms. Never Tell sued Jones, claiming that under the syndicate agree-ment it should have had the right to purchase the other syndicate members' interests in YOU AND I. With whom do you think the court sided in this case? Why? [*Never Tell Farm, LLC v. Airdrie Stud, Inc.,* 123 Fed. Appx. 194 (2005).]

10. Chic Miller operated a General Motors (GM) fran-chise car dealership. His written franchise agree-ment with GM stipulated that Miller had to maintain a floor-plan financing agreement with a lender to enable him to buy new cars from GM. Initially, Miller maintained a line of credit with a GM affiliate (GMAC), but he terminated the agreement because he felt that GMAC charged him an exorbitant inter-est rate. Miller was able to find another line of credit from Chase Manhattan Bank, but Chase withdrew its financing agreement with Miller after one year. Miller attempted to resume the agreement with GMAC, but GMAC refused. Miller alleged *ipse dixit* (an asser-tion without evidence) that GMAC discouraged other lenders from providing a line of credit to Miller. GM then notified Miller that it was terminating its franchise relationship with him because he failed to satisfy the financing stipulation of the written fran-chise agreement. Two months after receiving this notice from GM, Miller attempted to sell his fran-chise to Kenneth Crowley, the owner of another car dealership. GM rejected this sale, alleging that Miller no longer had a franchise to sell because GM had terminated the franchise agreement two months ear-lier. Miller sued GM for failing to help his franchise obtain floor-plan financing and for rejecting the sale of his franchise to Crowley. How do you think the court ruled in this case? What requirements must GM meet to lawfully terminate a franchise? Did GM meet those requirements? [*Chic Miller's Chevrolet, Inc. v. GMC,* 352 F. Supp. 2d 251 (2005).]

11. Margaret Miller operated an H&R Block tax-preparation franchise for 15 years. She hired William Hehlen as an income tax return preparer for five years, from 1997 to 2001. Each year, Miller and Hehlen signed an employment agreement drawn up by H&R Block. The 2001 agreement was between Hehlen and "Margaret Miller, doing business as H&R Block," and included stipulations prohibiting Hehlen from reproducing confidential business informa-tion and from soliciting clients away from Miller's business. Hehlen maintained on his home computer a spreadsheet of customer names that he obtained from Miller. In April 2001, H&R Block terminated its franchise agreement with Miller, and Miller sub-sequently operated her business as a sole proprietor-ship under the name "MJM & Associates." Hehlen's employment with Miller ended after the 2001 tax season. In December 2001, Miller sent advertising postcards to clients referring to Hehlen as one of her associates. When Hehlen, who went to work for another H&R Block office, learned of the postcards, he began telephoning the customers whose names he had obtained from Miller. Miller learned of the calls in February 2002 and filed a cease-and-desist action against Hehlen, arguing that Hehlen was violating his employment contract with Miller. Hehlen argued that his employment contract was with Miller's H&R Block franchise, which ceased to exist after April 2001. Do you think Hehlen's employment contract was signed with Miller's franchise or with Miller's sole proprietorship? If you think Hehlen's contract was with Miller's franchise, should Miller have the

right to enforce the contract provisions after H&R Block terminated her franchise agreement? Why or why not? [*Miller v. Hehlen,* 104 P.3d 193 (2005).]

12. Harvey Pierce was a work-release inmate from the local county jail who worked at an Arby's franchise restaurant owned by Dennis Rasmussen, Inc. (DRI). One day in June 1999, Pierce walked off the job without permission and crossed the street to wait for his former girlfriend, Robin Kerl, and her fiancé, David Jones, in the parking lot of the Walmart store where both Kerl and Jones worked. When Kerl and Jones exited the store, Pierce shot both of them in the head, killing Jones and seriously injuring and permanently disabling Kerl. Pierce then shot himself and died immediately. Kerl and Jones's estate sued Arby's and DRI for negligent supervision, hiring, and retention, arguing that Arby's, the franchisor, was vicariously liable for the negligence of DRI, the franchisee. Do you think Arby's should be vicariously liable for the negligence of its franchisee? Why or why not? [*Kerl v. DRI and Arby's, Inc.,* 682 N.W.2d 328 (2004).]

Looking for more review material?

The Online Learning Center at **www.mhhe.com/kubasekess2e** contains this chapter's "Assignment on the Internet" and also a list of URLs for more information, entitled "On the Internet." Find both of them in the Student Center portion of the OLC, along with quizzes and other helpful materials.

Partnerships

CASE OPENER

Rockwell and a Potential Partnership

Seth Rockwell filed a motion against Eric Swenson to try to receive lost wages and reimbursement for expenses he had incurred while working as Swenson's employee. Swenson immediately moved for summary judgment because Rockwell was supposedly his partner, not his employee. If Rockwell was Swenson's partner, it was possible that he would not be able to retrieve lost funds.

The district court found that Rockwell was Swenson's employee and not his partner. Swenson appealed the decision, continuing to argue that Rockwell was a partner who had only the right to request an accounting of the corporation. Depending on the appellate court's decision, Rockwell would be awarded $41,580 in unpaid wages and $10,896.39 in nonreimbursed expenses. Additionally, a potential maritime lien would be imposed on Swenson.

1. Why would a potential partnership between Rockwell and Swenson have any influence on the outcome of this case?
2. What could Swenson have done to avoid this suit?

LEARNING OBJECTIVES

After reading this chapter, you will be able to answer the following questions:

LO 21-1 What is a partnership?

LO 21-2 What are the different ways in which a partnership can be formed?

LO 21-3 What are the rights of partners as they interact with each other?

LO 21-4 Are all members of a partnership liable for interactions with third parties?

LO 21-5 What are the steps involved in the termination of a partnership?

LO 21-6 How is a limited partnership formed?

LO 21-7 What are the rights and privileges of a limited partner as opposed to a general partner?

The Uniform Partnership Act (UPA) is the main statute governing partnership law. If there is no express partnership agreement, UPA establishes the rules for the partnership.

This chapter discusses the creation and operation of the partnership, how partnerships are terminated, and special types of partnerships. The chapter begins by considering the nature of the partnership relationship. Then it explains how a partnership is created and how partnerships function. Next, it discusses how a partnership is terminated. The chapter concludes with a look at special types of partnerships.

LO 21-1

Nature of the Partnership

partnership

A voluntary association between two or more people who co-own a business for profit.

What exactly is a partnership? According to UPA Section 6, a **partnership** is "an association of two or more persons to carry on as co-owners a business for profit." It is important that we analyze all four parts of this definition in order to determine its exact meaning and implications.

First, by "association," UPA means that the partnership is a voluntary and consensual relationship. Thus, no one could force someone else to enter into a partnership with him. Second, a partnership requires "two or more persons." UPA defines *persons* as "individuals, partnerships, corporations, and other associations." Therefore, almost any individual or group of people could serve as a partner, but these persons must have the legal capacity to be partners. For example, although minors can serve as partners, the resulting partnership agreement is voidable.

Third, in a partnership, the partners must "carry on as co-owners of a business for profit." Here *business* is defined as any trade, occupation, or profession. "Carrying on" a business refers to making several transactions. Finally, UPA requires that the partners be "co-owners" of the business, meaning the partners must share the profits or losses of the business as well as share in the management of the business.

Fourth, the final element of the definition of partnership is that it be "for profit," meaning that the partners must be intending to make some kind of profit from the business.

To summarize, a partnership has the following characteristics:

- *Voluntary* and *consensual* relationship.
- Between two or more *individuals, partnerships, corporations,* or other forms of business organization.
- Who engage in *numerous business transactions* over a period of time.
- Intending *to make a profit.*
- And *share* the *profits* and *management* of the business.

When parties dispute whether a partnership relationship exists, the courts will look for those factors in the case. The relationship between Rockwell and Swenson in the Case Opener did not constitute a partnership because it did not meet these criteria. The two men had never voluntarily

or consensually entered into a partnership. There was no evidence that the profits or management duties were shared between the two men.

Probably the most important factor in determining whether a partnership exists is determining whether the profits from the business are shared. However, UPA has established several exceptions in which a sharing of profits does not constitute a partnership. For example, when an employer shares profits with an employee as payment for work, there is no partnership. Similarly, when a landlord accepts shares of profits for payment of rent, there is no partnership. If a party receives a share of profits for any of the following reasons, there is no partnership:

- Payment of a debt.
- Payment of an annuity to a widow or representative of a deceased partner.
- Payment from the sale of goodwill of a business or other property.
- Payment of interest on a loan.

Case 21-1 illustrates the court's analysis of whether a partnership relationship indeed exists.

> To see more about management and partnerships, please see the **Connecting to the Core** activity on the text's website at www.mhhe.com/kubasekess2e.

BROWN v. SWETT & CRAWFORD OF TEXAS, INC.
COURT OF APPEALS OF TEXAS, FIRST DISTRICT
178 S.W.3d 373 (2005)

FACTS: *Braden St. John Brown was a wholesale insurance broker. Wholesale brokers act as middlemen between retail insurance agents and insurance companies, and the insurance companies pay the wholesale broker a "gross commission," which is a percentage of the premium for each policy sold. Brown was a salaried at-will employee of IBS. Mr. Brown worked with his supervisor and friend, Mr. Galtney, and with Galtney shared commissions they received through their office. On July 31, 2000, IBS fired Brown after problems with his work. Brown sued, for the wrongful expulsion from a partnership he had with his boss at IBS. The district court dismissed his claim, so he appealed.*

ISSUE: Was Brown an employee or a partner?

REASONING: The Texas Revised Partnership Act (TRPA) sets forth five factors to consider in determining whether a partnership has been created. Those factors include (1) the receipt or right to receive a share of profits of the business; (2) the expression of an intent to be partners of the business; (3) the participation or right to participate in control of the business; (4) the sharing of or agreement to share losses of the business or liability for claims by third parties against the business; and (5) the contribution of or an agreement to contribute money or property to the business.

Specifically, Brown's partnership claims failed as a matter of law because the evidence conclusively established that he had no right to receive a share of the profits of the business because his salary and bonus compensation package was merely compensation for the services of an at-will employee. Brown was entitled to receive a base salary plus 42 percent of half of the gross commissions attributable to business written out of IBS's office. Brown's base salary cannot be considered a share of profits. Similarly, Brown's portion of the gross commissions was compensation for services rendered to IBS, not an interest in the overall profits of IBS.

DECISION AND REMEDY: The evidence showed that Brown was an employee with a fixed compensation and commission. He had not entered into a partnership with Galtney, so he had no claim against the value of a partnership. The trial court's ruling was affirmed.

SIGNIFICANCE OF THE CASE: This case should be a reminder that often people can be taken to court regarding partnership interests, even if they never entered into an explicit partnership agreement. Luckily for IBS, the court ruled in its favor. It is important for business managers to understand how a partnership is formed.

CRITICAL THINKING

What evidence led the court to hold that Brown was not a partner?

ETHICAL DECISION MAKING

Who are the relevant stakeholders that could potentially be affected by the court's decision?

Now that you know how the courts determine whether a partnership exists, what kind of legal status do partnerships have? Partnerships can be treated two different ways: as entities or as aggregates.

PARTNERSHIP AS A LEGAL ENTITY

legal entity
Any individual, proprietorship, partnership, corporation, association, or other organization that has, in the eyes of the law, the capacity to form an agreement and the ability to assume an obligation and to discharge an indebtedness.

In some respects, a partnership is treated as a **legal entity,** a person separate from the partnership. Thus, in some cases, the partnership has a life of its own.

First, a partnership is often considered a legal entity when it is sued or being sued. States determine when a partnership can or cannot be named in a suit. Second, under the doctrine of marshaling assets, assets are arranged in a certain order to pay for any outstanding debts. Partnership creditors have first priority in obtaining partnership assets, while individual personal creditors have first priority to the assets of the individual partners. Thus, the partnership assets are kept separate from the individual partners' assets.

Third, the title to property may be put in the partnership name. Therefore, the partnership may own property that individual partners do not hold. If the partners want to sell the partnership property to another party, all partners must participate in the transaction of the partnership property. Finally, every partner is considered to be an agent to the partnership, and every partner has a fiduciary relationship with the other partners.

PARTNERSHIP AS A LEGAL AGGREGATE

While in some cases the partnership is considered a separate legal entity, there are other cases in which the partnership is considered a legal aggregate of the partners. For instance, the debts of the partnership eventually become the debts of the individual partners. Furthermore, the partnership is not taxed as a separate being; instead, the partners pay taxes on the income generated through the partnership. Moreover, because the partnership ceases to exist when one of the partners dies (unless otherwise established by the partnership agreement), the partnership is considered an aggregate of the individual partners.

LO 21-2 Formation of the Partnership

While an explicit written agreement is not required to create a partnership, the partners are advised to create one. The written agreement ensures that the terms of the partnership will be upheld. For example, suppose that you and your partner orally agree that you will receive three-fourths of the profits because you are doing significantly more management tasks. However, when you distribute the funds, your partner sues you because you give him only one-fourth of the profits. Without a written partnership agreement, the courts will have a difficult time ruling in your favor. A written agreement that creates a partnership is called the **articles of partnership.**

articles of partnership
The written agreement that creates a partnership.

440

Forms of Partnerships in the ICT Sector in Developing Countries

In the information and communication technology (ICT) sector of developing countries, businesses are using partnerships between local and multinational companies to create a support structure for the ICT sector. Three forms of partnership are especially important: (1) industrial districts, (2) *keiretsus* (groups of businesses in which each individual business has a stake in the others), and (3) offshore partnerships.

Industrial districts are loosely structured collectives of small to medium-size firms located in a specific area. The firms are highly specialized in one or more phases of a production process. Industrial districts are coordinated through both personal relationships and marketlike mechanisms. One purpose of industrial districts is to pool local competencies.

Keiretsus bring foreign ICT companies into a partnership, and they serve as "hubs." Local ICT ventures serve the hubs. *Keiretsus* add the strength of a competent hub, but, over time, this strength could make it less likely that local firms will develop strength of their own.

Offshore partnerships combine the strengths of firms that operate in developing countries and firms that operate in countries that are foreign to the developing countries, for example, firms in the United States. Firms in developing countries use offshore partnerships to gain international exposure and technological competence. Foreign firms use offshore partnerships to gain (1) access to competent yet low-cost workers and (2) the opportunity to enter developing markets.

What kind of information do the articles of partnership usually include? First, the partners' names, as well as the name of the partnership, should be listed on the document. Second, the agreement should address the duration of the partnership. The agreement could include the date or event on which the partnership agreement would expire. Alternatively, the agreement could specify that the term of the partnership is indefinite. Third, the agreement should state the division of profits as well as losses. Fourth, the articles of partnership should establish the division of management duties. Fifth, the agreement should state exactly what capital contributions will be made by each partner. Creating articles of partnership can prevent legal problems by explicitly establishing the terms of the partnership agreement.

PARTNERSHIP BY ESTOPPEL

In some cases, parties who are not named in partnership agreements can be considered partners. How? Suppose you create a partnership agreement with your best friend. When you interact with your first potential customer, you tell this customer that your parents are also partners in this business. On the basis of your parents' participation in the partnership, the customer decides to place an order to purchase certain goods from you. Your parents discover that you have reported that they are your partners, but they do not contact the customer to tell her that they are not your partners. When your business cannot afford to purchase these goods to sell them to the customer, the customer sues you as well as your parents. Because your parents were aware of the misrepresentation but did not correct it, they will be estopped from denying they are your partners. While they will not be able to claim the rights associated with being a partner (e.g., sharing the profits), in many states they could be held liable for the costs of the damages to the customer.

Most states recognize two situations in which a partnership by estoppel exists. First, as in the example above, if a third party is aware of a misrepresentation of partnership and consents to the misrepresentation, a partnership by estoppel is present. Second, if a nonpartner has represented himself or herself as a partner and a third party *reasonably relies* on this information to his or her detriment, the nonpartner can be held liable for the third party's damages.

Interactions between Partners LO 21-3

The operation of the partnership encompasses two types of interactions: interactions between the partners and interactions between the partnership and third parties. The partners have certain rights and duties within each type of interaction.

Written Partnership Agreements in Russia

Russian law recognizes two different kinds of partnerships: the *full* partnership and the *simple* partnership. Full partnerships are similar to the traditional U.S. partnership in that they are ones whose participants are contractually engaged in entrepreneurial activities in the name of the partnership and are personally liable. In both the United States and Russia the partnership is relatively easy and inexpensive to form; however, Russian law requires much more written paperwork to form a partnership.

For example, although in the United States a written partnership agreement is highly recommended, no written contract or agreement is required. However, oral partnership agreements are not accepted in Russia, where partnerships must be based on a formal, written *founding contract*. In the United States no official founding documents are required aside from the Certificate of Doing Business, filed at the office of the County Clerk. However, in Russia, substantially more paperwork is required. Specifically, paperwork must be filed explaining in great detail the organization of the partnership, including how the partnership will be managed, the purposes of the partnership, the process by which the partnership will be created, and the process by which property is transferred to the partnership. Furthermore, financial details such as the terms and procedures for the distribution of profits and losses and the amount of partnership capital are required to be included in the documents.

You may have been initially surprised about how easy it is to create a partnership in the United States. But consider the advantages of having written partnership contracts. Can you create a list of reasons for why the U.S. legal system should require written partnership agreements? What are some of the disadvantages of requiring written agreements, as in Russia?

DUTIES OF PARTNERS TO ONE ANOTHER

Most of the duties that partners hold to one another involve a duty to be loyal. They include the fiduciary duty to the other partners, the duty of obedience, and the duty of care.

Perhaps the most important duty of the partners is their fiduciary duty. They must, in good faith, work for the benefit of the partnership. They should not take any kind of action that will undermine the partnership. Consequently, the partners must not engage in any business that competes with the partnership.

Partners must disclose any material facts affecting the business. If a partner derives some kind of benefit from the partnership without the consent of the other partners, he or she must notify the partners of this benefit.

The second duty that the partners have to each other is the duty of obedience, to obey the partnership agreement. If they do not obey the agreement, they can be held liable for any losses that the partnership incurs.

The third duty the partners have is a duty of care to the other partners. Each partner must perform her management functions to the best of her abilities. If a partner makes an honest mistake in fulfilling her responsibilities to the partnership, she will not be held liable for the mistake.

RIGHTS OF THE PARTNERS IN THEIR INTERACTIONS WITH OTHER PARTNERS

According to the law, partners have certain rights regarding their interactions with other partners.

Right to Share in Management Unless otherwise stated in the partnership agreement, all partners have a right to participate equally in the management of the partnership. Even if one partner has an unusually large proportion of the management duties, each partner has one vote in determining how the partnership is managed. While most decisions are made by majority vote, some decisions require agreement by all partners. For instance, if the partners are voting on whether to change some element of the partnership agreement, all partners must agree with the change. Other types of decisions that require a unanimous vote include a decision to admit new partners or a decision to alter the nature of the firm's business.

Right to Share in Profits Each partner is entitled to a share of the profits of the partnership. How big is each partner's share? If the partnership agreement does not establish a certain division of profits, all partners will share the profits equally. Similarly, partners must share in the losses of the partnership. Thus, if there is no statement of how the losses will be divided among the partners, the losses will be divided in a proportion identical to the sharing of the profits.

Right to Compensation Unless otherwise agreed, no partner will receive compensation for his or her participation in the business. In other words, the partner will not receive a salary regardless of the amount of time and effort he or she devotes to the business. Of course, the partners may agree to create salaries for certain partners, but no partner enters the partnership relationship with a right to compensation for his or her business activities. If a partner dies during the term of the partnership, the surviving partner is, however, entitled to compensation for services in closing the business affairs.

Property Rights Partners have three property rights associated with the partnership: (1) the right to participate in the management of the business (discussed earlier), (2) the right to specific partnership property, and (3) the right to her partnership interest. Here, we examine the latter two property rights.

First, partners own the partnership property as *tenants in common,* which means that the partners own the property as a group. Any property that is brought into or acquired by the partnership is considered property of the partnership. If property is in the name of an individual partner but was purchased with partnership funds, the property is considered partnership property.

One way to determine whether specific property will be considered a partnership asset is to determine the relationship of the asset to the partnership. If the asset is closely related to the business of the partnership, it will likely be considered a partnership asset.

Each partner has the right to possess partnership property. However, a partner cannot use this property to pay a personal debt. Similarly, a partner cannot sell or use the property if the purpose is outside the partnership interest.

What happens to the partnership property if a partner dies? According to the **right of survivorship,** the rights in specific partnership property pass to the surviving partner(s). However, the surviving partners must account to the deceased partner's estate for the value of that partner's interest in the specific property.

> **right of survivorship**
> The right that specific partnership property will pass on to the surviving partner(s).

Second, a partner has a right to an interest in the partnership. This interest, composed of a combination of the partner's share of the profits and a return of capital contributed by the partner, is part of the partner's personal property. If necessary, a partner can sell his or her interest in the partnership to a creditor. A partner's personal creditor cannot seize specific items of partnership property; however, the creditor can obtain a **charging order,** which entitles the creditor to the partner's profits. The charging order permits the partner to continue to act as a partner and engage in the partnership business; however, the creditor collects the partner's share of the profits.

> **charging order**
> An order that entitles a creditor to collect a partner's profits.

Right to Inspect Books Each partner has the right to receive full information regarding partnership matters. This right corresponds to the fiduciary duty of the partners to disclose any information affecting the partnership. Thus, partners must have access to all partnership books and records and be allowed to make copies of these records. Unless otherwise agreed, the records must be kept at the principal business office.

Right to an Account An **accounting** is a review and listing of all partnership assets and/or profit. The accounting typically lists the distribution of assets and profit to the partners. Each partner has a right to an accounting in four circumstances:

> **accounting**
> A review and listing of all partnership assets and/ or profit.

1. Whenever the partnership agreement provides for an account.
2. Whenever the copartners wrongfully exclude a partner from the partnership or from access to the books.

3. Whenever any partner fails to disclose a profit or benefit from the partnership, thus breaching his or her fiduciary duty.

4. Whenever circumstances render an account as "just and reasonable."

For example, in the Case Opener, Swenson argued that if Rockwell were a partner, he was not approaching the suit appropriately. If Rockwell were a partner and thought that Swenson was taking funds, Rockwell would have a partner's right to request an accounting to determine whether funds had been withheld.

LO 21-4 Interactions between Partners and Third Parties

Each partner can serve as an agent for the other partners as well as the partnership. Consequently, as long as a partner has authority to act, his act in performing business duties, as well as making agreements with third parties, is binding for the partnership. If the partner has authority to act and the partnership is bound by the act, each partner has unlimited personal liability for the obligation.

ACTUAL AUTHORITY OF THE PARTNERS

According to UPA, general agency principles establish that partners have the authority to bind a partnership in an agreement. Consequently, if a partner, following normal business procedures, establishes an agreement in which he or she binds the partnership to the agreement, both the partner and the partnership are liable for the obligation in the agreement.

Suppose Brittany is a partner in a firm. While allegedly carrying on partnership business, she engages in a business transaction and binds the partnership to the agreement. Yet suppose Brittany really didn't have authority to bind the partnership to the agreement with the third party. In this case, both Brittany and the firm are liable for the obligation.

However, suppose that the third party is aware that Brittany does not have the authority to bind the partnership to the agreement. Since the party is aware that the authority is absent, Brittany will be held liable for the obligation but the partnership will not be held liable.

IMPLIED AUTHORITY OF THE PARTNERS

Because of the nature of the partnership, partners generally have greater implied authority than do typical agents. The implied authority of the partners is usually determined by the nature of the business. For instance, a partner typically has the implied authority to enter into agreements necessary to carry on partnership business. Thus, a partner has the authority to purchase goods that are necessary to perpetuate the business. However, a partner does not have implied authority to sell any property without the consent of all other partners.

LIABILITY TO THIRD PARTIES

jointly liable
A term applied to partners who share liability for the partnership's debts.

joint and several liability
A type of liability in which a third party can choose to sue the partners separately or to sue all partners jointly in one action.

According to UPA, if a partnership is liable, each partner has unlimited personal liability. That is, all partners are **jointly liable** for the partnership's debts. Thus, if a party wants to bring a successful claim, the party must name all partners as defendants. Instead of naming every partner in a lawsuit, a party can simply name the partnership. If the party is successful at bringing his or her claim, each partner is liable for the judgment. If one partner pays the entire judgment, the other partners are required to indemnify, or reimburse, that partner.

If a partner commits a tort or a breach of trust, all partners are jointly and severally liable. **Joint and several liability** means that a third party can choose to sue the partners separately or all partners jointly in one action. Suppose William sues your partnership, which has four partners. William might name one of the partners in the first action. If the partner is found liable, William can sue all three other partners separately. However, if in the first claim the court ruled that the partnership was not liable in any form, William cannot bring a successful claim against a second partner on the issue of the partner's liability.

If William brings a successful claim against a partner, he can collect the judgment only on the assets of one partner. The partner is required to reimburse the partnership for the damages it pays to William. Case 21-2 considers how partners in a partnership can be held liable for the negligence of one partner.

CASE 21-2

ERIC JOHNSON & LORI JOHNSON v. ST. THERESE MEDICAL CENTER
APPELLATE COURT OF ILLINOIS, SECOND DISTRICT
296 Ill. App. 3d 341; 694 N.E.2d 1088; 1998 Ill. App. LEXIS 301

FACTS: *In November 1990, Eric and Lori Johnson brought their 22-month-old daughter, Erica, to St. Therese Medical Center, where she was treated and released by Dr. Bruce Sands. Dr. Sands was a partner of Northern Illinois Emergency Physicians, Ltd. Drs. Richard Keller, Michael Oster, Thomas Braniff, Rodney Haenschen, and Phillip Gillespie were the other partners in the partnership. The Johnsons filed suit against Dr. Sands and the partnership. They argued that Dr. Sands negligently caused the death of Erica and that the partnership was liable because St. Therese acted on behalf of the partnership. A jury gave the Johnsons a $4 million award against Dr. Sands, St. Therese, and the partnership. Dr. Sands later filed for bankruptcy. In February 1997, the trial court judge ruled that the Johnsons could proceed against the general partners individually if they were partners at the time of the incident. Consequently, the plaintiffs started motions to withhold the wages of all the partners. Various court proceedings ensued in which various partners argued that they should not be held personally liable. In June 1997, the trial court ruled that the assets of Keller, Haenschen, and Braniff be turned over to the Johnsons.*

ISSUE: Can a judgment against a partnership be enforced against the partners individually?

REASONING: Generally speaking, all partners are jointly and severally liable for everything chargeable to the partnership for the loss or injury of a third person due to any wrongful act or omission of any partner acting in the ordinary course of the business of the partnership. Additionally, a judgment against a partnership in its firm name does not bar an action to enforce the individual liability of any partner. The problem for the Johnsons comes when the court considers the *Cook* standard. In *Cook*, the court ruled that a judgment against a partnership in only the partnership's name did not provide notice to the individual partners that the individual partners' assets were at risk, and therefore it did not allow recovery of the judgment from the individual partners. In this case, the Johnsons sued the partnership in the partnership's name—not the partners individually. Hence, the individual partners were not provided notice that their personal assets were at risk, and thus they were not provided due process.

DECISION AND REMEDY: The court reversed the lower court's ruling.

SIGNIFICANCE OF THE CASE: This case demonstrates the importance of naming all relevant parties to a lawsuit. Had the Johnsons named the partnership *and* each individual partner as defendants in the original lawsuit, the Johnsons would likely have succeeded in collecting the judgment amount from the individual partners.

CRITICAL THINKING

The court seems to have relied heavily on a standard set in *Cook.* What information do you need to know about *Cook* to determine whether the court was drawing an apt or a faulty analogy?

ETHICAL DECISION MAKING

Suppose you were one of the partners in this case. If you were guided by duty ethics, would any of the details of the case described above be altered?

Silent Partnerships in Germany

The original intent behind silent partnerships was for two people to be able to engage in a partnership without having to inform the third party. Recently, both civil and common law countries have been moving away from this idea of total anonymity. For example, France permits the silent partner to choose whether he or she wants to disclose the relationship. Germany, however, has held to the original intent of silent partnerships.

Under German law, a contract is formed between the silent partner (usually the financier) and the proprietor of the business. In exchange for his or her investment, the silent partner receives a designated share of the profits. Enlisting a silent partner does not require registration, and the company should continue to operate under the proprietor's name.

Because business is conducted under the proprietor's name and because the partnership remains a secret to the third party, the silent partner is not held personally liable for damages incurred in the course of business. This non-liability factor makes silent partnerships less widely used in Germany than other countries. Nevertheless, the nonliability allows for unique situations. For instance, a proprietor could enlist his or her child as a silent partner. The child would collect assets while remaining anonymous and ineligible for any liability claims. Nonliability guards the interests of the silent partner.

In Germany, the benefits swing in favor of the silent partner. While the proprietor transacts all the business and the third party remains unaware of the existence of the partnership relationship, the silent partner enjoys minimal responsibility and no risk of personal liability.

You may be initially surprised that the silent-partner arrangement is legal in Germany. But as a critical thinker you have a responsibility to rethink your reasoning. Can you create a list of reasons for why the U.S. legal system should encourage silent partnerships?

LIABILITY OF INCOMING PARTNERS

When a partnership adds another partner, the new partner assumes limited liability for any obligations that occurred before she was added. The new partner cannot be held personally liable for these obligations, but the capital that the new partner adds can be used to pay off these obligations. Clearly, because an incoming partner assumes limited liability, the dates of agreements, as well as the date that the new partner was added, are extremely important.

The Revised Uniform Partnership Act

The majority of the states have adopted a revised version of the Uniform Partnership Act that is typically referred to as the Revised Uniform Partnership Act (RUPA). Just as the original Uniform Partnership Act governs partnerships in the absence of an express agreement, RUPA is an updated version that has significantly changed several of the laws that relate to partnerships. Since being approved in 1996, RUPA has been adopted in roughly half of the states. Since the other half of the states have not yet adopted RUPA, it is wise to determine whether the state in which a partnership was formed operates under UPA or RUPA. Although RUPA generally serves to expand UPA, there is some disagreement between UPA and RUPA about the rules of partnership.

So far, we've discussed what a partnership is, how a partnership is formed, and how a partnership operates. In most cases, a partnership will not last forever. That is why we now turn our attention to how a partnership ends.

LO 21-5

Termination of the Partnership

Before the termination of any partnership can be considered to be complete, a partnership must experience what are referred to as the *dissolution stage* and the *winding-up stage*. The first of these stages, dissolution, is considered complete when any partner stops fulfilling the role of a partner to the business (by choice or default). The second stage, the winding-up stage, is completed by taking account of the assets of the partner who has left the partnership and redistributing them among the other partners. The rest of this section explains the steps that must occur within the dissolution and winding-up stages for the termination of the partnership to be considered complete.

DISSOLUTION OF THE BUSINESS

Section 29 of UPA defines **dissolution** as "the change in the relation of the partners caused by any partner's ceasing to be associated with the carrying on, as distinguished from the winding up"—the activity of completing unfinished partnership business, collecting and paying debts, collecting partnership assets, and taking inventory—"of the business." What might cause the dissolution of the partnership? The dissolution may occur by an act of the partners, an operation of the law, or an act of the court.

dissolution
The change in the relation of partners caused by any partner's ceasing to be associated with the carrying on of the partnership's business.

Act of Partners The partnership is a voluntary and consensual relationship, so the partners have the power to dissolve the relationship at almost any time. There are many reasons why an act of the partners might lead to the dissolution of the partnership. First, the partners may simply agree that the partnership will terminate at a certain time. For example, suppose that Lisa and Jason, two partners in a college preparation business, are graduating from college. They are both planning to accept jobs at other firms; consequently, neither thinks that she or he will be able to continue the college preparation business. Perhaps, when their business was created, the partners might have agreed to dissolve the partnership when one of them graduated from college.

Alternatively, once partners reach a certain objective, they might agree to dissolve the partnership. As an illustration, consider a partnership to sell homes in a housing development. Once all of those homes are sold, the partners may agree to dissolve the partnership.

Let's return to the college preparation–business example. Suppose the original agreement was that the partnership would be terminated once either partner graduates from college. However, suppose the business is either a flop or an enormous success. The partners can then agree to dissolve the partnership early or extend the terms of the partnership after graduation.

What are the circumstances in which a partnership can be **rightfully dissolved,** meaning that the partnership dissolution does not violate the partnership agreement? We have established two of these circumstances above (dissolution after meeting an established objective and dissolution at the end of the term stated in the partnership agreement). The following are also circumstances in which the partnership can be rightfully terminated:

rightfully dissolved
A term applied to the dissolution of a partnership that does not violate its partnership agreement.

1. *A partner withdraws from the partnership at will.* (A *partnership at will* is an agreement that does not specify the objective or duration of the partnership.)

2. *A partner withdraws in accordance with the partnership agreement.* The partnership agreement may establish specific reasons that a partner may withdraw.

3. *A partner is expelled from the partnership in accordance with the partnership agreement.* Suppose you are a partner in a law firm and you steal some type of property from the partnership. The partnership agreement will usually determine the cases in which a partner may be removed from the partnership, and theft is often one of the reasons for removal. Thus, your stealing would likely lead to your expulsion from the partnership.

If a partnership is rightfully dissolved, all partners can demand that the partnership be wound up and can participate in the winding up. Moreover, if the partners unanimously agree, they can continue the business using the partnership's name.

However, if a partner dissolves the partnership in violation of the partnership agreement, the partner can be held liable for **wrongful dissolution.** If a partner has wrongfully dissolved the partnership, that partner cannot require that the business be wound up. Furthermore, that partner can be held liable for damages to the remaining partners. The remaining partners can choose to continue the business under the partnership name or to wind up the business.

wrongful dissolution
A dissolution of a partnership in violation of its partnership agreement.

Operation of Law Several circumstances provided by law dissolve a partnership: if a partner dies, if a partner is adjudicated bankrupt, or if the partnership business engages in an activity that suddenly becomes illegal. For example, suppose Congress decides that cigarettes are illegal. If the partnership manufactures and sells cigarettes, the partnership would be automatically dissolved.

CASE Nugget

When Does a Partnership Dissolve?

In re Leah Beth Woskob, Debtor; Alex Woskob; Helen Woskob; the Estate of Victor Woskob v. Leah Beth Woskob, Appellant
U.S. Court of Appeals for the Third Circuit

305 F.3d 177 (2002)

In 1996, Leah Beth Woskob and Victor Woskob formed a partnership, the Legends Partnership, to construct, own, and operate the Legends, an apartment building. They were married at the time that the partnership was formed; however, they separated and filed for divorce the following year. During the divorce proceedings, Victor prevented Leah from receiving any of the partnership proceeds. Leah was granted a petition for special relief and awarded the exclusive right to manage and derive income from the partnership. Shortly thereafter, Victor filed for bankruptcy. Leah continued to file tax returns on behalf of the partnership, each of which listed Victor as a general partner. When Victor died in a car accident in 1999, Leah gave his estate notice that she was exercising her right to buy out Victor's interest in the partnership. Victor's estate sued, claiming that the partnership had been dissolved previously and requesting that someone be appointed to oversee the winding up of the partnership and a full accounting of the company's assets. When Leah filed for bankruptcy, the suits were moved to the bankruptcy court. The bankruptcy court ruled in favor of Leah, finding that the partnership had dissolved on Victor's death. Victor's estate appealed to the district court, which found that the partnership had dissolved two years before Victor's death, making Leah's attempt to buy out Victor's interest untimely. Leah appealed.

The task before the appeals court was to determine the timeliness of Leah's attempt to buy out Victor's interest in the partnership, which depended entirely on the date of the dissolution of the partnership. The court looked to the Uniform Partnership Act (UPA), which defined the dissolution of a partnership as "the change in the relation of the partners caused by any partner ceasing to be associated in the carrying on, as distinguished from the winding up, of the business." Victor's estate claimed that the dissolution of the partnership occurred at any one of three points, each at least 18 months prior to Victor's death. First, Victor excluded Leah from the partnership after they separated; second, Leah excluded Victor from the partnership after seeking special relief from the Court of Common Pleas; third, Victor filed for bankruptcy.

The appeals court found that the exclusions of Leah and Victor from the partnership were not, in and of themselves, grounds for automatic dissolution of the partnership. Rather, the exclusions could have provided a basis for dissolution, had either Leah or Victor sought judicial decree of the dissolution after the exclusions. In addition, bankruptcy in and of itself is not grounds for automatic dissolution of the partnership. If the nondebtor partner does not consent to continue the partnership with the debtor, bankruptcy may be grounds for dissolution. However, Leah continued to list Victor as a general partner on the tax returns she filed for the partnership, even after he filed for bankruptcy. Thus, the appeals court found that the partnership had not dissolved prior to Victor's death in 1999 and that Leah's attempt to buy out Victor's interest in the partnership was therefore timely.

Act of the Court A partner may make application to the court to dissolve the partnership for several reasons. First, a partnership can be dissolved when a partner is adjudicated insane. Second, if it becomes impractical to carry out the business of the partnership (e.g., if the continuation of the partnership will result in lost profits only), the court will likely dissolve the partnership.

Termination of Partnerships in Spain

In Spain, there are four specific situations in which full dissolution is permitted (*full dissolution* simply means that the partnership ends without litigation or a waiting period): (1) if a partner dies, (2) if a partner is declared insane and unfit to manage the business, (3) if a partner is declared bankrupt, (4) if a partner requests that the partnership be terminated.

In Spain there are other situations that call for provisional dissolution of the partnership. *Provisional dissolution* is followed by litigation to determine the legitimacy of the termination request. There are six situations of provisional, or partial, dissolution: (1) A partner fails to comply with provisions of the contract, (2) a partner unexplainably abandons the partnership and does not return on request, (3) a partner fails to bring the capital he promised, (4) a partner is accused of fraud or mismanagement, (5) a partner exceeds the limits of her power, and (6) a partner uses capital belonging to the partnership in his own name.

In any of these circumstances, the partnership is temporarily dissolved pending the outcome of litigation. During partial dissolution, the accused is excluded from all managerial responsibilities and profits. He or she is also excluded from any liability to business conducted during this time.

The stage of provisional dissolution prevents those unfairly accused of certain behaviors from losing position in the partnership. The process, however, can be a tedious and lengthy one whether the partial dissolution is moved to complete termination or the partnership resumes.

Third, if a partner is incapable of carrying out his or her duties as established by the partnership agreement, the court can dissolve the partnership.

Fourth, the court can dissolve the partnership for other circumstances. For instance, suppose that the partners in the college preparation business begin bitterly disagreeing about how the business should be managed. The disagreement is contrary to the cooperation necessary for a partnership to exist. In this instance, the court can dissolve the partnership.

Exhibit 21-1 provides 13 reasons for dissolution of a partnership.

CONSEQUENCES OF DISSOLUTION

If a partner intends to dissolve or withdraw from the partnership, the partner must give the other partners notice of this intent. When the partnership is dissolved, the partner no longer has actual authority to bind the partnership. However, if the partnership does not notify third parties of the dissolution, the partner can still have implied authority to bind the partnership. Suppose that Lisa, one of the partners in the college preparation business, intends to dissolve the partnership. However, Lisa has not yet notified Jason of her intent, and Jason makes an agreement to begin

1. The term established in the partnership agreement expires.
2. The partnership meets its established objective.
3. A partner withdraws from the partnership at will.
4. A partner withdraws in accordance with the partnership agreement.
5. A partner is expelled from the partnership in accordance with the partnership agreement.
6. A partner dies.
7. A partner is adjudicated bankrupt.
8. The business of the partnership becomes illegal.
9. A partner is adjudicated insane.
10. A partner becomes incapable of performing the duties as established by the partnership agreement.
11. The business of the partnership can be carried on only at a loss of profits.
12. A disagreement between the partners is such that it undermines the nature of the partnership.
13. Other circumstances of the partnership necessitate the dissolution.

Exhibit 21-1

Reasons for Rightful Dissolution of a Partnership

working with five new students to prepare them for college. Because Lisa has not yet given notice of her intent to dissolve, she is still liable for the agreement Jason has made.

To ensure that a dissolving partner does not create additional liability for a partnership, partnerships usually take active steps to notify third parties about dissolution. They often place a notice in the newspaper, for example. However, a partnership must provide direct verbal or written notice to any third party that has provided credit to the partnership.

After the dissolution of the partnership, the partners' next step is either winding up the business or continuing the partnership or business after the dissolution. We'll discuss winding up the business first.

WINDING UP THE BUSINESS

winding up
The process of completing unfinished partnership business.

Once a partnership is liquidated, the partners begin the process of **winding up,** the activity of completing unfinished partnership business, collecting and paying debts, collecting partnership assets, and taking inventory. During the winding up, the partners must still fulfill their fiduciary duty to one another, in the sense that they must disclose all information about the partnership assets. However, during the winding-up process, the partners can now engage in business that competes with the partnership business.

Who can demand that the winding-up process begin? As we stated earlier, if a partnership has been rightfully dissolved, any partner can demand that the winding-up stage begin. However, if a partner wrongfully dissolves a partnership, that partner has no right to demand a winding up. In Case 21-3, the court considered a demand for an accounting in the winding-up phase.

CASE 21-3

ROBERT M. TAFOYA v. DEE S. PERKINS
COURT OF APPEALS OF COLORADO, DIVISION FOUR
932 P.2d 836; 1996 Colo. App. LEXIS 206; 20 BTR 1115

FACTS: *Robert Tafoya and Dee Perkins, brother and sister, entered into a partnership with Dee's husband, Eugene Perkins. The partnership involved the ownership and maintenance of an apartment complex. In 1979, the apartment complex was sold. The partnership took back a 10-year promissory note with a balloon payment due in 1989. Ten years later, when the balloon payment was due, Eugene Perkins purchased the apartments again at a foreclosure sale. In December 1989, Eugene Perkins issued a "Notice of Termination of Partnership" because of losses associated with the partnership. At the same time, Robert Tafoya ceased being associated with the partnership. In July 1990, Eugene Perkins died. The trial court ruled that Perkins's death, as well as Tafoya's separation from the partnership, was sufficient to dissolve the partnership. Dee Perkins continued to manage the property until January 1994, when she sold the property for a profit. Tafoya filed* his complaint before the sale of the property, arguing that Perkins had breached her fiduciary duty. Tafoya requested an accounting of the partnership's assets. The trial court found no breach of fiduciary duty, yet it concluded that Tafoya was entitled to an accounting and awarded him a share of the proceeds from the apartment complex sale. Dee Perkins appealed, arguing that Tafoya's claim was barred by a statute of limitations.

ISSUE: Is Tafoya's request for an accounting barred by a statute of limitations?

REASONING: In this case, regardless of the notice issued by Eugene Perkins, the partnership was dissolved when Tafoya ceased to be associated with the partnership. At the point that the partnership dissolved, the statute of limitations started to run. There is no clear statute of limitations for a request for an accounting. The court disagreed

with Tafoya's claim that the applicable statute of limitations was six years because that statute of limitations applied to an action to recover an unliquidated, determinable amount of money due to Tafoya. In this case, the amount of money due him was not determinable from the partnership agreement or a simple computation. Rather, Tafoya was requesting an accounting to determine the amount of money due him. Thus, the applicable statute of limitations was a "catch-all" two-year period from the time of dissolution. Tafoya ceased to be associated with the partnership in 1989, thus dissolving the partnership, and did not file this action until 1994.

DECISION AND REMEDY: Tafoya's request for an accounting was barred by a statute of limitations, which had lapsed three years before Tafoya's request. The trial court's ruling was reversed.

SIGNIFICANCE OF THE CASE: Tafoya attempted to exercise a partner's basic right: the right to an accounting. However, Tafoya waited five years before attempting to determine whether the partnership owed him money. This case demonstrates exiting partners' responsibility to make timely requests for an accounting and to finish all partnership-related business quickly.

CRITICAL THINKING

How do you react to the evidence in this case? Does it strike you as being seriously incomplete? What additional information would you have liked to have had were you asked to decide this case?

ETHICAL DECISION MAKING

What were the primary values upheld by the court in its decision? If you were the judge reviewing the case, which values would motivate your decision?

Once all the partnership assets have been gathered, the assets are distributed to the partners or any creditors that the partnership might have. If the partnership has been successful (i.e., has very little or no debt), the order of the distribution of assets is not too important. However, when the dissolved partnership has many creditors, the order of the distribution of the assets is immensely important. UPA establishes that when a partnership has debt, the distribution of liquidated assets must take the following order:

1. Payment to creditors of the partnership.
2. Payment of refunds or loans to partners for loans made to the firm.
3. Payment of partners for the capital they invested.
4. Payment of profits distributed to partners on the basis of the partnership agreement.

To see more about the management, accounting, and dissolution of partnerships, please see the **Connecting to the Core** activity on the text's website at www.mhhe.com/kubasekess2e.

If the partners' liabilities for the partnership are greater than their liquidated assets, the partners are liable for the losses. Each partner must contribute his or her share of the losses to pay the creditors. If one partner is unable to contribute his or her share and another partner covers the first partner's unpaid share, the second partner has a right of contribution against the partner who did not pay.

CONTINUING THE PARTNERSHIP AFTER DISSOLUTION

After a partnership is dissolved, the remaining partners have several options. One option is to continue the partnership after dissolution. What happens to the noncontinuing partner? Regardless of why the partner is noncontinuing, this partner must receive his or her interest in the partnership. For example, if a noncontinuing partner holds 20 percent of the partnership in which the assets are valued at $10,000, this partner must receive $2,000 after dissolution.

CASE Nugget

What Duties Do Partners Owe after Dissolution?

Sanfurd G. Bluestein and Sylvia Krugman v. Robert Olden
U.S. District Court for the Southern District of New York

2004 U.S. Dist. LEXIS 3631

In 1978, Bluestein, Krugman, and Olden formed a partnership, the principal asset of which was a building located in New York City. For 26 years, Olden operated Olden Camera and Lens Company, Inc., in part of the building. Olden Camera itself had been in the building for more than 60 years. In 2001, the plaintiffs sent a letter to Olden to terminate the partnership in accordance with the terms of the partnership agreement. After the letter was sent, the partnership continued to operate in dissolution. The partners agreed to sell the building, but they could not agree on whom to sell to and how much to charge. Olden offered $9 million for the plaintiff's combined interest in the partnership, but he added that the plaintiffs must release any claims against him and his business, as well as any claims to profits from the partnership for 2002–2003. A competing offer from a third party contained no requirements and offered $15,400,000 for the building, but it provided for a reduction of the purchase price by $200,000 if Olden's business remained in the building.

 The plaintiffs filed an order to show cause, requesting "1) the appointment of plaintiff Bluestein as Liquidating and/or Winding Up Partner of the general partnership; 2) a direction that Olden cooperate in the liquidation of the assets of the partnership; and 3) enjoining Olden from entering into any new leases or renewing any leases for space in the building." Because the partnership was terminated in accordance with the partnership agreement, the court ruled that Olden could not prevent maximization of the partnership's assets. Bluestein was appointed the liquidating partner and given sole authority to liquidate the partnership's assets and divide the proceeds after paying the partnership's debts. Olden was ordered to cooperate in the liquidation of the assets and enjoined from entering into or renewing any leases or agreements affecting the partnership's building in New York City. The court retained jurisdiction to ensure that the partners complied with its orders.

Perhaps the best way that partners can preserve a partnership business is through a *continuation agreement.* This agreement states that continuing partners can keep partnership property and carry on the partnership business, particularly in cases when a partner dies.

LO 21-6

Limited Partnerships

limited partnership (LP)
A partnership consisting of at least one general partner and at least one limited partner in which the general partners assume all liability for the partnership's debts and the limited partners assume no liability beyond their originally invested capital.

Chapter 20 introduced limited partnerships. Limited partnerships, also known as *special partnerships,* originated in Europe more than 500 years ago and have existed in the United States for nearly 200 years. Limited partnerships are attractive to potential investors because of the limited liability as well as the tax advantages associated with this form of business.

 Recall that the **limited partnership** is an agreement between at least one general partner and at least one limited partner. The general partner has management responsibility for the partnership and assumes unlimited personal liability for the debts of the partnership. In contrast, the limited partner assumes no liability for the partnership beyond the capital he or she invested in the business.

How the Internet Assists Business Owners Who Use Limited Partnerships

The Internet is making it easier for business owners to engage in business as limited partnerships. For example, at the Michigan Corporation Division page (www.michigan.gov/cis/0,1607,7-154-10557_12901-25254–,00.html), you can download a certificate of limited partnership.

Additionally, the Internet provides partnerships with an easy opportunity to advertise to the public when there is a change in the partnership. For example, when a partnership is in the dissolution stage, it must notify third parties of the dissolution of the partnership. Thus, the partnership can simply post information on the Internet explaining the dissolution. You can see a sample partnership dissolution notice at http://smallbusiness.findlaw.com/business-forms-contracts/be28_8_1.html.

Functioning as the equivalent of RUPA, the Revised Uniform Limited Partnership Act (RULPA) is the law governing limited partnerships. Like all law, RULPA is not static; it changes as lawmakers revise it to handle new issues that arise and to better achieve social goals. RULPA was originally drafted in 1976, revised in 1985, and revised again in 2001. About one-fourth of the states have adopted the 1976 version of RULPA, and about three-fourths have adopted the 1985 version. Only a handful of states have adopted the 2001 version. Louisiana is the only state not to have adopted any version of RULPA.

FORMATION OF THE LIMITED PARTNERSHIP

LO 21-7

How is a limited partnership created? In contrast to the often-informal partnership agreements described earlier in the chapter, the formation of a limited partnership must follow very specific statutory requirements. The general and limited partners must sign a **certificate of limited partnership** and file this certificate with the secretary of state. If the partners do not correctly fill out or do not file this certificate, the partners will not receive limited liability.

certificate of limited partnership
A document signed on the formation of a limited partnership and filed with the secretary of state.

RIGHTS AND LIABILITIES OF THE LIMITED PARTNERS AND THE GENERAL PARTNERS

Limited partners generally have all the rights given to partners in general partnerships, as discussed earlier. Thus, the limited partner (as well as the general partner) has the right to share in the profits of the business. Furthermore, the limited partner has the right to an account of the partnership. Moreover, if the general partner wants to add a partner to the partnership, the general partner must have the consent of all partners in the limited partnership. Finally, an additional right of limited partners is that they often recover their investment before general partners.

However, the limited partner has a few special rights under RULPA. For example, if a general partner fails to bring a suit on behalf of the limited partnership, the limited partner can bring the suit.

What about the duties and liabilities of the partnership? While there are not many distinctions between the rights of the general partner and those of the limited partner, there are numerous distinctions in the duties and liabilities of each partner.

For instance, the general partner has unlimited personal liability for the debts of the partnership. This broad liability is in contrast to the limited partner's limited liability, which is restricted to the amount of capital the partner has invested in the business. Thus, if you enter into a limited partnership by contributing $10,000 to the partnership, as a limited partner you cannot be held liable for more than $10,000.

A limited partner's limited personal liability depends on that partner's maintaining three conditions:

1. The limited partner has complied in good faith with the requirement that a certificate of limited partnership be filed.
2. The limited partner does not participate in the control of the business.
3. The limited partner's surname is not part of the partnership name.

Exhibit 21-2

Comparison of General Partners and Limited Partners

	GENERAL PARTNER	LIMITED PARTNER
Control of business	Has *all* rights associated with controlling the business	Has *no* right to participate in the management and control of the business
Liability	Has unlimited personal liability for all partnership debts	Has liability limited to the amount of capital the partner has contributed to the business
Agency of partnership	Acts as an agent of the partnership	Is not an agent of the partnership

If any of these conditions are violated, the limited partner surrenders his or her limited liability. For example, the general partner typically has exclusive control and management of the limited partnership. In contrast, the limited partner does not share in this control of the partnership. If the limited partner does share in the management of the company, the courts will likely rule that the partner has forfeited his or her limited liability. Exhibit 21-2 distinguishes several aspects of general partners and limited partners.

DISSOLUTION OF THE LIMITED PARTNERSHIP

Dissolution of the limited partnership is very similar to dissolution of the general partnership. The limited partner has no right or power to dissolve the partnership. While the death or bankruptcy of the limited partner rarely dissolves the partnership, the death of the general partner usually dissolves the partnership (unless the agreement specifies otherwise). According to RULPA, a limited partnership can be dissolved for the following reasons:

1. The expiration of the term established in the certificate of limited partnership.
2. The completion of the objective established in the certificate.
3. The unanimous written consent of all partners (limited and general).
4. The withdrawal of the general partner (unless the certificate establishes that other general partners will continue).
5. An act of the court.

If the limited partnership is dissolved, the limited partnership's assets are distributed in the same order as described earlier in this chapter (i.e., payment to third-party creditors, payment to partners who have loaned the partnership money, payment to the partners according to their investments in the partnership, and payment to the partners on the basis of their shares of the profits).

SUMMARY

Nature of the Partnership

The Uniform Partnership Act defines a partnership as "an association of two or more persons to carry on as co-owners a business for profit." An essential element in a partnership is the sharing of profits from the partnership.

Formation of the Partnership

A partnership is created by the articles of partnership, which should include the names of each partner and the partnership, the duration of the partnership, the way profits will be divided, the division of management duties, and the contributions to be made by each partner.

Interactions between Partners

Each partner has specific duties, including:

- Duty to be loyal
- Duty of obedience
- Duty of care

Each partner has specific rights, including:

- Right to share in management
- Right to inspect books
- Right to compensation
- Rights to partnership property

Interactions between Partners and Third Parties

If a partnership has a liability, each partner has unlimited personal liability. All partners are jointly and severally liable for the commission of a tort by any partner.

There is only implied liability when purchases are made to perpetuate the partnership's business.

The Revised Uniform Partnership Act

RUPA is a revised version of UPA, and its use varies from state to state.

Termination of the Partnership

Termination begins when a partnership dissolves. Once the partnership has been dissolved and the assets have been liquidated and distributed, the partnership has been terminated.

Dissolution refers to the ceasing of a partnership. Acts of partners, the operation of the law, and acts of the court can serve to rightfully dissolve a partnership.

- *Consequences of dissolution:* A partner who wishes to dissolve or withdraw from the partnership must give notice of his intent. Third parties are usually contacted promptly about a dissolving partner to prevent the creation of additional liability for the partnership.

Winding up is the activity of completing unfinished partnership business, collecting and paying debts, collecting partnership assets, and taking inventory.

Limited Partnerships

The limited partnership involves an agreement between at least one general partner and at least one limited partner. This partnership permits investors to share in the profits of the partnership, yet it limits these limited partners' liability to the amount they invest in the business.

Point/Counterpoint

Should a Partnership Be Allowed to Expel a Partner on the Basis of Illegal Personal Conduct Unrelated to the Terms of the Partnership Agreement?	
YES	NO
A partnership should be able to expel a partner on the basis of illegal personal conduct even when the illegal conduct isn't specified in the partnership agreement.	If a partner participates in an illegal activity unrelated to the partnership agreement, the partnership should not be allowed to expel the individual on the basis of his or her involvement in the illegal activity.

A partnership should be able to expel a partner on the basis of illegal personal conduct even when the illegal conduct isn't specified in the partnership agreement.

It would be nearly impossible to create a partnership agreement that dictated every possible situation that would allow for dissolution of the partnership. Individuals are always expected to conduct themselves within the bounds of national, state, and local laws. Any illegal behavior should have implications for the partnership as an ongoing business enterprise.

A partner's personal behavior affects the entire partnership and associated business in many different ways. A partner's behavior outside the business atmosphere can damage the reputation of the company. For example, if one partner of a five-partner law firm is arrested for smoking marijuana, clients will associate this marijuana-smoking partner with the entire firm. Clients may first begin to question the single partner's priorities and ethical beliefs: If he participates in this illegal activity, in which other

If a partner participates in an illegal activity unrelated to the partnership agreement, the partnership should not be allowed to expel the individual on the basis of his or her involvement in the illegal activity.

The partners had the opportunity when formulating the partnership agreement to include a stipulation for the dissolution of the partnership if a partner engaged in illegal activity.

If the agreement does not specify the relevant illegal activities, an individual is not aware of the potential impact of her actions on her status as a partner. Had she known the possible consequences regarding her participation in the partnership, she might have acted differently. However, she cannot be expected to abide by restrictions that are not stated.

The logic behind dissolving the partnership on the basis of an unrelated activity is faulty. Is it logical to revoke an individual's driver's license because she looked at pornography in a state where such an activity is illegal? Additionally, an individual can make a poor personal choice and still be capable of performing her

illegal activities does he partake? Does he keep faulty books? Will I be overcharged?

Next, clients (his clients and the other attorneys' clients) may begin to question the firm as a whole for allowing a man who partakes in illegal activities to remain a partner in the firm. Do all the attorneys participate in illegal activities?

While a partner may suffer personal legal consequences for his actions, the whole partnership suffers when one partner makes a poor personal choice. Therefore, the partnership should be able to decide the consequences.

expected duties. A rule allowing partnerships to expel a partner on the basis of unrelated illegal activity could be easily abused. Partnerships that want to expel a partner for other reasons (inconvenience, additional profit, etc.) could easily say she participated in illegal activity and expel her from the partnership for that reason alone. A partner should not be expelled from a partnership because she participates in unrelated criminal activity. The partner already suffers personal legal consequences and should not experience additional penalties for an activity that has no impact on the partnership.

Questions & Problems

1. Explain each element of UPA's definition of a partnership.

2. Explain the need for partnership by estoppel.

3. What are the possible problems with any single list of the legal liabilities of a partner?

4. Madison Real Estate is a limited partner of KanAm USA XIX Limited Partnership. The partnership agreement sets out the rights and obligations of the limited partners and the general partner and provides limited partners with a right to inspect the partnership's books of account. Specifically, it states: "The General Partner shall cause complete and accurate *books of account* to be kept for the Partnership, which shall be available for examination by the Partners during normal business hours. The fiscal year of the Partnership shall be the calendar year and the *books of account* shall be closed as of the end of each year."

Madison requested inspection of books and records from the partnership, including rent rolls for properties and terms and conditions of property debt. The purpose of the demand was for Madison to "properly value its investment in the partnership." KanAm refused. Madison sued, alleging that by refusing to make available the requested books and records, KanAm breached the Uniform Limited Partnership Act and the partnership agreement. The court had to consider whether the limited partner's primary purpose for inspecting the books was reasonably related to its limited partner interests and, thus, was a proper purpose for inspection. Do you think the purpose for inspecting the books was related to the interests of the limited partner? In other words, do you think the court said this limited partner should be allowed to inspect the books? Recall the differences between general and limited partners when you answer these

questions. [Civil Action No. 2863-VCP, Court of Chancery of Delaware, 2008 Del. Ch. LEXIS 201.]

5. Two brothers, Charles and William Hooper, entered into an oral partnership agreement for the purpose of carrying on the business of industrial scrap metal sales. Charles expressly offered William an equal partnership in the business, stating that he needed a partner, not an employee, and that he wanted William to be his partner. Charles and William were both injured in a car accident in 1984. William's injuries were very significant, requiring two major surgeries. At that time, Charles took control of the management of the partnership and its assets. Because of his injuries, William could not operate an automobile and was dependent on Charles to provide him with the information necessary for William to continue participating in the management of the partnership business. In early 1985, William tried to return to work, but he could not because of his injuries. Thereafter, William performed limited services for the business from his home. Sometime after that point, the two brothers fought over a partnership matter, and they became so angry that they did not speak and Charles refused to give William any information about the partnership. William filed suit, asking the court to order an accounting and to dissolve the partnership. Charles alleged that he was entitled to monetary compensation (on top of his share of the profits) for the services he performed for the partnership after William was injured because William was no longer doing his share of the work for the partnership. Do you think the court granted him this additional compensation? [*Hooper v. Hooper,* 2002 Cal. App. Unpub. LEXIS 835.]

6. The Vancouver Group is made up of five investors, Pietz, Wynne, Fordham, Indermuehle, and Smith.

The group entered into a partnership with Robert Berry for the joint purchase of the Sundance Hotel and Casino. The group and Berry made an offer to purchase the hotel. Pietz agreed to supply $500,000 to the deal and post a $285,000 letter of credit. However, after receiving information that caused him to doubt Berry, Pietz withdrew his interests from the partnership. Berry threatened to sue Pietz for breach of contract, fraud, and tortious breach of the covenant of good faith. Pietz and Berry settled, and Pietz subsequently sued the Vancouver Group for the cost of the settlement. The trial court rejected Pietz's claim of breach of fiduciary duty. He appealed the decision. How do you think the court decided? Was there a breach of fiduciary duty? [*Pietz v. Indermuehle,* 949 P.2d 449 (1998).]

7. Larry Buhman opened an upscale cigar shop called "The Smoke Ring." Buhman became dissatisfied with his partner's performance and decided to terminate the relationship. James McGaughy, who previously had been working part-time at The Smoke Ring, accepted what he believed was Buhman's oral offer to make him the new partner, but their agreement was not reduced to writing and its terms are hotly disputed. The parties agree only that McGaughy was to manage the store and was promised a 40 percent share of the profits with a guaranteed minimum of $2,000 per month. It is also undisputed that for several years McGaughy and Buhman used business cards that identified each as "Owner" of The Smoke Ring. Buhman paid for the cards. McGaughy identified himself as an owner or a partner in the business to his friends and family, and did so in Buhman's presence without correction. The Smoke Ring was also repeatedly reorganized into various business structures for tax advantages as directed by Buhman. At one time, the business was organized as a partnership, and Buhman identified McGaughy to the Internal Revenue Service as the owner of a 1 percent partnership interest; however, Buhman claimed 100 percent of the deductions arising from the business on his personal tax return. Later, Buhman became dissatisfied with McGaughy's performance and informed him that his employment was terminated. McGaughy sued Buhman to recover his share in the partnership he believed to exist. Buhman argued that there was no partnership agreement supported by consideration and that McGaughy was a contract laborer receiving 40 percent of the profits at the time he was terminated. Was McGaughy a partner of The Smoke Ring? Why or why not? [*Buhman v. McGaughy,* 2007 Tex. App. LEXIS 3177.]

8. Phillip Heller was a partner of the Pillsbury, Madison & Sutro law firm. The relationship between Heller and the firm was not strong, as Heller's work performance was unsatisfactory. He billed 1,000 hours fewer than he had estimated that he would produce, and he did not establish strong working relationships. Heller signed the partnership agreement in 1992. The agreement authorized the Executive Committee to expel partners. After Heller submitted a derogatory and lewd article entitled "Why I Fired My Secretary," the committee met and terminated Heller's partnership. Heller challenged the authority of the committee to expel him, regardless of whether he had signed the partnership agreement. Do you think the court agreed with him? Why or why not? [*Heller v. Pillsbury, Madison & Sutro,* 58 Cal. Rptr. 2d 336 (1996).]

9. Jones and Hardy entered into an oral partnership agreement. They planned to develop and lease certain areas of land. Together, they formed the Bloomington Knolls Association. Jones and Hardy began to experience financial problems, and they brought in a third partner, Jackson, to arrange additional financing for the project. Jones subsequently dissolved the partnership and requested that he be given a portion of the land as his share of the partnership assets. Jackson and Hardy did not honor his request, and Jones never received any assets of the partnership. Jones moved for an accounting and winding up of partnership affairs and brought the case to court. The district court entered judgment against Hardy and Jackson, jointly and severally, for an amount representative of Jones's interest in the partnership. Jackson and Hardy appealed the district court's decision. How do you think the court decided? [*MacKay v. Hardy,* 896 P.2d 626 (1995).]

10. Cider Mills, a limited partnership, was continued after the dissolution date for purposes of winding up. The partnership had entered into a contract for the sale of land three months prior to its dissolution date. The property was sold after the dissolution date. The parties disagreed as to the order in which payments would be made following the dissolution of the partnership. The limited partners argued that they should share in the profits from the sale. The court determined that the order of payment should be creditors, limited partners, general partners. Anthony Pappas, a limited partner, objected to the court's decision regarding the distribution of partnership assets. Do you think the court's decision was reversed on appeal? Why or why not? [*Pappas v. Arfaras,* 20 F. Supp. 2d 372 (1998).]

11. Richard H. Pettingell and Joseph A. Regan withdrew as partners from the Boston law firm of Morrison, Mahoney, & Miller. They brought an action to receive funds that they believed were due to them for voluntarily withdrawing from the firm. Pettingell and

Regan left the partnership to establish a new, competing firm. The partnership agreement states that if a partner voluntarily withdraws from the firm and "engages in any activities which are in competition with the then-current activities of the firm, he shall forfeit all of the benefits" that would be received if the employee were to voluntarily withdraw. There was no evidence to indicate that the establishment of the new firm had seriously affected the original firm. Pettingell and Regan disagreed with the forfeiture provision of the partnership agreement. How do you think the court decided? [*Pettingell v. Morrison, Mahoney, & Miller,* 687 N.E.2d 1237 (1997).]

12. After the dissolution of a partnership formed to develop the Four Seasons Resort, TSA International Limited brought an action against Shimizu Corporation alleging breach of fiduciary duty. TSA had approached Shimizu in 1986 with plans for developing the hotel. The two companies formed a partnership, and they began to make plans for several golf and hotel developments. The loans TSA and Shimizu had taken out soon became delinquent. The partners met to negotiate the payment of the hotel and golf course loans. At the request of Shimizu, the agreements were drafted in Japanese. TSA subsequently filed a complaint asserting, among other things, breach of fiduciary duty. When reaching the agreements, Shimizu had discouraged TSA from hiring its own accountants or legal counsel because of "the long-term relationship of trust between Shimizu and TSA." TSA also alleged that Shimizu arranged the agreement so that substantial tax advantages would be obtained. The circuit court found in favor of Shimizu. How do you think the case was decided on appeal? Did Shimizu breach its fiduciary duty? [*TSA Intern. Ltd. v. Shimizu Corp.,* 990 P.2d 713 (1999).]

13. North Port Golf Associates (NPGA) is a limited partnership involved in real estate and golf course development. NPGA contacted the Palmer Course Design Company (PCDC) and the Arnold Palmer Golf Management Company (APGMC) to design and manage two championship golf courses. As part of the agreement, NPGA was prohibited from using Arnold Palmer's name to promote any other business. A disclaimer was placed on the official investment summary brochure of NPGA stating, "As described herein, golf course design and management services will be provided to the partnership by PCDC and APGMC, respectively. Neither of these companies, nor Arnold Palmer, is affiliated with the partnership or general partners." PCDC completed the design of the golf course, but APGMC terminated its contract after NPGA refused to pay. After the failure of the project, NPGA alleged that Arnold Palmer, APGMC, and PCDC were partners by estoppel and were partially responsible for the interests of the limited partnership. Do you think the court agreed with NPGA? Why or why not?
[*Binkley v. Palmer,* 10 S.W.3d 166 (Mo. App. 1999).]

Looking for more review material?

The Online Learning Center at **www.mhhe.com/kubasekess2e** contains this chapter's "Assignment on the Internet" and also a list of URLs for more information, entitled "On the Internet." Find both of them in the Student Center portion of the OLC, along with quizzes and other helpful materials.

CHAPTER

Corporations: Formation and Organization

22

The Formation of Goodyear Tire & Rubber Company

The Goodyear Tire & Rubber Company is the world's largest tire manufacturer, generating net sales of approximately $20 billion in 2007. Named after Charles Goodyear, the inventor of vulcanized rubber, Goodyear Tire incorporated in 1898, largely through the efforts of promoters and subscribers. As a corporation, Goodyear Tire is an "artificial person," a status with legal implications for both the corporation and its owners.

1. What are the legal implications of Goodyear's status as a corporation?
2. How do corporations form? What factors should be considered by a businessperson interested in forming a corporation?

LEARNING OBJECTIVES

After reading this chapter, you will be able to answer the following questions:

LO 22-1 What are the powers granted to corporations by the states?

LO 22-2 How are corporations formed?

LO 22-3 What is the role of a director, an officer, and a shareholder?

LO 22-4 What are the duties of directors, officers, and shareholders?

LO 22-5 In what ways can a director, officer, and shareholder be held liable?

LO 22-6 What are the rights of directors, officers, and shareholders?

LO 22-7 What are mergers and consolidations?

This chapter explains the steps necessary to establish a corporate entity. Although state law generally governs corporations and each state has its own corporate regulatory statutes, the Revised Model Business Corporation Act (RMBCA) is the basis of most state statutes. More than 25 states have adopted at least part of RMBCA.

In addition, the chapter describes the legal relationships among the many groups of individuals with various priorities and agendas within a corporation. Not surprisingly, these priorities and agendas often come into conflict. To ensure that individuals, corporations, and the public achieve fair outcomes to conflicts within corporations, statutory laws have been designed to delegate particular roles, duties, and rights to each group of individuals within corporations.

Characteristics of Corporations

How are corporations different from other forms of business organization?

LEGAL ENTITY

In U.S. law, corporations are legal entities. In other words, corporations exist separately from their shareholders. Thus, corporations can sue or be sued by others.

RIGHTS AS A PERSON AND A CITIZEN

Courts consider corporations to be "legal persons." Thus, in most cases, corporations, like natural persons, have certain rights according to the Bill of Rights. Specifically, the Fifth and Fourteenth Amendments state that government cannot deprive any "person" of life, liberty, or property without due process. Courts have held that corporations are "persons" in this case and thus have a right to due process.

Furthermore, courts consider corporations to be persons with respect to the Fourth Amendment. Hence, the Fourth Amendment protects corporations from unreasonable searches and seizures. Finally, courts consider corporations to be persons that have free-speech rights protected by the First Amendment.

CREATURE OF THE STATE

State incorporation statutes establish the requirements for corporate formation. Each individual corporation's charter creates a contract between that corporation and the state.

LIMITED LIABILITY

Because corporations are legal entities distinct from their shareholders, corporations are liable for corporate actions. Shareholders' liability, therefore, is limited to their investment in the corporation. For example, in 1977 Big O Tire Dealers sued Goodyear Tire & Rubber Company. Big O Tire accused Goodyear of copying its BIGFOOT trademark on new tires. The court agreed and awarded Big O Tire several million dollars in damages. The Goodyear corporation, and not individual Goodyear shareholders, paid the damages. Although payment of damages to Big O Tire may have reduced the dividends shareholders received, the court did not hold the shareholders individually liable for any portion of the award.

FREE TRANSFERABILITY OF CORPORATE SHARES

Generally, shareholders can freely transfer their corporate shares. For example, shareholders can sell their shares or give them to charity.

PERPETUAL EXISTENCE

The life of a corporation does not end when the lives of its owners end. If shareholders die, corporations do not dissolve. Similarly, if corporate directors or officers withdraw or die, the corporation continues to exist. In some cases, the *articles of incorporation,* a document a corporation files with the state explaining its organization, may include a restriction on the duration of the corporation. Otherwise, in most states, corporations continue to exist indefinitely.

A small number of states, however, set a maximum length of existence for corporations. After the maximum duration expires, corporations must formally renew their corporate existence.

CENTRALIZED MANAGEMENT

Unless the articles of incorporation specify otherwise, shareholders do not participate in corporate management. Instead, shareholders elect a board of directors. The board, in turn, selects officers to manage the day-to-day business of the corporation.

CORPORATE TAXATION

Because corporations are separate legal entities, government taxes their income directly (S corporations are an exception; this chapter discusses them, and their tax advantages, in detail later). Corporations must pay federal and state taxes on their income.

Corporations, however, have control over their income. Corporations can distribute their income to shareholders in the form of **dividends,** although they do not receive tax deductions for distributing these dividends. When corporations distribute income to shareholders, the shareholders pay taxes on that income. Because the corporation pays income taxes and the shareholders are also paying taxes on their dividends, the dividends are subjected to double taxation, thus creating a disadvantage for corporations. Alternatively, corporations can keep profits, or **retained earnings,** to reinvest. Corporations' investment of retained earnings can lead to higher stock prices, thus benefiting shareholders when they sell their stock.

dividend
A distribution of corporate profits or income ordered by the directors and paid to the shareholders.

retained earnings
Profits that a corporation keeps.

LIABILITY FOR OFFICERS AND EMPLOYEES

Because the relationship between corporations and their directors, officers, and employees is an agency relationship, corporations are liable for torts and crimes committed by their agents during the scope of their employment. Courts refer to this liability as the doctrine of *respondeat superior* (Latin for "let the master answer"). Although in the past courts were reluctant to impose criminal liability on corporations, prosecutions today are much more common.

LO 22-1

Exhibit 22-1 presents a summary of nine characteristics of corporations.

Corporate Powers

Because corporations are creatures of the state, they have only those powers states grant them. States give powers to corporations through state incorporation statutes and through each corporation's articles of incorporation.

EXPRESS AND IMPLIED POWERS

State incorporation statutes typically grant the following express powers to corporations: the power to have perpetual existence, the power to sue and be sued in the corporation's name, the power to acquire property, the power to make contracts and borrow money, the power to lend money, the power to make charitable

Exhibit 22-1

Characteristics of Corporations

1. Separate legal entity
2. Status as "legal person" and "citizen"
3. Creature of the state
4. Limited liability of shareholders
5. Free transferability of corporate shares
6. Perpetual existence
7. Centralized management separate from owners
8. Unique taxation method
9. Corporate liability for torts and crimes of agents

donations, and the power to establish rules for managing the corporation. Additionally, corporations may take whatever actions are necessary to execute these express powers. Thus, corporations have implied powers. Generally, the statement of corporate purpose in each corporation's articles of incorporation gives each corporation its implied powers.

ULTRA VIRES ACT

If corporations act beyond their express and implied powers, the act is called an *ultra vires* (Latin for "beyond powers") act. Corporations commit *ultra vires* acts most frequently when they create contracts outside the scope of their powers.

Today, most state incorporation statutes permit businesses to incorporate for any lawful purpose, and thus most articles of corporation do not limit corporate powers. Hence, the doctrine of *ultra vires* is much less significant today than it was in the past because very few corporate acts qualify as *ultra vires*.

Historically, courts have ruled that *ultra vires* acts are null and void. More recently, however, courts have permitted corporations to use the *ultra vires* defense if neither party to the contract has performed the terms of the contract. Yet courts uphold *ultra vires* contracts if one of the parties has executed her or his part of the contract.

For example, suppose a timber corporation's articles of incorporation specified that the corporation's purpose was to harvest and sell timber. Suppose further that the directors of the corporation entered into an *ultra vires* contract with a machinery company to purchase machines to mine coal on the corporation's cleared land. As long as the machinery company has not delivered the machinery to the timber corporation, courts will hold the contract null and void. If, however, the machinery company has delivered the machinery to the timber corporation, courts will uphold the *ultra vires* contract and require that the timber corporation fulfill the terms of the contract. Can you see which party the court is trying to protect by upholding the *ultra vires* contract in this situation?

If a corporation commits an *ultra vires* act, RMBCA provides several remedies:

1. Shareholders may sue to prohibit the corporation from fulfilling the *ultra vires* contract.
2. The corporation or shareholders may sue corporate directors or officers for the damages caused by the *ultra vires* act.
3. The state attorney general can have the corporation dissolved or prevent the corporation from fulfilling the *ultra vires* contract.

Classification of Corporations

Corporations can be classified as public or private; profit or nonprofit; domestic, foreign, or alien; publicly or closely held; S corporations; or professional corporations.

public corporation
A corporation that is created by government to help administer law.

private corporation
A corporation that is created by private persons and does not have government duties.

PUBLIC OR PRIVATE

A **public corporation** is a corporation created by government to help administer law. Thus, public corporations often have specific government duties to fulfill. The Federal Deposit Insurance Corporation (FDIC) is an example of a public corporation. In contrast, private persons create **private corporations** for private purposes. Private corporations do not have government duties.

for-profit corporation
A corporation whose objective is to make a profit.

PROFIT OR NONPROFIT

Most corporations are **for-profit corporations**. Thus, their objective is to operate for profit. Shareholders seeking to make a profit purchase the stock these corporations issue. This profit can

take two forms. First, shareholders receive dividends from the corporation. Second, the market price of the stock can increase. Shareholders can then sell their stock at a higher price than the purchase price of the stock.

Nonprofit corporations may earn profits, but they do not distribute these profits to shareholders. In fact, nonprofit corporations do not have shareholders. More important, nonprofit corporations' objective is not to earn profit. They do not issue stock. Instead, nonprofit corporations provide services to their members (not shareholders). These corporations reinvest most of their profits in the business. Churches and charitable organizations are examples of nonprofit corporations.

nonprofit corporation
A corporation that operates for educational, charitable, social, religious, civic, or humanitarian purposes, rather than to earn a profit.

DOMESTIC, FOREIGN, AND ALIEN CORPORATIONS

Every corporation is incorporated in a particular state. A corporation is a **domestic corporation** in the state in which it is incorporated. Many corporations, however, do business in more than one state. A corporation that does business in states other than the state in which it is incorporated must obtain a certificate of authority in each state in which it does business. A corporation is a **foreign corporation** in states in which it conducts business but is not incorporated. For example, the McDonald's Corporation is incorporated in Delaware but does business in all 50 states. Thus, McDonald's is a domestic corporation in Delaware and a foreign corporation in the other 49 states.

An **alien corporation** is a business incorporated in another country. Thus, if a U.S. corporation wants to do business in Canada or Mexico, it is an alien corporation in those countries.

domestic corporation
A corporation in the state in which it is incorporated.

foreign corporation
A corporation in a state in which it conducts business but is not incorporated.

alien corporation
A business that is incorporated in a foreign country.

PUBLICLY HELD OR CLOSELY HELD

The stock of **publicly held corporations** is available to the public. Thus, if you want to invest in a corporation, you could purchase stock in a publicly held corporation. Most publicly held corporations have many shareholders, and managers of these corporations usually do not own large percentages of the corporation's stock. Shareholders wishing to sell their shares do not face many transfer restrictions.

In contrast, **closely held corporations** (also called *close, family,* or *privately held corporations*) generally do not offer stock to the general public. Shareholders are usually family members and friends who are often active in the business. Controlling shareholders typically manage closely held corporations. Because closely held corporations are often family businesses, they often maintain restrictions on the transfer of shares to prevent outsiders from obtaining control of the business. Although they account for only a small fraction of corporate assets and revenues, most U.S. corporations are closely held corporations.

publicly held corporation
A corporation whose stock is available to the public.

closely held corporation
A corporation that does not sell stock to the general public.

SUBCHAPTER S CORPORATION

S corporations are named after the subchapter of the Internal Revenue Code that provides for them. They are a particular type of closely held corporation. Government taxes S corporations differently from other corporations. Government taxes most corporations twice on their income: Corporations must pay income tax, and shareholders must pay taxes on dividends they receive. S corporations, however, enjoy the tax status of partnerships. Thus, shareholders of S corporations report their income from the corporation as personal income.

In addition to the avoidance of double taxation, S corporations offer two more important tax advantages. First, shareholders in an S corporation are allowed to deduct corporate losses from their personal income, ultimately lowering how much the shareholders have to pay in taxes. Second, depending on a shareholder's income, choosing to be an S corporation can result in the corporation's paying lower taxes.

To be classified as an S corporation, a corporation must meet certain requirements. First, it cannot have more than 100 shareholders. Second, only individuals, trusts, and (in certain circumstances) corporations can be shareholders (partnerships cannot be shareholders). Third,

S corporation
A corporation that enjoys the tax status of a partnership.

S corporations can issue only one class of shares, although not all shares must have identical voting rights. Fourth, all S corporations must be domestic corporations. Fifth, no shareholder of an S corporation can be a nonresident alien.

PROFESSIONAL CORPORATION

If a group of dentists, doctors, or other professionals wants to practice as a corporation, all 50 states permit them to incorporate. Because of the nature of professional work, however, courts sometimes alter the liability associated with such corporations. For example, courts often impose personal liability on doctors in professional corporations for medical malpractice performed under their oversight.

LO 22-2

Formation of the Corporation

The creation of a corporation involves two parts: general organizational activities and legal activities necessary for incorporation.

ORGANIZING AND PROMOTING THE CORPORATION

Two groups of important players are responsible for the organization of the corporation: promoters and subscribers.

promoter
A person who begins the corporate creation and organization process.

subscription agreement
An agreement between promoters (persons raising capital for a new corporation) and subscribers (investors), in which the subscribers agree to purchase stock in the new corporation.

subscriber
An investor who agrees to purchase stock in a new corporation.

Promoters **Promoters** begin the corporate creation and organization process by arranging for necessary capital, financing, and licenses. Promoters raise capital for the infant corporation by making **subscription agreements** with **subscribers** (investors) in which the subscribers agree to purchase stock in the new corporation.

Promoters have other organizational responsibilities besides making subscription agreements. For example, promoters prepare the corporation's incorporation papers. Promoters can also enter into contracts as needed to establish the new corporation. For example, promoters can purchase or lease buildings for the corporation. Frank Seiberling was the promoter who founded the Goodyear Tire & Rubber Company. In 1898, Seiberling purchased Goodyear's first plant in Akron, Ohio, with $3,500 borrowed from his brother-in-law. Seiberling also established Goodyear workers' hourly wages between 13 and 25 cents.

When problems with preincorporation contracts arise, courts generally hold promoters liable and rule that these contracts do not bind infant corporations. Courts usually hold that promoters are not agents of the infant corporation because promoters cannot serve as agents for a principal (the new corporation) that does not yet exist.

Once incorporated, however, corporations can accept or reject preincorporation agreements. However, even if a corporation accepts a preincorporation agreement, courts usually still hold promoters liable for the contract.

Subscribers Subscribers make offers to purchase stock in a corporation in the incorporation process. A subscriber becomes a shareholder once the corporation incorporates or accepts her purchase offer, whichever occurs first.

SELECTING A STATE FOR INCORPORATION

Next, an infant corporation must select a state in which to incorporate. Each state has different laws governing the incorporation process and different corporate tax rates. Other factors corporations consider when selecting a state for incorporation include the following:

• How much flexibility does the state grant to corporate management?

• What rights do state statutes give to shareholders?

- What restrictions does the state place on the distribution of dividends?

- Does the state offer any kind of protection against takeovers?

Although most corporations incorporate in the state in which they are located and do most of their business, more than half of all publicly held corporations, including more than half of the Fortune 500 companies, are incorporated in Delaware. Decades ago, Delaware law offered extremely low corporate tax rates and granted more extensive rights to management in the event of a takeover than did other states. Thus, in the 1940s and 1950s, many corporations changed their state of incorporation to Delaware. Since then, other states have made their corporate laws more attractive to corporations. Many corporations remain incorporated in Delaware, however, because Delaware courts are highly experienced in issues involving corporate law.

Closely held corporations and professional corporations, however, almost always incorporate in the state in which most of their stockholders live.

Although a corporation can incorporate in only one state, it can file a certificate of authority to do business in other states. Some states fine corporations that fail to obtain a certificate of authority before conducting business in the state. Other states fine directors and officers of these corporations directly and hold them personally liable for contracts made in the state.

Once a corporation chooses a state for incorporation, it can begin the formal legal process of incorporation.

Legal Process of Incorporation

SELECTION OF CORPORATE NAME

All state incorporation statutes require that corporations indicate in the name of the corporation that the business is incorporated. Every corporation must attach *Corporation, Company, Limited,* or *Incorporated,* or an abbreviation of one of these terms, to the end of its business name. Additionally, every corporation must distinguish its name from the names of all other domestic or foreign corporations licensed to do business within the state. This requirement protects third parties from confusion about similar names. Once the corporation has chosen a name, this name is subject to the approval of the state.

INCORPORATORS

An **incorporator** is an individual who applies to the state for incorporation on behalf of a corporation. RMBCA requires only one incorporator to incorporate a business, although it permits more. Generally, the incorporators' only duty is to sign the articles of incorporation.

incorporator
An individual who applies for incorporation on behalf of a corporation.

ARTICLES OF INCORPORATION

One of the most important elements of the corporate formation process is the **articles of incorporation,** a document providing basic information about the corporation. According to RMBCA, a corporation's articles of incorporation must include (1) the name of the corporation, (2) the address of the registered office, (3) the name of the registered agent (i.e., the specific person who receives legal documents on behalf of the corporation), and (4) the names and addresses of the incorporators.

The incorporators must execute and sign the articles of incorporation and file the document with the secretary of state, including the required filing fee, to legally form the corporation. Once the incorporators file the document, it governs the corporation. Next, the secretary of state usually issues a **certificate of incorporation,** a document certifying that the corporation is incorporated in the state and is authorized to conduct business.

articles of incorporation
A document that contains basic information about a corporation and is filed with the state.

certificate of incorporation
A document certifying that a corporation is incorporated in the state and is authorized to conduct business.

FIRST ORGANIZATIONAL MEETING

After the secretary of state issues the certificate of incorporation, the shareholders meet to elect the corporate board of directors, pass corporate bylaws, and carry out other corporate business. In some cases, however, shareholders name the board of directors before the first organizational meeting and list the board members in the articles of incorporation. In these situations, the directors usually run the meeting.

At the first organizational meeting, shareholders adopt a set of corporate bylaws, or rules and regulations that govern the corporation's internal management. The articles of incorporation determine who has the power to amend the corporate bylaws after the first organizational meeting: shareholders, directors, or both.

bylaws
Rules and regulations that govern a corporation's internal management.

Potential Problems with Formation of the Corporation

Most businesses incorporate to enjoy limited liability or the perpetual existence of the corporation. Shareholders enjoy these benefits, however, only if the promoters and incorporator formally and correctly incorporate the business. If the incorporator or promoters make an error or omission during the incorporation process, courts may rule that the organization is not a corporation. In this case, the organization is a **defective corporation.** Shareholders may be personally liable for a defective corporation's actions.

defective corporation
A corporation about which an error or omission was made during its incorporation process.

RESPONSES TO DEFECTIVE INCORPORATION

Suppose an incorporator incorrectly indicates the address of the corporate office in the articles of incorporation. Does the corporation still exist? Depending on the seriousness of the error, courts may disregard an error in the articles of incorporation by recognizing the corporation as a *de jure* or *de facto* corporation.

De Jure Corporations A *de jure* **corporation** (literally, a "lawful corporation") has met the substantial elements of the incorporation process. A corporation that has received its certificate of incorporation has met the mandatory statutory provisions and is thus a *de jure* corporation. Courts usually hold that corporations that make minor errors in the incorporation process still enjoy *de jure* corporate status. Figure 22-1 illustrates the process for creating a *de jure* corporation.

Thus, even if the incorporator wrote the incorrect address of the corporate office in the articles of incorporation, courts would not revoke the corporation's limited liability. No party can question a *de jure* corporation's status as a corporate entity in court.

de jure **corporation**
Latin for "lawful corporation"; a corporation that has met the mandatory statutory provisions and thus received its certificate of incorporation.

Figure 22-1

De Jure Corporation Formation

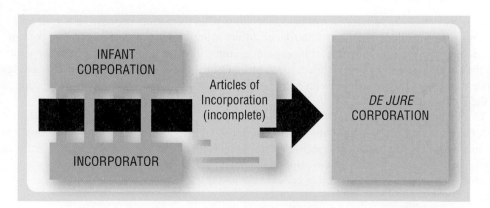

Corporate Structure in China

As you may expect, corporate governance varies among countries. Specifically, there are countries that have a one-tier board system (as in the United States), and there are others that have a two-tier board system. In a one-tier board all directors (both executive directors and nonexecutive directors) form one board. A two-tier board consists of a management board (all executive directors) and a separate supervisory board (all nonexecutive directors). German corporation law, for example, requires that all corporations have two boards.

In recent years, China has followed the German model and adopted a two-tier board structure, with both a board of directors and a supervisory board. Corporations following this model are required to provide in their annual reports a supervisory board report (SBR). In China, the supervisory board has significant power to supervise directors, examine financial documents, and convene shareholder meetings. In these respects, supervisors exercise substantial control over corporate managers.

Although corporations in China are not required to have a supervisory board (unlike the case in Germany), there is usually a supervisory board that consists of shareholder representatives and an employee representative. However, the supervisory board does not always function at the level that many envisioned it would. In practice, supervisory boards in China have not functioned effectively because they do not have genuine power to select or discipline directors and managers. Furthermore, some critics argue that there is some overlap between the function of the supervisory board and that of the board of directors. What do you think are the advantages and disadvantages of the two-tier board system?

De Facto Corporation Suppose, however, that the incorporator makes a more serious mistake or omission. For example, suppose the incorporator did not file the articles of incorporation with the secretary of state. In this case, courts may recognize the corporation as a *de facto* corporation (literally, a "corporation in fact"). A *de facto* corporation has not substantially met the requirements of the state incorporation statute, but courts recognize it as a corporation for most purposes to avoid unfairness to third parties who believed it was properly incorporated. *De facto* corporations, regardless of whether the state has a general corporation statute, must meet the following requirements:

de facto corporation

Latin for "corporation in fact"; a corporation that has not substantially met the requirements of the state incorporation statutes.

• The promoters, subscribers, and incorporator made a good-faith attempt to comply with the incorporation statute.

• The organization has already conducted business as a corporation.

The process for recognizing a corporation as a *de facto* corporation is depicted in Figure 22-2. Only the state can challenge a *de facto* corporation's existence as a corporate entity.

Figure 22-2 *De Facto* Corporation Recognition Process

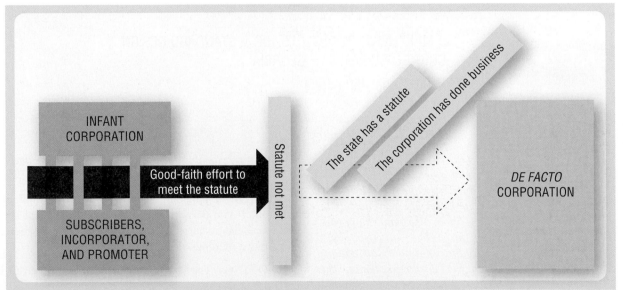

Corporation by Estoppel Defective corporations cannot escape corporate entity status due to mistakes or omissions in their incorporation procedures. For example, suppose a corporation's articles of incorporation do not include the name of its registered agent. Suppose further that the corporation's directors, managers, and shareholders are unaware of the mistake. If the corporation conducts business with a third party who later sues for breach of contract, the corporation cannot claim that it is not a corporate entity to escape liability.

In such cases, courts hold that the corporation is a **corporation by estoppel**; thus, courts *estop* (prevent) the corporation from denying its corporate status. Although a court ruling of corporation by estoppel prevents the business from denying corporate status, it does not remedy the error or grant the organization corporate status for conducting future business.

If a corporation makes a significant error in the incorporation process and is not a *de jure* or *de facto* corporation, and corporation by estoppel does not apply to the situation, courts usually deny the organization corporate entity status. Thus, the organization does not enjoy limited shareholder liability.

corporation by estoppel

A defective corporation that has conducted business with a third party and therefore cannot deny its status as a corporation to escape liability.

Piercing the Corporate Veil In some cases, courts will deny limited liability to a corporation that would normally have *de jure* or *de facto* status because shareholders have used the corporation to engage in illegal or wrongful acts. Shareholders attempt to hide behind the "corporate veil" of limited liability to protect themselves from personal liability. In these cases, courts *pierce the corporate veil,* or impose personal liability on shareholders. Courts are likely to pierce the corporate veil when:

- A corporation lacked adequate capital when it initially formed.
- A corporation did not follow statutory mandates regarding corporate business.
- Shareholders' personal interests and corporate interests are commingled such that the corporation has no separate identity.
- Shareholders attempt to commit fraud through a corporation.

For example, corporations must keep corporate funds and records separate from shareholder funds and records. If a corporation does not carefully maintain these separate records, courts may pierce the corporate veil and impose personal liability on shareholders, as Case 22-1 illustrates.

CASE 22-1

J-MART JEWELRY OUTLETS, INC. v. STANDARD DESIGN
COURT OF APPEALS OF GEORGIA
218 Ga. App. 459 (1995)

FACTS: *Jim Halter, the major shareholder of J-Mart Jewelry Outlets, Inc., and several other corporations, was aware that J-Mart was in financial trouble. Before J-Mart went out of business, Halter paid off his personal credit cards using corporate funds. Halter also paid the corporation $1 for a corporate car purchased with corporation funding. Four of J-Mart's creditors brought suit against Halter in an attempt to recover corporate funds. The trial court jury pierced the corporate veil to hold Halter* *personally responsible for the debts. Halter appealed the court's denial of his request for a directed verdict.*

ISSUE: Has the appellant used his position as the major shareholder of a corporation to disregard the legal separation between a shareholder and the corporation, thereby permitting a piercing of the corporate veil?

REASONING: The judge argued that for the veil to be pierced,

[t]here must be evidence of abuse of the corporate form. Plaintiff must show that the defendant disregarded the separateness of legal entities by commingling on an interchangeable or joint basis or confusing the otherwise separate properties, records or control. . . .

Halter knew as early as late April but not later than June 1991 that J-Mart would have to cease operations as a result of its financial difficulties. There was direct evidence that the $6,902.87 balance on Halter's American Express personal account was paid by J-Mart on December 23, 1991, eight days before it ceased doing business. The check was marked "PAYMENT IN FULL: JIM'S PERSONAL[,]" indicating that a material question of fact existed as to whether Halter used corporate funds to pay a personal debt. The evidence also established that J-Mart, with knowledge that it would soon cease doing business, purchased a new Cadillac for Halter's use. It thereafter made three payments on the vehicle before transferring it to Halter for

$1 and allowing him to assume the remaining payments, indicating the presence of further questions of material fact relative to a *de facto* unauthorized payment for Halter's personal benefit.

DECISION AND REMEDY: The court determined that "[i]n light of the evidence presented, the trial court properly denied the motion for a directed verdict upon the claim of Halter's personal liability for violation of the corporate form. . . . On appeal, we construe all the evidence most strongly in support of the verdict. . . . [T]he jury's verdict was proper and must stand."

SIGNIFICANCE OF THE CASE: This case illustrates the requirements that a plaintiff must meet to establish a basis for piercing the corporate veil and affirms the jury's role in judging material questions of fact in these cases.

CRITICAL THINKING

Given what you know of the facts of the case, is there any information Halter could have provided that would lead you to believe that he was not responsible for the debts? What would this information be?

ETHICAL DECISION MAKING

Describe the ethical conflict Halter was facing. For what purpose, or value, was he acting? Had Halter followed the Golden Rule, would he have chosen to act in the way he did? Given this information, what could have been done to convince Halter to refrain from using corporate funds to pay off his personal credit cards?

Corporate Financing

Corporations, like other businesses, need a source of funding. Corporations most commonly obtain financing by issuing and selling corporate securities: **debt securities** (bonds), which represent loans to a corporation, and **equity securities** (stocks), which represent ownership in a corporation.

debt securities
Securities that represent loans to a corporation.

DEBT SECURITIES

Debt securities, or bonds, represent loans to a corporation from another party. Bonds are usually long-term loans on which the corporation promises to pay interest. Bonds frequently list a maturity date on which the corporation must repay the face amount of the loan. Before the maturity date, however, corporations usually pay bondholders fixed-dollar interest payments on a scheduled basis. Hence, bonds are sometimes called *fixed-income securities.*

equity securities
Securities that represent ownership in a corporation.

EQUITY SECURITIES

Stocks and bonds are not identical. While bond owners have loaned money to a corporation, stock owners actually own part of a corporation. Thus, while bond owners have no voice in

corporate management, stockholders have a voice in control of the corporation. Not all corporations issue bonds, but all for-profit issue stock. Common stock and preferred stock are the two major types of stock.

preferred stock
Stock that conveys preferences to its holders with respect to assets and dividends.

Preferred Stock Owners of **preferred stock,** or *preferred shares,* enjoy preferences with respect to assets and dividends. Corporations often have several classes of preferred shares. Preferred stock shares many characteristics with bonds. For example, preferred stock owners usually receive a percentage of dividends associated with the face value of their preferred stock. Furthermore, corporations pay dividends to owners of preferred stock before they pay owners of common stock. Some corporations limit preferred stock owners' voting rights.

common stock
Corporate stock that does not convey any preferences to its holders.

Common Stock Owners of **common stock,** or *common shares,* own a portion of a corporation but do not enjoy any preferences. A common stock owner is entitled to a portion of the corporation's dividends in proportion to the number of shares of common stock she owns. Common stock owners also have the right to vote in corporate elections. Each share is usually worth one vote in corporate elections. Thus, if you own 20,000 common shares of a corporation, you have 20,000 votes. In some cases, however, most notably the election of the board of directors, corporations use a method called *cumulative voting* to increase the influence of shareholders who own a small number of shares.

Common stock owners have the lowest priority when a corporation distributes dividends. Creditors and preferred stock owners receive dividends first. Once a corporation pays these groups, however, common stock owners have a claim to the remainder of the corporate earnings.

Importance of Regulating Interactions among Directors, Officers, and Shareholders within a Corporation

The three major groups of individuals within a corporation are *directors, officers,* and *shareholders.* All three groups have different interests, and in many situations the interests of one group conflict with the interests of another. Statutory law provides rules to ensure that the directors, officers, and shareholders within a corporation work together to the benefit of all involved.

Although directors and officers play different roles within the corporation, they share the same goal. Both directors and officers attempt to ensure that their institution survives and that they keep their jobs. Shareholders, on the other hand, have a different agenda. Their goal is to raise the value of the company's stock.

These different agendas can lead to conflict within corporations. If a corporation has an opportunity to make a decision that will raise the value of its stock quickly, shareholders will push the directors and officers to make this decision. However, if the directors and officers believe that the decision might jeopardize their jobs, they will resist the pressure of the shareholders. To resolve these conflicts, the law gives legal duties and rights to different groups within the corporation.

LO 22-3

Roles of Directors, Officers, and Shareholders

Before discussing the duties and rights of each position within the corporation, it is important to understand the specific roles that directors, officers, and shareholders play. The rights and duties of each group of individuals are dependent on these roles.

DIRECTORS' ROLES

Directors play a vital role within every corporation. When a corporation faces important decisions, the board of directors meets to decide what course of action the corporation will take.

Elections Typically, shareholders use a majority vote to elect directors. The only exception occurs during incorporation. Because there are no shareholders in the beginning, either the incorporators appoint board members or the corporate articles name the board members. This first board then serves until the first shareholder meeting, at which the shareholders elect a new board. The corporate articles or bylaws specify the number of corporate directors.

In the past, the minimum number of directors required was three, but today many states allow fewer. In fact, if a corporation has fewer than 50 shareholders, Section 7.32 of RMBCA allows companies to eliminate the board of directors altogether.

Interestingly, almost anyone can become a director. The legal requirements for director qualification are incredibly lax. In most states, directors are not even required to own stock in the corporation. In some cases, however, statutory law and corporate bylaws require not only ownership but also a minimum age.

Directors typically serve for one year, but most state statutes allow for longer terms if the terms of the various directors are staggered. These terms can be terminated and the directors can be removed from their positions *for cause*—for failing to perform a required duty. Directors who are removed for cause, however, can ask the courts to review the legality of the removal.

Meetings and Voting A minimum number of directors, or a quorum, must be present at each meeting of the board of directors for decisions made at the meeting to be valid. Quorum requirements are different in each state, but most states leave the decision up to the corporation itself. Because a quorum is required at each meeting, directors are notified whenever special meetings are called. Directors vote in person, and each director has one vote. While ordinary decisions require a majority vote, more important decisions sometimes require a two-thirds vote.

Directors as Managers Although directors meet to vote on major decisions about the corporation, they are also responsible for many day-to-day managerial activities of the company. The directors appoint, supervise, and remove corporate officers as they see fit, and they declare and pay corporate dividends to shareholders. They are also responsible for making financial decisions and authorizing corporate policy decisions. Some directors are also officers or employees of the corporation; these directors are known as *inside directors*. Directors who are not officers or employees of the corporation are called *outside directors*. Outside directors are further divided into two groups: *affiliated directors* and *unaffiliated directors*. Affiliated directors have business contacts with the corporation, while unaffiliated directors do not.

Because the day-to-day tasks of a corporation can be overwhelming for a small board of directors that has larger issues to address, directors often appoint an executive committee to handle day-to-day responsibilities.

OFFICERS' ROLES

Officers are executive managers whom the board of directors hires to run the organization. While directors are in charge of major policy decisions, officers run the day-to-day business of the corporation. Officers act as agents of the corporation, and thus the rules of agency apply to their work.

Qualifications required of officers are set forth in the corporate articles and bylaws of each corporation, but in most cases an individual may serve as both a director and an officer. Many corporations find it beneficial to include an officer on their board of directors so that the board can stay in touch with the day-to-day operations of the company.

SHAREHOLDERS' ROLES

Shareholders own the firm. As soon as an individual purchases the stock of a particular corporation, she becomes an owner of the corporation. While she is not legally recognized as an owner of corporate property, she has an *equitable,* or ownership, interest in the company. Shareholders are not directly responsible for the daily management of the corporation, but they elect the directors who are responsible for that management.

Power of Shareholders The articles of incorporation established within each corporation and general incorporation law in each state grant shareholders certain powers within the institution. Because shareholders must approve major corporate decisions, they are in a sense empowered to make major decisions for the corporation.

Their most influential power, however, is the power to elect and remove members of the board of directors. The board of directors is responsible for making crucial policy decisions for the corporation, and the shareholders have the power to decide who the directors will be.

Shareholders also have the power to propose ideas for the corporation. If a shareholder feels that he has a worthwhile idea for the company, he can include his proposal in the *proxy materials* sent out to the shareholders before their annual meeting. The Securities and Exchange Commission (SEC) has established that any shareholder who owns more than $1,000 worth of stock in the corporation can submit proposals to be included in proxy materials.

Meetings Typically, shareholders meet once a year, but in emergencies they can meet more often. The board of directors, shareholders who own at least 10 percent of the corporation's outstanding shares, and others authorized in the articles of incorporation may call a special shareholder meeting. Before each meeting, each shareholder receives notice of the time and place of the meeting. If the meeting is a special meeting, the purpose of the meeting is also included in the notice.

Like directors' meetings, shareholder meetings require a quorum. Generally, a quorum of shareholders exists when shareholders holding more than 50 percent of the outstanding shares are present. Once a quorum is present, a majority vote of the shares represented at the meeting is required to pass resolutions. Occasionally, however, articles of incorporation include supermajority provisions, which state that more than a majority is needed to pass major corporate proposals, such as corporate merger or dissolution.

Voting Like directors, each shareholder is entitled to one vote per share in most instances. Corporations practice unique voting processes, however, that alter the influence of each shareholder's votes. These voting processes are especially important for minority shareholders within a corporation. One voting process required in most states, called *cumulative voting,* ensures that minority shareholders have a voice in electing the board of directors.

The cumulative-voting process divides shareholders into majority and minority shareholders, and each group has a certain number of votes to cast in the election. The number of votes is determined by multiplying the number of shares the group owns by the number of open director positions. If a company is electing eight directors and the minority shareholders own 2,000 shares, the minority shareholders get 16,000 votes to cast in the election. If the majority shareholders in the same corporation own 8,000 shares, they get 64,000 votes.

Although it may seem that the minority shareholders have little influence in the election, the cumulative-voting process permits them to vote at least one director onto the board because they can cast all of their votes for one candidate. If the majority shareholders wish to elect all eight directors from their nominees, each nominee must receive more than 16,000 votes in order to beat the 16,000 votes of the minority nominee. However, because the majority shareholders have only 64,000 votes to cast in the election, they cannot cast more than 16,000 votes for eight candidates ($16,000 \times 8 = 128,000$). Thus, if the minority shareholders cast all of their 16,000 votes for one candidate, they guarantee that candidate's election.

Cumulative voting is more egalitarian than simple majority voting because it ensures that every voice within the corporation is heard. Cumulative voting, however, occurs only when the corporation's articles of incorporation provide for it.

Exhibit 22-2 summarizes the respective roles of directors, officers, and shareholders.

POSITION	ROLES
Directors	Vote on important corporate decisions.
	Appoint and supervise officers.
	Declare and pay corporate dividends.
	Manage the corporation.
Officers	Run the day-to-day business of the firm.
	Act as agents of the corporation.
Shareholders	Elect a board of directors.
	Approve major decisions of the board.

Exhibit 22-2

Roles of
Directors, Officers,
and Shareholders

Duties of Directors, Officers, and Shareholders

LO 22-4

Because all individuals within a corporation depend on one another, the law requires that directors, officers, and shareholders perform certain duties within the business. In other words, individuals within the corporation have legal responsibilities to the corporation. These duties to the corporation are called *fiduciary duties.* Because individuals play different roles within the corporation, the fiduciary duties of individuals depend on whether they are directors, officers, or shareholders.

DUTIES OF DIRECTORS AND OFFICERS

Because the owners of the corporation, the shareholders, have little input in the day-to-day operations of the corporation, they trust the directors and officers to run the company to the best of their ability. Thus, directors and officers have duties to the shareholders and to the corporation. The two primary fiduciary duties of directors and officers are the duty of care and the duty of loyalty.

Duty of Care Directors and officers have a fiduciary *duty of care,* meaning that they must exercise *due care* when making decisions for the corporation. The phrase *due care* is ambiguous and various courts have interpreted it differently over time. In general, however, acting with due care requires that one exercise the care that an ordinary prudent person would exercise in the management of her own assets.

Because directors and officers have a duty to act in the best interest of the company, they must supervise, to a reasonable extent, employees who work for the corporation. They also have a duty to attend director and corporate business meetings. Most important, however, directors and officers have a fiduciary duty to make informed and reasonable business decisions.

The directors and officers of Enron failed in their duty of care with regard to their shareholders by not acting in the best interest of the company. The directors and officers continued to urge employees to invest in the employee stock-sharing options, even though it appears that the directors and officers knew the stock was drastically overpriced. Furthermore, the directors and officers failed in their duty of care regarding oversight. They either did not pay enough attention to see the collapse of the company's stock coming or purposely kept the information secret. Either way, the directors and officers at Enron breached their fiduciary duty of care and therefore are liable to their shareholders, many of whom were employees of Enron.

Directors and officers are expected to stay abreast of all important corporate matters. In other words, they must obtain information about business transactions, review contracts, read reports, and attend presentations. Because some directors are too busy to stay informed on every

When a B2B Company Cooks the Books

When a business student thinks about companies that "cook the books," it is not surprising that companies such as Enron, Tyco, and Adelphia come to mind. Issues related to the duty of care of officers and directors are expressed in questions such as, "Why did the officers and directors of the company fail to realize accountants were cooking company books? Were any officers or directors involved in the fraud?"

Students may have to revise their images of corrupt companies by adding business-to-business (B2B) e-commerce companies to their Enron-Tyco-Adelphia list. They may have to ask, "Why did the officers and directors of an *e-commerce business* fail to realize accountants were cooking company books? Were any officers or directors involved in the fraud?"

PurchasePro is one example of an e-commerce company that allegedly engaged in "overstating revenues, engaging in aggressive accounting practices and mismanaging corporate assets." Basically, the company manipulated its financial records to make it look far more successful than it really was. PurchasePro, which provided a business-to-business software application that gave companies access to an online marketplace, went bankrupt in September 2002.

Federal prosecutors charged company officers and directors with conspiracy, securities fraud, and obstruction of justice. Two senior officers, Jeffrey R. Anderson and Scott H. Miller, pleaded guilty to federal crimes in 2003. Their behavior was similar to that of officers of other, more well-known companies that have cooked the books—they had secret side deals with purchasers that gave the appearance of sales but the sales did not exist; they misrepresented the company's financial health, so investors could not make informed decisions; and, when news of alleged fraud surfaced, the officers used their energy to shred incriminating documents.

subject, RMBCA allows directors to make decisions on the basis of information gathered by other employees.

The decisions that corporate directors and officers make must not only be informed, however, but also be reasonable. If a director or officer is taken to court for breaching his duty of care by making an unreasonable decision, the court typically inquires whether the decision had any rational business purpose. In other words, the courts ask whether there was good reason to think that the decision *could* have helped the company.

Part of the duty of care a director or officer owes a corporation, as was previously stated, is to act in the corporation's best interest. Therefore, when the corporation is doing something the director or officer does not think is in its best interest, it is up to her to voice her dissent.

Duty of Loyalty Because directors and officers have great decision-making freedom, they have the power to make business decisions that will benefit themselves while harming the company. Thus, to protect shareholders, directors and officers have a fiduciary *duty of loyalty.* In other words, they have a fiduciary duty to put the corporation's interest above their own when making business decisions.

self-dealing

Any instance in which directors or officers make decisions that violate their corporate duty of loyalty.

When directors or officers violate their duty of loyalty, they are **self-dealing.** There are two types of self-dealing in which a director or officer can engage. The first form of self-dealing, called *business self-dealing,* occurs when a director or officer makes decisions that benefit other companies with which he has a relationship. The second form of self-dealing, called *personal self-dealing,* occurs when a director or officer makes business decisions that benefit her personally. When Enron directors and officers advocated that employees buy more Enron stock so that the directors and officers would make more money, they engaged in self-dealing in breach of their fiduciary duty of loyalty.

In many situations, when a director or officer is self-dealing, he forces the corporation into unfair business deals. Directors and officers can also breach their fiduciary duty of loyalty, however, by *preventing* corporate opportunity. This breach usually happens when directors or officers own other companies that compete with their corporation without the consent of the board of directors or the shareholders. If a director or officer uses corporate assets to start another business, goes into the same line of business, or uses her position in the company to develop a new business that the company might have pursued, she is preventing corporate opportunity and can be held liable for violating her fiduciary duty of loyalty.

CASE Nugget

How Should Directors Handle Personal Interests That Conflict with Corporate Interests?

Patrick v. Allen
United States District Court, S.D. New York

355 F. Supp. 2d 704 (2005)

RPO, a privately traded corporation, rented land to a private golf course of which several of RPO's directors were members. The directors charged the golf course enough rent to cover only the property taxes on the land. Patrick, a shareholder of RPO, brought a suit against the directors of RPO, alleging that RPO's directors breached their fiduciary duty of loyalty to the corporation by failing to maximize the value of the corporation for shareholders. The directors argued that they were exempt from liability under the business judgment rule. (The business judgment rule is covered in the section below entitled "Liabilities of Directors, Officers, and Shareholders.")

The U.S. District Court for the Southern District of New York ruled against the RPO's directors, holding:

> The business judgment rule will not protect a decision that was the product of fraud, self-dealing, or bad faith. Directors may benefit from the rule only if they possess a disinterested independence and do not stand in a dual relation which prevents a nonprejudicial exercise of judgment. It is black-letter, settled law that when a corporate director or officer has an interest in a decision, the business judgment rule does not apply. . . . A director is considered interested in a transaction if the director stands to receive a direct financial benefit from the transaction which is different from the benefit to shareholders generally. . . . The duty of loyalty requires a director to subordinate his own personal interests to the interest of the corporation.

A director or officer convicted of breaching his duty of loyalty is required to cede to the corporation all the profits he earned as a result of the breach. The goal of this rule is to create incentives that discourage breaches of the duty of loyalty by taking from the director or officer all the profits that he made.

The fiduciary duties of care and loyalty are rooted in ethics. Without these legal duties, directors and officers could pursue their own interests at the expense of others. Through these fiduciary duties, however, the law requires that directors and officers consider the interests of others. Think back to Chapter 1 and the different ethical guidelines used to make ethical decisions. Which ethical guideline is the legal system using when it delegates fiduciary duties?

Duty to Disclose Conflict of Interest Because there are many times when individual directors and officers may personally benefit from decisions made by the board of directors, the directors and officers have a fiduciary duty to fully disclose conflicts of interest that arise in corporate transactions. Moreover, if the board of directors addresses an issue that might personally benefit a particular director, the director is required not only to disclose the self-interest but also to abstain from voting on that issue. Note that a decision can be made that will personally benefit one director or officer as long as (1) there is full disclosure of the interest and (2) the disinterested board members and/or disinterested shareholders approve the decision.

DUTIES OF SHAREHOLDERS

Although shareholders typically have few legal duties, in rare instances majority shareholders have fiduciary duties to the corporation and to minority shareholders. In some corporations, the majority shareholder owns such a significant portion of the corporation's stock that she

essentially controls the firm. When the majority shareholder sells her shares, control of the company shifts to another individual. Thus, the majority shareholder in this situation has a fiduciary duty to act with care and loyalty when selling her shares.

As noted earlier, more than half of all U.S. publicly traded corporations are incorporated in Delaware. Thus, when Delaware courts rule on the duties of majority shareholders to minority shareholders, for example, the courts' rulings have a far-reaching impact. In Case 22-2, brought before the supreme court of Delaware, minority shareholders sued the majority shareholder within their corporation for violating its fiduciary duties.

CASE 22-2

FRIEDA H. RABKIN v. PHILIP A. HUNT CHEMICAL CORP.
SUPREME COURT OF DELAWARE
498 A.2d 1099 (1985)

FACTS: *On March 1, 1983, Olin Corporation bought 63.4 percent of the outstanding shares of Hunt Chemical Corporation from Turner and Newall Industries, Inc., at $25 per share, which moved Olin into the position of majority shareholder. Before Turner and Newall Industries sold the shares to Olin, it insisted that Olin agree to pay $25 per share if Olin acquired the remaining Hunt stock within one year. On July 5, 1984, Hunt merged into Olin by buying out the remaining stock for $20 a share. The minority shareholders of Hunt then filed a suit against Olin that challenged the Olin-Hunt merger on the grounds that the price offered was grossly inadequate because Olin unfairly manipulated the timing of the merger to avoid the one-year commitment and that specific language in Olin's Schedule 13D, filed when it purchased the Hunt stock, constituted a price commitment by which Olin failed to abide, contrary to its fiduciary obligations to the minority shareholders. The trial judge dismissed the complaint on grounds that the only remedy legally available to the minority shareholders was an appraisal. The plaintiffs then sought and were denied leave to amend their complaints. They appealed.*

ISSUE: Did the alleged acts by Olin constitute unfair dealing that breached its fiduciary duty?

REASONING: The judge found that the allegations related to Olin's attitude toward the minority owners, together with the absence of any meaningful negotiations as to price, raised unanswered questions about the extent to which Olin fulfilled its duty of loyalty to Hunt. The court found strong-enough allegations concerning the possible avoidance of the one-year commitment to "support a claim of unfair dealing sufficient to defeat dismissal at this stage of the proceedings."

DECISION AND REMEDY: The decision was reversed because the judge found that the material facts were serious enough that a motion to dismiss should have been denied. At minimum, they constituted overreaching.

SIGNIFICANCE OF THE CASE: This case illustrates the kind of fact pattern that causes legal examination of a possible breach of fiduciary duty, and it establishes the court's reluctance to permit majority shareholders to abuse their power in relation to minority shareholders.

CRITICAL THINKING

What reasons does the court give for its conclusion? Are you persuaded by those reasons?

ETHICAL DECISION MAKING

Clearly, the court explicitly emphasizes a particular value in its ruling. What is this value? The court's vigorous emphasis of this particular value makes it difficult for the court to consider other values. Which value(s) does this ruling tend to ignore?

Liabilities of Directors, Officers, and Shareholders

Because almost all individuals within a corporation have legal fiduciary duties to the corporation, almost all individuals within the firm can be held liable for harming the business by violating these duties. There are, however, certain instances in which directors, officers, and shareholders cannot be held liable for harming the business.

LIABILITY OF DIRECTORS AND OFFICERS

Directors and officers are held liable for many of the same actions because they have nearly identical fiduciary duties to the corporation. A shareholder can sue them if the shareholder feels that they have caused harm to the business by violating their fiduciary duties. Directors and officers can be held liable for the torts and crimes of their employees.

Liability for Torts and Crimes Although the corporations themselves are liable for the torts and crimes of their directors and officers, directors and officers can also be held personally responsible for their own torts and crimes. They can even be held personally responsible for the torts and crimes of other employees within the organization when they have failed to adequately supervise the employees' behavior.

According to the *responsible person doctrine,* a court may find a corporate officer criminally liable regardless of the extent to which the officer took part in the criminal activity. Even if the officer knew nothing about the criminal activity, the officer can still be held criminally liable if the court determines that a responsible person would have known about and could have prevented the illegal activity.

Corporate directors and officers may also be held liable for wrongful personal transactions involving company stock. Directors and officers who use inside information to trade the corporation's stock for a profit can be held liable for breaching their fiduciary duty to the shareholders from whom they purchase or to whom they sell the stock.

Business Judgment Rule Although directors and officers are expected to make decisions that are in the best interest of the corporation, they are not expected to make perfect decisions all the time. Many directors and officers make decisions that inadvertently harm the corporation. Although shareholders may want to hold their directors and officers liable for these decisions, the *business judgment rule* does not allow them to do so.

Under this rule, directors and officers are not liable for decisions that harm the corporation if they were acting in good faith at the time of the decision. In other words, if there was reason to believe that the decision was a good decision at the time, the directors and officers are not liable for the resulting harm.

Although the business judgment rule is not a statute, it is common law recognized by almost every court in the country. The rule is practical because it grants directors the freedom to work without constant fear of personal liability. The business judgment rule also encourages individuals to serve as directors by removing the threat of personal liability for inadvertent mistakes.

LIABILITY OF SHAREHOLDERS

The main liability that shareholders face is liability for the debts of the corporation. Because shareholders are the owners of the corporation, they are liable to the extent of their investment when the company loses money. There are rare instances, however, in which shareholders are personally liable.

For instance, in some cases, individuals sign stock subscription agreements before incorporation. Once an individual signs a stock subscription agreement, she is contractually obligated to purchase shares in the corporation. For **par-value shares,** or shares that have a fixed face value noted on the stock certificate, the shareholder must pay the corporation at least the par value of

par-value shares
Stock shares that have a fixed face value noted on the stock certificate.

the stock. For **no-par shares,** or shares without a par value, the shareholder must pay the corporation the fair market value of the shares. The shareholder is personally liable for breach of contract if she does not buy shares.

Alternatively, a shareholder can be held personally responsible if he receives **watered stock.** Watered stock is stock issued to individuals below its fair market value. When watered stock is issued to a shareholder, the shareholder is individually liable for paying the difference between the price he paid for the shares and the stated corporate value of the shares.

LO 22-6 Rights of Directors, Officers, and Shareholders

Along with their specific roles and duties, directors, officers, and shareholders have specific rights within the corporation. Because shareholders are in a position of limited decision-making power, they have rights that allow them to participate within the corporation. Directors and officers also have specific rights that allow them to perform their duties within the corporation to the best of their abilities.

DIRECTORS' RIGHTS

The unique responsibilities of corporate directors call for unique rights. Directors have four major rights within a corporation: rights of compensation, participation, inspection, and indemnification.

All corporate directors have a *right to compensation* for their work, and different corporations grant compensation in different ways. Most directors hold other managerial positions within their companies and receive their compensation through those positions. Another common avenue for compensating directors is paying them nominal sums as honorariums for their contributions to the company.

Because directors are required to make informed business decisions, they have the *rights of participation and inspection.* In other words, they have the right to get involved in and understand every aspect of the business. A corporate director has the right to be notified of all meetings and has access to all books and records.

Finally, because directors are in positions of great legal vulnerability, they have the *right to indemnification.* That is, they have the right to reimbursement for any legal fees incurred in lawsuits against them.

OFFICERS' RIGHTS

Because corporate officers are technically employees of the corporation, their rights are defined by employment contracts drawn up by the board of directors or the incorporators. They are in a contractual relationship with the corporation, and if they are removed from their positions in violation of the terms of the contract, the corporation may be liable for breach of contract.

SHAREHOLDERS' RIGHTS

Although shareholders' most powerful right is the right to vote at shareholders' meetings, they also possess many other rights.

Stock Certificates Some corporations issue **stock certificates** to shareholders as proof of ownership in the corporation. Each certificate includes the corporation's name and the number of shares represented by the certificate. An example of a stock certificate is shown in Figure 22-3. A shareholder's ownership in the corporation, however, does not depend on his possession of the physical stock certificate. For example, if the certificate is destroyed in a fire, the shareholder's ownership in the corporation is not destroyed.

Assigned Directors in Japan

A common corporate practice in Japan is for multiple corporations, banks, and companies to form hierarchical conglomerates known as *keiretsus*. There are two types of *keiretsus*. The first is a horizontal *keiretsu,* in which a powerful bank acts as the unifying agent under which several large corporations come together. With the exception of the bank, power is shared equally among the members. The second type is a vertical *keiretsu*. In contrast to horizontal *keiretsus,* vertical *keiretsu* are hierarchically ordered with an unequal distribution of power. Large corporations often control several hundred subordinate companies.

Power distribution within *keiretsus* plays a key role in determining the board of directors. Usually the main bank or parent corporation assigns its own executives to serve on the boards of the less powerful companies. The prosperity of these companies is important to the main banks and parent corporations. The assigned directors act as overseers, consultants, and mentors. They want to promote simultaneously the interests of the parent corporation and the growth of the subordinate ones. Thus, the subordinate companies do not view the assignment of directors as a sign of mistrust. To the Japanese the logic is patent: If the success of the *keiretsu* and the success of each company are reciprocal, all parties should work together to achieve the collective goal.

Preemptive Rights Under common law, shareholders have *preemptive rights.* Preemptive rights give preference to shareholders to purchase shares of a new issue of stock. Each shareholder receives preference in proportion to the percentage of stock she already owns.

For example, suppose that a shareholder owns 1,500 shares in a corporation with 5,000 outstanding shares. She owns 30 percent of the corporation's outstanding stock. Now suppose that the corporation decides to issue an additional 10,000 shares. If the corporation does not grant preemptive rights, her relative control of the corporation will fall because she now owns only 1,500 of the corporation's 15,000 outstanding shares, or 10 percent of its stock. In contrast, if the corporation does reserve preemptive rights, and the shareholder elects to purchase 3,000 shares of the newly issued stock, then she owns 4,500 shares of the corporation's 15,000 outstanding shares (30 percent). Thus, with preemptive rights, she can maintain her proportionate control of the corporation.

In most states, a corporation's bylaws can negate preemptive rights, so the corporation determines whether to grant preemptive rights. Preemptive rights are especially important

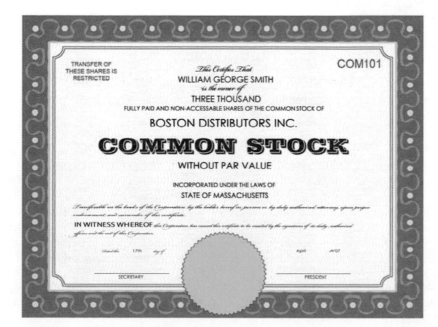

Figure 22-3

Example of a Stock Certificate

for individuals who own stock in close corporations due to the relatively small number of issued shares. If a close corporation issues additional shares, an individual shareholder may lose proportional control over the firm if he does not buy newly issued shares. However, if preemptive rights exist within the corporation, all shareholders receive **stock warrants,** which they can redeem for a certain number of shares at a specified price within a given time period.

Dividends If directors fail to declare and distribute dividends, shareholders have the right to take legal action to force the directors to declare the dividends. In many cases, however, directors have good reason to hold dividends for a limited amount of time to finance major undertakings such as research or expansion. Thus, shareholders must show that the directors are acting unreasonably and abusing their discretion in withholding the dividend.

Inspection Rights All shareholders have the right to inspection under both statutory and common law. A shareholder can, moreover, appoint an agent to conduct the inspection on her behalf. To prevent abuse, however, this right has many limitations. Shareholders can inspect records and books only if they ask in advance and have a *proper purpose.* Many states have other statutory limitations to this right. For example, some states allow only shareholders with a minimum number of shares to inspect. Other states require that the shareholder own stock for a minimum amount of time before inspection. Additionally, corporations can deny shareholders' right to inspect confidential corporate information, such as trade secrets.

Share Transfer The law generally permits property owners to transfer their property to another person, and, in most cases, stock is considered transferable property. In closely held corporations, however, the transfer of stock is usually restricted so that shareholders can choose the corporation's other shareholders.

One method of restricting stock transferability is called the **right of first refusal.** If a corporation establishes this right in its bylaws, the corporation or its shareholders have the right to purchase any shares of stock offered for resale by a shareholder within a specified period of time.

Corporate Dissolution Shareholders have the right to petition the court to dissolve their corporation if they feel the company cannot continue to operate profitably. According to Section 14.30 of RMBCA, if a corporation engages in any of the following behaviors, shareholders have a legal right to initiate dissolution.

1. Directors are deadlocked in managerial decisions and harming the corporation.
2. Directors are acting in illegal, oppressive, or fraudulent ways.
3. Assets are being wasted or used improperly.
4. Shareholders are deadlocked and cannot elect directors.

Once dissolution has taken place and the corporation has settled its debts with its creditors, shareholders have a right to receive the remaining assets of the company in proportion to the number of shares they own.

Shareholder's Derivative Suit One of the shareholder's most important rights is the right to a derivative suit. If corporate directors fail to sue when the corporation has been harmed by an individual, another corporation, or a director, individual shareholders can file a **shareholder's derivative suit** on behalf of the corporation. In most jurisdictions, to be able to file a shareholder's derivative suit, a shareholder must have held stock at the time of the alleged wrongdoing. Before filing the suit, the shareholder must file a complaint with the board of directors. If nothing is done in response to the complaint, the shareholder can proceed with the suit. Enron shareholders brought shareholder's derivative suits against various directors and officers of Enron.

Derivative suits are important when shareholders believe that directors of the corporation are harming the corporation. It seems highly unlikely that directors will sue themselves for damages

stock warrant
A type of security issued by a corporation (usually together with a bond or preferred stock) that gives the holder the right to purchase a certain amount of common stock at a stated price.

right of first refusal
A method of restricting stock transferability whereby a corporation or its shareholders have the right to purchase any shares of stock offered for resale by a shareholder within a specified time frame.

shareholder's derivative suit
A lawsuit filed by a shareholder on behalf of the corporation.

Exhibit 22-3

Rights of
Directors, Officers,
and Shareholders

POSITION	RIGHT
Directors	Right to compensation
	Right to participation
	Right to inspection
	Right to indemnification
Officers	Rights determined in employment contract
Shareholders	Right to have stock certificates
	Preemptive rights
	Right to dividends
	Right to transfer shares
	Inspection rights
	Right to corporate dissolution
	Right to file a derivative suit
	Right to file a direct suit

they cause in such cases. Thus, the shareholder's derivative suit is important for holding the directors accountable for their behavior. Because the shareholder files this suit on behalf of the corporation, all damages recovered are given to the corporation, not the individual shareholder.

Shareholder's Direct Suit In addition to their right to bring suit on behalf of the corporation, shareholders can also bring a direct suit against the corporation. In a **shareholder's direct suit,** the shareholder alleges that she has suffered damages caused by the corporation. For example, shareholders can bring a direct suit if the board of directors is improperly withholding dividends or if a shareholder is wrongly denied his right to inspect corporate records. If a court awards damages as a result of a shareholder's direct suit, the damages go to the shareholder personally.

Exhibit 22-3 summarizes the respective rights of directors, officers, and shareholders.

shareholder's direct suit

A lawsuit filed by a shareholder against the corporation.

Introduction to Mergers and Consolidations

LO 22-7

Although many people believe that *mergers* and *consolidations* are synonymous, they are in fact two legally distinct procedures. Nevertheless, in both mergers and consolidations, corporations, shareholders, and creditors have the same rights and liabilities.

MERGERS

A **merger** occurs when a legal contract combines two or more corporations and only one of the corporations continues to exist. A useful way to understand a merger is to think of one corporation absorbing another corporation (called an *absorbed corporation* or a *disappearing corporation*), yielding a single surviving corporation.

The surviving firm remains a single corporation, but it changes in several ways after the merger. First, its shareholders must amend its articles of incorporation according to the specific conditions of the merger. Second, the surviving corporation becomes liable for all debts and obligations of the absorbed corporation.

The surviving corporation also grows from the merger because it obtains the absorbed corporation's property and assets. Additionally, it acquires the absorbed corporation's rights, powers, and privileges.

merger

A combination of two or more corporations in which only one of the corporations continues to exist.

CONSOLIDATIONS

consolidation

A combination of two or more corporations in which the combining corporations cease to exist and a new corporation is formed.

Like mergers, **consolidations** legally combine two or more corporations. In a consolidation, however, neither of the original corporations continues to exist legally. Rather, they form an entirely new corporation with its own legal status.

Because the new corporation has independent legal status, the articles of incorporation of the original companies are void. The shareholders of the new corporation create new articles of incorporation, called *articles of consolidation,* according to the details of the consolidation.

The consolidated firm assumes the liabilities, debts, and obligations of the original corporations. The new corporation also acquires the original corporations' property and assets. Finally, the consolidated corporation takes on the rights, privileges, and powers of the original companies.

Today, consolidations are very rare. As Section 11.01 of RMBCA reads, "In modern corporate practice consolidation transactions are obsolete since it is nearly always advantageous for one of the parties in the transaction to be the surviving corporation."

THE RIGHTS OF SHAREHOLDERS

When shareholders invest in corporations, they expect the board of directors to handle daily business issues. They also expect, however, to vote on exceptional matters, including mergers, consolidations, changes in partners, sales or leases of the corporation, and exchanges of assets. Because shareholders have a vested interest in the survival and prosperity of the corporation, these matters are of great significance to them. Thus, the merger and consolidation procedures require shareholder approval.

APPRAISAL RIGHTS

appraisal right

A dissenting shareholder's right to have his or her shares appraised and to receive monetary compensation from the corporation for their value.

The law protects shareholders as a group from corporations, but it also protects individual shareholders from one another. Suppose that although an overwhelming majority of shareholders vote to approve a merger, a single shareholder dissents. In this situation, the law does not force the dissenting shareholder to become a shareholder in a corporation different from the one in which she originally invested. Thus, the law permits dissenting shareholders to exercise their appraisal rights. An **appraisal right** is a dissenting shareholder's right to have her shares appraised and to receive monetary compensation from the corporation for their value.

Strict procedures govern appraisal rights. Before a shareholder vote, dissenting shareholders must submit a notification of dissent. By conveying their disapproval before the vote, the dissenting shareholders may sway other shareholders to reconsider their decision. If, however, the shareholder vote approves the transaction, the dissenting shareholders must issue another statement demanding adequate compensation for their shares.

The corporation must then present the dissenting shareholders with a document stating the value of their shares. Shareholders and corporations often clash when determining the value of these shares. Generally, however, they use the value of the shares on the day before the shareholder vote. The language of the law is of little help; it ambiguously calls for the "fair value of shares" (RMBCA 13.01). If the dissenting shareholders and the corporation cannot reach an agreement, courts intervene to establish the shares' value.

Exhibit 22-4 summarizes the core concepts of corporation consolidations and mergers.

Exhibit 22-4

Review of Mergers and Consolidations

- A merger occurs when a legal contract combines two or more corporations and only one corporation continues to exist.
- A consolidation occurs when a legal contract combines two or more corporations and an entirely new corporation results.
- An appraisal right is a dissenting shareholder's right to have her or his shares appraised and to receive monetary compensation from the corporation for that value.

Purchase of Stock

Besides engaging in mergers and consolidations, corporations can extend their operations by purchasing another corporation's stock. An acquiring corporation, or *aggressor,* can buy any or all of another corporation's voting shares. Through such a stock purchase, the purchasing corporation gains control of the selling corporation in a corporate **takeover.**

The Nature of Takeovers

During the 1980s, not only did the number of corporate takeovers increase, but so too did the number of hostile takeovers. **Hostile takeovers** are takeovers to which the management of the target corporation objects. When a hostile takeover succeeds, the target corporation's management frequently compares the transition to a full-scale invasion characterized by layoffs and dramatic changes in company policy.

TYPES OF TAKEOVERS

To initiate a stock purchase, the aggressor must appeal directly to the shareholders of the corporation it hopes to buy, known as the *target corporation.* The aggressor can offer several types of deals to the target shareholders. It can make a **tender offer,** in which it offers target shareholders a price above the current market value of the stock. Aggressors, however, often require that they receive a certain number of shares within a certain time frame.

Alternatively, the aggressor may make an exchange tender offer. In an **exchange tender offer,** the aggressor offers to exchange target shareholders' current stock for stock in the aggressor's corporation. The aggressor may also make a **cash tender offer** to the target shareholders in which it pays them cash for their stock.

After acquiring a substantial number of the target corporation's shares, the aggressor initiates a proxy fight by fighting for control over target shareholders' proxies. Before an aggressor can gain control of the target corporation through proxies, it needs a key piece of information: a list of target shareholders. Although resistant target corporations often want to conceal this information, federal securities law requires that target corporations assist aggressors in some ways. Thus, to avoid lengthy and expensive lawsuits, target corporations often provide a list of shareholders voluntarily.

Those seeking to acquire corporations have developed tactics to overcome the law's rules encouraging cooperation from target corporations. Because contacting each individual target shareholder is expensive, aggressors often try to win the favor of a few institutional investors that own a large block of shares. If an aggressor can obtain the proxies of these investors, it can win control of the target corporation.

RESPONSE TO TAKEOVERS

Once an aggressor has presented its offer to the target corporation's shareholders, the target corporation's board of directors must inform shareholders of all facts pertinent to shareholders' votes. After reviewing these material facts, the directors vote to accept or reject the offer and advise shareholders accordingly.

If the directors conclude that a takeover is not in the company's best interest, the company may employ many methods of resistance. One common method is a **self-tender offer,** in which the target corporation offers to buy its shareholders' stock. If the shareholders accept the offer, the target corporation maintains control of the business.

Alternatively, target corporations may defend themselves using leveraged buyouts. A **leveraged buyout (LBO)** occurs when a group within a corporation (usually management) buys all the outstanding corporate stock held by the public. Thus, the group gains control over corporate operations by "going private," or becoming a privately held corporation.

takeover
The purchase of one corporation's stock by another corporation as a means of gaining control of the selling corporation.

hostile takeover
A takeover to which the management of the target corporation objects.

tender offer
A type of takeover in which the aggressor corporation offers the target shareholders a price above their stock's current market value.

exchange tender offer
A type of takeover in which the aggressor corporation offers to exchange the target shareholders' current stock for stock in the aggressor's corporation.

cash tender offer
A type of takeover in which the aggressor corporation offers to pay the target shareholders cash for their stock.

self-tender offer
A takeover-resistance strategy in which the target corporation offers to buy its shareholders' stock.

leveraged buyout (LBO)
A takeover-resistance strategy in which a group within the target corporation buys all the corporate stock held by the public, thereby turning the company into a privately held corporation.

LBOs are usually high-risk endeavors, however, because the target corporation must borrow money to purchase the outstanding stock. It may have to borrow money from an investment bank or issue corporate bonds.

In Case 22-3, the U.S. Court of Appeals for the Sixth Circuit considered the legality of a "golden parachute." A golden parachute is a clause in an executive's contract specifying that he

CASE 22-3

CAMPBELL, KESSER, AND WILLIAMS v. POTHAS CORPORATION
U.S. COURT OF APPEALS FOR THE SIXTH CIRCUIT
238 F.3d 792 (2001)

FACTS: *PCS, a Saskatchewan fertilizer corporation, approached Arcadian, a Tennessee fertilizer corporation, about a possible merger. They decided to merge, and Arcadian and PCS negotiated the terms of the merger and the severance agreements. The Arcadian board approved employment agreements for nine senior executives that included so-called golden parachutes. The "golden parachute" portion of the severance package provided a formula to compensate senior executives in case of a change in corporate control accompanied by a material change in the executive's position at the new company. In such a circumstance, the executive could leave the company and receive an aggregate payment in one lump sum. Three of the executives elected to take the severance package but were not compensated accordingly. Campbell (the former president and CEO), Kesser (the former vice president and general counsel), and Williams (the former vice president and CFO) sued PCS for breach of contract because PCS refused to make those severance payments to the executives. In response, PCS argued that the golden parachute agreements were not enforceable because they violated public policy.*

ISSUE: Are the "golden parachutes" offered to the three executives enforceable, or do they violate public policy?

REASONING: PCS argued that the golden parachutes violated public policy and therefore that the assumption agreement promising them is void. However, PCS offered golden parachutes to its own top managers. Hypocrisy aside, PCS cited no circuit case law supporting this proposition. Although the court has frowned on golden parachutes in past dicta, the court has never held that such severance packages were per se unlawful. Furthermore, PCS did not provide much reason to equate this type of executive compensation with contracts prohibited by public policy, such as ones to perform illegal acts. Although PCS cited a congressional committee report saying that golden parachutes should be discouraged, Congress decided to tax golden parachutes and not prohibit them. Therefore, PCS did not cite compelling evidence that the contracts were prohibited by public policy.

DECISION AND REMEDY: The court ruled that the golden parachutes did not violate public policy, and it subsequently ordered enforcement of the severance agreements. PCS already received the benefit of the bargain it struck concerning golden parachutes in having an orderly change in corporate control, and it cannot refuse payment in return.

SIGNIFICANCE OF THE CASE: This case illustrates the trouble firms can get into when they engage in mergers and severance packages. PCS made an agreement to secure the loyalty of its top management, but when the time came to fulfill its part of the bargain, the company tried to argue that enforcement of such a contract would be unfair and unenforceable.

CRITICAL THINKING

Is there any missing information you would ask for when considering the facts of this case? If you were to argue to reverse the trial court's decision, what reasons would you offer?

ETHICAL DECISION MAKING

Think about the WPH process of ethical decision making. What is the purpose of the court's decision? In other words, which value is upheld? What value is in conflict with the reasoning of the court?

or she will receive large benefits should the executive's employment be terminated. Management of the target firm in this case made an agreement with its top managers to win their cooperation in resisting a takeover.

Response to Termination

The "death" of a corporation occurs in two phases: *dissolution,* the legal termination of the corporation, and *liquidation,* the process by which the board of directors converts the corporation's assets into cash and distributes them among the corporation's creditors and shareholders.

DISSOLUTION

Dissolution may be voluntary or involuntary, depending on who initiates and compels the dissolution. *Voluntary dissolution* occurs when the directors or shareholders trigger the dissolution procedures. The directors can initiate the proposal and submit it to the shareholders for a vote, or the shareholders can begin dissolution procedures. *Involuntary dissolution* results when government or private parties successfully get a court order dissolving the corporation. Either way, for dissolution to be successful, shareholders must unanimously vote for the proposal.

Regardless of whether the directors or shareholders initiate dissolution, the corporation must follow specific procedures. First, the directors must file articles of dissolution with the secretary of state. These articles must include the company name, the date of dissolution, and the method of authorization of dissolution. Next, the directors must notify the shareholders. If shareholders or creditors have claims against the corporation, they must make them known within a stipulated time frame. Although the corporation establishes the time frame, the period must extend at least 120 days after the date of dissolution.

SUMMARY

Characteristics of Corporations	• Legal entity.
	• Rights as person and citizen.
	• Creature of the state.
	• Limited liability of shareholders.
	• Unrestricted transferability of corporate shares.
	• Perpetual existence.
	• Centralized management.
	• Corporate taxation.
	• Liability for corporate agents.
Corporate Powers	Corporations have both express and implied powers.
	An *ultra vires* act is a corporate action that is beyond the scope of the corporation's authority.
Classification of Corporations	• Public or private.
	• For profit or nonprofit.
	• Domestic, foreign, or alien.
	• Publicly held or closely held.
	• S corporations.
	• Professional corporations.
Formation of the Corporation	To create a corporation:
	• Promoters organize corporate formation.
	• Subscribers offer to purchase stock in the corporation during the formation process.
	• A state is selected for incorporation.

Legal Process of Incorporation	The legal requirements are: • Selecting the corporate name. • Drafting and filing the articles of incorporation. • Holding t he first organizational meeting.
Potential Problems with Formation of the Corporation	Remedies for defective incorporation include: • *De jure* corporations. • *De facto* corporations. • Corporations by estoppel. • Piercing the corporate veil.
Corporate Financing	• Debt securities (bonds). • Equity securities (preferred stock and common stock).
Roles of Directors, Officers, and Shareholders	Directors: • A minimum number must attend board of directors meetings. • They are legally responsible for day-to-day managerial activities. Officers: • Run the day-to-day business of the organization. • Act as agent of the corporation. Shareholders: • Approve major corporate decisions. • Elect and remove members of the board of directors.
Duties of Directors, Officers, and Shareholders	Directors and officers: • Duty of care. • Duty of loyalty. • Duty to disclose conflicts of interest. Majority shareholder: • Duty of care and loyalty when selling shares.
Liabilities of Directors, Officers, and Shareholders	Directors and officers: • Personally liable for their own torts and crimes. • Liable for torts and crimes of others when there was inadequate supervision. Shareholders: • Liable for debts of the corporation to the extent of their investment.
Rights of Directors, Officers, and Shareholders	Directors: • Compensation. • Participation. • Inspection. • Indemnification. Officers' rights are spelled out in their employment contract. Shareholders: • Right to vote at the shareholders' meeting. • Preemption. • Inspection. • Share transfer. • Petition for dissolution. • Direct and derivative suits against the corporation.

Introduction to Mergers and Consolidations	*Merger:* A legal contract whereby two or more corporations combine and only one of the corporations continues to exist.
	Consolidation: A legal contract whereby two or more corporations combine and an entirely new corporation results.
	Rights of shareholders: Shareholders vote only on exceptional matters regarding the corporation.
	Appraisal right: An appraisal right is the shareholder's right to have her or his shares appraised and to receive monetary compensation for their value
Purchase of Stock	An acquiring corporation can take control of another corporation by purchasing a substantial amount of its voting stock.
The Nature of Takeovers	A corporation can expand its size and operations by purchasing the stock of another firm.
	A *hostile takeover* is a takeover to which the management of the target corporation objects.
	Types of takeovers:
	• Tender offers.
	• Exchange offers.
	• Cash tender offers.
Response to Termination	*Response to takeovers:* Directors declare whether they accept or reject the offer. If they object to the offer, they can engage in methods of resistance.
	Dissolution is the legal death of a corporation.

Point/Counterpoint

Should Corporations Be Allowed the Status of "Legal Personhood" and Be Given Full Protection under the Bill of Rights as Persons?

YES	NO
On May 10, 1886, in the case of *Santa Clara County v. The Southern Pacific Railroad Company,* the Supreme Court clearly decided that "other corporations" deserved "equal protection of the laws," specifically the Fourteenth Amendment.	The Bill of Rights, including the Fourteenth Amendment, was created at a time when corporations clearly existed in the United States. However, a stipulation to include corporations *as a separate entity* was not included in the Bill of Rights. Clearly, the creators of the Bill of Rights were aware that corporations existed at the time. The corporations were not mentioned as having rights *independent of the natural persons associated with the corporations,* so the Bill of Rights was not designed to protect corporations as "legal persons."
Several reasons support the position that corporations should be considered legal persons. A corporation is created by and is composed of natural persons. Actions of the corporation directly affect the natural persons associated with the corporation. The rights of the creators and shareholders cannot be violated, and violating the rights of the corporation indirectly violates the rights of the persons who created and are part of the corporation. Further, additional limitations should not be placed on a group of people simply because they have combined their efforts and formed a corporation.	
Logical limitations are in place to restrict corporations' existence as "persons." Corporations cannot become official citizens and cannot vote. Even though the political system affects the corporation, the natural citizens involved with the corporation are	Further, classifying corporations as legal persons and allowing them protection under the Bill of Rights, although advantageous for corporate interests, is harmful to human interests. For example, corporate money speaks much louder than one person's letter as a means of influencing politicians.
	If corporations are given rights as a natural person, the individuals making decisions behind the corporation are not held accountable to the larger world community. The corporation is punished for a poor decision rather than the individual who used poor judgment. When the corporation is punished rather

expected to vote with the corporation's best interest in mind.

Finally, corporations deserve the same rights as natural persons because a corporation fulfills the same obligations as natural persons as an entity separate from the natural persons associated with the corporation. For example, corporations pay government taxes on profits; the shareholders also pay taxes.

than the individual who made the decision, the individual may not feel much, if any, of the consequences of his or her action.

Corporations should not be considered legal persons and protected as such because corporations do not face the same restrictions as a natural person. A natural person's life must end; however, a corporation is allowed perpetual existence.

Also, corporations do not face the same potential consequences as natural persons. A corporation cannot be sent to jail for its actions. A corporation cannot be rehabilitated and changed to become a profitable member of society if it breaks the law.

Questions & Problems

1. Name at least three characteristics that distinguish corporations from other forms of business organization.

2. How is an *ultra vires* act related to a corporation's powers?

3. Compare and contrast common stock and preferred stock.

4. Explain the primary duties of officers and directors.

5. What is the business judgment rule?

6. The Greek shipping company Ionia Management managed a 600-foot oil tanker that delivered oil to ports along the eastern seaboard of the United States. During these deliveries, Ionia's engine room crew, at the direction of their ship supervisors, regularly dumped oily waste into the ocean. To conceal the wrongdoing, the ship's crew falsified entries in its oil record book and lied to Coast Guard officials regarding the waste. The top executives and officials at Ionia did not know that employees were violating company policy and falsifying ship records to cover up their wrongdoing. A jury convicted Ionia of conspiracy, pollution, and obstruction of justice and the company was fined $4.9 million in addition to probation and assessments. The corporation appealed. Should the corporation be found criminally liable for the illegal actions of its lower-level employees under the doctrine of *respondeat superior?* Why or why not? [*United States v. Ionia Mgmt,* 555 F.3d 303 (2009).]

7. Peter Smejkal was a corporate officer and director of J.A. Morrissey, Inc. (JAM), a construction company. While employed at JAM, Smejkal had his own excavation business and secretly performed excavation work on JAM projects on his own behalf. On one occasion he also used JAM employees for

construction activities that were unrelated to JAM's projects. Additionally, Smejkal abused his position at the company and poisoned the relationship with three JAM clients while still an officer at JAM and then succeeded in obtaining those clients' projects for his own company after his termination from JAM. Did Smejkal owe duties of good faith and loyalty to JAM? If so, do you think Smejkal breached his duties of good faith an d loyalty to the corporation? Why or why not? [*J.A. Morrissey, Inc. v. Smejkal*, 6 A.3d 701 (Vt. 2010).]

8. The Metacon Gun Club operated an outdoor shooting range adjacent to a river, a golf course, a riding stable, several private homes, and a state park. The Simsbury-Avon Preservation Society, a corporation composed of homeowners who live adjacent to the gun club, sued Metacon, alleging that the discharge of chromium, lead, lead shot, lead bullets, ammunition fragments, and ammunition wadding had contaminated the groundwater. The members of the society depended on water resources in the vicinity of the gun club. Metacon argued that the society was not a corporation at the time it filed the suit because the state returned its paperwork several days later due to a missing address. Thus, Metacon argued, the society was not a legal entity and did not have standing to sue. How do you think the court ruled in this case? Why? [*Simsbury-Avon Pres. Soc'y, L.L.C. v. Metacon Gun Club, Inc.,* 2005 U.S. Dist. LEXIS 11699.]

9. Attorney Nicholas Kepple, the president of M&K Realty, drew up a contract for the sale of a parcel of land (Lot 5) from Howard Engelsen to M&K. To establish a purchase price for the sale, Engelsen had Lot 5 appraised. The appraisers based their appraisal of Lot 5 on several facts that Kepple and Engelsen

learned were incorrect after they signed the contract. These facts included the total acreage of Lot 5 and whether Lot 5 could be divided into two separate lots without the need for a subdivision approval from the planning and zoning commissioner. After learning that these facts were in error, Kepple saw that the original purchase price was well below the market price for Lot 5, and he attempted to complete the sale for the original purchase price. Engelsen informed Kepple that he would not complete the sale of Lot 5 because M&K had never legally formed as a corporation under the state incorporation statutes and thus lacked the capacity to enter the contract in the first place. Do you think the court agreed with Engelsen's argument? Why or why not? [*BRJM LLC v. Output Systems, Inc., et al.,* 2005 Conn. Super. LEXIS 1699.]

10. The Ray Griffith Company, Inc. (RGC) began in the 1950s in Columbia, Mississippi, when Ray Griffith purchased the rights to a patent to manufacture a pecan picker. In 1992, RGC was devised to Ray's two sons, Tom and Harry Griffith. Tom was given direct ownership of three shares of the company, and Harry was given direct ownership of two shares of the company. Additionally, a trust was set up in each son's name, with each trust holding 87½ shares. Over the years that followed, the dividends of the corporation decreased, until Tom discovered that the reason the corporation's expenses were increasing was that Harry was charging personal expenses to the corporation and charging expenses of his two other businesses to the corporation. Tom sued Harry for conversion and breach of fiduciary duty. However, Harry maintained that out of those personal expenses, his cell phone bill, car repairs, gas, and health insurance were "necessary business expenses." Tom disputed this assertion. Do you think Harry breached his fiduciary duty in his capacity as the president of the corporation? Why or why not? *Griffith v. Griffith,* 997 So. 2d 218 (2008).]

11. Lawrence Roseman was the sole corporate officer of RLG, Inc., the owner-operator of the Spring Valley Landfill in Wabash, Indiana. The Indiana Department of Environmental Management (IDEM) filed suit against RLG, seeking injunctive relief and civil penalties for violations of state environmental laws at Spring Valley. In response, RLG negotiated agreements to remedy the violations and to close the landfill and provide a postclosure plan. In return, IDEM agreed to drop its claim for other relief, including civil penalties. After the negotiations, an environmental scientist inspected the landfill and found that the initial violations had not been remedied and also that the subsequent agreements had been breached. A trial court found that RLG had failed to comply with the agreements in several respects. Then IDEM filed a second, amended complaint with an additional count seeking to impose personal liability on Roseman, based on his status as the sole corporate officer of RLG. How do you think the responsible person doctrine applies to this case? Should Roseman be held individually liable? [*Commissioner, Indiana Dep't of Envtl. Mgmt. v. RLG, Inc.,* 755 N.E.2d 556 (2001).]

Looking for more review material?

The Online Learning Center at **www.mhhe.com/kubasekess2e** contains this chapter's "Assignment on the Internet" and also a list of URLs for more information, entitled "On the Internet." Find both of them in the Student Center portion of the OLC, along with quizzes and other helpful materials.

CHAPTER

23 Securities Regulation

CASE OPENER

The Martha Stewart Case

On December 27, 2001, Martha Stewart's stockbroker, Peter Bacanovic, informed Stewart that two of his clients, Samuel Waksal, CEO of the biopharmaceutical company ImClone, and Waksal's daughter, had just sold all of their ImClone stock. Waksal secretly knew that the FDA was about to reject Erbitux, a key cancer drug ImClone had developed. Stewart did not know about the impending FDA rejection of Erbitux, and information about Waksal's sale of ImClone's stock was not available to the public. After receiving the information about Waksal's transaction, Stewart instructed her broker to sell all of her shares of ImClone stock. The following day, the FDA announced its rejection of Erbitux, and ImClone's stock price plummeted 16 percent. Stewart's timely trade allowed her to avoid a $45,673 loss.

Eighteen months later, the Securities and Exchange Commission (SEC) filed charges against Stewart and her broker for illegal insider trading and securities fraud.[1]

1. Did Martha Stewart violate federal securities law? Why or why not?
2. Did Martha Stewart's broker violate securities law? Why or why not?

[1] www.sec.gov/news/press/2003-69.htm.

LEARNING OBJECTIVES

After reading this chapter, you will be able to answer the following questions:

LO 23-1 What is a security?

LO 23-2 What requirements are imposed by the Securities Act of 1933?

LO 23-3 How does the Securities Exchange Act of 1934 regulate the trading of securities?

LO 23-4 How are investment companies regulated?

LO 23-5 How do states regulate securities?

Companies frequently need to raise money to expand. One way they raise money is by issuing securities. For example, corporations issue corporate **securities**—stocks and bonds—to raise capital for corporate expansion.

> **security**
> A financial instrument designated as a note, stock, or bond or any other instrument named in the Securities Act of 1933

However, a security is simply a piece of paper; it has no intrinsic value. Consequently, without securities regulations, corporations could easily commit fraud by issuing large numbers of securities and then refusing to repay them. Thus, the government heavily regulates securities issuance and trading.

Securities regulation is a relatively recent body of law. Before the Great Depression, government did not regulate securities, and fraudulent transactions occurred frequently. After the stock market crash in 1929, Congress passed several laws to regulate securities markets.

This chapter begins by defining *security.* It then examines federal securities regulations. Finally, the chapter briefly discusses state securities regulations.

What Is a Security?

Physically, a security is merely a piece of paper, as illustrated in Figure 22-3 of the previous chapter. But when investors buy securities, they are not buying a piece of paper. They are buying what the paper represents. The value of the security is based on what the paper represents.

Earlier, we loosely defined securities as stocks and bonds. To be more precise, securities include stocks, bonds, debentures, and warrants. Furthermore, certain items mentioned in securities acts, such as interests in oil and gas rights, are securities. In some cases, courts have even defined cosmetics, vacuum cleaners, and cemetery lots as securities. Finally, investment contracts, contracts in which individuals invest money with the expectation of making a profit, are securities. How can so many different things be securities?

The Securities Act of 1933 offers a complicated definition of *security,* and as a result, courts have struggled when determining whether a particular instrument is a security. In an effort to provide a framework for analysis, the U.S. Supreme Court stated in the 1985 case *Landreth Timber Co. v. Landreth* that courts should presumptively treat as a security any financial instrument designated as a note, stock, bond, or other instrument named in the 1933 act.

If the instrument in question does not have the characteristics of an instrument specifically named in the 1933 act, the courts apply a three-part test. In the classic 1946 case *SEC v. W. J. Howey Co.,*[2] the U.S. Supreme Court defined a security as an (1) investment in a common enterprise with the (2) reasonable expectation of profit gained (3) primarily or substantially from others' efforts. Anything that meets these three criteria is subject to security law. Case 23-1 illustrates how courts apply the *Howey* test.

[2] 328 U.S. 293, 66 S. Ct. 1100 (1946).

CASE 23-1	LIBERTY PROPERTY TRUST AND LIBERTY PROPERTY LIMITED PARTNERSHIP v. REPUBLIC PROPERTIES CORP. ET AL. U.S. COURT OF APPEALS FOR THE DISTRICT OF COLUMBIA CIRCUIT 577 F.3d 335 (2009)

FACTS: *Kramer, Grigg, and a third developer, Keller, formed Republic Property Trust in 2005. The trust was a real estate investment trust (REIT). Before the initial public offering, the trust established Republic Property Limited Partnership. The limited partnership was owned approximately 88% by the trust, which was also its sole general partner. Real estate investment trusts (REITs) with affiliated limited partnerships are called Umbrella Partnerships or UPREITs. In 2004, Republic Properties Corporation agreed to provide fee-based services to the City of*

West Palm Beach to design, develop, and construct a $100 million urban mixed-use development in West Palm Beach. The contract between the corporation and West Palm Beach Community Redevelopment Agency created a "Professional Services Agreement" which stated that the corporation would "at all times conduct business in a reputable manner" and that the corporation "had not employed or retained any company or person and had not agreed to pay any person, company, corporation, individual, or firm any fee, commission, percentage, gift, or any other consideration contingent upon or resulting from the award of making this agreement."

A month later Liberti, a member of the West Palm Beach Community Redevelopment Agency, was hired by the defendants as a consultant "to help win a construction contract for a teaching hospital at Florida Atlantic University." The corporation paid Liberti $5,000 a month and later $8,000 a month for a period of November 15, 2004–May 2006. Liberti's services were "limited to projects outside the city limits of the City of West Palm Beach." Then, as a voting member of the West Palm Beach Community Redevelopment Agency, Liberti voted in favor of approving and amending the Professional Services Agreement, which benefited the defendants.

In December 2005, the real estate investment trust was formed as an element of several transactions; one of these transactions was a "Contribution Agreement" in which the corporation sold its rights in the Professional Services Agreement to the limited partnership in exchange for limited partnership units, valued at $1.2 million. The corporation's rights were then transferred to an owned subsidiary of the limited partnership, Republic WPB LLC.

On May 5, 2006, Liberti was charged for accepting bribes and abusing his elected position by carrying out transactions not involved with the parties of this case. After the charges, "the city notified the corporation that it intended to terminate the Professional Services Agreement." The limited partnership then "entered into an assignment agreement with mutual releases, terminating the Professional Services Agreement and ending development with the West Palm Beach project."

The plaintiffs alleged securities fraud under rule 10b-5, control person liability. The plaintiffs argued that the "relationship between the corporation and Liberti was material information affecting the value of the Contribution Agreement"; however, the corporation, Kramer, and Grigg failed to disclose that relationship before assigning the Contribution Agreement to the limited partnership. The District Court held that the partnership units were not securities under the Howey test, so there was no liability; the court granted a motion to dismiss, and the plaintiffs appealed the motion.

ISSUE: Are the limited partnership units securities under Section 10(b) of the Securities Exchange Act?

REASONING: In the words of the court:

> In defining "security" for purposes of the Exchange Act, 15 U.S.C. § 78c(a)(10) provides a list of terms including "investment contract," that describe different types of securities. To determine whether the limited partnership units in this case are "investment contract[s]," we apply the test of *SEC v. W.J. Howey Co.* In *Howey,* the Supreme Court held an investment contract to be "a contract, transaction, or scheme whereby a person invests his money in a common enterprise and is led to expect profits solely from the efforts of the promoter or a third party." This court has repeatedly treated this test as met when profits are generated "predominantly" from the efforts of others.

Whether limited partnership units are securities is an issue of first impression in our Circuit. Other courts have considered this issue in different circumstances. In *Mayer v. Oil Field Systems Corp.,* 721 F.2d 59 (2d Cir. 1983), the Second Circuit noted that a limited partnership interest "generally is a security because such an interest involves investment 'in a common enterprise with profits to come solely from the efforts of others.'" Id. at 65 (quoting Howey, 328 U.S. at 301). The Third Circuit held limited partnership interests not to be securities when the limited partner owned 98.79% of the enterprise and therefore could exercise "pervasive control over the management of the Partnership." Steinhardt Group, Inc. v. Citigroup, 126 F.3d 144, 154 (3d Cir. 1997). In a case from the Southern District of New York predating both these decisions, limited partnership interests were held to be securities when bought by plaintiffs who simultaneously bought general partnership interests because the plaintiffs were not general [11] partners prior to the purchase. Hirsch v. duPont, 396 F. Supp. 1214, 1228 (S.D.N.Y. 1975), aff'd 553 F.2d 750 (2d Cir. 1977) (holding "plaintiffs' limited partnership interests may be considered separately from their general partnership interests purchased at the same time"). The principles courts have applied in these cases lead us to conclude that the limited partnership units in this case were securities.

DECISION AND REMEDY: The court found that the limited partnership units were securities under the Securities Exchange Act. Accordingly, the district court's motion to dismiss was reversed.

SIGNIFICANCE OF THE CASE: The case illustrates the application of the *Howey* doctrine and how it is used to identify securities.

(continued)

CRITICAL THINKING

Why might the ambiguity in the definition of *security* be a problem in securities regulation?

ETHICAL DECISION MAKING

You probably have a good idea of the ethical theory you agree with most. Under that ethical theory, what is your opinion of the business of Liberti and Republic Properties Corp.?

Securities Regulation

Two crucial acts regulate securities transactions. The Securities Act of 1933[3] regulates how companies issue corporate securities, while the Securities Exchange Act of 1934[4] oversees the purchase and sale of securities. Both attempt to provide greater stability to securities transactions. First, the acts mandate that investors have access to certain information when deciding whether to buy or sell securities. Second, the acts strive to curb fraudulent securities transactions.

THE SECURITIES AND EXCHANGE COMMISSION

The 1934 act created the Securities and Exchange Commission (SEC), an independent agency whose function is to administer federal securities laws. The SEC is headed by five individuals appointed by the president. These five individuals serve fixed five-year terms.

The SEC has a number of responsibilities. First, it is responsible for the enforcement of securities laws. Thus, in response to an allegation of violation of securities law, the SEC investigates and, if necessary, initiates an enforcement action against the violator. Enforcement actions often include penalties or injunctive remedies. If the violation is severe enough to warrant criminal prosecution, however, the Fraud Section of the Criminal Division Department of Justice will prosecute the alleged violator.

Second, the SEC interprets the securities acts and adopts rules to achieve the purposes of the acts. Thus, the SEC passes securities transaction regulations that have the force of law.

Third, the SEC regulates the activities of securities brokers, dealers, and advisers. All securities dealers and brokers must register with the SEC.

Fourth, the SEC regulates the trade of securities on securities exchanges. As you read about securities regulations in this chapter, remember that the SEC is responsible for their administration and enforcement. Exhibit 23-1 traces how the SEC's regulatory powers have evolved.

[3] 15 U.S.C. §§ 77a–77aa.
[4] 15 U.S.C. §§ 78a–78mm.

Exhibit 23-1

The Expansion of SEC Powers in the 1990s

Securities Enforcement Remedies and Penny Stock Reform Act of 1990

Permits the SEC to:

- Issue a cease-and-desist order against a violator of any federal securities law
- Seek civil money penalties against any violators
- Create rules to require that brokers and dealers provide information concerning prices and risk associated with the penny-stock market

National Securities Markets Improvement Act of 1996

Permits the SEC to exempt persons, securities, and transactions from securities regulations

Sarbanes-Oxley Act of 2002

- Increases corporate disclosure requirements
- Penalizes violators of securities laws more heavily
- Holds corporate executives responsible for errors in corporate reports filed with the SEC

Market Reform Act of 1990	• Requires earlier filing of financial and stock transaction reports
Allows the SEC to suspend securities trading if prices vary excessively in a short time period	• Creates and establishes SEC oversight over the Public Company Accounting Oversight Board to regulate public accounting firms
Securities Acts Amendments of 1990	
Permit the SEC to seek punishment of violators of foreign securities laws	

Other countries have bodies that serve functions similar to those of the SEC. In Singapore, for example, the government controls securities markets through the Securities Industry Council. The council is an advisory board to the minister of finance, who, on the basis of the council's advice, issues guidelines for exchanges, mergers, and trading.

LO 23-2 · The Securities Act of 1933

Congress passed the Securities Act of 1933 in reaction to the mistrust of securities transactions before the Great Depression. Thus, a function of the act was to legitimize security transactions by requiring the registration of securities offered to the public. Through the registration process, investors have more information to make better-informed decisions about their securities purchases.

Section 5 of the 1933 act mandates that any corporation, partnership, association, or individual that offers the sale of securities to the public through the use of mails or through any facility of interstate commerce must register that security unless it qualifies for an exemption (discussed later in this section). Any issuer of securities must file a written registration statement and a prospectus with the SEC.

REGISTRATION STATEMENT

Although the SEC requires that different types of companies complete slightly different registration forms, the SEC requires certain elements from all companies. The registration statement generally contains (1) a description of the securities offered for sale, (2) an explanation of how proceeds from the sale of the securities will be used, (3) a description of the registrant's business and properties, (4) information about the management of the company, (5) a description of any pending lawsuits in which the registrant is involved, and (6) financial statements certified by an independent public accountant.

Caution: Although the SEC requires the registration of securities, the SEC does not "approve" these securities. In other words, the SEC does not make any judgment about the worth of securities; it simply enforces the requirement that issuers provide certain information to potential buyers.

prospectus
A written document filed with the SEC that contains a description of a security and other financial information regarding the company offering the security; also distributed as an advertising tool to potential investors.

PROSPECTUS

Along with filing a registration statement, issuers of securities must also file a prospectus with the SEC. A **prospectus** is a written document that contains most of the information that appears in the registration statement. The prospectus is different from the registration statement, however, because it is an advertising tool that issuers distribute to potential investors, who rely on the prospectus to help decide whether they should buy the securities.

The SEC requires, but cannot guarantee, the accuracy of facts stated in the registration statement and prospectus. If an issuer makes a false or misleading statement in a registration statement, the issuer can be subject to criminal or civil penalties. These penalties are discussed later in the chapter.

To see an example of market failure, please see the **Connecting to the Core** activity on the text's website at www.mhhe.com/kubasekess2e.

China's Securities Regulation

The purpose of securities regulation in China is similar to that of the SEC in the United States. The Securities Law of the People's Republic of China, for example, contains 12 chapters that regulate items such as stock issuance, stock transactions, prohibited transactions, stock exchanges, securities companies, securities registration, and much more. The Securities Law of China does not approve registration of securities; instead, securities are approved by the regulatory body under the State Council of China.

PERIODS OF THE FILING PROCESS

The filing process consists of three periods: prefiling, waiting, and posteffective.

Prefiling Period The prefiling period begins when an issuer starts to think about issuing securities, and it ends when the issuer files the registration statement and prospectus with the SEC. Before filing these documents, the issuer cannot make any offers to sell securities. The issuer can, however, negotiate with *underwriters,* investment banking firms that purchase securities from the issuing corporation with the intent to sell them to brokerage houses, which then sell them to the public.

Because they cannot offer to sell securities during the prefiling period, issuers, officers, directors, and underwriters usually try to avoid generating publicity about possibly issuing securities because the SEC may construe such publicity as an attempt to condition the market to generate interest in the securities. In fact, the SEC could consider speeches or press releases mentioning the potential issuance of securities to be an offer. The issuing firm is permitted, however, to publish a notice about the prospective offering, including the name of the issuer as well as a description of the potential securities, but the notice may not include the name of the underwriter.

Waiting Period Once an issuer files a registration statement and prospectus, the waiting period begins. During this period, the SEC reviews the information filed by the issuing firm. Issuers must wait 20 days after the filing date to sell their securities. During the waiting period, issuers may make oral offers to sell the securities and may distribute a **red-herring prospectus**—a prospectus with a notice written in red print at the top of the page warning investors that the registration has been filed with the SEC but not yet approved. Moreover, the issuer may publish a **tombstone advertisement,** a brief ad with a format similar to that of a tombstone.

Posteffective Period The posteffective period begins when the SEC declares the registration statement effective, and it ends when the issuer sells all securities offered or withdraws them from sale. During this time, investors may buy and sell the securities, but purchasers must receive a final prospectus, a version of the prospectus the buyer must receive at the point of sale. If an issuer does not send the purchaser a final prospectus, the issuer has violated the 1933 Securities Act.

SPECIAL REGISTRATION PROVISIONS

Amendments to the 1933 act stipulate more relaxed registration requirements for companies that have consistently satisfied applicable registration requirements. For example, *shelf registrations* permit certain qualified issuers to register securities that they will sell "off the shelf" on a delayed or continuous basis in the future. SEC Rule 415 requires that corporations using shelf registrations keep information in the original registration accurate and up to date.

EXEMPTIONS UNDER THE 1933 ACT

Although these complex registration requirements are standard for most securities, they do not apply to all securities in all situations. Some securities are exempt because of the nature of the securities themselves—exe*mpt securities*—and others are exempt when exchanged in certain ways—exempt *transactions.*

red-herring prospectus

A prospectus with a warning written in red print at the top of the page telling investors that the registration has been filed with the SEC but not yet approved.

tombstone advertisement

A print advertisement that announces a forthcoming sale of securities in a format similar to that of a tombstone.

Exempt Securities The 1933 act provides that certain securities are exempt from the registration procedures described above. These securities are *unregistered unrestricted securities, an*d they include:

1. Securities issued by governments, including municipal, state, and federal governments.
2. Securities issued by nonprofit issuers, such as religious institutions or charitable organizations.
3. Securities issued by financial institutions supervised by banking associations.
4. Securities issued as a result of corporation reorganization in which one security is exchanged for another security.
5. Stock dividends and stock splits.
6. Insurance and annuity contracts issued by insurance companies.
7. Securities issued by federally regulated carriers (i.e., railways).
8. Short-term notes with a maturity date that does not exceed nine months.
9. Securities sold before July 27, 1933.
10. An issuer's offer of up to $5 million in securities in a 12-month period.

Although the last exemption permits the issuer to avoid the complex requirements of full registration, Regulation A nevertheless requires that the issuer file certain reports with the SEC. For example, the issuer must file a notice of issue and an offering circular and provide the offering circular to investors before sale of the securities. Even with these requirements, however, the registration process under Regulation A is much less burdensome than the full registration process. For example, Regulation A permits issuers to "test the waters" for interest in their securities before preparing the offering circular, selling any securities, or gaining the commitment of interested buyers.

Exempt Transactions If a security does not fall under one of the exempt categories described above, an issuer can nevertheless avoid registering the security by making certain exempt transactions. Such securities are *unregistered restricted securities.* Issuers might want to avoid the registration process because it can be costly, complicated, and time-consuming. Exempt transactions offer an opportunity to save time and money. Consequently, many issuers sell securities through exempt transactions.

Although these transactions are exempt from registration, issuers must still provide investors with information about the securities, such as annual reports and financial statements.

Exempt transactions include limited offers, intrastate issues, and resales of securities.

Limited Offers. Certain securities transactions known as *limited offers* are exempt from the registration process because they either involve small amounts of money or are offered only to sophisticated investors. The investors who participate in limited offers generally do not need the protection afforded by the registration process.

The SEC's Regulation D[6] enumerates three exemptions for limited offers (Rules 504, 505, and 506). Section 4(6) of the 1933 act contains an additional limited-offer exemption.

Private Placement Exemption (Rule 506) Issuers who make private offerings of securities are exempt from the registration process. These issuers, however, cannot advertise their private offerings to the general public. This exemption, usually referred to as the *private placement exemption,* allows firms to issue an unlimited number of securities to an unlimited number of accredited investors. Consequently, firms can easily raise large amounts of capital. Firms may not, however, issue to more than 35 unaccredited investors.

accredited investor

A private investor who is allowed to accept private securities offerings under certain specific guidelines set by the SEC.

The SEC defines an **accredited investor** as:[7]

1. Any natural person who has a net worth of at least $1 million.
2. Any natural person whose annual income has been at least $200,000 for the two previous years and expects to make at least $200,000 in the current year.
3. Any corporation or partnership with total assets in excess of $5 million.

[6] www.law.uc.edu/CCL/33ActRls/regD.html.
[7] SEC Rule 501.

4. Insiders of the issuers, such as executive officers or directors.

5. Registered investment companies, colleges and universities, banks, and insurance companies.

The SEC assumes that accredited investors are better able to evaluate the financial risk associated with buying securities. Consequently, government protection in the form of required registration is less imperative.

The SEC also requires that firms selling to unaccredited investors under Rule 506 believe that these investors have expertise regarding securities trading. The firms must believe that the investors, or their representatives, have reasonable ability to evaluate the financial risk associated with purchasing securities. If a firm privately offers any unaccredited investor the opportunity to purchase securities, all investors must receive the basic information contained in the registration statement (i.e., information about the issuing company and the securities). If no unaccredited investors are involved, however, the issuer does not have to disclose any information. While firms do not have to register these exempt securities with the SEC, they must notify the SEC of any sales made under the exemption.

The private placement exemption provides one of the easiest ways for firms to raise capital. Instead of making a public offering, firms can simply make a private offering to investors capable of ascertaining the risk associated with buying securities. The firms cannot, however, advertise the securities to the general public.

Rule 505 Rule 505 is very similar to Rule 506, but it has two important differences. First, according to Rule 505, a firm's private offerings may not exceed $5 million in a 12-month period, while under Rule 506, a firm may issue an unlimited number of securities. Second, according to Rule 506, if a firm issues securities to unaccredited investors, it must believe that they have the knowledge to evaluate the risk associated with the security. In contrast, under Rule 505, firms need not believe that investors have the reasonable ability to evaluate the risk of purchasing securities.

Rule 504 *Noninvestment firms*—firms that do not engage primarily in the buying and selling of securities—that offer no more than $1 million in securities over a 12-month period are exempt from registration. An unlimited number of both accredited and nonaccredited investors may purchase these securities; however, the firms must notify the SEC of their securities sales. Issuers need not disclose any information to investors.

Section 4(6) If a firm offers securities only to accredited investors for an amount less than $5 million, the issuer is exempt from registration. An unlimited number of accredited investors may participate in the transactions, but no unaccredited investors may buy these securities. Firms may not advertise these securities to the public. Issuers do not have to disclose any information to investors, but they must notify the SEC of any sales under this exemption. Moreover, investors who want to resell these securities must register them with the SEC.

Intrastate Issues. Under Section 3 of the 1933 act, any security offered or sold to a permanent resident of the single state where the issuer of the security resides and does business is exempt. Thus, local businesses can rely on local investors to raise an unlimited amount of capital without registration.

Courts and the SEC have interpreted this exemption very narrowly. Issuers must do at least 80 percent of their business within the state, receive at least 80 percent of their profits within the state, have at least 80 percent of their assets within the state, plan to use at least 80 percent of the profits within the state, and have their main offices in the state.

During the period of sale and at least nine months after the period of sale, buyers of these securities under the intrastate exemption may not resell them to nonresidents. Issuers must take precautions against interstate resales.

Resales. The 1933 Securities Act creates an exemption for "transactions by any person other than an issuer, underwriter, or dealer." Because another section of the act exempts dealers and brokers, only issuers and underwriters are not exempt from registering resales of securities.

Consequently, the average investor does not have to register securities when he or she wants to sell. If the investor acquired them through sales under Rule 505, Rule 506, or Section 4(6)

restricted securities
Securities that have limited transferability and are usually issued in a private placement.

(e.g., intrastate issues and limited offers), they are **restricted securities.** If an investor wants to resell a restricted security, she must register the securities unless she follows Rule 144 or Rule 144a.

Rule 144 Under Rule 144, any person wanting to resell a restricted security is exempt from registration if certain criteria are met. First, the public must have access to adequate current information about the issuer. Second, the person selling the restricted security must have owned the security for at least two years. Third, the seller must sell the restricted securities in limited amounts in unsolicited broker transactions. Fourth, the seller must notify the SEC of the sale.

If a seller is not an affiliate of the issuer and has owned the securities for three years, he or she may sell the securities in unlimited amounts and is not subject to any of the criteria under Rule 144 for an exemption. An *affiliate is a* person who controls, is controlled by, or is in common control with the issuer. The 1933 act restricts sales by affiliates much more than sales by non-affiliates. If an affiliate sells restricted or nonrestricted securities, he must meet all but one of the criteria to be exempt from registration. The affiliate does not need to hold a nonrestricted security for two years before reselling.

VIOLATIONS AND LIABILITY

If the SEC uncovers a potential violation of the 1933 act, it can (1) take administrative action, (2) take injunctive action, or (3) recommend criminal prosecution. If the SEC takes administrative action, it conducts a formal investigation of the potential violation by calling relevant witnesses to testify or produce evidence. If, through this investigation, the SEC uncovers evidence of a violation, the SEC may order an administrative proceeding before an administrative law judge, who can impose sanctions and even revoke a security's registration.

Usually the SEC takes injunctive action when it believes that a defendant is likely to continue to violate the law. Thus, the SEC may seek an injunction to prevent issuers from advertising securities by mail. In the Case Opener about Martha Stewart, the SEC sought an injunction prohibiting Stewart and her broker from violating securities laws and limiting her activities as an officer of a public company.

Finally, if the SEC recommends criminal action, the Department of Justice prosecutes criminal charges against the violators. Criminal penalties include a fine up to $10,000, imprisonment for up to five years, or both.

How might an issuing company violate the 1933 Securities Act? First, a company violates the act if it intentionally misleads investors by omitting or falsifying information on a registration statement or prospectus. Second, if a company is negligent in discovering a fraudulent statement, it can be liable. Third, an issuing company violates the act if it sells securities before the effective date of the registration statement.

Issuers charged with a violation of the 1933 act can raise several defenses. A company charged with the first or second violation described above may claim that the omitted or false statement was immaterial to the sale of the security. Similarly, if the issuer can prove that the plaintiff was aware of the omission or false statement when she bought the security, the defendant can avoid liability.

due diligence defense
A defense in which the defendant argues that he or she applied the appropriate degree of attention, care, and research expected of a party in a given situation and had reasonable grounds to believe that certain facts and statements were accurate and had no omission of material facts.

Any defendant except the issuer can assert the **due diligence defense.** This defense requires that the defendant demonstrate that she investigated the registration statement and had reasonable grounds to believe that the statement was accurate and had no omission of material facts.

If a defendant sold securities before the effective date of registration, however, she will almost certainly be liable because the 1933 act provides no defenses for this violation.

If an investor purchased securities and suffered damages as a result of an issuer's false or misleading statement, the investor is entitled to bring a civil suit to recover his losses. The burden of proof falls on the investor to demonstrate this incomplete or inaccurate disclosure of facts. Case 23-2 illustrates an investor's attempt to recover damages based on the omission of allegedly material facts from the prospectus and registration statement.

STEVEN KLEIN, WARREN BRANDWINE v. GENERAL NUTRITION COMPANIES, INC.

U.S. COURT OF APPEALS FOR THE THIRD CIRCUIT

186 F.3d 338 (1999)

FACTS: *Steven Klein and Warren Brandwine purchased shares of General Nutrition Companies (GNC) common stock between February and May 1996. During this time period, GNC sold over 1.5 million shares in a public offering, realizing proceeds of over $33 million. At the end of May 1996, GNC announced that its store sales would be 3 to 6 percent lower than the previous quarter. Consequently, the price of GNC stock fell from around $21.50 to $14. Klein and Brandwine asserted that GNC violated several securities regulations by failing to disclose material facts in its prospectus. They argued that GNC's failure to disclose this information led to an artificially inflated stock price for the offering of securities. Consequently, Klein and Brandwine sued GNC under Sections 11and 12(a)(2) of the Securities Act, which creates a private cause of action when a registration statement or prospectus omits a material fact that is required to make the other statements not misleading. The district court dismissed the case, and Klein and Brandwine appealed.*

ISSUE: Did the defendant's failure to disclose in the prospectus (1) a loss of third-party advertising support; (2) a worldwide shortage of deodorized distillate, a raw material used to produce vitamin E; and (3) the fact that GNC's new store openings would siphon business from existing stores violate Sections 11and 12 of the Securities Act?

REASONING: For a fact's nondisclosure to violate the act, the fact must be material, meaning that "there is a substantial likelihood that a reasonable [investor] would consider it important in deciding how to [act], . . . taking into account such factors as the certainty of the information,

its availability in the public domain, and the need for the information in light of cautionary statements being made."

Applying those factors, the nondisclosed information was immaterial. Regarding the loss of advertising support from third parties, the defendant simply had a concern that a decrease in sales by the third party might affect that party's ability to supply GNC with free advertising; a concern is not definite enough to require disclosure. Where an event is contingent or speculative in nature, it is difficult to ascertain whether the reasonable investor would have considered the omitted information significant at the time. The free advertising was actually not suspended until a month after the public offering.

The worldwide vitamin E shortage did not need to be disclosed because it was public knowledge, and, furthermore, it was expected to be temporary. Federal securities laws do not require that a company state the obvious.

Finally, the failure of the prospectus to disclose that, at the time of the public offering, same-store sales were being adversely affected by the opening of new stores in close proximity to existing locations was not a violation because the prospectus adequately cautioned investors that GNC's expansion plans might not be achieved and might not be profitable.

DECISION AND REMEDY: The court held that "[a]ll of the alleged omissions are immaterial as a matter of law." The judgment was affirmed in favor of the defendant.

SIGNIFICANCE OF THE CASE: The case helps illustrate the kind of information that must be disclosed in a prospectus.

CRITICAL THINKING

This case was based on omitted information. An important skill in critical thinking is being able to determine whether omitted information is important. Klein and Brandwine felt that the omitted information was important, while the court did not. With whom do you agree, and why?

ETHICAL DECISION MAKING

What stakeholders benefited from the court's decision? Using your favorite ethical perspectives, do you think that these stakeholders deserved the benefits they derived from the court's decision? Why?

LO 23-3 The Securities Exchange Act of 1934

While the 1933 Securities Act regulates the issuance of securities, the 1934 Securities Exchange Act regulates the subsequent trading (resale) of securities, chiefly through the required registration of securities exchanges, brokers, dealers, and national securities associations. Moreover, the act requires that certain issuers file periodic reports with the SEC. The 1934 act also permits the SEC to monitor securities markets for fraud and market manipulation.

In one of the most closely watched business cases in years, the Supreme Court, in a 5-3 decision, protected those who are only secondary players in securities fraud, as long as the public did not rely on any explicit statements or actions by the secondary players. The case appears to limit the liability of accountants, lawyers, and others who may know about questionably fraudulent corporate behavior but can establish that they are not directly involved in it. The Case Nugget explains this case.

CASE Nugget

Aiders and Abettors Get a Free Pass from the Supreme Court

Stoneridge Inv. Partners, LLC v. Scientific-Atlanta, Inc.
United States Supreme Court

128 S. Ct. 761 (2008)

The facts in the case are fairly straightforward. At the request of Charter, which in mid-2000 was falling short of its cash-flow target, Scientific-Atlanta and Motorola agreed to increase their prices for the cable boxes they sold to Charter and to use the extra money to buy advertising on Charter's cable stations. The arrangement allowed Charter to treat the advertising purchases as current revenue while listing the money spent on cable boxes as a capital expense. By recording the advertising purchases as millions in extra revenue, Charter fooled its auditor into approving a financial statement that showed it met projected revenue and operating cash-flow numbers.

In rejecting the shareholders' claim against Scientific-Atlanta, the Court majority said that bankers, lawyers, and other third parties who did not directly mislead investors but worked with corporations that did cannot be sued by shareholders. The Court reasoned that the key test for liability is whether investors relied on an entity's actions or statements, and in this case investors had no knowledge of deceptive acts during the time in question. The Court noted that the primary punishment of such secondary offenders would come from criminal prosecutions and enforcement actions by the SEC.

Shareholder activists are concerned that this decision, in effect, offers less protection to shareholders in a variety of situations. Their concerns were strengthened when less than a week after the Stoneridge case, the high court turned down an appeal in a class action case in which several plaintiffs alleged that three investment banks, Credit Suisse, Merrill Lynch, and Barclays Bank, had aided and abetted Enron in the fraudulent practices that led to the giant corporation's filing bankruptcy. The plaintiffs were seeking up to $40 million in damages. The court of appeals in the case held that the shareholders could not sue the banks for fraud because the banks did not have primary liability for the matter under federal law.

SECTION 10(B) AND RULE 10B-5

One of the most important sections of the 1934 act is Section 10(b), which prohibits the use of manipulative and deceptive devices to bypass SEC rules. Within this section, subsection 5 prohibits fraud associated with the purchase or sale of all securities. Thus, even though securities may be exempt from registration, they are still subject to Rule 10b-5:

> It shall be unlawful for any person, directly or indirectly, by use of any means or instrumentality of interstate commerce or of the mails, or of any facility of any national securities exchange,

a. to employ any device, scheme, or artifice to defraud,

b. to make any untrue statement of a material fact or to omit to state a material fact necessary in order to make the statements made, in light of circumstances under which they were made, not misleading, or

c. to engage in any act, practice, or course of business that operates or would operate as a fraud or deceit upon any person, in connection with the purchase or sale of any security.

Both Section 10(b) and Rule 10b-5 play an important role in preventing insider trading.

INSIDER TRADING

When a company employee or executive uses material inside information to make a profit, she or he is engaging in **insider trading.** Insider trading is illegal because it gives the violator an important advantage over the general public and shareholders.

Section 10(b) and Rule 10b-5 define *insiders* as corporate officers, directors, employees, lawyers, consultants, accountants, majority shareholders, or any other individuals who receive private information regarding the trading of securities.

A company employee or executive who has inside information may be liable depending on whether the information is material. If there is a material omission or misrepresentation during a securities transaction, the individual has violated Section 10(b) and Rule 10b-5. If the omission or misrepresentation is not material, however, the individual is not liable. Examples of material information include the following:

1. A change in the status of litigation against the company.
2. A change in dividends.
3. A contract for the sale of corporate assets or for the purchase of assets.
4. A new product, process, or discovery.
5. A significant change in the financial status of the company.

According to the SEC, an individual with material inside information should either refrain from using the information or disclose the information to the other parties involved in the transaction.[8] Case 23-3 is a classic example of how courts address insider trading.

insider trading
Illegal buying or selling of a corporation's stock or other securities by corporate insiders such as officers and directors, in breach of a fiduciary duty or some other relationship of trust and confidence, while in possession of material, nonpublic information about the security.

[8] Matter of Cady, Roberts & Co., 40 SEC 907 (1961).

CASE 23-3

SECURITIES AND EXCHANGE COMMISSION v. TEXAS GULF SULPHUR CO.
U.S. COURT OF APPEALS FOR THE SECOND CIRCUIT
401 F.2d 833 (1968)

FACTS: *In June 1963, Texas Gulf Sulphur (TGS) acquired the option to buy land in Timmons, Ontario. Preliminary drilling in November 1963 suggested that the land held great amounts of copper and zinc. This information was supposed to be kept secret; not even officers and executives at TGS were supposed to know about the results of the drilling. TGS acquired the land and resumed drilling in March 1964.*

From November 1963 to March 1964, certain directors, officers, and employees of TGS received "tips" and

purchased TGS stock or options to buy shares at a fixed price. When drilling began in November 1963, these people had owned 1,135 shares of TGS stock and possessed no calls; thereafter they owned a total of 8,235 shares and possessed 12,300 calls.

In April 1964, when rumors of a major mineral find appeared in newspapers, TGS publicly claimed that the rumors had no factual basis; a few days later TGS confirmed that the strike was expected to yield many million tons of ore. Between the days that TGS claimed the rumors were false and later confirmed the rumors, two defendants, Clayton and Crawford, ordered a combined total of 500 shares of TGS stock. The SEC brought suit against TGS and 13 of its directors, officers, and employees for violation of Section 10(b) of the Exchange Act and SEC Rule 10(b)-5, seeking an injunction to prevent TGS from publishing misleading press releases and requesting rescission of TGS's purchases and stock options. The district court dismissed the charges against all defendants but Clayton and Crawford, and the SEC appealed.

ISSUE: Did the corporate employees possess inside information that should have precluded them from trading in the company's stock?

REASONING: In the words of the court:

> The essence of the Rule is that anyone who, trading for his own account in the securities of a corporation has "access, directly or indirectly, to information intended to be available only for a corporate purpose and not for the personal benefit of anyone" may not take "advantage of such information knowing it is unavailable to those with whom he is dealing," i.e., the investing public. . . . Insiders, as directors or management officers are, of course, by this Rule, precluded from so unfairly dealing, but the Rule is also applicable to one possessing the information who may not be strictly termed an "insider" within the meaning of Sec. 16(b) of the Act. Thus, anyone in possession of material inside information must either disclose it to the investing public, or, if he is disabled from disclosing it in order to protect a corporate confidence, or he chooses not to do so,

must abstain from trading in or recommending the securities concerned while such inside information remains undisclosed. So, it is here no justification for insider activity that disclosure was forbidden by the legitimate corporate objective of acquiring options to purchase the land surrounding the exploration site; if the information was, as the SEC contends, material, its possessors should have kept out of the market until disclosure was accomplished. . . .

The basic test of materiality . . . is whether a *reasonable man* would attach importance . . . in determining his choice of action in the transaction in question. . . . This, of course, encompasses any fact ". . . which in reasonable and objective contemplation *might* affect the value of the corporation's stock or securities. . . ." . . . Such a fact is a material fact and must be effectively disclosed to the investing public prior to the commencement of insider trading in the corporation's securities . . . disclosing the earnings and distributions of a company but also those facts which affect the probable future of the company and those which may affect the desire of investors to buy, sell, or hold the company's securities. . . .

Here . . . knowledge of the possibility . . . of the existence of a mine of the vast magnitude indicated by the remarkably rich drill core located rather close to the surface . . . might well have affected the price of TGS stock and would certainly have been an important fact to a reasonable, if speculative, investor in deciding whether he should buy, sell, or hold.

DECISION AND REMEDY: The court found that the "transactions in TGS stock or calls by individuals apprised of the drilling results were made in violation of Rule 10b-5." The judgment was reversed in favor of the plaintiff.

SIGNIFICANCE OF THE CASE: The case is significant because it clarifies the type of information a person may possess that qualifies him as an "inside trader" for purposes of the law.

CRITICAL THINKING

Again, omitted information is the concern of this case. Can you make a distinction between the omitted information here and that in Case 23-2?

ETHICAL DECISION MAKING

What values are being emphasized by the prohibition on insider trading?

THE PRIVATE SECURITIES LITIGATION REFORM ACT OF 1995

Although Rule 10b-5 was designed to encourage disclosure of accurate information, one of its unintended side effects was the deterrence of forecasts. Shareholders who purchased stock in corporations with high earning forecasts often brought suit against the corporations' directors if actual corporate earnings fell short of forecast earnings, alleging that the directors violated Rule 10b-5 by disclosing misleading financial information.

Congress attempted to remedy this problematic side effect by passing the *Private Securities Litigation Reform Act (PSLRA) of 1995.* Among other things, the act provides a "safe harbor" from liability for publicly held issuers who make financial forecasts as long as the forecasts are "accompanied by meaningful cautionary statements identifying important factors that could cause actual results to differ materially from those in the forward-looking statement."[9]

Innovative shareholders attempted to subvert the PSLRA by suing corporate directors in state courts. Congress responded to these efforts by passing the *Securities Litigation Uniform Standards Act of 1998.* This act strictly limits shareholders' ability to bring class action suits against nationally traded corporations.

OUTSIDERS AND INSIDER TRADING

Not only may insiders be liable for omitting or misrepresenting material information, but certain "outsiders" may also be liable through two theories: *misappropriation theory* and the *tipper/ tippee theory.* Consider whether Martha Stewart is liable under either theory.

Misappropriation Theory In addition to being a theory of tort (see Chapter 6), misappropriation can establish liability for insider trading. **Misappropriation theory** holds that if an individual wrongfully acquires (misappropriates) and uses inside information for trading for her personal gain, she is liable for insider trading. Because she wrongfully acquires inside information, she is essentially stealing information to use for her benefit.

Because it expands the SEC's power, application of misappropriation theory to insider trading has not gone uncontested. The Case Nugget describes the first case in which the SEC convinced the courts to apply misappropriation theory to Rule 10b-5.

Over 10 years later, in *United States v. O'Hagan,*[10] the U.S. Supreme Court conclusively established that misappropriation theory is applicable to Rule 10b-5.

Tipper/Tippee Theory The **tipper/tippee theory** holds that any individual who acquires material inside information as a result of an insider's breach of duty has engaged in insider trading. This individual, one who has received a tip from an insider, is called a **tippee.** The insider who gives the inside tip is called the **tipper.**

Suppose that Jerry (the tipper) gives material inside information to Elaine (the tippee). Jerry is liable because he is passing on inside information. Furthermore, Elaine is liable if she makes trading decisions based on information that she should know is not public. Jerry is liable for any profits made by Elaine. Now suppose that Elaine passes the tip on to George. Elaine is now a tipper, and George is a tippee. Both Elaine and Jerry are liable for the profits made by George. George is liable for the profits of his transactions if he knew or should have known that the material information was not public.

SECTION 16(B)

Under Section 16(a) of the 1934 act, certain large stockholders, executive officers, and directors are considered **statutory insiders.** All statutory insiders must file a report detailing their ownership and trading of the corporation's securities.

To prevent statutory insiders from using inside information for their personal gain, Section 16(b) of the 1934 act requires that statutory insiders return all **short-swing profits,** or profits made from the sale of company stock within any six-month period by a statutory insider, to the company. Even if the insider did not use the inside information to make the transaction, all

misappropriation theory
A theory of insider trading which holds that if an individual wrongfully acquires (misappropriates) and uses inside information for trading for his or her personal gain, that person is liable for insider trading.

tipper/tippee theory
A theory of insider trading which holds that any individual (tippee) who acquires material inside information as a result of an insider's (tipper's) breach of duty has engaged in insider trading.

tippee
An individual who receives confidential information from an insider.

tipper
An insider who gives inside information to someone.

statutory insiders
Certain large stockholders, executive officers, and directors who are deemed insiders by the Securities Exchange Act of 1934.

short-swing profits
Profits made from the sale of company stock within any six-month period by a statutory insider.

[9] 15 U.S.C. § 77z-2 (2005).
[10] 117 S. Ct. 2199 (1997).

CASE Nugget

Using Misappropriation Theory to Establish a 10b-5 Violation

United States v. Carpenter
U.S. Court of Appeals for the Second Circuit

791 F.2d 1024 (1985)

In 1981, R. Foster Winans wrote the "Heard on the Street" column for *The Wall Street Journal.* He was aware of the *Journal's* policy that all news material gained by employees in the course of their employment was confidential. However, Winans and Carpenter, a news clerk at *The Wall Street Journal,* participated in a scheme with stockbrokers Felis and Brant. Winans provided the brokers with securities-related information that was about to be printed in the "Heard on the Street" column. Using this information, Felis and Brant would buy or sell the relevant securities. Carpenter was a messenger between Winans and the stockbrokers. The net profit on the use of the information for securities trading was $690,000. Felis's brokerage firm noticed a correlation between the "Heard on the Street" column and the trading in Felis's account. Although Felis denied the connection, he began making plans to cover up the trading. Soon, the SEC began an investigation. Later, Winans and Carpenter revealed the entire scheme to the SEC. The SEC sued under Section 10(b) of the Securities Exchange Act of 1934, arguing that the securities information had been misappropriated. The district court found Winans and Felis guilty of misappropriation under 10(b), and Carpenter was convicted for aiding and abetting the commission of securities fraud. They appealed.

The appellate court held that the newspaper employees and brokers, acting in concert, criminally violated the federal securities laws by misappropriating material, nonpublic information, in contravention of established policies of the newspapers, for their own profit in the purchase and sale of securities. This type of fraudulent act is the type of deceptive act that the securities laws are designed to protect against. It therefore falls under the broad prohibition of "any device, scheme, or artifice to defraud."

short-swing profits belong to the corporation. Section 16(b) imposes strict liability on statutory insiders who earn short-swing profits. In other words, violators cannot use lack of intent or lack of knowledge as a defense. Certain transactions, however, such as bankruptcy proceedings, are exempt from Section 16(b).

PROXY SOLICITATIONS

A **proxy** is a writing signed by a shareholder that authorizes the individual named in the writing to exercise the shareholder's votes (corresponding to his shares of stock) at a shareholders' meeting. Corporate managers often contact shareholders to request that they give a certain manager authority to vote on their behalf in an upcoming meeting. This process of obtaining authority to vote on behalf of shareholders is called **proxy solicitation.** Because the proxy solicitation process is potentially susceptible to fraud, the SEC regulates the proxy solicitation process.

Section 14(a) states that an issuer making proxy solicitations must also furnish a written proxy statement to shareholders. This statement must disclose to the shareholder all facts pertinent to the voting that will occur in the meeting. See Exhibit 23-2 for an excerpt from an example of a proxy statement that explains the purpose of the statement.

proxy

A writing signed by a shareholder that authorizes the individual named in the writing to exercise the shareholder's votes (corresponding to his or her shares of stock) at a shareholders' meeting.

proxy solicitation

The process of obtaining authority to vote on behalf of shareholders.

Exhibit 23-2

Proxy Statement Opening

Proxy Statement Excerpt

General Electric Company
3135 Easton Turnpike
Fairfield, Connecticut 06828

This proxy statement is furnished in connection with the solicitation of proxies by General Electric Company on behalf of the Board of Directors for the 2010 Annual Meeting of Shareowners. Distribution of this proxy statement and a proxy form to shareowners is scheduled to begin on or about March 9, 2010.

You can ensure that your shares are voted at the meeting by submitting your instructions by telephone or by Internet, or by completing, signing, dating and returning the enclosed proxy form in the envelope provided. Submitting your instructions or proxy by any of these methods will not affect your right to attend the meeting and vote. A shareowner who gives a proxy may revoke it at any time before it is exercised by voting in person at the annual meeting, by delivering a subsequent proxy or by notifying the inspectors of election in writing of such revocation.

Source: General Electric, "Notice of 2010 Annual Meeting and Proxy Statement," www.ge.com/pdf/investors/financial_reporting/proxy_statements/ge_proxy_2010.pdf.

VIOLATIONS OF THE 1934 ACT

The 1934 act authorizes both civil and criminal penalties. If an individual engages in insider trading, a violation of Section 10(b) or Rule 10b-5, she has committed a criminal offense punishable with a fine up to $1 million, a prison sentence up to 10 years, or both. If a defendant did not know of the rule she violated, she cannot be imprisoned. If a partnership or corporation engages in insider trading, it is subject to fines up to $2.5 million.

Both the SEC and private parties can bring civil actions against violators of the 1934 act. The SEC investigates alleged violations under the 1934 act. In the process of an investigation, the SEC can enter into consent orders with defendants or seek injunctions to stop certain actions by defendants.

Perhaps the most useful tool the SEC has for punishing those engaging in insider trading is the *Insider Trading Sanctions Act of 1984,* which permits the SEC to sue any individual who violates the 1934 act or who helps another person to engage in insider trading in violation of that act. If the SEC succeeds in demonstrating its claim, courts may assess a civil penalty up to triple the profits gained or losses avoided by the defendant.

Congress expanded the SEC's authority to punish violators of the 1934 act when it passed the *Insider Trading and Securities Fraud Enforcement Act of 1988.* This act subjects more individuals to civil liability for insider trading and grants the SEC power to award **bounty payments** (government rewards for acts beneficial to the public) to insider-trading whistle-blowers.

bounty payment
A government reward for an act that is beneficial to the public.

Private parties may also sue violators of the 1934 act. A private party may seek rescission of a contract to buy securities or may recover damages based on the violator's profits. If the court rules that an individual is liable for violations of the 1934 act, he can seek contribution from others, such as accountants or lawyers, who shared responsibility for the violation.

Regulation of Investment Companies

LO 23-4

In the past century, smaller investors have become important players in securities markets. Investment companies facilitate their involvement in securities markets by purchasing a large, diverse portfolio of securities and managing it on behalf of small investor-owners. However, because small investors often lack the resources and ability to adequately supervise investment companies, they can be subject to fraud and exploitation.

To prevent exploitation of small investors, Congress passed the *Investment Company Act of 1940,* providing for SEC regulation of investment companies. Congress later expanded the SEC's

E-COMMERCE and the Law

Marketing Securities on the Internet

Perhaps one of the most important and exciting developments in securities regulations is the explosion of the securities market on the Internet. The web permits companies to sell securities in an online initial public offering (IPO), thereby avoiding the expensive filing requirements of a traditional IPO. For example, some websites allow customers to buy and sell securities online. This technology, however, presents a greater opportunity for fraud because anyone can create a website. Several cases of securities fraud have occurred simply because a company has offered "free stock" over the Internet. The SEC has issued cease-and-desist orders against companies that illegally offered free stock on their websites because they had not registered their stocks with the SEC.

Another type of online fraud, called "pumping and dumping," occurs when an owner of a particular stock tells other investors about the virtues of the stock, artificially increasing demand for the stock and pumping up its price, only to sell (dump) it for a quick profit. Unregulated message boards on the Internet permit pumping and dumping on a fast and efficient basis. In response to the increasing use of this method of stock price manipulation, the SEC has pursued harsher and more frequent prosecution of individuals who engage in pumping and dumping online. The web also provides potential investors with access to enormous amounts of information about securities. For example, the SEC maintains the Electronic Data Gathering, Analysis, and Retrieval (EDGAR) database to help investors access information about IPOs and other documents filed with the SEC. Visit www.sec.gov/edgar.shtml to learn more about EDGAR.

SEC regulations apply to online advertising and securities transactions. When a company delivers a paperless prospectus, it is subject to the following rules:

1. The company must provide timely and adequate notice of the delivery of information.

2. The company must use an easily accessible communication system, such as the Internet.

3. The company must create evidence of the delivery of information.

power to regulate investment companies under the *Investment Company Act Amendments of 1970* and the *National Securities Markets Improvement Act of 1996.*

The Investment Company Act defines an *investment company* as any entity (1) that is engaged primarily in the business of investing, reinvesting, or trading in securities or (2) that is engaged in such business and in which more than 40 percent of the company's assets are investment securities. The act excludes a number of institutions, however, including banks, insurance companies, savings and loans, and finance companies.

The act requires that all investment companies file a notification of registration with the SEC. Additionally, they must file annual reports with the SEC and hold all securities in the custody of a bank or member of the stock exchange. The act prohibits investment companies from purchasing securities on the margin (borrowing money to purchase securities), selling short (selling securities that the company does not yet own), or participating in joint trading accounts.

LO 23-5 State Securities Laws

blue-sky law

A law that regulates the offering and sale of purely intrastate securities.

Not only must issuers obey federal securities regulations, but they are also subject to state securities laws, often referred to as **blue-sky laws.** These laws regulate the offering and sale of purely intrastate securities. Hence, although certain securities are exempt from federal securities regulation, they may be subject to state securities laws.

Many state securities laws serve functions similar to those of federal securities laws. For example, many states have laws requiring registration of securities issued within the state and requiring disclosure of certain information. Moreover, state laws regulate securities brokers and dealers. Although the purposes of state and federal securities regulations overlap, the specific regulations differ. Consequently, to encourage greater coordination between federal and state securities laws, most states have adopted the Uniform Securities Act.

SUMMARY

What Is a Security? As defined by the *Howey* test, a security is an investment in a common enterprise with the reasonable expectation of profit gained predominantly from others' efforts.

Securities Regulation The Securities and Exchange Commission (SEC) was created in 1934 to enforce securities laws, interpret provisions of securities acts, and regulate the trade of securities as well as the activities of securities brokers, dealers, and advisers.

The Securities Act of 1933 A *registration statement* is a document containing a description of the securities offered for sale, an explanation of how proceeds from the sale will be used, a description of the registrant's business and properties, information about the management of the company, a description of any pending lawsuits, and certified financial statements

A *prospectus* is a written document that is similar to a registration statement and is used as a selling tool for potential investors.

Periods of the filing process:

1. Prefiling period
2. Waiting period
3. Posteffective period

Unregistered unrestricted securities are exempt from the registration process. They include:

1. Securities issued by governments, including municipal, state, and federal governments.
2. Securities issued by nonprofit issuers, such as religious institutions or charitable organizations.
3. Securities issued by financial institutions supervised by banking associations.
4. Securities issued as a result of corporation reorganization in which one security is exchanged for another security.
5. Stock dividends and stock splits.
6. Insurance and annuity contracts issued by insurance companies.
7. Securities issued by federally regulated carriers (i.e., railways).
8. Short-term notes with a maturity date that does not exceed nine months.
9. Securities sold before July 27, 1933.
10. An issuer's offer of up to $5 million in securities in a 12-month period.

Certain kinds of transactions are exempt, including the following:

1. *Limited offers* involve small amounts of money or are offered only to sophisticated investors. There are four possible exemptions:
 a. *Private placement exemption:* Exempts private offerings of securities.
 b. *Rule 505:* States that private offerings may not exceed $5 million in a 12-month period and firms do not have to believe that investors have a reasonable ability to evaluate risk.
 c. *Rule 504:* Exempts noninvestment firms that offer no more than $1 million in securities in a 12-month period.
 d. *Section 4(6):* Exempts securities offered only to accredited investors for an amount less than $5 million.
2. *Intrastate issues* exempt local investors in local businesses.
3. *Resales* exempt transactions by any person other than an issuer, underwriter, or dealer.

Restricted securities are securities acquired under Rule 505, Rule 506, or Section 4(6) that must be registered for resale unless the investor follows Rule 144 or Rule 144(a).

Violations may result in:

1. Administrative action
2. Injunctive action
3. Criminal prosecution

The Securities Exchange Act of 1934 *Section 10(b):* Regulation that prohibits the use of manipulative and deceptive devices to bypass SEC rules.

Insider trading: Trading in which a company employee or executive uses material inside information to make a profit.

Misappropriation theory: Theory that an individual who wrongly acquires and uses inside information for profit is liable for insider trading.

Tipper/tippee theory: Theory that an individual who receives material inside information as a result of an insider's breach of duty is guilty of insider trading.

Statutory insiders: Certain stockholders, executive officers, and directors who must file a report detailing their ownership and trading of the corporation's securities.

Short-swing profits: Profits made from the sale of company stock within any six-month period by a statutory insider; according to Section 16(b), these profits must be returned to the company.

Proxy: Document that authorizes an individual to vote a shareholder's share of stocks at a shareholders' meeting.

Proxy solicitation: Process of obtaining the authority to vote on behalf of a shareholder.

Violations may result in:

1. Criminal penalties.
2. Civil penalties.
3. Suits against those involved in insider trading under the Insider Trading Sanctions Act of 1984.

Regulation of Investment Companies

The *Investment Company Act of 1940* provides for SEC regulation of investment companies.

The act requires that all investment companies file a notification of registration with the SEC, file annual reports with the SEC, and hold all securities in the custody of a bank or member of the stock exchange.

State Securities Laws

State securities laws serve functions similar to those of federal securities laws and include blue-sky laws.

Blue-sky laws regulate the offering and sale of securities within the state only.

Point/Counterpoint

Should the Government Decrease Regulation of Securities Markets?	
YES	NO
The government currently overregulates securities markets.	The government currently underregulates securities markets.
Government regulation is inefficient and perpetually behind the times. For example, some securities do not provide investors with dividends or bond payments until several years after their issue date. The nature of these securities renders investors susceptible to fraud, yet they might not discover the fraud until several years later, at a point when the trail is cold and government is impotent to remedy the situation. In another infamous example, a 15-year-old in New Jersey used Internet chat rooms to "pump and dump" securities. He was able to make off with over $800,000 before the SEC discovered what he had done.	A common and not unfounded perception of securities markets is that small investors frequently lose everything while big investors and insiders win big. Consider, for example, the corporate accounting scandals of the early 2000s. Insiders made off with millions of dollars, while many small investors lost their retirement savings. Unless the government does more to level the playing field, such scandals will continue to occur.
Left unregulated, securities markets will provide an efficient level of information and will punish those who commit securities fraud. Intelligent investors will refuse to purchase securities about which they have insufficient information and hence push companies that provide insufficient information out of the market.	Markets produce efficient results only when certain conditions exist. The online Connecting to the Core box for this chapter pointed out that securities markets are plagued by asymmetrical information: Investors almost always know less about securities than do issuers. If left unremedied, asymmetrical information leaves investors susceptible to many forms of securities fraud.
	Even if government is unable to catch every perpetrator of securities fraud, its ability to catch high-profile perpetrators and punish them heavily still serves as

Alternatively, if companies themselves refuse to provide information about securities they issue, investors will demand information from other sources. This investor demand will encourage development of markets providing information about securities. Indeed, these information markets already exist in the form of publications (e.g., *The Wall Street Journal* and *The Financial Times*) and professional services (e.g., stockbrokers and financial advisers).

Moreover, as the chapter pointed out, the five leaders of the SEC are unelected. As a result, they are insulated from democratic pressure to regulate securities markets in a manner consistent with voters' goals. Thus, even if more government regulation were desirable in theory, in practice the SEC is ill-equipped to provide it.

an effective deterrent to other potential violators. For example, the wide publicity of the Martha Stewart case, explained in the Case Opener, sent a strong message to investors that the SEC will punish outsiders who use even small pieces of inside information for personal gain.

Moreover, the unelected nature of SEC board members allows the president to appoint individuals with tremendous expertise. Perhaps Congress lacks the institutional competence to regulate complex securities markets efficiently, but experts who have spent their careers working with securities are more likely to be able to regulate effectively.

Government regulation of securities markets will never be perfect, but the appropriate comparison is not between government regulation and perfect regulation but between government regulation and available alternatives.

Questions & Problems

1. What was the stimulus for the creation of securities regulation? State the purposes of the two main federal securities laws.

2. What is the function of the SEC?

3. Explain the process of registering securities.

4. Why are certain securities transactions exempt from the registration process?

5. Why is it illegal to use inside information in making securities transactions?

6. How does the misappropriation theory apply to insider trading?

7. Alleging security fraud and breach of promissory notes under Section 10(b) of the federal Securities Exchange Act of 1934, plaintiff Dale LeBrun filed suit against the defendant, Kuswa. LeBrun was a vendor/supplier for Tomorrow Inc., a company that needed more capital to continue production of its products. LeBrun and his family and friends agreed to lend approximately $105,000 to Tomorrow Inc. For each of the six lenders, Kuswa drafted a document entitled "Agreement to Borrow Monies." The terms required that Kuswa repay the loan within 12 months and pay interest quarterly based on sales or pay 100 percent of the initial amount borrowed. The plaintiff continued to communicate with Kuswa through mail, but Kuswa did not make full payments on the loans within the specified year. The plaintiff argued that, under the Securities Exchange Act, the loans not repaid by the defendant were promissory notes that had matured a year ago. The defendant claimed that the promissory notes in question were not securities under the definition provided in the Securities Exchange Act and therefore no federal jurisdiction existed. How do you think the court decided? [*Lebrun v. Kuswa*, 24 F. Supp. 2d 641 (1998).]

8. Plaintiff Simmonds alleged that the defendant investment banks violated Section 16(b) of the Securities

Exchange Act by engaging in short-swing transactions with 54 defendant issuing companies. Simmonds asserted that the companies "engaged in improper research-related activities that were designed to inflate the market price of the shares and that these allegations establish that the Underwriters and Insiders acted as a group and coordinated their conduct with respect to acquiring the Issuing Companies' stock, holding the stock, and disposing of the stock to share in the profits gained." Thirty of the issuing companies (the moving issuers) argued that Simmond's claims of short-swing transactions were time-barred and that Simmonds failed to submit adequate demand letters to the companies before she filed suit against them. The district court granted the request of the moving issuers, "based on the inadequacy of Simmonds's demand letters." Simmonds appealed. The appellate court affirmed the district court's decision that Simmonds's demand letters to 30 of the issuing companies, the moving issuers, were inadequate. Do you agree with the ruling of the district court and appellate court? Why or why not? [*Simmonds v. Credit Suisse Secs.*, 2010 U.S. App. LEXIS 24634.]

9. Charles Zandford was a securities broker when he convinced William Wood to invest money with him that he would "conservatively" invest. The account would be for Wood and his daughter. Zandford sold shares of the Woods' mutual fund for his own benefit and wrote checks to himself from the Woods' account. Zandford generated the money in the Woods' account by selling securities. Zandford was convicted of 13 counts of wire fraud for the loss of $419,255 belonging to the Woods. The SEC subsequently filed a civil action against Zandford to prevent him from violating securities laws and to recover the gains Zandford had made on the Woods' account. Securities laws do not cover all types of fraud; rather, the laws cover only fraud that is sufficiently

connected to a securities transaction. That is, the laws cover fraud that occurred "in the offer or sale of any securities." The district court granted summary judgment for the SEC. Zandford appealed the decision. Did the court of appeals affirm or reverse Zandford's civil conviction? Why? [*Securities and Exchange Commission v. Charles Zandford,* 238 F.3d 559 (2001).]

10. The plaintiff commented that the defendants "intentionally or recklessly failed to disclose a change in Japanese regulations that predictably reduced demand for the corporation's products and services in Japan, a significant market for the company." The plaintiff further alleged that this information was material and that its nondisclosure by the defendants was misleading and grounds for illegal conduct under Sections 10(b) and 20(a) of the Securities Exchange Act, as insider trading. The district court dismissed the allegations for "failing to meet the strong inference of scienter set forth in the Private Securities Litigation Reform Act." The plaintiff appealed, and the appellate court affirmed the district court's dismissal of the insider-trading allegations. The appellate court concluded that "it would have been easy [for the defendants] to disclose the change in regulations. It was not unreasonable to be suspicious of why that was not done. But mere suspicion was not enough." Do you agree or disagree with the appellate court's ruling regarding the allegations of insider trading? Why? [*City of Dearborn Heights 345 Police & Fire Sys. v. Waters Corp.,* 632 F.3d 751 (2011).]

11. A corporation, Platforms, held stock that was not registered with the SEC under the Securities Act of 1933. William Martin provided consulting to Platforms as an employee of a sole proprietorship called Intermedia Video Marketing Company. Martin alleged that in exchange for the consulting services, Intermedia earned at least 17.45 million unregistered shares of Platforms stock but "these shares were not issued to Intermedia." The SEC filed a civil enforcement action against Platforms and Martin for violating Section 5 of the Securities Act by selling to the public the 17.45 million unregistered Platforms securities. The defendants did not dispute that the transactions were unregistered securities; however, the defendants did dispute whether the transactions qualified for an exemption from the registration requirement. The district court granted the SEC partial summary judgment on its Section 5 claim regarding unregistered securities. On appeal, the defendants alleged that there was a registration exception in this case: "[T]here is a genuine issue of material fact whether the issuance of shares by Platforms qualified for an exemption under Securities Act Section 4(2), because they took reasonable care to assure that Intermedia was not an underwriter." The appellate court denied the defendants this exception and affirmed the summary judgment of the district court. Why do you think the appellate court did not believe that the defendants qualified for the registration exception? [*SEC v. Platforms Wireless Int'l Corp.,* 617 F.3d 1072 (2010).]

12. Atul Bhagat was an employee of Nvidia Corporation. Nvidia successfully competed for a multimillion-dollar contract to develop the X-box video game console for Microsoft. Nvidia's CEO sent a companywide e-mail announcing that Nvidia had won the contract. The next morning, Nvidia's CEO sent several follow-up e-mails instructing Nvidia employees to keep the information about the contract confidential and prohibiting them from buying any Nvidia stock for several days. Later that morning, Bhagat purchased a large quantity of Nvidia stock. Four days later, after Nvidia publicly announced the contract with Microsoft, Bhagat sold his stock in the company for a substantial profit. When the SEC brought criminal charges against him for insider trading, Bhagat claimed he had not read the e-mails from Nvidia's CEO prior to making his purchases; thus, he had no insider information when he made his purchase. How do you think the court ruled? Why? [*United States v. Bhagat,* 2006 WL 288129 (2006).]

13. Investors brought a class action lawsuit against managers of a corporation, claiming that the managers made misleading statements that caused them to overpay for the corporation's stocks. An expert concluded that the fraud-on-the-market doctrine was applicable to "establish reliance and causation." The defendants argued that a class of action could not be certified unless the district court determined that the contested statements actually "caused material changes in the stock prices." The judge of the district court determined a class certification. The defendants appealed. The appellate court held that the corporation met the fraud-on-the-market requirements. When can a statement regarding the securities market be considered fraudulent or misleading? What conditions must be met to qualify as a "material change in the stock prices"? [*Schleicher v. Wendt et al.,* 618 F.3d 679, 2010 App. LEXIS 17367.]

Looking for more review material?

Employment and Discrimination Law

CASE OPENER

Brad Gets Fired from "So Clean!"

Brad has worked in the marketing department of "So Clean!" for the last five years. So Clean is a company that produces household cleaners. Brad is an excellent employee and was recently promoted. Shortly after his promotion, Brad decided to reveal publicly that he is homosexual. His family and most of his co-workers have been very supportive.

Soon after his promotion and announcement that he is gay, Brad began having problems with his boss, Jennifer. She began asking Brad questions about his personal life. At first it was small things, such as asking Brad if he was a smoker (he is, although only outside the workplace). Jennifer then began asking Brad very personal questions about his sexuality and told him she did not like weak men. The final straw for Brad occurred when Jennifer announced that she would "cure" his homosexuality and told him to come home with her that night after work or be fired. Jennifer was careful that there were never any witnesses around when she asked Brad personal questions or propositioned him. Brad refused Jennifer's advances and was fired. He filed an administrative complaint with the Equal Employment Opportunity Commission (EEOC) alleging wrongful termination, retaliation, sexual harassment, and sexual discrimination. Jennifer's response was that she fired Brad because of "creative" differences about how to run the marketing department and because he is a smoker. Jennifer denied Brad's accusations about sexual discrimination and harassment.

1. May an employer discriminate against an employee because he is gay?
2. May an employer fire an employee because the employee smokes outside the workplace?
3. May a man file a claim of sexual discrimination? Sexual harassment?
4. What defenses does an employer have to a charge of discrimination?

LEARNING OBJECTIVES

After reading this chapter, you will be able to answer the following questions:

LO 24-1 What does it mean to be an at-will employee?

LO 24-2 What are the federal laws governing employment discrimination?

LO 24-1 When May an Employee Be Fired?

During the 18th and 19th centuries in the United States, employees had no protection in the workplace. An employee who was injured could be fired. In fact, an employer could fire a worker for no reason at all. This concept came to be known as *at-will employment.*[1] At-will employment applied in all states with no exceptions until 1959.[2]

Today, any employee who is not employed under a contract for a set duration or under a collective bargaining agreement[3] is considered to be an at-will employee. This means that the employee may quit at any time for any reason or no reason at all, with no required notice to the employer.[4] Similarly, an employer may fire the employee at any time, with no notice, for almost any reason. For example, your employer could decide he doesn't like the color of your shirt and fire you on the spot! The exception to the at-will rule is that an employer may not fire an employee for an illegal reason. What is an illegal reason? Broadly, any termination based on a violation of a state statute, a state constitution, a federal law, the U.S. Constitution, or a public policy is illegal. Exceptions to at-will employment have also been found through breaches of implied contracts with employees that were based on employee handbooks.[5]

LO 24-2 Federal Employment Discrimination Laws Governing Employers

Employees are protected in the workplace by a number of both federal and state laws. Federal laws apply to everyone in the United States. Federal law may be described as a "minimum" level of protection for all workers. State laws may give employees more, but not less, protection than federal laws. Exhibit 24-1 is an overview of some of the most important federal employment discrimination laws.

[1] See *Toussaint v. Blue Cross & Blue Shield of Mich.,* 408 Mich. 579, 600, 292 N.W.2d 880, 885 (1980), for an extended discussion on the at-will rule.

[2] BambooWeb Dictionary, www.bambooweb.com/articles/a/t/At-Will_Employment.html. The first judicial exception to the at-will rule was created in *Peterman v. Intl. Bhd. of Teamsters, Chauffeurs, Warehousemen, and Helpers of Am., Local 396,* 174 Cal. App. 2d 184, 344 P.2d 44 (1959).

[3] Union employees are covered by collective bargaining agreements.

[4] Most employees do give an employer notice before leaving a job as a matter of professional courtesy. Such action, however, is not required under the law.

[5] "Some challenges and exceptions to at-will employment include breach of implied contracts through employee handbooks, public policy violations, reliance on an offer of employment, and intentional infliction of emotional distress" (Legal Database, www.legal-database .net/at-will.htm).

CASE Nugget

What Are the Limits to an At-Will Contract?

Brown v. Sabre, Inc.
Court of Appeals of Texas

173 S.W.3d 581 (Tx. Ct. App. 2005)

Brown was an employee of Sabre. After Sabre was sold to EDS, Brown and 4,000 other at-will employees had a choice of moving to EDS or quitting. Brown moved to EDS. In its handbook, the company reserved the right to alter, amend, modify, or terminate its policies at any time in its sole discretion. Under Sabre's vacation policy, vacation days were earned one year and taken the next year. Brown and others were told that EDS would honor this vacation policy, but then it changed the policy. Brown received pay for half his vacation days but lost the value of the other half of his vacation days. He sued for breach of contract.

 The district court rejected Brown's claim, so he appealed. The appellate court affirmed the decision of the district court, holding that any modification of an employee's at-will employment status must be an express, rather than an implied, agreement and that it must be clear and specific. Statements in employee handbooks and policy manuals are general guidelines and do not create implied contracts. Given the disclaimer in the employee handbook, the employer had the right to amend, modify, or terminate the policy at any time.

FEDERAL LEGISLATION	PURPOSE
Civil Rights Act (CRA) of 1964—Title VII (as amended by the Civil Rights Act of 1991)	Protects employees against discrimination based on race, color, religion, national origin, and sex; also prohibits harassment based on the same protected categories
Pregnancy Discrimination Act (PDA) of 1987	Amends Title VII of the CRA, expanding the definition of sex discrimination to include discrimination based on pregnancy
Age Discrimination in Employment Act (ADEA) of 1967	Prohibits employers from refusing to hire, discharging, or discriminating in terms and conditions of employment on the basis of an employee's or applicant's being age 40 or older
Americans with Disabilities Act (ADA) of 1990 (as amended in 2008)	Prohibits discrimination against employees and job applicants with disabilities
Equal Pay Act of 1963	Prohibits an employer from paying workers of one gender less than the wages paid to employees of the opposite gender for work that requires equal skill, effort, and responsibility

Exhibit 24-1

Federal Discrimination Laws

Civil Rights Act—Title VII

The Civil Rights Act is divided into sections, called *titles*. **Title VII of the Civil Rights Act (CRA) of 1964** deals with discrimination in employment. It prohibits employers from hiring, firing, or otherwise discriminating in terms and conditions of employment, and it prohibits segregating employees in a manner that would affect their employment opportunities on the basis of their race, color, religion, sex, or national origin. There are two ways to prove discrimination under Title VII—disparate treatment and disparate impact.

Title VII of CRA applies to employers who have 15 or more employees for 20 consecutive weeks within one year and who are engaged in a business that affects commerce. The U.S. government, corporations owned by the government, agencies of the District of Columbia, Indian tribes, private clubs, unions, and employment agencies are also covered by Title VII of CRA.

DISPARATE-TREATMENT DISCRIMINATION UNDER TITLE VII

In order to sue for **disparate treatment** under Title VII, the plaintiff must be a member of a protected class as listed in CRA. In other words, the employee must have been discriminated against on the basis of race, color, national origin, religion, or sex (i.e., gender). If the employee has been refused work, fired, denied a promotion, or the like, based on membership in a protected class, this is a form of intentional discrimination and qualifies the employee to sue for disparate-treatment discrimination. Proving disparate-treatment discrimination in employment under Title VII is a three-step process:

1. Plaintiff (the employee) must demonstrate a prima facie case of discrimination.
2. Defendant (the employer) must articulate a legitimate, nondiscriminatory business reason for the action.
3. Plaintiff (the employee) must show that the reason given by the defendant (the employer) is a mere pretext.[6]

After all the evidence has been presented, the trier of fact (a jury in most cases)[7] must decide whether discrimination has occurred. The burden of proof in a civil case is preponderance of the evidence (i.e., more likely than not). If the jury finds in favor of the plaintiff-employee, damages must be assessed. Damages under Title VII of CRA include up to two years of back pay, compensatory damages, punitive damages (limited in some cases), attorney fees, court costs, court orders (including reinstatement), and remedial seniority. If the jury finds in favor of the defendant-employer, the plaintiff-employee receives nothing.

DISPARATE-IMPACT DISCRIMINATION UNDER TITLE VII

Disparate-impact cases are sometimes called *unintentional-discrimination* cases. While it is very difficult to prove disparate treatment, it is even more difficult to prove disparate impact. Disparate-impact cases arise when a plaintiff attempts to establish that while an employer's policy or practice appears to apply to everyone equally, its actual effect is that it disproportionately limits employment opportunities for a protected class.

The plaintiff proves a case based on disparate impact by first establishing statistically that the rule disproportionately restricts employment opportunities for a protected class. The burden of proof then shifts to the defendant, who can avoid liability by demonstrating that the practice or policy is a business necessity. The plaintiff, at this point, can still recover by proving either that the "necessity" was promulgated as a pretext for discrimination or that an alternative employment practice had less discriminatory effect and the employer failed to adopt such practice.

The initial steps for proving a prima facie case of disparate impact were set forth in *Griggs v. Duke Power Co.*[8] In that case, the employer-defendant required that all applicants have a high

[6] *McDonnell Douglas v. Green,* 411 U.S. 792, 802 (1973).
[7] In a bench trial, the judge becomes the trier of fact as no jury is impaneled. A discrimination case could also be decided by a judge on a motion for summary judgment.
[8] *Griggs v. Duke Power,* 401 U.S. 424 (1971).

school diploma and a successful score on a professionally recognized intelligence test for all jobs except laborer. The stated purpose of these criteria was to upgrade the quality of the workforce.

The plaintiff statistically demonstrated the discriminatory impact by showing that 34 percent of the white males in the state had high school diplomas, whereas only 12 percent of the black males did, and by introducing evidence from an EEOC study showing that 58 percent of the whites, compared to 6 percent of the blacks, had passed tests similar to the one given by the defendant. Because the defendant could not demonstrate any business-related justification for either employment policy, the plaintiff was successful. Requiring a high IQ or high school or college diploma may be necessary for some jobs but not for all jobs at Duke Power.

SEXUAL HARASSMENT UNDER TITLE VII

Harassment first developed in the context of discrimination based on sex, and it evolved to become applicable to other protected classes. The definition of **sexual harassment** stated in the Equal Employment Opportunity Commission (EEOC) guidelines and accepted by the U.S. Supreme Court is "unwelcome sexual advances, requests for sexual favors, and other verbal or physical conduct of a sexual nature" that implicitly or explicitly makes submission a term or condition of employment; makes employment decisions related to the individual dependent on submission to or rejection of such conduct; or has the purpose or effect of creating an intimidating, hostile, or offensive work environment. In the Case Opener, did the actions of Jennifer create a sexually hostile environment for Brad?

Two distinct forms of sexual harassment are recognized. The first, and generally easiest to prove, is *quid pro quo*, which occurs when a supervisor makes a sexual demand on someone and this demand is reasonably perceived as a term or condition of employment. The second form of sexual harassment involves the creation of a hostile work environment. Case 24-1 demonstrates the standard used by the U.S. Supreme Court to determine whether an employer's conduct has created a hostile work environment.

> **sexual harassment**
> Unwelcome sexual advances, requests for sexual favors, and other verbal or physical conduct of a sexual nature that makes submission a condition of employment or a factor in employment decisions or that creates an intimidating, hostile, or offensive work environment. The two types are hostile environment and *quid pro quo*.

CASE 24-1

TERESA HARRIS v. FORKLIFT SYSTEMS, INC.
UNITED STATES SUPREME COURT
510 U.S.17, 114 S. Ct. 367 (1994)

FACTS: *During her tenure as a manager at defendant Forklift Systems, Inc., plaintiff Harris was repeatedly insulted by the defendant's president because of her gender and subjected to sexual innuendos. In front of other employees, the president frequently told Harris, "You're just a woman, what do you know?" He sometimes asked Harris and other female employees to remove coins from his pockets and made suggestive comments about their clothes. He suggested to Harris in front of others that they negotiate her salary at the Holiday Inn. When Harris complained, he said that he would stop, but he continued behaving in the same manner, so Harris quit. She then filed an action against the defendant for creating an abusive work environment on the basis of her gender. The district court found in favor of the defendant, holding that some of the comments were offensive to the plaintiff but were not so serious as to severely affect Harris's psychological well-being or interfere with her work performance. The court of appeals affirmed. Plaintiff Harris appealed to the U.S. Supreme Court.*

ISSUE: Must an employee suffer serious psychological damage in order to pursue damages for a claim of sexual harassment?

REASONING: In the court's own words:

As we made clear in *Meritor Savings Bank* v. *Vinson*, this language [of Title VII] "is not limited to 'economic' or 'tangible' discrimination. The phrase 'terms, conditions, or privileges of employment' evinces a congressional intent 'to strike at the entire spectrum of disparate treatment of men and women' in employment," which includes requiring people to work in a discriminatorily hostile or abusive environment. When the workplace is permeated with "discriminatory intimidation, ridicule,

and insult," that is "sufficiently severe or pervasive to alter the conditions of the victim's employment and create an abusive working environment."

This standard, which we reaffirm today, takes a middle path between making actionable any conduct that is merely offensive and requiring the conduct to cause a tangible psychological injury. As we pointed out in *Meritor,* "mere utterance of an . . . epithet which engenders offensive feelings in a employee," does not sufficiently affect conditions of employment to implicate Title VII. . . . Likewise, if the victim does not subjectively perceive the environment to be abusive, the conduct has not actually altered the conditions of the victim's employment, and there is no Title VII violation.

But Title VII comes into play before the harassing conduct leads to a nervous breakdown. A discriminatorily abusive work environment, even one that does not seriously affect employees' psychological well-being, can and often will detract from employees' job performance, discourage employees from remaining on the job, or keep them from advancing in their careers. Moreover, even without regard to these tangible effects, the very fact that the discriminatory conduct was so severe or pervasive that it created a work environment abusive to employees because of their race, gender, religion, or national origin offends Title VII's broad rule of workplace equality. The appalling conduct alleged in *Meritor,* and the reference in that case to environments "so heavily polluted with discrimination as to destroy completely the emotional and psychological stability of minority group workers," merely present some especially egregious examples of harassment. They do not mark the boundary of what is actionable.

. . . Certainly Title VII bars conduct that would seriously affect a reasonable person's psychological well-being, but the statute is not limited to such conduct. So long as the environment would reasonably be perceived, and is perceived, as hostile or abusive, there is no need for it also to be psychologically injurious.

This is not, and by its nature cannot be, a mathematically precise test. But we can say that whether an environment is "hostile" or "abusive" can be determined only by looking at all the circumstances. These may include the frequency of the discriminatory conduct; its severity; whether it is physically threatening or humiliating, or a mere offensive utterance; and whether it unreasonably interferes with an employee's work performance. The effect on the employee's psychological well-being is, of course, relevant to determining whether the plaintiff actually found the environment abusive. But while psychological harm, like any other relevant factor, may be taken into account, no single factor is required.

DECISION AND REMEDY: The lower court's decision was reversed and remanded, in favor of the plaintiff.

SIGNIFICANCE: In this case, the Supreme Court for the first time held that harassment in and of itself is illegal and actionable, regardless of the amount of damage to the victim.

CRITICAL THINKING

Identify the Court's reasons for its finding. Do you think these reasons were sufficient to overturn the previous ruling? Why or why not?

ETHICAL DECISION MAKING

Imagine that the judge is operating under a duty-based system of ethics. What duty is she advocating in terms of employer–employee relationships? Would this ruling serve well as a universal standard?

LO 24-3

Same-Sex Harassment—The Supreme Court Speaks Initially, same-sex harassment was not covered under CRA. By 1997, however, the courts were split on the issue. This issue was resolved in 1998 in *Oncale v. Sundowner Offshore Services, Inc.*[9] Oncale, a male, was forcibly subjected to sex-related, humiliating actions against him by other male employees. He was physically sexually assaulted and threatened with rape. He complained, to no avail, so he filed a lawsuit alleging discrimination based on sex. The district court granted a motion for summary judgment for the defendant employer, holding that a male had no cause of action under Title VII for harassment by male co-workers. The case was appealed to the U.S. Supreme Court, which concluded that sex discrimination consisting of same-sex sexual harassment is actionable under Title VII. The Court reversed the appellate court's order and remanded the case for further proceedings.

[9] 523 U.S. 75, 118 S. Ct. 998 (1998).

Harassment by Nonemployees under Title VII Employers may be held liable for harassment of their employees by nonemployees under very limited circumstances. If an employer knows that a customer repeatedly harasses an employee yet the employer does nothing to remedy the situation, the employer may be liable. For example, in *Lockhard v. Pizza Hut, Inc.*,[10] the franchise was held liable for the harassment of a waitress by two male customers because no steps had been taken to prevent the harassment.

HARASSMENT OF OTHER PROTECTED CLASSES UNDER TITLE VII

Hostile-environment issues have also been used in cases of discrimination based on religion and race. For example, in a 1986 case, *Snell v. Suffolk County*,[11] Hispanic and black corrections workers demonstrated that a hostile work environment existed by proving that they had been subjected to continuing verbal abuse and racial harassment by co-workers and that the county sheriff's department had done nothing to prevent the abuse. The white employees had continually used racial epithets and posted racially offensive materials on bulletin boards, such as a picture of a black man with a noose around his neck, cartoons favorably portraying the Ku Klux Klan, and a "black officers' study guide," consisting of children's puzzles. White officers once dressed a Hispanic inmate in a straw hat, sheet, and sign that said "spic." Such activities were found by the court to constitute a hostile work environment.

PREGNANCY DISCRIMINATION ACT OF 1987—AN AMENDMENT TO TITLE VII

In 1987, Title VII was amended by the Pregnancy Discrimination Act (PDA). This law expanded the definition of discrimination based on gender to include discrimination based on pregnancy. "Discrimination on the basis of pregnancy, childbirth or related medical conditions constitutes unlawful sex discrimination under Title VII."[12] Under the act, temporary disability caused by pregnancy must be treated the same as any other temporary disability.

DEFENSES TO CLAIMS UNDER TITLE VII

As a business owner or manager, how would you respond if one of your employees filed a lawsuit under Title VII? Are there any legal exceptions for discriminating against a protected class? The answer, surprising to many business owners and managers, is yes. The three most important defenses available to defendants in Title VII cases are the bona fide occupational qualification, merit, and seniority system defenses. These defenses are raised by the defendant after the plaintiff has established a prima facie case of discrimination based on either disparate treatment or disparate impact. They would obviously not be applicable to a claim based on harassment.

The Bona Fide Occupational Qualification Defense The bona fide occupational qualification (BFOQ) defense allows an employer to discriminate in hiring on the basis of sex, religion, or national origin (but not race or color) when doing so is necessary for the performance of the job. Necessity must be based on actual qualifications, not stereotypes about one group's abilities. For example, being a male cannot be a BFOQ for a job simply because it is a dirty job, although there may be a valid requirement that an applicant be able to lift a certain amount of weight if such lifting is a part of the job. Conversely, being a female may be a BFOQ for modeling female clothing. An employer would not be required or expected to hire a male for such a job. Employer arguments about inconvenience to the employer, such as having to provide two sets of restroom facilities, have not been persuasive in the courts. Nor have customer preferences to be served by a particular gender or nationality. The only exception to customer preference is sexual privacy (e.g., female restroom attendants in the women's restroom and male attendants in the men's room).[13]

[10] 162 F.3d 1062 (10th Cir. 1998).
[11] 782 F.2d 1094 (1986).
[12] EEOC, "Facts about Pregnancy Discrimination," www.eeoc.gov/facts/fs-preg.html.
[13] *In the Matter of the Accusation of the Department of Fair Employment and Housing v. San Luis Obispo Coastal Unified School District, Respondent; Marlene Anne Mendes, Complainant,* Case No. E95-96 L-0725-00s, 98-14 (October 7, 1998). See www.dfeh.ca.gov/PrecedentialD/1998-14.html.

The Merit Defense The merit defense is usually raised when hiring or promotion decisions are partially based on test scores. Professionally developed ability tests that are not designed, intended, or used to discriminate may be used. While these tests may have an adverse impact on a class, as long as they are manifestly related to job performance, they do not violate the act. Since 1978, the "Uniform Guidelines on Employee Selection Procedures" (UGESP) have guided government agencies charged with enforcing civil rights, and they provide guidance to employers and other interested persons about when ability tests are valid and job-related. Under these guidelines, tests must be validated in accordance with standards established by the American Psychological Association.

> To see more on the nondiscriminatory selection process, please see the **Connecting to the Core** activity on the text's website at www.mhhe.com/kubasekess2e.

Three types of validation are acceptable: (1) *criterion-related validity,* which is the statistical relationship between test scores and objective criteria of job performance; (2) *content validity,* which isolates some skill used on the job and directly tests that skill; and (3) *construct validity,* wherein a psychological trait needed to perform the job is measured. A test that required a word processor to use a computer would be content-valid. A test of patience for a teacher would be construct-valid.

The Seniority System Defense A bona fide seniority system is a legal defense under Title VII. Even though a seniority system, in which employees are given preferential treatment based on their length of service, may perpetuate past discrimination, such systems are considered bona fide and are thus not illegal if (1) the system applies equally to all persons; (2) the seniority units follow industry practices; (3) the seniority system did not have its genesis in discrimination; and (4) the system is maintained free of any illegal discriminatory purpose.

REMEDIES UNDER TITLE VII

A plaintiff may seek both equitable and legal remedies for violations of Title VII. Courts have ordered parties to engage in diverse activities ranging from publicizing their commitment to minority hiring to establishing special training programs for minorities. A successful plaintiff may recover back pay for up to two years from the time of the discriminatory act.

A plaintiff who was not hired for a job because of a Title VII violation may also receive remedial seniority dating back to the time when the plaintiff was discriminated against; compensatory damages, including those for pain and suffering; and, in some cases, punitive damages.

In cases based on discrimination other than race, however, punitive damages are capped at $300,000 for employers of more than 500 employees, $100,000 for firms with 101 to 200 employees, and $50,000 for firms with 100 or fewer employees. An employer will not be held vicariously liable for punitive damages as long as it made "good-faith efforts" to comply with federal law.

Attorney fees may be awarded to a successful plaintiff in Title VII cases. They are typically denied only when special circumstances would render the award unjust. If it is determined that the plaintiff's action was frivolous, unreasonable, or without foundation, the courts may award attorney fees to the prevailing defendant. For more information on Title VII, visit the EEOC website at www.eeoc.gov.

PROCEDURE FOR FILING A CLAIM UNDER TITLE VII

Filing a claim under Title VII is much more complicated than simply filing a lawsuit. Failure to follow the proper procedures within the strict time framework may result in a plaintiff's losing his or her right to file a lawsuit under Title VII.

The first step in initiating a Title VII action is the aggrieved party's filing of a charge with the state Equal Opportunity Commission or, if no such agency exists, the federal EEOC. A *charge* is a sworn statement that states the name of the charging party, the name(s) of the defendant(s), and the nature of the discriminatory act. Title VII charges must be filed with the EEOC within 180 days of the alleged discriminatory act.

Within 10 days of receiving the charge, the EEOC must notify the alleged violator of the charge. Then the EEOC investigates the matter to determine whether there is "reasonable cause" to believe that a violation has occurred. If the EEOC does find such reasonable cause, it attempts to eliminate the discriminatory practice through conciliation, that is, by trying to negotiate a settlement between the two parties. If unsuccessful, the EEOC *may* file suit against the alleged discriminator in federal district court. Failure to file suit does not necessarily mean that the EEOC thinks the plaintiff does not have a valid claim; the EEOC may simply feel that the claim is not the type it wishes to use its limited resources on pursuing.

If the EEOC decides not to sue, it notifies the plaintiff of his or her right to file an action and issues the plaintiff a *right-to-sue letter,* which is not intended to be anything other than a statement that the plaintiff has followed the proper initial procedures and therefore may file a lawsuit. The plaintiff must have this letter in order to file a private action.

Discrimination Based on Sexual Orientation—Actionable?

There is currently no federal legislation that prohibits discrimination based on sexual orientation. However, state laws prohibiting such discrimination exist in 20 states and one district.

What do these laws mean to Brad, the employee in our Case Opener? It depends on where Brad lives. If Brad lives in Texas and is fired for being gay, he has absolutely no legal rights and cannot sue his employer. Conversely, if Brad lives in California, he may sue Jennifer and So Clean, his employer, for discrimination based on sexual orientation. In California and a handful of other states, discriminating in terms of employment (i.e., failure to hire, firing, failure to promote) based on a person's sexual orientation is prohibited.

Age Discrimination in Employment Act of 1967

LO 24-4

The **Age Discrimination in Employment Act (ADEA) of 1967** was enacted to prohibit employers from refusing to hire, discharging, or discriminating in terms and conditions of employment against employees or applicants age 40 or older. The language describing the prohibited conduct is virtually the same as that of Title VII, except that age is the prohibited basis for discrimination. ADEA applies to employers having 20 or more employees.

Americans with Disabilities Act

The goal of the **Americans with Disabilities Act (ADA)** is preventing employers from discriminating against employees and applicants with disabilities. ADA attempts to attain this objective by requiring that employers make reasonable accommodations to the known physical or mental disabilities of an otherwise-qualified person with a disability unless the necessary accommodation would impose an undue burden on the employer's business.

> When the ADA was before Congress, some members predicted a flood of lawsuits that would bankrupt or at least overburden business. . . . Studies have shown, however, that businesses have adapted to the ADA much more easily—and inexpensively—than the doomsayers predicted. . . . Law Professor Peter Blanck of the University of Iowa has studied business compliance with the ADA, including Sears Roebuck and many other large businesses, and found that compliance was often as easy as raising or lowering a desk, installing a ramp, or modifying a dress code. Another survey found that three-quarters of all changes cost less than $100. Moreover, the predicted flood of lawsuits proved to be imaginary. Almost 90 percent of the cases brought before the Equal Employment

Age Discrimination in Employment Act (ADEA) of 1967
Federal law that prohibits employers from refusing to hire, discharging, or discriminating in terms and conditions of employment on the basis of an employee's or applicant's being age 40 or older.

Americans with Disabilities Act (ADA)
Federal law that prohibits discrimination against employees and job applicants with disabilities.

Opportunity Commission are thrown out. And only about 650 lawsuits were filed in the ADA's first five years—a small number compared to 6 million businesses, 666,000 public and private employers, and 80,000 units of state and local governments that must comply. The American Bar Association recently conducted a survey and learned that, of the cases that actually go to court, 98 percent are decided in favor of the defendants, usually businesses.[14]

ADA is enforced by the EEOC in the same way that Title VII is enforced. To bring a successful claim under ADA, the plaintiff must show that he or she meets all of the following:

- Had a disability.
- Was otherwise qualified for the job.
- Suffered an adverse employment decision because of that disability.

Remedies for ADA violations are similar to those available under Title VII. A successful plaintiff may recover reinstatement, back pay, and injunctive relief. In cases of intentional discrimination, limited compensatory and punitive damages are also available. An employer who has repeatedly violated the act may be subject to fines of up to $100,000.

May an Employer Discriminate against a Smoker?

In the Case Opener, Jennifer discovered that Brad was a smoker. Later, she fired him. One of Jennifer's given reasons for terminating Brad's employment was that he was a smoker. May Jennifer and So Clean legally fire an employee for smoking outside the workplace? The answer is, "It depends!"

A recent trend has been for employers to consider a potential employee's lifestyle when deciding whether to hire that person. Employers argue that smokers have higher health care costs and miss more work, lowering productivity.

The Centers for Disease Control and Prevention estimated that $75 billion is spent annually on medical expenses attributed to smoking. Businesses lose $82 billion in lost productivity from smokers. And smokers take about 6.5 more sick days a year than nonsmokers. About one in five Americans—or 46 million people—smoke.[15]

As a result, some companies either won't hire smokers or are threatening to fire current employees who will not or are unable to quit smoking. In 2005, Michigan-based Weyco, Inc., announced that it would terminate all workers who did not stop smoking.[16] Many states have passed laws preventing companies from engaging in such action.

Michigan, with 1.9 million smokers and one of the highest cigarette taxes in the nation, has no "smoker's rights law" found in 29 other states, so there isn't much that employees can do. Weyco terminated four of its employees after they refused to submit to a smoking breath test in light of the company's new policy that bans tobacco use among its 200 employees during work and even when they are off the clock. "We are saying people can smoke if they choose to smoke. That's their choice," said Gary Climes, Weyco's chief financial officer. "But they just can't work for us."[17]

If Brad works in Michigan, Jennifer and So Clean may legally terminate him for smoking outside the workplace. Conversely, if Brad works in any of the 29 states with "smoker's rights laws," he could not be legally terminated for smoking outside the workplace. Finally, employers should be aware that giving breaks on health care plans to employees who are nonsmokers could be in violation of a "smoker's rights law."

[14] Center for an Accessible Society, "Disability Issues Information for Journalists," www.accessiblesociety.org/topics/ada.
[15] "Workers Fume as Firms Ban Smoking at Home," www.detnews.com/2005/business/0501/27/A01-71823.htm.
[16] Ibid.
[17] Ibid.

Equal Pay Act of 1963

While we generally think of Title VII as being the primary means of protecting women from discrimination, an earlier law actually was designed specifically to protect women from wage discrimination: the **Equal Pay Act (EPA) of 1963.** When EPA was passed, the average wages of women were less than 60 percent of those of men. The primary purpose of the law was to eliminate situations in which women, working alongside men or replacing men, would be paid lower wages for doing substantially the same job. EPA prohibits any employer from discriminating within any "establishment . . . between employees on the basis of sex by paying wages to employees in such establishment at a rate less than the rate at which he pays wages to employees of the opposite sex . . . for equal work on jobs the performance of which requires equal skill, effort, and responsibility, and which are performed under similar working conditions, except where payment is made pursuant to (i) a seniority system; (ii) a merit system; (iii) a system which measures earnings by quantity or quality of production; or (iv) differential based on any factor other than sex."[18]

Equal Pay Act (EPA) of 1963

Federal law that prohibits an employer from paying workers of one gender less than the wages paid to employees of the opposite gender for work that requires equal skill, effort, and responsibility.

Additional Laws Governing the Employment Relationship

LO 24-5

There are several major categories of state and federal laws that cover employee rights with regard to wages, benefits, and health and safety standards. Exhibit 24-2 lists significant state and federal legislation protecting employees.

LAW	IMPACT
Wage and hour laws	Federal and state laws that impose minimum-wage and hour requirements for employees.
Family and Medical Leave Act (FMLA)	Federal act requiring that certain employers establish a policy that provides all eligible employees with up to 12 weeks of unpaid leave during any 12-month period for several family-related occurrences (e.g., birth of a child, care of a sick spouse).
Unemployment compensation	State system, created by the Federal Unemployment Tax Act (FUTA), that provides unemployment compensation to qualified employees who lose their jobs.
Consolidated Omnibus Budget Reconciliation Act (COBRA)	Federal law that ensures that when employees lose their jobs or have their hours reduced to a level at which they would not be eligible to receive medical, dental, or optical benefits from their employer, the employees will be able to continue receiving benefits under the employers' policy for up to 18 months by paying the premiums for the policy.
Employee Retirement Income Security Act (ERISA)	Federal law that sets minimum standards for most voluntarily established pension and health plans in private industry to provide protection for individuals in these plans. HIPAA and COBRA are amendments to ERISA.
Occupational Safety and Health Act (OSHA) of 1970	Federal law that established the Occupational Safety and Health Administration, the agency responsible for setting safety standards under the act, as well as enforcing the act through inspections and the levying of fines against violators.

Exhibit 24-2

Significant Laws Governing the Employment Relationship

[18] 29 U.S.C. § 206(d)1.

FAIR LABOR STANDARDS ACT

Fair Labor Standards Act (FLSA)

Federal law which requires that a minimum wage of a specified amount be paid to all employees in covered industries; also mandates that employees who work more than 40 hours in a week be paid no less than 1½ times their regular wage for all hours beyond 40 worked in a given week.

The **Fair Labor Standards Act (FLSA)** requires that a minimum wage of a specified amount be paid to all employees in covered industries. The specified amount is periodically raised by Congress to compensate for increases in the cost of living caused by inflation. In the summer of 2009, the federal minimum wage was raised to $7.25. This was the first increase in almost 10 years.

FLSA mandates that employees who work more than 40 hours in a week be paid no less than one and one-half times their regular wage for all the hours beyond 40 that they work during a given week. Four categories of employees are excluded:

- Executives
- Administrative employees
- Professional employees
- Outside salespersons

FAMILY AND MEDICAL LEAVE ACT

Family and Medical Leave Act (FMLA)

Federal act requiring that employers provide all eligible employees with up to 12 weeks of leave during any 12-month period for several family-related occurrences (e.g., birth of a child, care of a sick spouse).

When the **Family and Medical Leave Act (FMLA)** went into effect in 1993, it was hailed by its supporters as a "breakthrough" in American law and feared by its opponents as an unwieldy encumbrance on business. FMLA covers all public employers, as well as private employers with 50 or more employees. It guarantees all eligible employees (those who have worked at least 25 hours a week for each of 12 months prior to the leave) up to 12 weeks of *unpaid* leave during any 12-month period for any of the following family-related occurrences:

- The birth of a child.
- The adoption of a child.
- The placement of a foster child in the employee's care.
- The care of a seriously ill spouse, parent, or child.
- A serious health condition that renders the employee unable to perform any of the essential functions of his or her job.

UNEMPLOYMENT COMPENSATION

unemployment compensation

A state system, created by the Federal Unemployment Tax Act (FUTA), that provides unemployment compensation to qualified employees who lose their jobs.

While FMLA in some cases helps employees retain their jobs, what happens if they lose their jobs? The Federal Unemployment Tax Act (FUTA),[19] passed in 1935, created a state system to provide **unemployment compensation** to qualified employees who lose their jobs. Under this law, employers pay taxes to the states, which deposit the money into the federal government's Unemployment Insurance Fund. Each state has an account from which it can access the money in the fund in accordance with the rules the state establishes for eligibility. States have different minimum standards for qualifying for unemployment compensation, although almost all states require that the applicant did not voluntarily quit or get fired for cause.

WORKERS' COMPENSATION LAWS

workers' compensation laws

State laws that provide for financial compensation to employees or their dependents when a covered employee is injured on the job.

Unlike many other laws affecting the employment relationship, workers' compensation legislation is purely state law. Our coverage of this topic must therefore be rather generalized. Prudent businesspeople will familiarize themselves with the workers' compensation statutes of the states within which their companies operate.

Workers' compensation laws ensure that covered workers who are injured on the job can receive financial compensation through an administrative procedure, rather than having to sue their employer. For administrative convenience, most states exclude certain types of businesses and small firms from coverage. Some states also allow businesses that have sufficient resources to be self-insured, rather than participate in the state program.

[19] 26 U.S.C. §§ 3301–3310.

Parental Leave in the United Kingdom

Benefits are relative. Many in the United Kingdom compare their benefits to those of parents in France and feel they receive inadequate benefits; but in comparison to what parents in the United States receive, parents, especially mothers, in the United Kingdom are treated quite well. Women are entitled to 26 weeks off, regardless of how long they have worked for their employer. Statutory maternity pay (SMP) is paid for 36 weeks. For the first six weeks SMP is paid at 90 percent of average earnings, and for the remaining 30 weeks SMP is £108 a week or 90 percent of average weekly earnings if this is less.

Women can take another 26 weeks of additional maternity leave if they have completed 26 weeks' continuous service with their employer by the beginning of the 14th week before their expected week of childbirth. This leave is unpaid, but many employers provide some financial compensation during this period.

Fathers are entitled to two weeks' paid paternity leave that may be taken any time from the date of birth to eight weeks from the birth. Fathers get statutory paternity pay (SPP) of £108 a week or 90 percent of their average weekly earnings, whichever is less, for the two weeks.

CONSOLIDATED OMNIBUS BUDGET RECONCILIATION ACT OF 1985

The **Consolidated Omnibus Budget Reconciliation Act (COBRA)** ensures that employees who lose their jobs or have their hours reduced to a level at which they are no longer eligible to receive medical, dental, or optical benefits can pay to continue receiving benefits for themselves and their dependents under the employer's policy. The employee must pay the premiums for the policy, plus up to a 2 percent administration fee, to maintain the coverage for up to 18 months, or 29 months for a disabled worker. This is often quite expensive. An employee has 60 days after coverage would ordinarily terminate to decide whether to maintain the coverage.

This obligation does *not* arise under either of two conditions:

1. The employee is fired for gross misconduct.
2. The employer decides to eliminate benefits for all current employees.

Consolidated Omnibus Budget Reconciliation Act (COBRA)

Federal law which ensures that when employees lose their jobs or have their hours reduced to a level at which they would not be eligible to receive medical, dental, or optical benefits from their employer, the employees will be able to continue receiving benefits under the employer's policy for up to 18 months by paying the premiums for the policy.

EMPLOYEE RETIREMENT INCOME SECURITY ACT OF 1974

The **Employee Retirement Income Security Act (ERISA)** is "a federal law that sets minimum standards for most voluntarily established pension and health plans in private industry to provide protection for individuals in these plans."[20] Under ERISA, employers must provide participants with all the following:

1. Plan information (i.e., features and funding).
2. Assurances of the fiduciary responsibility of those in charge of managing and controlling the plan assets.
3. A grievance and appeals process for participants to get benefits from their plans.
4. The right to sue for benefits and breaches of fiduciary duty.[21]

Employers are required to provide to employees, free of charge, a *summary plan description (SPD),* which provides information on how the plan operates, the benefits under the plan, how to apply for such benefits, when such benefits vest, and when benefits may be paid out.

Employee Retirement Income Security Act (ERISA)

Federal law that sets minimum standards for most voluntarily established pension and health plans in private industry to provide protection for individuals in these plans.

OCCUPATIONAL SAFETY AND HEALTH ACT OF 1970

The federal government regulates workplace safety primarily through the **Occupational Safety and Health Act (OSHA) of 1970,** which requires that every employer "furnish to each of his

Occupational Safety and Health Act (OSHA) of 1970

Federal law that established the Occupational Safety and Health Administration, the agency responsible for setting safety standards under the act and enforcing the act through inspections and the levying of fines against violators.

[20] Department of Labor, Employee Retirement Income Security Act, www.dol.gov/dol/topic/health-plans/erisa.htm.
[21] Ibid.

employees . . . employment . . . free from recognized hazards that are likely to cause death or serious physical harm." The Occupational Safety and Health Administration (abbreviated OSHA, the same as the act) is the agency that is responsible for promulgating workplace safety standards, inspecting facilities to ensure compliance with the standards, and bringing enforcement actions against violators. In addition, OSHA undertakes educational programs for employers and employees.

LO 24-6 Employee Privacy in the Workplace

With the rapid expansion of technology, new issues related to workplace privacy have evolved. Technology has stimulated the growth of such issues in a number of ways. On the one hand, technology has given employers new ways to gather information about employees. On the other hand, new technologies have provided more temptations for employees to be "off the job" at work, thus creating a stimulus for more employer monitoring. For example, surveys have shown that 90 percent of employees with Internet access at work look at non-work-related websites at least once a day,[22] 90 percent receive non-work-related e-mail,[23] and 84 percent send non-work-related e-mail.[24] Given such statistics, it is understandable that employers would want to monitor what employees are doing when they are supposed to be on the job.

ELECTRONIC MONITORING AND COMMUNICATION

Omnibus Crime Control and Safe Streets Act of 1968

Federal statute banning employers from listening to the private telephone conversations of employees or disclosing the contents of these conversations. Employers may ban personal calls and monitor calls for compliance as long as they discontinue listening to any conversation once they determine it is personal.

Electronic Communications Privacy Act (ECPA) of 1986

Federal law that extended employees' privacy rights to electronic forms of communication, including e-mail and cellular phones; outlaws the intentional interception of electronic communications and the intentional disclosure or use of the information obtained through such interception.

Business owners need to understand the extent to which they can monitor employees' telephone conversations, read their e-mail, and listen to their voice mail. Questions related to such monitoring primarily involve the common law tort of invasion of privacy and two federal statutes: the Omnibus Crime Control and Safe Streets Act of 1968,[25] as amended by the Electronic Communications Privacy Act of 1986.[26]

Under the **Omnibus Crime Control and Safe Streets Act of 1968,** employers cannot listen to the private telephone conversations of employees or disclose the contents of these conversations. They may, however, ban personal calls and monitor calls for compliance as long as they discontinue listening to any conversation once they determine it is personal. Violators may be subject to fines of up to $10,000. Under the **Electronic Communications Privacy Act (ECPA) of 1986,** employee's privacy rights were extended to electronic forms of communication including e-mail and cellular phones. ECPA outlaws the intentional interception of electronic communications and the intentional disclosure or use of the information obtained through such interception.

In recognition of the fact that employers may sometimes need to monitor employee conversations for the purpose of improving employee performance or protecting employees from harassing calls, ECPA includes a "business-extension exemption" that allows employers to monitor employee telephone conversations in the ordinary course of their employment. This exception is subject to the constraint that the employer cannot continue to listen to conversations after it becomes apparent that they are personal. Also, monitoring is allowed when employees give their prior consent.

The key question in cases involving employer monitoring and interception of employee communications via e-mail, telephone, or voice mail is whether the employee had a *reasonable expectation of privacy* with respect to the communication in question. Employers are in the strongest position if they have a clear policy establishing that there is no reasonable expectation of privacy. Employment law experts advise that having a clear employee privacy policy that employees sign will minimize the likelihood of being sued by employees for invasion of

[22] Dyland Loeb McClain, "I'll Be Right with You, Boss, as Soon as I Finish My Shopping," *New York Times,* January 10, 2001, p. G1.
[23] Ibid.
[24] Ibid.
[25] 18 U.S.C. § 2210 et seq.
[26] 18 U.S.C. §§ 2510–2521.

CASE Nugget

When Can Employees Be Forced to Take a Lie Detector Test?

Polkey v. Transtrecs Corp.
U.S. Court of Appeals for the Eleventh Circuit

404 F.3d 1264 (11th Cir. 2005)

Polkey was a supervisor in the mailroom at Pensacola Naval Air Station. The mailroom was run by a company called Transtrecs. After discovering that some mail had been tampered with, Polkey reported it to her supervisor. Transtrecs asked all six employees, including Polkey, to take a lie detector (i.e., polygraph) test. The employee most suspected was tested first, and the lie detector test indicated that he might have been the one who tampered with the mail. Polkey and the remaining employees then refused to take the lie detector test. Transtrecs fired Polkey. She sued for violation of the Employee Polygraph Protection Act (EPPA). The district court granted summary judgment for Polkey. Transtrecs appealed.

On appeal, the district court's judgment was affirmed. The court held that Transtrecs violated EPPA by requesting and even suggesting that the employees take a polygraph test. Transtrecs argued that it was exempt because of national security, but the appellate court said that this applies only to the government. Transtrecs was merely a contractor for the government. Transtrecs also argued that it was exempt because the polygraph was part of an ongoing investigation of Polkey and that she was under suspicion. For this exemption to apply, an employer must have an articulable basis in fact to indicate that the employee was involved in or responsible for an economic loss. Transtrecs could make no such showing. Polkey prevailed.

privacy. These policies should be spelled out in the employee handbook, as well as explained to employees. At a minimum, employer privacy policies should cover the following issues:

1. Employer monitoring of telephone conversations.
2. Employer surveillance policies.
3. Employee access to medical and personnel records.
4. Drug testing policies.
5. Lie detector policies.
6. Ownership of computers and all issues unique to the electronic workplace.

Labor Laws and Unions LO 24-7

Many people would argue that the laws that improved workers' conditions most significantly were not any of those previously discussed but, rather, were the laws that gave employees the right to organize and bargain collectively over wages and terms and conditions of employment. During the Great Depression, workers were first given the right to organize, and since that time unionization rates have varied significantly. During the post-World War II period, over one-third of American workers were organized. Yet by 2005, only 12.5 percent of workers were unionized.[27]

[27] Bureau of Labor Statistics, www.bls.gov/news.release/union2.nr0.htm.

Not all occupations are equally organized, with the main base of unions being in the industrial sector. Unions, however, are increasingly organizing professionals and those in the service industry. Today, nearly 4 in 10 government workers belong to a union, and protective service workers, a group that includes police and firefighters, had the highest unionization rate of all occupations during 2005: 37 percent.[28]

Labor-management relations in the United States today are governed by three major pieces of legislation:

1. The Wagner Act of 1935.
2. The Taft-Hartley Act of 1947.
3. The Landrum-Griffin Act of 1959.

The Taft-Hartley Act amended the Wagner Act, and they are jointly referred to as the *National Labor Relations Act (NLRA)*.

THE WAGNER ACT OF 1935

The first major piece of federal legislation adopted explicitly to encourage the formation of labor unions and provide for **collective bargaining** between employers and unions as a means of obtaining the peaceful settlement of labor disputes was the **Wagner Act.** Collective bargaining "consists of negotiations between an employer and a group of employees so as to determine the conditions of employment."[29]

The Wagner Act also created an administrative agency, the *National Labor Relations Board (NLRB),* to interpret and enforce the NLRA. Finally, the act provides for judicial review in designated federal courts of appeal.

THE TAFT-HARTLEY ACT OF 1947

The 12 years between passage of the Wagner Act and that of the Taft-Hartley Act saw a huge growth in unionization, which resulted in an increase in workers' power. Public perception of this trend led to the passage of the **Taft-Hartley Act,** also known as the Labor-Management Relations Act, which was designed to curtail some of the powers the unions had acquired under the Wagner Act.

THE LANDRUM-GRIFFIN ACT OF 1959

The **Landrum-Griffin Act** primarily governs the internal operations of labor unions. This act, which was a response to evidence of certain undesirable internal labor union practices, requires certain financial disclosures by unions and establishes civil and criminal penalties for financial abuses by union officials. "Labor's Bill of Rights," contained in the act, protects employees from their own unions.

THE NATIONAL LABOR RELATIONS BOARD

The **National Labor Relations Board (NLRB)** is the administrative agency that interprets and enforces the *National Labor Relations Act (NLRA)*. The NLRB's three primary functions are to:

1. Monitor the conduct of the employer and the union during an election to determine whether workers want to be represented by a union.
2. Prevent and remedy unfair labor practices by employers or unions.
3. Establish rules interpreting the NLRA.

The NLRB has jurisdiction over all employees *except* those who work in federal, state, and local government and those covered by the Railway Labor Act (employees in the transportation

collective bargaining
The process whereby workers organize collectively and bargain with employers regarding the workplace.

Wagner Act
The first major piece of federal legislation adopted explicitly to encourage the formation of labor unions and provide for collective bargaining between employers and unions as a means of obtaining the peaceful settlement of labor disputes.

Taft-Hartley Act
Federal legislation designed to curtail some of the powers that unions had acquired under the Wagner Act; designates certain union actions as unfair. Also called *Labor-Management Relations Act.*

Landrum-Griffin Act
Federal legislation that primarily governs the internal operations of labor unions. It requires financial disclosures by unions, establishes penalties for financial abuses by union officials, and includes "Labor's Bill of Rights" to protect employees from their own unions.

National Labor Relations Board (NLRB)
An administrative agency created by the Wagner Act to interpret and enforce the National Labor Relations Act.

[28] Ibid.
[29] Legal Information Institute, www.law.cornell.edu/topics/collective_bargaining.html.

CASE Nugget

May an Employee Be Fired for Trashing Her Employer on Facebook?

Fair Labor Standards Board [on behalf of Dawnmarie Souza] v. American Medical Response of Connecticut
Unpublished

Case settled by unpublished agreement between parties, February 2011

Dawnmarie Souza was employed by American Medical Response (AMR) of Connecticut. A customer complained about her work, and she was required to prepare a response. Her supervisor refused to permit a representative of the Teamsters, the union representing the company's workers, to help prepare her response. Souza then mocked her supervisor on Facebook, reportedly using several vulgarities to ridicule him. According to copies of Souza's Facebook posts obtained by CNET, she called her supervisor a "dick" in one and "a scumbag" in another. The Connecticut ambulance company fired Souza on December 1, 2009. The National Labor Relations Board (NLRB) sued AMR of Connecticut on October 27, 2010, claiming the employee, Dawnmarie Souza, was illegally fired and denied union representation.

The closely watched case touched on whether employers have the right to discipline employees for comments they make on social-networking sites. The NLRB complaint said that Souza "engaged in concerted activities with other employees by criticizing respondent's supervisor . . . on her Facebook page" on November 8, 2009. In response to the NLRB complaint, AMR claimed Souza's comments were not protected activity. However, the NLRB contended that AMR's termination of Souza's employment violated the National Labor Relations Act, which allows employees to discuss the terms and conditions of their employment with co-workers and others.

In February 2011, the case was settled. Under the terms of the settlement, AMR agreed to revise "overly broad rules" in the employee handbook regarding how employees can communicate on the Internet and with co-workers regarding their work conditions. According to the FLSB, the company also agreed to not discipline employees for requesting union representation. The allegations regarding Souza's discharge were resolved in a separate, private agreement between Souza and AMR. Financial terms were not revealed.

Sources: Steven Musil, "Company Settles Facebook Firing Case," February 7, 2011, http://news.cnet.com/8301-1023_3-20030955-93.html; see also Erline Aguiluz, "AMR Settles Dawnmarie Souza's Wrongful Termination Lawsuit," February 11, 2011, http://philadelphiaemploymentlawnews.com/2011/02/amr-settles-dawnmarie-souzas-wrongful-termination-lawsuit.html.

industry); independent contractors; agricultural workers; household domestics; persons employed by a spouse or parent; and supervisors, managerial employees, and confidential employees. In the case above, the NLRB brought a lawsuit against a company after the company fired an employee for posting negative comments about a supervisor on Facebook.

THE COLLECTIVE BARGAINING PROCESS

Once the union has been certified, union and management must begin to bargain in good faith about wages, hours, and other terms and conditions of work. Note that the NLRB can order only that the parties bargain in good faith; it cannot order them to reach an agreement with respect to any contract term.

Both the employer and the bargaining-unit representative are required by the NLRA to bargain collectively in good faith with respect to wages, hours, and other terms and conditions of employment

SUMMARY

When May an Employee Be Fired?	*At-will employment* means that any employee who is not employed under a contract or a collective bargaining agreement may quit at any time for any reason or no reason at all, with no required notice to the employer. Moreover, the employer may fire the employee at any time, with no notice, for almost any reason.
Federal Employment Discrimination Laws Governing Employers	Federal law may be described as a "minimum" level of protection for all workers. State laws may give employees more, but not less, protection than federal laws. Some of the most important federal employment discrimination laws are the Civil Rights Act (CRA) of 1964—Title VII (as amended by the Civil Rights Act of 1991); Pregnancy Discrimination Act (PDA) of 1987; Age Discrimination in Employment Act (ADEA) of 1967; Americans with Disabilities Act; and Equal Pay Act of 1963.
Civil Rights Act— Title VII	Title VII of CRA (1964, as amended by the Civil Rights Act of 1991) protects employees against discrimination based on race, color, religion, national origin, and sex. It also prohibits harassment based on the same protected categories. Defenses to a charge of discrimination under Title VII include *merit, seniority system,* and *bona fide occupational qualification (BFOC)*.

- *Disparate treatment:* If the employee has been hired, fired, denied a promotion, and so on, based on membership in a protected class under Title VII, this is a form of intentional discrimination and qualifies the employee to sue for disparate-treatment discrimination.
- *Disparate impact: Disparate-impact cases arise when a plaintiff attempts to establish that while an employer's policy or practice appears to apply to everyone equally, its actual effect is that it disproportionately limits employment opportunities for a protected class.*
- *Sexual harassment:* Sexual harassment includes unwelcome sexual advances, requests for sexual favors, and other verbal or physical conduct of a sexual nature that implicitly or explicitly makes submission a term or condition of employment; makes employment decisions related to the individual dependent on submission to or rejection of such conduct; or has the purpose or effect of creating an intimidating, hostile, or offensive work environment. Two recognized forms are *hostile environment* and *quid pro quo harassment.*

Pregnancy Discrimination Act of 1987: PDA amended Title VII of CRA, expanding the definition of sex discrimination to include discrimination based on pregnancy.

Equal Employment Opportunity Commission: The EEOC is the federal agency charged with overseeing Title VII of the Civil Rights Act. Administrative complaints must be filed with the EEOC (or an equivalent state agency) prior to filing a lawsuit for discrimination or harassment.

Discrimination Based on Sexual Orientation— Actionable?	There is currently no federal legislation that prohibits discrimination based on sexual orientation. What does exist are individual state laws that prohibit such discrimination. State laws prohibiting discrimination based on sexual orientation exist in 17 states.
Age Discrimination in Employment Act of 1967	ADEA prohibits employers from refusing to hire, discharging, or discriminating in terms and conditions of employment on the basis of an employee's or applicant's being age 40 or older.
Americans with Disabilities Act	ADA prohibits discrimination against employees and job applicants with disabilities.
May an Employer Discriminate against a Smoker?	Some companies either won't hire smokers or are threatening to fire current employees who will not or are unable to quit smoking. Many states have passed laws preventing companies from engaging in such action.
Equal Pay Act of 1963	EPA prohibits an employer from paying workers of one gender less than the wages paid to employees of the opposite gender for work that requires equal skill, effort, and responsibility.
Additional Laws Governing the Employment Relationship	*Fair Labor Standards Act:* Employers must follow federal minimum-wage and hour laws. FLSA covers all employers engaged in interstate commerce or the production of goods for interstate commerce and requires that a "minimum wage" of a specified amount be paid to all employees in covered industries. The specified amount is periodically raised by Congress to

compensate for increases in the cost of living caused by inflation. The current minimum wage is $7.25.

Family and Medical Leave Act: The FMLA covers all public employers, as well as private employers with 50 or more employees. It guarantees all eligible employees (those who have worked at least 25 hours a week for each of 12 months prior to the leave) up to 12 weeks of unpaid leave during any 12-month period for any of the following family-related occurrences: the birth of a child; the adoption of a child; the placement of a foster child in the employee's care; the care of a seriously ill spouse, parent, or child; or a serious health condition that renders the employee unable to perform any of the essential functions of his or her job.

Unemployment compensation: The Federal Unemployment Tax Act (FUTA) created a state system that provides unemployment compensation to qualified employees who lose their jobs.

Workers' compensation laws: State laws provide for financial compensation to employees or their dependents when a covered employee is injured on the job.

Consolidated Omnibus Budget Reconciliation Act: COBRA ensures that when employees lose their jobs or have their hours reduced to a level at which they would not be eligible to receive medical, dental, or optical benefits from their employer, the employees will be able to continue receiving benefits under the employer's policy for up to 18 months by paying the premiums for the policy.

Employee Retirement Income Security Act: ERISA sets minimum standards for most voluntarily established pension and health plans in private industry to provide protection for individuals in these plans.

Occupational Safety and Health Act of 1970: The Occupational Safety and Health Administration is responsible for setting safety standards under OSHA, as well as enforcing the act through inspections and the levying of fines against violators.

Employee Privacy in the Workplace

Privacy issues are of increasing importance in the workplace. Privacy policies should cover matters such as employer surveillance policies, control of and access to medical and personnel records, drug testing, and e-mail policies.

Omnibus Crime Control and Safe Streets Act of 1968: Employers cannot listen to the private telephone conversations of employees or disclose the contents of these conversations. They may, however, ban personal calls and monitor calls for compliance as long as they discontinue listening to any conversation once they determine it is personal. Violators may be subject to fines of up to $10,000.

Electronic Communications Privacy Act of 1986: Under ECPA, employees' privacy rights were extended to electronic forms of communication including e-mail and cellular phones. ECPA outlaws the intentional interception of electronic communications and the intentional disclosure or use of the information obtained through such interception.

Labor Laws and Unions

Wagner Act of 1935: The Wagner Act was the first major piece of federal legislation adopted explicitly to encourage the formation of labor unions and provide for collective bargaining between employers and unions as a means of obtaining the peaceful settlement of labor disputes.

Collective bargaining: Collective bargaining consists of negotiations between an employer and a group of employees to determine the conditions of employment.

National Labor Relations Board: The Wagner Act created the NLRB, an administrative agency, to interpret and enforce the National Labor Relations Act (NLRA) and to provide for judicial review in designated federal courts of appeal.

Taft-Hartley Act of 1947: Also known as the Labor-Management Relations Act, the Taft-Hartley Act was designed to curtail some of the powers the unions had acquired under the Wagner Act. Just as the Wagner Act designated certain employer actions as unfair, the Taft-Hartley Act designated certain union actions as unfair.

Landrum-Griffin Act of 1959: The Landrum-Griffin Act primarily governs the internal operations of labor unions. It requires certain financial disclosures by unions and establishes civil and criminal penalties for financial abuses by union officials. "Labor's Bill of Rights," contained in the act, protects employees from their own unions.

Point/Counterpoint

Should Employers Be Permitted to Fire Employees for Activities, Such as Smoking, That They Do Outside Working Hours?	
YES	**NO**
The Centers for Disease Control and Prevention estimated that $75 billion is spent annually on medical expenses attributed to smoking. Businesses lose $82 billion in lost productivity from smokers. Smokers take about 6.5 more sick days a year than nonsmokers.	Employers should have no say in what employees do outside the workplace. Forcing employees to take tests to reveal whether they are smokers is an invasion of the employees' privacy. Many employees are addicted to cigarettes and would unfairly lose badly needed employment if unable to quit smoking.

Questions & Problems

1. Name five statutes that prohibit discrimination in employment.

2. Does Title VII apply to same-sex harassment?

3. What is the current amount of the federal minimum wage? When was the last time the federal minimum wage was increased?

4. What is required for an employee to be eligible for benefits under the Family and Medical Leave Act?

5. Whom does the Age Discrimination in Employment Act protect?

6. List the protected classes under the Civil Rights Act of 1964 (as amended in 1991).

7. Machinchick worked for PB Power for six years. He received excellent reviews. Two years after beginning work, he was promoted to vice president. Four years after his promotion, Machinchick got a new supervisor and the company adopted a new management approach. The new supervisor, Knowlton, stated his plan to "hand-pick employees whose mindset resides in the 21st Century." On April 7, 2002, Knowlton sent an e-mail in which he stated that he wanted to "strategically hire some younger engineers and designers." Two days later, Knowlton sent an e-mail to the Human Resources Department criticizing Machinchick's performance. A short time later, Machinchick, age 63, was fired. He was told to turn over his client base to Betz, age 42. Machinchick sued PB Power, alleging it had violated the Age Discrimination in Employment Act. The trial court granted a motion for summary judgment in favor of PB Power. Machinchick appealed. How should the appellate court decide? Has Machinchick shown enough evidence of age discrimination to warrant allowing the case to be heard by a jury? Explain your decision. [*Machinchick v. PB Power, Inc.,* 398 F.3d 345 (5th Cir. 2005).]

8. Cheryl Hall maintains that she was fired by Nalco Company for taking time off from work to undergo in vitro fertilization after being diagnosed with infertility. She filed suit under Title VII of the Civil Rights Act of 1964, as amended by the Pregnancy Discrimination Act (PDA), alleging her termination constituted discrimination on the basis of sex. The district court concluded that Hall's allegations did not state a Title VII claim because infertility is a gender-neutral condition entitled to no protection under the language of the PDA. The case went up on appeal. Do you agree with the district court that infertility is a gender-neutral condition? Or should the appellate court reverse the district court and hold that Hall was discriminated against on the basis of sex? Explain your reasoning. [*Cheryl Hall v. Nalco Company,* 534 F.3d 644 (2008).]

9. Jennifer Erickson was employed by Bartell Drug Company. Jennifer sued the company because its insurance plan failed to provide coverage for prescription contraceptives. She alleged that this was a form of sex discrimination under Title VII and a violation of the Pregnancy Discrimination Act (PDA). Her employer defended by arguing that its failure to

provide coverage for prescription contraceptives did not violate Title VII or the PDA because contraceptives were voluntary, were preventive, and did not treat or prevent an illness or disease and because control of one's fertility was not pregnancy, childbirth, or a related medical condition under PDA. If you were the court, how would you decide? Is failure to provide insurance coverage of prescription contraceptives a form of sex discrimination? Or pregnancy discrimination? Both? Neither? Explain the reasons for your answer. [*Erickson v. Bartell Drug Co.,* 141 F. Supp. 2d 1266 (U.S. Dist. Ct., Wash., 2001).]

10. Baxter Pharmacy paid its pharmacists a salary but no overtime pay. Under the Fair Labor Standards Act (FLSA), employers must pay employees overtime for hours worked in excess of 40 hours per week. Baxter Pharmacy believes that the pharmacists are exempt under FLSA because they are "professionals." The pharmacists disagree. Is being a professional an exemption from the requirement to pay overtime under FLSA? Are pharmacists professionals? How do you think the court ruled? [*De Jesus-Rentas v. Baxter Pharmacy Services Corp.,* 400 F.3d 72 (1st Cir. 2005).]

11. Antonucci worked as a dental assistant. She was stuck in the thumb with an instrument twice during a period of two months. Antonucci claimed that she feared for her health and safety. She quit her job and applied for unemployment compensation. Did Antonucci have "good cause" to quit her job? Should Antonucci be permitted to collect unemployment compensation? How do you think this matter was decided by the court? [*Antonucci v. State of Florida,* 793 So. 2d 1116 (Fla. Dist. Ct. App. 2001).]

12. Cynthia Anderson worked for the city of Columbus, Georgia, answering telephone calls from citizens. Anderson knew that calls from citizens were recorded, but she was unaware that due to a glitch, the telephone system continued to record her statements through her headset after a call was terminated. Anderson made disparaging remarks about the city manager's office, and her employment was terminated. Anderson sued the city, alleging that it had no right to record her private conversations with coworkers, which were unrelated to city business. Who should prevail? Why? [*Anderson v. City of Columbus, Georgia,* 2005 U.S. Dist. LEXIS 12612.]

13. Meadows worked as an assistant manager at a Dollar General store. While she was ringing up an order for a customer, he became verbally abusive. After she finished ringing up the sale, the customer threw the bag, containing a can of motor oil, at Meadows, hitting her in the eye. Meadows suffered a detached retina. The trial court awarded Meadows permanent partial disability under workers' compensation for her injury. Dollar General appealed the decision, arguing that the injury did not occur in the "course of employment." Do you believe that Meadows's injury occurred during the course of her employment? Why or why not? Was the trial court correct in granting her permanent partial disability, or did the appeals court overturn that decision? [*Dollar General Corp. v. Meadows,* 63 P.3d 548 (2002 WL 31991909, Okla. Ct. Civ. App. 2002).]

14. Occupational exposure to lead entails health risks, including the risk of harm to any fetus carried by a woman subjected to such exposure. Eight employees of an employer, in whose battery manufacturing process lead was a primary ingredient, became pregnant while maintaining blood-lead levels in excess of the level that appeared to be the critical level noted by the Occupational Safety and Health Administration (OSHA) for a woman who was planning to have a family. Afterward, the employer announced a policy barring all women, except those whose inability to bear children was medically documented, from jobs involving exposure or potential exposure to lead at a level exceeding OSHA standards. A group of employees who had been affected by the employer's fetal-protection policy filed, in the U.S. District Court for the Eastern District of Wisconsin, a class action challenging the policy as sex discrimination that violated Title VII of the Civil Rights Act of 1964, as amended, which prohibits sex-based classifications in terms and conditions of employment, in hiring and discharge decisions, and in other employment decisions. May the employer defend by arguing that being male is a bona fide occupational qualification for the job of manufacturing batteries? Or does the employer's action violate Title VII? Explain your reasoning. [*International Union, United Automobile, Aerospace & Agricultural Implement Workers of America, UAW et al., Petitioners v. Johnson Controls, Inc.,* 499 U.S. 187 (1991).]

15. Anthony Romeo was an openly gay student at Seton Hall, a Catholic university. He claimed that he elected to attend Seton Hall in part because of its published antidiscrimination policy. In 2003, he applied to the Seton Hall University Department of Student Affairs for provisional recognition of a gay and lesbian student organization. Dr. Laura Wankel, vice president of student affairs at Seton Hall, responded to Romeo's application in a letter, stating in pertinent part: "I am informing you that your application for provisional recognition has been denied. No organization based solely upon sexual orientation may receive formal University recognition." Wankel went on to say that "the Division of Student Affairs remains prepared

to work with gay and lesbian students to meet their needs. I am committed to working collaboratively with you and other students in fostering a positive, safe and caring community." Wankel then made a modest proposal giving the group some rights. The proposal, however, was not satisfactory to the students, and Romeo filed his complaint alleging violations of New Jersey's Law against Discrimination. He also cited Seton Hall's nondiscrimination policy: "No person may be denied employment or related benefits or admission to the University or to any of its programs or activities, either academic or nonacademic, curricular or extracurricular, because of race, color, religion, age, national origin, gender, sexual orientation, handicap and disability, or veteran's status." How should the court rule? May a Catholic university prevent recognition of a gay and lesbian student organization? Does the university's nondiscrimination policy make a difference? Why or why not? [*Romeo v. Seton Hall University,* 2005 N.J. Super. LEXIS 197.]

Looking for more review material?

The Online Learning Center at **www.mhhe.com/kubasekess2e** contains this chapter's "Assignment on the Internet" and also a list of URLs for more information, entitled "On the Internet." Find both of them in the Student Center portion of the OLC, along with quizzes and other helpful materials.

Chapter

25

Consumer Law

The Firestone Recall

On August 9, 2000, Bridgestone/Firestone Inc. announced a recall of 14.4 million tires, including all 15-inch Firestone ATX, ATX II, and 15-inch Wilderness AT tires used by Ford Motor Company on its popular SUVs. This announcement came 10 years after the first suit was filed against these companies for defective tires. Secrecy and protective orders within the courts kept this information hush-hush for 10 years until a local news station in Houston, Texas, got word in 1999 that Ford was replacing tires on Explorers in Saudi Arabia through what it called a "customer notification enhancement action." In response, the National Highway Traffic Safety Administration opened an investigation of the cases associated with these tires.[1]

In the original recall press release, Ford and Firestone claimed that they had each just been made aware of the safety problem and were consequently recalling the tires. However, some have argued that Ford and Firestone knew about the safety problems with the tires as much as 10 years earlier but did not inform the National Highway Traffic Safety Administration of the potential danger. Ford had been replacing tires not only in Saudi Arabia but also in Venezuela and Thailand.[2]

1. Suppose you were a member of Congress when this case emerged. What action would you take to ensure that situations such as this would not occur again?

2. Suppose you were the manager of Ford or Firestone. Would you have handled the situation differently, and if so, why?

[1] Terril Yue Jones, "Cause of Tire Failures Still a Matter of Dispute," *Los Angeles Times*, October 22, 2000, p. C1.
[2] Michael B. Bowden, "Firestone Tire Recall Could Have Broad Impact on Litigation," 2000 LWUSA 842 (2000).

After reading this chapter, you will be able to answer the following questions:

LO 25-1 What is the purpose of the Federal Trade Commission Act?

LO 25-2 How does the Federal Trade Commission determine what constitutes deceptive advertising?

LEARNING OBJECTIVES

LO 25-3 What is the purpose of labeling and packaging laws?

LO 25-4 What are the different acts that provide credit protection?

LO 25-5 What are the different laws that help ensure consumer health and safety?

consumer law

A statute or administrative rule serving to protect consumer interests.

Consumers buy products and services from sellers every day. In some instances, however, consumers do not have as much power in the transaction as the seller has. As we see in the Firestone case, the seller had more knowledge about the product, how it was made, and pricing strategies than did the consumers. Because Congress recognized the opportunities for sellers to take advantage of buyers in this way, it created laws that regulate transactions between consumers and sellers. A **consumer law** is a statute or administrative rule serving to protect consumer interests.

Various state and federal consumer laws protect consumers from unfair trade practices of sellers as well as unsafe products. Although the laws differ among the states, many of the state laws provide consumer protection exceeding that guaranteed by federal law. This chapter explores a range of consumer laws concerning deceptive advertising, product labeling, sales procedures, health and product safety, and consumer credit. First, however, it discusses a federal agency that is one of the most important creators and enforcers of consumer protection laws—the Federal Trade Commission.

LO 25-1

The Federal Trade Commission

Congress created the Federal Trade Commission (FTC) through the Federal Trade Commission Act of 1914.[3]

The FTC is an independent federal agency with five commissioners appointed by the president and confirmed by the Senate. Each commissioner serves a seven-year term. The president chooses one commissioner to serve as chair of the FTC.

How does the FTC meet its goal of protecting consumers? The FTC helps to protect consumers through two methods: (1) consumer education and (2) legal action. First, the FTC creates campaigns to educate consumers about laws that protect them. Second, the FTC educates businesses to help them comply voluntarily with consumer laws. For example, the FTC creates **industry guides,** interpretations of consumer laws, to encourage businesses to stop unlawful behavior. When businesses follow the FTC guidelines, they can cut potentially steep costs associated with violating consumer laws.

industry guides

Interpretations of consumer laws created by the FTC to encourage businesses to stop unlawful behavior.

HOW THE FTC BRINGS AN ACTION

The FTC receives a variety of complaints about businesses from consumer groups and individuals. When a consumer files a complaint with the FTC, he or she triggers a chain of events that could lead to an FTC action against the violator. The FTC typically begins a nonpublic investigation of the company.

If, after its investigation, the FTC believes that a company violated the law, the FTC sends a complaint to the alleged violator. At that time, the FTC may settle the complaint through a consent order with the company. A **consent order** is a statement in which the company agrees to stop the disputed behavior but does not admit that it broke the law. Should the company violate the consent order, it will usually be forced to pay a fine.

consent order

A statement in which a company agrees to stop disputed behavior but does not admit that it broke the law.

If the company refuses to enter into a consent agreement, the FTC may then decide to issue a formal administrative complaint. The issuing of this complaint leads to a hearing before an administrative law judge. If the judge decides that the company has violated the law, the FTC

[3] 15 U.S.C. §§ 41–58.

issues a **cease-and-desist order,** requiring that the company stop the illegal behavior. However, the company may appeal this decision to the five commissioners. If the commissioners uphold the ruling, the company may appeal to the U.S. court of appeals and, finally, to the Supreme Court. If the courts uphold the FTC's decision, the company must follow the cease-and-desist order. If the company violates the order, the FTC can seek an injunction against the company or fine the company up to $10,000 per violation.

cease-and-desist order
An FTC order requiring that a company stop its illegal behavior.

TRADE REGULATION RULES

Bringing an action may be effective in protecting consumers from the activities of one company, but how can the FTC protect consumers if most companies within one industry are using the same unfair or deceptive practices? Bringing actions against all of these companies would be costly and time-consuming.

An alternative method of addressing these practices is through trade regulation rules. If the FTC finds that deception is pervasive in an industry, the FTC can recommend rule making. An administrative rule has the effect of law. Furthermore, the FTC can bring legal action against those who violate FTC rules.

Deceptive Advertising

LO 25-2

Section 5 of the Federal Trade Commission Act prohibits deceptive and unfair acts in commercial settings, including consumer purchases. This section of the chapter specifically analyzes **deceptive advertising,** the practice of advertising with claims that mislead or could mislead a reasonable consumer. **Puffing,** the use of generalities and clear exaggerations, is permissible.

The FTC decides whether an advertisement is deceptive on a case-by-case basis. Deceptive claims have three elements:[4] (1) a *material* misrepresentation, omission, or practice that is (2) *likely to mislead* (3) a *reasonable* consumer. When an advertised claim appears to be authentic but in fact is not, the advertising is deceptive. While the FTC has the power to determine whether an advertisement is deceptive or just mere puffing, courts often have to make that determination as well. Sometimes companies seek injunctive relief for false advertising of their competitors under the Lanham Act. The Lanham Act was intended, in part, to protect persons engaged in commerce against false advertising and unfair competition. In Case 25-1, the court considers whether statements made by a business were deceptive advertising under the Lanham Act or mere puffing.

deceptive advertising
The practice of advertising with claims that mislead or could mislead a reasonable consumer.

puffing
The use of generalities and clear exaggerations.

[4] FTC, "Policy Statement on Deception," 1983.

CASE 25-1

AMERICAN ITALIAN PASTA COMPANY v. NEW WORLD PASTA COMPANY
U.S. COURT OF APPEALS FOR THE EIGHTH CIRCUIT
371 F.3d 387 (2004)

FACTS: *In the fall of 2000, American Italian Pasta Company purchased Mueller's brand dried pasta from Best Foods and assumed all packaging, distributing, pricing, and marketing for the brand. American placed the phrase "America's Favorite Pasta" on Mueller's packaging. On various packages, the phrase "Quality Since 1867," "Made from 100% Semolina," or "Made with Semolina" accompanies the phrase "America's Favorite Pasta." The packaging also contains a paragraph in which the phrase* "America's Favorite Pasta" appears. The paragraph (1) states pasta lovers have enjoyed Mueller's pasta for 130 years; (2) claims Mueller's "pasta cooks to perfect tenderness every time," because Mueller's uses "100% pure semolina milled from the highest quality durum wheat"; and (3) encourages consumers to "taste why Mueller's is America's favorite pasta." A pasta competitor, New World, demanded that American cease the use of such phrase, and American filed the litigation seeking a declaration

(continued)

from the Court that such phrase was not false and misleading advertising but was instead mere puffery.

ISSUE: Is the phrase "America's favorite pasta" deceptive advertising or mere puffery?

REASONING:

Puffery exists in two general forms: (1) exaggerated statements of bluster or boast upon which no reasonable consumer would rely; and (2) vague or highly subjective claims of product superiority, including bald assertions of superiority. Puffery and statements of fact are mutually exclusive. If a statement is a specific, measurable claim or can be reasonably interpreted as being a factual claim, i.e., one capable of verification, the statement is one of fact. Conversely, if the statement is not specific and measurable, and cannot be reasonably interpreted as providing a benchmark by which the veracity of the statement can be ascertained, the statement constitutes puffery. Defining puffery broadly provides advertisers and manufacturers considerable leeway to craft their statements, allowing the free market to hold advertisers and manufacturers accountable for their statements, ensuring vigorous competition, and protecting legitimate commercial speech.

The statement "America's Favorite Pasta" is not a specific, measurable claim and cannot be reasonably interpreted as an objective fact. "Well liked" and "admired" [part of the definition of "favorite"] are entirely subjective and vague. Neither the words "well liked" nor "admired" provide an empirical benchmark by which the claim can be measured. "Well liked" and "admired" do not convey a quantifiable threshold in sheer number, percentage, or place in a series. A product may be well liked or admired, but the product may not dominate in sales or market share.

DECISION AND REMEDY: The court found that the phrase was mere puffery and not deceptive advertising because no statements of fact were made regarding the product. A reasonable person would not intrepret the phrase in dispute as an objective fact.

SIGNIFICANCE OF THE CASE: The line between deceptive advertising and mere puffery is vague and uncertain and has to be determined on a case-by-case basis. Businesses should be careful to consult with attorneys if a phrase has the potential to mislead or might be considered deceptive advertising.

CRITICAL THINKING

What is the court's reasoning for concluding that the statement in question was puffing? How strong do you find the reasoning?

ETHICAL DECISION MAKING

What values does the court promote in its decision to rule in the manner it did? How does the decision promote those values?

half-truth

Information that is true but is not complete.

ad substantiation

An FTC standard requiring that advertisers have a reasonable basis for the claims made in their ads.

If the advertisement is a **half-truth**—that is, the information presented is true but incomplete—the advertiser is deceiving the consumer. To combat deceptive advertisements and half-truths, the FTC requires **ad substantiation,** requiring that advertisers have a reasonable basis for the claims made in their advertisements. As Exhibit 25-1 points out, many have argued that "Made in the USA" labels are deceptive advertising.

Exhibit 25-1

"Made in the USA" Labels and the FTC

Many companies boast that their products are "Made in the USA." But what exactly does it mean to be "Made in the USA"? The FTC is charged with setting forth standards to avoid deception and false advertising about products that are supposedly made in the United States.

In the past, the FTC stated that "Made in the USA" should not be used "unless all, or virtually all, of the components and labor are of U.S. origin." Thus, if a company assembled a product in the United States but shipped in some components from out of the country, the FTC would argue that "Made in the USA" should not be used.

The FTC's definition of the phrase was stricter than others' definitions. For example, NAFTA defines "Made in the USA" as a product for which at least 55 percent of the labor and components are from Canada, Mexico, or the United States. Customs draws the line at 50 percent.

In 1997, the FTC decided to continue enforcing the "all or virtually all" standard. Those with strong union ties had argued against any weaker definition, such as the 75 percent the FTC had been debating.

Source: Federal Trade Commission, FTC Consumer Report, "Complying with the Made in the USA Standard," www.ftc.gov/bcp/conline/pubs/buspubs/madeusa.shtm.

Deceptive Advertising in China

Although puffery is allowed in advertising in the United States, not all countries universally accept puffery as an acceptable form of advertising. For example, China has greater restrictions on advertising than the United States. Problematic advertising claims in China fall largely into two groups: (1) unsubstantiated, clearly deceptive claims that are also unacceptable in the United States and (2) claims such as puffery, comparisons, and statistics, which are okay in the United States but are prohibited or restricted by Chinese law. Specifically, in China there is a statutory ban on puffery due to its deceptive nature. The ban has the potential to affect commerce and trade of global brands that have a standardized approach in their international advertising and do not take into careful consideration the Chinese regulations. In such cases, Chinese regulators of advertisements rarely accept the puffery defense.

However, the supreme court of China does exonerate commercial claims that employ obvious exaggerations but are unlikely to mislead the public, slightly contradicting the statutory ban on puffery (China Supreme People's Court, 2007). Because the terms *misleading* and *deceptive* are subjective, sometimes judges in China determine on a case-by-case basis what constitutes obvious exaggerations that are unlikely to mislead, just as U.S. judges often face this question. To help judges determine whether illegal puffing has occurred, the China Supreme People's Court advises the lower courts to consider factors such as daily life experience, the general understanding of the relevant public, people being misled, and the situation of the target consumer.

Source: Zhihong Gao, "Controlling Deceptive Advertising in China: An Overview," *Journal of Public Policy & Marketing,* Fall 2008, pp. 165–177.

An example of an FTC claim of deceptive advertising involved Body Wise International, Inc.'s "AG-Immune" dietary supplement. In 1995, Body Wise was prohibited from using false or unsubstantiated claims while advertising *any* of its products as part of its settlement with the FTC for using deceptive advertising to market a different dietary supplement. Body Wise then entered into a contract with Dr. Stoff to market AG-Immune. Stoff was paid royalties on every bottle of AG-Immune that Body Wise sold. However, no connection between Body Wise and Stoff was ever admitted in any of the advertisements for the product.

The FTC then alleged that Body Wise violated the 1995 order with its advertisements for AG-Immune. According to the FTC, Body Wise advertised that AG-Immune was able to "prevent or treat numerous diseases or conditions, including cancer, HIV/AIDS, heart disease, chronic fatigue syndrome, and asthma" and that scientific research supported the claims. Body Wise also allegedly claimed that AG-Immune improved the immune system's "ability to prevent or treat the aforementioned and many other diseases and conditions."[5] The FTC also argued that Stoff falsely claimed that the advertisements were supported by scientific data and that he was in a professional position to assess the efficacy of AG-Immune.

Body Wise and Stoff both agreed to settle with the FTC out of court. Both parties were responsible for paying hefty fines to the FTC for their deceptive advertisements. The main thrust of the FTC's argument was related to the fact that no scientific data existed to back Body Wise's claims regarding AG-Immune.

The existence of deceptive advertisements is not enough alone to prove damages for recovery when individual civil suits are filed. For example, in *Oliveira v. Amoco Oil Co.,*[6] a class action suit was brought against Amoco for deceptive advertisements. Amoco had made many claims over a seven-year period about the superiority of its premium gasoline. However, according to the plaintiffs, no scientific evidence supported Amoco's claims. The plaintiffs argued that the advertisements created a higher demand for Amoco gas, creating artificially high gas prices that hurt consumers regardless of specific reliance on the advertisements. The court rejected this argument, ruling that a "market theory" of causation is not enough to establish damages in an individual case. Moreover, reliance on the advertisements is a crucial element in establishing liability.

This case illustrates the importance of understanding specific consumer protection laws. Future business managers need to understand what kinds of advertising claims are permissible in our legal environment. To simplify this understanding for consumers and business owners, the FTC has classified certain types of deceptive or unfair advertising practices and created specific rules defining and prohibiting violations of these rules. The next section examines these classifications.

[5] FTC, "Body Wise International to Pay over $3.5 Million to Settle Federal and State Deceptive Advertising Charges for 'AG-Immune' Dietary Supplement," January 18, 2005, www.ftc.gov/opa/2005/01/bodywise.htm.
[6] 201 Ill. 2d 134 (2002).

BAIT-AND-SWITCH ADVERTISING

When sellers advertise a low price for an item generally unavailable to the consumer and then push the consumer to buy a more expensive item, they are engaging in **bait-and-switch advertising.** The low advertised price "baits" the consumer. Then the salesperson "switches" the consumer to a higher-priced item. In 1968, the FTC prohibited bait-and-switch advertising.

According to the FTC's "Guides against Bait Advertising," a seller can engage in bait-and-switch advertising in several ways. For instance, the seller might advertise a low price but have too little of the advertised good in stock, or the seller might discourage employees from selling the advertised item. These bait-and-switch advertising techniques violate FTC rules.

CASE Nugget

Are "No-Annual-Fee" Offers Bait-and-Switch Advertising?

Paula E. Rossman, Individually and for All Others Similarly Situated v. Fleet Bank (R.I.) National Association et al.
U.S. Court of Appeals for the Third Circuit

280 F.3d 384 (2002)

In 1999, Paula Rossman received a credit card offer from Fleet Bank, advertising the "Fleet Platinum MasterCard" with a low annual percentage rate and no annual fee. A few months after Rossman's account was opened, Fleet imposed an annual fee. Fleet sent a letter to Rossman stating that a $35 annual fee would be charged to her account annually on the anniversary of her account's opening; however, a second letter notified Rossman that the annual fee would be charged to her account within months. Rossman sued Fleet, claiming that Fleet had violated the disclosure requirements of the Truth in Lending Act (TILA) and engaged in a bait-and-switch advertising scheme. The district court dismissed Rossman's TILA claim for failing to state a claim on which relief could be granted. Rossman appealed to the Third Circuit Court of Appeals.

The appeals court applied a two-part test to determine whether Fleet's statement that the card had no annual fee was lawful. "First, it must have disclosed all of the information required by the statute. And second, it must have been true—i.e., an accurate representation of the legal obligations of the parties at that time—when the relevant solicitation was mailed." Rossman claimed that Fleet was required to disclose all fees that were currently imposed, as well as any fees that may be imposed later. Rossman also claimed that Fleet's disclosure was misleading by suggesting that there would never be an annual fee. Additionally, Rossman claimed that Fleet engaged in a bait-and-switch scheme, using the "no-annual-fee" provision to lure consumers into a contract when Fleet had no intention of honoring that provision.

Fleet argued that it was not required to disclose any future fees that may be imposed, but only those that currently existed. Fleet also turned to a clause in the solicitation disclosure insert that stated it "reserve[d] the right to change the benefit features associated with your Card at any time." The court found that Fleet's disclosure, as placed and worded, did not adequately link itself to the no-annual-fee provision. Thus, if the annual fee was permitted to be changed within the first annual term of the agreement, the court found that the statement "no annual fee" was an inadequate disclosure.

Turning its attention to Rossman's claim that Fleet had engaged in a bait-and-switch advertising scheme, the court did not see Fleet's behavior as resembling the classic bait-and-switch design. Ordinarily, consumers are baited with certain terms, but the switch for less enticing products or terms is made before the consumer enters into an agreement or contract. Rather, the court found Fleet's behavior to be even more egregious because Fleet actually bound the consumer in a contract before making the switch to charging an annual fee. Thus, Fleet had violated the provisions of TILA. The appeals court reversed the district court's ruling and remanded for proceedings.

FTC ACTIONS AGAINST DECEPTIVE ADVERTISING

If the FTC takes actions against a company and proves the advertising is deceptive, the FTC may issue a cease-and-desist order. To go a step beyond cease-and-desist orders, the FTC may also issue multiple-product orders. A **multiple-product order** is a form of cease-and-desist order issued by the FTC that applies not only to the product that was the subject of the action but also to other products produced by the same firm. Alternatively, the FTC may require that the company engage in **corrective advertising** (or *counteradvertising*), running advertisements in which the company explicitly states that the formerly advertised claims were untrue.

The rationale for corrective advertising is that consumers who saw the previous ads will see the new ads; the new ads will then correct the deceptive advertising. In a commission decision regarding the deceptive advertising of Doan's Pills, Commissioner Sheila Anthony described the characteristics of a situation requiring corrective advertising:

> Requiring the dissemination of a truthful message to counteract beliefs created or reinforced by a respondent's deceptive message is an appropriate method of restoring the *status quo ante* and denying a respondent the ability to continue to profit from its deception. . . . Corrective advertising is an appropriate remedy if (1) the challenged ads have substantially created or reinforced a misbelief; and (2) the misbelief is likely to linger into the future.[7]

However, some companies—and even one of the commissioners of the FTC—argued that corrective advertising is a form of compelled speech and thus violates the First Amendment right to engage in free speech.

multiple-product order

A form of cease-and-desist order issued by the FTC that applies not only to a specified product but also to other products produced by the same firm.

To see more about the FTC's regulation of advertising and how it helps prevent market failures, please see the **Connecting to the Core** activity on the text's website at www.mhhe.com/kubasekess2e.

corrective advertising

Advertising in which the company explicitly states that formerly advertised claims were untrue. Also called *counteradvertising*.

TELEMARKETING AND ELECTRONIC ADVERTISING

Consumer law, like all law, is dynamic, and technology is often a driving force of change in consumer law. Although technological developments provide consumers with a host of benefits, these developments are often prone to abuses not covered by existing consumer law. For example, telephones and fax machines facilitate fast and inexpensive communication around the world, but telemarketers can use these technologies to deceive consumers and invade their privacy. Hence, lawmakers have passed new laws to address these issues.

Two major acts regulate advertising by telephone and fax, the Telephone Consumer Protection Act (TCPA) of 1991 and the Telemarketing and Consumer Fraud and Abuse Prevention Act of 1994.[8] TCPA, which the Federal Communications Commission (FCC) enforces, forbids phone solicitation using an automatic telephone dialing system or a prerecorded voice. TCPA also makes it illegal to transmit advertisements via fax unless the recipient agrees to the fax transmission. TCPA allows consumers to obtain a private right to legal action. In other words, the act gives consumers the right to recover for their losses. If a telemarketer violates TCPA, the consumer can recover either monetary losses or $500 per violation. However, if the telemarketer willfully violated the act, the court can decide to triple the amount owed to the consumer.

Sometimes laws are ineffective in achieving their goals, however, so legislatures draft new laws to supplement existing law. Thus, even though the goals of consumer laws may not change, specific rules and provisions do. For example, despite the protection of TCPA, consumers still lost an estimated $40 billion in telemarketing fraud after the act went into effect.

To give consumers more protection against deceptive and abusive telemarketing practices, Congress enacted the Telemarketing and Consumer Fraud and Abuse Prevention Act of 1994.[9] Through this act, Congress asked the FTC to define "deceptive and abusive" telemarketing practices and required that the FTC create and enforce rules governing telemarketing that would prohibit such practices. Consequently, the FTC created the Telemarketing Sales Rule of 1995,[10]

[7] FTC, "Doan's Pills Must Run Corrective Advertising: FTC Ads Claiming Doan's Is Superior in Treating Back Pain Were Unsubstantiated" (press release), May 27, 1999.
[8] 47 U.S.C. § 227.
[9] 15 U.S.C. §§ 6101–6108.
[10] 16 C.F.R. § 310.

Respecting Languages of the Consumer

U.S. consumers often purchase products that are labeled or give directions in various languages, such as Spanish and French. The United States does not require that other publications, such as billboards, restaurant menus, or television advertisements, be multilingual. However, such requirements do exist in France, Canada, and Quebec.

During the early 1970s, French consumers voiced concern about foreign imports. Most of those products were labeled in languages other than French, so it became difficult to read directions or determine the content and function of a product. The government responded by passing a law in 1975 that regulates the labels and advertising of imported goods. The law mandates that French and English have to be the languages used for product labels, instructions, and all forms of advertising.

Canada passed a similar decree concerning the use of the French language. The Consumer Packaging and Labeling Act of Canada requires that all goods be labeled in both French and English.

While France and Canada were legislating the inclusion of both languages, Quebec legislated the exclusion of English. The Charter of the French Language, drafted by the Quebec government, requires that all public signs and advertisements be solely in French. If a product is produced and sold in Quebec, its packaging and product instructions are also to be in French alone.

which requires that telemarketers (1) identify the call as a sales call; (2) identify the product name and seller; (3) tell the total cost of goods being sold; (4) notify the listener or reader of whether the sale is nonrefundable; and (5) remove the consumer's name from the potential contact list if the consumer so requests.

Moreover, the FTC established that certain telemarketing behaviors are abusive, such as using profane or obscene language toward a customer and calling a person who previously requested to be taken off the particular seller's calling list. Additionally, if the telemarketer calls a residence before 8 a.m. or after 9 p.m., the telemarketer is engaging in abusive behavior. If a telemarketer violates the rule, the FTC or the state attorney general may bring an action against the telemarketer. If the action is successful, the telemarketer can face fines up to $10,000 per violation.

While reviewing and amending the Telemarketing Sales Rule in 2002, the FTC created a "Do Not Call" registry. The FTC states that the purpose of the Do Not Call registry is to give consumers a choice regarding telemarketing calls. The registry makes it illegal for telemarketers to call any number that has been registered for more than 31 days. The registration lasts for five years, and it can be completed online through the FTC's website. Both the FTC and the FCC are responsible for maintaining the list, with help from local state law enforcement officials.

The Global Context box discusses different restrictions placed on advertisements in other countries.

TOBACCO ADVERTISING

The tobacco industry's advertising is regulated through two acts: the Public Health Cigarette Smoking Act[11] of 1970 and the Smokeless Tobacco Health Education Act[12] of 1986. The Public Health Cigarette Smoking Act prohibits radio and television cigarette advertisements, and the Smokeless Tobacco Act imposes the same restrictions for smokeless tobacco ads.

LO 25-3 # Labeling and Packaging Laws

When consumers examine a product to decide whether to buy it, the label often influences the decision to purchase. For example, many of us have purchased food because the label said the food was "low fat." Unfortunately, manufacturers can include or omit information on labels that misleads consumers.

[11] 15 U.S.C. § 1331.
[12] 15 U.S.C. §§ 4401–4408.

Consequently, federal and state governments have passed laws that regulate product labeling. These laws generally require that the manufacturer provide accurate, understandable information on the label. Furthermore, if the product is potentially harmful, the manufacturer must make the consumer aware of the harm.

Several federal laws regulate product labeling. The Wool Products Labeling Act of 1939[13] requires accurate labeling of wool products. Similarly, the Fur Products Labeling Act of 1951[14] requires the accurate labeling of fur products. The Flammable Fabrics Act of 1953[15] makes it illegal to produce or distribute clothing "so highly flammable as to be dangerous when worn." The Fair Packaging and Labeling Act of 1966[16] requires that products carry labels that identify the product and provide specific information about the contents, such as the quantity of the contents and the size of a serving, if the number of servings is stated. Moreover, under this act, food product labels must show the nutritional content of the product. Similarly, the Nutrition Labeling and Education Act of 1990[17] requires that standard nutrition information (i.e., calories and fat) be provided on food labels. Additionally, this act defines the words *fresh* and *low fat.* In 1994, the FTC issued a statement saying that it would apply these label restrictions to food advertising to prevent deceptive advertising. Thus, not only do sellers need to be concerned about the use of *high, low,* and *light* on labels, but they are also required to use these words in particular ways in advertisements.

The goal of these laws is to provide consumers with specific information about product content. However, Congress has passed several laws that require information about the potential harms associated with a product. For example, the Federal Hazardous Substances Act of 1960 requires that all items containing dangerous substances carry warning labels.

Canada's cigarette labeling requirements are even more stringent than the U.S. requirements. In Canada, approximately 40 percent of cigarette packaging must be devoted to health warnings.[18] The Canadian Bureau of Tobacco Control, however, has proposed a new rule requiring that manufacturers dedicate 50 percent of cigarette packages to such warnings, which would include explicit pictures and images of mouth cancer or other severe diseases caused by cigarette use.[19]

Sales

The FTC and other government agencies have the power to regulate sales. For example, the Federal Reserve Board of Governors has the power to govern credit provisions related to sales contracts through its Regulation Z.[20] The FTC has created rules that govern specific types of sales in which the consumer is in a more vulnerable position compared to a consumer who walks into a traditional retail setting. This section examines FTC regulation of three of these uncommonly vulnerable commercial settings: door-to-door, telephone, and mail-order sales.

DOOR-TO-DOOR SALES

Imagine that you hear a knock at your door, open it, and discover a salesperson for an Internet provider. The person who knocked knows that you have just purchased a computer and are interested in learning about the Internet. The salesperson explains the price of various programs by which you can become familiar with the Internet. You listen, but decide that you would like to get additional information from an alternative provider. However, the salesperson is extremely pushy; to get the salesperson out of your house, you decide to purchase one of his plans.

[13] 15 U.S.C. §§ 1331–1341.
[14] 15 U.S.C. § 69.
[15] 15 U.S.C. § 1191.
[16] 15 U.S.C. §§ 1451 et seq.
[17] 21 U.S.C. § 343-1.
[18] Tobacco Products Control Regulations, SOR/89-21.
[19] Action on Smoking and Health, "Majority of Canadians Want Larger Warnings on Cigarette Packages" (press release), October 2000.
[20] 12 C.F.R. § 225.

In most door-to-door sales, the consumer does not have a chance to compare products and services to find the best service for his or her money. In addition, many consumers find it difficult to escape a salesperson in their homes. It is much easier to walk out of a store. Because the consumer is in a particularly vulnerable position in a door-to-door sale, the FTC has created special rules for such sales.

The FTC created the Cooling-Off Rule, giving consumers three days to cancel purchases they make from salespeople who come to their homes. Moreover, the salesperson must notify the consumer, both verbally and in writing, that the sales transaction may be canceled. The FTC rule also requires that the consumer be notified in writing in the same language in which the oral negotiations were conducted, thereby preventing unscrupulous businesses from taking advantage of non-English speakers.

The following case provides an example of the kinds of pressures that the FTC is trying to offset: Consolidated Promotions offered consumers a free gift for setting up a meeting in their home to discuss Consolidated products. This in-home meeting was in fact a sales pitch for Consolidated's photography packages, which included film and discounted photo processing. These packages cost from $1,200 to $2,500. When Consolidated Promotions refused to cancel some of the consumers' contracts, the FTC approved a complaint and referred it to the Department of Justice. The FTC alleged that the company violated the Cooling-Off Rule by "1) failing to honor valid cancellation notices; 2) misrepresenting consumers' rights to cancel their contracts; and 3) failing to inform each buyer orally of his or her right to cancel the order."[21] The FTC proposed that Consolidated Promotions enter into a consent decree whereby Consolidated would be required to send notice to all customers who bought a photography package after July 1, 1996, giving them an opportunity to cancel their contracts.

TELEPHONE AND MAIL-ORDER SALES

Most consumers have purchased at least one item from a catalog. Unfortunately, telephone and mail-order purchases trigger more complaints than do traditional retail or door-to-door sales. Suppose the office manager of a small accounting firm ordered five new chairs for the office through a catalog. The writing in the catalog indicated that the chairs would arrive within two weeks. The office manager called in the chair order, but six weeks later he had heard nothing from the company. What rights does he have in this situation?

The FTC originally addressed problems with mail-order sales through the 1975 Mail-Order Rule.[22] The Mail or Telephone Order Merchandise Rule of 1993 amended the 1975 Mail-Order Rule to extend protections to consumers who purchase goods over phone lines, including through computers and fax machines.

The 1993 rule established three key guidelines. First, sellers must ship items within the time promised. If they do not specify a time, the seller is limited to 30 days from receipt of the order. Second, if the seller cannot ship the item within the promised time, the seller must notify the customer in writing and offer an opportunity to cancel. Third, if a customer decides to cancel the order, the seller must refund the customer's money within a specified period of time.

Unsolicited Merchandise When a consumer goes to her mailbox only to discover that a company has sent her a book, must she pay for the book? Anyone who receives unsolicited merchandise may treat the item as a gift. The recipient may keep or dispose of the merchandise without any obligation to the sender. In accordance with the Postal Reorganization Act of 1970,[23] any unsolicited merchandise sent by mail is free to be used by the recipient as he or she sees fit with no obligation by the recipient to the sender.

[21] FTC, "FTC Settlement Protects Door-to-Door Sales Consumers" (press release), May 2, 2000.
[22] 16 C.F.R. §§ 435.1–435.2.
[23] 16 C.F.R. § 256.

FTC REGULATION OF SALES IN SPECIFIC INDUSTRIES

In certain industries, sellers have extensive opportunities to take advantage of customers. Thus, the FTC—and in some cases, Congress—creates special rules for certain sales practices specific to certain industries.

Used-Car Sales Consumers who purchase a used car often have very little information about the car's history. For instance, they do not know whether the car has been in an accident or whether there are any serious problems that are not visible.

To protect used-car buyers, Congress passed the Odometer Act of 1973, which protects against odometer fraud in used-car sales. The FTC extended that act's protection through the 1984 Used Motor Vehicle Registration Rule.[24] Under this rule, a dealer must attach a buyer's guide label to any used car he or she is attempting to sell. The label must state that the car is being sold "as is." This label is a warning to the customer that the seller is not guaranteeing anything at all about the performance of the car. Furthermore, the label must include a suggestion that the buyer obtain an inspection for the used car before any decision to purchase.

Consumer protections against fraud in used-car sales vary widely from state to state. During the 1960s and 1970s there was widespread pressure to reform our legislative system to protect consumers from fraud; many states responded more favorably to that pressure than did others. All states enacted the Uniform Commercial Code (UCC), but in each case the UCC was enacted with significant variations. The difference between states was also heightened in that each state had unique nonuniform consumer protection statutes. Consequently, the consumer protection laws against used-car fraud (also known as "lemon laws") vary from state to state. Some states provide minimum protection, while others states, such as Minnesota, presume that one unsuccessful effort to repair a used car demonstrates nonrepairability. Minnesota's laws also extend statutory protection to potential buyers of returned vehicles by banning resale of automobiles returned because of major safety defects.[25]

Funeral Home Services Consumers who must purchase goods and services for a funeral and burial are often vulnerable for several reasons. The consumer is usually preoccupied with his or her loss of a relative or friend and is unlikely to "comparison shop." Additionally, grieving consumers can be more readily persuaded to purchase unnecessary, expensive items for this last tribute to their loved ones. To prevent funeral homes from taking advantage of these customers, the FTC created the 1984 Funeral Rule and revised it in 1994. The rule requires that those who operate funeral homes provide customers with itemized price information about funeral goods and services. Furthermore, funeral homes may not misrepresent legal or cemetery requirements or require that the customer buy certain funeral goods and services as a condition for receiving other funeral goods and services.

Real Estate Sales Because real estate purchases are probably one of the largest purchases a consumer will make, Congress passed several acts requiring that sellers disclose certain information about the property. First, the Interstate Land Sales Full Disclosure Act,[26] passed in 1968, requires disclosure of information to consumers so that they can make informed decisions about real estate purchases. Under this act, anyone planning to sell or lease 100 or more lots of unimproved land through a common promotional plan must file an initial statement of record with the Department of Housing and Urban Development's (HUD's) Office of Interstate Land Sales Registration. Before the developer can offer land for sale, HUD must approve the initial statement.

[24] 16 C.F.R. §§ 455.1–455.5.
[25] David A. Rice, "Product Quality Laws and the Economics of Federalism," *Boston University Law Review,* 65 (1985), p. 1.
[26] 15 U.S.C. §§ 1701–1720.

Congress provided more protection for people purchasing homes in the Real Estate Settlement Procedures Act of 1974[27] and its 1976 amendments. This act requires the disclosure of information regarding mortgage loans to the buyer. For example, the lender must give the buyer an estimate of the costs for finalizing the real estate purchase.

Online Sales With the ever-expanding reach of the Internet, there has been an increase in business-to-consumer (B2C) sales transactions. Anyone with an Internet connection can make purchases from his or her favorite stores, from Barnes & Noble to Macy's. Most existing consumer protection laws were developed to protect consumers in their interactions with businesses face-to-face. Hence, protecting consumers online requires new approaches. Although not a specific industry, the Internet facilitates such a huge volume of commerce that additional focused protective legislation is needed.

Despite the difficulty of prosecuting online fraud, the FTC has brought a number of enforcement actions against online businesses. The federal statutes already in existence prohibiting wire fraud apply to online transactions. In addition, several states have begun to amend statutes to explicitly protect online consumers.

LO 25-4 Credit Protection

The widespread use of credit to purchase goods and services means that consumer credit protection has become increasingly important. This section explores three key federal laws regulating the credit industry to protect consumers: the Truth-in-Lending Act, the Fair Credit Reporting Act, and the Fair Debt Collection Practices Act.

THE TRUTH IN LENDING ACT

One of the earliest, most significant statutes regulating credit is Title I of the Consumer Credit Protection Act (CCPA), referred to as the *Truth in Lending Act (TILA)*.[28] The purpose of the act is to require that sellers disclose the terms of the credit or loan to help consumers compare a variety of credit lines or loans. More important, consumers must be able to understand this disclosure of terms. TILA is administered, in part, by the Federal Reserve Board through the previously mentioned Regulation Z.

Suppose your business extends credit to customers. Are your credit lines through your business subject to TILA? First, TILA applies to consumer loans only. Second, TILA applies to those who lend money or arrange for credit through the ordinary course of business. Third, the credit or loan must be in the amount of $25,000 or less, unless the loan is secured by a mortgage on real estate. Fourth, the creditor must be making the loan to a natural person, not a legal entity. Fifth, the credit or loan must be subject to a finance charge or must have repayments of more than four installments.

All creditors subject to TILA must disclose the finance charge and the annual percentage rate of the credit or loan. This information must be disclosed in a meaningful way, which prevents creditors from burying the information in a large paragraph unrelated to the credit terms.

Consider the following example: In May 1999, a jury heard *Carlisle v. Whirlpool Financial National Bank*.[29] According to the case facts, Gulf Coast Electric's salespeople traveled door-to-door, selling satellite dishes through financing. The price of the satellite dish was $1,100. However, consumers could purchase this dish for approximately $200 in stores. The consumers argued that the salespeople hid the number of payments the buyers would have to pay, thereby violating TILA. The jury found in favor of the customers and awarded them $581 million.

[27] 12 U.S.C. §§ 2501–2517.
[28] 15 U.S.C. §§ 1601–1693r.
[29] No. 97-068, Cir. Ct., Hale Co., Ala.

Types of Loans under TILA TILA includes three categories of loans: open-end credit, closed-end credit, and credit card applications and solicitations. Each category has specific disclosure requirements. For example, an *open-end credit line* permits repeated transactions and assesses a finance charge on unpaid balances. A creditor of an open-end credit line is required to disclose information in periodic statements. In contrast, a *closed-end credit line* is one for a loan given for a specific amount of time. The creditor of a closed-end credit line must disclose the total amount financed and the number, amount, and due dates of payments. Finally, *credit card applications and solicitations* must include the APR, annual fees, and the grace period for paying without a finance charge.

Unauthorized Charges and Disputes TILA establishes certain consumer protection rules regarding unauthorized charges to credit cards. If your credit card is stolen and someone makes unauthorized purchases on your account, your liability for those charges cannot exceed $50 per card if prompt notification of the theft is made to the credit card company. If you notify the credit card company before unauthorized charges are made, you cannot be held liable for any of the charges. Similarly, if a credit card company sends you an unsolicited card in the mail and the card is stolen, you cannot be held liable for any of the charges.

TILA offers another protection to consumers who unknowingly purchase damaged goods using a credit card. If three requirements are met, consumers will not be obligated to pay for the good. First, the consumer must purchase the item near her home (i.e., the business is in the same state as the consumer's home or within 100 miles of the home). Second, the item must cost more than $50. Third, the consumer must make a good-faith effort to resolve the dispute, such as asking the store for a refund. If these requirements are met, the credit card company cannot bill the consumer for the damaged item.

Consumer Leasing Act In 1988, the Consumer Leasing Act (CLA)[30] amended TILA to provide greater protection for people leasing automobiles and other goods. CLA applies to those who lease goods as part of their regular business. For CLA to apply, the lease must be for a minimum of four months and the price must not exceed $25,000. Under CLA and its controlling regulation, Regulation M,[31] anyone leasing goods must disclose up front, in writing, all the material terms and conditions of the lease.

Equal Credit Opportunity Act In the 1970s, a woman old enough to have children would have had difficulty securing credit because creditors believed that married women with children would be less likely to pay their debts. In response to this discrimination, Congress passed the Equal Credit Opportunity Act (ECOA)[32] as a 1974 amendment to TILA. This amendment makes it illegal for creditors to deny credit to individuals on the basis of race, religion, national origin, color, sex, marital status, or age. When determining the creditworthiness of a credit applicant, the creditor cannot use information about the applicant's marital status, nor can the creditor require that a spouse co-sign the application. Finally, the act prohibits creditors from denying credit on the basis of whether the applicant receives public assistance benefits.

THE FAIR CREDIT REPORTING ACT

If you own a credit card, you also have a credit report. If you apply for a new credit card or a loan, the creditor will check your credit history to make a judgment about your creditworthiness by examining a copy of your credit report. This report contains information about your financial transactions, such as payments on credit, debt collection, and other financial information the creditor needs to know about if entering a business transaction with you.

Because credit bureaus influence consumers' ability to make purchases and secure loans, Congress passed the Fair Credit Reporting Act (FCRA)[33] of 1970 to ensure accurate credit reporting. FCRA regulates the issuance of credit reports for limited business purposes, such as

[30] 15 U.S.C. §§ 1667–1667e.
[31] 12 C.F.R. Part 213.
[32] 15 U.S.C. §§ 1691–1691f.
[33] 15 U.S.C. §§ 1681–1681t.

CASE Nugget

What Does the Law Require of a Loan Company?

Alvin Ricciardi, Appellant, v. Ameriquest Mortgage Company
U.S. Court of Appeals for the Third Circuit

164 Fed. Appx. 221 (2006)

Alvin Ricciardi bought a home in May 2001, took out a home equity loan, and then applied for a loan to refinance the two mortgages through Ameriquest. Ricciardi closed the loan in September 2002, at which point he received the "Borrower's Acknowledgment of Final Loan Terms." The acknowledgment stated the terms of the loan that Ricciardi had originally requested, as well as the final terms of the loan. Ricciardi signed all the documents presented during the closing. Eight months later, Ricciardi filed suit against Ameriquest for violating the Equal Credit Opportunity Act, the Truth in Lending Act, and the Pennsylvania Unfair Trade Practices Act and Consumer Protection Law. The district court granted summary judgment regarding Ricciardi's ECOA claim, finding for Ameriquest. At a later nonjury trial, the court ruled in favor of Ameriquest on all counts of Ricciardi's claim as well as Ameriquest's counterclaim. Ricciardi appealed.

Ricciardi's appeal put forth three arguments. First, Ricciardi argued that the district court erred in granting summary judgment in favor of Ameriquest on his ECOA claim because Ameriquest failed to provide notice of its counteroffer before the closing of the loan. Second, Ricciardi argued that the district court erred in its adverse credibility finding. Third, Ricciardi argued that Ameriquest violated TILA by overcharging him for insurance and thereby gave him the right to rescind the loan. The appeals court rejected each of Ricciardi's arguments, affirming the ruling of the district court.

The appeals court addressed each of Ricciardi's arguments in turn. First, TILA requires that a creditor respond to an applicant within 30 days of receipt of a completed loan application. Ameriquest did respond to Ricciardi within 30 days. Contrary to Ricciardi's claim, Ameriquest was not required to respond in the form of a counteroffer. Additionally, there is no requirement that a counteroffer be received before the closing of the loan. Thus, Ricciardi's argument was without merit. Second, the appeals court found that the district court had not erred in its adverse credibility finding. Ricciardi contradicted himself numerous times on the record, in addition to committing fraud by misrepresenting his occupation and income on the loan application to Ameriquest. Third, the appeals court found that Ricciardi had not presented sufficient evidence to substantiate his claim that Ameriquest had overcharged him for insurance. In Pennsylvania, state-mandated insurance rates are published in the *Rate Manual*. The rates decrease if the property is being refinanced and was previously insured. Ricciardi failed to show that the property was previously insured; thus, the district court correctly found that there was no evidence that Ameriquest had overcharged Ricciardi.

a determination of credit or insurance eligibility, employment, and licensing. If a credit bureau issues a consumer credit report for a reason not specified by FCRA, it may be held liable for damages and additional fines. Furthermore, anyone who uses a credit report for purposes other than those specified in the act may be held liable for damages.

In Case 25-2, a husband and wife sued banks that offered them preapproved credit cards but then rejected their applications. The couple argued that by rejecting the applications for the preapproved credit cards, the banks ultimately obtained their credit reports under false pretenses under FCRA.

RICHARD D. KENNEDY AND SALLY S. KENNEDY v. CHASE MANHATTAN BANK, USA, N.A., ET AL.

U.S. COURT OF APPEALS FOR THE FIFTH CIRCUIT

369 F.3d 833 (2004)

FACTS: *Richard and Sally Kennedy received prequalified offers for credit card accounts from Chase Manhattan and Bank of America (BOA). On the basis of the representations made by the banks, the Kennedys believed they were preapproved for credit, and they accepted the offers by returning the applications. The banks, however, obtained consumer credit reports from Experian and Transunion and notified the Kennedys that, on the basis of the information in these reports, the banks would not open credit card accounts for the Kennedys. The Kennedys contended that the banks violated Section 1681q of the Fair Credit Reporting Act by obtaining information under the act under false pretenses. The banks filed for summary judgment, and the district court granted all the motions. The Kennedys appealed.*

ISSUE: After giving a "prequalified offer," may a bank obtain an individual's credit report to determine whether to extend credit?

REASONING: Section 1681q of the Fair Credit Reporting Act allows individuals to sue when banks obtain their credit information under false pretenses. To succeed in this case, the Kennedys needed to prove that the banks had an impermissible purpose in obtaining their credit reports. Section 1681q of the act allows banks to obtain consumer credit reports in connection with a credit transaction not initiated by the consumer if the transaction consists of a firm offer of credit or the consumer authorizes the report. In this case, the credit card offers sent to the Kennedys stated that the offered credit may not be extended if, after the Kennedys returned the applications, the banks obtained the Kennedys' credit reports and determined that the Kennedys did not meet the banks' standards for creditworthiness. The Kennedys signed the credit card offers, acknowledging notice that the banks would check their credit history and also authorizing the banks to access their credit information.

DECISION AND REMEDY: The credit card offers signed by the Kennedys showed that the banks did not obtain the Kennedys' credit information under false pretenses. The district court's ruling was affirmed, in favor of the defendants.

SIGNIFICANCE OF THE CASE: This case shows that banks may send "prequalified" offers for credit cards without committing to extend credit to every customer. Banks are permitted to screen potential customers' credit history before deciding to extend credit—granted that those customers agree to the terms of the prequalified offer.

CRITICAL THINKING

Explain how rival causes affect this case. Considering the information available to you, what do you think is the most likely cause leading to the banks' obtaining the Kennedys' credit information?

ETHICAL DECISION MAKING

Who are the primary stakeholders affected by the facts in this case? How would it affect the quality of the decision making if judges were to simply forget about some of these stakeholders?

This case illustrates one application of the Fair Credit Reporting Act. FCRA establishes other duties for credit reporting. For example, a credit bureau cannot report obsolete information. (General credit information is considered obsolete after seven years.) However, a bankruptcy will be reported for 10 years. Also, any time a credit applicant is denied credit, the applicant has a right to the name and address of the credit bureau that reported the information. Finally, FCRA imposes a duty on the reporting agency to ensure that its information is as accurate as possible. Consequently, if a consumer reports an error in his or her credit report, the credit bureau is required to investigate the error and make the corrections in the report, if necessary.

THE FAIR DEBT COLLECTION PRACTICES ACT

Suppose a consumer owes $3,000 on his credit card and has not been able to make monthly payments for the past six months. The credit card company will likely refer the case to a collection agency, which will notify the consumer in an attempt to get him to pay the debt. The collection agency then may start calling the consumer regularly to discuss the debt. Next, the agency might start contacting the consumer's acquaintances, telling them about the debt in an effort to pressure the consumer into paying the debt.

This type of debt-collecting behavior is prohibited by the Fair Debt Collection Practices Act (FDCPA).[34] This act applies only to debt collectors who regularly attempt to collect debts on behalf of others. The following collection behaviors are expressly prohibited by FDCPA:

1. Contacting a debtor at work if the debtor's employer objects.
2. Contacting a debtor who has notified the collection agency that he or she wants no contact with the agency.
3. Contacting the debtor before 8 a.m. or after 9 p.m.
4. Contacting third parties about the debt (exceptions: contacting the debtor's parents, spouse, or financial adviser).
5. Using obscene or threatening language when communicating with the debtor.
6. Misrepresenting the collection agency as a lawyer or a police officer.

THE CREDIT CARD FRAUD ACT

Credit card fraud is a serious problem in the United States, costing consumers millions of dollars per year. Accordingly, Congress passed the Credit Card Fraud Act of 1984[35] to close existing loopholes in federal laws that allowed credit card fraud to be pervasive. The Credit Card Fraud Act states that it is unlawful to (1) possess an unauthorized credit card, (2) counterfeit or alter a credit card, (3) use the account number of another's credit card to perpetuate fraud, and (4) use a credit card obtained from a third party with his or her consent, even if the third party conspires to report the card as stolen. The act also increases the penalty for committing credit card fraud.

THE FAIR CREDIT BILLING ACT

Did your credit card company fail to extend your credit when it informed you that your credit would be extended? Were you ever charged for merchandise you did not purchase or receive? Were you ever charged twice for one purchase? If so, you have been the victim of a credit billing error. The Fair Credit Billing Act (FCBA) of 1986[36] was created to handle such billing errors, as well as many others.

FCBA, enforced by the FTC, creates procedures consumers are to follow in filing complaints when billing errors occur. FCBA also requires that the creditor explain to the consumer and FTC why the error occurred and promptly fix the error. When a complaint is filed, the creditor may not try to collect on the disputed amount or take any action against the consumer until the complaint is answered.

THE FAIR AND ACCURATE CREDIT TRANSACTIONS ACT

The Fair and Accurate Credit Transactions Act (FACTA) of 2003[37] was passed in response to the growing number of identity-theft cases. If someone thinks he is a victim of identity theft, he may contact the FTC, and an alert will be placed in his credit files. The credit files then serve as a national fraud alert system to better enable authorities to catch those who are stealing identities.

Several other requirements created by the act protect consumers. First, major credit reporting agencies are required to provide consumers with a free copy of their credit reports every 12 months. Second, receipts from credit card purchases are to list an abbreviated version of the card

[34] 15 U.S.C. § 1692.
[35] 18 U.S.C. § 1029(a)(1–4).
[36] 15 U.S.C. § 1601.
[37] Pub. L. No. 108–159, 117 Stat. 1952.

number to protect consumer accounts. Third, financial institutions must work with the FTC to "red-flag" suspicious transactions that might be a sign of identity theft. Fourth, assistance will be provided to victims of identity theft to help them rebuild their credit. Fifth, victims of identity theft may report fraud directly to creditors to protect their credit ratings.

Consumer Health and Safety

<div align="right">LO 25-5</div>

The legislation and rules we have examined regulate the advertising, labeling, and sale of products. Now we turn to legislation regarding product safety. This legislation is directly related to the Firestone-Ford investigation. The purpose of such regulations is to ensure that companies like Firestone and Ford produce safe products for consumers who do not have all the information. The two main federal statutes that address product safety are the Federal Food, Drug, and Cosmetic Act and the Consumer Product Safety Act.

THE FEDERAL FOOD, DRUG, AND COSMETIC ACT

In 1906, Congress created the first federal legislation regulating food and drugs, the Pure Food and Drugs Act. Subsequently, Congress amended the Pure Food and Drugs Act when it created the Federal Food, Drug, and Cosmetic Act (FFDCA)[38] in 1938 to protect consumers against misbranded or adulterated food, drugs, medical devices, or cosmetics. The U.S. Food and Drug Administration (FDA), the agency responsible for administering FFDCA, creates standards to regulate food and drugs, thus protecting consumers. Specifically, the FDA must ensure that food, drugs, cosmetics, and medical devices meet specific safety standards.

Under FFDCA, the FDA must follow a set of procedures to determine whether a drug is safe to enter the market. Recently, the Supreme Court ruled on the issue of whether the FDA has the authority to regulate tobacco (see Case 25-3). According to the FDA, it (1) has authority to regulate drugs and (2) considers nicotine a drug.

[38] 21 U.S.C. §§ 301–393.

CASE 25-3

FOOD AND DRUG ADMINISTRATION ET AL. v. BROWN & WILLIAMSON TOBACCO CORPORATION ET AL.

UNITED STATES SUPREME COURT

120 S. Ct. 1291 (2000)

FACTS: *Before 1995, the FDA consistently stated that it did not have the power to regulate tobacco. However, in 1995, the FDA established that nicotine is a "drug" and cigarettes and smokeless tobacco are "devices" for administering the drug. FFDCA grants the FDA authority to regulate drugs and devices. Consequently, in August 1996, the FDA issued a rule with restrictions on the sale, promotion, and labeling of tobacco products, directed at behaviors marketed to kids. A group of tobacco manufacturers, retailers, and advertisers filed suit against the FDA, arguing that it did not have authority to regulate tobacco products and that the advertising restrictions were not permissible under the Constitution. The district court ruled that FFDCA authorizes the FDA to regulate tobacco products and that*

the labeling requirements were permitted. The Fourth Circuit Court of Appeals reversed, finding Congress did not give the FDA jurisdiction to regulate tobacco products.

ISSUE: Does the FDA have jurisdiction to regulate tobacco products?

REASONING: The majority (five justices) saw a fatal contradiction in the FDA's case. The FDA has jurisdiction to regulate products that are safe for their intended use. If the FDA has determined that nicotine and cigarettes are unsafe when used for their intended purposes, the FDA has a duty to ban those products—which has been explicitly prohibited by Congress. (Four dissenting justices believed that the FDA did have authority to regulate tobacco products because the FDA has authority

to regulate articles intended to affect the structure or any function of the body.) Further, the majority looked to Congress's tobacco-specific legislation. Congress explicitly prohibits federal agencies from imposing health-related labeling requirements on tobacco products. (The dissenting justices believed that the majority overlooked the very purpose of FFDCA: to protect public health. Given the purpose of the statute, the FDA should be permitted to regulate tobacco products.)

DECISION AND REMEDY: The FDA does not have jurisdiction over tobacco products. The appellate court's ruling was affirmed.

SIGNIFICANCE OF THE CASE: The obvious significance of this case is that the FDA was not allowed to protect children from tobacco advertisements, but this case is also a good example of the conflict between the letter of the law and the purpose of the law. The majority of the justices based their ruling on the letter of the law: what Congress had previously said about the FDA's authority to regulate tobacco products, which led the majority to one conclusion. The minority of the justices based their dissent on the purpose of the law: the FDA's ability to protect the public's health, which led the minority to a different conclusion.

CRITICAL THINKING

The first reason the majority offers for its conclusion that the FDA does not have authority to regulate tobacco is that the regulation of tobacco does not "fit" with the FDA's scheme for evaluating drugs. Consequently, the FDA would be forced to ban tobacco. What evidence does the court offer for this reason? Are you persuaded by the evidence?

ETHICAL DECISION MAKING

Consider both the majority and dissenting opinions. Who are the primary stakeholders affected by the decision that the FDA cannot regulate tobacco?

This case demonstrates the significant influence the FDA has over the lives and health of American citizens. It also illustrates the problems with some of its regulation devices. The Food and Drug Administration Modernization Act of 1997 amended FFDCA to help improve the regulation process, particularly for drugs and medical devices. For example, the 1997 act reauthorized a drug program that cut the time required for a drug review from 30 months to 15 months. The act also increased patient access to experimental drugs and accelerated the review of important new medications.

THE CONSUMER PRODUCT SAFETY ACT

In the Consumer Product Safety Act of 1972 Congress created and directed the Consumer Product Safety Commission (CPSC) to "protect the public against unreasonable risks of injuries and deaths associated with consumer products."[39]

The CPSC protects the public from injuries associated with consumer products in several ways. First, the CPSC issues and enforces mandatory standards regarding product safety. Similarly, the commission works with industries to develop voluntary product standards. If the CPSC cannot establish a standard that would adequately protect the public, it can ban consumer products from the market. In addition, the CPSC can administer existing product safety legislation. Examples of such legislation include the Child Protection and Toy Safety Act of 1969[40] and the Federal Hazardous Substance Act of 1960.[41]

Second, the CPSC can arrange for a recall of products. Although the CPSC has the authority to issue product recalls on its own, usually the CPSC works with companies that are voluntarily issuing recalls for dangerous products. For example, in August 2006, both Dell and Apple issued

[39] 15 U.S.C. § 2051.
[40] Amendments to 15 U.S.C. §§ 1251, 1252, and 1274.
[41] 15 U.S.C. §§ 1251–1277.

Exhibit 25-2

Other Consumer
Protection Laws

STATUTE	PURPOSE
Pure Food and Drugs Act of 1906 (amended by the Federal Food, Drug, and Cosmetic Act)	Forbids the adulteration and mislabeling of food and drugs
Meat Inspection Act of 1906	Provides for meat inspection
Wholesome Meat Act of 1967	Amended the Meat Inspection Act to promulgate standards for animal slaughter for meat
Flammable Fabrics Act of 1953	Prohibits the sale of highly flammable clothing
Child Protection and Toy Safety Act of 1969	Requires childproof devices and toy labeling
Toy Safety Act of 1984	Permits the Consumer Product Safety Commission to recall toys and other articles used by children
Drug-Price Competition and Patent-Term Restoration Act of 1984	Simplifies the Food and Drug Administration's process of approving generic drugs

voluntary recalls, with the help of the CPSC, for lithium ion batteries sold in their laptops. Both companies received several separate complaints about their batteries overheating, and thus the CPSC aided the companies in the battery recall.

Third, the commission conducts research regarding potentially hazardous products. The National Highway Traffic Safety Administration (NHTSA) is similar to the CPSC in that it too conducts investigations about the safety of potentially hazardous products. The NHTSA, however, focuses primarily on motor vehicles. The NHTSA was the agency that investigated the Ford-Firestone case to determine exactly what was causing the tire blowouts in Ford Explorers.

Fourth, the CPSC educates consumers about product safety. One important way the CPSC offers this education is through the National Injury Information Clearinghouse.

This section examined two of the most significant laws governing the safety of consumer products. Exhibit 25-2 lists six additional consumer product safety laws.

SUMMARY

The Federal Trade Commission

How the FTC brings an action:

1. FTC conducts an investigation.
2. FTC sends a complaint to the violator.
3. FTC and the violator settle the complaint through a consent agreement.
4. If the company refuses to enter the consent agreement, the FTC may issue a formal administrative complaint, which leads to an administrative hearing.
5. If the company has violated the law, the FTC issues a cease-and-desist order.

If the company violates the order, the FTC can seek an injunction against the company or fine the company up to $10,000 per violation.

Deceptive Advertising

Bait-and-switch advertising: Advertising a low price to "bait" the consumer into the store only so that the salesperson can "switch" the consumer to another, higher-priced item.

FTC actions against deceptive advertising:

- *Cease-and-desist actions:* Court orders requiring that firms stop their current advertising behavior.
- *Multiple-product orders:* Court orders requiring that firms stop current advertisements on numerous products, as opposed to one specified product.
- *Corrective advertising:* Advertising in which the company explicitly states that the formerly advertised claims were untrue.

Telemarketing and electronic advertising:

- *1991 Telephone Consumer Protection Act:* Telemarketers cannot use an automatic telephone dialing system or a prerecorded voice.
- *Telemarketing and Consumer Fraud and Abuse Prevention Act of 1994:* This act created certain requirements regarding when and how telemarketers may make calls.
- *Federal Do Not Call registry:* Telemarketers cannot call consumers who have voluntarily placed their phone numbers on the federal Do Not Call list.

Tobacco advertising: Cigarette and smokeless-tobacco advertising is restricted.

Labeling and Packaging Laws

Federal and state governments have passed laws requiring that manufacturers provide accurate, understandable information on labels. Furthermore, if a product is potentially harmful, the manufacturer must make the consumer aware of the harm.

Sales

Door-to-door sales: The Cooling-Off Rule gives consumers three days to cancel purchases they make from salespeople who come to their homes.

Telephone and mail-order sales: The *Mail or Telephone Order Merchandise Rule of 1993* extends protections to those who purchase over the phone or by fax.

Unsolicited merchandise: Anyone receiving such merchandise may treat it as a gift.

FTC regulation of specific industries:

1. Used-car sales
2. Funeral home services
3. Real estate sales
4. Online sales

Credit Protection

The Truth in Lending Act requires that sellers disclose the terms of the credit or loan to facilitate the consumer's comparison of a variety of credit lines or loans.

The Fair Credit Reporting Act ensures accurate credit reporting.

The Fair Debt Collection Practices Act regulates the actions of debt collectors that regularly attempt to collect debts on behalf of others.

The Credit Card Fraud Act closes loopholes in federal laws to further punish people who commit credit card fraud.

The Fair Credit Billing Act seeks to rectify problems and abuses associated with credit billing errors.

The Fair and Accurate Credit Transactions Act takes affirmative actions to control and prosecute identity theft.

Consumer Health and Safety

The Federal Food, Drug, and Cosmetic Act protects consumers against misbranded or adulterated food, drugs, medical devices, and cosmetics.

The Consumer Product Safety Act created the Consumer Product Safety Commission (CPSC) to "protect the public against unreasonable risks of injuries and deaths associated with consumer products."

Point/Counterpoint

Should Firms Be Prevented from Concealing Valuable Product Information from Consumers?

YES	NO
Consumer protection legislation should protect consumers against sellers who want to sell goods and services under cover of deception.	The best way to protect consumers is by placing responsibility on them to ask the right questions. They and only they know what they are seeking from a good or service. No regulatory agency understands why consumers are purchasing a particular product.
The great benefit of markets is that they satisfy consumers. But a consumer cannot be sovereign when he is asked to purchase a tainted version of the good he thought he was buying.	

When firms conceal information that they well know would affect the likelihood of a sale, they are encouraging a culture of mistrust. They are saying by their behavior that it is appropriate business behavior to deceive in the interest of encouraging an exchange.

To try to protect consumers against any and all possible harm is to treat them as if they were infants, incapable of watching out for themselves.

A business firm should not be required to mention every attribute possessed by a product just to satisfy some utopian goal of full disclosure.

Questions & Problems

1. What is the goal of the FTC, and how does it achieve its goal? What are some pieces of legislation that enable the FTC to achieve its goal?

2. What are the elements of a deceptive advertisement, and how does the FTC prove an ad is deceptive?

3. What are the main provisions of the Truth in Lending Act, and how does it aid consumers?

4. Until 2002, the City of Bethlehem contractually retained the private law firm of Portnoff Law Associates, Ltd. (PLA) to collect payment for overdue water and sewer obligations. The city notified PLA of delinquent water and sewer assessments, and PLA then contacted homeowners in attempts to collect on those claims. On February 20, 2002, the city notified PLA of a delinquent water service obligation of Bridget and Michael Piper in the amount of $252.71. PLA sent numerous letters, some on its letterhead and some on the city's letterhead, as well as made a number of telephone calls to the Piper residence in an effort to secure payment of the delinquent water service fees. PLA has never disputed that the letters it sent to the Pipers failed to include the debt verification language required by Section 1692(g) of FDCPA. PLA has likewise never disputed that its letters did not state they were sent by a debt collector, the debt collector was attempting to collect a debt, and any information obtained by PLA would be used for that purpose, as required by Section 1692(e)(11) of FDCPA. Bridget Piper filed suit against PLA and two of its attorneys in the U.S. District Court for the Eastern District of Pennsylvania. The complaint alleged that PLA's attempts to collect payment of water and sewer bills owed to the city violated FDCPA. The complaint alleged that PLA violated this statute by failing to include statutory disclosures required for communications sent to consumers, by falsely representing or implying that the letters were from an attorney, and by collecting and attempting to collect fees not permitted by the agreement creating the debt or by law. Were the Pipers successful in their suit against PLA? Why? [*Piper v. Portnoff Law Assocs.*, 396 F.3d 227 (2005).]

5. On March 7, 2001, the U.S. District Court for the Eastern District of Virginia, after finding that H&R Block had willfully and maliciously engaged in a false and misleading advertising campaign aimed at preventing Liberty Tax Service and 13 of its franchisees from competing for customers, entered a permanent nationwide injunction against H&R Block requiring, among other things, that its advertisements "clearly and prominently" disclose whether an advertised product is actually a loan. On October 10, 2001, and January 10, 2002, Liberty filed two separate civil contempt motions alleging that H&R Block was in violation of the district court's injunction because its "Instant Money" advertisements used much smaller type and less apparent color print for the term *loan* than for terms such as *refund, check today,* and *instant money.* Liberty further alleged that H&R Block's advertisements failed to "clearly and prominently" disclose whether an advertised product was a loan because the loan disclosures contained therein were placed in areas that increased the likelihood they would go unnoticed and consequently unread. Liberty argued that the injunction's "clearly and prominently" language required that H&R Block's loan disclosures be presented in a manner that made them immediately noticeable to consumers. The district court ruled in favor of H&R Block because the reasonable person reading the H&R Block ads would be able to tell that the "Instant Money" campaign actually referred to loans taken out against an expected refund. Liberty appealed. Was Liberty successful on appeal? Why? [*JTH Tax, Inc. v. H&R Block E. Tax Servs.*, 359 F.3d 699 (2004).]

6. Brenda Laramore receives federal assistance pursuant to Section Eight of the United States Housing Act. "Section [Eight] is a federal program designed to assist the elderly, low income, and disabled pay rent for privately owned housing." The assistance generally comes in the form of a voucher the recipient can use to pay a portion of his or her rent. On October 21, 2002, Laramore telephoned Ritchie, the company responsible for managing the apartment in question, to request an application for a lease. The woman who

took the call initially told Laramore the apartment was available to rent. After Laramore informed her she intended to use a Section 8 voucher to pay a portion of the rent, however, the woman told Laramore the apartment was not available to persons using Section 8 vouchers. On February 21, 2003, Laramore filed suit claiming that Ritchie violated ECOA by denying her a rental application because she receives public assistance. Ritchie moved to dismiss the complaint on the ground that a rental application is not a credit transaction under ECOA. The district court agreed with Ritchie and dismissed the suit. Laramore appealed. Did Ritchie violate ECOA? Should ECOA apply to rental applications? [*Laramore v. Ritchie Realty Mgmt. Co.,* 397 F.3d 544 (2005).]

7. In August 1999, United Artists contracted with ABF, a company in the business of distributing advertisements by fax, to send a one-page advertisement for discount movie ticket packages. The following month, ABF transmitted the advertisement to about 90,000 fax machines in the Phoenix area. United Artists received $12,080 through the ad, and paid ABF $3,375 for its services. ESI is the only recipient that complained to United Artists about receiving the advertisement. After ESI received the faxed advertisement, it filed a complaint, alleging violation of the Telephone Consumer Protection Act (TCPA), which makes it unlawful for persons within the United States to, among other things, "use any telephone facsimile machine, computer, or other device to send an unsolicited advertisement to a telephone facsimile machine." ESI requested statutory damages of $500 per violation, with possible trebling (tripling) of those damages, and injunctive relief. ESI sought to represent a class consisting of "all persons and entities who received on a telephone facsimile machine" the particular advertisement sent by ABF for United Artists. United Artists objected to the class certification, arguing, among other things, that a class action suit could lead to liability against United Artists disproportionate to the harm caused. ESI offered to waive the statutory minimum recovery of $500 per violation and to reduce damages to $90 or, alternatively, to modify and reduce the number of the class. The trial court denied ESI's motion for certification of the class. ESI appealed the trial court's ruling. Should United Artists be required to pay for sending out its one-page fax? If you were on the court, how would you rule? Why? [*ESI Ergonomic Solutions, LLC v. UA Theatre Circuit, Inc.,* 50 P.3d 844 (2002).]

8. American Collections Enterprise, Inc. (ACEI) is a debt collector that contracted with Capital One in 2001 to provide debt collection services. Under the terms of the collection agreement, Capital One assigned delinquent accounts to ACEI for collection, and ACEI collected these debts on a contingent-fee basis. Pooja Goswami owed approximately $900 on her Capital One credit card and failed to pay. Capital One referred that debt to ACEI for collection on March 20, 2001, and ACEI pursued Goswami's delinquent account. It sent a collection notice letter to Goswami on December 7, 2001. A second form letter was sent on January 25, 2002, more than 180 days after the debt had been referred to ACEI. The second letter was sent to Goswami in an envelope that bore a half-inch-thick blue bar, across the entire envelope, containing the words "Priority Letter" in white. ACEI admitted that the markings on the envelope had been developed to entice debtors to open the letter. The letter itself contained a second blue bar and "Priority Letter" marking as a header. After receiving the letter, Goswami filed a complaint alleging violation of FDCPA, in particular 15 U.S.C. Sections 1692f(8) and 1692e(10). Goswami complained that the markings on the envelope violate Section 1692f(8), which prohibits any markings on debt collection letter envelopes besides the name and address of the sender and the addressee. She further complained that the contents of the letter were deceptive, in violation of Section 1692e(10). ACEI moved for summary judgment, arguing that neutral or benign expressions on an envelope, such as "priority letter," that in no way indicate it is a collection letter are not banned by FDCPA. The district court agreed, granted the defendant's summary judgment motion, and dismissed the case. Goswami appealed. Are the markings on the envelope and letter misleading and a violation of FDCPA? Why? [*Goswami v. Am. Collections Enter.,* 377 F.3d 488 (2004).]

9. CEU's sole business activity was the collection of dishonored checks received by area merchants. When a check was dishonored, a merchant would forward the check to CEU, who would then send out a series of notices to the check writer, usually using a letterhead of the Sheriff's Department in that area. However, only after three notices are sent does CEU actually notify the Sheriff's Department about the bad check. Sherri Gradisher wrote a bad check, and CEU sent three notices to Gradisher for the $81.30 bounced check. The notices were all on the letterhead of the Muskegon county sheriff. (The sheriff previously agreed to allow CEU to use its letterhead for debt collection purposes.) The notices contained the telephone number and address that Gradisher could use to contact CEU to pay or dispute the debt, but they did not state the name of the company anywhere. The letters also stated, "Failure to Make Payment Can Result in a Warrant for Your Arrest." Gradisher sued

CEU, contending that it violated the Fair Debt Collection Practices Act by using the letterhead of the Sheriff's Department. She alleged that the letterhead gave the false and misleading impression that the notices were from the sheriff and that the letters did not disclose the true name of the debt collector. Did the letters CEU sent violate FDCPA? Why or why not? [*Gradisher v. Check Enforcement Unit, Inc.*, 210 F. Supp. 2d 907 (2002).]

10. Aroma Housewares Co. is a California corporation that distributes electric kitchen appliances. Aroma distributed between 30,000 and 40,000 juice extractors in the United States. The juicers employed a rapidly spinning metal grater, whose sharp teeth pulverized fruits and vegetables that were inserted through a plastic chute. Aroma began receiving consumer reports of failed juicers. Exploding juicers, the reports claimed, "[threw] with great violence pieces of the clear plastic cover and shreds of the razor-sharp separator screen as far as eight feet." One consumer called the juicer "an unsafe and dangerous machine which exploded in [his] face." A flying blade sliced the hand of another. And one injured woman was taken by ambulance to the hospital, where she stayed overnight, and she sustained permanent damage to her fingers, hand, and arm. In all, Aroma received complaints from 23 consumers. Aroma tested the juicers but was unable to replicate the malfunctions. It reported none of this to the Consumer Product Safety Commission. But some of the consumers did. Alerted to the problems, the commission asked the company to report what it knew about the dangers posed by its juicers. Aroma disclosed the consumer complaints, as well as the results of its own tests. A few months later, Aroma and the commission jointly announced that the juicers were being recalled. The United States subsequently sued Aroma, alleging that the company had violated the reporting requirements of the Consumer Product Safety Act. The district court granted partial summary judgment for the United States. Aroma appealed. Did Aroma violate CPSA? Should Aroma have reported the defective juicers even though it could not replicate the malfunctions? [*U.S. v. Mirama Enters.*, 387 F.3d 983 (2004).]

11. Microprocessors are a computer part commonly referred to as the "brain" of the computer. Intel, a microprocessor manufacturer, introduced the Pentium 4 microprocessor in November 2000. Computers with a Pentium 4 processor were priced, at least initially, at a premium over similarly equipped computers containing a Pentium III processor. However, the actual superiority of the Pentium 4 over the Pentium III processor was in doubt. A class action suit occurred in which consumers alleged that the manufacturer falsely represented that its newest microprocessor was the best and fastest processor on the market. The basic message plaintiffs challenge was at the core of Intel's billion-dollar marketing campaign: "4 is better than 3." "Better" and "best" are used repeatedly in the marketing materials; one expert elaborated that Intel positioned the Pentium 4 as its "best," Pentium III as "better," and Celeron as "good." Suppose it is established that the Pentium 4 was not faster than the Pentium III processor. Were Intel's claims actionable? In other words, were Intel's claims of the processor being better or best deceptive advertising or mere puffery? [*Barbara's Sales, Inc. v. Intel Corp.*, 879 N.E.2d 910 (2007).]

12. Delores Villegas was having problems paying her debts, so she filed for bankruptcy. Weinstein, a debt collector handling some of her debt, sent a letter to the lawyer representing Villegas in bankruptcy. The letter discussed the debt and advised the attorney that the debt might be nondischargeable and the company would like to settle the matter if counsel did not believe that there was a defense to the claim. After discovering a letter was sent to a third party instead of her, Villegas sued Weinstein for violation of the Fair Debt Collection Practices Act. Do you think the debt collector violated the FDCPA by contacting her bankruptcy attorney instead of Villegas? Why or why not? [*Villegas v. Weinstein & Riley*, 723 F. Supp. 2d 755 (2010).]

13. As part of its ongoing efforts to uncover overhyped health claims in food advertising, the Federal Trade Commission issued an administrative complaint charging the maker of POM Wonderful 100% Pomegranate Juice with making false and unsubstantiated claims that its products will prevent or treat heart disease. The ads in question appeared in national publications such as *Parade, Fitness, The New York Times,* and *Prevention.* Furthermore, executives at POM made statements, in some instances through an expert endorser, that clinical studies, research, and/or trials prove that drinking 8 ounces of POM juice daily prevents or reduces the risk of heart disease and treats heart disease by decreasing arterial plaque and improving blood flow to the heart. However, the FTC alleges that clinical studies, research, and/or trials do not prove these things. Among other things, large studies that POM funded showed no significant difference between consumption of pomegranate juice and that of a control beverage in thickness of arteries and reduction of plaque. Furthermore, two smaller studies funded by POM Wonderful or its agents showed no significant difference between consumption of pomegranate juice and that of a control beverage on measures of cardiovascular function, and multiple studies

funded by POM Wonderful or its agents did not show that POM products reduce blood pressure. The FTC complaint alleges that POM Wonderful's heart disease claims are false and unsubstantiated because many of the scientific studies conducted by POM Wonderful did not show heart disease benefit from use of its products. How do you think this FTC case will turn out? In other words, do you think POM's actions violate Section 5 of the Federal Trade Commission Act? Why or why not? If so, what possible penalties could POM face? [FTC complaint available at www.ftc.gov/os/caselist/0823122/100927pomcmpt.pdf (2010).]

Looking for more review material?

The Online Learning Center at **www.mhhe.com/kubasekess2e** contains this chapter's "Assignment on the Internet" and also a list of URLs for more information, entitled "On the Internet." Find both of them in the Student Center portion of the OLC, along with quizzes and other helpful materials.

The Constitution of the United States of America

Preamble

We the People of the United States, in Order to form a more perfect Union, establish Justice, insure domestic Tranquility, provide for the common defense, promote the general Welfare, and secure the Blessings of Liberty to ourselves and our Posterity, do ordain and establish this Constitution for the United States of America.

Article I

Section 1 All legislative Powers herein granted shall be vested in a Congress of the United States, which shall consist of a Senate and House of Representatives.

Section 2 The House of Representatives shall be composed of Members chosen every second Year by the People of the several States, and the Electors in each State shall have the Qualifications requisite for Electors of the most numerous Branch of the State Legislature.

No Person shall be a Representative who shall not have attained to the age of twenty five Years, and been seven Years a Citizen of the United States, and who shall not, when elected, be an Inhabitant of that State in which he shall be chosen.

Representatives and direct Taxes shall be apportioned among the several States which may be included within this Union, according to their respective Numbers, which shall be determined by adding to the whole Number of free Persons, including those bound to Service for a Term of Years, and excluding Indians not taxed, three fifths of all other Persons.[1] The actual Enumeration shall be made within three Years after the first Meeting of the Congress of the United States, and within every subsequent Term of ten Years, in such Manner as they shall by Law direct. The Number of Representatives shall not exceed one for every thirty Thousand, but each State shall have at Least one Representative, and until such enumeration shall be made, the State of New Hampshire shall be entitled to choose three, Massachusetts eight, Rhode-Island and Providence Plantations one, Connecticut five, New York six, New Jersey four, Pennsylvania eight, Delaware one, Maryland six, Virginia ten, North Carolina five, South Carolina five, and Georgia three.

When vacancies happen in the Representation from any State, the Executive Authority thereof shall issue Writs of Election to fill such Vacancies.

The House of Representatives shall chuse their Speaker and other Officers; and shall have the sole Power of Impeachment.

Section 3 The Senate of the United States shall be composed of two Senators from each State, chosen by the Legislature thereof,[2] for six Years; and each Senator shall have one Vote.

Immediately after they shall be assembled in Consequence of the first Election, they shall be divided as equally as may be into three Classes. The Seats of the Senators of the first Class shall be vacated at the Expiration of the second Year, of the second Class at the Expiration of the fourth Year, and of the third Class at the Expiration of the sixth Year, so that one third may be chosen every second Year; and if Vacancies happen by Resignation, or otherwise, during the Recess of the Legislature of any State, the Executive thereof may make temporary Appointments until the next Meeting of the Legislature, which shall then fill such Vacancies.[3]

No Person shall be a Senator who shall not have attained to the Age of thirty Years, and been nine Years a Citizen of the United States, and who shall not, when elected, be an Inhabitant of that State for which he shall be chosen.

The Vice President of the United States shall be President of the Senate, but shall have no Vote, unless they be equally divided.

The Senate shall chuse their other Officers, and also a President pro tempore, in the Absence of the Vice President, or when he shall exercise the Office of President of the United States.

The Senate shall have the sole Power to try all Impeachments. When sitting for that Purpose, they shall be on Oath or Affirmation. When the President of the United States is tried, the Chief Justice shall preside: And no Person shall be convicted without the Concurrence of two thirds of the Members present.

[1] Changed by the Fourteenth Amendment.

[2] Changed by the Seventeenth Amendment.
[3] Changed by the Seventeenth Amendment.

Judgment in Cases of Impeachment shall not extend further than to removal from Office, and disqualification to hold and enjoy any Office of honor, Trust or Profit under the United States: but the Party convicted shall nevertheless be liable and subject to Indictment, Trial, Judgment and Punishment, according to Law.

Section 4 The Times, Places and Manner of holding Elections for Senators and Representatives, shall be prescribed in each State by the Legislature thereof; but the Congress may at any time by Law make or alter such Regulations, except as to the Places of chusing Senators.

The Congress shall assemble at least once in every Year, and such Meeting shall be on the first Monday in December, unless they shall by Law appoint a different Day.[4]

Section 5 Each House shall be the Judge of the Elections, Returns and Qualifications of its own Members, and a Majority of each shall constitute a Quorum to do Business; but a smaller Number may adjourn from day to day, and may be authorized to compel the Attendance of absent Members, in such Manner, and under such Penalties as each House may provide.

Each House may determine the Rules of its Proceedings, punish its Members for disorderly Behaviour, and with the Concurrence of two thirds, expel a Member.

Each House shall keep a Journal of its Proceedings, and from time to time publish the same, excepting such Parts as may in their Judgment require Secrecy; and the Yeas and Nays of the Members of either House on any question shall, at the Desire of one fifth of those Present, be entered on the Journal.

Neither House, during the Session of Congress, shall, without the Consent of the other, adjourn for more than three days, nor to any other Place than that in which the two Houses shall be sitting.

Section 6 The Senators and Representatives shall receive a Compensation for their Services, to be ascertained by Law, and paid out of the Treasury of the United States. They shall in all Cases, except Treason, Felony and Breach of the Peace, be privileged from Arrest during their Attendance at the Session of their respective Houses, and in going to and returning from the same; and for any Speech or Debate in either House, they shall not be questioned in any other Place.

No Senator or Representative shall, during the Time for which he was elected, be appointed to any civil Office under the Authority of the United States, which shall have been created, or the Emoluments whereof shall have been encreased during such time; and no Person holding any Office under the United States, shall be a Member of either House during his Continuance in Office.

Section 7 All Bills for raising Revenue shall originate in the House of Representatives; but the Senate may propose or concur with Amendments as on other Bills.

Every Bill which shall have passed the House of Representatives and the Senate, shall, before it becomes a Law, be presented to the President of the United States; If he approves he shall sign it, but if not he shall return it, with his Objections to that House in which it shall have originated, who shall enter the Objections at large on their Journal, and proceed to reconsider it. If after such Reconsideration two thirds of that House shall agree to pass the Bill, it shall be sent, together with the Objections, to the other House, by which it shall likewise be reconsidered, and if approved by two thirds of that House, it shall become a Law. But in all such Cases the Votes of both Houses shall be determined by Yeas and Nays, and the Names of the Persons voting for and against the Bill shall be entered on the Journal of each House respectively. If any Bill shall not be returned by the President within ten Days (Sundays excepted) after it shall have been presented to him, the Same shall be a Law, in like Manner as if he had signed it, unless the Congress by their Adjournment prevent its Return, in which Case it shall not be a Law.

Every Order, Resolution, or Vote to which the Concurrence of the Senate and House of Representatives may be necessary (except on a question of Adjournment) shall be presented to the President of the United States; and before the Same shall take Effect, shall be approved by him, or being disapproved by him, shall be repassed by two thirds of the Senate and House of Representatives, according to the Rules and Limitations prescribed in the Case of a Bill.

Section 8 The Congress shall have Power To lay and collect Taxes, Duties, Imposts and Excises, to pay the Debts and provide for the common Defence and general Welfare of the United States; but all Duties, Imposts and Excises shall be uniform throughout the United States.

To borrow Money on the credit of the United States;

To regulate Commerce with foreign Nations, and among the several States, and with the Indian Tribes;

To establish an uniform Rule of Naturalization, and uniform Laws on the subject of Bankruptcies throughout the United States;

To coin Money, regulate the Value thereof, and of foreign Coin, and fix the Standard of Weights and Measures;

To provide for the Punishment of counterfeiting the Securities and current Coin of the United States;

To establish Post Offices and post Roads;

To promote the Progress of Science and useful Arts, by securing for limited Times to Authors and Inventors the exclusive Right to their respective Writings and Discoveries;

To constitute Tribunals inferior to the supreme Court;

To define and punish Piracies and Felonies committed on the high Seas, and Offences against the Law of Nations;

[4] Changed by the Twentieth Amendment.

To declare War, grant Letters of Marque and Reprisal, and make Rules concerning Captures on Land and Water;

To raise and support Armies, but no Appropriation of Money to that Use shall be for a longer Term than two Years;

To provide and maintain a Navy;

To make Rules for the Government and Regulation of the land and naval Forces;

To provide for calling forth the Militia to execute the Laws of the Union, suppress Insurrections and repel Invasions;

To provide for organizing, arming, and disciplining, the Militia, and for governing such Part of them as may be employed in the Service of the United States, reserving to the States respectively, the Appointment of the Officers, and the Authority of training the Militia according to the discipline prescribed by Congress;

To exercise exclusive Legislation in all Cases whatsoever, over such District (not exceeding ten Miles square) as may, by Cession of particular States, and the Acceptance of Congress, become the Seat of the Government of the United States, and to exercise like Authority over all Places purchased by the Consent of the Legislature of the State in which the Same shall be, for the Erection of Forts, Magazines, Arsenals, dock-Yards, and other needful Buildings;—And

To make all Laws which shall be necessary and proper for carrying into Execution the foregoing Powers, and all other Powers vested by this Constitution in the Government of the United States, or in any Department or Officer thereof.

Section 9 The Migration or Importation of such Persons as any of the States now existing shall think proper to admit, shall not be prohibited by the Congress prior to the Year one thousand eight hundred and eight, but a Tax or duty may be imposed on such Importation, not exceeding ten dollars for each Person.

The Privilege of the Writ of Habeas Corpus shall not be suspended, unless when in Cases of Rebellion or Invasion the public Safety may require it.

No Bill of Attainder or ex post facto Law shall be passed.

No Capitation, or other direct, Tax shall be laid, unless in Proportion to the Census of Enumeration herein before directed to be taken.[5]

No Tax or Duty shall be laid on Articles exported from any State.

No Preference shall be given by any Regulation of Commerce or Revenue to the Ports of one State over those of another: nor shall Vessels bound to, or from, one State, be obliged to enter, clear, or pay Duties in another.

No Money shall be drawn from the Treasury, but in Consequence of Appropriations made by Law; and a regular Statement and Account of the Receipts and Expenditures of all public Money shall be published from time to time.

No Title of Nobility shall be granted by the United States: And no Person holding any Office of Profit or Trust under them, shall, without the Consent of the Congress, accept of any present, Emolument, Office, or Title, of any kind whatever, from any King, Prince, or foreign State.

Section 10 No State shall enter into any Treaty, Alliance, or Confederation; grant Letters of Marque and Reprisal; coin Money; emit Bills of Credit; make any Thing but gold and silver coin a Tender in Payment of Debts; pass any Bill of Attainder, ex post facto Law, or Law impairing the Obligation of Contracts, or grant any Title of Nobility.

No State shall, without the Consent of the Congress, lay any Imposts or Duties on Imports or Exports, except what may be absolutely necessary for executing its inspection Laws: and the net Produce of all Duties and Imposts, laid by any State on Imports or Exports, shall be for the Use of the Treasury of the United States; and all such Laws shall be subject to the Revision and Controul of the Congress.

No State shall, without the consent of Congress, lay any Duty of Tonnage, keep Troops, or Ships of War in time of Peace, enter into any Agreement or Compact with another State, or with a foreign Power, or engage in War, unless actually invaded, or in such imminent Danger as will not admit of delay.

Article II

Section 1 The executive Power shall be vested in a President of the United States of America. He shall hold his Office during the Term of four Years, and, together with the Vice President, chosen for the same Term, be elected, as follows

Each state shall appoint, in such Manner as the Legislature thereof may direct, a Number of Electors, equal to the whole Number of Senators and Representatives to which the State may be entitled in Congress: but no Senator or Representative, or Person holding an Office of Trust or Profit under the United States, shall be appointed an Elector.

The Electors shall meet in their respective States, and vote by Ballot for two Persons, of whom one at least shall not be an inhabitant of the same State with themselves. And they shall make a List of all the Persons voted for, and of the Number of Votes for each; which List they shall sign and certify, and transmit sealed to the Seat of the Government of the United States, directed to the President of the Senate. The President of the Senate shall, in the Presence of the Senate and House of Representatives, open all the Certificates, and the Votes shall then be counted. The Person having the greatest Number of Votes shall be the President, if such Number be a Majority of the whole Number of

[5] Changed by the Sixteenth Amendment.

Electors appointed; and if there be more than one who have such Majority, and have an equal Number of Votes, then the House of Representatives shall immediately chuse by Ballot one of them for President; and if no Person have a Majority, then from the five highest on the List the said House shall in like Manner chuse the President. But in chusing the President, the Votes shall be taken by States, the Representation from each State having one Vote; A quorum for this purpose shall consist of a Member or Members from two thirds of the States, and a Majority of all the States shall be necessary to a Choice. In every Case, after the Choice of the President, the Person having the greatest Number of Votes of the Electors shall be the Vice President. But if there should remain two or more who have equal Votes, the Senate shall chuse from them by Ballot the Vice President.[6]

The Congress may determine the Time of chusing the Electors, and the Day on which they shall give their Votes; which Day shall be the same throughout the United States.

No Person except a natural born Citizen, or a Citizen of the United States, at the time of the Adoption of this Constitution, shall be eligible to the Office of President; neither shall any Person be eligible to that Office who shall not have attained to the Age of thirty five Years, and been fourteen Years a Resident within the United States.

In Case of the Removal of the President from Office, or of his Death, Resignation, or Inability to discharge the Powers and Duties of the said Office, the Same shall devolve on the Vice President, and the Congress may by Law provide for the Case of Removal, Death, Resignation or Inability, both of the President and Vice President, declaring what Officer shall then act as President, and such Officer shall act accordingly, until the Disability be removed, or a President shall be elected.[7]

The President shall, at stated Times, receive for his Services, a Compensation, which shall neither be encreased nor diminished during the Period for which he shall have been elected, and he shall not receive within that Period any other Emolument from the United States, or any of them.

Before he enter on the Execution of his Office, he shall take the following Oath or Affirmation:—"I do solemnly swear (or affirm) that I will faithfully execute the Office of President of the United States, and will to the best of my Ability, preserve, protect, and defend the Constitution of the United States."

Section 2 The President shall be Commander in Chief of the Army and Navy of the United States, and of the Militia of the several States, when called into the actual Service of the United States; he may require the Opinion, in writing, of the principal Officer in each of the executive Departments, upon any Subject relating to the Duties of their respective Offices, and he shall have Power to grant Reprieves and Pardons for Offences against the United States, except in Cases of Impeachment.

He shall have Power, by and with the Advice and Consent of the Senate, to make Treaties, provided two thirds of the Senators present concur; and he shall nominate, and by and with the Advice and Consent of the Senate, shall appoint Ambassadors, other public Ministers and Consuls, Judges of the supreme Court, and all other Officers of the United States, whose Appointments are not herein otherwise provided for, and which shall be established by Law; but the Congress may by Law vest the Appointment of such inferior Officers, as they think proper, in the President alone, in the Courts of Law, or in the Heads of Departments.

The President shall have Power to fill up all Vacancies that may happen during the Recess of the Senate, by granting Commissions which shall expire at the End of their next Session.

Section 3 He shall from time to time give to the Congress Information of the State of the Union, and recommend to their Consideration such Measures as he shall judge necessary and expedient; he may, on extraordinary Occasions, convene both Houses, or either of them, and in Case of Disagreement between them, with Respect to the Time of Adjournment, he may adjourn them to such Time as he shall think proper; he shall receive Ambassadors and other public Ministers; he shall take Care that the Laws be faithfully executed, and shall Commission all the Officers of the United States.

Section 4 The President, Vice President and all civil Officers of the United States, shall be removed from Office on Impeachment for, and Conviction of, Treason, Bribery, or other high Crimes and Misdemeanors.

Article III

Section 1 The judicial Power of the United States, shall be vested in one supreme Court, and in such inferior Courts as the Congress may from time to time ordain and establish. The Judges, both of the supreme and inferior Courts, shall hold their Offices during good Behaviour, and shall, at stated Times, receive for their Services, a Compensation, which shall not be diminished during their Continuance in Office.

Section 2 The judicial Power shall extend to all Cases, in Law and Equity, arising under this Constitution, the Laws of the United States, and Treaties made, or which shall be made, under their Authority;—to all Cases affecting Ambassadors, other public Ministers and Consuls;—to all Cases of admiralty and maritime Jurisdiction;—to Controversies to which the United States shall be a party;—to Controversies between two or more States;—between

[6] Changed by the Twelfth Amendment.
[7] Changed by the Twenty-fifth Amendment.

a State and Citizens of another State;[8]—between Citizens of different States;—between Citizens of the same State claiming Lands under Grants of different States, and between a State, or the Citizens thereof, and foreign States, Citizens or Subjects.

In all Cases affecting Ambassadors, other public Ministers and Consuls, and those in which a State shall be Party, the supreme Court shall have original Jurisdiction. In all the other Cases before mentioned, the supreme Court shall have appellate Jurisdiction, both as to Law and Fact, with such Exceptions, and under such Regulations as the Congress shall make.

The Trial of all Crimes, except in Cases of Impeachment, shall be by Jury: and such Trial shall be held in the State where the said Crimes shall have been committed; but when not committed within any State, the Trial shall be at such Place or Places as the Congress may by Law have directed.

Section 3 Treason against the United States, shall consist only in levying War against them, or in adhering to their Enemies, giving them Aid and Comfort. No Person shall be convicted of Treason unless on the Testimony of two Witnesses to the same overt Act, or on Confession in open Court.

The Congress shall have Power to declare the Punishment of Treason, but no Attainder of Treason shall work Corruption of Blood, or Forfeiture except during the Life of the Person attainted.

Article IV

Section 1 Full Faith and Credit shall be given in each State to the public Acts, Records, and judicial Proceedings of every other State. And the Congress may by general Laws prescribe the Manner in which such Acts, Records and Proceedings shall be proved, and the Effect thereof.

Section 2 The Citizens of each State shall be entitled to all Privileges and Immunities of Citizens in the several States.

A Person charged in any State with Treason, Felony, or other Crime, who shall flee from Justice, and be found in another State, shall on Demand of the executive Authority of the State from which he fled, be delivered up, to be removed to the State having Jurisdiction of the Crime.

No Person held to Service or Labour in one State, under the Laws thereof, escaping into another, shall, in Consequence of any Law or Regulation therein, be discharged from such Service or Labour, but shall be delivered up on Claim of the Party to whom such Service or Labour may be due.[9]

Section 3 New States may be admitted by the Congress into this Union; but no new State shall be formed or erected within the Jurisdiction of any other State; nor any State be formed by the Junction of two or more States, or Parts of States, without the Consent of the Legislatures of the States concerned as well as of the Congress.

The Congress shall have Power to dispose of and make all needful Rules and Regulations respecting the Territory or other Property belonging to the United States; and nothing in this Constitution shall be so construed as to Prejudice any Claims of the United States, or of any particular State.

Section 4 The United States shall guarantee to every State in this Union a Republican Form of Government, and shall protect each of them against Invasion; and on Application of the Legislature, or of the Executive (when the Legislature cannot be convened) against domestic Violence.

Article V

The Congress, whenever two thirds of both Houses shall deem it necessary, shall propose Amendments to this Constitution, or, on the Application of the Legislatures of two thirds of the several States, shall call a Convention for proposing Amendments, which, in either Case, shall be valid to all Intents and Purposes, as Part of this Constitution, when ratified by the legislatures of three fourths of the several States, or by Conventions in three fourths thereof, as the one or the other Mode of Ratification may be proposed by the Congress; Provided that no Amendment which may be made prior to the Year One thousand eight hundred and eight shall in any Manner affect the first and fourth Clauses in the Ninth Section of the first Article; and that no State, without its Consent, shall be deprived of its equal Suffrage in the Senate.

Article VI

All Debts contracted and Engagements entered into, before the Adoption of this Constitution, shall be as valid against the United States under this Constitution, as under the Confederation.

The Constitution, and the Laws of the United States which shall be made in Pursuance thereof; and all Treaties made, or which shall be made, under the Authority of the United States, shall be the supreme Law of the Land; and the Judges in every State shall be bound thereby, any Thing in the Constitution or Laws of any State to the Contrary notwithstanding.

The Senators and Representatives before mentioned, and the Members of the several State Legislatures, and all executive and judicial Officers, both of the United States and of the several States, shall be bound by Oath or Affirmation, to support this Constitution; but no religious Test shall ever be required as a Qualification to any Office or public Trust under the United States.

[8] Changed by the Eleventh Amendment.
[9] Changed by the Thirteenth Amendment.

Article VII

The Ratification of the Conventions of nine States, shall be sufficient for the Establishment of this Constitution between the States so ratifying the Same.

Done in Convention by the Unanimous Consent of the States present the Seventeenth Day of September in the Year of our Lord one thousand seven hundred and eighty seven and of the Independance of the United States of America the Twelfth. In witness whereof We have hereunto subscribed our Names.

Amendments

[The first 10 amendments are known as the "Bill of Rights."]

Amendment I (Ratified 1791) Congress shall make no law respecting an establishment of religion, or prohibiting the free exercise thereof; or abridging the freedom of speech, or of the press; or the right of the people peaceably to assemble, and to petition the Government for a redress of grievances.

Amendment 2 (Ratified 1791) A well regulated Militia, being necessary to the security of a free State, the right of the people to keep and bear Arms, shall not be infringed.

Amendment 3 (Ratified 1791) No Soldier shall, in time of peace be quartered in any house, without the consent of the Owner, nor in time of war, but in a manner to be prescribed by law.

Amendment 4 (Ratified 1791) The right of the people to be secure in their persons, houses, papers, and effects, against unreasonable searches and seizures, shall not be violated, and no Warrants shall issue, but upon probable cause, supported by Oath or affirmation, and particularly describing the place to be searched, and the persons or things to be seized.

Amendment 5 (Ratified 1791) No person shall be held to answer for a capital, or otherwise infamous crime, unless on a presentment or indictment of a Grand Jury, except in cases arising in the land or naval forces, or in the Militia, when in actual service in time of War or public danger; nor shall any person be subject for the same offence to be twice put in jeopardy of life or limb; nor shall be compelled in any criminal case to be a witness against himself, nor be deprived of life, liberty, or property, without due process of law; nor shall private property be taken for public use, without just compensation.

Amendment 6 (Ratified 1791) In all criminal prosecutions, the accused shall enjoy the right to a speedy and public trial, by an impartial jury of the State and district wherein the crime shall have been committed, which district shall have been previously ascertained by law, and to be informed of the nature and cause of the accusation; to be confronted with the witnesses against him; to have compulsory process for obtaining Witnesses in his favor, and to have assistance of counsel for his defence.

Amendment 7 (Ratified 1791) In Suits at common law, where the value in controversy shall exceed twenty dollars, the right of trial by jury shall be preserved, and no fact tried by a jury, shall be otherwise re-examined in any Court of the United States, than according to the rules of the common law.

Amendment 8 (Ratified 1791) Excessive bail shall not be required, nor excessive fines imposed, nor cruel and unusual punishments inflicted.

Amendment 9 (Ratified 1791) The enumeration in the Constitution, of certain rights, shall not be construed to deny or disparage others retained by the people.

Amendment 10 (Ratified 1791) The powers not delegated to the United States by the Constitution, nor prohibited by it to the States, are reserved to the States respectively, or to the people.

Amendment 11 (Ratified 1795) The Judicial power of the United States shall not be construed to extend to any suit in law or equity, commenced or prosecuted against one of the United States by Citizens of another State, or by Citizens or Subjects of any Foreign State.

Amendment 12 (Ratified 1804) The Electors shall meet in their respective states, and vote by ballot for President and Vice-President, one of whom, at least, shall not be an inhabitant of the same state with themselves; they shall name in their ballots the person voted for as President, and in distinct ballots the person voted for as Vice-President, and they shall make distinct lists of all persons voted for as President, and of all persons voted for as Vice-President, and of the number of votes for each, which lists they shall sign and certify, and transmit sealed to the seat of the government of the United States, directed to the President of the Senate;— The President of the Senate shall, in the presence of the Senate and House of Representatives, open all the certificates and the votes shall then be counted;—The person having the greatest number of votes for President, shall be the President, if such number be a majority of the whole number of Electors appointed; and if no person have such majority, then from the persons having the highest numbers not exceeding three on the list of those voted for as President, the House of Representatives shall choose immediately, by ballot, the President.

But in choosing the President, the votes shall be taken by states, the representation from each state having one vote; a quorum for this purpose shall consist of a member or members from two-thirds of the states, and a majority of all the states shall be necessary to a choice. And if the House of Representatives shall not choose a President whenever the right of choice shall devolve upon them, before the fourth day of March next following, then the Vice-President shall act as president, as in the case of the death or other constitutional disability of the President.[10]—The person having the greatest number of votes as Vice-President, shall be the Vice-President, if such number be a majority of the whole number of Electors appointed, and if no person have a majority, then from the two highest numbers on the list, the Senate shall choose the Vice-President; a quorum for the purpose shall consist of two-thirds of the whole number of Senators, and a majority of the whole number shall be necessary to a choice. But no person constitutionally ineligible to the office of President shall be eligible to that of Vice-President of the United States.

Amendment 13 (Ratified 1865)

Section 1 Neither slavery nor involuntary servitude, except as a punishment for crime whereof the party shall have been duly convicted, shall exist within the United States, or any place subject to their jurisdiction.

Section 2 Congress shall have power to enforce this article by appropriate legislation.

Amendment 14 (Ratified 1868)

Section 1 All persons born or naturalized in the United States, and subject to the jurisdiction thereof, are citizens of the United States and of the State wherein they reside. No State shall make or enforce any law which shall abridge the privileges or immunities of citizens of the United States; nor shall any State deprive any person of life, liberty, or property, without due process of law; nor deny to any person within its jurisdiction the equal protection of the laws.

Section 2 Representatives shall be apportioned among the several States according to their respective numbers, counting the whole number of persons in each State, excluding Indians not taxed. But when the right to vote at any election for the choice of electors for President and Vice President of the United States, Representatives in Congress, the Executive and Judicial officers of a State, or the members of the Legislature thereof, is denied to any of the male inhabitants of such State, being twenty-one[11] years of age, and citizens of the United States, or in any way abridged except for participation in rebellion, or other crime, the basis of representation therein shall be reduced in the proportion which the number of such male citizens shall bear to the whole number of male citizens twenty-one years of age in such State.

Section 3 No person shall be a Senator or Representative in Congress, or elector of President and Vice President, or hold any office, civil or military, under the United States, or under any State, who, having previously taken an oath, as a member of Congress, or as an officer of the United States, or as a member of any State legislature, or as an executive or judicial officer of any State, to support the Constitution of the United States, shall have engaged in insurrection or rebellion against the same, or given aid or comfort to the enemies thereof. But Congress may by a vote of two-thirds of each House, remove such disability.

Section 4 The validity of the public debt of the United States, authorized by law, including debts incurred for payment of pensions and bounties for services in suppressing insurrection or rebellion, shall not be questioned. But neither the United States nor any State shall assume or pay any debt or obligation incurred in aid of insurrection or rebellion against the United States, or any claim for the loss or emancipation of any slave; but all such debts, obligations and claims shall be held illegal and void.

Section 5 The Congress shall have power to enforce, by appropriate legislation, the provisions of this article.

Amendment 15 (Ratified 1870)

Section 1 The right of citizens of the United States to vote shall not be denied or abridged by the United States or by any State on account of race, color, or previous condition of servitude.

Section 2 The Congress shall have power to enforce this article by appropriate legislation.

Amendment 16 (Ratified 1913)
The Congress shall have power to lay and collect taxes on incomes, from whatever source derived, without apportionment among the several States, and without regard to any census or enumeration.

Amendment 17 (Ratified 1913)
The Senate of the United States shall be composed of two Senators from each State, elected by the people thereof, for six years; and each Senator shall have one vote. The electors in each State shall have the qualifications requisite for electors of the most numerous branch of the State legislatures.

When vacancies happen in the representation of any State in the Senate, the executive authority of such State shall issue writs of election to fill such vacancies: *Provided,* That the legislature of any State may empower the executive thereof to make temporary appointments until the people fill the vacancies by election as the legislature may direct.

[10] Changed by the Twentieth Amendment.
[11] Changed by the Twenty-sixth Amendment.

This amendment shall not be so construed as to affect the election or term of any Senator chosen before it becomes valid as part of the Constitution.

Amendment 18 (Ratified 1919; Repealed 1933)

Section 1 After one year from the ratification of this article the manufacture, sale, or transportation of intoxicating liquors within, the importation thereof into, or the exportation thereof from the United States and all territory subject to the jurisdiction thereof for beverage purposes is hereby prohibited.

Section 2 The Congress and the several States shall have concurrent power to enforce this article by appropriate legislation.

Section 3 This article shall be inoperative unless it shall have been ratified as an amendment to the Constitution by the legislatures of the several States, as provided in the Constitution, within seven years from the date of the submission hereof to the States by the Congress.[12]

Amendment 19 (Ratified 1920)
The right of citizens of the United States to vote shall not be denied or abridged by the United States or by any State on account of sex.

Congress shall have power to enforce this article by appropriate legislation.

Amendment 20 (Ratified 1933)

Section 1 The terms of the President and Vice President shall end at noon on the 20th day of January, and the terms of Senators and Representatives at noon on the 3d day of January, of the years in which such terms would have ended if this article had not been ratified; and the terms of their successors shall then begin.

Section 2 The Congress shall assemble at least once in every year, and such meeting shall begin at noon on the 3d day of January, unless they shall by law appoint a different day.

Section 3 If, at the time fixed for the beginning of the term of the President, the President elect shall have died, the Vice President elect shall become President. If a President shall not have been chosen before the time fixed for the beginning of his term, or if the President elect shall have failed to qualify, then the Vice President elect shall act as President until a President shall have qualified; and the Congress may by law provide for the case wherein neither a President elect nor a Vice President elect shall have qualified, declaring who shall then act as President, or the manner in which one who is to act shall be selected, and such person shall act accordingly until a President or Vice President shall have qualified.

Section 4 The Congress may by law provide for the case of the death of any of the persons from whom the House of Representatives may choose a President whenever the right of choice shall have devolved upon them, and for the case of the death of any of the persons from whom the Senate may choose a Vice President whenever the right of choice shall have devolved upon them.

Section 5 Sections 1 and 2 shall take effect on the 15th day of October following the ratification of this article.

Section 6 This article shall be inoperative unless it shall have been ratified as an amendment to the Constitution by the legislatures of three-fourths of the several States within seven years from the date of its submission.

Amendment 21 (Ratified 1933)

Section 1 The eighteenth article of amendment to the Constitution of the United States is hereby repealed.

Section 2 The transportation or importation into any State, Territory, or possession of the United States for delivery or use therein of intoxicating liquors, in violation of the laws thereof, is hereby prohibited.

Section 3 This article shall be inoperative unless it shall have been ratified as an amendment to the Constitution by conventions in the several States, as provided in the Constitution, within seven years from the date of the submission hereof to the States by the Congress.

Amendment 22 (Ratified 1951)

Section 1 No person shall be elected to the office of the President more than twice, and no person who has held the office of President, or acted as President, for more than two years of a term to which some other person was elected President shall be elected to the office of the President more than once. But this Article shall not apply to any person holding the office of President when this Article was proposed by the Congress, and shall not prevent any person who may be holding the office of President, or acting as President, during the term within which this Article becomes operative from holding the office of President or acting as President during the remainder of such term.

Section 2 This Article shall be inoperative unless it shall have been ratified as an amendment to the Constitution by the legislatures of three-fourths of the several States within seven years from the date of its submission to the States by the Congress.

Amendment 23 (Ratified 1961)

Section 1 The District constituting the seat of Government of the United States shall appoint in such manner as the Congress may direct:

[12] Repealed by the Twenty-first Amendment.

A number of electors of President and Vice President equal to the whole number of Senators and Representatives in Congress to which the District would be entitled if it were a State, but in no event more than the least populous State; they shall be in addition to those appointed by the States, but they shall be considered, for the purposes of the election of President and Vice President, to be electors appointed by a State; and they shall meet in the District and perform such duties as provided by the twelfth article of amendment.

Section 2 The Congress shall have power to enforce this article by appropriate legislation.

Amendment 24 (Ratified 1964)

Section 1 The right of citizens of the United States to vote in any primary or other election for President or Vice President, for electors for President or Vice President, or for Senator or Representative in Congress, shall not be denied or abridged by the United States or any State by reason of failure to pay any poll tax or other tax.

Section 2 The Congress shall have power to enforce this article by appropriate legislation.

Amendment 25 (Ratified 1967)

Section 1 In case of the removal of the President from office or of his death or resignation, the Vice President shall become President.

Section 2 Whenever there is a vacancy in the office of the Vice President, the President shall nominate a Vice President who shall take office upon confirmation by a majority vote of both Houses of Congress.

Section 3 Whenever the President transmits to the President pro tempore of the Senate and the Speaker of the House of Representatives his written declaration that he is unable to discharge the powers and duties of his office, and until he transmits to them a written declaration to the contrary, such powers and duties shall be discharged by the Vice President as Acting President.

Section 4 Whenever the Vice President and a majority of either the principal officers of the executive departments or of such other body as Congress may by law provide, transmit to the President pro tempore of the Senate and the Speaker of the House of Representatives their written declaration that the President is unable to discharge the powers and duties of his office, the Vice President shall immediately assume the powers and duties of the office as Acting President.

Thereafter, when the President transmits to the President pro tempore of the Senate and the Speaker of the House of Representatives his written declaration that no inability exists, he shall resume the powers and duties of his office unless the Vice President and a majority of either the principal officers of the executive department or of such other body as Congress may by law provide, transmit within four days to the President pro tempore of the Senate and the Speaker of the House of Representatives their written declaration that the President is unable to discharge the powers and duties of his office. Thereupon Congress shall decide the issue, assembling within forty-eight hours for that purpose if not in session. If the Congress, within twenty-one days after receipt of the latter written declaration, or, if Congress is not in session, within twenty-one days after Congress is required to assemble, determines by two-thirds vote of both Houses that the President is unable to discharge the powers and duties of his office, the Vice President shall continue to discharge the same as Acting President; otherwise, the President shall resume the powers and duties of his office.

Amendment 26 (Ratified 1971)

Section 1 The right of citizens of the United States, who are eighteen years of age or older, to vote shall not be denied or abridged by the United States or by any State on account of age.

Section 2 The Congress shall have power to enforce this article by appropriate legislation.

Amendment 27 (Ratified 1992)

No law, varying the compensation for the services of the Senators and Representatives, shall take effect, until an election of Representatives shall have intervened.

Uniform Commercial Code

Article 2–Sales

Part 1: Short Title, General Construction and Subject Matter

§ 2–101. Short Title. This Article shall be known and may be cited as Uniform Commercial Code—Sales.

§ 2–102. Scope; Certain Security and Other Transactions Excluded from This Article. Unless the context otherwise requires, this Article applies to transactions in goods; it does not apply to any transaction which although in the form of an unconditional contract to sell or present sale is intended to operate only as a security transaction nor does this Article impair or repeal any statute regulating sales to consumers, farmers or other specified classes of buyers.

§ 2–103. Definitions and Index of Definitions.

(1) In this Article unless the context otherwise requires
 (a) "Buyer" means a person who buys or contracts to buy goods.
 (b) "Good faith" in the case of a merchant means honesty in fact and the observance of reasonable commercial standards of fair dealing in the trade.
 (c) "Receipt" of goods means taking physical possession of them.
 (d) "Seller" means a person who sells or contracts to sell goods.

(2) Other definitions applying to this Article or to specified Parts thereof, and the sections in which they appear are:

"Acceptance"	Section 2–606.
"Banker's credit"	Section 2–325.
"Between merchants"	Section 2–104.
"Cancellation"	Section 2–106(4).
"Commercial unit"	Section 2–105.
"Confirmed credit"	Section 2–325.
"Conforming to contract"	Section 2–106.
"Contract for sale"	Section 2–106.
"Cover"	Section 2–712.

"Entrusting"	Section 2–403.
"Financing agency"	Section 2–104.
"Future goods"	Section 2–105.
"Goods"	Section 2–105.
"Identification"	Section 2–501.
"Installment contract"	Section 2–612.
"Letter of Credit"	Section 2–325.
"Lot"	Section 2–105.
"Merchant"	Section 2–104.
"Overseas"	Section 2–323.
"Person in position of seller"	Section 2–707.
"Present sale"	Section 2–106.
"Sale"	Section 2–106.
"Sale on approval"	Section 2–326.
"Sale or return"	Section 2–326.
"Termination"	Section 2–106.

(3) The following definitions in other Articles apply to this Article:

"Check"	Section 3–104.
"Consignee"	Section 7–102.
"Consignor"	Section 7–102.
"Consumer goods"	Section 9–109.
"Dishonor"	Section 3–502.
"Draft"	Section 3–104.

(4) In addition Article 1 contains general definitions and principles of construction and interpretation applicable throughout this Article.

As amended in 1994.
 See Appendix XI for material relating to changes made in text in 1994.

§ 2–104. Definitions: "Merchant"; "Between Merchants"; "Financing Agency".

(1) "Merchant" means a person who deals in goods of the kind or otherwise by his occupation holds himself out as having knowledge or skill peculiar to the practices

or goods involved in the transaction or to whom such knowledge or skill may be attributed by his employment of an agent or broker or other intermediary who by his occupation holds himself out as having such knowledge or skill.

(2) "Financing agency" means a bank, finance company or other person who in the ordinary course of business makes advances against goods or documents of title or who by arrangement with either the seller or the buyer intervenes in ordinary course to make or collect payment due or claimed under the contract for sale, as by purchasing or paying the seller's draft or making advances against it or by merely taking it for collection whether or not documents of title accompany the draft. "Financing agency" includes also a bank or other person who similarly intervenes between persons who are in the position of seller and buyer in respect to the goods (Section 2–707).

(3) "Between merchants" means in any transaction with respect to which both parties are chargeable with the knowledge or skill of merchants.

§ 2–105. Definitions: "Transferability"; "Goods"; "Future" Goods; "Lot"; "Commercial Unit".

(1) "Goods" means all things (including specially manufactured goods) which are movable at the time of identification to the contract for sale other than the money in which the price is to be paid, investment securities (Article 8) and things in action. "Goods" also includes the unborn young of animals and growing crops and other identified things attached to realty as described in the section on goods to be severed from realty (Section 2–107).

(2) Goods must be both existing and identified before any interest in them can pass. Goods which are not both existing and identified are "future" goods. A purported present sale of future goods or of any interest therein operates as a contract to sell.

(3) There may be a sale of a part interest in existing identified goods.

(4) An undivided share in an identified bulk of fungible goods is sufficiently identified to be sold although the quantity of the bulk is not determined. Any agreed proportion of such a bulk or any quantity thereof agreed upon by number, weight or other measure may to the extent of the seller's interest in the bulk be sold to the buyer who then becomes an owner in common.

(5) "Lot" means a parcel or a single article which is the subject matter of a separate sale or delivery, whether or not it is sufficient to perform the contract.

(6) "Commercial unit" means such a unit of goods as by commercial usage is a single whole for purposes of sale and division of which materially impairs its character or value on the market or in use. A commercial unit may be a single article (as a machine) or a set

of articles (as a suite of furniture or an assortment of sizes) or a quantity (as a bale, gross, or carload) or any other unit treated in use or in the relevant market as a single whole.

§ 2–106. Definitions: "Contract"; "Agreement"; "Contract for Sales"; "Sale"; "Present Sale"; "Conforming" to Contract; "Termination"; "Cancellation".

(1) In this Article unless the context otherwise requires "contract" and "agreement" are limited to those relating to the present or future sale of goods. "Contract for sale" includes both a present sale of goods and a contract to sell goods at a future time. A "sale" consists in the passing of title from the seller to the buyer for a price (Section 2–401). A "present sale" means a sale which is accomplished by the making of the contract.

(2) Goods or conduct including any part of a performance are "conforming" or conform to the contract when they are in accordance with the obligations under the contract.

(3) "Termination" occurs when either party pursuant to a power created by agreement or law puts an end to the contract otherwise than for its breach. On "termination" all obligations which are still executory on both sides are discharged but any right based on prior breach or performance survives.

(4) "Cancellation" occurs when either party puts an end to the contract for breach by the other and its effect is the same as that of "termination" except that the cancelling party also retains any remedy for breach of the whole contract or any unperformed balance.

§ 2–107. Goods to Be Severed from Realty: Recording.

(1) A contract for the sale of minerals or the like (including oil and gas) or a structure or its materials to be removed from realty is a contract for the sale of goods within this Article if they are to be severed by the seller but until severance a purported present sale thereof which is not effective as a transfer of an interest in land is effective only as a contract to sell.

(2) A contract for the sale apart from the land of growing crops or other things attached to realty and capable of severance without material harm thereto but not described in subsection (1) or of timber to be cut is a contract for the sale of goods within this Article whether the subject matter is to be severed by the buyer or by the seller even though it forms part of the realty at the time of contracting, and the parties can by identification effect a present sale before severance.

(3) The provisions of this section are subject to any third party rights provided by the law relating to realty records, and the contract for sale may be executed and recorded as a document transferring an interest in land and shall then constitute notice to third parties of the buyer's rights under the contract for sale. As amended in 1972.

Part 2: Form, Formation and Readjustment of Contract

§ 2–201. Formal Requirements; Statute of Frauds.

(1) Except as otherwise provided in this section a contract for the sale of goods for the price of $500 or more is not enforceable by way of action or defense unless there is some writing sufficient to indicate that a contract for sale has been made between the parties and signed by the party against whom enforcement is sought or by his authorized agent or broker. A writing is not insufficient because it omits or incorrectly states a term agreed upon but the contract is not enforceable under this paragraph beyond the quantity of goods shown in such writing.

(2) Between merchants if within a reasonable time a writing in confirmation of the contract and sufficient against the sender is received and the party receiving it has reason to know its contents, it satisfies the requirements of subsection (1) against such party unless written notice of objection to its contents is given within 10 days after it is received.

(3) A contract which does not satisfy the requirements of subsection (1) but which is valid in other respects is enforceable

 (a) if the goods are to be specially manufactured for the buyer and are not suitable for sale to others in the ordinary course of the seller's business and the seller, before notice of repudiation is received and under circumstances which reasonably indicate that the goods are for the buyer, has made either a substantial beginning of their manufacture or commitments for their procurement; or

 (b) if the party against whom enforcement is sought admits in his pleading, testimony or otherwise in court that a contract for sale was made, but the contract is not enforceable under this provision beyond the quantity of goods admitted; or

 (c) with respect to goods for which payment has been made and accepted or which have been received and accepted (Section 2–606).

§ 2–202. Final Written Expression: Parol or Extrinsic Evidence.
Terms with respect to which the confirmatory memoranda of the parties agree or which are otherwise set forth in a writing intended by the parties as a final expression of their agreement with respect to such terms as are included therein may not be contradicted by evidence of any prior agreement or of a contemporaneous oral agreement but may be explained or supplemented

 (a) by course of dealing or usage of trade (Section 1–205) or by course of performance (Section 2–208); and

 (b) by evidence of consistent additional terms unless the court finds the writing to have been intended

also as a complete and exclusive statement of the terms of the agreement.

§ 2–203. Seals Inoperative.
The affixing of a seal to a writing evidencing a contract for sale or an offer to buy or sell goods does not constitute the writing a sealed instrument and the law with respect to sealed instruments does not apply to such a contract or offer.

§ 2–204. Formation in General.

(1) A contract for sale of goods may be made in any manner sufficient to show agreement, including conduct by both parties which recognizes the existence of such a contract.

(2) An agreement sufficient to constitute a contract for sale may be found even though the moment of its making is undetermined.

(3) Even though one or more terms are left open a contract for sale does not fail for indefiniteness if the parties have intended to make a contract and there is a reasonably certain basis for giving an appropriate remedy.

§ 2–205. Firm Offers.
An offer by a merchant to buy or sell goods in a signed writing which by its terms gives assurance that it will be held open is not revocable, for lack of consideration, during the time stated or if no time is stated for a reasonable time, but in no event may such period of irrevocability exceed three months; but any such term of assurance on a form supplied by the offeree must be separately signed by the offeror.

§ 2–206. Offer and Acceptance in Formation of Contract.

(1) Unless otherwise unambiguously indicated by the language or circumstances

 (a) an offer to make a contract shall be construed as inviting acceptance in any manner and by any medium reasonable in the circumstances;

 (b) an order or other offer to buy goods for prompt or current shipment shall be construed as inviting acceptance either by a prompt promise to ship or by the prompt or current shipment of conforming or non-conforming goods, but such a shipment of non-conforming goods does not constitute an acceptance if the seller seasonably notifies the buyer that the shipment is offered only as an accommodation to the buyer.

(2) Where the beginning of a requested performance is a reasonable mode of acceptance an offeror who is not notified of acceptance within a reasonable time may treat the offer as having lapsed before acceptance.

§ 2–207. Additional Terms in Acceptance or Confirmation.

(1) A definite and seasonable expression of acceptance or a written confirmation which is sent within a reasonable

time operates as an acceptance even though it states terms additional to or different from those offered or agreed upon, unless acceptance is expressly made conditional on assent to the additional or different terms.

(2) The additional terms are to be construed as proposals for addition to the contract. Between merchants such terms become part of the contract unless:

 (a) the offer expressly limits acceptance to the terms of the offer;

 (b) they materially alter it; or

 (c) notification of objection to them has already been given or is given within a reasonable time after notice of them is received.

(3) Conduct by both parties which recognizes the existence of a contract is sufficient to establish a contract for sale although the writings of the parties do not otherwise establish a contract. In such case the terms of the particular contract consist of those terms on which the writings of the parties agree, together with any supplementary terms incorporated under any other provisions of this Act.

§ 2–208. Course of Performance or Practical Construction.

(1) Where the contract for sale involves repeated occasions for performance by either party with knowledge of the nature of the performance and opportunity for objection to it by the other, any course of performance accepted or acquiesced in without objection shall be relevant to determine the meaning of the agreement.

(2) The express terms of the agreement and any such course of performance, as well as any course of dealing and usage of trade, shall be construed whenever reasonable as consistent with each other; but when such construction is unreasonable, express terms shall control course of performance and course of performance shall control both course of dealing and usage of trade (Section 1-205).

(3) Subject to the provisions of the next section on modification and waiver, such course of performance shall be relevant to show a waiver or modification of any term inconsistent with such course of performance.

§ 2–209. Modification, Rescission and Waiver.

(1) An agreement modifying a contract within this Article needs no consideration to be binding.

(2) A signed agreement which excludes modification or rescission except by a signed writing cannot be otherwise modified or rescinded, but except as between merchants such a requirement on a form supplied by the merchant must be separately signed by the other party.

(3) The requirements of the statute of frauds section of this Article (Section 2–201) must be satisfied if the contract as modified is within its provisions.

(4) Although an attempt at modification or rescission does not satisfy the requirements of subsection (2) or (3) it can operate as a waiver.

(5) A party who has made a waiver affecting an executory portion of the contract may retract the waiver by reasonable notification received by the other party that strict performance will be required of any term waived, unless the retraction would be unjust in view of a material change of position in reliance on the waiver.

§ 2–210. Delegation of Performance; Assignment of Rights.

(1) A party may perform his duty through a delegate unless otherwise agreed or unless the other party has a substantial interest in having his original promisor perform or control the acts required by the contract. No delegation of performance relieves the party delegating of any duty to perform or any liability for breach.

(2) Unless otherwise agreed all rights of either seller or buyer can be assigned except where the assignment would materially change the duty of the other party, or increase materially the burden or risk imposed on him by his contract, or impair materially his chance of obtaining return performance. A right to damages for breach of the whole contract or a right arising out of the assignor's due performance of his entire obligation can be assigned despite agreement otherwise.

(3) Unless the circumstances indicate the contrary a prohibition of assignment of "the contract" is to be construed as barring only the delegation to the assignee of the assignor's performance.

(4) An assignment of "the contract" or of "all my rights under the contract" or an assignment in similar general terms is an assignment of rights and unless the language or the circumstances (as in an assignment for security) indicate the contrary, it is a delegation of performance of the duties of the assignor and its acceptance by the assignee constitutes a promise by him to perform those duties. This promise is enforceable by either the assignor or the other party to the original contract.

(5) The other party may treat any assignment which delegates performance as creating reasonable grounds for insecurity and may without prejudice to his rights against the assignor demand assurances from the assignee (Section 2–609).

Part 3: General Obligation and Construction of Contract

§ 2–301. General Obligations of Parties. The obligation of the seller is to transfer and deliver and that of the buyer is to accept and pay in accordance with the contract.

§ 2–302. Unconscionable Contract or Clause.

(1) If the court as a matter of law finds the contract or any clause of the contract to have been unconscionable at the time it was made the court may refuse to enforce the contract, or it may enforce the remainder of the contract without the unconscionable clause, or it may so limit the application of any unconscionable clause as to avoid any unconscionable result.

(2) When it is claimed or appears to the court that the contract or any clause thereof may be unconscionable the parties shall be afforded a reasonable opportunity to present evidence as to its commercial setting, purpose and effect to aid the court in making the determination.

§ 2–303. Allocation or Division of Risks.
Where this Article allocates a risk or a burden as between the parties "unless otherwise agreed", the agreement may not only shift the allocation but may also divide the risk or burden.

§ 2–304. Price Payable in Money, Goods, Realty, or Otherwise.

(1) The price can be made payable in money or otherwise. If it is payable in whole or in part in goods each party is a seller of the goods which he is to transfer.

(2) Even though all or part of the price is payable in an interest in realty the transfer of the goods and the seller's obligations with reference to them are subject to this Article, but not the transfer of the interest in realty or the transferor's obligations in connection therewith.

§ 2–305. Open Price Term.

(1) The parties if they so intend can conclude a contract for sale even though the price is not settled. In such a case the price is a reasonable price at the time for delivery if
 (a) nothing is said as to price; or
 (b) the price is left to be agreed by the parties and they fail to agree; or
 (c) the price is to be fixed in terms of some agreed market or other standard as set or recorded by a third person or agency and it is not so set or recorded.

(2) A price to be fixed by the seller or by the buyer means a price for him to fix in good faith.

(3) When a price left to be fixed otherwise than by agreement of the parties fails to be fixed through fault of one party the other may at his option treat the contract as cancelled or himself fix a reasonable price.

(4) Where, however, the parties intend not to be bound unless the price be fixed or agreed and it is not fixed or agreed there is no contract. In such a case the buyer must return any goods already received or if unable so to do must pay their reasonable value at the time of delivery and the seller must return any portion of the price paid on account.

§ 2–306. Output, Requirements and Exclusive Dealings.

(1) A term which measures the quantity by the output of the seller or the requirements of the buyer means such actual output or requirements as may occur in good faith, except that no quantity unreasonably disproportionate to any stated estimate or in the absence of a stated estimate to any normal or otherwise comparable prior output or requirements may be tendered or demanded.

(2) A lawful agreement by either the seller or the buyer for exclusive dealing in the kind of goods concerned imposes unless otherwise agreed an obligation by the seller to use best efforts to supply the goods and by the buyer to use best efforts to promote their sale.

§ 2–307. Delivery in Single Lot or Several Lots.
Unless otherwise agreed all goods called for by a contract for sale must be tendered in a single delivery and payment is due only on such tender but where the circumstances give either party the right to make or demand delivery in lots the price if it can be apportioned may be demanded for each lot.

§ 2–308. Absence of Specified Place for Delivery.
Unless otherwise agreed
 (a) the place for delivery of goods is the seller's place of business or if he has none his residence; but
 (b) in a contract for sale of identified goods which to the knowledge of the parties at the time of contracting are in some other place, that place is the place for their delivery; and
 (c) documents of title may be delivered through customary banking channels.

§ 2–309. Absence of Specific Time Provisions; Notice of Termination.

(1) The time for shipment or delivery or any other action under a contract if not provided in this Article or agreed upon shall be a reasonable time.

(2) Where the contract provides for successive performances but is indefinite in duration it is valid for a reasonable time but unless otherwise agreed may be terminated at any time by either party.

(3) Termination of a contract by one party except on the happening of an agreed event requires that reasonable notification be received by the other party and an agreement dispensing with notification is invalid if its operation would be unconscionable.

§ 2–310. Open Time for Payment or Running of Credit; Authority to Ship Under Reservation.
Unless otherwise agreed
 (a) payment is due at the time and place at which the buyer is to receive the goods even though the place of shipment is the place of delivery; and

(b) if the seller is authorized to send the goods he may ship them under reservation, and may tender the documents of title, but the buyer may inspect the goods after their arrival before payment is due unless such inspection is inconsistent with the terms of the contract (Section 2–513); and

(c) if delivery is authorized and made by way of documents of title otherwise than by subsection (b) then payment is due at the time and place at which the buyer is to receive the documents regardless of where the goods are to be received; and

(d) where the seller is required or authorized to ship the goods on credit the credit period runs from the time of shipment but postdating the invoice or delaying its dispatch will correspondingly delay the starting of the credit period.

§ 2–311. Options and Cooperation Respecting Performance.

(1) An agreement for sale which is otherwise sufficiently definite (subsection (3) of Section 2–204) to be a contract is not made invalid by the fact that it leaves particulars of performance to be specified by one of the parties. Any such specification must be made in good faith and within limits set by commercial reasonableness.

(2) Unless otherwise agreed specifications relating to assortment of the goods are at the buyer's option and except as otherwise provided in subsections (1)(c) and (3) of Section 2–319 specifications or arrangements relating to shipment are at the seller's option.

(3) Where such specification would materially affect the other party's performance but is not seasonably made or where one party's cooperation is necessary to the agreed performance of the other but is not seasonably forthcoming, the other party in addition to all other remedies

(a) is excused for any resulting delay in his own performance; and

(b) may also either proceed to perform in any reasonable manner or after the time for a material part of his own performance treat the failure to specify or to cooperate as a breach by failure to deliver or accept the goods.

§ 2–312. Warranty of Title and Against Infringement; Buyer's Obligation Against Infringement.

(1) Subject to subsection (2) there is in a contract for sale a warranty by the seller that

(a) the title conveyed shall be good, and its transfer rightful; and

(b) the goods shall be delivered free from any security interest or other lien or encumbrance of which the buyer at the time of contracting has no knowledge.

(2) A warranty under subsection (1) will be excluded or modified only by specific language or by circumstances which give the buyer reason to know that the person selling does not claim title in himself or that he is purporting to sell only such right or title as he or a third person may have.

(3) Unless otherwise agreed a seller who is a merchant regularly dealing in goods of the kind warrants that the goods shall be delivered free of the rightful claim of any third person by way of infringement or the like but a buyer who furnishes specifications to the seller must hold the seller harmless against any such claim which arises out of compliance with the specifications.

§ 2–313. Express Warranties by Affirmation, Promise, Description, Sample.

(1) Express warranties by the seller are created as follows:

(a) Any affirmation of fact or promise made by the seller to the buyer which relates to the goods and becomes part of the basis of the bargain creates an express warranty that the goods shall conform to the affirmation or promise.

(b) Any description of the goods which is made part of the basis of the bargain creates an express warranty that the goods shall conform to the description.

(c) Any sample or model which is made part of the basis of the bargain creates an express warranty that the whole of the goods shall conform to the sample or model.

(2) It is not necessary to the creation of an express warranty that the seller use formal words such as "warrant" or "guarantee" or that he have a specific intention to make a warranty, but an affirmation merely of the value of the goods or a statement purporting to be merely the seller's opinion or commendation of the goods does not create a warranty.

§ 2–314. Implied Warranty: Merchantability; Usage of Trade.

(1) Unless excluded or modified (Section 2–316), a warranty that the goods shall be merchantable is implied in a contract for their sale if the seller is a merchant with respect to goods of that kind. Under this section the serving for value of food or drink to be consumed either on the premises or elsewhere is a sale.

(2) Goods to be merchantable must be at least such as

(a) pass without objection in the trade under the contract description; and

(b) in the case of fungible goods, are of fair average quality within the description; and

(c) are fit for the ordinary purposes for which such goods are used; and

(d) run, within the variations permitted by the agreement, of even kind, quality and quantity within each unit and among all units involved; and

(e) are adequately contained, packaged, and labeled as the agreement may require; and

(f) conform to the promise or affirmations of fact made on the container or label if any.

(3) Unless excluded or modified (Section 2–316) other implied warranties may arise from course of dealing or usage of trade.

§ 2–315. Implied Warranty: Fitness for Particular Purpose.

Where the seller at the time of contracting has reason to know any particular purpose for which the goods are required and that the buyer is relying on the seller's skill or judgment to select or furnish suitable goods, there is unless excluded or modified under the next section an implied warranty that the goods shall be fit for such purpose.

§ 2–316. Exclusion or Modification of Warranties.

(1) Words or conduct relevant to the creation of an express warranty and words or conduct tending to negate or limit warranty shall be construed wherever reasonable as consistent with each other; but subject to the provisions of this Article on parol or extrinsic evidence (Section 2–202) negation or limitation is inoperative to the extent that such construction is unreasonable.

(2) Subject to subsection (3), to exclude or modify the implied warranty of merchantability or any part of it the language must mention merchantability and in case of a writing must be conspicuous, and to exclude or modify any implied warranty of fitness the exclusion must be by a writing and conspicuous. Language to exclude all implied warranties of fitness is sufficient if it states, for example, that "There are no warranties which extend beyond the description on the face hereof."

(3) Notwithstanding subsection (2)

(a) unless the circumstances indicate otherwise, all implied warranties are excluded by expressions like "as is", "with all faults" or other language which in common understanding calls the buyer's attention to the exclusion of warranties and makes plain that there is no implied warranty; and

(b) when the buyer before entering into the contract has examined the goods or the sample or model as fully as he desired or has refused to examine the goods there is no implied warranty with regard to defects which an examination ought in the circumstances to have revealed to him; and

(c) an implied warranty can also be excluded or modified by course of dealing or course of performance or usage of trade.

(4) Remedies for breach of warranty can be limited in accordance with the provisions of this Article on liquidation or limitation of damages and on contractual modification of remedy (Sections 2–718 and 2–719).

§ 2–317. Cumulation and Conflict of Warranties Express or Implied.

Warranties whether express or implied shall be construed as consistent with each other and as cumulative, but if such construction is unreasonable the intention of the parties shall determine which warranty is dominant. In ascertaining that intention the following rules apply:

(a) Exact or technical specifications displace an inconsistent sample or model or general language of description.

(b) A sample from an existing bulk displaces inconsistent general language of description.

(c) Express warranties displace inconsistent implied warranties other than an implied warranty of fitness for a particular purpose.

§ 2–318. Third Party Beneficiaries of Warranties Express or Implied.

Note: *If this Act is introduced in the Congress of the United States this section should be omitted. (States to select one alternative.)*

Alternative A

A seller's warranty whether express or implied extends to any natural person who is in the family or household of his buyer or who is a guest in his home if it is reasonable to expect that such person may use, consume or be affected by the goods and who is injured in person by breach of the warranty. A seller may not exclude or limit the operation of this section.

Alternative B

A seller's warranty whether express or implied extends to any natural person who may reasonably be expected to use, consume or be affected by the goods and who is injured in person by breach of the warranty. A seller may not exclude or limit the operation of this section.

Alternative C

A seller's warranty whether express or implied extends to any person who may reasonably be expected to use, consume or be affected by the goods and who is injured by breach of the warranty. A seller may not exclude or limit the operation of this section with respect to injury to the person of an individual to whom the warranty extends. As amended in 1966.

§ 2–319. F.O.B. and F.A.S. Terms.

(1) Unless otherwise agreed the term F.O.B. (which means "free on board") at a named place, even though used only in connection with the stated price, is a delivery term under which

(a) when the term is F.O.B. the place of shipment, the seller must at that place ship the goods in the

manner provided in this Article (Section 2–504) and bear the expense and risk of putting them into the possession of the carrier; or

(b) when the term is F.O.B. the place of destination, the seller must at his own expense and risk transport the goods to that place and there tender delivery of them in the manner provided in this Article (Section 2–503);

(c) when under either (a) or (b) the term is also F.O.B. vessel, car or other vehicle, the seller must in addition at his own expense and risk load the goods on board. If the term is F.O.B. vessel the buyer must name the vessel and in an appropriate case the seller must comply with the provisions of this Article on the form of bill of lading (Section 2–323).

(2) Unless otherwise agreed the term F.A.S. vessel (which means "free alongside") at a named port, even though used only in connection with the stated price, is a delivery term under which the seller must

(a) at his own expense and risk deliver the goods alongside the vessel in the manner usual in that port or on a dock designated and provided by the buyer; and

(b) obtain and tender a receipt for the goods in exchange for which the carrier is under a duty to issue a bill of lading.

(3) Unless otherwise agreed in any case falling within subsection (1)(a) or (c) or subsection (2) the buyer must seasonably give any needed instructions for making delivery, including when the term is F.A.S. or F.O.B. the loading berth of the vessel and in an appropriate case its name and sailing date. The seller may treat the failure of needed instructions as a failure of cooperation under this Article (Section 2–311). He may also at his option move the goods in any reasonable manner preparatory to delivery or shipment.

(4) Under the term F.O.B. vessel or F.A.S. unless otherwise agreed the buyer must make payment against tender of the required documents and the seller may not tender nor the buyer demand delivery of the goods in substitution for the documents.

§ 2–320. C.I.F. and C. & F. Terms.

(1) The term C.I.F. means that the price includes in a lump sum the cost of the goods and the insurance and freight to the named destination. The term C. & F. or C.F. means that the price so includes cost and freight to the named destination.

(2) Unless otherwise agreed and even though used only in connection with the stated price and destination, the term C.I.F. destination or its equivalent requires the seller at his own expense and risk to

(a) put the goods into the possession of a carrier at the port for shipment and obtain a negotiable bill

or bills of lading covering the entire transportation to the named destination; and

(b) load the goods and obtain a receipt from the carrier (which may be contained in the bill of lading) showing that the freight has been paid or provided for; and

(c) obtain a policy or certificate of insurance, including any war risk insurance, of a kind and on terms then current at the port of shipment in the usual amount, in the currency of the contract, shown to cover the same goods covered by the bill of lading and providing for payment of loss to the order of the buyer or for the account of whom it may concern; but the seller may add to the price the amount of the premium for any such war risk insurance; and

(d) prepare an invoice of the goods and procure any other documents required to effect shipment or to comply with the contract; and

(e) forward and tender with commercial promptness all the documents in due form and with any indorsement necessary to perfect the buyer's rights.

(3) Unless otherwise agreed the term C. & F. or its equivalent has the same effect and imposes upon the seller the same obligations and risks as a C.I.F. term except the obligation as to insurance.

(4) Under the term C.I.F. or C. & F. unless otherwise agreed the buyer must make payment against tender of the required documents and the seller may not tender nor the buyer demand delivery of the goods in substitution for the documents.

§ 2–321. C.I.F. or C. & F.: "Net Landed Weights"; "Payment on Arrival"; Warranty of Condition on Arrival. Under a contract containing a term C.I.F. or C. & F.

(1) Where the price is based on or is to be adjusted according to "net landed weights", "delivered weights", "out turn" quantity or quality or the like, unless otherwise agreed the seller must reasonably estimate the price. The payment due on tender of the documents called for by the contract is the amount so estimated, but after final adjustment of the price a settlement must be made with commercial promptness.

(2) An agreement described in subsection (1) or any warranty of quality or condition of the goods on arrival places upon the seller the risk of ordinary deterioration, shrinkage and the like in transportation but has no effect on the place or time of identification to the contract for sale or delivery or on the passing of the risk of loss.

(3) Unless otherwise agreed where the contract provides for payment on or after arrival of the goods the seller must before payment allow such preliminary inspection as is feasible; but if the goods are lost delivery of

the documents and payment are due when the goods should have arrived.

§ 2–322. Delivery "Ex-Ship".

(1) Unless otherwise agreed a term for delivery of goods "ex-ship" (which means from the carrying vessel) or in equivalent language is not restricted to a particular ship and requires delivery from a ship which has reached a place at the named port of destination where goods of the kind are usually discharged.

(2) Under such a term unless otherwise agreed

 (a) the seller must discharge all liens arising out of the carriage and furnish the buyer with a direction which puts the carrier under a duty to deliver the goods; and

 (b) the risk of loss does not pass to the buyer until the goods leave the ship's tackle or are otherwise properly unloaded.

§ 2–323. Form of Bill of Lading Required in Overseas Shipment; "Overseas".

(1) Where the contract contemplates overseas shipment and contains a term C.I.F. or C. & F. or F.O.B. vessel, the seller unless otherwise agreed must obtain a negotiable bill of lading stating that the goods have been loaded in board or, in the case of a term C.I.F. or C. & F., received for shipment.

(2) Where in a case within subsection (1) a bill of lading has been issued in a set of parts, unless otherwise agreed if the documents are not to be sent from abroad the buyer may demand tender of the full set; otherwise only one part of the bill of lading need be tendered. Even if the agreement expressly requires a full set

 (a) due tender of a single part is acceptable within the provisions of this Article on cure of improper delivery (subsection (1) of Section 2–508); and

 (b) even though the full set is demanded, if the documents are sent from abroad the person tendering an incomplete set may nevertheless require payment upon furnishing an indemnity which the buyer in good faith deems adequate.

(3) A shipment by water or by air or a contract contemplating such shipment is "overseas" insofar as by usage of trade or agreement it is subject to the commercial, financing or shipping practices characteristic of international deep water commerce.

§ 2–324. "No Arrival, No Sale" Term. Under a term "no arrival, no sale" or terms of like meaning, unless otherwise agreed,

 (a) the seller must properly ship conforming goods and if they arrive by any means he must tender them on arrival but he assumes no obligation that the goods will arrive unless he has caused the non-arrival; and

 (b) where without fault of the seller the goods are in part lost or have so deteriorated as no longer to conform to the contract or arrive after the contract time, the buyer may proceed as if there had been casualty to identified goods (Section 2–613).

§ 2–325. "Letter of Credit" Term; "Confirmed Credit".

(1) Failure of the buyer seasonably to furnish an agreed letter of credit is a breach of the contract for sale.

(2) The delivery to seller of a proper letter of credit suspends the buyer's obligation to pay. If the letter of credit is dishonored, the seller may on seasonable notification to the buyer require payment directly from him.

(3) Unless otherwise agreed the term "letter of credit" or "banker's credit" in a contract for sale means an irrevocable credit issued by a financing agency of good repute and, where the shipment is overseas, of good international repute. The term "confirmed credit" means that the credit must also carry the direct obligation of such an agency which does business in the seller's financial market.

§ 2–326. Sale on Approval and Sale or Return; Consignment Sales and Rights of Creditors.

(1) Unless otherwise agreed, if delivered goods may be returned by the buyer even though they conform to the contract, the transaction is

 (a) a "sale on approval" if the goods are delivered primarily for use, and

 (b) a "sale or return" if the goods are delivered primarily for resale.

(2) Except as provided in subsection (3), goods held on approval are not subject to the claims of the buyer's creditors until acceptance; goods held on sale or return are subject to such claims while in the buyer's possession.

(3) Where goods are delivered to a person for sale and such person maintains a place of business at which he deals in goods of the kind involved, under a name other than the name of the person making delivery, then with respect to claims of creditors of the person conducting the business the goods are deemed to be on sale or return. The provisions of this subsection are applicable even though an agreement purports to reserve title to the person making delivery until payment or resale or uses such words as "on consignment" or "on memorandum". However, this subsection is not applicable if the person making delivery

 (a) complies with an applicable law providing for a consignor's interest or the like to be evidenced by a sign, or

 (b) establishes that the person conducting the business is generally known by his creditors to be

substantially engaged in selling the goods of others, or

(c) complies with the filing provisions of the Article on Secured Transactions (Article 9).

(4) Any "or return" term of a contract for sale is to be treated as a separate contract for sale within the statute of frauds section of this Article (Section 2–201) and as contradicting the sale aspect of the contract within the provisions of this Article on parol or extrinsic evidence (Section 2–202).

§ 2–327. Special Incidents of Sale on Approval and Sale or Return.

(1) Under a sale on approval unless otherwise agreed
 (a) although the goods are identified to the contract the risk of loss and the title do not pass to the buyer until acceptance; and
 (b) use of the goods consistent with the purpose of trial is not acceptance but failure seasonably to notify the seller of election to return the goods is acceptance, and if the goods conform to the contract acceptance of any part is acceptance of the whole; and
 (c) after due notification of election to return, the return is at the seller's risk and expense but a merchant buyer must follow any reasonable instructions.

(2) Under a sale or return unless otherwise agreed
 (a) the option to return extends to the whole or any commercial unit of the goods while in substantially their original condition, but must be exercised seasonably; and
 (b) the return is at the buyer's risk and expense.

§ 2–328. Sale by Auction.

(1) In a sale by auction if goods are put up in lots each lot is the subject of a separate sale.

(2) A sale by auction is complete when the auctioneer so announces by the fall of the hammer or in other customary manner. Where a bid is made while the hammer is falling in acceptance of a prior bid the auctioneer may in his discretion reopen the bidding or declare the goods sold under the bid on which the hammer was falling.

(3) Such a sale is with reserve unless the goods are in explicit terms put up without reserve. In an auction with reserve the auctioneer may withdraw the goods at any time until he announces completion of the sale. In an auction without reserve, after the auctioneer calls for bids on an article or lot, that article or lot cannot be withdrawn unless no bid is made within a reasonable time. In either case a bidder may retract his bid until the auctioneer's announcement of completion of the sale, but a bidder's retraction does not revive any previous bid.

(4) If the auctioneer knowingly receives a bid on the seller's behalf or the seller makes or procures such a bid, and notice has not been given that liberty for such bidding is reserved, the buyer may at his option avoid the sale or take the goods at the price of the last good faith bid prior to the completion of the sale. This subsection shall not apply to any bid at a forced sale.

Part 4: Title, Creditors and Good Faith Purchasers

§ 2–401. Passing of Title; Reservation for Security; Limited Application of This Section.
Each provision of this Article with regard to the rights, obligations and remedies of the seller, the buyer, purchasers or other third parties applies irrespective of title to the goods except where the provision refers to such title. Insofar as situations are not covered by the other provisions of this Article and matters concerning title become material the following rules apply:

(1) Title to goods cannot pass under a contract for sale prior to their identification to the contract (Section 2–501), and unless otherwise explicitly agreed the buyer acquires by their identification a special property as limited by this Act. Any retention or reservation by the seller of the title (property) in goods shipped or delivered to the buyer is limited in effect to a reservation of a security interest. Subject to these provisions and to the provisions of the Article on Secured Transactions (Article 9), title to goods passes from the seller to the buyer in any manner and on any conditions explicitly agreed on by the parties.

(2) Unless otherwise explicitly agreed title passes to the buyer at the time and place at which the seller completes his performance with reference to the physical delivery of the goods, despite any reservation of a security interest and even though a document of title is to be delivered at a different time or place; and in particular and despite any reservation of a security interest by the bill of lading
 (a) if the contract requires or authorizes the seller to send the goods to the buyer but does not require him to deliver them at destination, title passes to the buyer at the time and place of shipment; but
 (b) if the contract requires delivery at destination, title passes on tender there.

(3) Unless otherwise explicitly agreed where delivery is to be made without moving the goods,
 (a) if the seller is to deliver a document of title, title passes at the time when and the place where he delivers such documents; or
 (b) if the goods are at the time of contracting already identified and no documents are to be delivered, title passes at the time and place of contracting.

(4) A rejection or other refusal by the buyer to receive or retain the goods, whether or not justified, or a justified

revocation of acceptance revests title to the goods in the seller. Such revesting occurs by operation of law and is not a "sale".

§ 2–402. Rights of Seller's Creditors Against Sold Goods.

(1) Except as provided in subsections (2) and (3), rights of unsecured creditors of the seller with respect to goods which have been identified to a contract for sale are subject to the buyer's rights to recover the goods under this Article (Sections 2–502 and 2–716).

(2) A creditor of the seller may treat a sale or an identification of goods to a contract for sale as void if as against him a retention of possession by the seller is fraudulent under any rule of law of the state where the goods are situated, except that retention of possession in good faith and current course of trade by a merchant-seller for a commercially reasonable time after a sale or identification is not fraudulent.

(3) Nothing in this Article shall be deemed to impair the rights of creditors of the seller
 (a) under the provisions of the Article on Secured Transactions (Article 9); or
 (b) where identification to the contract or delivery is made not in current course of trade but in satisfaction of or as security for a pre-existing claim for money, security or the like and is made under circumstances which under any rule of law of the state where the goods are situated would apart from this Article constitute the transaction a fraudulent transfer or voidable preference.

§ 2–403. Power to Transfer; Good Faith Purchase of Goods; "Entrusting".

(1) A purchaser of goods acquires all title which his transferor had or had power to transfer except that a purchaser of a limited interest acquires rights only to the extent of the interest purchased. A person with voidable title has power to transfer a good title to a good faith purchaser for value. When goods have been delivered under a transaction of purchase the purchaser has such power even though
 (a) the transferor was deceived as to the identity of the purchaser, or
 (b) the delivery was in exchange for a check which is later dishonored, or
 (c) it was agreed that the transaction was to be a "cash sale", or
 (d) the delivery was procured through fraud punishable as larcenous under the criminal law.

(2) Any entrusting of possession of goods to a merchant who deals in goods of that kind gives him power to transfer all rights of the entruster to a buyer in ordinary course of business.

(3) "Entrusting" includes any delivery and any acquiescence in retention of possession regardless of any condition expressed between the parties to the delivery or acquiescence and regardless of whether the procurement of the entrusting or the possessor's disposition of the goods have been such as to be larcenous under the criminal law. *[Publisher's Editorial Note: If a state adopts the repealer of Article 6—Bulk Transfers (Alternative A), subsec. (4) should read as follows:]*

(4) The rights of other purchasers of goods and of lien creditors are governed by the Articles on Secured Transactions (Article 9) and Documents of Title (Article 7). *[Publisher's Editorial Note: If a state adopts Revised Article 6—Bulk Sales (Alternative B), subsec. (4) should read as follows:]*

(5) The rights of other purchasers of goods and of lien creditors are governed by the Articles on Secured Transactions (Article 9), Bulk Sales (Article 6) and Documents of Title (Article 7).

As amended in 1988.

For material relating to the changes made in text in 1988, see section 3 of Alternative A (Repealer of Article 6—Bulk Transfers) and Conforming Amendment to Section 2–403 following end of Alternative B (Revised Article 6—Bulk Sales).

Part 5: Performance

§ 2–501. Insurable Interest in Goods; Manner of Identification of Goods.

(1) The buyer obtains a special property and an insurable interest in goods by identification of existing goods as goods to which the contract refers even though the goods so identified are non-conforming and he has an option to return or reject them. Such identification can be made at any time and in any manner explicitly agreed to by the parties. In the absence of explicit agreement identification occurs
 (a) when the contract is made if it is for the sale of goods already existing and identified;
 (b) if the contract is for the sale of future goods other than those described in paragraph (c), when goods are shipped, marked or otherwise designated by the seller as goods to which the contract refers;
 (c) when the crops are planted or otherwise become growing crops or the young are conceived if the contract is for the sale of unborn young to be born within twelve months after contracting or for the sale of crops to be harvested within twelve months or the next normal harvest season after contracting whichever is longer.

(2) The seller retains an insurable interest in goods so long as title to or any security interest in the goods remains in him and where the identification is by the seller alone he may until default or insolvency or notification to the buyer that the identification is final substitute other goods for those identified.

(3) Nothing in this section impairs any insurable interest recognized under any other statute or rule of law.

§ 2–502. Buyer's Right to Goods on Seller's Insolvency.

(1) Subject to subsection (2) and even though the goods have not been shipped a buyer who has paid a part or all of the price of goods in which he has a special property under the provisions of the immediately preceding section may on making and keeping good a tender of any unpaid portion of their price recover them from the seller if the seller becomes insolvent within ten days after receipt of the first installment on their price.

(2) If the identification creating his special property has been made by the buyer he acquires the right to recover the goods only if they conform to the contract for sale.

§ 2–503. Manner of Seller's Tender of Delivery.

(1) Tender of delivery requires that the seller put and hold conforming goods at the buyer's disposition and give the buyer any notification reasonably necessary to enable him to take delivery. The manner, time and place for tender are determined by the agreement and this Article, and in particular

 (a) tender must be at a reasonable hour, and if it is of goods they must be kept available for the period reasonably necessary to enable the buyer to take possession; but

 (b) unless otherwise agreed the buyer must furnish facilities reasonably suited to the receipt of the goods.

(2) Where the case is within the next section respecting shipment tender requires that the seller comply with its provisions.

(3) Where the seller is required to deliver at a particular destination tender requires that he comply with subsection (1) and also in any appropriate case tender documents as described in subsections (4) and (5) of this section.

(4) Where goods are in the possession of a bailee and are to be delivered without being moved

 (a) tender requires that the seller either tender a negotiable document of title covering such goods or procure acknowledgment by the bailee of the buyer's right to possession of the goods; but

 (b) tender to the buyer of a non-negotiable document of title or of a written direction to the bailee to deliver is sufficient tender unless the buyer seasonably objects, and receipt by the bailee of notification of the buyer's rights fixes those rights as against the bailee and all third persons; but risk of loss of the goods and of any failure by the bailee to honor the non-negotiable document of title or to obey the direction remains on the seller until the buyer has had a reasonable time to present the document or direction, and a refusal by the bailee to honor the document or to obey the direction defeats the tender.

(5) Where the contract requires the seller to deliver documents

 (a) he must tender all such documents in correct form, except as provided in this Article with respect to bills of lading in a set (subsection (2) of Section 2–323); and

 (b) tender through customary banking channels is sufficient and dishonor of a draft accompanying the documents constitutes non-acceptance or rejection.

§ 2–504. Shipment by Seller.

Where the seller is required or authorized to send the goods to the buyer and the contract does not require him to deliver them at a particular destination, then unless otherwise agreed he must

 (a) put the goods in the possession of such a carrier and make such a contract for their transportation as may be reasonable having regard to the nature of the goods and other circumstances of the case; and

 (b) obtain and promptly deliver or tender in due form any document necessary to enable the buyer to obtain possession of the goods or otherwise required by the agreement or by usage of trade; and

 (c) promptly notify the buyer of the shipment.

Failure to notify the buyer under paragraph (c) or to make a proper contract under paragraph (a) is a ground for rejection only if material delay or loss ensues.

§ 2–505. Seller's Shipment Under Reservation.

(1) Where the seller has identified goods to the contract by or before shipment:

 (a) his procurement of a negotiable bill of lading to his own order or otherwise reserves in him a security interest in the goods. His procurement of the bill to the order of a financing agency or of the buyer indicates in addition only the seller's expectation of transferring that interest to the person named.

 (b) a non-negotiable bill of lading to himself or his nominee reserves possession of the goods as security but except in a case of conditional delivery (subsection (2) of Section 2–507) a non-negotiable bill of lading naming the buyer as consignee reserves no security interest even though the seller retains possession of the bill of lading.

(2) When shipment by the seller with reservation of a security interest is in violation of the contract for sale it constitutes an improper contract for transportation

within the preceding section but impairs neither the rights given to the buyer by shipment and identification of the goods to the contract nor the seller's powers as a holder of a negotiable document.

§ 2–506. Rights of Financing Agency.

(1) A financing agency by paying or purchasing for value a draft which relates to a shipment of goods acquires to the extent of the payment or purchase and in addition to its own rights under the draft and any document of title securing it any rights of the shipper in the goods including the right to stop delivery and the shipper's right to have the draft honored by the buyer.

(2) The right to reimbursement of a financing agency which has in good faith honored or purchased the draft under commitment to or authority from the buyer is not impaired by subsequent discovery of defects with reference to any relevant document which was apparently regular on its face.

§ 2–507. Effect of Seller's Tender; Delivery on Condition.

(1) Tender of delivery is a condition to the buyer's duty to accept the goods and, unless otherwise agreed, to his duty to pay for them. Tender entitles the seller to acceptance of the goods and to payment according to the contract.

(2) Where payment is due and demanded on the delivery to the buyer of goods or documents of title, his right as against the seller to retain or dispose of them is conditional upon his making the payment due.

§ 2–508. Cure by Seller of Improper Tender or Delivery; Replacement.

(1) Where any tender or delivery by the seller is rejected because non-conforming and the time for performance has not yet expired, the seller may seasonably notify the buyer of his intention to cure and may then within the contract time make a conforming delivery.

(2) Where the buyer rejects a non-conforming tender which the seller had reasonable grounds to believe would be acceptable with or without money allowance the seller may if he seasonably notifies the buyer have a further reasonable time to substitute a conforming tender.

§ 2–509. Risk of Loss in the Absence of Breach.

(1) Where the contract requires or authorizes the seller to ship the goods by carrier
 (a) if it does not require him to deliver them at a particular destination, the risk of loss passes to the buyer when the goods are duly delivered to the carrier even though the shipment is under reservation (Section 2–505); but

 (b) if it does require him to deliver them at a particular destination and the goods are there duly tendered while in the possession of the carrier, the risk of loss passes to the buyer when the goods are there duly so tendered as to enable the buyer to take delivery.

(2) Where the goods are held by a bailee to be delivered without being moved, the risk of loss passes to the buyer
 (a) on his receipt of a negotiable document of title covering the goods; or
 (b) on acknowledgment by the bailee of the buyer's right to possession of the goods; or
 (c) after his receipt of a non-negotiable document of title or other written direction to deliver, as provided in subsection (4)(b) of Section 2–503.

(3) In any case not within subsection (1) or (2), the risk of loss passes to the buyer on his receipt of the goods if the seller is a merchant; otherwise the risk passes to the buyer on tender of delivery.

(4) The provisions of this section are subject to contrary agreement of the parties and to the provisions of this Article on sale on approval (Section 2–327) and on effect of breach on risk of loss (Section 2–510).

§ 2–510. Effect of Breach on Risk of Loss.

(1) Where a tender or delivery of goods so fails to conform to the contract as to give a right of rejection the risk of their loss remains on the seller until cure or acceptance.

(2) Where the buyer rightfully revokes acceptance he may to the extent of any deficiency in his effective insurance coverage treat the risk of loss as having rested on the seller from the beginning.

(3) Where the buyer as to conforming goods already identified to the contract for sale repudiates or is otherwise in breach before risk of their loss has passed to him, the seller may to the extent of any deficiency in his effective insurance coverage treat the risk of loss as resting on the buyer for a commercially reasonable time.

§ 2–511. Tender of Payment by Buyer; Payment by Check.

(1) Unless otherwise agreed tender of payment is a condition to the seller's duty to tender and complete any delivery.

(2) Tender of payment is sufficient when made by any means or in any manner current in the ordinary course of business unless the seller demands payment in legal tender and gives any extension of time reasonably necessary to procure it.

(3) Subject to the provisions of this Act on the effect of an instrument on an obligation (Section 3-310), payment by check is conditional and is defeated as

between the parties by dishonor of the check on due presentment.

As amended in 1994.

See Appendix XI for material relating to changes made in text in 1994.

§ 2–512. Payment by Buyer Before Inspection. 1995 *Amendments to text indicated by strikeout and underline*

(1) Where the contract requires payment before inspection non-conformity of the goods does not excuse the buyer from so making payment unless
 (a) the non-conformity appears without inspection; or
 (b) despite tender of the required documents the circumstances would justify injunction against honor under this Act (Section 5-109(b)).
(2) Payment pursuant to subsection (1) does not constitute an acceptance of goods or impair the buyer's right to inspect or any of his remedies.

As amended in 1995.

See Appendix XIV for material relating to changes made in text in 1995.

§ 2–513. Buyer's Right to Inspection of Goods.

(1) Unless otherwise agreed and subject to subsection (3), where goods are tendered or delivered or identified to the contract for sale, the buyer has a right before payment or acceptance to inspect them at any reasonable place and time and in any reasonable manner. When the seller is required or authorized to send the goods to the buyer, the inspection may be after their arrival.
(2) Expenses of inspection must be borne by the buyer but may be recovered from the seller if the goods do not conform and are rejected.
(3) Unless otherwise agreed and subject to the provisions of this Article on C.I.F. contracts (subsection (3) of Section 2–321), the buyer is not entitled to inspect the goods before payment of the price when the contract provides
 (a) for delivery "C.O.D." or on other like terms; or
 (b) for payment against documents of title, except where such payment is due only after the goods are to become available for inspection.
(4) A place or method of inspection fixed by the parties is presumed to be exclusive but unless otherwise expressly agreed it does not postpone identification or shift the place for delivery or for passing the risk of loss. If compliance becomes impossible, inspection shall be as provided in this section unless the place or method fixed was clearly intended as an indispensable condition failure of which avoids the contract.

§ 2–514. When Documents Deliverable on Acceptance; When on Payment. Unless otherwise agreed documents against which a draft is drawn are to be delivered to the drawee on acceptance of the draft if it is payable more than three days after presentment; otherwise, only on payment.

§ 2–515. Preserving Evidence of Goods in Dispute. In furtherance of the adjustment of any claim or dispute

 (a) either party on reasonable notification to the other and for the purpose of ascertaining the facts and preserving evidence has the right to inspect, test and sample the goods including such of them as may be in the possession or control of the other; and
 (b) the parties may agree to a third party inspection or survey to determine the conformity or condition of the goods and may agree that the findings shall be binding upon them in any subsequent litigation or adjustment.

Part 6: Breach, Repudiation and Excuse

§ 2–601. Buyer's Rights on Improper Delivery. Subject to the provisions of this Article on breach in installment contracts (Section 2–612) and unless otherwise agreed under the sections on contractual limitations of remedy (Sections 2–718 and 2–719), if the goods or the tender of delivery fail in any respect to conform to the contract, the buyer may

 (a) reject the whole; or
 (b) accept the whole; or
 (c) accept any commercial unit or units and reject the rest.

§ 2–602. Manner and Effect of Rightful Rejection.

(1) Rejection of goods must be within a reasonable time after their delivery or tender. It is ineffective unless the buyer seasonably notifies the seller.
(2) Subject to the provisions of the two following sections on rejected goods (Sections 2–603 and 2–604),
 (a) after rejection any exercise of ownership by the buyer with respect to any commercial unit is wrongful as against the seller; and
 (b) if the buyer has before rejection taken physical possession of goods in which he does not have a security interest under the provisions of this Article (subsection (3) of Section 2–711), he is under a duty after rejection to hold them with reasonable care at the seller's disposition for a time sufficient to permit the seller to remove them; but
 (c) the buyer has no further obligations with regard to goods rightfully rejected.
(3) The seller's rights with respect to goods wrongfully rejected are governed by the provisions of this Article on Seller's remedies in general (Section 2–703).

§ 2–603. Merchant Buyer's Duties as to Rightfully Rejected Goods.

(1) Subject to any security interest in the buyer (subsection (3) of Section 2–711), when the seller has no

agent or place of business at the market of rejection a merchant buyer is under a duty after rejection of goods in his possession or control to follow any reasonable instructions received from the seller with respect to the goods and in the absence of such instructions to make reasonable efforts to sell them for the seller's account if they are perishable or threaten to decline in value speedily. Instructions are not reasonable if on demand indemnity for expenses is not forthcoming.

(2) When the buyer sells goods under subsection (1), he is entitled to reimbursement from the seller or out of the proceeds for reasonable expenses of caring for and selling them, and if the expenses include no selling commission then to such commission as is usual in the trade or if there is none to a reasonable sum not exceeding ten per cent on the gross proceeds.

(3) In complying with this section the buyer is held only to good faith and good faith conduct hereunder is neither acceptance nor conversion nor the basis of an action for damages.

§ 2–604. Buyer's Options as to Salvage of Rightfully Rejected Goods.

Subject to the provisions of the immediately preceding section on perishables if the seller gives no instructions within a reasonable time after notification of rejection the buyer may store the rejected goods for the seller's account or reship them to him or resell them for the seller's account with reimbursement as provided in the preceding section. Such action is not acceptance or conversion.

§ 2–605. Waiver of Buyer's Objections by Failure to Particularize.

(1) The buyer's failure to state in connection with rejection a particular defect which is ascertainable by reasonable inspection precludes him from relying on the unstated defect to justify rejection or to establish breach

 (a) where the seller could have cured it if stated seasonably; or

 (b) between merchants when the seller has after rejection made a request in writing for a full and final written statement of all defects on which the buyer proposes to rely.

(2) Payment against documents made without reservation of rights precludes recovery of the payment for defects apparent on the face of the documents.

§ 2–606. What Constitutes Acceptance of Goods.

(1) Acceptance of goods occurs when the buyer

 (a) after a reasonable opportunity to inspect the goods signifies to the seller that the goods are conforming or that he will take or retain them in spite of their non-conformity; or

 (b) fails to make an effective rejection (subsection (1) of Section 2–602), but such acceptance does not occur until the buyer has had a reasonable opportunity to inspect them; or

 (c) does any act inconsistent with the seller's ownership; but if such act is wrongful as against the seller it is an acceptance only if ratified by him.

(2) Acceptance of a part of any commercial unit is acceptance of that entire unit.

§ 2–607. Effect of Acceptance; Notice of Breach; Burden of Establishing Breach After Acceptance; Notice of Claim or Litigation to Person Answerable Over.

(1) The buyer must pay at the contract rate for any goods accepted.

(2) Acceptance of goods by the buyer precludes rejection of the goods accepted and if made with knowledge of a non-conformity cannot be revoked because of it unless the acceptance was on the reasonable assumption that the non-conformity would be seasonably cured but acceptance does not of itself impair any other remedy provided by this Article for non-conformity.

(3) Where a tender has been accepted

 (a) the buyer must within a reasonable time after he discovers or should have discovered any breach notify the seller of breach or be barred from any remedy; and

 (b) if the claim is one for infringement or the like (subsection (3) of Section 2–312) and the buyer is sued as a result of such a breach he must so notify the seller within a reasonable time after he receives notice of the litigation or be barred from any remedy over for liability established by the litigation.

(4) The burden is on the buyer to establish any breach with respect to the goods accepted.

(5) Where the buyer is sued for breach of a warranty or other obligation for which his seller is answerable over

 (a) he may give his seller written notice of the litigation. If the notice states that the seller may come in and defend and that if the seller does not do so he will be bound in any action against him by his buyer by any determination of fact common to the two litigations, then unless the seller after seasonable receipt of the notice does come in and defend he is so bound.

 (b) if the claim is one for infringement or the like (subsection (3) of Section 2–312) the original seller may demand in writing that his buyer turn over to him control of the litigation including settlement or else be barred from any remedy over and if he also agrees to bear all expense and to satisfy any adverse judgment, then unless the buyer after seasonable receipt of the demand does turn over control the buyer is so barred.

(6) The provisions of subsections (3), (4) and (5) apply to any obligation of a buyer to hold the seller harmless against infringement or the like (subsection (3) of Section 2–312).

§ 2–608. Revocation of Acceptance in Whole or in Part.

(1) The buyer may revoke his acceptance of a lot or commercial unit whose non-conformity substantially impairs its value to him if he has accepted it

 (a) on the reasonable assumption that its non-conformity would be cured and it has not been seasonably cured; or

 (b) without discovery of such non-conformity if his acceptance was reasonably induced either by the difficulty of discovery before acceptance or by the seller's assurances.

(2) Revocation of acceptance must occur within a reasonable time after the buyer discovers or should have discovered the ground for it and before any substantial change in condition of the goods which is not caused by their own defects. It is not effective until the buyer notifies the seller of it.

(3) A buyer who so revokes has the same rights and duties with regard to the goods involved as if he had rejected them.

§ 2–609. Right to Adequate Assurance of Performance.

(1) A contract for sale imposes an obligation on each party that the other's expectation of receiving due performance will not be impaired. When reasonable grounds for insecurity arise with respect to the performance of either party the other may in writing demand adequate assurance of due performance and until he receives such assurance may if commercially reasonable suspend any performance for which he has not already received the agreed return.

(2) Between merchants the reasonableness of grounds for insecurity and the adequacy of any assurance offered shall be determined according to commercial standards.

(3) Acceptance of any improper delivery or payment does not prejudice the aggrieved party's right to demand adequate assurance of future performance.

(4) After receipt of a justified demand failure to provide within a reasonable time not exceeding thirty days such assurance of due performance as is adequate under the circumstances of the particular case is a repudiation of the contract.

§ 2–610. Anticipatory Repudiation. When either party repudiates the contract with respect to a performance not yet due the loss of which will substantially impair the value of the contract to the other, the aggrieved party may

 (a) for a commercially reasonable time await performance by the repudiating party; or

 (b) resort to any remedy for breach (Section 2–703 or Section 2–711), even though he has notified the repudiating party that he would await the latter's performance and has urged retraction; and

 (c) in either case suspend his own performance or proceed in accordance with the provisions of this Article on the seller's right to identify goods to the contract notwithstanding breach or to salvage unfinished goods (Section 2–704).

§ 2–611. Retraction of Anticipatory Repudiation.

(1) Until the repudiating party's next performance is due he can retract his repudiation unless the aggrieved party has since the repudiation cancelled or materially changed his position or otherwise indicated that he considers the repudiation final.

(2) Retraction may be by any method which clearly indicates to the aggrieved party that the repudiating party intends to perform, but must include any assurance justifiably demanded under the provisions of this Article (Section 2–609).

(3) Retraction reinstates the repudiating party's rights under the contract with due excuse and allowance to the aggrieved party for any delay occasioned by the repudiation.

§ 2–612. "Installment Contract"; Breach.

(1) An "installment contract" is one which requires or authorizes the delivery of goods in separate lots to be separately accepted, even though the contract contains a clause "each delivery is a separate contract" or its equivalent.

(2) The buyer may reject any installment which is non-conforming if the non-conformity substantially impairs the value of that installment and cannot be cured or if the non-conformity is a defect in the required documents; but if the non-conformity does not fall within subsection (3) and the seller gives adequate assurance of its cure the buyer must accept that installment.

(3) Whenever non-conformity or default with respect to one or more installments substantially impairs the value of the whole contract there is a breach of the whole. But the aggrieved party reinstates the contract if he accepts a non-conforming installment without seasonably notifying of cancellation or if he brings an action with respect only to past installments or demands performance as to future installments.

§ 2–613. Casualty to Identified Goods. Where the contract requires for its performance goods identified when the contract is made, and the goods suffer casualty without fault of either party before the risk of loss passes to the buyer, or in a proper case under a "no arrival, no sale" term (Section 2–324) then

(a) if the loss is total the contract is avoided; and

(b) if the loss is partial or the goods have so deteriorated as no longer to conform to the contract the buyer may nevertheless demand inspection and at his option either treat the contract as avoided or accept the goods with due allowance from the contract price for the deterioration or the deficiency in quantity but without further right against the seller.

§ 2–614. Substituted Performance.

(1) Where without fault of either party the agreed berthing, loading, or unloading facilities fail or an agreed type of carrier becomes unavailable or the agreed manner of delivery otherwise becomes commercially impracticable but a commercially reasonable substitute is available, such substitute performance must be tendered and accepted.

(2) If the agreed means or manner of payment fails because of domestic or foreign governmental regulation, the seller may withhold or stop delivery unless the buyer provides a means or manner of payment which is commercially a substantial equivalent. If delivery has already been taken, payment by the means or in the manner provided by the regulation discharges the buyer's obligation unless the regulation is discriminatory, oppressive or predatory.

§ 2–615. Excuse by Failure of Presupposed Conditions.
Except so far as a seller may have assumed a greater obligation and subject to the preceding section on substituted performance:

(a) Delay in delivery or non-delivery in whole or in part by a seller who complies with paragraphs (b) and (c) is not a breach of his duty under a contract for sale if performance as agreed has been made impracticable by the occurrence of a contingency the non-occurrence of which was a basic assumption on which the contract was made or by compliance in good faith with any applicable foreign or domestic governmental regulation or order whether or not it later proves to be invalid.

(b) Where the causes mentioned in paragraph (a) affect only a part of the seller's capacity to perform, he must allocate production and deliveries among his customers but may at his option include regular customers not then under contract as well as his own requirements for further manufacture. He may so allocate in any manner which is fair and reasonable.

(c) The seller must notify the buyer seasonably that there will be delay or non-delivery and, when allocation is required under paragraph (b), of the estimated quota thus made available for the buyer.

§ 2–616. Procedure on Notice Claiming Excuse.

(1) Where the buyer receives notification of a material or indefinite delay or an allocation justified under the preceding section he may by written notification to the seller as to any delivery concerned, and where the prospective deficiency substantially impairs the value of the whole contract under the provisions of this Article relating to breach of installment contracts (Section 2–612), then also as to the whole,

(a) terminate and thereby discharge any unexecuted portion of the contract; or

(b) modify the contract by agreeing to take his available quota in substitution.

(2) If after receipt of such notification from the seller the buyer fails so to modify the contract within a reasonable time not exceeding thirty days the contract lapses with respect to any deliveries affected.

(3) The provisions of this section may not be negated by agreement except in so far as the seller has assumed a greater obligation under the preceding section.

Part 7: Remedies

§ 2–701. Remedies for Breach of Collateral Contracts Not Impaired.
Remedies for breach of any obligation or promise collateral or ancillary to a contract for sale are not impaired by the provisions of this Article.

§ 2–702. Seller's Remedies on Discovery of Buyer's Insolvency.

(1) Where the seller discovers the buyer to be insolvent he may refuse delivery except for cash including payment for all goods theretofore delivered under the contract, and stop delivery under this Article (Section 2–705).

(2) Where the seller discovers that the buyer has received goods on credit while insolvent he may reclaim the goods upon demand made within ten days after the receipt, but if misrepresentation of solvency has been made to the particular seller in writing within three months before delivery the ten day limitation does not apply. Except as provided in this subsection the seller may not base a right to reclaim goods on the buyer's fraudulent or innocent misrepresentation of solvency or of intent to pay.

(3) The seller's right to reclaim under subsection (2) is subject to the rights of a buyer in ordinary course or other good faith purchaser under this Article (Section 2–403). Successful reclamation of goods excludes all other remedies with respect to them.

As amended in 1966.

§ 2–703. Seller's Remedies in General.
Where the buyer wrongfully rejects or revokes acceptance of goods or fails to make a payment due on or before delivery or repudiates

with respect to a part or the whole, then with respect to any goods directly affected and, if the breach is of the whole contract (Section 2–612), then also with respect to the whole undelivered balance, the aggrieved seller may

 (a) withhold delivery of such goods;

 (b) stop delivery by any bailee as hereafter provided (Section 2–705);

 (c) proceed under the next section respecting goods still unidentified to the contract;

 (d) resell and recover damages as hereafter provided (Section 2–706);

 (e) recover damages for non-acceptance (Section 2–708) or in a proper case the price (Section 2–709);

 (f) cancel.

§ 2–704. Seller's Right to Identify Goods to the Contract Notwithstanding Breach or to Salvage Unfinished Goods.

(1) An aggrieved seller under the preceding section may

 (a) identify to the contract conforming goods not already identified if at the time he learned of the breach they are in his possession or control;

 (b) treat as the subject of resale goods which have demonstrably been intended for the particular contract even though those goods are unfinished.

(2) Where the goods are unfinished an aggrieved seller may in the exercise of reasonable commercial judgment for the purposes of avoiding loss and of effective realization either complete the manufacture and wholly identify the goods to the contract or cease manufacture and resell for scrap or salvage value or proceed in any other reasonable manner.

§ 2–705. Seller's Stoppage of Delivery in Transit or Otherwise.

(1) The seller may stop delivery of goods in the possession of a carrier or other bailee when he discovers the buyer to be insolvent (Section 2–702) and may stop delivery of carload, truckload, planeload or larger shipments of express or freight when the buyer repudiates or fails to make a payment due before delivery or if for any other reason the seller has a right to withhold or reclaim the goods.

(2) As against such buyer the seller may stop delivery until

 (a) receipt of the goods by the buyer; or

 (b) acknowledgment to the buyer by any bailee of the goods except a carrier that the bailee holds the goods for the buyer; or

 (c) such acknowledgment to the buyer by a carrier by reshipment or as warehouseman; or

 (d) negotiation to the buyer of any negotiable document of title covering the goods.

(3) (a) To stop delivery the seller must so notify as to enable the bailee by reasonable diligence to prevent delivery of the goods.

 (b) After such notification the bailee must hold and deliver the goods according to the directions of the seller but the seller is liable to the bailee for any ensuing charges or damages.

 (c) If a negotiable document of title has been issued for goods the bailee is not obliged to obey a notification to stop until surrender of the document.

 (d) A carrier who has issued a non-negotiable bill of lading is not obliged to obey a notification to stop received from a person other than the consignor.

§ 2–706. Seller's Resale Including Contract for Resale.

(1) Under the conditions stated in Section 2–703 on seller's remedies, the seller may resell the goods concerned or the undelivered balance thereof. Where the resale is made in good faith and in a commercially reasonable manner the seller may recover the difference between the resale price and the contract price together with any incidental damages allowed under the provisions of this Article (Section 2–710), but less expenses saved in consequence of the buyer's breach.

(2) Except as otherwise provided in subsection (3) or unless otherwise agreed resale may be at public or private sale including sale by way of one or more contracts to sell or of identification to an existing contract of the seller. Sale may be as a unit or in parcels and at any time and place and on any terms but every aspect of the sale including the method, manner, time, place and terms must be commercially reasonable. The resale must be reasonably identified as referring to the broken contract, but it is not necessary that the goods be in existence or that any or all of them have been identified to the contract before the breach.

(3) Where the resale is at private sale the seller must give the buyer reasonable notification of his intention to resell.

(4) Where the resale is at public sale

 (a) only identified goods can be sold except where there is a recognized market for a public sale of futures in goods of the kind; and

 (b) it must be made at a usual place or market for public sale if one is reasonably available and except in the case of goods which are perishable or threaten to decline in value speedily the seller must give the buyer reasonable notice of the time and place of the resale; and

 (c) if the goods are not to be within the view of those attending the sale the notification of sale must state the place where the goods are located and provide for their reasonable inspection by prospective bidders; and

 (d) the seller may buy.

(5) A purchaser who buys in good faith at a resale takes the goods free of any rights of the original buyer even though the seller fails to comply with one or more of the requirements of this section.

(6) The seller is not accountable to the buyer for any profit made on any resale. A person in the position of a seller (Section 2–707) or a buyer who has rightfully rejected or justifiably revoked acceptance must account for any excess over the amount of his security interest, as herein after defined (subsection (3) of Section 2–711).

§ 2–707. "Person in the Position of a Seller".

(1) A "person in the position of a seller" includes as against a principal an agent who has paid or become responsible for the price of goods on behalf of his principal or anyone who otherwise holds a security interest or other right in goods similar to that of a seller.

(2) A person in the position of a seller may as provided in this Article withhold or stop delivery (Section 2–705) and resell (Section 2–706) and recover incidental damages (Section 2–710).

§ 2–708. Seller's Damages for Non-acceptance or Repudiation.

(1) Subject to subsection (2) and to the provisions of this Article with respect to proof of market price (Section 2–723), the measure of damages for non-acceptance or repudiation by the buyer is the difference between the market price at the time and place for tender and the unpaid contract price together with any incidental damages provided in this Article (Section 2–710), but less expenses saved in consequence of the buyer's breach.

(2) If the measure of damages provided in subsection (1) is inadequate to put the seller in as good a position as performance would have done then the measure of damages is the profit (including reasonable overhead) which the seller would have made from full performance by the buyer, together with any incidental damages provided in this Article (Section 2–710), due allowance for costs reasonably incurred and due credit for payments or proceeds of resale.

§ 2–709. Action for the Price.

(1) When the buyer fails to pay the price as it becomes due the seller may recover, together with any incidental damages under the next section, the price

 (a) of goods accepted or of conforming goods lost or damaged within a commercially reasonable time after risk of their loss has passed to the buyer; and

 (b) of goods identified to the contract if the seller is unable after reasonable effort to resell them at a reasonable price or the circumstances reasonably indicate that such effort will be unavailing.

(2) Where the seller sues for the price he must hold for the buyer any goods which have been identified to the contract and are still in his control except that if resale becomes possible he may resell them at any time prior to the collection of the judgment. The net proceeds of any such resale must be credited to the buyer and payment of the judgment entitles him to any goods not resold.

(3) After the buyer has wrongfully rejected or revoked acceptance of the goods or has failed to make a payment due or has repudiated (Section 2–610), a seller who is held not entitled to the price under this section shall nevertheless be awarded damages for non-acceptance under the preceding section.

§ 2–710. Seller's Incidental Damages.
Incidental damages to an aggrieved seller include any commercially reasonable charges, expenses or commissions incurred in stopping delivery, in the transportation, care and custody of goods after the buyer's breach, in connection with return or resale of the goods or otherwise resulting from the breach.

§ 2–711. Buyer's Remedies in General; Buyer's Security Interest in Rejected Goods.

(1) Where the seller fails to make delivery or repudiates or the buyer rightfully rejects or justifiably revokes acceptance then with respect to any goods involved, and with respect to the whole if the breach goes to the whole contract (Section 2–612), the buyer may cancel and whether or not he has done so may in addition to recovering so much of the price as has been paid

 (a) "cover" and have damages under the next section as to all the goods affected whether or not they have been identified to the contract; or

 (b) recover damages for non-delivery as provided in this Article (Section 2–713).

(2) Where the seller fails to deliver or repudiates the buyer may also

 (a) if the goods have been identified recover them as provided in this Article (Section 2–502); or

 (b) in a proper case obtain specific performance or replevy the goods as provided in this Article (Section 2–716).

(3) On rightful rejection or justifiable revocation of acceptance a buyer has a security interest in goods in his possession or control for any payments made on their price and any expenses reasonably incurred in their inspection, receipt, transportation, care and custody and may hold such goods and resell them in like manner as an aggrieved seller (Section 2–706).

§ 2–712. "Cover"; Buyer's Procurement of Substitute Goods.

(1) After a breach within the preceding section the buyer may "cover" by making in good faith and without unreasonable delay any reasonable purchase of or contract to purchase goods in substitution for those due from the seller.

(2) The buyer may recover from the seller as damages the difference between the cost of cover and the contract price together with any incidental or consequential damages as hereinafter defined (Section 2–715), but less expenses saved in consequence of the seller's breach.

(3) Failure of the buyer to effect cover within this section does not bar him from any other remedy.

§ 2–713. Buyer's Damages for Non-delivery or Repudiation.

(1) Subject to the provisions of this Article with respect to proof of market price (Section 2–723), the measure of damages for non-delivery or repudiation by the seller is the difference between the market price at the time when the buyer learned of the breach and the contract price together with any incidental and consequential damages provided in this Article (Section 2–715), but less expenses saved in consequence of the seller's breach.

(2) Market price is to be determined as of the place for tender or, in cases of rejection after arrival or revocation of acceptance, as of the place of arrival.

§ 2–714. Buyer's Damages for Breach in Regard to Accepted Goods.

(1) Where the buyer has accepted goods and given notification (subsection (3) of Section 2–607) he may recover as damages for any non-conformity of tender the loss resulting in the ordinary course of events from the seller's breach as determined in any manner which is reasonable.

(2) The measure of damages for breach of warranty is the difference at the time and place of acceptance between the value of the goods accepted and the value they would have had if they had been as warranted, unless special circumstances show proximate damages of a different amount.

(3) In a proper case any incidental and consequential damages under the next section may also be recovered.

§ 2–715. Buyer's Incidental and Consequential Damages.

(1) Incidental damages resulting from the seller's breach include expenses reasonably incurred in inspection, receipt, transportation and care and custody of goods rightfully rejected, any commercially reasonable charges, expenses or commissions in connection with effecting cover and any other reasonable expense incident to the delay or other breach.

(2) Consequential damages resulting from the seller's breach include
 (a) any loss resulting from general or particular requirements and needs of which the seller at the time of contracting had reason to know and which could not reasonably be prevented by cover or otherwise; and
 (b) injury to person or property proximately resulting from any breach of warranty.

§ 2–716. Buyer's Right to Specific Performance or Replevin.

(1) Specific performance may be decreed where the goods are unique or in other proper circumstances.

(2) The decree for specific performance may include such terms and conditions as to payment of the price, damages, or other relief as the court may deem just.

(3) The buyer has a right of replevin for goods identified to the contract if after reasonable effort he is unable to effect cover for such goods or the circumstances reasonably indicate that such effort will be unavailing or if the goods have been shipped under reservation and satisfaction of the security interest in them has been made or tendered.

§ 2–717. Deduction of Damages from the Price.
The buyer on notifying the seller of his intention to do so may deduct all or any part of the damages resulting from any breach of the contract from any part of the price still due under the same contract.

§ 2–718. Liquidation or Limitation of Damages; Deposits.

(1) Damages for breach by either party may be liquidated in the agreement but only at an amount which is reasonable in the light of the anticipated or actual harm caused by the breach, the difficulties of proof of loss, and the inconvenience or nonfeasibility of otherwise obtaining an adequate remedy. A term fixing unreasonably large liquidated damages is void as a penalty.

(2) Where the seller justifiably withholds delivery of goods because of the buyer's breach, the buyer is entitled to restitution of any amount by which the sum of his payments exceeds
 (a) the amount to which the seller is entitled by virtue of terms liquidating the seller's damages in accordance with subsection (1), or
 (b) in the absence of such terms, twenty per cent of the value of the total performance for which the buyer is obligated under the contract or $500, whichever is smaller.

(3) The buyer's right to restitution under subsection (2) is subject to offset to the extent that the seller establishes

(a) a right to recover damages under the provisions of this Article other than subsection (1), and

(b) the amount or value of any benefits received by the buyer directly or indirectly by reason of the contract.

(4) Where a seller has received payment in goods their reasonable value or the proceeds of their resale shall be treated as payments for the purposes of subsection (2); but if the seller has notice of the buyer's breach before reselling goods received in part performance, his resale is subject to the conditions laid down in this Article on resale by an aggrieved seller (Section 2–706).

§ 2–719. Contractual Modification or Limitation of Remedy.

(1) Subject to the provisions of subsections (2) and (3) of this section and of the preceding section on liquidation and limitation of damages,

(a) the agreement may provide for remedies in addition to or in substitution for those provided in this Article and may limit or alter the measure of damages recoverable under this Article, as by limiting the buyer's remedies to return of the goods and repayment of the price or to repair and replacement of non-conforming goods or parts; and

(b) resort to a remedy as provided is optional unless the remedy is expressly agreed to be exclusive, in which case it is the sole remedy.

(2) Where circumstances cause an exclusive or limited remedy to fail of its essential purpose, remedy may be had as provided in this Act.

(3) Consequential damages may be limited or excluded unless the limitation or exclusion is unconscionable. Limitation of consequential damages for injury to the person in the case of consumer goods is prima facie unconscionable but limitation of damages where the loss is commercial is not.

§ 2–720. Effect of "Cancellation" or "Rescission" on Claims for Antecedent Breach.
Unless the contrary intention clearly appears, expressions of "cancellation" or "rescission" of the contract or the like shall not be construed as a renunciation or discharge of any claim in damages for an antecedent breach.

§ 2–721. Remedies for Fraud.
Remedies for material misrepresentation or fraud include all remedies available under this Article for non-fraudulent breach. Neither rescission or a claim for rescission of the contract for sale nor rejection or return of the goods shall bar or be deemed inconsistent with a claim for damages or other remedy.

§ 2–722. Who Can Sue Third Parties for Injury to Goods.
Where a third party so deals with goods which have been identified to a contract for sale as to cause actionable injury to a party to that contract

(a) a right of action against the third party is in either party to the contract for sale who has title to or a security interest or a special property or an insurable interest in the goods; and if the goods have been destroyed or converted a right of action is also in the party who either bore the risk of loss under the contract for sale or has since the injury assumed that risk as against the other;

(b) if at the time of the injury the party plaintiff did not bear the risk of loss as against the other party to the contract for sale and there is no arrangement between them for disposition of the recovery, his suit or settlement is, subject to his own interest, as a fiduciary for the other party to the contract;

(c) either party may with the consent of the other sue for the benefit of whom it may concern.

§ 2–723. Proof of Market Price: Time and Place.

(1) If an action based on anticipatory repudiation comes to trial before the time for performance with respect to some or all of the goods, any damages based on market price (Section 2–708 or Section 2–713) shall be determined according to the price of such goods prevailing at the time when the aggrieved party learned of the repudiation.

(2) If evidence of a price prevailing at the times or places described in this Article is not readily available the price prevailing within any reasonable time before or after the time described or at any other place which in commercial judgment or under usage of trade would serve as a reasonable substitute for the one described may be used, making any proper allowance for the cost of transporting the goods to or from such other place.

(3) Evidence of a relevant price prevailing at a time or place other than the one described in this Article offered by one party is not admissible unless and until he has given the other party such notice as the court finds sufficient to prevent unfair surprise.

§ 2–724. Admissibility of Market Quotations.
Whenever the prevailing price or value of any goods regularly bought and sold in any established commodity market is in issue, reports in official publications or trade journals or in newspapers or periodicals of general circulation published as the reports of such market shall be admissible in evidence. The circumstances of the preparation of such a report may be shown to affect its weight but not its admissibility.

§ 2–725. Statute of Limitations in Contracts for Sale.

(1) An action for breach of any contract for sale must be commenced within four years after the cause of action

has accrued. By the original agreement the parties may reduce the period of limitation to not less than one year but may not extend it.

(2) A cause of action accrues when the breach occurs, regardless of the aggrieved party's lack of knowledge of the breach. A breach of warranty occurs when tender of delivery is made, except that where a warranty explicitly extends to future performance of the goods and discovery of the breach must await the time of such performance the cause of action accrues when the breach is or should have been discovered.

(3) Where an action commenced within the time limited by subsection (1) is so terminated as to leave available a remedy by another action for the same breach such other action may be commenced after the expiration of the time limited and within six months after the termination of the first action unless the termination resulted from voluntary discontinuance or from dismissal for failure or neglect to prosecute.

(4) This section does not alter the law on tolling of the statute of limitations nor does it apply to causes of action which have accrued before this Act becomes effective.

Article 2A—Leases

Part 1: General Provisions

§ 2A–101. Short Title. This Article shall be known and may be cited as the Uniform Commercial Code—Leases.

> *See Appendix VI [following Amendment 24 therein] for material relating to changes in the Official Comment to conform to the 1990 amendments to various sections of Article 2A.*

§ 2A–102. Scope. This Article applies to any transaction, regardless of form, that creates a lease.

§ 2A–103. Definitions and Index of Definitions.

(1) In this Article unless the context otherwise requires:

(a) "Buyer in ordinary course of business" means a person who in good faith and without knowledge that the sale to him [or her] is in violation of the ownership rights or security interest or leasehold interest of a third party in the goods buys in ordinary course from a person in the business of selling goods of that kind but does not include a pawnbroker. "Buying" may be for cash or by exchange of other property or on secured or unsecured credit and includes receiving goods or documents of title under a preexisting contract for sale but does not include a transfer in bulk or as security for or in total or partial satisfaction of a money debt.

(b) "Cancellation" occurs when either party puts an end to the lease contract for default by the other party.

(c) "Commercial unit" means such a unit of goods as by commercial usage is a single whole for purposes of lease and division of which materially impairs its character or value on the market or in use. A commercial unit may be a single article, as a machine, or a set of articles, as a suite of furniture or a line of machinery, or a quantity, as a gross or carload, or any other unit treated in use or in the relevant market as a single whole.

(d) "Conforming" goods or performance under a lease contract means goods or performance that are in accordance with the obligations under the lease contract.

(e) "Consumer lease" means a lease that a lessor regularly engaged in the business of leasing or selling makes to a lessee who is an individual and who takes under the lease primarily for a personal, family, or household purpose [if the total payments to be made under the lease contract, excluding payments for options to renew or buy, do not exceed $_____].

(f) "Fault" means wrongful act, omission, breach, or default.

(g) "Finance lease" means a lease with respect to which:

(i) the lessor does not select, manufacture, or supply the goods;

(ii) the lessor acquires the goods or the right to possession and use of the goods in connection with the lease; and

(iii) one of the following occurs:

(A) the lessee receives a copy of the contract by which the lessor acquired the goods or the right to possession and use of the goods before signing the lease contract;

(B) the lessee's approval of the contract by which the lessor acquired the goods or the right to possession and use of the goods is a condition to effectiveness of the lease contract;

(C) the lessee, before signing the lease contract, receives an accurate and complete statement designating the promises and warranties, and any disclaimers of warranties, limitations or modifications of remedies, or liquidated damages, including those of a third party, such as the manufacturer of the goods, provided to the lessor by the person supplying the goods in connection with or as part of the contract by which the lessor acquired the goods or the right to possession and use of the goods; or

(D) if the lease is not a consumer lease, the lessor, before the lessee signs the

lease contract, informs the lessee in writing (a) of the identity of the person supplying the goods to the lessor, unless the lessee has selected that person and directed the lessor to acquire the goods or the right to possession and use of the goods from that person, (b) that the lessee is entitled under this Article to the promises and warranties, including those of any third party, provided to the lessor by the person supplying the goods in connection with or as part of the contract by which the lessor acquired the goods or the right to possession and use of the goods, and (c) that the lessee may communicate with the person supplying the goods to the lessor and receive an accurate and complete statement of those promises and warranties, including any disclaimers and limitations of them or of remedies.

(h) "Goods" means all things that are movable at the time of identification to the lease contract, or are fixtures (Section 2A–309), but the term does not include money, documents, instruments, accounts, chattel paper, general intangibles, or minerals or the like, including oil and gas, before extraction. The term also includes the unborn young of animals.

(i) "Installment lease contract" means a lease contract that authorizes or requires the delivery of goods in separate lots to be separately accepted, even though the lease contract contains a clause "each delivery is a separate lease" or its equivalent.

(j) "Lease" means a transfer of the right to possession and use of goods for a term in return for consideration, but a sale, including a sale on approval or a sale or return, or retention or creation of a security interest is not a lease. Unless the context clearly indicates otherwise, the term includes a sublease.

(k) "Lease agreement" means the bargain, with respect to the lease, of the lessor and the lessee in fact as found in their language or by implication from other circumstances including course of dealing or usage of trade or course of performance as provided in this Article. Unless the context clearly indicates otherwise, the term includes a sublease agreement.

(l) "Lease contract" means the total legal obligation that results from the lease agreement as affected by this Article and any other applicable rules of law. Unless the context clearly indicates otherwise, the term includes a sublease contract.

(m) "Leasehold interest" means the interest of the lessor or the lessee under a lease contract.

(n) "Lessee" means a person who acquires the right to possession and use of goods under a lease. Unless the context clearly indicates otherwise, the term includes a sublessee.

(o) "Lessee in ordinary course of business" means a person who in good faith and without knowledge that the lease to him [or her] is in violation of the ownership rights or security interest or leasehold interest of a third party in the goods, leases in ordinary course from a person in the business of selling or leasing goods of that kind but does not include a pawnbroker. "Leasing" may be for cash or by exchange of other property or on secured or unsecured credit and includes receiving goods or documents of title under a preexisting lease contract but does not include a transfer in bulk or as security for or in total or partial satisfaction of a money debt.

(p) "Lessor" means a person who transfers the right to possession and use of goods under a lease. Unless the context clearly indicates otherwise, the term includes a sublessor.

(q) "Lessor's residual interest" means the lessor's interest in the goods after expiration, termination, or cancellation of the lease contract.

(r) "Lien" means a charge against or interest in goods to secure payment of a debt or performance of an obligation, but the term does not include a security interest.

(s) "Lot" means a parcel or a single article that is the subject matter of a separate lease or delivery, whether or not it is sufficient to perform the lease contract.

(t) "Merchant lessee" means a lessee that is a merchant with respect to goods of the kind subject to the lease.

(u) "Present value" means the amount as of a date certain of one or more sums payable in the future, discounted to the date certain. The discount is determined by the interest rate specified by the parties if the rate was not manifestly unreasonable at the time the transaction was entered into; otherwise, the discount is determined by a commercially reasonable rate that takes into account the facts and circumstances of each case at the time the transaction was entered into.

(v) "Purchase" includes taking by sale, lease, mortgage, security interest, pledge, gift, or any other voluntary transaction creating an interest in goods.

(w) "Sublease" means a lease of goods the right to possession and use of which was acquired by the lessor as a lessee under an existing lease.

(x) "Supplier" means a person from whom a lessor buys or leases goods to be leased under a finance lease.

(y) "Supply contract" means a contract under which a lessor buys or leases goods to be leased.

(z) "Termination" occurs when either party pursuant to a power created by agreement or law puts an end to the lease contract otherwise than for default.

(2) Other definitions applying to this Article and the sections in which they appear are:

"Accessions"	Section 2A–310(1).
"Construction mortgage"	Section 2A–309(1) (d).
"Encumbrance"	Section 2A–309(1) (e).
"Fixtures"	Section 2A–309(1) (a).
"Fixture filing"	Section 2A–309(1) (b).
"Purchase money lease"	Section 2A–309(1) (c).

(3) The following definitions in other Articles apply to this Article:

"Account"	Section 9–106.
"Between merchants"	Section 2–104(3).
"Buyer"	Section 2–103(1) (a).
"Chattel paper"	Section 9–105(1) (b).
"Consumer goods"	Section 9–109(1).
"Document"	Section 9–105(1) (f).
"Entrusting"	Section 2–403(3).
"General intangibles"	Section 9–106.
"Good faith"	Section 2–103(1) (b).
"Instrument"	Section 9–105(1) (i).
"Merchant"	Section 2–104(1).
"Mortgage"	Section 9–105(1) (j).
"Pursuant to commitment"	Section 9–105(1) (k).
"Receipt"	Section 2–103(1) (c).
"Sale"	Section 2–106(1).
"Sale on approval"	Section 2–326.
"Sale or return"	Section 2–326.
"Seller"	Section 2–103(1) (d).

(4) In addition Article 1 contains general definitions and principles of construction and interpretation applicable throughout this Article.

As amended in 1990.

§ 2A–104. Leases Subject to Other Law.

(1) A lease, although subject to this Article, is also subject to any applicable:

(a) certificate of title statute of this State: (list any certificate of title statutes covering automobiles, trailers, mobile homes, boats, farm tractors, and the like);

(b) certificate of title statute of another jurisdiction (Section 2A–105); or

(c) consumer protection statute of this State, or final consumer protection decision of a court of this State existing on the effective date of this Article.

(2) In case of conflict between this Article, other than Sections 2A–105, 2A–304(3), and 2A–305(3), and a statute or decision referred to in subsection (1), the statute or decision controls.

(3) Failure to comply with an applicable law has only the effect specified therein.

As amended in 1990.

§ 2A–105. Territorial Application of Article to Goods Covered by Certificate of Title.
Subject to the provisions of Sections 2A–304(3) and 2A–305(3), with respect to goods covered by a certificate of title issued under a statute of this State or of another jurisdiction, compliance and the effect of compliance or noncompliance with a certificate of title statute are governed by the law (including the conflict of laws rules) of the jurisdiction issuing the certificate until the earlier of (a) surrender of the certificate, or (b) four months after the goods are removed from that jurisdiction and thereafter until a new certificate of title is issued by another jurisdiction.

§ 2A–106. Limitation on Power of Parties to Consumer Lease to Choose Applicable Law and Judicial Forum.

(1) If the law chosen by the parties to a consumer lease is that of a jurisdiction other than a jurisdiction in which the lessee resides at the time the lease agreement becomes enforceable or within 30 days thereafter or in which the goods are to be used, the choice is not enforceable.

(2) If the judicial forum chosen by the parties to a consumer lease is a forum that would not otherwise have jurisdiction over the lessee, the choice is not enforceable.

§ 2A–107. Waiver or Renunciation of Claim or Right After Default.
Any claim or right arising out of an alleged default or breach of warranty may be discharged in whole or in part without consideration by a written waiver or renunciation signed and delivered by the aggrieved party.

§ 2A–108. Unconscionability.

(1) If the court as a matter of law finds a lease contract or any clause of a lease contract to have been unconscionable at the time it was made the court may refuse to enforce the lease contract, or it may enforce the remainder of the lease contract without the unconscionable clause, or it may so limit the application of any unconscionable clause as to avoid any unconscionable result.

(2) With respect to a consumer lease, if the court as a matter of law finds that a lease contract or any clause of

a lease contract has been induced by unconscionable conduct or that unconscionable conduct has occurred in the collection of a claim arising from a lease contract, the court may grant appropriate relief.

(3) Before making a finding of unconscionability under subsection (1) or (2), the court, on its own motion or that of a party, shall afford the parties a reasonable opportunity to present evidence as to the setting, purpose, and effect of the lease contract or clause thereof, or of the conduct.

(4) In an action in which the lessee claims unconscionability with respect to a consumer lease:

(a) If the court finds unconscionability under subsection (1) or (2), the court shall award reasonable attorney's fees to the lessee.

(b) If the court does not find unconscionability and the lessee claiming unconscionability has brought or maintained an action he [or she] knew to be groundless, the court shall award reasonable attorney's fees to the party against whom the claim is made.

(c) In determining attorney's fees, the amount of the recovery on behalf of the claimant under subsections (1) and (2) is not controlling.

§ 2A–109. Option to Accelerate at Will.

(1) A term providing that one party or his [or her] successor in interest may accelerate payment or performance or require collateral or additional collateral "at will" or "when he [or she] deems himself [or herself] insecure" or in words of similar import must be construed to mean that he [or she] has power to do so only if he [or she] in good faith believes that the prospect of payment or performance is impaired.

(2) With respect to a consumer lease, the burden of establishing good faith under subsection (1) is on the party who exercised the power; otherwise the burden of establishing lack of good faith is on the party against whom the power has been exercised.

Part 2: Formation and Construction of Lease Contract

§ 2A–201. Statute of Frauds.

(1) A lease contract is not enforceable by way of action or defense unless:

(a) the total payments to be made under the lease contract, excluding payments for options to renew or buy, are less than $1,000; or

(b) there is a writing, signed by the party against whom enforcement is sought or by that party's authorized agent, sufficient to indicate that a lease contract has been made between the parties and to describe the goods leased and the lease term.

(2) Any description of leased goods or of the lease term is sufficient and satisfies subsection (1) (b), whether or not it is specific, if it reasonably identifies what is described.

(3) A writing is not insufficient because it omits or incorrectly states a term agreed upon, but the lease contract is not enforceable under subsection (1) (b) beyond the lease term and the quantity of goods shown in the writing.

(4) A lease contract that does not satisfy the requirements of subsection (1), but which is valid in other respects, is enforceable:

(a) if the goods are to be specially manufactured or obtained for the lessee and are not suitable for lease or sale to others in the ordinary course of the lessor's business, and the lessor, before notice of repudiation is received and under circumstances that reasonably indicate that the goods are for the lessee, has made either a substantial beginning of their manufacture or commitments for their procurement;

(b) if the party against whom enforcement is sought admits in that party's pleading, testimony or otherwise in court that a lease contract was made, but the lease contract is not enforceable under this provision beyond the quantity of goods admitted; or

(c) with respect to goods that have been received and accepted by the lessee.

(5) The lease term under a lease contract referred to in subsection (4) is:

(a) if there is a writing signed by the party against whom enforcement is sought or by that party's authorized agent specifying the lease term, the term so specified;

(b) if the party against whom enforcement is sought admits in that party's pleading, testimony, or otherwise in court a lease term, the term so admitted; or

(c) a reasonable lease term.

§ 2A–202. Final Written Expression: Parol or Extrinsic Evidence.
Terms with respect to which the confirmatory memoranda of the parties agree or which are otherwise set forth in a writing intended by the parties as a final expression of their agreement with respect to such terms as are included therein may not be contradicted by evidence of any prior agreement or of a contemporaneous oral agreement but may be explained or supplemented:

(a) by course of dealing or usage of trade or by course of performance; and

(b) by evidence of consistent additional terms unless the court finds the writing to have been intended also as a complete and exclusive statement of the terms of the agreement.

§ 2A–203. Seals Inoperative.
The affixing of a seal to a writing evidencing a lease contract or an offer to enter into a lease contract does not render the writing a sealed

instrument and the law with respect to sealed instruments does not apply to the lease contract or offer.

§ 2A–204. Formation in General.

(1) A lease contract may be made in any manner sufficient to show agreement, including conduct by both parties which recognizes the existence of a lease contract.

(2) An agreement sufficient to constitute a lease contract may be found although the moment of its making is undetermined.

(3) Although one or more terms are left open, a lease contract does not fail for indefiniteness if the parties have intended to make a lease contract and there is a reasonably certain basis for giving an appropriate remedy.

§ 2A–205. Firm Offers.

An offer by a merchant to lease goods to or from another person in a signed writing that by its terms gives assurance it will be held open is not revocable, for lack of consideration, during the time stated or, if no time is stated, for a reasonable time, but in no event may the period of irrevocability exceed 3 months. Any such term of assurance on a form supplied by the offeree must be separately signed by the offeror.

§ 2A–206. Offer and Acceptance in Formation of Lease Contract.

(1) Unless otherwise unambiguously indicated by the language or circumstances, an offer to make a lease contract must be construed as inviting acceptance in any manner and by any medium reasonable in the circumstances.

(2) If the beginning of a requested performance is a reasonable mode of acceptance, an offeror who is not notified of acceptance within a reasonable time may treat the offer as having lapsed before acceptance.

§ 2A–207. Course of Performance or Practical Construction.

(1) If a lease contract involves repeated occasions for performance by either party with knowledge of the nature of the performance and opportunity for objection to it by the other, any course of performance accepted or acquiesced in without objection is relevant to determine the meaning of the lease agreement.

(2) The express terms of a lease agreement and any course of performance, as well as any course of dealing and usage of trade, must be construed whenever reasonable as consistent with each other; but if that construction is unreasonable, express terms control course of performance, course of performance controls both course of dealing and usage of trade, and course of dealing controls usage of trade.

(3) Subject to the provisions of Section 2A–208 on modification and waiver, course of performance is relevant to show a waiver or modification of any term inconsistent with the course of performance.

§ 2A–208. Modification, Rescission and Waiver.

(1) An agreement modifying a lease contract needs no consideration to be binding.

(2) A signed lease agreement that excludes modification or rescission except by a signed writing may not be otherwise modified or rescinded, but, except as between merchants, such a requirement on a form supplied by a merchant must be separately signed by the other party.

(3) Although an attempt at modification or rescission does not satisfy the requirements of subsection (2), it may operate as a waiver.

(4) A party who has made a waiver affecting an executory portion of a lease contract may retract the waiver by reasonable notification received by the other party that strict performance will be required of any term waived, unless the retraction would be unjust in view of a material change of position in reliance on the waiver.

§ 2A–209. Lessee Under Finance Lease as Beneficiary of Supply Contract.

(1) The benefit of a supplier's promises to the lessor under the supply contract and of all warranties, whether express or implied, including those of any third party provided in connection with or as part of the supply contract, extends to the lessee to the extent of the lessee's leasehold interest under a finance lease related to the supply contract, but is subject to the terms of the warranty and of the supply contract and all defenses or claims arising therefrom.

(2) The extension of the benefit of a supplier's promises and of warranties to the lessee (Section 2A–209(1)) does not: (i) modify the rights and obligations of the parties to the supply contract, whether arising therefrom or otherwise, or (ii) impose any duty or liability under the supply contract on the lessee.

(3) Any modification or rescission of the supply contract by the supplier and the lessor is effective between the supplier and the lessee unless, before the modification or rescission, the supplier has received notice that the lessee has entered into a finance lease related to the supply contract. If the modification or rescission is effective between the supplier and the lessee, the lessor is deemed to have assumed, in addition to the obligations of the lessor to the lessee under the lease contract, promises of the supplier to the lessor and warranties that were so modified or rescinded as they existed and were available to the lessee before modification or rescission.

(4) In addition to the extension of the benefit of the supplier's promises and of warranties to the lessee under subsection (1), the lessee retains all rights that the

lessee may have against the supplier which arise from an agreement between the lessee and the supplier or under other law.

As amended in 1990.

§ 2A–210. Express Warranties.

(1) Express warranties by the lessor are created as follows:

 (a) Any affirmation of fact or promise made by the lessor to the lessee which relates to the goods and becomes part of the basis of the bargain creates an express warranty that the goods will conform to the affirmation or promise.

 (b) Any description of the goods which is made part of the basis of the bargain creates an express warranty that the goods will conform to the description.

 (c) Any sample or model that is made part of the basis of the bargain creates an express warranty that the whole of the goods will conform to the sample or model.

(2) It is not necessary to the creation of an express warranty that the lessor use formal words, such as "warrant" or "guarantee," or that the lessor have a specific intention to make a warranty, but an affirmation merely of the value of the goods or a statement purporting to be merely the lessor's opinion or commendation of the goods does not create a warranty.

§ 2A–211. Warranties Against Interference and Against Infringement; Lessee's Obligation Against Infringement.

(1) There is in a lease contract a warranty that for the lease term no person holds a claim to or interest in the goods that arose from an act or omission of the lessor, other than a claim by way of infringement or the like, which will interfere with the lessee's enjoyment of its leasehold interest.

(2) Except in a finance lease there is in a lease contract by a lessor who is a merchant regularly dealing in goods of the kind a warranty that the goods are delivered free of the rightful claim of any person by way of infringement or the like.

(3) A lessee who furnishes specifications to a lessor or a supplier shall hold the lessor and the supplier harmless against any claim by way of infringement or the like that arises out of compliance with the specifications.

§ 2A–212. Implied Warranty of Merchantability.

(1) Except in a finance lease, a warranty that the goods will be merchantable is implied in a lease contract if the lessor is a merchant with respect to goods of that kind.

(2) Goods to be merchantable must be at least such as

 (a) pass without objection in the trade under the description in the lease agreement;

 (b) in the case of fungible goods, are of fair average quality within the description;

 (c) are fit for the ordinary purposes for which goods of that type are used;

 (d) run, within the variation permitted by the lease agreement, of even kind, quality, and quantity within each unit and among all units involved;

 (e) are adequately contained, packaged, and labeled as the lease agreement may require; and

 (f) conform to any promises or affirmations of fact made on the container or label.

(3) Other implied warranties may arise from course of dealing or usage of trade.

§ 2A–213. Implied Warranty of Fitness for Particular Purpose.
Except in a finance lease, if the lessor at the time the lease contract is made has reason to know of any particular purpose for which the goods are required and that the lessee is relying on the lessor's skill or judgment to select or furnish suitable goods, there is in the lease contract an implied warranty that the goods will be fit for that purpose.

§ 2A–214. Exclusion or Modification of Warranties.

(1) Words or conduct relevant to the creation of an express warranty and words or conduct tending to negate or limit a warranty must be construed wherever reasonable as consistent with each other; but, subject to the provisions of Section 2A–202 on parol or extrinsic evidence, negation or limitation is inoperative to the extent that the construction is unreasonable.

(2) Subject to subsection (3), to exclude or modify the implied warranty of merchantability or any part of it the language must mention "merchantability", be by a writing, and be conspicuous. Subject to sub-section (3), to exclude or modify any implied warranty of fitness the exclusion must be by a writing and be conspicuous. Language to exclude all implied warranties of fitness is sufficient if it is in writing, is conspicuous and states, for example, "There is no warranty that the goods will be fit for a particular purpose".

(3) Notwithstanding subsection (2), but subject to subsection (4),

 (a) unless the circumstances indicate otherwise, all implied warranties are excluded by expressions like "as is," or "with all faults," or by other language that in common understanding calls the lessee's attention to the exclusion of warranties and makes plain that there is no implied warranty, if in writing and conspicuous;

 (b) if the lessee before entering into the lease contract has examined the goods or the sample or model as fully as desired or has refused to examine the goods, there is no implied warranty with regard to defects that an examination ought in the circumstances to have revealed; and

(c) an implied warranty may also be excluded or modified by course of dealing, course of performance, or usage of trade.

(4) To exclude or modify a warranty against interference or against infringement (Section 2A–211) or any part of it, the language must be specific, be by a writing, and be conspicuous, unless the circumstances, including course of performance, course of dealing, or usage of trade, give the lessee reason to know that the goods are being leased subject to a claim or interest of any person.

§ 2A–215. Cumulation and Conflict of Warranties Express or Implied.

Warranties, whether express or implied, must be construed as consistent with each other and as cumulative, but if that construction is unreasonable, the intention of the parties determines which warranty is dominant. In ascertaining that intention the following rules apply:

(a) Exact or technical specifications displace an inconsistent sample or model or general language of description.

(b) A sample from an existing bulk displaces inconsistent general language of description.

(c) Express warranties displace inconsistent implied warranties other than an implied warranty of fitness for a particular purpose.

§ 2A–216. Third Party Beneficiaries of Express and Implied Warranties.

Alternative A

A warranty to or for the benefit of a lessee under this Article, whether express or implied, extends to any natural person who is in the family or household of the lessee or who is a guest in the lessee's home if it is reasonable to expect that such person may use, consume, or be affected by the goods and who is injured in person by breach of the warranty. This section does not displace principles of law and equity that extend a warranty to or for the benefit of a lessee to other persons. The operation of this section may not be excluded, modified, or limited, but an exclusion, modification, or limitation of the warranty, including any with respect to rights and remedies, effective against the lessee is also effective against any beneficiary designated under this section.

Alternative B

A warranty to or for the benefit of a lessee under this Article, whether express or implied, extends to any natural person who may reasonably be expected to use, consume, or be affected by the goods and who is injured in person by breach of the warranty. This section does not displace principles of law and equity that extend a warranty to or for the benefit of a lessee to other persons. The operation of this section may not be excluded, modified, or limited, but an exclusion, modification, or limitation of the warranty,

including any with respect to rights and remedies, effective against the lessee is also effective against the beneficiary designated under this section.

Alternative C

A warranty to or for the benefit of a lessee under this Article, whether express or implied, extends to any person who may reasonably be expected to use, consume, or be affected by the goods and who is injured by breach of the warranty. The operation of this section may not be excluded, modified, or limited with respect to injury to the person of an individual to whom the warranty extends, but an exclusion, modification, or limitation of the warranty, including any with respect to rights and remedies, effective against the lessee is also effective against the beneficiary designated under this section.

§ 2A–217. Identification.

Identification of goods as goods to which a lease contract refers may be made at any time and in any manner explicitly agreed to by the parties. In the absence of explicit agreement, identification occurs:

(a) when the lease contract is made if the lease contract is for a lease of goods that are existing and identified;

(b) when the goods are shipped, marked, or otherwise designated by the lessor as goods to which the lease contract refers, if the lease contract is for a lease of goods that are not existing and identified; or

(c) when the young are conceived, if the lease contract is for a lease of unborn young of animals.

§ 2A–218. Insurance and Proceeds.

(1) A lessee obtains an insurable interest when existing goods are identified to the lease contract even though the goods identified are nonconforming and the lessee has an option to reject them.

(2) If a lessee has an insurable interest only by reason of the lessor's identification of the goods, the lessor, until default or insolvency or notification to the lessee that identification is final, may substitute other goods for those identified.

(3) Notwithstanding a lessee's insurable interest under subsections (1) and (2) , the lessor retains an insurable interest until an option to buy has been exercised by the lessee and risk of loss has passed to the lessee.

(4) Nothing in this section impairs any insurable interest recognized under any other statute or rule of law.

(5) The parties by agreement may determine that one or more parties have an obligation to obtain and pay for insurance covering the goods and by agreement may determine the beneficiary of the proceeds of the insurance.

§ 2A–219. Risk of Loss.

(1) Except in the case of a finance lease, risk of loss is retained by the lessor and does not pass to the lessee.

In the case of a finance lease, risk of loss passes to the lessee.

(2) Subject to the provisions of this Article on the effect of default on risk of loss (Section 2A–220), if risk of loss is to pass to the lessee and the time of passage is not stated, the following rules apply:

(a) If the lease contract requires or authorizes the goods to be shipped by carrier

(i) and it does not require delivery at a particular destination, the risk of loss passes to the lessee when the goods are duly delivered to the carrier; but

(ii) if it does require delivery at a particular destination and the goods are there duly tendered while in the possession of the carrier, the risk of loss passes to the lessee when the goods are there duly so tendered as to enable the lessee to take delivery.

(b) If the goods are held by a bailee to be delivered without being moved, the risk of loss passes to the lessee on acknowledgment by the bailee of the lessee's right to possession of the goods.

(c) In any case not within subsection (a) or (b), the risk of loss passes to the lessee on the lessee's receipt of the goods if the lessor, or, in the case of a finance lease, the supplier, is a merchant; otherwise the risk passes to the lessee on tender of delivery.

§ 2A–220. Effect of Default on Risk of Loss.

(1) Where risk of loss is to pass to the lessee and the time of passage is not stated:

(a) If a tender or delivery of goods so fails to conform to the lease contract as to give a right of rejection, the risk of their loss remains with the lessor, or, in the case of a finance lease, the supplier, until cure or acceptance.

(b) If the lessee rightfully revokes acceptance, he [or she], to the extent of any deficiency in his [or her] effective insurance coverage, may treat the risk of loss as having remained with the lessor from the beginning.

(2) Whether or not risk of loss is to pass to the lessee, if the lessee as to conforming goods already identified to a lease contract repudiates or is otherwise in default under the lease contract, the lessor, or, in the case of a finance lease, the supplier, to the extent of any deficiency in his [or her] effective insurance coverage may treat the risk of loss as resting on the lessee for a commercially reasonable time.

§ 2A–221. Casualty to Identified Goods. If a lease contract requires goods identified when the lease contract is made, and the goods suffer casualty without fault of the lessee, the lessor or the supplier before delivery, or the goods suffer casualty before risk of loss passes to the lessee pursuant to the lease agreement or Section 2A–219, then:

(a) if the loss is total, the lease contract is avoided; and

(b) if the loss is partial or the goods have so deteriorated as to no longer conform to the lease contract, the lessee may nevertheless demand inspection and at his [or her] option either treat the lease contract as avoided or, except in a finance lease that is not a consumer lease, accept the goods with due allowance from the rent payable for the balance of the lease term for the deterioration or the deficiency in quantity but without further right against the lessor.

Part 3: Effect of Lease Contract

§ 2A–301. Enforceability of Lease Contract. Except as otherwise provided in this Article, a lease contract is effective and enforceable according to its terms between the parties, against purchasers of the goods and against creditors of the parties.

§ 2A–302. Title to and Possession of Goods. Except as otherwise provided in this Article, each provision of this Article applies whether the lessor or a third party has title to the goods, and whether the lessor, the lessee, or a third party has possession of the goods, notwithstanding any statute or rule of law that possession or the absence of possession is fraudulent.

§ 2A–303. Alienability of Party's Interest Under Lease Contract or of Lessor's Residual Interest in Goods; Delegation of Performance; Transfer of Rights.

(1) As used in this section, "creation of a security interest" includes the sale of a lease contract that is subject to Article 9, Secured Transactions, by reason of Section 9–102(1) (b).

(2) Except as provided in subsections (3) and (4), a provision in a lease agreement which (i) prohibits the voluntary or involuntary transfer, including a transfer by sale, sublease, creation or enforcement of a security interest, or attachment, levy, or other judicial process, of an interest of a party under the lease contract or of the lessor's residual interest in the goods, or (ii) makes such a transfer an event of default, gives rise to the rights and remedies provided in subsection (5), but a transfer that is prohibited or is an event of default under the lease agreement is otherwise effective.

(3) A provision in a lease agreement which (i) prohibits the creation or enforcement of a security interest in an interest of a party under the lease contract or in the lessor's residual interest in the goods, or (ii) makes such a transfer an event of default, is not enforceable unless, and then only to the extent that, there is an actual

transfer by the lessee of the lessee's right of possession or use of the goods in violation of the provision or an actual delegation of a material performance of either party to the lease contract in violation of the provision. Neither the granting nor the enforcement of a security interest in (i) the lessor's interest under the lease contract or (ii) the lessor's residual interest in the goods is a transfer that materially impairs the prospect of obtaining return performance by, materially changes the duty of, or materially increases the burden or risk imposed on, the lessee within the purview of subsection (5) unless, and then only to the extent that, there is an actual delegation of a material performance of the lessor.

(4) A provision in a lease agreement which (i) prohibits a transfer of a right to damages for default with respect to the whole lease contract or of a right to payment arising out of the transferor's due performance of the transferor's entire obligation, or (ii) makes such a transfer an event of default, is not enforceable, and such a transfer is not a transfer that materially impairs the prospect of obtaining return performance by, materially changes the duty of, or materially increases the burden or risk imposed on, the other party to the lease contract within the purview of subsection (5).

(5) Subject to subsections (3) and (4):

(a) if a transfer is made which is made an event of default under a lease agreement, the party to the lease contract not making the transfer, unless that party waives the default or otherwise agrees, has the rights and remedies described in Section 2A–501(2);

(b) if paragraph (a) is not applicable and if a transfer is made that (i) is prohibited under a lease agreement or (ii) materially impairs the prospect of obtaining return performance by, materially changes the duty of, or materially increases the burden or risk imposed on, the other party to the lease contract, unless the party not making the transfer agrees at any time to the transfer in the lease contract or otherwise, then, except as limited by contract, (i) the transferor is liable to the party not making the transfer for damages caused by the transfer to the extent that the damages could not reasonably be prevented by the party not making the transfer and (ii) a court having jurisdiction may grant other appropriate relief, including cancellation of the lease contract or an injunction against the transfer.

(6) A transfer of "the lease" or of "all my rights under the lease", or a transfer in similar general terms, is a transfer of rights and, unless the language or the circumstances, as in a transfer for security, indicate the contrary, the transfer is a delegation of duties by the transferor to the transferee. Acceptance by the transferee constitutes a promise by the transferee to perform those duties. The promise is enforceable by either the transferor or the other party to the lease contract.

(7) Unless otherwise agreed by the lessor and the lessee, a delegation of performance does not relieve the transferor as against the other party of any duty to perform or of any liability for default.

(8) In a consumer lease, to prohibit the transfer of an interest of a party under the lease contract or to make a transfer an event of default, the language must be specific, by a writing, and conspicuous.

As amended in 1990.

§ 2A–304. Subsequent Lease of Goods by Lessor.

(1) Subject to Section 2A–303, a subsequent lessee from a lessor of goods under an existing lease contract obtains, to the extent of the leasehold interest transferred, the leasehold interest in the goods that the lessor had or had power to transfer, and except as provided in subsection (2) and Section 2A–527(4), takes subject to the existing lease contract. A lessor with voidable title has power to transfer a good leasehold interest to a good faith subsequent lessee for value, but only to the extent set forth in the preceding sentence. If goods have been delivered under a transaction of purchase, the lessor has that power even though:

(a) the lessor's transferor was deceived as to the identity of the lessor;

(b) the delivery was in exchange for a check which is later dishonored;

(c) it was agreed that the transaction was to be a "cash sale"; or

(d) the delivery was procured through fraud punishable as larcenous under the criminal law.

(2) A subsequent lessee in the ordinary course of business from a lessor who is a merchant dealing in goods of that kind to whom the goods were entrusted by the existing lessee of that lessor before the interest of the subsequent lessee became enforceable against that lessor obtains, to the extent of the leasehold interest transferred, all of that lessor's and the existing lessee's rights to the goods, and takes free of the existing lease contract.

(3) A subsequent lessee from the lessor of goods that are subject to an existing lease contract and are covered by a certificate of title issued under a statute of this State or of another jurisdiction takes no greater rights than those provided both by this section and by the certificate of title statute.

As amended in 1990.

§ 2A–305. Sale or Sublease of Goods by Lessee.

(1) Subject to the provisions of Section 2A–303, a buyer or sublessee from the lessee of goods under an existing lease contract obtains, to the extent of the interest

transferred, the leasehold interest in the goods that the lessee had or had power to transfer, and except as provided in subsection (2) and Section 2A–511(4), takes subject to the existing lease contract. A lessee with a voidable leasehold interest has power to transfer a good leasehold interest to a good faith buyer for value or a good faith sublessee for value, but only to the extent set forth in the preceding sentence. When goods have been delivered under a transaction of lease the lessee has that power even though:

 (a) the lessor was deceived as to the identity of the lessee;

 (b) the delivery was in exchange for a check which is later dishonored; or

 (c) the delivery was procured through fraud punishable as larcenous under the criminal law.

(2) A buyer in the ordinary course of business or a sublessee in the ordinary course of business from a lessee who is a merchant dealing in goods of that kind to whom the goods were entrusted by the lessor obtains, to the extent of the interest transferred, all of the lessor's and lessee's rights to the goods, and takes free of the existing lease contract.

(3) A buyer or sublessee from the lessee of goods that are subject to an existing lease contract and are covered by a certificate of title issued under a statute of this State or of another jurisdiction takes no greater rights than those provided both by this section and by the certificate of title statute.

§ 2A–306. Priority of Certain Liens Arising by Operation of Law. If a person in the ordinary course of his [or her] business furnishes services or materials with respect to goods subject to a lease contract, a lien upon those goods in the possession of that person given by statute or rule of law for those materials or services takes priority over any interest of the lessor or lessee under the lease contract or this Article unless the lien is created by statute and the statute provides otherwise or unless the lien is created by rule of law and the rule of law provides otherwise.

§ 2A–307. Priority of Liens Arising by Attachment or Levy on, Security Interests in, and Other Claims to Goods.

(1) Except as otherwise provided in Section 2A–306, a creditor of a lessee takes subject to the lease contract.

(2) Except as otherwise provided in subsections (3) and (4) and in Sections 2A–306 and 2A–308, a creditor of a lessor takes subject to the lease contract unless:

 (a) the creditor holds a lien that attached to the goods before the lease contract became enforceable;

 (b) the creditor holds a security interest in the goods and the lessee did not give value and receive delivery of the goods without knowledge of the security interest; or

 (c) the creditor holds a security interest in the goods which was perfected (Section 9–303) before the lease contract became enforceable.

(3) A lessee in the ordinary course of business takes the leasehold interest free of a security interest in the goods created by the lessor even though the security interest is perfected (Section 9–303) and the lessee knows of its existence.

(4) A lessee other than a lessee in the ordinary course of business takes the leasehold interest free of a security interest to the extent that it secures future advances made after the secured party acquires knowledge of the lease or more than 45 days after the lease contract becomes enforceable, whichever first occurs, unless the future advances are made pursuant to a commitment entered into without knowledge of the lease and before the expiration of the 45-day period.

As amended in 1990.

§ 2A–308. Special Rights of Creditors.

(1) A creditor of a lessor in possession of goods subject to a lease contract may treat the lease contract as void if as against the creditor retention of possession by the lessor is fraudulent under any statute or rule of law, but retention of possession in good faith and current course of trade by the lessor for a commercially reasonable time after the lease contract becomes enforceable is not fraudulent.

(2) Nothing in this Article impairs the rights of creditors of a lessor if the lease contract (a) becomes enforceable, not in current course of trade but in satisfaction of or as security for a preexisting claim for money, security, or the like, and (b) is made under circumstances which under any statute or rule of law apart from this Article would constitute the transaction a fraudulent transfer or voidable preference.

(3) A creditor of a seller may treat a sale or an identification of goods to a contract for sale as void if as against the creditor retention of possession by the seller is fraudulent under any statute or rule of law, but retention of possession of the goods pursuant to a lease contract entered into by the seller as lessee and the buyer as lessor in connection with the sale or identification of the goods is not fraudulent if the buyer bought for value and in good faith.

§ 2A–309. Lessor's and Lessee's Rights When Goods Become Fixtures.

(1) In this section:

 (a) goods are "fixtures" when they become so related to particular real estate that an interest in them arises under real estate law;

(b) a "fixture filing" is the filing, in the office where a mortgage on the real estate would be filed or recorded, of a financing statement covering goods that are or are to become fixtures and conforming to the requirements of Section 9–402(5);

(c) a lease is a "purchase money lease" unless the lessee has possession or use of the goods or the right to possession or use of the goods before the lease agreement is enforceable;

(d) a mortgage is a "construction mortgage" to the extent it secures an obligation incurred for the construction of an improvement on land including the acquisition cost of the land, if the recorded writing so indicates; and

(e) "encumbrance" includes real estate mortgages and other liens on real estate and all other rights in real estate that are not ownership interests.

(2) Under this Article a lease may be of goods that are fixtures or may continue in goods that become fixtures, but no lease exists under this Article of ordinary building materials incorporated into an improvement on land.

(3) This Article does not prevent creation of a lease of fixtures pursuant to real estate law.

(4) The perfected interest of a lessor of fixtures has priority over a conflicting interest of an encumbrancer or owner of the real estate if:

(a) the lease is a purchase money lease, the conflicting interest of the encumbrancer or owner arises before the goods become fixtures, the interest of the lessor is perfected by a fixture filing before the goods become fixtures or within ten days thereafter, and the lessee has an interest of record in the real estate or is in possession of the real estate; or

(b) the interest of the lessor is perfected by a fixture filing before the interest of the encumbrancer or owner is of record, the lessor's interest has priority over any conflicting interest of a predecessor in title of the encumbrancer or owner, and the lessee has an interest of record in the real estate or is in possession of the real estate.

(5) The interest of a lessor of fixtures, whether or not perfected, has priority over the conflicting interest of an encumbrancer or owner of the real estate if:

(a) the fixtures are readily removable factory or office machines, readily removable equipment that is not primarily used or leased for use in the operation of the real estate, or readily removable replacements of domestic appliances that are goods subject to a consumer lease, and before the goods become fixtures the lease contract is enforceable; or

(b) the conflicting interest is a lien on the real estate obtained by legal or equitable proceedings after the lease contract is enforceable; or

(c) the encumbrancer or owner has consented in writing to the lease or has disclaimed an interest in the goods as fixtures; or

(d) the lessee has a right to remove the goods as against the encumbrancer or owner. If the lessee's right to remove terminates, the priority of the interest of the lessor continues for a reasonable time.

(6) Notwithstanding subsection (4)(a) but otherwise subject to subsections (4) and (5), the interest of a lessor of fixtures, including the lessor's residual interest, is subordinate to the conflicting interest of an encumbrancer of the real estate under a construction mortgage recorded before the goods become fixtures if the goods become fixtures before the completion of the construction. To the extent given to refinance a construction mortgage, the conflicting interest of an encumbrancer of the real estate under a mortgage has this priority to the same extent as the encumbrancer of the real estate under the construction mortgage.

(7) In cases not within the preceding subsections, priority between the interest of a lessor of fixtures, including the lessor's residual interest, and the conflicting interest of an encumbrancer or owner of the real estate who is not the lessee is determined by the priority rules governing conflicting interests in real estate.

(8) If the interest of a lessor of fixtures, including the lessor's residual interest, has priority over all conflicting interests of all owners and encumbrancers of the real estate, the lessor or the lessee may (i) on default, expiration, termination, or cancellation of the lease agreement but subject to the agreement and this Article, or (ii) if necessary to enforce other rights and remedies of the lessor or lessee under this Article, remove the goods from the real estate, free and clear of all conflicting interests of all owners and encumbrancers of the real estate, but the lessor or lessee must reimburse any encumbrancer or owner of the real estate who is not the lessee and who has not otherwise agreed for the cost of repair of any physical injury, but not for any diminution in value of the real estate caused by the absence of the goods removed or by any necessity of replacing them. A person entitled to reimbursement may refuse permission to remove until the party seeking removal gives adequate security for the performance of this obligation.

(9) Even though the lease agreement does not create a security interest, the interest of a lessor of fixtures, including the lessor's residual interest, is perfected by filing a financing statement as a fixture filing for leased goods that are or are to become fixtures in accordance with the relevant provisions of the Article on Secured Transactions (Article 9).

As amended in 1990.

§ 2A–310. Lessor's and Lessee's Rights When Goods Become Accessions.

(1) Goods are "accessions" when they are installed in or affixed to other goods.

(2) The interest of a lessor or a lessee under a lease contract entered into before the goods became accessions is superior to all interests in the whole except as stated in subsection (4).

(3) The interest of a lessor or a lessee under a lease contract entered into at the time or after the goods became accessions is superior to all subsequently acquired interests in the whole except as stated in subsection (4) but is subordinate to interests in the whole existing at the time the lease contract was made unless the holders of such interests in the whole have in writing consented to the lease or disclaimed an interest in the goods as part of the whole.

(4) The interest of a lessor or a lessee under a lease contract described in subsection (2) or (3) is subordinate to the interest of

 (a) a buyer in the ordinary course of business or a lessee in the ordinary course of business of any interest in the whole acquired after the goods became accessions; or

 (b) a creditor with a security interest in the whole perfected before the lease contract was made to the extent that the creditor makes subsequent advances without knowledge of the lease contract.

(5) When under subsections (2) or (3) and (4) a lessor or a lessee of accessions holds an interest that is superior to all interests in the whole, the lessor or the lessee may (a) on default, expiration, termination, or cancellation of the lease contract by the other party but subject to the provisions of the lease contract and this Article, or (b) if necessary to enforce his [or her] other rights and remedies under this Article, remove the goods from the whole, free and clear of all interests in the whole, but he [or she] must reimburse any holder of an interest in the whole who is not the lessee and who has not otherwise agreed for the cost of repair of any physical injury but not for any diminution in value of the whole caused by the absence of the goods removed or by any necessity for replacing them. A person entitled to reimbursement may refuse permission to remove until the party seeking removal gives adequate security for the performance of this obligation.

§ 2A–311. Priority Subject to Subordination.
Nothing in this Article prevents subordination by agreement by any person entitled to priority.

As added in 1990.

Part 4: Performance of Lease Contract: Repudiated, Substituted and Excused

§ 2A–401. Insecurity: Adequate Assurance of Performance.

(1) A lease contract imposes an obligation on each party that the other's expectation of receiving due performance will not be impaired.

(2) If reasonable grounds for insecurity arise with respect to the performance of either party, the insecure party may demand in writing adequate assurance of due performance. Until the insecure party receives that assurance, if commercially reasonable the insecure party may suspend any performance for which he [or she] has not already received the agreed return.

(3) A repudiation of the lease contract occurs if assurance of due performance adequate under the circumstances of the particular case is not provided to the insecure party within a reasonable time, not to exceed 30 days after receipt of a demand by the other party.

(4) Between merchants, the reasonableness of grounds for insecurity and the adequacy of any assurance offered must be determined according to commercial standards.

(5) Acceptance of any nonconforming delivery or payment does not prejudice the aggrieved party's right to demand adequate assurance of future performance.

§ 2A–402. Anticipatory Repudiation.
If either party repudiates a lease contract with respect to a performance not yet due under the lease contract, the loss of which performance will substantially impair the value of the lease contract to the other, the aggrieved party may:

 (a) for a commercially reasonable time, await retraction of repudiation and performance by the repudiating party;

 (b) make demand pursuant to Section 2A–401 and await assurance of future performance adequate under the circumstances of the particular case; or

 (c) resort to any right or remedy upon default under the lease contract or this Article, even though the aggrieved party has notified the repudiating party that the aggrieved party would await the repudiating party's performance and assurance and has urged retraction. In addition, whether or not the aggrieved party is pursuing one of the foregoing remedies, the aggrieved party may suspend performance or, if the aggrieved party is the lessor, proceed in accordance with the provisions of this Article on the lessor's right to identify goods to the lease contract notwithstanding default or to salvage unfinished goods (Section 2A–524).

§ 2A–403. Retraction of Anticipatory Repudiation.

(1) Until the repudiating party's next performance is due, the repudiating party can retract the repudiation unless, since the repudiation, the aggrieved party has cancelled the lease contract or materially changed the aggrieved party's position or otherwise indicated that the aggrieved party considers the repudiation final.

(2) Retraction may be by any method that clearly indicates to the aggrieved party that the repudiating party intends to perform under the lease contract and includes any assurance demanded under Section 2A–401.

(3) Retraction reinstates a repudiating party's rights under a lease contract with due excuse and allowance to the aggrieved party for any delay occasioned by the repudiation.

§ 2A–404. Substituted Performance.

(1) If without fault of the lessee, the lessor and the supplier, the agreed berthing, loading, or unloading facilities fail or the agreed type of carrier becomes unavailable or the agreed manner of delivery otherwise becomes commercially impracticable, but a commercially reasonable substitute is available, the substitute performance must be tendered and accepted.

(2) If the agreed means or manner of payment fails because of domestic or foreign governmental regulation:

(a) the lessor may withhold or stop delivery or cause the supplier to withhold or stop delivery unless the lessee provides a means or manner of payment that is commercially a substantial equivalent; and

(b) if delivery has already been taken, payment by the means or in the manner provided by the regulation discharges the lessee's obligation unless the regulation is discriminatory, oppressive, or predatory.

§ 2A–405. Excused Performance. Subject to Section 2A–404 on substituted performance, the following rules apply:

(a) Delay in delivery or nondelivery in whole or in part by a lessor or a supplier who complies with paragraphs (b) and (c) is not a default under the lease contract if performance as agreed has been made impracticable by the occurrence of a contingency the nonoccurrence of which was a basic assumption on which the lease contract was made or by compliance in good faith with any applicable foreign or domestic governmental regulation or order, whether or not the regulation or order later proves to be invalid.

(b) If the causes mentioned in paragraph (a) affect only part of the lessor's or the supplier's capacity to perform, he [or she] shall allocate production and deliveries among his [or her] customers but at his [or her] option may include regular customers not then under contract for sale or lease as well as his [or her] own requirements for further manufacture. He [or she] may so allocate in any manner that is fair and reasonable.

(c) The lessor seasonally shall notify the lessee and in the case of a finance lease the supplier seasonably shall notify the lessor and the lessee, if known, that there will be delay or nondelivery and, if allocation is required under paragraph (b), of the estimated quota thus made available for the lessee.

§ 2A–406. Procedure on Excused Performance.

(1) If the lessee receives notification of a material or indefinite delay or an allocation justified under Section 2A–405, the lessee may by written notification to the lessor as to any goods involved, and with respect to all of the goods if under an installment lease contract the value of the whole lease contract is substantially impaired (Section 2A–510):

(a) terminate the lease contract (Section 2A–505(2)); or

(b) except in a finance lease that is not a consumer lease, modify the lease contract by accepting the available quota in substitution, with due allowance from the rent payable for the balance of the lease term for the deficiency but without further right against the lessor.

(2) If, after receipt of a notification from the lessor under Section 2A–405, the lessee fails so to modify the lease agreement within a reasonable time not exceeding 30 days, the lease contract lapses with respect to any deliveries affected.

§ 2A–407. Irrevocable Promises: Finance Leases.

(1) In the case of a finance lease that is not a consumer lease the lessee's promises under the lease contract become irrevocable and independent upon the lessee's acceptance of the goods.

(2) A promise that has become irrevocable and independent under subsection (1):

(a) is effective and enforceable between the parties, and by or against third parties including assignees of the parties; and

(b) is not subject to cancellation, termination, modification, repudiation, excuse, or substitution without the consent of the party to whom the promise runs.

(3) This section does not affect the validity under any other law of a covenant in any lease contract making the lessee's promises irrevocable and independent upon the lessee's acceptance of the goods.

As amended in 1990.

Part 5: Default

§ 2A–501. Default: Procedure.

(1) Whether the lessor or the lessee is in default under a lease contract is determined by the lease agreement and this Article.

(2) If the lessor or the lessee is in default under the lease contract, the party seeking enforcement has rights and remedies as provided in this Article and, except as limited by this Article, as provided in the lease agreement.

(3) If the lessor or the lessee is in default under the lease contract, the party seeking enforcement may reduce the party's claim to judgment, or otherwise enforce the lease contract by self-help or any available judicial procedure or nonjudicial procedure, including administrative proceeding, arbitration, or the like, in accordance with this Article.

(4) Except as otherwise provided in Section 1–106(1) or this Article or the lease agreement, the rights and remedies referred to in subsections (2) and (3) are cumulative.

(5) If the lease agreement covers both real property and goods, the party seeking enforcement may proceed under this Part as to the goods, or under other applicable law as to both the real property and the goods in accordance with that party's rights and remedies in respect of the real property, in which case this Part does not apply.

As amended in 1990.

§ 2A–502. Notice After Default.
Except as otherwise provided in this Article or the lease agreement, the lessor or lessee in default under the lease contract is not entitled to notice of default or notice of enforcement from the other party to the lease agreement.

§ 2A–503. Modification or Impairment of Rights and Remedies.

(1) Except as otherwise provided in this Article, the lease agreement may include rights and remedies for default in addition to or in substitution for those provided in this Article and may limit or alter the measure of damages recoverable under this Article.

(2) Resort to a remedy provided under this Article or in the lease agreement is optional unless the remedy is expressly agreed to be exclusive. If circumstances cause an exclusive or limited remedy to fail of its essential purpose, or provision for an exclusive remedy is unconscionable, remedy may be had as provided in this Article.

(3) Consequential damages may be liquidated under Section 2A–504, or may otherwise be limited, altered, or excluded unless the limitation, alteration, or exclusion is unconscionable. Limitation, alteration, or exclusion of consequential damages for injury to the person in the case of consumer goods is prima facie unconscionable but limitation, alteration, or exclusion of damages where the loss is commercial is not prima facie unconscionable.

(4) Rights and remedies on default by the lessor or the lessee with respect to any obligation or promise collateral or ancillary to the lease contract are not impaired by this Article.

As amended in 1990.

§ 2A–504. Liquidation of Damages.

(1) Damages payable by either party for default, or any other act or omission, including indemnity for loss or diminution of anticipated tax benefits or loss or damage to lessor's residual interest, may be liquidated in the lease agreement but only at an amount or by a formula that is reasonable in light of the then anticipated harm caused by the default or other act or omission.

(2) If the lease agreement provides for liquidation of damages, and such provision does not comply with subsection (1), or such provision is an exclusive or limited remedy that circumstances cause to fail of its essential purpose, remedy may be had as provided in this Article.

(3) If the lessor justifiably withholds or stops delivery of goods because of the lessee's default or insolvency (Section 2A–525 or 2A–526), the lessee is entitled to restitution of any amount by which the sum of his [or her] payments exceeds:

(a) the amount to which the lessor is entitled by virtue of terms liquidating the lessor's damages in accordance with subsection (1); or

(b) in the absence of those terms, 20 percent of the then present value of the total rent the lessee was obligated to pay for the balance of the lease term, or, in the case of a consumer lease, the lesser of such amount or $500.

(4) A lessee's right to restitution under subsection (3) is subject to offset to the extent the lessor establishes:

(a) a right to recover damages under the provisions of this Article other than subsection (1); and

(b) the amount or value of any benefits received by the lessee directly or indirectly by reason of the lease contract.

§ 2A–505. Cancellation and Termination and Effect of Cancellation, Termination, Rescission, or Fraud on Rights and Remedies.

(1) On cancellation of the lease contract, all obligations that are still executory on both sides are discharged, but any right based on prior default or performance survives, and the cancelling party also retains any remedy for default of the whole lease contract or any unperformed balance.

(2) On termination of the lease contract, all obligations that are still executory on both sides are discharged but any right based on prior default or performance survives.

(3) Unless the contrary intention clearly appears, expressions of "cancellation," "rescission," or the like of the lease contract may not be construed as a renunciation or discharge of any claim in damages for an antecedent default.

(4) Rights and remedies for material misrepresentation or fraud include all rights and remedies available under this Article for default.

(5) Neither rescission nor a claim for rescission of the lease contract nor rejection or return of the goods may bar or be deemed inconsistent with a claim for damages or other right or remedy.

§ 2A–506. Statute of Limitations.

(1) An action for default under a lease contract, including breach of warranty or indemnity, must be commenced within 4 years after the cause of action accrued. By the original lease contract the parties may reduce the period of limitation to not less than one year.

(2) A cause of action for default accrues when the act or omission on which the default or breach of warranty is based is or should have been discovered by the aggrieved party, or when the default occurs, whichever is later. A cause of action for indemnity accrues when the act or omission on which the claim for indemnity is based is or should have been discovered by the indemnified party, whichever is later.

(3) If an action commenced within the time limited by subsection (1) is so terminated as to leave available a remedy by another action for the same default or breach of warranty or indemnity, the other action may be commenced after the expiration of the time limited and within 6 months after the termination of the first action unless the termination resulted from voluntary discontinuance or from dismissal for failure or neglect to prosecute.

(4) This section does not alter the law on tolling of the statute of limitations nor does it apply to causes of action that have accrued before this Article becomes effective.

§ 2A–507. Proof of Market Rent: Time and Place.

(1) Damages based on market rent (Section 2A–519 or 2A–528) are determined according to the rent for the use of the goods concerned for a lease term identical to the remaining lease term of the original lease agreement and prevailing at the times specified in Sections 2A–519 and 2A–528.

(2) If evidence of rent for the use of the goods concerned for a lease term identical to the remaining lease term of the original lease agreement and prevailing at the times or places described in this Article is not readily available, the rent prevailing within any reasonable time before or after the time described or at any other place or for a different lease term which in commercial judgment or under usage of trade would serve as a reasonable substitute for the one described may be used, making any proper allowance for the difference, including the cost of transporting the goods to or from the other place.

(3) Evidence of a relevant rent prevailing at a time or place or for a lease term other than the one described in this Article offered by one party is not admissible unless and until he [or she] has given the other party notice the court finds sufficient to prevent unfair surprise.

(4) If the prevailing rent or value of any goods regularly leased in any established market is in issue, reports in official publications or trade journals or in newspapers or periodicals of general circulation published as the reports of that market are admissible in evidence. The circumstances of the preparation of the report may be shown to affect its weight but not its admissibility.

As amended in 1990.

§ 2A–508. Lessee's Remedies.

(1) If a lessor fails to deliver the goods in conformity to the lease contract (Section 2A–509) or repudiates the lease contract (Section 2A–402), or a lessee rightfully rejects the goods (Section 2A–509) or justifiably revokes acceptance of the goods (Section 2A–517), then with respect to any goods involved, and with respect to all of the goods if under an installment lease contract the value of the whole lease contract is substantially impaired (Section 2A–510), the lessor is in default under the lease contract and the lessee may:

(a) cancel the lease contract (Section 2A–505(1));

(b) recover so much of the rent and security as has been paid and is just under the circumstances;

(c) cover and recover damages as to all goods affected whether or not they have been identified to the lease contract (Sections 2A–518 and 2A–520), or recover damages for nondelivery (Sections 2A–519 and 2A–520);

(d) exercise any other rights or pursue any other remedies provided in the lease contract.

(2) If a lessor fails to deliver the goods in conformity to the lease contract or repudiates the lease contract, the lessee may also:

(a) if the goods have been identified, recover them (Section 2A–522); or

(b) in a proper case, obtain specific performance or replevy the goods (Section 2A–521).

(3) If a lessor is otherwise in default under a lease contract, the lessee may exercise the rights and pursue the remedies provided in the lease contract, which may include a right to cancel the lease, and in Section 2A–519(3).

(4) If a lessor has breached a warranty, whether express or implied, the lessee may recover damages (Section 2A–519(4)).

(5) On rightful rejection or justifiable revocation of acceptance, a lessee has a security interest in goods in the lessee's possession or control for any rent and security that has been paid and any expenses reasonably incurred in their inspection, receipt, transportation, and care and custody and may hold those goods and dispose of them in good faith and in a commercially reasonable manner, subject to Section 2A–527(5).

(6) Subject to the provisions of Section 2A–407, a lessee, on notifying the lessor of the lessee's intention to do so, may deduct all or any part of the damages resulting from any default under the lease contract from any part of the rent still due under the same lease contract.

As amended in 1990.

§ 2A–509. Lessee's Rights on Improper Delivery; Rightful Rejection.

(1) Subject to the provisions of Section 2A–510 on default in installment lease contracts, if the goods or the tender or delivery fail in any respect to conform to the lease contract, the lessee may reject or accept the goods or accept any commercial unit or units and reject the rest of the goods.

(2) Rejection of goods is ineffective unless it is within a reasonable time after tender or delivery of the goods and the lessee seasonably notifies the lessor.

§ 2A–510. Installment Lease Contracts: Rejection and Default.

(1) Under an installment lease contract a lessee may reject any delivery that is nonconforming if the nonconformity substantially impairs the value of that delivery and cannot be cured or the nonconformity is a defect in the required documents; but if the nonconformity does not fall within subsection (2) and the lessor or the supplier gives adequate assurance of its cure, the lessee must accept that delivery.

(2) Whenever nonconformity or default with respect to one or more deliveries substantially impairs the value of the installment lease contract as a whole there is a default with respect to the whole. But, the aggrieved party reinstates the installment lease contract as a whole if the aggrieved party accepts a nonconforming delivery without seasonably notifying of cancellation or brings an action with respect only to

past deliveries or demands performance as to future deliveries.

§ 2A–511. Merchant Lessee's Duties as to Rightfully Rejected Goods.

(1) Subject to any security interest of a lessee (Section 2A–508(5)), if a lessor or a supplier has no agent or place of business at the market of rejection, a merchant lessee, after rejection of goods in his [or her] possession or control, shall follow any reasonable instructions received from the lessor or the supplier with respect to the goods. In the absence of those instructions, a merchant lessee shall make reasonable efforts to sell, lease, or otherwise dispose of the goods for the lessor's account if they threaten to decline in value speedily. Instructions are not reasonable if on demand indemnity for expenses is not forthcoming.

(2) If a merchant lessee (subsection (1)) or any other lessee (Section 2A–512) disposes of goods, he [or she] is entitled to reimbursement either from the lessor or the supplier or out of the proceeds for reasonable expenses of caring for and disposing of the goods and, if the expenses include no disposition commission, to such commission as is usual in the trade, or if there is none, to a reasonable sum not exceeding 10 percent of the gross proceeds.

(3) In complying with this section or Section 2A–512, the lessee is held only to good faith. Good faith conduct hereunder is neither acceptance or conversion nor the basis of an action for damages.

(4) A purchaser who purchases in good faith from a lessee pursuant to this section or Section 2A–512 takes the goods free of any rights of the lessor and the supplier even though the lessee fails to comply with one or more of the requirements of this Article.

§ 2A–512. Lessee's Duties as to Rightfully Rejected Goods.

(1) Except as otherwise provided with respect to goods that threaten to decline in value speedily (Section 2A–511) and subject to any security interest of a lessee (Section 2A–508(5)):

(a) the lessee, after rejection of goods in the lessee's possession, shall hold them with reasonable care at the lessor's or the supplier's disposition for a reasonable time after the lessee's seasonable notification of rejection;

(b) if the lessor or the supplier gives no instructions within a reasonable time after notification of rejection, the lessee may store the rejected goods for the lessor's or the supplier's account or ship them to the lessor or the supplier or dispose of them for the lessor's or the supplier's account with reimbursement in the manner provided in Section 2A–511; but

(c) the lessee has no further obligations with regard to goods rightfully rejected.

(2) Action by the lessee pursuant to subsection (1) is not acceptance or conversion.

§ 2A–513. Cure by Lessor of Improper Tender or Delivery; Replacement.

(1) If any tender or delivery by the lessor or the supplier is rejected because nonconforming and the time for performance has not yet expired, the lessor or the supplier may seasonably notify the lessee of the lessor's or the supplier's intention to cure and may then make a conforming delivery within the time provided in the lease contract.

(2) If the lessee rejects a nonconforming tender that the lessor or the supplier had reasonable grounds to believe would be acceptable with or without money allowance, the lessor or the supplier may have a further reasonable time to substitute a conforming tender if he [or she] seasonably notifies the lessee.

§ 2A–514. Waiver of Lessee's Objections.

(1) In rejecting goods, a lessee's failure to state a particular defect that is ascertainable by reasonable inspection precludes the lessee from relying on the defect to justify rejection or to establish default:

 (a) if, stated seasonably, the lessor or the supplier could have cured it (Section 2A–513); or

 (b) between merchants if the lessor or the supplier after rejection has made a request in writing for a full and final written statement of all defects on which the lessee proposes to rely.

(2) A lessee's failure to reserve rights when paying rent or other consideration against documents precludes recovery of the payment for defects apparent on the face of the documents.

§ 2A–515. Acceptance of Goods.

(1) Acceptance of goods occurs after the lessee has had a reasonable opportunity to inspect the goods and

 (a) the lessee signifies or acts with respect to the goods in a manner that signifies to the lessor or the supplier that the goods are conforming or that the lessee will take or retain them in spite of their nonconformity; or

 (b) the lessee fails to make an effective rejection of the goods (Section 2A–509(2)).

(2) Acceptance of a part of any commercial unit is acceptance of that entire unit.

§ 2A–516. Effect of Acceptance of Goods; Notice of Default; Burden of Establishing Default After Acceptance; Notice of Claim or Litigation to Person Answerable Over.

(1) A lessee must pay rent for any goods accepted in accordance with the lease contract, with due allowance for goods rightfully rejected or not delivered.

(2) A lessee's acceptance of goods precludes rejection of the goods accepted. In the case of a finance lease, if made with knowledge of a nonconformity, acceptance cannot be revoked because of it. In any other case, if made with knowledge of a nonconformity, acceptance cannot be revoked because of it unless the acceptance was on the reasonable assumption that the nonconformity would be seasonably cured. Acceptance does not of itself impair any other remedy provided by this Article or the lease agreement for nonconformity.

(3) If a tender has been accepted:

 (a) within a reasonable time after the lessee discovers or should have discovered any default, the lessee shall notify the lessor and the supplier, if any, or be barred from any remedy against the party not notified;

 (b) except in the case of a consumer lease, within a reasonable time after the lessee receives notice of litigation for infringement or the like (Section 2A–211) the lessee shall notify the lessor or be barred from any remedy over for liability established by the litigation; and

 (c) the burden is on the lessee to establish any default.

(4) If a lessee is sued for breach of a warranty or other obligation for which a lessor or a supplier is answerable over the following apply:

 (a) The lessee may give the lessor or the supplier, or both, written notice of the litigation. If the notice states that the person notified may come in and defend and that if the person notified does not do so that person will be bound in any action against that person by the lessee by any determination of fact common to the two litigations, then unless the person notified after seasonable receipt of the notice does come in and defend that person is so bound.

 (b) The lessor or the supplier may demand in writing that the lessee turn over control of the litigation including settlement if the claim is one for infringement or the like (Section 2A–211) or else be barred from any remedy over. If the demand states that the lessor or the supplier agrees to bear all expense and to satisfy any adverse judgment, then unless the lessee after seasonable receipt of the demand does turn over control the lessee is so barred.

(5) Subsections (3) and (4) apply to any obligation of a lessee to hold the lessor or the supplier harmless against infringement or the like (Section 2A–211).

As amended in 1990.

§ 2A–517. Revocation of Acceptance of Goods.

(1) A lessee may revoke acceptance of a lot or commercial unit whose nonconformity substantially impairs its value to the lessee if the lessee has accepted it:

 (a) except in the case of a finance lease, on the reasonable assumption that its nonconformity would be cured and it has not been seasonally cured; or

 (b) without discovery of the nonconformity if the lessee's acceptance was reasonably induced either by the lessor's assurances or, except in the case of a finance lease, by the difficulty of discovery before acceptance.

(2) Except in the case of a finance lease that is not a consumer lease, a lessee may revoke acceptance of a lot or commercial unit if the lessor defaults under the lease contract and the default substantially impairs the value of that lot or commercial unit to the lessee.

(3) If the lease agreement so provides, the lessee may revoke acceptance of a lot or commercial unit because of other defaults by the lessor.

(4) Revocation of acceptance must occur within a reasonable time after the lessee discovers or should have discovered the ground for it and before any substantial change in condition of the goods which is not caused by the nonconformity. Revocation is not effective until the lessee notifies the lessor.

(5) A lessee who so revokes has the same rights and duties with regard to the goods involved as if the lessee had rejected them.

As amended in 1990.

§ 2A–518. Cover; Substitute Goods.

(1) After a default by a lessor under the lease contract of the type described in Section 2A–508(1) , or, if agreed, after other default by the lessor, the lessee may cover by making any purchase or lease of or contract to purchase or lease goods in substitution for those due from the lessor.

(2) Except as otherwise provided with respect to damages liquidated in the lease agreement (Section 2A–504) or otherwise determined pursuant to agreement of the parties (Sections 1–102(3) and 2A–503), if a lessee's cover is by a lease agreement substantially similar to the original lease agreement and the new lease agreement is made in good faith and in a commercially reasonable manner, the lessee may recover from the lessor as damages (i) the present value, as of the date of the commencement of the term of the new lease agreement, of the rent under the new lease agreement applicable to that period of the new lease term which is comparable to the then remaining term of the original lease agreement minus the present value as of the same date of the total rent for the then remaining lease term of the original lease agreement, and (ii) any incidental or consequential damages, less expenses saved in consequence of the lessor's default.

(3) If a lessee's cover is by lease agreement that for any reason does not qualify for treatment under subsection (2), or is by purchase or otherwise, the lessee may recover from the lessor as if the lessee had elected not to cover and Section 2A–519 governs.

As amended in 1990.

§ 2A–519. Lessee's Damages for Nondelivery, Repudiation, Default, and Breach of Warranty in Regard to Accepted Goods.

(1) Except as otherwise provided with respect to damages liquidated in the lease agreement (Section 2A–504) or otherwise determined pursuant to agreement of the parties (Sections 1–102(3) and 2A–503), if a lessee elects not to cover or a lessee elects to cover and the cover is by lease agreement that for any reason does not qualify for treatment under Section 2A–518(2), or is by purchase or otherwise, the measure of damages for nondelivery or repudiation by the lessor or for rejection or revocation of acceptance by the lessee is the present value, as of the date of the default, of the then market rent minus the present value as of the same date of the original rent, computed for the remaining lease term of the original lease agreement, together with incidental and consequential damages, less expenses saved in consequence of the lessor's default.

(2) Market rent is to be determined as of the place for tender or, in cases of rejection after arrival or revocation of acceptance, as of the place of arrival.

(3) Except as otherwise agreed, if the lessee has accepted goods and given notification (Section 2A–516(3)), the measure of damages for nonconforming tender or delivery or other default by a lessor is the loss resulting in the ordinary course of events from the lessor's default as determined in any manner that is reasonable together with incidental and consequential damages, less expenses saved in consequence of the lessor's default.

(4) Except as otherwise agreed, the measure of damages for breach of warranty is the present value at the time and place of acceptance of the difference between the value of the use of the goods accepted and the value if they had been as warranted for the lease term, unless special circumstances show proximate damages of a different amount, together with incidental and consequential damages, less expenses saved in consequence of the lessor's default or breach of warranty.

As amended in 1990.

§ 2A–520. Lessee's Incidental and Consequential Damages.

(1) Incidental damages resulting from a lessor's default include expenses reasonably incurred in inspection,

receipt, transportation, and care and custody of goods rightfully rejected or goods the acceptance of which is justifiably revoked, any commercially reasonable charges, expenses or commissions in connection with effecting cover, and any other reasonable expense incident to the default.

(2) Consequential damages resulting from a lessor's default include:

 (a) any loss resulting from general or particular requirements and needs of which the lessor at the time of contracting had reason to know and which could not reasonably be prevented by cover or otherwise; and

 (b) injury to person or property proximately resulting from any breach of warranty.

§ 2A–521. Lessee's Right to Specific Performance or Replevin.

(1) Specific performance may be decreed if the goods are unique or in other proper circumstances.

(2) A decree for specific performance may include any terms and conditions as to payment of the rent, damages, or other relief that the court deems just.

(3) A lessee has a right of replevin, detinue, sequestration, claim and delivery, or the like for goods identified to the lease contract if after reasonable effort the lessee is unable to effect cover for those goods or the circumstances reasonably indicate that the effort will be unavailing.

§ 2A–522. Lessee's Right to Goods on Lessor's Insolvency.

(1) Subject to subsection (2) and even though the goods have not been shipped, a lessee who has paid a part or all of the rent and security for goods identified to a lease contract (Section 2A–217) on making and keeping good a tender of any unpaid portion of the rent and security due under the lease contract may recover the goods identified from the lessor if the lessor becomes insolvent within 10 days after receipt of the first installment of rent and security.

(2) A lessee acquires the right to recover goods identified to a lease contract only if they conform to the lease contract.

§ 2A–523. Lessor's Remedies.

(1) If a lessee wrongfully rejects or revokes acceptance of goods or fails to make a payment when due or repudiates with respect to a part or the whole, then, with respect to any goods involved, and with respect to all of the goods if under an installment lease contract the value of the whole lease contract is substantially impaired (Section 2A–510), the lessee is in default under the lease contract and the lessor may:

 (a) cancel the lease contract (Section 2A–505(1));

 (b) proceed respecting goods not identified to the lease contract (Section 2A–524);

 (c) withhold delivery of the goods and take possession of goods previously delivered (Section 2A–525);

 (d) stop delivery of the goods by any bailee (Section 2A–526);

 (e) dispose of the goods and recover damages (Section 2A–527), or retain the goods and recover damages (Section 2A–528), or in a proper case recover rent (Section 2A–529);

 (f) exercise any other rights or pursue any other remedies provided in the lease contract.

(2) If a lessor does not fully exercise a right or obtain a remedy to which the lessor is entitled under subsection (1), the lessor may recover the loss resulting in the ordinary course of events from the lessee's default as determined in any reasonable manner, together with incidental damages, less expenses saved in consequence of the lessee's default.

(3) If a lessee is otherwise in default under a lease contract, the lessor may exercise the rights and pursue the remedies provided in the lease contract, which may include a right to cancel the lease. In addition, unless otherwise provided in the lease contract:

 (a) if the default substantially impairs the value of the lease contract to the lessor, the lessor may exercise the rights and pursue the remedies provided in subsections (1) or (2); or

 (b) if the default does not substantially impair the value of the lease contract to the lessor, the lessor may recover as provided in subsection (2).

As amended in 1990.

§ 2A–524. Lessor's Right to Identify Goods to Lease Contract.

(1) After default by the lessee under the lease contract of the type described in Section 2A–523(1) or 2A–523(3)(a) or, if agreed, after other default by the lessee, the lessor may:

 (a) identify to the lease contract conforming goods not already identified if at the time the lessor learned of the default they were in the lessor's or the supplier's possession or control; and

 (b) dispose of goods (Section 2A–527(1)) that demonstrably have been intended for the particular lease contract even though those goods are unfinished.

(2) If the goods are unfinished, in the exercise of reasonable commercial judgment for the purposes of avoiding loss and of effective realization, an aggrieved lessor or the supplier may either complete manufacture and wholly identify the goods to the lease contract or cease

manufacture and lease, sell, or otherwise dispose of the goods for scrap or salvage value or proceed in any other reasonable manner.

As amended in 1990.

§ 2A–525. Lessor's Right to Possession of Goods.

(1) If a lessor discovers the lessee to be insolvent, the lessor may refuse to deliver the goods.

(2) After a default by the lessee under the lease contract of the type described in Section 2A–523(1) or 2A–523(3) (a) or, if agreed, after other default by the lessee, the lessor has the right to take possession of the goods. If the lease contract so provides, the lessor may require the lessee to assemble the goods and make them available to the lessor at a place to be designated by the lessor which is reasonably convenient to both parties. Without removal, the lessor may render unusable any goods employed in trade or business, and may dispose of goods on the lessee's premises (Section 2A–527).

(3) The lessor may proceed under subsection (2) without judicial process if it can be done without breach of the peace or the lessor may proceed by action.

As amended in 1990.

§ 2A–526. Lessor's Stoppage of Delivery in Transit or Otherwise.

(1) A lessor may stop delivery of goods in the possession of a carrier or other bailee if the lessor discovers the lessee to be insolvent and may stop delivery of carload, truckload, planeload, or larger shipments of express or freight if the lessee repudiates or fails to make a payment due before delivery, whether for rent, security or otherwise under the lease contract, or for any other reason the lessor has a right to withhold or take possession of the goods.

(2) In pursuing its remedies under subsection (1), the lessor may stop delivery until

 (a) receipt of the goods by the lessee;

 (b) acknowledgment to the lessee by any bailee of the goods, except a carrier, that the bailee holds the goods for the lessee; or

 (c) such an acknowledgment to the lessee by a carrier via reshipment or as warehouseman.

(3) **(a)** To stop delivery, a lessor shall so notify as to enable the bailee by reasonable diligence to prevent delivery of the goods.

 (b) After notification, the bailee shall hold and deliver the goods according to the directions of the lessor, but the lessor is liable to the bailee for any ensuing charges or damages.

 (c) A carrier who has issued a nonnegotiable bill of lading is not obliged to obey a notification to stop received from a person other than the consignor.

§ 2A–527. Lessor's Rights to Dispose of Goods.

(1) After a default by a lessee under the lease contract of the type described in Section 2A–523(1) or 2A–523(3) (a) or after the lessor refuses to deliver or takes possession of goods (Section 2A–525 or 2A–526), or, if agreed, after other default by a lessee, the lessor may dispose of the goods concerned or the undelivered balance thereof by lease, sale, or otherwise.

(2) Except as otherwise provided with respect to damages liquidated in the lease agreement (Section 2A–504) or otherwise determined pursuant to agreement of the parties (Sections 1–102(3) and 2A–503), if the disposition is by lease agreement substantially similar to the original lease agreement and the new lease agreement is made in good faith and in a commercially reasonable manner, the lessor may recover from the lessee as damages (i) accrued and unpaid rent as of the date of the commencement of the term of the new lease agreement, (ii) the present value, as of the same date, of the total rent for the then remaining lease term of the original lease agreement minus the present value, as of the same date, of the rent under the new lease agreement applicable to that period of the new lease term which is comparable to the then remaining term of the original lease agreement, and (iii) any incidental damages allowed under Section 2A–530, less expenses saved in consequence of the lessee's default.

(3) If the lessor's disposition is by lease agreement that for any reason does not qualify for treatment under subsection (2), or is by sale or otherwise, the lessor may recover from the lessee as if the lessor had elected not to dispose of the goods and Section 2A–528 governs.

(4) A subsequent buyer or lessee who buys or leases from the lessor in good faith for value as a result of a disposition under this section takes the goods free of the original lease contract and any rights of the original lessee even though the lessor fails to comply with one or more of the requirements of this Article.

(5) The lessor is not accountable to the lessee for any profit made on any disposition. A lessee who has rightfully rejected or justifiably revoked acceptance shall account to the lessor for any excess over the amount of the lessee's security interest (Section 2A–508(5)).

As amended in 1990.

§ 2A–528. Lessor's Damages for Nonacceptance, Failure to Pay, Repudiation, or Other Default.

(1) Except as otherwise provided with respect to damages liquidated in the lease agreement (Section 2A–504) or otherwise determined pursuant to agreement of the parties (Sections 1–102(3) and 2A–503), if a lessor elects to retain the goods or a lessor elects to dispose

of the goods and the disposition is by lease agreement that for any reason does not qualify for treatment under Section 2A–527(2), or is by sale or otherwise, the lessor may recover from the lessee as damages for a default of the type described in Section 2A–523(1) or 2A–523(3) (a), or, if agreed, for other default of the lessee, (i) accrued and unpaid rent as of the date of default if the lessee has never taken possession of the goods, or, if the lessee has taken possession of the goods, as of the date the lessor repossesses the goods or an earlier date on which the lessee makes a tender of the goods to the lessor, (ii) the present value as of the date determined under clause (i) of the total rent for the then remaining lease term of the original lease agreement minus the present value as of the same date of the market rent at the place where the goods are located computed for the same lease term, and (iii) any incidental damages allowed under Section 2A–530, less expenses saved in consequence of the lessee's default.

(2) If the measure of damages provided in subsection (1) is inadequate to put a lessor in as good a position as performance would have, the measure of damages is the present value of the profit, including reasonable overhead, the lessor would have made from full performance by the lessee, together with any incidental damages allowed under Section 2A–530, due allowance for costs reasonably incurred and due credit for payments or proceeds of disposition.

As amended in 1990.

§ 2A–529. Lessor's Action for the Rent.

(1) After default by the lessee under the lease contract of the type described in Section 2A–523(1) or 2A–523(3) (a) or, if agreed, after other default by the lessee, if the lessor complies with subsection (2), the lessor may recover from the lessee as damages:

(a) for goods accepted by the lessee and not repossessed by or tendered to the lessor, and for conforming goods lost or damaged within a commercially reasonable time after risk of loss passes to the lessee (Section 2A–219), (i) accrued and unpaid rent as of the date of entry of judgment in favor of the lessor, (ii) the present value as of the same date of the rent for the then remaining lease term of the lease agreement, and (iii) any incidental damages allowed under Section 2A–530, less expenses saved in consequence of the lessee's default; and

(b) for goods identified to the lease contract if the lessor is unable after reasonable effort to dispose of them at a reasonable price or the circumstances reasonably indicate that effort will be unavailing, (i) accrued and unpaid rent as of the date of entry of judgment in favor of the lessor, (ii) the present

value as of the same date of the rent for the then remaining lease term of the lease agreement, and (iii) any incidental damages allowed under Section 2A–530, less expenses saved in consequence of the lessee's default.

(2) Except as provided in subsection (3), the lessor shall hold for the lessee for the remaining lease term of the lease agreement any goods that have been identified to the lease contract and are in the lessor's control.

(3) The lessor may dispose of the goods at any time before collection of the judgment for damages obtained pursuant to subsection (1). If the disposition is before the end of the remaining lease term of the lease agreement, the lessor's recovery against the lessee for damages is governed by Section 2A–527 or Section 2A–528, and the lessor will cause an appropriate credit to be provided against a judgment for damages to the extent that the amount of the judgment exceeds the recovery available pursuant to Section 2A–527 or 2A–528.

(4) Payment of the judgment for damages obtained pursuant to subsection (1) entitles the lessee to the use and possession of the goods not then disposed of for the remaining lease term of and in accordance with the lease agreement.

(5) After default by the lessee under the lease contract of the type described in Section 2A–523(1) or Section 2A–523(3) (a) or, if agreed, after other default by the lessee, a lessor who is held not entitled to rent under this section must nevertheless be awarded damages for nonacceptance under Section 2A–527 or Section 2A–528.

As amended in 1990.

§ 2A–530. Lessor's Incidental Damages.

Incidental damages to an aggrieved lessor include any commercially reasonable charges, expenses, or commissions incurred in stopping delivery, in the transportation, care and custody of goods after the lessee's default, in connection with return or disposition of the goods, or otherwise resulting from the default.

§ 2A–531. Standing to Sue Third Parties for Injury to Goods.

(1) If a third party so deals with goods that have been identified to a lease contract as to cause actionable injury to a party to the lease contract (a) the lessor has a right of action against the third party, and (b) the lessee also has a right of action against the third party if the lessee:

(i) has a security interest in the goods;

(ii) has an insurable interest in the goods; or

(iii) bears the risk of loss under the lease contract or has since the injury assumed that risk as against the lessor and the goods have been converted or destroyed.

(2) If at the time of the injury the party plaintiff did not bear the risk of loss as against the other party to the lease contract and there is no arrangement between them for disposition of the recovery, his [or her] suit or settlement, subject to his [or her] own interest, is as a fiduciary for the other party to the lease contract.

(3) Either party with the consent of the other may sue for the benefit of whom it may concern.

§ 2A–532. Lessor's Rights to Residual Interest. In addition to any other recovery permitted by this Article or other law, the lessor may recover from the lessee an amount that will fully compensate the lessor for any loss of or damage to the lessor's residual interest in the goods caused by the default of the lessee.

As added in 1990.

Sarbanes-Oxley Act of 2002

Note: **Only some sections are represented in this appendix. The full act can be found as a link on the text's Website at www.mhhe.com/kubasekess2e.**

Section 1. Short Title

(a) Short Title. This Act may be cited as the "Sarbanes-Oxley Act of 2002."

Title I—Public Company Accounting Oversight Board

Title II—Auditor Independence

Title III— Corporate Responsibility

Title IV—Enhanced Financial Disclosures

Title V—Analyst Conflicts of Interest

Title VI—Commission Resources and Authority

Title VII—Studies and Reports

Sec. 302. Corporate Responsibility for Financial Reports.

(a) **Regulations Required.** The Commission shall, by rule, require, for each company filing periodic reports under section 13(a) or 15(d) of the Securities Exchange Act of 1934 (15 U.S.C. 78m, 78o(d)), that the principal executive officer or officers and the principal financial officer or officers, or persons performing similar functions, certify in each annual or quarterly report filed or submitted under either such section of such Act that—

(1) the signing officer has reviewed the report;

(2) based on the officer's knowledge, the report does not contain any untrue statement of a material fact or omit to state a material fact necessary in order to make the statements made, in light of the circumstances under which such statements were made, not misleading;

(3) based on such officer's knowledge, the financial statements, and other financial information included in the report, fairly present in all material respects the financial condition and results of operations of the issuer as of, and for, the periods presented in the report;

(4) the signing officers—

 (A) are responsible for establishing and maintaining internal controls;

 (B) have designed such internal controls to ensure that material information relating to the issuer and its consolidated subsidiaries is made known to such officers by others within those entities, particularly during the period in which the periodic reports are being prepared;

 (C) have evaluated the effectiveness of the issuer's internal controls as of a date within 90 days prior to the report; and

 (D) have presented in the report their conclusions about the effectiveness of their internal controls based on their evaluation as of that date;

(5) the signing officers have disclosed to the issuer's auditors and the audit committee of the board of directors (or persons fulfilling the equivalent function)—

 (A) all significant deficiencies in the design or operation of internal controls which could adversely affect the issuer's ability to record, process, summarize, and report financial data and have identified for the issuer's auditors any material weaknesses in internal controls; and

 (B) any fraud, whether or not material, that involves management or other employees who have a significant role in the issuer's internal controls; and

(6) the signing officers have indicated in the report whether or not there were significant changes in internal controls or in other factors that could significantly affect internal controls subsequent to the date of their evaluation, including any corrective actions with regard to significant deficiencies and material weaknesses.

(b) Foreign Reincorporations Have No Effect. Nothing in this section 302 shall be interpreted or applied in any way to allow any issuer to lessen the legal force of the statement required under this section 302, by an issuer having reincorporated or having engaged in any other transaction that resulted in the transfer of the corporate domicile or offices of the issuer from inside the United States to outside of the United States.

(c) Deadline. The rules required by subsection (a) shall be effective not later than 30 days after the date of enactment of this Act.

Sec. 306. Insider Trades during Pension Fund Blackout Periods.

(a) Prohibition of Insider Trading during Pension Fund Blackout Periods.

(1) IN GENERAL—Except to the extent otherwise provided by rule of the Commission pursuant to paragraph (3), it shall be unlawful for any director or executive officer of an issuer of any equity security (other than an exempted security), directly or indirectly, to purchase, sell, or otherwise acquire or transfer any equity security of the issuer (other than an exempted security) during any blackout period with respect to such equity security if such director or officer acquires such equity security in connection with his or her service or employment as a director or executive officer.

(2) REMEDY—

(A) IN GENERAL—Any profit realized by a director or executive officer referred to in paragraph (1) from any purchase, sale, or other acquisition or transfer in violation of this subsection shall inure to and be recoverable by the issuer, irrespective of any intention on the part of such director or executive officer in entering into the transaction.

(B) ACTIONS TO RECOVER PROFITS—An action to recover profits in accordance with this subsection may be instituted at law or in equity in any court of competent jurisdiction by the issuer, or by the owner of any security of the issuer in the name and in behalf of the issuer if the issuer fails or refuses to bring such action within 60 days after the date of request, or fails diligently to prosecute the action thereafter, except that no such suit shall be brought more than 2 years after the date on which such profit was realized.

(3) RULEMAKING AUTHORIZED—The Commission shall, in consultation with the Secretary of Labor, issue rules to clarify the application of this subsection and to prevent evasion thereof. Such rules shall provide for the application of the requirements of paragraph (1) with respect to entities treated as a single employer with respect to an issuer under section 414(b), (c), (m), or (o) of the Internal Revenue Code of 1986 to the extent necessary to clarify the application of such requirements and to prevent evasion thereof. Such rules may also provide for appropriate exceptions from the requirements of this subsection, including exceptions for purchases pursuant to an automatic dividend reinvestment program or purchases or sales made pursuant to an advance election.

(4) BLACKOUT PERIOD—For purposes of this subsection, the term "blackout period," with respect to the equity securities of any issuer—

(A) means any period of more than 3 consecutive business days during which the ability of not fewer than 50 percent of the participants or beneficiaries under all individual account plans maintained by the issuer to purchase, sell, or otherwise acquire or transfer an interest in any equity of such issuer held in such an individual account plan is temporarily suspended by the issuer or by a fiduciary of the plan; and

(B) does not include, under regulations which shall be prescribed by the Commission—

(i) a regularly scheduled period in which the participants and beneficiaries may not purchase, sell, or otherwise acquire or transfer an interest in any equity of such issuer, if such period is—

(I) incorporated into the individual account plan; and

(II) timely disclosed to employees before becoming participants under the individual account plan or as a subsequent amendment to the plan; or

(ii) any suspension described in subparagraph (A) that is imposed solely in connection with persons becoming participants or beneficiaries, or ceasing to be participants or beneficiaries, in an individual account plan by reason of a corporate merger, acquisition, divestiture, or similar transaction involving the plan or plan sponsor.

(5) INDIVIDUAL ACCOUNT PLAN—For purposes of this subsection, the term "individual account plan" has the meaning provided in section 3(34) of the Employee Retirement Income Security Act of 1974 (29 U.S.C. 1002(34), except that such term shall not

include a one-participant retirement plan (within the meaning of section 101(i)(8)(B) of such Act (29 U.S.C. 1021(i)(8)(B))).

(6) NOTICE TO DIRECTORS, EXECUTIVE OFFICERS, AND THE COMMISSION—In any case in which a director or executive officer is subject to the requirements of this subsection in connection with a blackout period (as defined in paragraph (4)) with respect to any equity securities, the issuer of such equity securities shall timely notify such director or officer and the Securities and Exchange Commission of such blackout period.

(b) Notice Requirements to Participants and Beneficiaries under ERISA.

(1) IN GENERAL—Section 101 of the Employee Retirement Income Security Act of 1974 (29 U.S.C. 1021) is amended by redesignating the second subsection (h) as subsection (j), and by inserting after the first subsection (h) the following new subsection:

(i) Notice of Blackout Periods to Participant or Beneficiary under Individual Account Plan.

"**(1)** DUTIES OF PLAN ADMINISTRATOR—In advance of the commencement of any blackout period with respect to an individual account plan, the plan administrator shall notify the plan participants and beneficiaries who are affected by such action in accordance with this subsection.

"**(2)** NOTICE REQUIREMENTS—

"**(A)** IN GENERAL—The notices described in paragraph (1) shall be written in a manner calculated to be understood by the average plan participant and shall include—

"**(i)** the reasons for the blackout period,

"**(ii)** an identification of the investments and other rights affected,

"**(iii)** the expected beginning date and length of the blackout period,

"**(iv)** in the case of investments affected, a statement that the participant or beneficiary should evaluate the appropriateness of their current investment decisions in light of their inability to direct or diversify assets credited to their accounts during the blackout period, and

"**(v)** such other matters as the Secretary may require by regulation.

"**(B)** NOTICE TO PARTICIPANTS AND BENEFICIARIES—Except as otherwise provided in this subsection, notices described in paragraph (1) shall be furnished to all participants and beneficiaries under the plan to whom the blackout period

applies at least 30 days in advance of the blackout period.

"**(C)** EXCEPTION TO 30-DAY NOTICE REQUIREMENT—In any case in which—

"**(i)** a deferral of the blackout period would violate the requirements of subparagraph (A) or (B) of section 404(a)(1), and a fiduciary of the plan reasonably so determines in writing, or

"**(ii)** the inability to provide the 30-day advance notice is due to events that were unforeseeable or circumstances beyond the reasonable control of the plan administrator, and a fiduciary of the plan reasonably so determines in writing, subparagraph (B) shall not apply, and the notice shall be furnished to all participants and beneficiaries under the plan to whom the blackout period applies as soon as reasonably possible under the circumstances unless such a notice in advance of the termination of the blackout period is impracticable.

"**(D)** WRITTEN NOTICE—The notice required to be provided under this subsection shall be in writing, except that such notice may be in electronic or other form to the extent that such form is reasonably accessible to the recipient.

"**(E)** NOTICE TO ISSUERS OF EMPLOYER SECURITIES SUBJECT TO BLACKOUT PERIOD—In the case of any blackout period in connection with an individual account plan, the plan administrator shall provide timely notice of such blackout period to the issuer of any employer securities subject to such blackout period.

"**(3)** EXCEPTION FOR BLACKOUT PERIODS WITH LIMITED APPLICABILITY—In any case in which the blackout period applies only to 1 or more participants or beneficiaries in connection with a merger, acquisition, divestiture, or similar transaction involving the plan or plan sponsor and occurs solely in connection with becoming or ceasing to be a participant or beneficiary under the plan by reason of such merger, acquisition, divestiture, or transaction, the requirement of this subsection that the notice be provided to all participants and beneficiaries shall be treated as met if the notice required under paragraph (1) is provided to such participants or beneficiaries to whom the blackout period applies as soon as reasonably practicable.

"**(4)** CHANGES IN LENGTH OF BLACKOUT PERIOD—If, following the furnishing of the notice pursuant to this subsection, there is a change in the beginning date or length of the blackout period (specified in such notice pursuant to paragraph (2)(A)(iii)),

the administrator shall provide affected participants and beneficiaries notice of the change as soon as reasonably practicable. In relation to the extended blackout period, such notice shall meet the requirements of paragraph (2)(D) and shall specify any material change in the matters referred to in clauses (i) through (v) of paragraph (2)(A).

"**(5)** REGULATORY EXCEPTIONS—The Secretary may provide by regulation for additional exceptions to the requirements of this subsection which the Secretary determines are in the interests of participants and beneficiaries.

"**(6)** GUIDANCE AND MODEL NOTICES—The Secretary shall issue guidance and model notices which meet the requirements of this subsection.

"**(7)** BLACKOUT PERIOD—For purposes of this subsection—

"**(A)** IN GENERAL—The term 'blackout period' means, in connection with an individual account plan, any period for which any ability of participants or beneficiaries under the plan, which is otherwise available under the terms of such plan, to direct or diversify assets credited to their accounts, to obtain loans from the plan, or to obtain distributions from the plan is temporarily suspended, limited, or restricted, if such suspension, limitation, or restriction is for any period of more than 3 consecutive business days.

"**(B)** EXCLUSIONS—The term 'blackout period' does not include a suspension, limitation, or restriction—

"**(i)** which occurs by reason of the application of the securities laws (as defined in section 3(a)(47) of the Securities Exchange Act of 1934),

"**(ii)** which is a change to the plan which provides for a regularly scheduled suspension, limitation, or restriction which is disclosed to participants or beneficiaries through any summary of material modifications, any materials describing specific investment alternatives under the plan, or any changes thereto, or

"**(iii)** which applies only to 1 or more individuals, each of whom is the participant, an alternate payee (as defined in section 206(d)(3)(K)), or any other beneficiary pursuant to a qualified domestic relations order (as defined in section 206(d)(3)(B)(i)).

"**(8)** INDIVIDUAL ACCOUNT PLAN—

"**(A)** IN GENERAL—For purposes of this subsection, the term 'individual account plan' shall have the meaning provided such term in section 3(34), except that such term shall not include a one-participant retirement plan.

"**(B)** ONE-PARTICIPANT RETIREMENT PLAN—For purposes of subparagraph (A), the term 'one-participant retirement plan' means a retirement plan that—

"**(i)** on the first day of the plan year—

"**(I)** covered only the employer (and the employer's spouse) and the employer owned the entire business (whether or not incorporated), or

"**(II)** covered only one or more partners (and their spouses) in a business partnership (including partners in an S or C corporation (as defined in section 1361(a) of the Internal Revenue Code of 1986)),

"**(ii)** meets the minimum coverage requirements of section 410(b) of the Internal Revenue Code of 1986 (as in effect on the date of the enactment of this paragraph) without being combined with any other plan of the business that covers the employees of the business,

"**(iii)** does not provide benefits to anyone except the employer (and the employer's spouse) or the partners (and their spouses),

"**(iv)** does not cover a business that is a member of an affiliated service group, a controlled group of corporations, or a group of businesses under common control, and

"**(v)** does not cover a business that leases employees."

(2) ISSUANCE OF INITIAL GUIDANCE AND MODEL NOTICE—The Secretary of Labor shall issue initial guidance and a model notice pursuant to section 101(i)(6) of the Employee Retirement Income Security Act of 1974 (as added by this subsection) not later than January 1, 2003. Not later than 75 days after the date of the enactment of this Act, the Secretary shall promulgate interim final rules necessary to carry out the amendments made by this subsection.

(3) CIVIL PENALTIES FOR FAILURE TO PROVIDE NOTICE—Section 502 of such Act (29 U.S.C. 1132) is amended—

(A) in subsection (a)(6), by striking "(5), or (6)" and inserting "(5), (6), or (7)";

(B) by redesignating paragraph (7) of subsection (c) as paragraph (8); and

(C) by inserting after paragraph (6) of subsection (c) the following new paragraph:

"**(7)** The Secretary may assess a civil penalty against a plan administrator of up to $100 a day from the date of the plan administrator's failure or refusal to provide notice to participants and beneficiaries in accordance with section 101(i). For purposes of this paragraph, each violation with respect to any single participant or beneficiary shall be treated as a separate violation."

(3) PLAN AMENDMENTS—If any amendment made by this subsection requires an amendment to any plan, such plan amendment shall not be required to be made before the first plan year beginning on or after the effective date of this section, if—

 (A) during the period after such amendment made by this subsection takes effect and before such first plan year, the plan is operated in good faith compliance with the requirements of such amendment made by this subsection, and

 (B) such plan amendment applies retroactively to the period after such amendment made by this subsection takes effect and before such first plan year.

(c) EFFECTIVE DATE—The provisions of this section (including the amendments made thereby) shall take effect 180 days after the date of the enactment of this Act. Good faith compliance with the requirements of such provisions in advance of the issuance of applicable regulations thereunder shall be treated as compliance with such provisions.

Sec. 402. Enhanced Conflict of Interest Provisions.

(a) Prohibition on Personal Loans to Executives. Section 13 of the Securities Exchange Act of 1934 (15 U.S.C. 78m), as amended by this Act, is amended by adding at the end the following:

"(k) Prohibition on Personal Loans to Executives.

"**(1)** IN GENERAL—It shall be unlawful for any issuer (as defined in section 2 of the Sarbanes-Oxley Act of 2002), directly or indirectly, including through any subsidiary, to extend or maintain credit, to arrange for the extension of credit, or to renew an extension of credit, in the form of a personal loan to or for any director or executive officer (or equivalent thereof) of that issuer. An extension of credit maintained by the issuer on the date of enactment of this subsection shall not be subject to the provisions of this subsection, provided that there is no material modification

to any term of any such extension of credit or any renewal of any such extension of credit on or after that date of enactment.

"**(2)** LIMITATION—Paragraph (1) does not preclude any home improvement and manufactured home loans (as that term is defined in section 5 of the Home Owners' Loan Act (12 U.S.C. 1464)), consumer credit (as defined in section 103 of the Truth in Lending Act (15 U.S.C. 1602)), or any extension of credit under an open end credit plan (as defined in section 103 of the Truth in Lending Act (15 U.S.C. 1602)), or a charge card (as defined in section 127(c)(4)(e) of the Truth in Lending Act (15 U.S.C. 1637(c)(4)(e)), or any extension of credit by a broker or dealer registered under section 15 of this title to an employee of that broker or dealer to buy, trade, or carry securities, that is permitted under rules or regulations of the Board of Governors of the Federal Reserve System pursuant to section 7 of this title (other than an extension of credit that would be used to purchase the stock of that issuer), that is—

 "**(A)** made or provided in the ordinary course of the consumer credit business of such issuer;

 "**(B)** of a type that is generally made available by such issuer to the public; and

 "**(C)** made by such issuer on market terms, or terms that are no more favorable than those offered by the issuer to the general public for such extensions of credit.

"**(3)** Rule of Construction for Certain Loans—Paragraph (1) does not apply to any loan made or maintained by an insured depository institution (as defined in section 3 of the Federal Deposit Insurance Act (12 U.S.C. 1813)), if the loan is subject to the insider lending restrictions of section 22(h) of the Federal Reserve Act (12 U.S.C. 375b)."

Sec. 403. Disclosures of Transactions Involving Management and Principal Stockholders.

(a) Amendment. Section 16 of the Securities Exchange Act of 1934 (15 U.S.C. 78p) is amended by striking the heading of such section and subsection (a) and inserting the following:

"Sec. 16. Directors, Officers, and Principal Stockholders.
"(a) Disclosures Required.

"**(1)** DIRECTORS, OFFICERS, AND PRINCIPAL STOCKHOLDERS REQUIRED TO FILE—Every person who is directly or indirectly the beneficial

owner of more than 10 percent of any class of any equity security (other than an exempted security) which is registered pursuant to section 12, or who is a director or an officer of the issuer of such security, shall file the statements required by this subsection with the Commission (and, if such security is registered on a national securities exchange, also with the exchange).

"(2) TIME OF FILING—The statements required by this subsection shall be filed—

"(A) at the time of the registration of such security on a national securities exchange or by the effective date of a registration statement filed pursuant to section 12(g);

"(B) within 10 days after he or she becomes such beneficial owner, director, or officer;

"(C) if there has been a change in such ownership, or if such person shall have purchased or sold a security-based swap agreement (as defined in section 206(b) of the Gramm-Leach-Bliley Act (15 U.S.C. 78c note)) involving such equity security, before the end of the second business day following the day on which the subject transaction has been executed, or at such other time as the Commission shall establish, by rule, in any case in which the Commission determines that such 2-day period is not feasible.

"(3) CONTENTS OF STATEMENTS—A statement filed—

"(A) under subparagraph (A) or (B) of paragraph (2) shall contain a statement of the amount of all equity securities of such issuer of which the filing person is the beneficial owner; and

"(B) under subparagraph (C) of such paragraph shall indicate ownership by the filing person at the date of filing, any such changes in such ownership, and such purchases and sales of the security-based swap agreements as have occurred since the most recent such filing under such subparagraph.

"(4) ELECTRONIC FILING AND AVAILABILITY— Beginning not later than 1 year after the date of enactment of the Sarbanes-Oxley Act of 2002—

"(A) a statement filed under subparagraph (C) of paragraph (2) shall be filed electronically;

"(B) the Commission shall provide each such statement on a publicly accessible Internet site not later than the end of the business day following that filing; and

"(C) the issuer (if the issuer maintains a corporate website) shall provide that statement on that corporate website, not later than the end of the business day following that filing."

(b) Effective Date. The amendment made by this section shall be effective 30 days after the date of the enactment of this Act.

Sec. 404. Management Assessment of Internal Controls.

(a) Rules Required. The Commission shall prescribe rules requiring each annual report required by section 13(a) or 15(d) of the Securities Exchange Act of 1934 (15 U.S.C. 78m or 78o(d)) to contain an internal control report, which shall—

(1) state the responsibility of management for establishing and maintaining an adequate internal control structure and procedures for financial reporting; and

(2) contain an assessment, as of the end of the most recent fiscal year of the issuer, of the effectiveness of the internal control structure and procedures of the issuer for financial reporting.

(b) Internal Control Evaluation and Reporting. With respect to the internal control assessment required by subsection (a), each registered public accounting firm that prepares or issues the audit report for the issuer shall attest to, and report on, the assessment made by the management of the issuer. An attestation made under this subsection shall be made in accordance with standards for attestation engagements issued or adopted by the Board. Any such attestation shall not be the subject of a separate engagement.

Sec. 802. Criminal Penalties for Altering Documents.

(a) In General. Chapter 73 of title 18, United States Code, is amended by adding at the end the following:

"Sec. 1519. Destruction, alteration, or falsification of records in Federal investigations and bankruptcy

"Whoever knowingly alters, destroys, mutilates, conceals, covers up, falsifies, or makes a false entry in any record, document, or tangible object with the intent to impede, obstruct, or influence the investigation or proper administration of any matter within the jurisdiction of any department or agency of the United States or any case filed under title 11, or in relation to or contemplation of any such matter or case, shall be fined under this title, imprisoned not more than 20 years, or both.

"Sec. 1520. Destruction of corporate audit records

"**(a)(1)** Any accountant who conducts an audit of an issuer of securities to which section 10A(a) of the Securities

Exchange Act of 1934 (15 U.S.C. 78j-1(a)) applies, shall maintain all audit or review workpapers for a period of 5 years from the end of the fiscal period in which the audit or review was concluded.

"**(2)** The Securities and Exchange Commission shall promulgate, within 180 days, after adequate notice and an opportunity for comment, such rules and regulations, as are reasonably necessary, relating to the retention of relevant records such as workpapers, documents that form the basis of an audit or review, memoranda, correspondence, communications, other documents, and records (including electronic records) which are created, sent, or received in connection with an audit or review and contain conclusions, opinions, analyses, or financial data relating to such an audit or review, which is conducted by any accountant who conducts an audit of an issuer of securities to which section 10A(a) of the Securities Exchange Act of 1934 (15 U.S.C. 78j-1(a)) applies. The Commission may, from time to time, amend or supplement the rules and regulations that it is required to promulgate under this section, after adequate notice and an opportunity for comment, in order to ensure that such rules and regulations adequately comport with the purposes of this section.

"**(b)** Whoever knowingly and willfully violates subsection (a)(1), or any rule or regulation promulgated by the Securities and Exchange Commission under subsection (a)(2), shall be fined under this title, imprisoned not more than 10 years, or both.

"**(c)** Nothing in this section shall be deemed to diminish or relieve any person of any other duty or obligation imposed by Federal or State law or regulation to maintain, or refrain from destroying, any document."

Sec. 804. Statute of Limitations for Securities Fraud.

(a) In General. Section 1658 of title 28, United States Code, is amended—

(1) by inserting "(a)" before "Except"; and

(2) by adding at the end the following:

"**(b)** Notwithstanding subsection (a), a private right of action that involves a claim of fraud, deceit, manipulation, or contrivance in contravention of a regulatory requirement concerning the securities laws, as defined in section 3(a)(47) of the Securities Exchange Act of 1934 (15 U.S.C. 78c(a)(47)), may be brought not later than the earlier of—

"**(1)** 2 years after the discovery of the facts constituting the violation; or

"**(2)** 5 years after such violation."

(b) Effective Date. The limitations period provided by section 1658(b) of title 28, United States Code, as added by this section, shall apply to all proceedings addressed by this section that are commenced on or after the date of enactment of this Act.

(c) No Creation of Actions. Nothing in this section shall create a new, private right of action.

Sec. 806. Protection for Employees of Publicly Traded Companies Who Provide Evidence of Fraud.

(a) In General. Chapter 73 of title 18, United States Code, is amended by inserting after section 1514 the following:

"**Sec. 1514A. Civil action to protect against retaliation in fraud cases**

"**(a) Whistleblower Protection for Employees of Publicly Traded Companies.** No company with a class of securities registered under section 12 of the Securities Exchange Act of 1934 (15 U.S.C. 78l), or that is required to file reports under section 15(d) of the Securities Exchange Act of 1934 (15 U.S.C. 78o(d)), or any officer, employee, contractor, subcontractor, or agent of such company, may discharge, demote, suspend, threaten, harass, or in any other manner discriminate against an employee in the terms and conditions of employment because of any lawful act done by the employee—

"**(1)** to provide information, cause information to be provided, or otherwise assist in an investigation regarding any conduct which the employee reasonably believes constitutes a violation of section 1341, 1343, 1344, or 1348, any rule or regulation of the Securities and Exchange Commission, or any provision of Federal law relating to fraud against shareholders, when the information or assistance is provided to or the investigation is conducted by—

 "**(A)** a Federal regulatory or law enforcement agency;

 "**(B)** any Member of Congress or any committee of Congress; or

 "**(C)** a person with supervisory authority over the employee (or such other person working for the employer who has the authority to investigate, discover, or terminate misconduct); or

"**(2)** to file, cause to be filed, testify, participate in, or otherwise assist in a proceeding filed or about to be filed (with any knowledge of the employer) relating to an alleged violation of section 1341, 1343, 1344, or 1348, any rule or regulation of the Securities and

Exchange Commission, or any provision of Federal law relating to fraud against shareholders.

"(b) Enforcement Action.

"(1) IN GENERAL—A person who alleges discharge or other discrimination by any person in violation of subsection (a) may seek relief under subsection (c), by—

"(A) filing a complaint with the Secretary of Labor; or

"(B) if the Secretary has not issued a final decision within 180 days of the filing of the complaint and there is no showing that such delay is due to the bad faith of the claimant, bringing an action at law or equity for de novo review in the appropriate district court of the United States, which shall have jurisdiction over such an action without regard to the amount in controversy.

"(2) PROCEDURE—

"(A) IN GENERAL—An action under paragraph (1)(A) shall be governed under the rules and procedures set forth in section 42121(b) of title 49, United States Code.

"(B) EXCEPTION—Notification made under section 42121(b)(1) of title 49, United States Code, shall be made to the person named in the complaint and to the employer.

"(C) BURDENS OF PROOF—An action brought under paragraph (1)(B) shall be governed by the legal burdens of proof set forth in section 42121(b) of title 49, United States Code.

"(D) STATUTE OF LIMITATIONS—An action under paragraph (1) shall be commenced not later than 90 days after the date on which the violation occurs.

"(c) Remedies.

"(1) IN GENERAL—An employee prevailing in any action under subsection (b)(1) shall be entitled to all relief necessary to make the employee whole.

"(2) COMPENSATORY DAMAGES—Relief for any action under paragraph (1) shall include—

"(A) reinstatement with the same seniority status that the employee would have had, but for the discrimination;

"(B) the amount of back pay, with interest; and

"(C) compensation for any special damages sustained as a result of the discrimination, including litigation costs, expert witness fees, and reasonable attorney fees.

"(d) Rights Retained by Employee. Nothing in this section shall be deemed to diminish the rights, privileges, or remedies of any employee under any Federal or State law, or under any collective bargaining agreement."

(b) Clerical Amendment. The table of sections at the beginning of chapter 73 of title 18, United States Code, is amended by inserting after the item relating to section 1514 the following new item:

"1514A. Civil action to protect against retaliation in fraud cases."

Sec. 807. Criminal Penalties for Defrauding Shareholders of Publicly Traded Companies.

(a) In General. Chapter 63 of title 18, United States Code, is amended by adding at the end the following:

"Sec. 1348. Securities fraud

"Whoever knowingly executes, or attempts to execute, a scheme or artifice—

"(1) to defraud any person in connection with any security of an issuer with a class of securities registered under section 12 of the Securities Exchange Act of 1934 (15 U.S.C. 78l) or that is required to file reports under section 15(d) of the Securities Exchange Act of 1934 (15 U.S.C. 78o(d)); or

"(2) to obtain, by means of false or fraudulent pretenses, representations, or promises, any money or property in connection with the purchase or sale of any security of an issuer with a class of securities registered under section 12 of the Securities Exchange Act of 1934 (15 U.S.C. 78l) or that is required to file reports under section 15(d) of the Securities Exchange Act of 1934 (15 U.S.C. 78o(d));

shall be fined under this title, or imprisoned not more than 25 years, or both."

Sec. 906. Corporate Responsibility for Financial Reports.

(a) In General. Chapter 63 of title 18, United States Code, is amended by inserting after section 1349, as created by this Act, the following:

"Sec. 1350. Failure of corporate officers to certify financial reports

"(a) Certification of Periodic Financial Reports. Each periodic report containing financial statements filed by an issuer with the Securities Exchange Commission pursuant to section 13(a) or 15(d) of the Securities Exchange Act of

1934 (15 U.S.C. 78m(a) or 78o(d)) shall be accompanied by a written statement by the chief executive officer and chief financial officer (or equivalent thereof) of the issuer.

"(b) Content. The statement required under subsection (a) shall certify that the periodic report containing the financial statements fully complies with the requirements of section 13(a) or 15(d) of the Securities Exchange Act pf 1934 (15 U.S.C. 78m or 78o(d)) and that information contained in the periodic report fairly presents, in all material respects, the financial condition and results of operations of the issuer.

"(c) Criminal Penalties. Whoever—
"(1) certifies any statement as set forth in subsections (a) and (b) of this section knowing that the periodic report accompanying the statement does not comport with all the requirements set forth in this section shall be fined not more than $1,000,000 or imprisoned not more than 10 years, or both; or

"(2) willfully certifies any statement as set forth in subsections (a) and (b) of this section knowing that the periodic report accompanying the statement does not comport with all the requirements set forth in this section shall be fined not more than $5,000,000, or imprisoned not more than 20 years, or both."

(b) Clerical Amendment. The table of sections at the beginning of chapter 63 of title 18, United States Code, is amended by adding at the end the following:

"1350. Failure of corporate officers to certify financial reports."

Glossary

A

absolute privilege A special right, immunity, permission, or benefit given to certain individuals that allows them to make any statements about someone without being held liable for defamation for any false statement made, regardless of intent or knowledge of the falsity of the claim.

acceptance A key factor in the agreement element of a contract; consists of the agreement of one party, the offeree, to the terms of the offer in the contract made by the other party, the offeror.

acceptor A person (drawee) who accepts and signs a draft to agree to pay the draft when it is presented.

accommodation party A party who signs an instrument to provide credit for another party who has also signed the instrument.

accord and satisfaction An arrangement between contracting parties whereby one of the parties substitutes a different performance for his or her original duty under the contract. The promise to perform the new duty is the *accord*, and the actual performance of that new duty is the *satisfaction*.

accounting A review and listing of all partnership assets and/ or profit.

accredited investor A private investor who is allowed to accept private securities offerings under certain specific guidelines set by the SEC.

actual cause The determination that the defendant's breach of duty resulted directly in the plaintiff's injury.

actual malice In defamation, either a person's knowledge that his or her statement or published material is false or the person's reckless disregard for whether it is false.

actual notice Notice of agency termination that is given by directly informing third parties, either orally or in writing.

actus reus Latin for "guilty act"; a wrongful behavior that is associated with the physical act of a declared crime.

ad substantiation An FTC standard requiring that advertisers have a reasonable basis for the claims made in their ads.

adhesion contract A contract created by a party to an agreement that is presented to the other party on a take-it-or-leave-it basis. Such contracts are legal but are sometimes rescinded on the grounds of unconscionability and the absence of one party's free will to enter a contract.

administrative agency Any government body created by the legislative branch (e.g., Congress, a state legislature, or a city council) to carry out specific duties.

administrative law The collection of rules and decisions made by administrative agencies to fill in particular details missing from constitutions and statutes.

administrative law judge (ALJ) A judge who presides over an administrative hearing; may attempt to get the parties to settle but has the power to issue a binding decision.

Administrative Procedures Act (APA) Federal legislation that places limitations on how agencies are run and contains very specific guidelines on rule making by agencies.

admission A statement made in court, under oath, or at some stage during a legal proceeding in which a party against whom charges have been brought admits that an oral contract existed, even though the contract was required to be in writing.

adverse possession An involuntary property transfer in which a person acquires ownership of property by treating a piece of real property as his or her own, without protest or permission from the owner.

affirm An appellate court decision that accepts a lower court's judgment in a case that has been appealed.

after-acquired property Property acquired by a debtor after the security arrangement is made.

Age Discrimination in Employment Act (ADEA) of 1967 Federal law that prohibits employers from refusing to hire, discharging, or discriminating in terms and conditions of employment on the basis of an employee's or applicant's being age 40 or older.

agency The fiduciary relationship that arises when one person consents to have another act on his behalf and subject to his control and the other consents to do so.

agency by agreement See **expressed agency**.

agency by estoppel See **apparent agency**.

agency by ratification An agency relationship that arises when an individual misrepresents himself or herself as an agent for another party and that party accepts the unauthorized act.

agency coupled with an interest An agency relationship that is created for the benefit of the agent, not the principal.

agency relationship The association between one party and an agent who acts on behalf of that party.

agent A party who has the authority to act on behalf of and bind another party.

agreement One of the four elements necessary for a contract; consists of an offer made by one party, the offeror, and the acceptance of the offer by another party, the offeree.

alien corporation A business that is incorporated in a foreign country.

allonge Accompanying a negotiable instrument, a piece of paper that provides room for an endorsement if no room is available on the instrument itself.

alteration An unauthorized change to an instrument that modifies the obligation of a party to the instrument.

alternative dispute resolution (ADR) The resolution of legal problems through methods other than litigation.

Americans with Disabilities Act (ADA) Federal law that prohibits discrimination against employees and job applicants with disabilities.

answer The response of the defendant to the plaintiff's complaint.

apparent agency An agency relationship created by operation of law when one party, by his actions, causes a third party to believe someone is his agent when that person actually has no authority. Also called *agency by estoppel*.

appellate court A higher court, usually consisting of more than one judge, that reviews the decision and results of a lower court (either a trial court or a lower-level appellate court) when a losing party files for an appeal. Appellate courts do not hold trials but may request additional oral and written arguments from each party; they issue written decisions, which collectively constitute case law or the common law. Also called *court of appellate jurisdiction*.

appraisal right A dissenting shareholder's right to have his or her shares appraised and to receive monetary compensation from the corporation for their value.

arbitration A type of alternative dispute resolution in which disputes are submitted for resolution to private nonofficial persons selected in a manner provided by law or the agreement of the parties.

arraignment The first appearance in court by the defendant, at which the defendant is advised of the pending charges, the right to counsel, and the right to trial by jury and he or she enters a plea to the charge.

arrest The action in which a police officer or a person acting under the law seizes, holds, or takes an individual into custody.

articles of incorporation A document that contains basic information about a corporation and is filed with the state.

articles of partnership The written agreement that creates a partnership.

assault A civil wrong that occurs when one person intentionally and voluntarily places another in fear or apprehension of an immediate, offensive physical harm. Assault does not require actual contact.

assignee In a contract, the party who receives the rights of another party (an assignor) to collect what was contractually agreed on in the original contract.

assignment A contracting party's (an assignor's) transfer of his or her rights to a contract to a third party (an assignee).

assignor In a contract, the party who transfers his or her rights to the contract to a third party (an assignee), giving the assignee the right to collect what was contractually agreed on in the original contract.

assumption of the risk A defense whereby the defendant must prove that the plaintiff voluntarily assumed the risk the defendant caused.

attachment The point at which a creditor becomes the secured party that has a security interest in the collateral.

automatic stay After bankruptcy has been filed, a moratorium during which creditors cannot bring or continue action against the debtor or his or her property.

B

bail A thing of value, such as a money bail bond or any other form of property, that is given to the court to temporarily allow a person's release from jail and to ensure his or her appearance in court.

bait-and-switch advertising A deceptive practice in which a seller advertises a low-priced item, generally unavailable to the consumer, and then pushes the consumer to buy a more expensive item.

Bankruptcy Abuse Prevention and Consumer Protection Act (BAPCPA) of 2005 A renovation in the system of bankruptcy enacted to address increased numbers of bankruptcy filings, significant losses associated with bankruptcy filings, loopholes and incentives that allowed for abuse, and the financial ability of debtors.

bankruptcy estate The assets that are collected from a debtor who files for bankruptcy.

battery A civil wrong that occurs when one person intentionally and voluntarily brings about a nonconsented harmful or offensive contact with a person or something closely associated with him or her. Battery requires an actual contact.

bearer instrument An instrument payable to cash or to whoever is in possession of the instrument.

bench trial A trial before a judge, with the judgment decided by the judge rather than a jury; occurs when the defendant has waived his or her right to a jury trial.

beneficiary A person who can expect to benefit from a relationship.

bilateral contract A promise exchanged for a promise.

binding arbitration clause A contract provision mandating that all disputes arising under the contract must be settled by arbitration.

blank endorsement A payee's or last endorsee's signature on a negotiable instrument.

blue-sky law A law that regulates the offering and sale of purely intrastate securities.

booking After an individual is arrested, the procedure during which the name of the defendant and the alleged crime are recorded in the investigating agency's or police department's records.

bounty payment A government reward for an act that is beneficial to the public.

bribery A corrupt and illegal activity in which a person offers, gives, solicits, or receives money, services, or anything of value in order to gain an illicit advantage.

brief A written legal argument, which a party presents to a court, that explains why that party to the case should prevail.

burden of proof The duty of the plaintiff or prosecution to establish a claim or allegation by admissible evidence and to prove that the defendant committed all the essential elements of the crime to the jury's or court's satisfaction beyond any reasonable doubt, in order to convict the defendant.

business ethics The use of ethics and ethical principles to solve business dilemmas.

business law The enforceable rules of conduct that govern the actions of buyers and sellers in market exchanges.

business trust A business organization governed by a group of trustees, who operate the trust for beneficiaries.

buyer in the ordinary course of business A person who routinely buys goods in good faith from a person who routinely sells such goods.

bylaws Rules and regulations that govern a corporation's internal management.

C

capacity The legal ability to enter into a binding contract.

case law The collection of legal interpretations made by judges. They are considered to be law unless otherwise revoked by a statutory law. Also known as *common law*.

case or controversy A term used in the U.S. Constitution to describe the structure and requirements of conflicting claims of individuals that can be brought before a federal court for resolution. A case or controversy requires an actual dispute between parties over their legal rights that remains in conflict at the time the case is presented and that is a proper matter for judicial determination. Also referred to as *justifiable controversy*.

cash tender offer A type of takeover in which the aggressor corporation offers to pay the target shareholders cash for their stock.

cashier's check A check for which both drawer and drawee are the same bank.

cease-and-desist order An FTC order requiring that a company stop its illegal behavior.

certificate of deposit A document whereby a bank promises to pay a payee a certain amount of money at a future time.

certificate of incorporation A document certifying that a corporation is incorporated in the state and is authorized to conduct business.

certificate of limited partnership A document signed on the formation of a limited partnership and filed with the secretary of state.

certified check A check that is accepted by the bank from which the funds are drawn.

chain-style business operation A type of franchise in which the franchise operates under the franchisor's business name and is required to follow the franchisor's standards and methods of business operation.

charging order An order that entitles a creditor to collect a partner's profits.

chattel paper A writing that indicates both a monetary obligation and a security interest in specific goods.

check A special draft that orders a bank (the drawee) to pay a specified sum of money to the payee from the drawer's account.

civil law The body of laws that govern the rights and responsibilities either between persons or between persons and their government.

closely held corporation A corporation that does not sell stock to the general public.

collateral The property that is subject to a secured interest.

collective bargaining The process whereby workers organize collectively and bargain with employers regarding the workplace.

commerce clause Clause 3 of Article I, Section 8, of the U.S. Constitution, which authorizes Congress to "regulate Commerce with foreign Nations, and among the several States, and with the Indian Tribes."

commercial reasonableness Reasonable commercial standards of fair dealing, required of merchants in addition to honesty in fact.

commercial speech Speech made by businesses about commercial matters, such as the sale of goods and services. It is protected by the First Amendment.

common-carrier delivery contract A type of contract in which purchased goods are delivered to the buyer via an independent contractor, such as a trucking line.

common law See **case law**.

common stock Corporate stock that does not convey any preferences to its holders.

compensatory damages Money awarded to a plaintiff as reimbursement for her or his losses; based on the amount of actual damage or harm to property, lost wages or profits, pain and suffering, medical expenses, disability, etc.

complaint A formal written document that begins a civil lawsuit; contains the plaintiff's list of allegations against the defendant, along with the damages the plaintiff seeks.

complete performance Contract performance that occurs when all aspects of the parties' duties under the contract are carried out perfectly.

computer crime Crime committed using a computer.

concealment The active hiding of the truth about a material fact.

concurrent conditions In a contract, terms under which each party's performance is conditioned on the performance of the other; occur only when the parties are required to perform for each other simultaneously.

condemnation The legal process by which a transfer of property is made against the protest of the property owner.

condition precedent In a contract, an event that must occur in order for a party's duty to arise.

condition subsequent In a contract, a future event that terminates the obligations of the parties when it occurs.

conditional contract A contract that becomes enforceable only on the happening or termination of a specified condition.

conditional estate An ownership interest in which the holder has the same interest as that in a fee simple absolute except that this interest is subject to a condition.

conditional privilege A special right, immunity, permission, or benefit given to certain individuals that allows them to make any statements about someone without being held liable for defamation for any false statement made without actual malice.

conditional sales contract A type of contract in which the sale itself is contingent on approval; can be either a sale-on-approval contract or a sale-or-return contract.

conforming goods Goods that conform to contract specifications.

consent order A statement in which a company agrees to stop disputed behavior but does not admit that it broke the law.

consequential damages In a contract, foreseeable damages that result from special facts and circumstances arising outside the contract itself. The damages must be within the

contemplation of the parties at the time the breach occurs. Also called *special damages*.

consideration The bargained-for exchange; what each party gets in exchange for his or her promise under a contract.

Consolidated Omnibus Budget Reconciliation Act (COBRA) Federal law that ensures that when employees lose their jobs or have their hours reduced to a level at which they would not be eligible to receive medical, dental, or optical benefits from their employer, the employees will be able to continue receiving benefits under the employer's policy for up to 18 months by paying the premiums for the policy.

consolidation A combination of two or more corporations in which the combining corporations cease to exist and a new corporation is formed.

constitutional law The general limits and powers of a government as interpreted from its written constitution.

constructive notice Notice of agency termination that is usually given by publishing an announcement in a newspaper.

constructive trust An equitable trust imposed on a person who wrongfully obtains or holds legal right to property he or she should not possess.

consumer good A good used or bought for use primarily for personal, family, or household purposes.

consumer law A statute or administrative rule serving to protect consumer interests.

contract A promise or set of promises for the breach of which the law gives a remedy or the performance of which the law in some way recognizes a duty.

contract clause The clause in the U.S. Constitution that prohibits the government from unreasonably interfering with an existing contract.

contract under seal A contract that has a seal certifying its legality. Such contracts require no consideration for them to be legal.

contractual capacity The legal ability to enter into a binding agreement.

contributory negligence A defense to negligence whereby the defendant can escape all liability by proving that the plaintiff failed to act in a way that would protect him or her from an unreasonable risk of harm and that the plaintiff's negligent behavior contributed in some way to the plaintiff's accident.

conversion Permanent interference with another's use and enjoyment of his or her personal property.

cooperative An organization formed by individuals to market new products. Individuals in a cooperative pool their resources together to gain an advantage in the market.

copyright The protection of the expression of a creative work; i.e., protection of the fixed form that expresses the ideas.

corporation A legal entity formed by issuing stock to investors, who are the owners of the corporation.

corporation by estoppel A defective corporation that has conducted business with a third party and therefore cannot deny its status as a corporation to escape liability.

corrective advertising Advertising in which the company explicitly states that formerly advertised claims were untrue. Also called *counteradvertising*.

cost-benefit analysis An economic school of jurisprudence in which all costs and benefits of a law are given monetary values. Laws with the highest ratios of benefits to costs are then preferable to those with lower ratios.

counterclaim A claim made by the defendant against the plaintiff that is filed along with the defendant's answer.

course of dealing Previous commercial transactions between the same parties.

course of performance The history of dealings between the parties in the particular contract at issue.

court of appellate jurisdiction See **appellate court**.

court of original jurisdiction See **trial court**.

covenant not to compete An agreement not to compete against a party for a set period of time within a designated geographic area.

cover A buyer's right to substitute goods for those due under a sales or lease agreement when the seller provides nonconforming goods.

creditor An entity to which a debtor owes money.

creditor beneficiary A third party who benefits from a contract in which the promisor agrees to pay the promisee's debt.

creditors' meeting A meeting of all the creditors listed in the Chapter 7 required schedule for liquidation.

criminal law The body of laws that involve the rights and responsibilities an individual has with respect to the public as a whole.

critical thinking in the legal context Examining a legal opinion to search for potential problems in the reasoning.

critical thinking skills The ability to understand the structure and worth of an argument by evaluating the facts, issue, reasons, and conclusion of that argument.

cross-licensing An illegal contractual arrangement in which two or more parties license each other to use their specified intellectual property *only* on the condition that neither licenses anyone else to use the property without the other's consent.

cure A breaching party's right to provide conforming goods when nonconforming goods were initially delivered; subject to a reasonable time test.

custom See **historical school**.

cyber terrorist A hacker whose intention is the exploitation of a target computer or network to create a serious impact, such as the crippling of a communications network or the sabotage of a business or organization, which may have an impact on millions of citizens if the terrorist's attack is successful.

D

de facto **corporation** Latin for "corporation in fact"; a corporation that has not substantially met the requirements of the state incorporation statutes.

de jure **corporation** Latin for "lawful corporation"; a corporation that has met the mandatory statutory provisions and thus received its certificate of incorporation.

debt securities Securities that represent loans to a corporation.

debtor A party that owes money to another party.

deceptive advertising The practice of advertising with claims that mislead or could mislead a reasonable consumer.

defamation A false statement or an action that harms the reputation or character of an individual, business, product, group, government, or nation.

default Failure to make payments on a loan.

default judgment Judgment for the plaintiff that occurs when the defendant fails to respond to the complaint.

defective corporation A corporation about which an error or omission was made during its incorporation process.

defendant The person or party against whom a civil or criminal lawsuit is filed in a court of law.

delegatee A third party who is not part of the original contract but to whom duties to perform are transferred by one of the contracting parties (a delegator).

delegation A contracting party's (a delegator's) transfer of his or her duty to perform to a third party who is not part of the original contract (a delegatee).

delegator A party in a contract who transfers his or her duties to perform to a third party who is not a part of the original contract (a delegatee).

demand instrument A type of draft that allows the payee to demand payment at any time from a holder.

deposition A pretrial sworn and recorded testimony of a witness that is acquired out of court with no judge present.

digital cash Money stored electronically in place of physical currency.

directed verdict A ruling by the judge, after the plaintiff has put forward his or her case but before any evidence is put forward by the defendant, in favor of the defendant because the plaintiff has failed to present the minimum amount of evidence necessary to establish his or her claim.

discharge A written federal court order signed by a bankruptcy judge stating that the debtor is immune from creditor actions to collect debt; i.e., a release from liability.

discharged Released from liability for a negotiable instrument.

disclosed principal A principal whose identity is known to a third party. The third party is aware that the agent is making an agreement on behalf of the principal.

discovery The pretrial phase in a lawsuit during which each party requests relevant documents and other evidence from the other side in an attempt to "discover" pertinent facts and avoid any surprises in the courtroom during the trial. Discovery tools include requests for admissions, interrogatories, depositions, requests for inspection, and document production requests.

dishonored Refused; specifically, a payment that has been refused despite a holder's presenting an instrument in a timely and proper manner.

disparagement A business tort that occurs when a statement is intentionally used to defame a business product or service.

disparate impact A form of discrimination that arises when an employer's policy or practice appears to apply to everyone equally but its actual effect is that it disproportionately limits employment opportunities for a protected class.

disparate treatment A form of intentional discrimination in which an employee is hired, fired, denied a promotion, or the like, based on membership in a protected class. This is a form of intentional discrimination.

dissolution The change in the relation of partners caused by any partner's ceasing to be associated with the carrying on of the partnership's business.

distributorship A type of franchise in which the franchisor manufactures a product and licenses a dealer to sell the product in an exclusive territory.

dividend A distribution of corporate profits or income ordered by the directors and paid to the shareholders.

domestic corporation A corporation in the state in which it is incorporated.

donee beneficiary A third party who benefits from a contract in which a promisor agrees to give a gift to the third party.

dormant commerce clause A restriction on states' authority that is implied in the commerce clause of the U.S. Constitution: The power given to Congress to enact legislation that affects interstate commerce in effect prohibits a state from passing legislation that improperly burdens interstate commerce.

draft An instrument validating an order by a drawer to a drawee to pay a payee.

drawee The party that must obey an order. In the context of banking, the drawee is the bank that must pay the funds ordered by a customer's check.

drawer The party that writes an order or the person who writes a check.

due diligence defense A defense in which the defendant argues that he or she applied the appropriate degree of attention, care, and research expected of a party in a given situation and had reasonable grounds to believe that certain facts and statements were accurate and had no omission of material facts.

due process clause A clause in the Fifth Amendment of the U.S. Constitution providing that the government cannot deprive an individual of life, liberty, or property without a fair and just hearing.

durable power of attorney A document that specifies that an agent's authority is intended to continue beyond the principal's incapacitation.

duress Any unlawful act or threat exercised on a person whereby the person is forced to enter into an agreement or to perform some other act against his or her will.

duty of accounting An agent's obligation to keep an accurate account of the transactions of money and property made on behalf of the principal.

duty of cooperation A principal's obligation to assist an agent in the performance of the agent's duties and not to interfere with reasonable conduct of the agent.

duty of loyalty An agent's obligation to act in the interest of the principal.

duty of notification An agent's obligation to inform the principal of the agent's actions on the principal's behalf and of all relevant information.

duty of obedience An agent's obligation to follow the lawful instruction and direction of the principal.

duty of performance An agent's obligation to perform the duties specified in the agency agreement and to do so with reasonable skill and care.

duty of reimbursement and indemnification A principal's obligation to reimburse an agent for any expenses or losses incurred by the agent on the principal's behalf.

duty to compensate A principal's obligation to pay an agent for his or her services.

duty to provide safe working conditions A principal's obligation to provide proper equipment, suitable premises, and a safe working environment in accordance with federal and state statutes.

E

e-money Electronic money.

easement An irrevocable right to use some part of another's land for a specific purpose without taking anything from it.

Electronic Communications Privacy Act (ECPA) of 1986 Federal law that extended employees' privacy rights to electronic forms of communication, including e-mail and cellular phones; outlaws the intentional interception of electronic communications and the intentional disclosure or use of the information obtained through such interception.

electronic fund transfer (EFT) The transfer of funds by an electronic terminal, telephone, or computer.

embezzlement A wrongful conversion of another's funds or property by one who is lawfully in possession of those funds or that property.

Employee Retirement Income Security Act (ERISA) Federal law that sets minimum standards for most voluntarily established pension and health plans in private industry to provide protection for individuals in these plans.

enabling legislation A statute that specifies the name, functions, and specific powers of an administrative agency and grants the agency broad powers for the purpose of serving the public interest, convenience, and necessity.

endorsee One who receives an endorsement.

endorser One who issues an endorsement.

English rule A rule that states that the first assignee to give notice of assignment to the obligor is the party with rights to the contract.

entrustment The transfer of goods to a merchant who ordinarily deals in that type of goods. If the merchant subsequently sells them to a good-faith third-party purchaser, the buyer acquires good title to the goods.

equal dignity rule A rule requiring that contracts that would normally fall under the statute of frauds and need a writing if negotiated by the principal must be in writing even if negotiated by an agent.

Equal Pay Act (EPA) of 1963 Federal law that prohibits an employer from paying workers of one gender less than the wages paid to employees of the opposite gender for work that requires equal skill, effort, and responsibility.

equal protection clause A clause in the Fourteenth Amendment of the U.S. Constitution that prevents states from denying "the equal protection of the laws" to any citizen. This clause implies that all citizens are created equal.

equity securities Securities that represent ownership in a corporation.

establishment clause One of two provisions in the First Amendment of the U.S. Constitution that protect citizens' freedom of religion. It prohibits (1) the establishment of a national religion by Congress and (2) the preference of one religion over another or of religion over nonreligious philosophies in general.

ethical dilemma A question about how one should behave that requires one to reflect on the advantages and disadvantages of the optional choices for various stakeholders.

ethical guideline A simple tool that helps determine whether an action is moral.

ethics The study and practice of decisions about what is good or right.

exchange tender offer A type of takeover in which the aggressor corporation offers to exchange the target shareholders' current stock for stock in the aggressor's corporation.

exculpatory clause A statement in a contract that frees one party (usually the drafter of the agreement) from all liability arising out of performance of the contract; generally based on factors such as consumer ignorance or a great deal of unexplained fine print that serve to deprive the less powerful party of a meaningful choice.

executed A term applied to a contract in which all of the terms have been fully performed.

executive agency An agency that is typically located within the executive branch, under one of the cabinet-level departments. The agency head is appointed by the president with the advice and consent of the Senate.

executory A term applied to a contract in which not all of the terms have been fully performed.

express authority The authority of an agent that arises when the principal explicitly instructs the agent to do something. Also called *actual authority*.

express condition A condition specifically and explicitly stated in a contract and usually preceded by words such as *conditioned on, if, provided that,* or *when.*

express contract A contract in which all the terms are clearly set forth in either written or spoken words.

express warranty Any description of a good's physical nature or its use, in either general or specific circumstances, that becomes part of a contract.

expressed agency An agency created in a written or oral agreement. Also called *agency by agreement.*

extortion A criminal offense in which a person obtains money, property, and/or services from another by wrongfully threatening or inflicting harm on the other's person, property, or reputation. Also called *blackmail.*

F

Fair Labor Standards Act (FLSA) Federal law that requires that a minimum wage of a specified amount be paid to all

employees in covered industries; also mandates that employees who work more than 40 hours in a week be paid no less than 1½ times their regular wage for all hours beyond 40 worked in a given week.

fair-use doctrine The lawful use of a limited, noncommercial portion of another's work for purposes of criticism, comment, news reporting, teaching, scholarship, and research.

False Claims Act An act that allows employees to sue employers on behalf of the federal government for fraud against the government. The employee retains a share of the recovery as a reward for his or her efforts.

false pretense The illegal obtaining of another's property by making a materially false representation of an existing fact, with knowledge of the falsity of the representation and with the intent to defraud.

Family and Medical Leave Act (FMLA) Federal act requiring that employers provide all eligible employees with up to 12 weeks of leave during any 12-month period for several family-related occurrences (e.g., birth of a child, care of a sick spouse).

federal preemption A principle asserting the supremacy of federal legislation over state legislation when both pertain to the same matter.

Federal Register The government publication in which an agency publishes each proposed rule, along with an explanation of the legal authority for issuing the rule and a description of how the public can participate in the rule-making process, and later publishes the final rule.

federalism A system of government in which power is divided between a central authority and constituent political units.

fee simple absolute An ownership interest in which the holder has exclusive rights to ownership and possession of the land; the most comprehensive type of estate.

felony A serious crime, such as murder, rape, or robbery, that is punishable by imprisonment for more than one year or death.

fictitious payee Someone having no right to payment. The UCC fictitious-payee rule governs the liability of companies and their endorsed checks: Any check made out to a fictitious payee and endorsed must be honored and is not considered a forgery.

fiduciary A person who has a duty to act primarily for another person's benefit.

financing statement A document that lists the names and addresses of all the parties involved in the transaction, a description of the collateral, and the signature of the debtor.

firm offer An offer made in writing and giving assurances that it will be irrevocable for not longer than three months despite a lack of consideration for the irrevocability.

first appearance The initial appearance of an arrested individual before a judge who determines whether there was probable cause for the arrest. If the judge ascertains that probable cause did not exist, the individual is freed.

first-assignment-in-time rule A rule that states that the first party granted the assignment is the party correctly entitled to the contractual right.

food disparagement A tort that provides ranchers and farmers with a cause of action when someone spreads false information about the safety of a food product.

for-profit corporation A corporation whose objective is to make a profit.

foreign corporation A corporation in a state in which it conducts business but is not incorporated.

forgery A criminal falsification by imitating, impersonating, or altering a real document with the intent to deceive or defraud.

formal contract A contract that must have a special form or must be created in a specific manner.

formal rule making A type of rule making that is used when legislation requires a formal hearing process with a complete transcript; consists of publication of the proposed rule in the *Federal Register*, a public hearing, publication of formal findings, and publication of the final rule if adopted.

franchise A business arrangement between an owner of a trade name or trademark and a person who sells goods or services under the trade name or trademark.

franchise agreement A contract whereby a company (the franchisor) grants permission (a license) to another entity (the franchisee) to use the franchisor's name, trademark, or copyright in the operation of a business and associated sale of goods in return for payment.

franchisee The seller of goods or services under a trade name or trademark in a franchise.

franchisor The owner of the trade name or trademark in a franchise.

fraud An intentional deception that causes harm to another.

fraud in the factum A liability defense available to a party who signs a negotiable instrument without knowing that it is a negotiable instrument.

fraudulent misrepresentation (1) The tort that occurs when a misrepresentation is made with the intent to facilitate personal gain and with the knowledge that it is false. (2) In contracts, a false representation of a material fact that is consciously false and is intended to mislead the other party.

fraudulent transfer A transfer of property made with intent to defraud creditors or made for an amount significantly lower than the property's fair market value within two years of filing for bankruptcy.

free-exercise clause A clause in the First Amendment of the U.S. Constitution that states that government (state and federal) cannot make a law "prohibiting the free exercise" of religion. This clause is interpreted to include absolute freedom to believe and freedom to act that may face state restriction.

Freedom of Information Act (FOIA) Federal legislation that mandates and facilitates public access to government information and records, including records about oneself. Sensitive information (e.g., on national security) is excluded.

full faith and credit clause The clause of the U.S. Constitution (Article IV, Section 1) mandating that each state must recognize, respect, and enforce the public records, legislative acts, and judicial decisions of the other states.

future interest A person's present right to property ownership and possession in the future.

G

gambling An agreement in which a party pays consideration (money placed during bets) for the chance, or opportunity, to obtain an amount of money or property.

general partnership A partnership in which the partners divide profits and management responsibility and share unlimited personal liability for the partnership's debts.

good faith Honesty in fact.

Good Samaritan statute A statute that exempts from liability a person, such as a physician passerby, who voluntarily renders aid to an injured person but negligently, but not unreasonably negligently, causes injury while rendering the aid.

good title Title acquired from someone who already owns the goods free and clear.

goods All physically existing things that are movable at the time of identification to the contract for sale.

goods-in-bailment contract A type of contract in which the purchased goods are in some kind of storage under the control of a third party, such as a warehouseman.

gratuitous agent An agent who acts without being paid for his or her services.

gross negligence An action committed with extreme reckless disregard for the property or life of another person.

H

hacker A person who illegally accesses or enters another person's or a company's computer system to obtain information or to steal money.

half-truth Information that is true but is not complete.

historical school A school of jurisprudence that uses traditions as the model for future laws and behavior. Also called *tradition* or *custom*.

holder A party in possession of a negotiable instrument.

holder in due course (HDC) An individual who acquires a negotiable instrument in good faith.

hostile takeover A takeover to which the management of the target corporation objects.

hybrid agency An agency that has characteristics of both executive and independent agencies.

hybrid rule making A type of rule making that combines features of formal and informal rule making; consists of publication in the *Federal Register*, a written-comment period, and an informal public hearing with restricted cross-examination.

I

identification with the vulnerable A school of jurisprudence that holds that society should be fair. Particular attention is therefore paid to the poor, the ill, and the elderly.

illusory promise A situation in which a party appears to commit to something but really has not committed to anything. It is not a promise and thus not consideration.

implied authority The authority of an agent that arises by inference from the words and actions of the principal.

implied condition A condition that is not specifically and explicitly stated but is inferred from the nature and language of the contract.

implied contract A contract that arises not from words of agreement but from the conduct of the parties.

implied warranty of fitness for a particular purpose An assurance, inferred in any UCC sale, whereby when a seller or lessor knows or has reason to know (1) why the buyer or lessee is purchasing or leasing the goods in question and (2) that the buyer or lessee is relying on him or her to make the selection, the buyer or lessee has an enforceable warranty if such assurance is false.

implied warranty of merchantability An assurance, inferred in every sale unless clearly disclaimed, that merchantable goods will conform to a reasonable performance expectation. The purchaser must have purchased or leased the good from a merchant.

implied warranty of trade usage An assurance, inferred in the context of certain UCC sales, depending on the circumstances, that can be created through a well-accepted course of dealing or trade usage.

imposter rule A rule that holds that if one obtains a negotiable instrument by impersonating another and endorses it with the impersonated party's signature, the loss falls on the drawer of the instrument.

in pari delicto In equal fault.

in personam **jurisdiction** The power of a court to require that a party (usually the defendant) or a witness come before the court. The court must have personal jurisdiction to enforce its judgments or orders against a party. *In personam* jurisdiction extends only to the state's borders in the state court system and across the court's geographic district in the federal system.

in rem **jurisdiction** The power of a court over the property or status of an out-of-state defendant when that property or status is located within the court's jurisdiction area.

incidental beneficiary One who unintentionally gains a benefit from a contract between other parties.

incorporator An individual who applies for incorporation on behalf of a corporation.

independent agency An agency that is typically not located within a government department. It is governed by a board of commissioners, who are appointed by the president with the advice and consent of the Senate.

independent contractor A person who is hired to perform a task for another but who is not the other's employee.

indictment Finding by the grand jury that there is adequate evidence to charge the defendant and bring him or her to trial.

indivisible contract A contract that requires complete performance by both parties.

industry guides Interpretations of consumer laws created by the FTC to encourage businesses to stop unlawful behavior.

informal contract A contract that requires no formalities.

informal rule making A type of rule making in which an agency publishes a proposed rule in the *Federal Register*,

considers public comments, and then publishes the final rule. Also called *notice-and-comment rule making.*

information A document, prepared by the prosecutor and presented to the magistrate, which demonstrates that there is enough evidence to charge the defendant and bring him or her to trial.

injunction A court order either forcing a party to do something or prohibiting a party from doing something.

innocent misrepresentation A false statement about a fact material to an agreement that the person who made the statement believed to be true.

insider trading Illegal buying or selling of a corporation's stock or other securities by corporate insiders such as officers and directors, in breach of a fiduciary duty or some other relationship of trust and confidence, while in possession of material, nonpublic information about the security.

insolvent debtor A debtor who cannot pay debts in a timely fashion.

instrument A writing that serves as evidence of the right to payment of money.

integrated contract A written contract intended to be the complete and final representation of the parties' agreement.

intellectual property Intangible property that is the product of one's mind and not one's hands.

intended beneficiary A third party to a contract whom the contracting parties intended to benefit directly from their contact.

intent The intended purpose or goal of an action, especially in a contract.

intentional interference with contract The tort that occurs when someone intentionally takes an action that will cause a person to breach a contract that she or he has with another.

intentional misrepresentation In a contract, a false representation of a material fact made by a party who either knows or believes that the factual claim is false or knows that there is no basis for the assertion. Scienter is clear.

intentional tort A civil wrong resulting from an intentional act committed on the person, property, or economic interest of another. Intentional torts include assault, battery, conversion, false imprisonment, intentional infliction of emotional distress, trespass to land, and trespass to chattels.

intermediate scrutiny A standard of review under which a law must be necessary to achieve a substantial, or important, government interest and it must be narrowly tailored to that interest.

interpretive rule A rule that does not create any new rights or duties but is merely a detailed statement of an agency's interpretation of an existing law, including the actions a party is to take to be in compliance with the law.

interrogatories A formal set of written questions that one party to a lawsuit asks the opposing party as part of the pretrial discovery process in order to clarify matters of evidence and help determine in advance what facts will be presented at any trial in the case. The questions must be answered in writing under oath or under penalty of perjury within a specified time. Also called *requests for further information.*

Interstate Commerce Commission (ICC) The first federal administrative agency; created to regulate the anticompetitive conduct of railroads.

J

joint and several liability A type of liability in which a third party can choose to sue the partners separately or to sue all partners jointly in one action.

joint stock company A partnership agreement in which company members hold transferable shares while all the goods of the company are held in the names of the partners.

joint venture An association between two or more parties wherein the parties share profits and management responsibilities with respect to a specific project.

jointly liable A term applied to partners who share liability for the partnership's debts.

judicial review The power of a court to review legislative and executive actions, such as a law or an official act of a government employee or agent, to determine whether they are constitutional.

L

lack of genuine assent A defense to the agreement of a contract in which the offeree claims that the offeror secured the agreement through improper means, such as duress, fraud, undue influence, or misrepresentation.

Landrum-Griffin Act Federal legislation that primarily governs the internal operations of labor unions. It requires financial disclosures by unions, establishes penalties for financial abuses by union officials, and includes "Labor's Bill of Rights" to protect employees from their own unions.

last-clear-chance doctrine A doctrine used by the plaintiff when the defendant establishes contributory negligence. If the plaintiff can establish that the defendant had the last opportunity to avoid the accident, the plaintiff may still recover, despite being contributorily negligent.

law Rules of conduct in any organized society that are enforced by the governing authority of the community.

lease A transfer of the right to possession and use of goods for a term in return for consideration.

leasehold A possessory interest, but not an ownership interest, transferred by contract.

legal entity Any individual, proprietorship, partnership, corporation, association, or other organization that has, in the eyes of the law, the capacity to form an agreement and the ability to assume an obligation and to discharge an indebtedness.

legal object A purpose that does not violate a statute or public policy.

legal positivism A school of jurisprudence that holds that because society requires authority, a legal and authoritarian hierarchy should exist. When a law is made, therefore, obedience is expected because authority created it.

legal realism A school of jurisprudence that holds that context must be considered as well as law. Context includes factors such as economic conditions and social conditions.

lessee A person who acquires the right to possession and use of goods under a lease.

lessor A person who transfers the right to possession and use of goods under a lease.

letter of credit A binding document that a buyer can request from a bank to guarantee that the payment for goods will be made to the seller.

leveraged buyout (LBO) A takeover-resistance strategy in which a group within the target corporation buys all the corporate stock held by the public, thereby turning the company into a privately held corporation.

liability without fault A legal term that imposes responsibility for damages regardless of the existence of negligence. Also called *strict liability*.

license A revocable right to temporarily use another's property.

life estate An ownership interest in which the holder has the right to possess the property until her or his death.

limited liability company (LLC) An unincorporated business that is taxed like a partnership, with the members paying personal income taxes, and has the limited liability of a corporation.

limited liability partnership (LLP) A partnership in which all the partners assume liability for any partner's professional malpractice to the extent of the partnership's assets.

limited partnership (LP) A partnership consisting of at least one general partner and at least one limited partner in which the general partners assume all liability for the partnership's debts and the limited partners assume no liability beyond their originally invested capital.

liquidated damages Damages specified as a term of the contract, before a breach of contract occurs.

liquidated debt Debt for which there is no dispute between the parties about the fact that money is owed and the amount of money owed.

liquidation The process in which a debtor turns over all assets to a trustee.

long-arm statute A statute that enables a court to obtain jurisdiction against an out-of-state defendant as long as the defendant has sufficient minimum contacts within the state, such as committing a tort or doing business in the state.

M

mailbox rule The principle that holds that an acceptance is valid when it is placed in the mailbox, whereas a revocation is effective only when received by the offeree. In some jurisdictions the mailbox rule has been expanded to faxes.

maker A person who has promised to pay a set sum to the holder of a promissory note or certificate of deposit.

manufacturing arrangement A type of franchise in which the franchisor provides the franchisee with a formula or necessary ingredient to manufacture a product.

material breach A substantial breach of a significant term or terms of a contract that excuses the nonbreaching party from further performance under the contract and gives the nonbreaching party the right to recover damages.

med-arb A type of dispute resolution process in which both parties agree to start out in mediation and, if unsuccessful, to move on to arbitration.

mediation A type of intensive negotiation in which disputing parties select a neutral party to help facilitate communication and suggest ways for the parties to solve their dispute.

mens rea Latin for "guilty mind"; the mental state accompanying a wrongful behavior.

merchant Under the UCC, a person who regularly sells goods as his or her business or trade or employs people to sell those goods; anyone who works for a person selling those goods; or anyone who holds himself or herself out as a "merchant" or a "dealer."

merger A combination of two or more corporations in which only one of the corporations continues to exist.

merger clause A clause in a written agreement within the statute of frauds that states that the written agreement accurately reflects the final, complete version of the agreement.

minitrial A type of conflict resolution in which lawyers for each side present their arguments to a neutral adviser, who then offers an opinion as to what the verdict would be if the case went to trial. This decision is not binding.

Miranda rights The rights that are read to an arrested individual by a law enforcement agent before the individual is questioned about the commission of a crime.

mirror-image rule The principle that holds that the terms of the acceptance must mirror the terms of the offer; if the terms of the acceptance do not mirror the terms of the offer, no contract is formed and the attempted acceptance is a counteroffer.

misappropriation theory A theory of insider trading that holds that if an individual wrongfully acquires (misappropriates) and uses inside information for trading for his or her personal gain, that person is liable for insider trading.

misdemeanor A crime that is less serious than a felony and is punishable by a fine and/or imprisonment for less than one year.

misrepresentation An untruthful assertion by one of the parties about a material fact.

mistake An erroneous belief about the facts of a contract at the time the contract is concluded. When a mistake occurs, legal assent is absent.

mixed sale A contract that combines a good with a service or real estate.

mock trial A contrived or imitation trial, with a jury recruited by a jury selection firm, that attorneys sometimes use in preparing for an actual trial to test theories, experiment with arguments, and try to predict the outcome of the real trial.

model laws See **uniform laws**.

modified comparative negligence A defense accepted in some states whereby the defendant is not liable for the percentage of harm that he or she can prove is due to the plaintiff's own negligence if the plaintiff's negligence is responsible for less than 50 percent of the harm; if the defendant establishes that the plaintiff's negligence caused more than 50 percent of the harm, the defendant has no liability.

modify An appellate court decision that grants an alternative remedy in a case; rendered when the court finds that the decision of the lower court was correct but the remedy was not.

motion An application by a party to a judge or a court in a civil case requesting an order in favor of the applicant.

motion for judgment on the pleadings In a civil case, a request made by either party, after pleadings have been entered, that asks a judge or a court to issue a judgment.

motion for summary judgment In a civil case, a request made by either party that asks a judge or a court to promptly and expeditiously dispose of a case without a trial. Any evidence or information that would be admissible at trial under the rules of evidence, such as affidavits, interrogatories, depositions, and admissions, may be considered on a motion for summary judgment. A court may hold oral arguments or decide the motion on the basis of the parties' briefs and supporting documentation alone.

motion to dismiss A request by the defendant that asks a judge or a court in a civil case to dismiss the case because even if all the allegations are true, the plaintiff is not entitled to any legal relief. Also called *demurrer*.

movability The quality of a negotiable instrument that ensures it is mobile and available.

multiple-product order A form of cease-and-desist order issued by the FTC that applies not only to a specified product but also to other products produced by the same firm.

mutual mistake The result of an error by both parties about a material fact, i.e., one that is important in the context of a particular contract.

N

National Labor Relations Board (NLRB) An administrative agency created by the Wagner Act to interpret and enforce the National Labor Relations Act.

natural law A school of jurisprudence that recognizes the existence of higher law, or law that is morally superior to human laws.

negligence Behavior that creates an unreasonable risk of harm to others.

negligence per se A doctrine that allows a judge or jury to infer duty and breach of duty from the fact that a defendant violated a criminal statute that was designed to prevent the type of harm that the plaintiff incurred.

negligent misrepresentation A false statement of material fact made by a party who thinks it is true but who would have known the truth about the fact had he or she used reasonable care to discover or reveal it.

negligent tort A civil wrong that occurs when the defendant acts in a way that subjects other people to an unreasonable risk of harm (i.e., the defendant is careless, to someone else's detriment). Negligence claims are usually used to achieve compensation for accidents and injuries.

negotiable instrument A written document signed by a person who makes an unconditional promise to pay a specific sum of money on demand or at a certain time to the holder of the instrument; an acceptable medium for exchanging value from one person to another.

negotiation (1) A bargaining process in which disputing parties interact informally to attempt to resolve their dispute. (2) The transferring of the rights to a negotiable instrument from one party to another.

no-par shares Stock shares that do not have a par value.

nolo contendere A plea in which the defendant does not admit guilt but agrees not to contest the charges.

nominal damages Monetary damages awarded to a plaintiff in a very small amount, typically $1 to $5, to signify that the plaintiff has been wronged by the defendant even though the plaintiff suffered no compensable harm.

nondisclosure A failure to provide pertinent information about a projected contract.

nonprofit corporation A corporation that operates for educational, charitable, social, religious, civic, or humanitarian purposes, rather than to earn a profit.

note A promise by the maker of the note to pay the payee of the note.

notice-and-comment rule making See **informal rule making**.

novation In a contract, the substitution of a third party for one of the original parties; the duties remain the same under the contract, but one original party is discharged and the third party takes that original party's place.

O

obligee A contractual party who agreed to receive something from the other party.

obligor A contractual party who agreed to do something for the other party.

Occupational Safety and Health Act (OSHA) of 1970 Federal law that established the Occupational Safety and Health Administration, the agency responsible for setting safety standards under the act and enforcing the act through inspections and the levying of fines against violators.

offer A key factor is the agreement element of a contract; consists of the terms and conditions set by one party, the offeror, and presented to another party, the offeree.

Omnibus Crime Control and Safe Streets Act of 1968 Federal statute banning employers from listening to the private telephone conversations of employees or disclosing the contents of these conversations. Employers may ban personal calls and monitor calls for compliance as long as they discontinue listening to any conversation once they determine it is personal.

option contract An agreement whereby the offeree gives the offeror a piece of consideration in exchange for the offeror's agreement to hold the offer open for the specified period of time.

order A binding decision rendered by a judge.

order instrument An instrument payable to a specific, named payee.

order of relief An order stating that bankruptcy proceedings can continue.

output contract An agreement whereby the seller guarantees to sell everything he or she produces to one buyer and no quantity is stated; valid under the UCC but not under common law.

P

par-value shares Stock shares that have a fixed face value noted on the stock certificate.

parol evidence rule A common law rule that states that oral evidence of an agreement made prior to or contemporaneously with a written agreement is inadmissible when the parties intend

to have the written agreement be the complete and final version of their agreement.

partial performance An exception to the statute of frauds in which the performance of portions of an unwritten agreement by one or both parties can constitute proof that an oral contract exists between the parties.

partially disclosed principal A principal whose identity is not known by a third party, although the third party is aware that the agent is making an agreement on behalf of a principal. Also called *unidentified principal*.

partnership A voluntary association between two or more people who co-own a business for profit.

patent Protection that grants the holder the exclusive right to produce, sell and use the object of the patent for 20 years; can be obtained for a product, process, invention, machine, or a plant produced by asexual reproduction.

payee The party that receives the benefit of an order (check, etc.).

peremptory challenge In a jury trial, the right of the plaintiff and the defendant in jury selection to reject, without stating a reason, a certain number of potential jurors who appear to have an unfavorable bias.

perfect tender rule Requirement that the seller deliver the goods in conformity with the contract, down to the last detail.

perfection The series of legal steps a secured party takes to protect its right in the collateral from the other creditors who want to have their debt returned through the same collateral.

personal defense A liability defense that is not applicable to holders in due course.

personal property Any property that is not land or permanently affixed to the land.

petit jury A group of 6 or 12 citizens who are summoned to and sworn by the court to hear evidence presented by both sides and render a verdict in a trial.

petty offense A minor crime that is punishable by a small fine and/or imprisonment for less than six months in a jail.

plaintiff The person or party who initiates a lawsuit (also known as an *action*) before a court by filing a complaint with the clerk of the court against the defendant(s). Also known as *claimant* or *complainant*.

plea bargain An agreement in which the prosecutor agrees to reduce charges, drop charges, or recommend a certain sentence if the defendant pleads guilty.

pledge The transfer of collateral to the secured party.

police power Power retained by each state to pass laws that protect the health, safety, and welfare of its citizens.

policy statement A general statement about the directions in which an agency intends to proceed with respect to its rule-making or enforcement activities; has no binding impact on anyone.

political speech Speech that is used to support political candidates or referenda. It is given a high level of protection by the First Amendment as compared to other types of speech.

power of attorney A specific form of express authority that grants an agent specific powers.

precedent A tool used by judges to make rulings on cases on the basis of key similarities to previous cases.

preexisting duty A promise to do something that one is already obligated to do. It is not considered valid consideration.

preferential payment A payment made by an insolvent debtor that gives preferential treatment to one creditor over another.

preferred stock Stock that conveys preferences to its holders with respect to assets and dividends.

prejudicial error An error of law that is so significant that it affects the outcome of the case.

prenuptial agreement An agreement two parties enter into before marriage that clearly states the ownership rights each party enjoys in the other party's property. To be enforceable, the agreement must be in writing.

presentment The act of making a demand for the drawee to pay.

presentment warranty A warranty covering the parties accepting an instrument for payment; created to ensure that the accepting or paying party is paying the proper party.

pretrial conference An informal meeting of the judge with the attorneys representing the parties before the actual trial begins.

primarily liable Liable for paying the amount designated on an instrument when it is presented for payment.

principal The party that an agent's authority can bind or act on behalf of.

principle of rights The principle that judges the morality of a decision on the basis of how it affects the rights of all those involved.

private corporation A corporation that is created by private persons and does not have government duties.

private law Law that involves suits between private individuals or groups.

private nuisance A nuisance that affects only a single person or a very limited number of individuals.

private trial An ADR method in which a referee is selected and paid by the disputing parties to offer a legally binding judgment in a dispute.

privileges and immunities clause Clause in the U.S. Constitution requiring that a state grant citizens of other states the same legal benefits that it grants its own citizens.

probable cause Any essential element and/or standard by which a lawful officer may make a valid arrest, conduct a personal or property search, or obtain a warrant.

procedural due process The requirement that a government must use fair procedures before depriving a person of his or her life, liberty, or property.

procedural unconscionability Unconscionability that derives from the process of making a contract.

proceeds Something that is exchanged for a debtor's sold collateral.

profit The right to go onto someone's land and take part of the land or a product of it away from the land.

promisee In a third-party beneficiary contract, the party to the contract who owes something to the promisor in exchange for the promise made to the third-party.

promisor In a third-party beneficiary contract, the party to the contract who made the promise that benefits the third party.

promissory estoppel The legal enforcement of an otherwise unenforceable contract due to a party's detrimental reliance on the contract.

promoter A person who begins the corporate creation and organization process.

prospectus A written document filed with the SEC that contains a description of a security and other financial information regarding the company offering the security; also distributed as an advertising tool to potential investors.

proximate cause The extent to which, as a matter of policy, a defendant may be held liable for the consequences of his or her actions. In the majority of states, proximate cause requires that the plaintiff and the plaintiff's damages were foreseeable at the time of the accident. In the minority of states, proximate cause exists if the defendant's actions led to the plaintiff's harm.

proxy A writing signed by a shareholder that authorizes the individual named in the writing to exercise the shareholder's votes (corresponding to his or her shares of stock) at a shareholders' meeting.

proxy solicitation The process of obtaining authority to vote on behalf of shareholders.

public corporation A corporation that is created by government to help administer law.

public figure privilege A special right, immunity, or permission given to people that allows them to make any statements about public figures, typically politicians and entertainers, without being held liable for defamation for any false statement made without malice.

public law Law that involves suits between private individuals or groups and their government.

publicly held corporation A corporation whose stock is available to the public.

puffing The use of generalities and clear exaggerations.

punitive damages Compensation awarded to a plaintiff that goes beyond reimbursement for actual losses and is imposed to punish the defendant and deter such conduct in the future.

purchase-money security interest (PMSI) A security interest formed when a debtor uses borrowed money from the secured party to buy the collateral.

pure comparative negligence A defense accepted in some states whereby the defendant is not liable for the percentage of harm that he or she can prove is due to the plaintiff's own negligence.

Q

quasi-contract A court-imposed contractual obligation to prevent unjust enrichment.

quasi *in rem* jurisdiction A type of jurisdiction exercised by a court over an out-of-state defendant's property that is within the jurisdictional boundaries of the court. It applies to personal suits against the defendant in which the property is not the source of the conflict but is sought as compensation by the plaintiff. Also called *attachment jurisdiction*.

question of fact A question about an event or characteristic in a case.

question of law An issue concerning the interpretation or application of a law.

R

Racketeer Influenced and Corrupt Organizations (RICO) Act A U.S. law that provides extended penalties for criminal acts performed as part of an ongoing criminal organization.

ratify To approve an unauthorized agent's signature on an instrument.

rational-basis test The lowest standard of review; requires that a law be designed to protect a legitimate state interest and be rationally related to that interest.

reaffirmation agreement An agreement in which the debtor agrees to pay a debt even though it could have been discharged in bankruptcy.

real defense A liability defense that applies universally to all parties.

real property Land and everything permanently attached to it.

reasonable person standard A measurement of the way members of society expect an individual to act in a given situation.

recognizance An obligation in which a party acknowledges in court that he or she will perform some specified act and/or pay a price on failure to do so.

red-herring prospectus A prospectus with a warning written in red print at the top of the page telling investors that the registration has been filed with the SEC but not yet approved.

reg-neg A type of rule making in which representatives of concerned interest groups and of the involved government agency participate in mediated bargaining sessions to reach an agreement, which is forwarded to the agency.

relative permanence The quality of a negotiable instrument that ensures its longevity.

remand An appellate court decision that returns a case to the trial court for a new trial or for limited hearing on a specified subject matter; rendered when the court decides that an error was committed that may have affected the outcome of a case.

reply A response by the plaintiff to the defendant's counterclaim.

request to produce documents In a lawsuit, the right of a party to examine and copy papers of the opposing party that are relevant to the case. A legal request may be made and the categories of the documents must be stated to allow the other party to know what documents he or she must produce.

requirement contract An agreement whereby the buyer agrees to purchase all of his or her goods from one seller and no quantity is stated in the contract; valid under the UCC but not under common law.

res ipsa loquitur A doctrine that allows the judge or jury to infer that, more likely than not, the defendant's negligence was the cause of the plaintiff's harm, even though there is no direct evidence of the defendant's lack of due care.

rescind To cancel a contract.

rescission The termination of a contract.

respondeat superior Latin for "let the superior speak"; the principle by which liability for harm caused by an agent/employee is held by the principal/employer.

Restatements of the Law Summaries of common law rules in a particular area of the law. Restatements do not carry the weight of law but can be used to guide interpretations of particular cases.

restitution The return of any property given up under a contract.

restricted securities Securities that have limited transferability and are usually issued in a private placement.

retained earnings Profits that a corporation keeps.

reverse An appellate court decision that overturns the judgment of a lower court, concluding that the lower court was incorrect and its verdict cannot be allowed to stand.

revocation Termination of a contract that occurs when an offeror takes back the initial offer and annuls the opportunity for the offeree to accept the offer.

RICO Act See **Racketeer Influenced and Corrupt Organizations (RICO) Act**.

right of first refusal A method of restricting stock transferability whereby a corporation or its shareholders have the right to purchase any shares of stock offered for resale by a shareholder within a specified time frame.

right of survivorship The right that specific partnership property will pass on to the surviving partner(s).

rightfully dissolved A term applied to the dissolution of a partnership that does not violate its partnership agreement.

ripeness The readiness of a case for a decision to be made. The goal is to prevent premature litigation for a dispute that is insufficiently developed. A claim is not ripe for litigation if it rests on contingent future events that may not occur as anticipated or may not occur at all.

S

S corporation A corporation that enjoys the tax status of a partnership.

Sabbath laws Laws prohibiting the performance of certain activities on Sundays.

sale The passing of title from a seller to a buyer for a price.

sale-on-approval contract A contract in which the seller allows the buyer to take possession of the goods before deciding whether to complete the contract by making the purchase.

sale-or-return contract A contract in which the buyer and seller agree that the buyer may return the goods at a later time.

Sarbanes-Oxley Act An act that criminalizes specific nonaudit services when provided by a registered accounting firm to an audit client; also increases the punishment for a number of white-collar offenses. Also known as the *Public Company Accounting Reform and Investor Protection Act of 2002*.

scienter Deliberately or knowingly.

search warrant A court order that authorizes law enforcement agents to search for or seize items specifically described in the warrant.

secondarily liable Liable for paying the amount designated on an instrument should the primarily liable party default.

secured interest An interest in personal property or fixtures that secures payment or performance to a creditor.

secured party The party that holds the interest in a secured property.

secured transaction A transaction in which the payment of a debt is guaranteed by personal property owned by the debtor.

security A financial instrument designated as a note, stock, or bond or any other instrument named in the Securities Act of 1933.

security agreement An agreement in which the debtor gives the secured interest to the secured party.

self-dealing Any instance in which directors or officers make decisions that violate their corporate duty of loyalty.

self-tender offer A takeover-resistance strategy in which the target corporation offers to buy its shareholders' stock.

service of process The procedure by which a court delivers a copy of the statement of claim or other legal documents, such as a summons, complaint, or subpoena, to the defendant.

severable contract A contract that contains multiple parts that can each be performed separately.

sexual harassment Unwelcome sexual advances, requests for sexual favors, and other verbal or physical conduct of a sexual nature that makes submission a condition of employment or a factor in employment decisions or that creates an intimidating, hostile, or offensive work environment. The two types are hostile environment and *quid pro quo*.

shadow jury An unofficial jury, provided by a jury selection firm, that sits in during the actual trial and deliberates at the end of each day to evaluate for the attorneys how each side is doing.

shareholders Investors in a corporation, who own the corporation.

shareholder's derivative suit A lawsuit filed by a shareholder on behalf of the corporation.

shareholder's direct suit A lawsuit filed by a shareholder against the corporation.

shelter principle The principle that when an item is transferred, the transferee acquires all the rights the transferor had to the item.

short-swing profits Profits made from the sale of company stock within any six-month period by a statutory insider.

signature liability Liability attributed because of a party's signature on an instrument.

simple delivery contract Type of contract in which purchased goods are transferred to the buyer from the seller either at the time of the sale or at some time later by the seller's delivery.

slander of quality A business tort that occurs when false spoken statements criticize a business product or service and result in a loss of sales.

slander of title A business tort that occurs when false published statements are related to the ownership of the business property.

social responsibility of business The expectations that a community places on the actions of firms inside that community's borders.

sole proprietor The single person at the head of a sole proprietorship.

sole proprietorship A business in which one person (sole proprietor) is in control of the management and profits.

special damages See **consequential damages**.

special endorsement An endorser's signature accompanied by the name of the endorsee.

specific performance An order of the court requiring that a nonbreaching party fulfill the terms of the contract.

stakeholders The groups of people affected by a firm's decisions.

stale check A check that is not presented to a bank within six months of its date.

standing The legal right of a party or an individual to bring a lawsuit by demonstrating to the court sufficient connection to and harm from the law or action challenged (i.e., the plaintiff has to demonstrate that he or she is harmed or will be harmed). Otherwise, the court will dismiss the case, ruling that the plaintiff "lacks standing" to bring the suit.

stare decisis "Standing by the decision"; a principle stating that rulings made in higher courts are binding precedent for lower courts.

statute of frauds State-level legislation that addresses the enforceability of contracts that fail to meet the requirements set forth in the statute; serves to protect promisors from poorly considered oral contracts by requiring that certain contracts be in writing.

statutory insiders Certain large stockholders, executive officers, and directors who are deemed insiders by the Securities Exchange Act of 1934.

statutory law The assortment of rules and regulations put forth by legislatures.

stock certificate A document that serves as a stockholder's proof of ownership in a corporation.

stock warrant A type of security issued by a corporation (usually together with a bond or preferred stock) that gives the holder the right to purchase a certain amount of common stock at a stated price.

stop-payment order An order by a drawer that instructs the drawee bank not to pay an issued check.

stored-value card A plastic card that contains data regarding the value of the card, thereby allowing EFTs to be made.

strict liability Liability in which responsibility for damages is imposed regardless of the existence of negligence. Also called *liability without fault*.

strict-liability offense Offense for which no *mens rea* is required.

strict-liability tort A civil wrong that occurs when the defendant takes an action that is inherently dangerous and cannot ever be undertaken safely, no matter what precautions the defendant takes. In such situations, a defendant is liable for the plaintiff's damages without any requirement that the plaintiff prove that the defendant was negligent.

strict scrutiny The most exacting standard of review used by the courts in determining the constitutionality of a statute; requires a compelling government interest and the least restrictive means of attaining that objective.

subject-matter jurisdiction The power of a court over the type of case presented to it.

subpoena An order to appear at a particular time and place and provide testimony.

subpoena *duces tecum* An order to appear and bring specified documents.

subscriber An investor who agrees to purchase stock in a new corporation.

subscription agreement An agreement between promoters (persons raising capital for a new corporation) and subscribers (investors), in which the subscribers agree to purchase stock in the new corporation.

substantial evidence Refers to evidence that a reasonable mind could accept as adequate to support a conclusion. It is defined as "more than a scintilla but less than preponderance" and consists of "such relevant evidence as a reasonable person would accept as adequate to support a conclusion."

substantial impairment A concept, used to modify the perfect tender rule, whereby a buyer can revoke acceptance of goods and, with installment contracts, a buyer/lessee can reject an installment of a particular item only if the defects substantially impair the value of the goods.

substantial performance Contract performance that occurs when nearly all the terms of the agreement have been met, there has been an honest effort to complete all the terms, and there has been no willful departure from the terms of the agreement.

substantive due process The requirement that laws depriving an individual of life, liberty, or property be fair and not arbitrary.

substantive unconscionability Unconscionability that derives from one-sided, unjust, or overly harsh substance in a contract.

summary jury trial An abbreviated trial that leads to a nonbinding jury verdict.

summons A legal document issued by a court and addressed to a defendant that notifies him or her of the lawsuit and how and when to respond to the complaint. A summons may be used in both civil and criminal proceedings.

supremacy clause Article VI, Paragraph 2, of the U.S. Constitution, which states that the Constitution and all laws and treaties of the United States constitute the supreme law of the land. Thus, any state or local law that directly conflicts with the U.S. Constitution or federal laws or treaties is void.

syndicate An investment group that comes together for the explicit purpose of financing a specific large project.

T

Taft-Hartley Act Federal legislation designed to curtail some of the powers that unions had acquired under the Wagner Act; designates certain union actions as unfair. Also called *Labor-Management Relations Act*.

takeover The purchase of one corporation's stock by another corporation as a means of gaining control of the selling corporation.

takings clause A clause in the Fifth Amendment of the U.S. Constitution requiring that when government uses its power to

take private property for public use, it must pay the owner just compensation, or fair market value, for the property.

tender An offer by a party in a contract to perform, along with being ready, willing, and able to perform, a duty outlined in that contract.

tender of delivery Requirement that the seller or lessor have and hold conforming goods at the disposal of the buyer or lessee and give the buyer or lessee reasonable notification to enable him or her to take delivery.

tender offer A type of takeover in which the aggressor corporation offers the target shareholders a price above their stock's current market value.

termination statement An amendment to a financing statement that states that the debtor has no obligation to the secured party.

third-party beneficiary contract A contract created when two parties enter into a contract agreement with the intended purpose of benefiting a third party.

time instrument A type of draft that allows the payee to collect payment only at a specific time in the future.

tippee An individual who receives confidential information from an insider.

tipper An insider who gives inside information to someone.

tipper/tippee theory A theory of insider trading that holds that any individual (tippee) who acquires material inside information as a result of an insider's (tipper's) breach of duty has engaged in insider trading.

Title VII of the Civil Rights Act (CRA) of 1964 Federal law (amended by the Civil Rights Act of 1991) that protects employees against discrimination based on race, color, religion, national origin, and sex; also prohibits harassment based on the same protected categories.

tombstone advertisement A print advertisement that announces a forthcoming sale of securities in a format similar to that of a tombstone.

tort A violation of another person's rights or a civil wrongdoing that does not arise out of a contract or statute; primary types are intentional, negligent, and strict-liability torts.

tortfeasor A person who commits an intentional or through-negligence tort that causes a harm or loss for which a civil remedy may be sought.

trade dress The overall appearance and image of a product.

trade libel A business tort that occurs when false printed statements criticize a business product or service and result in a loss of sales.

trade secret A process, product, method of operation, or compilation of information that gives a businessperson an advantage over his or her competitors.

trademark A distinctive mark, word, design, picture, or arrangement that is used by a producer in conjunction with a product and tends to cause consumers to identify the product with the producer.

tradition See **historical school**.

transfer warranties Warranties regarding a negotiable instrument and its transfer; created by a party who transfers the instrument.

traveler's check An order that is payable on demand, is drawn on or through a bank, is designated by the phrase *traveler's check*, and requires a countersignature by the person whose signature appears on the check.

trespass to personal property Temporary interference with another's use or enjoyment of his or her personal property.

trespass to realty A tort that occurs when someone goes on another's property without permission or places something on another's property without permission.

trial court A court in which most civil or criminal cases start when they first enter the legal system. The parties present evidence and call witnesses to testify. Trial courts are referred to as *courts of common pleas* or *county courts* in state court systems and as *district courts* in the federal system. Also called *court of original jurisdiction* and *court of first instance*.

trustee (1) In bankruptcy proceedings, an individual who takes over administration of a debtor's estate. (2) A person who operates a trust for beneficiaries in a business trust.

tying arrangement Illegal agreement in which the sale of one product is tied to the sale of another.

U

unconscionability Grounds for rescinding an unconscionable contract.

unconscionable A term applied to a contract in which one party has so much more bargaining power than the other party that the powerful party dictates the terms of the agreement and eliminates the other party's free will.

undisclosed principal A principal whose existence is not known by a third party. That is, the third party does not know an agent is acting on behalf of a principal.

undue influence The situation in which one person has taken advantage of his or her dominant position in a relationship to unduly persuade the other person to the extent that the dominant person's persuasive efforts have interfered with the other person's ability to make his or her own decision.

unemployment compensation A state system, created by the Federal Unemployment Tax Act (FUTA), that provides unemployment compensation to qualified employees who lose their jobs.

unenforceable A term applied to a contract that, because of a law, cannot be enforced by the courts.

unfair competition The act of competing with another not to make a profit but for the sole purpose of driving that other out of business.

unforeseen circumstances Events that a reasonable person would not be expected to anticipate.

unidentified principal See **partially disclosed principal**.

Uniform Commercial Code (UCC) A statutory source of contract law in the United States applicable to transactions involving the sale of goods. The UCC was created in 1952 and adopted by all 50 states, the District of Columbia, and the Virgin Islands; it may be modified by each state to reflect the wishes of the state legislature.

uniform laws Laws created to account for the variability of laws among states. These laws serve to standardize the otherwise different interstate laws. Also called *model laws*.

unilateral contract A promise exchanged for an act.

unilateral mistake The result of an error by one party about a material fact, i.e., one that is important in the context of a particular contract.

United Nations Convention on Contracts for the International Sale of Goods (CISG) The legal structure for international sales, including business-to-business sales contracts.

universalization test The ethical guideline that urges us to consider, before we do an action, what the world would be like if everyone acted in this way.

unliquidated debt Debt for which the parties either dispute the fact that any money is owed or agree that some money is owed but dispute the amount.

usage of trade Any practice that members of an industry expect to be part of their dealings.

usury The lending of money at an exorbitant or unlawful rate of interest.

V

valid A term applied to a contract that includes all four elements of a contract: agreement (offer and acceptance), consideration, contractual capacity, and legal object.

values Positive abstractions that capture our sense of what is good and desirable.

venue (1) The place where a hearing takes place. Its geographic location is determined by each state's statutes and based on where the parties live or where the event occurred or the alleged wrong was committed. (2) A legal doctrine relating to the selection of a court with subject-matter and personal jurisdiction that is the most appropriate geographic location for the resolution of the dispute.

vest To mature, as in the maturing of rights such that a party can legally act on the rights.

vicarious liability The liability or responsibility imposed on a person, a party, or an organization for damages caused by another; most commonly used in relation to employment, with the employer held vicariously liable for damages caused by its employees.

virus A computer program that rearranges, damages, destroys, or replaces computer data.

void A term applied to a contract that is not valid because its object is illegal or it has some defect that is so serious that it is not a contract.

void title Not true title; e.g., the title held by someone who knowingly or unknowingly purchased stolen goods.

voidable A term applied to a contract that one or both parties have the ability to either withdraw from or enforce.

voidable title Title that occurs in situations in which the contract between the original parties would be void but the goods have already been sold to a third party.

voir dire The process of questioning potential jurors to ensure that the jury will be made up of nonbiased individuals.

W

Wagner Act The first major piece of federal legislation adopted explicitly to encourage the formation of labor unions and provide for collective bargaining between employers and unions as a means of obtaining the peaceful settlement of labor disputes.

warranty An assurance, either express or implied, by one party that the other party can rely on its representations of fact; in sales, a binding promise regarding a product in the event that the product does not meet the manufacturer's or seller's promises.

warranty liability Liability attributed when the transfer of an instrument breaches a warranty associated with an instrument.

warranty of title An assurance, inferred in every UCC sales transaction, that the seller has good and valid title to the goods and has the right to transfer title free and clear of any liens, judgments, or infringements of intellectual property rights of which the buyer does not have knowledge.

watered stock Stock that is issued to individuals below its fair market value.

white-collar crime A variety of nonviolent illegal acts against society that occur most frequently in the business context.

winding up The process of completing unfinished partnership business.

workers' compensation laws State laws that provide for financial compensation to employees or their dependents when a covered employee is injured on the job.

WPH approach (to ethical decision making) A set of ethical guidelines that urges us to consider whom an action affects, the purpose of the action, and how we view its morality.

writ of certiorari A Supreme Court order, issued after the Court decides to hear an appeal, mandating that the lower court send to the Supreme Court the record of the appealed case.

writing A type of documentation that shows contractual intent and satisfies the statute of frauds requirement.

wrongful dissolution A dissolution of a partnership in violation of its partnership agreement.

Credits

Name Index

Page numbers followed by n refer to notes.

Subject Index

Page numbers followed by n refer to notes.